# KEY TO WORLD MAP PAGES

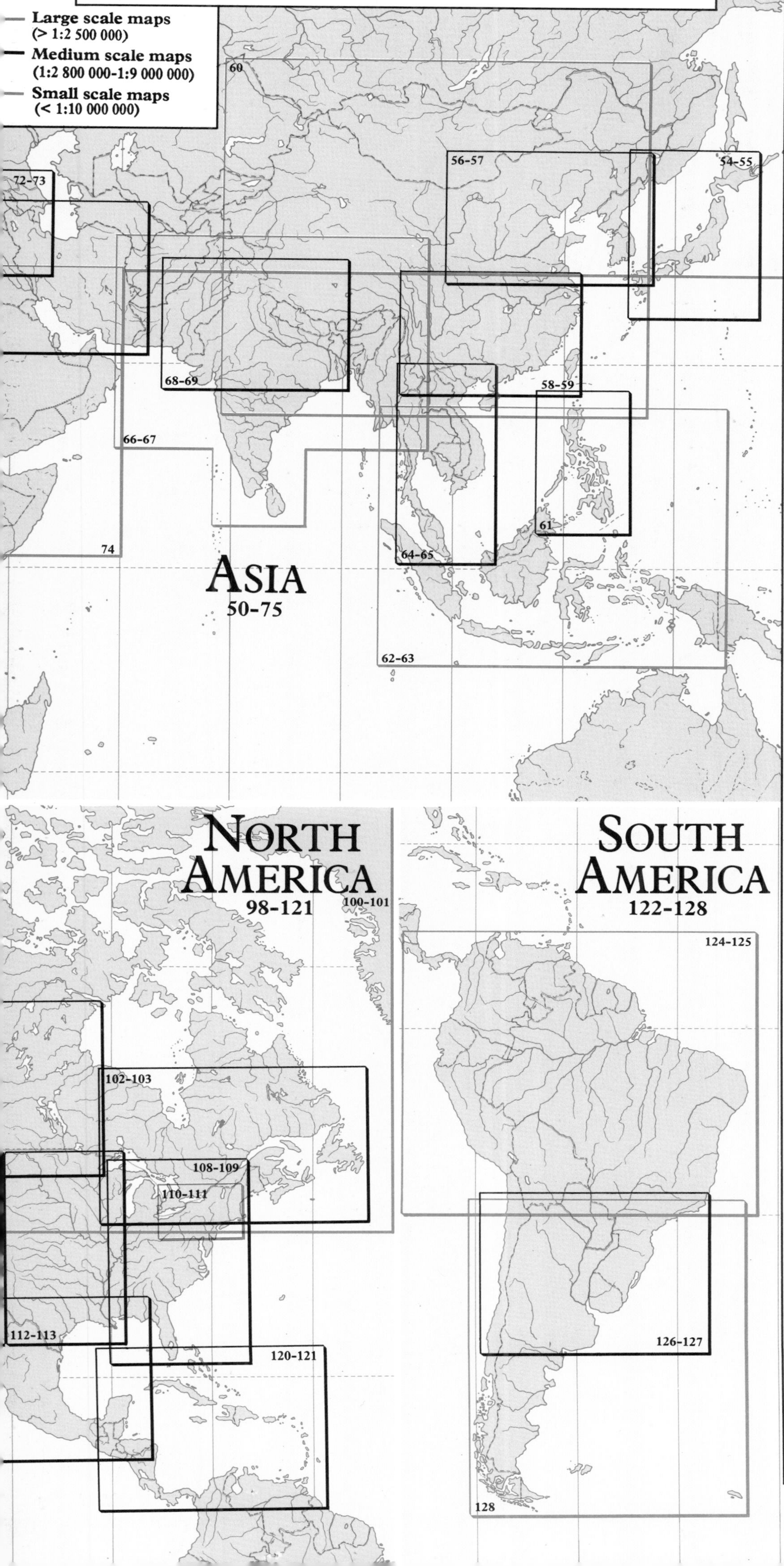
Large scale maps
(> 1:2 500 000)
Medium scale maps
(1:2 800 000–1:9 000 000)
Small scale maps
(< 1:10 000 000)
ASIA
50-75
NORTH AMERICA
98-121
SOUTH AMERICA
122-128
60
56-57
54-55
72-73
68-69
58-59
66-67
61
74
64-65
62-63
100-101
124-125
102-103
108-109
110-111
112-113
120-121
126-127
128

# COU


| | |
|---|---|
| Afghanistan | |
| Albania | |
| Algeria | |
| Angola | |
| Argentina | |
| Armenia | |
| Australia | |
| Austria | 26–27 |
| Azerbaijan | 73 |
| Bahamas | 120–121 |
| Bahrain | 71 |
| Bangladesh | 67 |
| Barbados | 121 |
| Belarus | 46–47 |
| Belgium | 17 |
| Belize | 120 |
| Benin | 83 |
| Bhutan | 67 |
| Bolivia | 124 |
| Bosnia-Herzegovina | 29, 40 |
| Botswana | 88–89 |
| Brazil | 124–127 |
| Brunei | 78 |
| Bulgaria | 40–41 |
| Burkina Faso | 82–83 |
| Burma | 67 |
| Burundi | 86 |
| Cambodia | 64–65 |
| Cameroon | 84 |
| Canada | 100–101 |
| Central African Republic | 84 |
| Chad | 79 |
| Chile | 124, 128 |
| China | 56–60 |
| Colombia | 124 |
| Congo | 84 |
| Congo, Dem. Rep. of the | 84–85 |
| Costa Rica | 120 |
| Croatia | 29, 42 |
| Cuba | 120–121 |
| Cyprus | 36 |
| Czech Republic | 26–27 |
| Denmark | 11 |
| Djibouti | 74 |
| Dominican Republic | 121 |
| Ecuador | 124 |
| Egypt | 80 |
| El Salvador | 120 |
| England | 12–13 |
| Equatorial Guinea | 84 |
| Eritrea | 80–81 |
| Estonia | 46 |
| Ethiopia | 74, 81 |
| Fiji | 91 |
| Finland | 8–9 |
| France | 18–21 |
| French Guiana | 125 |
| Gabon | 84 |
| Gambia | 82 |
| Georgia | 73 |
| Germany | 24–25 |
| Ghana | 82–83 |
| Greece | 38–41 |
| Greenland | 4 |
| Guatemala | 120 |
| Guinea | 82 |
| Guinea-Bissau | 82 |
| Guyana | 124 |
| Haiti | 121 |
| Honduras | 120 |
| Hungary | 42 |
| Iceland | 8 |
| India | 66–69 |
| Indonesia | 62–63 |
| Iran | 70–71 |
| Iraq | 70–71 |
| Irish Republic | 15 |
| Israel | 75 |
| Italy | 28–31 |
| Ivory Coast | 82 |
| Jamaica | 120 |
| Japan | 54–55 |
| Jordan | 75 |
| Kazakstan | 50 |
| Kenya | 86 |
| Korea, North | 57 |
| Korea, South | 57 |
| Liberia | 82 |
| Libya | 79 |
| Lithuania | 46 |
| Luxembourg | 17 |
| Macedonia | 40 |
| Madagascar | 89 |
| Malawi | 87 |
| Malaysia | 62–63 |
| Mali | 78, 82–83 |
| Malta | 36 |
| Mauritania | 78, 82 |
| Mauritius | 77 |
| Mexico | 118–119 |
| Moldova | 43 |
| Mongolia | 60 |
| Morocco | 78 |
| Mozambique | 85, 87 |
| Namibia | 88 |
| Nepal | 69 |
| Netherlands | 17 |
| New Zealand | 91 |
| Nicaragua | 120 |
| Niger | 83 |
| Nigeria | 83 |
| Northern Ireland | 15 |
| Norway | 8–9 |
| Oman | 74 |
| Pakistan | 68 |
| Panama | 120 |
| Papua New Guinea | 90 |
| Paraguay | 126–127 |
| Peru | 124 |
| Philippines | 61 |
| Poland | 44–45 |
| Portugal | 34–35 |
| Puerto Rico | 121 |
| Qatar | 71 |
| Romania | 42–43 |
| Russia | 50–51 |
| Rwanda | 86 |
| Saudi Arabia | 74 |
| Scotland | 14 |
| Senegal | 82 |
| Sierra Leone | 82 |
| Singapore | 65 |
| Slovak Republic | 27 |
| Slovenia | 29 |
| Somali Republic | 74 |
| South Africa | 88–89 |
| Spain | 32–35, 37 |
| Sri Lanka | 66 |
| Sudan | 79, 81 |
| Surinam | 124–125 |
| Swaziland | 89 |
| Sweden | 8–9 |
| Switzerland | 25 |
| Syria | 72–73 |
| Taiwan | 59 |
| Tajikistan | 50 |
| Tanzania | 86–87 |
| Thailand | 64–65 |
| Togo | 83 |
| Trinidad and Tobago | 121 |
| Tunisia | 78–79 |
| Turkey | 72–73 |
| Turkmenistan | 50 |
| Uganda | 86 |
| Ukraine | 47 |
| United Arab Emirates | 71 |
| United Kingdom | 12–15 |
| USA | 106–117 |
| Uruguay | 126–127 |
| Uzbekistan | 50 |
| Venezuela | 124 |
| Vietnam | 64–65 |
| Wales | 12–13 |
| Yemen | 74 |
| Yugoslavia | 40, 42 |
| Zambia | 84–85, 87 |
| Zimbabwe | 87 |

# PHILIP'S

# WORLD TRAVELLER'S ATLAS

# PHILIP'S

# WORLD TRAVELLER'S ATLAS

IN ASSOCIATION WITH
**THE ROYAL GEOGRAPHICAL SOCIETY**
WITH THE INSTITUTE OF BRITISH GEOGRAPHERS

## PICTURE ACKNOWLEDGEMENTS

**WORLD EXPLORER:**
© *CORBIS* 26 bottom, 27 bottom, /Adam Woolfitt 5 centre right, 30 centre left, /AFP 24 top, 25 bottom, /Angelo Hornak 29 centre left, /Australian Picture Library 13 top, /Bob Krist 14 top, /Bob Winsett 20 top, /Brandon D. Cole 11 bottom, /Buddy Mays 26 centre, 22 bottom, /Catherine Karnow 19 bottom, /Charles and Josette Lenars 30 bottom right, /Charles O'Rear 23 left, /Clem Haagner; Gallo Images 10 centre, /Dave G. Houser 30 top, /David Muench 4 left, /Dean Conger 15 bottom, /Derek Hall; Frank Lane Picture Agency 3 centre, /Douglas Peebles 32 bottom, /Duomo 20 right, /Enzo and Paolo Ragazzini 16 bottom, /Galen Rowell 2 left, 9 bottom, 21 top, /George H. H. Huey 4 top, /George Lepp 12 bottom, /Hans Georg Roth 5 top, /Inge Yspeert 10 bottom right, /James Marshall 6 centre right, /John Dakers; Eye Ubiquitous 25 right, /Kevin Schafer 13 bottom, /Marc Muench 20 left, /Michael and Patricia Fogden 8 /Michael Busselle 3 top, /Michael S. Yamashita 22 top, /Milepost 92½ 15 top, /Mimmo Jodice 29 bottom, /Morton Beebe, S. F. 24 centre right, /Nik Wheeler 19 top, /O. Alamany and E. Vicens 5 bottom, /Patrick Ward 7 bottom, 16 centre right, /Peter Johnson 10 top, /Peter Wilson 28 bottom, /Premium Stock 28 top, /Quadrillion 31 bottom, /Raymond Gehman 2 top, 6 top, /Rick Doyle 23 bottom, /Robert Holmes 16 top, /Roger Ressmeyer 3 bottom, /Roger Tidman 9 left, /Stephanie Maze 24 bottom, /Stephen Frink 12 top, 13 centre, /Steve Kaufman 6 bottom, /Tim Thompson 14 centre right, 14 bottom, /Tiziana and Gianni Baldizzone 7 centre right, /Tom Bean 8 bottom, /Tom Brakefield 11 top, /Tom Nebbia 17 right, /Tony Arruza 23 top, /Vanni Archive 29 top, /W. Cody 18 right, 27 top, /Wild Country 26 top, /Wolfgang Kaehler 17 top, 18 top and bottom, 8 top.
© *ALTON TOWERS* 32 left.

**CITY GAZETTEER:**
© *CORBIS* /Bettmann 41 bottom right, /Carmen Redondo 44 centre left, /Charles E. Rotkin 40 top right, /Chris Lisle 47 centre top, /Hubert Stadler 41 centre top, /John Heseltine 42 top right, /Larry Lee 46 bottom right, /Lindsay Hebberd 42 left, /Patrick Ward 44 bottom right, /Paul A. Souders 47 bottom right, /Richard T. Nowitz 43 bottom centre, /Tim Thompson 41 left, /Todd Gipstein 44 centre top, /Wolfgang Kaehler 45 top right, /Yann Arthus-Bertrand 46 top left.
© *MIKE MOULE* 40 left, 43 top left and centre right, 45 left, 46 centre, 48 centre and right.

## CITY MAPS
**Cartography by Philip's**

PAGE 11, DUBLIN: The town plan of Dublin is based on Ordnance Survey Ireland by permission of the Government Permit Number 7516. © Ordnance Survey Ireland and Government of Ireland.

PAGE 11, EDINBURGH, and PAGE 15, LONDON:
This product includes mapping data licensed from Ordnance Survey® with the permission of the Controller of Her Majesty's Stationery Office. © Crown copyright 2002. All rights reserved. Licence number 100011710.

VECTOR DATA: Courtesy of Gräfe and Unser Verlag GmbH, München, Germany (city centre maps of Bangkok, Beijing, Cape Town, Jerusalem, Mexico City, Moscow, Singapore, Sydney, Tokyo and Washington D.C.)

> **NOTE:**
> For reasons of safety or politics, there may be times when it is not advisable, or desirable, to visit one or more of the places described in the World Explorer and City Gazetteer sections. If in doubt, please check with the Foreign Office.

Published in Great Britain in 2002 by Philip's, a division of Octopus Publishing Group Limited, 2–4 Heron Quays, London E14 4JP

Copyright © 2002 Philip's

Cartography by Philip's

ISBN 0–540–08264–3

A CIP catalogue record for this book is available from the British Library.

Printed in Hong Kong

Details of other Philip's titles and services can be found on our website at: www.philips-maps.co.uk

Philip's World Atlases are published in association with The Royal Geographical Society (with The Institute of British Geographers).

The Society was founded in 1830 and given a Royal Charter in 1859 for 'the advancement of geographical science'. It holds historical collections of national and international importance, many of which relate to the Society's association with and support for scientific exploration and research from the 19th century onwards. It was pivotal in establishing geography as a teaching and research discipline in British universities close to the turn of the century, and has played a key role in geographical and environmental education ever since.

Today the Society is a leading world centre for geographical learning – supporting education, teaching, research and expeditions, and promoting public understanding of the subject.

The Society welcomes those interested in geography as members. For further information, please visit the website at: www.rgs.org

# Philip's World Maps

The reference maps which form the main body of this atlas have been prepared in accordance with the highest standards of international cartography to provide an accurate and detailed representation of the Earth. The scales and projections used have been carefully chosen to give balanced coverage of the world, while emphasizing the most densely populated and economically significant regions. A hallmark of Philip's mapping is the use of hill shading and relief colouring to create a graphic impression of landforms: this makes the maps exceptionally easy to read. However, knowledge of the key features employed in the construction and presentation of the maps will enable the reader to derive the fullest benefit from the atlas.

## MAP SEQUENCE

The atlas covers the Earth continent by continent: first Europe; then its land neighbour Asia (mapped north before south, in a clockwise sequence), then Africa, Australia and Oceania, North America and South America. This is the classic arrangement adopted by most cartographers since the 16th century. For each continent, there are maps at a variety of scales. First, physical relief and political maps

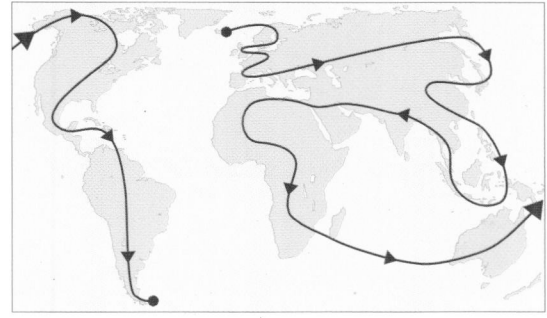

of the whole continent; then a series of larger-scale maps of the regions within the continent, each followed, where required, by still larger-scale maps of the most important or densely populated areas. The governing principle is that by turning the pages of the atlas, the reader moves steadily from north to south through each continent, with each map overlapping its neighbours.

## MAP PRESENTATION

With very few exceptions (e.g. for the Arctic and Antarctic), the maps are drawn with north at the top, regardless of whether they are presented upright or sideways on the page. In the borders will be found the map title; a locator diagram showing the area covered and the page numbers for maps of adjacent areas; the scale; the projection used; the degrees of latitude and longitude; and the letters and figures used in the index for locating place names and geographical features. Physical relief maps also have a height reference panel identifying the colours used for each layer of contouring.

## MAP SYMBOLS

Each map contains a vast amount of detail which can only be conveyed clearly and accurately by the use of symbols. Points and circles of varying sizes locate and identify the relative importance of towns and cities; different styles of type are employed for administrative, geographical and regional place names to aid identification. A variety of pictorial symbols denote landscape features such as glaciers, marshes and coral reefs, and man-made structures including roads, railways, airports, canals and dams. International borders are shown by red lines. Where neighbouring countries are in dispute, for example in parts of the Middle East, the maps show the *de facto* boundary between nations, regardless of the legal or historical situation. The symbols are explained on the first page of the *World Maps* section of the atlas.

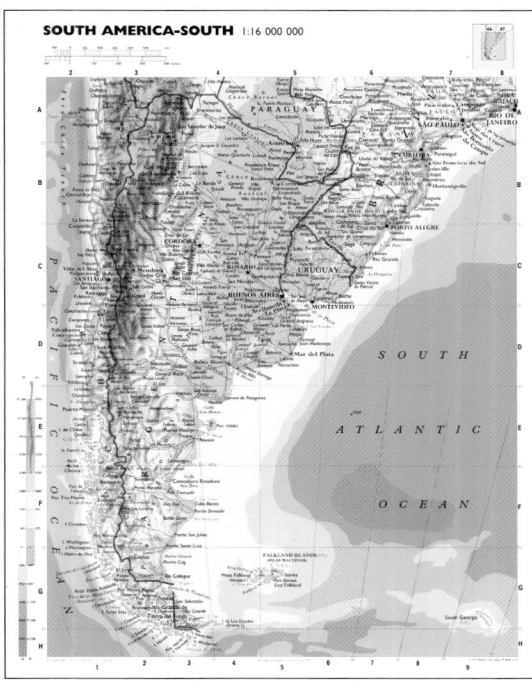

## MAP SCALES

| 1:16 000 000 |
|---|
| 1 inch = 252 statute miles |

The scale of each map is given in the numerical form known as the 'representative fraction'. The first figure is always one, signifying one unit of distance on the map; the second figure, usually in millions, is the number by which the map unit must be multiplied to give the equivalent distance on the Earth's surface. Calculations can easily be made in centimetres and kilometres, by dividing the Earth units figure by 100 000 (i.e. deleting the last five 0s). Thus 1:1 000 000 means 1 cm = 10 km. The calculation for inches and miles is more laborious, but 1 000 000 divided by 63 360 (the number of inches in a mile) shows that 1:1 000 000 means approximately 1 inch = 16 miles. The table below provides distance equivalents for scales down to 1:50 000 000.

| LARGE SCALE | | |
|---|---|---|
| 1:1 000 000 | 1 cm = 10 km | 1 inch = 16 miles |
| 1:2 500 000 | 1 cm = 25 km | 1 inch = 39.5 miles |
| 1:5 000 000 | 1 cm = 50 km | 1 inch = 79 miles |
| 1:6 000 000 | 1 cm = 60 km | 1 inch = 95 miles |
| 1:8 000 000 | 1 cm = 80 km | 1 inch = 126 miles |
| 1:10 000 000 | 1 cm = 100 km | 1 inch = 158 miles |
| 1:15 000 000 | 1 cm = 150 km | 1 inch = 237 miles |
| 1:20 000 000 | 1 cm = 200 km | 1 inch = 316 miles |
| 1:50 000 000 | 1 cm = 500 km | 1 inch = 790 miles |
| SMALL SCALE | | |

## MEASURING DISTANCES

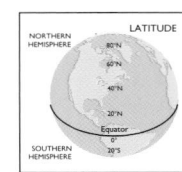

Although each map is accompanied by a scale bar, distances cannot always be measured with confidence because of the distortions involved in portraying the curved surface of the Earth on a flat page. As a general rule, the larger the map scale (i.e. the lower the number of Earth units in the representative fraction), the more accurate and reliable will be the distance measured. On small-scale maps such as those of the world and of entire continents, measurement may only

be accurate along the 'standard parallels', or central axes, and should not be attempted without considering the map projection.

## MAP PROJECTIONS

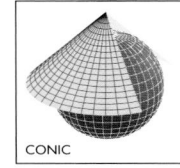  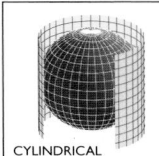

Unlike a globe, no flat map can give a true scale representation of the world in terms of area, shape and position of every region. Each of the numerous systems that have been devised for projecting the curved surface of the Earth on to a flat page involves the sacrifice of accuracy in one or more of these elements. The variations in shape and position of landmasses such as Alaska, Greenland and Australia, for example, can be quite dramatic when different projections are compared.

For this atlas, the guiding principle has been to select projections that involve the least distortion of size and distance. The projection used for each map is noted in the border. Most fall into one of three categories – conic, azimuthal or cylindrical – whose basic concepts are shown above. Each involves plotting the forms of the Earth's surface on a grid of latitude and longitude lines, which may be shown as parallels, curves or radiating spokes.

## LATITUDE AND LONGITUDE

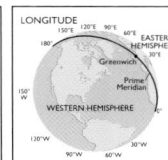 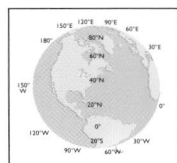

Accurate positioning of individual points on the Earth's surface is made possible by reference to the geometrical system of latitude and longitude. Latitude *parallels* are drawn west–east around the Earth and numbered by degrees north and south of the Equator, which is designated 0° of latitude. Longitude *meridians* are drawn north–south and numbered by degrees east and west of the *prime meridian*, 0° of longitude, which passes through Greenwich in England. By referring to these co-ordinates and their subdivisions of minutes (1/60th of a degree) and seconds (1/60th of a minute), any place on Earth can be located to within a few hundred metres. Latitude and longitude are indicated by blue lines on the maps; they are straight or curved according to the projection employed. Reference to these lines is the easiest way of determining the relative positions of places on different maps, and for plotting compass directions.

## NAME FORMS

For ease of reference, both English and local name forms appear in the atlas. Oceans, seas and countries are shown in English throughout the atlas; country names may be abbreviated to their commonly accepted form (e.g. Germany, not The Federal Republic of Germany). Conventional English forms are also used for place names on the smaller-scale maps of the continents. However, local name forms are used on all large-scale and regional maps, with the English form given in brackets only for important cities – the large-scale map of Russia and Central Asia thus shows Moskva (Moscow). For countries which do not use a Roman script, place names have been transcribed according to the systems adopted by the British and US Geographic Names Authorities. For China, the Pin Yin system has been used, with some more widely known forms appearing in brackets, as with Beijing (Peking). Both English and local names appear in the index, the English form being cross-referenced to the local form.

# Contents

# WORLD MAPS

# Europe

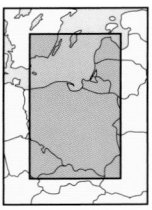
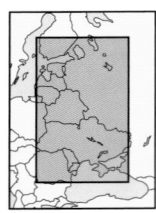
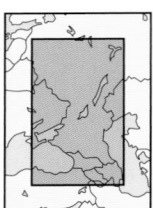
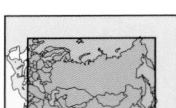

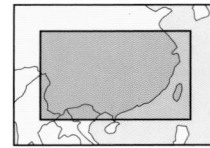
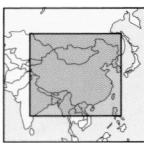
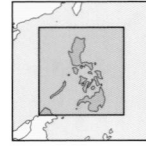
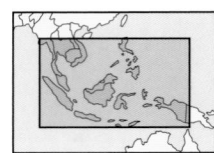
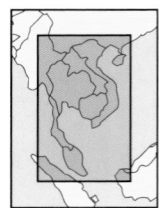
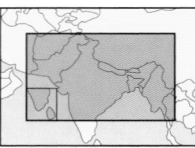
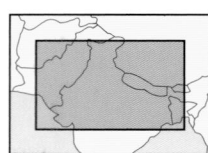
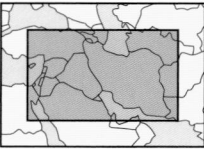
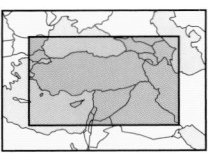
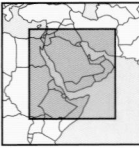
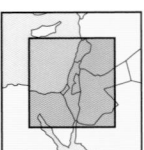
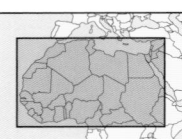
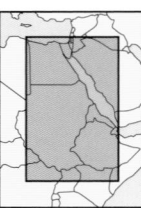
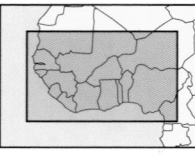
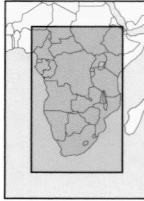

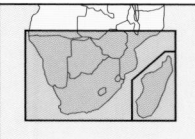

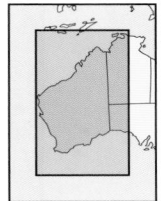
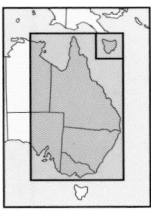
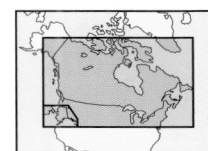
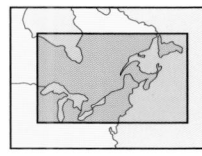

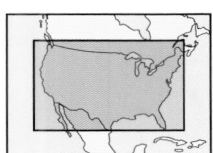
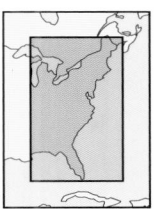
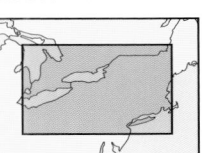
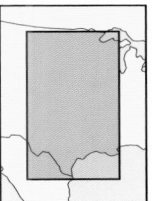
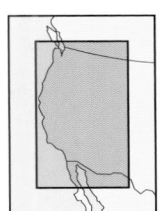
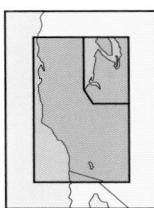
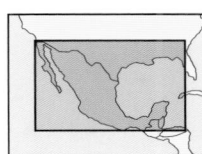
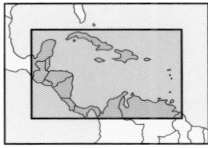

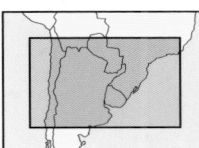
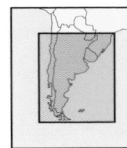

# World Statistics: Countries

This alphabetical list includes all the countries and territories of the world. If a territory is not completely independent, the country it is associated with is named. The area figures give the total area of land, inland water and ice.

The population figures are 2001 estimates. The annual income is the Gross Domestic Product per capita† in US dollars. The figures are the latest available, usually 2000 estimates.

| Country/Territory | Area km² Thousands | Area miles² Thousands | Population Thousands | Capital | Annual Income US $ |
|---|---|---|---|---|---|
| Afghanistan | 652 | 252 | 26,813 | Kabul | 800 |
| Albania | 28.8 | 11.1 | 3,510 | Tirana | 3,000 |
| Algeria | 2,382 | 920 | 31,736 | Algiers | 5,500 |
| American Samoa (US) | 0.2 | 0.08 | 67 | Pago Pago | 8,000 |
| Andorra | 0.45 | 0.17 | 68 | Andorra La Vella | 18,000 |
| Angola | 1,247 | 481 | 10,366 | Luanda | 1,000 |
| Anguilla (UK) | 0.1 | 0.04 | 12 | The Valley | 8,200 |
| Antigua & Barbuda | 0.44 | 0.17 | 67 | St John's | 8,200 |
| Argentina | 2,767 | 1,068 | 37,385 | Buenos Aires | 12,900 |
| Armenia | 29.8 | 11.5 | 3,336 | Yerevan | 3,000 |
| Aruba (Netherlands) | 0.19 | 0.07 | 70 | Oranjestad | 28,000 |
| Australia | 7,687 | 2,968 | 19,358 | Canberra | 23,200 |
| Austria | 83.9 | 32.4 | 8,151 | Vienna | 25,000 |
| Azerbaijan | 86.6 | 33.4 | 7,771 | Baku | 3,000 |
| Azores (Portugal) | 2.2 | 0.87 | 243 | Ponta Delgada | 11,040 |
| Bahamas | 13.9 | 5.4 | 298 | Nassau | 15,000 |
| Bahrain | 0.68 | 0.26 | 645 | Manama | 15,900 |
| Bangladesh | 144 | 56 | 131,270 | Dhaka | 1,570 |
| Barbados | 0.43 | 0.17 | 275 | Bridgetown | 14,500 |
| Belarus | 207.6 | 80.1 | 10,350 | Minsk | 7,500 |
| Belgium | 30.5 | 11.8 | 10,259 | Brussels | 25,300 |
| Belize | 23 | 8.9 | 256 | Belmopan | 3,200 |
| Benin | 113 | 43 | 6,591 | Porto-Novo | 1,030 |
| Bermuda (UK) | 0.05 | 0.02 | 64 | Hamilton | 33,000 |
| Bhutan | 47 | 18.1 | 2,049 | Thimphu | 1,100 |
| Bolivia | 1,099 | 424 | 8,300 | La Paz/Sucre | 2,600 |
| Bosnia-Herzegovina | 51 | 20 | 3,922 | Sarajevo | 1,700 |
| Botswana | 582 | 225 | 1,586 | Gaborone | 6,600 |
| Brazil | 8,512 | 3,286 | 174,469 | Brasília | 6,500 |
| Brunei | 5.8 | 2.2 | 344 | Bandar Seri Begawan | 17,600 |
| Bulgaria | 111 | 43 | 7,707 | Sofia | 6,200 |
| Burkina Faso | 274 | 106 | 12,272 | Ouagadougou | 1,000 |
| Burma (= Myanmar) | 677 | 261 | 41,995 | Rangoon | 1,500 |
| Burundi | 27.8 | 10.7 | 6,224 | Bujumbura | 720 |
| Cambodia | 181 | 70 | 12,492 | Phnom Penh | 1,300 |
| Cameroon | 475 | 184 | 15,803 | Yaoundé | 1,700 |
| Canada | 9,976 | 3,852 | 31,593 | Ottawa | 24,800 |
| Canary Is. (Spain) | 7.3 | 2.8 | 1,577 | Las Palmas/Santa Cruz | 17,100 |
| Cape Verde Is. | 4 | 1.6 | 405 | Praia | 1,700 |
| Cayman Is. (UK) | 0.26 | 0.1 | 36 | George Town | 24,500 |
| Central African Republic | 623 | 241 | 3,577 | Bangui | 1,700 |
| Chad | 1,284 | 496 | 8,707 | Ndjaména | 1,000 |
| Chile | 757 | 292 | 15,328 | Santiago | 10,100 |
| China | 9,597 | 3,705 | 1,273,111 | Beijing | 3,600 |
| Colombia | 1,139 | 440 | 40,349 | Bogotá | 6,200 |
| Comoros | 2.2 | 0.86 | 596 | Moroni | 720 |
| Congo | 342 | 132 | 2,894 | Brazzaville | 1,100 |
| Congo (Dem. Rep. of the) | 2,345 | 905 | 53,625 | Kinshasa | 600 |
| Cook Is. (NZ) | 0.24 | 0.09 | 21 | Avarua | 5,000 |
| Costa Rica | 51.1 | 19.7 | 3,773 | San José | 6,700 |
| Croatia | 56.5 | 21.8 | 4,334 | Zagreb | 5,800 |
| Cuba | 111 | 43 | 11,184 | Havana | 1,700 |
| Cyprus | 9.3 | 3.6 | 763 | Nicosia | 13,800 |
| Czech Republic | 78.9 | 30.4 | 10,264 | Prague | 12,900 |
| Denmark | 43.1 | 16.6 | 5,353 | Copenhagen | 25,500 |
| Djibouti | 23.2 | 9 | 461 | Djibouti | 1,300 |
| Dominica | 0.75 | 0.29 | 71 | Roseau | 4,000 |
| Dominican Republic | 48.7 | 18.8 | 8,581 | Santo Domingo | 5,700 |
| East Timor | 14.9 | 5.7 | 737 | Dili | N/A |
| Ecuador | 284 | 109 | 13,184 | Quito | 2,900 |
| Egypt | 1,001 | 387 | 69,537 | Cairo | 3,600 |
| El Salvador | 21 | 8.1 | 6,238 | San Salvador | 4,000 |
| Equatorial Guinea | 28.1 | 10.8 | 486 | Malabo | 2,000 |
| Eritrea | 94 | 36 | 4,298 | Asmara | 710 |
| Estonia | 44.7 | 17.3 | 1,423 | Tallinn | 10,000 |
| Ethiopia | 1,128 | 436 | 65,892 | Addis Ababa | 600 |
| Faroe Is. (Denmark) | 1.4 | 0.54 | 46 | Tórshavn | 20,000 |
| Fiji | 18.3 | 7.1 | 844 | Suva | 7,300 |
| Finland | 338 | 131 | 5,176 | Helsinki | 22,900 |
| France | 552 | 213 | 59,551 | Paris | 24,400 |
| French Guiana (France) | 90 | 34.7 | 178 | Cayenne | 6,000 |
| French Polynesia (France) | 4 | 1.5 | 254 | Papeete | 10,800 |
| Gabon | 268 | 103 | 1,221 | Libreville | 6,300 |
| Gambia, The | 11.3 | 4.4 | 1,411 | Banjul | 1,100 |
| Gaza Strip (OPT)* | 0.36 | 0.14 | 1,178 | – | 1,000 |
| Georgia | 69.7 | 26.9 | 4,989 | Tbilisi | 4,600 |
| Germany | 357 | 138 | 83,030 | Berlin | 23,400 |
| Ghana | 239 | 92 | 19,894 | Accra | 1,900 |
| Gibraltar (UK) | 0.007 | 0.003 | 28 | Gibraltar Town | 17,500 |
| Greece | 132 | 51 | 10,624 | Athens | 17,200 |
| Greenland (Denmark) | 2,176 | 840 | 56 | Nuuk (Godthåb) | 20,000 |
| Grenada | 0.34 | 0.13 | 89 | St George's | 4,400 |
| Guadeloupe (France) | 1.7 | 0.66 | 431 | Basse-Terre | 9,000 |
| Guam (US) | 0.55 | 0.21 | 158 | Agana | 21,000 |
| Guatemala | 109 | 42 | 12,974 | Guatemala City | 3,700 |
| Guinea | 246 | 95 | 7,614 | Conakry | 1,300 |
| Guinea-Bissau | 36.1 | 13.9 | 1,316 | Bissau | 850 |
| Guyana | 215 | 83 | 697 | Georgetown | 4,800 |
| Haiti | 27.8 | 10.7 | 6,965 | Port-au-Prince | 1,800 |
| Honduras | 112 | 43 | 6,406 | Tegucigalpa | 2,700 |
| Hong Kong (China) | 1.1 | 0.4 | 7,211 | – | 25,400 |
| Hungary | 93 | 35.9 | 10,106 | Budapest | 11,200 |
| Iceland | 103 | 40 | 278 | Reykjavik | 24,800 |
| India | 3,288 | 1,269 | 1,029,991 | New Delhi | 2,200 |
| Indonesia | 1,890 | 730 | 227,701 | Jakarta | 2,900 |
| Iran | 1,648 | 636 | 66,129 | Tehran | 6,300 |
| Iraq | 438 | 169 | 23,332 | Baghdad | 2,500 |
| Ireland | 70.3 | 27.1 | 3,841 | Dublin | 21,600 |
| Israel | 20.6 | 7.96 | 5,938 | Jerusalem | 18,900 |
| Italy | 301 | 116 | 57,680 | Rome | 22,100 |
| Ivory Coast (= Côte d'Ivoire) | 322 | 125 | 16,393 | Yamoussoukro | 1,600 |
| Jamaica | 11 | 4.2 | 2,666 | Kingston | 3,700 |
| Japan | 378 | 146 | 126,772 | Tokyo | 24,900 |
| Jordan | 89.2 | 34.4 | 5,153 | Amman | 3,500 |
| Kazakstan | 2,717 | 1,049 | 16,731 | Astana | 5,000 |
| Kenya | 580 | 224 | 30,766 | Nairobi | 1,500 |
| Kiribati | 0.72 | 0.28 | 94 | Tarawa | 850 |
| Korea, North | 121 | 47 | 21,968 | Pyŏngyang | 1,000 |
| Korea, South | 99 | 38.2 | 47,904 | Seoul | 16,100 |
| Kuwait | 17.8 | 6.9 | 2,042 | Kuwait City | 15,000 |
| Kyrgyzstan | 198.5 | 76.6 | 4,753 | Bishkek | 2,700 |
| Laos | 237 | 91 | 5,636 | Vientiane | 1,700 |
| Latvia | 65 | 25 | 2,385 | Riga | 7,200 |

*OPT = Occupied Palestinian Territory  N/A = Not Available

| Country/Territory | Area km² Thousands | Area miles² Thousands | Population Thousands | Capital | Annual Income US $ |
|---|---|---|---|---|---|
| Lebanon | 10.4 | 4 | 3,628 | Beirut | 5,000 |
| Lesotho | 30.4 | 11.7 | 2,177 | Maseru | 2,400 |
| Liberia | 111 | 43 | 3,226 | Monrovia | 1,100 |
| Libya | 1,760 | 679 | 5,241 | Tripoli | 8,900 |
| Liechtenstein | 0.16 | 0.06 | 33 | Vaduz | 23,000 |
| Lithuania | 65.2 | 25.2 | 3,611 | Vilnius | 7,300 |
| Luxembourg | 2.6 | 1 | 443 | Luxembourg | 36,400 |
| Macau (China) | 0.02 | 0.006 | 454 | – | 17,500 |
| Macedonia (FYROM) | 25.7 | 9.9 | 2,046 | Skopje | 4,400 |
| Madagascar | 587 | 227 | 15,983 | Antananarivo | 800 |
| Madeira (Portugal) | 0.81 | 0.31 | 259 | Funchal | 12,120 |
| Malawi | 118 | 46 | 10,548 | Lilongwe | 900 |
| Malaysia | 330 | 127 | 22,229 | Kuala Lumpur | 10,300 |
| Maldives | 0.3 | 0.12 | 311 | Malé | 2,000 |
| Mali | 1,240 | 479 | 11,009 | Bamako | 850 |
| Malta | 0.32 | 0.12 | 395 | Valletta | 14,300 |
| Marshall Is. | 0.18 | 0.07 | 71 | Dalap-Uliga-Darrit | 1,670 |
| Martinique (France) | 1.1 | 0.42 | 418 | Fort-de-France | 11,000 |
| Mauritania | 1,030 | 398 | 2,747 | Nouakchott | 2,000 |
| Mauritius | 2 | 0.72 | 1,190 | Port Louis | 10,400 |
| Mayotte (France) | 0.37 | 0.14 | 163 | Mamoundzou | 600 |
| Mexico | 1,958 | 756 | 101,879 | Mexico City | 9,100 |
| Micronesia, Fed. States of | 0.7 | 0.27 | 135 | Palikir | 2,000 |
| Moldova | 33.7 | 13 | 4,432 | Chişinău | 2,500 |
| Monaco | 0.002 | 0.001 | 32 | Monaco | 27,000 |
| Mongolia | 1,567 | 605 | 2,655 | Ulan Bator | 1,780 |
| Montserrat (UK) | 0.1 | 0.04 | 8 | Plymouth | 5,000 |
| Morocco | 447 | 172 | 30,645 | Rabat | 3,500 |
| Mozambique | 802 | 309 | 19,371 | Maputo | 1,000 |
| Namibia | 825 | 318 | 1,798 | Windhoek | 4,300 |
| Nauru | 0.02 | 0.008 | 12 | Yaren District | 5,000 |
| Nepal | 141 | 54 | 25,284 | Katmandu | 1,360 |
| Netherlands | 41.5 | 16 | 15,981 | Amsterdam/The Hague | 24,400 |
| Netherlands Antilles (Neths) | 0.99 | 0.38 | 212 | Willemstad | 11,400 |
| New Caledonia (France) | 18.6 | 7.2 | 205 | Nouméa | 15,000 |
| New Zealand | 269 | 104 | 3,864 | Wellington | 17,700 |
| Nicaragua | 130 | 50 | 4,918 | Managua | 2,700 |
| Niger | 1,267 | 489 | 10,355 | Niamey | 1,000 |
| Nigeria | 924 | 357 | 126,636 | Abuja | 950 |
| Northern Mariana Is. (US) | 0.48 | 0.18 | 75 | Saipan | 12,500 |
| Norway | 324 | 125 | 4,503 | Oslo | 27,700 |
| Oman | 212 | 82 | 2,622 | Muscat | 7,700 |
| Pakistan | 796 | 307 | 144,617 | Islamabad | 2,000 |
| Palau | 0.46 | 0.18 | 19 | Koror | 7,100 |
| Panama | 77.1 | 29.8 | 2,846 | Panamá | 6,000 |
| Papua New Guinea | 463 | 179 | 5,049 | Port Moresby | 2,500 |
| Paraguay | 407 | 157 | 5,734 | Asunción | 4,750 |
| Peru | 1,285 | 496 | 27,484 | Lima | 4,550 |
| Philippines | 300 | 116 | 82,842 | Manila | 3,800 |
| Poland | 313 | 121 | 38,634 | Warsaw | 8,500 |
| Portugal | 92.4 | 35.7 | 9,444 | Lisbon | 15,800 |
| Puerto Rico (US) | 9 | 3.5 | 3,939 | San Juan | 10,000 |
| Qatar | 11 | 4.2 | 769 | Doha | 20,300 |
| Réunion (France) | 2.5 | 0.97 | 733 | St-Denis | 4,800 |
| Romania | 238 | 92 | 22,364 | Bucharest | 5,900 |
| Russia | 17,075 | 6,592 | 145,470 | Moscow | 7,700 |
| Rwanda | 26.3 | 10.2 | 7,313 | Kigali | 900 |
| St Kitts & Nevis | 0.36 | 0.14 | 39 | Basseterre | 7,000 |
| St Lucia | 0.62 | 0.24 | 158 | Castries | 4,500 |
| St Vincent & Grenadines | 0.39 | 0.15 | 116 | Kingstown | 2,800 |
| Samoa | 2.8 | 1.1 | 179 | Apia | 3,200 |
| San Marino | 0.06 | 0.02 | 27 | San Marino | 32,000 |
| São Tomé & Príncipe | 0.96 | 0.37 | 165 | São Tomé | 1,100 |
| Saudi Arabia | 2,150 | 830 | 22,757 | Riyadh | 10,500 |
| Senegal | 197 | 76 | 10,285 | Dakar | 1,600 |
| Seychelles | 0.46 | 0.18 | 80 | Victoria | 7,700 |
| Sierra Leone | 71.7 | 27.7 | 5,427 | Freetown | 510 |
| Singapore | 0.62 | 0.24 | 4,300 | Singapore | 26,500 |
| Slovak Republic | 49 | 18.9 | 5,415 | Bratislava | 10,200 |
| Slovenia | 20.3 | 7.8 | 1,930 | Ljubljana | 12,000 |
| Solomon Is. | 28.9 | 11.2 | 480 | Honiara | 2,000 |
| Somalia | 638 | 246 | 7,489 | Mogadishu | 600 |
| South Africa | 1,220 | 471 | 43,586 | C. Town/Pretoria/Bloem. | 8,500 |
| Spain | 505 | 195 | 38,432 | Madrid | 18,000 |
| Sri Lanka | 65.6 | 25.3 | 19,409 | Colombo | 3,250 |
| Sudan | 2,506 | 967 | 36,080 | Khartoum | 1,000 |
| Surinam | 163 | 63 | 434 | Paramaribo | 3,400 |
| Swaziland | 17.4 | 6.7 | 1,104 | Mbabane | 4,000 |
| Sweden | 450 | 174 | 8,875 | Stockholm | 22,200 |
| Switzerland | 41.3 | 15.9 | 7,283 | Bern | 28,600 |
| Syria | 185 | 71 | 16,729 | Damascus | 3,100 |
| Taiwan | 36 | 13.9 | 22,370 | Taipei | 17,400 |
| Tajikistan | 143.1 | 55.2 | 6,579 | Dushanbe | 1,140 |
| Tanzania | 945 | 365 | 36,232 | Dodoma | 710 |
| Thailand | 513 | 198 | 61,798 | Bangkok | 6,700 |
| Togo | 56.8 | 21.9 | 5,153 | Lomé | 1,500 |
| Tonga | 0.75 | 0.29 | 104 | Nuku'alofa | 2,200 |
| Trinidad & Tobago | 5.1 | 2 | 1,170 | Port of Spain | 9,500 |
| Tunisia | 164 | 63 | 9,705 | Tunis | 6,500 |
| Turkey | 779 | 301 | 66,494 | Ankara | 6,800 |
| Turkmenistan | 488.1 | 188.5 | 4,603 | Ashkhabad | 4,300 |
| Turks & Caicos Is. (UK) | 0.43 | 0.17 | 18 | Cockburn Town | 7,300 |
| Tuvalu | 0.03 | 0.01 | 11 | Fongafale | 1,100 |
| Uganda | 236 | 91 | 23,986 | Kampala | 1,100 |
| Ukraine | 603.7 | 233.1 | 48,760 | Kiev | 3,850 |
| United Arab Emirates | 83.6 | 32.3 | 2,407 | Abu Dhabi | 22,800 |
| United Kingdom | 243.3 | 94 | 59,648 | London | 22,800 |
| United States of America | 9,373 | 3,619 | 278,059 | Washington, DC | 36,200 |
| Uruguay | 177 | 68 | 3,360 | Montevideo | 9,300 |
| Uzbekistan | 447.4 | 172.7 | 25,155 | Tashkent | 2,400 |
| Vanuatu | 12.2 | 4.7 | 193 | Port-Vila | 1,300 |
| Vatican City | 0.0004 | 0.0002 | 0.89 | Vatican City | N/A |
| Venezuela | 912 | 352 | 23,917 | Caracas | 6,200 |
| Vietnam | 332 | 127 | 79,939 | Hanoi | 1,950 |
| Virgin Is. (UK) | 0.15 | 0.06 | 21 | Road Town | 16,000 |
| Virgin Is. (US) | 0.34 | 0.13 | 122 | Charlotte Amalie | 15,000 |
| Wallis & Futuna Is. (France) | 0.2 | 0.08 | 15 | Mata-Utu | 2,000 |
| West Bank (OPT)* | 5.86 | 2.26 | 2,091 | – | 1,500 |
| Western Sahara | 266 | 103 | 251 | El Aaiún | N/A |
| Yemen | 528 | 204 | 18,078 | Sana | 820 |
| Yugoslavia (Serbia & Montenegro) | 102.3 | 39.5 | 10,677 | Belgrade | 2,300 |
| Zambia | 753 | 291 | 9,770 | Lusaka | 880 |
| Zimbabwe | 391 | 151 | 11,365 | Harare | 2,500 |

† Gross Domestic Product per capita has been measured using the purchasing power parity method. This enables comparisons to be made between countries through their purchasing power (in US dollars), showing real price levels of goods and services rather than using currency exchange rates.

# World Statistics: Cities

This list shows the principal cities with more than 500,000 inhabitants (only cities with more than 1 million inhabitants are included for Brazil, China, Indonesia, Japan and Russia). The figures are taken from the most recent census or estimate available, and as far as possible are the population of the metropolitan area, e.g. greater New York, Mexico or Paris. All the figures are in thousands. Local name forms have been used for the smaller cities (e.g. Kraków).

**AFGHANISTAN**
Kabul — 1,565
**ALGERIA**
Algiers — 1,722
Oran — 664
**ANGOLA**
Luanda — 2,250
**ARGENTINA**
Buenos Aires — 10,990
Córdoba — 1,198
Rosario — 1,096
Mendoza — 775
La Plata — 640
San Miguel de Tucumán — 622
Mar del Plata — 520
**ARMENIA**
Yerevan — 1,256
**AUSTRALIA**
Sydney — 4,041
Melbourne — 3,417
Brisbane — 1,601
Perth — 1,364
Adelaide — 1,093
**AUSTRIA**
Vienna — 1,560
**AZERBAIJAN**
Baku — 1,713
**BANGLADESH**
Dhaka — 7,832
Chittagong — 2,041
Khulna — 877
Rajshahi — 517
**BELARUS**
Minsk — 1,717
Homyel — 502
**BELGIUM**
Brussels — 948
**BENIN**
Cotonou — 537
**BOLIVIA**
La Paz — 1,126
Santa Cruz — 767
**BOSNIA-HERZEGOVINA**
Sarajevo — 526
**BRAZIL**
São Paulo — 10,434
Rio de Janeiro — 5,858
Salvador — 2,443
Belo Horizonte — 2,239
Fortaleza — 2,141
Brasília — 2,051
Curitiba — 1,587
Recife — 1,423
Manaus — 1,406
Pôrto Alegre — 1,361
Belém — 1,281
Goiânia — 1,093
Guarulhos — 1,073
**BULGARIA**
Sofia — 1,139
**BURKINA FASO**
Ouagadougou — 690
**BURMA (MYANMAR)**
Rangoon — 2,513
Mandalay — 533
**CAMBODIA**
Phnom Penh — 570
**CAMEROON**
Douala — 1,200
Yaoundé — 800
**CANADA**
Toronto — 4,881
Montréal — 3,511
Vancouver — 2,079
Ottawa–Hull — 1,107
Calgary — 972
Edmonton — 957
Québec — 693
Winnipeg — 685
Hamilton — 681
**CENTRAL AFRICAN REPUBLIC**
Bangui — 553
**CHAD**
Ndjaména — 530
**CHILE**
Santiago — 4,691
**CHINA**
Shanghai — 15,082
Beijing — 12,362
Tianjin — 10,687
Hong Kong (SAR)* — 6,502
Chongqing — 3,870
Shenyang — 3,762
Wuhan — 3,520
Guangzhou — 3,114
Harbin — 2,505
Nanjing — 2,211
Xi'an — 2,115
Chengdu — 1,933
Dalian — 1,855
Changchun — 1,810
Jinan — 1,660
Taiyuan — 1,642
Qingdao — 1,584
Zibo — 1,346
Zhengzhou — 1,324
Lanzhou — 1,296
Anshan — 1,252
Fushun — 1,246
Kunming — 1,242
Changsha — 1,198
Hangzhou — 1,185
Nanchang — 1,169
Shijiazhuang — 1,159
Guiyang — 1,131
Ürümqi — 1,130
Jilin — 1,118
Tangshan — 1,110
Qiqihar — 1,104
Baotou — 1,033
**COLOMBIA**
Bogotá — 6,005
Cali — 1,986
Medellín — 1,971
Barranquilla — 1,158
Cartagena — 813
Cúcuta — 589
Bucaramanga — 508
**CONGO**
Brazzaville — 938
Pointe-Noire — 576
**CONGO (DEM. REP.)**
Kinshasa — 2,664
Lubumbashi — 565
**CROATIA**
Zagreb — 868
**CUBA**
Havana — 2,204
**CZECH REPUBLIC**
Prague — 1,203
**DENMARK**
Copenhagen — 1,362
**DOMINICAN REPUBLIC**
Santo Domingo — 2,135
Stgo. de los Caballeros — 691
**ECUADOR**
Guayaquil — 2,070
Quito — 1,574
**EGYPT**
Cairo — 6,800
Alexandria — 3,339
El Gîza — 2,222
Shubra el Kheima — 871
**EL SALVADOR**
San Salvador — 1,522
**ETHIOPIA**
Addis Ababa — 2,316
**FINLAND**
Helsinki — 532
**FRANCE**
Paris — 11,175
Lyons — 1,648
Marseilles — 1,516
Lille — 1,143
Toulouse — 965
Nice — 933
Bordeaux — 925
Nantes — 711
Strasbourg — 612
Toulon — 565
Douai — 553
Rennes — 521
Rouen — 518
Grenoble — 515
**GEORGIA**
Tbilisi — 1,253
**GERMANY**
Berlin — 3,426
Hamburg — 1,705
Munich — 1,206
Cologne — 964
Frankfurt — 644
Essen — 609
Dortmund — 595
Stuttgart — 585
Düsseldorf — 571
Bremen — 547
Duisburg — 529
Hanover — 521
**GHANA**
Accra — 1,781
**GREECE**
Athens — 3,097
**GUATEMALA**
Guatemala — 1,167
**GUINEA**
Conakry — 1,508
**HAITI**
Port-au-Prince — 885
**HONDURAS**
Tegucigalpa — 814
**HUNGARY**
Budapest — 1,885
**INDIA**
Mumbai (Bombay) — 16,368
Kolkata (Calcutta) — 13,217
Delhi — 12,791
Chennai (Madras) — 6,425
Bangalore — 5,687
Hyderabad — 5,534
Ahmadabad — 4,519
Pune — 3,756
Surat — 2,811
Kanpur — 2,690
Jaipur — 2,324
Lucknow — 2,267
Nagpur — 2,123
Patna — 1,707
Indore — 1,639
Vadodara — 1,492
Bhopal — 1,455
Coimbatore — 1,446
Ludhiana — 1,395
Cochin — 1,355
Vishakhapatnam — 1,329
Agra — 1,321
Varanasi — 1,212
Madurai — 1,195
Meerut — 1,167
Nasik — 1,152
Jabalpur — 1,117
Jamshedpur — 1,102
Asansol — 1,090
Faridabad — 1,055
Allahabad — 1,050
Amritsar — 1,011
Vijayawada — 1,011
Rajkot — 1,002
**INDONESIA**
Jakarta — 11,500
Surabaya — 2,701
Bandung — 2,368
Medan — 1,910
Semarang — 1,366
Palembang — 1,352
Tangerang — 1,198
Ujung Pandang — 1,092
**IRAN**
Tehran — 6,759
Mashhad — 1,887
Esfahan — 1,266
Tabriz — 1,191
Shiraz — 1,053
Karaj — 941
Ahvaz — 805
Qom — 778
Bakhtaran — 693
**IRAQ**
Baghdad — 3,841
As Sulaymaniyah — 952
Arbil — 770
Al Mawsil — 664
Al Kazimiyah — 521
**IRELAND**
Dublin — 1,024
**ISRAEL**
Tel Aviv-Yafo — 1,880
Jerusalem — 591
**ITALY**
Rome — 2,654
Milan — 1,306
Naples — 1,050
Turin — 923
Palermo — 689
Genoa — 659
**IVORY COAST**
Abidjan — 2,500
**JAMAICA**
Kingston — 644
**JAPAN**
Tokyo — 17,950
Yokohama — 3,427
Osaka — 2,599
Nagoya — 2,171
Sapporo — 1,822
Kobe — 1,494
Kyoto — 1,468
Fukuoka — 1,341
Kawasaki — 1,250
Hiroshima — 1,126
Kitakyushu — 1,011
Sendai — 1,008
**JORDAN**
Amman — 1,752
**KAZAKSTAN**
Almaty — 1,151
Qaraghandy — 574
**KENYA**
Nairobi — 2,000
Mombasa — 600
**KOREA, NORTH**
Pyóngyang — 2,741
Hamhung — 710
Chóngjin — 583
**KOREA, SOUTH**
Seoul — 10,231
Pusan — 3,814
Taegu — 2,449
Inch'on — 2,308
Taejón — 1,272
Kwangju — 1,258
Ulsan — 967
Sóngnam — 869
Puch'on — 779
Suwón — 756
Anyang — 590
Chónju — 563
Chóngju — 531
Ansan — 510
P'ohang — 509
**KYRGYZSTAN**
Bishkek — 589
**LAOS**
Vientiane — 532
**LATVIA**
Riga — 811
**LEBANON**
Beirut — 1,500
Tripoli — 500
**LIBERIA**
Monrovia — 962
**LIBYA**
Tripoli — 960
**LITHUANIA**
Vilnius — 580
**MACEDONIA**
Skopje — 541
**MADAGASCAR**
Antananarivo — 1,053
**MALAYSIA**
Kuala Lumpur — 1,145
**MALI**
Bamako — 810
**MAURITANIA**
Nouakchott — 735
**MEXICO**
Mexico City — 15,643
Guadalajara — 2,847
Monterrey — 2,522
Puebla — 1,055
León — 872
Ciudad Juárez — 798
Tijuana — 743
Culiacán — 602
Mexicali — 602
Acapulco — 592
Mérida — 557
Chihuahua — 530
San Luis Potosí — 526
Aguascalientés — 506
**MOLDOVA**
Chişinău — 658
**MONGOLIA**
Ulan Bator — 673
**MOROCCO**
Casablanca — 2,943
Rabat-Salé — 1,220
Marrakesh — 602
Fès — 564
**MOZAMBIQUE**
Maputo — 2,000
**NEPAL**
Katmandu — 535
**NETHERLANDS**
Amsterdam — 1,115
Rotterdam — 1,086
The Hague — 700
Utrecht — 557
**NEW ZEALAND**
Auckland — 1,090
**NICARAGUA**
Managua — 864
**NIGERIA**
Lagos — 10,287
Ibadan — 1,432
Ogbomosho — 730
Kano — 674
**NORWAY**
Oslo — 502
**PAKISTAN**
Karachi — 9,269
Lahore — 5,064
Faisalabad — 1,977
Rawalpindi — 1,406
Multan — 1,182
Hyderabad — 1,151
Gujranwala — 1,125
Peshawar — 988
Quetta — 560
Islamabad — 525
**PARAGUAY**
Asunción — 945
**PERU**
Lima — 6,601
Arequipa — 620
Trujillo — 509
**PHILIPPINES**
Manila — 8,594
Quezon City — 1,989
Caloocan — 1,023
Davao — 1,009
Cebu — 662
Zamboanga — 511
**POLAND**
Warsaw — 1,626
Lódz — 815
Kraków — 740
Wroclaw — 641
Poznań — 580
**PORTUGAL**
Lisbon — 2,561
Oporto — 1,174
**ROMANIA**
Bucharest — 2,028
**RUSSIA**
Moscow — 8,405
St Petersburg — 4,216
Nizhniy Novgorod — 1,371
Novosibirsk — 1,367
Yekaterinburg — 1,275
Samara — 1,170
Omsk — 1,158
Kazan — 1,085
Chelyabinsk — 1,084
Ufa — 1,082
Perm — 1,025
Rostov — 1,023
Volgograd — 1,005
**SAUDI ARABIA**
Riyadh — 1,800
Jedda — 1,500
Mecca — 630
**SENEGAL**
Dakar — 1,905
**SIERRA LEONE**
Freetown — 505
**SINGAPORE**
Singapore — 3,866
**SOMALIA**
Mogadishu — 997
**SOUTH AFRICA**
Cape Town — 2,350
Johannesburg — 1,196
Durban — 1,137
Pretoria — 1,080
Port Elizabeth — 853
Vanderbijlpark–Vereeniging — 774
Soweto — 597
Sasolburg — 540
**SPAIN**
Madrid — 3,030
Barcelona — 1,615
Valencia — 763
Sevilla — 720
Zaragoza — 608
Málaga — 532
**SRI LANKA**
Colombo — 1,863
**SUDAN**
Omdurman — 1,271
Khartoum — 925
Khartoum North — 701
**SWEDEN**
Stockholm — 727
**SWITZERLAND**
Zürich — 733
**SYRIA**
Aleppo — 1,813
Damascus — 1,394
Homs — 659
**TAIWAN**
T'aipei — 2,596
Kaohsiung — 1,435
T'aichung — 858
T'ainan — 708
Panch'iao — 539
**TAJIKISTAN**
Dushanbe — 524
**TANZANIA**
Dar-es-Salaam — 1,361
**THAILAND**
Bangkok — 7,507
**TOGO**
Lomé — 590
**TUNISIA**
Tunis — 1,827
**TURKEY**
Istanbul — 8,506
Ankara — 3,294
Izmir — 2,554
Bursa — 1,485
Adana — 1,273
Konya — 1,140
Mersin (Içel) — 956
Gaziantep — 867
Antalya — 867
Kayseri — 862
Diyarbakir — 833
Urfa — 785
Manisa — 696
Kocaeli — 629
Antalya — 591
Samsun — 590
Kahramanmaras — 551
Balikesir — 538
Eskisehir — 519
Erzurum — 512
Malatya — 510
**TURKMENISTAN**
Ashkhabad — 536
**UGANDA**
Kampala — 954
**UKRAINE**
Kiev — 2,621
Kharkov — 1,521
Dnepropetrovsk — 1,122
Donetsk — 1,065
Odessa — 1,027
Zaporizhzhya — 863
Lviv — 794
Kryvyy Rih — 720
Mykolayiv — 518
Mariupol — 500
**UNITED ARAB EMIRATES**
Abu Dhabi — 928
Dubai — 674
**UNITED KINGDOM**
London — 8,089
Birmingham — 2,373
Manchester — 2,353
Liverpool — 852
Glasgow — 832
Sheffield — 661
Nottingham — 649
Newcastle — 617
Bristol — 552
Leeds — 529
**UNITED STATES**
New York — 21,200
Los Angeles — 16,374
Chicago–Gary — 9,158
Washington–Baltimore — 7,608
San Francisco–San Jose — 7,039
Philadelphia–Atlantic City — 6,188
Boston–Worcester — 5,819
Detroit–Flint — 5,456
Dallas–Fort Worth — 5,222
Houston–Galveston — 4,670
Atlanta — 4,112
Miami–Fort Lauderdale — 3,876
Seattle–Tacoma — 3,554
Phoenix–Mesa — 3,252
Minneapolis–St Paul — 2,969
Cleveland–Akron — 2,946
San Diego — 2,814
St Louis — 2,604
Denver–Boulder — 2,582
San Juan — 2,450
Tampa–Saint Petersburg — 2,396
Pittsburgh — 2,359
Portland–Salem — 2,265
Cincinnati–Hamilton — 1,979
Sacramento–Yolo — 1,797
Kansas City — 1,776
Milwaukee–Racine — 1,690
Orlando — 1,645
Indianapolis — 1,607
San Antonio — 1,592
Norfolk–Virginia Beach–Newport News — 1,570
Las Vegas — 1,563
Columbus, OH — 1,540
Charlotte–Gastonia — 1,499
New Orleans — 1,338
Salt Lake City — 1,334
Greensboro–Winston Salem–High Point — 1,252
Austin–San Marcos — 1,250
Nashville — 1,231
Providence–Fall River — 1,189
Raleigh–Durham — 1,188
Hartford — 1,183
Buffalo–Niagara Falls — 1,170
Memphis — 1,136
West Palm Beach — 1,131
Jacksonville, FL — 1,100
Rochester — 1,098
Grand Rapids — 1,089
Oklahoma City — 1,083
Louisville — 1,026
Richmond–Petersburg — 997
Greenville — 962
Dayton–Springfield — 951
Fresno — 923
Birmingham — 921
Honolulu — 876
Albany–Schenectady — 876
Tucson — 844
Tulsa — 803
Syracuse — 732
Omaha — 717
Albuquerque — 713
Knoxville — 687
El Paso — 680
Bakersfield — 662
Allentown — 638
Harrisburg — 629
Scranton — 625
Toledo — 618
Baton Rouge — 603
Youngstown–Warren — 595
Springfield, MA — 592
Sarasota — 590
Little Rock — 584
McAllen — 569
Stockton–Lodi — 564
Charleston — 549
Wichita — 545
Mobile — 540
Columbia, SC — 537
Colorado Springs — 517
Fort Wayne — 502
**URUGUAY**
Montevideo — 1,379
**UZBEKISTAN**
Tashkent — 2,118
**VENEZUELA**
Caracas — 1,975
Maracaibo — 1,706
Valencia — 1,263
Barquisimeto — 811
Ciudad Guayana — 642
Petare — 176
Maracay — 459
**VIETNAM**
Ho Chi Minh City — 4,322
Hanoi — 3,056
Haiphong — 783
**YEMEN**
Sana' — 972
Aden — 562
**YUGOSLAVIA**
Belgrade — 1,598
**ZAMBIA**
Lusaka — 982
**ZIMBABWE**
Harare — 1,189
Bulawayo — 622

\* SAR = Special Administrative Region of China

# World Statistics: Distances

The table shows air distances in miles and kilometres between 30 major cities. Known as 'Great Circle' distances, these measure the shortest routes between the cities, which aircraft use wherever possible. The maps show the world centred on six cities, and illustrate, for example, why direct flights from Japan to northern America and Europe are across the Arctic regions. The maps have been constructed on an Azimuthal Equidistant projection, on which all distances measured through the centre point are true to scale. The red lines are drawn at 5,000, 10,000 and 15,000 km from the central city.

Upper-right triangle = **Kms**; lower-left triangle = **Miles**; diagonal = city name.

| | Beijing | Bombay | Buenos Aires | Cairo | Calcutta | Caracas | Chicago | Hong Kong | Honolulu | Johannesburg | Lagos | London | Los Angeles | Mexico City | Moscow | Nairobi | New York | Paris | Rio de Janeiro | Rome | Singapore | Sydney | Tokyo | Wellington |
|---|---|---|---|---|---|---|---|---|---|---|---|---|---|---|---|---|---|---|---|---|---|---|---|---|
| Beijing | **Beijing** | 2956 | 11972 | 4688 | 2031 | 8947 | 6588 | 1220 | 5070 | 7276 | 7119 | 5057 | 6251 | 7742 | 3600 | 5727 | 6828 | 5106 | 10773 | 5049 | 2783 | 5561 | 1304 | 6700 |
| Bombay | 4757 | **Bombay** | 9275 | 2706 | 1034 | 9024 | 8048 | 2683 | 8024 | 4334 | 4730 | 4467 | 8700 | 9728 | 3126 | 2816 | 7793 | 4356 | 8332 | 3837 | 2432 | 6313 | 4189 | 7686 |
| Buenos Aires | 19268 | 14925 | **Buenos Aires** | 7341 | 10268 | 3167 | 5599 | 11481 | 7558 | 5025 | 4919 | 6917 | 6122 | 4591 | 8374 | 6463 | 5298 | 6867 | 1214 | 6929 | 9867 | 7332 | 11410 | 6202 |
| Cairo | 7544 | 4355 | 11814 | **Cairo** | 3541 | 6340 | 6127 | 5064 | 8838 | 3894 | 2432 | 2180 | 7580 | 7687 | 1803 | 2197 | 5605 | 1994 | 6149 | 1325 | 5137 | 8959 | 5947 | 10268 |
| Calcutta | 3269 | 1664 | 16524 | 5699 | **Calcutta** | 9609 | 7978 | 1653 | 7048 | 5256 | 5727 | 4946 | 8152 | 9494 | 3438 | 3839 | 7921 | 4883 | 9366 | 4486 | 1800 | 5678 | 3195 | 7055 |
| Caracas | 14399 | 14522 | 5096 | 10203 | 15464 | **Caracas** | 2502 | 10166 | 6009 | 6847 | 4810 | 4664 | 3612 | 2228 | 6175 | 7173 | 2131 | 4738 | 2825 | 5196 | 11407 | 9534 | 8801 | 8154 |
| Chicago | 10603 | 12953 | 9011 | 3206 | 12839 | 4027 | **Chicago** | 7783 | 4247 | 8689 | 5973 | 3949 | 1742 | 1694 | 4971 | 8005 | 711 | 4132 | 5311 | 4809 | 9369 | 9243 | 6299 | 8358 |
| Hong Kong | 1963 | 4317 | 18478 | 8150 | 2659 | 16360 | 12526 | **Hong Kong** | 5543 | 6669 | 7360 | 5980 | 7232 | 8775 | 4439 | 5453 | 8047 | 5984 | 11001 | 5769 | 1615 | 4582 | 1786 | 5857 |
| Honolulu | 8160 | 12914 | 12164 | 14223 | 11343 | 9670 | 6836 | 8921 | **Honolulu** | 11934 | 10133 | 7228 | 2558 | 3781 | 7036 | 10739 | 4958 | 7437 | 8290 | 8026 | 6721 | 5075 | 3854 | 4669 |
| Johannesburg | 11710 | 6974 | 8088 | 6267 | 8459 | 11019 | 13984 | 10732 | 19206 | **Johannesburg** | 2799 | 5637 | 10362 | 9063 | 5692 | 1818 | 7979 | 5426 | 4420 | 4811 | 5381 | 6860 | 8418 | 7308 |
| Lagos | 11457 | 7612 | 7916 | 3915 | 9216 | 7741 | 9612 | 11845 | 16308 | 4505 | **Lagos** | 3118 | 7713 | 6879 | 3886 | 2366 | 5268 | 2929 | 3750 | 2510 | 6925 | 9643 | 8376 | 9973 |
| London | 8138 | 7190 | 11131 | 3508 | 7961 | 7507 | 6356 | 9623 | 11632 | 9071 | 5017 | **London** | 5442 | 5552 | 1552 | 4237 | 3463 | 212 | 5778 | 889 | 6743 | 10558 | 5942 | 11691 |
| Los Angeles | 10060 | 14000 | 9852 | 12200 | 13120 | 5812 | 2804 | 11639 | 4117 | 16676 | 12414 | 8758 | **Los Angeles** | 1549 | 6070 | 9659 | 2446 | 5645 | 6310 | 6331 | 8776 | 7502 | 5475 | 6719 |
| Mexico City | 12460 | 15656 | 7389 | 12372 | 15280 | 3586 | 2726 | 14122 | 6085 | 14585 | 11071 | 8936 | 2493 | **Mexico City** | 6664 | 9207 | 2090 | 5717 | 4780 | 6365 | 10321 | 8058 | 7024 | 6897 |
| Moscow | 5794 | 5031 | 13477 | 2902 | 5534 | 9938 | 8000 | 7144 | 11323 | 9161 | 6254 | 2498 | 9769 | 10724 | **Moscow** | 3942 | 4666 | 1545 | 7184 | 1477 | 5237 | 9008 | 4651 | 10283 |
| Nairobi | 9216 | 4532 | 10402 | 3536 | 6179 | 11544 | 12883 | 8776 | 17282 | 2927 | 3807 | 6819 | 15544 | 14818 | 6344 | **Nairobi** | 7358 | 4029 | 5548 | 3350 | 4635 | 7552 | 6996 | 8490 |
| New York | 10988 | 12541 | 8526 | 9020 | 12747 | 3430 | 1145 | 12950 | 7980 | 12841 | 8477 | 5572 | 3936 | 3264 | 7510 | 11842 | **New York** | 3626 | 4832 | 4280 | 9531 | 9935 | 6741 | 8951 |
| Paris | 8217 | 7010 | 11051 | 3210 | 7858 | 7625 | 6650 | 9630 | 11968 | 8732 | 4714 | 342 | 9085 | 9200 | 2486 | 6485 | 5836 | **Paris** | 5708 | 687 | 6671 | 10539 | 6038 | 11798 |
| Rio de Janeiro | 17338 | 13409 | 1953 | 9896 | 15073 | 4546 | 8547 | 17704 | 13342 | 7113 | 6035 | 9299 | 10155 | 7693 | 11562 | 8928 | 7777 | 9187 | **Rio de Janeiro** | 5725 | 9763 | 8389 | 11551 | 7367 |
| Rome | 8126 | 6175 | 11151 | 2133 | 7219 | 8363 | 7739 | 9284 | 12916 | 7743 | 4039 | 1431 | 10188 | 10243 | 2376 | 5391 | 6888 | 1105 | 9214 | **Rome** | 6229 | 10143 | 6127 | 11523 |
| Singapore | 4478 | 3914 | 15879 | 8267 | 2897 | 18359 | 15078 | 2599 | 10816 | 8660 | 11145 | 10852 | 14123 | 16610 | 8428 | 7460 | 15339 | 10737 | 15712 | 10025 | **Singapore** | 3915 | 3306 | 5298 |
| Sydney | 8949 | 10160 | 11800 | 14418 | 9138 | 15343 | 14875 | 7374 | 8168 | 11040 | 15519 | 16992 | 12073 | 12969 | 14497 | 12153 | 15989 | 16962 | 13501 | 16324 | 6300 | **Sydney** | 4861 | 1383 |
| Tokyo | 2099 | 6742 | 18362 | 9571 | 5141 | 14164 | 10137 | 2874 | 6202 | 13547 | 13480 | 9562 | 8811 | 11304 | 7485 | 11260 | 10849 | 9718 | 18589 | 9861 | 5321 | 7823 | **Tokyo** | 5762 |
| Wellington | 10782 | 12370 | 9981 | 16524 | 11354 | 13122 | 13451 | 9427 | 7513 | 11761 | 16050 | 18814 | 10814 | 11100 | 16549 | 13664 | 14405 | 18987 | 11855 | 18545 | 8526 | 2226 | 9273 | **Wellington** |

## Northern Hemisphere

MEXICO CITY
19 26°N 99 4°W

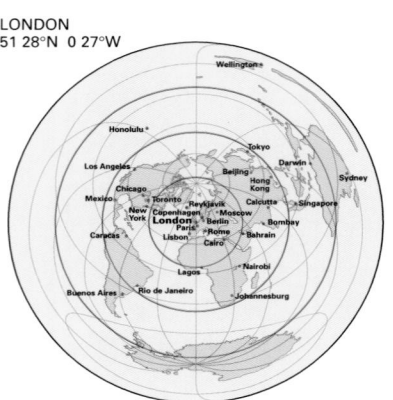

LONDON
51 28°N 0 27°W

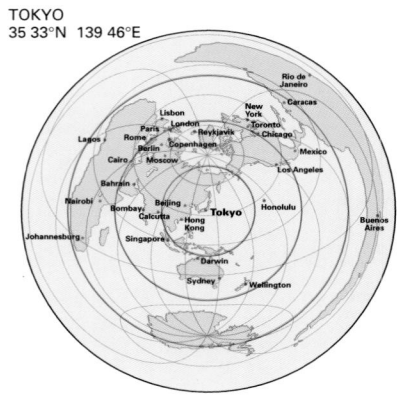

TOKYO
35 33°N 139 46°E

## Southern Hemisphere

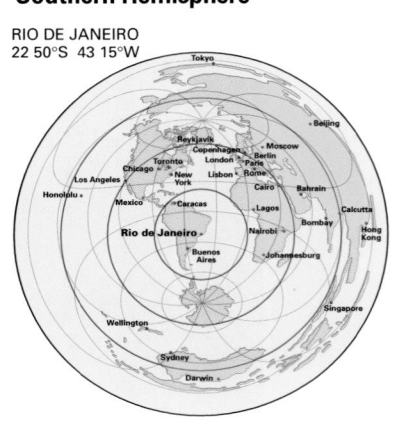

RIO DE JANEIRO
22 50°S 43 15°W

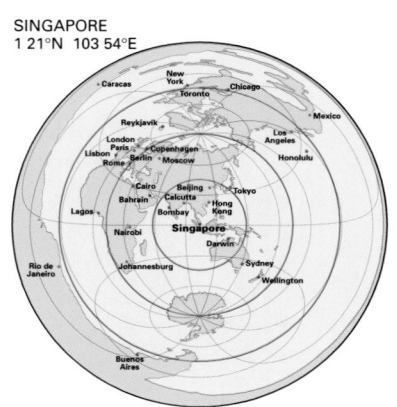

SINGAPORE
1 21°N 103 54°E

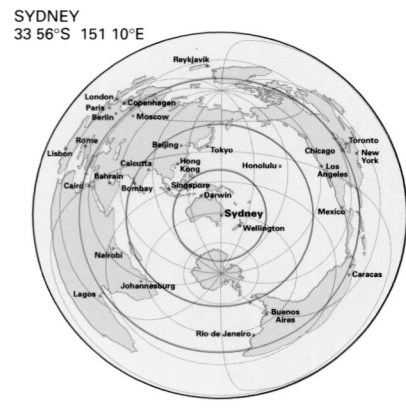

SYDNEY
33 56°S 151 10°E

# World Statistics: Climate

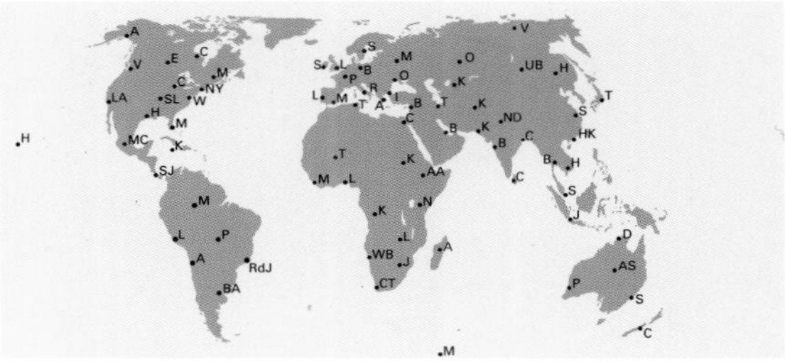

Rainfall and temperature figures are provided for more than 70 cities around the world. As climate is affected by altitude, the height of each city is shown in metres beneath its name. For each month, the figures in blue show the total rainfall or snow in millimetres, and in red the average temperature in degrees Celsius; the total annual rainfall and average annual temperature are at the end of the rows.

| EUROPE | Jan. | Feb. | Mar. | Apr. | May | June | July | Aug. | Sept. | Oct. | Nov. | Dec. | Year |
|---|---|---|---|---|---|---|---|---|---|---|---|---|---|
| **Athens, Greece** | 62 | 37 | 37 | 23 | 23 | 14 | 6 | 7 | 15 | 51 | 56 | 71 | 402 |
| 107 m | 10 | 10 | 12 | 16 | 20 | 25 | 28 | 28 | 24 | 20 | 15 | 11 | 18 |
| **Berlin, Germany** | 46 | 40 | 33 | 42 | 49 | 65 | 73 | 69 | 48 | 49 | 46 | 43 | 603 |
| 55 m | –1 | 0 | 4 | 9 | 14 | 17 | 19 | 18 | 15 | 9 | 5 | 1 | 9 |
| **Istanbul, Turkey** | 109 | 92 | 72 | 46 | 38 | 34 | 34 | 30 | 58 | 81 | 103 | 119 | 816 |
| 14 m | 5 | 6 | 7 | 11 | 16 | 20 | 23 | 23 | 20 | 16 | 12 | 8 | 14 |
| **Lisbon, Portugal** | 111 | 76 | 109 | 54 | 44 | 16 | 3 | 4 | 33 | 62 | 93 | 103 | 708 |
| 77 m | 11 | 12 | 14 | 16 | 17 | 20 | 22 | 23 | 21 | 18 | 14 | 12 | 17 |
| **London, UK** | 54 | 40 | 37 | 37 | 46 | 45 | 57 | 59 | 49 | 57 | 64 | 48 | 593 |
| 5 m | 4 | 5 | 7 | 9 | 12 | 16 | 18 | 17 | 15 | 11 | 8 | 5 | 11 |
| **Málaga, Spain** | 61 | 51 | 62 | 46 | 26 | 5 | 1 | 3 | 29 | 64 | 64 | 62 | 474 |
| 33 m | 12 | 13 | 16 | 17 | 19 | 29 | 25 | 26 | 23 | 20 | 16 | 13 | 18 |
| **Moscow, Russia** | 39 | 38 | 36 | 37 | 53 | 58 | 88 | 71 | 58 | 45 | 47 | 54 | 624 |
| 156 m | –13 | –10 | –4 | 6 | 13 | 16 | 18 | 17 | 12 | 6 | –1 | –7 | 4 |
| **Odesa, Ukraine** | 57 | 62 | 30 | 21 | 34 | 34 | 42 | 37 | 37 | 13 | 35 | 71 | 473 |
| 64 m | –3 | –1 | 2 | 9 | 15 | 20 | 22 | 22 | 18 | 12 | 9 | 1 | 10 |
| **Paris, France** | 56 | 46 | 35 | 42 | 57 | 54 | 59 | 64 | 55 | 50 | 51 | 50 | 619 |
| 75 m | 3 | 4 | 8 | 11 | 15 | 18 | 20 | 19 | 17 | 12 | 7 | 4 | 12 |
| **Rome, Italy** | 71 | 62 | 57 | 51 | 46 | 37 | 15 | 21 | 63 | 99 | 129 | 93 | 744 |
| 17 m | 8 | 9 | 11 | 14 | 18 | 22 | 25 | 25 | 22 | 17 | 13 | 10 | 16 |
| **Shannon, Irish Republic** | 94 | 67 | 56 | 53 | 61 | 57 | 77 | 79 | 86 | 86 | 96 | 117 | 929 |
| 2 m | 5 | 5 | 7 | 9 | 12 | 14 | 16 | 16 | 14 | 11 | 8 | 6 | 10 |
| **Stockholm, Sweden** | 43 | 30 | 25 | 31 | 34 | 45 | 61 | 76 | 60 | 48 | 53 | 48 | 554 |
| 44 m | –3 | –3 | –1 | 5 | 10 | 15 | 18 | 17 | 12 | 7 | 3 | 0 | 7 |
| **ASIA** | | | | | | | | | | | | | |
| **Bahrain** | 8 | 18 | 13 | 8 | <3 | 0 | 0 | 0 | 0 | 0 | 18 | 18 | 81 |
| 5 m | 17 | 18 | 21 | 25 | 29 | 32 | 33 | 34 | 31 | 28 | 24 | 19 | 26 |
| **Bangkok, Thailand** | 8 | 20 | 36 | 58 | 198 | 160 | 160 | 175 | 305 | 206 | 66 | 5 | 1,397 |
| 2 m | 26 | 28 | 29 | 30 | 29 | 29 | 28 | 28 | 28 | 28 | 26 | 25 | 28 |
| **Beirut, Lebanon** | 191 | 158 | 94 | 53 | 18 | 3 | <3 | <3 | 5 | 51 | 132 | 185 | 892 |
| 34 m | 14 | 14 | 16 | 18 | 22 | 24 | 27 | 28 | 26 | 24 | 19 | 16 | 21 |
| **Bombay, India** | 3 | 3 | 3 | <3 | 18 | 485 | 617 | 340 | 264 | 64 | 13 | 3 | 1,809 |
| 11 m | 24 | 24 | 26 | 28 | 30 | 29 | 27 | 27 | 27 | 28 | 27 | 26 | 27 |
| **Calcutta, India** | 10 | 31 | 36 | 43 | 140 | 297 | 325 | 328 | 252 | 114 | 20 | 5 | 1,600 |
| 6 m | 20 | 22 | 27 | 30 | 30 | 30 | 29 | 29 | 29 | 28 | 23 | 19 | 26 |
| **Colombo, Sri Lanka** | 89 | 69 | 147 | 231 | 371 | 224 | 135 | 109 | 160 | 348 | 315 | 147 | 2,365 |
| 7 m | 26 | 26 | 27 | 28 | 28 | 27 | 27 | 27 | 27 | 27 | 26 | 26 | 27 |
| **Harbin, China** | 6 | 5 | 10 | 23 | 43 | 94 | 112 | 104 | 46 | 33 | 8 | 5 | 488 |
| 160 m | –18 | –15 | –5 | 6 | 13 | 19 | 22 | 21 | 14 | 4 | –6 | –16 | 3 |
| **Ho Chi Minh, Vietnam** | 15 | 3 | 13 | 43 | 221 | 330 | 315 | 269 | 335 | 269 | 114 | 56 | 1,984 |
| 9 m | 26 | 27 | 29 | 30 | 29 | 28 | 28 | 28 | 27 | 27 | 27 | 26 | 28 |
| **Hong Kong, China** | 33 | 46 | 74 | 137 | 292 | 394 | 381 | 361 | 257 | 114 | 43 | 31 | 2,162 |
| 33 m | 16 | 15 | 18 | 22 | 26 | 28 | 28 | 28 | 27 | 25 | 21 | 18 | 23 |
| **Jakarta, Indonesia** | 300 | 300 | 211 | 147 | 114 | 97 | 64 | 43 | 66 | 112 | 142 | 203 | 1,798 |
| 8 m | 26 | 26 | 27 | 27 | 27 | 27 | 27 | 27 | 27 | 27 | 27 | 26 | 27 |
| **Kabul, Afghanistan** | 31 | 36 | 94 | 102 | 20 | 5 | 3 | 3 | <3 | 15 | 20 | 10 | 338 |
| 1,815 m | –3 | –1 | 6 | 13 | 18 | 22 | 25 | 24 | 20 | 14 | 7 | 3 | 12 |
| **Karachi, Pakistan** | 13 | 10 | 8 | 3 | 3 | 18 | 81 | 41 | 13 | <3 | 3 | 5 | 196 |
| 4 m | 19 | 20 | 24 | 28 | 30 | 31 | 30 | 29 | 28 | 28 | 24 | 20 | 26 |
| **Kazalinsk, Kazakstan** | 10 | 10 | 13 | 13 | 15 | 5 | 5 | 8 | 8 | 10 | 13 | 15 | 125 |
| 63 m | –12 | –11 | –3 | 6 | 18 | 23 | 25 | 23 | 16 | 8 | –1 | –7 | 7 |
| **New Delhi, India** | 23 | 18 | 13 | 8 | 13 | 74 | 180 | 172 | 117 | 10 | 3 | 10 | 640 |
| 218 m | 14 | 17 | 23 | 28 | 33 | 34 | 31 | 30 | 29 | 26 | 20 | 15 | 25 |
| **Omsk, Russia** | 15 | 8 | 8 | 13 | 31 | 51 | 51 | 51 | 28 | 25 | 18 | 20 | 318 |
| 85 m | –22 | –19 | –12 | –1 | 10 | 16 | 18 | 16 | 10 | 1 | –11 | –18 | –1 |
| **Shanghai, China** | 48 | 58 | 84 | 94 | 94 | 180 | 147 | 142 | 130 | 71 | 51 | 36 | 1,135 |
| 7 m | 4 | 5 | 9 | 14 | 20 | 24 | 28 | 28 | 23 | 19 | 12 | 7 | 16 |
| **Singapore** | 252 | 173 | 193 | 188 | 173 | 173 | 170 | 196 | 178 | 208 | 254 | 257 | 2,413 |
| 10 m | 26 | 27 | 28 | 28 | 28 | 28 | 28 | 27 | 27 | 27 | 27 | 27 | 27 |
| **Tehran, Iran** | 46 | 38 | 46 | 36 | 13 | 3 | 3 | 3 | 3 | 8 | 20 | 31 | 246 |
| 1,220 m | 2 | 5 | 9 | 16 | 21 | 26 | 30 | 29 | 25 | 18 | 12 | 6 | 17 |
| **Tokyo, Japan** | 48 | 74 | 107 | 135 | 147 | 165 | 142 | 152 | 234 | 208 | 97 | 56 | 1,565 |
| 6 m | 3 | 4 | 7 | 13 | 17 | 21 | 25 | 26 | 23 | 17 | 11 | 6 | 14 |
| **Ulan Bator, Mongolia** | <3 | <3 | 3 | 5 | 10 | 28 | 76 | 51 | 23 | 5 | 5 | 3 | 208 |
| 1,325 m | –26 | –21 | –13 | –1 | 6 | 14 | 16 | 14 | 8 | –1 | –13 | –22 | –3 |
| **Verkhoyansk, Russia** | 5 | 5 | 3 | 5 | 8 | 23 | 28 | 25 | 13 | 8 | 8 | 5 | 134 |
| 100 m | –50 | –45 | –32 | –15 | 0 | 12 | 14 | 9 | 2 | –15 | –38 | –48 | –17 |
| **AFRICA** | | | | | | | | | | | | | |
| **Addis Ababa, Ethiopia** | <3 | 3 | 25 | 135 | 213 | 201 | 206 | 239 | 102 | 28 | <3 | 0 | 1,151 |
| 2,450 m | 19 | 20 | 20 | 20 | 19 | 18 | 18 | 19 | 21 | 22 | 21 | 20 | 20 |
| **Antananarivo, Madagas.** | 300 | 279 | 178 | 53 | 18 | 8 | 8 | 10 | 18 | 61 | 135 | 287 | 1,356 |
| 1,372 m | 21 | 21 | 21 | 19 | 18 | 15 | 14 | 15 | 17 | 19 | 21 | 21 | 19 |
| **Cairo, Egypt** | 5 | 5 | 5 | 3 | 3 | <3 | 0 | 0 | <3 | <3 | 3 | 5 | 28 |
| 116 m | 13 | 15 | 18 | 21 | 25 | 28 | 28 | 28 | 26 | 24 | 20 | 15 | 22 |
| **Cape Town, South Africa** | 15 | 8 | 18 | 48 | 79 | 84 | 89 | 66 | 43 | 31 | 18 | 10 | 508 |
| 17 m | 21 | 21 | 20 | 17 | 14 | 13 | 12 | 13 | 14 | 16 | 18 | 19 | 17 |
| **Johannesburg, S. Africa** | 114 | 109 | 89 | 38 | 25 | 8 | 8 | 8 | 23 | 56 | 107 | 125 | 709 |
| 1,665 m | 20 | 20 | 18 | 16 | 13 | 10 | 11 | 13 | 16 | 18 | 19 | 20 | 16 |
| **Khartoum, Sudan** | <3 | <3 | <3 | <3 | 3 | 8 | 53 | 71 | 18 | 5 | <3 | 0 | 158 |
| 390 m | 24 | 25 | 28 | 31 | 33 | 34 | 32 | 31 | 32 | 32 | 28 | 25 | 29 |
| **Kinshasa, Congo (D.R.)** | 135 | 145 | 196 | 196 | 158 | 8 | 3 | 3 | 31 | 119 | 221 | 142 | 1,354 |
| 325 m | 26 | 26 | 27 | 27 | 26 | 24 | 23 | 24 | 25 | 26 | 26 | 26 | 25 |
| **Lagos, Nigeria** | 28 | 46 | 102 | 150 | 269 | 460 | 279 | 64 | 140 | 206 | 69 | 25 | 1,836 |
| 3 m | 27 | 28 | 29 | 28 | 28 | 26 | 26 | 25 | 26 | 26 | 28 | 28 | 27 |
| **Lusaka, Zambia** | 231 | 191 | 142 | 18 | 3 | <3 | <3 | 0 | <3 | 10 | 91 | 150 | 836 |
| 1,277 m | 21 | 22 | 21 | 21 | 19 | 16 | 16 | 18 | 22 | 24 | 23 | 22 | 21 |
| **Monrovia, Liberia** | 31 | 56 | 97 | 216 | 516 | 973 | 996 | 373 | 744 | 772 | 236 | 130 | 5,138 |
| 23 m | 26 | 26 | 27 | 27 | 26 | 25 | 24 | 25 | 25 | 25 | 26 | 26 | 26 |
| **Nairobi, Kenya** | 38 | 64 | 125 | 211 | 158 | 46 | 15 | 23 | 31 | 53 | 109 | 86 | 958 |
| 1,820 m | 19 | 19 | 19 | 19 | 18 | 16 | 16 | 16 | 18 | 19 | 18 | 18 | 18 |
| **Timbuktu, Mali** | <3 | <3 | 3 | <3 | 5 | 23 | 79 | 81 | 38 | 3 | <3 | <3 | 231 |
| 301 m | 22 | 24 | 28 | 32 | 34 | 35 | 32 | 30 | 32 | 31 | 28 | 23 | 29 |
| **Tunis, Tunisia** | 64 | 51 | 41 | 36 | 18 | 8 | 3 | 8 | 33 | 51 | 48 | 61 | 419 |
| 66 m | 10 | 11 | 13 | 16 | 19 | 23 | 26 | 27 | 25 | 20 | 16 | 11 | 18 |
| **Walvis Bay, Namibia** | <3 | 5 | 8 | 3 | 3 | <3 | <3 | 3 | <3 | <3 | <3 | <3 | 23 |
| 7 m | 19 | 19 | 19 | 18 | 17 | 16 | 15 | 14 | 14 | 15 | 17 | 18 | 18 |
| **AUSTRALIA, NEW ZEALAND AND ANTARCTICA** | | | | | | | | | | | | | |
| **Alice Springs, Australia** | 43 | 33 | 28 | 10 | 15 | 13 | 8 | 8 | 8 | 18 | 31 | 38 | 252 |
| 579 m | 29 | 28 | 25 | 20 | 15 | 12 | 12 | 14 | 18 | 23 | 26 | 28 | 21 |
| **Christchurch, N. Zealand** | 56 | 43 | 48 | 48 | 66 | 66 | 69 | 48 | 46 | 43 | 48 | 56 | 638 |
| 10 m | 16 | 16 | 14 | 12 | 9 | 6 | 6 | 7 | 9 | 12 | 14 | 16 | 11 |
| **Darwin, Australia** | 386 | 312 | 254 | 97 | 15 | 3 | <3 | 3 | 13 | 51 | 119 | 239 | 1,491 |
| 30 m | 29 | 29 | 29 | 29 | 28 | 26 | 25 | 26 | 28 | 29 | 30 | 29 | 28 |
| **Mawson, Antarctica** | 11 | 30 | 20 | 10 | 44 | 180 | 4 | 40 | 3 | 20 | 0 | 0 | 362 |
| 14 m | 0 | –5 | –10 | –14 | –15 | –16 | –18 | –18 | –19 | –13 | –5 | –1 | –11 |
| **Perth, Australia** | 8 | 10 | 20 | 43 | 130 | 180 | 170 | 149 | 86 | 56 | 20 | 13 | 881 |
| 60 m | 23 | 23 | 22 | 19 | 16 | 14 | 13 | 13 | 15 | 16 | 19 | 22 | 18 |
| **Sydney, Australia** | 89 | 102 | 127 | 135 | 127 | 117 | 117 | 76 | 73 | 71 | 73 | 73 | 1,181 |
| 42 m | 22 | 22 | 21 | 18 | 15 | 13 | 12 | 13 | 15 | 18 | 19 | 21 | 17 |
| **NORTH AMERICA** | | | | | | | | | | | | | |
| **Anchorage, Alaska, USA** | 20 | 18 | 15 | 10 | 13 | 18 | 41 | 66 | 66 | 56 | 25 | 23 | 371 |
| 40 m | –11 | –8 | –5 | 2 | 7 | 12 | 14 | 13 | 9 | 2 | –5 | –11 | 2 |
| **Chicago, Illinois, USA** | 51 | 51 | 66 | 71 | 86 | 89 | 84 | 81 | 79 | 66 | 61 | 51 | 836 |
| 251 m | –4 | –3 | 2 | 9 | 14 | 20 | 23 | 22 | 19 | 12 | 5 | –1 | 10 |
| **Churchill, Man., Canada** | 15 | 13 | 18 | 23 | 32 | 44 | 46 | 58 | 51 | 43 | 39 | 21 | 402 |
| 13 m | –28 | –26 | –20 | –10 | –2 | 6 | 12 | 11 | 5 | –2 | –12 | –22 | –7 |
| **Edmonton, Alta., Canada** | 25 | 19 | 19 | 22 | 43 | 77 | 89 | 78 | 39 | 17 | 16 | 25 | 466 |
| 676 m | –15 | –10 | –5 | 4 | 11 | 15 | 17 | 16 | 11 | 6 | –4 | –10 | 3 |
| **Honolulu, Hawaii, USA** | 104 | 66 | 79 | 48 | 25 | 18 | 23 | 28 | 36 | 48 | 64 | 104 | 643 |
| 12 m | 23 | 18 | 19 | 20 | 22 | 24 | 25 | 26 | 26 | 24 | 22 | 19 | 22 |
| **Houston, Texas, USA** | 89 | 76 | 84 | 91 | 119 | 117 | 99 | 99 | 104 | 94 | 89 | 109 | 1,171 |
| 12 m | 12 | 13 | 17 | 21 | 24 | 27 | 28 | 29 | 26 | 22 | 16 | 12 | 21 |
| **Kingston, Jamaica** | 23 | 15 | 23 | 31 | 102 | 89 | 38 | 91 | 99 | 180 | 74 | 36 | 800 |
| 34 m | 25 | 25 | 25 | 26 | 26 | 28 | 28 | 28 | 27 | 27 | 26 | 26 | 26 |
| **Los Angeles, Calif., USA** | 79 | 76 | 71 | 25 | 10 | 3 | <3 | <3 | 5 | 15 | 31 | 66 | 381 |
| 95 m | 13 | 14 | 14 | 16 | 17 | 19 | 21 | 22 | 21 | 18 | 16 | 14 | 17 |
| **Mexico City, Mexico** | 13 | 5 | 10 | 20 | 53 | 119 | 170 | 152 | 130 | 51 | 18 | 8 | 747 |
| 2,309 m | 12 | 13 | 16 | 18 | 19 | 19 | 17 | 18 | 18 | 16 | 14 | 13 | 16 |
| **Miami, Florida, USA** | 71 | 53 | 64 | 81 | 173 | 178 | 155 | 160 | 203 | 234 | 71 | 51 | 1,516 |
| 8 m | 20 | 20 | 22 | 23 | 25 | 27 | 28 | 28 | 27 | 25 | 22 | 21 | 24 |
| **Montréal, Que., Canada** | 72 | 65 | 74 | 74 | 66 | 82 | 90 | 92 | 88 | 76 | 81 | 87 | 946 |
| 57 m | –10 | –9 | –3 | –6 | 13 | 18 | 21 | 20 | 15 | 9 | 2 | –7 | 6 |
| **New York City, N.Y., USA** | 94 | 97 | 91 | 81 | 81 | 84 | 107 | 109 | 86 | 89 | 76 | 91 | 1,092 |
| 96 m | –1 | –1 | 3 | 10 | 16 | 20 | 23 | 23 | 21 | 15 | 7 | 2 | 11 |
| **St Louis, Mo., USA** | 58 | 64 | 89 | 97 | 114 | 114 | 89 | 86 | 81 | 74 | 71 | 64 | 1,001 |
| 173 m | 0 | 1 | 7 | 13 | 19 | 24 | 26 | 26 | 22 | 15 | 8 | 2 | 14 |
| **San José, Costa Rica** | 15 | 5 | 20 | 46 | 229 | 241 | 211 | 241 | 305 | 300 | 145 | 41 | 1,798 |
| 1,146 m | 19 | 19 | 21 | 21 | 22 | 21 | 21 | 21 | 21 | 20 | 20 | 19 | 20 |
| **Vancouver, B.C., Canada** | 154 | 115 | 101 | 60 | 52 | 45 | 32 | 41 | 67 | 114 | 150 | 182 | 1,113 |
| 14 m | 3 | 5 | 6 | 9 | 12 | 15 | 17 | 17 | 14 | 10 | 6 | 4 | 10 |
| **Washington, D.C., USA** | 86 | 76 | 91 | 84 | 94 | 99 | 112 | 109 | 94 | 74 | 66 | 79 | 1,064 |
| 22 m | 1 | 2 | 7 | 12 | 18 | 23 | 25 | 24 | 20 | 14 | 8 | 3 | 13 |
| **SOUTH AMERICA** | | | | | | | | | | | | | |
| **Antofagasta, Chile** | 0 | 0 | 0 | <3 | <3 | 3 | 5 | 3 | <3 | 3 | <3 | 0 | 13 |
| 94 m | 21 | 21 | 20 | 18 | 16 | 15 | 14 | 14 | 15 | 16 | 18 | 19 | 17 |
| **Buenos Aires, Argentina** | 79 | 71 | 109 | 89 | 76 | 61 | 56 | 61 | 79 | 86 | 84 | 99 | 950 |
| 27 m | 23 | 23 | 21 | 17 | 13 | 9 | 10 | 11 | 13 | 15 | 19 | 22 | 16 |
| **Lima, Peru** | 3 | <3 | <3 | <3 | 5 | 5 | 8 | 8 | 8 | 3 | 3 | <3 | 41 |
| 120 m | 23 | 24 | 24 | 22 | 19 | 17 | 17 | 16 | 17 | 18 | 19 | 21 | 20 |
| **Manaus, Brazil** | 249 | 231 | 262 | 221 | 170 | 84 | 58 | 38 | 46 | 107 | 142 | 203 | 1,811 |
| 44 m | 28 | 28 | 28 | 27 | 28 | 28 | 28 | 28 | 29 | 29 | 29 | 28 | 28 |
| **Paraná, Brazil** | 287 | 236 | 239 | 102 | 13 | <3 | 3 | 5 | 28 | 127 | 231 | 310 | 1,582 |
| 260 m | 23 | 23 | 23 | 23 | 23 | 21 | 21 | 22 | 24 | 24 | 24 | 23 | 23 |
| **Rio de Janeiro, Brazil** | 125 | 122 | 130 | 107 | 79 | 53 | 41 | 43 | 66 | 79 | 104 | 137 | 1,082 |
| 61 m | 26 | 26 | 25 | 24 | 22 | 21 | 21 | 21 | 21 | 22 | 23 | 25 | 23 |

# World Statistics: Physical Dimensions

Each topic list is divided into continents and within a continent the items are listed in order of size. The order of the continents is as in the atlas, Europe through to South America. The lists down to this mark > are complete; below they are selective. The world top ten are shown in square brackets; in the case of mountains this has not been done because the world top 30 are all in Asia. The figures are rounded as appropriate.

## WORLD, CONTINENTS, OCEANS

| THE WORLD | km² | miles² | % |
|---|---|---|---|
| The World | 509,450,000 | 196,672,000 | – |
| Land | 149,450,000 | 57,688,000 | 29.3 |
| Water | 360,000,000 | 138,984,000 | 70.7 |
| | | | |
| Asia | 44,500,000 | 17,177,000 | 29.8 |
| Africa | 30,302,000 | 11,697,000 | 20.3 |
| North America | 24,241,000 | 9,357,000 | 16.2 |
| South America | 17,793,000 | 6,868,000 | 11.9 |
| Antarctica | 14,100,000 | 5,443,000 | 9.4 |
| Europe | 9,957,000 | 3,843,000 | 6.7 |
| Australia & Oceania | 8,557,000 | 3,303,000 | 5.7 |
| | | | |
| Pacific Ocean | 179,679,000 | 69,356,000 | 49.9 |
| Atlantic Ocean | 92,373,000 | 35,657,000 | 25.7 |
| Indian Ocean | 73,917,000 | 28,532,000 | 20.5 |
| Arctic Ocean | 14,090,000 | 5,439,000 | 3.9 |

## SEAS

| PACIFIC | km² | miles² |
|---|---|---|
| South China Sea | 2,974,600 | 1,148,500 |
| Bering Sea | 2,268,000 | 875,000 |
| Sea of Okhotsk | 1,528,000 | 590,000 |
| East China & Yellow | 1,249,000 | 482,000 |
| Sea of Japan | 1,008,000 | 389,000 |
| Gulf of California | 162,000 | 62,500 |
| Bass Strait | 75,000 | 29,000 |

| ATLANTIC | km² | miles² |
|---|---|---|
| Caribbean Sea | 2,766,000 | 1,068,000 |
| Mediterranean Sea | 2,516,000 | 971,000 |
| Gulf of Mexico | 1,543,000 | 596,000 |
| Hudson Bay | 1,232,000 | 476,000 |
| North Sea | 575,000 | 223,000 |
| Black Sea | 462,000 | 178,000 |
| Baltic Sea | 422,170 | 163,000 |
| Gulf of St Lawrence | 238,000 | 92,000 |

| INDIAN | km² | miles² |
|---|---|---|
| Red Sea | 438,000 | 169,000 |
| The Gulf | 239,000 | 92,000 |

## MOUNTAINS

| EUROPE | | m | ft |
|---|---|---|---|
| Elbrus | Russia | 5,642 | 18,510 |
| Mont Blanc | France/Italy | 4,807 | 15,771 |
| Monte Rosa | Italy/Switzerland | 4,634 | 15,203 |
| Dom | Switzerland | 4,545 | 14,911 |
| Liskamm | Switzerland | 4,527 | 14,852 |
| Weisshorn | Switzerland | 4,505 | 14,780 |
| Taschorn | Switzerland | 4,490 | 14,730 |
| Matterhorn/Cervino | Italy/Switz. | 4,478 | 14,691 |
| Mont Maudit | France/Italy | 4,465 | 14,649 |
| Dent Blanche | Switzerland | 4,356 | 14,291 |
| Nadelhorn | Switzerland | 4,327 | 14,196 |
| > Grandes Jorasses | France/Italy | 4,208 | 13,806 |
| Jungfrau | Switzerland | 4,158 | 13,642 |
| Barre des Ecrins | France | 4,103 | 13,461 |
| Gran Paradiso | Italy | 4,061 | 13,323 |
| Piz Bernina | Italy/Switzerland | 4,049 | 13,284 |
| Eiger | Switzerland | 3,970 | 13,025 |
| Monte Viso | Italy | 3,841 | 12,602 |
| Grossglockner | Austria | 3,797 | 12,457 |
| Wildspitze | Austria | 3,772 | 12,382 |
| Monte Disgrazia | Italy | 3,678 | 12,066 |
| Mulhacén | Spain | 3,478 | 11,411 |
| Pico de Aneto | Spain | 3,404 | 11,168 |
| Marmolada | Italy | 3,342 | 10,964 |
| Etna | Italy | 3,340 | 10,958 |
| Zugspitze | Germany | 2,962 | 9,718 |
| Musala | Bulgaria | 2,925 | 9,596 |
| Olympus | Greece | 2,917 | 9,570 |
| Triglav | Slovenia | 2,863 | 9,393 |
| Monte Cinto | France (Corsica) | 2,710 | 8,891 |
| Gerlachovka | Slovak Republic | 2,655 | 8,711 |
| Ben Nevis | UK | 1,343 | 4,406 |

| ASIA | | m | ft |
|---|---|---|---|
| Everest | China/Nepal | 8,850 | 29,035 |
| K2 (Godwin Austen) | China/Kashmir | 8,611 | 28,251 |
| Kanchenjunga | India/Nepal | 8,598 | 28,208 |
| Lhotse | China/Nepal | 8,516 | 27,939 |
| Makalu | China/Nepal | 8,481 | 27,824 |
| Cho Oyu | China/Nepal | 8,201 | 26,906 |
| Dhaulagiri | Nepal | 8,172 | 26,811 |
| Manaslu | Nepal | 8,156 | 26,758 |
| Nanga Parbat | Kashmir | 8,126 | 26,660 |
| Annapurna | Nepal | 8,078 | 26,502 |
| Gasherbrum | China/Kashmir | 8,068 | 26,469 |
| Broad Peak | China/Kashmir | 8,051 | 26,414 |
| Xixabangma | China | 8,012 | 26,286 |
| Kangbachen | India/Nepal | 7,902 | 25,925 |
| Jannu | India/Nepal | 7,902 | 25,925 |
| Gayachung Kang | Nepal | 7,897 | 25,909 |
| Himalchuli | Nepal | 7,893 | 25,896 |
| Disteghil Sar | Kashmir | 7,885 | 25,869 |
| Nuptse | Nepal | 7,879 | 25,849 |
| Khunyang Chhish | Kashmir | 7,852 | 25,761 |
| Masherbrum | Kashmir | 7,821 | 25,659 |
| Nanda Devi | India | 7,817 | 25,646 |
| Rakaposhi | Kashmir | 7,788 | 25,551 |
| Batura | Kashmir | 7,785 | 25,541 |
| Namche Barwa | China | 7,756 | 25,446 |
| Kamet | India | 7,756 | 25,446 |
| Soltoro Kangri | Kashmir | 7,742 | 25,400 |
| Gurla Mandhata | China | 7,728 | 25,354 |
| Trivor | Pakistan | 7,720 | 25,328 |
| > Kongur Shan | China | 7,719 | 25,324 |
| Tirich Mir | Pakistan | 7,690 | 25,229 |
| K'ula Shan | Bhutan/China | 7,543 | 24,747 |
| Pik Kommunizma | Tajikistan | 7,495 | 24,590 |
| Demavend | Iran | 5,604 | 18,386 |
| Ararat | Turkey | 5,165 | 16,945 |
| Gunong Kinabalu | Malaysia (Borneo) | 4,101 | 13,455 |
| Yu Shan | Taiwan | 3,997 | 13,113 |
| Fuji-San | Japan | 3,776 | 12,388 |

| AFRICA | | m | ft |
|---|---|---|---|
| Kilimanjaro | Tanzania | 5,895 | 19,340 |
| Mt Kenya | Kenya | 5,199 | 17,057 |
| Ruwenzori | | | |
| (Margherita) | Uganda/Congo (D.R.) | 5,109 | 16,762 |
| Ras Dashan | Ethiopia | 4,620 | 15,157 |
| Meru | Tanzania | 4,565 | 14,977 |
| Karisimbi | Rwanda/Congo (D.R.) | 4,507 | 14,787 |
| Mt Elgon | Kenya/Uganda | 4,321 | 14,176 |
| Batu | Ethiopia | 4,307 | 14,130 |
| Guna | Ethiopia | 4,231 | 13,882 |
| Toubkal | Morocco | 4,165 | 13,665 |
| Irhil Mgoun | Morocco | 4,071 | 13,356 |
| Mt Cameroon | Cameroon | 4,070 | 13,353 |
| Amba Ferit | Ethiopia | 3,875 | 13,042 |
| Pico del Teide | Spain (Tenerife) | 3,718 | 12,198 |
| Thabana Ntlenyana | Lesotho | 3,482 | 11,424 |
| Emi Koussi | Chad | 3,415 | 11,204 |
| > Mt aux Sources | Lesotho/S. Africa | 3,282 | 10,768 |
| Mt Piton | Réunion | 3,069 | 10,069 |

| OCEANIA | | m | ft |
|---|---|---|---|
| Puncak Jaya | Indonesia | 5,029 | 16,499 |
| Puncak Trikora | Indonesia | 4,750 | 15,584 |
| Puncak Mandala | Indonesia | 4,702 | 15,427 |
| Mt Wilhelm | Papua NG | 4,508 | 14,790 |
| > Mauna Kea | USA (Hawaii) | 4,205 | 13,796 |
| Mauna Loa | USA (Hawaii) | 4,169 | 13,681 |
| Mt Cook (Aoraki) | New Zealand | 3,753 | 12,313 |
| Mt Balbi | Solomon Is. | 2,439 | 8,002 |
| Orohena | Tahiti | 2,241 | 7,352 |
| Mt Kosciuszko | Australia | 2,237 | 7,339 |

| NORTH AMERICA | | m | ft |
|---|---|---|---|
| Mt McKinley | | | |
| (Denali) | USA (Alaska) | 6,194 | 20,321 |
| Mt Logan | Canada | 5,959 | 19,551 |
| Citlaltepetl | Mexico | 5,700 | 18,701 |
| Mt St Elias | USA/Canada | 5,489 | 18,008 |
| Popocatepetl | Mexico | 5,452 | 17,887 |

| NORTH AMERICA (continued) | | m | ft |
|---|---|---|---|
| Mt Foraker | USA (Alaska) | 5,304 | 17,401 |
| Ixtaccihuatl | Mexico | 5,286 | 17,342 |
| Lucania | Canada | 5,227 | 17,149 |
| Mt Steele | Canada | 5,073 | 16,644 |
| Mt Bona | USA (Alaska) | 5,005 | 16,420 |
| Mt Blackburn | USA (Alaska) | 4,996 | 16,391 |
| Mt Sanford | USA (Alaska) | 4,940 | 16,207 |
| Mt Wood | Canada | 4,848 | 15,905 |
| Nevado de Toluca | Mexico | 4,670 | 15,321 |
| Mt Fairweather | USA (Alaska) | 4,663 | 15,298 |
| Mt Hunter | USA (Alaska) | 4,442 | 14,573 |
| Mt Whitney | USA | 4,418 | 14,495 |
| Mt Elbert | USA | 4,399 | 14,432 |
| Mt Harvard | USA | 4,395 | 14,419 |
| Mt Rainier | USA | 4,392 | 14,409 |
| > Blanca Peak | USA | 4,372 | 14,344 |
| Longs Peak | USA | 4,345 | 14,255 |
| Tajumulco | Guatemala | 4,220 | 13,845 |
| Grand Teton | USA | 4,197 | 13,770 |
| Mt Waddington | Canada | 3,994 | 13,104 |
| Mt Robson | Canada | 3,954 | 12,972 |
| Chirripó Grande | Costa Rica | 3,837 | 12,589 |
| Pico Duarte | Dominican Rep. | 3,175 | 10,417 |

| SOUTH AMERICA | | m | ft |
|---|---|---|---|
| Aconcagua | Argentina | 6,960 | 22,834 |
| Bonete | Argentina | 6,872 | 22,546 |
| Ojos del Salado | Argentina/Chile | 6,863 | 22,516 |
| Pissis | Argentina | 6,779 | 22,241 |
| Mercedario | Argentina/Chile | 6,770 | 22,211 |
| Huascaran | Peru | 6,768 | 22,204 |
| Llullaillaco | Argentina/Chile | 6,723 | 22,057 |
| Nudo de Cachi | Argentina | 6,720 | 22,047 |
| Yerupaja | Peru | 6,632 | 21,758 |
| N. de Tres Cruces | Argentina/Chile | 6,620 | 21,719 |
| Incahuasi | Argentina/Chile | 6,601 | 21,654 |
| Cerro Galan | Argentina | 6,600 | 21,654 |
| Tupungato | Argentina/Chile | 6,570 | 21,555 |
| > Sajama | Bolivia | 6,542 | 21,463 |
| Illimani | Bolivia | 6,485 | 21,276 |
| Coropuna | Peru | 6,425 | 21,079 |
| Ausangate | Peru | 6,384 | 20,945 |
| Cerro del Toro | Argentina | 6,380 | 20,932 |
| Siula Grande | Peru | 6,356 | 20,853 |
| Chimborazo | Ecuador | 6,267 | 20,561 |
| Alpamayo | Peru | 5,947 | 19,511 |
| Cotapaxi | Ecuador | 5,896 | 19,344 |
| Pico Colon | Colombia | 5,800 | 19,029 |
| Pico Bolivar | Venezuela | 5,007 | 16,427 |

| ANTARCTICA | | m | ft |
|---|---|---|---|
| Vinson Massif | | 4,897 | 16,066 |
| Mt Kirkpatrick | | 4,528 | 14,855 |
| Mt Markham | | 4,349 | 14,268 |

## OCEAN DEPTHS

| ATLANTIC OCEAN | m | ft | |
|---|---|---|---|
| Puerto Rico (Milwaukee) Deep | 9,220 | 30,249 | [7] |
| Cayman Trench | 7,680 | 25,197 | [10] |
| Gulf of Mexico | 5,203 | 17,070 | |
| Mediterranean Sea | 5,121 | 16,801 | |
| Black Sea | 2,211 | 7,254 | |
| North Sea | 660 | 2,165 | |
| Baltic Sea | 463 | 1,519 | |
| Hudson Bay | 258 | 846 | |

| INDIAN OCEAN | m | ft |
|---|---|---|
| Java Trench | 7,450 | 24,442 |
| Red Sea | 2,635 | 8,454 |
| Persian Gulf | 73 | 239 |

| PACIFIC OCEAN | m | ft | |
|---|---|---|---|
| Mariana Trench | 11,022 | 36,161 | [1] |
| Tonga Trench | 10,882 | 35,702 | [2] |
| Japan Trench | 10,554 | 34,626 | [3] |
| Kuril Trench | 10,542 | 34,587 | [4] |
| Mindanao Trench | 10,497 | 34,439 | [5] |
| Kermadec Trench | 10,047 | 32,962 | [6] |

## PACIFIC OCEAN (continued)

| | m | ft | |
|---|---|---|---|
| Peru–Chile Trench | 8,050 | 26,410 | [8] |
| Aleutian Trench | 7,822 | 25,662 | [9] |

## ARCTIC OCEAN

| | m | ft |
|---|---|---|
| Molloy Deep | 5,608 | 18,399 |

## LAND LOWS

| | | m | ft |
|---|---|---|---|
| Dead Sea | Asia | −403 | −1,322 |
| Lake Assal | Africa | −156 | −512 |
| Death Valley | N. America | −86 | −282 |
| Valdés Peninsula | S. America | −40 | −131 |
| Caspian Sea | Europe | −28 | −92 |
| Lake Eyre North | Oceania | −16 | −52 |

## RIVERS

### EUROPE

| | | km | miles | |
|---|---|---|---|---|
| Volga | Caspian Sea | 3,700 | 2,300 | |
| Danube | Black Sea | 2,850 | 1,770 | |
| Ural | Caspian Sea | 2,535 | 1,575 | |
| Dnepr (Dnipro) | Black Sea | 2,285 | 1,420 | |
| Kama | Volga | 2,030 | 1,260 | |
| Don | Black Sea | 1,990 | 1,240 | |
| Petchora | Arctic Ocean | 1,790 | 1,110 | |
| Oka | Volga | 1,480 | 920 | |
| Belaya | Kama | 1,420 | 880 | |
| Dnister (Dniester) | Black Sea | 1,400 | 870 | |
| Vyatka | Kama | 1,370 | 850 | |
| Rhine | North Sea | 1,320 | 820 | |
| N. Dvina | Arctic Ocean | 1,290 | 800 | |
| Desna | Dnepr (Dnipro) | 1,190 | 740 | |
| Elbe | North Sea | 1,145 | 710 | |
| Wisla | Baltic Sea | 1,090 | 675 | |
| Loire | Atlantic Ocean | 1,020 | 635 | |

### ASIA

| | | km | miles | |
|---|---|---|---|---|
| Yangtze | Pacific Ocean | 6,380 | 3,960 | [3] |
| Yenisey–Angara | Arctic Ocean | 5,550 | 3,445 | [5] |
| Huang He | Pacific Ocean | 5,464 | 3,395 | [6] |
| Ob–Irtysh | Arctic Ocean | 5,410 | 3,360 | [7] |
| Mekong | Pacific Ocean | 4,500 | 2,795 | [9] |
| Amur | Pacific Ocean | 4,400 | 2,730 | [10] |
| Lena | Arctic Ocean | 4,400 | 2,730 | |
| Irtysh | Ob | 4,250 | 2,640 | |
| Yenisey | Arctic Ocean | 4,090 | 2,540 | |
| Ob | Arctic Ocean | 3,680 | 2,285 | |
| Indus | Indian Ocean | 3,100 | 1,925 | |
| Brahmaputra | Indian Ocean | 2,900 | 1,800 | |
| Syrdarya | Aral Sea | 2,860 | 1,775 | |
| Salween | Indian Ocean | 2,800 | 1,740 | |
| Euphrates | Indian Ocean | 2,700 | 1,675 | |
| Vilyuy | Lena | 2,650 | 1,645 | |
| Kolyma | Arctic Ocean | 2,600 | 1,615 | |
| Amudarya | Aral Sea | 2,540 | 1,575 | |
| Ural | Caspian Sea | 2,535 | 1,575 | |
| Ganges | Indian Ocean | 2,510 | 1,560 | |
| Si Kiang | Pacific Ocean | 2,100 | 1,305 | |
| Irrawaddy | Indian Ocean | 2,010 | 1,250 | |
| Tarim–Yarkand | Lop Nor | 2,000 | 1,240 | |
| Tigris | Indian Ocean | 1,900 | 1,180 | |

### AFRICA

| | | km | miles | |
|---|---|---|---|---|
| Nile | Mediterranean | 6,670 | 4,140 | [1] |
| Congo | Atlantic Ocean | 4,670 | 2,900 | [8] |
| Niger | Atlantic Ocean | 4,180 | 2,595 | |
| Zambezi | Indian Ocean | 3,540 | 2,200 | |
| Oubangi/Uele | Congo (D.R.) | 2,250 | 1,400 | |
| Kasai | Congo (D.R.) | 1,950 | 1,210 | |
| Shaballe | Indian Ocean | 1,930 | 1,200 | |
| Orange | Atlantic Ocean | 1,860 | 1,155 | |
| Cubango | Okavango Swamps | 1,800 | 1,120 | |
| Limpopo | Indian Ocean | 1,600 | 995 | |
| Senegal | Atlantic Ocean | 1,600 | 995 | |
| Volta | Atlantic Ocean | 1,500 | 930 | |

### AUSTRALIA

| | | km | miles |
|---|---|---|---|
| Murray–Darling | Indian Ocean | 3,750 | 2,330 |
| Darling | Murray | 3,070 | 1,905 |
| Murray | Indian Ocean | 2,575 | 1,600 |
| Murrumbidgee | Murray | 1,690 | 1,050 |

### NORTH AMERICA

| | | km | miles | |
|---|---|---|---|---|
| Mississippi–Missouri | Gulf of Mexico | 6,020 | 3,740 | [4] |
| Mackenzie | Arctic Ocean | 4,240 | 2,630 | |
| Mississippi | Gulf of Mexico | 3,780 | 2,350 | |
| Missouri | Mississippi | 3,780 | 2,350 | |
| Yukon | Pacific Ocean | 3,185 | 1,980 | |
| Rio Grande | Gulf of Mexico | 3,030 | 1,880 | |

### NORTH AMERICA (continued)

| | | km | miles |
|---|---|---|---|
| Arkansas | Mississippi | 2,340 | 1,450 |
| Colorado | Pacific Ocean | 2,330 | 1,445 |
| Red | Mississippi | 2,040 | 1,270 |
| Columbia | Pacific Ocean | 1,950 | 1,210 |
| Saskatchewan | Lake Winnipeg | 1,940 | 1,205 |
| Snake | Columbia | 1,670 | 1,040 |
| Churchill | Hudson Bay | 1,600 | 990 |
| Ohio | Mississippi | 1,580 | 980 |
| Brazos | Gulf of Mexico | 1,400 | 870 |
| St Lawrence | Atlantic Ocean | 1,170 | 730 |

### SOUTH AMERICA

| | | km | miles | |
|---|---|---|---|---|
| Amazon | Atlantic Ocean | 6,450 | 4,010 | [2] |
| Paraná–Plate | Atlantic Ocean | 4,500 | 2,800 | |
| Purus | Amazon | 3,350 | 2,080 | |
| Madeira | Amazon | 3,200 | 1,990 | |
| São Francisco | Atlantic Ocean | 2,900 | 1,800 | |
| Paraná | Plate | 2,800 | 1,740 | |
| Tocantins | Atlantic Ocean | 2,750 | 1,710 | |
| Paraguay | Paraná | 2,550 | 1,580 | |
| Orinoco | Atlantic Ocean | 2,500 | 1,550 | |
| Pilcomayo | Paraná | 2,500 | 1,550 | |
| Araguaia | Tocantins | 2,250 | 1,400 | |
| Juruá | Amazon | 2,000 | 1,240 | |
| Xingu | Amazon | 1,980 | 1,230 | |
| Ucayali | Amazon | 1,900 | 1,180 | |
| Marañón | Amazon | 1,600 | 990 | |
| Uruguay | Plate | 1,600 | 990 | |

## LAKES

### EUROPE

| | | km² | miles² |
|---|---|---|---|
| Lake Ladoga | Russia | 17,700 | 6,800 |
| Lake Onega | Russia | 9,700 | 3,700 |
| Saimaa system | Finland | 8,000 | 3,100 |
| Vänern | Sweden | 5,500 | 2,100 |
| Rybinskoye Res. | Russia | 4,700 | 1,800 |

### ASIA

| | | km² | miles² | |
|---|---|---|---|---|
| Caspian Sea | Asia | 371,800 | 143,550 | [1] |
| Lake Baykal | Russia | 30,500 | 11,780 | [8] |
| Aral Sea | Kazakhstan/Uzbekistan | 28,687 | 11,086 | [10] |
| Tonlé Sap | Cambodia | 20,000 | 7,700 | |
| Lake Balqash | Kazakhstan | 18,500 | 7,100 | |
| Lake Dongting | China | 12,000 | 4,600 | |
| Lake Ysyk | Kyrgyzstan | 6,200 | 2,400 | |
| Lake Orumiyeh | Iran | 5,900 | 2,300 | |
| Lake Koko | China | 5,700 | 2,200 | |
| Lake Poyang | China | 5,000 | 1,900 | |
| Lake Khanka | China/Russia | 4,400 | 1,700 | |
| Lake Van | Turkey | 3,500 | 1,400 | |

### AFRICA

| | | km² | miles² | |
|---|---|---|---|---|
| Lake Victoria | E. Africa | 68,000 | 26,000 | [3] |
| Lake Tanganyika | C. Africa | 33,000 | 13,000 | [6] |
| Lake Malawi/Nyasa | E. Africa | 29,600 | 11,430 | [9] |
| Lake Chad | C. Africa | 25,000 | 9,700 | |
| Lake Turkana | Ethiopia/Kenya | 8,500 | 3,300 | |
| Lake Volta | Ghana | 8,500 | 3,300 | |
| Lake Bangweulu | Zambia | 8,000 | 3,100 | |
| Lake Rukwa | Tanzania | 7,000 | 2,700 | |
| Lake Mai-Ndombe | Congo (D.R.) | 6,500 | 2,500 | |
| Lake Kariba | Zambia/Zimbabwe | 5,300 | 2,000 | |
| Lake Albert | Uganda/Congo (D.R.) | 5,300 | 2,000 | |
| Lake Nasser | Egypt/Sudan | 5,200 | 2,000 | |
| Lake Mweru | Zambia/Congo (D.R.) | 4,900 | 1,900 | |
| Lake Cabora Bassa | Mozambique | 4,500 | 1,700 | |
| Lake Kyoga | Uganda | 4,400 | 1,700 | |
| Lake Tana | Ethiopia | 3,630 | 1,400 | |

### AUSTRALIA

| | | km² | miles² |
|---|---|---|---|
| Lake Eyre | Australia | 8,900 | 3,400 |
| Lake Torrens | Australia | 5,800 | 2,200 |
| Lake Gairdner | Australia | 4,800 | 1,900 |

### NORTH AMERICA

| | | km² | miles² | |
|---|---|---|---|---|
| Lake Superior | Canada/USA | 82,350 | 31,800 | [2] |
| Lake Huron | Canada/USA | 59,600 | 23,000 | [4] |
| Lake Michigan | USA | 58,000 | 22,400 | [5] |
| Great Bear Lake | Canada | 31,800 | 12,280 | [7] |
| Great Slave Lake | Canada | 28,500 | 11,000 | |
| Lake Erie | Canada/USA | 25,700 | 9,900 | |
| Lake Winnipeg | Canada | 24,400 | 9,400 | |
| Lake Ontario | Canada/USA | 19,500 | 7,500 | |
| Lake Nicaragua | Nicaragua | 8,200 | 3,200 | |
| Lake Athabasca | Canada | 8,100 | 3,100 | |
| Smallwood Reservoir | Canada | 6,530 | 2,520 | |
| Reindeer Lake | Canada | 6,400 | 2,500 | |
| Nettilling Lake | Canada | 5,500 | 2,100 | |
| Lake Winnipegosis | Canada | 5,400 | 2,100 | |

### SOUTH AMERICA

| | | km² | miles² |
|---|---|---|---|
| Lake Titicaca | Bolivia/Peru | 8,300 | 3,200 |
| Lake Poopo | Peru | 2,800 | 1,100 |

## ISLANDS

### EUROPE

| | | km² | miles² | |
|---|---|---|---|---|
| Great Britain | UK | 229,880 | 88,700 | [8] |
| Iceland | Atlantic Ocean | 103,000 | 39,800 | |
| Ireland | Ireland/UK | 84,400 | 32,600 | |
| Novaya Zemlya (N.) | Russia | 48,200 | 18,600 | |
| W. Spitzbergen | Norway | 39,000 | 15,100 | |
| Novaya Zemlya (S.) | Russia | 33,200 | 12,800 | |
| Sicily | Italy | 25,500 | 9,800 | |
| Sardinia | Italy | 24,000 | 9,300 | |
| N.E. Spitzbergen | Norway | 15,000 | 5,600 | |
| Corsica | France | 8,700 | 3,400 | |
| Crete | Greece | 8,350 | 3,200 | |
| Zealand | Denmark | 6,850 | 2,600 | |

### ASIA

| | | km² | miles² | |
|---|---|---|---|---|
| Borneo | S. E. Asia | 744,360 | 287,400 | [3] |
| Sumatra | Indonesia | 473,600 | 182,860 | [6] |
| Honshu | Japan | 230,500 | 88,980 | [7] |
| Sulawesi (Celebes) | Indonesia | 189,000 | 73,000 | |
| Java | Indonesia | 126,700 | 48,900 | |
| Luzon | Philippines | 104,700 | 40,400 | |
| Mindanao | Philippines | 101,500 | 39,200 | |
| Hokkaido | Japan | 78,400 | 30,300 | |
| Sakhalin | Russia | 74,060 | 28,600 | |
| Sri Lanka | Indian Ocean | 65,600 | 25,300 | |
| Taiwan | Pacific Ocean | 36,000 | 13,900 | |
| Kyushu | Japan | 35,700 | 13,800 | |
| Hainan | China | 34,000 | 13,100 | |
| Timor | Indonesia | 33,600 | 13,000 | |
| Shikoku | Japan | 18,800 | 7,300 | |
| Halmahera | Indonesia | 18,000 | 6,900 | |
| Ceram | Indonesia | 17,150 | 6,600 | |
| Sumbawa | Indonesia | 15,450 | 6,000 | |
| Flores | Indonesia | 15,200 | 5,900 | |
| Samar | Philippines | 13,100 | 5,100 | |
| Negros | Philippines | 12,700 | 4,900 | |
| Bangka | Indonesia | 12,000 | 4,600 | |
| Palawan | Philippines | 12,000 | 4,600 | |
| Panay | Philippines | 11,500 | 4,400 | |
| Sumba | Indonesia | 11,100 | 4,300 | |
| Mindoro | Philippines | 9,750 | 3,800 | |

### AFRICA

| | | km² | miles² | |
|---|---|---|---|---|
| Madagascar | Indian Ocean | 587,040 | 226,660 | [4] |
| Socotra | Indian Ocean | 3,600 | 1,400 | |
| Réunion | Indian Ocean | 2,500 | 965 | |
| Tenerife | Atlantic Ocean | 2,350 | 900 | |
| Mauritius | Indian Ocean | 1,865 | 720 | |

### OCEANIA

| | | km² | miles² | |
|---|---|---|---|---|
| New Guinea | Indon./Papua NG | 821,030 | 317,000 | [2] |
| New Zealand (S.) | Pacific Ocean | 150,500 | 58,100 | |
| New Zealand (N.) | Pacific Ocean | 114,700 | 44,300 | |
| Tasmania | Australia | 67,800 | 26,200 | |
| New Britain | Papua NG | 37,800 | 14,600 | |
| New Caledonia | Pacific Ocean | 19,100 | 7,400 | |
| Viti Levu | Fiji | 10,500 | 4,100 | |
| Hawaii | Pacific Ocean | 10,450 | 4,000 | |
| Bougainville | Papua NG | 9,600 | 3,700 | |
| Guadalcanal | Solomon Is. | 6,500 | 2,500 | |
| Vanua Levu | Fiji | 5,550 | 2,100 | |
| New Ireland | Papua NG | 3,200 | 1,200 | |

### NORTH AMERICA

| | | km² | miles² | |
|---|---|---|---|---|
| Greenland | Atlantic Ocean | 2,175,600 | 839,800 | [1] |
| Baffin Is. | Canada | 508,000 | 196,100 | [5] |
| Victoria Is. | Canada | 212,200 | 81,900 | [9] |
| Ellesmere Is. | Canada | 212,000 | 81,800 | [10] |
| Cuba | Caribbean Sea | 110,860 | 42,800 | |
| Newfoundland | Canada | 110,680 | 42,700 | |
| Hispaniola | Dom. Rep./Haiti | 76,200 | 29,400 | |
| Banks Is. | Canada | 67,000 | 25,900 | |
| Devon Is. | Canada | 54,500 | 21,000 | |
| Melville Is. | Canada | 42,400 | 16,400 | |
| Vancouver Is. | Canada | 32,150 | 12,400 | |
| Somerset Is. | Canada | 24,300 | 9,400 | |
| Jamaica | Caribbean Sea | 11,400 | 4,400 | |
| Puerto Rico | Atlantic Ocean | 8,900 | 3,400 | |
| Cape Breton Is. | Canada | 4,000 | 1,500 | |

### SOUTH AMERICA

| | | km² | miles² |
|---|---|---|---|
| Tierra del Fuego | Argentina/Chile | 47,000 | 18,100 |
| Falkland Is. (East) | Atlantic Ocean | 6,800 | 2,600 |
| South Georgia | Atlantic Ocean | 4,200 | 1,600 |
| Galapagos (Isabela) | Pacific Ocean | 2,250 | 870 |

# World: Regions in the News

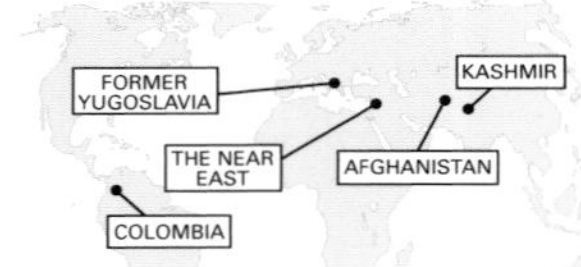

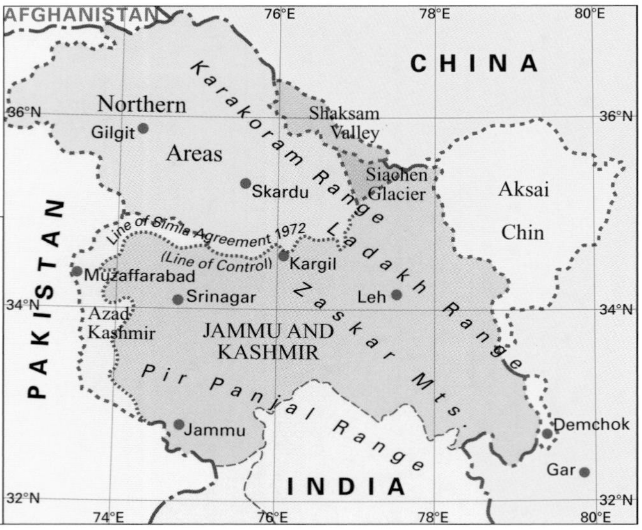

## KASHMIR

0    100    200 km

- Aksai Chin – Administered by China, claimed by India
- Shaksam Valley – Administered by China, claimed by India
- Azad Kashmir – Administered by Pakistan, claimed by India
- Northern Areas – Administered by Pakistan, claimed by India
- Siachen Glacier – Administered by India, claimed by Pakistan
- Jammu and Kashmir – Administered by India

*(Kashmir map)* AFGHANISTAN, 76°E, 78°E, 80°E, CHINA, Northern Areas, Gilgit, Shaksam Valley, 36°N, Skardu, Siachen Glacier, Aksai Chin, Line of Simla Agreement 1972, (Line of Control), Muzaffarabad, Kargil, Karakoram Range, Ladakh Range, 34°N, Azad Kashmir, Srinagar, Leh, Zaskar Mts, JAMMU AND KASHMIR, Pir Panjal Range, Jammu, Demchok, 32°N, PAKISTAN, INDIA, Gar, 74°E, 76°E, 78°E, 80°E

## YUGOSLAVIA
**POPULATION:** 10,677,000
(Serb 62.6%, Albanian 16.5%, Montenegrin 5%, Hungarian 3.3%, Muslim 3.2%)
**Serbia POPULATION:** 5,799,800
(Serb 87.7%, excluding the provinces of Kosovo and Vojvodina)
**Kosovo POPULATION:** 2,084,4000
(Albanian 81.6%, Serb 9.9%)
**Vojvodena POPULATION:** 1,980,800
(Serb 56.8%, Hungarian 16.9%)
**Montenegro POPULATION:** 635,000
(Montenegrin 61.9%, Muslim 14.6%, Albanian 7%)

## CROATIA
**POPULATION:** 4,334,000
(Croat 78.1%, Serb 12.2%)

## SLOVENIA
**POPULATION:** 1,930,000
(Slovene 88%, Croat 3%, Serb 2%)

## MACEDONIA (FYROM)
**POPULATION:** 2,046,000
(Macedonian 64%, Albanian 21.7%, Turkish 5%, Romanian 3%, Serb 2%)

## BOSNIA-HERZEGOVINA
**POPULATION:** 3,922,000
(Muslim 49%, Serb 31.2%, Croat 17.2%)

### FORMER YUGOSLAVIA

- International boundaries
- Republic boundaries
- Province boundaries
- Capital cities
- Dayton Peace Agreement Boundary
- Muslim–Croat Federation
- Bosnian Serb Republic

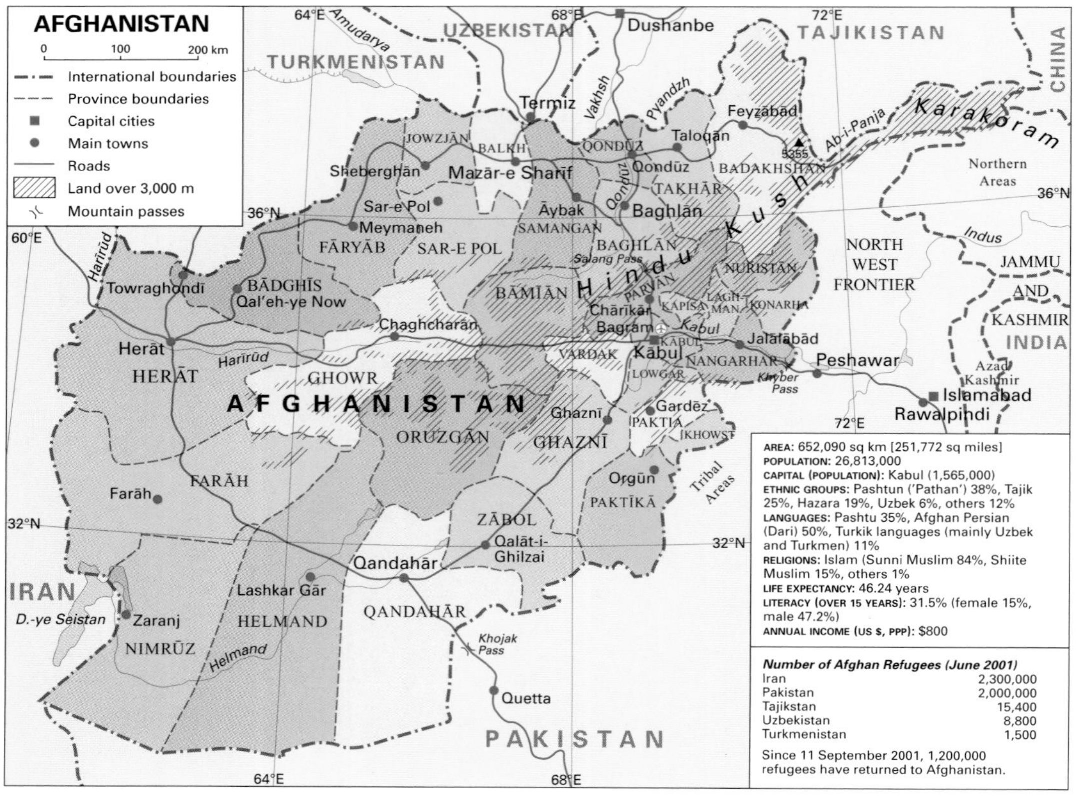

0    100    200 km

*(Former Yugoslavia map labels)* AUSTRIA, HUNGARY, Maribor, Ljubljana, SLOVENIA, Zagreb, Drava, Subotica, ROMANIA, CROATIA, Osijek, Vojvodina, Timişoara, Rijeka, Vukovar, Novi Sad, Zrenjanin, Bihać, Banja Luka, Beograd (Belgrade), BOSNIA-HERZEGOVINA, Zenica, Tuzla, Danube, Smederevo, Sarajevo, Srebrenica, YUGOSLAVIA, Kragujevac, Split, Goražde, SERBIA, Mostar, Kraljevo, Morava, Novi Pazar, Nikšić, Niš, MONTENEGRO, Leskovac, Dubrovnik, Podgorica, Priština, Vranje, Dakovica, Kosovo, Prizren, Skopje, Shkodër, Kukës, Tetovo, ADRIATIC SEA, Durrës, Tirana, ALBANIA, MACEDONIA, Prilep, ITALY, Bitola, GREECE, BULGARIA

## AFGHANISTAN

0    100    200 km

- International boundaries
- Province boundaries
- Capital cities
- Main towns
- Roads
- Land over 3,000 m
- Mountain passes

*(Afghanistan map labels)* TURKMENISTAN, UZBEKISTAN, Dushanbe, TAJIKISTAN, CHINA, Amudarya, Termiz, Vakhsh, Pyandzh, Feyzābād, JOWZJĀN, BALKH, QONDUZ, Taloqan, Karakoram, Sheberghān, Mazār-e Sharif, Qonduz, BADAKHSHAN, Northern Areas, Sar-e Pol, Āybak, Baghlān, TAKHĀR, Meymaneh, SAMANGAN, FĀRYĀB, SAR-E POL, BAGHLĀN, Salang Pass, Indus, NORTH WEST FRONTIER, Towraghondi, BĀDGHĪS, Qal'eh-ye Now, BĀMIĀN, Hindu Kush, NURISTAN, JAMMU AND KASHMIR, Chaghcharān, KĀPĪSĀ, LAGH MAN, KONARHA, Herāt, Harirūd, Bāgrām, Kābul, Jalālābād, Peshawar, HERĀT, GHOWR, Kābul, NANGARHAR, Azad Kashmir, GHOR, AFGHANISTAN, VARDAK, LOWGAR, Khyber Pass, Farāh, Ghaznī, Gardēz, Islamabad, FARĀH, ORUZGĀN, GHAZNĪ, PAKTIA, [KHOWST], Rawalpindi, Orgūn, Tribal Areas, ZĀBOL, PAKTĪKĀ, Qalāt-i-Ghilzai, Lashkar Gāh, Qandahār, IRAN, D.-ye Seistan, Zaranj, HELMAND, QANDAHĀR, Khojak Pass, NIMRŪZ, Helmand, Quetta, PAKISTAN

**AREA:** 652,090 sq km [251,772 sq miles]
**POPULATION:** 26,813,000
**CAPITAL (POPULATION):** Kabul (1,565,000)
**ETHNIC GROUPS:** Pashtun ('Pathan') 38%, Tajik 25%, Hazara 19%, Uzbek 6%, others 12%
**LANGUAGES:** Pashtu 35%, Afghan Persian (Dari) 50%, Turkik languages (mainly Uzbek and Turkmen) 11%
**RELIGIONS:** Islam (Sunni Muslim 84%, Shiite Muslim 15%, others 1%
**LIFE EXPECTANCY:** 46.24 years
**LITERACY (OVER 15 YEARS):** 31.5% (female 15%, male 47.2%)
**ANNUAL INCOME (US $, PPP):** $800

*Number of Afghan Refugees (June 2001)*
| | |
|---|---|
| Iran | 2,300,000 |
| Pakistan | 2,000,000 |
| Tajikstan | 15,400 |
| Uzbekistan | 8,800 |
| Turkmenistan | 1,500 |

Since 11 September 2001, 1,200,000 refugees have returned to Afghanistan.

## COLOMBIA

0    200    400 km

- International boundaries
- Province boundaries
- FARC Demilitarized Zone
- Land over 3,000 m
- Capital cities
- Main towns

**POPULATION:** 40,349,388 (Mestizo 58%, White 20%, Mulatto 14%, Black 4%, Mixed Black-Amerindian 3%, Amerindian 1%)
**RELIGIONS:** Roman Catholic 90%
**FARC MEMBERS:** 18,000 (Revolutionary Armed Forces of Colombia)
**CIVILIANS IN FARC ZONE:** 90,000
**AID RECEIVED (US) 2000:** US $1.3 billion
**AID RECEIVED (US) 2002:** US $0.3 billion

*(Colombia map labels)* CARIBBEAN SEA, Barranquilla, GUAJIRA, ATLANTICO, Caracas, Cartagena, MAGDALENA, CÉSAR, 10°N, PANAMA, BOLÍVAR, VENEZUELA, Panamá, CÓRDOBA, SUCRE, SANTANDER, ARAUCA, PACIFIC OCEAN, ANTIOQUIA, Medellín, CHOCÓ, BOYACÁ, CASANARE, Bogotá, CALDAS, 5°N, VALLE DEL CAUCA, Cali, TOLIMA, META, VICHADA, CAUCA, HUILA, Uribe, San Vicente del Caguán, GUAVIARE, NARIÑO, FARC Demilitarized Zone, GUAINÍA, PUTUMAYO, CAQUETÁ, VAUPÉS, Equator, Quito, ECUADOR, AMAZONAS, BRAZIL, PERU, Amazon

## THE NEAR EAST

0    25    50 km

- 1949 Armistice Line
- 1974 Cease-fire Line
- Palestinian control
- Joint Israeli/Palestinian control
- *Efrata* Main Jewish settlements in the West Bank and Gaza Strip
- *Halhul* Main Palestinian Arab towns in the West Bank and Gaza Strip
- Road corridor linking Gaza and West Bank

*(Near East map labels)* LEBANON, Beqaa Valley, Saydā, 35°E, Litani, Sūr (Tyre), Qiryat Shemona, SYRIA, Nahariyya, 33°N, Akko, Zefat, Yam Kinneret, Golan Heights, Hefa, Terverya, Hadera, Nazerat, Netanya, Jenin, West, Tūlkarm, Shavel Shomron, Tūbās, Kedumim, Elon More, Qalqilya, Natulus, Karne Shomron, Emanuel, Kfar Tapuah, Tel Aviv-Yafo, Elkana, Ariel, Shiloh, Bank, Rehovot, Rām, Beit El, As Salt, Ashdod, Beit Horon, Al Birah, El-Arihā (Jericho), Ammān, Jerusalem, Maale Adumim, Ashqelon, Bayt Lahm (Bethlehem), Alei Sinai, Effata, Tkoa, Gaza, Nisanit, Halhul, Dead Sea, Gaza Strip, Netzarin, Al Khalil (Hebron), Qiryat Arba, Kfar Darom, Be'er Sheva, Gadid, Khān Yūnis, MEDITERRANEAN SEA, EGYPT, JORDAN, Irbid, 32°N

**ISRAEL**
**POPULATION:** 5,938,000 (inc. East Jerusalem and Jewish settlers in the areas under Israeli administration. Jewish 82%, Arab Muslim 13.8%, Arab Christian 2.5%, Druze 1.7%)

**West Bank**
**POPULATION:** 2,091,000 (Palestinian Arab 97% [of whom Arab Muslim 85%, Jewish 7%, Christian 8%])

**Gaza Strip**
**POPULATION:** 1,178,000 (Arab 98%)

**JORDAN**
**POPULATION:** 5,153,000 (Arab 99% [of whom about 50% are Palestinian Arab])

**LEBANON**
**POPULATION:** 3,628,000 (Arab 93% [of whom 83% are Lebanese Arab and 10% Palestinian Arab])

# WORLD EXPLORER

## CONTENTS

# Mountains and volcanoes

The world's mountains provide a huge variety of magnificent scenery, ranging from the tree-covered Blue Mountains of Australia, little more than 1,070 m (3,500 ft) high, to the towering snow-covered Himalayan peaks of Nepal and China, several of which are over 8,000 m (26,000 ft) high. Many are accessible by road, or sometimes by train or cable car, but walking, even if only a short distance, is usually the best way to experience the breathtaking views that they offer.

◄ **Rocky Mountains, Banff National Park, Canada**
Pointed peaks and sheer cliffs contribute to a magnificent land-scape. Over 1,600 km (1,000 miles) of trails pass by glaciers, turquoise lakes and forests of pine, fir and spruce. In the town of Banff a cable car rises to the top of Sulfur Mountain, 2,263 m (7,440 ft) high.
*Best time to visit:* June–September

## THE AMERICAS

### Mount McKinley, Denali National Park, Alaska, USA
The USA's highest mountain at 6,194 m (20,321 ft) is in a spectacular wilderness of snow-covered peaks and glaciers with wildlife that includes brown bears, caribou, moose and marmots. Activities include river rafting and sightseeing by plane.
*Best time to visit:* June–August

### Popocatepetl Volcano ('Smoking Mountain'), Sierra Nevada, Mexico
A cloud of smoke often hovers above the massive crater of Popocatepetl, which is 5,452 m (17,887 ft) high. It is possible to climb and descend the mountain in one very long day with the aid of a guide.
*Best time to climb:* November–March

### Cotopaxi and Chimborazo Volcanoes, Ecuador
The two highest active volcanoes in the world are in a country where the main road is known as the 'Avenue of the Volcanoes'. Non-mountaineers can climb Cotopaxi (5,896 m/19,344 ft) and get near to the top of Chimborazo (6,267 m/20,561 ft).
*Best time to climb:* January–April

### Cordillera Blanca, Huascaran National Park, Peru
With 663 glaciers, the peaks of the Cordillera Blanca, more than 50 of which rise to heights of between 5,000 and 6,000 m (16,500 and 19,700 ft), are a great attraction for ice climbers. Huarez is the main climbing centre. An alternative for those who prefer to trek is the richly glaciated Huayhuash range.
*Best time to visit:* July–September

## EUROPE

### Landmannalaugar, Iceland
A combination of volcanic and geothermal activity has produced a unique landscape in Landmannalaugar, where mountain peaks (little more than 1,070 m/3,500 ft high) rise above a landscape of convoluted lava fields and blue mountain lakes, and hot springs provide open-air baths.
*Best time to visit:* July–early September

### Mount Vesuvius, Italy
The volcano of Vesuvius dominates the landscape around Naples. Although it lost its plume of smoke after erupting in 1944, it is still active. A bus from Pompeii goes to within 1.5 km (1 mile) of the summit (1,277 m/4,189 ft).
*Time to visit:* All seasons

## AFRICA

### Atlas Mountains, Morocco
Canyons with dramatic rock formations are to be found in these rugged mountains that rise to a height of over 3,900 m (13,000 ft). Organized treks pass by numerous isolated Berber villages, far from the road from Marrakech, which winds up to a mountain pass 2,275 m (7,467 ft) high.
*Best time to visit:* June–October

### Mount Kilimanjaro, Tanzania
Africa's highest mountain rises majestically to 5,895 m (19,340 ft) above the plains of Amboseli National Park. It is possible to trek to the top for stunning views over Kenya and Tanzania, along

▲ **Sierra Nevada, Yosemite National Park, USA**
The Californian Yosemite National Park is famous for its sheer-sided granite domes, such as the Half Dome and the 1,066 m (3,500 ft) high El Capitan, which rise above forests and emerald lakes. Among the many species of flowers and trees to be found in the park are ancient giant sequoias over 60 m (200 ft) high, one of which is estimated to be 2,700 years old. An added attraction are the Yosemite Falls which, with a drop of 739 m (2,425 ft), are the highest in North America. Walkers can escape the summer crowds by using the 1,280 km (800 miles) of trails.
*Best time to visit:* May–September

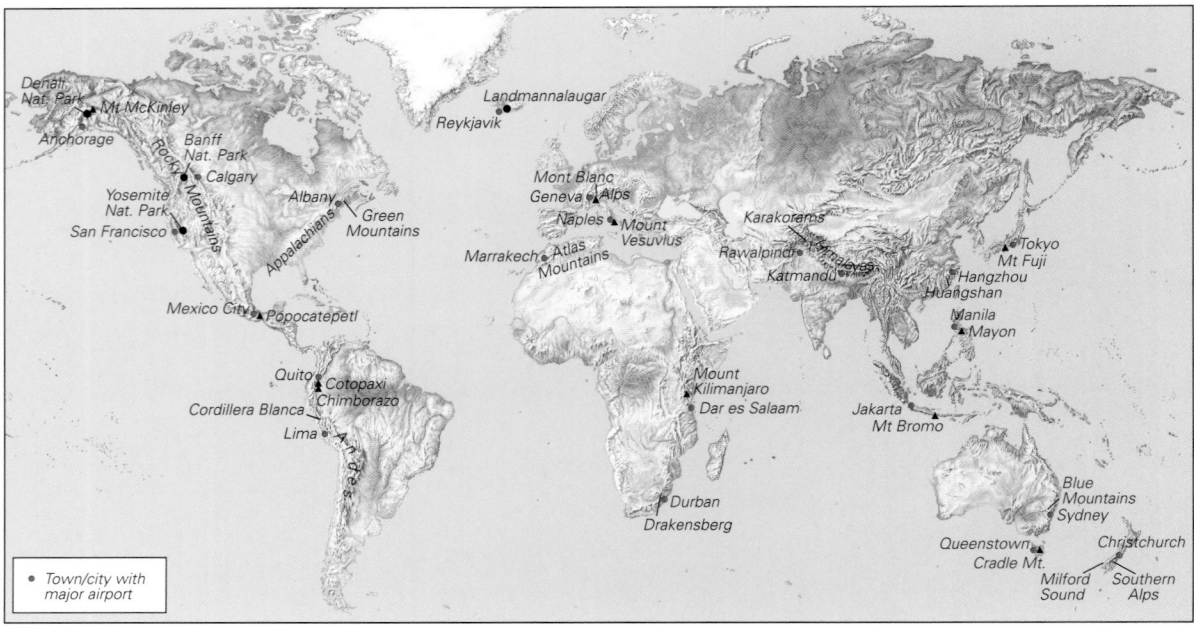

● *Town/city with major airport*

Denali Nat. Park · Mt McKinley · Anchorage · Banff Nat. Park · Calgary · Landmannalaugar · Reykjavik · Yosemite Nat. Park · San Francisco · Albany · Green Mountains · Appalachians · Rockies · Mexico City · Popocatepetl · Quito · Cotopaxi · Chimborazo · Cordillera Blanca · Lima · Andes · Mont Blanc · Geneva · Alps · Naples · Mount Vesuvius · Marrakech · Atlas Mountains · Karakorams · Himalayas · Rawalpindi · Katmandu · Tokyo · Mt Fuji · Hangzhou · Huangshan · Manila · Mayon · Mount Kilimanjaro · Dar es Salaam · Jakarta · Mt Bromo · Durban · Drakensberg · Blue Mountains · Sydney · Queenstown · Cradle Mt. · Christchurch · Milford Sound · Southern Alps

**▲ Mont Blanc, Alps, France**
Europe's highest mountain rises to a height of 4,807 m (15,760 ft). A splendid view of it can be had from the peak of the Aiguille de Midi, a granite spear 3,840 m (12,600 ft) high, that is reached by a steep 3 km (2-mile) ascent in a cable car from Chamonix. Below Mont Blanc is the start of a long-distance ski and walking route, which passes ten of the 12 highest peaks in the Alps on its way to the Matterhorn in Switzerland and Italy.
*Best time for walking:* May–September

**▼ Mt Bromo, Java**
A crater within a vast outer crater, Bromo emits white smoke, as does Mount Semeru, seen here in the distance. Visitors usually stay overnight in a village at the rim of the outer crater, from where it is possible to walk to Bromo at dawn to watch the sun rise up over the outer crater.
*Best time to visit:* April–October

routes that pass through farmland and lush forest before reaching alpine-like vegetation and snow-covered rock.
*Best time to climb:* mid January–late February and late August–September

**Drakensberg Mountains, South Africa**
Vast pinnacles and blocks of basalt rise to a height of over 3,475 m (11,400 ft) in this range of mountains that also runs through Lesotho. Snowcapped in winter, many of the peaks are an enormous challenge for mountaineers. The Royal Natal National Park has numerous hiking trails.
*Best time to visit:* April–October

## ASIA

### Himalayas, Nepal
Within the Himalayas in Nepal are ten of the world's 14 peaks with a height of over 8,000 m (26,000 ft), including Everest (8,850 m/29,035 ft). Far below the snow-capped peaks are terraced hillsides dotted with villages, while above a height of about 2,700 m (9,000 ft) are forests in which rhododendrons bloom between February and April. The most popular base for exploring the mountains is Pokhara. The famous ten-day trek to the mountain town of Jomsom begins here, as does the three-to four-day Annapurna Skyline Trek which provides superb views while being easy enough to be undertaken with children.
*Best time to visit:* October–April

### Karakorams, Pakistan
The jagged peaks of the Karakorams include K2, the world's second highest mountain (8,611 m/28,400 ft). A journey along the Karakoram Highway follows the route of the old Silk Road along the Indus Valley from Rawalpindi to Kashgar in China, sometimes clinging to cliff faces as it winds its way through the mountains up to the Khunjerab Pass at 4,934 m (16,280 ft).
*Best time to visit:* May–August

**Great mountain treks**
*The following is a selection of great mountain treks that take four or more days. The months given are those in which it is best to undertake each trek.*

**Long Trail, Vermont, USA** (424 km/265 miles; 16–21 days; May–Sept) Easily reached by road, the trail through Vermont's Green Mountains can be walked in sections. It is part of the 3,456 km (2,160-mile) long Appalachian Trail, whose most demanding section is through New Hampshire's White Mountains.
**Inca Trail, Peru** (4–5 days; April–Sept) By far the best way to approach the spectacular Inca site of Machu Picchu (see *Historic Sites of the Americas*), the Inca Trail begins some distance from Cuzco.
**Mont Blanc Circuit, France and Switzerland** (10 days; July–Sept) Possibly the finest walk in Europe, it usually starts from Chamonix. With an average altitude of 1,525 m (5,000 ft), it links the seven valleys surrounding Mont Blanc.

**Annapurna Circuit, Nepal** (17 days; Oct–Nov and March–April) Regarded as Nepal's classic trek, it goes through many types of landscape *(see picture below)*, and reaches a height of 5,416 m (17,765 ft), as well as providing superb views of Annapurna and Dhaulagiri.
**Everest Trek, Nepal** (14–16 days; Oct–Nov and March–April) A trek from Jiri to the Everest Base Camp on the Khumbu Glacier provides wonderful views of Everest. It is possible to fly back to Katmandu from Lukla, three days' walk away.
**Milford Track, New Zealand** (54 km/34 miles; 4 days; Oct–April) A walk that is regarded as a must by most New Zealanders ends at the breathtaking Milford Sound (see *Sea and ocean cruises*). The number of walkers is limited and booking well ahead is necessary.

### Mayon Volcano, Philippines
Often described as the world's most perfect volcano cone, Mayon (2,462 m/8,075 ft) is still very active. An eruption in 1993 killed 70 people. It can be climbed in two days but it is essential to do so with a guide.
*Best time to climb:* December–May

### Mt Kinabalu, Borneo, Malaysia
It is possible to walk rather than climb to the top of the highest mountain in South-east Asia (4,010 m/13,455 ft). It does, however, take two days and hiring a guide is compulsory. The view from the top some-times stretches to the Philippines.
*Best time to climb:* April–September

### Huangshan, China
The Chinese regard the 72-peak Huang-shan range as one of the great natural attractions of their country. Some 30 peaks rise to over 1,500 m (4,900 ft ). There are two main walking routes up the side of the

range, and an eight-minute cable car ride from Yungusi to the top.
*Best time to visit:* spring and autumn

### Mt Fuji, Japan
The perfectly symmetrical cone of Japan's highest mountain (3,776 m/12,388 ft), which last erupted in 1707, is climbed by people of all ages in the summer. A road goes to the fourth and fifth 'stations', from where it takes four or five hours to climb to the crater. This is best reached at dawn, before the clouds gather.
*Best time to climb:* July–August

## AUSTRALASIA

### Blue Mountains, New South Wales, Australia
Reaching a height of just over 1,070 m (3,500 ft), the Blue Mountains – with their densely forested slopes, sandstone chasms, dramatic rock formations and waterfalls – provide a beautiful environment in which to drive and walk. As well as a network of trails there are a number of interesting villages and towns, of which the largest, Katoomba, is served by a railway from Sydney just 80 km (50 miles) away.
*Time to visit:* All seasons

### Cradle Mountain/Lake St Clair National Park, Tasmania, Australia
Australia's best mountain trails and rugged alpine scenery are to be found around Cradle Mountain. Jagged peaks, the highest of which is Mt Ossa (1,617 m/5,300 ft), rise above tarns and lakes in deep valleys.
*Best time to visit:* November–March

# Deserts and canyons

For the adventurous traveller, the stunning landscapes of rock and sand which make up some of the world's most inhospitable environments offer a challenge not to be missed. From the vast sand seas of the Sahara Desert to the deep canyons and distinctive rock formations of the south-western United States, there is an extraordinary range of landforms to explore.

## NORTH AMERICA

### Bryce Canyon, Utah, USA

On a more human scale than the Grand Canyon, Bryce Canyon is not really a canyon at all but a natural amphitheatre filled with dazzling orange, red and pink rock pinnacles – known as 'hoodoos' – overlooking spectacularly colourful ravines. This surreal landscape can be explored on foot along a network of marked trails, or simply enjoyed from one of the viewpoints along the rim of the amphitheatre.

### Monument Valley, Arizona, USA

With its majestic rock pillars towering over a barren, desert landscape, Monument Valley is an awe-inspiring sight. It has been made famous as a backdrop to numerous Hollywood westerns and is now part of the Navajo Reservation. A 27 km (17-mile) road tour of the valley takes two to three hours and offers stunning views of this unforgettable place.

### Zion Canyon, Utah, USA

The road through the steep-sided Zion Canyon can become crowded in summer, and it is worth leaving the car to follow one of the short trails to the Emerald Pools or the hanging gardens at Weeping Rock. Longer trails lead from the canyon to the desert plateau above and offer spectacular views of the contrasting landscapes.

## SOUTH AMERICA

### Colca Canyon, Peru

High in the Andes the River Colca runs through a gorge which is twice the depth of the Grand Canyon, past ancient Inca granaries cut into the rock and green slopes covered by pre-Inca terracing. This astonishingly beautiful landscape, complete with smoking volcano in the background, is home to the Collagua and Cabana people, whose traditional way of life is punctuated with lively festivals.

### Atacama Desert, Chile

Overlooked by a ruined pre-Inca fortress, the picturesque oasis village of San Pedro de Atacama, with its adobe buildings and excellent archeological museum, makes a good base for exploring the canyons, saltpans and stark landscapes of the surrounding desert. One of the most beautiful places to visit is the Valle de la Luna, where the multi-coloured desert formations are a magnet for photographers and filmmakers.

## EUROPE

### Almerían Desert, Spain

The setting for the film *Lawrence of Arabia* as well as many 'spaghetti westerns', the Almerían Desert is an extraordinary, almost lunar landscape of sand dunes dissected by dried-up river beds and littered with sandstone cones. Film sets are open to the public at Mini-Hollywood.

### Timanfaya National Park, Lanzarote, Canary Islands

On an island where it rarely rains, a series of volcanic eruptions in the 1730s created an extraordinary apocalyptic landscape. Guided tours go to an area of solidified lava and volcanic cones, aptly called the Mountains of Fire, where a dry bush dropped into a crevice will burst into flames and meals at a solitary restaurant are barbecued on a volcano.

## AFRICA

### Draa Valley, the Sahara, Morocco

From the town of Ouarzazate, with its dramatic kasbah, the Draa river runs south-east through a rich landscape of dramatic gorges, agricultural land and kasbahs towards the Sahara. After around 160 km (100 miles), the river reaches the former frontier fort of Zagora, which makes a good base for exploring the desert.

▲ **Grand Canyon, Arizona, USA**
Carved by the Colorado River out of the multi-coloured rock of the Arizona Desert, the Grand Canyon is one of North America's most awe-inspiring natural features. Drives and trails around its rim – 443 km (277 miles) in length – provide stunning views. Visitors can walk or ride mules down one of the vertiginous trails to the valley floor, 1.7 km (1 mile) below, or try rafting on the river.

▲ **Sonoran Desert, USA/Mexico**
Almost encircling the Gulf of California and covering 310,000 sq km (120,00 sq miles), the Sonoran Desert is the hottest of North America's deserts. Tucson, Arizona, serves as a base for tours into the desert, including archaeological tours. Nearby are the excellent Arizona-Sonora Desert Museum and the protected desert habitat of Organ Pipe Cactus National Monument where visitors can see the giant saguaro and organ pipe cacti which have come to symbolize the area. There are good trails and scenic drives around the park, and plenty of desert wildlife to watch.

Town/city with major airport

**Saharan oases, Tunisia**
The shifting sand dunes around the town of Douz are an excellent example of the landscape popularly associated with the Sahara Desert. In fact the desert, which covers an area of 8,600,000 sq km (3,320,000 sq miles), has extensive stony plains, rock-strewn plateaux, mountains and large oasis depressions as well as seas of sand. Douz is a good base for camel safaris and for exploring the more isolated southern oases. To the north-west the town of Tozeur, with its beautiful 12th-century mosque, is set beside a vast oasis fed by over 200 springs. It serves as an excellent starting point for four-wheel-drive tours into the desert and to the nearby beautiful mountain oases, such as Tamerza, Mides and Chebika.

Guided expeditions of up to a week can include camel riding and stargazing under the immense Saharan sky.

**Ténéré Desert, Niger**
For desert purists the seemingly endless sea of sand that is the Ténéré Desert is perhaps the most beautiful part of the Sahara. A two-week round trip from the desert city of Agadez might pass through a massive dinosaur cemetery on the way to the classic oasis town of Bilma and the prehistoric cave paintings of the Djado Plateau. Crossing the Ténéré is notoriously challenging and often dangerous, but the experience is unforgettable.

**Sinai Desert, Egypt**
Inland from the coastal resorts of the Sinai Peninsula is a hot, desolate wilderness sprinkled with oases and ancient settlements. They include the 6th-century monastery of St Catherine, which stands at the foot of Mount Sinai, where Moses is said to have received the Ten Commandments from God. Camel treks and jeep safaris take visitors into the aptly-named Wilderness of Wanderings, in the centre of the peninsula.

**North Kenyan Desert**
In sharp contrast to the developed south of Kenya, the North Kenyan Desert is a vast tract of scrubland inhabited by ancient nomadic tribes whose way of life has changed little over the centuries. A rich diversity of desert landscapes here includes scrub desert – which bursts into colour after rainfall – and lunar, volcanic areas. There are lush oases and river-cut canyons too, but the reason most people come here is to see the 'Jade Sea', Lake Turkana, with its profusion of birdlife, hippos and Nile crocodiles.

**Namib Desert, Namibia**
Stretching for 1,930 km (1,200 miles) down the length of the Namibian coastline to the mouth of the Orange River in South Africa, the Namib is a strip of desert with an average width of 110 km (70 miles). The highest sand dunes in the world – sometimes exceeding 244 m (800 ft) – are to be found at Sossus Vlei, in the Namib-Naukluft National Park. The northern section is known as Skeleton Coast because of the many shipwrecks that lie on the ocean bed nearby.

**Blyde River Canyon, South Africa**
The view over the canyon from the spot known as God's Window is one of the highlights of any visit to the beautiful Blyde River Nature Reserve, in the Drakensberg. There are two trails down into the canyon – which in some places is over 700 m (2,300 ft) deep – from Bourke's Luck Portholes, where strange natural rock formations can be seen.

## ASIA AND AUSTRALASIA

### Thar Desert, Rajasthan, India
Within the Rajasthan Desert National Park two areas of interest to tourists can be reached easily from the attractive city of Jaisalmer with its 12th-century fort. One is the Akal Fossil Park where the petrified trunks of 25 trees once covered by the sea lie on a bare hillside. The second is the 3 km (2-mile) long Sam Dunes, just 40 km (25 miles) from Jaisalmer. The dunes are usually crowded with tourists taking camel rides, but it is possible to escape the crowds and go on safaris of several days, by either jeep or camel.

### Gobi Desert, Mongolia
For 70 years part of the Soviet Union, the Gobi Desert has only recently become accessible to western travellers. Its greatest attraction is the red sandstone Flaming Cliffs, 80 km (50 miles) north-west of Dalandzadgad, which became famous in the 1920s when the explorer and scientist Roy Chapman Andrews (on whom the character of Indiana Jones was based) discovered fossilized dinosaur remains there. Still rich in dinosaur fossils, the cliffs are just north of the vast Three Beauties National Park with a landscape of mountains, canyons, gravel and sand.

▼ **Wadi Rum, Jordan**
Soaring vertically from the desert floor of Wadi Rum are the massive rock formations known as jebels for which the area is famous. Vehicles and camels can be hired in the Bedouin settlement of Rum, but it is hard to beat the experience of walking through this extraordinary, silent landscape and sleeping out in the desert under the stars.

◄ **Uluru National Park, Northern Territory, Australia**
The largest sandstone monolith in the world, Uluru (Ayers Rock) is a magnificent sight, particularly at sunset when it appears to burn from within. Some 40 km (25 miles) to the west are the Olgas – 36 enormous granite domes – which, like Uluru, are an important Aboriginal site. Access is restricted, but visitors can experience their haunting beauty by following the trail through the Valley of the Winds.

# Lakes and waterfalls

From the azure tranquillity of Lake Garda in Italy to the thundering roar of Zimbabwe's Victoria Falls, the great lakes and waterfalls of the world are set amidst dramatically beautiful scenery. Many resorts offer watersports as well as long-distance trails for ramblers and horse-riders.

▶ **Lake Maligne, Jasper National Park, Canada**
The glacier-fed Lake Maligne – shown here at dawn – is set among the snow-covered peaks of Jasper National Park, the biggest and wildest of Canada's four Rocky Mountain national parks at 10,400 sq km (4,000 sq miles). Boat and hiking tours, fishing, rafting and riding are available, while the independent explorer can hire a boat or walk along the excellent network of trails.

▼ **Angel Falls, Venezuela**
The world's highest waterfall with an uninterrupted drop of 2,650 ft (807 m), Angel Falls are 16 times the height of Niagara Falls. Although often shrouded in mist, the Falls are at their most spectacular during the rainy season (June–November) when the volume of water is greatest and when visitors can travel by motorized canoe along the river to Devil's Canyon at the foot of the Falls.

▼ **Lake Argentino, Argentina**
The south-western arm of Lake Argentino is periodically dammed by the Moreno Glacier, from which icebergs regularly break off and crash into the channel below. Visitors can see, hear and photograph the glacier in safety from a series of platforms and viewing points. The massive Upsala Glacier on the northern arm of the lake can be reached by boat from Puerto Bandera.

## NORTH AMERICA

### Niagara Falls, Canada/USA
The most-visited waterfall in the world, Niagara Falls has been developed as a tourist attraction offering every possible viewing experience, including cable cars, helicopter rides, viewing towers, boats and even tunnels in the rockface. Despite the commercialization, this massive, perpetual curtain of falling water lives up to its reputation as one of the wonders of the natural world.

### Waterton-Glacier Park, Montana and Alberta, Canada/USA
Silver lakes are a major feature of the landscape of mountain peaks, waterfalls and hanging valleys, carved by glaciers 10,000 years ago, in the Waterton-Glacier Park. There are spectacular trails for walkers of all levels, and the Going-to-the-Sun Road through the park is considered to be one of the USA's driving highlights.

### Lake Tahoe, California, USA
High in the Sierra Nevada mountains on the border between California and Nevada, Lake Tahoe is a popular year-round holiday destination. In winter the area is packed with skiers (see *Winter sports*) while summer brings people seeking the cooler temperatures of the mountains and the crystal waters and sandy beaches of the lake. On the California side, there is swimming, boating, fishing and walking, while the Nevada side offers a glittering nightlife of restaurants and casinos.

## SOUTH AMERICA

### Iguaçu Falls, Brazil
The torrential waters of the Iguaçu River plunge more than 75 m (250 ft) over a huge, crescent-shaped cliff into the gorge below in a series of some 275 separate waterfalls. Surrounded by lush rainforest, the 4 km (2.5-mile) wide cascades can be viewed from platforms and paths on both sides of the Falls.

### Lake Titicaca, Bolivia
High in the Altiplano the clear blue waters of Lake Titicaca bring an oasis of life and colour to the parched landscape. At 8,340 sq km (3,220 sq miles), it is the largest lake in South America, with many lakeside settlements. Boat trips can be made to the floating reed islands inhabited by the Uros, and to ancient Inca ruins on the sacred islands of the Sun and Moon.

### Lake Llanquihue, Chile
A reflection of the perfect cone of Volcano Orsono can be seen in this immense lake which lies amid gently rolling pastureland. Towns on the shore include Frutillar Bajo, a popular summer resort with black-sand beaches, and Puerto Varas, a centre for 'adventure' activities such as rafting, riding, hiking and climbing.

## EUROPE

### Lake Siljan, Sweden
In a land of around 96,000 lakes, Siljan is noted as a centre of Swedish folk tradition

and art. Locals and visitors arrive in boats reminiscent of Viking longships during midsummer celebrations at the lakeside church of Rättvik, and traditional mystery plays are performed annually in the open-air theatre at Leksand. Visitors can watch traditional painted wooden horses being made at Nusnäs, and visit the studio of the painter Anders Zorn, who lived in the lakeside town of Mora.

### Lake District, England
Famous as the haunt of the Romantic Poets, the Lake District is a beautiful and varied landscape of hills, mountains, lakes and rivers, encompassing a wide range of scenery within a relatively small area. The southern lakes – including Windermere, Coniston and Grasmere – are surrounded by gentle green slopes and attract enormous numbers of visitors in summer.

The wilder north, with its sheer, forbidding crags is more spectacular and much less crowded. Boating is popular on the larger lakes, and a network of paths makes the area a haven for walkers and climbers.

### Lake Lucerne, Switzerland
The picturesque medieval town of Lucerne with its famous Kapellbrücke bridge makes an excellent base for exploring this beautiful lake and its mountain surroundings. Visitors can go on a lake cruise and stop off at some of the peaceful villages along the shore, or take the oldest mountain railway in Europe to Mount Rigi for wonderful views of the Alpine scenery.

### Lake Garda, Italy
The largest of Italy's lakes, Lake Garda is certainly one of its most beautiful. Sheltered from the north-east by the Dolomites, its climate is particularly gentle, with orange and lemon groves flourishing on its banks. Dotted around the lake are many attractive and historic resort towns – some dating back to Roman times – and romantic hillside villas.

## AFRICA

### Lake Bosumtwi, Ghana
Sacred to the Asante people, the crater lake of Bosumtwi is the deepest natural lake in Ghana, and its waters are still rising. Its beautiful setting among thickly wooded crater walls makes it a relaxing place to go fishing, boating and swimming. Motorboat trips across the lake are available, and walks around the shore can include visits to lakeside villages.

### Murchison Falls, Uganda
The sheer force of the Nile as it shoots through a narrow cleft in the rocks and crashes over a 30 m (100 ft) precipice is what makes Murchison Falls so spectacular. A journey up the river from Paraa Camp to the base of the falls is also an excellent way to see some of the wildlife of the Murchison Falls National Park, including crocodiles, elephants, hippos, giraffes, buffalo, waterbucks and many bird species.

### Lake Baringo, Kenya
Encircled by mountains and rich in bird and animal life, Lake Baringo is a fascinating and beautiful place to visit. The shoreline is home to crocodiles and herds of hippos and the area is famous for its hundreds of bird species, attracting birdwatchers from all over the world. A resident ornithologist offers guided walks, and there are also horse rides, camel rides and boat trips to the lake's islands.

## ASIA

### Lake Toba, Sumatra
Encircled by steep crags – once the rim of an enormous ancient volcano – Lake Toba is the largest crater lake in the world. The area is home to the Toba Batak people, whose brightly painted houses with distinctive crescent-shaped roofs can be seen around the lake. The beautiful island of Samosir is a popular tourist destination

with excellent trekking and rafting as well as interesting megalithic tombs to visit.

### Lake Batur, Bali
The largest lake in Bali, Lake Batur is a crater lake and is sacred to the Balinese as the home of the goddess Dewi Danu. The hot springs at Toya Bungkah are said to have healing properties, and the lakeside temple of Pura Jati presides over a holy bathing place. From Toyah Bungkah there are trekking routes up to the summit of Gunung Batur, the soaring 1,717 m (5,630 ft) high volcano which dominates the lake.

### Lake Karakul, Tajikistan
At a height of 3,600 m (11,800 ft) in the foothills of the Pamir mountains, Lake Karakul's setting is remote and beautiful. Flanked by the massive Mount Kongur to the north and the magnificent Mount Muztaghata to the south, Karakul is the home of the Kirgiz people and their herds of sheep, goats, horses and camels. It takes a day to walk around the lake, after which walkers can stay overnight in a traditional felt-covered *yurt* at the visitors' camp.

### Lake Chuzenji-ko and Kegon Waterfall, Japan
Visitors to Lake Chuzenji-ko and the dramatic Kegon Waterfall are well provided for with cable cars and platforms from which to gaze at the spectacular view, especially popular in autumn when the

leaves are changing colour. Beside the lake is a colourful shrine after which both the town and lake are named.

## AUSTRALASIA

### Lake Rotorua, New Zealand
Bubbling hot springs, vertical jets of steam and scalding geysers make Rotorua an exciting place to visit. There are lakeside bath houses where visitors can sample the waters, as well as cruises and facilities for a wide range of watersports on the lake and nearby rivers. Maoris have lived beside the lake for around 700 years, and there are many cultural attractions on offer, some more authentic than others.

**▲ Keli Mutu, Flores, Indonesia**
An extinct volcano, Keli Mutu has three extraordinary crater lakes. Not only is each lake a different colour, but the colours change over decades from vivid green through to deep red and intense turquoise as mineral layers dissolve.

**◄ Victoria Falls, Zimbabwe**
The 1.7 km (1-mile) wide Victoria Falls are made up of five separate waterfalls which plummet more than 100 m (320 ft) into the gorge below. The Falls are a popular base for adrenaline-boosting activities, such as bungee jumping, white-water rafting and riverboarding, and tours of every description can be taken from operators based in Victoria Falls town.

# Wildlife in the Americas and Europe

From the bears and moose of the Alaskan wilderness, to the jaguars and toucans of the Central American forests, to the condors and rheas of Patagonia, the Americas have an amazing variety of wildlife. Europe by contrast is famed for its seabirds, and the vast flocks of migrant wildfowl that gather in its wetlands.

**▶ Torres del Paine National Park, Chile**
An awe-inspiring landscape of forests, glaciers, shimmering lakes, thundering cascades and soaring granite pillars, Torres del Paine National Park in Patagonia is a haven for wildlife, including guanacos, rheas, flamingos, condors and the shy huemul (Chilean deer). There is an excellent network of short- and long-distance trails through the park.

**▼ Wrangell-St Elias National Park, Alaska, USA**
Of all the Alaskan national parks, Wrangell-St Elias is the best for wildlife watching. This vast landscape of mountains and glaciers is home to moose, wolves, wolverines, bears, beavers and herds of caribou. There are several campsites but few other facilities for visitors in this true wilderness park.

## NORTH AMERICA

### Wood Buffalo National Park, Alberta/NW Territories, Canada
Canada's largest national park, Wood Buffalo is famous for its free-roaming buffalo herd. Among other inhabitants are lynx, bears and hundreds of bird species, including a river rookery of rare white pelicans and the few remaining whooping cranes in the world. Fort Smith has some accommodation, but canoeing along the rivers and camping are perhaps the best ways to explore this wilderness of forest, marsh and grassland.

### Yellowstone National Park, Wyoming, USA
Famous for its many geothermal geysers and hot springs, Yellowstone Park is also home to one of the largest and most diverse populations of mammals in North America. Inhabitants include bison, moose, elks, Bighorn sheep, beavers and marmots as well as lynx, bobcats, wolves and coyotes. Millions of visitors flock to Yellowstone every year, but despite the inevitable tourist development, most of the park is still a true wilderness.

### Everglades National Park, Florida, USA
The largest sub-tropical wilderness on the North American mainland, Everglades National Park is a vast area of swamps, mangrove forests and grasslands. It is the only place in the world where alligators and crocodiles live side by side, and there are still a few panthers and black bears. Canoe trails and boat tours are the best way to view the abundant wildlife, which includes a huge variety of bird species.

## CENTRAL AMERICA

### Braulio Carrillo Park, Costa Rica
Many different habitats exist in Braulio Carrillo, a large area of rainforest covering a range of altitudes from just above sea level to 3,000 m (9,850 ft). Each has its own distinct flora and fauna, although the astonishingly lush vegetation can make spotting animals such as tapirs, sloths, ocelots, jaguars and pumas difficult. The park's abundant birdlife includes toucans, quetzels, umbrella birds, guans and eagles.

### Corcovado National Park, Costa Rica
Set on the remote Osa peninsula, Corcovado National Park encompasses coastal mangrove swamps, pristine cloud forests and rocky canyons. Many of Costa Rica's endangered species live here, including tapirs, caymans and jaguars, while crocodiles swim in its waters and turtles lay their eggs on the park's deserted beaches. Ranger stations provide simple accommodation and advice.

### Darién National Park, Panama
More than 500 bird species have been seen in the pristine rainforest of Darién National Park, among them many endangered species such as the harpy eagle. Indeed, Cerro Pirre mountain is considered by many birdwatchers to be one of the best sites in the world. Boat trips and forest walks are ideal ways to view the abundant wildlife, although visitors should seek advice on when it is safe to travel because of possible paramilitary activity.

### Cockscomb Basin Wildlife Sanctuary, Belize
Beneath the peaks of the Cockscomb mountain range, the dense rainforest of the Cockscomb Basin is home to around 600 jaguars as well as tapirs, anteaters, armadillos and otters. Nearly 300 bird species have been reported in this lush jungle, and a wide variety of reptiles and amphibians are readily visible. Excellent forest trails make this a very rewarding place for wildlife watchers.

## SOUTH AMERICA

### Podocarpus National Park, Ecuador
Encompassing a wide range of habitats at different altitudes, Podocarpus (near Loja) has many rare plant and animal species, such as the Andean fox, the Andean speckled bear and the mountain tapir. Birdlife is abundant, and it is easy to see many fascinating species. This is, however, a park in peril, with the authorities struggling to protect the environment from poachers, loggers and others. For visitors prepared to rough it, there is much to enjoy in this landscape of lakes, mountains and rainforest.

### Manu Biosphere Reserve, Peru
Altitudes range from 200 m (650 ft) to over 4,000 m (13,000 ft) in this area of rainforest near Cuzco. An astonishing 850 bird species are found here, and mammals include jaguars, ocelots, otters and many primate species. The reserve is divided into zones, with restricted visitor access in some areas. A stay in the Reserved Zone, which is set aside for ecotourism and research, must be arranged in advance, but offers the best jungle experience.

**▲ Monteverde Cloud Forest Reserve, Costa Rica**
Festooned with bromeliads and orchids, the towering rainforest trees of Monteverde Cloud Forest provide shelter for an enormous variety of wildlife including tapirs, monkeys, coatimundis and armadillos, as well as more than 400 bird species. The reserve was established in 1950 by a group of Quakers, who have developed a range of unobtrusive facilities for visitors, including simple accommodation and excellent guided walks.

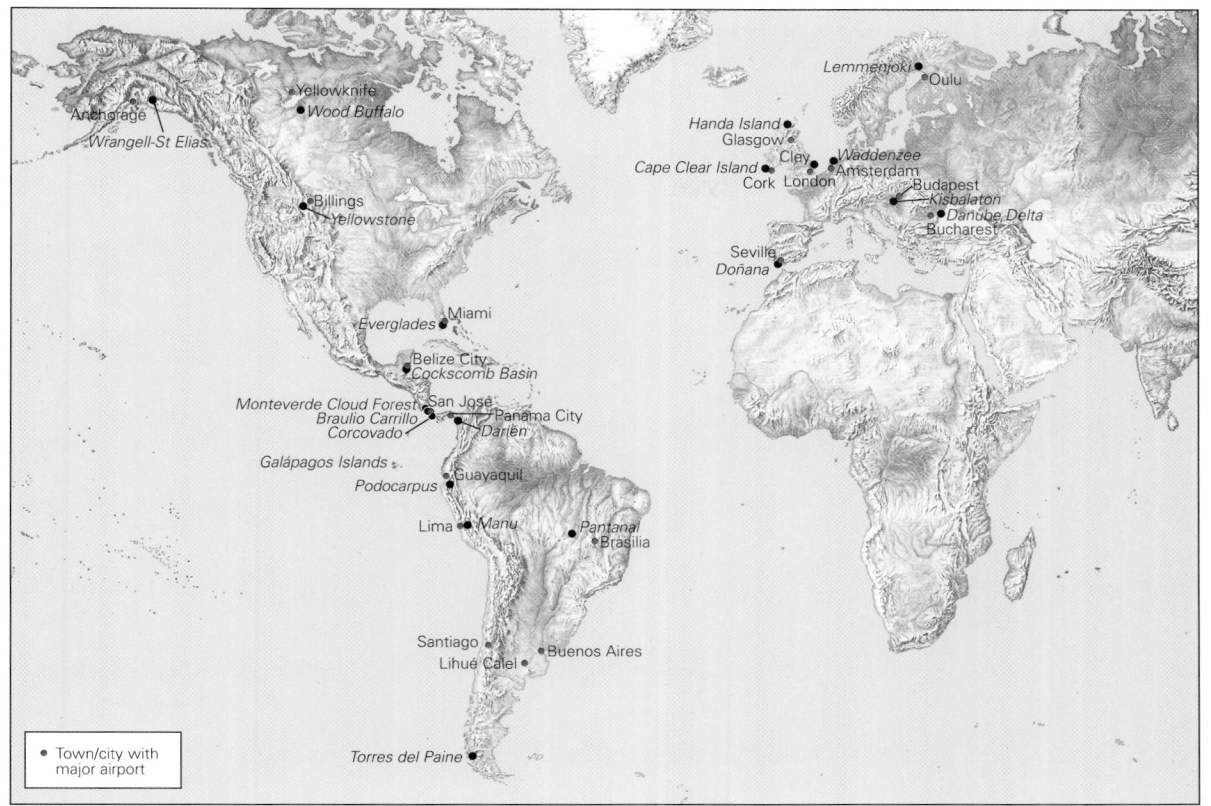

● Town/city with major airport

## ▶ Handa Island, Scotland

The sea cliffs of Handa Island are one of north-west Europe's largest seabird nesting sites, with the high cliff ledges attracting guillemots, razorbills and kittiwakes in enormous numbers. Fulmars, puffins and shags also nest here, while the island's moorland is home to great and Arctic skuas, red-throated divers, shelducks, ringed plovers, wheatears, meadow pipits and skylarks. The island can be visited for the day by boat from the mainland village of Tarbet, near Loch Laxford.

### Pantanal, Brazil

A vast swamp covering an area the size of Great Britain, the Pantanal is perhaps the best place to see wildlife in the Americas. Animals wander freely around the wide open spaces, making it relatively easy for visitors to spot such creatures as alligators, jaguars and anacondas, and birds such as the giant red-necked stork. There are organized tours by boat or jeep and on horseback, with overnight accommodation at converted ranch houses.

### Lihué Calel National Park, Argentina

An arid landscape of low, pink granite mountains and scrub forest, Lihué Calel (south-west of Santa Rosa) is home to several wild cat species and other mammals such as guanacos, Patagonian foxes, Patagonian hares and chinchillas. Birdlife is plentiful, too, and includes many species of birds of prey. The park has an excellent campsite and visitor centre.

## EUROPE

### Lemmenjoki National Park, Lappland, Finland

Lemmenjoki (near Inarijärvi) is one of the most extensive areas of uninhabited, forested wilderness in Europe (2,855 sq km/1,102 sq miles). Wide rivers flow through a landscape of peatland and spruce- and birch-forested hills, home to brown bears, golden eagles, foxes, lynx, wolverines and moose. There are also plenty of semi-domesticated reindeer.

### Cape Clear Island, Ireland

Ireland's southernmost inhabited island, tiny Cape Clear is famous for its birds. It has breeding populations of chough, black guillemot and rock dove and is visited by many migrant species in August–October, including the rare bee-eater, little bittern, night and purple herons, and great reed warbler, as well as many seabirds. The Bird Observatory has a full-time bird-warden and offers simple accommodation.

### Cley Marshes, Norfolk, England

One of Britain's leading birdwatching reserves, Cley Marshes (near Sheringham) has many thatched hides offering excellent views of thousands of water birds. Migrating waders stop in the area on their way to and from their Arctic breeding grounds, and in summer bitterns and avocets breed here. Wildfowl such as teals, widgeons and shovelers are plentiful in winter.

### Waddenzee, The Netherlands

Regarded by birdwatchers as the most important intertidal area in Europe, Waddenzee has huge populations of waders and wildfowl. One of the best areas to see the birds is around Schiermonnikoog, particularly at high tide. Among the birds present in summer are avocets, godwits and ruffs, while in winter they include Bewick's swans, barnacle geese, marsh and hen harriers and white-tailed eagles.

### Kisbalaton Reserve, Lake Balaton, Hungary

With its reed beds, the Kisbalaton Reserve provides the perfect environment for marsh birds to breed. Night, purple and squacco herons are all to be found here along with little and great white egrets, spoonbills, marsh harriers and several warblers. From October huge flocks of migrating ducks and geese stop in the reserve on their journey south.

### Danube Delta, Romania

One of Europe's last unspoiled ecosystems, consisting of forest, lakes, reed beds and marshland, the Danube Delta is home to huge numbers of birds. Due to the lack of tourist facilities, it is probably best-visited in an organized group, ideally from late May–June. Species include bitterns, pygmy cormorants, white pelicans, night, purple and squacco herons, spoonbills, ruddy shelducks, honey buzzards, bee-eaters and white-tailed eagles.

### Doñana National Park, Spain

Huge sand dunes and the seasonally flooded plains (*marismas*) behind them provide ideal conditions for a great variety of birdlife in one of Europe's most important wildlife habitats. Peregrines, stone-curlews and short-toed eagles are to be seen in the dunes, while the marismas are feeding grounds for white storks, spoonbills, night and purple herons and colonies of little and cattle egrets.

### Galápagos Islands and ecotourism

Lying 960 km (600 miles) off the coast of Ecuador, the fragile wilderness of the Galápagos Islands provides a habitat for a surprising combination of penguins and corals as well as giant tortoises, land and marine iguanas, sperm whales, sea lions, fur seals, orca whales, sharks and a variety of tropical fish. Many of the species living here are found nowhere else in the world, making the Galápagos a vital laboratory for the study of animal and plant life. Access to the islands is strictly controlled and limited to 50 designated visitor sites. The development of ecotourism in the Galápagos Islands aims to ensure the preservation of the habitats and wildlife while enabling tourists to visit and learn about this unique environment.

# Wildlife in Africa, Asia and Australasia

An African safari is one of the world's great wildlife-watching experiences. Vast stretches of open savanna are home to the 'big five' – lion, leopard, elephant, rhinoceros and buffalo – as well as herds of zebra and gazelle. The endangered Indian tiger and exotic komodo dragon are just two of the animals that attract visitors to Asia, while Australia has its own unique fauna, including kangaroo, koala and duck-billed platypus.

## AFRICA

### Abuko Nature Reserve, Gambia
In this small reserve, mangroves, gallery forest and savanna combine to attract over 270 bird species – including the world's largest and smallest kingfishers – making it one of the best birdwatching sites in West Africa. Abuko is also known for its troops of colobus, patas and vervet monkeys.

### Niokolo-Koba National Park, Senegal
Some 80 mammal species, including lions, leopards, elephants, waterbucks, bushbucks, baboons and chimpanzees live in Niokolo-Koba, along with around 350 bird species. The best time to see the animals is when they gather at waterholes during the hot season in April and May.

### Tsavo (East and West), Kenya
Tsavo East and Tsavo West combine to make one of the world's biggest national parks, covering an area of 21,000 sq km (8,000 sq miles). As well as the 'big five', the animals include cheetahs, giraffes, zebras, crocodiles, hippos, porcupines and mongooses. Tsavo East is a popular safari destination while at Tsavo West the excellent facilities include underwater hides for hippo watching.

◀ **Masai Mara National Reserve, Kenya**
Kenya's greatest concentration of wildlife can be seen in Masai Mara, where cheetahs, hyenas, zebras, hartebeest, hippos and crocodiles share the territory with the 'big five'. During the summer enormous herds of wildebeest, zebras and gazelles arrive from the Serengeti on the first stage of their dramatic annual migration.

### Ngorongoro Crater, Tanzania
Protected within a circle of thickly-forested crater walls, Ngorongoro Crater is an expanse of grassland and forest measuring 14 km (9 miles) across and teeming with wildlife. Elephants, leopards, hyenas, bushbucks, buffalo, wildebeest, elands, warthogs, gazelles and ostriches live alongside the rare black rhinoceros and the handsome black-maned lion, while Lake Makat is home to flocks of flamingos and other water birds.

### Jozani Reserve, Zanzibar, Tanzania
The largest remaining area of indigenous forest on Zanzibar, Jozani Reserve is home to a variety of birds and butterflies, as well as a number of rare mammals, including the red colobus monkey, which can only be found here.

### Bwindi National Park, Uganda
Half of all the world's endangered mountain gorillas live in Bwindi National Park, an area of hilly rainforest. The park supports a rich variety of animal life including chimpanzees, golden cats, civets, leopards, bushpigs and giant forest hogs. Small groups of visitors who have booked several months in advance can go on guided gorilla-tracking expeditions.

### Chobe National Park, Botswana
Encompassing habitats that range from marshland to forest, Chobe is home to a great variety of wildlife, including the rare puku and red lechwe antelope. Other inhabitants include lions, cheetahs, buffalo, giraffes, elephants, zebras, jackals, warthogs, hippos, crocodiles, hyenas, antelopes and wildebeest, as well as an abundance of birdlife. The animals can be viewed from boats on the Chobe River.

### Kruger National Park, South Africa
A vast game reserve covering almost 20,000 sq km (7,400 sq miles), Kruger Park is home to around 137 mammal species, including lions, elephants, rhinoceros, leopards, buffalo, zebras, giraffes, impalas, wildebeest, hippos and crocodiles, as well as the rare roan and sable antelopes and oribi. The northern part is especially noted for its birdlife, including the highest density of birds of prey anywhere in the world.

### Bird Island, Seychelles
Huge colonies of seabirds nest on the tiny, coral Bird Island. The sooty tern, fairy tern and common noddy are everywhere, while passing migrants add to the interest for birdwatchers. The island is also home to large numbers of giant turtles.

▼ **Serengeti National Park, Tanzania**
Covering 14,763 sq km (5,700 sq miles) and including woodland and mountains, as well as huge tracts of open grassland, the Serengeti is home to the 'big five' plus cheetahs, hyenas, zebras, giraffes, gazelles and many others. It also has around 500 bird species. It is most famous for the spectacular summer migration of gazelles, wildebeest and zebras, when around 2 million animals set off on a 800 km (500-mile) trek to fresh feeding grounds.

▲ **Etosha National Park, Namibia**
One of the most important game reserves in Africa, Etosha covers a vast 20,000 sq km (7,720 sq miles) of woodland and grassland surrounding the Etosha Pan – an immense saline desert. Animals living here include springboks, impalas, kudu, wildebeest, hartebeest, roan antelopes, elands, zebras, elephants and the rare white rhinoceros, as well as predators such as lions, leopards, cheetahs, caracals, jackals and hyenas. There are around 340 bird species, including eagles, ostriches and secretary birds. Accommodation to suit all budgets is available.

## ASIA

### Kaziranga National Park, Assam, India

Famous as the home of the rare one-horned Great Indian Rhinoceros – most of the surviving 1,500 are here – Kaziranga (east of Gauhati) also has tigers, bears, elephants, bison and many bird species. A good way to travel around the tall-grass and swampy terrain is on an elephant. The park is only open from November to April.

### Keoladeo Ghana National Park, Rajasthan, India

Formerly known as the Bharatpur Bird Sanctuary, Keoladeo is famous for its breeding populations of native water birds as well as its thousands of migrating birds which arrive every year from China and Siberia, including herons, storks, snake birds and the rare Siberian crane. The best time to visit is from October to February, when the migratory birds are in residence.

### Sundarbans Wildlife Sanctuary, India/Bangladesh

Home to one of the largest remaining tiger populations in India, the Sundarbans Wildlife Sanctuary covers 6,695 sq km (2,585 sq miles) of mangrove swamp in the vast Ganges delta. Tigers are not often spotted by visitors, but a boat excursion through the peaceful mangroves will reveal many other animals – monkeys, wild pigs, spotted deer, crocodiles and fishing cats, as well as a profusion of birdlife.

### Kanha National Park, Madhya Pradesh, India

Kipling set his *Jungle Book* in this beautiful landscape of forests, rivers and grasslands (near Mandla). Kanha is the only home of the barasingha (swamp deer) and it also plays an important role in the preservation of the tiger, leopard, chital, sambar and gaur (Indian bison). The park is open November–May, with sightings increasing from March onwards as the hot weather brings out the animals in search of water. Excursions are available.

### Khao Yai National Park, Thailand

Encompassing a variety of habitats, from mountains clad in evergreen forest to lowland scrub and grassland, Khao Yai (north-east of Bangkok) has an abundance of wildlife, including elephants, gibbons, porcupines, tigers, leopards, Indian munjaks, Malaysian sun bears and several species of deer and monkey. There are over 250 bird species here, too, including the great hornbill and many colourful parrots and parakeets. Visitors can venture deep into the forest on several excellent trails, some of which require guides.

### Taman Negara, Malaysia

Covering 4,340 sq km (1,676 sq miles) of ancient tropical rainforest, Taman Negara is a haven for hundreds of species of birds and animals, while its vegetation includes some of the world's rarest orchids. Inhabitants include tapirs, bears, elephants and gibbons. The park, which is the most visited in Pahang, has an elevated canopy walkway, and jungle hides in the trees, where visitors can spend the night.

### Komodo National Park, Indonesia

The world's largest lizard, the astonishing 3 m (10 ft) long Komodo dragon, is found only on Komodo and a few neighbouring small islands. Guided treks usually include visits to dragon feeding places, and allow visitors to see some of the other wildlife of the park, such as wild pigs, deer, monkeys, water buffalo and eagles.

### Ujung Kulon National Park, Indonesia

The last remaining low-relief forest on Java, in the far west, Ujung Kulon National Park is the only home of the one-horned Javan rhinoceros. Other inhabitants include the Javan gibbon, Javan tiger, muntjac (barking deer), chevrotain (mouse deer), green sea turtle and crocodile.

## AUSTRALASIA

### Eungella National Park, Queensland, Australia

With its tall, ancient rainforest trees, rocky creeks and spectacular waterfalls, Eungella is an extraordinarily beautiful place to watch wildlife. Among its inhabitants are kangaroos, possums, feathertail gliders, pythons and the native Eungella honeyeater, but the star attraction is the shy duck-billed platypus, which can be seen around the riverbanks at dawn and dusk.

### Otago Peninsula, New Zealand

A remarkable variety of wildlife is concentrated on the Otago Peninsula. Seals and other marine life can be seen along the rocky coastline, while the inlets and beaches shelter numerous waders and waterfowl. A protected albatross nesting-site at Taiaroa Head is open to the public once the eggs are laid, and yellow-eyed penguins can be seen at close quarters from an excellent conservation reserve.

### Catlins Forest Park, New Zealand

Ancient rainforest runs down to the rocky inlets and estuaries of the coast, offering a variety of habitats for some of New Zealand's rarest plants and animals. There are colonies of Hooker's sea lion and yellow-eyed penguin, and much birdlife. Two- and four-day ecotours are available.

◄ **Royal Chitwan National Park, Nepal**
With its lush sub-tropical jungle and floodplain swamp, Chitwan National Park is a natural habitat for animals such as the tiger, Indian rhinoceros and leopard. Tours on foot, by jeep or on the back of an elephant are best undertaken between October and March.

▼ **Kakadu National Park, Northern Territory, Australia**
Australia's largest national park, Kakadu encompasses a spectacular collection of rainforest, ravines and wetlands along the South Alligator River. These varied habitats shelter a vast array of wildlife, including 1,500 species of butterflies and moths, 75 reptile species, including crocodiles, 25 species of frog and one third of all Australia's bird species. Mammals include kangaroos, wallabies, walleroos, dingoes and many species of bat.

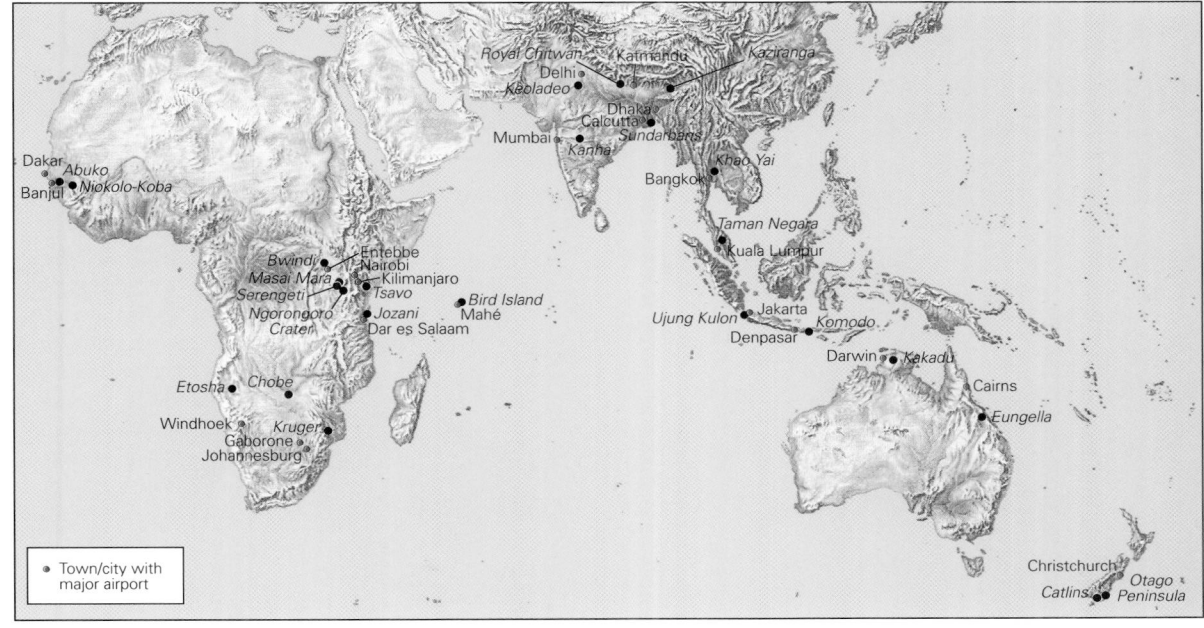

Town/city with major airport

# Marine wildlife

With whale numbers recovering strongly following the world ban on hunting, many seaports in North America, South Africa and Australasia offer boat trips to watch whales and other large fish and mammals. In the warm waters of the tropics, coral reefs teeming with vividly coloured sealife can be explored by scuba divers and snorkellers or viewed from the comfort of a glass-bottomed boat.

◀ **Florida Keys, USA**
Among many places in the Caribbean that serve as a base for viewing or swimming with dolphins is Florida Keys. Consisting of 45 islands surrounded by spectacular corals, Florida Keys also provides a perfect environment for scuba diving.

## THE AMERICAS

### Johnstone Strait, Canada
The sea between Vancouver Island and the mainland is one of the best places in the world to see orcas (killer whales), the largest and most powerful predators on earth, and minke whales.

### Hudson Bay, Canada
Beluga whales can be seen in June, July and August in the bay's Arctic waters. Particularly large numbers spend these months in the Churchill River estuary, an area famous for its polar bears.

### Cape Breton and Grand Manan Islands, Canada
Whale-watching boat trips take place around both islands. Off Grand Manan, in the Bay of Fundy, up to 20 whale species, including the rare northern right whale and the finback, can be seen.

### Massachusetts Bay, USA
Stellwagen Bank in Massachusetts Bay is a feeding ground for humpback, finback and minke whales from April to October. It is a world-renowned whale-watching area, attracting around 1.5 million whale watchers a year. The coastal towns of New England offer a range of boat trips.

### Caribbean Sea, Cayman Islands
The islands are famous among scuba divers for their exceptionally clear waters and deep diving with spectacular sponge colonies and a wide range of reef fish. Those interested in larger species can see dolphins, barracudas and sharks – including silky sharks – here.

### Caribbean Sea, Belize
The barrier reef of Belize is the largest in the western hemisphere, and second only to Australia's in the world. Between the reef and the mainland lie more than 175 cays and atolls (coral islands and rings) offering some of the best diving opportunities in the world. The extraordinary Blue Hole at the centre of Lighthouse Reef is a circular shaft over 120 m (395 ft) deep which was once a cavern underneath the sea bed. Half Moon Caye offers one of Belize's most spectacular wall dives, with an almost sheer drop overhung with wonderful coral spurs, rich in marine life.

### Caribbean Sea, Venezuela
There is good diving to be had around the offshore islands of Venezuela, especially in the archipelago of Los Roques with its white sand beaches and beautiful coral reefs. The Parque Nacional Morrocoy on the north-west coast of Venezuela is very popular for snorkelling.

### Paracas National Park, Peru
A boat trip around the offshore islands within this national park provides an opportunity to see dolphins, seals and sea lions, as well as pelicans and the great Andean condors that inhabit the cliffs.

## AFRICA AND THE INDIAN OCEAN

### Canary Islands
The waters around the islands provide sheltered feeding grounds for pilot whales, not usually seen so close to shore, and there are many boat trips available from Tenerife. Unfortunately, whale watching is not properly regulated here and whales have been injured by the boats.

### Red Sea, Egypt
Hurghada is a good base for snorkelling and diving around the coral reefs of the Red Sea. Jolanda Reef, at the tip of the Sinai Peninsula in the Ras Muhammad National Park, is a spectacular column of coral 800 m (2,625 ft) high. The park is best approached from the Sharm el Sheikh resort.

▲ **Point Reyes, California, USA**
Grey whales can be seen from Point Reyes, north of San Francisco, between October and January as they migrate down the coast of Canada and the USA to the Gulf of California. Between December and March they can be found at Guerrero Negro in Mexico, where they gather to calve.

Whale watching
Diving
Other

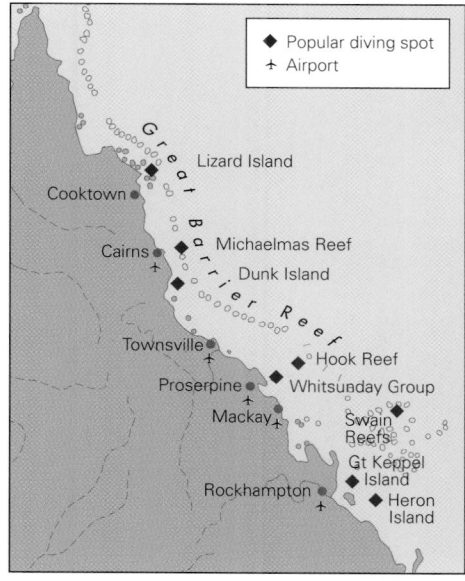

## Pemba, Zanzibar and Mafia, Tanzania

The three main islands off the Tanzanian coast are surrounded by spectacular coral reefs which are home to a wide variety of marine species including bat fish, lion fish, turtles and rays. They offer some of the best diving opportunities in the world from August to December. Mafia Island is also a favourite breeding ground for giant turtles.

## Cape of Good Hope, South Africa

In a country which has the strictest whale protection laws in the world, most whale watching takes place from the shore. The 'Whale Route' is a spectacularly scenic road along the coast from Cape Town, around the Cape of Good Hope, to the Indian Ocean, with many official whale-viewing sites. The town of Hermanus (the self-proclaimed 'whale capital' of South Africa) makes a good base. From June to October southern right whales, once hunted to near-extinction, can be seen swimming in these waters.

## Seychelles

The outlying islands in particular offer world-class diving. The reef-ringed shores are a paradise for snorkellers, with over 150 species of tropical reef fish and 30 species of coral. Dophins, porpoises, sharks and barracudas can also be seen. There are four marine national parks and diving schools with good facilities.

## Maldives

Without doubt the Maldives are the best place in the Indian Ocean for diving. There are hundreds of diving sites, with something for everyone from beginners to experts. The more adventurous can explore shipwrecks as well as spectacular caves and terraces of coral. There is also plenty of scope for snorkellers.

▶ **Tortuguero Park, Costa Rica**
In the company of a guide, limited numbers of visitors can watch green turtles at their largest nesting site in the western hemisphere. The turtles lay their eggs on the beach between July and October, the peak time being late August.

### Australia's Great Barrier Reef

The Great Barrier Reef is the largest structure on earth made by living organisms. It is a chain of coral reefs 2,000 km (1,200 miles) long, encompassing more than 600 islands and cays. About 20 of these islands have resort facilities, with Heron Island and Lizard Island both especially popular with divers. There are around 2,000 species of fish living on the reef and the area is home to many marine mammals, including the rare dugong and several species of whale. The best time to visit the reef is between April and December. Cairns is the mainland base for most reef activities and offers all kinds of tours.

## ASIA

### Ang Thong National Marine Park, Thailand

Boat trips around 42 limestone islands, many eroded into fantastic shapes, provide opportunities for seeing a variety of wildlife – including dolphins, turtles and sea otters – and for snorkelling and diving.

### Surin Islands, Thailand

The Surin Islands are noted for diving in moonlight. The wildlife that may be encountered includes wahoo turtles, moray eels, black tip sharks and bat fish.

### Sipadan Island, Sabah, Malaysia

An amazing undersea 'wall', teeming with marine life that includes whale sharks, manta rays, turtles and tuna, makes Sipadan one of the world's great diving destinations. The island is the tip of an underwater mountain, making it possible to dive from the beach.

### Bunaken Island, Sulawesi, Indonesia

Perhaps the most famous marine destination in Indonesia, Bunaken Island near Manado serves as the main base for exploring the stunning coral reefs known as the 'sea gardens of Sulawesi'.

## AUSTRALASIA AND THE PACIFIC

### Kaikoura, New Zealand

A world-famous whale-watching centre, Kaikoura caters for 30,000 whale watchers

a year. The deepwater canyons near the shore are home to sperm whales.

### Hawaii, USA

The extraordinary song of the humpback whale can be heard in the waters around Hawaii from November to May, after which these rare animals return to their summer feeding grounds in the near-polar waters of the north Pacific. Whale watching is strictly regulated, but there are plenty of boat trips on offer. Hawaii also has coral reefs, though with fewer species than on other Indo-Pacific reefs. Diving is popular, with lessons being provided in the crater lake of the extinct Molokini volcano. Excursions in submarines down to a depth of 50 m (160 ft) offer superb views of the underwater world through portholes.

### Rangiroa, Tuamotu Islands

Among many excellent diving sites in French Polynesia, this is possibly the best, with outstanding coral, sharks, dolphins, barracudas and rays.

### Marquesas Islands

The oxygen-rich water around the islands, which is thick with plankton, supports a variety of marine creatures, including hammerhead and white-tipped sharks, leopard and manta rays, tuna and barracudas. There are around 20 dive sites, including some impressive caves.

▲ **Malindi and Wasini Island, Kenya**
One of a number of good diving and snorkelling spots in Kenya, Malindi also offers excursions in glass-bottomed boats to the nearby coral reef. The Kisite Marine National Park on Wasini Island, in the far south, provides spectacular diving safaris.

# Great railway journeys

From the luxury of the Orient-Express to the spartan rigours of the Trans-Siberian Railway, the world's great train journeys exert an irresistible lure for many travellers, passing through spectacular landscapes. Journeys vary in length from a few hours to a fortnight, and the more sought-after trains must be booked well in advance.

## NORTH AMERICA

**Green Mountain Flyer, Vermont, USA**
**Distance: 21 km (13 miles)**
A vintage train takes passengers through the beautiful Vermont countryside, running alongside the Connecticut River for part of the way. Largely a tourist service, the peak period is during October when the autumn colours are at their best.

**Coast Starlight, USA**
**Distance: 2,235 km (1,389 miles)**
A journey from Seattle to Los Angeles, through the magnificent landscapes of the west coast of the USA, includes amongst its highlights the mountains of the Oregon Cascades and the Californian Coast Range. South of Oakland the track runs along the edge of the Pacific Ocean, passing several of California's most popular beaches.

**Los Mochis to Chihuahua, Mexico**
**Distance: 655 km (407 miles)**
This 14-hour journey is one of contrasting landscapes, from the tropical Pacific coastlands to the high northern plateau by way of the magnificent Copper Canyon (Barranca del Cobre). Longer and deeper than Arizona's Grand Canyon, this is an area of steeply wooded gorges and spectacular mountain peaks.

## SOUTH AMERICA

**Guayaquil to Quito, Ecuador**
**Distance: 463 km (288 miles)**
For those who relish danger as well as breathtaking scenery, this line – which has been called 'the world's greatest roller-

**▶ Palace on Wheels**
India's most luxurious train, originally hauled by the *Desert Queen*, takes passengers on an eight-day tour that begins and ends in Delhi. It includes Jaipur and the other major cities of Rajasthan, and Agra.

coaster' – is a must. It climbs high into the Andes, zigzagging perilously to an altitude of 3,609 m (11,840 ft) and passing directly under a waterfall. Trains are erratic and often break down.

**Central Railway, Peru**
**Distance: 335 km (208 miles)**
The highest railway in the world, this takes passengers on an eight- to nine-hour journey across the Andes, from Lima to Huancayo. Dizzy heights, sheer drops, zigzags, loops and tunnels abound.

## EUROPE

**Flåm Railway, Norway**
**Distance: 20 km (12 miles)**
Dropping 865 m (2,838 ft) in just 20 km (12 miles), this is one of the steepest non-rack railways in the world. Beginning with a view over the Kjosfossen lake and waterfall, the train weaves its way from Myrdal towards Aurlands Fjord and Flåm through a series of tunnels, with spectacular views between tunnels and snow shelters.

**West Highland Line, Scotland**
**Distance: 264 km (164 miles)**
Running between Glasgow and Mallaig, this line provides one of the most spectacular railway journeys in Britain. The route is particularly dramatic between Fort William and Mallaig, with a series of viaducts and tunnels through the mountains high above the Atlantic coast.

**Venice Simplon-Orient-Express, Europe**
**Distance: 1,714 km (1,065 miles)**
Passengers travel in style on a train that re-creates the romance of the golden age of rail as it crosses Europe from London to Venice, via Paris, Zürich, Innsbruck and Verona, in 32 hours. Orient-Express trains also run to Rome and Istanbul on a variety of routes that go through Venice, Florence, Lucerne, Budapest and Bucharest.

**Andalusian Express, Spain**
**Distance: 740 km (460 miles)**
The luxurious *Al Andalus* follows a circular route from Seville through the beautiful Andalusian countryside, with its citrus and olive groves, vineyards and hilltop villages. There are opportunities to stop off and see the sites at Córdoba, Granada, Antequera and Ronda.

**◀ Glacier Express, Switzerland**
**Distance: 290 km (180 miles)**
An exhilarating seven-and-a-half hour journey in the Swiss Alps, between the ski resorts of St Moritz and Zermatt, is provided by this train. Extraordinary feats of engineering are displayed as it weaves its way through the mountains, travelling through 91 tunnels, crossing 291 bridges and negotiating hairpin bends and steep ascents.

**▲ Canadian, Canada**
**Distance: 2,776 miles (4,4467 km)**
On a 69-hour journey that begins in Toronto, this train passes through some of the most beautiful scenery on earth. The prairie lands of Manitoba and Saskatchewan give way to the cattle ranches of Alberta, from where the train climbs into the Rockies. Here it passes lakes, glaciers and the dramatic Fraser Canyon before reaching Vancouver.

**Useful web addresses**
all preceded by www.

Canadian trains:
cwrr.com
viarail.ca

US trains:
amtrak.com

European trains:
raileurope.com

Orient-Express:
orient-expresstrains.com

Pride of Africa:
rovos.co.za

Palace on Wheels:
palaceonwheels.net

Eastern and Oriental Express:
diethelm-travel.com/eastern.htm

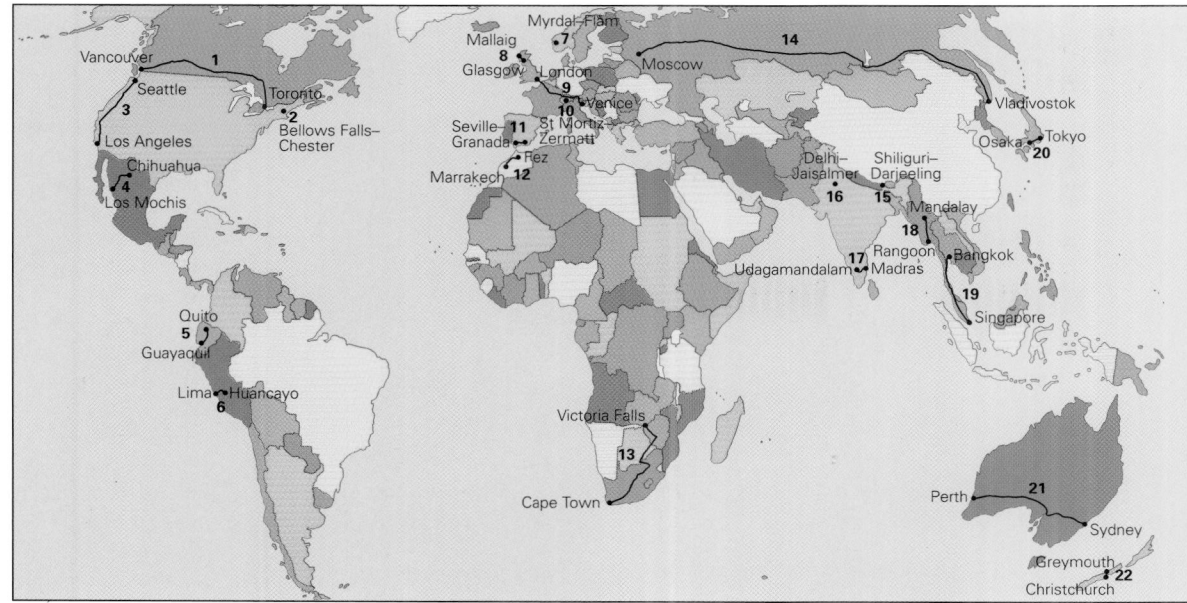

| | |
|---|---|
| 1 | Canadian, Canada |
| 2 | Green Mountain Flyer, USA |
| 3 | Coast Starlight, USA |
| 4 | Los Mochis to Chihuahua, Mexico |
| 5 | Guayaquil to Quito, Ecuador |
| 6 | Central Railway, Peru |
| 7 | Flåm Railway, Norway |
| 8 | West Highland Line, Scotland |
| 9 | Venice Simplon-Orient-Express, Europe |
| 10 | Glacier Express, Switzerland |
| 11 | Andalusian Express, Spain |
| 12 | Marrakech Express, Morocco |
| 13 | Pride of Africa, Southern Africa |
| 14 | Trans-Siberian Railway, Russia |
| 15 | Darjeeling Himalayan Railway, India |
| 16 | Palace on Wheels, India |
| 17 | Madras to Udagamandalam, India |
| 18 | Mandalay Express, Burma (Myanmar) |
| 19 | Eastern Oriental Express, Thailand and Malaysia |
| 20 | Tokyo to Osaka, Japan |
| 21 | Indian–Pacific, Australia |
| 22 | TranzAlpine Express, New Zealand |

## AFRICA

### Marrakech Express, Morocco
**Distance: 583 km (362 miles)**

Passing through Morocco's four imperial cities, this nine-hour journey begins in Marrakech, near the foot of the High Atlas Mountains, and travels north through the desert to Casablanca. From here the line follows the Atlantic coast to Rabat then gradually heads back inland through orchards and olive groves to Meknès and on to Fès.

### Pride of Africa, Southern Africa
**Distance: 3,2000 km (2,000 miles)**

The journey from Cape Town in this luxurious train is full of romance and drama. In the early stages the train travels through a landscape of vineyards and farmland and across the Karoo Desert to Pretoria. Passengers can enjoy watching wildlife as the journey continues through the African bush across Botswana and Zimbabwe to the spectacular Victoria Falls on the Zambian border.

## ASIA

### Madras to Udagamandalam, India
**Distance: 640 km (400 miles)**

This 16-hour journey takes travellers from the plains of Madras through a colourful rural landscape and up into the beautiful Nilgiri hills to the famous hill station of Udagamandalam, formerly known as Ootacamund, or Ooty. The train passes through some of the most dramatic scenery India has to offer, climbing steeply on India's only rack railway to the gentler landscapes of the Deccan Plateau.

### Darjeeling Himalayan Railway, India
**Distance: 88 km (55 miles)**

The tiny engine used on this railway, which is a UNESCO heritage site, takes passengers from Shiliguri on the hot Bengal plains to the mountain climate of Darjeeling in the Himalayas. The journey involves steep ascents and precipitous curves, climbing 2,164 m (7,100 ft). On the way the train passes through Ghoom, which is the second highest station in the world at 2,258 m (7,408 ft) above sea level.

### Mandalay Express, Burma (Myanmar)
**Distance: 616 km (385 miles)**

By no means a tourist train, the Express offers the traveller a truly local experience as it makes its way slowly north from Yangon (formerly Rangoon) through a landscape of rice fields and golden-spired pagodas. The crowded train makes numerous – often unscheduled – stops along the way, making it an unpredictable and colourful journey. Best undertaken between November and February, the journey takes around 16 hours.

### Eastern and Oriental Express, Thailand and Malaysia
**Distance: 1,943 km (1,207 miles)**

Starting in Bangkok, this train takes 52 hours to travel south through the terraced farmlands of Thailand and the rubber plantations and jungles of Malaysia to Singapore. It represents the height of luxury in train travel, while International Express trains that follow the same route provide a more down-to-earth experience.

## AUSTRALASIA

### Indian–Pacific, Australia
**Distance: 3,960 km (2,461 miles)**

This three-day transcontinental service from Perth to Sydney includes the longest stretch of straight railway track in the world (462 km/287 miles) across the vast expanse of the Nullarbor Plain, offering the traveller a rare sense of space and distance. The mountains of the Flinders and Gawler ranges provide a stunning contrast, while the Blue Mountains (see *Mountains and volcanoes*) offer a spectacular finale.

◀ **Tokyo to Osaka, Japan**
**Distance: 518 km (322 miles)**

The Nozomi Express – the fastest scheduled train service in the world – travels at speeds of up to 300 km/h (186 mph) along this line. Not quite as fast, the Hikari Express completes the journey in just over three hours. However, the scenery, which includes Mount Fuji, can best be appreciated from the slower 'bullet' trains.

### TranzAlpine Express, New Zealand
**Distance: 233 km (154 miles)**

Travelling from Christchurch on the South Island's east coast to Greymouth on the west coast, the Express takes passengers on a four-and-a-half hour journey through a variety of landscapes. After crossing the farmlands of the Canterbury Plains it follows the Waimakariri River gorge into the mountainous Arthur's Pass National Park, where it enters the long Otira tunnel. From here the line descends through lush rainforest, passing lakes Poerua and Brunner, to Greymouth.

### Trans-Siberian Railway, Russia
**Distance: 9,297 km (5,776 miles)**

The southern shore of Lake Baikal is on the route of the Trans-Siberian Railway, the world's longest, and possibly most famous, railway. The eight-day journey takes passengers from Moscow to Vladivostok via the Urals, the forested wilderness of Siberia, and the Transbaikalian Mountains.

In the early days of the railway, built between 1891 and 1916, a ferry was used in summer to carry the train across Lake Baikal, while in winter, when the lake froze, temporary rails were laid over the ice. The Siberian landscape is particularly beautiful in winter when it is covered with snow. In the spring there are carpets of wild flowers while in autumn there are the golden colours of the birch forests.

# River and canal journeys

The world's great boat journeys give travellers a unique perspective on the countries through which they pass: rivers and canals were the highways of the past, and there are often opportunities to visit historic sites or natural habitats. Whether you are steaming down the Mississippi in a paddleboat, gliding through the French countryside past castles and vineyards or exploring the tributaries of the Amazon, the pace of the journey gives ample time to enjoy the beauty of the surroundings.

## NORTH AMERICA

### St Lawrence, Canada

From Kingston, where Lake Ontario flows into the majestic St Lawrence River, a six-night journey can be made on a replica steamboat to Montréal (see *World Cities*) and Québec (see *Historic sites in the Americas*). Just east of Kingston the river is dotted with literally a Thousand Islands, many of which have summer houses and opulent mansions set amid forests of yellow birch, silver maple and red and white trillium. In the spring the trillium trees are covered by white blossom.

### Upper Mississippi, USA

In the summer months, seven-day cruises by paddleboat run between Minneapolis/St Paul and St Louis. There are also three-day cruises between St Louis and Memphis. The upper river, flowing through relatively flat countryside, is wide, slow moving and dotted with islands, but the stretch immediately below St Louis flows between rocky bluffs. Days spent cruising are alternated with sightseeing tours of such places as the boyhood home of Mark Twain, in Hannibal, Memphis, and a historic Native American site in Burlington, Iowa.

► **St Petersburg to Moscow, Russia**
This seven-day cruise passes through a network of rivers, lakes and canals in the richly wooded region of Southern Karelia, and down the upper reaches of the Volga River. Ports of call include the ancient town of Yaroslavl, the attractive Karelian capital of Petrozavodsk, and the Church of the Transfiguration on the island of Kizhi in Lake Onega, with its 22 wooden domes, constructed without a single nail.

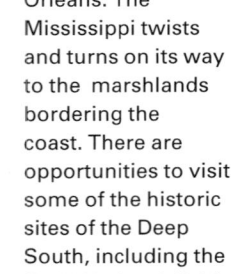

◄ **Lower Mississippi, USA**
A seven-day cruise by paddleboat can be taken from Memphis to New Orleans. The Mississippi twists and turns on its way to the marshlands bordering the coast. There are opportunities to visit some of the historic sites of the Deep South, including the Civil War battlefields of Vicksburg, and the elegant mansion at Oak Alley Plantation, and to sample some of the local Creole and Cajun cuisine.

## CENTRAL AND SOUTH AMERICA

### Amazon, Peru and Brazil

Cruises of between three and ten days along the Amazon River, starting from the remote but elegant Peruvian town of Iquitos, or from the brash and bustling Manaus in Brazil, are a relatively comfortable way to see the abundant wildlife of the rainforest. Many companies adopt an educational approach and include lectures on the local flora and fauna. Some include an opportunity to explore smaller tributaries by canoe. For the adventurous independent traveller who is prepared to rough it, a six-day journey by local riverboat from the Atlantic port of Belém to Manaus offers an unforgettable experience of local life and culture.

### Orinoco Delta, Venezuela

The vast Orinoco Delta – a maze of channels running between countless forested islands – is one of Venezuela's wildest regions. The area is home to the indigenous Warao people, known for their skilled carving and basketwork, whose houses on stilts can be seen on the

riverbanks. Boat tours into the delta can be arranged from the town of Tucupita, and usually last for between two and four days.

## EUROPE

### Shropshire Union Canal, UK

From Autherley, a 100 km (60-mile) journey can be taken on a slow-moving barge along the Shropshire Union Canal. Deep wooded cuttings, peaceful rural landscapes, medieval market towns and quiet villages are all passed at little more than walking pace. The ancient city of Chester, with its Roman ruins and medieval city walls, is a highlight of the journey. The canal ends at Ellesmere Port on the River Mersey, where there is an excellent boating museum.

### Rhine, Switzerland, Germany and the Netherlands

A ten-day journey down the Rhine from Basel to Arnhem combines stunning scenery with a chance to visit the historic towns and cities along its banks. After flowing through the German Black Forest, the river passes romantic clifftop castles, sloping vineyards and picturesque villages on its way to the cities of the north: Bonn, Cologne and Düsseldorf. A detour up the River Neckar to the historic town of Heidelberg is often included.

▲ **The Burgundy Canal, France**
Passing through a landscape of wooded valleys and sleepy villages, the six-day journey on a barge from Tonnere to Dijon along the Burgundy Canal provides an opportunity to see the beautiful 16th-century chateaux of Tanlay and Ancy le Franc and the 12th-century Cistercian Abbey of Fontenay. The region is famous for its *grand cru* vineyards and its robust cuisine, and there are plenty of opportunities to enjoy both along the way.

## Douro, Portugal

Most cruises on the Douro are round trips of seven to nine days, beginning and ending in Porto. Once the boat leaves the coastal plain, it passes between spectacularly terraced vineyards, in an area unspoilt by major roads. Ports of call include the picturesque towns of Lamego and Vila Real. The region is the centre of Portugal's port wine production, and all cruises include a visit to a vineyard to sample the local produce.

## Danube, Hungary, Slovak Republic, Austria and Germany

A Danube cruise of around eight days combines sightseeing tours of some of Central Europe's most historic towns and cities with an opportunity to relax on board, watching rich farmland and terraced slopes slip past. A cruise up-river from Budapest to Regensburg includes frequent stops, enabling passengers to explore Bratislava, Vienna, Linz and Passau, and to visit the sumptuous Baroque palace of Schönbrunn and the Benedictine Abbey in Melk. Since the boat berths overnight, passengers can also enjoy some nightlife ashore, and attend specially organized classical concerts.

## AFRICA

### River Gambia National Park, Gambia

A day trip on the river from Janjanbureh (Georgetown) or Kuntaur provides an opportunity to view crocodiles and hippos at close range. As the rice fields and coconut trees on the banks give way to dense forest, it may also be possible to glimpse monkeys, baboons and many species of birds.

### Niger, Mali

A journey along the River Niger as it curves through the semi-desert of the Sahel is the classic way to see and experience the life of this area. Local passenger boats are scheduled to take seven days, but can take as long as 14 to travel between Gao and Koulikoro. The most popular section is the two days or so between Mopti and Korioumé, the stopping point for visits to the ancient desert city of Timbuktu. Also highly recommended is a detour up the River Bani to the beautiful old town of Djenné, where the mosque is a stunning example of construction using mud bricks and render.

## ASIA AND AUSTRALASIA

### Backwaters of Kerala, India

The eight-hour journey through the backwaters of Kerala, from Kollam (Quilon) to Alappuzha, is popular with tourists. Passengers are transported along a network of rivers, canals and lagoons, overhung with dense tropical foliage that every so often gives way to open paddy fields. Brightly coloured birds and ancient buildings can be glimpsed on the banks, and the Keralan people can be seen going about their daily lives.

### Gorges of the Yangtze, China

Time is running out for those who want to experience the ferocious pounding of the Yangtze River as it passes between the rocky pinnacles of the Three Gorges. In 2008 the controversial Three Gorges Dam is due to be completed, creating the world's largest reservoir. Until then it is still possible to travel by steamship from Chongqing to Shanghai in a week, passing through the Qutang, Wuhang, and Xiling gorges, stopping off at the small town of Badong, perched precariously on the cliffs, and out into the wider, slower-moving lower reaches of the river.

### Sepik, Papua New Guinea

The Sepik River twists and turns its way from the central mountains of Papua New Guinea through jungles, swamps and grasslands to the sea. Most cruises start from a remote inland location, to which passengers are transferred from Port Moresby by small plane. There is then a leisurely journey through the rainforest, with stops at riverside villages, some of which are on stilts. The people of the region are renowned for their woodcarving and traditional art, each village having its own distinctive style.

### Murray, South Australia

A six-day cruise on a paddleboat, beginning and ending at Mannum, passes through colourful scenery, including verdant wetlands, brick-red plains, sandstone cliffs and deep blue lagoons. The cruise may also include a visit to the old river port of Morgan and an opportunity to hear about Aboriginal customs from elders at the Ngaut Ngaut Conservation Park.

◄ **Nile, Egypt**
A week-long cruise up the Nile from Luxor to Aswan and back combines visits to magnificent historic sites – such as the huge temple of Karnak and the tombs in the Valley of the Kings at Luxor – with periods of relaxation on board an air-conditioned riverboat. There are also opportunities to take camel rides into the desert that lies beyond the narrow fertile strip on either side of the river. From Aswan, where it is possible to sail on the river in a *felucca* (pictured here), a short flight takes passengers to the splendid temple of Abu Simbel, above the shores of Lake Nasser. Abu Simbel can also be reached by taking a luxury three-day cruise on the lake. Created by the building of the Aswan Dam, the lake itself is an impressive sight.

**Useful web addresses**
all preceded by www.
fieldingtravel.com
cruise-tours.com
goway.com/cruises
burgundy-canal.com
cruiselocator.com

▼ **Li, China**
The 80 km (50-mile) journey down the Li River from Guilin to the beautiful town of Yangshuo passes through a landscape of precipitous peaks, with names such as Paint Brush Hill and Five Tigers Catch a Goat Hill. Gliding past bamboo-lined riverbanks and picturesque villages, the trip and a bus-ride back to Guilin takes one day.

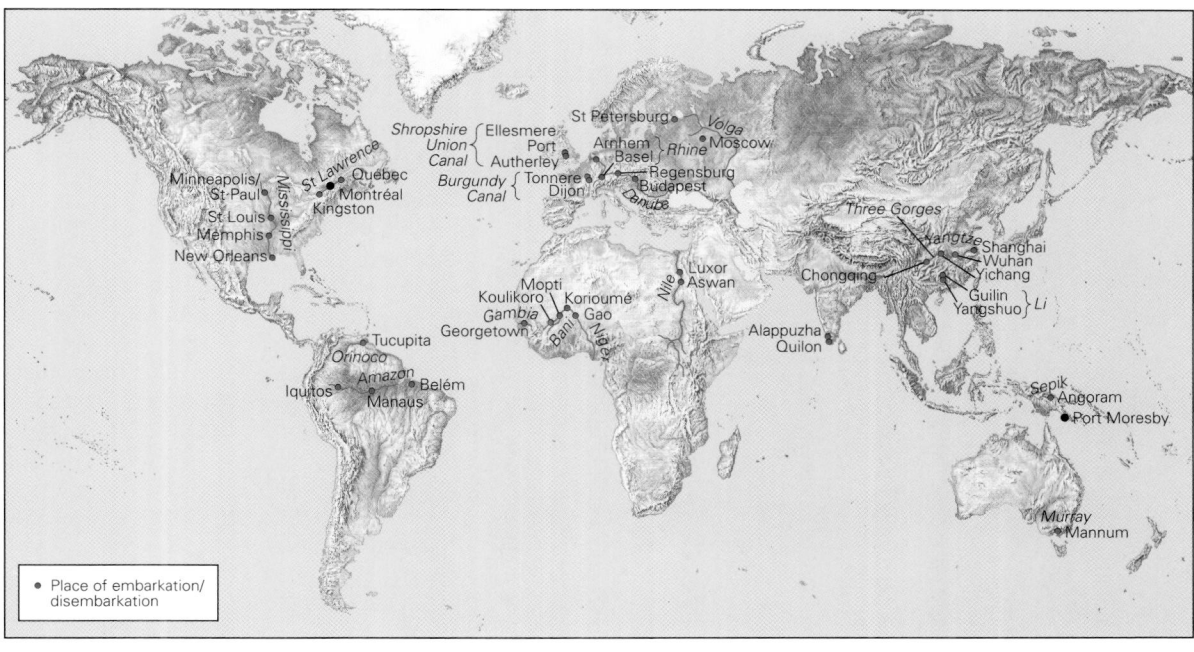

• Place of embarkation/ disembarkation

# Sea and ocean cruises

Cruises attract all kinds of travellers and cater for an increasingly wide range of tastes. The steep-sided inlets of Alaska, Chile, Norway and New Zealand allow cruise liners to hug the coast, providing matchless views of these dramatic landscapes. Caribbean cruises allow almost daily shore visits, for shopping and exploring. Transatlantic cruises provide lavish on-board entertainment during the long sea passages. Cruise companies also vary in their appeal: some include lectures on the places they visit; others take a far less serious approach!

**◄ The Caribbean**
There are numerous variations on the Caribbean cruise, but virtually all have relatively short sea passages and a visit to a different island almost every day. There are organized trips to the rain-forests of Puerto Rico and sites of European colonial history. Some passengers, however, prefer to spend their time simply enjoying the islands' magnificent beaches.

## NORTH AMERICA AND THE ATLANTIC

### Alaska/British Columbia
The main attractions of a cruise in this area are the spectacular mountain scenery and the opportunity to see whales and seals, bears and birds of prey at close hand. Ships hug the coastline, entering steep-sided fjords and sailing close to the mouths of glaciers. Ports of call include Juneau, Alaska's capital, the 'gold rush' town of Skagway, and the Russian settlement of Sitka, with its onion domes.

### Mexican Riviera
Mexico's west coast is becoming an increasingly popular area for relatively short cruises to catch the late-summer sunshine. For some tourists, the attractions are miles of unspoilt beaches fringed by jungle, such as those at Manzanillo and Zihuatanejo, and being able to go marlin fishing. For others they are the opportunities to experience Mexican culture and to visit the chic resort of Puerto Vallarta.

### Atlantic Isles (Canaries, Madeira)
The Atlantic Isles are a popular cruise destination, particularly in winter and spring, when the lower mountain slopes are brilliant with flowers. Shore visits in Madeira usually include the novelty of a ride in a bullock cart or wicker sled on the mountain roads, while a trip to the summit of Tenerife's Mount Teide (3,718 m/12,000 ft) provides spectacular views of the surrounding islands.

### Transatlantic cruises
Cruises link Europe with New York or Boston, with ports further south, such as Miami, and also with various Caribbean islands. The most direct, more northerly, route is for those wishing to enjoy the elaborate onboard entertainment, high standard of cuisine, and formal social life that are typical of the transatlantic liner. On ships plying more southerly waters, passengers can combine a luxury lifestyle with sunbathing, swimming and other deck activities.

## SOUTH AMERICA

### Chilean fjords
Cruises along the most southern 1,000 km (625 miles) of Chile's coastline provide magnificent views of mountains and glaciers. The further south, the colder and less predictable the weather becomes, but for many the thrill of travelling the route of Darwin's *Beagle* and visiting Tierra del Fuego outweighs the risk of storms.

## EUROPE

### Norwegian fjords
Those cruising the fjords of Norway do so primarily to enjoy the majestic mountain scenery. Waterfalls, glaciers and wildlife can all be viewed from the comfort of the ship, while shore visits include a ride on a spectacular mountain railway from Flåm (see *Great railway journeys*). Some cruises extend as far as Europe's most northern point, where passengers can experience the midnight sun.

### Western Mediterranean
One of the joys of a cruise in the Western Mediterranean is the opportunity to sample the local cuisine and wines. Most cruises include a day in the vibrant Spanish city of Barcelona. In Italy, there are brief organized trips to view the art treasures of Pisa and Florence, and the Roman remains of Pompeii (see *Historic sites in Europe*). There are also opportunities to enjoy the high-life in some of the fashionable resorts of the French Riviera, such as St Tropez, to visit the casinos of Monte Carlo, and to watch the Spanish flamenco dancers in Cartagena. Some cruises extend as far as the Adriatic, call in at the fortress town of Dubrovnik and include a day's sightseeing in Venice.

### Eastern Mediterranean
A region rich in the remains of earlier civilizations, the Eastern Mediterranean provides much of historic interest, and many cruises have on-board experts to give background lectures. Some of the main sites visited include the Roman town of Ephesus in Turkey, the Ancient Greek ruins of Delos, the Crusader castle of Krak des Chevaliers in Syria, and the pyramids in Egypt (see *Historic sites in Africa*). Most cruises also include opportunities for swimming, snorkelling and sunbathing.

**▼ Antarctic**
Many of the 'expedition cruises' to the Antarctic use converted research ships or ice breakers, which offer less luxurious accommodation than other cruise ships. Passengers are taken ashore in small inflatable craft, and are thus able to get close to the teeming wildlife. There is always the chance of encountering whales in the surrounding seas, as well as sighting beautifully sculpted icebergs.

**▲ North-east America**
The north-eastern seaboard of America offers areas of great natural beauty such as Acadia National Park in Maine, whose fall colours are the focus of October cruises. There is also an opportunity to see the whales that frequent the waters of Stellwagen Bank off the coast of Massachusetts. Included in a wide variety of shore visits are the Canadian fishing town of Lunenburg, the popular US resort of Martha's Vineyard, and the cities of Boston and New York.

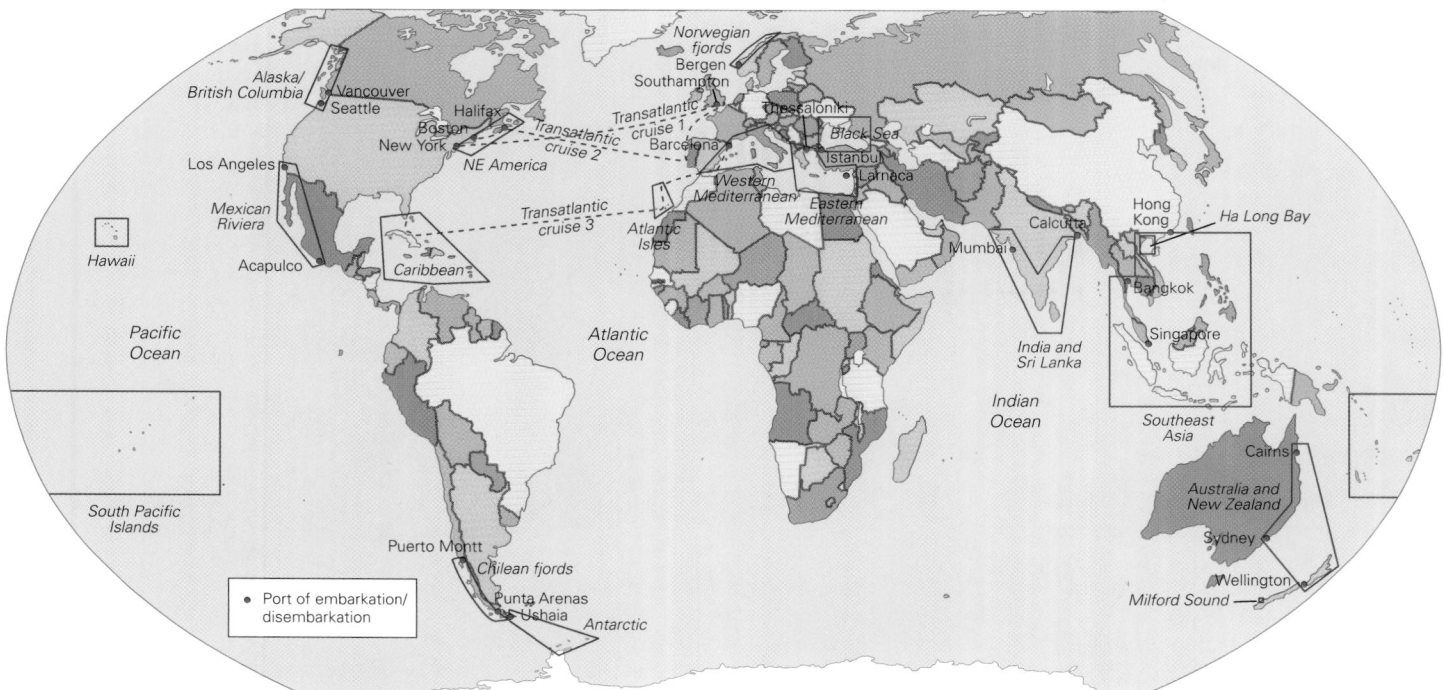

▼ Black Sea

**▼ Black Sea**
A day in Istanbul (see *World Cities*) is included in most cruises of the Black Sea. The countries bordering the Black Sea provide a rich variety of historic sites, from the medieval churches of Nesebúr in Bulgaria, to the 19th-century opera house in Ukrainian Odessa, the 18th-century palace of Tsar Alexander II on the Crimean peninsula, and the abandoned Byzantine monastery of Sumela, high above the Turkish port of Trabzon.

## AFRICA, ASIA AND THE INDIAN OCEAN

### India and Sri Lanka

Cruises around the Indian subcontinent provide an opportunity to visit a number of historic sites without the strain of overland travel. A day's sightseeing is followed by a day's relaxation in the relatively cool sea breezes. Many of the sites visited are from India's colonial past – the Dutch fort at Cochin, the former Portuguese colony of Goa, remnants of the British Raj in Madras – but there are also trips to some indigenous sites, such as the Hindu cave temples of Mumbai (Bombay).

### South-east Asia

With such a wealth of possible sights and exciting ports of call, there are many varieties of the South-east Asian cruise, which is a popular option for the Christmas break. Most shore visits consist of whistle-stop tours of the port of call, but there are also more adventurous expeditions, such as a visit to an orang-utan sanctuary in Sarawak, or a trek to catch a glimpse of the famous 'Komodo dragon' (see *Wildlife in Asia*). Many of the cruises visit Bali, with its sandy beaches, terraced rice fields and ornate Hindu temples.

## AUSTRALASIA AND THE PACIFIC

### Australia and New Zealand

Most cruises of Australia's east coast provide more than one opportunity to stop on the 2,000 km (1,250-mile) long Great Barrier Reef (see *Marine wildlife*). By way of contrast, the natural wonders of New Zealand include the spouting geysers and boiling mud of Rotorua (see *Lakes and waterfalls*), and the dolphins, whales and penguins of the verdant Bay of Islands.

### Milford Sound, New Zealand

Milford Sound is perfect for a cruise of just a few hours. It is possible to enjoy lunch while gazing out at towering granite peaks and glaciers, and, on the lower slopes, thick beech forests and waterfalls. There is always the chance of sighting the dolphins, seals, penguins and other sea birds that inhabit the sheltered inlet.

### Hawaii, USA

The mountainous Hawaiian island chain was formed by a series of volcanoes, many of which are still active. Trips to Volcanoes National Park and the world's most active volcano usually include the memorable experience of getting as close as is safe to the actual lava flow. The lower slopes of the mountains are covered in rainforest, home to 20,000 species of orchid and echoing to the sound of waterfalls. Hawaii is a port of call for most Pacific cruises, but it is also possible to take a cruise exclusively of the islands, and so be able to enjoy some of the dramatic beaches and the local culture.

### Where, when and for how long?

| | Main season | Duration of cruise (in days) |
|---|---|---|
| Alaska | May–Sept | 7–14 |
| NE America | Aug–Oct | 7–14 |
| Mexican Riviera | Sept–Oct | 7–10 |
| Atlantic Islands | Apr–Dec | 9–14 |
| Transatlantic | April and Sep–Nov | 14 |
| Caribbean | Oct–Dec | 3–23 |
| Chilean fjords | Oct–May | 3–7 |
| Antarctica | mid-Oct– early March | 9–12 |
| Norwegian fjords | May–July | 7–14 |
| Western Mediterranean | Apr–Nov | 12–14 |
| Eastern Mediterranean | Aug–Dec | 10–14 |
| Black Sea | Aug–Oct | 14 |
| India/Sri Lanka | Dec–Feb | 14 |
| Southeast Asia | Dec–Feb | 8–17 |
| Ha Long, Vietnam | All year | 1 |
| Australia/ New Zealand | Nov–Apr | 14 |
| Milford Sound | Nov–Apr | half day |
| Hawaii | Sept–Oct | 7–14 |

**Useful web addresses**
all preceded by www.

travelshop.de/english/ cruises.html

cruises.about.com/travel /cruises/mbody.htm

fieldingtravel.com

cruiselocator.com

cruiseweb.com

cruiseinformationservice .co.uk

**◄ Ha Long Bay, Gulf of Tonkin, Vietnam**
'Ha Long' means 'where the dragon plunged into the sea', and the bay contains around 3,000 islands, famous for their sheer, limestone cliffs with honeycombs of caves. A day trip from Haiphong (by motorboat or slower junk) is included in the itineraries of long-distance cruises as well as being available to the independent traveller.

# Winter sports

Mountain resorts all over the world are upgrading their facilities: constructing 'ski parks' for snowboarders, installing faster ski-lifts to cut queuing times, and using snow cannons to guarantee good conditions. Now that many of the top resorts can be reached by long-haul flights from either hemisphere, it is possible to enjoy 'winter sports' at any time of year.

### THE AMERICAS

### Whistler, British Columbia, Canada

Considered one of the top ski resorts in the world, the resort provides access to two mountains with vertical drops of around 1,500 m (5,000 ft). As well as a wide variety of runs, Whistler's crowning glory is its five bowls, which provide plenty of scope for expert skiers and boarders, the latter being well catered for. The base village, which is pedestrian-only, has over 100 restaurants.

### Banff, Alberta, Canada

The city of Banff is the gateway to three resorts that are linked by a shuttle bus and share a lift pass. **Lake Louise**, a particularly beautiful resort, is a good choice for families of mixed ability, with a beginners' run from the top of every chair lift. **Sunshine Village** includes 'Delirium Dive', one of the most challenging runs in North America. **Mt Norquay/Mystic Ridge** has a number of runs for the very best skiers and also offers night skiing.

### Killington, Vermont, USA

The largest ski area in the eastern USA, Killington spreads over seven mountains. It caters for every level of skier, but is especially suitable for beginners, who have their own network of pistes, and for snowboarders who are provided with their own trail map. Snow cannons ensure good coverage throughout an extended season.

**▼ Jackson Hole, Wyoming, USA**
One of the most spectacular mountain resorts in the United States, Jackson Hole is most suited to the experienced skier or snowboarder. A 60-person cable car transports skiers from Teton Village to Mount Rendezvous, from where the skilled and intrepid can experience some of the most difficult piste skiing in the world. Other attractions include trips into Yellowstone Park, a swim at 2,460 m (8,000 ft) in the Granite Hot Springs, and sleigh rides to view a huge elk herd.

### Lake Tahoe (Squaw Valley, Heavenly) California/Nevada, USA

Lake Tahoe is surrounded by ski resorts. **Squaw Valley** comprises six inter-linked mountain areas, some of which are still open in June. It has excellent facilities for children, including a family fun snow park. **Heavenly** has a spectacular setting, with something to suit skiers and snowboarders of all abilities. Snowboarders are further catered for by specially constructed mountainside features and by a dedicated fun park. A single ski pass is available for all resorts in the area.

### Aspen, Colorado, USA

Long considered the smartest ski resort in the United States, Aspen provides an enormous range of facilities and entertainment, including opera. A linked ticket gives access to four mountains. Aspen Mountain and Aspen Highlands are most suitable for intermediates and experts, Buttermilk for beginners, and Snowmass for all levels. Snowboarding is allowed on all but Aspen Mountain.

### Valle Nevado, Chile

A purpose-built resort in the Andes, at an altitude of 2,900 m (9,500 ft), Valle Nevado has wide, open pistes and spectacular views. It is also possible to heli-ski.

### Gran Catedral (Bariloche), Argentina

Perched on Catedral Mountain, overlooking Lake Nahuel Huapi, Gran Catedral (formerly Bariloche) is Argentina's best-known and most extensive resort. Many visitors are attracted to the area in August for the National Snow Party.

### EUROPE

### Geilo, Norway

On the edge of the Hardanger plateau, Geilo provides uncomplicated downhill skiing as well as extensive cross-country trails. It is an excellent family resort, with ski schools giving tuition (in English) in snowboarding and cross-country skiing, as well as alpine skiing.

### Soldeu/El Tarter, Andorra

For those on a budget, Andorra is a good option, and Soldeu/El Tarter the best of its resorts. Its reputable ski school and gentle slopes make it ideal for the beginner. A drag lift linking it with the neighbouring resorts of Pas de la Casa/Grau Roig has expanded the quality and quantity of runs available for the more experienced skier.

**◄ Vail, Colorado, United States**
Vail has runs for all abilities and a special family skiing area. Snowboarders are provided with dedicated pistes, a half-pipe and two fun parks. Numerous winter sports are possible, including dog sledding and snowmobiling.

### Three Valleys, France

The vast inter-linked ski area of the Three Valleys can be accessed from several resorts. **Courchevel** provides varied skiing, including wooded slopes, but intrepid skiers can also make their way across the whole Three Valleys system. **Méribel** is conveniently placed in the centre of the system. **Val Thorens**, which at 2,320 m (7,544 ft) is Europe's highest ski resort, has three lifts still open in summer.

### Chamonix, France

Chamonix is an attractive town set in a steep-sided valley and dominated by Mont Blanc (see *Mountains and volcanoes*). There is extensive, varied skiing on both sides of the valley, linked by bus services. The most famous run, the Vallée Blanche, involves a cable-car ride up to the Aiguille du Midi, followed by a tough walk to the top of the glacier, and a 20 km (13-mile) run down to the valley. The Mont Blanc Ski Pass includes other resorts, giving access to 1,000 km (625 miles) of piste.

**▲ Val d'Isère/Tignes, France**
Snowboarders and off-piste skiiers are among those well catered for by the huge inter-linked system of L'Espace Killy. The system is served by a number of modern resorts. The largest is **Val d'Isère**, which is better suited to more advanced skiers than to beginners, since its easiest skiing is inconveniently located on the upper slopes. **Tignes**, a collection of villages clustered around a mountain lake, offers skiing all year round. The lift pass provides access to the whole Espace Killy, as well as a day's skiing at nearby Les Arcs or La Plagne.

## Skiing and snowboarding resorts

Level: B = Beginner  I = Intermediate  A = Advanced  Sb = Snowboarding

| Resort | Main season | Skiable area or distance | Best-suited level(s) |
|---|---|---|---|
| **NORTH AMERICA** | | | |
| Whistler | Nov–Apr | 2,863 ha (7,071 acres) | I/A/Sb |
| Banff | Dec–Apr | 100 km (62 miles) | I |
| Killington | Oct–Apr | 152 km (95 miles) | B/Sb |
| Squaw Valley | Nov–May | 1,600 ha (4,000 acres) | I/A/Sb |
| Heavenly | Nov–May | 1,942 ha (4,800 acres) | I/A |
| Jackson Hole | Dec–Apr | 1,011 ha (2,500 acres) | A |
| Aspen | late Nov–Apr | 1,936 ha (4,785 acres) | all |
| Vail | early Nov–late May | 1,879 ha (4,644 acres) | all |
| Valle Nevado | mid-June–mid-Oct | 64 km (40 miles) | I/A |
| Gran Catedral | mid-June–end Sept | 640 ha (1,600 acres) | I |
| **EUROPE** | | | |
| Geilo | Nov–May | 25 km (16 miles) / 250 km (156 miles) cross-country | B/I |
| Soldeu/El Tarter | Dec–Mar | 74 km (46 miles) | B/I |
| Three Valleys | Dec–Apr | 300 km (187 miles) | all/Sb |
| Val d'Isère/Tignes | Dec–Apr | 300 km (187 miles) | I/A/Sb |
| Chamonix | Dec–Apr | 140 km (87 miles) | A/Sb |
| Zermatt | Dec–Apr | 150 km (93 miles) | I/A |
| Cervinia | Dec–Mar | 80 km (50 miles) | B/I |
| Wengen/Grindelwald | Dec–Mar | 195 km (121 miles) | B/I |
| St Moritz | Dec–Mar | 80 km (50 miles) | I |
| St Anton | Dec–Apr | 170 km (106 miles) | I/A |
| Söll, Ski-Welt | Dec–Mar | 250 km (156 miles) | B/I |
| Cortina | Dec–Mar | 140 km (87 miles) | all |
| **ASIA AND AUSTRALASIA** | | | |
| Hakuba | Dec–Apr | c. 500 ha (1,250 acres) | all |
| Perisher Blue | June–Oct | 1,250 ha (3,100 acres) | I |
| The Remarkables | June–Oct | 220 ha (550 acres) | I |
| Coronet Peak | June–Oct | 280 ha (700 acres) | I |

◄ **Matterhorn (Zermatt, Cervinia), Switzerland/Italy**
The visitor to the Matterhorn area has the choice of staying in the expensive, car-free, Swiss resort of **Zermatt**, or the cheaper, more lively, Italian resort of **Cervinia**. The lift systems of the two resorts are linked. Zermatt provides a huge variety of skiing, from the wooded slopes immediately above the town to the steep runs below the Kleine Matterhorn. The sunny, south-facing slopes of Cervinia provide plenty of runs of intermediate standard. Summer skiing is possible on the highest slopes.

### Jungfrau (Wengen, Grindelwald), Switzerland

The slopes of this famous mountain are served by two of Switzerland's best-known resorts. **Wengen**, which considers itself the 'birthplace of Alpine skiing', is an attractive town whose charm is enhanced by a lack of cars (a mountain railway providing the only access). **Grindelwald** is a larger, livelier town. The two are linked by a lift system that provides access to wonderfully varied skiing.

### St Moritz, Switzerland

Famous in particular for its glamorous nightlife, St Moritz serves as a gateway to two major lift systems. Corvatsch/Furtshellas provides an opportunity for glacier skiing in both winter and summer. Corviglia provides varied skiing, interspersed by numerous restaurants in spectacular locations.

### St Anton, Austria

St Anton attracts skiers from all over the world to its challenging ski runs, with cannon ensuring a good snow coverage. Dramatic off-piste skiing adds to its attraction for the experienced skier and boarder, but there is little for the beginner.

### Söll, Ski-Welt, Austria

Söll provides good family skiing. It is ideal for the beginner and intermediate skier,
but is not for the adventurous. Its low altitude results in a short season, although snow cannons have been installed.

### Cortina, Italy

Surrounded by the distinctive rocky outcrops of the Dolomites, Cortina provides skiing in five main areas. There are runs for a range of skills, including a difficult descent from the Tofana bowl, and the gentle runs of the Socrepes–Pocol area. Cortina is the smartest of the Italian resorts, with a lively nightlife. Activities off the slopes include ice-skating.

## ASIA AND AUSTRALASIA

### Hakuba, Japan

The village of Hakuba (near Nagano) is the gateway to seven ski areas, providing runs for different standards of skiers, with beginners and intermediates best served
by **Hakuba Goryu-Toomi**, and more advanced skiers by Happo'one (where night skiing is possible) and **Hakuba 47**.

### Perisher Blue, Australia

This winter sports area comprises four resorts, spread over seven mountain peaks, accessed by an underground alpine railway and covered by one ski pass. There is a Nordic Ski Centre at Guthega, and 90 km (55 miles) of cross-country skiing. The main resort town is Jindabyne.

### Queenstown (Coronet Peak, The Remarkables), New Zealand

Queenstown provides a residential base for two winter sports areas, The Remarkables and Coronet Peak, with shuttles operating between them. As well as good skiing, both areas offer facilities for snowboarders, including pipes and a terrain park. Families are well catered for, with good ski schools. Heli-skiing is also available.

# Great beaches

▶ **Negril, Jamaica**
Negril beach is 11 km (7 miles) long and fringed by trees that hide low-rise hotels and restaurants. While definitely a tourist resort, it still retains a laid-back Jamaican character. Growing environmentalism has led to planning restrictions and active preservation of the surrounding area, including the creation of the Negril Marine Park. This encompasses the Great Morass swamp behind the beach, and the coral reef, cliffs and grottoes that make Negril so popular with scuba divers and snorkellers.

From California to the Caribbean to Australia, the lure of the beach still has a part in most holiday plans. The range is endless – chic and cosmopolitan in the Mediterranean, wild and rugged along the Atlantic shores or palm-fringed coral in the South Pacific. This small selection highlights some of the great beaches that can be linked into a round-the-world trip – whether for the exhilaration of surfing or sailing, or just to do absolutely nothing.

## NORTH AMERICA

### Venice Beach, Los Angeles, USA
Venice Beach is famous not so much for its wide stretch of sand as for its curving 'boardwalk'. Here, some of LA's more flamboyant citizens display themselves – on foot, skateboard, rollerblade and cycle. The area was originally developed to imitate its European namesake and, although there is no comparison, it is pleasant to stroll along its canals.

### Assateague Island, Maryland/Virginia, USA
Assateague Island National Seashore on the Atlantic coast of the Chesapeake Peninsula consists of 60 km (37 miles) of pristine sandy beach, fringed by pine forest and salt marsh. Only a small area of it is accessible by car and the rest of the beach is deserted, except for the more intrepid campers, many of whom come for the fishing and birdwatching. Herds of wild ponies roam the island.

### Sanibel Island, Florida, USA
Sanibel's 19 km (12 miles) of beaches are famous for their seashells. Visitors can be seen scouring the seashore or taking boat trips to more remote locations to find the best shells. Around 40% of the island, which can be toured on rented bicycles, is a wildlife preserve and it is also within striking distance of the Florida Everglades (see *Wildlife in the Americas*).

### Puerto Escondido, Mexico
The resort of Puerto Escondido has a beach to suit every taste. 'Playa Zicatela' is considered one of the best surfing beaches in North America, but is suitable only for the strongest swimmers. 'Playa Principal' is a more urban beach, with pleasure craft and waterfront restaurants, while the small coves just out of town provide perfect swimming conditions.

## THE CARIBBEAN AND SOUTH AMERICA

### Magens Bay, St Thomas, US Virgin Islands
The heart-shaped Magens Bay contains a gently sloping sandy beach, surrounded by overhanging trees that provide welcome shade. Protected from the winds and currents, the bay is safe for bathing. Although nude bathing is not allowed on the main beach, it is permitted on the nearby Little Magens Beach. Interesting rock formations on the fringes of the bay are good for snorkelling. The beach is well served by restaurants and bars, carefully hidden among the trees.

### Copacabana Beach, Rio de Janeiro, Brazil
Copacabana's 4 km (2.5 miles) of sand is fringed by a wavy black and white mosaic walkway. The beach is provided with modern amenities, such as public showers, kiosks and restaurants, and the shopping centre is only a short walk away. As well as attracting tourists, the beach is a meeting place for the citizens of Rio, and is the focus of the New Year celebrations. It is framed on one side by a huge granite headland and on the other by an imposing World War I fort, below which is an area from which local fishermen still operate.

### Viña del Mar, Chile
Known as 'the Garden City' because of the luscious, tropical foliage that lines its boulevards, Viña del Mar also has a beautiful beach. Visitors who tire of the soft white sand and rolling surf can enjoy a tour of the town by horse-drawn carriage, visit the art museum and the extensive botanical gardens. Evening entertainment comes in the form of gourmet restaurants, casinos, discos and concerts.

▲ **Oahu, Hawaiian Islands, USA**
Most visitors to the island of Oahu flock to the string of connected beaches in the resort of Waikiki, just to the east of Honolulu, where the curving sand, studded with palm trees, is backed by a towering wall of high-rise hotels. Those looking for a more peaceful holiday, however, head further around the coast and seek out Waimanalo Beach (above), with its gently shelving, near-white sand and mountain backdrop. On the north coast the calm waters of Waimea Bay in summer also provide excellent swimming, but in winter months it is the centre of the surfing scene, as 10 m (30 ft) waves roll in across the Pacific.

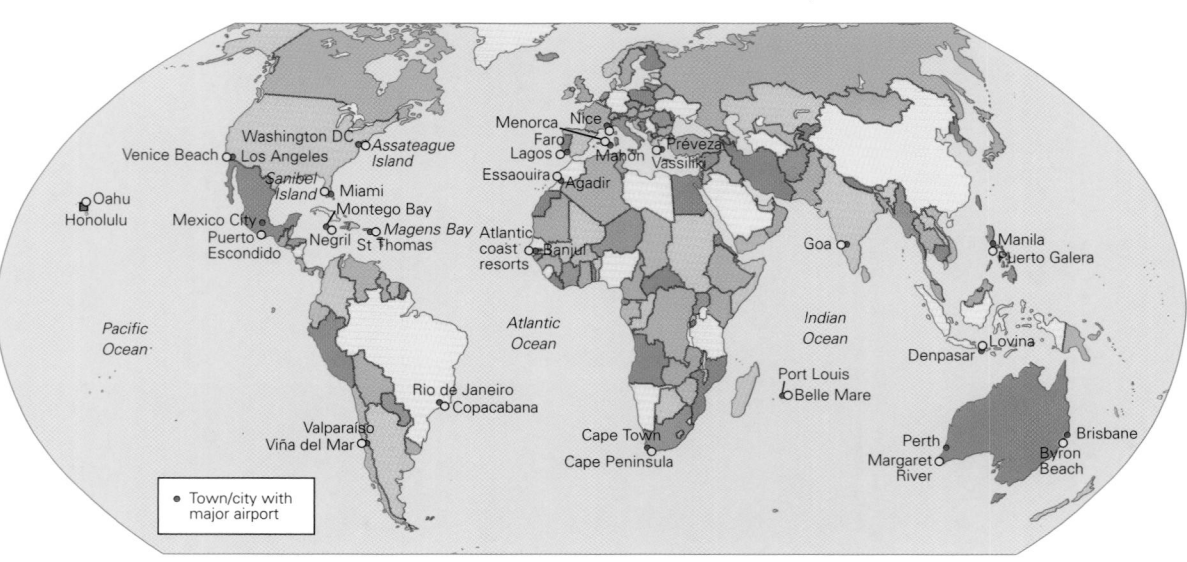

• Town/city with major airport

## EUROPE

### Nice, France
Nice is the largest town on the Côte d'Azur, renowned for the clarity of its light and the colour of its sea. Many famous artists have been inspired by the region, and some are represented in the town's art gallery. The long curved beach is rather pebbly, but its surroundings are attractive, with a wide esplanade on which 'to see and be seen'.

### Santa Galdana, Menorca
The Balearic Island least affected by tourism, Menorca is famous for its beaches. The main beach at Santa Galdana can be very crowded in summer, but it is still possible to find relatively unspoilt coves nearby. Just a 1 km (0.5-mile) walk east is the wood-lined sandy beach of Cala Mirjana, where the favourite sport is to jump from rocks into crystal-clear water.

### Vassiliki, Levkás, Greece
The small resort of Vassiliki is one of the foremost windsurfing and dinghy sailing centres in the eastern Mediterranean. Set in a bay that provides some shelter for the beginner, it is blessed with reliable winds. The lighter breezes of the morning are followed, after a brief lunchtime lull, by winds strong enough to delight the expert.

## AFRICA AND THE INDIAN OCEAN

### Essaouira, Morocco
The ancient town of Essaouira provides a fascinating backdrop to 3 km (2 miles) of

**▲ Cape Peninsula, South Africa**
Among the many beaches on the narrow peninsula south of Cape Town is Boulders Beach, so named because of the huge rocks that provide shelter from the wind. Here, visitors share the sands with a colony of jack-ass penguins. Other resorts on the peninsula, where the ocean water to the west is considerably colder than that of False Bay to the east, include some, such as Fish Hoek, which cater specifically for families, and some, such as the fashionable Clifton area, which attract the young and wealthy. Surfers head for the remote Long Beach at Kommetjie.

sandy shoreline. The commercial life of the town tends to spill over on to the beach, with fishermen offering to cook their catch and camel drivers selling rides, although it is possible to find more secluded areas. The town is the centre of the craft of wood inlay, the local Thuya trees providing the raw material.

### Atlantic coast resorts, Gambia
The resorts of Kololi, Kotu, Fajara and Bakau, strung out along a 10 km (6-mile) coastal strip, provide a full range of amenities, including golf courses, equipment for water sports, and swimming pools. Although the sea is relatively safe, there are times when the conditions are unsuitable for all but the strongest swimmer. For those seeking a more authentic African experience, the market town of Serekunda is nearby.

### Belle Mare, Mauritius
The coral reef that surrounds much of the island of Mauritius provides a natural breakwater, ensuring calm inshore waters. The beaches are all beautiful, although some have been over-developed or have areas cordoned off by hotels. However, Belle Mare, on the less-developed east coast, still has plenty of public areas. There are also the attractions of a mixed French, Indian and Chinese culture, evident in the island's architecture and cuisine.

## ASIA

### Goa, India
The dozens of beaches on Goa's 100 km (62-mile) coastline provide plenty of choice. Calangute and Colva, to which young people flocked in the 1970s, are now tourist resorts. However, at both the northern and southern ends of the Goan coast are many relatively unspoilt beaches, including Arambol and Palolem, where beach huts and tree houses provide the main accommodation. At Palolem visitors can take dolphin-watching boat trips.

### Puerto Galera, Mindoro, Philippines
A resort area comprising 12 separate coastal districts, Puerto Galera is renowned for its pristine sandy coves, sheltered by a rugged, jungle-covered coastline. Accommodation ranges from

bamboo beach huts to air-conditioned bungalows and family-run hotels. The rich marine life of the area attracts scuba-divers, and equipment for underwater and other marine activities is available for hire.

### Lovina, Bali
Although second in size only to Kuta, famous for its surf, Lovina manages to retain the relaxed atmosphere its larger rival has long since lost. Situated on Bali's rugged northern coast, the resort comprises six villages, dotted along 8 km (5 miles) of black-sand beach. Those who enjoy some lively nightlife make for the village of Kalibukbuk. Beach-centred activities include snorkelling and dolphin watching. Excursions can be made inland to nearby hot springs and a Buddhist temple, or further afield to the volcanic regions of Bedugul and Batur.

## AUSTRALASIA

### Byron Beach, New South Wales, Australia
Byron Beach offers a wide range of beaches. Main Beach is ideal for families, with a life-guard patrol and play equipment shaded by trees, while those wishing for more seclusion head for the smaller coves out on Cape Byron. The area also provides some good surfing and the opportunity to watch passing whales and dolphins. The town itself is less commercial, and better suited to those seeking an alternative lifestyle, than the popular resort of Gold Coast, 50 km (30 miles) to the north.

**◄ Lagos, Portugal**
Lagos is a busy fishing port and one of the Algarve's oldest settlements, with a long maritime tradition. To the east lie miles of sand dunes and the gently sloping Meia beach. West of the town, the dramatically eroded sandstone cliffs typical of the region form numerous small coves, some of which are only accessible from the sea. Lagos is an excellent base for surfers, who can travel the short distance to Portugal's west-facing beaches if local surf fails. The town provides plenty of interest, from seafood restaurants and bars to the curiosities of the local museum.

**▼ Margaret River, Western Australia**
Margaret River is among the best surfing areas in Australia, providing conditions to suit both beginners and experts. It also has much for the non-surfer to enjoy, including swimming beaches, river canoeing trips, and visits to local vineyards to taste some of Australia's best wines.

# Festivals

Whether sacred or profane, festivals throughout the world bring thousands of participants and spectators out on to the streets with grand processions and dazzling displays of music and dance, drama and sporting prowess.

◄ **Palio, Siena, Italy**
Celebrated every year on 2 July and 16 August, the Palio is a bare-back horserace that dates from the 16th century. Ten horses, each representing one of Siena's *contrade*, or districts, race three times around the crowded central piazza, sometimes barging into each other and unseating their riders. Before the race there is a procession in which men dressed in medieval clothes whirl and twist the *palio*, or flag, of their *contrada*, to the accompaniment of drummers.

## THE AMERICAS

▼ **Chinese New Year, San Francisco, California, USA**
For Chinese communities everywhere, the New Year is a week-long festival. Many celebrations are family-based, but they lead up to a very public grand finale. Chinatown in San Francisco is taken over by the Golden Dragon Parade when hundreds of people, including drummers and other musicians, accompany a 23 m (75 ft) dragon through the streets. The Chinese follow a lunar calendar, which means that their New Year occurs in late January or early February.

### Corn Dance Festival, Santa Domingo, New Mexico, USA
At Santa Domingo (near Albuquerque) the Pueblo people honour the harvest goddess, Iyatiko, in the Corn Dance Festival. Celebrants, known as the *koshare*, dress in cornhusks and animal skins to enact the history of their people on a day that is filled with drumming, dancing and feasting. The festival which, unlike many Pueblo ceremonies, is a public event, is always held on 4 August.

### Heritage and Jazz Festival, New Orleans, Louisiana, USA
Jazz evolved in New Orleans during the late 19th and early 20th centuries, but the first jazz festival was not until 1968. A major event in the musical calendar and organized by the Heritage and Jazz Festival, it runs over two weekends in April or May. Musicians from all over the world perform in large tents at the Fair Grounds and in smaller venues – clubs, theatres and halls – throughout the city.

### Fisherman's Festival, Jamaica
29 June is Saint Peter's day. He is the patron saint of fishermen, and in the fishing ports of Jamaica boats are drawn up to the beach where the owners decorate them with shells and flowers. Long processions follow priests to the edge of the sea where they bless the boats, and the beaches become crowded with steel bands, dancers and family picnics.

### Urkupina, Calvario Hill, Bolivia
Early in the 20th century a girl tending her sheep on Calvario Hill had a vision of the Virgin Mary. Now, on 15 August, thousands of pilgrims carrying candles and flowers, and accompanied by musicians, performers and vendors, climb the hill to pay homage to the Virgin. The festivities that follow last for three days.

### National Rodeo Festival, Rancagua, Chile
Rodeos take place all over the country and, in late March, the best competitors go to the National Rodeo in Rancagua. This event celebrates the Chilean *huaso* or cowboy. Thousands come to watch as huasos, wearing traditional costume and the heavy spurs unique to Chile, provide exhibitions of horsemanship. The town is given over to feasts of cowboy food and *la cueca*, the erotic folk dance of Chile.

## EUROPE

### Puck Fair, Killorglin, Ireland
A billygoat, King Puck – adorned with ribbons and a crown – opens the three-day Puck Fair every year on 2 August. Musicians from all over Europe perform, and Romanies are among those who entertain the crowds with Irish jigs and stories. The billy is honoured because in the 17th century a herd of goats warned the village of an impending English attack.

### Oktober Bierfest, Munich, Germany
The Oktober Bierfest has been an annual event since 1835. It is an important festival for most young visitors to the city and is a huge celebration in honour of beer. It lasts for 16 days from 17 October, and vast beer tents that each house 5,000 drinkers are erected. Food stalls and funfairs add to the festive atmosphere.

### Lajkonic, Kraków, Poland
Every year, usually in June, a man dressed as a Tartar rides a mock horse through the streets, accompanied by trumpeters and citizens dressed in medieval costume. He does so in memory of Lajkonic, who in the 13th century killed a Tartar and put on the dead man's clothing before riding into the city to warn that the Tartars were about to attack. The resulting defeat of the Tartars is now celebrated with much pageantry.

### San Fermin, Pamplona, Spain
Starting on 6 July and running for eight days, the festival is held in honour of Fermin, patron saint of bullfighters. Each day starts with the playing of drums and pipes, and an effigy of the saint is followed by a procession of matadors and horses, dressed and decorated for the occasion. A rocket signals the release of the bulls from their pen to race through the streets to the bullring. Men run and leap ahead of them, a practice that more than once has resulted in someone being killed. Bull fights and parties fill the evenings.

### Mardi Gras Carnaval, Rio de Janeiro, Brazil
All over the Catholic Christian world, there are festivals at Mardi Gras, the last day before the 40 days of Lenten fasting. The Mardi Gras Carnaval in Rio de Janeiro is the most famous. Over the course of two nights the city's 14 main samba schools compete with each other by dancing and parading down the 1 km (0.5-mile) long Sambadrome, watched by thousands of spectators. Each school's parade consists of around 4,000 people in lavish, often extravagant, costumes, accompanied by enormous and elaborate floats, and a band of over 500 drummers. The judging takes place a few days later. Broadcast live on television, it is followed by great celebrations.

## Aksu Black Sea Festival, Turkey

The origins of this July festival are very old, dating back to pre-Christian fertility rites. Cybele, the fertility goddess, wore a pebble in her crown and women still throw pebbles into the Black Sea in the hope that this will help them conceive. The highlight of the festival is a performance by male dancers dressed in black and silver, and other artists – musicians, potters, painters and weavers – flock to the site where they perform or sell their work.

## AFRICA

### Odwira, Ghana

The Asante calendar is filled with religious days and ceremonies, of which the Odwira, usually in August or September, is one of the most important. The high chiefs and priests are involved for some days in secret and sacred rituals, and then the roll of drums announces the start of feasting. It all ends with a grand procession, in which the chiefs are carried in splendid palanquins.

### Abu El-Haggag, Luxor, Egypt

Among the ancient ruins of Luxor is a small mosque dedicated to a 12th-century Muslim saint, El-Haggag. Each year, in October or November, thousands of people crowd into Luxor for the saint's *mulid*, or festival, during which Sufis and floats parade the streets. Three model boats are carried about by groups of men, though whether this is in memory of the Ancient Egyptian journey into the Underworld, or of the time when the pilgrimage to Mecca involved a sea crossing, is uncertain.

### Timket, Ethiopia

Ethiopian Christians celebrate the baptism of Christ for three days starting on 19 January. The priests, after all-night prayers, emerge from churches carrying holy tabots – caskets holding sacred texts – followed by singing children. Multicoloured umbrellas, signifying high office and authority, are held above the priests. After this religious ceremony, a party mood takes over and there are huge communal meals, music, and excited horse races which sometimes lurch into the spectators.

### ▶ Ganesh Festival, Mumbai, India

Chowpatty Beach is crowded for ten days in August through to September. Families exchange gifts and women decorate shrines to Shiva, mother of the Hindu elephant-headed god Ganesh. On the tenth day a huge effigy of Ganesh is carried through the streets to be cast into the sea. Drummers and pipers announce its passage, which is followed by a large procession of people dancing and singing.

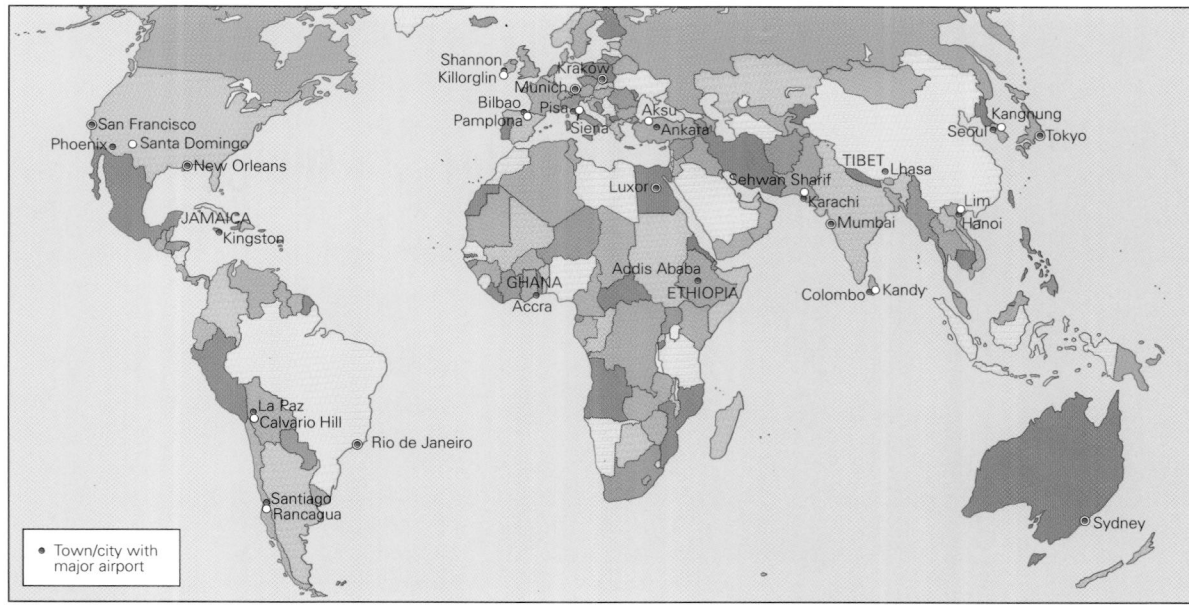

## ASIA AND AUSTRALIA

### Urs to Lal Shahbaz Qalandar, Sehwan Sharif, Pakistan

All over Pakistan, Muslims celebrate holy men with *urs*, or saints' days. One of the most popular, attracting many thousands of pilgrims, is held in Sehwan Sharif, around the tomb of the 12th-century Iranian scholar-poet Lal Shahbaz Qalandar. For three days, in October or November, Sufis perform their holy, trance-like dances, while drums and gongs beat hour after hour. The entire crowd dances and chants, and many offer votive offerings to the tomb.

### Festival of the Tooth, Kandy, Sri Lanka

In the Esala Perhera temple in Kandy is the Tooth Relic of the Buddha. Usually in July, but occasionally in August, there is a spectacular festival in which there are festive meals and dances to celebrate the relic and Buddha. At the festival's climax a great procession of dancers, drummers, temple chieftains, and over 50 elephants in ceremonial attire, goes to the temple, followed by huge crowds of pilgrims.

### Ho Lim, Lim, Vietnam

Singers from all over Vietnam pour into the village of Lim (near Bac Ninh) seven days after Tet, the Chinese New Year, in January or February. They participate in a folk-singing contest, and competition is fierce. The crowds who come to listen are also entertained by a circus, street performers, wrestling competitions, and chess games in which people play the parts of the pieces.

### Losar, Tibet

The calendar in Tibet follows the lunar cycle. There are two 'New Year' days, but the significant one is Gyalpo Losar, the King's New Year, which is usually in April. People wear new, decorative clothing; the priests fill the temples with chanting, the beating of gongs and the ringing of bells, and new prayer flags are lifted above the temple roofs. Throughout the city, street theatres and musicians perform while people party and play dice in the parks.

### Tano, Kangnung, South Korea

This spring festival, usually in April or May, traditionally involved displays of the Korean form of wrestling, *ssirum*, even in the most remote villages. Now, many Koreans spend the holiday watching *ssirum* on television, except in the village of Kangnung. Here they celebrate for five days, not only with wrestling matches but also with performances of the traditional dance called *nong-ak*. The huge crowds also enjoy a spring drink, *chehotang*.

### Gay and Lesbian Mardi Gras, Sydney, Australia

Participants pride themselves on outrageous displays and flamboyant costumes during the annual Mardi Gras parade. The street procession ends in a huge party at the RAS Show Ground in Moore Park, which is restricted to ticket holders. However, revellers throughout the city regard this as an opportunity to party until dawn and beyond.

**▲ Sanja Matsuri, Tokyo, Japan**
*Matsuri* – festivals where shrines, or *mikoshi*, believed to contain a god-spirit, are carried through towns and villages – take place all over Japan. However, the biggest event is in Tokyo in April or May. Here the *mikoshi* weigh about 1 tonne each, and 50 men are needed to hoist one through the streets to the Asakusa Temple. Groups of costumed figures, and musicians playing flutes and beating drums, accompany the *mikoshi* on its journey.

# Historic sites in the Americas

Amid the rocky canyons of New Mexico, Arizona and Colorado, the dense jungle of Central America and the towering peaks of the Andes lie the spectacular ruins of civilizations that flourished long before 1500 and the arrival of the Europeans. Scattered throughout the continent are the mansions, churches, cathedrals and forts built by European settlers and their descendants since the 16th century.

### Mesa Verde and the Anasazi

Mesa Verde National Park in Colorado, USA, contains the ruins of spectacular Anasazi complexes of multi-storey apartments constructed on natural or artificial platforms on the face of canyon cliffs. They are among the remains of hundreds of villages that were built by the Anasazi from the 8th century onwards in south-western USA. Called pueblos by the Spanish, they took various forms. In Chaco Canyon, for example, elaborate complexes of adjoining rooms surrounded circular subterranean ceremonial structures known as *kivas*. The Anasazi began to abandon their pueblos in the 15th century, eventually settling along the Rio Grande. There are many impressive sites worth visiting, but they are usually in remote locations.
*Peak season:* May–October
*Nearest airports:* Albuquerque, Santa Fe

## NORTH AMERICA

### Québec, Canada

Founded by the French in 1608 and now the only walled city in the Americas north of Mexico, Québec has several 17th- and 18th-century buildings. The area by the St Lawrence River has the general appearance of 1759, when the city was captured by the British. On the cliff-top above is the citadel of Cap Diamant, dating from 1820.

### Plymouth Plantation, Massachusetts, USA

Costumed actors re-create the life and times of the first permanent colony and a Native American encampment in New England at Plymouth Plantation, a historical theme park. Visitors can go aboard the *Mayflower II*, a reconstruction of the ship that brought the original settlers from England in 1620.

### Historic Triangle, Virginia, USA

The colonial towns of Williamsburg, Jamestown and Yorktown comprise the Historic Triangle. **Williamsburg**, Virginia's capital 1699–1780, has a large restored historic district of 17th- and 18th-century buildings with tours led by costumed guides. **Jamestown**, founded in 1607, has some 17th-century ruins, a reconstruction of the 1607 James Fort and full-scale replicas of 17th-century ships. **Yorktown**, the site of the last major battle (1781) in the American Revolution, and besieged during the Civil War, contains fortifications dating from both wars. Other historic sites in Virginia include Thomas Jefferson's house, **Monticello**, George Washington's house, **Mount Vernon**, the plantation house, **Shirley Plantation**, built in the 1660s, and Civil War sites in **Richmond**.

### Pueblo de Taos, New Mexico, USA

The largest, multi-storied, adobe (sun-dried brick) structure in the USA, Pueblo de Taos dates from around 1450 and is still inhabited by 1,500 Native Americans. In the town of Taos is the home of Kit Carson, the famous 19th-century mountain man.

### Chaco Culture National Historic Park, New Mexico, USA

Impressive Anasazi ruins are to be found in this remote park. Among them is the site of Pueblo Bonito, with remains of a massive plaza surrounded by a semi-circular, five-storey tiered complex of some 200 rooms which once housed up to 1,200 people.

### Charleston, USA

A historic centre of Southern culture, Charleston has many colonial buildings. The military relics of the Battery overlook the harbour, while 5 km (3 miles) away is Fort Sumter where the first shot of the Civil War was fired.

### San Miguel de Allende, Mexico

An almost totally colonial town, San Miguel de Allende has many attractive houses and churches dating from the 18th century. It is also an important artistic centre, where painting, pottery, sculpture, drama, music and literature all flourish.

### Guanajuato, Mexico

A former silver-mining town, founded in the 16th century, Guanajuato has colonial buildings dating from the 17th and 18th centuries among its narrow streets with houses painted in bright colours.

### Teotíhuacán, Mexico

Impressive ruins are all that remain of a city which in AD 500 was the sixth largest in the world, with a population of around

**▲ Savannah, Georgia, USA**
The Cotton Exchange is just one of over 1,000 splendid 18th- and 19th-century buildings that have been restored in the historic downtown district of Savannah. Others include the US Customs House and the gold-domed City Hall. Near the city are the Civil War forts of Old Fort Jackson and Fort Pulaski.

### Chichén-Itzá and the Maya

Chichén-Itzá in Mexico is a particularly impressive Mayan site that is unique because it displays many features of the Toltecs who occupied the city in the 10th century. Among them is the reclining sculpture of the Toltec rain god. The magnificent remains of the literate Mayan civilization are scattered throughout southern Mexico, Guatemala, Belize and Honduras. Mayan cities expanded rapidly in the 7th and 8th centuries but were then abandoned between the 9th and 13th centuries. Their ruins often include stone-built pyramids crowned by temples and palaces, and courts used in a ritual ball game that involved the sacrifice of the losing team.

There are numerous Mayan sites worth visiting, and it is possible to spend two to three weeks following a route that links the most important in Mexico, Guatemala and Belize.
*Peak season:* November–April
*Nearest airports:* See map of 'Mayan Route'

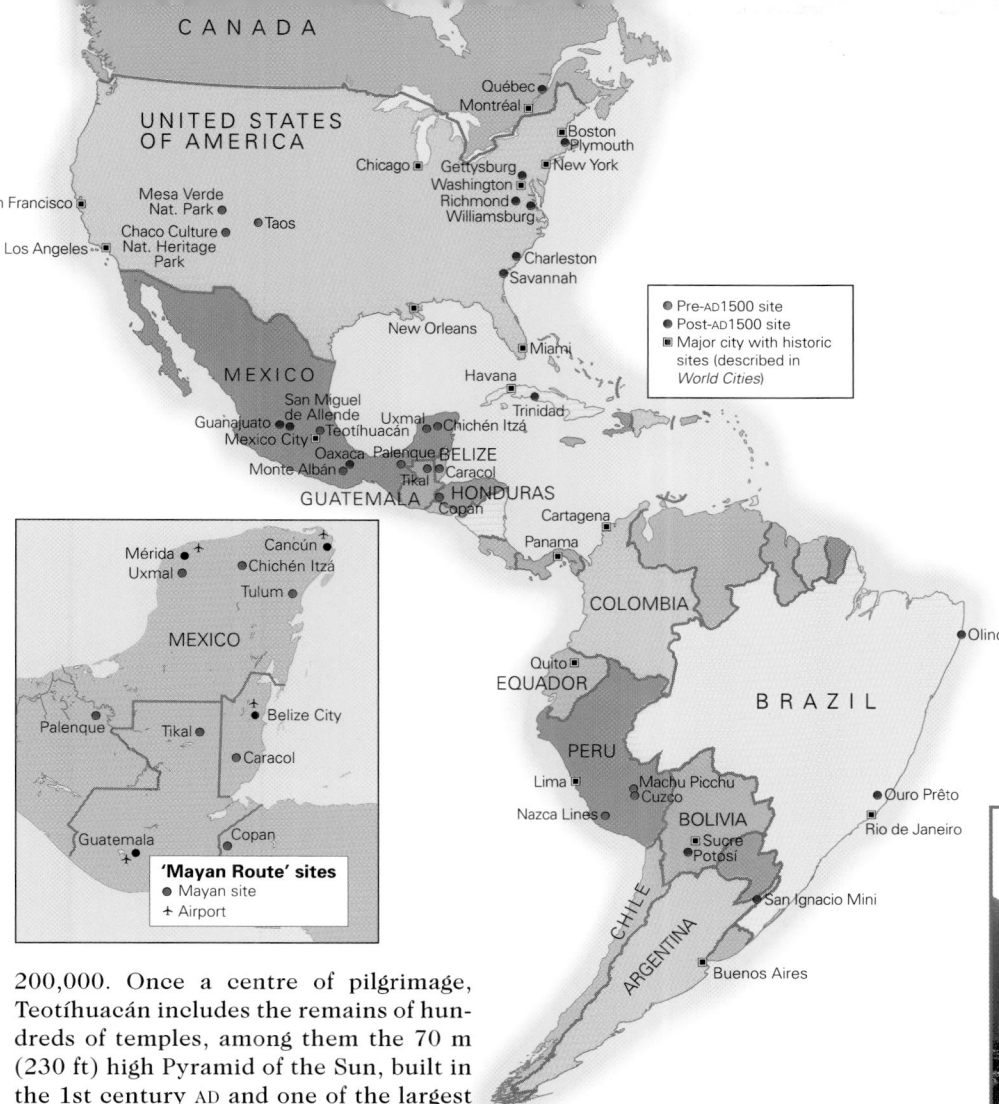

**▲ Gettysburg National Cemetery, Pennsylvania, USA** The burial place of 979 Union soldiers killed in the Civil War battle of 1863 is also the site of President Lincoln's famous Gettysburg Address. Tours include the 91 m (300 ft) National Tower and the Cyclorama Center, where a film about the battle is shown.

200,000. Once a centre of pilgrimage, Teotíhuacán includes the remains of hundreds of temples, among them the 70 m (230 ft) high Pyramid of the Sun, built in the 1st century AD and one of the largest buildings in the New World before 1500.

### Oaxaca and Monte Albán, Mexico
Oaxaca is a well-preserved colonial town with a cathedral and many other buildings dating from the 16th century onwards. Just 10 km (6 miles) away are the impressive ruins of Monte Albán, which from the 7th century BC served as a centre of worship for many different peoples, including the Maya. Surrounding a huge man-made plateau are the remains of pyramids, a ball court, burial chambers with beautiful murals, and carvings of dancers.

### Palenque, Mexico
A Mayan site in a clearing in the jungle, Palenque has numerous buildings with particularly beautiful decoration. They include the Temple of Inscriptions, a stepped pyramid with a 25 m (80 ft) tunnel that leads to a crypt containing the sarcophagus of a 7th-century Mayan king.

### Uxmal, Mexico
One of the most beautiful pre-1500 sites in Mexico, Uxmal has Classical Maya architecture. The chief building is the smooth-sided El Adivino, or Pyramid of the Soothsayer, up which there is an almost vertical climb to the 35 m (115 ft) high summit that is crowned by a temple. Nearby is the Governor's Palace, which features a frieze with 103 masks.

## CENTRAL AMERICA AND THE CARIBBEAN

### Caracol, Belize
An amazing Mayan site deep in the rainforest, Caracol is still being excavated. The ruins, whose full extent has only recently become apparent, include a pyramid 42 m (140 ft) high.

### Tikal, Guatemala
Possibly the greatest Mayan site, Tikal is surrounded on all sides by jungle. The remains of 3,000 buildings can be seen, some with painted carvings. The pyramid-like Temple of the Great Jaguar, built in AD 700, is considered the world's best example of Mayan temple construction.

### Trinidad, Cuba
Cuba's best-preserved colonial town, Trinidad has many buildings that reflect the town's prosperity as a centre of the sugar trade in the 18th and 19th centuries.

## SOUTH AMERICA

### Cuzco and the Urubumba Valley, Peru
Former capital of the Incas high in the Andes, Cuzco contains extensive Inca ruins mixed with colonial churches, palaces, houses and a 17th-century cathedral. An attractive and lively town, it is the main starting point for people visiting Machu Picchu (by train or a four-day trek) and other Inca ruins in the Urubumba Valley.

### Nazca Lines, Peru
People of the Nazca culture (375 BC–AD 650) created gigantic lines by removing stones to expose the desert soil beneath. The lines, which depict geometrical shapes, birds – one with a wing-span of over 100 m (328 ft) – and animals, are best seen from the air, in a local plane.

### Potosí, Bolivia
Founded in 1545 as a silver-mining town, Potosí was the largest city in the Americas in the early 17th century. Today it has over 2,000 colonial buildings, including several 18th-century Baroque churches.

### Machu Picchu and the Incas
Machu Picchu in Peru is the most spectacular of many Inca sites in the Andes. Tier upon tier of houses, palaces, temples and defensive walls rise up the side of a high mountain ridge overlooked by the granite pinnacle of Huayana Picchu. The Spaniards failed to find the site in the 16th century, and it was mysteriously abandoned and forgotten until the early 20th century. The Incas developed an enormous empire between the 14th and 15th centuries that extended from modern Ecuador, through Peru to southern Chile. It was conquered by the Spaniards in the 1530s.
*Peak season:* April–October
*Nearest airport:* Lima

### Olinda, Brazil
One of the best-preserved colonial cities in Brazil, on a hill overlooking the Atlantic, Olinda has many 16th- to 18th-century buildings. It is a major cultural centre, with art galleries, music and festivals.

### Ouro Prêto, Brazil
A beautiful colonial town founded in 1711, Ouro Prêto has cobblestone roads, statues, fountains, churches, a palace and a theatre. It also serves as a base for exploring other colonial towns in Minas Gerais province, such as Diamantina.

### San Ignacio Mini, Argentina
The most impressive of the ruins of Jesuit mission villages in the Misiones region, San Ignacio Mini had 4,356 Guarani inhabitants before the Jesuits were expelled from Spanish territory in 1767. The ruins of only three other missions indicate their former splendour: Sao Miguel in Brazil, and Jesús and Trinidad in Paraguay.

**Major cities with historic sites**
(see *World Cities*)
• Boston
• Buenos Aires
• Cartagena
• Chicago
• Havana
• Lima
• Los Angeles
• Miami
• Mexico City
• Montréal
• New Orleans
• New York
• Panama
• Quito
• Rio de Janeiro
• San Francisco
• Sucre
• Washington

# Historic sites in Europe

There is a huge variety of historic sites in Europe, ranging from prehistoric monuments over 5,000 years old to 19th-century castles. Ruins of the architectural achievements of the Classical Greek and Roman civilizations contrast with what are often perfectly preserved cathedrals, churches, monasteries, castles, palaces and civic buildings dating from the 11th century onwards.

### ◄ Neuschwanstein Castle, Germany
The ultimate fairytale castle, Neuschwanstein (near Fussen) was built in 1869–86 and is the most famous of Ludwig II's castles inspired by Wagner's vision of medieval Germany. It has a wide range of architectural styles, and its tall white marble towers topped by cone-shaped pinnacles, which have been copied by Disneyworld, are instantly recognizable.

### Rock of Cashel, Ireland
Poised dramatically above the town of Cashel in County Tipparary stands a limestone outcrop, 109 m (358 ft) high, known as the Rock of Cashel. It is topped by a group of medieval ecclesiastical ruins, which include a bishop's palace, the 13th-century St Patrick's Cathedral, and the adjoining 12th-century Romanesque St Cormac's chapel.

### Caernarfon Castle, Wales
Considered to be the finest of the castles built by Edward I of England after his conquest of Wales in 1283, Caernarfon Castle is exceptionally well preserved. Constructed as a royal palace as well as a military stronghold, it dominates the surrounding walled town, which was also founded by Edward.

### Stonehenge, England
The most famous prehistoric monument in Europe, Stonehenge is a circular arrangement of massive standing stones, surrounded by earthworks, whose function is a subject of controversy. Built in stages between c. 3100 BC and c. 1000 BC, it may have been an astronomical observatory, a temple or a secular ceremonial centre. Its distinctive stone trilithons – pairs of uprights topped with horizontal lintels – are an impressive landmark on the Salisbury Plain.

### ▼ Meteora, Greece
Perched on top of natural rock pinnacles which rise hundreds of metres from the flat plain of Thessaly, near Tríkkala, is a group of Greek orthodox monasteries, some of which are still inhabited today. The highest of these – at 533 m (1,749 ft) is Great Meteoron, which was built from 1356 with a domed church added in the 16th century.

### Bruges, Belgium
Once one of Europe's greatest trading centres, Bruges is a well-preserved medieval city with narrow streets and canals spanned by picturesque bridges. Within its 13th-century walls are many historic buildings, including the magnificent Gothic Town Hall and the medieval Cloth Hall. The Groeninge Museum contains paintings by the 15th-century Flemish masters.

### Mont-St-Michel, France
Rising dramatically out of the Bay of St-Michel is a steep, rocky island with a medieval abbey on its summit. Buildings and fortifications have been added since the 11th century, resulting in a mixture of styles and shapes which culminate in the 19th-century spire of the church.

### Versailles, France
Built for Louis XIV, the 'Sun King', the vast Baroque palace of Versailles was the envy of all Europe in the 17th century. Today, visitors flock to see the Hall of Mirrors – where the Treaty of Versailles was signed at the end of World War I – and to wander between the elaborate fountains in the magnificent formal gardens.

### Heidelberg, Germany
Majestically set on the banks of the River Neckar and dominated by the romantic ruins of the castle, Heidelberg is one of Germany's most beautiful and best preserved historic towns, with many fascinating buildings. Its 600-year-old university provides a youthful atmosphere on the streets, especially in the evenings.

### Petrodvorets, Russia
An imperial palace in the Baroque style, Petrodvorets was built by Peter the Great after he had visited Versailles. It is set in beautiful parkland interwoven by a system of fountains, cascades and waterways connected to the sea.

- ● Pre-AD 500 site
- ● Post-AD 500 site
- ■ Major city with historic sites (described in *World Cities*)

## Salzburg, Austria

Set in a magnificent subalpine landscape, Salzburg is a picturesque city with many fine Baroque churches and a grand Italianate cathedral, the first of its kind to be built north of the Alps. The simple apartment where Mozart was born is a place of pilgrimage for music lovers.

## Český Krumlov, Czech Republic

One of Europe's most picturesque towns, Český Krumlov has hardly changed since the 18th century. Its beautiful medieval and Renaissance buildings are almost encircled by the Vltava River and overlooked by a magnificent castle. Originally a Gothic fortress, Krumlov Castle was rebuilt in the 16th century as a fortified palace.

## Évora, Portugal

An attractive city with a history dating back to Roman times, Évora has a walled medieval centre with a distinctly Moorish atmosphere, and many fine Renaissance buildings from its time as a royal residence. The church of São Francisco is a good example of the Portuguese Manueline style of architecture, combining Gothic and Moorish influences.

## Toledo, Spain

An ancient city of steep, winding streets lined with elegant if sombre buildings, Toledo is a splendid monument to the many cultures that have flourished here in the past. Moorish, Jewish and Christian traditions are all represented, and parts of the city walls date from the 6th century, when the Visigoths made Toledo their capital. The cathedral is a particularly fine example of the Spanish Gothic.

## Segovia, Spain

Set on a rock, Segovia is a delightful old town with a fairytale castle and a 1st-century Roman aqueduct. Other notable buildings include the palace of La Granja, the 16th-century Gothic cathedral and the 12-sided, 13th-century Templar church of Vera Cruz.

## Pisa, Italy

The famous Leaning Tower of Pisa is just one of a quartet of ecclesiastical buildings which make up the beautiful Campo dei Miracoli (Field of Miracles) in this medieval walled city. The black and white marble facades of the Duomo and Baptistery, decorated by a succession of distinguished sculptors, are perfect examples of the Pisan Romanesque style, while the cloistered cemetery of Camposanto contains 14th-century frescoes.

## Siena, Italy

Surrounded by city walls, Siena's medieval centre, with its narrow, winding streets, fine buildings and palaces, is wonderfully preserved. It is dominated by the Piazza del Campo, a large, shell-shaped square where the spectacular horserace known as the Corsa del Palio is held (see *Festivals*).

## Delphi, Greece

In a stunning location, at the foot of Mount Parnassós, lie the impressive ruins of a sanctuary dedicated to Apollo, whose oracle was the most important in Classical Greece. The ruins include the 4th-century BC Temple of Apollo, the Doric Treasury of Athens, a theatre restored by the Romans, and a well-preserved stadium where the Pythian games were held.

## Knossós, Crete

The ruined palace of Knossós is one of the few remains of the Minoan civilization, which flourished c. 3000–1100 BC. The first palace at Knossós was built around 2000 BC, and was rebuilt after an earthquake in c. 1720 BC. Excavations have revealed workshops, storerooms, dwellings and ceremonial rooms, one of which contains a gypsum throne.

## Dubrovnik, Croatia

The fortifications of the ancient port of Dubrovnik rise straight from the Adriatic, and the double line of city walls encompass two palaces, two monasteries and many churches and other historic buildings, mostly dating from the 15th and 16th centuries. The narrow, winding streets of the old city are free from motor vehicles.

## Ephesus, Turkey

The extensive and well-preserved ruins of the ancient city of Ephesus are one of Turkey's most popular historic sites, containing buildings from ancient Greek, Roman and Byzantine times. Among those dating from the Roman period are several temples, a theatre, a library, terraced houses, public baths and latrines, as well as some fine mosaics and wall paintings.

**▲ Chartres Cathedral, France**
Built in the middle of the 13th century, and almost unaltered since, the great cathedral of Notre Dame at Chartres is an exceptionally fine example of high Gothic architecture, with its flying buttresses, vaulted ceilings, intricate stonework and beautifully detailed stained glass. A rare 13th-century labyrinth design on the floor, a Renaissance choir screen and the glowing stained glass of the rose window all add to the beauty and impact of the building.

### Pompeii and the Romans

Pompeii is an exceptional historic site because, when the eruption of Vesuvius in AD 79 engulfed the city in volcanic debris, the life of the people, their homes and streets, public spaces and palaces were preserved as if frozen in time. Excavations have revealed a wealth of detailed information about the everyday life of citizens of the Roman Empire, including their public notices, graffiti, brothels, latrines, furnishings and food. At its greatest extent, in the 1st–4th centuries AD, the Roman Empire encircled the Mediterranean Sea, reaching north as far as Britain and south into Egypt. Remains of Roman theatres, temples, baths, arenas, villas and other buildings can be found at sites throughout Europe and north Africa.

**▲ The Alhambra, Granada, Spain**
The most splendid example of Moorish architecture in Spain is the hilltop Alhambra palace, which was built in the 13th–14th centuries. The unassuming fortress walls contain a richly decorated interior made up of many halls and courtyards, with fountains and pools throughout.

**Major cities with historic sites**
(see *World Cities*)
- Amsterdam
- Athens
- Barcelona
- Berlin
- Brussels
- Budapest
- Copenhagen
- Dublin
- Edinburgh
- Florence
- Geneva
- Hamburg
- Helsinki
- Istanbul
- Kraków
- Lisbon
- London
- Luxembourg
- Madrid
- Milan
- Moscow
- Munich
- Oslo
- Paris
- Prague
- Reykjavik
- Riga
- Rome
- St Petersburg
- Stockholm
- Vienna
- Warsaw
- Venice

# Historic sites in Africa, Asia and Australasia

Africa is the home of the imposing ruins of ancient Egypt – one of the world's first civilizations. With the Middle East, it also has historic sites that reflect the competing influences of Christianity and Islam. In Asia, vast temple complexes, often adorned with wonderful sculptures, are among the remains of great empires, while in Australia, Aboriginal rock paintings are evidence of a culture that flourished long before the Europeans arrived.

## AFRICA AND THE MIDDLE EAST

### Dogon cliffside villages, Mali
Built among the rocks at the foot of the Bandiagara escarpment are the picturesque traditional houses, temples, granaries and meeting places of the Dogon people, whose culture has survived since the 14th century. The area can be reached only on foot and conditions can be gruelling. The best time to visit is December, for the harvest celebrations.

### Rock churches of Lalibela, Ethiopia
Carved out of the red volcanic rock of the central highlands are 11 extraordinary medieval churches containing rare and beautiful frescoes, elaborate carvings and bas-reliefs. A complex network of tunnels and passageways connects the churches, some of which are hidden in deep trenches while others have been cut into the cliff face. The best time to visit is the Ethiopian Christmas (7 January) and Easter.

### Kilwa Kisiwani, Tanzania
Once an Islamic city-state, the island of Kilwa Kisiwani has extensive ruins, which include a 12th-century mosque, several palaces and grand houses, and a 15th-century Portuguese fort. The impressive 14th-century cliff-top palace of Husuni Kubwa has a 30 m (98 ft) high dome and over 100 rooms.

### Zanzibar, Tanzania
The buildings of Zanzibar Town's 'old quarter', Stone Town, reflect its colourful history as an important trading centre, particularly in the 19th century. A maze of narrow streets contain a sultan's palace, an ochre-coloured Arab fort, and the home of the notorious slave trader Tippu Tip, as well as numerous bazaars.

### Great Zimbabwe, Zimbabwe
The extensive ruins of a major medieval city dating from the 10th century onwards, Great Zimbabwe is made up of curved stone walls and enclosures which incorporate features of the landscape into their design. The Elliptical Building, with an unusual conical tower and a diameter of almost 100 m (328 ft), is the largest ancient structure in sub-Saharan Africa.

### Akko, Israel
The ancient walled port of Akko contains many relics of its long and distinguished history, including the underground 12th-century Crusader vaults and halls, the Ottoman Turkish citadel, and the beautiful 18th-century El Jazzar mosque. A remarkable 18th-century Turkish bathhouse has been sensitively restored.

### Petra, Jordan
Carved out of red sandstone mountains, the majestic remains of the desert city of Petra include two theatres, the High Place of Sacrifice, a temple and many elaborate tombs. The majority date from the period c. 100 BC –AD 150, when Petra was at the height of its prosperity as an important centre of trade. It had strong links with the Greek Hellenistic world, which are reflected in the Classical facades of its tombs.

## ASIA

### Mohenjodaro, Pakistan
The excavated remains of a city, Mohenjodaro is the most impressive of all the sites relating to the civilization that flourished in the Indus Valley c. 2600–1800 BC. The site consists of a raised citadel, with public buildings that include an assembly hall and a Great Bath, and a lower town containing residential and industrial areas.

◄ **Angkor, Cambodia** The magnificent ruins at Angkor, capital of the Khmer empire, merit more than one day of sight-seeing. The best-preserved of the buildings is the 12th-century sandstone temple of Angkor Wat, which symbolizes the Hindu universe. Surrounded by pools, it is lavishly decorated with statues and bas-reliefs that are the longest in the world. Around 1.5 km (1 mile) away is the temple complex of Angkor Thom, within which is the Buddhist temple of Bayon with reliefs depicting everyday life.

▼ **Ajanta and Ellora Caves, near Aurangabad, India** Cut into a spectacular horseshoe-shaped cliff, the Buddhist temples and monasteries of Ajanta are decorated with wall-paintings which are among the greatest examples of early Indian art. The series of rock-cut temples at Ellora includes the 8th-century Hindu Kailasa temple which is renowned for its exceptional sculptures of gods and mythological figures.

### The Pyramids and Ancient Egypt
Khafre's Sphinx, 73 m (240 ft) in length and carved from a limestone outcrop, stands near the three pyramids at Giza. The most famous of the Egyptian pyramids, they were built as spectacular royal tombs over 4,500 years ago, during the period of the Old Kingdom. The largest at Giza is nearly 150 m (500 ft) high. The last of the Old Kingdom dynasties collapsed c. 2180 BC, but central government was restored by the dynasties of the Middle Kingdom (c. 2055–1650 BC) and New Kingdom (c. 1550–1070 BC). In the era of the New Kingdom, vast temples and lavishly painted royal tombs were constructed, most notably those either side of the River Nile at Luxor and overlooking Lake Nasser at Abu Simbel (see *River and canal journeys*).

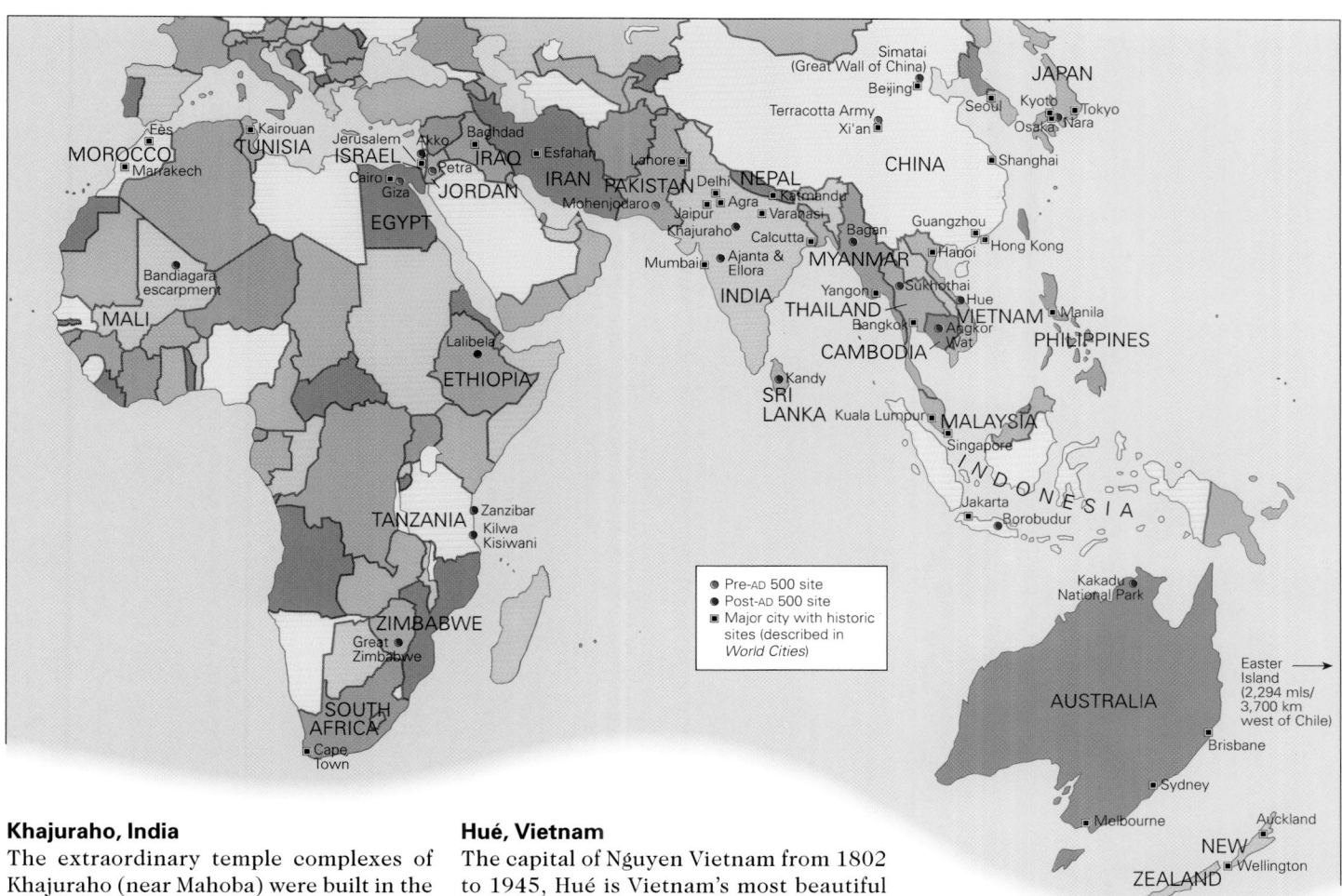

### Khajuraho, India

The extraordinary temple complexes of Khajuraho (near Mahoba) were built in the 10th and 11th centuries by the Hindu Chandela dynasty, but were abandoned in the 14th century. Rediscovered in the jungle in 1838, they were carefully restored and are now famous for their sensual and erotic sculptures depicting human, divine, animal and mythological subjects.

### Kandy and the Cultural Triangle, Sri Lanka

Famous for its temple and Festival of the Tooth (see *Festivals*), Kandy is one of three former Sinhalese capitals that together form a 'Cultural Triangle'. The other two are Anuradhapura, a huge site with the remains of palaces and temples dating back to the 3rd century BC, and the more compact and better-preserved Polonnaruwa, around 1,000 years old. Within the triangle is the 1st-century BC cave-temple of Dambulla, with 150 Buddha images, and the impressive 6th-century palace-fortress of Sigiriya. Built on top of 'Lion Rock', this is decorated with frescoes and includes a water garden.

### Bagan, Burma (Myanmar)

Built between the 11th and the 13th centuries, Bagan (Pagan, near Pakkoku) became known as 'the city of 4 million pagodas', and was the capital of a vast realm. Today it is an important archeological site covering about 40 sq km (15 sq miles) with over 2,000 structures still standing. Among the most impressive are the Temple of Ananda and the Shwezigon Pagoda, with glazed plaques showing scenes from the life of Buddha.

### Old Sukhothai, Thailand

The ruins of the 13th-century capital of the Sukhothai empire have been preserved as a 70 sq km (27 sq mile) historical park. They contain numerous temples set in a landscape of lakes, trees and lawns. The most impressive is Wat Mahathat, with fine stucco work and carved Buddhas.

### Hué, Vietnam

The capital of Nguyen Vietnam from 1802 to 1945, Hué is Vietnam's most beautiful city. The magnificent moated citadel with its ten fortified gates contains a palace, a mandarin hall and a museum. In the hills to the south of the city there are seven elaborate royal tombs.

### Borobudur, Java, Indonesia

Rising like a squat pyramid from the Kedu Plain, Borobudur (near Yogyakarta) is a colossal 9th-century Buddhist stupa (temple) built by the Sailendra dynasty. The largest monument in the southern hemisphere, it covers 200 sq m (2,153 sq ft) and includes over 500 shrines with seated Buddhas. The walls of the stupa, which has five square and four circular terraces, are decorated with bas-reliefs.

### Great Wall of China, Simatai, China

Stretching from the Central Asian desert to the Yellow Sea, the Great Wall is over 2,240 km (1,400 miles) long, averages over 6 m (20 ft) in height, and has a central walkway nearly 4 m (13 ft) wide. Much of what exists today dates from the 14th–16th centuries. The Wall can be visited at Badaling, just 70 km (45 miles) from Beijing. However, a less crowded section is at Simatai, 110 km (68 miles) from Beijing, where there are wonderful views to the distant mountains.

### Nara, Japan

The ancient city of Nara has many beautiful pagodas, shrines, gardens and temples, the most famous of which is the 8th-century Eastern Great Temple, the Tadai-Ji. Its Great Buddha Hall houses Japan's largest bronze statue of Buddha; the hall itself is the largest wooden building in the world.

## AUSTRALASIA AND THE PACIFIC

### Kakadu National Park, Australia

Thousands of Aboriginal rock paintings cover the walls of the caves and cliffs of the ancient Aboriginal lands in Kakadu National Park (see also *Wildlife in Australasia*). The paintings, some of which are estimated to be over 20,000 years old, provide a continuous link with the past for the several hundred Aboriginal people who still live there today.

### Easter Island statues, Polynesia

The extraordinary stone statues of Easter Island are the legacy of a lost culture which flourished on the island between around AD 400 and 1600. More than 800 colossal stone heads were erected all around the island's coast. The volcanic crater from which the stone was quarried still contains hundreds of unfinished statues, including the 20 m (65 ft) high El Gigante.

◄ **Army of Terracotta Warriors, near Xi'an, China** The massive underground mausoleum of China's first emperor, Shi Huang Di, who died in 210 BC, contains an army of around 7,500 life-size terracotta soldiers. Standing in military formation, they are a unique sight.

# Theme parks

Inspired by the phenomenon of Disneyland, Los Angeles, the top theme parks around the world are irresistible to children both young and old, as well as adults. The combination of charm and fantasy with white-knuckle rides and superb service guarantees a successful family visit, and since most are located near major cities it is easy to incorporate them into a longer itinerary.

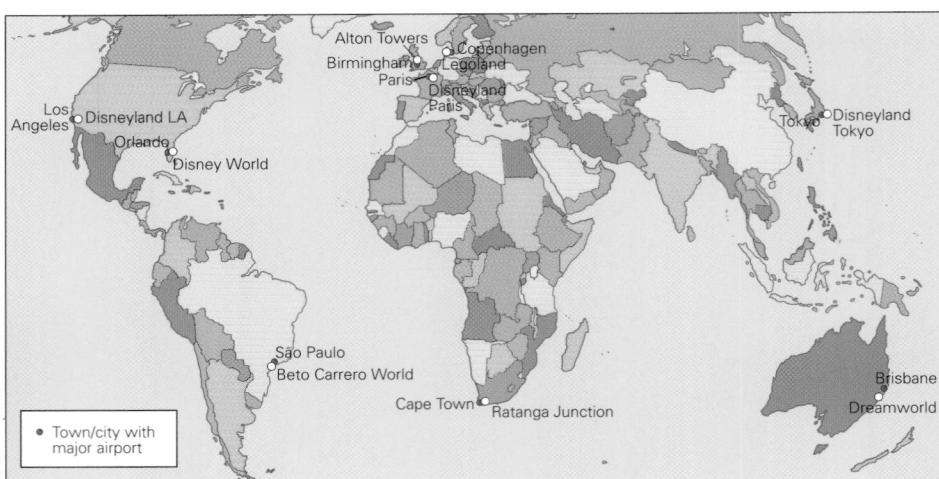

• Town/city with major airport

**▲ Alton Towers, England**

The combination of a ruined stately home, wooded parkland and over 100 rides means that Alton Towers (in Staffordshire) provides entertainment for all tastes. For the benefit of its younger visitors it puts on shows featuring characters from storybooks and songs, such as 'Peter Rabbit and Friends on Ice'. Its more challenging rides have a much darker theme, with names such as Nemesis and Oblivion.

### Disneyland, Los Angeles, USA

Disneyland, founded in 1955, is the original Disney theme park, and Mainstreet, Frontierland and Fantasyland – representations of American life and its dreams – have been duplicated in Disney theme parks around the world. Visitors are attracted not only by rides like the runaway train of Big Thunder Mountain, the parade of Disney characters and the famous nightly firework show, but also out of nostalgia and a desire to experience what is itself now a historic site.

### Beto Carrero World, Santa Catarina, Brazil

The most extensive theme park in Brazil, Beto Carrero World (near Itajai) combines thrilling rides, shows and a zoo. Its themed areas cover a range of cultures, including a German House complete with beer cellar, a Viking longboat and a Wild West area. Its shows are similarly wide-ranging and feature the legend of Excalibur. Its white-knuckle rides include the free-falling Tower of Terror, and Star World Mountain, with two 360-degree loops. The animal park includes African wildlife and a large collection of cobras.

### Disneyland Paris, France

Although based on the same formula as the Los Angeles theme park, the marketing for Disneyland Paris emphasizes the educational element. There are 'Discovery rides', such as the 'Mississippi Steamboat' which provides information about life in frontier towns, while the Swiss Family Robinson tree-house demonstrates practical survival tips. Most visitors, however, go for the glamour of the shows and parades, and the thrill of the rides. These include being catapulted 'From the Earth to the Moon' on a Jules Verne style rocket.

### Legoland, Billund, Denmark

Legoland, in which everything is built out of lego, is divided into themed areas, such as Pirateland and Castleland, where children recognize, and are able to interact with, their favourite lego characters. Although the park is aimed primarily at children, providing them with opportunities to play creatively, adults are also charmed by the intricate scale models of real, if somewhat idealized, scenes.

### Ratanga Junction, Cape Town, South Africa

Africa's first theme park opened in the late 1990s. It takes as its theme the wildlife of Africa, with rides such as The Cobra, Monkey Falls, and Crocodile Gorge, in which visitors can experience white-water rafting in controlled conditions. A diamond mine is featured, with an underground runaway mine train providing the thrills. There are also less alarming rides for all the family, and 'interactive play areas' for young children.

### Disneyland Tokyo, Japan

With many of the same attractions as other Disney theme parks, Disneyland Tokyo is unashamedly American in its culture, although it also offers a journey through Japanese history in Tomorrow Land. The Disney Parade celebrates '100 years of magic', with characters from the earliest cartoons through to the present day, and attempts to predict those of the future.

### Dreamworld, Queensland, Australia

Thrilling rides and shows are combined with a wildlife park and conservation zone in Dreamworld (near Gold Coast). The Tower of Terror roller coaster reaches speeds of 160 km (100 miles) per hour as it descends from a height of 115 m (375 ft). The Giant Drop uses the same structure to release passengers vertically so that they experience momentary weightlessness. In an 'interactive tiger exhibition' tigers swim with their trainers, while in the Koala Park visitors can handle koalas and watch other native Australian animals.

**Walt Disney World, Orlando, Florida, USA**
The massive Walt Disney World in Florida encompasses four separate theme parks. At Magic Kingdom there are rides graded for every taste, from those in Fantasyland aimed specifically at younger children, to the Space Mountain rocket trip, which is not for the faint-hearted. The Epcot Centre aims to re-create the atmosphere and architecture of different countries, including Norway, China and Italy. Visitors can eat food typical of the region, and enjoy themed rides, shows and videos. Disney MGM re-creates urban areas, such as New York Street and Hollywood Boulevard, and uses computer technology to enable visitors to come face to face with characters from recent films. The newest of the parks, Animal Kingdom, combines a safari park with typical Disney features, including thrilling rides, exhibitions and shows.

# WORLD CITIES

## CITY MAPS

## City Maps

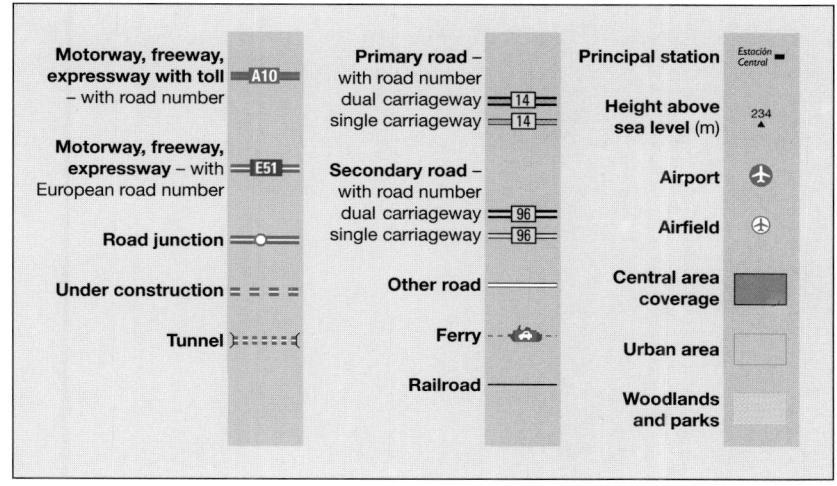

## Central Area Maps

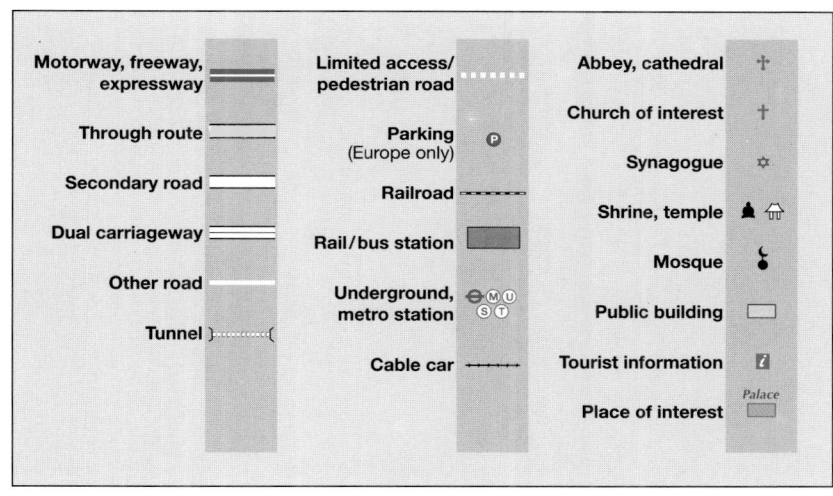

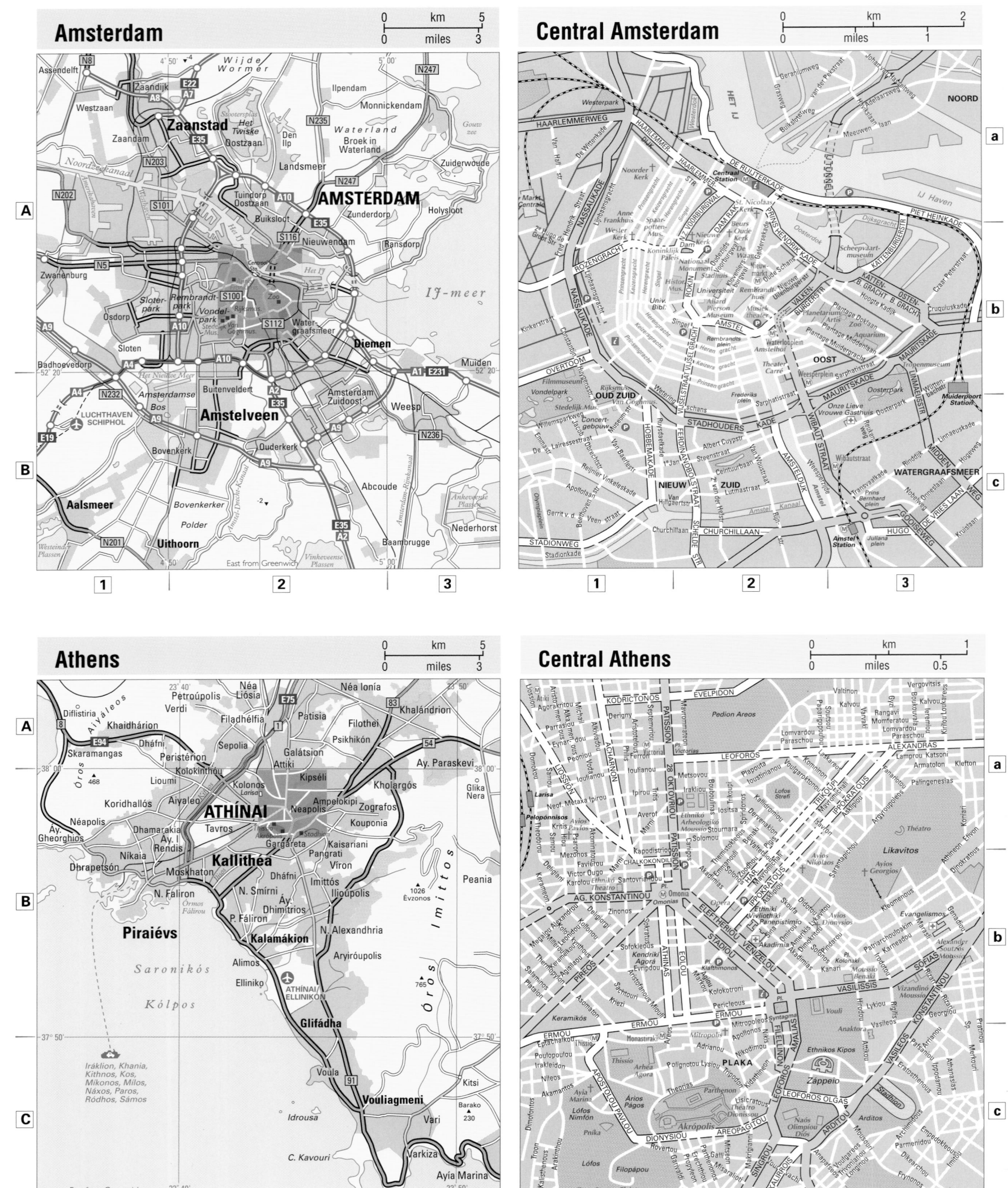

### Amsterdam

km 5
miles 3

N8 Assendelft
Zaandijk E22
A8 A7
Westzaan
Zaanstad E35
Zaandam Oostzaan
Noordzeekanaal N203
N202
N5 Zwanenburg
S101 Tuindorp Oostzaan
A Buiksloot
Badhoevedorp
A4 A10
N232 Amsterdamse Bos
LUCHTHAVEN SCHIPHOL A9
E19 Amstelveen
Bovenkerk
Aalsmeer
N201 Uithoorn
Westeindér Plassen

Wijde Wormer
Ilpendam
Monnickendam
N235
Waterland
Broek in Waterland
N247
Landsmeer
AMSTERDAM
Nieuwendam
Het IJ
Diemen
Amsterdam Zuidoost
Ouderkerk
Bovenkerker Polder
Vinkeveense Plassen

Gouw zee
Zuiderwoude
Holysloot
Ransdorp
IJ-meer
Müiden
Weesp
N236
Abcoude
Baambrugge
E35 A2
Nederhorst
Ankeveense Plassen

### Athens

km 5
miles 3

Diflistiria
Khaidhárion
Skaramangas
Óros Aiyáleos
Néapolis
Ay. Gheorghios
Koridhallós
Níkaia
Dhrapetsón
Piraiévs
N. Fáliron
Saronikós Kólpos
Iráklion, Khania, Kíthnos, Kos, Mílos, Náxos, Paros, Ródhos, Sámos
Idrousa

Petroúpolis
Verdi
Dháfni
Peristérion
Lioumi
Aiyáleo
Dhamarakia
Ay. Rendis
Tavros
Moskhaton
Kallithéa
N. Smírni
P. Fáliron
Kalamákion
Alimos
Elliniko
ATHÍNAI ELLINIKON
Glifádha
Voula

Néa Liósia
Filadhélfia
Sepolia
Kolokinthoú
Kolonos Larisa
Neapolis
ATHÍNAI
Gargáreta
Dháfni
Áy. Dhimítrios
N. Alexandhria
91
Vari
Varkiza

Patisia
Galátsion
Attiki
Kipséli
Ampelokipi
Zografos
Kaisariani
Víron
Imittós
Ilioúpolis
Aryiroúpolis

Néa Ionía
Filothéi
Psikhikón
Kholargós
Glika Nera
Ay. Paraskevi
1026 Evzonos
765
Óros Imittós
Peania
Barako 230
Ayia Marina

### Central Amsterdam

km 2
miles 1

### Central Athens

km 1
miles 0.5

## Atlanta

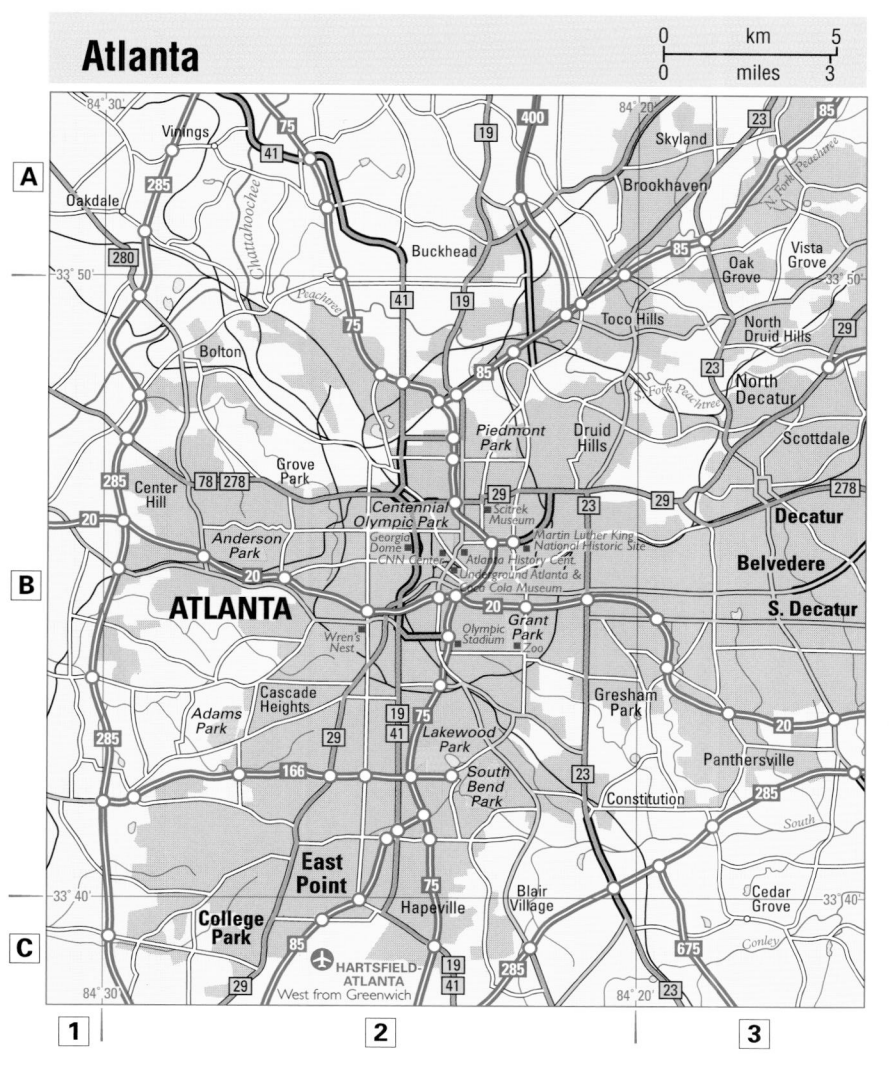

## Baghdad

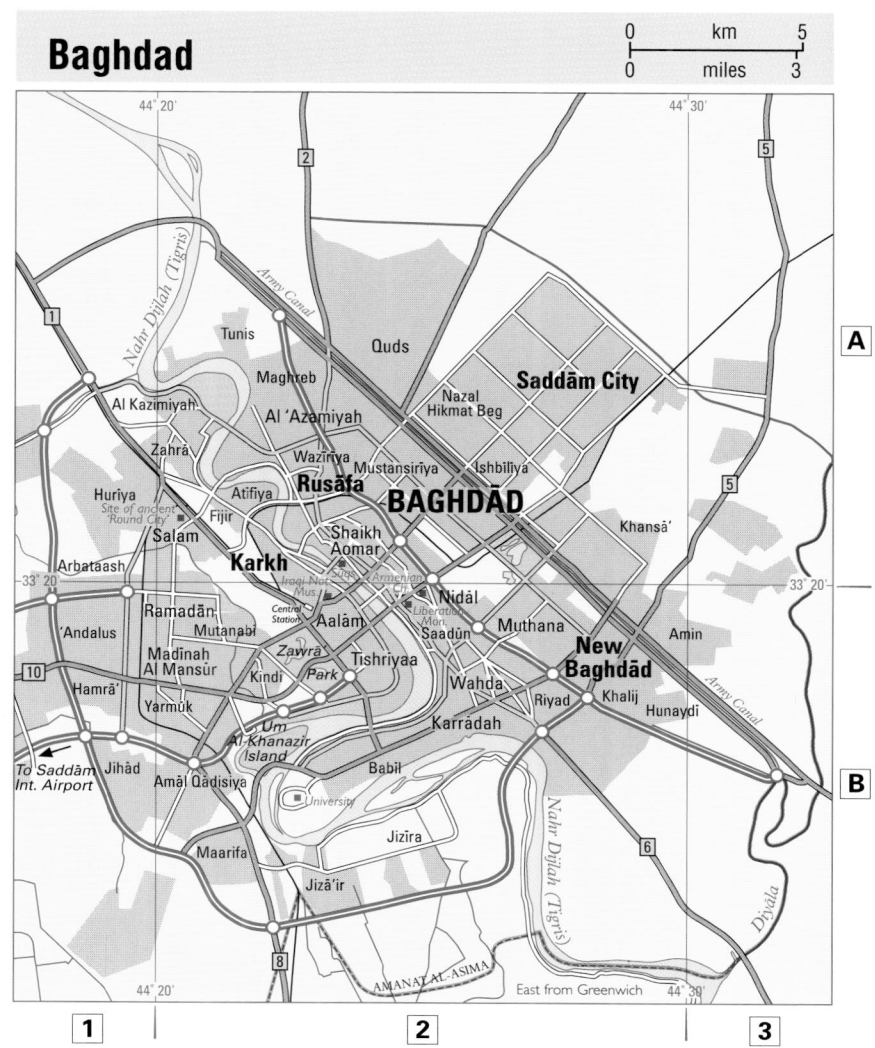

## Bangkok

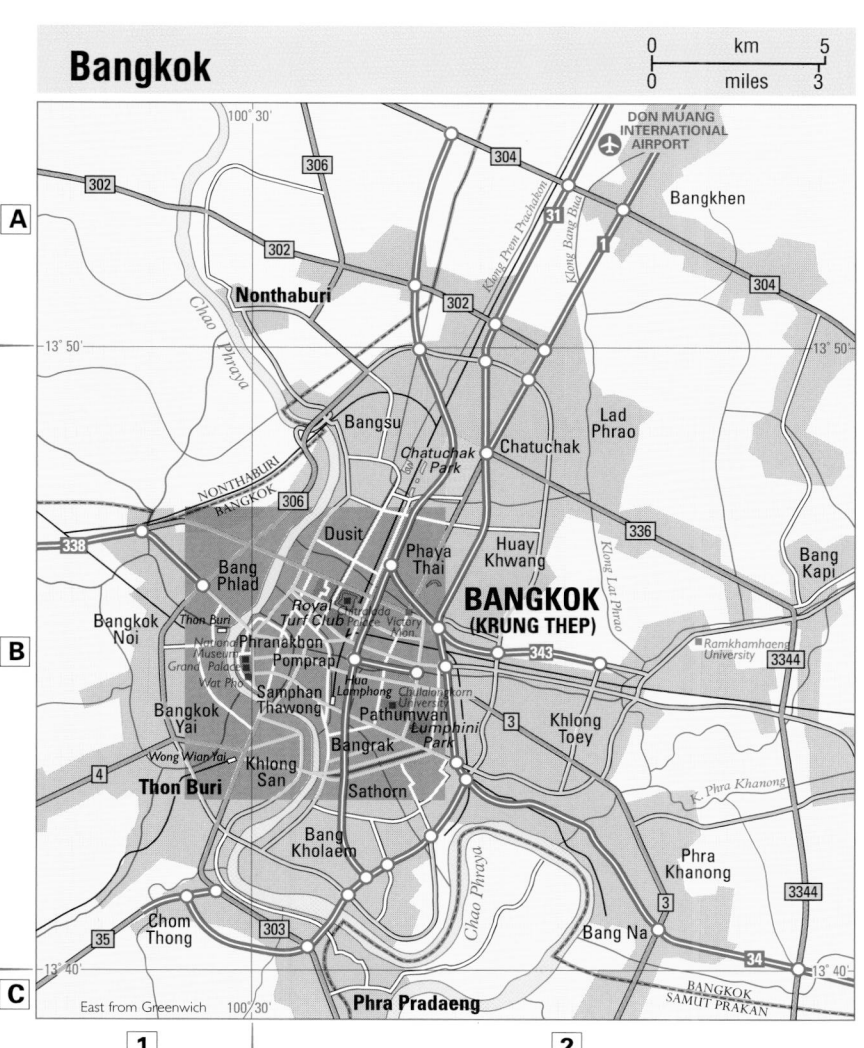

## Central Bangkok

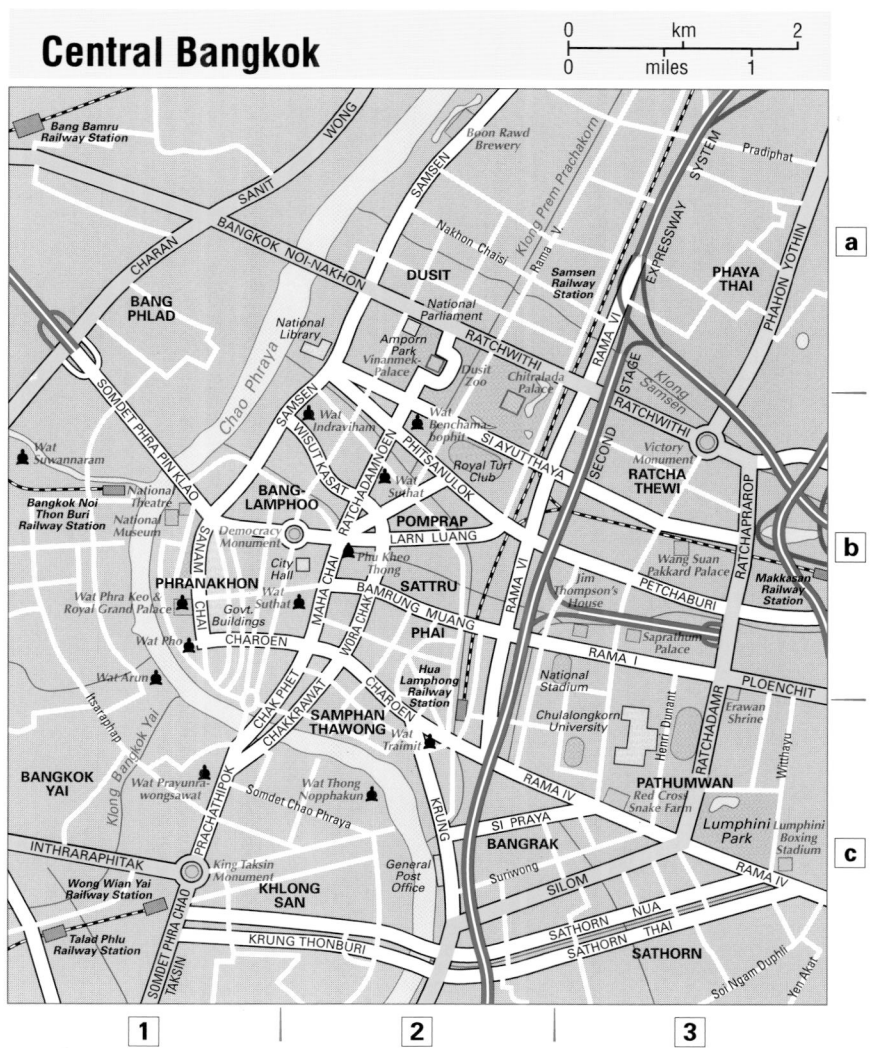

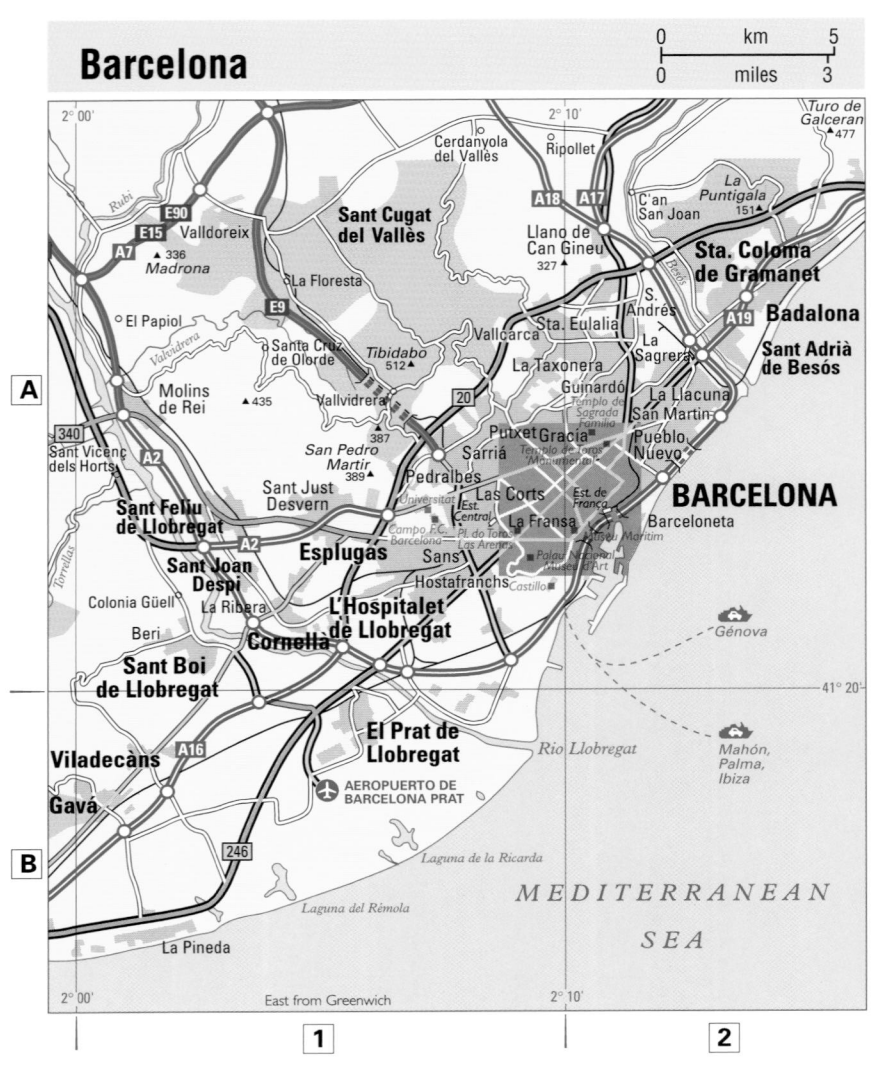

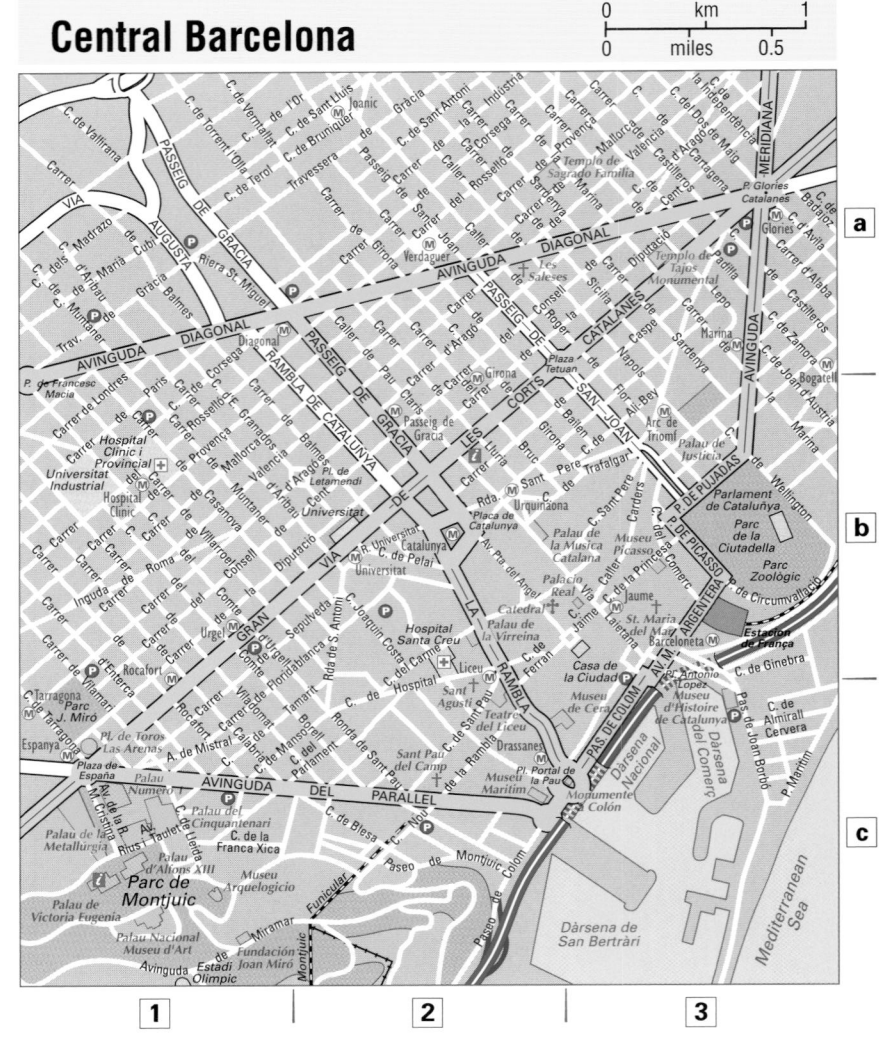

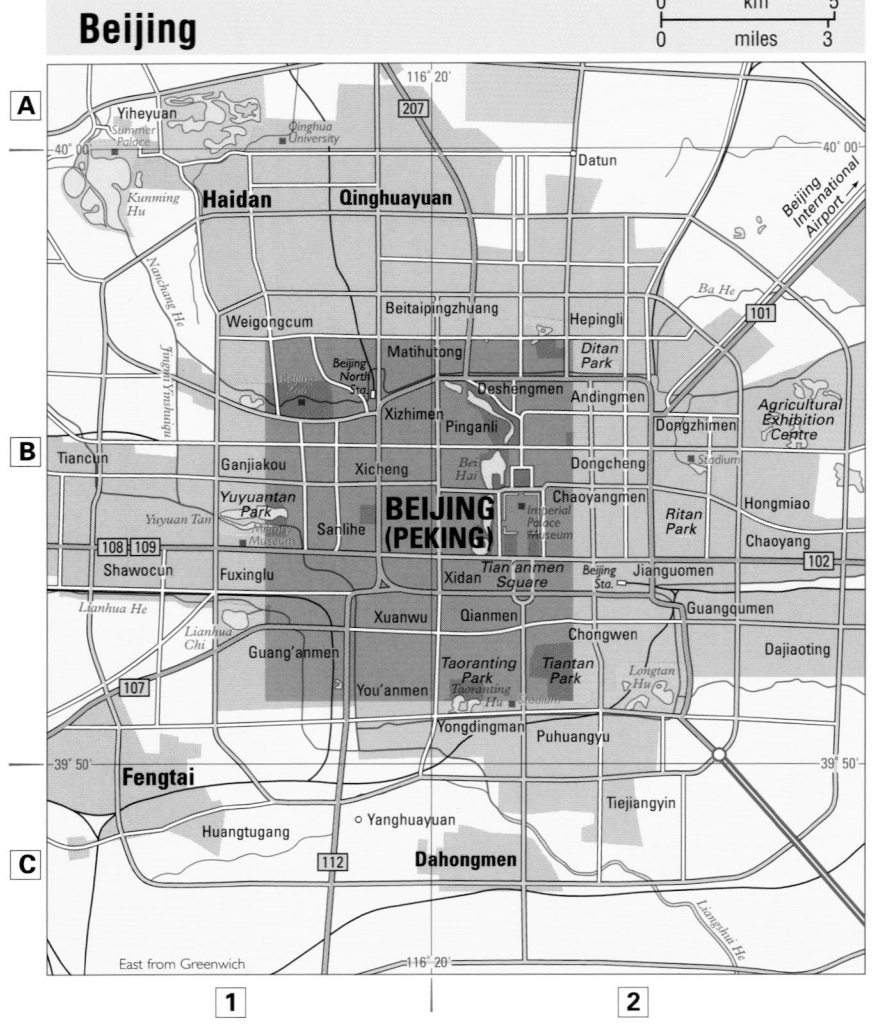

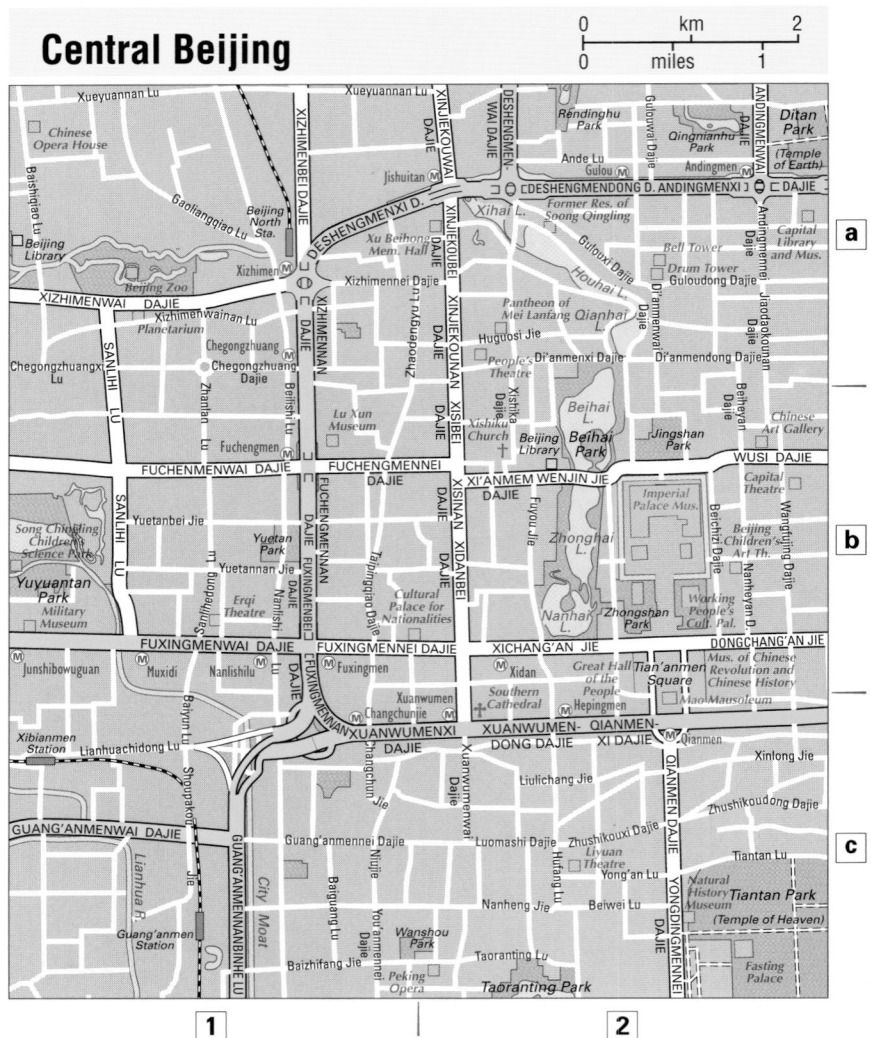

# Berlin

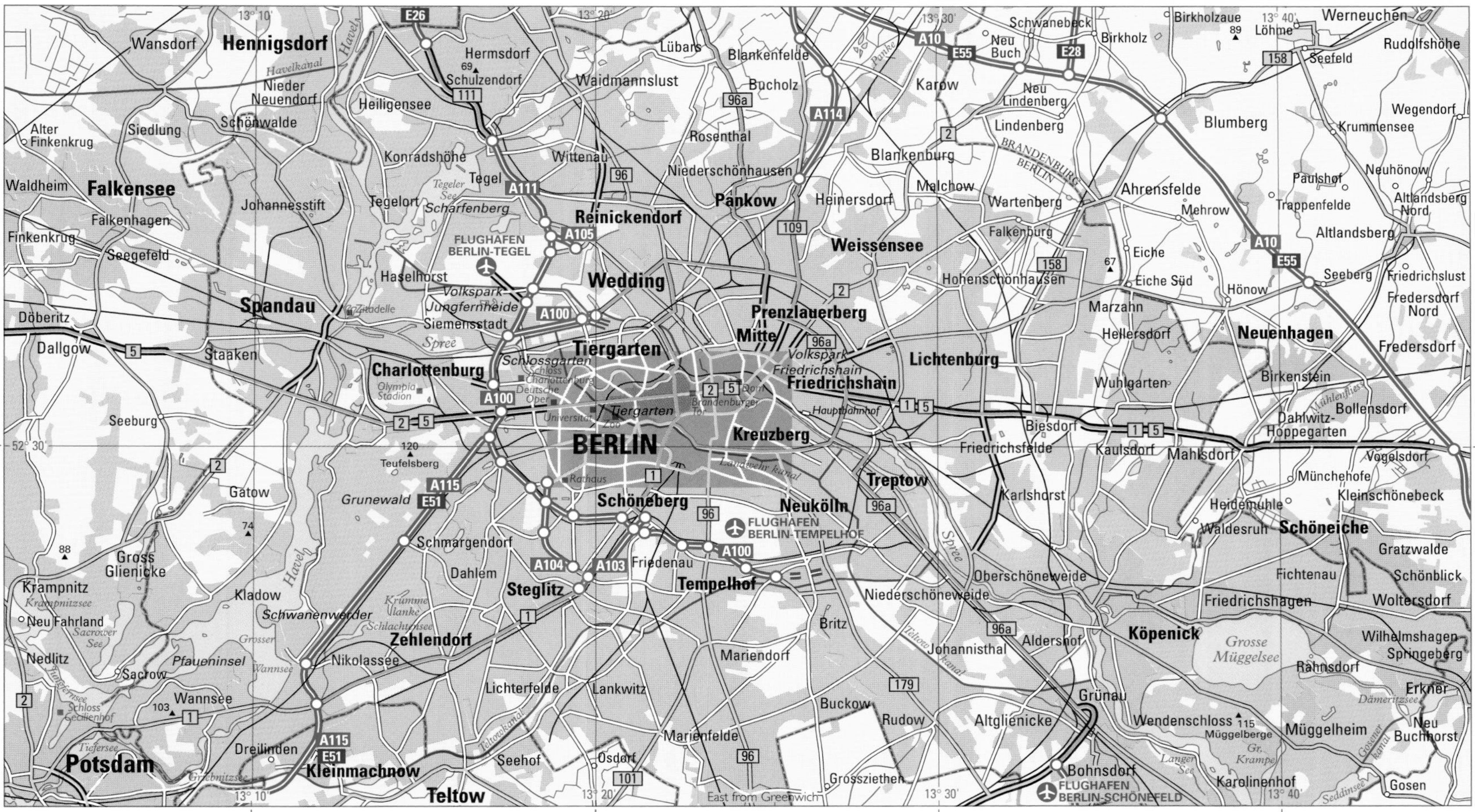

# Central Berlin

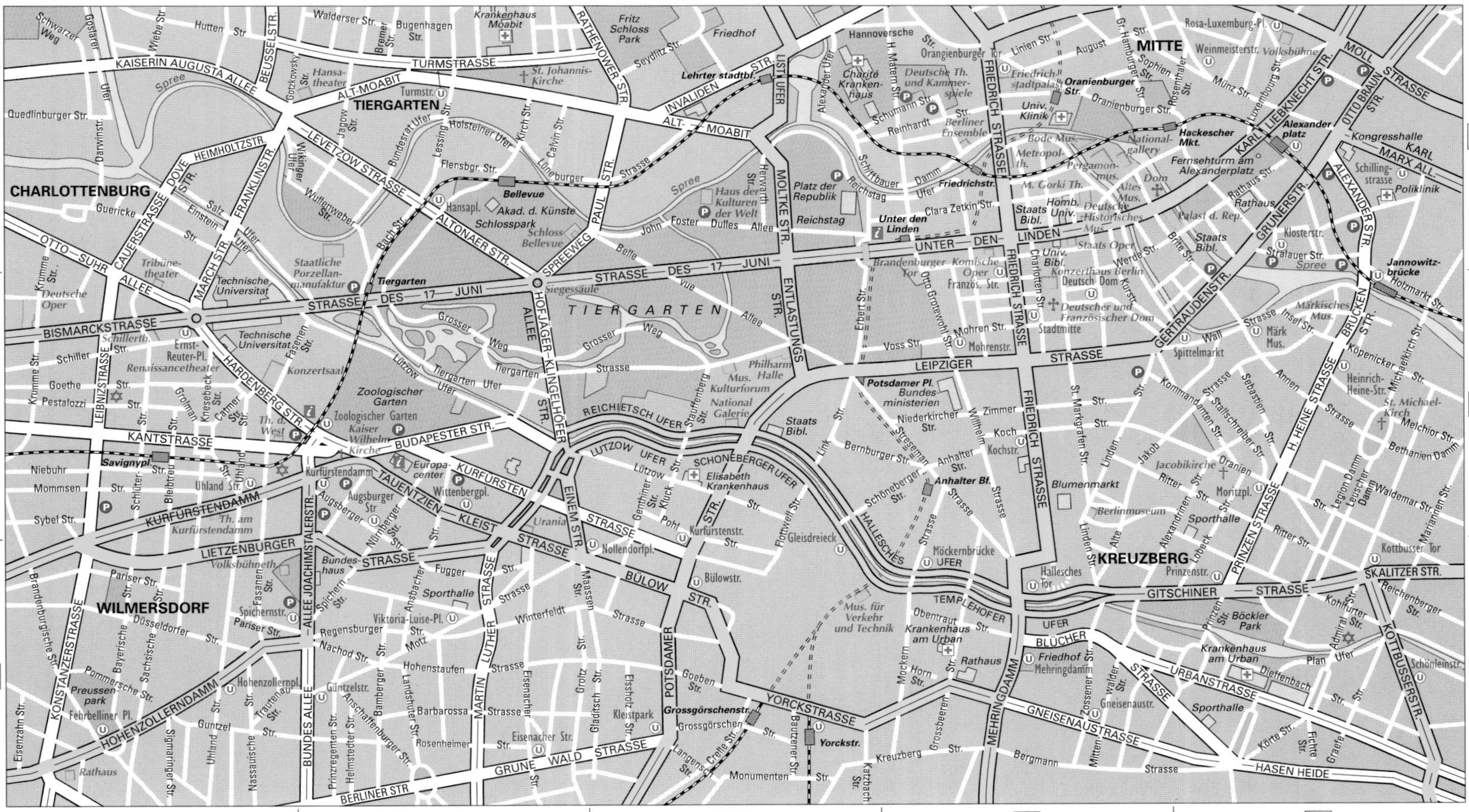

## Boston

0 km 5
0 miles 3

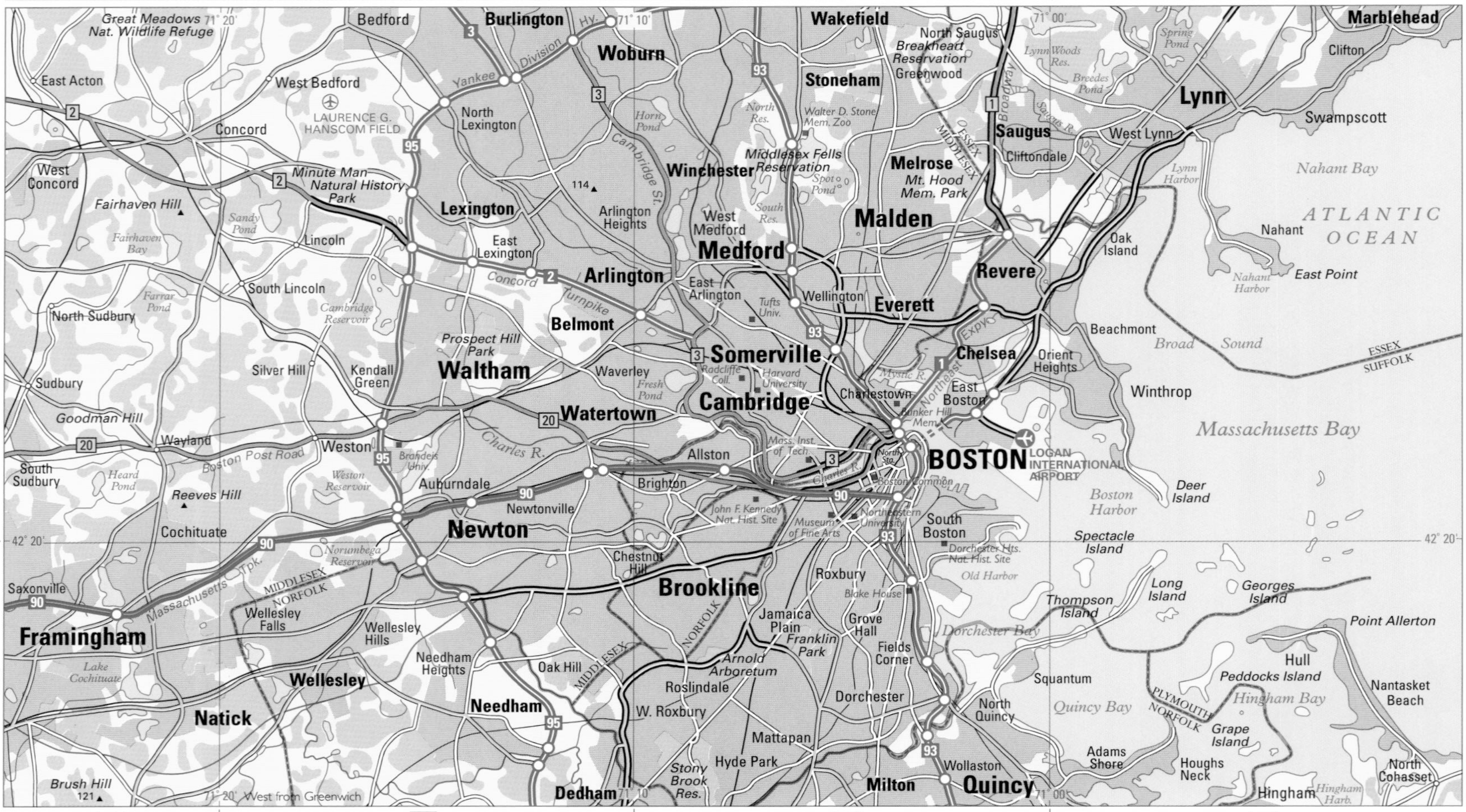

Great Meadows 71° 20'
Nat. Wildlife Refuge
Bedford
Burlington
Wakefield
Marblehead

East Acton
West Bedford
Woburn
North Saugus
Breakheart
Reservation
Greenwood
Clifton

LAURENCE G.
HANSCOM FIELD
Concord
Stoneham
Lynn
Swampscott

West
Concord
North Lexington
Walter D. Stone
Mem. Zoo
Saugus
West Lynn

Minute Man
Natural History
Park
Middlesex Fells
Reservation
Melrose
Mt. Hood
Mem. Park
ATLANTIC
OCEAN

Fairhaven Hill
Sandy Pond
Lincoln
Lexington
Winchester
West
Medford
Malden
Nahant

**A**
Fairhaven
Bay
South Lincoln
East
Lexington
Arlington
Heights
Arlington St.
Medford
Revere
Nahant
East Point
**A**

North Sudbury
Cambridge
Reservoir
Prospect Hill
Park
East
Arlington
East
Arlington
Tufts Univ.
Everett
Beachmont
Broad
Sound
ESSEX
SUFFOLK

Sudbury
Silver Hill
Kendall
Green
Belmont
Waverley
Fresh Pond
Radcliffe Coll.
Harvard University
Somerville
Chelsea
Orient
Heights
Winthrop

Goodman Hill
Waltham
Watertown
Cambridge
Charlestown
East
Boston
LOGAN
INTERNATIONAL
AIRPORT

South
Sudbury
Wayland
Weston
Auburndale
Charles R.
Allston
Brighton
Mass. Inst.
of Tech.
BOSTON
Boston
Harbor
Deer
Island
Massachusetts Bay

Cochituate
Newton
Newtonville
John F. Kennedy
Nat. Hist. Site
Northeastern University
Museum
of Fine Arts
South
Boston
Spectacle
Island

Saxonville
Framingham
Brookline
Roxbury
Blake House
Grove
Hall
Dorchester Hts.
Nat. Hist. Site
Old Harbor
Dorchester Bay
Long
Island
Georges
Island
Point Allerton

**B**
Lake
Cochituate
Wellesley
Falls
Wellesley
Hills
Needham
Heights
Jamaica
Plain
Franklin
Park
Fields
Corner
Thompson
Island
Hull
Peddocks Island
Nantasket
Beach
**B**

Natick
Wellesley
Needham
Oak Hill
Roslindale
W. Roxbury
Dorchester
North
Quincy
Squantum
Quincy Bay
PLYMOUTH
NORFOLK
Grape
Island

Brush Hill
Stony
Brook
Res.
Hyde Park
Mattapan
Milton
Wollaston
Quincy
Adams
Shore
Houghs
Neck
Hingham
Harb.
North
Cohasset

Dedham

## Brussels

0 km 5
0 miles 3

Oppem
Grimbergen
Vilvoorde

Mollem
Meise
Peutie
Perk

Bollebeek
Brussegem
Melsbroek
Wambeek

Kobbegem
Hamme
Wemmel
Strombeek-
Bever
Machelen
Steenokkerzeel

**A**
Atomium
Jette
Haren
Diegem
BRUSSEL NAT.
LUCHTHAVEN
Zaventem
**A**

Ganshoren
Evere
St-Stevens-
Woluwe

Berchem-
Ste-Agathe
Koekelberg
Schaerbeek
St-Joost-
Ten-Noode
Kraainem
Wezembeek-
Oppem

Dilbeek
Molenbeek-
St-Jean
Woluwe-St-
Lambert
Park van
Tervuren

Anderlecht
Woluwe-
St-Pierre

**B**
St-Pieters-
Leeuw
Ixelles
Etterbeek
Auderghem
**B**

St-Gilles
Forest
Watermael-
Boitsfort
BRUSSEL
BRUXELLES

Uccle
Forêt de
Soignes
Overijse

Vlezenbeek
Drogenbos
Linkebeek
Hoeilaart

Ruisbroek
Lot
Beersel
Sint-
Genesius-
Rode
Groenendaal

Halle
Buizingen
Holzingen
Alsemberg
La Hulpe

Waterloo
Dworp
Le Chenoi
Joli-Bois
Ransbèche
Rixensart

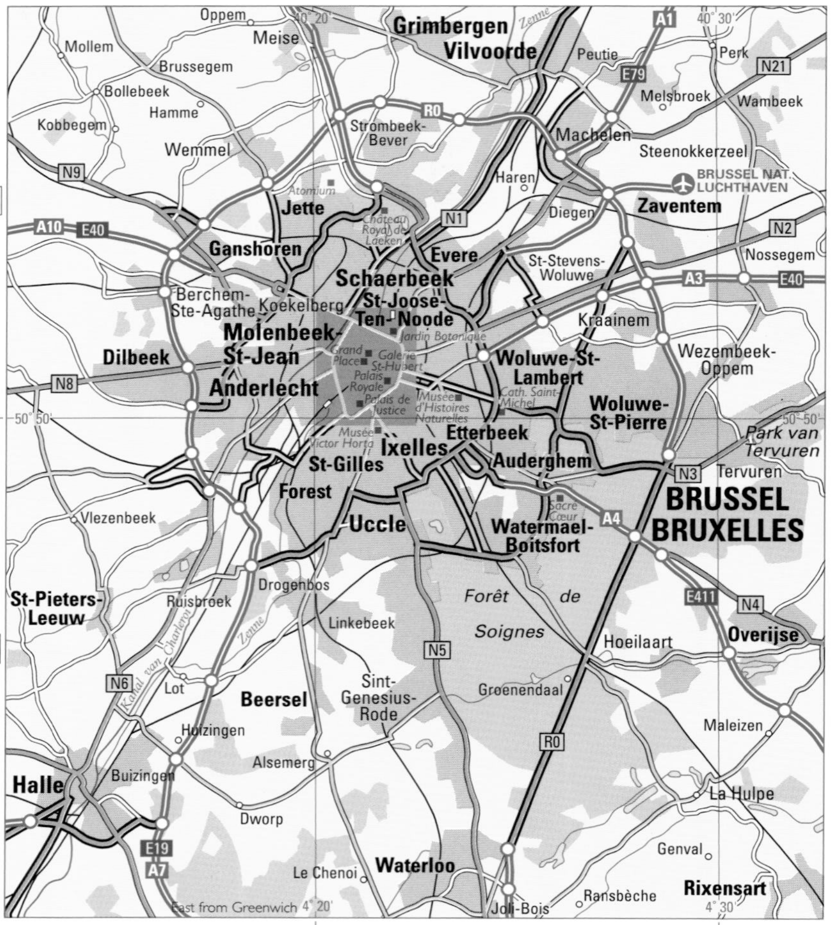

## Central Brussels

0 km 1
0 miles 0.5

Gare
du Nord

**a**

Jardin
Botanique

**b**

**c**

ST-GILLES
Gare
du Midi
(Eurostar)
IXELLES

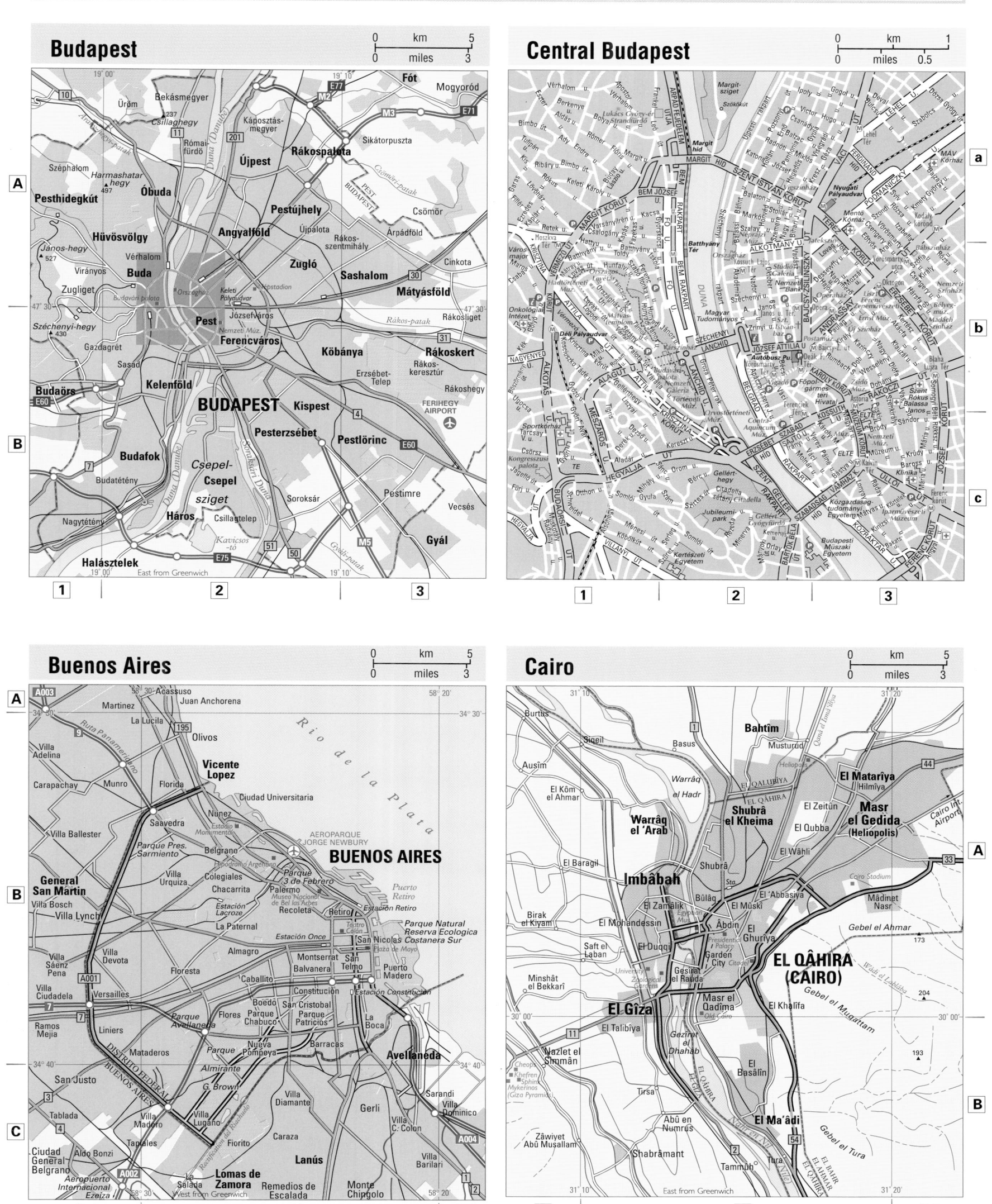

## Calcutta

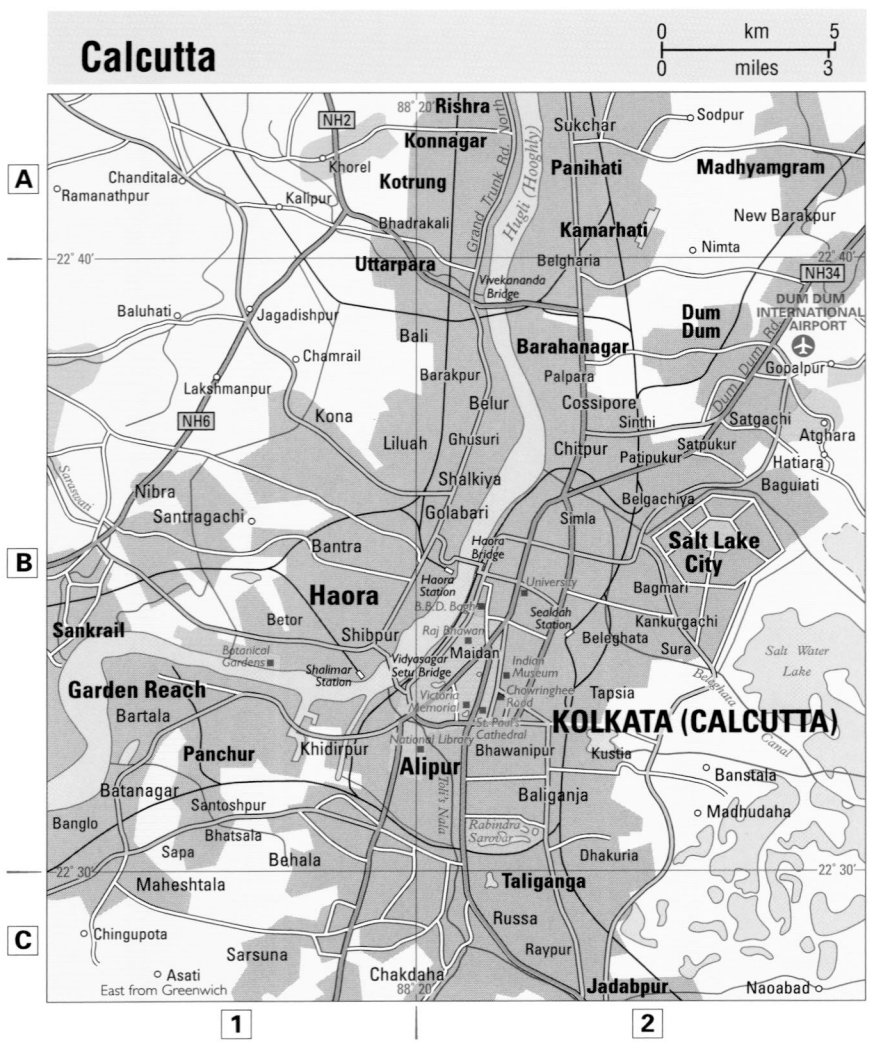

## Canton

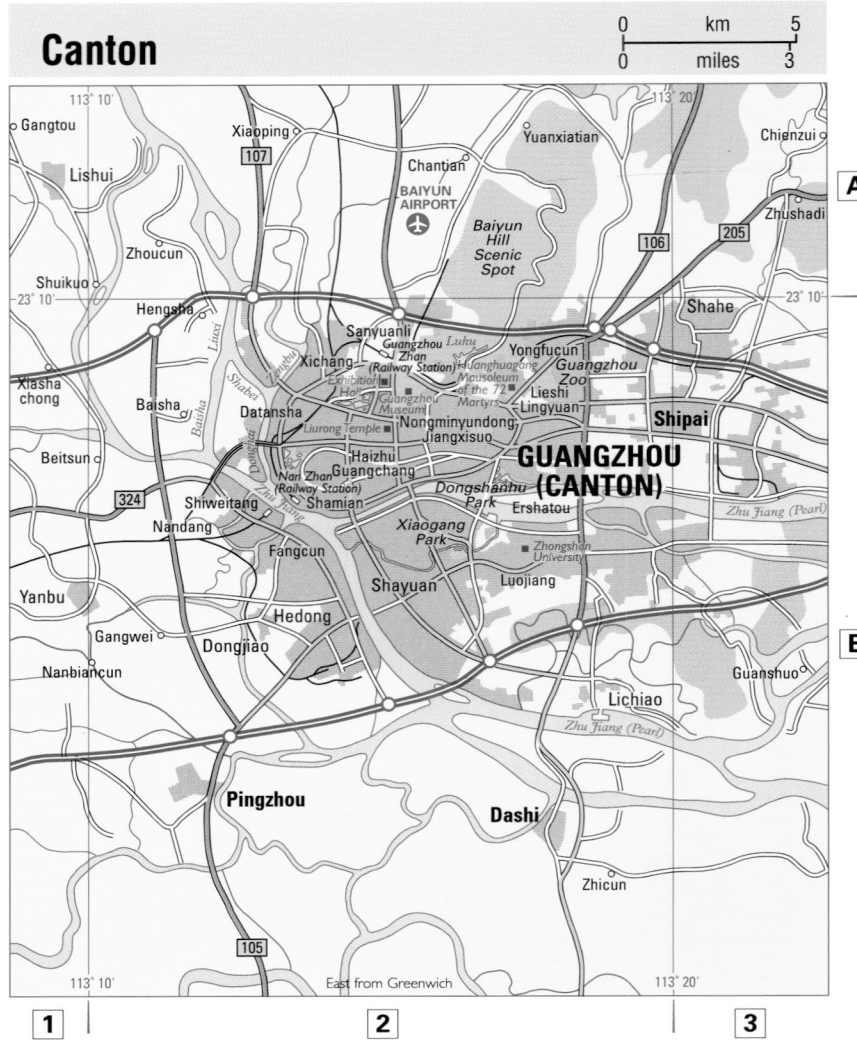

## Cape Town

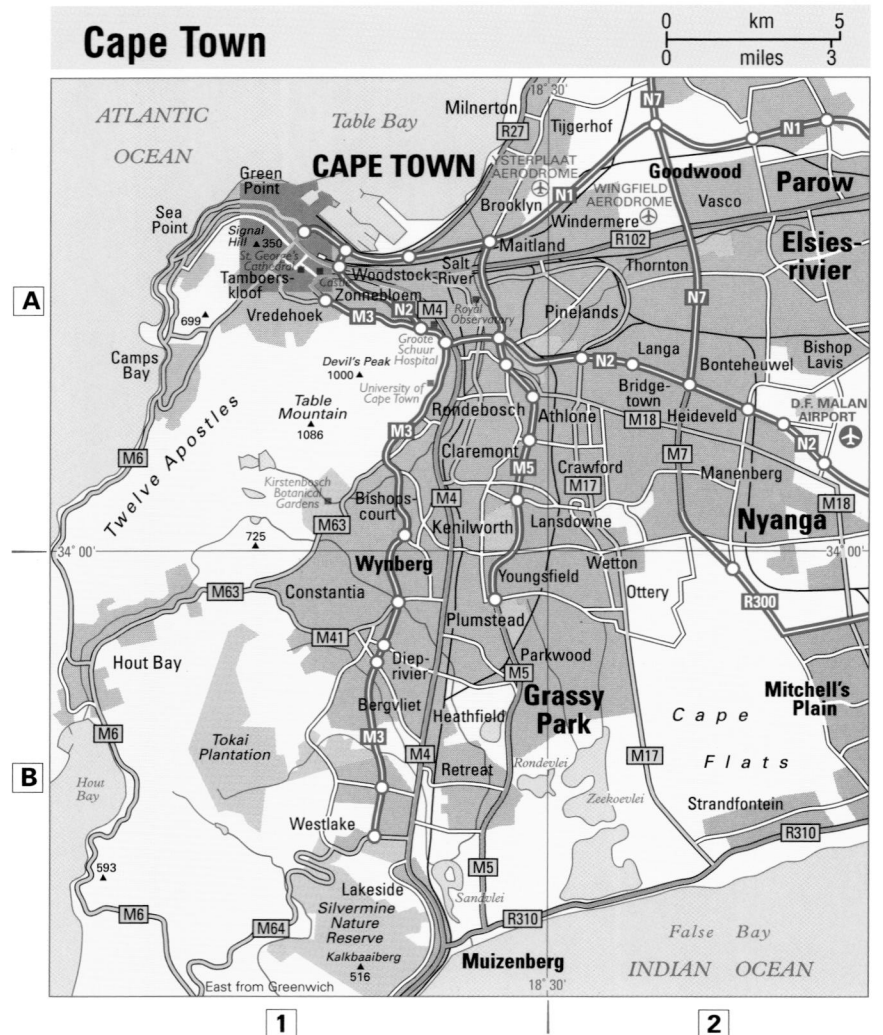

## Central Cape Town

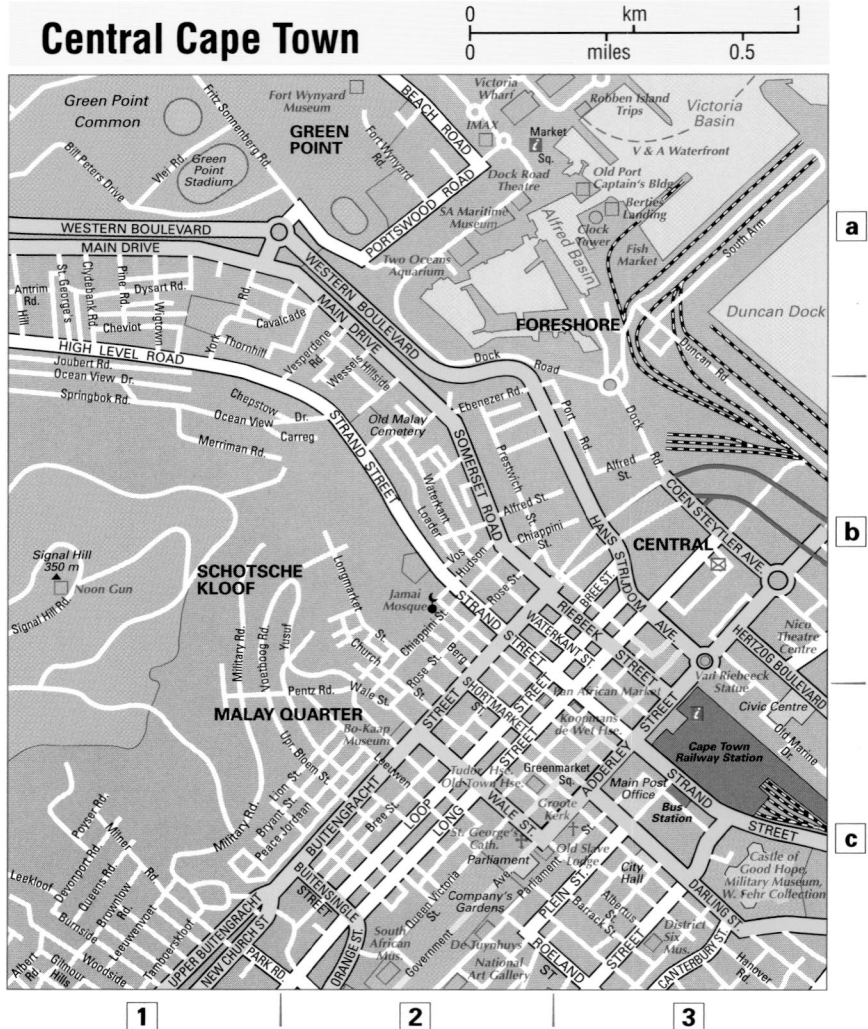

## Chicago

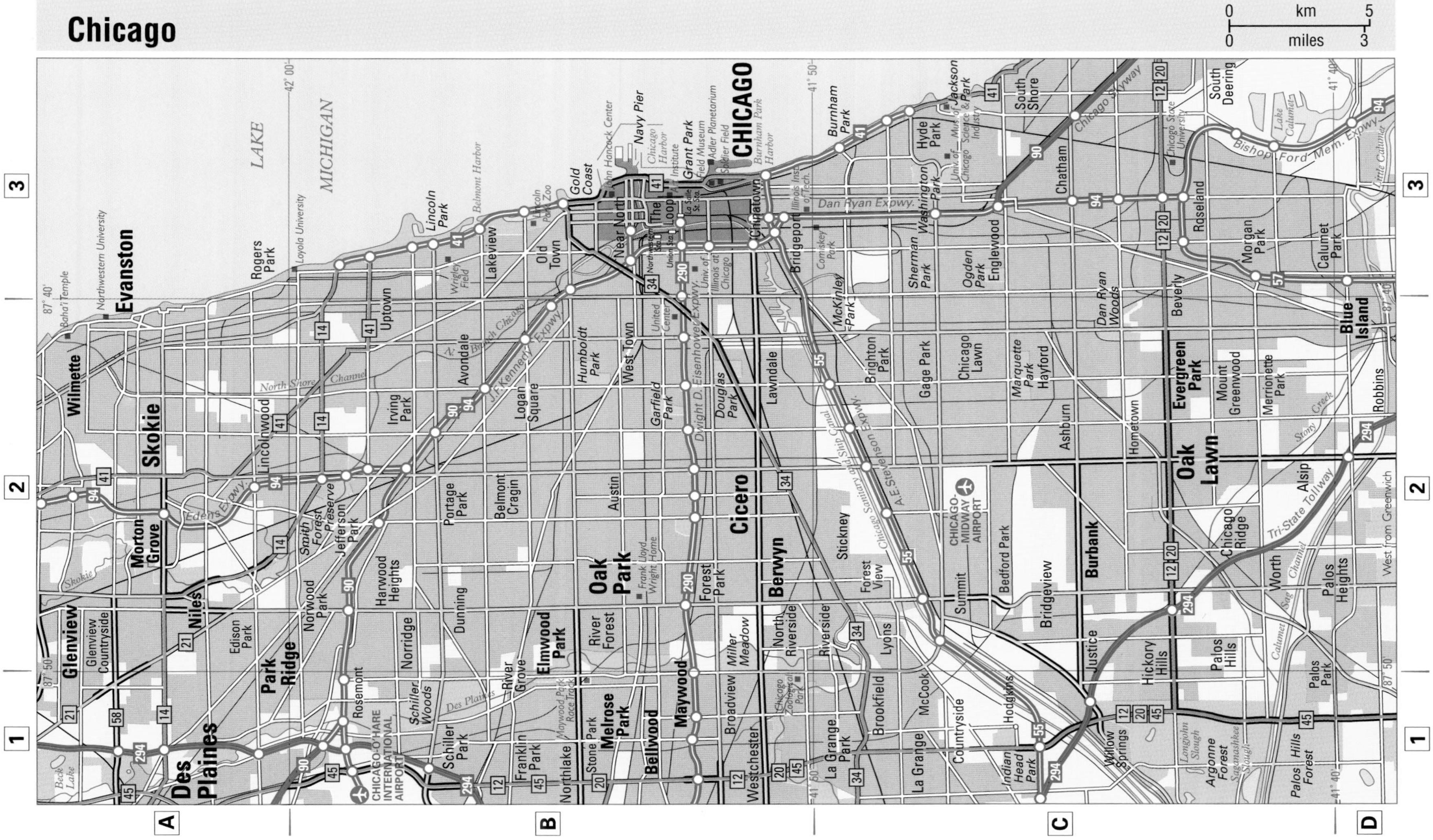

km 0 — 5
miles 0 — 3

LAKE MICHIGAN

Evanston
Wilmette
Skokie
Morton Grove
Glenview
Glenview Countryside
Niles
Park Ridge
Des Plaines
Northwestern University
Bahá'í Temple
Loyola University
Rogers Park
Uptown
Lincolnwood
Lakeview
Old Town
Gold Coast
Lincoln Park
Lincoln Park Zoo
Belmont Harbor
Wright's Field
Irving Park
Avondale
Logan Square
Humboldt Park
West Town
Near North
The Loop
CHICAGO
Chinatown
Bridgeport
Grant Park
Navy Pier
John Hancock Center
Art Institute
Field Museum
Adler Planetarium
Shedd Aquarium
Soldier Field
Burnham Park
Burnham Harbor
Hyde Park
Univ. of Chicago
Museum of Science & Industry
South Shore
South Deering
Lake Calumet
Edens Expwy.
Eden's Expressway
North Shore Channel
North Branch Chicago River
J.F. Kennedy Expwy.
Portage Park
Belmont Cragin
Austin
Garfield Park
Douglas Park
Lawndale
Dwight D. Eisenhower Expwy.
Cicero
Oak Park
Elmwood Park
River Forest
Maywood
Melrose Park
Bellwood
Broadview
Westchester
Forest Park
North Riverside
Riverside
Lyons
Brookfield
La Grange Park
La Grange
Countryside
Hodgkins
McCook
Summit
Bedford Park
Bridgeview
Justice
Hickory Hills
Palos Hills
Palos Park
Palos Heights
Argonne Forest
Sagananshkee Slough
Long John Slough
Worth
Chicago Ridge
Oak Lawn
Burbank
Ashburn
Hometown
Evergreen Park
Mount Greenwood
Merrionette Park
Robbins
Blue Island
Calumet Park
Morgan Park
Beverly
Roseland
Chatham
Englewood
Washington Park
Sherman Park
Ogden Park
Gage Park
Chicago Lawn
Marquette Park
Hayford
Brighton Park
McKinley Park
Comiskey Park
Dan Ryan Expwy.
Dan Ryan Woods
Chicago Sanitary & Ship Canal
Chicago Skyway
Bishop Ford Mem. Expwy.
Tri-State Tollway
A.E. Stevenson Expwy.
Calumet Sag Channel
Stickney
Forest View
Chicago Midway Airport
Chicago O'Hare International Airport
Schiller Park
Franklin Park
Northlake
Stone Park
River Grove
Schiller Woods
Harwood Heights
Norwood Park
Norridge
Dunning
Jefferson Park
Smith Forest Preserve
Frank Lloyd Wright Home
Miller Meadow
Chicago Zoological Park
Maywood Park Race Track
Edison Park
Rosemont
Des Plaines River
Skokie Lagoons
Indian Head Park
Willow Springs
Palos Hills Forest
Streamwood

## Central Chicago

km 0 — 1
miles 0 — 0.5

Outer Harbor
Navy Pier
Olive Park
Ohio St. Beach
Streeter Dr
Lake Point Tower
LAKE MICHIGAN
Chicago Harbor
Chicago Yacht Club
Adler Planetarium
Shedd Aquarium
Field Museum of Nat. History
Burnham Park
Soldier Field
Burnham Park Harbor
Merrill C. Meigs Field
McCormack Place East
McCormack Place West
E. Solidarity Dr
SOUTH LAKE SHORE DRIVE EAST
SOUTH LAKE SHORE DRIVE WEST
LAKE SHORE DRIVE
N LAKE SHORE DRIVE
Grant Park
Buckingham Fountain
Columbus Drive
Roosevelt Road Sta.
Gold Coast
Oak St. Beach
Oak St.
John Hancock Center
Water Tower Place
Water Tower
Northwestern Memorial Hosp.
McClurg Court
Tribune Tower
Wrigley Bldg.
Marshall Field's
Prudential Building
Sears Tower
Merchandise Mart
Union Sta.
Northwestern Sta.
Randolph St. Sta.
Van Buren Sta.
La Salle St. Sta.
Main Post Office
City Hall & County Bldg.
Civic Opera Ho.
Near North
River North
Gold Coast
The Loop
Printer's Row
South Loop
Chinatown
Chicago River
South Branch
North Branch
N Larrabee Street
N Hudson Avenue
New Orleans St.
N Kingsbury St.
N Kinzie St.
N Dearborn St.
N Clark St.
N LaSalle St.
N Wells St.
N Oak St.
N Locust St.
E Division St.
E Oak St.
E Delaware Pl.
E Chestnut St.
E Chicago Ave
E Superior St.
E Huron St.
E Erie St.
E Ontario St.
E Ohio St.
E Grand Ave
E Illinois St.
N Rush St.
N Wabash
N St. Clair St.
N Fairbanks Court
N McClurg Court
N Columbus Drive
N Michigan Avenue
E Randolph Drive
E Lake St.
E Wacker Drive
N Wacker Dr.
W Wacker Dr.
W Lake St.
W Randolph St.
W Washington St.
W Madison St.
W Monroe St.
W Adams St.
W Jackson Blvd.
Congress Pkwy.
W Van Buren St.
W Harrison St.
W Polk St.
W Taylor St.
S Canal St.
S Clinton St.
S Franklin St.
S Wells St.
S LaSalle St.
S Clark St.
S Dearborn St.
S State St.
S Wabash Ave
S Michigan Avenue
S Columbus Drive
S Prairie Ave
S Calumet Ave
S Indiana Ave
E 14th St.
E 16th St.
E 18th St.
E 21st St.
W Roosevelt Road
W Cermak Rd.
S Wentworth Ave
SOUTH STATE STREET
SOUTH MICHIGAN
SOUTH INDIANA
SOUTH WABASH AVE
E Balbo Ave

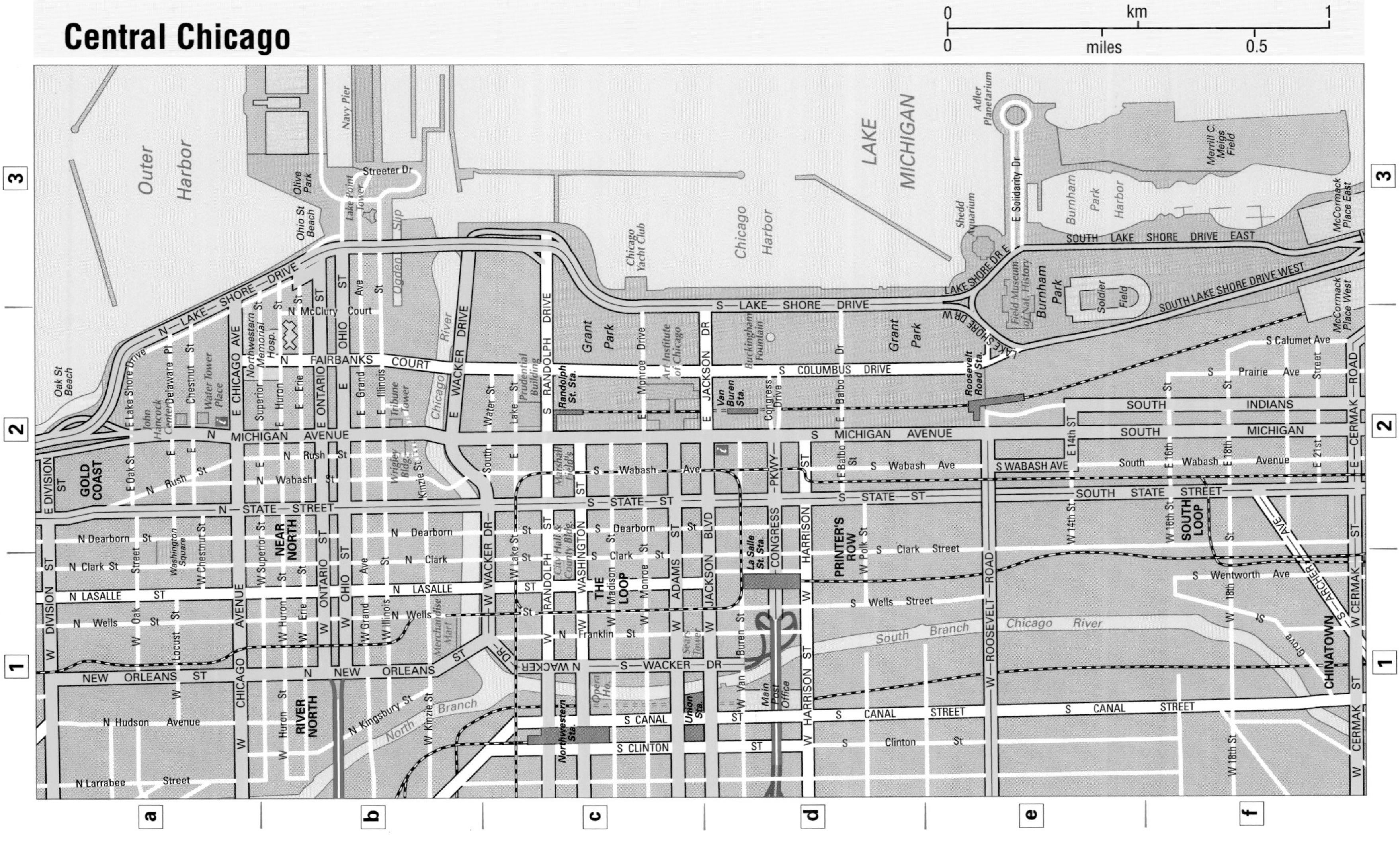

COPYRIGHT GEORGE PHILIP LTD.

## Copenhagen

km 0 — 5
miles 0 — 3

A

B

1 2 3

Øresund

Furesø

Lundtofte
Hjortekær
Kongens Lyngby
Tårbæk
Klampenborg
Jægersborg Dyrehave
Skovshoved
Ordrup
Jægersborg
Vangede
Gentofte
Hellerup
Charlottenlund
Buddinge
Søborg
Svanemøllen
Gladsakse
Hjortespring
Herlev
Husum
Bispebjerg
Skovlunde
Islev
Brønshøj
Fælled-parken
KØBENHAVN
Refshaleøen
Ballerup
Pederstrup
Ågerup
Eiby
Vanløse
Rosenborg Have
Amalienborg
Frederiksberg
Christianshavn
Herstedøster
Rødovre
Zoo
Vestskoven
Glostrup
Valby
Sundbyerne
Brøndbyøster
Albertslund
Saltholm
Tåstrup
Vallensbæk
Hvidovre
Øresund Bridge
Kastrup
Brøndby-vester
Avedøre
KØBENHAVN/KASTRUP LUFTHAVN
Ishøj Strand
Brøndby Strand
Tårnby
Amager
Hundige
Vallensbæk Strand
Store Magleby
Dragør
Hundige Strand
Greve Strand
Ullerup
Sydstranden
Søvang
Køge Bugt
Kongelunden
Aflandshage

Jonstrup
Måløv
Kirke Værløse
Lille Værløse
Frederiksdal
Virum
Brede
Store Hareskov ▲42
Hareskovby
Bagsværd
Bagsværd
Frederiksværk
Sønderso
Oslo
Rønne
Swinoujscie
Klaipeda

East from Greenwich

## Central Copenhagen

km 0 — 1
miles 0 — 0.5

a
b
c

1 2 3

ØSTERBRO
NØRREBRO
CHRISTIANSHAVN
Botanisk Have
Rosenborg Have
Kongens Have
Tivoli
Hovedbane Gaard.
Den lille Havfrue (Little Mermaid)
Kastellet
Amalienborg
Inderhavnen
Østerport Sta.
Nørreport Sta.
Vesterport Sta.
Universitet
Rosenborg Slot
Rundetaarn
Domkirken
Raadhus Pladsen
Christiansborg
Amager Boulevard

## Delhi

km 0 — 5
miles 0 — 3

A

B

1 2

Daulatpur
Shamapur
NH1
Subhepur
Loni
Badli
Mukandpur
Jagatpur
Rampur
Rithala
Bhalswa
Jahangirpuri
Wazirabad
Haidarpur
Coronation Memorial
UTTAR PRADESH
DELHI
Pitampura
Mangolpuri
Shakurbasti
Wazirpur
Ghonda
Babarpur
Mandoli
Saboli
NH10 Rohtak Road
Shastrinagar
Rajpura
Punjabi Bagh
Sabzi Mand
Civil Lines
Grand Trunk Road
NH124
Shahdara
Jwalahari
Patel Nagar
Karol Bagh
Silampur
IS Bus Terminal
Red Fort
Tilak Nagar
DELHI
New Delhi Station
Connaught Place
Ghazipur
Mandaoli
Jamakpuri
263
The Ridge
IG Stadium
Khichripur
Naraina
India Gate
New Delhi
Kondli
Noida
Chanakyapuri
Safdarjang Tomb
Humayun's Tomb
Chilla Saroda
Mehram Nagar
SAFDAR JANG AIRPORT
Nehru Stadium
INDIRA GANDHI INTERNATIONAL AIRPORT
Moti Bagh
Lodi Estate
Mujahidpur
Okha
Nangal Dewat
Ramakrishna Puram
Lotus Temple
Hauz Khas
Mehpalpur
Kalkaji
NH8
Qutb Minar
Rangpuri
Mahrauli
Tughlakabad
NH2

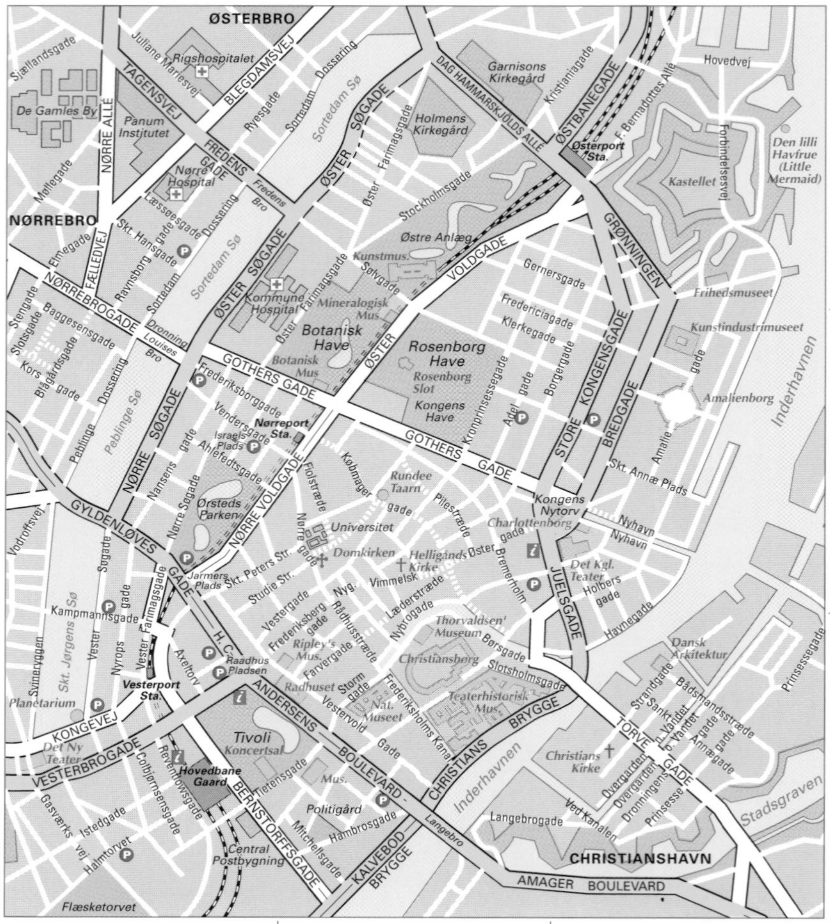

East from Greenwich

## Central Delhi

km 0 — 2
miles 0 — 1

a
b
c

1 2 3

Yamuna River
BOULEVARD ROAD
Interstate Bus Terminal
KALI DAS MARG
ZORAWAR SINGH MARG
St. Stephen's
Nicholson Road
St. James
GRAND TRUNK RD
OLD CITY
AZAD MARKET
DELHI CLOTH MILL RD
SADAR BAZAR
Old Delhi Station
SHYAMA PRASAD MUKHERJI MARG
Mahatma Gandhi Park
DARYA GANJ
MAHARAJA AGGARSAIN MARG
NEW ROHTAK ROAD
RANI JHANSI ROAD
QUTAB ROAD
Jain
Library
Town Hall
Jama Mandir
CHANDNI CHAUK
Lal Qila (Red Fort)
Vijay Ghat
Ajmal Khan Park
Fathehpur
Sunehri
Sisganj
Gauri Shankar
Kasturba Hospital
MAHATMA GANDHI MARG
EAST PARK ROAD
Idgah
SHARDHANAN D
Ajmer Gate
Kalan
Ghaziuddin
DESH-BANDHU-GUPTA ROAD
Holy Trinity
Delhi Gate
Bagh Ghat
LINK RD
RIDGE RD
New Delhi Station
JAWAHARLAL NEHRU MARG
ASAF ALI ROAD
Gandhi Museum
Kotla Firoz Shah Fort
BAHADUR SHAH ZAFAR MARG
PANCHKUIAN MARG
Main Bazar Road
Northern Railway
Mirdard Marg
CHELMSFORD ROAD
Jhandewalan
Doll Museum
CONNAUGHT PLACE
DEEN DAYAL UPADHYAYA MARG
RING ROAD
Indira Gandhi Indoor Stadium
Laxmi Narayan
Shaheed Bhagat Singh Marg
Rama Krishna Ashram Marg
BARAKHAMBA ROAD
Velodrome
Cathedral of the Sacred Heart
CONNAUGHT CIRCUS
VIVEKANAND MARG
Natural History Museum
VIKAS MARG
Dr R. M. Lohia
New Delhi GPO
SIKANDRA ROAD
MANDIR MARG
SINGH MARG
ASHOKA ROAD
Babar Rd
Supreme Court
PARK ST
KALI BARI RD
Jantar Mantar
TOLSTOY MARG
FIROZ SHAH ROAD
COPERNICUS MARG
Church of the Redemption
TALKATORA ROAD
JANPATH
PARLIAMENT ST
Halley Rd
KASTURBA GANDHI ROAD
Mughal Gardens
RAISINA RD
Lok Sabha (Parliament House)
Indira Gandhi Centre of Arts
TILAK MARG
Rashtrapati Bhawan (President's Res.)
MOTILAL NEHRU MARG
Rajpath
AKBAR ROAD
National Museum
India Gate
MATHURA ROAD
National Stadium
Dalhousie Road
KAMRAJ MG
Maulana
SHANTI PATH
Purana Qila (Old Fort)
South Ave
Thyagraj Mg
SHERSHAH RD
NEW DELHI

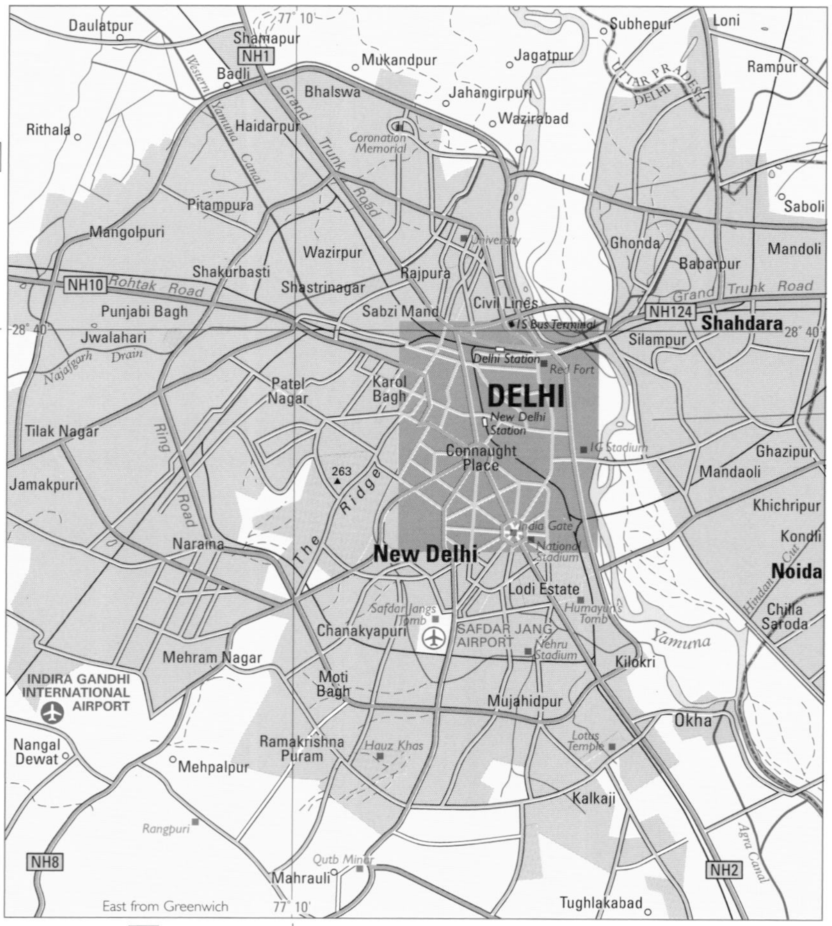

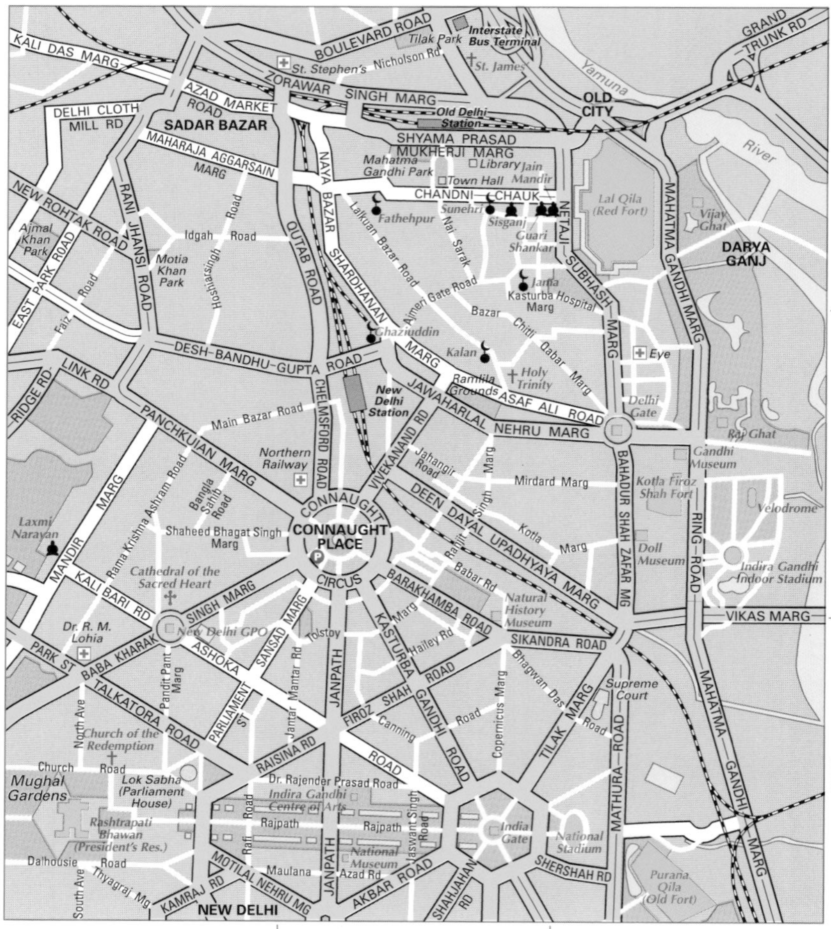

## Dublin

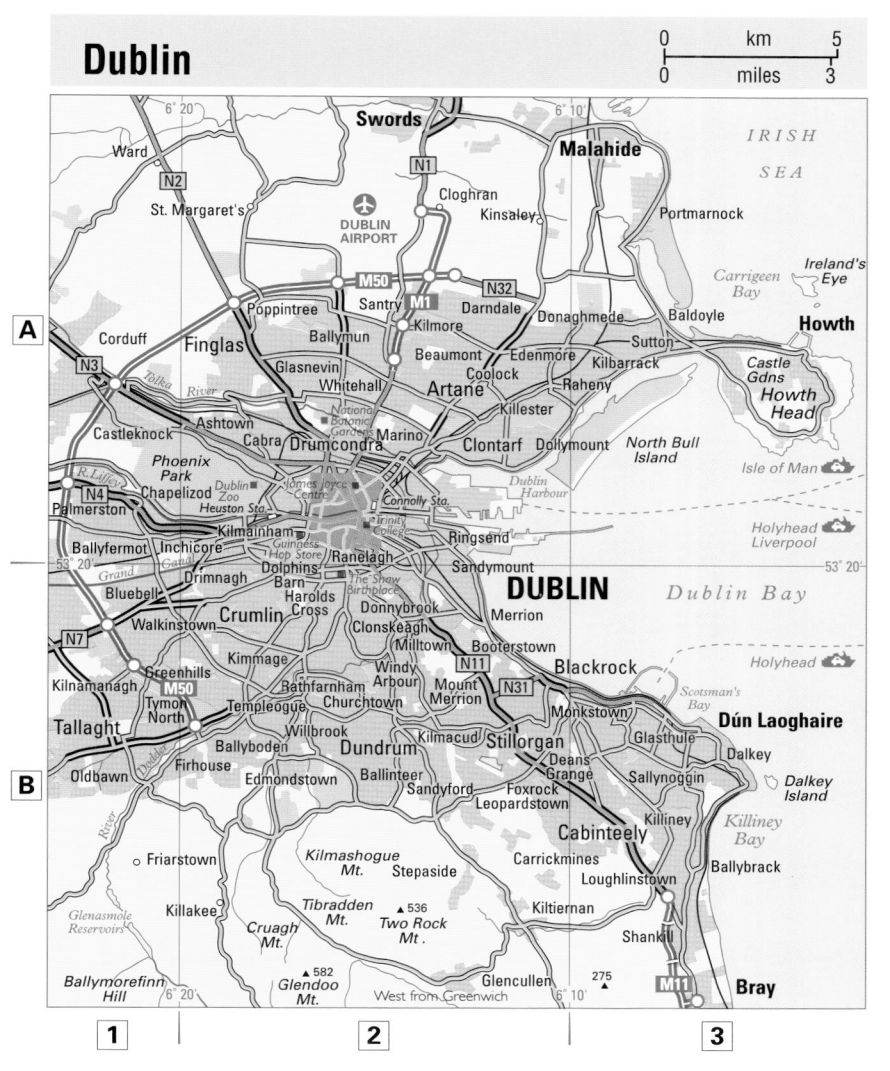

## Central Dublin

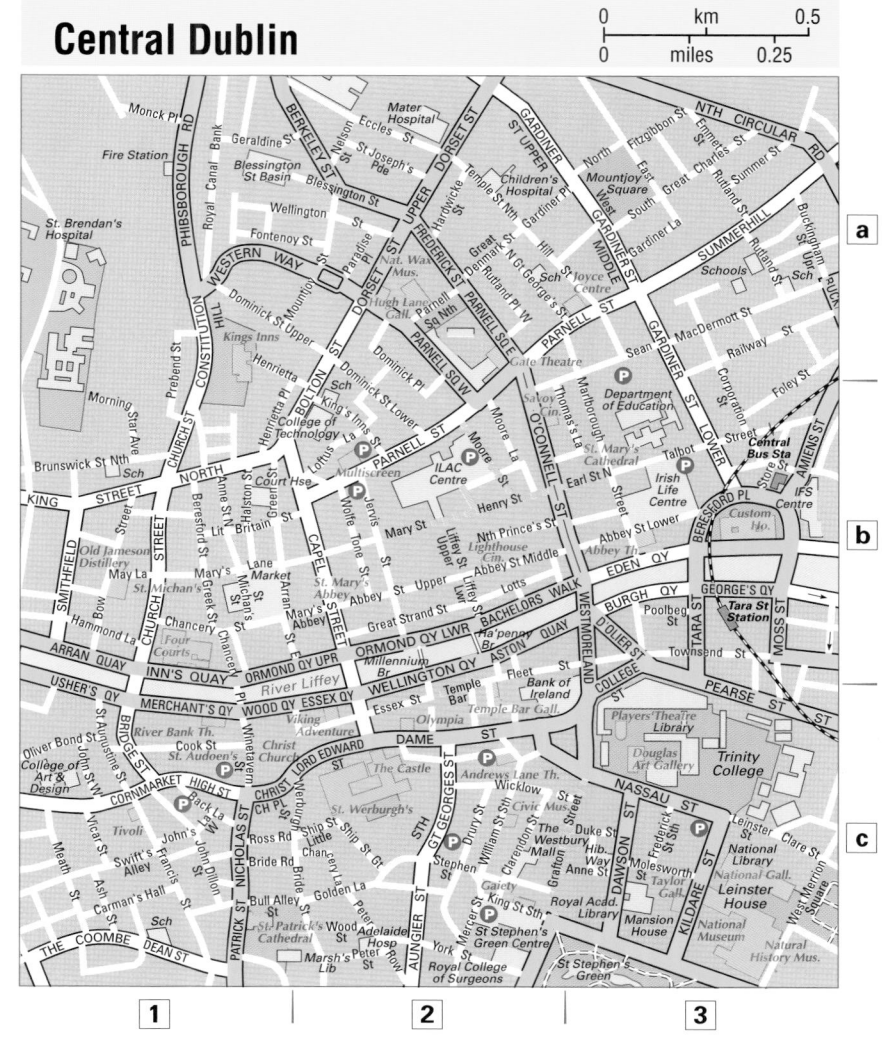

## Edinburgh

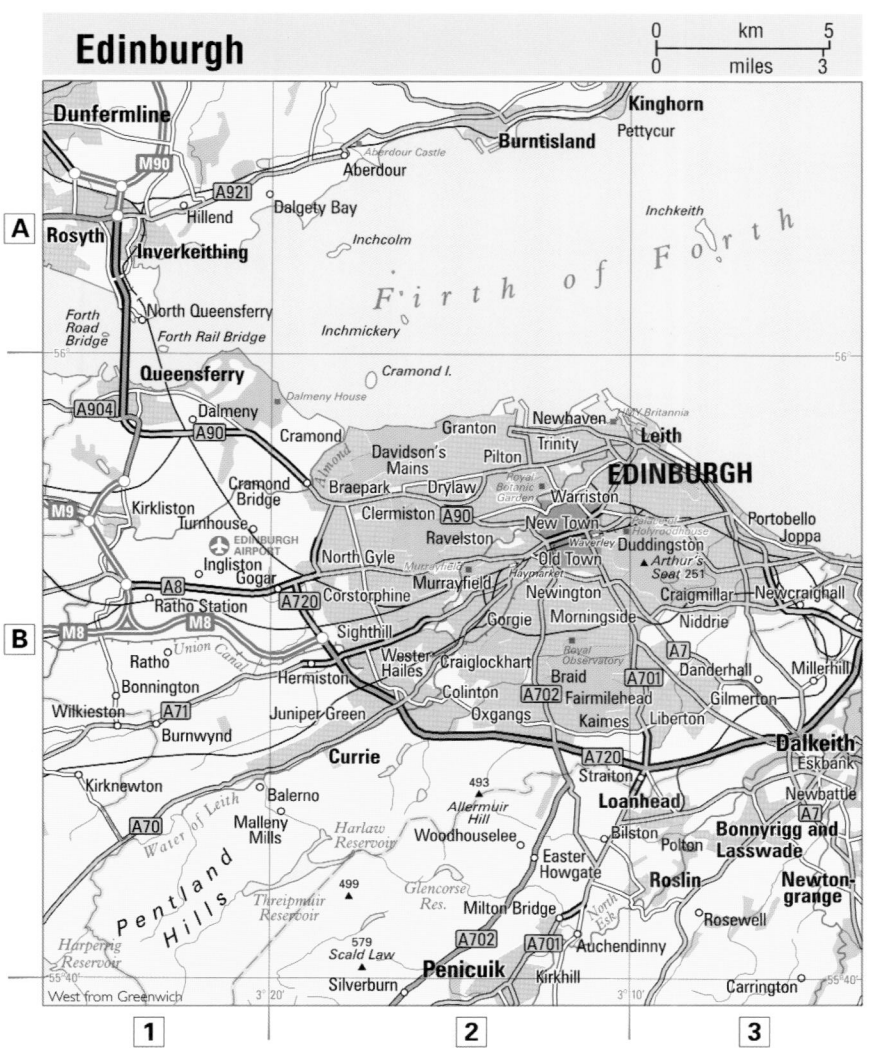

## Central Edinburgh

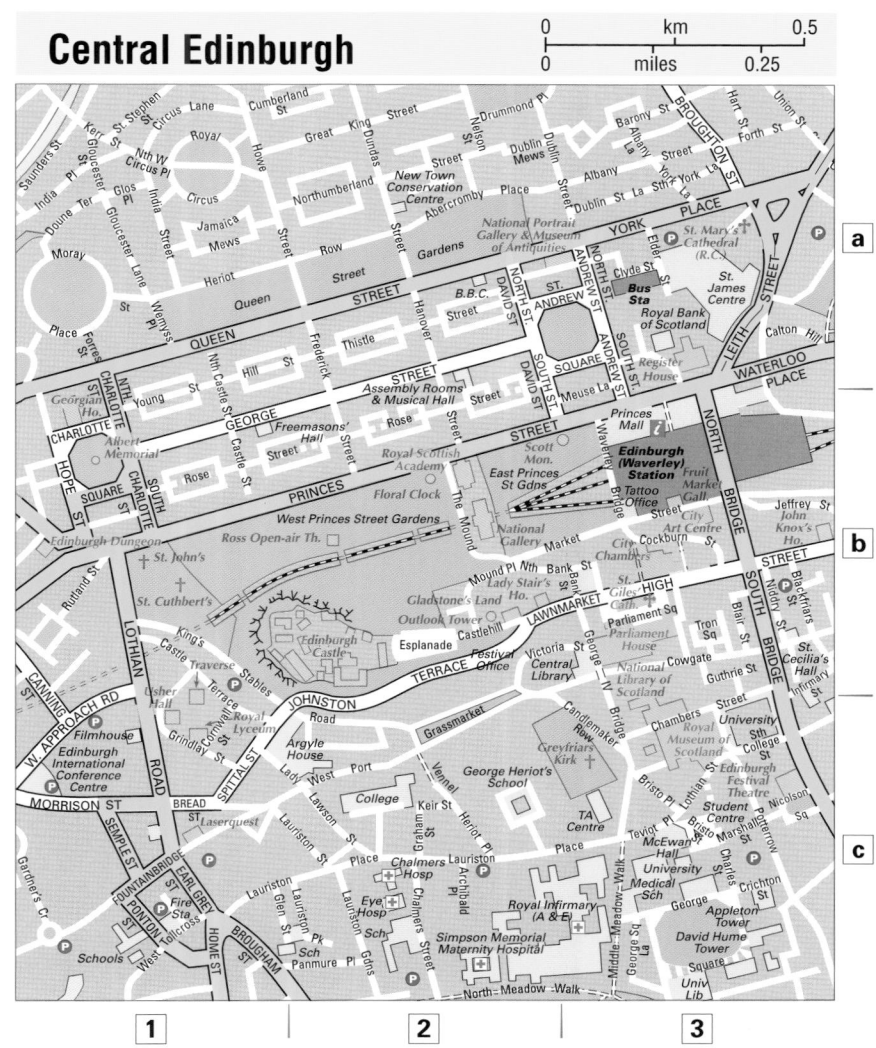

## Helsinki

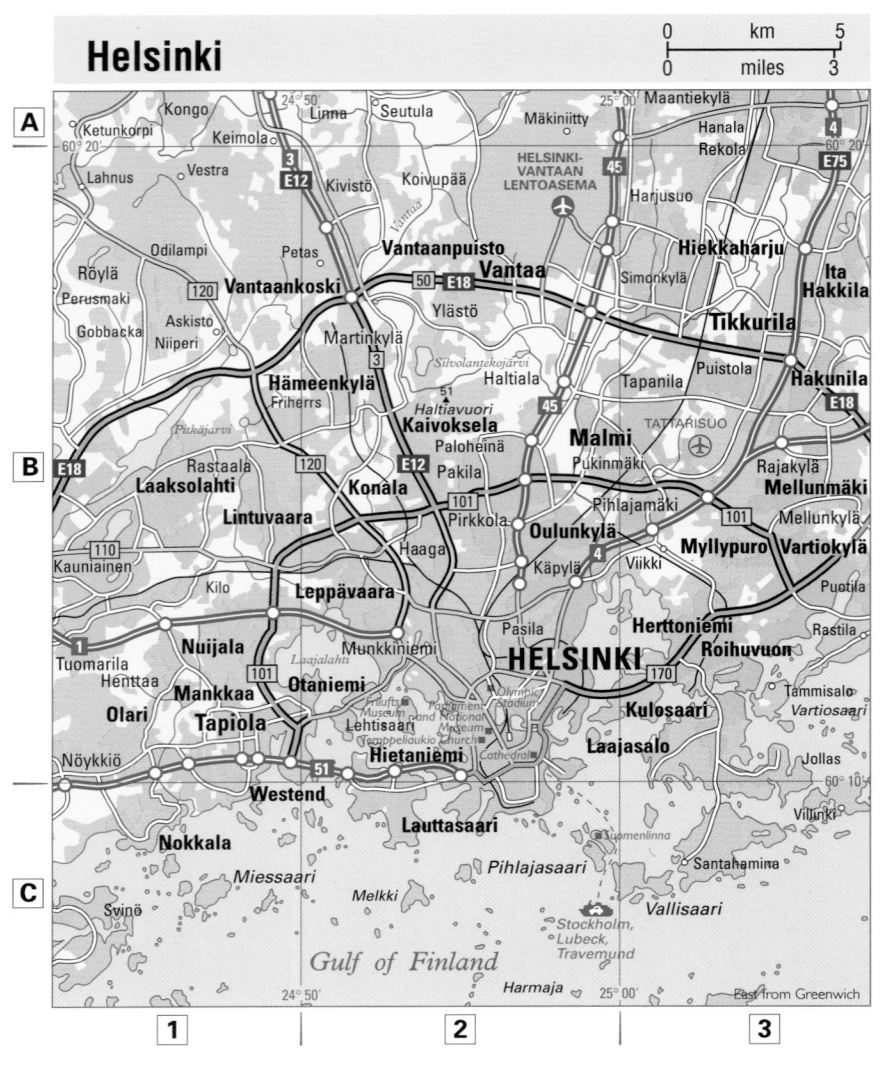

## Istanbul

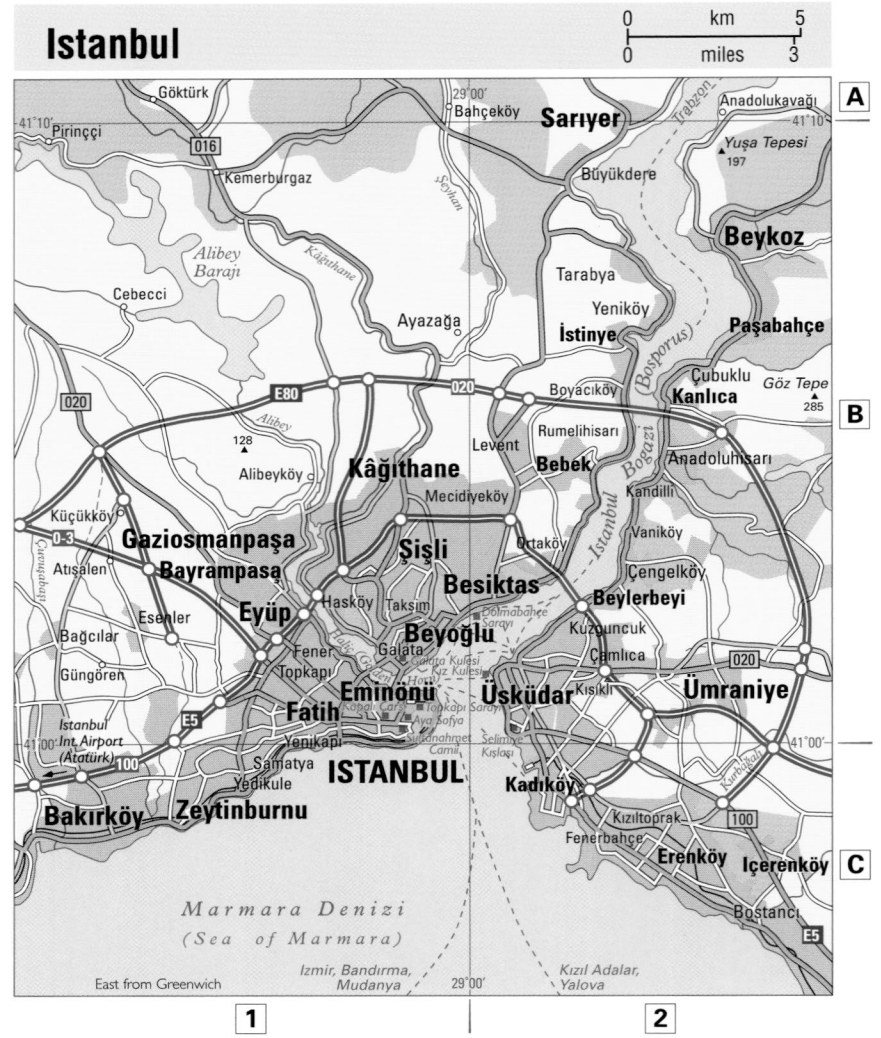

## Hong Kong

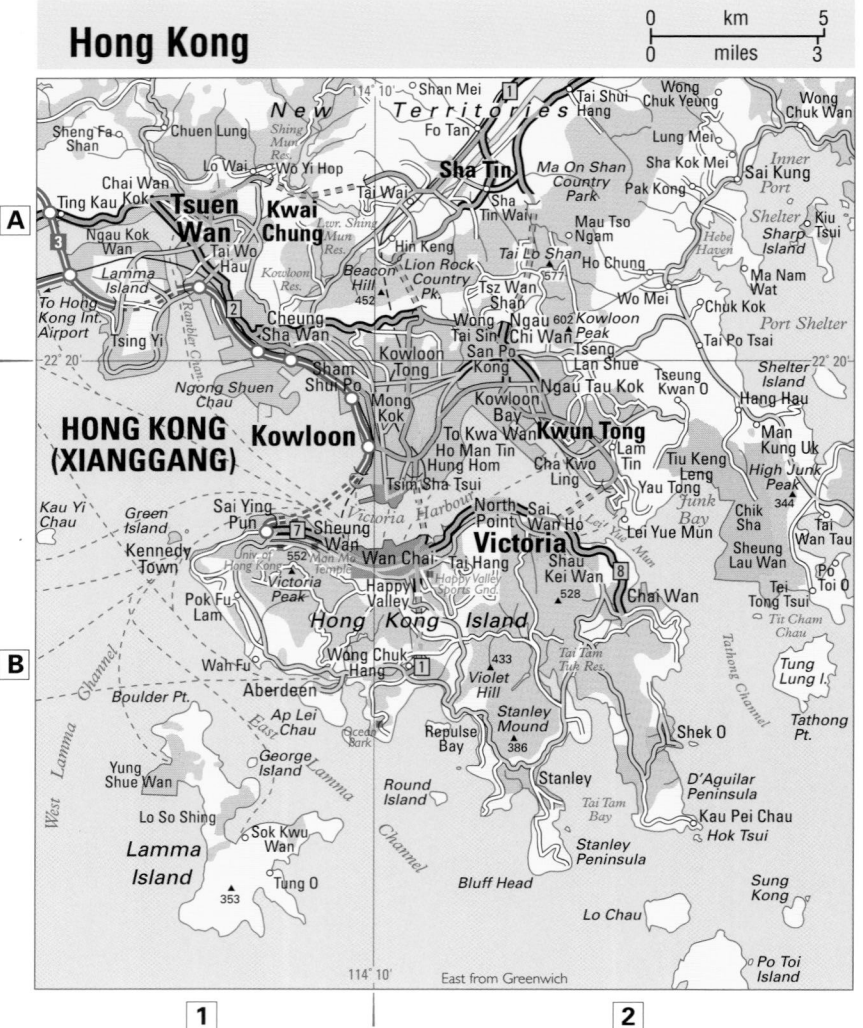

## Central Hong Kong

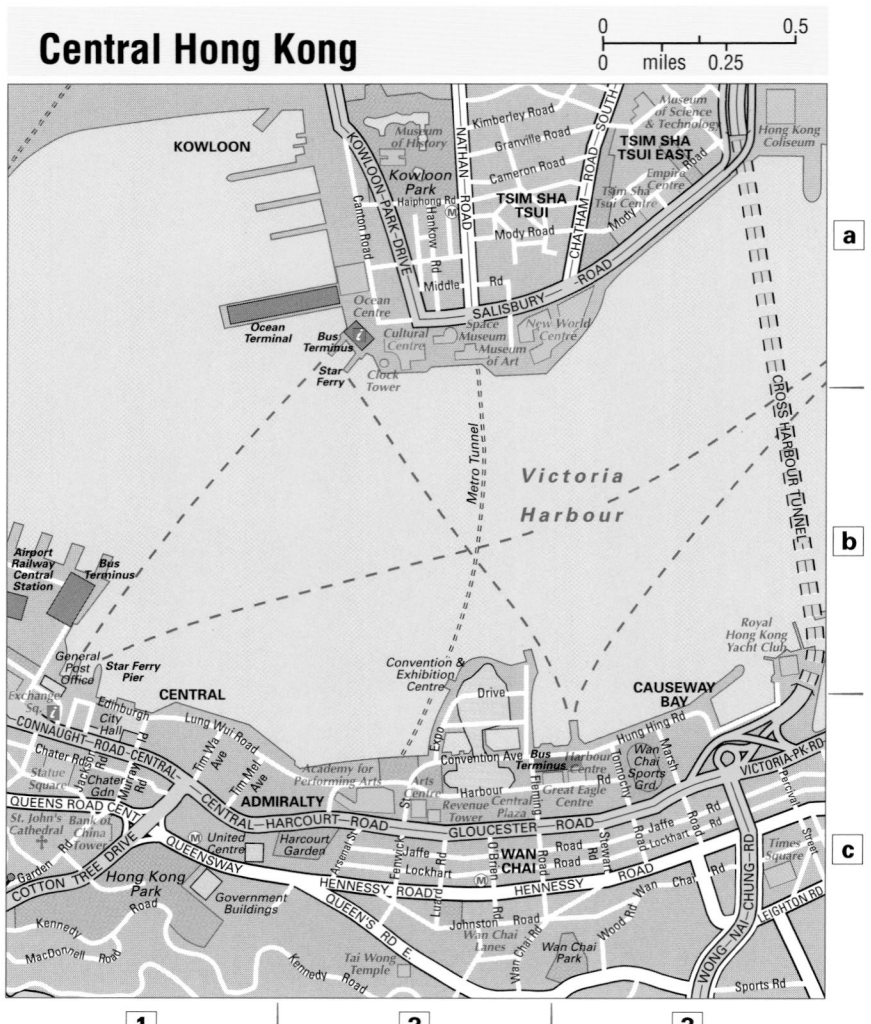

## Jerusalem

0 km 5
0 miles 3

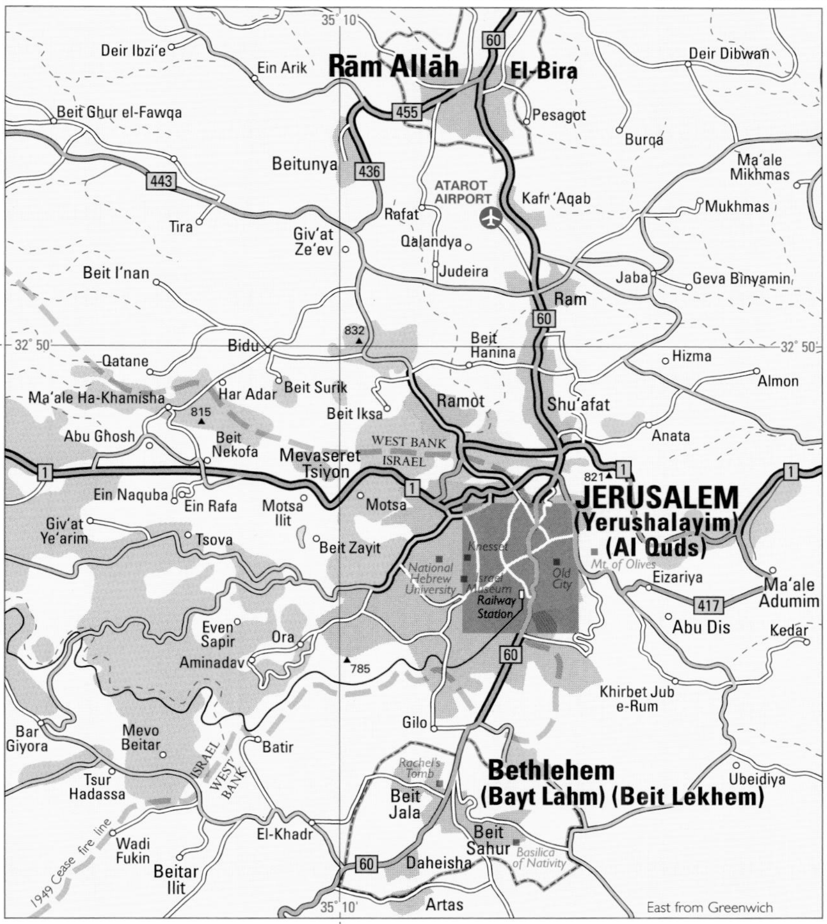

Deir Ibzi'e
Ein Arik
**Rām Allāh**   **El-Bira**
60
Deir Dibwan
455
Beit Ghur el-Fawqa
Pesagot
Burqa
Ma'ale Mikhmas
Beitunya
443
436
Beit I'nan
Tira
Giv'at Ze'ev
Rafat
Kafr 'Aqab
Mukhmas
ATAROT AIRPORT
Qalandya
Judeira
Jaba
Geva Binyamin
Bidu
832
Ram
Beit Hanina
Hizma
Almon
35° 10'
32° 50'
Qatane
Ma'ale Ha-Khamisha
Har Adar
Beit Surik
Beit Iksa
Ramot
Shu'afat
Anata
Abu Ghosh
815
Beit Nekofa
Mevaseret Tsiyon
WEST BANK
ISRAEL
Ein Naquba
Ein Rafa
Motsa Ilit
Motsa
821
**JERUSALEM (Yerushalayim) (Al Quds)**
Giv'at Ye'arim
Tsova
Beit Zayit
Eizariya
Ma'ale Adumim
785
417
Abu Dis
Kedar
Even Sapir
Ora
Aminadav
Khirbet Jub e-Rum
Bar Giyora
Mevo Beitar
Batir
Gilo
**Bethlehem (Bayt Laḥm) (Beit Lekhem)**
Ubeidiya
Tsur Hadassa
Rachel's Tomb
Beit Jala
Beit Sahur
Daheisha
Basilica of Nativity
Wadi Fukin
El-Khadr
60
Beitar Ilit
Artas
1949 Cease fire line
WEST BANK ISRAEL
East from Greenwich

## Central Jerusalem

0 km 1
0 miles 0.5

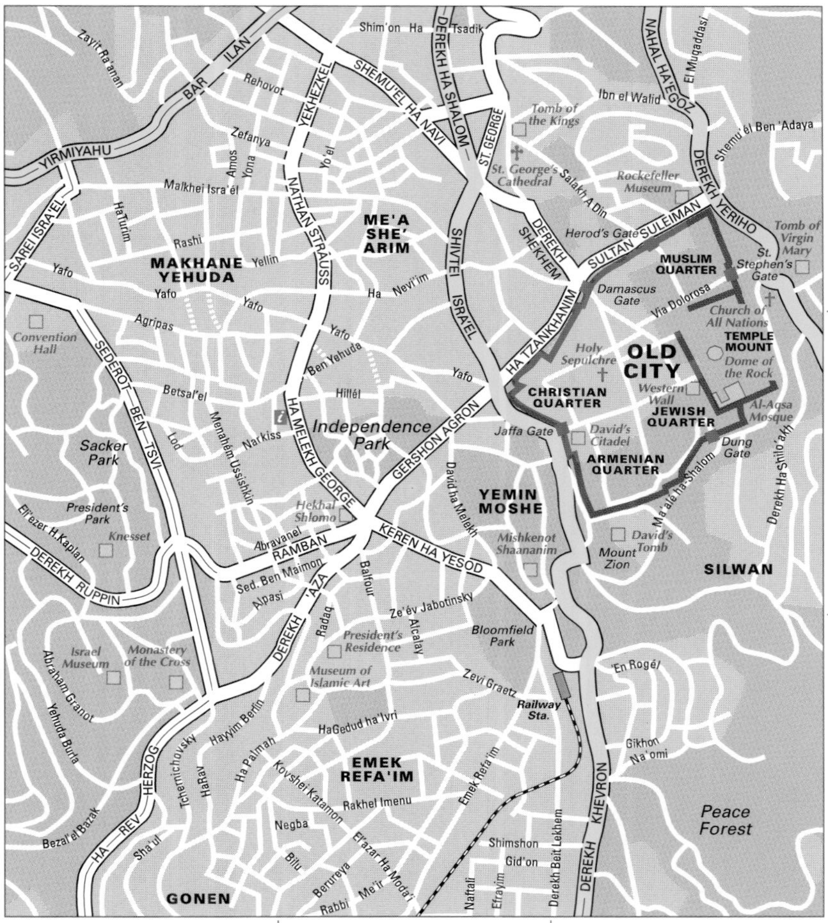

Tomb of the Kings
St. George's Cathedral
Rockefeller Museum
Tomb of the Virgin Mary
**MEA SHE'ARIM**
**MAKHANE YEHUDA**
Herod's Gate
St. Stephen's Gate
**MUSLIM QUARTER**
Damascus Gate
Via Dolorosa
Church of All Nations
Convention Hall
Holy Sepulchre
**OLD CITY**
**TEMPLE MOUNT** Dome of the Rock
Al-Aqsa Mosque
Sacker Park
Independence Park
**CHRISTIAN QUARTER**
Jaffa Gate
David's Citadel
Western Wall
**JEWISH QUARTER**
Dung Gate
President's Park
Knesset
**ARMENIAN QUARTER**
**YEMIN MOSHE**
Mishkenot Shaananim
Mount Zion
David's Tomb
**SILWAN**
Israel Museum
Monastery of the Cross
Bloomfield Park
President's Residence
Museum of Islamic Art
Railway Sta.
En Rogel
Peace Forest
**EMEK REFA'IM**
**GONEN**

## Jakarta

0 km 5
0 miles 3

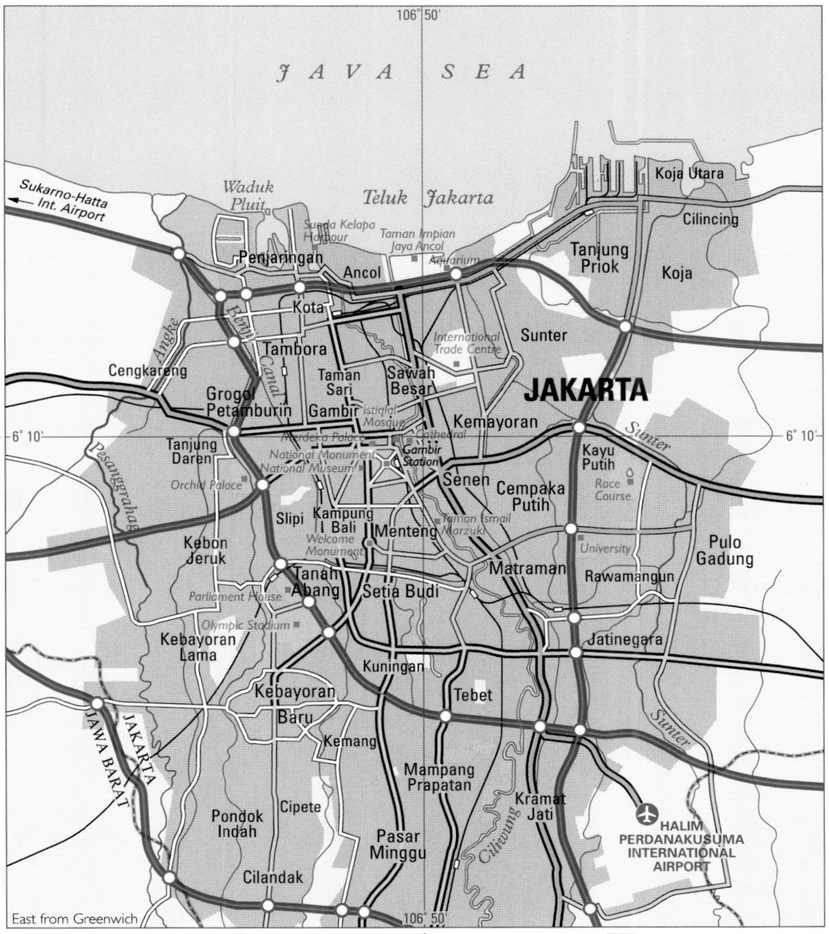

*J A V A   S E A*
106° 50'
*Teluk Jakarta*
Koja Utara
Waduk Pluit
Penjaringan
Sunda Kelapa Harbour
Taman Impian Jaya Ancol
Cilincing
Ancol
Atharium
Tanjung Priok
Koja
Cengkareng
Kota
Tambora
Taman Sari
International Trade Centre
Sunter
Grogol Petamburin
Gambir
Sawah Besar
Kemayoran
**JAKARTA**
Sukarno-Hatta Int. Airport
Tanjung Daren
National Monument
Gambir Station
Kayu Putih
6° 10'
Slipi
Kampung Bali
Senen
Cempaka Putih
Race Course
Pulo Gadung
Kebon Jeruk
Welcome Monument
Menteng
Taman Ismail Marzuki
Matraman
Rawamangun
Parliament House
Tanah Abang
Setia Budi
Olympic Stadium
Orchid Palace
University
Kebayoran Lama
Kuningan
Jatinegara
Kebayoran Baru
Tebet
Kemang
Mampang Prapatan
Kramat Jati
Pondok Indah
Cipete
Pasar Minggu
HALIM PERDANAKUSUMA INTERNATIONAL AIRPORT
Cilandak
106° 50'
JAKARTA BARAT
East from Greenwich

## Johannesburg

0 km 5
0 miles 3

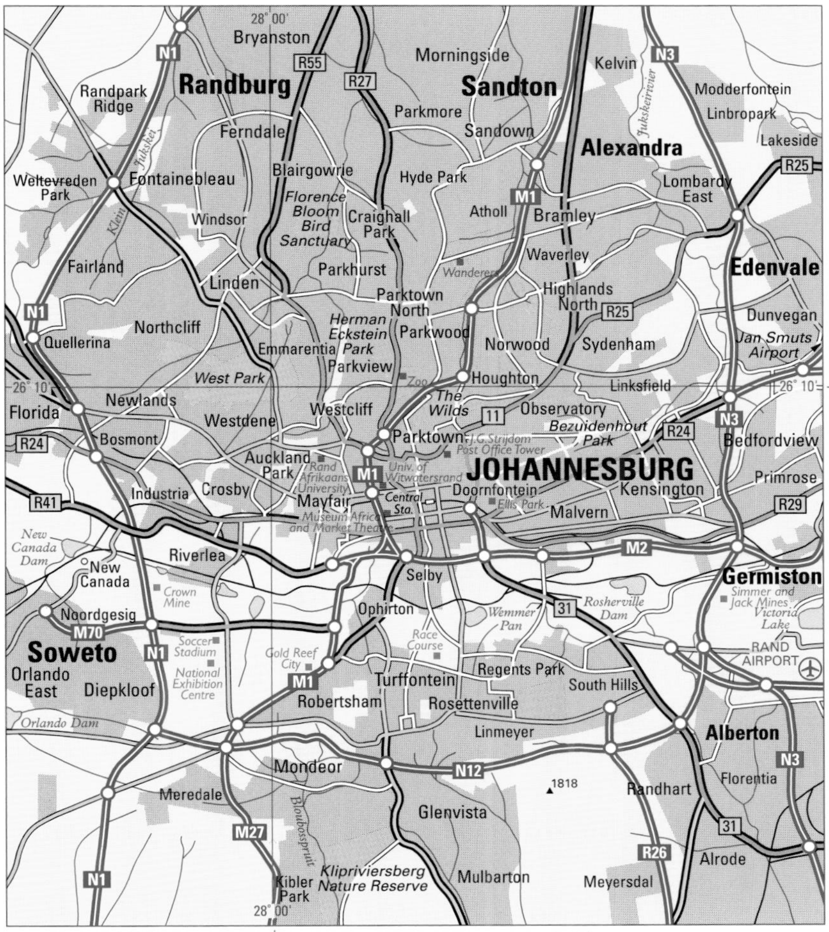

28° 00'
N1
Bryanston
R55
R27
**Randburg**
Morningside
Kelvin
N3
Randpark Ridge
Parkmore
**Sandton**
Modderfontein
Linbropark
Weltevreden Park
Ferndale
Fontainebleau
Sandown
**Alexandra**
Lakeside
Windsor
Blairgowrie
Hyde Park
M1
Lombardy East
Fairland
Florence Bloom Bird Sanctuary
Craighall Park
Atholl
Bramley
**Edenvale**
Linden
Parkhurst
Waverley
Quellerina
Northcliff
Parktown North
Highlands North
R25
Dunvegan
Jan Smuts Airport
West Park
Herman Eckstein Park
Parkwood
Norwood
Sydenham
26° 10'
Florida
Newlands
Westdene
Westcliff
Emmarentia Park
Parkview
Houghton
Linksfield
N1
Bosmont
The Wilds
Observatory
Bezuidenhout Park
N3
Bedfordview
R24
Auckland Park
Parktown
Strijdom Post Office Tower
**JOHANNESBURG**
Kensington
Primrose
R41
Industria
Crosby
M1
Central Sta.
Doornfontein
Ellis Park
R29
New Canada Dam
Mayfair
Museum Africa and Market Theatre
Malvern
M2
Riverlea
Selby
**Germiston**
New Canada
Crown Mine
Ophirton
Rosherville Dam
Simmer and Jack Mines
Victoria Lake
Noordgesig
M70
Soccer City Stadium
Wemmer Pan
Race Course
RAND AIRPORT
**Soweto**
Orlando East
Diepkloof
N1
National Exhibition Centre
Gold Reef City
Turffontein
Regents Park
South Hills
M1
Robertsham
Rosettenville
Linmeyer
**Alberton**
Orlando Dam
Mondeor
N12
1818
Randhart
N3
Meredale
Glenvista
Florentia
M27
Klipriviersberg Nature Reserve
Kibler Park
Mulbarton
Meyersdal
Alrode
R26
28° 00'
N1
31

COPYRIGHT GEORGE PHILIP LTD.

## Karachi

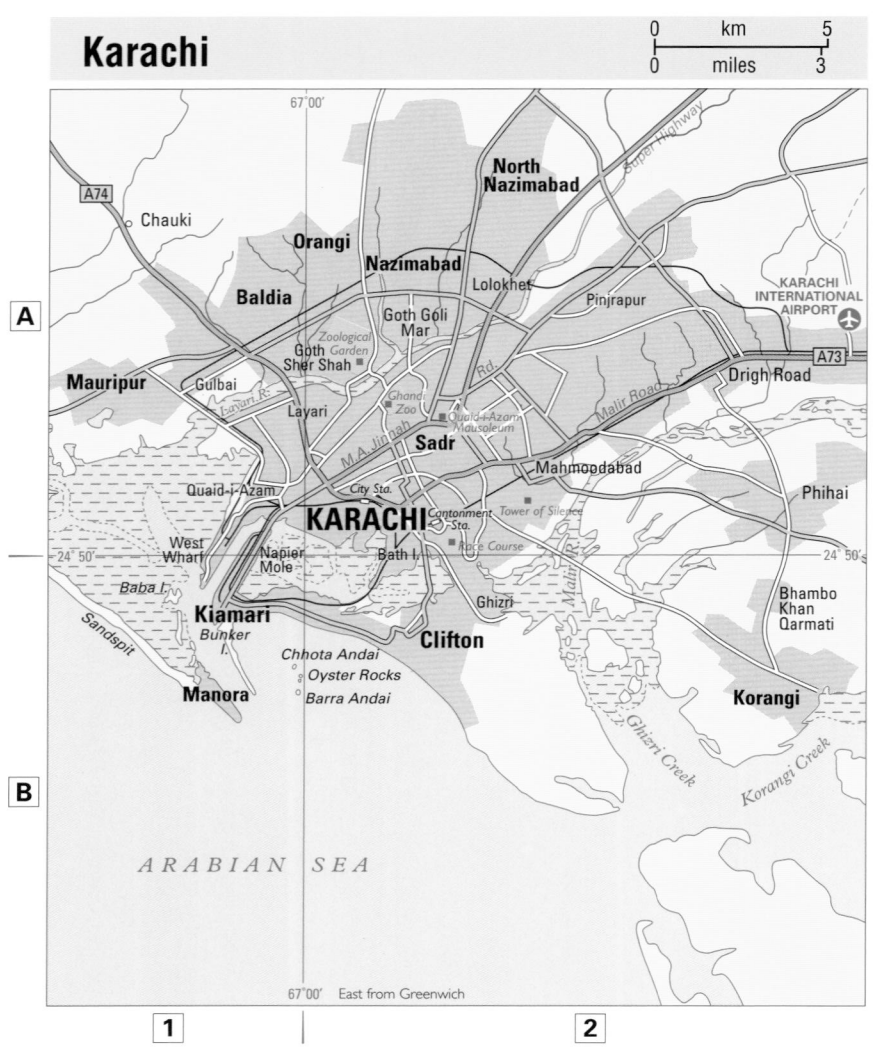

## Lagos

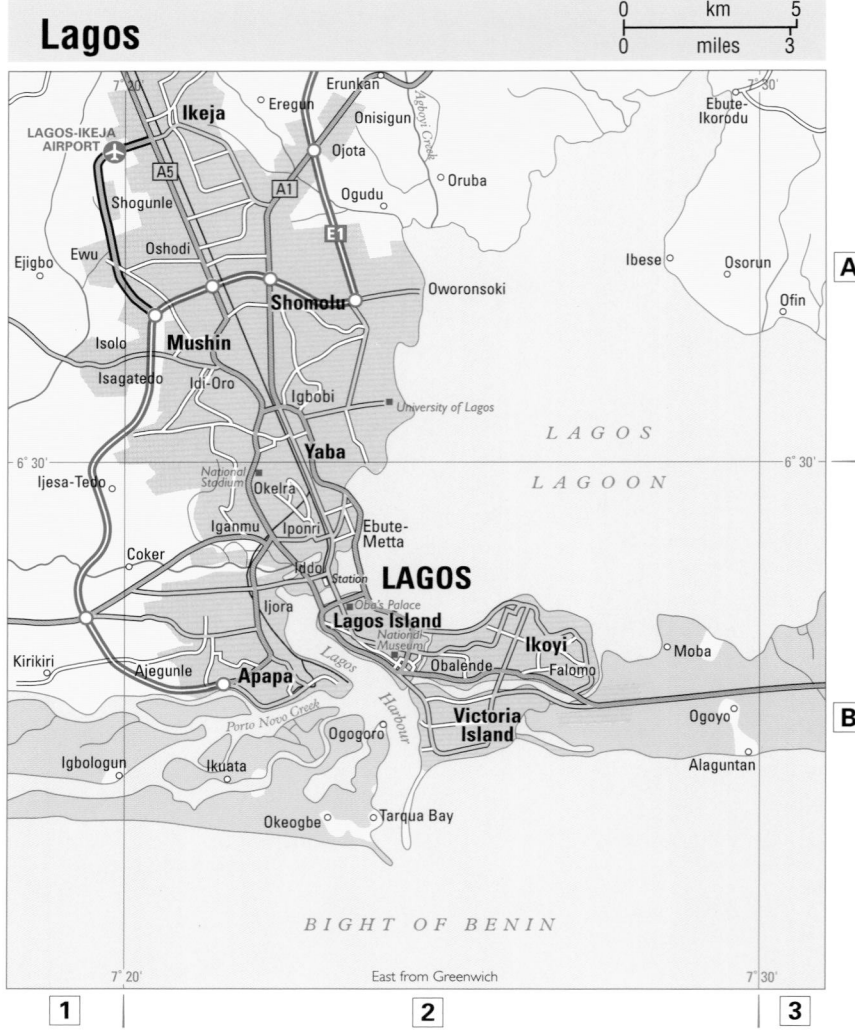

## Lisbon

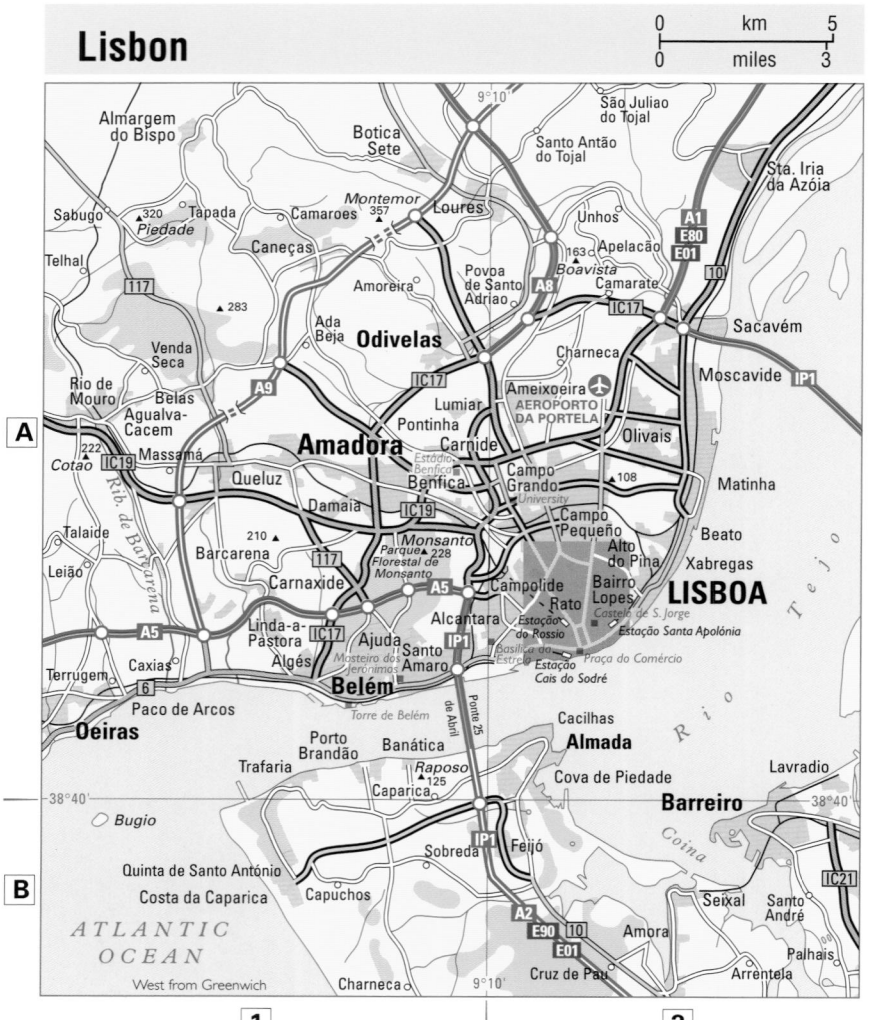

## Central Lisbon

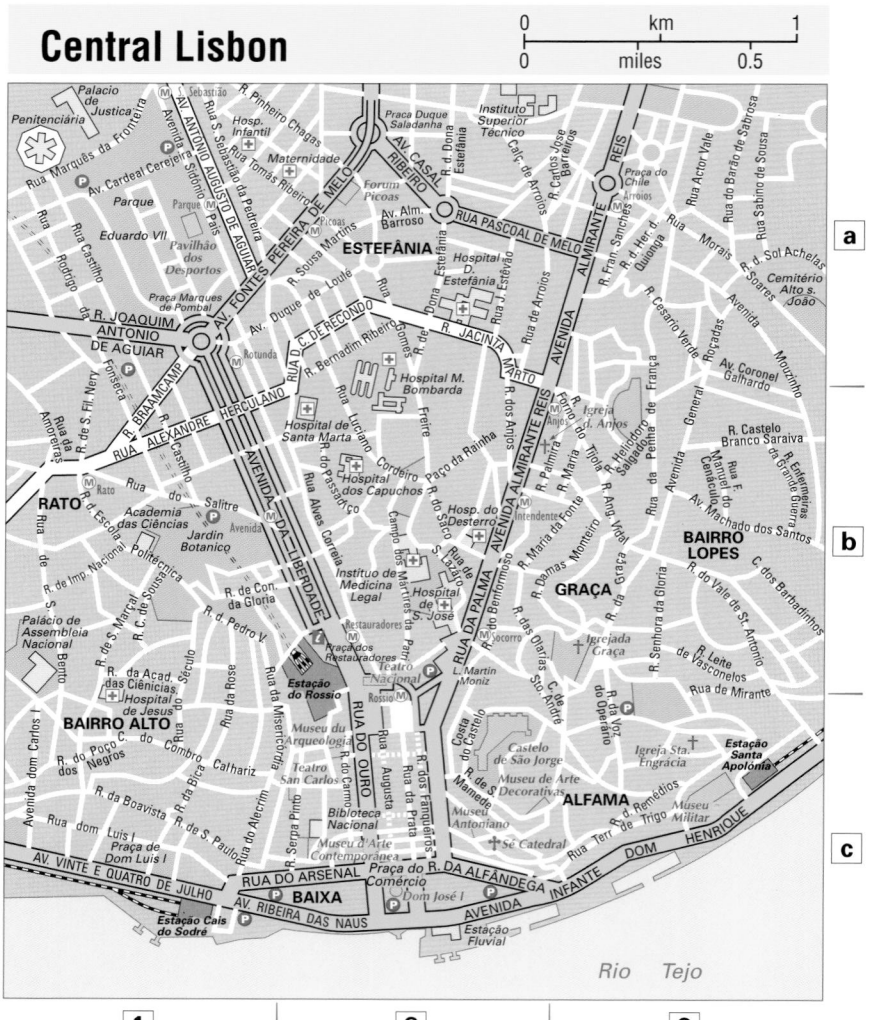

# London

km 0 5
miles 0 3

Northwood Stanmore Barnet Finchley Waltham Forest Woodford Havering-atte-Bower Harold Hill
Pinner Green Burnt Oak Mill Hill Colney Hatch Woodford Bridge Hainault Romford
Hatch End Belmont Church End Muswell Hill Wood Green Woodford Gidea Park Gallows Corner
Ruislip Common Pinner Queensbury Hendon East Finchley Hornsey Clayhall Barkingside Collier Row
Eastcote Wealdstone Kingsbury Golders Green Highgate Crouch End Wanstead Newbury Park Elm Park Hornchurch
**Harrow** Greenhill Hampstead Garden Suburb Finsbury Park Leyton Leytonstone **Redbridge** Seven Kings Chadwell Heath
Rayners Lane West Harrow Harrow on the Hill Hampstead **Brent Res.** Tufnell Park Stoke Newington **Hackney** Ilford Manor Park Goodmayes **Havering**
Hillingdon Ruislip South Harrow Roxeth Sudbury **Brent** Alperton Willesden Green Kentish Town Highbury Clapton **Tower** West Ham East Ham **Barking** **Dagenham** South Hornchurch
Cowley Perivale Neasden Kensal Green **Camden** **Islington** Dalston Bethnal Green **Hamlets** Poplar **Newham** Beckton **Rainham**
Hayes End Greenford **Ealing** Acton Maida Vale Paddington Holborn Shoreditch Stepney Wapping Canning Town **LONDON CITY** North Woolwich
Hayes Southall Hanwell **A40(M)** Notting Hill **Westminster** **City** Isle of Dogs Millennium Dome Thamesmead
**Heston** Chiswick **Hammersmith** **Kensington** Hyde Park **Southwark** Bermondsey Rotherhithe **Greenwich** Charlton Plumstead West Heath Belvedere
**HEATHROW AIRPORT** Isleworth Brentford Kew **Chelsea** **LONDON** Deptford Greenwich Observatory Woolwich East Wickham Northumberland Heath Erith
**Hounslow** Twickenham Barnes **Fulham** Battersea **Lambeth** Camberwell New Cross Blackheath Kidbrooke Welling Barnehurst Slade Green
West Bedfont Whitton Mortlake Putney Clapham Brixton Peckham **Lewisham** Lee Eltham Blackfen Bexleyheath Crayford
**Richmond upon Thames** Roehampton **Wandsworth** Balham Herne Hill Dulwich Forest Hill Catford Hither Green Mottingham Sidcup **Bexley** **Dartford**
Feltham Richmond Park Southfields Earlsfield Tooting Streatham West Norwood South Sydenham New Eltham Coldblow Wilmington
Ashford Teddington Wimbledon Common Wimbledon Tennis Club Upper Tooting Upper Norwood Penge Sydenham Bellingham Grove Park Chislehurst North Cray Hawley Swanley Village
Hampton Kingston Vale New Malden Colliers Wood Streatham Vale Thornton Heath South Norwood Beckenham Shortlands Bickley St Paul's Cray **Swanley** Hextable
Sunbury-on-Thames West Molesey Surbiton Morden Mitcham Common Selhurst Woodside Elmers End Upper Elmers End **Bromley** St-Mary-Cray Crockenhill Farningham
Littleton Shepperton Hampton Court Palace Long Ditton Tolworth Motspur Park Mitcham Gatwick Airport Beddington Corner North Cheam **Sutton** Hackbridge Addiscombe Eden Park Petts Wood Orpington **GREATER LONDON KENT**
Weybridge Walton on Thames Esher Hook Worcester Park **Croydon** Shortlands Bromley Common **M25 M20**

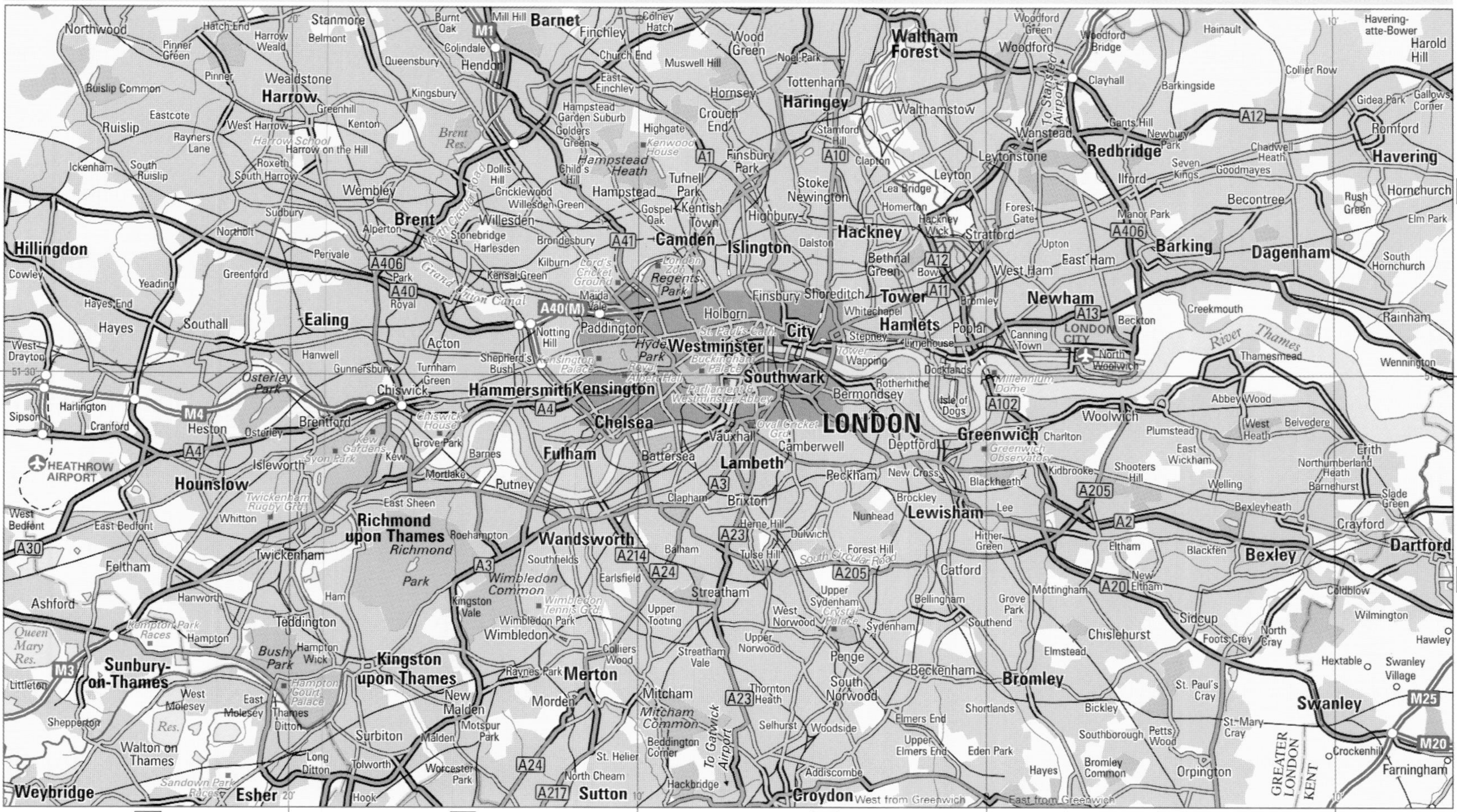

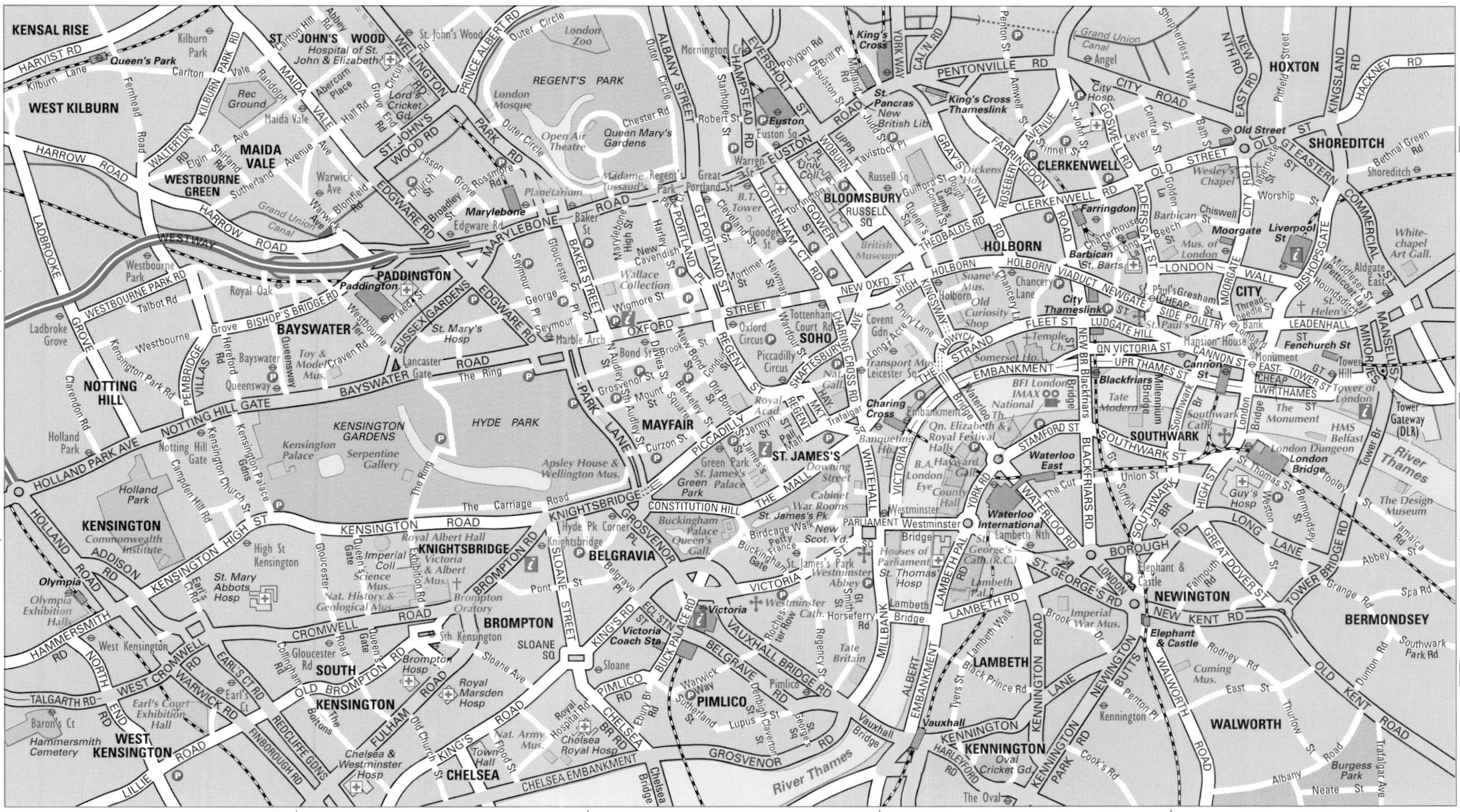

A1 Barnet Finchley... (grid references A, B; columns 1–5)

# Central London

0 km 2
0 miles 1

KENSAL RISE ST. JOHN'S WOOD King's Cross HOXTON
WEST KILBURN Queen's Park SHOREDITCH
MAIDA VALE CLERKENWELL Old Street
WESTBOURNE GREEN BLOOMSBURY HOLBORN Barbican LIVERPOOL ST Whitechapel Art Gall.
PADDINGTON Euston RUSSELL SQ Farringdon Moorgate CITY
BAYSWATER MARYLEBONE OXFORD STREET SOHO Covent Garden FLEET ST St Paul's Bank Fenchurch St
NOTTING HILL NOTTING HILL GATE HYDE PARK MAYFAIR PICCADILLY Charing Cross STRAND Blackfriars SOUTHWARK The Monument Tower of London Tower Gateway (DLR)
KENSINGTON KENSINGTON GARDENS Kensington Palace ST. JAMES'S Waterloo East London Dungeon London Bridge River Thames
Holland Park KNIGHTSBRIDGE BELGRAVIA Buckingham Palace WHITEHALL Waterloo International The Cuts Guy's Hosp The Design Museum
Olympia KENSINGTON KNIGHTSBRIDGE Victoria Houses of Parliament Westminster BOROUGH NEWINGTON BERMONDSEY
BROMPTON BELGRAVIA PIMLICO LAMBETH Imperial War Mus. Elephant & Castle
WEST KENSINGTON SOUTH KENSINGTON Victoria Coach Sta CHELSEA Vauxhall KENNINGTON WALWORTH
HAMMERSMITH Chelsea Royal Hosp CHELSEA EMBANKMENT River Thames The Oval Burgess Park

## Los Angeles

0 km 5
0 miles 3

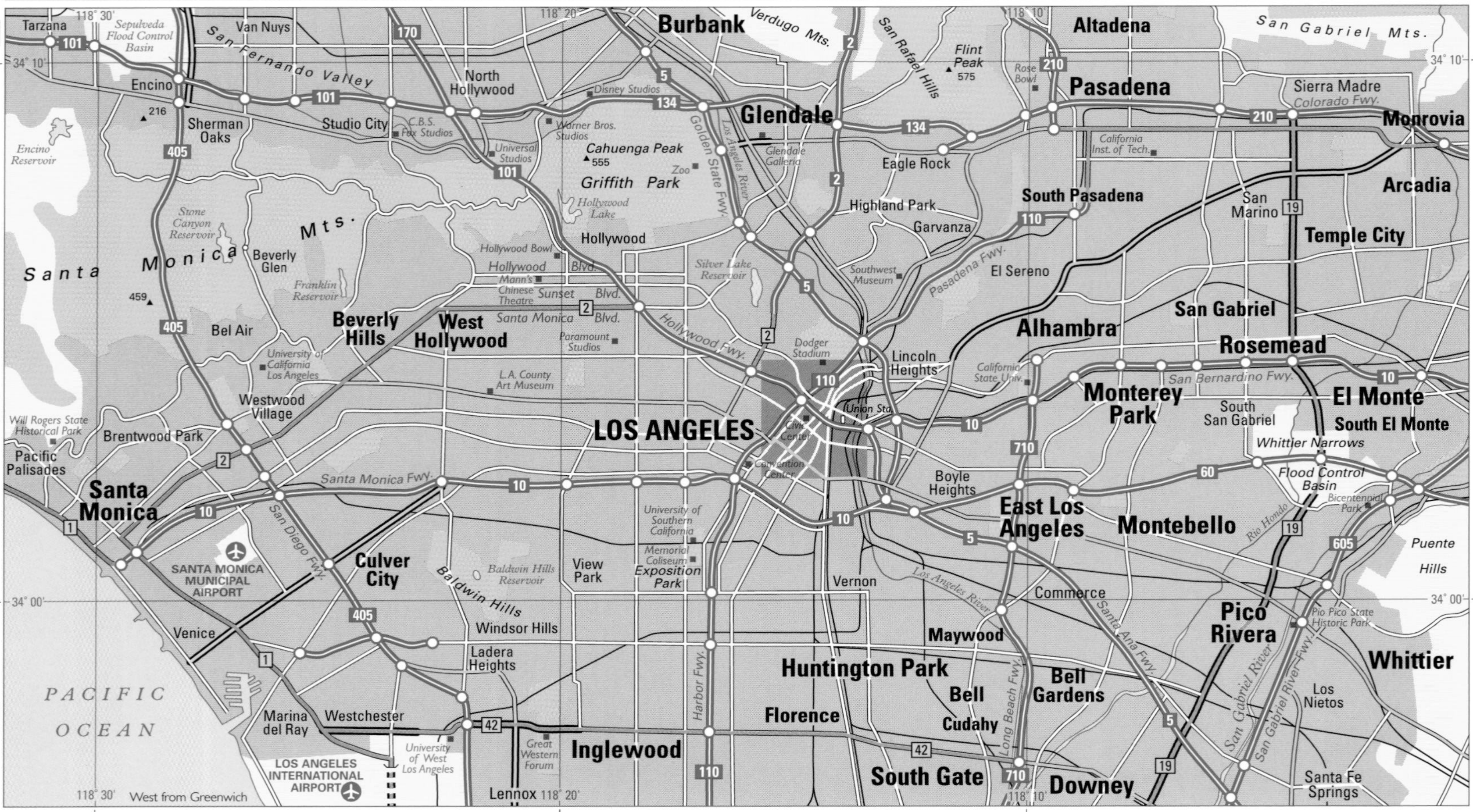
A
B
C
1
2
3
4
118° 30'
118° 20'
118° 10'
34° 10'
34° 00'
West from Greenwich
Tarzana
Sepulveda Flood Control Basin
Van Nuys
San Fernando Valley
Burbank
Verdugo Mts.
San Rafael Hills
Flint Peak 575
Altadena
San Gabriel Mts.
North Hollywood
Disney Studios
Rose Bowl
Pasadena
Sierra Madre
Colorado Fwy.
Encino
216
Sherman Oaks
Studio City
C.B.S. Fox Studios
Warner Bros. Studios
Glendale
Glendale Galleria
Monrovia
Encino Reservoir
Universal Studios
Cahuenga Peak 555
Griffith Park
Zoo
Eagle Rock
California Inst. of Tech.
Arcadia
Golden State Fwy.
Los Angeles River
Hollywood Lake
Highland Park
South Pasadena
San Marino
Stone Canyon Reservoir
Santa Monica Mts.
Garvanza
Temple City
Hollywood
Beverly Glen
Hollywood Bowl
Hollywood Blvd.
Mann's Chinese Theatre
Sunset Blvd.
Silver Lake Reservoir
Southwest Museum
Pasadena Fwy.
El Sereno
Franklin Reservoir
459
Santa Monica Blvd.
San Gabriel
Bel Air
Beverly Hills
West Hollywood
Paramount Studios
Hollywood Fwy.
Dodger Stadium
Lincoln Heights
Alhambra
Rosemead
University of California Los Angeles
L.A. County Art Museum
California State Univ.
San Bernardino Fwy.
Westwood Village
Monterey Park
El Monte
Will Rogers State Historical Park
Brentwood Park
LOS ANGELES
Civic Center
Union Sta.
South San Gabriel
South El Monte
Pacific Palisades
Whittier Narrows
Santa Monica
Santa Monica Fwy.
Convention Center
Boyle Heights
Flood Control Basin
Bicentennial Park
University of Southern California
East Los Angeles
Montebello
Rio Hondo
Memorial Coliseum
Exposition Park
Puente Hills
SANTA MONICA MUNICIPAL AIRPORT
San Diego Fwy.
Culver City
Baldwin Hills Reservoir
View Park
Vernon
Los Angeles River
Commerce
Hills
Baldwin Hills
Santa Ana Fwy.
Pico Rivera
Pio Pico State Historic Park
Venice
Windsor Hills
Maywood
Ladera Heights
Huntington Park
Bell Gardens
Whittier
PACIFIC OCEAN
Harbor Fwy.
Bell
Long Beach Fwy.
San Gabriel River
San Gabriel River Fwy.
Los Nietos
Marina del Ray
Westchester
Florence
Cudahy
University of West Los Angeles
Great Western Forum
Inglewood
LOS ANGELES INTERNATIONAL AIRPORT
South Gate
Downey
Santa Fe Springs
Lennox
101
405
170
134
5
2
210
110
19
10
60
605
1
42
710

## Lima

0 km 5
0 miles 3

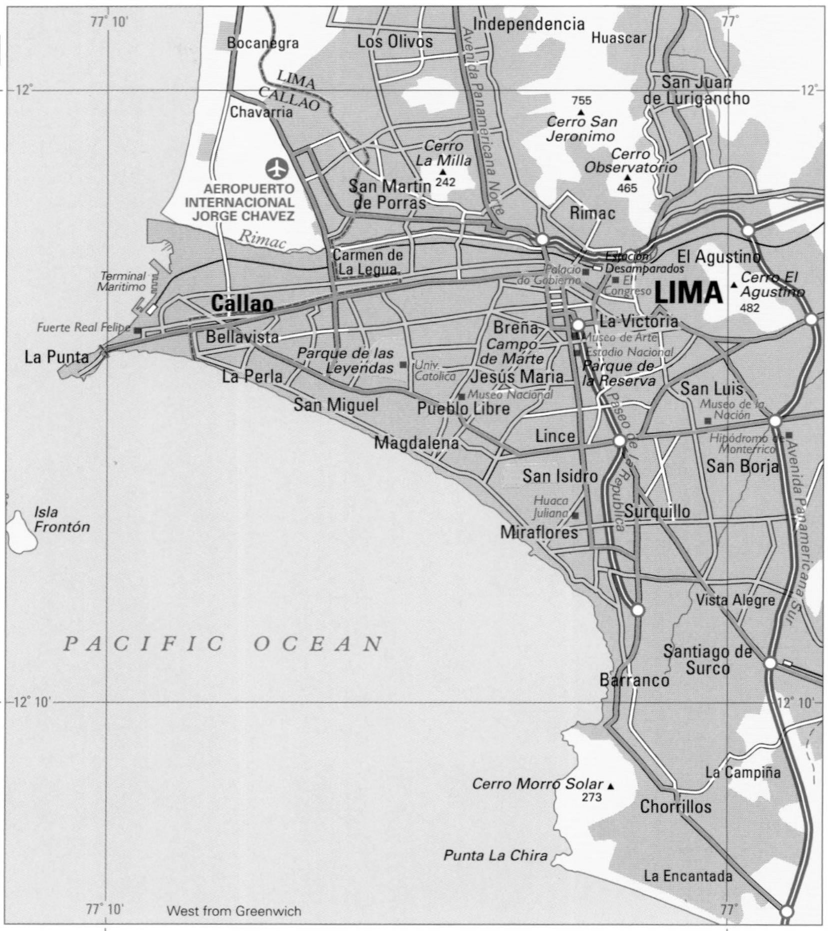
A
B
C
1
2
3
77° 10'
77°
12°
12° 10'
West from Greenwich
Bocanegra
Los Olivos
Independencia
Huascar
Avenida Panamericana Norte
San Juan de Lurigancho
LIMA
CALLAO
Chavarria
755
Cerro San Jeronimo
Cerro La Milla 242
Cerro Observatorio 465
AEROPUERTO INTERNACIONAL JORGE CHAVEZ
San Martin de Porras
Rimac
Rimac
Estación Desamparados
El Agustino
Carmen de La Legua
Palacio de Gobierno
El Congreso
Cerro El Agustino 482
Terminal Maritimo
Callao
LIMA
La Victoria
Fuerte Real Felipe
Bellavista
Breña
Museo de Arte
Estadio Nacional
La Punta
Parque de las Leyendas
Campo de Marte
Parque de la Reserva
La Perla
Univ. Católica
Jesús Maria
San Luis
Museo Nacional
Museo de la Nación
San Miguel
Pueblo Libre
Lince
Hipódromo de Monterrico
Magdalena
San Borja
San Isidro
Avenida Panamericana Sur
Paseo de la República
Huaca Juliana
Surquillo
Isla Frontón
Miraflores
Vista Alegre
PACIFIC OCEAN
Santiago de Surco
Barranco
La Campiña
Cerro Morro Solar 273
Chorrillos
Punta La Chira
La Encantada

## Central Los Angeles

0 km 1
0 miles 0.5

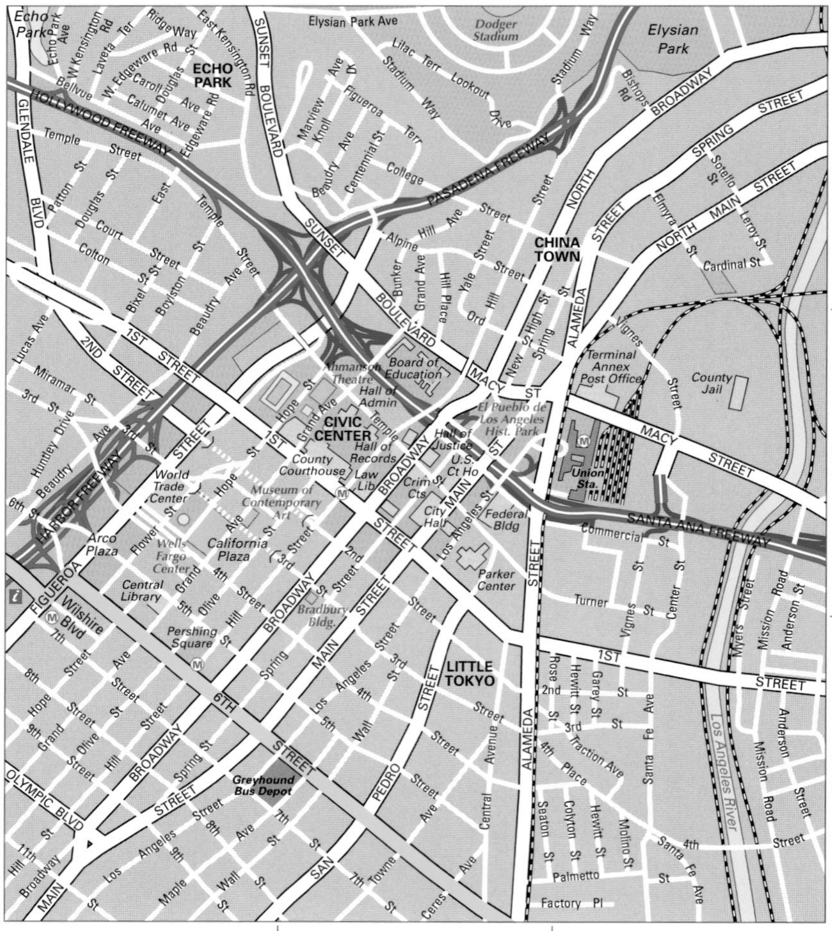
a
b
c
1
2
3
Echo Park
Elysian Park Ave
Dodger Stadium
Elysian Park
ECHO PARK
SUNSET BOULEVARD
HOLLYWOOD FREEWAY
PASADENA FREEWAY
Stadium Way
BROADWAY
SPRING STREET
NORTH MAIN STREET
GLENDALE BLVD
Temple St
CHINA TOWN
Cardinal St
ALAMEDA STREET
Terminal Annex Post Office
County Jail
MACY STREET
Board of Education
Ahmanson Theatre
Hall of Admin
CIVIC CENTER
El Pueblo de Los Angeles Hist. Park
Hall of Justice
Hall of Records
County Courthouse
Law Lib
U.S. Ct Ho
Union Sta.
World Trade Center
Museum of Contemporary Art
Crim Cts
City Hall
Federal Bldg
SANTA ANA FREEWAY
HARBOR FREEWAY
Arco Plaza
Wells Fargo Center
California Plaza
Parker Center
Commercial St
Central Library
Bradbury Bldg
FIGUEROA
Wilshire Blvd
Pershing Square
LITTLE TOKYO
1ST STREET
Los Angeles River
Greyhound Bus Depot
OLYMPIC BLVD
Santa Fe Ave
Mission Road
Anderson St
Traction Ave
Palmetto St
Factory Pl
SAN PEDRO STREET
CENTRAL AVENUE
Towne Ave
Ceres Ave
Maple Ave
Wall St
Los Angeles St
MAIN ST
Hill St
6TH STREET
7th St
8th St
9th St
11th St
Olive St
Grand Ave
Hope St
Flower St
2ND STREET
3rd St
4th St
5th St
Lucas Ave
Beaudry Ave
Miramar St
Huntley Dr
Turner St
Vignes St
Center St
Myers St

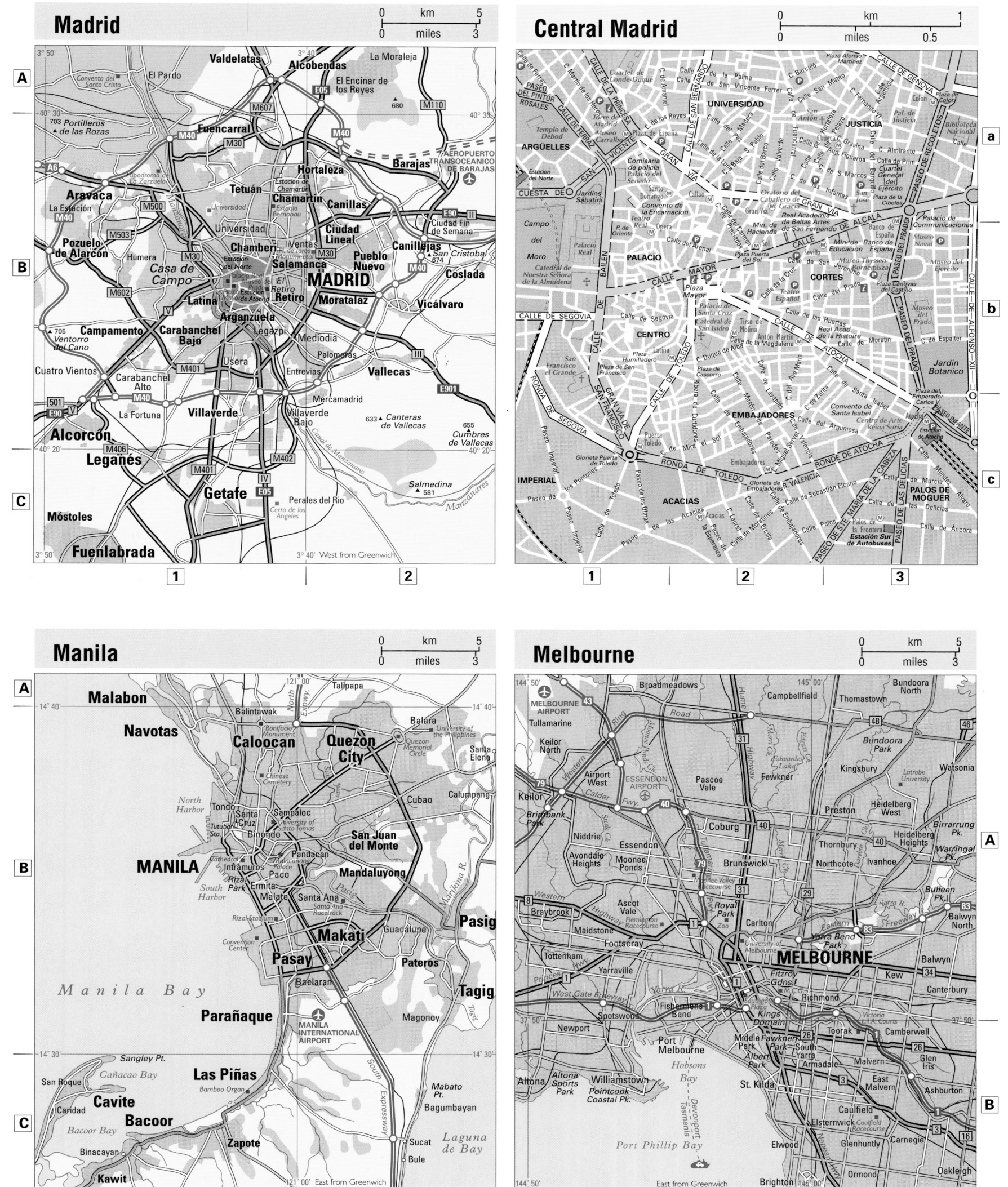

## Madrid

0 km 5
0 miles 3

## Central Madrid

0 km 1
0 miles 0.5

## Manila

0 km 5
0 miles 3

## Melbourne

0 km 5
0 miles 3

COPYRIGHT GEORGE PHILIP LTD.

## Mexico City

km 5 / miles 3

A B C rows; columns 1 2

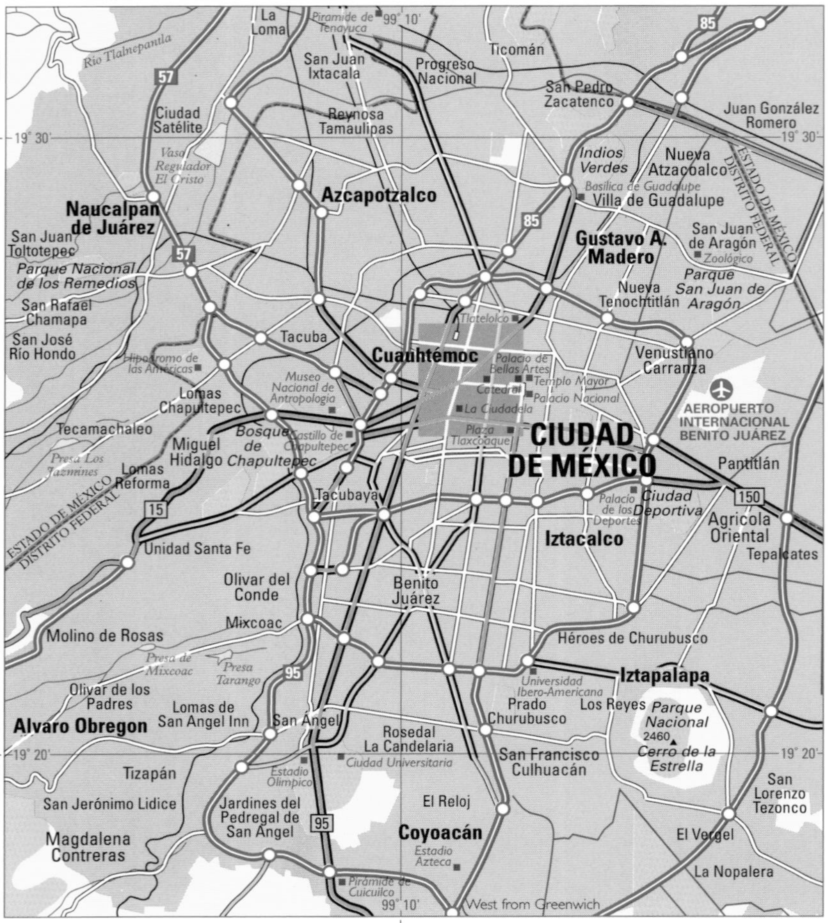

La Loma, Pirámide de Tenayuca, 99°10', Ticomán, 85, Río Tlalnepantla, 57, Ciudad Satélite, Progreso Nacional, San Juan Ixtacala, Reynosa Tamaulipas, San Pedro Zacatenco, Juan González Romero, 19°30', Vaso Regulador El Cristo, Naucalpan de Juárez, Azcapotzalco, Indios Verdes, Nueva Atzacoalco, Villa de Guadalupe, San Juan de Aragón, San Juan Toltotepec, 57, 85, Gustavo A. Madero, Parque Zoológico, Parque San Juan de Aragón, Parque Nacional de los Remedios, San Rafael Chamapa, Tacuba, Nueva Tenochtitlán, San José Río Hondo, Cuauhtémoc, Distrito Federal, Estado de México, Lomas Chapultepec, Tecamachalco, Miguel Hidalgo, Bosque de Chapultepec, Castillo de Chapultepec, Museo Nacional de Antropología, Palacio de Bellas Artes, Templo Mayor, Catedral, Plaza Tlaxcoaque, CIUDAD DE MÉXICO, Venustiano Carranza, AEROPUERTO INTERNACIONAL BENITO JUÁREZ, Lomas Reforma, Presa Las Jazmines, 15, Tacubaya, Ciudad de los Deportes Ciudad Deportiva, Pantitlán, Unidad Santa Fe, Iztacalco, Agrícola Oriental, Tepalates, 150, Olivar del Conde, Benito Juárez, Mixcoac, Molino de Rosas, Presa Tarango, Presa de Mixcoac, 95, Héroes de Churubusco, Olivar de los Padres, Lomas de San Angel Inn, San Angel, Prado Churubusco, Universidad Ibero-Americana, Los Reyes, Iztapalapa, Parque Nacional 2460 Cerro de la Estrella, Alvaro Obregón, Tizapán, Rosedal La Candelaria, Ciudad Universitaria, San Francisco Culhuacán, 19°20', San Jerónimo Lídice, Estadio Olímpico, El Reloj, San Lorenzo Tezonco, Jardines del Pedregal de San Angel, 95, Coyoacán, Estadio Azteca, El Vergel, Magdalena Contreras, Pirámide de Cuicuilco, La Nopalera, 99°10', West from Greenwich

## Central Mexico City

km 1 / miles 0.5

a b c rows; columns 1 2 3

Sta. María, Rosains, Estación FFCC Nacionales Buenavista, EJE CENT. LÁZARO CÁRDENAS, Monumento a Cuitláhuac, PASEO DE LA REFORMA, González Bocanegra, PERAVILLO, CARRANZA, Naranjo, Cipres, J. A. ALZATE, GUERRERO, Camelia, SANTA MARÍA, A. Nervo, Guerrero, Monumento a Gen. San Martín, ARGENTINA, Castellanos Tames, Tofieras, Sor Juana Inés de la Cruz, AVE. INSURGENTES NORTE, Degollado, Rep. de Honduras, Santa Catarina, San Cosme, Museo del Chapo, Revolución, Monumento a Simón Bolívar, Rep. de Perú, Santo Domingo, M. Schultz, Herrera, PUENTE ALVARADO, San Fernando, Belisario Domínguez, Museo Nacional de Arte, Secretaría de Educación Pública, Carmen, Monumento a la Revolución, Santa Veracruz, Bellas Artes, Antonio Caso, Pl. de la República, AVENIDA, HIDALGO, Palacio de Bellas Artes, ALLENDE, TACUBA, Templo Mayor, AVENIDA, JUARE[Z], 5 de Mayo, Iglesia de la Profesa, Catedral Metropolitana, Museo de Artes e Industrias Populares, Torre Latino-americana, MADER, Pal. de Iturbide, Zócalo, Palacio Nacional, Monumento a Colón, Av. Morelos, CENTRO, Victoria, V. Carranza, Zócalo, Versalles, Luis Moya, Isabel la Católica, 16 de Febrero, Museo de la Ciudad de México, Londres, Liverpool, Abraham Gonzáles, Biblioteca Nacional, 20 DE NOVIEMBRE, Iglesia y Fuente del Salto del Agua, PINO SUÁREZ, Salvador, Nápoles, BUCARELI, Balderas, ARCOS DE BELEN, N. S. de Merceditas, Iglesia de Regina, Isabel la Católica, Chimalpopoca, CHAPULTEPEC, Puebla, Arena México, DR. RÍO DE LA LOZA, IZAZAGA, Pino Suárez, Plaza Tlaxcoaque, AVENIDA CUAUHTÉMOC, Avenida Durango, Colima, Dr. Navarro, Dr. Barragán, Dr. Liceaga, C. F. SERVANDO TERESA DE MIER, ESPERANZA, ROMA, Dr. Velasco, Dr. Claudio Bernard, Niños Héroes, Bolívar, Isabel la Católica, 9°10' East from Greenwich

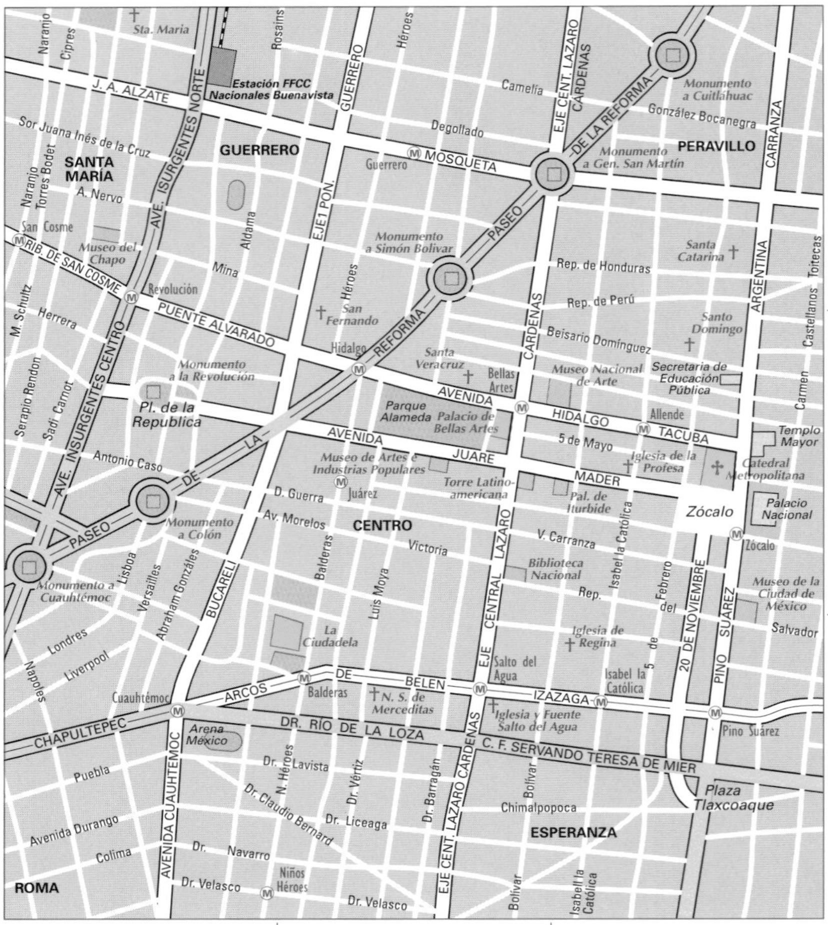

## Miami

km 5 / miles 3

A B rows; columns 1 2

821, Snake Creek Canal, 817, 95, 860, 826, Carol City, North Miami Beach, 826, 1, OPA-LOCKA AIRPORT, Opa-Locka, 826, North Miami, Museum of Contemporary Art, 75, 916, Bay Harbour Islands, Bal Harbor, 924, Biscayne Park, Surfside, Pinewood, Indian Creek Village, 27, Hialeah, 9, 817, Miami Shores, El Portal, North South Expressway, Miami Canal, 25°50', Little Haiti, North Bay Village, 95, Biscayne Bay, MIAMI BEACH, Virginia Gardens, Miami Springs, 27, Railway Station, American Police Hall of Fame, 195, Art Deco Historic District, Palmetto Expressway, 948, 953, 817, MIAMI INTERNATIONAL AIRPORT, 9, Venetian Islands, 826, 836, Little Havana, Metro-Dade Cultural Center, Orange Bowl Stadium, 41, 41, 41, West Miami, Coral Gables, 9, 817, 95, MIAMI, Fisher Island, 973, Vizcaya Museum and Gardens, Biscayne Bay, Virginia Key, 976, South Miami, 1, Barnacle State Historic Site, West from Greenwich, 80°15', Key Biscayne, Seaquarium, ATLANTIC OCEAN

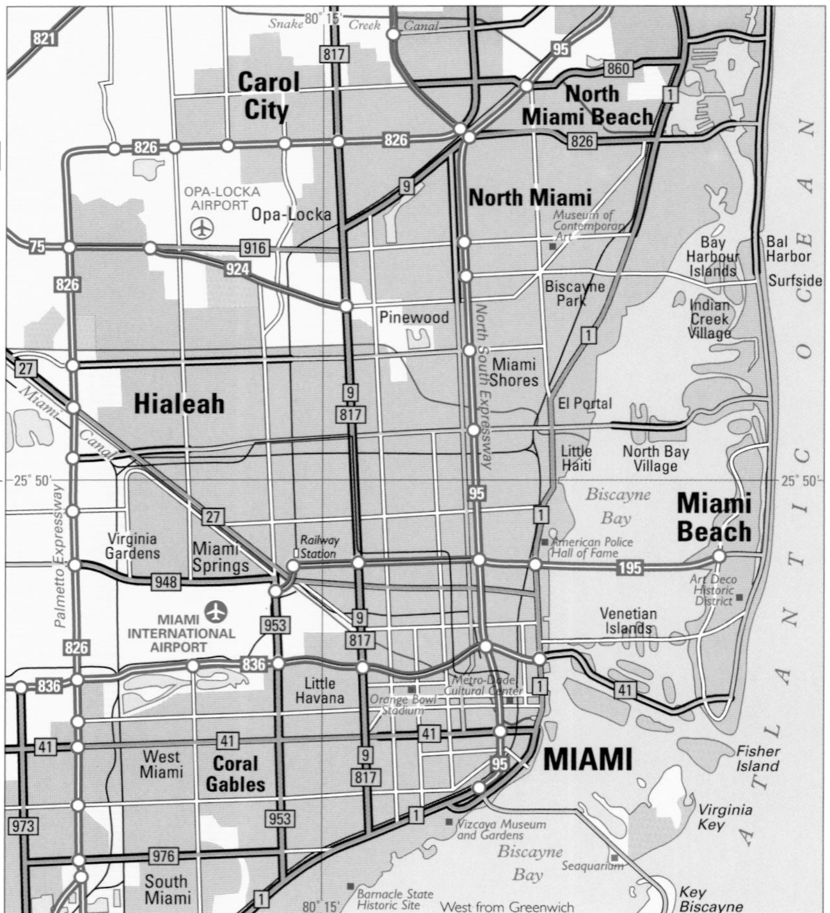

## Milan

km 5 / miles 3

A B rows; columns 1 2

Coronno, Cesate, Limbiate, Varedo, 527, Muggiò, Concorezzo, Autodromo, Pertusella, Garbagnate Milanese, Palazzolo, Nova Milanese, Monza, Lainate, 233, Senago, Cassina Amata, Dugnano, San Fruttuoso, 527, A52, Paderno, Cinisello Balsamo, 36, A51, E66, A4, Bollate, Cusano Milanino, Brughério, Passirana, Arese, Cormano, Bresso, San Maurizio al Lambro, A8, Bruzzano, Parco Regionale, Rho, Terrazzano, Ospiate, Affori, Greco, Cologno Monzèse, Sesto San Giovanni, Precotto, Crescenzago, Vimodrone, Cornaredo, A4, Pero, Novate Milanese, Bovisa, Musocco, Loreto, Lambrate, Milano Due, Pioltello, Vighignolo, Figino, Trenno, Boldinasco, Centrale, Parco Lambro, Settimo Milanese, E35, A50, 11, Stadio San Siro, MILANO, Lambrate, Segrate, San Siro, Fiera Camp., Ortica, Milano San Felice, Quinto Romano, Castello Sforzesco, Città degli Studi, San Bòvio, Assiano, Monzoro, Bàggio, La Scala, Duomo, Basilica di S. Ambrogio, Calvairate, AEROPORTO INTERNAZ. DI LINATE, Cusago, Quartiere Zingone, Moravione, A51, Mezzate, Cesano Boscone, San Cristóforo, Gambolóita, Peschiera Borromeo, 494, Vigentino, A7, Triulzo, 415, Córsico, Chiaravalle Milanese, Metanópoli, San Donato Milanese, Romano Banco, Assago, Gratosóglio, 412, Trezzano sul Naviglio, A1, 9, San Giuliano Milanese, Gaggiano, Buccinasco, Poasco, Quinto de Stampi, E35, Mediglia, San Novo, Rozzano, Opera, Sesto Ulteriano, A50, Zivido, Barate, San Pietro Cúsico, Gudo Gamb., Pontesesto, Pizzonasco, Zibido San Giacomo, Noviglio, Mairano, Tolcinasco, Locate di Triulzi, Zúnico, 9°10' East from Greenwich

# Moscow

0 km 5
0 miles 3

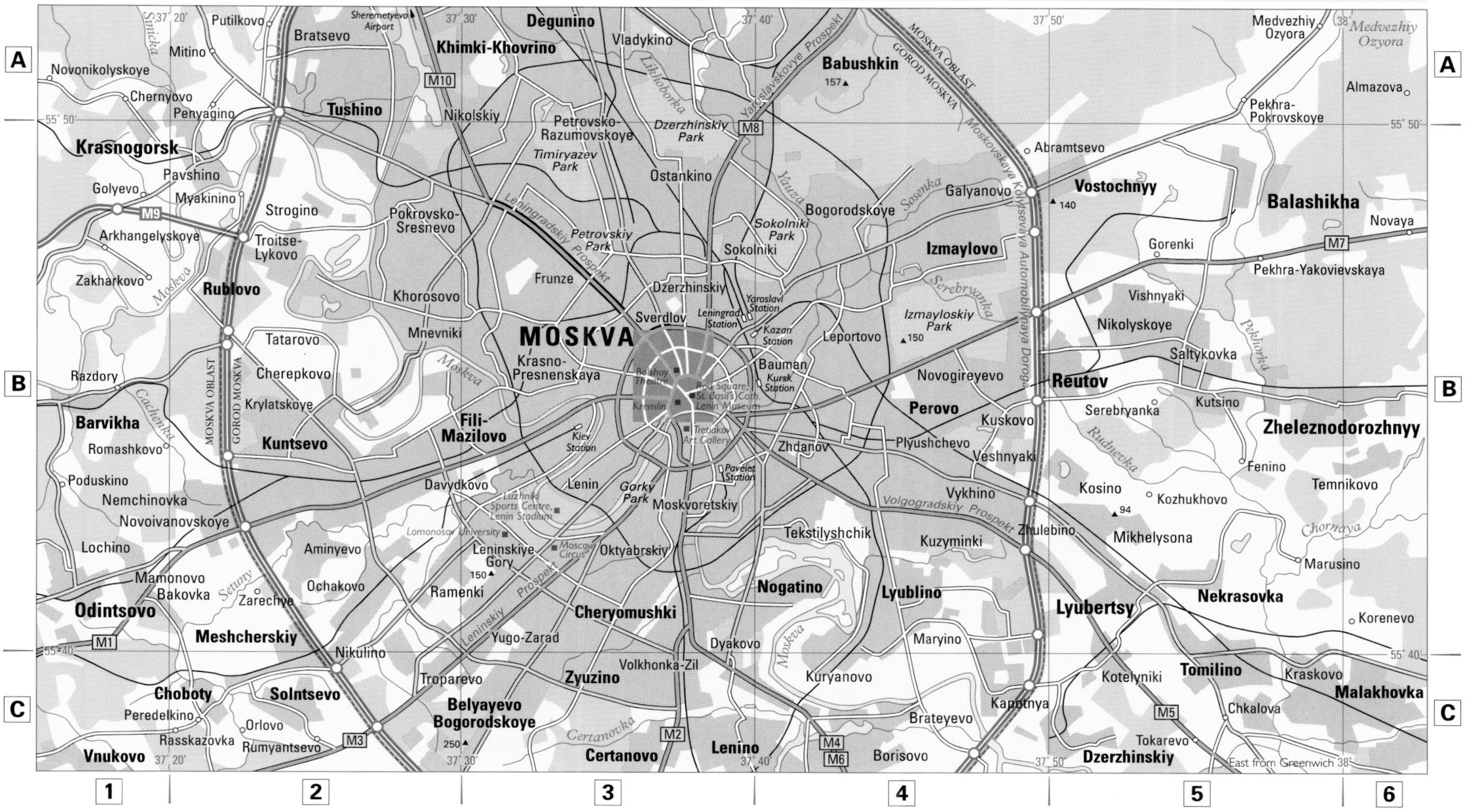

Novonikolyskoye, Putilkovo, Mitino, Bratsevo, Khimki-Khovrino, Vladykino, Degunino, Babushkin, Medvezhiy Ozyora, Almazova, Medvezhiy Ozyora
Chernyovo, Penyagino, Tushino, Nikolskiy, Petrovsko-Razumovskoye, Dzerzhinskiy Park, Ostankino, Abramtsevo, Pekhra-Pokrovskoye
Krasnogorsk, Pavshino, Timiryazev Park, Bogorodskoye, Galyanovo, Vostochnyy, Balashikha, Novaya
Golyevo, Myakinino, Strogino, Pokrovsko-Sresnevo, Petrovskiy Park, Sokolniki Park, Izmaylovo, Gorenki, Nikolyskoye, Pekhra-Yakovievskaya
Arkhangelskoye, Troitse-Lykovo, Frunze, Sokolniki, Izmayloskiy Park, Vishnyaki
Zakharkovo, Rublovo, Khorosovo, MOSKVA, Sverdlov, Leningrad Station, Kazan Station, Yaroslavl Station, Leportovo, Saltykovka
Razdory, Tatarovo, Cherepkovo, Krasno-Presnenskaya, Bauman, Kursk Station, Novogireyevo, Perovo, Reutov, Serebryanka, Kutsino, Zheleznodorozhnyy
Barvikha, Romashkovo, Krylatskoye, Fili-Mazilovo, Kiev Station, Red Square, St Basil's Cath, Lenin Museum, Kremlin, Tretiakov Art Gallery, Zhdanov, Plyushchevo, Veshnyaki, Fenino, Temnikovo
Poduskino, Kuntsevo, Davydkovo, Lenin, Gorky Park, Moskvoretskiy, Pavelet Station, Vykhino, Kosino, Kozhukhovo, Marusino
Nemchinovka, Novoivanovskoye, Aminyevo, Lenin Stadium, Lomonosov University, Leninskiye Gory, Moscow Circus, Oktyabrskiy, Tekstilyshchik, Kuzyminki, Zhulebino, Mikhelysona, Marusino
Lochino, Odintsovo, Meshcherskiy, Ochakovo, Zarechye, Ramenki, Yugo-Zarad, Cheryomushki, Nogatino, Lyublino, Lyubertsy, Nekrasovka, Korenevo
Choboty, Solntsevo, Nikulino, Troparevo, Zyuzino, Volkhonka-Zil, Dyakovo, Maryino, Tomilino, Kraskovo, Malakhovka
Peredelkino, Orlovo, Belyayevo Bogorodskoye, Kuryanovo, Kotelyniki, Chkalova
Vnukovo, Rasskazovka, Rumyantsevo, Certanovo, Lenino, Borisovo, Brateyevo, Kapotnya, Tokarevo, Dzerzhinskiy

# Montréal

0 km 5 / 0 miles 3

Île Jésus, Rivière-des-Prairies, Pointe-Aux-Trembles, Boucherville, St-Vincent-de-Paul, Montréal Nord, Anjou, Montréal Est, Vimont, Duvernay, St-Léonard, Boucherville, Laval, Bélanger, Pont-Viau, Sault-au-Récollet, St-Michel, Longue-Pointe, Îles de Boucherville, Abord-à-Plouffe, Rosemont, Parc Maisonneuve, Maisonneuve, Cartierville, Ahuntsic, Hochelaga, MONTRÉAL, Île Ste Hélène, Jacques Cartier, St-Laurent, Parc Lafontaine, Outremont, Mont-Royal, Parc Mont-Royal, Parc Hélène de Champlain, Île Notre-Dame, Longueuil, Mackayville, St-Lambert, Hampstead, Univ McGill, Palais des Congrès, Gare Central, Lemoyne, St-Hubert, Westmount, Côte-St-Luc, Notre-Dame-de-Grace, Musée des beaux Arts, Forum de Montréal, Gare Windsor, Pont Victoria, Préville, Greenfield Park, Notre Dame, St-Pierre, Brossard, Montréal Ouest, Verdun, Île des Soeurs, Lachine, Lasalle, Île aux Herons, Canal de Lachine, St. Laurent (St-Laurent), Pont Honoré Mercier, La Prairie, Kahnawake, Ste-Catherine, Candiac

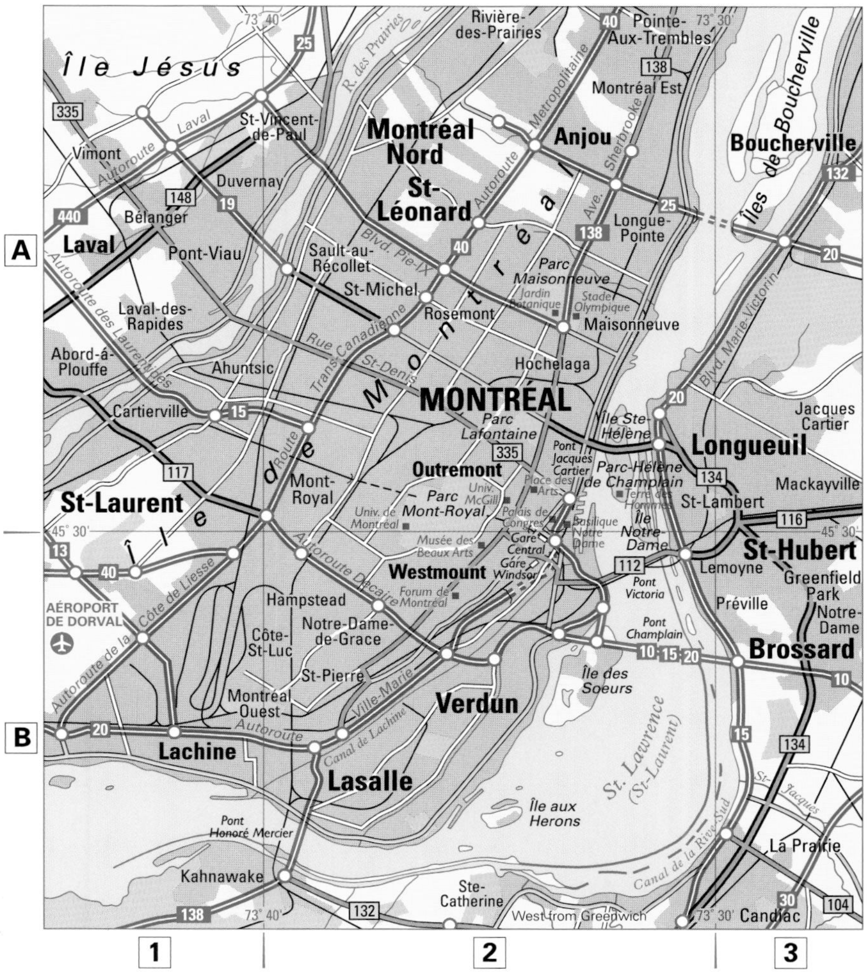

# Central Moscow

0 km 1 / 0 miles 0.5

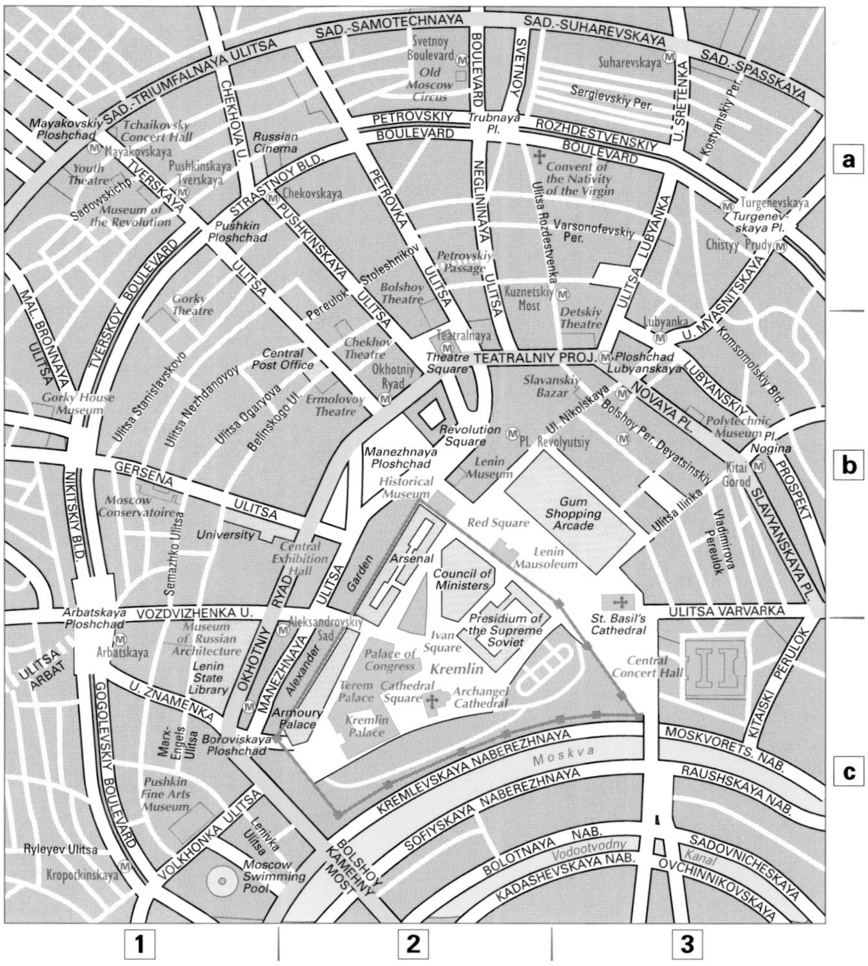

SAD-SAMOTECHNAYA, SAD-SUHAREVSKAYA, SAD-SPASSKAYA, Svetnoy Boulevard, Old Moscow Circus, Suharevskaya, Sergievskiy Per, Krestovskiy Per, Mayakovskiy Ploshchad, Tchaikovsky Concert Hall, Russian Cinema, PETROVSKY BOULEVARD, ROZHDESTVENSKY BOULEVARD, Convent of the Nativity of the Virgin, Turgenevskaya, Youth Theatre, Pushkinskaya, Chekhovskaya, Pushkin Ploshchad, Petrovsky Passage, Chisty Prudy, Museum of the Revolution, Gorky Theatre, Bolshoy Theatre, Sretenka, Lubyanka, Detskiy Mir, Bolshoy Theatre, Gorky House Museum, Chekhov Theatre, Central Post Office, Okhotny Ryad, Teatralniy Proj, Ploshchad Lubyanskaya, Slavanskiy Bazar, Polytechnic Museum, Nogina, Moscow Conservatoire, Ermolovo Theatre, Revolution Square, Lenin Museum, Gum Shopping Arcade, Kitai Gorod, University, Manezhnaya Ploshchad, Historical Museum, Red Square, Central Exhibition Hall, Manezhnaya, Arsenal, Lenin Mausoleum, Arbatskaya, Council of Ministers, St. Basil's Cathedral, Central Concert Hall, Museum of Russian Architecture, Aleksandrovskiy Sad, Presidium of the Supreme Soviet, ULITSA VARVARKA, Lenin State Library, Palace of Congress, Ivan Square, Terem Palace, Cathedral Square, Archangel Cathedral, Kremlin, Armoury Palace, Kremlin Palace, Pushkin Fine Arts Museum, Moskva, Moscow Swimming Pool, KREMLEVSKAYA NABEREZHNAYA, SOFYISKAYA NAB, MOSKVORETS NAB, RAUSHSKAYA NAB, BOLOTNAYA NAB, KADASHEVSKAYA NAB, OVCHINNIKOVSKAYA NAB, SADOVNICHESKAYA

COPYRIGHT GEORGE PHILIP LTD.

## Mumbai

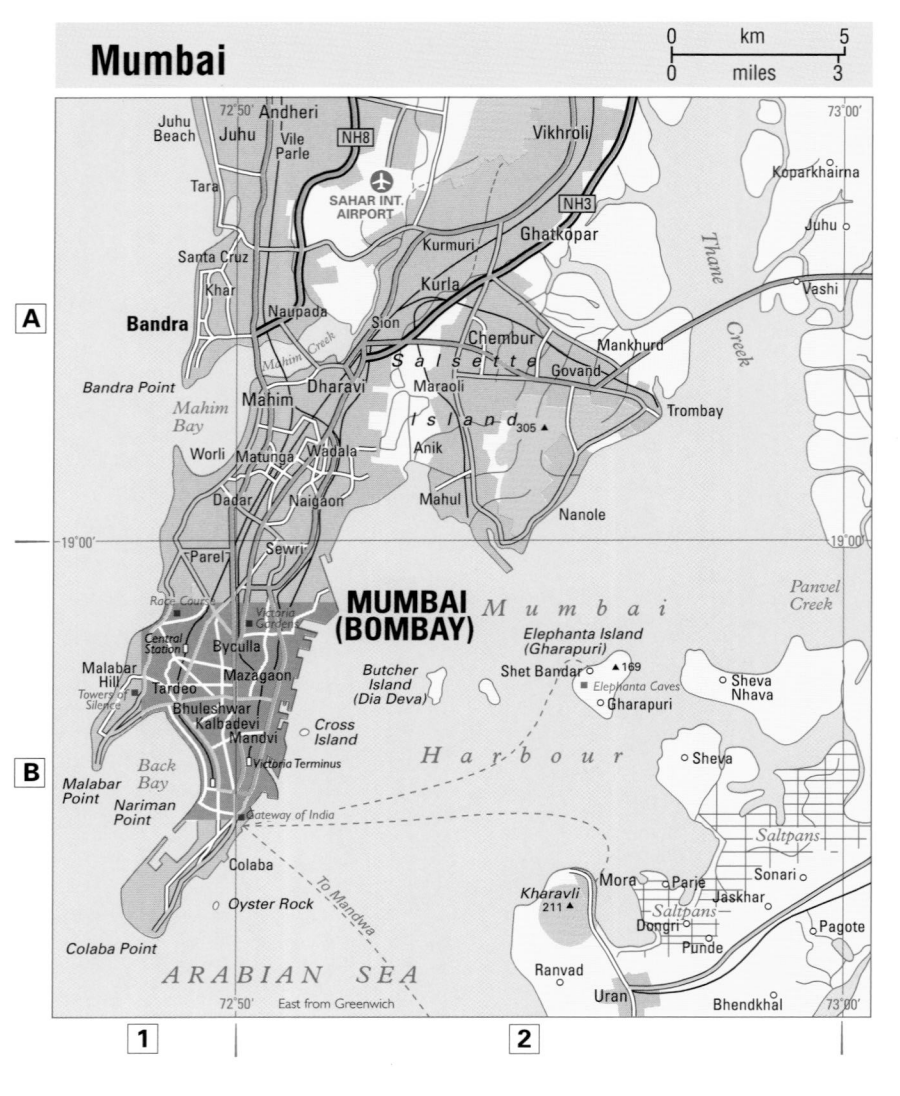

## Central Mumbai

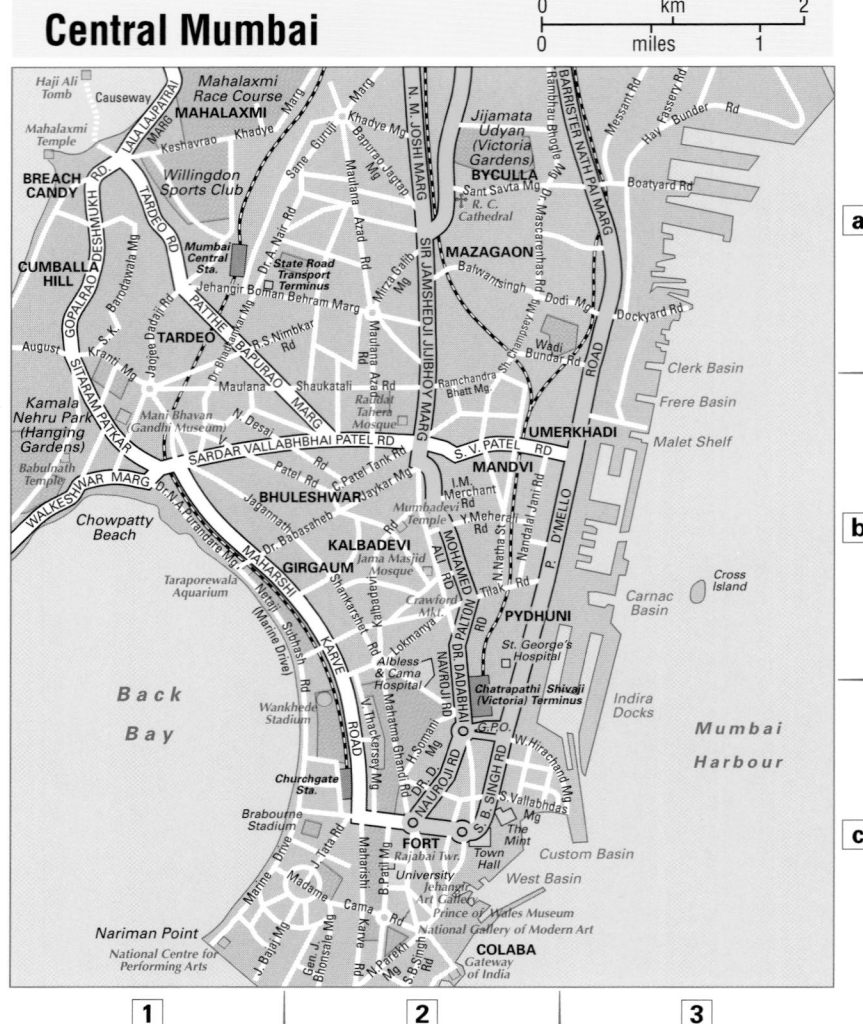

## Munich

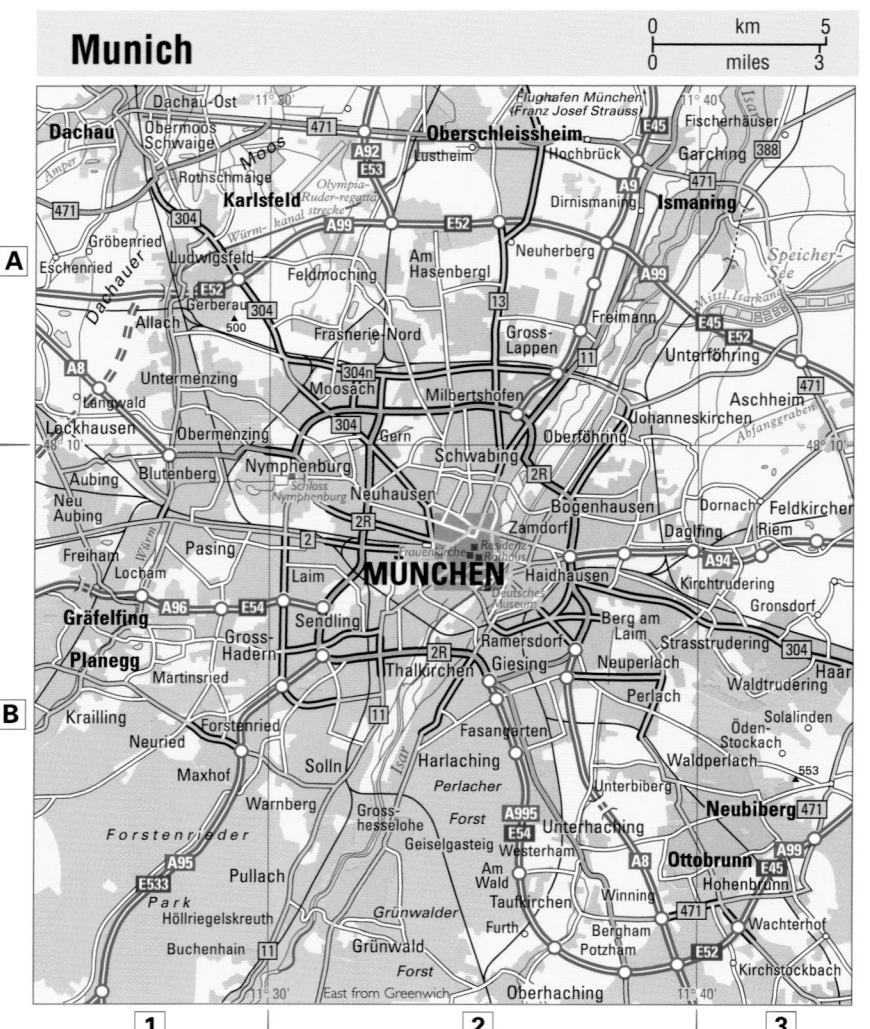

## Central Munich

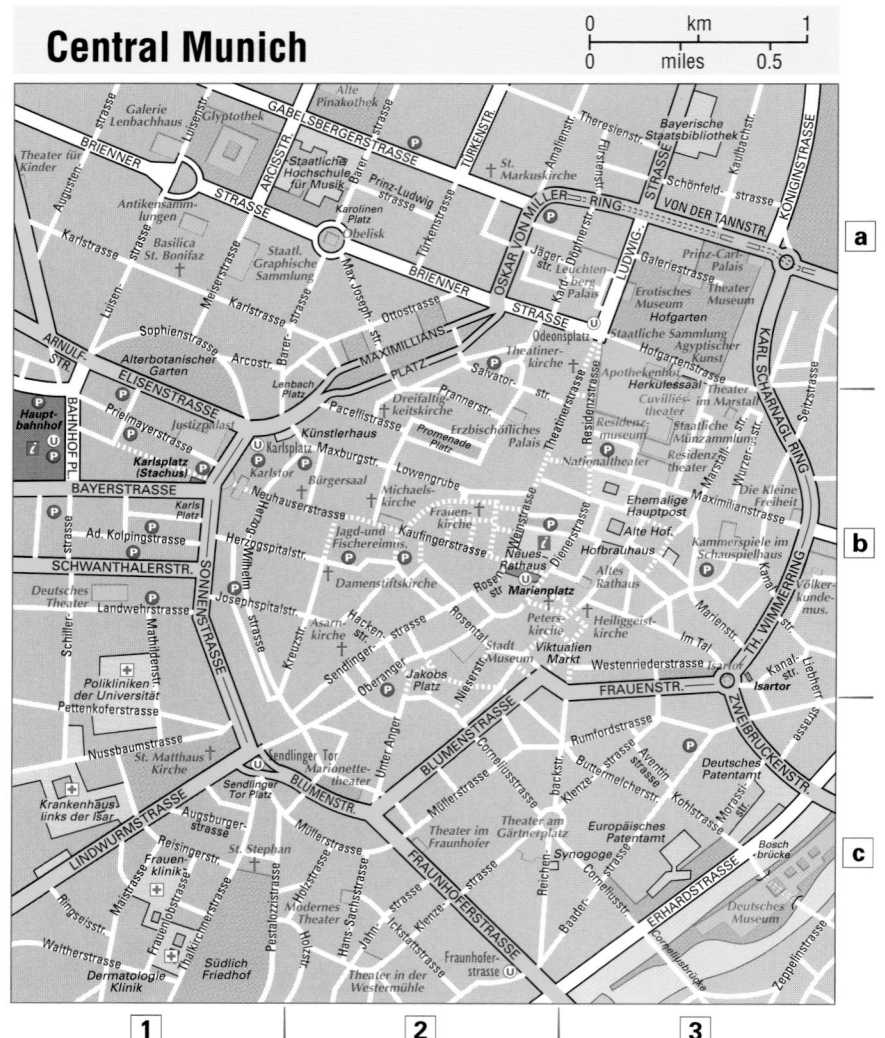

## New York

0 km 5
0 miles 3

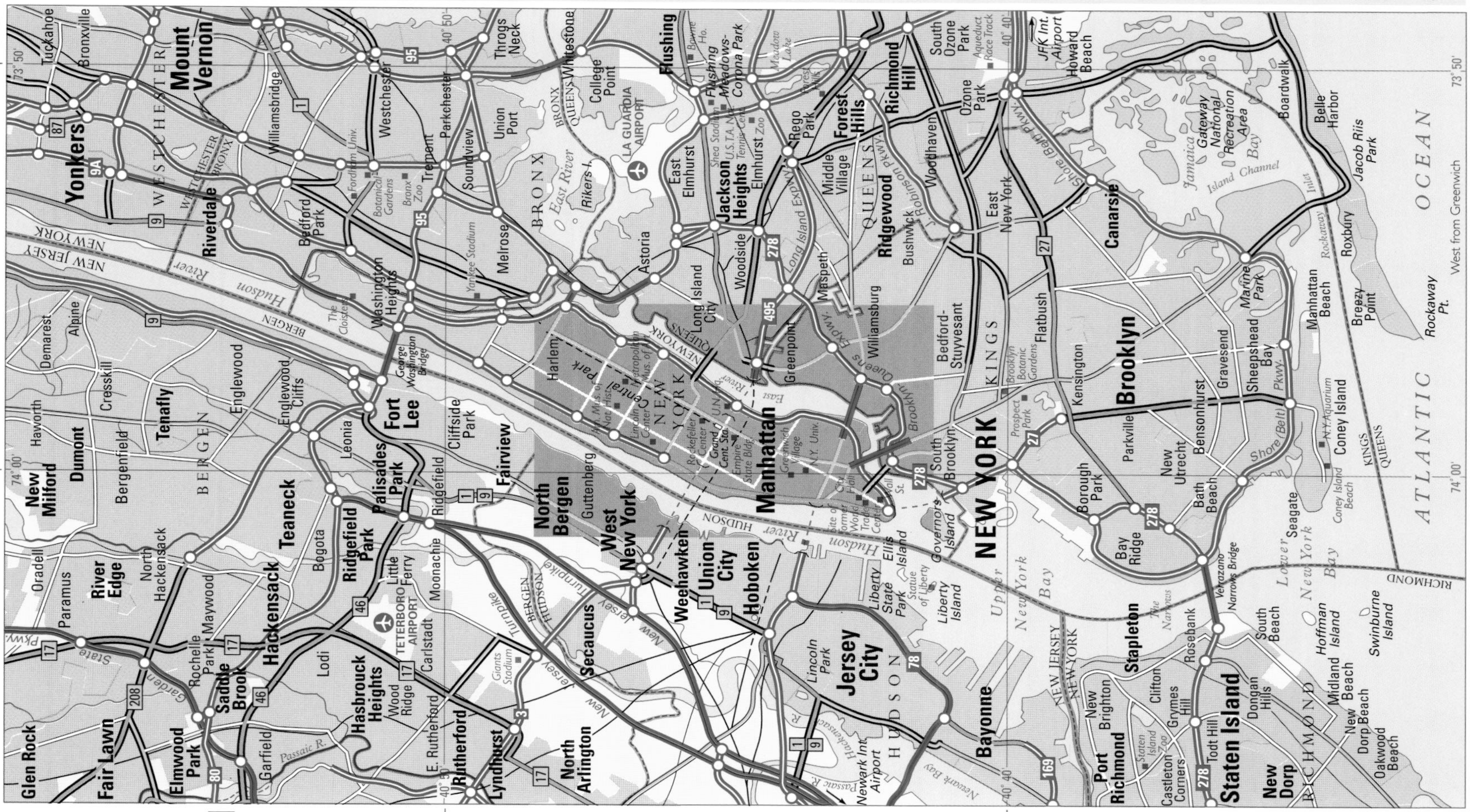
Yonkers
Mount Vernon
Tuckahoe
Bronxville
Riverdale
Washington Heights
Fort Lee
Harlem
Manhattan
Astoria
Long Island City
Jackson Heights
Flushing
Forest Hills
Richmond Hill
Ridgewood
Williamsburg
Greenpoint
Brooklyn
NEW YORK
Canarsie
Jersey City
Hoboken
Union City
Weehawken
West New York
North Bergen
Secaucus
Hackensack
Teaneck
Englewood
Tenafly
Bayonne
Stapleton
Staten Island
Port Richmond
New Dorp
Rockaway Pt.
ATLANTIC OCEAN
JFK Int. Airport
LA GUARDIA AIRPORT
TETERBORO AIRPORT
Newark Int. Airport
Upper New York Bay
Lower New York Bay
Hudson River
East River
West from Greenwich

1 2 3 A B C

## Central New York

0 km 2
0 miles 1

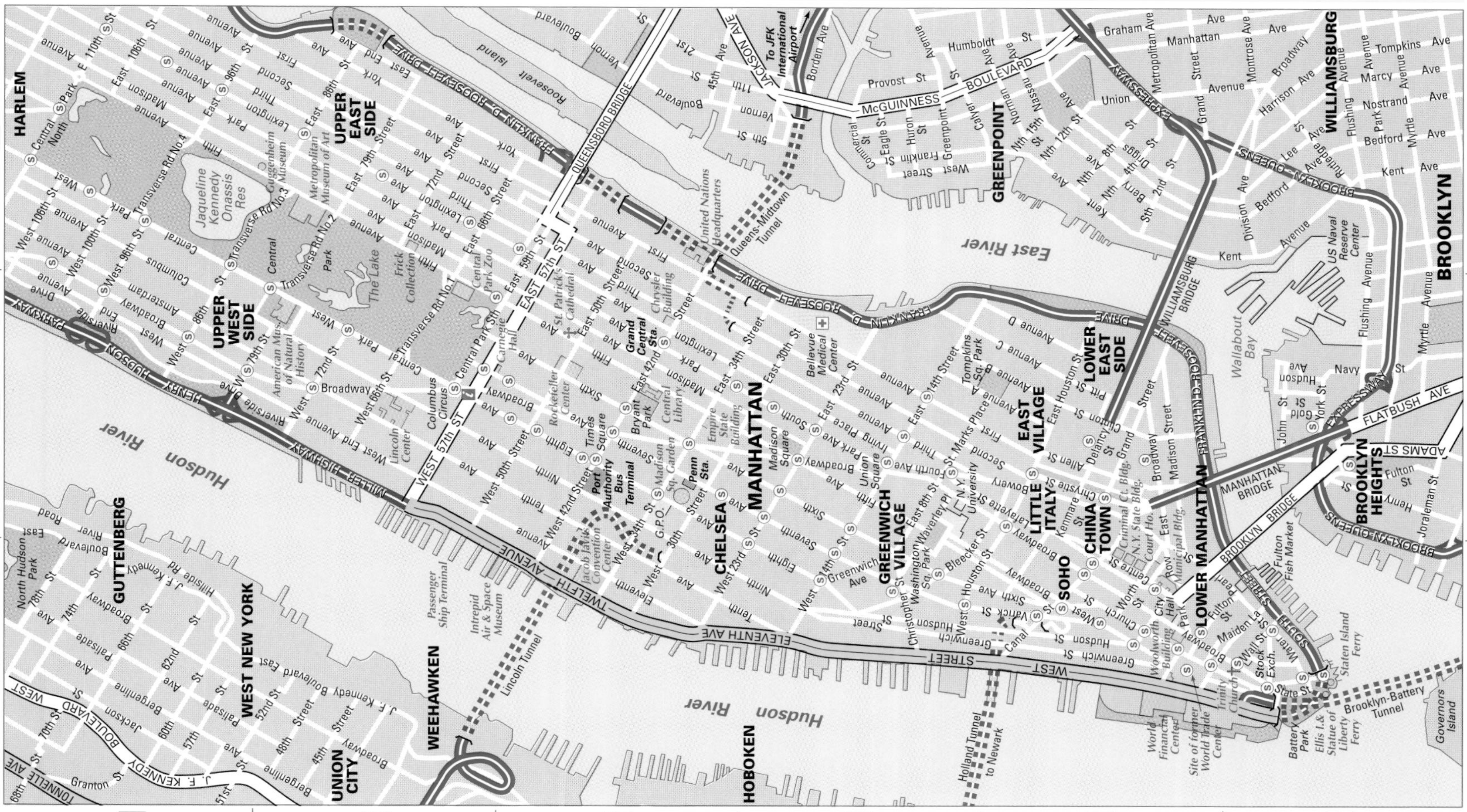
HARLEM
UPPER WEST SIDE
UPPER EAST SIDE
Central Park
MANHATTAN
CHELSEA
GREENWICH VILLAGE
SOHO
LITTLE ITALY
CHINA TOWN
LOWER EAST SIDE
EAST VILLAGE
LOWER MANHATTAN
GREENPOINT
WILLIAMSBURG
BROOKLYN
BROOKLYN HEIGHTS
GUTTENBERG
WEST NEW YORK
WEEHAWKEN
UNION CITY
HOBOKEN
Hudson River
East River
Roosevelt Island
Lincoln Tunnel
Holland Tunnel to Newark
Queens-Midtown Tunnel
Brooklyn-Battery Tunnel
QUEENSBORO BRIDGE
WILLIAMSBURG BRIDGE
MANHATTAN BRIDGE
BROOKLYN BRIDGE
Governors Island
Statue of Liberty
Ellis I.

a b c d e f 1 2 3

## Osaka

km 5
miles 3

Hirakata
509
Funasaka
Takarazuka
Arima
135°20'
135°30'
Karato
462
Senriyama
Yamada
Kori
598
722
Itami
OSAKA INTERNATIONAL AIRPORT
Toyonaka
Settsu
Neyagawa
Rokkō-Zan 932
Iwazono
Kwansei Gakuin University
171
Kadoma
Shijonawate
Tanigami
Rokkō Tunnel
Hirota
Suita
170
428
Obu-tōge
Maya-Zan 699
Kōbe University
Nishinomiya
173
Higashiyodogawa
Asahi
Moriguchi
365
Okamoto
Ashiaya
Daitō
Ōbu
Nada
43 Naruo
Amagasaki
Jūsō
Oyodo
Miyakojima
Kōnoike
403
Fukiai
Higashinada
2
Umeda
Kita
Jōtō
Ishikiri
Ikuta
Nishiyodogawa
Fukushima
Higashi
308
KŌBE
Rokkō Island
Konohana
Aji
Nishi
Minami
Higashinari
Nagata
Port Island
Minato
Nanwa
Ikuno
ŌSAKA
Higashiōsaka
Suma
Kōbe Harbour
Ōsaka Aquarium Suntory Museum
Tennōji
Abeno
Kizuri
Kyūhōji
Yamamoto
Ōsaka Harbour
Taishō
Liberty Museum
Shitennōji Temple
Yao
Nishinari
Higashisumiyoshi
Onchi
Sakai Harbour
Sumiyoshi Shrine
Sumiyoshi
25
Tainaka
YAO AIRPORT
Kashiwara
26
Ikeuchi
Fujidera
Matsubara
Sakai

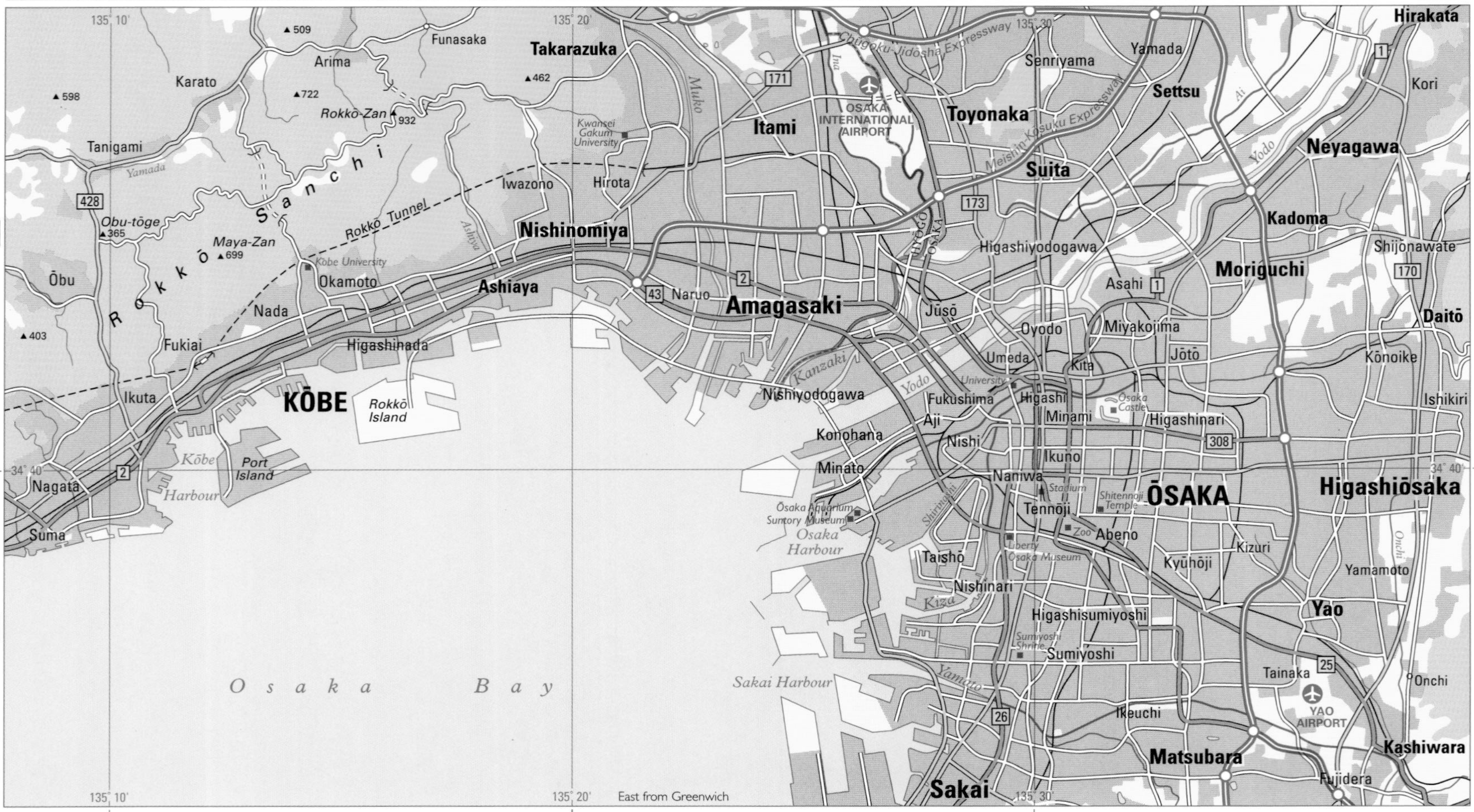

Osaka Bay

East from Greenwich

## Oslo

km 5
miles 3

OSLO AKERSHUS
Tryvannshøgda 531
Maridalen
Maridalsvatnet
418
Bogstadvatn
Holmenkollen
Alnsjøen
Gorud
Burudvatn
Sognsvatn
Kjelsås
Bærums Verk
Ila
Røa
Ris
Rødtvet
Bryn
Lijordet
Ullevål
4
163
168
OSLO
Sinsen
Kolsås
Haslum
Øya
Alna
E6
379
Ullern
160
Stabekk
Universitet Vestbane sta.
Tøyen
Bryn
Bærum
Høvik
Lysaker
Slottet Sentralsta.
164
Norsk Folke Museum
Akershus Slott
Oppsal
Bøler
Tanum
E18
166
Bygdøy
Hovedøya
Ryen
E18
E6
Slependen
Sandvika
Snarøya
Lindøya
Bekkelaget
165
Nesøya
Frederikshaven Helsingborg København Hirtshals, Kiel
Nesoddtangen
Lambertseter
Østmark kapellet
Hvalstad Nesbru
Ostøya
Ormøya
Nordstrand
Brønnøya
Malmøya
Asker
Flaskebekk
Skøkelfall
Ljabru
Klemetsrud
167
Vollen
Holmenfjorden
Bunnefjorden
155
Hauketo
Blåkstad
157
215
Torvvik
Ingierstrand
Kolbotn
E6
Slemmestad
Nesodden
Svestad
Hasle
156
Myrvoll
Oppegård
Vollen
Fjellstrand
Blyleget
Garder
134
Oppegård
Oslofjorden
Gjersjøen
Nærsnes
E18
East from Greenwich

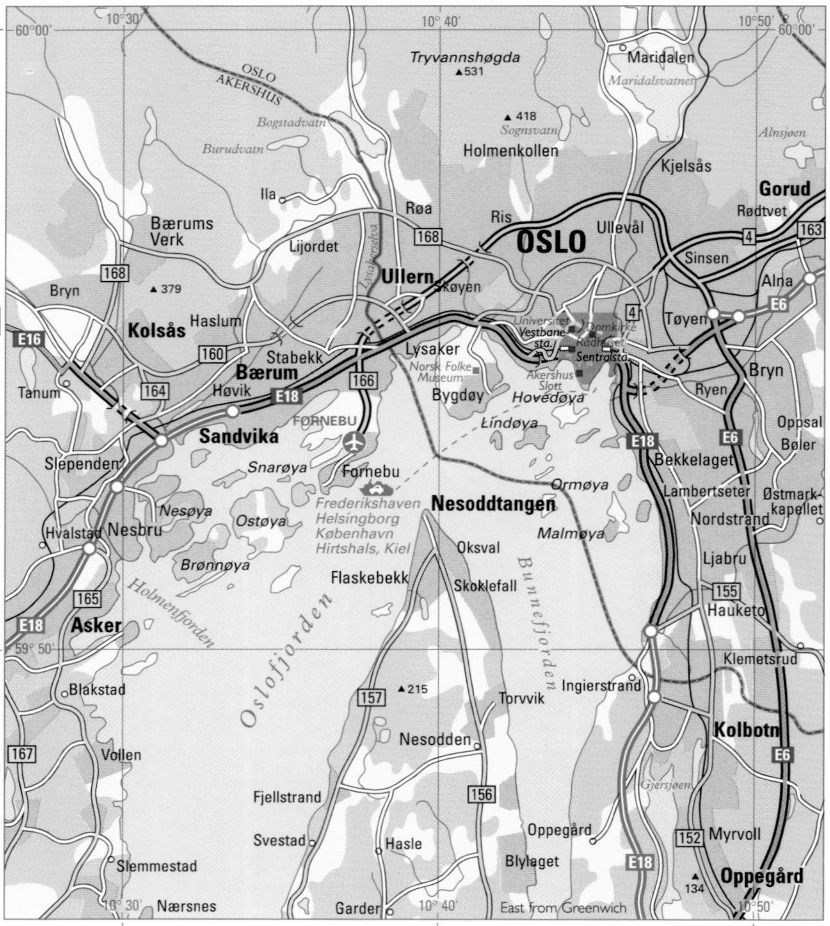

## Central Oslo

km 0.5
miles 0.25

Rikshospitalet
Vår Frelsers Gravlund
Nordre gate
PARKVEIEN
Wethaves gate
Steensberg g.
Westye Egebergs gate
Korsgata
Markveien
HEGDEHAUGSVEIEN
WERGELANDSVEIEN
Vor Frue hospitalet
Damstredet
Rostedsgt.
Torvald Meyers gate
Slotts parken
Kunstindustri mus.
St. Olavs-kirche
Akerselva
Det Kongelige Slottet
St. Olavs gate
Deichmanske bibliotek
KRISTIAN FREDERIKS GATE
Historisk museum
Møllergata
a
DRAMMENSVEIEN
Dronningparken
Nasjonal galleriet
Kristian Augusts gate
Keysersgt.
Apotekergata
RING 1
Universitet
HENRIK IBSEN
PILES FREDET
Ibsen-museet
National-theatret
National theatret
Det Norske Teater
VATERLANDS TUNNELEN
Oslo Spektrum
Stenersen-museet
Klingenbergata
Fridtjof Nansens plass
Operaen
STENERSGATA
Ruseløkk
Konserthuset
Stortinget
MØLLERGATA
Youngs-torget
GRENSEN
b
RING 1
Vestbane stasjonen
Karl Johans gate
Domkirke
Jernbane Torget
Busstorminalen
MUNKEDAMSVEIEN
Rådhuset
Hovedpost kontoret
Sentralstasjon
Dokkveien
Rådhusgata
Christiania torv
Havnegata
NYLANDSVEIEN
Teater-museet
Arkitekt museet
Børsen
BISPEGATA
OSLOTUNNELEN
Hjemmefront-museet
Myntgata
Astrup Fearnley museet
Bispelokket
Museet for samtidskunst
Akershus Slott og festning
Palékaia
Bispevika
Pipervika
Forsvars-museet
Bjørvika
Frederikshaven Helsingborg Hirtshals Kiel København

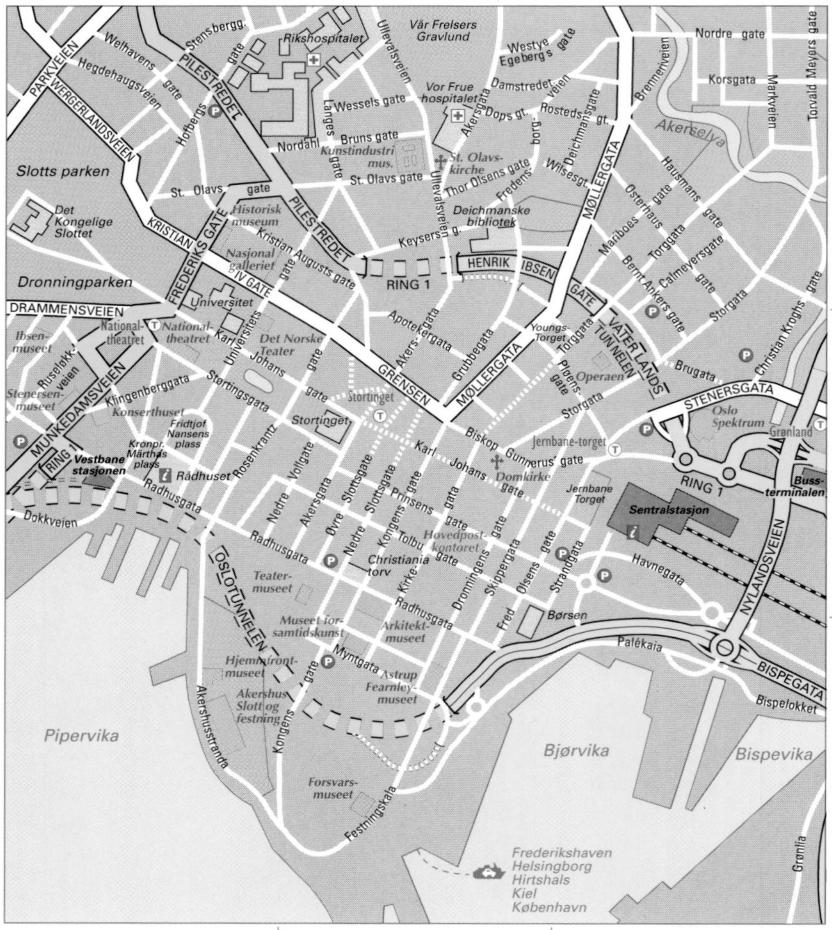

# Paris

km 5
miles 3

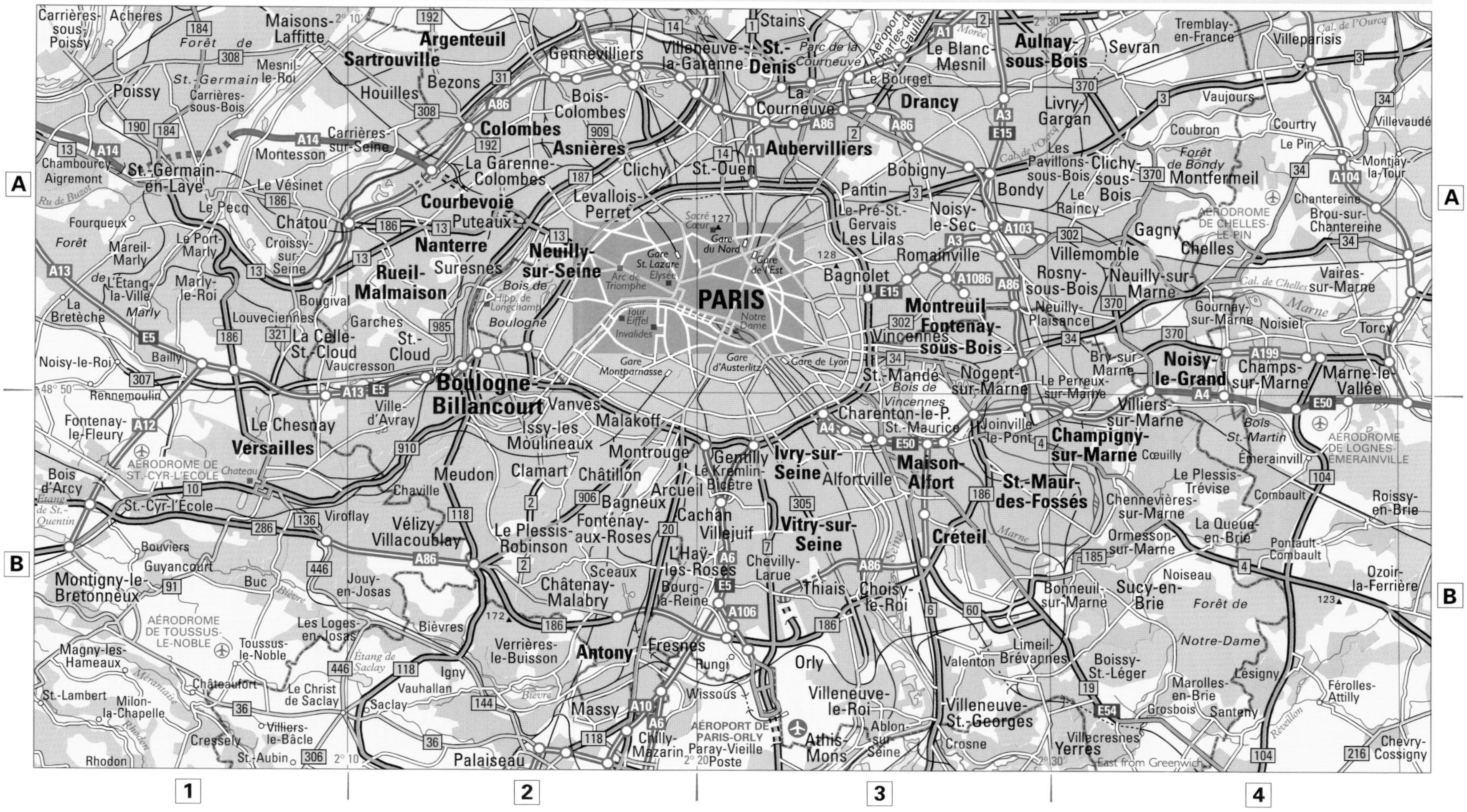

Carrières-sous-Poissy · Achères · Maisons-Laffitte · Argenteuil · Sartrouville · Gennevilliers · Villeneuve-la-Garenne · St.-Denis · Stains · Parc de la Courneuve · Le Blanc Mesnil · Aulnay-sous-Bois · Sevran · Tremblay-en-France · Villeparisis
Poissy · Mesnil-le-Roi · Houilles · Bezons · Bois-Colombes · La Courneuve · Le Bourget · Drancy · Livry-Gargan · Vaujours · Coubron · Courtry · Le Pin · Forêt de Bondy · Montfermeil · Villevaudé
St.-Germain-en-Laye · Le Vésinet · Colombes · Asnières · Clichy · St.-Ouen · Pantin · Aubervilliers · Bobigny · Noisy-le-Sec · Les Lilas · Romainville · Villemomble · Gagny · Chelles · Chantereine · Brou-sur-Chantereine
Courbevoie · Puteaux · La Garenne-Colombes · Levallois-Perret · Le Pré-St.-Gervais · Bagnolet · Rosny-sous-Bois · Neuilly-sur-Marne · Vaires-sur-Marne
Nanterre · Neuilly-sur-Seine · Sacré Cœur · Gare St.-Lazare · Gare du Nord · Gare de l'Est · **PARIS** · Montreuil · Fontenay-sous-Bois · Vincennes · Neuilly-Plaisance · Bry-sur-Marne · Noisy-le-Grand · Champs-sur-Marne · Marne-la-Vallée
Rueil-Malmaison · Suresnes · Arc de Triomphe · Tour Eiffel · Invalides · Gare de Lyon · St.-Mandé · Nogent-sur-Marne · Le Perreux-sur-Marne · Villiers-sur-Marne · Torcy
St.-Cloud · Vaucresson · Boulogne-Billancourt · Vanves · Malakoff · Gare Montparnasse · Gare d'Austerlitz · Charenton-le-P. · St.-Maurice · Joinville-le-Pont · Champigny-sur-Marne · Cœuilly · Émerainville
Versailles · Le Chesnay · Ville-d'Avray · Issy-les-Moulineaux · Montrouge · Gentilly · Le Kremlin-Bicêtre · Ivry-sur-Seine · Alfortville · Maisons-Alfort · St.-Maur-des-Fossés · Le Plessis-Trévise · Chennevières-sur-Marne · La Queue-en-Brie · Roissy-en-Brie
St.-Cyr-l'École · Meudon · Clamart · Châtillon · Bagneux · Arcueil · Cachan · Villejuif · Vitry-sur-Seine · Créteil · Ormesson-sur-Marne
Montigny-le-Bretonneux · Guyancourt · Vélizy-Villacoublay · Le Plessis-Robinson · Fontenay-aux-Roses · Sceaux · L'Haÿ-les-Roses · Bourg-la-Reine · Chevilly-Larue · Thiais · Choisy-le-Roi · Bonneuil-sur-Marne · Sucy-en-Brie · Forêt de Notre-Dame · Ozoir-la-Ferrière
Magny-les-Hameaux · Toussus-le-Noble · Châtenay-Malabry · Verrières-le-Buisson · Antony · Fresnes · Rungis · Orly · Valenton · Limeil-Brévannes · Boissy-St.-Léger
St.-Lambert · Milon-la-Chapelle · Le Christ de Saclay · Igny · Vauhallan · Saclay · Wissous · Villeneuve-le-Roi · Ablon-sur-Seine · Crosne · Villecresnes · Marolles-en-Brie · Grosbois · Santeny
Rhodon · Cressely · Villiers-le-Bâcle · St.-Aubin · Palaiseau · Massy · Chilly-Mazarin · Paray-Vieille-Poste · AÉROPORT DE PARIS-ORLY · Athis-Mons · Villeneuve-St.-Georges · Yerres · Chevry-Cossigny

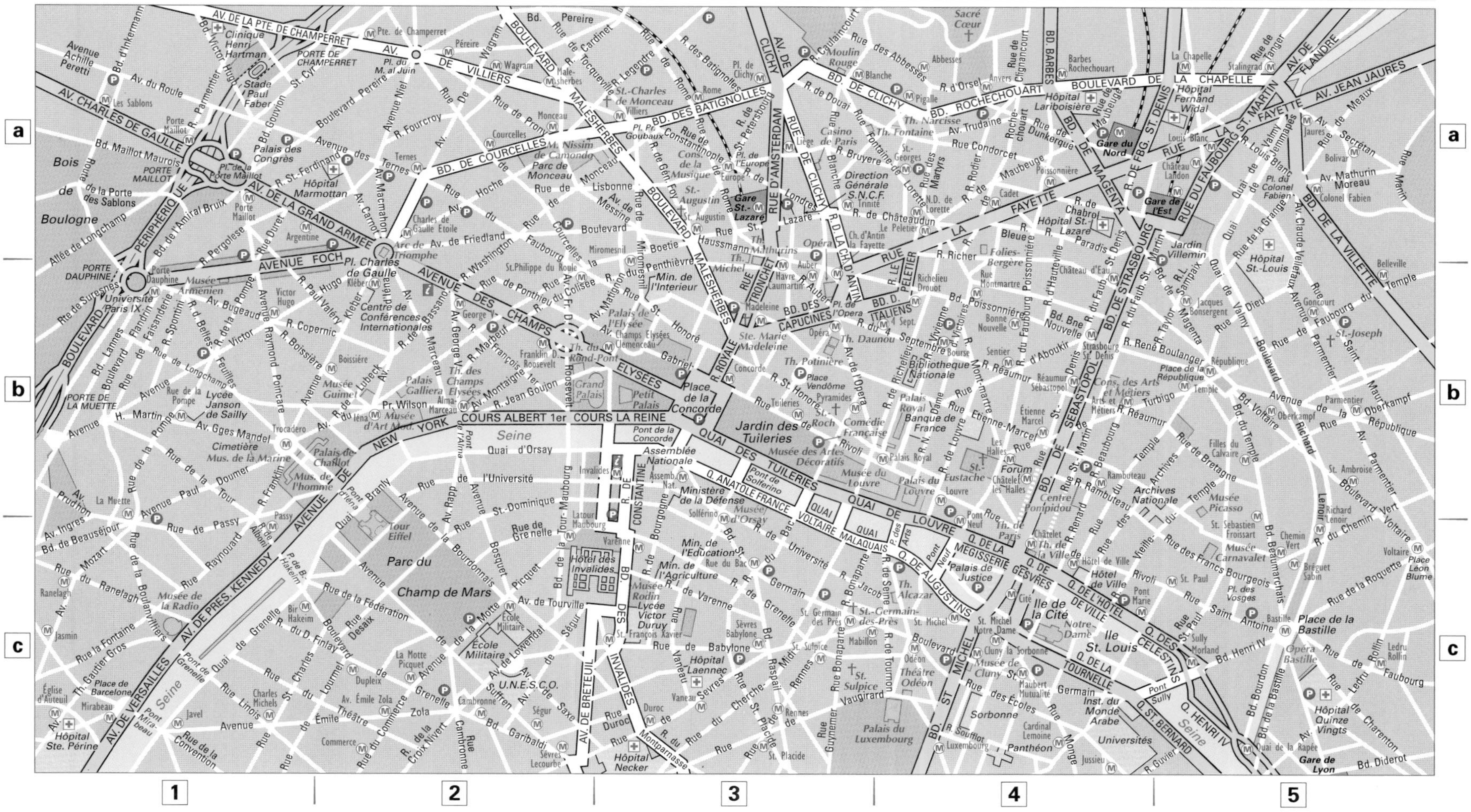

# Central Paris

km 1
miles 0.5

Bois de Boulogne · Porte Dauphine · Av. Foch · Arc de Triomphe · Place Charles de Gaulle Étoile · Av. des Champs Élysées · Gare St.-Lazare · Gare du Nord · Gare de l'Est
Palais des Congrès · Parc Monceau · Opéra · La Chapelle
Trocadéro · Palais de Chaillot · Place de la Concorde · Jardin des Tuileries · Palais du Louvre · Centre Pompidou · Musée Picasso
Tour Eiffel · Champ de Mars · École Militaire · U.N.E.S.C.O. · Hôtel des Invalides · Musée d'Orsay · St.-Germain-des-Prés · Île de la Cité · Notre Dame · Île St.-Louis · Place de la Bastille · Opéra Bastille
Palais du Luxembourg · Panthéon · Universités · Gare de Lyon

## Prague

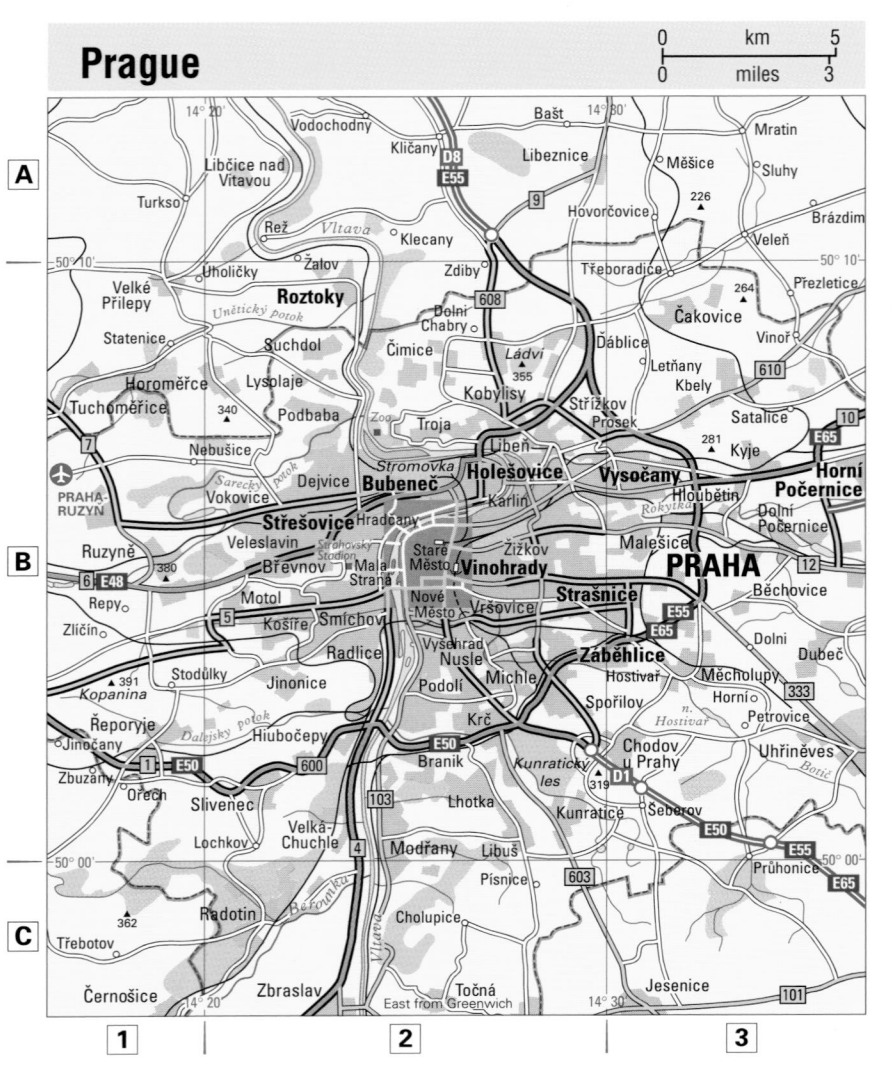

## Central Prague

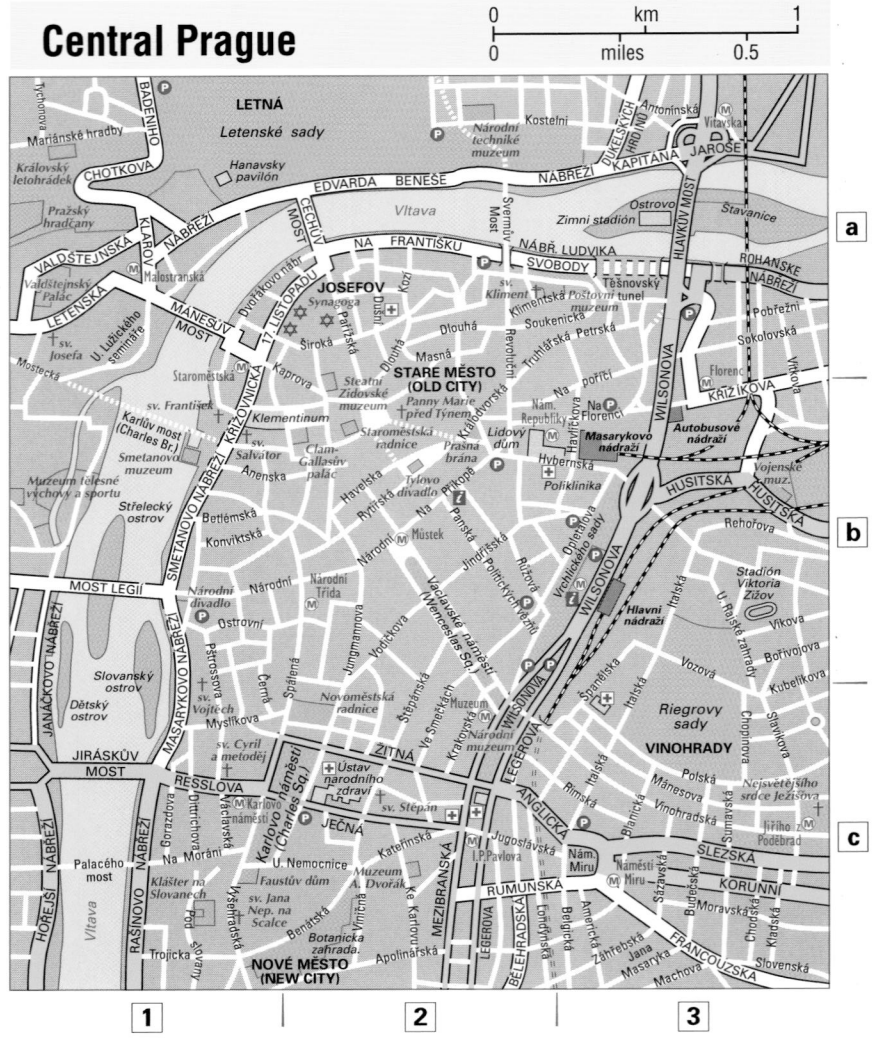

## Rio de Janeiro

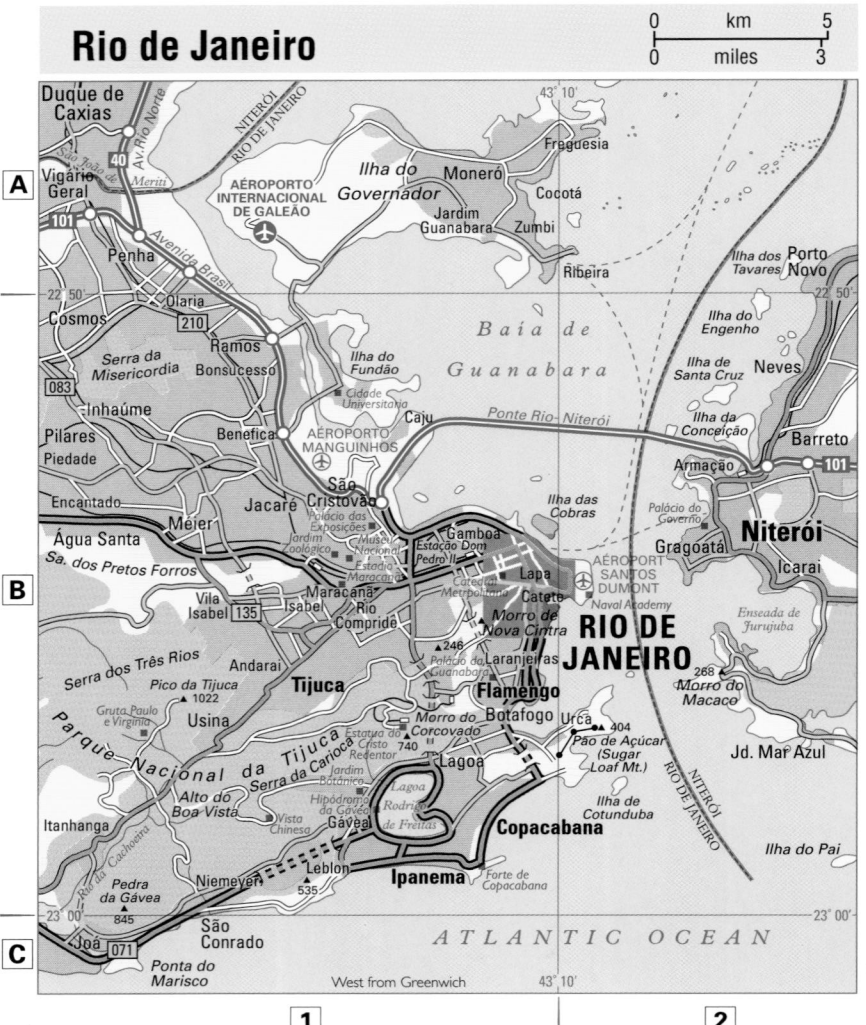

## Central Rio de Janeiro

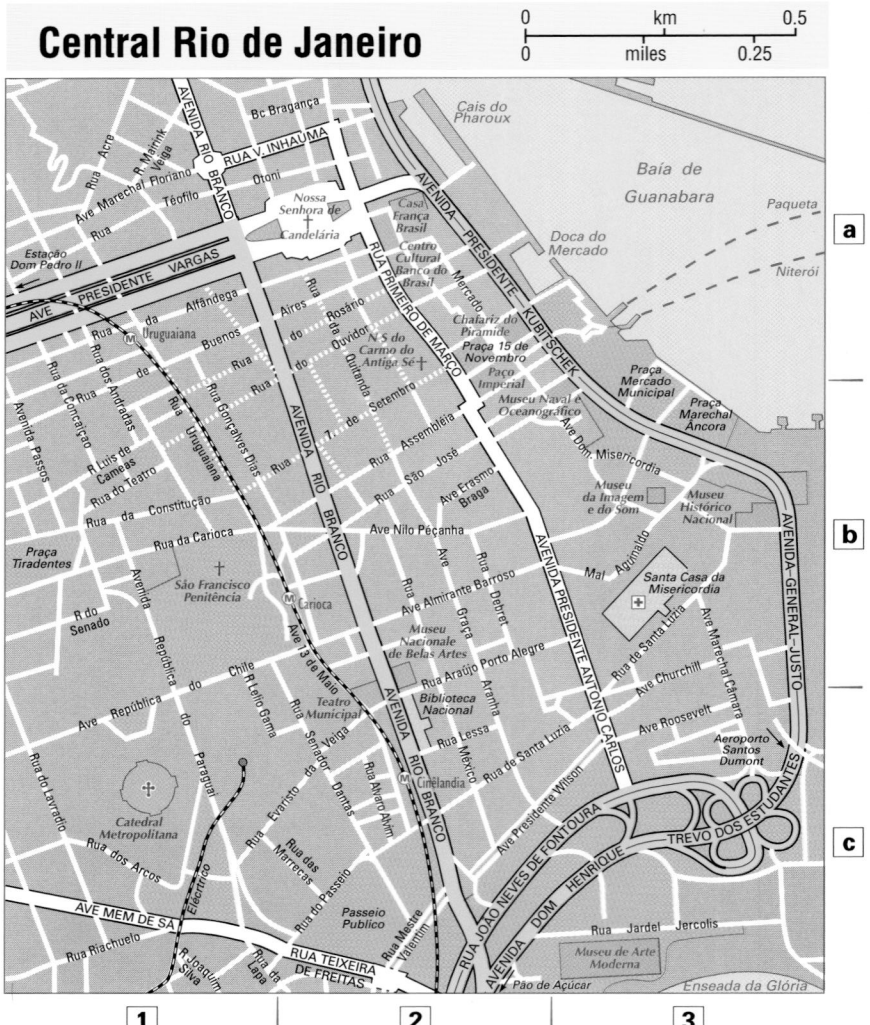

## Rome

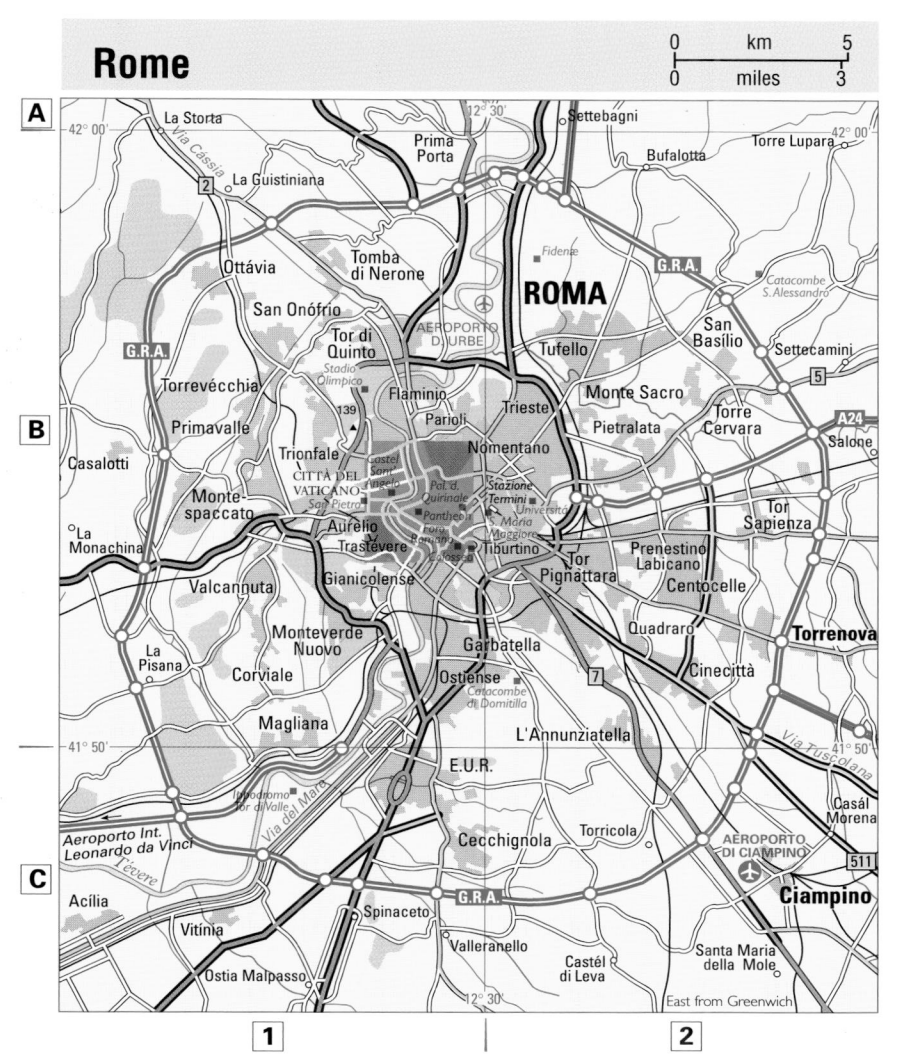

## Central Rome

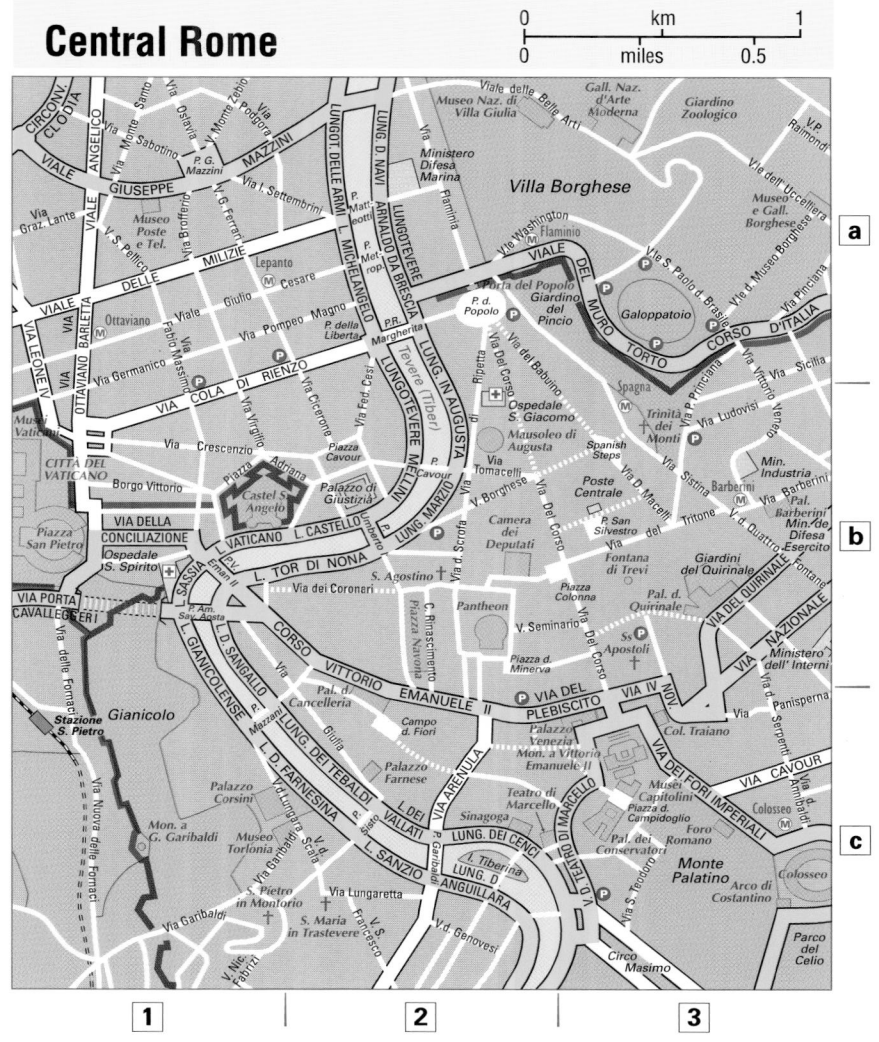

## San Francisco

## Central San Francisco

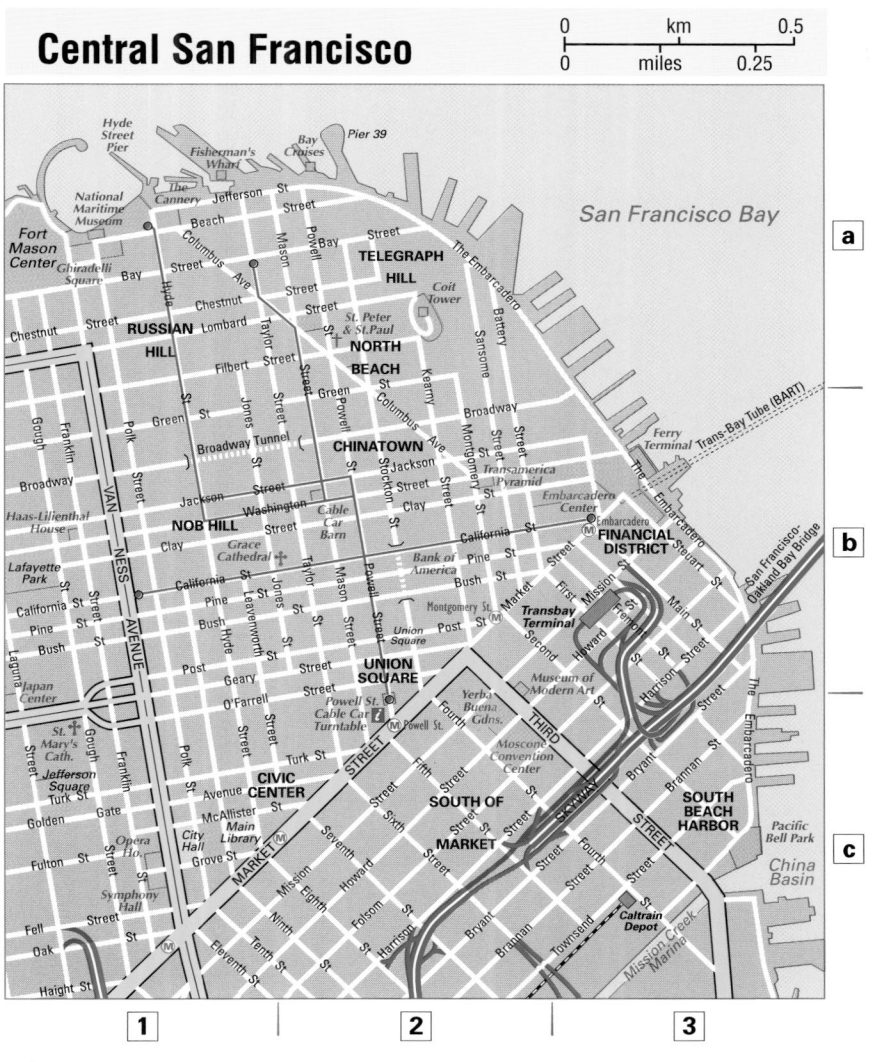

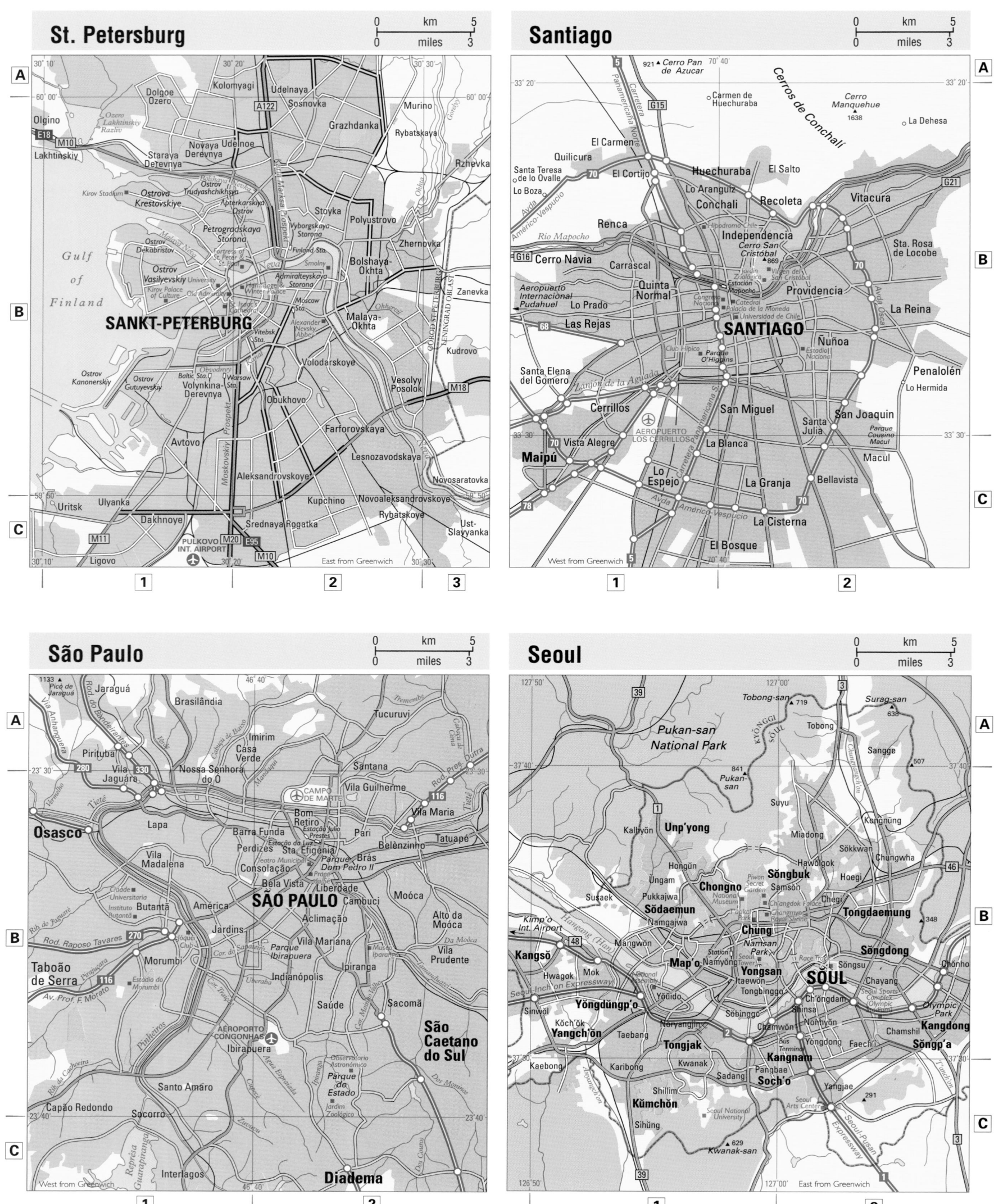

COPYRIGHT GEORGE PHILIP LTD.

## Shanghai

0 km 5
0 miles 3

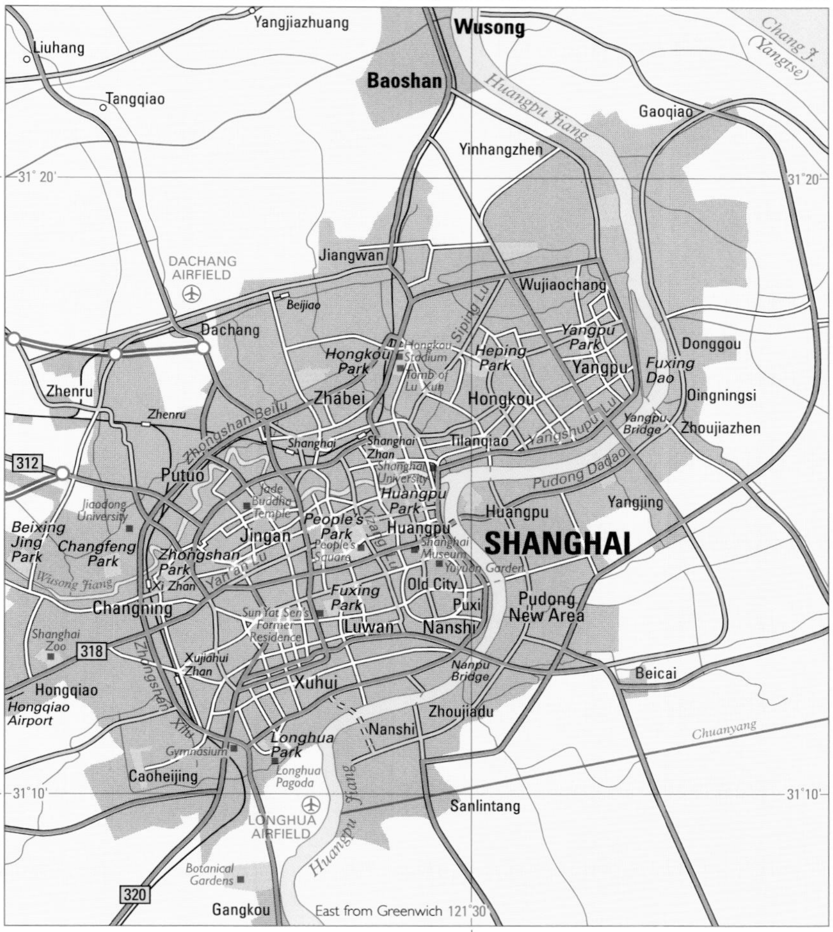

A

Liuhang
Yangjiazhuang
Wusong
Tangqiao
Baoshan
Huangpu Jiang
Chang J. (Yangtse)
Yinhangzhen
Gaoqiao
31° 20'

Dachang Airfield
Jiangwan
Wujiaochang
Donggou

Zhenru
Dachang
Beijiao
Hongkou Park
Heping Park
Yangpu
Fuxing Dao
Zhabei
Yangpu
Hongkou
Qingningsi
Zhoujiazhen
Yangjing

B
312
Putuo
Jiaodong University
Zhenru
Hongkou
Tilangiao
Yangpu Bridge
Pudong Dadao

Beixing Jing Jing Park
Changfeng Park
Jingan
Huangpu Park
People's Park
Huangpu
SHANGHAI
Huangpu
Yangjing

Shanghai Zoo
Zhongshan Park
Xi Zhan
Yan'an
People's Square
Old City
Fuxing Park
Puxi
Pudong New Area
Beicai

Changning
Xuihui
Xuhui
Nanshi
Nanpu Bridge
Zhoujiadu

318
Caoheijing
Longhua Park
Longhua Pagoda
Nanshi
Zhoujiadu

C
31° 10'
LONGHUA AIRFIELD
Sanlintang
Chuanyang

320
Botanical Gardens
Gangkou
East from Greenwich 121° 30'

1    2

## Central Singapore

0 km 1
0 miles 0.5

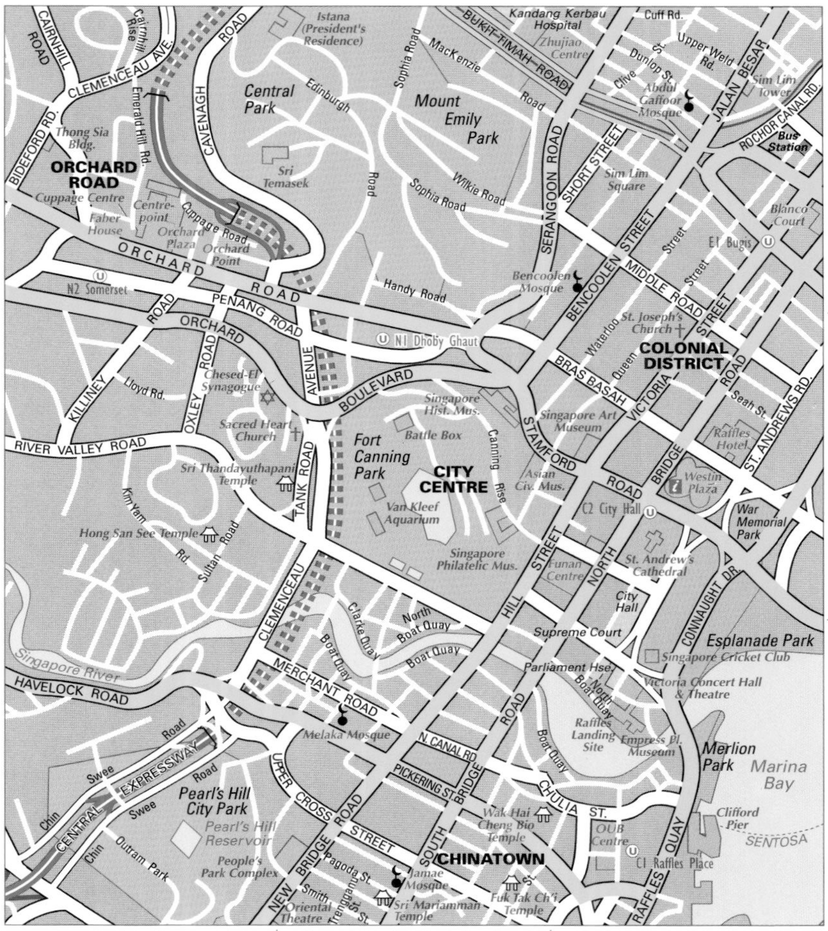

CAIRNHILL ROAD
CLEMENCEAU AVE
Istana (President's Residence)
Kandang Kerbau Hospital
Cuff Rd
BUKIT TIMAH ROAD
Zhujiao Centre
Upper Weld Rd
ROCHOR CANAL RD

a
BIDEFORD RD
Thong Sia Bldg.
Central Park
Edinburgh
Mount Emily Park
Sophia Road
MacKenzie
Sophia Road
SERANGOON ROAD
SHORT STREET
Sim Lim Tower
Abdul Gaffoor Mosque
JALAN BESAR
Bus Station

ORCHARD ROAD
Cuppage Centre
Centre-point
Faber House
Emerald Hill Rd
Sri Temasek
Wilkie Road
Sophia Road
Sim Lim Square
Blanco Court

N2 Somerset
ORCHARD ROAD
Cuppage Road
Orchard Point
Handy Road
BENCOOLEN STREET
MIDDLE ROAD
Bencoolen Mosque
St. Joseph's Church
COLONIAL DISTRICT

b
PENANG ROAD
N1 Dhoby Ghaut
BRAS BASAH ROAD
Singapore Art Museum
VICTORIA STREET
Raffles Hotel

KILLINEY ROAD
ORCHARD
Chesed-El Synagogue
Lloyd Rd
OXLEY
PENANG ROAD
AVENUE
BOULEVARD
Singapore Hist. Mus.
Battle Box
Singapore Art Museum
Asian Civ. Mus.

RIVER VALLEY ROAD
Sacred Heart Church
Sri Thandayuthapani Temple
Fort Canning Park
STAMFORD ROAD
CITY CENTRE
City Hall
St. Andrew's Cathedral
War Memorial Park

TANK ROAD
Canning Rise
HILL STREET
NORTH BRIDGE ROAD
City Hall
Westin Plaza

Hong San See Temple
Van Kleef Aquarium
Singapore Philatelic Mus.
CLEMENCEAU

c
Clarke Quay
Singapore River
North Boat Quay
Boat Quay
Supreme Court
Parliament Hse.
Raffles Landing Site
Empress Pl.
Victoria Concert Hall & Theatre
Esplanade Park
Singapore Cricket Club

HAVELOCK ROAD
MERCHANT ROAD
Melaka Mosque
Merlion Park
Marina Bay

EXPRESSWAY
Swee
Pearl's Hill City Park
Pearl's Hill Reservoir
PICKERING ST.
UPPER CROSS ROAD
SOUTH BRIDGE
N CANAL RD
Wak Hai Cheng Bio Temple
CHULIA ST.
Raffles Quay
OUB Centre
Clifford Pier
SENTOSA

CENTRAL
Chin
Swee
People's Park Complex
Chin
NEW BRIDGE
Pagoda St.
CHINATOWN
Jamae Mosque
Sri Mariamman Temple
Fuk Tak Chi Temple
Cl Raffles Place

Oriental Theatre

1    2    3

## Singapore

0 km 10
0 miles 6

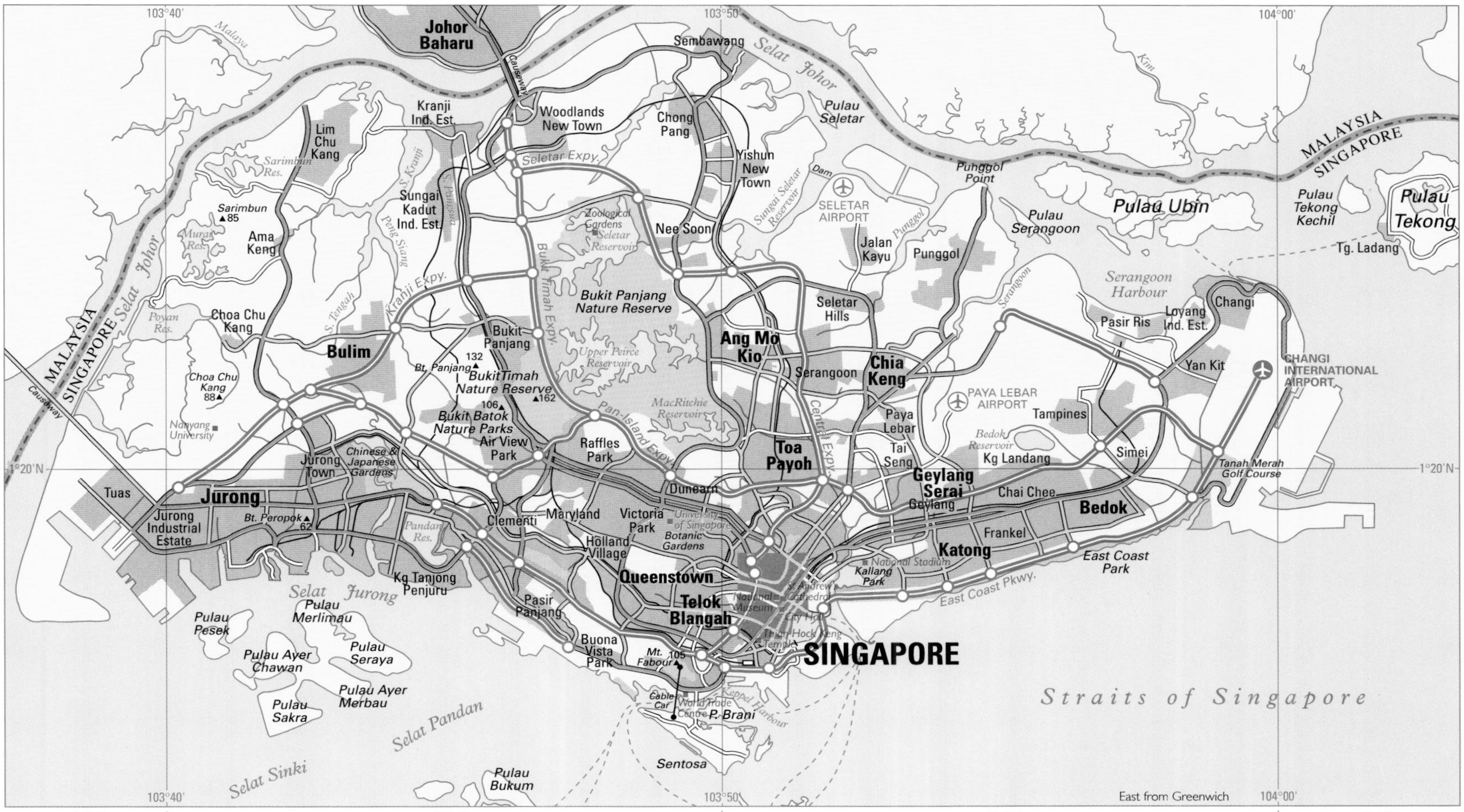

103° 40'
Malaya
Johor Baharu
Sembawang
Selat Johor
104° 00'
MALAYSIA SINGAPORE

Causeway
Kranji Ind. Est.
Woodlands New Town
Chong Pang
Pulau Seletar
Punggol Point
Pulau Tekong Kechil
Pulau Tekong

A
MALAYSIA SINGAPORE
Selat Johor
Lim Chu Kang
Sarimbun Res.
Sungai Kadut Ind. Est.
Yishun New Town
Zoological Gardens
Seletar Reservoir
SELETAR AIRPORT
Pulau Serangoon
Pulau Ubin
Serangoon Harbour
Changi
Pulau Tekong
Tg. Ladang
A

Sarimbun 85
Ama Keng
Sungei Seletar Reservoir
Nee Soon
Jalan Kayu
Punggol
Loyang Ind. Est.
Pasir Ris

Murai Res.
Choa Chu Kang
Poyan Res.
Bukit Panjang Nature Reserve
Upper Peirce Reservoir
Seletar Hills
Serangoon
Bukit Panjang
Bt. Panjang 132
Bukit Timah Nature Reserve
MacRitchie Reservoirs
Ang Mo Kio
Chia Keng
Paya Lebar
PAYA LEBAR AIRPORT
CHANGI INTERNATIONAL AIRPORT

Nanyang University
Bulim
Choa Chu Kang 88
Bukit Batok Nature Parks
Air View Park
Bt. Timah 162
Raffles Park
Serangoon
Toa Payoh
Paya Lebar
Tai Seng
Tampines
Yan Kit

Jurong Town
Chinese & Japanese Gardens
Dunearn
Geylang Serai
Kg Landang
Bedok Reservoir
Simei
Tanah Merah Golf Course

1° 20'N
Jurong
Bt. Peropok 62
Clementi
Maryland
Victoria Park
University of Singapore Botanic Gardens
Geylang
Chai Chee
Bedok
1° 20'N

Tuas
JURONG INDUSTRIAL ESTATE
Pandan Res.
Holland Village
Queenstown
Telok Blangah
Katong
Frankel
East Coast Park

Kg Tanjong Penjuru
Pasir Panjang
Buona Vista Park
Mt. Faber 106
Kallang Park
National Stadium
East Coast Pkwy.

B
Selat Jurong
Pulau Merlimau
Pulau Pesek
Cable Car
World Trade Centre
P. Brani
SINGAPORE
Straits of Singapore
B

Pulau Ayer Chawan
Pulau Seraya
Pulau Ayer Merbau
Pulau Sakra
Selat Pandan
Sentosa

Selat Sinki
Pulau Bukum
103° 40'
103° 50'
East from Greenwich
104° 00'

1    2    3    4

## Stockholm

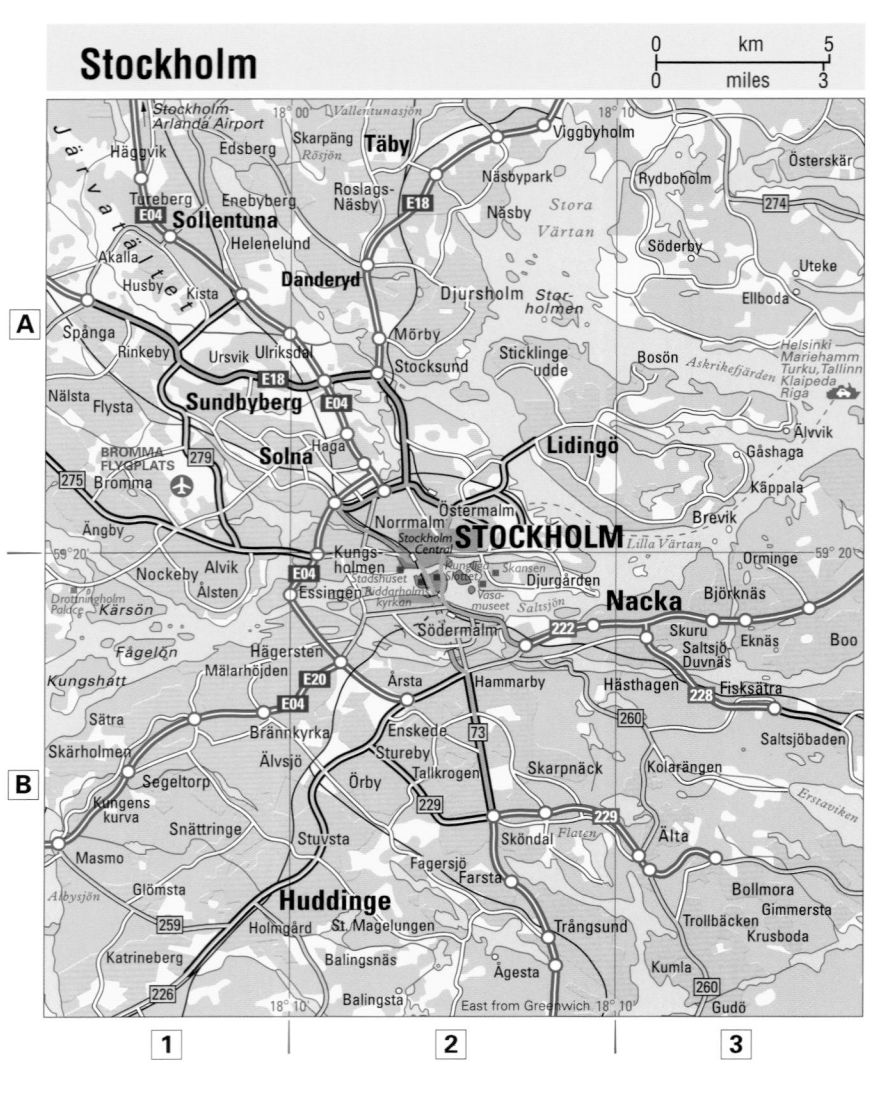

## Central Stockholm

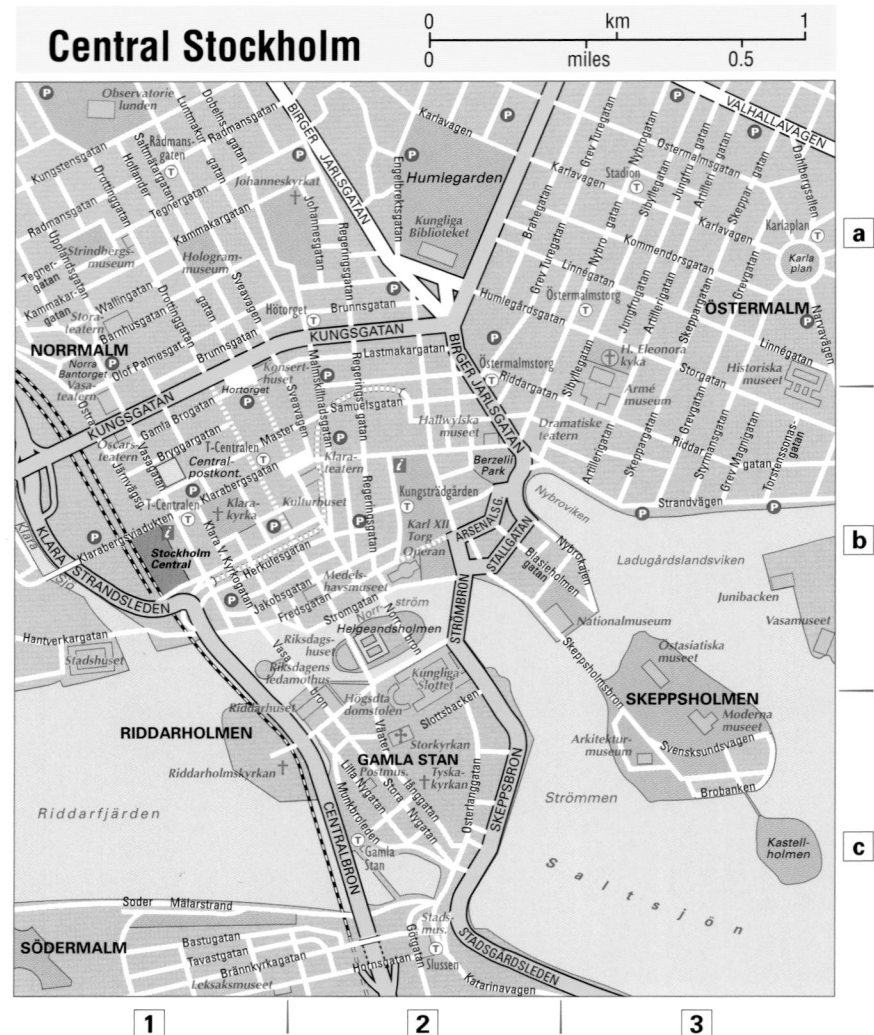

## Sydney

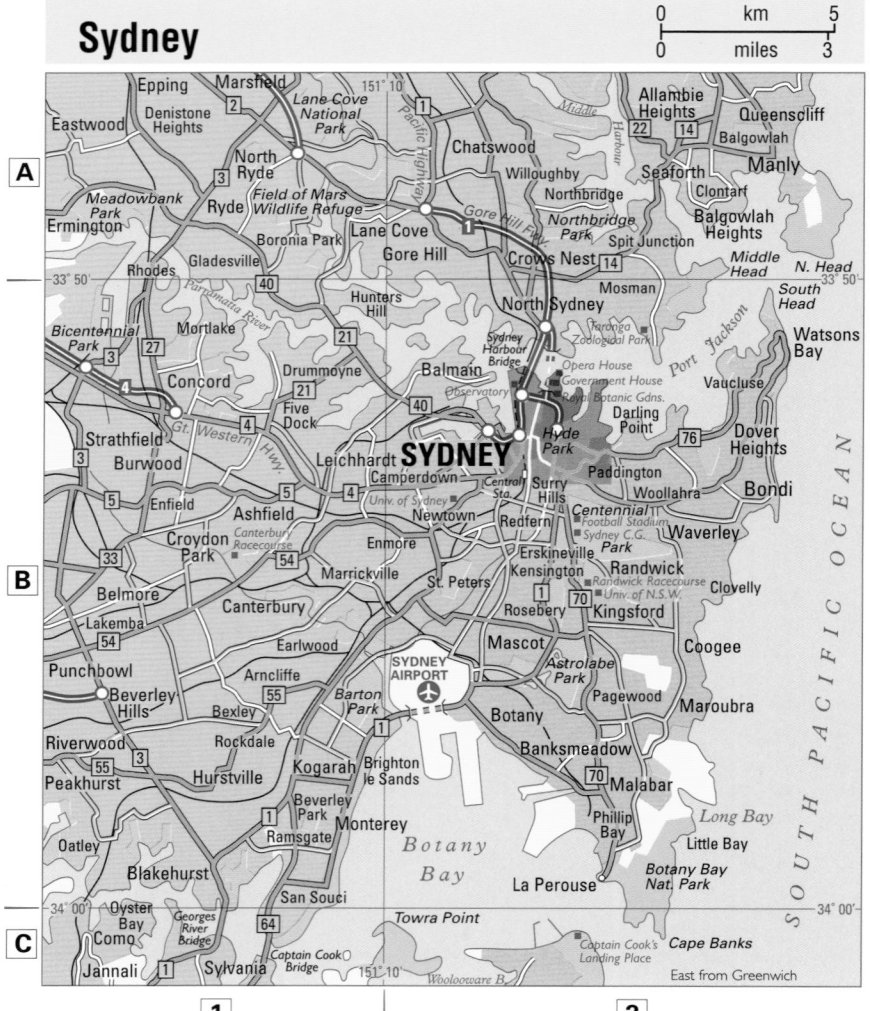

## Central Sydney

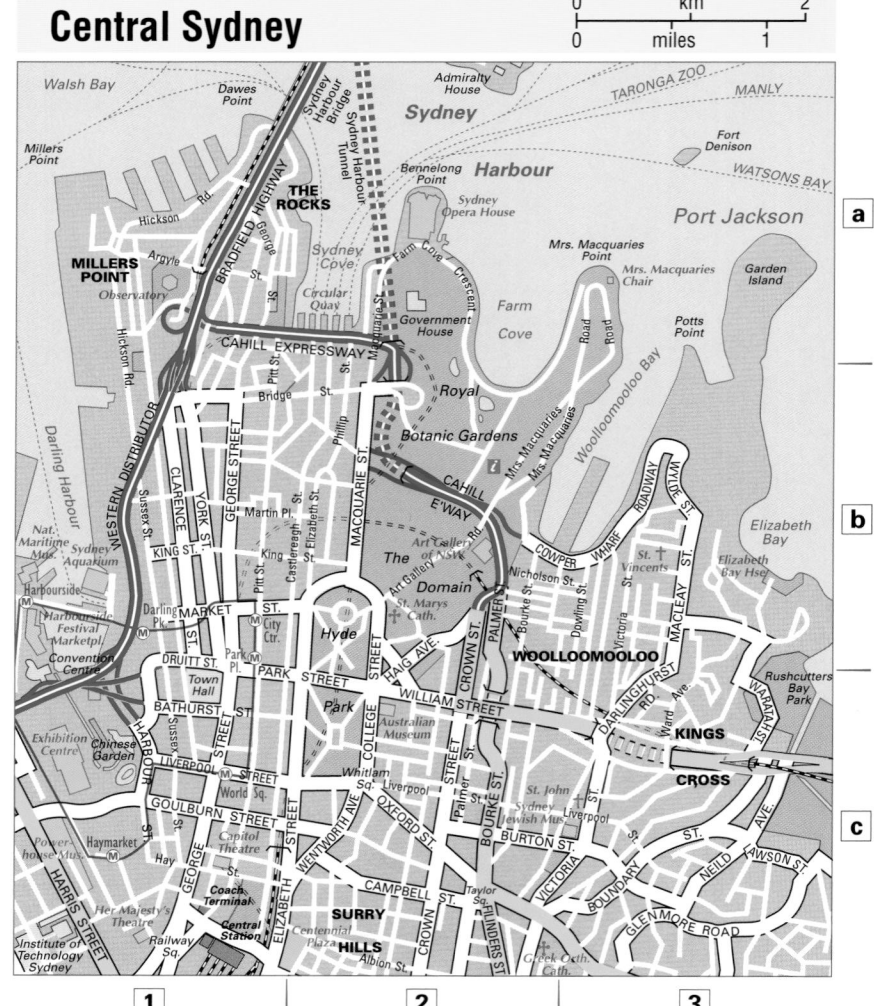

# Tokyo

0 km 5
0 miles 3

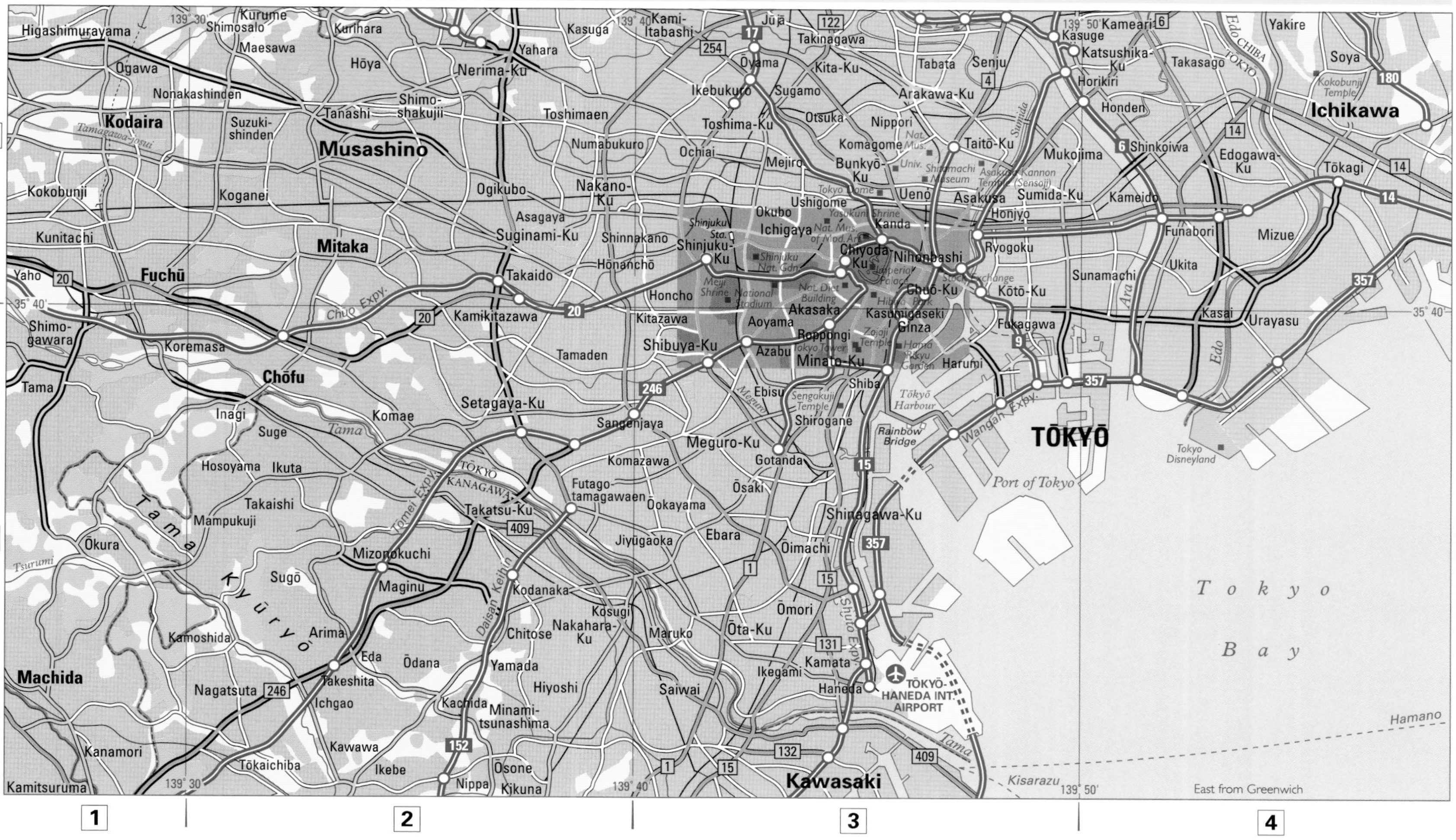

A

Higashimurayama · Kurume · Shimosalo · Shimosa · Kasuga · Jūjō · Kami-Itabashi · 122 · Takinagawa · Kameari · Kasuge · Katsushika-Ku · Takasago · Soya · Yakire · Tokagi

Kodaira · Ogawa · Nonakashinden · Maesawa · Kurihara · Yahara · Nerima-Ku · Ōyama · Kita-Ku · Tabata · Senju · Horikiri · Honden · Kokubunji Temple · 180 · Ichikawa

Musashino · Hōya · Suzuki-shinden · Tanashi · Shimo-shakujii · Ikebukuro · Sugamo · Otsuka · Nippori · Komagome · Mukojima · Shinkoiwa · Edogawa-Ku · 14

Kokubunji · Koganei · Ogikubo · Nakano-Ku · Numabukuro · Ochiai · Mejiro · Bunkyō-Ku · Univ. · Asakusa · Sumida-Ku · Kameido · Mizue · 14

Kunitachi · Mitaka · Asagaya · Suginami-Ku · Shinnakano · Honanchō · Okubo · Ichigaya · Kanda · Honjyo · Ryogoku · Funabori · Tōkagi

Yaho · Fuchū · Takaido · 20 · Kamikitazawa · Kitazawa · Shibuya-Ku · Aoyama · Roppongi · Ginza · Kōtō-Ku · Sunamachi · Kasai · Urayasu · 357

Shimo-gawara · Koremasa · Tama · Chōfu · Tamaden · 246 · Azabu · Minato-Ku · Shiba · Harumi · Wangan Expy. · TŌKYŌ · Tokyo Disneyland

Inagi · Suge · Setagaya-Ku · Sangenjaya · Komazawa · Meguro-Ku · Ebisu · Shirogane · Tōkyō Harbour · Rainbow Bridge · Port of Tokyo

Hosoyama · Ikuta · Komae · Futago-tamagawaen · Ōokayama · Gotanda · Shinagawa-Ku

Takaishi · Mampukuji · Mizonokuchi · Takatsu-Ku · 409 · Kodanaka · Ōsaki · Ōimachi · 357 · Tokyo Bay

Ōkura · Sugō · Maginu · Chitose · Nakahara-Ku · Ōmori

Kamoshida · Arima · Eda · Kosugi · Kata · Ōta-Ku · Kamata · Ikegami

Machida · Nagatsuta · 246 · Takeshita · Ōdana · Yamada · Hiyoshi · Saiwai · Minami-tsunashima · Haneda · TŌKYŌ HANEDA INT. AIRPORT

Kanamori · Ichgao · Kawawa · Kachida · Hamano

Kamitsuruma · Tōkaichiba · Ikebe · 152 · Ōsone · Nippa · Kikuna · Kawasaki · Kisarazu · East from Greenwich

1 2 3 4

# Central Tokyo

0 km 1
0 miles 0.5

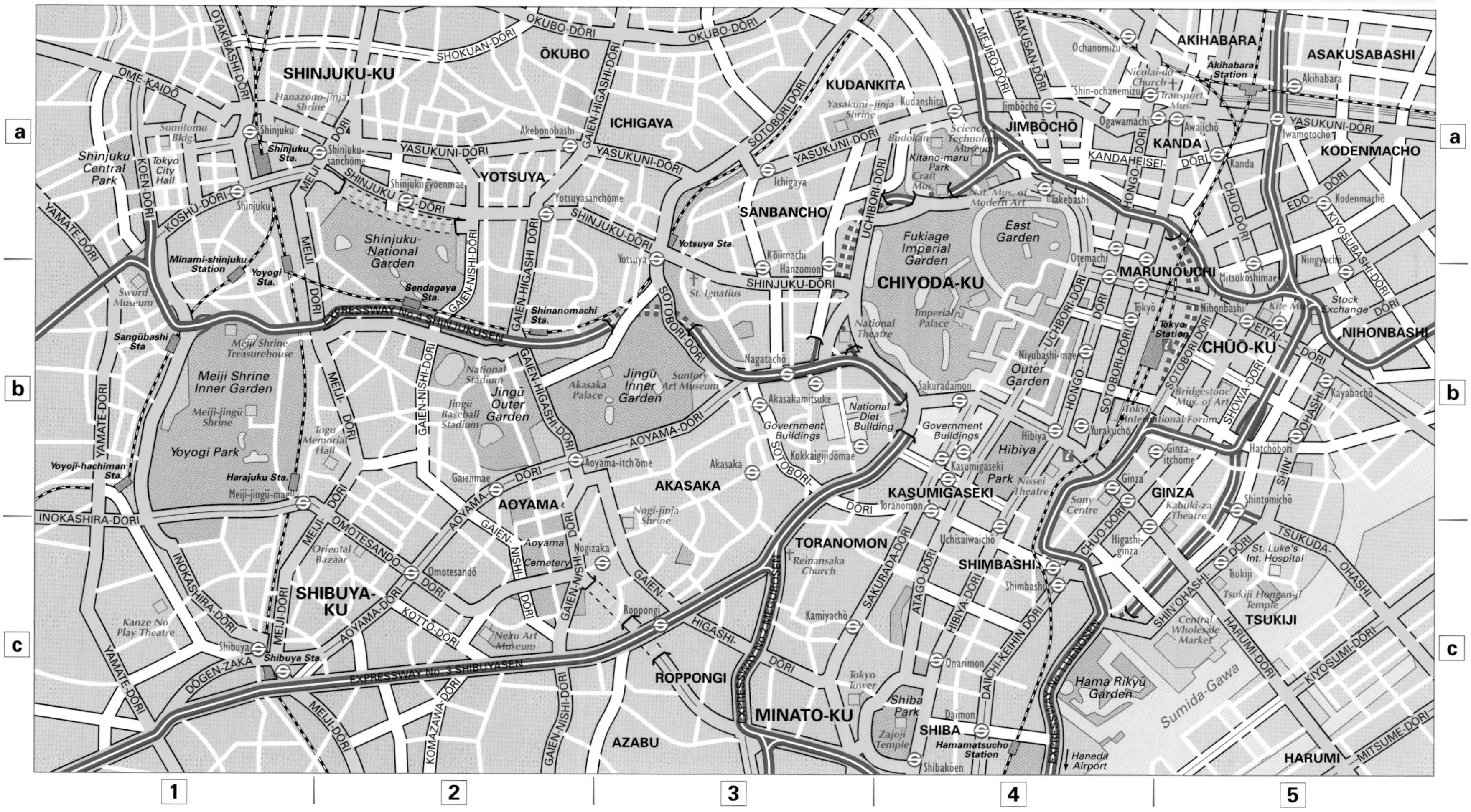

a

ŌKUBO · SHINJUKU-KU · OKUBO-DORI · KUDANKITA · AKIHABARA · ASAKUSABASHI

ICHIGAYA · YOTSUYA · SANBANCHO · JIMBŌCHŌ · KANDA · KODENMACHO

Shinjuku Sta. · Shinjuku-National Garden · Fukiage Imperial Garden · East Garden · MARUNOUCHI · NIHONBASHI

b

Meiji Shrine Inner Garden · Jingū Outer Garden · Jingū Inner Garden · Akasaka Palace · CHIYODA-KU · Imperial Palace · CHŪO-KU

Yoyogi Park · AOYAMA · AKASAKA · National Diet Building · KASUMIGASEKI · Hibiya · GINZA

SHIBUYA-KU · ROPPONGI · TORANOMON · SHIMBASHI · TSUKIJI

c

MINATO-KU · AZABU · SHIBA · HARUMI · Hama Rikyū Garden · Sumida-Gawa

1 2 3 4 5

## Tehran

0 — km — 5
0 — miles — 3

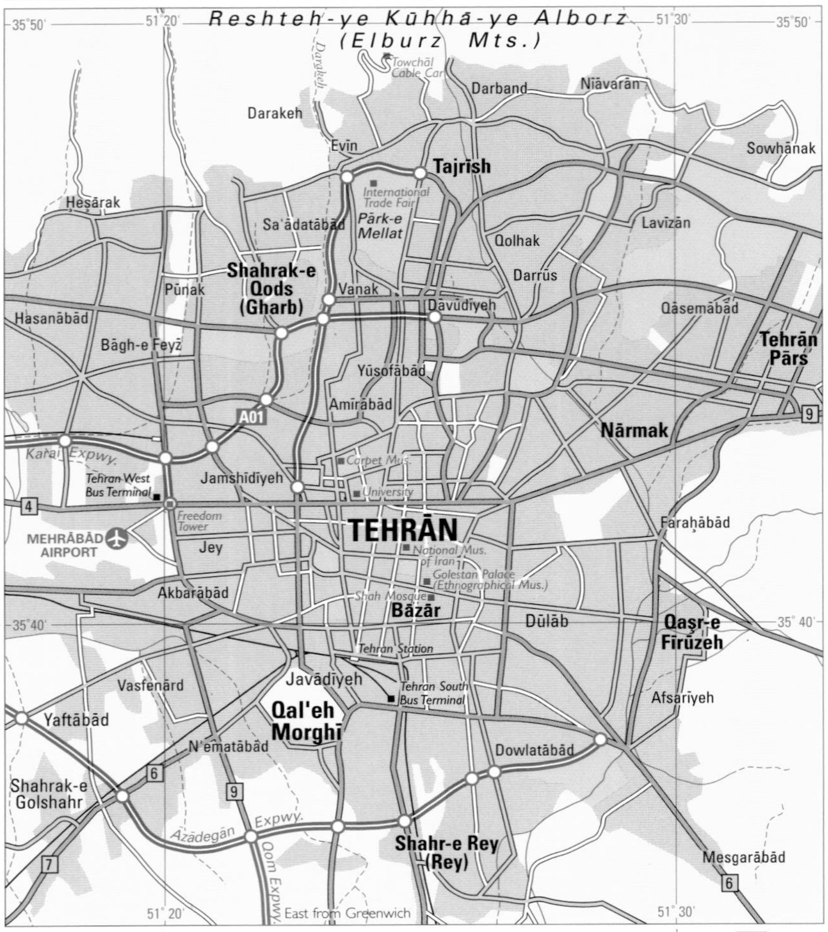

*Reshteh-ye Kūhhā-ye Alborz (Elburz Mts.)*

35°50' — 51°20' — 51°30' — 35°50'

Towchál Cable Car
Darakeh
Darband
Niāvárān
Darband
Evin
Sowhānak
**Tajrīsh**
International Trade Fair
Pārk-e Mellat
Qolhak
Lavīzān
Heşārak
Sa'ādatābād
Darrūs
Pūnak
**Shahrak-e Qods (Gharb)**
Vanak
Dāvūdīyeh
Qāsemābād
**A**
Hasanābād
**Tehrān Pārs**
Bāgh-e Feyż
Yūsofābād
Amīrābād
A01
**Nārmak**
9
Karaj Expwy.
Carpet Mus.
Tehran West Bus Terminal
Jamshīdīyeh
University
4
**MEHRĀBĀD AIRPORT**
Freedom Tower
Jey
**TEHRĀN**
National Mus. of Iran
Farahābād
Golestan Palace (Ethnographical Mus.)
Shah Mosque
Akbarābād
**Bāzār**
Dūlāb
**Qaşr-e Fīrūzeh**
35°40'
Tehran Station
Javādīyeh
Afsarīyeh
Vasfenārd
Tehran South Bus Terminal
**Qal'eh Morghī**
**B**
Yaftābād
N'ematābād
Dowlatābād
6
**Shahrak-e Golshahr**
9
Āzādegān
Qom Expwy.
Mesgarābād
7
**Shahr-e Rey (Rey)**
6
51°20' — East from Greenwich — 51°30'

**1** **2** **3**

## Tianjin

0 — km — 5
0 — miles — 3

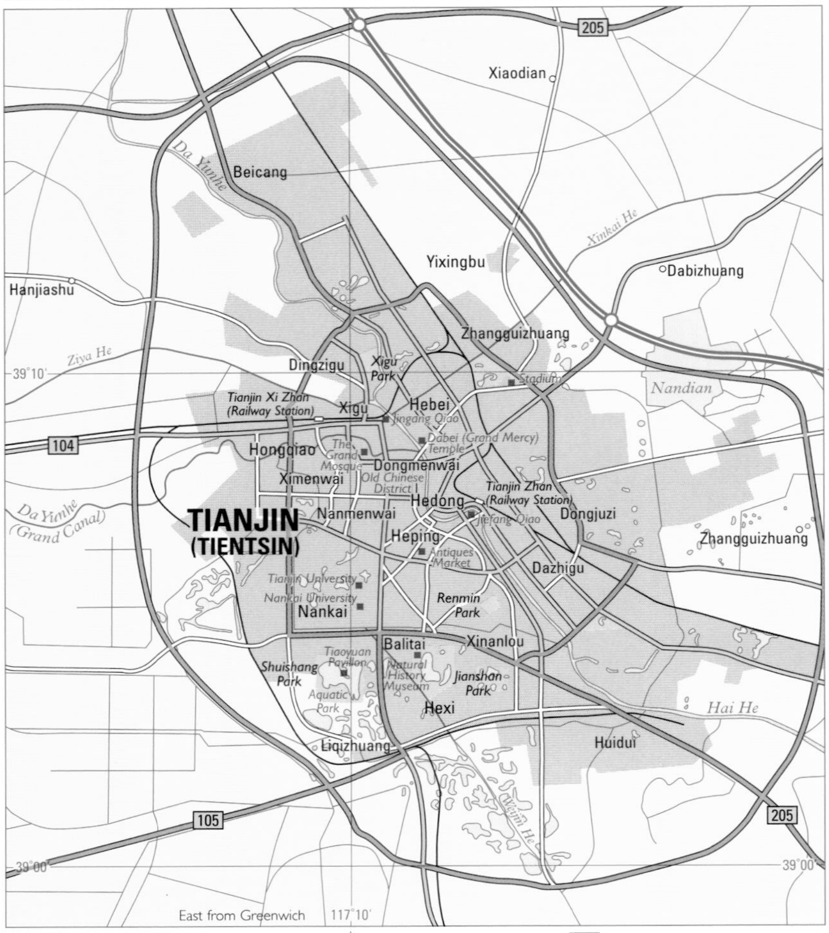

205
Xiaodian
Da Yunhe
Beicang
**A**
Hanjiashū
Yixingbu
Dabizhuang
Zhangguizhuang
39°10' — Ziya He
Dingzigu
Xigu Park
Zhangguizhuang
Tianjin Xi Zhan (Railway Station)
Xigu
Hebei
Nandian
Stadium
104
Hongqiao
Ximenwai
Hedong
Tianjin Zhan (Railway Station)
Dongjuzi
Da Yunhe (Grand Canal)
**TIANJIN (TIENTSIN)**
Nanmenwai
Dazhigu
Zhangguizhuang
Tianjin University
Nankai University
**B**
Nankai
Heping
Renmin Park
Xinanlou
Shuishang Park
Balitai
Natural History Museum
Jianshan Park
Aquatic Park
Hexi
Hai He
Liqizhuang
Huidui
105
39°00'
205
117°10' — East from Greenwich
**C**

**1** **2**

## Toronto

0 — km — 5
0 — miles — 3

79°40' — 79°30' — 79°20' — 79°10' — Fairport
27
407
Metro Toronto Zoo
Rouge
2A
401
Rouge Hill
West Rouge
407
Thornhill
Concord
East Don
**Markham**
Brown
Port Union
YORK TORONTO
Newtonbrook
48
Highland Creek
Pine Grove
Edgeley
404
Agincourt
Malvern
**Woodbridge**
Fisherville
Willowdale
11
Woburn
West Hill
York University
Humber Summit
Northmount
Bendale
Black Creek Pioneer Village
Lansing
401
Wexford
**Scarborough**
Beaumonte Heights
**North York**
York Mills
**A**
Thistletown
400
Armour Heights
Don Mills
Cliffside
Kipling Heights
DOWNSVIEW AIRPORT
Downsview
Lawrence Heights
Wilket Creek Park
427
Rexdale
Humberlea
401
Ontario Science Centre
Danforth
Malton
27
Weston
Thorncliffe
2
Woodbine Race Track
Leaside
Dentonia Park
409
Forest Hill
11
Birch Cliff
401
Humber Valley Village
Mount Dennis
5
**East York**
**TORONTO INTERNATIONAL AIRPORT (LESTER B. PEARSON)**
**York**
Casa Loma
Riverdale Park
Kew Gardens
43°40'
University of Toronto
Don Valley Pkwy.
**Etobicoke**
Lambton Mills
Swansea
Parliament Buildings
City Hall
427
Islington
Kingsway
High Park
CN Tower & SkyDome
Old Fort York
Union Sta.
**TORONTO**
Markland Wood
TORONTO YORK
Humber Bay
Parkdale
Exhibition Place
TORONTO CITY CENTRE AIRPORT
Gardiner Expy.
**B**
Burnhamthorpe
Sumerville
Humber Bay
Ontario Place
Toronto Harbour
**LAKE ONTARIO**
Hanlon
Elizabeth
Mimico
Toronto Islands
Island Park
Gibraltar Point
79°40' — New Toronto — 79°30' — West from Greenwich — 79°20' — 79°10'
2
Cooksville
**Mississauga**
Long Branch

**1** **2** **3** **4**

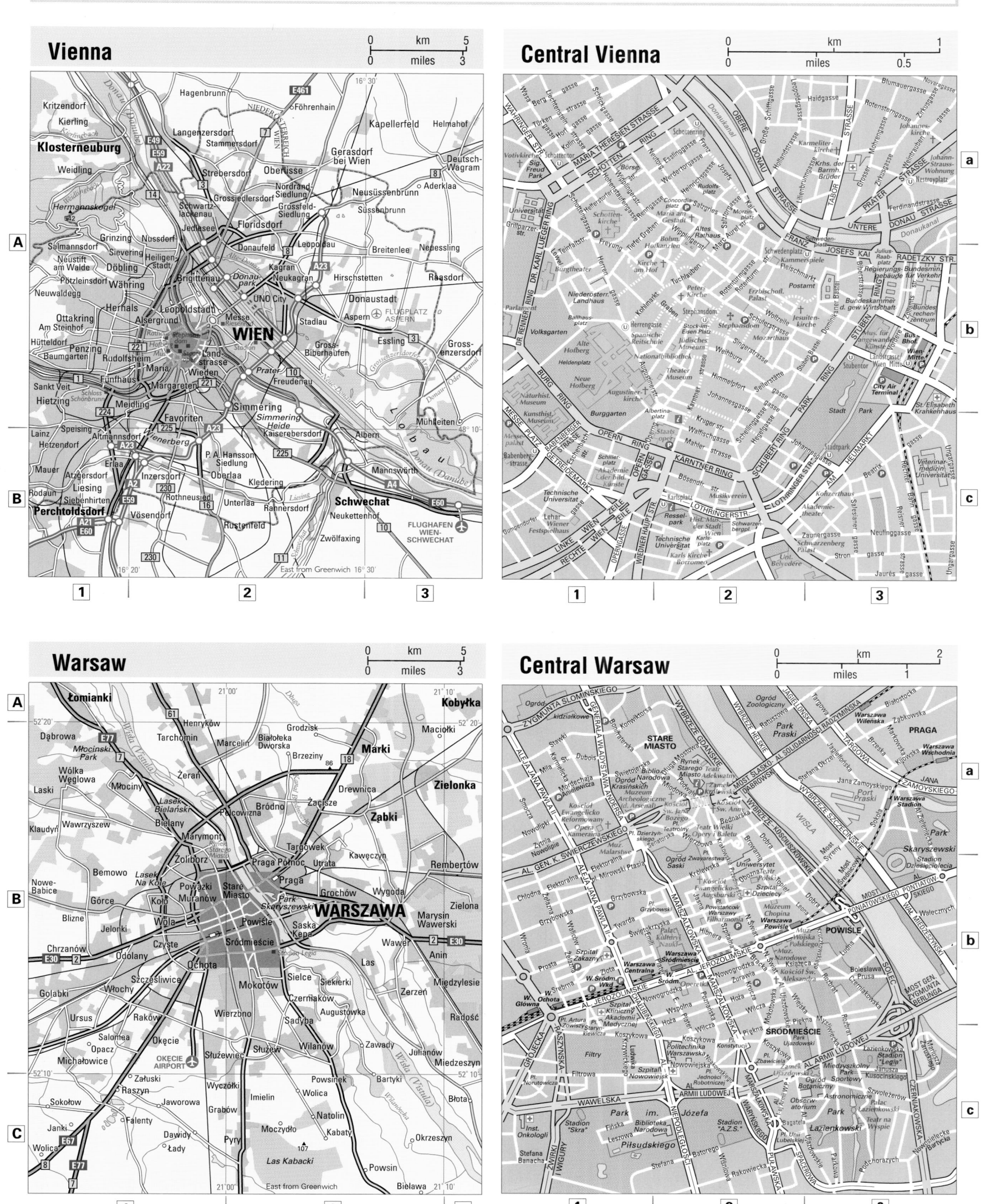

# Washington

km 5
miles 3

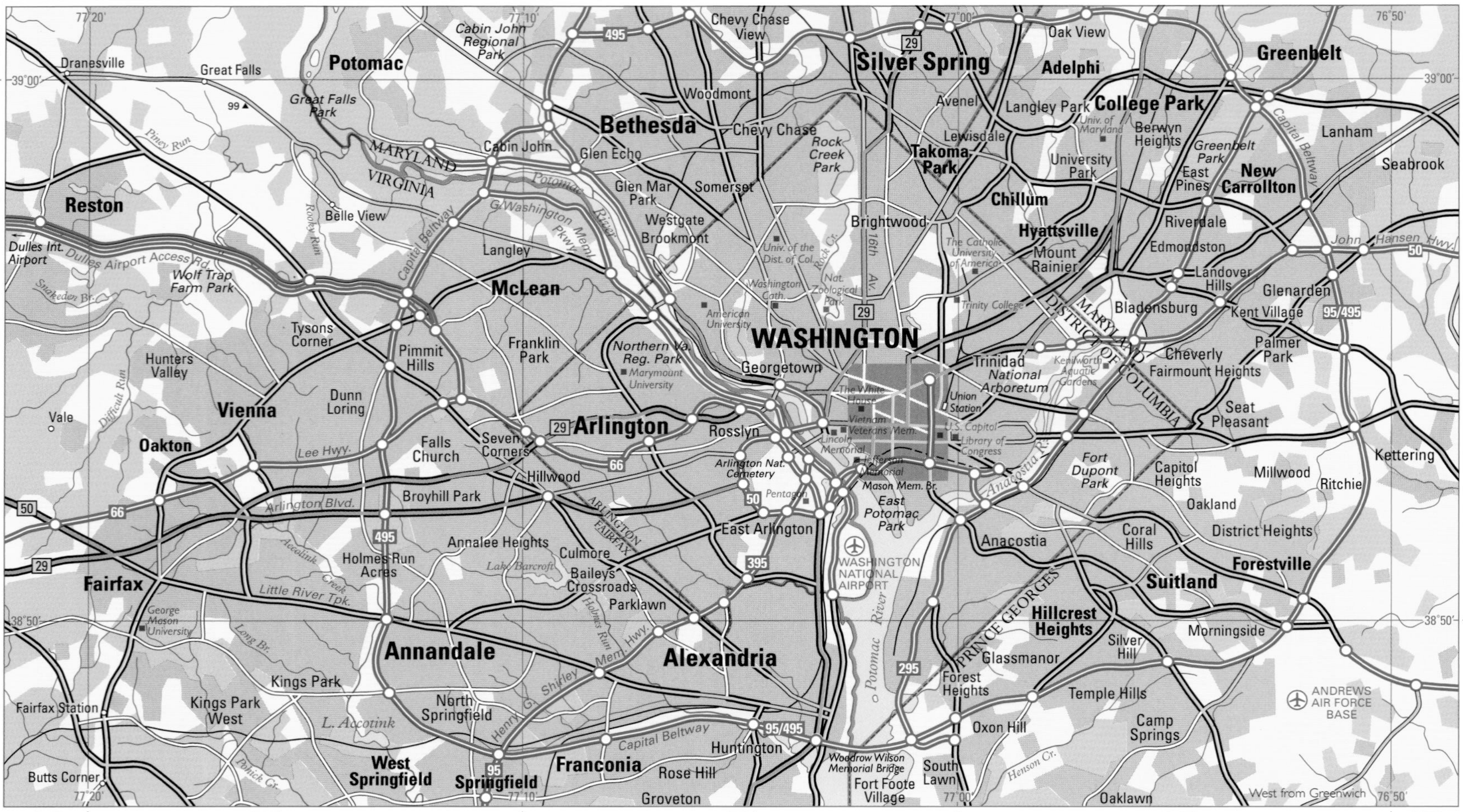

Dranesville · Great Falls · **Potomac** · Cabin John Regional Park · Chevy Chase View · **Silver Spring** · Oak View · **Greenbelt** · 29 · 495

Great Falls Park · 99 · **Bethesda** · Woodmont · Chevy Chase · **Adelphi** · Avenel · Langley Park · **College Park** · Lanham

**Reston** · Cabin John · Glen Echo · Rock Creek Park · Univ. of Maryland · Berwyn Heights · New Pines · **New Carrollton** · Seabrook

Glen Mar Park · Somerset · **Takoma Park** · Univ. of the Dist. of Col. · Greenbelt Park · Riverdale · Edmonston · 50

Belle View · Westgate · Brookmont · Brightwood · Nat. Zoological Park · The Catholic University of America · Mount Rainier · **Hyattsville** · Landover Hills · Glenarden · 95/495

**McLean** · Langley · **WASHINGTON** · Washington Cath. · Trinity College · **Chillum** · Bladensburg · Kent Village

Hunters Valley · Tysons Corner · Pimmit Hills · Franklin Park · Northern Va. Reg. Park · American University · **Georgetown** · The Mall White House · Union Station · Trinidad National Arboretum · Cheverly · Fairmount Heights · Palmer Park

**Vienna** · Dunn Loring · Marymount University · Lincoln Memorial Vietnam Vets Mem. · U.S. Capitol Library of Congress · Kenilworth Aquatic Gardens · Seat Pleasant

**Oakton** · 29 · **Arlington** · Rosslyn · Kettering · Fort Dupont Park · Capitol Heights · Millwood · Ritchie

Lee Hwy. · Seven Corners · Falls Church · Hillwood · Arlington Nat. Cemetery · Pentagon · Mason Mem. Br. · East Potomac Park · Anacostia · Oakland · District Heights

**Fairfax** · Arlington Blvd. · Broyhill Park · 66 · 50 · 395 · Coral Hills · **Forestville**

George Mason University · Annalee Heights · Holmes Run Acres · Baileys Crossroads · Culmore · East Arlington · WASHINGTON NATIONAL AIRPORT · **Suitland** · 95/495

Little River Tpk. · Parklawn · Prince Georges · **Hillcrest Heights** · Glassmanor · Silver Hill · Morningside · 38°50′

**Annandale** · Kings Park · North Springfield · **Alexandria** · L. Accotink · Forest Heights · Temple Hills · Camp Springs · **ANDREWS AIR FORCE BASE**

Fairfax Station · Kings Park West · **Franconia** · Huntington · 295 · Oxon Hill · 95/495

Butts Corner · **West Springfield** · **Springfield** · 95 · Rose Hill · Groveton · Woodrow Wilson Memorial Bridge · Fort Foote Village · South Lawn · Oaklawn · West from Greenwich

Potomac River · Anacostia R.

A · B · C · 1 · 2 · 3 · 4 · 5

---

# Central Washington

km 1
miles 0.5

P St. · 16th St. · Logan Circle · Island Ave. · NEW JERSEY AVE. · NORTH CAPITOL ST.

CONNECTICUT AVE. · RHODE ISLAND AVE. · Scott Circle · 13th St. · 12th St. · 10th St. · 8th St. · 6th St. · **NORTH WEST**

N St. · Thomas Circle · M St. · Mt. Vernon Sq.-UDC · NEW YORK AVE.

VERMONT AVE. · MASSACHUSETTS AVE. · M St. · Farragut North · Mt. Vernon Square · L St. · McPherson Sq. · Franklin Square · Convention Center · Metro Center · Gallery Place · Union Station · Columbus Circle

PENNSYLVANIA AVE. · Farragut West · 17th St. · Lafayette Square · H St. · Franklin Square · K St. · MASSACHUSETTS AVE. · LOUISIANA AVE.

World Bank · 18th St. · The White House · Nat. Mus. of American Art · Fords Theater · Judiciary Sq. · D St. · Union Station Plaza

Dept. of the Interior · E St. · Zero Milestone · The Ellipse · 14th St. · Federal Triangle · National Place · PENNSYLVANIA AVE. · Archives-Navy Memorial · CONSTITUTION

Reflecting Pool · D.C. War Memorial · CONSTITUTION AVE. · Nat. Museum of American History · Madison Dr · 7th St. · National Gallery of Art · National Air & Space Museum · 3RD ST. · Supreme Court · U.S. Capitol · Library of Congress · Botanic Gardens

Nat. Museum of Natural History · Washington Monument · The Mall · Smithsonian Institution · Jefferson Dr · Hirshhorn Museum · Grant Statue · INDEPENDENCE AVE.

INDEPENDENCE AVE. · US Holocaust Memorial Museum · L'Enfant Plaza · Federal Center SW · Tidal Basin

Jefferson Memorial · Outlet Bridge · 14TH ST. · E St. · **SOUTH WEST** · SOUTHWEST FREEWAY · NEW JERSEY AVE.

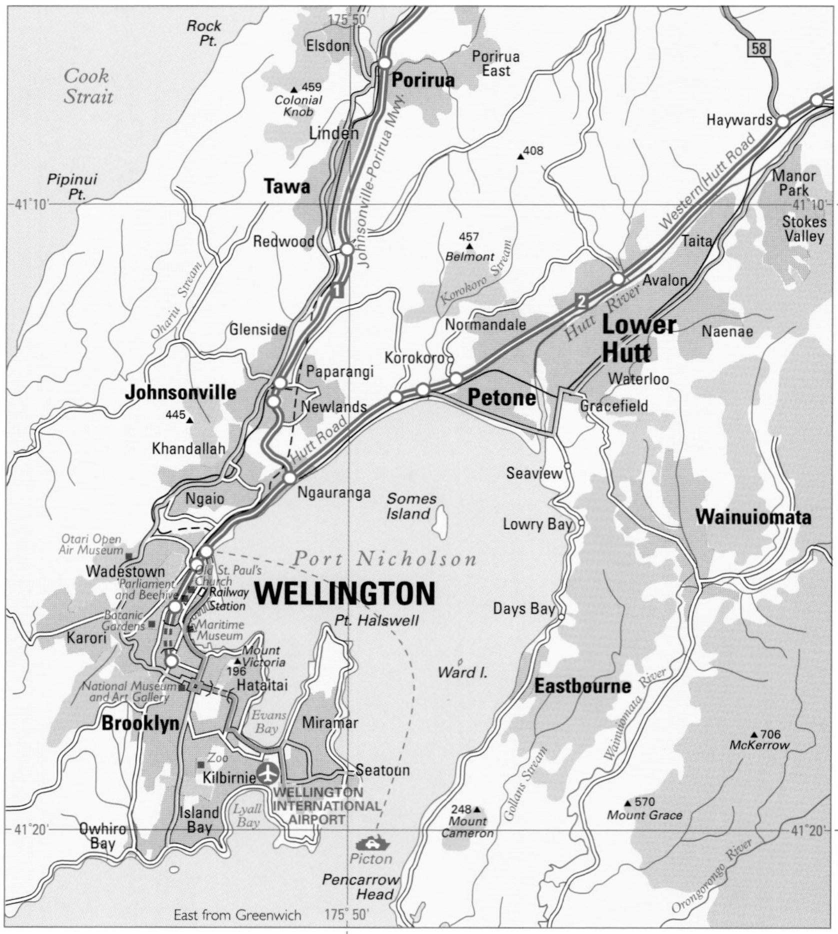

Potomac R. · East Potomac Park · Francis Case Mem. Bridge · MAINE AVE. · 7TH ST. · G St. · Waterfront · Washington Channel · SOUTH CAPITOL ST.

a · b · c · 1 · 2 · 3

---

# Wellington

km 5
miles 3

Rock Pt. · Elsdon · 175°50′ · Porirua East · 58 · **Cook Strait**

459 Colonial Knob · **Porirua** · Linden · Haywards · 408

Pipinui Pt. · **Tawa** · Manor Park · 41°10′ · Stokes Valley

Redwood · 457 Belmont · Korokoro Stream · Taita · Avalon

Glenside · Normandale · **Lower Hutt** · Naenae

**Johnsonville** · 445 · Paparangi · Korokoro · Waterloo · Western Hutt Road · Gracefield

Khandallah · Ngaio · Newlands · Ngauranga · **Petone** · Hutt Road · Seaview

Somes Island · Lowry Bay · **Wainuiomata**

Otari Open Air Museum · Wadestown · Parliament and Beehive · Railway Station · Port Nicholson · Days Bay

Karori · St Paul's Church · Maritime Museum · **WELLINGTON** · Pt. Halswell · Ward I. · **Eastbourne**

National Museum and Art Gallery · Botanic Gardens · Mount Victoria 196 · Hataitai · Evans Bay · Miramar · 706 McKerrow

**Brooklyn** · Zoo · Kilbirnie · Seatoun · 248 Mount Cameron · 570 Mount Grace

Owhiro Bay · Island Bay · Lyall Bay · **WELLINGTON INTERNATIONAL AIRPORT** · Picton · Pencarrow Head · 41°20′ · East from Greenwich · 175°50′

A · B · C · 1 · 2

# INDEX TO CITY MAPS

The index contains the names of all the principal places and features shown on the City Maps. Each name is followed by an additional entry in italics giving the name of the City Map within which it is located.

The number in bold type which follows each name refers to the number of the City Map page where that feature or place will be found.

The letter and figure which are immediately after the page number give the grid square on the map within which the feature or place is situated. The letter represents the latitude and the figure the longitude. Upper case letters refer to the City Maps, lower case letters to the Central Area Maps. The full geographic reference is provided in the border of the City Maps.

The location given is the centre of the city, suburb or feature and is not necessarily the name. Rivers, canals and roads are indexed to their name. Rivers carry the symbol → after their name.

An explanation of the alphabetical order rules and a list of the abbreviations used are to be found at the beginning of the World Map Index.

## A


Aalām, *Baghdad* 3 B2
Aalsmeer, *Amsterdam* 2 B1
Abbey Wood, *London* 15 B4
Abcoude, *Amsterdam* 2 B2
Âbdin, *Cairo* 7 A2
Abeno, *Osaka* 22 B4
Aberdeen, *Hong Kong* 12 B2
Aberdour, *Edinburgh* 11 A2
Aberdour Castle, *Edinburgh* 11 A2
Abfanggraben →, *Munich* 20 A3
Ablon-sur-Seine, *Paris* 23 B3
Abord-à-Plouffe, *Montreal* 19 A1
Abramtsevo, *Moscow* 19 B4
Abu Dis, *Jerusalem* 13 B2
Abû en Numrus, *Cairo* 7 B2
Abu Ghosh, *Jerusalem* 13 B1
Acacias, *Madrid* 17 c2
Acassuso, *Buenos Aires* 7 A1
Accotink Cr. →, *Washington* 32 B2
Acheres, *Paris* 23 A1
Acília, *Rome* 25 C1
Aclimação, *São Paulo* 26 B2
Acton, *London* 15 A2
Açúcar, Pão de, *Rio de Janeiro* 24 B2
Ada Beja, *Lisbon* 14 A1
Adams Park, *Atlanta* 3 B2
Adams Shore, *Boston* 6 B4
Addiscombe, *London* 15 B3
Adelphi, *Washington* 32 A4
Aderklaa, *Vienna* 31 A3
Admiralteyskaya Storona, *St. Petersburg* 26 B2
Áffori, *Milan* 18 A2
Aflandshage, *Copenhagen* 10 B3
Afsarīyeh, *Tehran* 30 B2
Agboyi Cr. →, *Lagos* 14 A2
Ågerup, *Copenhagen* 10 A1
Ågesta, *Stockholm* 28 B2
Agincourt, *Toronto* 30 A3
Agora, Arhéa, *Athens* 2 c1
Agra Canal, *Delhi* 10 B2
Agricola Oriental, *Mexico City* 18 B2
Agua Espraiada →, *São Paulo* 26 B2
Agualva-Cacem, *Lisbon* 14 A1
Agustino, Cerro El, *Lima* 16 B2
Ahrensfelde, *Berlin* 5 A4
Ahuntsic, *Montreal* 19 A1
Ai →, *Osaka* 22 A4
Aigremont, *Paris* 23 A1
Air View Park, *Singapore* 27 A2
Airport West, *Melbourne* 17 A1
Aiyaleo, *Athens* 2 B2
Aiyáleos, Óros, *Athens* 2 B1
Ajegunle, *Lagos* 14 B2
Aji, *Osaka* 22 A3
Ajuda, *Lisbon* 14 A1
Akalla, *Stockholm* 28 A1
Akasaka, *Tokyo* 29 b3
Akbarābād, *Tehran* 30 A2
Akershus Slott, *Oslo* 22 A3
Akihabara, *Tokyo* 29 a5
Akrópolis, *Athens* 2 c2
Al 'Azamiyah, *Baghdad* 3 A2
Al Quds = Jerusalem, *Jerusalem* 13 B2
Alaguntan, *Lagos* 14 B2
Alameda, *San Francisco* 25 B3
Alameda, Parque, *Mexico City* 18 b2
Alameda Memorial State Beach Park, *San Francisco* 25 B3
Albern, *Vienna* 31 B2
Albert Park, *Melbourne* 17 B1
Alberton, *Johannesburg* 13 B2
Albertslund, *Copenhagen* 10 B2
Albysjön, *Stockholm* 28 B1
Alcantara, *Lisbon* 14 A1
Alcatraz I., *San Francisco* 25 B2
Alcobendas, *Madrid* 17 A2
Alcorcón, *Madrid* 17 B1
Aldershof, *Berlin* 5 B4
Aldo Bonzi, *Buenos Aires* 7 C1
Aleksandrovskoye, *St. Petersburg* 26 B2
Alexander Nevsky Abbey, *St. Petersburg* 26 B2
Alexander Soutzos Moussío, *Athens* 2 b3
Alexandra, *Johannesburg* 13 A2
Alexandra, *Singapore* 27 B2
Alexandria, *Washington* 32 C3
Alfama, *Lisbon* 14 c3
Alfortville, *Paris* 23 B3
Algés, *Lisbon* 14 A1
Alhambra, *Los Angeles* 16 B4
Alibey →, *Istanbul* 12 B1
Alibey Barajı, *Istanbul* 12 B1
Alibeyköy, *Istanbul* 12 B1
Alimos, *Athens* 2 B2
Alipur, *Calcutta* 8 B1
Allach, *Munich* 20 A1
Allambie Heights, *Sydney* 28 A2
Allard Pierson Museum, *Amsterdam* 2 b2
Allermuir Hill, *Edinburgh* 11 B2
Allerton, Pt., *Boston* 6 B4
Allston, *Boston* 6 A3
Almada, *Lisbon* 14 A2
Almagro, *Buenos Aires* 7 B2
Almargem do Bispo, *Lisbon* 14 A1
Almazovo, *Moscow* 19 A6
Almirante G. Brown, Parque, *Buenos Aires* 7 C2
Almon, *Jerusalem* 13 B2
Almond →, *Edinburgh* 11 B2
Alnabru, *Oslo* 22 A4
Alnsjøen, *Oslo* 22 A4
Alperton, *London* 15 A2
Alpine, *New York* 21 A2
Alrode, *Johannesburg* 13 B2
Alsemerg, *Brussels* 6 B1
Alsergrund, *Vienna* 31 A2
Alsip, *Chicago* 9 C2
Ålsten, *Stockholm* 28 B1
Älta, *Stockholm* 28 B3
Altadena, *Los Angeles* 16 A4
Alte-Donau →, *Vienna* 31 A2
Alte Hofburg, *Vienna* 31 b1
Alter Finkenkrug, *Berlin* 5 A1
Altes Rathaus, *Munich* 20 b3
Altglienicke, *Berlin* 5 B4
Altlandsberg, *Berlin* 5 A5
Altlandsberg Nord, *Berlin* 5 A5
Altmannsdorf, *Vienna* 31 B1
Alto da Moóca, *São Paulo* 26 B2
Alto do Pina, *Lisbon* 14 A2
Altona, *Melbourne* 17 B1
Alvaro Obregon, *Mexico City* 18 B1
Alvik, *Stockholm* 28 B1
Älvsjo, *Stockholm* 28 B2
Älvvik, *Stockholm* 28 A3
Am Hasenbergl, *Munich* 20 A2
Am Steinhof, *Vienna* 31 A1
Am Wald, *Munich* 20 B2
Ama Keng, *Singapore* 27 A2
Amadora, *Lisbon* 14 A1
Amagasaki, *Osaka* 22 A3
Amager, *Copenhagen* 10 B3
Amāl Qādisiya, *Baghdad* 3 B2
Amalienborg, *Copenhagen* 10 b3
Amata, *Milan* 18 A1
Ameixoeira, *Lisbon* 14 A2
América, *São Paulo* 26 B1
Amin, *Baghdad* 3 B2
Aminadov, *Jerusalem* 13 B1
Aminyevo, *Moscow* 19 B2
Amīrābād, *Tehran* 30 A2
Amora, *Lisbon* 14 B2
Amoreira, *Lisbon* 14 A1
Ampelokipi, *Athens* 2 B2
Amper →, *Munich* 20 A1
Amstel, *Amsterdam* 2 b2
Amstel →, *Amsterdam* 2 c2
Amstel-Drecht-Kanaal, *Amsterdam* 2 B2
Amstel Station, *Amsterdam* 2 c3
Amstelhof, *Amsterdam* 2 b2
Amstelveen, *Amsterdam* 2 B2
Amsterdam, *Amsterdam* 2 A2
Amsterdam-Rijnkanaal, *Amsterdam* 2 B3
Amsterdam Zoo, *Amsterdam* 2 b3
Amsterdam Zuidoost, *Amsterdam* 2 B2
Amsterdamse Bos, *Amsterdam* 2 B1
Anacostia, *Washington* 32 B4
Anadoluhisarı, *Istanbul* 12 B2
Anadolukavağı, *Istanbul* 12 A2
Anata, *Jerusalem* 13 B2
Ancol, *Jakarta* 13 A1
'Andalus, *Baghdad* 3 B1
Andarai, *Rio de Janeiro* 24 B1
Anderlecht, *Brussels* 6 A1
Anderson Park, *Atlanta* 3 B2
Andingmen, *Beijing* 4 B2
Andrews Air Force Base, *Washington* 32 C4
Ang Mo Kio, *Singapore* 27 A3
Ängby, *Stockholm* 28 A1
Angel I., *San Francisco* 25 A2
Angel Island State Park, *San Francisco* 25 A2
Angke, Kali →, *Jakarta* 13 A1
Angyalföld, *Budapest* 7 A2
Anik, *Mumbai* 20 A2
Anin, *Warsaw* 31 B2
Anjou, *Montreal* 19 A2
Annalee Heights, *Washington* 32 B2
Annandale, *Washington* 32 C2
Anne Frankhuis, *Amsterdam* 2 a1
Antony, *Paris* 23 B2
Anyangch'on, *Seoul* 26 C1
Aoyama, *Tokyo* 29 b2
Ap Lei Chau, *Hong Kong* 12 B1
Apapa, *Lagos* 14 B2
Apelacão, *Lisbon* 14 A2
Apterkarskiy Ostrov, *St. Petersburg* 26 B2
Ar Kazimiyah, *Baghdad* 3 B1
Ara →, *Tokyo* 29 A4
Arakawa-Ku, *Tokyo* 29 A3
Arany-hegyi-patak →, *Budapest* 7 A2
Aravaca, *Madrid* 17 B1
Arbataash, *Baghdad* 3 A1
Arc de Triomphe, *Paris* 23 a2
Arcadia, *Los Angeles* 16 B4
Arceuil, *Paris* 23 B2
Arco Plaza, *Los Angeles* 16 b1
Arese, *Milan* 18 A1
Arganzuela, *Madrid* 17 B1
Argenteuil, *Paris* 23 A2
Argonne Forest, *Chicago* 9 C1
Argüelles, *Madrid* 17 a1
Arima, *Osaka* 22 A2
Arima, *Tokyo* 29 B2
Ários Págos, *Athens* 2 c1
Arkhangelyskoye, *Moscow* 19 B1
Arlington, *Boston* 6 A2
Arlington, *Washington* 32 B3
Arlington Heights, *Boston* 6 A2
Arlington Nat. Cemetery, *Washington* 32 B3
Armação, *Rio de Janeiro* 24 B2
Armadale, *Melbourne* 17 B2
Armenian Quarter, *Jerusalem* 13 b3
Armour Heights, *Toronto* 30 A2
Arncliffe, *Sydney* 28 B1
Arnold Arboretum, *Boston* 6 B3
Árpádföld, *Budapest* 7 A3
Arrentela, *Lisbon* 14 B2
Årsta, *Stockholm* 28 B2
Art Institute, *Chicago* 9 c2
Artane, *Dublin* 11 A2
Artas, *Jerusalem* 13 B2
Arthur's Seat, *Edinburgh* 11 B3
Aryiróupolis, *Athens* 2 B2
Asagaya, *Tokyo* 29 A2
Asahi, *Osaka* 22 A4
Asakusa, *Tokyo* 29 A3
Asakusabashi, *Tokyo* 29 a5
Asati, *Calcutta* 8 C1
Aschheim, *Munich* 20 A3
Ascot Vale, *Melbourne* 17 A1
Ashburn, *Chicago* 9 C2
Ashburton, *Melbourne* 17 B2
Ashfield, *Sydney* 28 B1
Ashford, *London* 15 B1
Ashiya, *Osaka* 22 A2
Ashiya →, *Osaka* 22 A2
Ashtown, *Dublin* 11 A2
Askisto, *Helsinki* 12 B1
Askrikefjärden, *Stockholm* 28 A3
Asnières, *Paris* 23 A2
Aspern, *Vienna* 31 A2
Aspern, Flugplatz, *Vienna* 31 A3
Assago, *Milan* 18 B1
Assemblée Nationale, *Paris* 23 b3
Assendelft, *Amsterdam* 2 A1
Assiano, *Milan* 18 B1
Astoria, *New York* 21 B2
Astrolabe Park, *Sydney* 28 B2
Atarot Airport, *Jerusalem* 13 A2
Atghara, *Calcutta* 8 B2
Athens = Athínai, *Athens* 2 B2
Athínai, *Athens* 2 B2
Athinai-Ellinikón Airport, *Athens* 2 B2
Athis-Mons, *Paris* 23 B3
Athlone, *Cape Town* 8 A2
Atholl, *Johannesburg* 13 A2
Atīfīya, *Baghdad* 3 A2
Atişalen, *Istanbul* 12 B1
Atlanta, *Atlanta* 3 B2
Atlanta History Center, *Atlanta* 3 B2
Atomium, *Brussels* 6 A2
Attiki, *Athens* 2 A2
Atzgersdorf, *Vienna* 31 B1
Aubervilliers, *Paris* 23 A3
Aubing, *Munich* 20 B1
Auburndale, *Boston* 6 A2
Aucherdinny, *Edinburgh* 11 B2
Auckland Park, *Johannesburg* 13 B2
Auderghem, *Brussels* 6 B2
Augusta, Mausoleo di, *Rome* 25 b2
Augustówka, *Warsaw* 31 B2
Aulnay-sous-Bois, *Paris* 23 A3
Aurelio, *Rome* 25 B1
Ausîm, *Cairo* 7 A1
Austerlitz, Gare d', *Paris* 23 A3
Austin, *Chicago* 9 B2
Avalon, *Wellington* 32 B2
Avedøre, *Copenhagen* 10 B2
Avellaneda, *Buenos Aires* 7 C2
Avenel, *Washington* 32 B4
Avondale, *Chicago* 9 B2
Avondale Heights, *Melbourne* 17 A1
Avtovo, *St. Petersburg* 26 B1
Ayazağa, *Istanbul* 12 B1
Ayer Chawan, P., *Singapore* 27 B2
Ayer Merbau, P., *Singapore* 27 B2
Ayía Marina, *Athens* 2 C3
Ayía Paraskevi, *Athens* 2 A2
Áyios Dhimitrios, *Athens* 2 B2
Áyios Ioánnis Rendis, *Athens* 2 B1
Azabu, *Tokyo* 29 c3
Azcapotzalco, *Mexico City* 18 B1
Azteca, Estadia, *Mexico City* 18 C2
Azucar, Cerro Pan de, *Santiago* 26 A1


## B


Baambrugge, *Amsterdam* 2 B2
Baba I., *Karachi* 14 B1
Babarpur, *Delhi* 10 A2
Babushkin, *Moscow* 19 A4
Back B., *Mumbai* 20 B1
Baclaran, *Manila* 17 B2
Bacoor, *Manila* 17 C1
Bacoor B., *Manila* 17 C1
Badalona, *Barcelona* 4 A2
Badhoevedorp, *Amsterdam* 2 A1
Badli, *Delhi* 10 A1
Bærum, *Oslo* 22 A2
Bağcılar, *Istanbul* 12 B1
Bággio, *Milan* 18 B1
Bāgh-e-Feyz, *Tehran* 30 A1
Baghdād, *Baghdad* 3 A2
Bagmari, *Calcutta* 8 B2
Bagneux, *Paris* 23 B2
Bagnolet, *Paris* 23 A3
Bagsværd, *Copenhagen* 10 A2
Bagsværd Sø, *Copenhagen* 10 A2
Baguiati, *Calcutta* 8 B2
Bagumbayan, *Manila* 17 C2
Bahçeköy, *Istanbul* 12 A1
Bahtîm, *Cairo* 7 A2
Baileys Crossroads, *Washington* 32 B3
Bailly, *Paris* 23 A1
Bairro Alto, *Lisbon* 14 c1
Bairro Lopes, *Lisbon* 14 b3
Baisha, *Canton* 8 B2
Baisha →, *Canton* 8 B2
Baixa, *Lisbon* 14 c2
Baiyun Airport, *Canton* 8 A2
Baiyun Hill Scenic Spot, *Canton* 8 B2
Bakırköy, *Istanbul* 12 C1
Bakovka, *Moscow* 19 B2
Bal Harbor, *Miami* 18 A2
Balara, *Manila* 17 B2
Balashikha, *Moscow* 19 B5
Baldia, *Karachi* 14 A1
Baldoyle, *Dublin* 11 A3
Baldwin Hills, *Los Angeles* 16 B2
Baldwin Hills Res., *Los Angeles* 16 B2
Balgowlah, *Sydney* 28 A2
Balgowlah Heights, *Sydney* 28 A2
Balham, *London* 15 B3
Bali, *Calcutta* 8 B1
Baliganja, *Calcutta* 8 B2
Balingsnäs, *Stockholm* 28 B2
Balingsta, *Stockholm* 28 B2
Balintawak, *Manila* 17 B1
Balitai, *Tianjin* 30 B2
Ballerup, *Copenhagen* 10 A2
Ballinteer, *Dublin* 11 B2
Ballyboden, *Dublin* 11 B2
Ballybrack, *Dublin* 11 B3
Ballyfermot, *Dublin* 11 A1
Ballymorefinn Hill, *Dublin* 11 B1
Ballymun, *Dublin* 11 A2
Balmain, *Sydney* 28 B2
Baluhati, *Calcutta* 8 B1
Balvanera, *Buenos Aires* 7 B2
Balwyn, *Melbourne* 17 A2
Balwyn North, *Melbourne* 17 A2
Banática, *Lisbon* 14 A1
Banco do Brasil, Centro Cultural, *Rio de Janeiro* 24 a2
Bandra, *Mumbai* 20 A1
Bandra Pt., *Mumbai* 20 A1
Bang Kapi, *Bangkok* 3 B2
Bang Kholaem, *Bangkok* 3 A2
Bang Na, *Bangkok* 3 B2
Bang Phlad, *Bangkok* 3 a1
Bangkhen, *Bangkok* 3 A2
Bangkok = Krung Thep, *Bangkok* 3 B2
Bangkok Noi, *Bangkok* 3 B1
Bangkok Yai, *Bangkok* 3 B1
Banglamphoo, *Bangkok* 3 b2
Banglo, *Calcutta* 8 B1
Bangrak, *Bangkok* 3 B2
Bangsu, *Bangkok* 3 B2
Bank, *London* 15 b5
Bank of America, *San Francisco* 25 b2
Bank of China Tower, *Hong Kong* 12 c1
Banks, C., *Sydney* 28 C2
Banksmeadow, *Sydney* 28 B2
Banstala, *Calcutta* 8 B2
Bantra, *Calcutta* 8 B1
Baoshan, *Shanghai* 27 A1
Bar Giyora, *Jerusalem* 13 B1
Barahanagar, *Calcutta* 8 B2
Barajas, *Madrid* 17 B2
Barajas, Aeropuerto Transoceanico de, *Madrid* 17 B2
Barakpur, *Calcutta* 8 A2
Barberini, Palazzo, *Rome* 25 b3
Barbican, *London* 15 a4
Barcarena, *Lisbon* 14 A1
Barcarena, Rib. de →, *Lisbon* 14 A1
Barcelona, *Barcelona* 4 A2
Barcelona-Prat, Aeropuerta de, *Barcelona* 4 B1
Barceloneta, *Barcelona* 4 A2
Barking, *London* 15 A4
Barkingside, *London* 15 A4
Barnes, *London* 15 B2
Barnet, *London* 15 A2
Barra Andai, *Karachi* 14 B2
Barra Funda, *São Paulo* 26 B2
Barracas, *Buenos Aires* 7 B2
Barranco, *Lima* 16 B2
Barreiro, *Lisbon* 14 B2
Barreto, *Rio de Janeiro* 24 B2
Bartala, *Calcutta* 8 B1
Barton Park, *Sydney* 28 B1
Bartyki, *Warsaw* 31 C2
Barvikha, *Moscow* 19 B1
Bastille, Place de la, *Paris* 23 c5
Basus, *Cairo* 7 A2
Batanagar, *Calcutta* 8 B1
Bath Beach, *New York* 21 C1
Bath I., *Karachi* 14 B2
Batir, *Jerusalem* 13 B1
Batok, Bukit, *Singapore* 27 A2
Battersea, *London* 15 B3
Battery Park, *New York* 21 f1
Bauman, *Moscow* 19 B4
Baumgarten, *Vienna* 31 A1
Bay Harbour Islands, *Miami* 18 A2
Bay Ridge, *New York* 21 C1
Bayonne, *New York* 21 B1
Bayshore, *San Francisco* 25 B3
Bayswater, *London* 15 b2
Bayt Lahm = Bethlehem, *Jerusalem* 13 B2
Bayview, *San Francisco* 25 B2
Bāzār, *Tehran* 30 A2
Beachmont, *Boston* 6 A4
Beacon Hill, *Hong Kong* 12 A2
Beato, *Lisbon* 14 A2
Beaumont, *Dublin* 11 A2
Beaumonte Heights, *Toronto* 30 A1
Bebek, *Istanbul* 12 B2
Běchovice, *Prague* 24 B3
Beck L., *Chicago* 9 A1
Beckenham, *London* 15 B3
Beckton, *London* 15 A4
Becontree, *London* 15 A4
Beddington Corner, *London* 15 B3
Bedford, *Boston* 6 A2
Bedford Park, *Chicago* 9 C2
Bedford Park, *New York* 21 A2
Bedford Stuyvesant, *New York* 21 B2
Bedford View, *Johannesburg* 13 B2
Bedok, *Singapore* 27 B3
Bedok, Res., *Singapore* 27 A3
Beersel, *Brussels* 6 B1
Behala, *Calcutta* 8 B1
Bei Hai, *Beijing* 4 B2
Beicai, *Shanghai* 27 B2
Beicang, *Tianjin* 30 A1
Beihai Park, *Beijing* 4 b2
Beijing, *Beijing* 4 B1
Beit Ghur el-Fawqa, *Jerusalem* 13 A1
Beit Hanina, *Jerusalem* 13 B2
Beit Iksa, *Jerusalem* 13 B2
Beit I'nan, *Jerusalem* 13 A1
Beit Jala, *Jerusalem* 13 B2
Beit Lekhem = Bethlehem, *Jerusalem* 13 B2
Beit Nekofa, *Jerusalem* 13 B1
Beit Sahur, *Jerusalem* 13 B2
Beit Surik, *Jerusalem* 13 B1
Beit Zayit, *Jerusalem* 13 B1
Beitaipingzhuan, *Beijing* 4 B1
Beitar Ilit, *Jerusalem* 13 B1
Beitsun, *Canton* 8 B2
Beitunya, *Jerusalem* 13 A2
Beixing Jing Park, *Shanghai* 27 B1
Békásmegyer, *Budapest* 7 A2
Bekkelaget, *Oslo* 22 A3
Bel Air, *Los Angeles* 16 B2
Bela Vista, *São Paulo* 26 B2
Bélanger, *Montreal* 19 A1
Belas, *Lisbon* 14 A1
Belas Artes, Museu Nacionale de, *Rio de Janeiro* 24 b2
Beleghata, *Calcutta* 8 B2
Belém, *Lisbon* 14 A1
Belém, Torre de, *Lisbon* 14 A1
Belènzinho, *São Paulo* 26 B2
Belgachiya, *Calcutta* 8 B2
Belgharia, *Calcutta* 8 B2
Belgrano, *Buenos Aires* 7 B2
Belgravia, *London* 15 c3
Bell, *Los Angeles* 16 C3
Bell Gardens, *Los Angeles* 16 C4
Bell Tower, *Beijing* 4 a2
Bellavista, *Lima* 16 B2
Bellavista, *Santiago* 26 C2
Belle Harbor, *New York* 21 C2
Belle View, *Washington* 32 B2
Bellevue, Schloss, *Berlin* 5 a2
Bellingham, *London* 15 B3
Bellwood, *Chicago* 9 B1
Belmont, *Boston* 6 A2
Belmont, *London* 15 A2
Belmont, *Wellington* 32 B2
Belmont Harbor, *Chicago* 9 B3
Belmore, *Sydney* 28 B1
Belur, *Calcutta* 8 B2
Belvedere, *Atlanta* 3 B3
Belvedere, *London* 15 B4
Belvedere, *San Francisco* 25 A2
Belyayevo Bogorodskoye, *Moscow* 19 C3
Bemowo, *Warsaw* 31 B1
Benaki, Moussío, *Athens* 2 b3
Bendale, *Toronto* 30 A3
Bendkhal, *Mumbai* 20 B2
Benefica, *Rio de Janeiro* 24 B1
Benfica, *Lisbon* 14 A1
Benito Juárez, *Mexico City* 18 B2
Benito Juárez, Aeropuerto Int., *Mexico City* 18 B2
Bensonhurst, *New York* 21 C2
Berchem-Sainte-Agathe, *Brussels* 6 A1
Berg am Laim, *Munich* 20 B2
Bergenfield, *New York* 21 A2
Bergham, *Munich* 20 B2
Bergvliet, *Cape Town* 8 B1
Beri, *Barcelona* 4 A1
Berkeley, *San Francisco* 25 A3
Berlin, *Berlin* 5 A3
Bermondsey, *London* 15 B3
Bernabeu, Estadio, *Madrid* 17 B1
Bernal Heights, *San Francisco* 25 B2
Berwyn, *Chicago* 9 B2
Berwyn Heights, *Washington* 32 B4
Besiktas, *Istanbul* 12 B2
Besós →, *Barcelona* 4 A2
Bethesda, *Washington* 32 B3
Bethlehem, *Jerusalem* 13 B2
Bethnal Green, *London* 15 A3
Betor, *Calcutta* 8 B1
Beurs, *Amsterdam* 2 b2
Beverley Hills, *Sydney* 28 B1
Beverley Park, *Sydney* 28 B1
Beverly, *Chicago* 9 C3
Beverly Glen, *Los Angeles* 16 B2
Beverly Hills, *Los Angeles* 16 B2
Bexley, *London* 15 B4
Bexley, *Sydney* 28 B1
Bexleyheath, *London* 15 B4
Beykoz, *Istanbul* 12 B2
Beylerbeyi, *Istanbul* 12 B2
Beyoğlu, *Istanbul* 12 B1
Bezons, *Paris* 23 A2
Bezuidenhout Park, *Johannesburg* 13 B2
Bhadrakali, *Calcutta* 8 A2
Bhalswa, *Delhi* 10 A2
Bhambo Khan Qarmati, *Karachi* 14 B2
Bhatsala, *Calcutta* 8 B1
Bhawanipur, *Calcutta* 8 B2
Bhuleshwar, *Mumbai* 20 b2
Białołeka Dworska, *Warsaw* 31 B2
Biblioteca Nacional, *Rio de Janeiro* 24 c2
Bicentennial Park, *Sydney* 28 B1
Bickley, *London* 15 B4
Bidu, *Jerusalem* 13 B1
Bielany, *Warsaw* 31 B1
Bielawa, *Warsaw* 31 C2
Biesdorf, *Berlin* 5 A4
Bièvre →, *Paris* 23 B1
Bièvres, *Paris* 23 B2
Bilston, *Edinburgh* 11 B2
Binacayan, *Manila* 17 C1
Binondo, *Manila* 17 B1
Birak el Kiyam, *Cairo* 7 A1
Birch Cliff, *Toronto* 30 A3
Birkenstein, *Berlin* 5 A5
Birkholz, *Berlin* 5 A4
Birkholzaue, *Berlin* 5 A4
Birrarrung Park, *Melbourne* 17 A2
Biscayne Bay, *Miami* 18 B2
Biscayne Park, *Miami* 18 A2
Bishop Lavis, *Cape Town* 8 A2
Bishopscourt, *Cape Town* 8 A1
Bispebjerg, *Copenhagen* 10 A3
Biwon Secret Garden, *Seoul* 26 B1
Björknas, *Stockholm* 28 B3
Black Cr. →, *Toronto* 30 A2
Blackfen, *London* 15 B4
Blackheath, *London* 15 B4
Blackrock, *Dublin* 11 B2
Bladensburg, *Washington* 32 B4
Blair Village, *Atlanta* 3 C2
Blairgowrie, *Johannesburg* 13 A2
Blakehurst, *Sydney* 28 B1
Blakstad, *Oslo* 22 B1
Blankenburg, *Berlin* 5 A3
Blankenfelde, *Berlin* 5 A3
Blizne, *Warsaw* 31 B1
Bloomsbury, *London* 15 a3
Błota, *Warsaw* 31 C3
Blue Island, *Chicago* 9 C2
Bluebell, *Dublin* 11 B1
Bluff Hd., *Hong Kong* 12 B2
Blumberg, *Berlin* 5 A4
Blunt Pt., *San Francisco* 25 A2
Blutenberg, *Munich* 20 B1
Blylaget, *Oslo* 22 B3
Bo-Kaap Museum, *Cape Town* 8 c2
Boa Vista, Alto do, *Rio de Janeiro* 24 B1
Boardwalk, *New York* 21 C3
Boavista, *Lisbon* 14 A2
Bobigny, *Paris* 23 A3
Bocanegra, *Lima* 16 A2
Boedo, *Buenos Aires* 7 B2
Bogenhausen, *Munich* 20 B2
Bogorodskoye, *Moscow* 19 B4
Bogota, *New York* 21 A1
Bogstadvatnet, *Oslo* 22 A2
Bohnsdorf, *Berlin* 5 B4
Bois-Colombes, *Paris* 23 A2
Bois-d'Arcy, *Paris* 23 B1
Boissy-St.-Léger, *Paris* 23 B4
Boldinasco, *Milan* 18 B1
Bøler, *Oslo* 22 A4
Bollate, *Milan* 18 A1
Bollebeek, *Brussels* 6 A1
Bollensdorf, *Berlin* 5 A5
Bollmora, *Stockholm* 28 B3
Bolshaya-Okhta, *St. Petersburg* 26 B2
Bolton, *Atlanta* 3 B2
Bom Retiro, *São Paulo* 26 B2
Bombay = Mumbai, *Mumbai* 20 B2
Bondi, *Sydney* 28 B2
Bondy, *Paris* 23 A3
Bondy, Forêt de, *Paris* 23 A4
Bonifacio Monument, *Manila* 17 B1
Bonneuil-sur-Marne, *Paris* 23 B4
Bonnington, *Edinburgh* 11 B1
Bonnyrig and Lasswade, *Edinburgh* 11 B3
Bonsucesso, *Rio de Janeiro* 24 B1
Bonteheuwel, *Cape Town* 8 A2
Boo, *Stockholm* 28 A3
Booterstown, *Dublin* 11 B2
Borisovo, *Moscow* 19 C4
Borle, *Mumbai* 20 A2
Boronia Park, *Sydney* 28 A1
Borough Park, *New York* 21 C2
Bosmont, *Johannesburg* 13 B1
Bosön, *Stockholm* 28 A3
Bosporus = Istanbul Boğazi, *Istanbul* 12 B2
Bostancı, *Istanbul* 12 C2
Boston Harbor, *Boston* 6 A4
Botafogo, *Rio de Janeiro* 24 B1
Botanisk Have, *Copenhagen* 10 b2
Botany, *Sydney* 28 B2
Botany B., *Sydney* 28 B2
Botany Bay Nat. Park, *Sydney* 28 B2
Botič →, *Prague* 24 B3
Botica Sete, *Lisbon* 14 A1
Boucherville, *Montreal* 19 A3
Boucherville, Îs. de, *Montreal* 19 A3
Bougival, *Paris* 23 A1
Boulder Pt., *Hong Kong* 12 B1
Boulogne, Bois de, *Paris* 23 A2
Boulogne-Billancourt, *Paris* 23 A2
Bourg-la-Reine, *Paris* 23 B2
Bouviers, *Paris* 23 B1
Bovenkerk, *Amsterdam* 2 B2
Bovenkerker Polder, *Amsterdam* 2 B2
Bovisa, *Milan* 18 A2
Bow, *London* 15 A3
Bowery, *New York* 21 e2
Boyacıköy, *Istanbul* 12 B2
Boyle Heights, *Los Angeles* 16 B3
Bradbury Building, *Los Angeles* 16 b2
Braepark, *Edinburgh* 11 B2
Braid, *Edinburgh* 11 B2
Bramley, *Johannesburg* 13 A2
Brandenburger Tor, *Berlin* 5 A3
Brani, P., *Singapore* 27 B3
Branik, *Prague* 24 B2
Brännkyrka, *Stockholm* 28 B2
Brás, *São Paulo* 26 B2
Brasilândia, *São Paulo* 26 A1
Brateyevo, *Moscow* 19 C4
Bratsevo, *Moscow* 19 A2
Bray, *Dublin* 11 B3
Braybrook, *Melbourne* 17 A1
Brázdim, *Prague* 24 A3
Breach Candy, *Mumbai* 20 a1
Breakheart Reservation, *Boston* 6 A3
Brede, *Copenhagen* 10 A3
Breeds Pond, *Boston* 6 A4
Breezy Point, *New York* 21 C2
Breitenlee, *Vienna* 31 A3
Breña, *Lima* 16 B2
Brent, *London* 15 A2
Brent Res., *London* 15 A2
Brentford, *London* 15 B2
Brentwood Park, *Los Angeles* 16 B2
Brera, *Milan* 18 B2
Bresso, *Milan* 18 A2
Brevik, *Stockholm* 28 A3
Břevnov, *Prague* 24 B2
Bridgeport, *Chicago* 9 B3
Bridgetown, *Cape Town* 8 A2
Bridgeview, *Chicago* 9 C2
Brighton, *Boston* 6 A3
Brighton, *Melbourne* 17 B1
Brighton le Sands, *Sydney* 28 B1
Brighton Park, *Chicago* 9 C2
Brightwood, *Washington* 32 B3
Brigittenau, *Vienna* 31 A2
Brimbank Park, *Melbourne* 17 A1
Brisbane, *San Francisco* 25 B2
British Museum, *London* 15 a3
Britz, *Berlin* 5 B3
Brixton, *London* 15 B3
Broad Sd., *Boston* 6 A4
Broadmeadows, *Melbourne* 17 A1
Broadmoor, *San Francisco* 25 B2
Broadview, *Chicago* 9 B1
Broadway, *New York* 21 e1
Brockley, *London* 15 B3
Bródno, *Warsaw* 31 B2
Bródnowski, Kanal, *Warsaw* 31 B2
Broek in Waterland, *Amsterdam* 2 A2
Bromley, *London* 15 B4
Bromley Common, *London* 15 B4
Bromma, *Stockholm* 28 A1
Bromma flygplats, *Stockholm* 28 A1
Brompton, *London* 15 c2
Brøndby Strand, *Copenhagen* 10 B2
Brøndbyøster, *Copenhagen* 10 B2
Brøndbyvester, *Copenhagen* 10 B2
Brondesbury, *London* 15 A2
Brønnøya, *Oslo* 22 A2
Brønshøj, *Copenhagen* 10 A2

Kapellerfeld 35


Fawkner Park, *Melbourne* 17 B1
Feijó, *Lisbon* 14 B2
Feldkirchen, *Munich* 20 B3
Feldmoching, *Munich* 20 A2
Feltham, *London* 15 B1
Fener, *Istanbul* 12 B1
Fenerbahçe, *Istanbul* 12 C2
Fengtai, *Beijing* 4 C1
Fenino, *Moscow* 19 B5
Ferencváros, *Budapest* 7 B2
Ferihegyi Airport, *Budapest* 7 B3
Ferndale, *Johannesburg* 13 A2
Férolles-Attilly, *Paris* 23 B4
Fichtenau, *Berlin* 5 B5
Fields Corner, *Boston* 6 B3
Fiera Camp, *Milan* 18 B1
Fifth Avenue, *New York* 21 b3
Figino, *Milan* 18 B1
Fijir, *Baghdad* 3 A2
Filadhélfia, *Athens* 2 A2
Fili-Mazilovo, *Moscow* 19 B2
Filothei, *Athens* 2 A2
Finchley, *London* 15 A2
Finglas, *Dublin* 11 A2
Finsbury, *London* 15 A3
Finsbury Park, *London* 15 A3
Fiorito, *Buenos Aires* 7 C2
Firhouse, *Dublin* 11 B2
Fischerhäuser, *Munich* 20 A3
Fisher Island, *Miami* 18 B2
Fishermans Bend, *Melbourne* 17 A1
Fisherman's Wharf, *San Francisco* 25 a1
Fisherville, *Toronto* 30 A2
Fisksätra, *Stockholm* 28 B3
Fitzroy Gardens, *Melbourne* 17 A1
Five Dock, *Sydney* 28 B1
Fjellstrand, *Oslo* 22 B2
Flamengo, *Rio de Janeiro* 24 B1
Flaminio, *Rome* 25 B1
Flaskebekk, *Oslo* 22 A2
Flatbush, *New York* 21 C2
Flaten, *Stockholm* 28 B2
Flemington Racecourse, *Melbourne* 17 A1
Flint Pk., *Los Angeles* 16 B3
Florence, *Los Angeles* 16 C3
Florence Bloom Bird Sanctuary, *Johannesburg* 13 A2
Florentia, *Johannesburg* 13 B2
Flores, *Buenos Aires* 7 B2
Floresta, *Buenos Aires* 7 B2
Florida, *Buenos Aires* 7 B2
Florida, *Johannesburg* 13 B1
Floridsdorf, *Vienna* 31 A2
Flushing, *New York* 21 B3
Flushing Meadows Corona Park, *New York* 21 B2
Flysta, *Stockholm* 28 A1
Fo Tan, *Hong Kong* 12 A2
Föhrenhain, *Vienna* 31 A2
Fontainebleau, *Johannesburg* 13 A1
Fontenay-aux-Roses, *Paris* 23 B2
Fontenay-le-Fleury, *Paris* 23 B1
Fontenay-sous-Bois, *Paris* 23 A3
Foots Cray, *London* 15 B4
Footscray, *Melbourne* 17 A1
Foreshore, *Cape Town* 8 a3
Forest, *Brussels* 6 B1
Forest Gate, *London* 15 A4
Forest Heights, *Washington* 32 C3
Forest Hill, *London* 15 B3
Forest Hill, *Toronto* 30 A2
Forest Hills, *New York* 21 B2
Forest Park, *Chicago* 9 B2
Forest View, *Chicago* 9 C2
Forestville, *Washington* 32 B4
Fornebu, *Oslo* 22 A2
Fornebu Airport, *Oslo* 22 A2
Foro Romano, *Rome* 25 c3
Forstenried, *Munich* 20 B1
Forstenrieder Park, *Munich* 20 B1
Fort, *Mumbai* 20 c2
Fort Canning Park, *Singapore* 27 b2
Fort Dupont Park, *Washington* 32 B4
Fort Foote Village, *Washington* 32 C3
Fort Lee, *New York* 21 A2
Fort Mason Center, *San Francisco* 25 a1
Forth, Firth of, *Edinburgh* 11 A2
Forth Rail Bridge, *Edinburgh* 11 A1
Forth Road Bridge, *Edinburgh* 11 A1
Fót, *Budapest* 7 A3
Fourqueux, *Paris* 23 A1
Foxrock, *Dublin* 11 B2
Framingham, *Boston* 6 B1
Franconia, *Washington* 32 C3
Frankel, *Singapore* 27 B3
Franklin Park, *Boston* 6 B3
Franklin Park, *Chicago* 9 B1
Franklin Park, *Washington* 32 B3
Franklin Res., *Los Angeles* 16 B2
Frauenkirche, *Munich* 20 b2
Frederiksberg, *Copenhagen* 10 A3
Frederiksdal, *Copenhagen* 10 A2
Fredersdorf, *Berlin* 5 A5
Freguesia, *Rio de Janeiro* 24 A1
Freidrichshain, Volkspark, *Berlin* 5 A3
Freiham, *Munich* 20 B1
Freimann, *Munich* 20 A2
Fresh Pond, *Boston* 6 A3
Fresnes, *Paris* 23 B2
Freudenau, *Vienna* 31 A2
Friarstown, *Dublin* 11 B1
Frick Collection, *New York* 21 b3
Friedenau, *Berlin* 5 B3
Friedrichsfelde, *Berlin* 5 B4
Friedrichshagen, *Berlin* 5 B4
Friedrichshain, *Berlin* 5 A3
Friedrichslust, *Berlin* 5 A5
Friherrs, *Helsinki* 12 B1
Frontón, I., *Lima* 16 B1
Frunze, *Moscow* 19 B3
Fuchū, *Tokyo* 29 A1
Fuencarral, *Madrid* 17 B1
Fuenlabrada, *Madrid* 17 C1
Fujidera, *Osaka* 22 B4
Fukagawa, *Tokyo* 29 B3
Fukiage Imperial Garden, *Tokyo* 29 a4
Fukiai, *Osaka* 22 A2
Fukushima, *Osaka* 22 A3
Fulham, *London* 15 B2
Funabori, *Tokyo* 29 A4
Funasaka, *Osaka* 22 A2
Fundão, I. do, *Rio de Janeiro* 24 B1
Fünfhaus, *Vienna* 31 A2
Furesø, *Copenhagen* 10 A2
Furth, *Munich* 20 B2
Futago-tamagawaen, *Tokyo* 29 B2
Fuxing Dao, *Shanghai* 27 B2
Fuxing Park, *Shanghai* 27 B1
Fuxinglu, *Beijing* 4 B1

# G

Gage Park, *Chicago* 9 C2
Gagny, *Paris* 23 A4
Galata, *Istanbul* 12 B1
Galátsion, *Athens* 2 A2
Galeão, Aéroporto Int. de, *Rio de Janeiro* 24 A1
Galyanovo, *Moscow* 19 B4
Gambir, *Jakarta* 13 A1
Gamboa, *Rio de Janeiro* 24 B1
Gambolóita, *Milan* 18 B2
Gamla Stan, *Stockholm* 28 c2
Gamlebyen, *Oslo* 22 A3
Gangtou, *Canton* 8 A1
Gangwei, *Canton* 8 B2
Ganjiakou, *Beijing* 4 B1
Ganshoren, *Brussels* 6 A1
Gants Hill, *London* 15 A4
Gaoqiao, *Shanghai* 27 A2
Garbagnate Milanese, *Milan* 18 A1
Garbatella, *Rome* 25 B2
Garches, *Paris* 23 A2
Garching, *Munich* 20 A3
Garden City, *Cairo* 7 A2
Garden Reach, *Calcutta* 8 B1
Garder, *Oslo* 22 B2
Garfield, *New York* 21 A1
Garfield Park, *Chicago* 9 B2
Gargareta, *Athens* 2 B2
Garvanza, *Los Angeles* 16 B3
Gåshaga, *Stockholm* 28 A3
Gateway National Recreation Area, *New York* 21 C2
Gateway of India, *Mumbai* 20 B2
Gatow, *Berlin* 5 B1
Gávea, *Rio de Janeiro* 24 B1
Gávea, Pedra da, *Rio de Janeiro* 24 B1
Gazdagrét, *Budapest* 7 B1
Gebel el Ahmar, *Cairo* 7 A2
Gebel el Muqattam, *Cairo* 7 A2
Gebel el Tura, *Cairo* 7 B2
Geiselgasteig, *Munich* 20 B2
General San Martin, *Buenos Aires* 7 B1
Gennevilliers, *Paris* 23 A2
Gentilly, *Paris* 23 B3
Gentofte, *Copenhagen* 10 A3
Genval, *Brussels* 6 B2
George I., *Hong Kong* 12 B1
Georges I., *Boston* 6 B4
Georges River Bridge, *Sydney* 28 C1
Georgetown, *Washington* 32 B3
Georgia Dome, *Atlanta* 3 B2
Gerasdorf bei Wien, *Vienna* 31 A2
Gerberau, *Munich* 20 A1
Gerli, *Buenos Aires* 7 C2
Germiston, *Johannesburg* 13 B2
Gern, *Munich* 20 B2
Gesîrat el Rauda, *Cairo* 7 A2
Getafe, *Madrid* 17 C1
Geva Binyamin, *Jerusalem* 13 A2
Geylang Serai, *Singapore* 27 B3
Gezîrat el Dhahab, *Cairo* 7 B2
Gharapuri, *Mumbai* 20 B2
Ghatkopar, *Mumbai* 20 A2
Ghazipur, *Delhi* 10 B2
Ghizri, *Karachi* 14 B2
Ghizri Cr. →, *Karachi* 14 B2
Ghonda, *Delhi* 10 A2
Ghusuri, *Calcutta* 8 B2
Gianicolense, *Rome* 25 B1
Gianicolo, *Rome* 25 c1
Gibraltar Pt., *Toronto* 30 B2
Gidea Park, *London* 15 A5
Giesing, *Munich* 20 B2
Gilmerton, *Edinburgh* 11 B3
Gilo, *Jerusalem* 13 B2
Gimmersta, *Stockholm* 28 B3
Ginza, *Tokyo* 29 b5
Girgaum, *Mumbai* 20 b2
Giv'at Ye'arim, *Jerusalem* 13 B1
Giv'at Ze'ev, *Jerusalem* 13 A2
Giza Pyramids = Pyramids, *Cairo* 7 B1
Gjersjøen, *Oslo* 22 B3
Gladesville, *Sydney* 28 B1
Gladsakse, *Copenhagen* 10 A2
Glasnevin, *Dublin* 11 A2
Glassmanor, *Washington* 32 C3
Glasthule, *Dublin* 11 B3
Glen Iris, *Melbourne* 17 B2
Glen Mar Park, *Washington* 32 B3
Glen Rock, *New York* 21 A1
Glenarden, *Washington* 32 B4
Glenasmole Reservoirs, *Dublin* 11 B1
Glencorse Res., *Edinburgh* 11 B2
Glencullen, *Dublin* 11 B2
Glendale, *Los Angeles* 16 B3
Glendoo Mt., *Dublin* 11 B2
Glenhuntly, *Melbourne* 17 B2
Glenside, *Wellington* 32 B1
Glenview, *Chicago* 9 A2
Glenview Countryside, *Chicago* 9 A2
Glenvista, *Johannesburg* 13 B2
Glifádha, *Athens* 2 B2
Glömsta, *Stockholm* 28 B1
Glostrup, *Copenhagen* 10 B2
Gogar, *Edinburgh* 11 B2
Göktürk, *Istanbul* 12 A1
Golabari, *Calcutta* 8 B2
Golabki, *Warsaw* 31 B1
Gold Coast, *Chicago* 9 a2
Golden Gate, *San Francisco* 25 B2
Golden Gate Bridge, *San Francisco* 25 B2
Golden Gate Park, *San Francisco* 25 B2
Golden Horn, *Istanbul* 12 B1
Golders Green, *London* 15 A2
Gollans Stream →, *Wellington* 32 B2
Golyevo, *Moscow* 19 B1
Goodman Hill, *Boston* 6 A1
Goodmayes, *London* 15 A4
Goodwood, *Cape Town* 8 A2
Gopalpur, *Calcutta* 8 B2
Górce, *Warsaw* 31 B1
Gore Hill, *Sydney* 28 A2
Gorelyy →, *St. Petersburg* 26 A3
Gorenki, *Moscow* 19 B5
Gorgie, *Edinburgh* 11 B2
Gorky Park, *Moscow* 19 B3
Gosen, *Berlin* 5 B5
Gosener kanal, *Berlin* 5 B5
Gospel Oak, *London* 15 A3
Gotanda, *Tokyo* 29 B3
Goth Goli Mar, *Karachi* 14 A2
Goth Sher Shah, *Karachi* 14 A1
Gournay-sur-Marne, *Paris* 23 A4
Governador, I. do, *Rio de Janeiro* 24 A1
Governor's I., *New York* 21 B1
Graben, *Vienna* 31 b2
Grabów, *Warsaw* 31 C1
Graça, *Lisbon* 14 b3
Grace, Mt., *Wellington* 32 B2
Grace Cathedral, *San Francisco* 25 b1
Gracefield, *Wellington* 32 B2
Gracia, *Barcelona* 4 A2
Gräfelfing, *Munich* 20 B1
Gragoatá, *Rio de Janeiro* 24 B2
Grand Cemtral Station, *New York* 21 c2
Grand Union Canal, *London* 15 A2
Grande Place, *Brussels* 6 b2
Grant Park, *Atlanta* 3 B2
Grant Park, *Chicago* 9 c2
Granton, *Edinburgh* 11 B2
Grape I., *Boston* 6 B4
Grassy Park, *Cape Town* 8 B2
Gratosóglio, *Milan* 18 B2
Gratzwalde, *Berlin* 5 B5
Gravesend, *New York* 21 C2
Grazhdanka, *St. Petersburg* 26 B2
Great Falls, *Washington* 32 B2
Great Falls Park, *Washington* 32 B2
Great Hall of the People, *Beijing* 4 b2
Great Meadows National Wildlife Refuge, *Boston* 6 A1
Greco, *Milan* 18 A2
Green I., *Hong Kong* 12 B1
Green Point, *Cape Town* 8 A1
Greenbelt, *Washington* 32 A4
Greenbelt Park, *Washington* 32 B4
Greenfield Park, *Montreal* 19 B3
Greenford, *London* 15 A1
Greenhill, *London* 15 A2
Greenhills, *Dublin* 11 B1
Greenmarket Square, *Cape Town* 8 c2
Greenpoint, *New York* 21 B2
Greenwich, *London* 15 B3
Greenwich Observatory, *London* 15 B3
Greenwich Village, *New York* 21 B2
Greenwood, *Boston* 6 A3
Grefsen, *Oslo* 22 A3
Gresham Park, *Atlanta* 3 B2
Greve Strand, *Copenhagen* 10 B1
Greyfriars Kirk, *Edinburgh* 11 c2
Griebnitzsee, *Berlin* 5 B1
Griffen Park, *Los Angeles* 16 B3
Grimbergen, *Brussels* 6 A2
Grinzing, *Vienna* 31 A2
Gröbenried, *Munich* 20 A1
Grochów, *Warsaw* 31 B2
Grodzisk, *Warsaw* 31 B2
Groenendaal, *Brussels* 6 B2
Grogol Petamburin, *Jakarta* 13 A1
Gronsdorf, *Munich* 20 B3
Grorud, *Oslo* 22 A4
Gross Glienicke, *Berlin* 5 B1
Gross-Hadern, *Munich* 20 B1
Gross-Lappen, *Munich* 20 A2
Grosse Krampe, *Berlin* 5 B5
Grosse Müggelsee, *Berlin* 5 B4
Grossenzersdorf, *Vienna* 31 A3
Grossenzersdorfer Arm →, *Vienna* 31 A3
Grosser Biberhaufen, *Vienna* 31 A2
Grosser Wannsee, *Berlin* 5 B2
Grossfeld-Siedlung, *Vienna* 31 A2
Grosshesselohe, *Munich* 20 B2
Grossjedlersdorf, *Vienna* 31 A2
Grossziethen, *Berlin* 5 B3
Grove Hall, *Boston* 6 B3
Grove Park, *Atlanta* 3 B2
Grove Park, *London* 15 B4
Grove Park, *London* 15 B2
Groveton, *Washington* 32 C3
Grünau, *Berlin* 5 B4
Grunewald, *Berlin* 5 B2
Grünwald, *Munich* 20 B2
Grünwalder Forst, *Munich* 20 B2
Grymes Hill, *New York* 21 C1
Guadalupe, *Manila* 17 B2
Guadalupe, Basilica de, *Mexico City* 18 B2
Guanabara, B. de, *Rio de Janeiro* 24 B1
Guanabara, Jardim, *Rio de Janeiro* 24 A1
Guanabara, Palácio da, *Rio de Janeiro* 24 B1
Guang'anmen, *Beijing* 4 B1
Guangqumen, *Beijing* 4 B2
Guangzhou, *Canton* 8 B2
Guanshuo, *Canton* 8 B3
Gudö, *Stockholm* 28 B3
Güell, Parque de, *Barcelona* 4 A2
Guerrero, *Mexico City* 18 a1
Guggenheim Museum, *New York* 21 b3
Guinardó, *Barcelona* 4 A2
Gulbai, *Karachi* 14 A1
Güngören, *Istanbul* 12 B1
Gunnersbury, *London* 15 B2
Gustavo A. Madero, *Mexico City* 18 B2
Guttenberg, *New York* 21 B1
Gutuyevskiy, Ostrov, *St. Petersburg* 26 B1
Guyancourt, *Paris* 23 B1
Gyál, *Budapest* 7 B3
Gyáli-patak →, *Budapest* 7 B2

# H

Haaga, *Helsinki* 12 B2
Haar, *Munich* 20 B3
Hackbridge, *London* 15 B3
Hackensack, *New York* 21 A1
Hackensack →, *New York* 21 B1
Hackney, *London* 15 A3
Hackney Wick, *London* 15 A3
Haga, *Stockholm* 28 A2
Hagenbrunn, *Vienna* 31 A2
Hägersten, *Stockholm* 28 B1
Häggvik, *Stockholm* 28 A1
Hai He →, *Tianjin* 30 B2
Haidan, *Beijing* 4 B1
Haidarpur, *Delhi* 10 A1
Haidhausen, *Munich* 20 B2
Haight-Ashbury, *San Francisco* 25 B2
Hainault, *London* 15 A4
Haizhu Guangchang, *Canton* 8 B2
Hakunila, *Helsinki* 12 B3
Halásztelek, *Budapest* 7 B1
Haliç = Golden Horn, *Istanbul* 12 B1
Halim Perdanakusuma International Airport, *Jakarta* 13 B2
Halle, *Brussels* 6 B1
Haltiala, *Helsinki* 12 B2
Haltiavuori, *Helsinki* 12 B2
Ham, *London* 15 B2
Hämeenkylä, *Helsinki* 12 B1
Hammarby, *Stockholm* 28 B2
Hamme, *Brussels* 6 A1
Hammersmith, *London* 15 B2
Hampstead, *London* 15 A2
Hampstead, *Montreal* 19 B2
Hampstead Garden Suburb, *London* 15 A2
Hampstead Heath, *London* 15 A2
Hampton, *London* 15 B1
Hampton Court Palace, *London* 15 B1
Hampton Wick, *London* 15 B2
Hamrā', *Baghdad* 3 B1
Hanala, *Helsinki* 12 A3
Haneda, *Tokyo* 29 B3
Hang Hau, *Hong Kong* 12 B2
Hanging Gardens, *Mumbai* 20 b1
Hanjiashu, *Tianjin* 30 A1
Hanlon, *Toronto* 30 B1
Hanwell, *London* 15 A1
Hanworth, *London* 15 B1
Haora, *Calcutta* 8 B1
Hapeville, *Atlanta* 3 C2
Happy Valley, *Hong Kong* 12 B2
Har Adar, *Jerusalem* 13 B1
Haren, *Brussels* 6 A2
Hareskovby, *Copenhagen* 10 A2
Haringey, *London* 15 A3
Harjusuo, *Helsinki* 12 B3
Harlaching, *Munich* 20 B2
Harlaw Res., *Edinburgh* 11 B2
Harlem, *New York* 21 B2
Harlesden, *London* 15 A2
Harlington, *London* 15 B1
Harmaja, *Helsinki* 12 C2
Harmashatar hegy, *Budapest* 7 A2
Harolds Cross, *Dublin* 11 B2
Háros, *Budapest* 7 B2
Harperrig Reservoir, *Edinburgh* 11 B1
Harrow, *London* 15 A1
Harrow on the Hill, *London* 15 A1
Harrow School, *London* 15 A1
Harrow Weald, *London* 15 A1
Hartsfield-Atlanta International Airport, *Atlanta* 3 C2
Harumi, *Tokyo* 29 c5
Harvard Univ., *Boston* 6 A3
Harwood Heights, *Chicago* 9 B2
Hasanābād, *Tehran* 30 A1
Hasbrouck Heights, *New York* 21 A1
Haselhorst, *Berlin* 5 A2
Hasköy, *Istanbul* 12 B1
Hasle, *Oslo* 22 B2
Haslum, *Oslo* 22 A2
Hästhagen, *Stockholm* 28 B2
Hataitai, *Wellington* 32 B1
Hatch End, *London* 15 A1
Hatiara, *Calcutta* 8 B2
Hauketo, *Oslo* 22 A3
Havel →, *Berlin* 5 A2
Havelkanal, *Berlin* 5 A2
Havering, *London* 15 A5
Havering-atte-Bower, *London* 15 A5
Hawŏlgok, *Seoul* 26 B2
Haworth, *New York* 21 A2
Hayes, *London* 15 B4
Hayes, *London* 15 A1
Hayes End, *London* 15 A1
Hayford, *Chicago* 9 C2
Haywards, *Wellington* 32 A2
Heard Pond, *Boston* 6 A1
Heathfield, *Cape Town* 8 B1
Heathrow Airport, *London* 15 B1
Hebe Haven, *Hong Kong* 12 A2
Hebei, *Tianjin* 30 B2
Hedong, *Canton* 8 B2
Hedong, *Tianjin* 30 B2
Heidelberg Heights, *Melbourne* 17 A2
Heidelberg West, *Melbourne* 17 A2
Heidemühle, *Berlin* 5 B5
Heideveld, *Cape Town* 8 A2
Heiligensee, *Berlin* 5 A2
Heiligenstadt, *Vienna* 31 A2
Heinersdorf, *Berlin* 5 A3
Heldenplatz, *Vienna* 31 b1
Hélène Champlain, Parc, *Montreal* 19 A2
Helenelund, *Stockholm* 28 A1
Heliopolis = Masr el Gedida, *Cairo* 7 A2
Hellersdorf, *Berlin* 5 A4
Hellerup, *Copenhagen* 10 A3
Helmahof, *Vienna* 31 A3
Helsingfors = Helsinki, *Helsinki* 12 B2
Helsinki, *Helsinki* 12 B2
Helsinki Airport, *Helsinki* 12 B2
Hendon, *London* 15 A2
Hengsha, *Canton* 8 B2
Hennigsdorf, *Berlin* 5 A2
Henryków, *Warsaw* 31 B1
Henson Cr. →, *Washington* 32 C4
Henttaa, *Helsinki* 12 B1
Heping, *Tianjin* 30 B2
Heping Park, *Shanghai* 27 B2
Hepingli, *Beijing* 4 B2
Herlev, *Copenhagen* 10 A2
Herman Eckstein Park, *Johannesburg* 13 A2
Hermannskogel, *Vienna* 31 A1
Hermiston, *Edinburgh* 11 B2
Hermitage and Winter Palace, *St. Petersburg* 26 B1
Hermsdorf, *Berlin* 5 A2
Hernals, *Vienna* 31 A2
Herne Hill, *London* 15 B3
Héroes de Churubusco, *Mexico City* 18 B2
Herons, Î. aux, *Montreal* 19 B2
Herstedøster, *Copenhagen* 10 A2
Herttoniemi, *Helsinki* 12 B3
Ḩeşārak, *Tehran* 30 A1
Heston, *London* 15 B1
Hetzendorf, *Vienna* 31 B1
Hexi, *Tianjin* 30 B2
Hextable, *London* 15 B5
Hialeah, *Miami* 18 A1
Hickory Hills, *Chicago* 9 C2
Hiekkaharju, *Helsinki* 12 B3
Hietaniemi, *Helsinki* 12 B2
Hietzing, *Vienna* 31 A1
Higashi, *Osaka* 22 A4
Higashimurayama, *Tokyo* 29 A1
Higashinada, *Osaka* 22 A2
Higashinari, *Osaka* 22 A4
Higashiōsaka, *Osaka* 22 B4
Higashisumiyoshi, *Osaka* 22 B4
Higashiyodogawa, *Osaka* 22 A3
High Park, *Toronto* 30 B2
Highbury, *London* 15 A3
Highgate, *London* 15 A3
Highland Cr. →, *Toronto* 30 A3
Highland Creek, *Toronto* 30 A3
Highland Park, *Los Angeles* 16 B3
Highlands North, *Johannesburg* 13 A2
Hillcrest Heights, *Washington* 32 C4
Hillend, *Edinburgh* 11 A1
Hillingdon, *London* 15 A1
Hillwood, *Washington* 32 B3
Hilmîya, *Cairo* 7 A2
Hin Keng, *Hong Kong* 12 A2
Hingham, *Boston* 6 B4
Hingham B., *Boston* 6 B4
Hingham Harbor, *Boston* 6 B4
Hirakata, *Osaka* 22 A4
Hirota, *Osaka* 22 A3
Hirschstetten, *Vienna* 31 A2
Histórico Nacional, Museu, *Rio de Janeiro* 24 b3
Hither Green, *London* 15 B3
Hiyoshi, *Tokyo* 29 B2
Hizma, *Jerusalem* 13 B2
Hjortekær, *Copenhagen* 10 A3
Hjortespring, *Copenhagen* 10 A2
Hlubočepy, *Prague* 24 B2
Ho Chung, *Hong Kong* 12 A2
Ho Man Tin, *Hong Kong* 12 B2
Hoboken, *New York* 21 B1
Hobsons B., *Melbourne* 17 B1
Hochbrück, *Munich* 20 A2
Hochelaga, *Montreal* 19 A2
Hodgkins, *Chicago* 9 C1
Hoegi, *Seoul* 26 B2
Hoeilaart, *Brussels* 6 B2
Hofberg, *Vienna* 31 A2
Hoffman I., *New York* 21 C1
Hofgarten, *Munich* 20 a3
Högsdtadomstolen, *Stockholm* 28 c2
Hohenbrunn, *Munich* 20 B3
Hohenschönhausen, *Berlin* 5 A4
Holborn, *London* 15 a4
Holešovice, *Prague* 24 B2
Holland Village, *Singapore* 27 B2
Höllriegelskreuth, *Munich* 20 B1
Hollywood, *Los Angeles* 16 B3
Holmenkollen, *Oslo* 22 A3
Holmes Run Acres, *Washington* 32 B2
Holmgård, *Stockholm* 28 B1
Holysloot, *Amsterdam* 2 A3
Homerton, *London* 15 A3
Hometown, *Chicago* 9 C2
Hōnanchō, *Tokyo* 29 A2
Honcho, *Tokyo* 29 A3
Honden, *Tokyo* 29 A4
Hondo, Rio →, *Los Angeles* 16 B4
Hong Kong, *Hong Kong* 12 B1
Hong Kong, Univ. of, *Hong Kong* 12 B1
Hong Kong I., *Hong Kong* 12 B2
Hong Kong Park, *Hong Kong* 12 c1
Hongkou, *Shanghai* 27 B1
Hongkou Park, *Shanghai* 27 B1
Hongmiao, *Beijing* 4 B2
Hongqiao, *Shanghai* 27 B1
Hongqiao, *Tianjin* 30 B1
Hongqiao Airport, *Shanghai* 27 B1
Hongŭn, *Seoul* 26 B1
Honjyo, *Tokyo* 29 A3
Honoré Mercier, Pont, *Montreal* 19 B1
Hönow, *Berlin* 5 A4
Hooghly = Hugli →, *Calcutta* 8 A2
Hook, *London* 15 B2
Horikiri, *Tokyo* 29 A4
Horn Pond, *Boston* 6 A2
Hornchurch, *London* 15 A5
Horni, *Prague* 24 B3
Horni Počernice, *Prague* 24 B3
Hornsey, *London* 15 A3
Horoměřice, *Prague* 24 B1
Hortaleza, *Madrid* 17 B2
Hosoyama, *Tokyo* 29 B2
Hostafranchs, *Barcelona* 4 A1
Hostivař, *Prague* 24 B3
Hôtel des Invalides, *Paris* 23 c2
Houbětin, *Prague* 24 B3
Houghs Neck, *Boston* 6 B4
Houghton, *Johannesburg* 13 B2
Houilles, *Paris* 23 A2
Hounslow, *London* 15 B1
Houses of Parliament, *London* 15 c3
Hout Bay, *Cape Town* 8 B1
Hove Å →, *Copenhagen* 10 A1
Hovedøya, *Oslo* 22 A3
Høvik, *Oslo* 22 A2
Hovorčovice, *Prague* 24 A3
Howard Beach, *New York* 21 C2
Howth, *Dublin* 11 A3
Howth Head, *Dublin* 11 A3
Hoxton, *London* 15 a5
Hōya, *Tokyo* 29 A2
Hradčany, *Prague* 24 B2
Huanghuagang Mausoleum of the 72 Martyrs, *Canton* 8 B2
Huangpu, *Shanghai* 27 B2
Huangpu Jiang →, *Shanghai* 27 B1
Huangpu Park, *Shanghai* 27 B1
Huangtugang, *Beijing* 4 C1
Huascar, *Lima* 16 A2
Huay Khwang, *Bangkok* 3 B2
Huddinge, *Stockholm* 28 B2
Hudson →, *New York* 21 A2
Huechuraba, *Santiago* 26 B1
Huertas de San Beltran, *Barcelona* 4 A1
Hugli →, *Calcutta* 8 A2
Huidui, *Tianjin* 30 B2
Huizingen, *Brussels* 6 B1
Hull, *Boston* 6 B4
Humber →, *Toronto* 30 A1
Humber B., *Toronto* 30 B2
Humber Bay, *Toronto* 30 B2
Humber Summit, *Toronto* 30 A1
Humber Valley Village, *Toronto* 30 A1
Humberlea, *Toronto* 30 A1
Humboldt Park, *Chicago* 9 B2
Humera, *Madrid* 17 B1
Hunaydī, *Baghdad* 3 B2
Hundige, *Copenhagen* 10 B1
Hundige Strand, *Copenhagen* 10 B2
Hung Hom, *Hong Kong* 12 B2
Hunters Hill, *Sydney* 28 B1
Hunters Pt., *San Francisco* 25 B2
Hunters Valley, *Washington* 32 B2
Huntington, *Washington* 32 C3
Huntington Park, *Los Angeles* 16 C3
Hurīya, *Baghdad* 3 A1
Hurstville, *Sydney* 28 B1
Husby, *Stockholm* 28 A1
Husum, *Copenhagen* 10 A2
Hutt R. →, *Wellington* 32 B2
Hütteldorf, *Vienna* 31 A1
Hüvösvölgy, *Budapest* 7 A2
Hvalstad, *Oslo* 22 A1
Hvalstrand, *Oslo* 22 A2
Hvidovre, *Copenhagen* 10 B2
Hwagok, *Seoul* 26 B1
Hyattsville, *Washington* 32 B4
Hyde Park, *Boston* 6 B3
Hyde Park, *Chicago* 9 C3
Hyde Park, *Johannesburg* 13 A2
Hyde Park, *London* 15 A2
Hyde Park, *Sydney* 28 B2

# I

Ibese, *Lagos* 14 A2
Ibirapuera, *São Paulo* 26 B1
Ibirapuera, Parque, *São Paulo* 26 B2
Icarai, *Rio de Janeiro* 24 B2
Içerenköy, *Istanbul* 12 C2
Ichgao, *Tokyo* 29 B2
Ichigaya, *Tokyo* 29 a3
Ichikawa, *Tokyo* 29 A4
Ickenham, *London* 15 A1
Iddo, *Lagos* 14 B2
Idi-Oro, *Lagos* 14 A2
Iganmu, *Lagos* 14 B2
Igbobi, *Lagos* 14 A2
Igbologun, *Lagos* 14 B1
Igny, *Paris* 23 B2
IJ, Het →, *Amsterdam* 2 A2
IJ-meer, *Amsterdam* 2 A3
Ijesa-Tedo, *Lagos* 14 B1
Ijora, *Lagos* 14 B2
IJtunnel, *Amsterdam* 2 a3
Ikebe, *Tokyo* 29 B2
Ikebukuro, *Tokyo* 29 A3
Ikegami, *Tokyo* 29 B3
Ikeja, *Lagos* 14 A2
Ikeuchi, *Osaka* 22 B4
Ikoyi, *Lagos* 14 B2
Ikuata, *Lagos* 14 B2
Ikuno, *Osaka* 22 A4
Ikuta, *Osaka* 22 A2
Ikuta, *Tokyo* 29 B2
Ila, *Oslo* 22 A2
Ilford, *London* 15 A4
Ilioúpolis, *Athens* 2 B2
Ilpendam, *Amsterdam* 2 A2
Ilsós →, *Athens* 2 B2
Imagem e do Som, Museu da, *Rio de Janeiro* 24 b3
Imbâbah, *Cairo* 7 A2
Imielin, *Warsaw* 31 C2
Imirim, *São Paulo* 26 A2
Imittós, *Athens* 2 B2
Imittoś, Óros, *Athens* 2 B2
Imperial Palace Museum, *Beijing* 4 b2
Inagi, *Tokyo* 29 B2
Inchcolm, *Edinburgh* 11 A2
Inchicore, *Dublin* 11 A1
Inchkeith, *Edinburgh* 11 A3
Inchmickery, *Edinburgh* 11 A2
Incirano, *Milan* 18 A1
Independencia, *Lima* 16 A2
Independencia, *Santiago* 26 B2
India Gate, *Delhi* 1 c2
Indian Creek Village, *Miami* 18 A2
Indian Head Park, *Chicago* 9 C1
Indianópolis, *São Paulo* 26 B2
Indios Verdes, *Mexico City* 18 B2
Indira Ghandi International Airport, *Delhi* 10 B1
Industria, *Johannesburg* 13 B1
Ingierstrand, *Oslo* 22 B3
Inglewood, *Los Angeles* 16 C3
Ingliston, *Edinburgh* 11 B1
Inhaúme, *Rio de Janeiro* 24 B1
Inner Port Shelter, *Hong Kong* 12 A2
Interlagos, *São Paulo* 26 C1
Intramuros, *Manila* 17 B1
Invalides, *Paris* 23 A2
Inverkeithing, *Edinburgh* 11 A1
Inzersdorf, *Vienna* 31 B2
Ipanema, *Rio de Janeiro* 24 B1
Ipiranga, *São Paulo* 26 B2
Ipiranga →, *São Paulo* 26 B2
Iponri, *Lagos* 14 B2
Ireland's Eye, *Dublin* 11 A3
Irving Park, *Chicago* 9 B2
Isabel, *Rio de Janeiro* 24 B1
Isagatedo, *Lagos* 14 A1
Isar →, *Munich* 20 A3
Ishbīlīya, *Baghdad* 3 A2
Ishikiri, *Osaka* 22 A4
Ishøj Strand, *Copenhagen* 10 B2
Island Bay, *Wellington* 32 B1
Island Park, *Toronto* 30 B2
Isle of Dogs, *London* 15 B3
Islev, *Copenhagen* 10 A2
Isleworth, *London* 15 B2
Islington, *London* 15 A3
Islington, *Toronto* 30 B1
Ismaning, *Munich* 20 A3
Ismayloskiy Park, *Moscow* 19 B4
Isolo, *Lagos* 14 A1
Issy-les-Moulineaux, *Paris* 23 B2
Istanbul, *Istanbul* 12 C1
Istanbul Boğazi, *Istanbul* 12 B2
Istinye, *Istanbul* 12 B2
Itä Hakkila, *Helsinki* 12 B3
Itaewŏn, *Seoul* 26 B1
Itahanga, *Rio de Janeiro* 24 B1
Itami, *Osaka* 22 A3
Ivanhoe, *Melbourne* 17 A2
Ivry-sur-Seine, *Paris* 23 B3
Iwazono, *Osaka* 22 A2
Ixelles, *Brussels* 6 B2
Izmaylovo, *Moscow* 19 B4
Iztacalco, *Mexico City* 18 B2
Iztapalapa, *Mexico City* 18 B2

# J

Jaba, *Jerusalem* 13 A2
Jababpur, *Calcutta* 8 C2
Jacaré, *Rio de Janeiro* 24 B1
Jackson Heights, *New York* 21 B2
Jackson Park, *Chicago* 9 C3
Jacques Cartier, *Montreal* 19 A3
Jacques Cartier, Pont, *Montreal* 19 A2
Jade Buddha Temple, *Shanghai* 27 B1
Jægersborg, *Copenhagen* 10 A3
Jægersborg Dyrehave, *Copenhagen* 10 A3
Jagadishpur, *Calcutta* 8 B1
Jagatpur, *Delhi* 10 A2
Jaguaré, Rib. do →, *São Paulo* 26 B1
Jahangirpur, *Delhi* 10 A2
Jakarta, *Jakarta* 13 A2
Jakarta, Teluk, *Jakarta* 13 A1
Jalan Kayu, *Singapore* 27 A3
Jamaica B., *New York* 21 C3
Jamaica Plain, *Boston* 6 B3
Jamakpuri, *Delhi* 10 B1
Jamshīdīyeh, *Tehran* 30 A2
Janki, *Warsaw* 31 C1
Jannali, *Sydney* 28 C1
Japan Center, *San Francisco* 25 c1
Jaraguá, *São Paulo* 26 A1
Jaraguá, Pico de, *São Paulo* 26 A1
Jardim Paulista, *São Paulo* 26 B1
Jardin Botanique, *Brussels* 6 a3
Järvatältet, *Stockholm* 28 A1
Jaskhar, *Mumbai* 20 B2
Jatinegara, *Jakarta* 13 B2
Javādīyeh, *Tehran* 30 B2
Jaworowa, *Warsaw* 31 C1
Jedlesee, *Vienna* 31 A2
Jefferson Memorial, *Washington* 32 c1
Jefferson Park, *Chicago* 9 B2
Jelonki, *Warsaw* 31 B1
Jerónimos, Mosteiro dos, *Lisbon* 14 A1
Jersey City, *New York* 21 B1
Jerusalem, *Jerusalem* 13 B2
Jésus, Î., *Montreal* 19 A1
Jesús Maria, *Lima* 16 B2
Jette, *Brussels* 6 A1
Jewish Quarter, *Jerusalem* 13 b3
Jey, *Tehran* 30 B2
Jianguomen, *Beijing* 4 B2
Jiangwan, *Shanghai* 27 B1
Jianshan Park, *Tianjin* 30 B2
Jihād, *Baghdad* 3 B1
Jim Thompson's House, *Bangkok* 3 b3
Jimbōchō, *Tokyo* 29 a4
Jingan, *Shanghai* 27 B1
Jingu Outer Garden, *Tokyo* 29 b2
Jinočany, *Prague* 24 B1
Jinonice, *Prague* 24 B2
Jiyūgaoka, *Tokyo* 29 B3
Jizā'ir, *Baghdad* 3 B2
Jizīra, *Baghdad* 3 B2
Johannesburg, *Johannesburg* 13 B2
Johanneskirchen, *Munich* 20 A2
Johannesstift, *Berlin* 5 A2
Johannisthal, *Berlin* 5 B4
John Hancock Center, *Chicago* 9 a2
John McLaren Park, *San Francisco* 25 B2
Johnsonville, *Wellington* 32 B1
Joinville-le-Pont, *Paris* 23 B3
Joli-Bois, *Brussels* 6 B2
Jollas, *Helsinki* 12 B3
Jonstrup, *Copenhagen* 10 A2
Joppa, *Edinburgh* 11 B3
Jorge Chavez, Aeropuerto Int., *Lima* 16 B2
Jorge Newbury, Aeroparque, *Buenos Aires* 7 B2
Jósefa Piłsudskiego Park, *Warsaw* 31 B1
Jōtō, *Osaka* 22 A4
Jouy-en-Josas, *Paris* 23 B2
Juan Anchorena, *Buenos Aires* 7 A2
Juan González Romero, *Mexico City* 18 A2
Judeira, *Jerusalem* 13 A2
Juhu, *Mumbai* 20 A2
Jūjā, *Tokyo* 29 A3
Jukskeirivier →, *Johannesburg* 13 A2
Julianów, *Warsaw* 31 B2
Jungfernheide, Volkspark, *Berlin* 5 A2
Jungfernsee, *Berlin* 5 B1
Juniper Green, *Edinburgh* 11 B2
Junk B., *Hong Kong* 12 B2
Jurong, *Singapore* 27 B2
Jurong, Selat, *Singapore* 27 B2
Jurong Industrial Estate, *Singapore* 27 B1
Jurujuba, Enseada de, *Rio de Janeiro* 24 B2
Jūsō, *Osaka* 22 A3
Justice, *Chicago* 9 C2
Justicia, *Madrid* 17 a3
Jwalahari, *Delhi* 10 B1

# K

Kabaty, *Warsaw* 31 C2
Kadıköy, *Istanbul* 12 C2
Kadoma, *Osaka* 22 A4
Kaebong, *Seoul* 26 C1
Kafr 'Aqab, *Jerusalem* 13 A2
Kâğıthane, *Istanbul* 12 B1
Kâğıthane →, *Istanbul* 12 B1
Kagran, *Vienna* 31 A2
Kahnawake, *Montreal* 19 B1
Kaimes, *Edinburgh* 11 B2
Kaisariani, *Athens* 2 B2
Kaiser Wilhelm Kirche, *Berlin* 5 b2
Kaiserebersdorf, *Vienna* 31 B2
Kaivoksela, *Helsinki* 12 B2
Kalamákion, *Athens* 2 B2
Kalbadevi, *Mumbai* 20 b2
Kalhyŏn, *Seoul* 26 B1
Kalipur, *Calcutta* 8 A1
Kalkaji, *Delhi* 10 B2
Kallithéa, *Athens* 2 B2
Kalveboderne, *Copenhagen* 10 B3
Kamarhati, *Calcutta* 8 A2
Kamata, *Tokyo* 29 B3
Kameari, *Tokyo* 29 A4
Kameido, *Tokyo* 29 A4
Kami-Itabashi, *Tokyo* 29 A3
Kamikitazawa, *Tokyo* 29 B2
Kamitsuruma, *Tokyo* 29 B1
Kamoshida, *Tokyo* 29 B2
Kampong Landang, *Singapore* 27 A3
Kampong Tanjong Penjuru, *Singapore* 27 B2
Kampung Bali, *Jakarta* 13 B1
Kanamori, *Tokyo* 29 B1
Kanda, *Tokyo* 29 a5
Kandilli, *Istanbul* 12 B2
Kangdong, *Seoul* 26 B2
Kangnam, *Seoul* 26 B1
Kangsŏ, *Seoul* 26 B1
Kankurgachi, *Calcutta* 8 B2
Kanlıca, *Istanbul* 12 B2
Kanonerskiy, Ostrov, *St. Petersburg* 26 B1
Kanzaki →, *Osaka* 22 A3
Kapellerfeld, *Vienna* 31 A2

## S

## T

# CITY GAZETTEER

*The entries below provide information on places of interest in cities throughout the world that have particularly large numbers of visitors, whether in a business or tourist capacity. The map page reference at the start of an entry indicates that one or more relevant maps are included in the City Maps section.*

## Accra, Ghana

Accra is not the most beautiful city in West Africa, but its people are considered to be among the friendliest and best educated. It has several lively markets and a National Museum with displays of West African art and artefacts. Near the city are some beautiful sandy beaches, although visitors should be alert to the powerful undertow. Further along the coast are forts and castles that once served as slave-trading centres, including St George's Castle at Elmina, the oldest European structure in sub-Saharan Africa.

## Agra, India

Agra is visited primarily for its architectural wonders, especially the 17th-century Taj Mahal. This magical building, a symbol of Mughal emperor Shah Jahan's love for his favourite wife, Mumtaz Mahal, captures the imagination even when crowded with tourists in the heat of the day. Agra's 16th-century Red Fort contains elaborately decorated royal apartments and gardens that give a vivid impression of life at the Mughal court. Just 40 km (25 miles) away is the Mughal 'ghost city' of Fatehpur Sikri which was abandoned almost immediately after it had been built in the 1570s.

Taj Mahal, Agra

## Amsterdam, The Netherlands     *Map page 2*

In the centre of Amsterdam is a network of canals, crossed by around a thousand bridges and edged with tree-lined streets of 17th- and 18th-century gabled houses. Canal cruises are an excellent way to get to know the city, and visitors can also hire bicycles – a major form of transport in Amsterdam. Among the museums are the Rijksmuseum, with its famous art collection, the Van Gogh Museum, and the Stedelijk Museum, housing modern art. The heart of the city is Dam Square, with the royal palace and Anne Frank's house (now a museum) close by. Rembrandt's house can also be visited in an area full of bars, nightclubs and restaurants.

## Athens, Greece     *Map page 2*

Athens is a curious mixture of ancient and modern, where ugly concrete tower blocks rub shoulders with Classical monuments. Dominating the centre of the city are the ruins on the Acropolis, dating from the 5th century BC and crowned by the magnificent Parthenon. Other interesting ruins include the Temple of Olympian Zeus, the largest temple in Greece. The National Archaeological Museum houses gold artefacts from Mycenae and spectacular Minoan frescoes.

Nestling beneath the Acropolis is the engaging Pláka quarter, with its small Byzantine churches and bustling tavernas. For most visitors the centre of Athens is Sindagma Square, with its large hotels, banks and open-air cafés. Ferries to the islands depart from the port of Piraeus, 10 km (6 miles) from the square.

## Atlanta, Georgia, USA     *Map page 3*

Beneath the glittering high-rise buildings of Atlanta's modern financial centre lies 'Underground Atlanta' – the revitalized old centre, complete with cobbled, gas-lit streets and packed with shops and restaurants. The piazza above it is filled with street entertainers and flanked by the Coca-Cola Museum. Atlanta is most famously associated with Martin Luther King, and an area of the city is devoted to his memory and to the history of the civil rights movement. The Centennial Olympic Park, with its Fountain of Rings, is an entertaining outdoor venue, and the adjacent CNN Center provides an interesting studio tour.

## Auckland, New Zealand

The heart of Auckland is the magnificent Waitemata Harbour, where sailing is a popular pastime. The city is not renowned for its nightlife, but it is pleasant to walk its streets, perhaps following the 13 km (8-mile) Coast-to-Coast Walkway from the Ferry Building to Manukau Harbour. On the route, in an area of parkland known as The Domain, is the Auckland Museum, with a unique collection of Maori and Pacific Island artefacts. Beyond is the inner suburb of Parnell, with its colonial buildings, east of which is Underwater World, a particularly impressive aquarium. There are several city beaches, and surfing beaches beyond the Waitakere Ranges.

## Baghdad, Iraq     *Map page 3*

Baghdad is a city where modern shops and restaurants rub shoulders with bazaars. Buildings dating from as early as the 13th century include the Abbasid Palace and an Islamic Law School (the Mustansiriyah), both now museums. The National Museum contains artefacts from ancient civilizations, including Mesopotamia and Babylonia. At the time of writing, Baghdad is effectively closed to Western visitors.

## Bangkok, Thailand     *Map page 3*

With its choking traffic, Bangkok can be both a daunting and an exhilarating city for short-stay visitors. Something of the old Siam can be uncovered by using the river-bus service to visit the Royal Grand Palace and the ornate Temple of the Emerald Buddha (Wat Phra Keo). Other Buddhist temples include the Temple of the Dawn (Wat Arun), whose 82 m (266 ft) high gilded stupa is best seen from the Chao Phraya River. At Jim Thompson's House there is an extraordinary private museum of Thai domestic architecture. The network of canals, with their floating markets, is well worth exploring, as are the shops for silk and other textiles, clothes, jewellery and handicrafts. Night-time entertainment includes traditional dancing and Thai boxing.

Floating market, Bangkok

## Barcelona, Spain     *Map page 4*

The capital of Catalonia and Spain's second city, Barcelona is a major port with a fashionable, cosmopolitan cultural life. Particularly enjoyable is strolling along the Ramblas, a broad avenue which bisects central Barcelona, and has a vibrant street life. At the southern end is the renovated harbour area, with shops, restaurants and tapas bars. The district of greatest historic interest is the Barri Gòtic, where medieval houses cluster around the great Gothic cathedral, La Seu. Barcelona has over 50 museums and galleries, including world-class museums dedicated to the works of Picasso and Miró, but it is the buildings of Antonio Gaudí that are most often associated with the city. His incomplete Sagrada Família Cathedral has become a symbol for Barcelona, and is perhaps the most fantastic of all his eccentric creations.

## Beijing, China     *Map page 4*

Despite Beijing's daunting scale, extreme climate and heavy traffic, its sights are well worth visiting. They include the massive Tiananmen Square, the Mao Mausoleum, the Great Hall of the People, the Imperial Palace (Forbidden City), the buildings of the Summer Palace along the shore of Kunming Lake, and the 15th-century Temple of Heaven. Beijing has many interesting parks, including Beihai Park with its historic buildings and exquisite Jade Island. However, perhaps the most famous attraction of all is the Great Wall, which can be visited at Badaling, just 70 km (40 miles) north-west of the city, on a trip that also takes in the Ming tombs in the Shisan Ling Valley.

## Berlin, Germany     *Map page 5*

After decades of being divided into West and East Berlin, the city is once again the capital of a united Germany. From the modern dome on the renovated Reichstag building there are fine views of the new buildings rising in the former no-man's-land between the two sectors, whose distinct character can still be felt. The city's youthful 'alternative' scene also continues to thrive, as does its famous nightlife in and around, for example, Savignyplatz in the west and the Scheunenviertel in the east. To the east of the Brandenburg Gate is an area of grand old squares and streets containing Berlin's main museums, including the Pergamon, with its collection of Ancient, Oriental and Islamic art. To the west is the landscaped Tiergarten, the famous zoo, with its exotic pastiche architecture, and the wealthy, modern heart of former West Berlin.

### Boston, Massachusetts, USA  *Map page 6*

The oldest areas of Boston have a European feel, their street plan based on meandering farm tracks. The Beacon Hill district contains splendid 19th-century brick houses and narrow alleyways, and the Massachusetts State House. A 'Freedom Trail', marked by a line of red bricks, takes the visitor past 17th- and 18th-century buildings, some of which are associated with the American Revolution. There are also guided tours of the USA's oldest surviving battleship – the USS *Constitution*, built in 1797 – moored in Boston Harbour. Across the Charles River lies Cambridge, with Harvard University and Square. Boston is a relatively unthreatening city for visitors, with a lively intellectual and artistic life, and a 'necklace' of city parks and tree-lined streets within a compact central area.

### Brisbane, Queensland, Australia

The relaxed atmosphere and compactness of its centre make Brisbane a pleasant place to stroll around. Its historic precinct, next to the Botanic Gardens, contains some fine 19th-century buildings, among them the Treasury. South of the River Brisbane is the State Art Gallery and the Cultural Centre, which includes two theatres and a superb concert hall. Day trips are possible to the beaches of the Gold and Sunshine Coasts.

### Brussels, Belgium  *Map page 6*

The centre of government for the European Union, Brussels is renowned for its excellent restaurants and shops, with everything from flea markets to the designer boutiques in the Galéries St Hubert. The imposing Hôtel de Ville, the gilded 17th-century houses and the Maison du Roi make the Grand-Place one of the world's most beautiful central squares. To the east lies the Gothic cathedral, the Palais Royale and the Royal Art Museums, containing both ancient and modern art. The city is full of fine examples of Art Nouveau architecture, including the museum dedicated to the founder of the movement, Victor Horta. A popular tourist site is the irreverent 17th-century statue, Manneken Pis.

### Budapest, Hungary  *Map page 7*

The Danube and Parliament building, Budapest

Formerly two cities, Buda and Pest, on opposite sides of the Danube, the capital of Hungary is a fascinating destination. The Castle Hill district of Buda includes the cobbled streets and medieval houses of the Old Town, and the Royal Palace (Budavári palota), containing the national art gallery and museum. The Fishermen's Bastion gives sweeping views over the city. A network of grand 19th-century boulevards forms the centre of the larger, more cosmopolitan Pest, with its imposing Parliament building (Orzságház).

There are many elegant spa baths (gyógyfürdo) dotted around the city, and extensive Roman remains, including an amphitheatre, at Óbuda and Rómaifürdo. Famous for its cafés, Budapest has excellent restaurants and offers a huge range of entertainment, including opera, jazz and discos.

### Buenos Aires, Argentina  *Map page 7*

The centre of Buenos Aires is laid out on a grand scale, with wide boulevards, imposing 19th-century buildings, modern tower blocks, and spacious plazas. Around this area, however, are the more intimate districts (*barrios*), each with its distinctive character. San Telmo is the artists' quarter, while La Boca, with its brightly painted houses, is the city's port district. The most fashionable district, Recoleta, houses the National Museum of Art, but is best known for the ornate tombs of its cemetery.

La Boca, Buenos Aires

### Cairo, Egypt  *Map page 7*

The largest city in Africa, Cairo is full of hooting taxis and bustling crowds. Modern buildings have risen next to the minarets of the old mosques, while a maze of markets provide potential bargains. The Pyramids of Giza are visible from the upper storeys of buildings all over the city. Famous worldwide for its unrivalled collection of antiquities, the Egyptian Museum houses the treasures of the Pharaoh Tutankhamun, and more than 100,000 other relics and antiquities from all periods of ancient Egyptian history. Experiences not to be missed include the *Son et Lumière* that takes place daily by the Sphinx at Giza, and drifting on the Nile in a *felucca* while watching the sun sink below the Cairo skyline.

### Calcutta (Kolkata), India  *Map page 8*

The capital of West Bengal, Calcutta (Kolkata) is regarded by many as the cultural and intellectual centre of India. It also has a reputation for extreme poverty and squalor. One of the great colonial cities of Asia, its main historic sites date from the days of the British Raj and include the white marble Victoria Memorial, the neo-Gothic St Paul's Cathedral, and the Indian Museum, with sculptures from all over India. These buildings are all in the vicinity of the Maidan, one of the largest city parks in the world, where hundreds of different interests – among them yoga, cricket and riding – are regularly pursued, and live entertainment is provided.

### Canton (Guangzhou), China  *Map page 8*

An economic success but a planning disaster, Guangzhou holds more attraction for the business traveller than for those seeking historic sites.

There are, however, numerous decaying French and British colonial buildings on Shamian Island, which provides a haven of peace from the bustle of Guangzhou's streets. A climb to the top of the 11th-century Temple of Six Banyan Trees provides a fine view. Another way of seeing the city is to take a cruise on the Pearl River.

### Cape Town, South Africa  *Map page 8*

South Africa's oldest city, Cape Town has several buildings of historic interest, including the Castle of Good Hope, the Old Town House, the Tuynhuis and the Parliament building. Artefacts from all over Africa are sold at the Saturday market in Greenmarket Square. The city lies below the spectacular Table Mountain, accessible by cable car. There are numerous good beaches, such as those at Clifton and Camps Bay on the cold Atlantic Ocean, and at Muizenberg and Fishoek on the warmer Indian Ocean. The old docks have been developed as the Victoria and Albert Waterfront, which boasts a range of restaurants. Boat trips run from here to the infamous Robben Island, where Nelson Mandela was imprisoned.

### Cartagena, Colombia

Several impressive 16th-century forts overlook the channel leading to the bay of Cartagena, evidence of the city's origins as an imperial Spanish stronghold. Huge 17th- and 18th-century walls surround narrow streets, palaces, churches, monasteries and plazas. The Palace of the Inquisition is a fine example of colonial architecture, with its magnificent Baroque gateway.

### Chicago, Illinois, USA  *Map page 9*

Built on the shore of Lake Michigan, Chicago played a key role in the economic development of the USA, serving as a railhead for the cattle trade of the Midwest. Its skyline includes skyscrapers dating from the 1890s, buildings in the International Style of the 1950s, and particularly fine examples of more recent architecture. The Sears Tower provides fantastic views of four states from its Space Deck. A closer view can be had on a boat trip up the Chicago River or from 'The Loop', an elevated railway that lends its name to the area it encircles. There are several important museums, including the vast Museum of Science and Industry and the Art Institute of Chicago. For outdoor pursuits, there is the extensive Grant Park, bordering the lake. The city is renowned for its rich musical life and, as well as a world-class symphony orchestra, there is a multitude of clubs offering blues, jazz, rock and folk music.

Skyline with Sears Tower, Chicago

## Cologne, Germany

Despite the almost total destruction of central Cologne during World War II, many historic buildings have been restored to their former glory, including the massive and beautiful twin-towered Gothic cathedral (Dom). Among the museums and art galleries are the Roman-Germanic Museum and the Imhoff-Stollwek Museum of Chocolate. The city's unique beer, *kslsch*, can be sampled in the numerous beer halls. Short boat trips on the Rhine provide views of the impressive riverfront, while longer boat excursions go to, for example, Königswinter and Linz.

## Copenhagen, Denmark     *Map page 10*

Scandinavia's largest and liveliest city, Copenhagen has excellent art collections, royal palaces, churches and other historic buildings as well as entertainment late into the night. Punctuated by parks, lakes, fountains and squares, the city is easily explored on foot or bicycle. The old harbour of Nyhavn, with its tall, brightly painted buildings, is packed with pavement cafés and bars, while the Latin Quarter is good for restaurants. From the top of the Round Tower (Rundee Taarn), Europe's oldest functioning observatory, there are magnificent views over the city. The famous Tivoli Gardens is a delightfully varied amusement park dating from 1843. A bridge now links Copenhagen to the attractive Swedish city of Malmö.

## Delhi, India     *Map page 10*

Red Fort, Delhi

The capital of India, Delhi is a city with two centres: New Delhi, which was established by the British in 1911, and Old Delhi, whose present layout dates from the 17th century. The streets of the old town, and in particular Chandni Chauk, are famously frenetic. The massive walls of the Red Fort and the Lahore Gate enclose a host of palace buildings, although many have been stripped of their fine decoration. India's largest mosque, the Jama Masjid, is also in the old town. The new city, with its broad avenues and imposing marble buildings, contains some older sites, including the 16th-century tomb of Humayun and the 12th-century Qutb Minar tower.

## Dublin, Ireland     *Map page 11*

Built on the River Liffey, Ireland's capital contains elegant 18th-century buildings, two Norman cathedrals, a castle, and some fine museums, three of them in Leinster House. One of the oldest books in the world, the 9th-century illuminated Book of Kells, is housed in Trinity College library, while the Writers' Museum pays homage to local literary figures such as W. B. Yeats, James Joyce and Oscar Wilde. Dublin has a relaxed, friendly atmosphere, and plenty of pubs and restaurants. In summer, outdoor events are often held in Phoenix Park. The famous Easter Uprising of 1916 is commemorated at Kilmainham Jail, where many heroes of Irish independence were once incarcerated.

## Edinburgh, Scotland     *Map page 11*

Set on a dramatic rock that soars 76 m (250 ft) from the valley floor, the Old Town of Edinburgh is a collection of historic buildings, towering tenements and narrow passages huddling beneath a romantic castle. The Royal Mile, lined with 16th- and 17th-century buildings, leads from the castle to the royal residence of Holyrood. The Royal Museum lies to its south, as does the lively Grassmarket district with its bars and restaurants. The small but elegant National Gallery sits in Princes Street Gardens to the north. Beyond lie graceful Georgian squares, terraces and crescents of the New Town. Scotland's capital has a rich cultural life, including the world-famous International and Fringe festivals.

## Esfahan, Iran

On the four sides of the vast central square of Esfahan, with its formal lawns and pool, are the delicately tiled façades of public buildings. These include the opulent Royal Mosque and the magnificent entrance to the bazaar, whose crowded streets twist and turn towards the steps of the Great Mosque, a complex of buildings spanning a 700-year period. Among other historic sites are the shrine of Imamzadeh Ahmad and several royal palaces. Esfahan's high altitude keeps it relatively cool, making it pleasant to stroll through the streets and parks, and sample the many teahouses.

## Fès, Morocco

The old part of Fès – Fès el-Bali – is one of the largest living medieval cities in the world. A fascinating labyrinth of some 94,000 streets and lanes, its covered bazaars are crammed with every conceivable sort of craft workshop, restaurants and market stalls, as well as extensive dye pits and tanneries. On the edge of the old town, the Museum of Moroccan Arts houses a splendid collection of artefacts, including colourful tribal carpets and the city's famous blue pottery.

## Florence, Italy

The pedestrianized streets in the beautiful centre of Florence enable visitors to wander about freely, visiting such well-known Renaissance sites as the cathedral, with its red-roofed dome, and the spacious Piazza della Signoria, dominated by the crenellated Palazzo Vecchio. Between the piazza and the River Arno is the Uffizi Gallery, containing famous works by Botticelli and Titian among many others. The 14th-century Ponte Vecchio bridge, lined on both sides with jewellery and gift shops, provides a route to the imposing Pitti Palace. The city's churches range in style from the exquisite San Miniato, through the austere Santo Croce to the classically inspired San Lorenzo. Of the many religious frescoes, those by Fra Angelico in the monastery of San Marco, and by Masaccio in the church of Santa Maria del Carmine, stand out. The Bargello has a fine collection of sculpture, while the Accademia houses Michelangelo's *David*.

Cathedral with Brunelleshci's dome, Florence

## Geneva, Switzerland

Geneva enjoys one of the world's most dramatic locations, straddling the Rhône where it leaves Lake Geneva, and overlooked by the Alps on one side and the Jura mountains on the other. A cosmopolitan, French-speaking city, it is a world centre for banking and commerce as well as for international organizations, such as the Red Cross. South of the river, the oldest part has excellent museums, galleries and historic buildings, including St Peter's Cathedral, where John Calvin preached. Geneva lives up to its reputation for efficiency, cleanliness and safety, but all this comes at a price: restaurants, clubs and other entertainments are smart and expensive.

## Hamburg, Germany

Germany's largest port (there are daily harbour tours from March to November), Hamburg combines its busy commercial life with a graceful, old-world charm. Situated on the River Elbe and criss-crossed by a network of canals, at its heart is the Alster lake, where boating is a popular pastime in the summer. The city has many extensive parks, stylish shopping arcades, elegant boulevards, museums and art galleries, among them the Kunsthalle with a fine collection of art spanning several centuries. There are numerous inviting café-bars and all-night entertainment, most notably in the St Pauli Quarter, where The Beatles famously performed in the 1960s.

## Hanoi, Vietnam

Built on the Red River, around several large lakes, Hanoi has both peaceful tree-lined avenues and parks, and a bustling old city where almost anything can be purchased, including silk, lacquerware, puppets and jewellery. Bikes are the main form of transport. The city's many religious buildings include the One-Pillar Pagoda and the 11th-century Temple of Literature. Ho Chi Minh's mausoleum provides a memorable experience, with visitors being escorted to view the embalmed body. A day trip can be made to the Perfume Pagoda – actually a complex of pagodas and Buddhist shrines carved out of limestone cliffs. A cruise from Haiphong around the limestone islands of Halong Bay is also recommended.

## Havana, Cuba

Ironically for a country that is proud of its independence from imperialism, one of the main attractions of Cuba's capital is its colonial past. The vast open space of Plaza de la Revolución and the post-colonial buildings of the Vedado district are worth seeing, but it is the boulevards and squares of Old Havana that are most fascinating.

The palaces surrounding the Plaza de Armas, the Baroque cathedral and the elegant thoroughfare 'The Paseo' are all fine examples of colonial architecture. There are few cars on the streets, but many bicycles. There are also many nightclubs, where salsa is the predominant dance style.

Capitol building and Grand Theatre, Havana

## Helsinki, Finland · Map page 12

Helsinki is almost surrounded by water and is full of the sounds and scents of the sea. Among its architectural gems are the 19th-century Neo-classical buildings of Senate Square – which also contains the blue-domed Lutheran Cathedral – and the rock-hewn church of Temppeliauko (1969) where many concerts are held. Although its combination of attractive buildings, good restaurants and excellent art galleries and museums make it a year-round tourist destination, Helsinki really comes to life in summer, with open-air cafés, concerts, and boat trips to the ruined fortress on nearby Suomenlinna Island.

## Hong Kong, China · Map page 12

Most visitors to Hong Kong take the short ferry ride from Kowloon across the harbour, with its spectacular view of the high-rise buildings on the waterfront of Hong Kong Island. A visit to the Man Mo temple, with its ornate interior, provides a complete contrast. A funicular goes to the top of Victoria Peak where there are shady paths through lush vegetation. The Tsim Sha Tsui area of Kowloon contains a group of modern exhibition buildings, including the Space Museum and the Hong Kong Museum of History, as well as air-conditioned shopping malls. A ferry goes to the islands of Lamma, where there are relatively uncrowded beaches, country walks and seafood restaurants. A hydrofoil goes to Macau.

## Istanbul, Turkey · Map page 12

Formerly known as Constantinople, Istanbul has an imperial history dating back to the time of the Roman Empire. Its strategic position straddling the Bosporus Strait makes it both a European and an Asian city. Among the churches built in the 6th century by Emperor Constantine is the domed Hagia Sophia (Aya Sofya), which was converted into a mosque in 1453 and is now a museum. The 17th-century Blue Mosque (Sultanahmet Camii) is a masterpiece of Ottoman architecture, while the Topkapi Palace, with its imperial treasury stuffed with gold and jewels, is on every itinerary. In old Istanbul is the labyrinthine Kapali Carsi (the world's largest covered bazaar) where more than 4,000 shops and stalls sell carpets, jewellery, ceramics, brass and leatherware. A fascinating mixture of both the ancient and modern, Istanbul also has a renowned cuisine.

## Jaipur, India

Known as the 'Pink City' because of the salmon-coloured wash applied to many of its buildings, Jaipur is the capital of the colourful state of Rajasthan. It is divided into areas dedicated to specialist activities, such as elephant-handling or the sale of textiles, silver or gems. Within the walled town are the Palace of Winds (Hawa Mahal), with its delicately screened windows, the City Palace – now a museum – and Jai Singh's extraordinary Observatory, with its huge angular stone instruments. Nearby is the hill town and Rajput palace complex of Amber.

## Jakarta, Indonesia · Map page 13

Jakarta's glinting high-rise office blocks contrast sharply with the cobbled square at the heart of what was 18th-century Batavia (now known as Kota). Much can be discovered of this colonial period at the dock of Sunda Kelapa, where many magnificent schooners are moored and a maritime museum has been created in an old warehouse. The National Museum has excellent displays on Indonesia's ethnic groups. There is a theme park at Taman Impian Jaya Ancol, and Balinese dancing and traditional music at Taman Ismail Marzuki. Jakarta also offers a fine range of restaurants.

## Jerusalem, Israel · Map page 13

The focus of most visits to Jerusalem is the Old City with its different quarters. The heart of the Christian quarter is the Church of the Holy Sepulchre, the site of Christ's crucifixion. This is reached along the Via Dolorosa, much of which passes through the Muslim quarter, with its impressive Mamluk architecture. The Western (Wailing) Wall is in the Jewish quarter, which also contains the multi-layered Temple Mount Excavations. The Armenian quarter, the centre of the Armenian Church, contains the impressive Citadel. Towering over all these is the golden Dome of the Rock, a sacred Muslim site in the Temple Mount compound.

Dome of the Rock, Jerusalem

## Johannesburg, South Africa · Map page 13

The richest city in Africa, Johannesburg is also a lively centre of South African culture. Museum-Africa has collections relating to the history and art of all sections of the community, while the nearby Market Theatre Complex, which contains four theatres, is an attractive place in which to eat and drink, and listen to music. Visitors, however, should be aware of the high crime rate in the downtown area, and enjoy instead the restaurants and gardens of northern suburbs such as Rosebank and Melville. Outside the city is Soweto, the vast black township which has a lively music and theatre scene but is best visited on a guided tour.

## Kairouan, Tunisia

An important centre for the Muslim faith, Tunisia's holy city has over 130 mosques, including the 9th-century Great Mosque, which once doubled as a fortress. A special permit is required to visit the holy sites. Kairouan's maze of buildings and narrow, winding streets is enclosed by ancient city walls, and it is a fascinating place in which to stroll. Artisans carry out the traditional trades of weaving and carpentry, and carpet sellers try to attract visitors to their stalls in the souk (bazaar).

## Karachi, Pakistan · Map page 14

Developed as a city by the British from the 1840s, Karachi is a business rather than a tourist centre. It does, however, have many colourful bazaars in Saddar, the central district, which specialize in such products as jewellery, cloth, dried fruit and bottles. It also has a fascinating coastline which can be viewed on a traditional lateen-sailed boat trip from the harbour. Clifton Beach, with its camel rides and fairground, is well equipped for families, while other, rather less commercialized beaches are a short drive away.

## Katmandu, Nepal

Street scene, Katmandu

Katmandu is a popular holiday destination – an intriguing mixture of modern buildings and narrow, traffic-clogged streets with intricately carved temples and shrines. Many of these ancient buildings are grouped around Durbar Square, including the Jaganath Temple, with its erotic carvings. The Old Royal Palace houses an interesting museum. Jochne, better known as 'Freak Street', is a focal point for many visitors, with its fascinating shops, cheap hotels and restaurants. Outside the city are three huge temples: the Hindu Pashupatinath complex, with its riverside ghats, and the Buddhist stupas of Boudhanath and Swayambunath.

## Kraków, Poland

Having come through World War II virtually unscathed, and with not a high-rise building in sight, Kraków's densely packed old centre is full of historic churches and picturesque streets and squares. The central market square, which is reputed to be the largest medieval town square in Europe, contains a number of interesting buildings, among them the largely 16th-century Cloth Hall. The square is also the focus of the city's vigorous cultural life. There are several jazz and cabaret clubs in the Old Town, as well as numerous attractive cafés, bars and restaurants. To the south are the castle and cathedral of Wawel, behind which lies Kazimierz, the gradually reviving Jewish district.

### Kuala Lumpur, Malaysia

A city that has sprung up since the 1860s, Kuala Lumpur is short on historic sites but has plenty to offer the visitor. Its colonial, 19th-century heart is Merdeka Square. Nearby is the most spectacular of the city's mosques, Masjid Jamek. Chinatown and Little India provide much of interest, and Malaysian craftwork and antiques can be bought at the Art Deco Central Market. The 'Golden Triangle' business area includes the Petronas Tower, the world's tallest building. The Lake Gardens contain a Bird Park, Orchid Garden and Butterfly Park. A half-hour drive outside the city are the Batu Caves, used as Hindu temples. Day trips can be made to the historic city of Malacca and the Genting Highlands Casino Complex.

### Kyoto, Japan

Japan's capital for over 1,000 years, Kyoto has numerous Buddhist temples, Shinto shrines, palaces and gardens. Despite extensive modern development, there are still traditional wooden houses and craft shops in the back streets. A city that is particularly spectacular when clad in either cherry blossom or autumnal colours, its main sights include the 1,001 gilded statues of Buddha lined up in the Hall of the Thirty-Three Bays, the view from the temple of Kiyomizu-dera, and the intriguing gardens of Ginkaku-ji. Other famous gardens include the lake-garden of Kinkaku-ji, and the 500-year-old garden of Ryoan-ji. The city of Nara, 35 km (22 miles) south, contains the huge bronze Buddha of Todai-ji, and other fine examples of early Japanese art and architecture.

Temple of Kiyomizu-dera, Kyoto

### Lagos, Nigeria
*Map page 14*

Although no longer the capital of Nigeria, Lagos is by far the largest city in West Africa. At its heart lies Lagos Island, a business centre whose skyline is spiked by skyscrapers. The National Museum provides a fascinating insight into the country's cultural heritage and includes works of art dating back 2,800 years, including beautiful Benin bronzes. The city's main attraction, however, is modern African music, and many of the country's best-known singers have nightclubs here.

### Lahore, Pakistan

Lahore is renowned for its Mughal architecture. The most attractive of its many mosques is that of Wazir Kahn, covered in intricate glazed mosaic tiles, but the largest is the Badshahi Mosque. The massive walls of Lahore Fort surround a compound of elegant buildings. Away from the centre is Jahangir's tomb and the Shalimar Garden, with its geometrically arranged terraces, ponds, fountains and, in February and March, its spectacular flowers.

### Las Vegas, Nevada, USA

A city whose population grew from 30 to half a million in just 90 years, Las Vegas is continually reinventing itself, with the casinos on The Strip providing ever bigger and better spectacles. The most famous is Caesar's Palace, with staff dressed as centurions and Cleopatra lookalikes. New York, New York entices with its replica skyscrapers and a Statue of Liberty. Treasure Island has a mock sea battle, Mirage an erupting volcano and Circus Circus live fire-eaters. Food and lodging are cheap, particularly midweek, with the real profits being made on the gambling tables and slot machines. Las Vegas is popular for outrageous weddings, with services being conducted in the most unlikely places – in a 'drive-through' chapel, the nearby Grand Canyon, or even in mid-air.

The Strip, Las Vegas

### Lima, Peru
*Map page 16*

A once-beautiful city, Lima has suffered badly at the hands of modern developers. It is worth visiting primarily for its fine museums, which provide background information about Peru's Inca sites. It is also a useful base from which to explore the surrounding countryside, including the beautiful beaches to the south, over which towers the temple complex of Pachacamac.

### Lisbon, Portugal
*Map page 14*

There are many hills to climb and much to see in Portugal's capital. Stretching north from the Rio Tejo, the Baixa district – rebuilt after the devastating earthquake of 1755 – contains many of the city's museums and theatres. The old Moorish area, the Alfama, survived the earthquake and its warren of narrow streets, stairways and squares leads up to the hilltop Castle of St George, with magnificent views. On the edge of the city the Belém area contains fine examples of 16th-century architecture, including the marvellous Jerônimos Monastery and the famous white Belém Tower. At night the haunting traditional *fado* music is played in bars in, for example, the Bairro Alto district. Day trips can be made to the hill town of Sintra or to the beaches on the Estoril coast.

### London, England
*Map page 15*

Europe's largest city, London is a lively, cosmopolitan metropolis, offering a huge range of attractions to the visitor. From the grand squares of Knightsbridge and Belgravia to the business district of the City, central London is made up of a mosaic of areas, each with its own distinctive atmosphere and architectural style. Historic buildings include the Tower of London (containing the Crown Jewels), St Paul's Cathedral, Westminster Abbey, the Houses of Parliament and Buckingham Palace. Among the many art galleries are the new Tate Modern, housed in a converted power station on the South Bank of the River Thames, and The National Gallery, overlooking Trafalgar Square. The British Museum contains a monumental collection of Egyptian, Greek and Roman artefacts. Soho, Piccadilly and Covent Garden form the heart of the theatre district, with numerous restaurants, clubs and bars. Day excursions can be made to Hampton Court Palace, Windsor Castle, Canterbury Cathedral, the Royal Pavilion in Brighton, and the historic university towns of Oxford and Cambridge.

### Los Angeles, California, USA
*Map page 16*

Among the skyscrapers in Los Angeles' downtown area are some notable public buildings, including the Museum of Contemporary Art. To the southwest is Exposition Park, home to three museums, including the interactive California Space Center. Most visitors, however, flock to Hollywood in search of film stars, although the big names have long since left for more salubrious neighbourhoods, such as Beverly Hills and elegant Bel Air. Other attractions include the Warner Bros. Studio Tour, and the thrilling rides at Universal Studios. On the coast, the long sandy beach linking Santa Monica and Venice is a magnet for Los Angeles' more colourful characters.

### Luxembourg City, Luxembourg

The picturesque old walled city of Luxembourg perches above the Pétrusse and Alzette valleys, overlooked by the ruins of its ancient fortress with a labyrinth of defensive tunnels and underground chambers (the casemates), which is a UNESCO World Heritage Site. Running between the Citadelle du St Esprit, which provides spectacular views, and the Grand Ducal Palace is the elegant Chemin de la Corniche, one of Europe's most beautiful pedestrian promenades.

### Madrid, Spain
*Map page 17*

Spain's capital is a huge metropolis with a remarkable collection of museums and art galleries, beautiful parks and a famously vibrant nightlife centred on Plaza de Santa Ana. The city is made up of a number of districts (*barrios*), each with its own distinct character. The area of most interest to visitors is around the 17th-century Plaza Mayor, with the elaborately decorated Royal Palace, the Opera House (Teatro Real) and the famous Prado Museum all within easy reach. The city has a vivacious character and a buzzing street life. Tapas bars are everywhere, and shoppers can explore the busy Gran Via or the atmospheric Rastro flea market centred on Plaza de Cascorro. Excursions can be made to the austere monastery of El Escorial and to the historic towns of Toledo, Segovia, Avila and Aranjuez.

Plaza Mayor, Madrid

## Manila, Philippines
*Map page 17*

Many people visit Manila purely for its bars and nightlife, and the city provides plenty to choose from in the business district of Makati and the streets behind Roxes Boulevard. The walled area known as Intramuros contains the most significant historic sites, including Fort Santiago and the imposing Romanesque cathedral. Rizal Park, projecting out into Manila Bay, contains a lagoon, a spectacular fountain, a replica of Beijing's Summer Palace, a Japanese Garden and planetarium. Manila's Chinatown (on the border of Santa Cruz and Binondo) is the place to go for silk, porcelain and Chinese dumplings.

## Marrakech, Morocco

Famous for its lively street life, Marrakech is also known for the pink colour that dominates the city from the earth walls around the old town centre to the flat-roofed houses. Every evening in Djemaa El Fna, the old town's central square, acrobats, snake charmers and storytellers perform. Nearby is the labyrinthine souk (bazaar), with its hundreds of small shops selling jewellery, carpets, metalware and leather. There are several beautiful gardens, and the Museum of Arts contains a magnificent display of carpets. Just an hour's drive away are the spectacular High Atlas mountains.

The souk, Marrakech

## Melbourne, Victoria, Australia
*Map page 17*

Central Melbourne, on the north bank of the River Yarra, is a striking blend of past and present. Ornate 19th-century buildings sit alongside towering skyscrapers, as in Collins Street where the 1980s Rialto Towers provide splendid views from an Observation Deck. Elsewhere, the Old Melbourne Gaol is a major historic attraction and there are many fine parks and gardens, including the outstanding Botanic Gardens. The city's multi-ethnic nature is apparent in the popular Queen Victoria Market and in the huge variety of restaurants. Outside the centre several inner suburbs, each with a distinct character, can be explored by tram. Places of interest nearby include the Yarra Valley with its wineries and wildlife sanctuaries, and Phillip Island with its penguins.

## Mexico City, Mexico
*Map page 18*

It is worth braving the traffic and pollution of Mexico City to see the impressive architecture of the buildings surrounding the main square (Zócalo), including the National Palace, with its murals by Diego Rivera. Nearby are the fascinating excavations of an Aztec temple (Templo Mayor). Bosque de Chapultepec, with its boating lakes, gardens and zoo, provides some relief from the hectic street life. It is also home to the outstanding

Museo de Antropologia, whose indoor and outdoor exhibition spaces house the world's greatest collection of Mexican art and artefacts. Just 48 km (30 miles) away from the centre are the splendid ruins of the ancient city of Teotihuacán.

## Miami, Florida, USA
*Map page 18*

Miami is spread out along the fragmented coastline of Biscayne Bay. The Spanish language predominates and the downtown area, with its modern tower blocks, is greatly enlivened by the Latin American street life. Little Havana and Little Haiti are two areas worth visiting for their strong culture. The city's most elegant neighbourhood is Coral Gables, built as a 'model suburb' in the 1920s. Miami Beach, on an island linked to the mainland by causeways, has many fine examples of Art Deco buildings and miles of sandy beaches, hotels and bars.

## Milan, Italy
*Map page 18*

Famous as a world centre for design and fashion, and for its grand opera house, La Scala, Milan has many historic buildings alongside its modern skyscrapers. The enormous Gothic cathedral dominates the main square, Piazza del Duomo, and the nearby convent of Santa Maria delle Grazie houses Leonardo da Vinci's fresco *The Last Supper*. Italy's most beautiful shopping arcade, the Galleria Vittorio Emanuele II, runs between the cathedral and La Scala. The Castello Sforzesco, a striking red-brick castle which was once the seat of the Dukes of Milan, houses the excellent municipal art collections. Excursions can be made to the old university town of Pavia and to the lake resorts such as Varenna and Bellagio on Lake Como, and Stresa on Lake Maggiore.

## Montréal, Québec, Canada
*Map page 19*

Situated on the St Lawrence River, Montréal is Canada's second-largest city. The multi-ethnic nature of its population, of whom around 60% are French-speaking, is evident in the diversity of its cuisine and cultural festivals. The Parisian-style old city has numerous 17th-, 18th- and 19th-century buildings, among them the Neo-gothic Basilique Notre-Dame. By the river a public space has been created out of the old shipyards, complete with exhibitions and amusements. Boat trips can be taken up and down the St Lawrence, including one through the Lachine Rapids. The collection in the Art Museum is wide-ranging and includes a display of Inuit art. There are also particularly interesting Botanic Gardens.

## Moscow, Russia
*Map page 19*

Moscow radiates outwards from the Kremlin in a series of rings, of which the innermost is of greatest interest to visitors and is small enough to be explored on foot. Among the buildings enclosed by the thick red-brick walls of the Kremlin are three imposing palaces and the Archangel Cathedral. Outside is Red Square, with the exotic, multi-coloured domes of St Basil's Cathedral, the Lenin Mausoleum, the Historical Museum and the magnificent 19th-century state department store, GUM, facing each other across the famous cobbled parade ground. There are also numerous literary museums and art galleries. The palatial metro system with its glittering chandeliers and fabulous marble architecture should not be missed.

St Basil's Cathedral, Moscow

## Mumbai (Bombay), India
*Map page 20*

Home to India's thriving film industry, Mumbai also has the largest slum area of any city in Asia. The influence of the British colonial heritage is apparent in the Victorian Gothic buildings of the Fort district, the triumphal Gateway of India arch, and the red double-decker buses. The frenetic streets and bazaars are, however, pure India. Malabar Hill, with its Hanging Gardens, provides some relief from the crowds, as do the Mahatma Gandhi Museum and an impressive new National Gallery of Modern Art. Most visitors take a boat trip across the large harbour to Elephanta Island, to see the Hindu temples hewn out of the rock.

## Munich, Germany
*Map page 20*

Munich is a cosmopolitan city, close to the Bavarian Alps, with many beautiful buildings and a wide variety of theatres, museums, galleries and restaurants. In the centre of the old town is the Marienplatz with its famous old town hall (Rathaus), and several historic churches. Many visitors shop in the glamorous Maximilianstrasse and spend an evening at the opera or drink in one of the city's many historic beer cellars, such as the famous Hofbräuhaus. Another attraction is the beer festival in October. Just outside the city is the Baroque palace of Nymphenburg.

## Nairobi, Kenya

East Africa's most modern city has broad streets lined with jacaranda trees. The compact city centre can be walked in 20 minutes, but visitors should be aware that street robberies are a growing problem. The National Museum details the history of Kenyan tribal groups. Close to the city is the Bomas of Kenya, where traditional dances and songs are performed, and the Nairobi National Park where zebras, giraffes, lions, leopards and rhinos are among the animals that can be seen, particularly from July to September.

## New Orleans, Louisiana, USA

Its fantastic mix of cultures – French, Spanish, Native American, African and Caribbean – makes New Orleans one of America's most stimulating cities. It is famous as the 'cradle of jazz', and trad jazz is still played in Preservation Hall. The best way to see the elegant architecture of the French Quarter is on foot, starting in Jackson Square – a park that is surrounded by some of the city's most important public buildings, including the Louisiana State Museum. Many visitors go to New Orleans simply to enjoy its restaurants, including the Creole and Cajun cuisines, both variations on the French. Popular times to visit are during the Mardi Gras carnival in February or March, and the annual Jazz Festival in April or May.

## New York, NY, USA     *Map page 21*

Manhattan and the Statue of Liberty, New York

New York is the ultimate destination for those who love cities, with most of its main attractions on Manhattan Island. However, its famous skyline was changed forever following the destruction of the twin towers of the World Trade Center on 11 September 2001; the 1930s Empire State Building is now the city's tallest building. The dozens of art galleries include the Metropolitan Museum of Art and the Guggenheim Museum of predominantly 20th-century art. The ferry to Staten Island provides panoramic views of Manhattan, while the Circle Line runs ferries across the harbour to the Statue of Liberty and Ellis Island. Districts to be toured on foot include Greenwich Village, with its cafés, SoHo, renowned for its art galleries and boutiques, and Little Italy. Some visitors are drawn to the city by stores such as Bloomingdales, others by its nightlife. Providing a haven from the big-city traffic is Central Park, where there is often live entertainment.

## Osaka, Japan     *Map page 22*

The Japanese city most welcoming to foreign visitors, Osaka is enjoyed mainly for its lively nightlife and varied cuisine. It has some fine historic sites, such as the castle and the red-painted Sumiyoshi Shinto shrine to the gods of the sea. Its museums include the Liberty Osaka Museum of Human Rights and the Suntory Museum of 20th-century graphic art. The spectacular Osaka Aquarium is another attraction.

## Oslo, Norway     *Map page 22*

The oldest of Scandinavia's capitals, Oslo is an attractive city situated at the head of Oslofjord. The impressive medieval Akershus castle contains grand staterooms, dungeons and the Norwegian Resistance Museum. The Munch Museum has over 5,000 drawings and paintings by Edvard Munch, while in the beautiful Vigeland Park, sculptures by Gustav Vigeland are on permanent display. Across the harbour is the Bygdøy peninsula with good beaches, an open-air folk museum and maritime museums containing Viking ships as well as Thor Heyerdahl's raft, *Kon-Tiki*.

## Panama City, Panama

Bristling with skyscrapers and fronted by palm-fringed beaches, Panama is a thriving modern city. In the Casco Viejo district, grand Spanish colonial buildings overlook the Bay of Panama from the tip of a fortified peninsula. The old sea wall provides excellent views across the bay and there are restaurants in its restored colonial dungeons. Other attractions include the 17th-century Presidential Palace, the cathedral and the Panama Canal. The 16th-century ruins of Old Panama (Panamá Viejo) lie 6.5 km (4 miles) to the east.

## Paris, France     *Map page 23*

Famously beautiful in springtime, Paris is fascinating at any time of year. Packed with historic buildings, world-famous art collections, fine restaurants and street cafés, it is one of the world's most elegant cities. Compact enough to explore on foot, the centre is made up of a number of distinct areas or *quartiers*, each with its own character. On a hill crowned by the basilica of Sacré-Coeur is Montmartre, with its village-like atmosphere, street artists, nearby flea markets and a splendid view over the city. The Notre Dame Cathedral and Sainte Chapelle are on the peaceful Île de la Cité, an island in the River Seine. The Picasso Museum is set among the beautiful old houses and courtyards of the Marais. The colourful Pompidou Centre looms above the galleries and cafés of the Beaubourg. The Louvre occupies a vast stretch of the Right Bank of the Seine, and there is a magnificent unbroken view through the Tuileries gardens and along the Champs Elysées to the Arc de Triomphe. Attractions on the Left Bank include the Musée d'Orsay – containing a huge collection of Impressionist art – and the Eiffel Tower. Excursions can be made to the royal palaces of Versailles and Fontainebleu, Monet's house at Giverney, and the beautiful cathedral at Chartres.

The Seine and Notre Dame, Paris

## Perth, Western Australia, Australia

Situated on a sweep of the Swan River, Perth has lots of sunshine and an easy-going atmosphere. Its centre is relatively compact and dominated by skyscrapers, among which are scattered some Victorian buildings, such as the ornate Government House and the Old Flour Mill. A few miles to the west lie excellent sandy beaches and opportunities for surfing, while cruise companies offer dolphin- and whale-watching trips. The port of Fremantle, just 20 km (12 miles) away, is worth visiting, as is Rottnest Island.

## Prague, Czech Republic     *Map page 24*

With a centre full of beautiful buildings covering 900 years of architecture it is easy to see why Prague, on the River Vitava, is one of Europe's top tourist attractions. Prague Castle (Prazsky Hrad), encompassing the 10th-century Church of St George and the Gothic St Vitus' Cathedral, is the focus of most visits to the city. Other architectural treasures include Baroque and Rococo palaces and the Neoclassical National Theatre (Náordní divadlo). The Old Jewish Quarter (Josefov) contains the Jewish Cemetery and several synagogues, including the Old-New Synagogue (Staranová). Prague's rich cultural life centres especially on its music – it is home to two fine orchestras. It is also arguably the beer-drinking capital of the world, and has several famous beer halls as well as numerous pubs and bars.

## Quito, Ecuador

At a height of 2,850 m (9,350 ft), Quito escapes the oppressive temperature and pollution of many Latin American cities. The historic centre, with its whitewashed buildings and red roofs, is a UNESCO heritage site and includes a 16th-century monastery and cathedral, as well as a number of museums. There is also a fascinating vivarium, with displays of many of Ecuador's reptiles, both living and dead.

## Reykjavik, Iceland

The world's northernmost capital, Reykjavik is a small modern city with colourful buildings, fashionable shops and a lively nightlife. The Arni Magnússon Institute houses a famous collection of Icelandic saga manuscripts, while the National Museum in the Old Town displays relics from the earliest days of settlement. The modern church of Hallgrímskirkja is built in the shape of a lava mountain and offers excellent views over the city from its 75 m (246 ft) high tower.

## Riga, Latvia

A bustling industrial city, Riga also has a waterfront castle, a medieval centre and a lively cultural life. Places to visit include the cavernous Dome Cathedral, the Riga Motor Museum, an open-air ethnographical museum and St Peter's Church – with a view over Old Riga from the spire, which is reached by a lift. To the west, a string of resort towns known collectively as Jurmala stretches for 20 km (12 miles) along the coast, with peaceful beaches and good restaurants.

## Rio de Janeiro, Brazil     *Map page 24*

With a spectacular location at the entrance to a bay, Rio has two famous landmarks that provide breathtaking views: Corcovado Mountain, topped by a huge statue of Christ, and Sugar Loaf Mountain. There are many museums, including the National Historical and the wide-ranging National. The city is best known, however, for its lively beaches, including Copacabana, and the more upmarket Ipanema. At night, the bars, clubs and discos of Rio resound to jazz and rock. There are samba shows primarily for tourists as well as more authentic dancehalls. A particularly popular time to visit is during the spectacular Mardi Gras Carnaval, in February or March.

View from Sugar Loaf Mountain, Rio de Janeiro

## Rome, Italy     *Map page 25*

The historic capital of the Roman Empire, of Latin Christendom and now of Italy, Rome is exceptionally rich in treasures from many eras. Ancient buildings include the Colosseum, the Arch of Constantine, Trajan's Column, the Roman Forum

and the Pantheon. Among the early Christian sites are the famous catacombs and the basilicas of Santa Maria Maggiore and San Giovanni in Laterano (near the Colosseum). Michelangelo's Piazza del Campidoglio – bordered by three palaces – is a fine example of Renaissance town planning, but Rome is known more for its Baroque buildings and squares, and landmarks such as the Trevi Fountain and the Spanish Steps. In the centre of Rome, the Vatican City is the world's smallest independent state, containing St Peter's Square, St Peter's Basilica, the Sistine Chapel and ten museums. Increased pedestrianization of the centre has made it easier to enjoy the exuberant street life for which the city is famous.

### St Petersburg, Russia          Map page 26

Situated in the Neva River delta, St Petersburg is a city of canals, bridges and elegant architecture. Founded in 1703 by Peter the Great, its oldest landmark is the massive Peter-Paul Fortress, with the slender spire of the Cathedral of St Peter and St Paul rising above it. At the heart of the city is Palace Square, dominated by the pastel-coloured façade of the Winter Palace. The palace is part of the Hermitage Museum, which contains one of the world's greatest collections of European art. Along the Nevsky Prospekt are the former homes of many famous Russians as well as several palaces, department stores, theatres, restaurants, churches and the richly decorated Kazan Cathedral. Day trips can be taken to several summer palaces, among them Pushkin and Petrodvorets.

### San Francisco, California, USA          Map page 25

One of the USA's most spectacular cities, San Francisco's trademarks are its elegant suspension bridges (Golden Gate and Oakland Bay Bridge) and the street cars that service the steep streets. It is also famous as America's gay capital, the main focus of the gay community being the Castro district. The city has a thriving Chinatown, and its North Beach area (between Russian and Telegraph hills) has long been associated with alternative culture. The northern waterfront includes the famous and crowded Fisherman's Wharf development, with its numerous restaurants. The Golden Gate Park is home to several specialist gardens, art galleries and museums. A boat takes visitors to Alcatraz, the notorious island prison.

### Santiago, Chile          Map page 26

Santiago is a sprawling city set on a wide plain at the foot of the Andes. However, its central area is relatively compact, and its tree-lined streets and landscaped parks are pleasant to explore on foot, with diversions to the Museum of Pre-Colombian Art in the Real Casa de Aduana and the Santiago Museum, close to the cathedral. A funicular goes to the peak of San Cristóbal and the Pablo Neruda Museum. Day trips can be made to the beaches of Valparaiso and the ski resort of Valle Nevado.

### São Paulo, Brazil          Map page 26

Although much of São Paulo is modern, the area around the central square (Praça da Sé) contains several interesting old buildings, such as the whitewashed Palácio do Colégio, (a 19th-century replica of Baroque buildings), the Igreja de Santo Antônio and the Solar da Marquesa de Santos. The city has plenty of nightlife and a varied cuisine, some of its best bars and restaurants being in the suburb known as the Jardins. The nearby Parque do Ibirapuera is a centre for sporting activities and home to several of the city's museums, as well as providing a haven of peace in its 'reading woods'.

### Seattle, Washington, USA

The sparkling skyscrapers of downtown Seattle, including the trademark 'flying saucer' of the Space Needle, rise from the shores of Elliott Bay against the spectacular backdrop of the snowy peak of Mount Rainier. A recent surge in the city's prosperity (Seattle is home to the Microsoft Corporation) has led to much new building and the restoration of the historic centre. The city is a centre for contemporary arts and music, the embodiment of which is the high-tech Experience Music Project building. It also contains the headquarters of the Boeing Corporation, whose out-of-town Museum of Flight is a popular attraction.

### Seoul, South Korea          Map page 26

Secret Garden of palace of Ch'angdok , Seoul

Selected as the site of the ruling dynasty's capital in 1394, Seoul today consists of a series of linked districts, each with its own centre. The National Assembly and financial institutions are on the small island of Youido. Spread around the old centre is a series of royal palaces, the best preserved of which is Ch'angdok, with its Secret Garden of wooded hills and ponds. T'apkol Park is a good place to meet the locals, while Namsan Park is home to the Botanic Gardens, and also to Seoul Tower, which provides a fine view of the city.

### Shanghai, China          Map page 27

Rapidly regaining its status as a major trading and commercial centre, Shanghai's colonial past is clearly visible in the massive 1920s Neoclassical buildings of its waterfront trading area, famous as 'The Bund'. The maze of narrow streets in the Old City and the crowded bazaar of Yuyuan Park provide a complete contrast. Chinese culture is celebrated in the impressive collection of paintings, ceramics, calligraphy, and sculpture in the new Shanghai Museum. Just 80 km (50 miles) away are the famous city gardens of Suzhou, some of which are over 1,000 years old.

### Singapore City, Singapore          Map page 27

Singapore is a popular 'stopover' city because it is relatively compact, has an efficient infrastructure and its shopping malls are a source of bargains. Amid the high-rise developments are colonial, Chinese, Malay and Indian enclaves that have retained their character, and some fine historic buildings, such as Coleman's Parliament building, the Buddhist Temple of Heavenly Happiness (Thian Hock Keng Temple) and the colourful Sri Mariamman Hindu Temple. On the riverside are the restored old shops of Boat and Clarke Quays, both of which are relatively lively nightspots. To the south a cable car and causeway go to the island of Sentosa, which has beaches and attractions such as the impressive Underwater World, while to the north is the well-designed zoo, which features a night safari park. To the west attractions include the Jurong Bird Park and Tang Dynasty City.

### Stockholm, Sweden          Map page 28

Built on 14 islands, between Lake Mälaren and the Baltic Sea, Stockholm is a beautiful city with numerous parks. It has an essentially modern feel, with many fine 20th-century buildings, although there is still a medieval Old Town (Gamla Stan), with narrow streets and a 15th-century cathedral (Storkyrkan). A ferry goes to Drottningholm – the royal family's island castle, complete with lakeside gardens and an 18th-century theatre. The island of Djurgarden is home to an open-air museum of Swedish vernacular architecture (Skansen) and the cathedral-like building that covers the *Vasa* – a beautifully restored 17th-century warship.

### Sydney, NSW, Australia          Map page 28

Australia's oldest and largest city is built around a beautiful harbour that is both a major port and recreational area. Best known for its sail-shaped opera house and striking steel-arched harbour bridge, Sydney also has excellent beaches such as Manly, which can be reached by ferry, and the famous Bondi. In the centre, ferries and harbour cruises set out from Circular Quay, near which is The Rocks, with a restored historic quarter. Another area of waterside redevelopment is Darling Harbour, not far from which is the bustling Sydney Fish Market. Away from the harbour, inner suburbs worth visiting include Glebe, Newtown and Paddington, each with a distinct character and attractive 19th-century terraced houses. With an exciting mix of Asian and European cultures, the city offers a cosmopolitan choice of restaurants, theatres and music. The many museums and art galleries include the Australian Museum, which has a gallery devoted to Aboriginal history. A day trip can be made by train to the spectacular Blue Mountains only 80 km (50 miles) away.

Opera House, Sydney

### Tehran, Iran          Map page 30

Most visitors to Tehran concentrate on its excellent museums. The National Museum and the Golestan Palace Museum house many ancient objects, including those taken from famous sites such as Persepolis. The Museum of Glass and Ceramics is well designed and organized, and the Reza Abbasis Museum displays Islamic art. For those willing to brave the heat and noise, Iran has an extensive bazaar.

## Tianjin, China
Map page 30

The centre of Tianjin, for decades an important trading port, is a mixture of international architectural styles – British, French, German and Japanese – from the late 19th century. The Ancient Culture Street, a major draw for visitors, is an attempt to re-create the feel of ancient China. For a more authentic experience of Chinese culture, it is worth going to the Antiques Market and taking a walk through the Hai River Park.

## Tokyo, Japan
Map page 29

Visitors to Tokyo, faced with a vast urban sprawl, normally work outwards from the Imperial Palace and the surrounding gardens, which contain the remains of Edo Castle. Immediately to the east is the downtown area, with a wide choice of restaurants and shops and some fine examples of modern architecture, including the Tokyo International Forum, with a 60 m (200 ft) high glass atrium. To the west is the Meijii Shrine, set in attractive gardens. The city centre has many art galleries, exhibiting both Japanese and European art. However, many of the largest museums, including the Tokyo National Museum, are further north, in Ueno. The adjacent Asakusa district reveals a more tranquil world of wooden houses, temples and shrines, including the magnificent temple of Senso-ji.

## Toronto, Ontario, Canada
Map page 30

Standing on the shore of Lake Ontario, Toronto is Canada's leading commercial city. In its centre is the tallest free-standing structure in the world: the CN Tower. Glass-fronted lifts transport visitors to the Space Deck, 442 m (1,400 ft high), from where it is possible to see as far as Niagara Falls. The city's museums include the Royal Ontario Museum and the Gallery of Inuit Art. Along the waterfront an area of old warehouses has been developed as the Harbourfront Park, with hotels, theatres, shops and restaurants. Toronto's large immigrant population has helped create a vibrant city culture, with a thriving music scene.

## Vancouver, British Columbia, Canada

Built around a natural harbour, Vancouver is a major port and city of inlets and green spaces, set against a mountain backdrop. The downtown area contains a cluster of sparkling, glass-fronted skyscrapers. Vancouver has a thriving Chinatown and a dynamic artistic and musical scene that encompasses classical, jazz and rock music. Of the many museums, the Museum of Anthropology is the finest. Stanley Park – a peninsula containing a large area of semi-wilderness – has three of Vancouver's many city beaches and the Vancouver Aquarium. Nearby is Vancouver Island, with its rainforest and glacial mountain peaks.

## Varanasi, India

Built on the banks of the sacred River Ganges, Varanasi is famous for the flights of stone steps (ghats), lining 5 km (3 miles) of the river banks, where Hindu pilgrims bathe in the waters and cremate their dead. The old town consists of a maze of narrow alleyways at the heart of which is the Golden Temple, dedicated to the god Shiva. The city is also sacred for Buddhists, and at nearby Sarnath there is a collection of restored temples.

## Venice, Italy

Distant view of Church of Santa Maria delle Salute, Venice

Built on a collection of islands and criss-crossed by 177 canals, Venice is a city like no other, where boats are the only means of transport. A journey by gondola or vaporetto along the Grand Canal passes many grand palaces, including the Gothic Ca' d'Oro and Ca' Foscari, the Renaissance Palazzo Grimani and the Baroque Rezzonico. The familiar landmark of the Rialto Bridge presides over the busiest shopping area in Venice. Around St Mark's Square is the stunning 11th-century Byzantine Basilica, the Pala d'Oro, and the Doge's Palace. A lift to the top of the towering Campanile provides exceptional views over the city and the lagoon, across which lies the Lido, with beaches and hotels. The Accademia contains the world's most comprehensive collection of Venetian art, including paintings by Titian, while the Peggy Guggenheim collection is one of the most important of 20th-century art outside the USA.

## Vienna, Austria
Map page 31

Formerly the capital of the Habsburg and Austro-Hungarian empires, today's Vienna preserves an atmosphere of historic grandeur. A city of cafés, beer cellars, parks and elegant boulevards, it has a centre, the Innere Stadt, that is sufficiently compact to be explored on foot. It contains numerous Baroque churches and palaces, the magnificent Gothic St Stephen's Cathedral, and the Hofburg – the Habsburgs' imperial palace, which is now home to the famous Spanish Riding School. Among the city's many museums are the Kunsthistorisches (Art History Museum), with an unrivalled collection of paintings by Peter Breugel the Elder, and the fine 18th-century Belvedere palace complex which features paintings by Klimt and Schiele among others. Outside the centre is Schönbrunn, the Habsburgs' impressive summer palace, and the Prater (in Leopoldstadt), a vast park featuring Vienna's giant ferris wheel. To the north the hills of Kahlenberg and Leopoldsberg provide magnificent views over the city.

## Warsaw, Poland
Map page 31

The old centre of Warsaw, on the left bank of the River Vistula, was reduced to rubble during World War II, but it has been meticulously rebuilt and is now a UNESCO World Heritage site. All the buildings appear to date from the 18th century or earlier. They include St John's Cathedral and the Renaissance and Baroque merchants' houses surrounding the Old Market Square (Rynek Starego Miasta). There is also the excellent Historical Museum of Warsaw, many lively cafés and some fine restaurants. Outside the Old Town is the beautiful Lazienki park and palace complex and, 6 km (4 miles) further south, the restored Baroque Wilanów park and palace.

## Washington DC, USA
Map page 32

The main public buildings of Washington DC are grouped on and around the National Mall – a broad swathe of parkland containing the Washington Monument, the Lincoln and Jefferson memorials, and the V-shaped polished black stone wall incised with thousands of names, which commemorates the Americans who fell in Vietnam. On the north side of the Mall is the White House, and over-looking all from the eastern end is the Capitol building, with its 55 m (180 ft) high rotunda. Home to the House of Representatives and the Senate, it is open to visitors. The National Gallery of Art and the National Air and Space Museum are two of the many museums. Central Washington DC can be dangerous at night. Georgetown is more relaxed, with its restaurants, bars and handsome streets. Within easy reach of the city are Chesapeake Bay and several Civil War battle sites.

## Wellington, New Zealand
Map page 32

Overlooked by Mount Victoria, Wellington is the political and commercial capital of New Zealand. Wooden Victorian houses climb the steep hills surrounding the magnificent harbour of Port Nicholson, and a cable car provides a spectacular view of the city. Among the historic buildings in the centre are the Old Government Buildings, while the city's museums include the recently opened Museum of New Zealand (Te Papa). A lively, cosmopolitan city, Wellington has an exciting cultural scene, as evidenced in February and March by the annual Fringe Festival and the biennial International Festival of the Arts.

View over the harbour, Wellington

## Xi'an, China

As well as being a base from which to visit the famous Army of Terracotta Warriors, Xi'an possesses its own historic sites. These include the impressive city walls that all but surround the old town, and the 64 m (200 ft) high Big Goose Pagoda. Xi'an also has a strong Islamic culture and its Great Mosque is the largest in China. The Shaanxi Provincial Museum presents a fascinating history of the Silk Road.

## Yangon (Rangoon), Burma (Myanmar)

The main focus of any visit to Yangon will be the magnificent Shwedagon stupa. The stupa is 90 m (290 ft) high and shaped like a bell. Completely covered in gold, it is surrounded by a host of smaller gilded stupas, statues, temples and pavilions. Of the many other Buddhist sites around the city, the huge reclining Buddha at Chaukhtatgyi Paya is the most impressive. Two large lakes provide areas of recreation, and the many tree-lined streets and areas of near-jungle give some parts an almost rural feel.

# WORLD MAPS

## SETTLEMENTS

▣ **PARIS**     ▣ **Berne**     ◉ **Livorno**     ◉ **Brugge**     ◉ Algeciras     ○ *Frejus*     ○ *Oberammergau*     ○ *Thira*

Settlement symbols and type styles vary according to the scale of each map and indicate the importance
of towns on the map rather than specific population figures

∴    Ruins or Archæological Sites          ⌄    Wells in Desert

## ADMINISTRATION

——— International Boundaries      ⬭ National Parks      Administrative Area Names

– – – International Boundaries (Undefined or Disputed)      Country Names    **NICARAGUA**      KENT    CALABRIA

··········· Internal Boundaries

International boundaries show the *de facto* situation where there are rival claims to territory

## COMMUNICATIONS

——— Principal Roads      ⊕ Airfields      ——— Other Railways

——— Other Roads      ——— Principal Railways      –⊦··⊦ Railway Tunnels

–⊦··⊦ Road Tunnels      – –～– Railways Under Construction      ············ Principal Canals

⌣ Passes

## PHYSICAL FEATURES

～～ Perrenial Streams      ⬚ Intermittent Lakes      ▲ 8848 Elevations in metres

– ～ – Intermittent Streams      ⬚ Swamps and Marshes      ▼ 8500 Sea Depths in metres

⬭ Perennial Lakes      ⬚ Permanent Ice and Glaciers      *1134* Height of Lake Surface Above Sea Level in metres

## ELEVATION AND DEPTH TINTS

**Height of Land above Sea Level**      **Land Below Sea Level**    **Depth of Sea**

in feet

| 6000 | 4000 | 3000 | 2000 | 1500 | 1000 | 400 | 200 | 0 |
| | | | | | | | | 6000 | 12 000 | 15 000 | 18 000 | 24 000 | in feet |

in metres

| 18 000 | 12 000 | 9000 | 6000 | 4500 | 3000 | 1200 | 600 |
| | | | | | | | 0 | 200 | 2000 | 4000 | 5000 | 6000 | 8000 | in metres |

Some of the maps have different contours to highlight and clarify the principal relief features

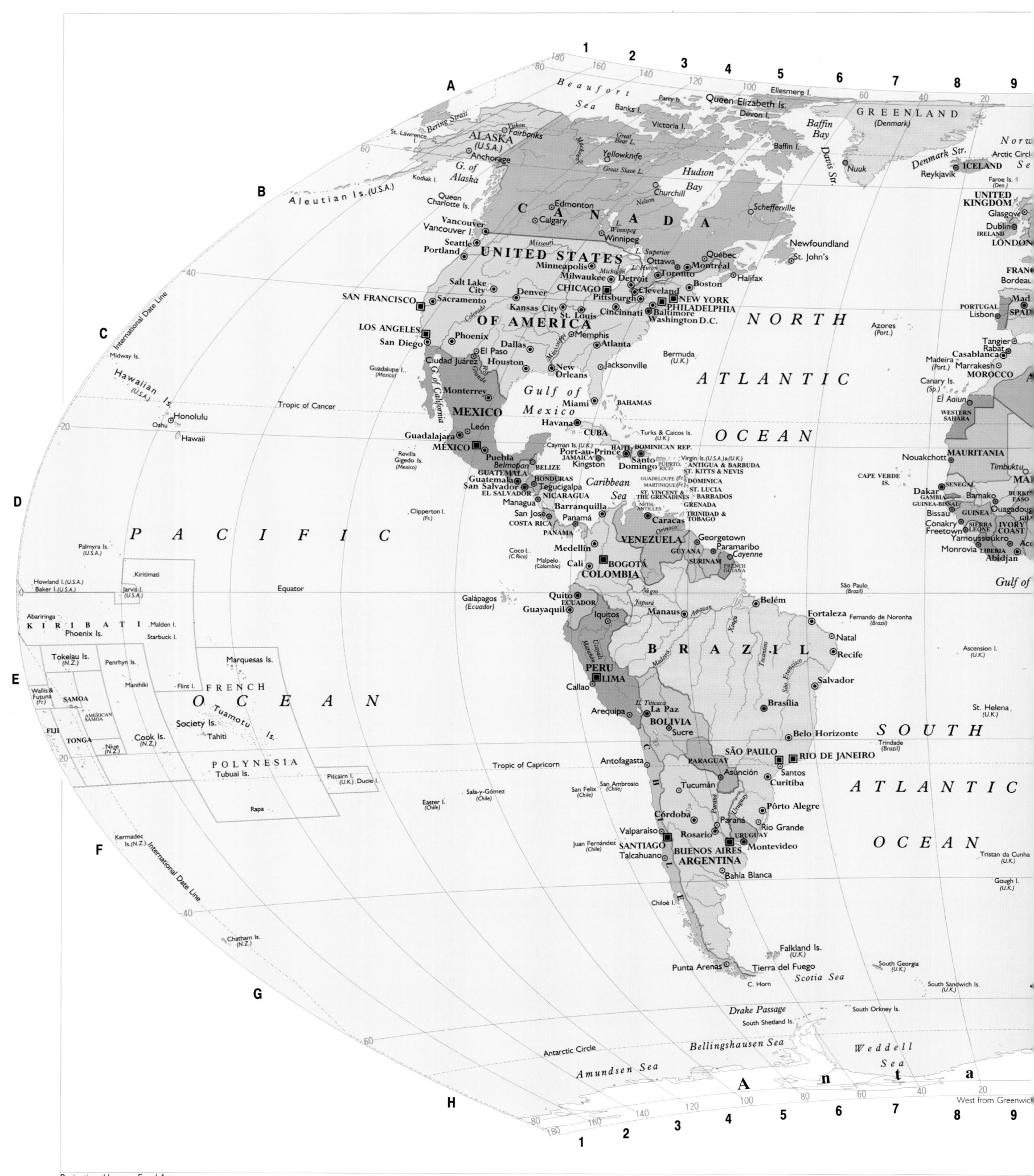

Projection: Hammer Equal Area

100 0 200 400 600 800 1000 1200 1400 km
100 0 200 400 600 800 1000 miles

Maximum extent of sea ice

Summer extent of sea ice

Ice caps and permanent ice shelf

Projection : Zenithal Equidistant

West from Greenwich   East from Greenwich

COPYRIGHT GEORGE PHILIP LTD

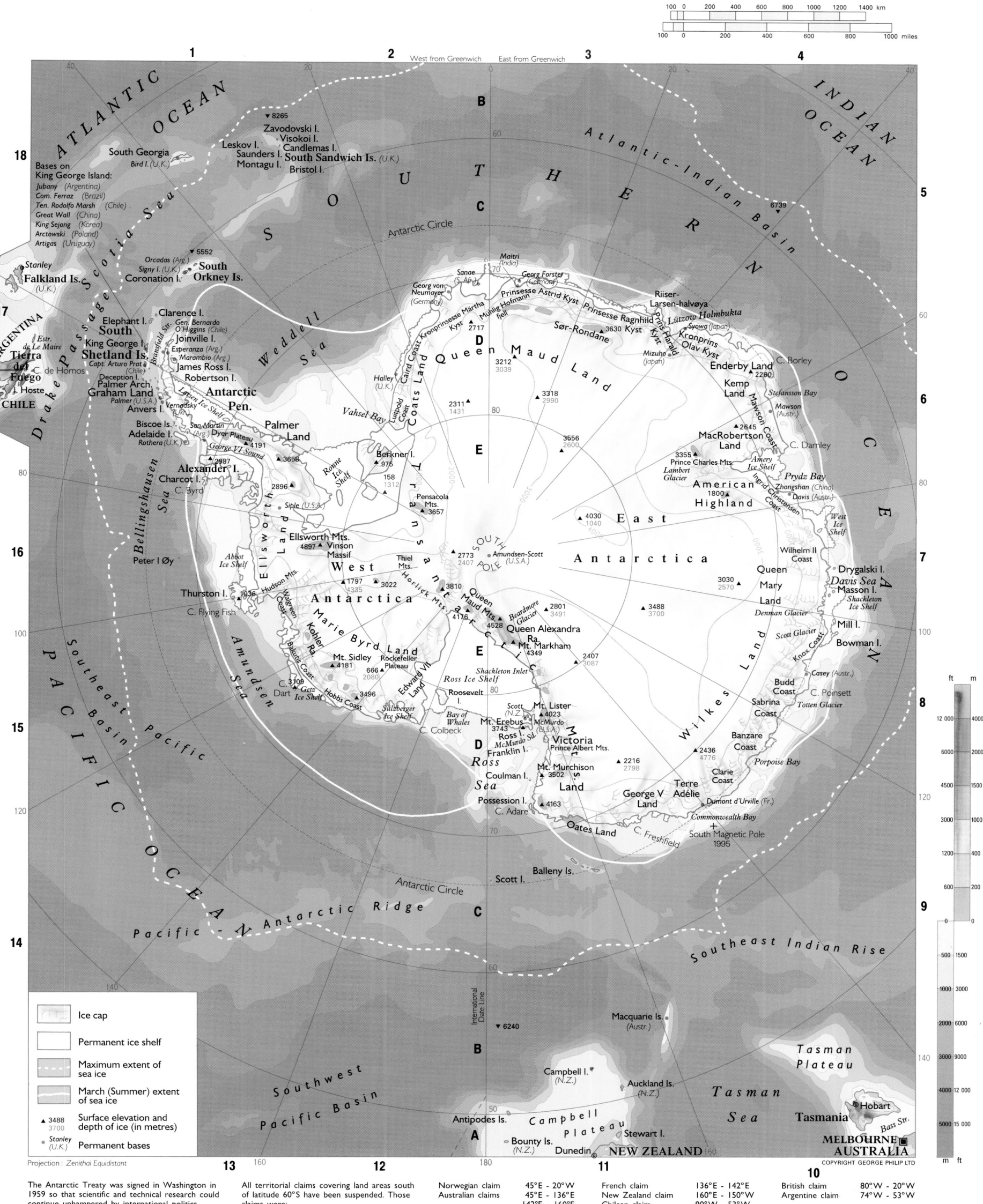

The Antarctic Treaty was signed in Washington in 1959 so that scientific and technical research could continue unhampered by international politics.

All territorial claims covering land areas south of latitude 60°S have been suspended. Those claims were:

| | | | |
|---|---|---|---|
| Norwegian claim | 45°E - 20°W | French claim | 136°E - 142°E |
| Australian claims | 45°E - 136°E | New Zealand claim | 160°E - 150°W |
| | 142°E - 160°E | Chilean claim | 90°W - 53°W |
| | | British claim | 80°W - 20°W |
| | | Argentine claim | 74°W - 53°W |

Projection: Zenithal Equidistant

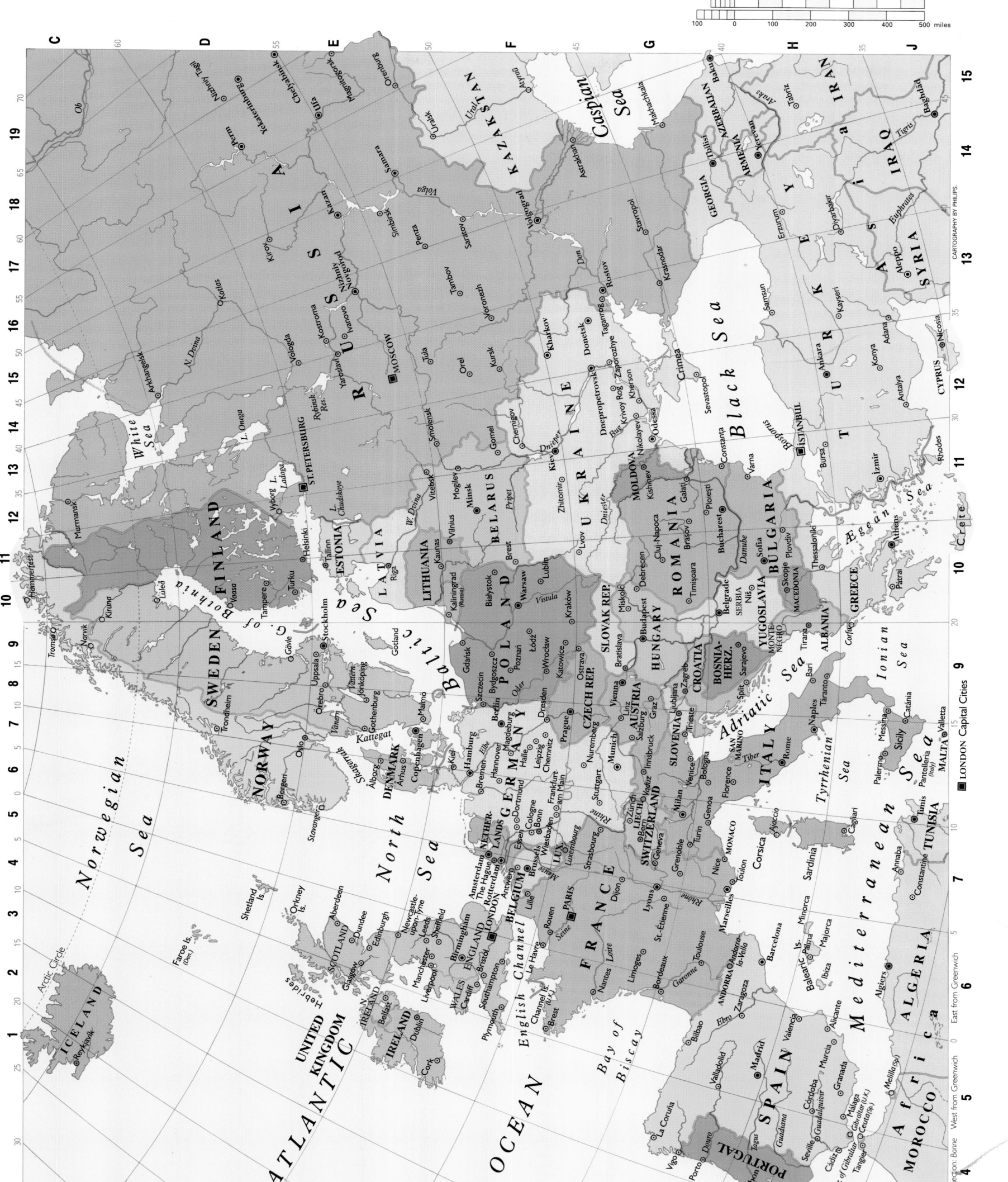

100  0  100  200  300  400  500  600  700  800 km
100  0  100  200  300  400  500 miles

**CARTOGRAPHY BY PHILIPS**

□ LONDON Capital Cities

# SCANDINAVIA 1:4 400 000

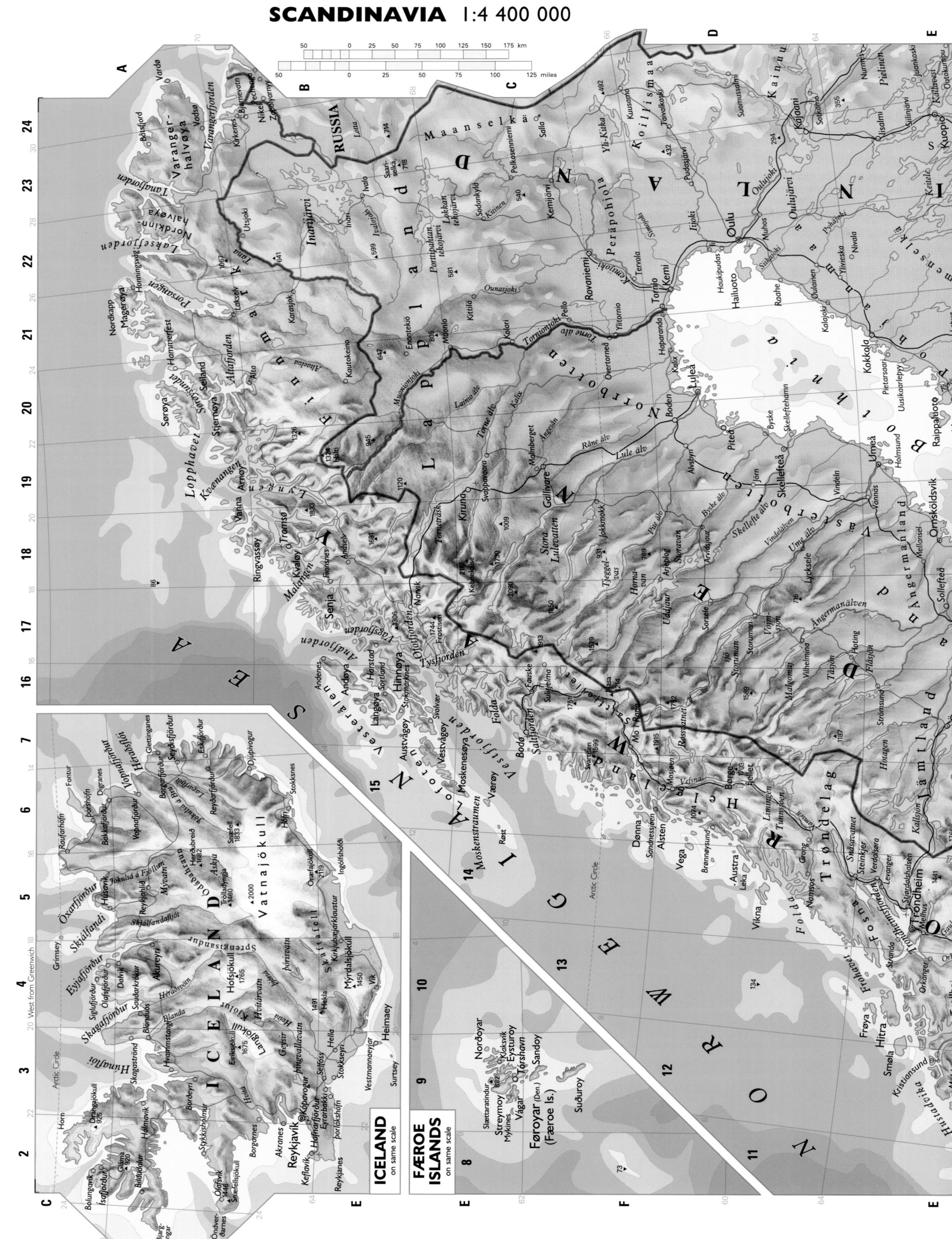

# Countries and Seas

**NORWAY** • **SWEDEN** • **FINLAND** • **ESTONIA** • **LATVIA** • **LITHUANIA** • **RUSSIA** • **BELARUS** • **POLAND** • **DENMARK** • **GERMANY**

**Gulf of Finland** • **Gulf of Riga** • **BALTIC SEA** • **Gulf of Bothnia** • **Kattegat** • **Skagerrak** • **Ålands hav**

## Finland

Varkaus, Savonlinna, Mikkeli, Saimaa, Lappeenranta, Heinola, Kouvola, Kotka, Hamina, Kymijoki, Lahti, Lovisa, Porvoo, Helsinki (Helsingfors), Espoo, Vantaa, Kerava, Hyvinkää, Hämeenlinna, Tampere, Nokia, Valkeakoski, Forssa, Salo, Turku (Åbo), Pori, Rauma, Uusikaupunki, Kristiinankaupunki, Kaskinen, Seinäjoki, Vaasa, Jyväskylä, Äänekoski, Keuruu, Mänttä, Jämsä, Parkano, Ilmajoki, Kurikka, Alavus, Kauhajoki, Jalasjärvi, Kankaanpää, Parkano, Naantali, Hanko, Tammisaari

## Estonia

Tallinn, Tartu, Narva, Pärnu, Viljandi, Rakvere, Paide, Põltsamaa, Haapsalu, Kuressaare, Hiiumaa (Dago), Saaremaa (Ösel), Muhu, Kärdla, Kunda, Ozero Chudskoye, Võrts Järv

## Latvia

Riga, Jūrmala, Jelgava, Daugavpils, Rēzekne, Valmiera, Cēsis, Sigulda, Limbaži, Tukums, Dobele, Saldus, Talsi, Ventspils, Kuldīga, Liepāja, Bauska, Jēkabpils, Gulbene, Alūksne, Madona, Ogre, Daugava, Roja

## Lithuania

Vilnius, Kaunas, Panevėžys, Šiauliai, Klaipėda, Palanga, Telšiai, Plungė, Kretinga, Šilutė, Tauragė, Jurbarkas, Marijampolė, Alytus, Varėna, Utena, Ukmergė, Kėdainiai, Jonava, Radviliškis, Mažeikiai, Skuodas, Kaliningrad (Russia), Sovetsk, Zelenogradsk, Neman, Gusev, Chernyakhovsk, Bagrationovsk

## Russia / Belarus

Pskov, Ostrov, Daugavpils, Braslaw, Vidzy, Lida, Lyntupy, Ashmiany

## Poland

Gdańsk, Gdynia, Sopot, Elbląg, Malbork, Słupsk, Koszalin, Kołobrzeg, Darłowo, Wejherowo, Lębork, Bytów, Tczew, Starogard, Gdański, Wisła, Augustów, Suwałki, Ełk, Giżycko, Kętrzyn

## Sweden

STOCKHOLM, Uppsala, Västerås, Eskilstuna, Södertälje, Norrköping, Linköping, Örebro, Gävle, Sundsvall, Härnösand, Hudiksvall, Söderhamn, Falun, Borlänge, Karlstad, Göteborg (Gothenburg), Borås, Jönköping, Växjö, Kalmar, Halmstad, Helsingborg, Malmö, Lund, Kristianstad, Karlskrona, Karlshamn, Visby, Gotland, Öland, Gotska Sandön, Fårö, Mora, Sala, Nyköping, Katrineholm, Motala, Mjölby, Nässjö, Västervik, Oskarshamn, Trollhättan, Vänersborg, Lidköping, Skövde, Mariestad, Falköping, Ulricehamn, Varberg, Ängelholm, Landskrona, Trelleborg, Ystad, Simrishamn, Vänern, Vättern, Mälaren, Dalälven, Svealand, Götaland, Norrland, Dalarna, Värmland, Uppland, Södermanland, Östergötland, Småland, Skåne, Halland, Blekinge, Bohuslän, Dalsland, Västmanland

## Norway

Oslo, Bergen, Stavanger, Kristiansand, Drammen, Sarpsborg, Fredrikstad, Moss, Tønsberg, Sandefjord, Larvik, Skien, Porsgrunn, Arendal, Grimstad, Hamar, Lillehammer, Gjøvik, Hønefoss, Kongsberg, Notodden, Haugesund, Ålesund, Molde, Flekkefjord, Egersund, Mandal, Oslofjorden, Sognefjorden, Hardangerfjorden, Jotunheimen, Dovrefjell, Gudbrandsdalen, Østerdalen, Telemark, Valdres, Rondane, Hallingdal, Hardangervidda

## Denmark

KØBENHAVN (Copenhagen), Århus, Ålborg, Odense, Esbjerg, Randers, Kolding, Vejle, Horsens, Silkeborg, Viborg, Herning, Fredericia, Roskilde, Helsingør, Næstved, Slagelse, Svendborg, Nykøbing, Sjælland, Fyn, Lolland, Falster, Langeland, Møn, Bornholm, Rønne, Frederikshavn, Hjørring, Skagen, Grenen, Læsø, Anholt, Thisted, Skive, Holstebro, Ringkøbing, Haderslev, Åbenrå, Sønderborg, Tønder, Little Bælt, Store Bælt, Lillebælt

## Germany

Kiel, Lübeck, Rostock, Wismar, Flensburg, Schleswig, Neumünster, Rendsburg, Itzehoe, Cuxhaven, Husum, Rügen, Usedom, Greifswald, Stralsund, Sassnitz, Fehmarn, Holstein, Nordfriesische Inseln, Ostfriesische Inseln, Helgoland, Deutsche Bucht, Mecklenburger Bucht, Kieler Bucht, Elbe, Sylt, Föhr, Amrum

Projection: Conical with two standard parallels

East from Greenwich

ft / m scale:
6000, 4500, 3000, 1500, 600, 200, 0, 200, 500, 1000, 1500, 2000, 3000, 6000
2000, 1500, 1000, 500, 200, 100, 0, 50, 150, 300, 600, 1500, 2000, 4000

Gulf of Bothnia

VÄSTER-NORRLANDS LÄN

NORRLANDS LÄN

Medelpad

Hälsingland

GÄVLEBORGS LÄN

Gästrikland

JÄMTLANDS LÄN

Härjedalen

KOPPARBERGS LÄN

Dalarna

Siljan

UPPSALA LÄN

Uppland

STOCKHOLMS LÄN

STOCKHOLM

Mälaren

VÄSTMANLANDS LÄN

SÖDERMANLANDS LÄN

Östersund

Storsjön

SÖR-TRØNDELAG

HEDMARK

Dovrefjell

Rondane

Jotunheimen

OPPLAND

ØSTERDALEN

Glåma

VÄRMLANDS LÄN

ÖREBRO LÄN

Närke

Örebro

Karlstad

Klarälven

Siljan

Falun

Borlänge

Gävle

Sandviken

Hudiksvall

Söderhamn

Sundsvall

Härnösand

Trondheim

MØRE OG ROMSDAL

TROLLHEIMEN

BUSKERUD

TELEMARK

VESTFOLD

ØSTFOLD

AKERSHUS

Oslo

Drammen

Fredrikstad

Hamar

Mjøsa

Lillehammer

Hallingdal

Numedal

Valdres

m  6000 4500 3000 1500 600 300 0
ft

km  10 0 10 20 30 40 50 60 70 80 90
miles  10 0 10 20 30 40 50 60

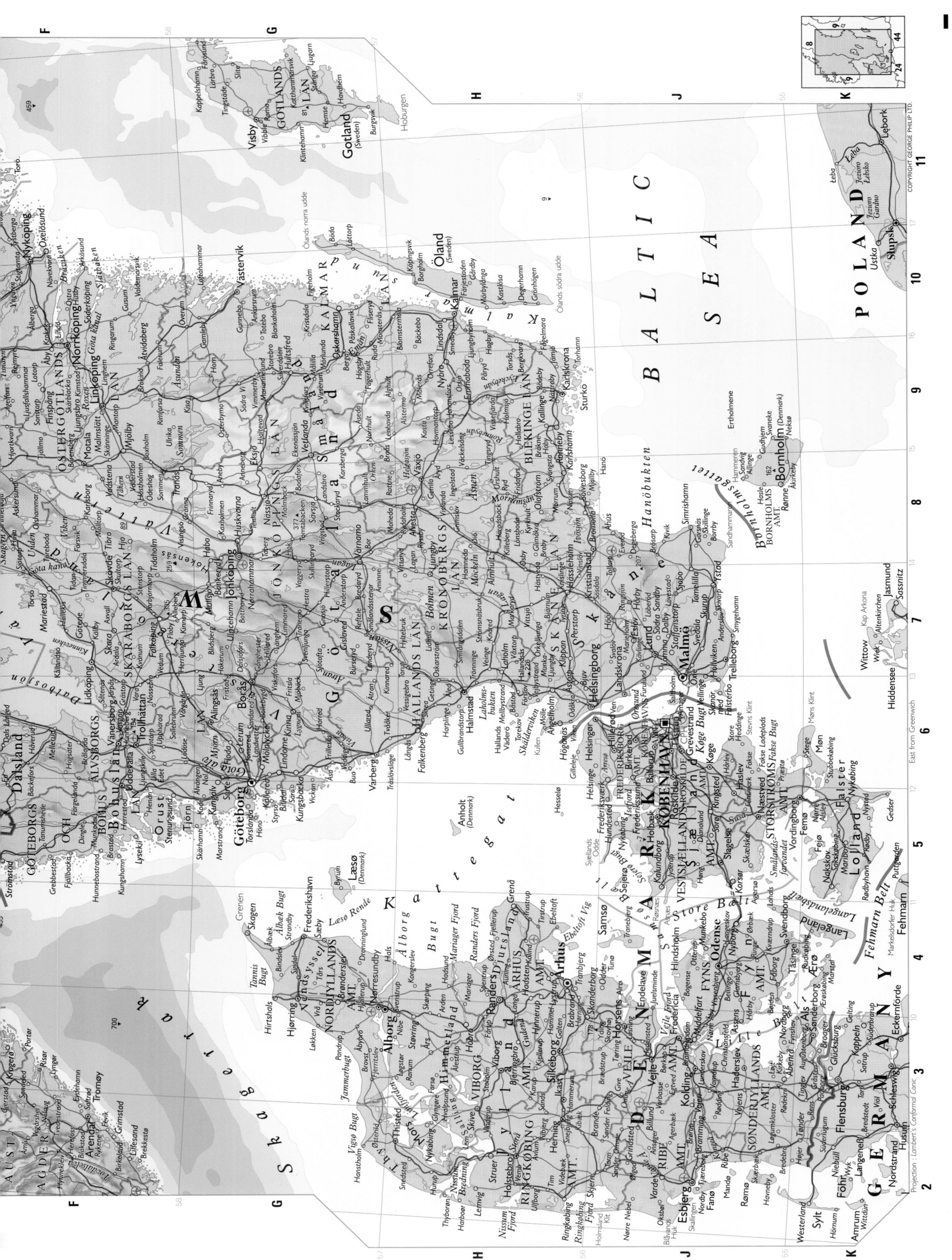

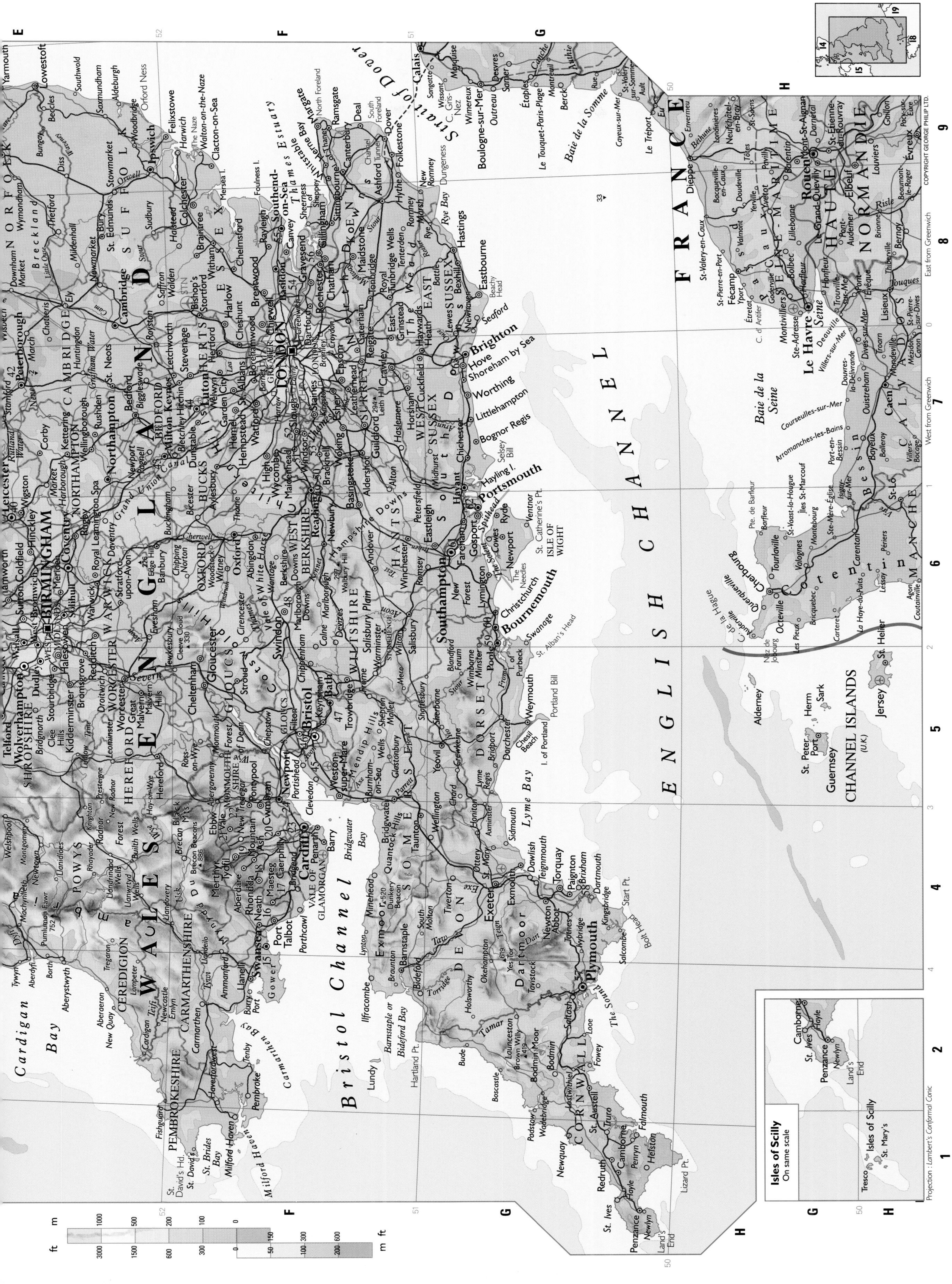

**ENGLAND**

**WALES**

**FRANCE**

**NORMANDIE**

**HAUTE-SEINE-MARITIME**

**CALVADOS**

**MANCHE**

**ENGLISH CHANNEL**

**Bristol Channel**

**Cardigan Bay**

**Baie de la Seine**

**Lyme Bay**

**CHANNEL ISLANDS (U.K.)**

Strait of Dover — Pas de Calais

Major cities and towns: London, Birmingham, Bristol, Cardiff, Plymouth, Portsmouth, Southampton, Bournemouth, Brighton, Exeter, Gloucester, Oxford, Cambridge, Ipswich, Colchester, Chelmsford, Canterbury, Dover, Folkestone, Hastings, Eastbourne, Worthing, Newport, Swansea, Hereford, Worcester, Coventry, Leicester, Northampton, Peterborough, Reading, Guildford, Maidstone, Newbury, Salisbury, Bath, Taunton, Torquay, Truro, Penzance, St. Ives, Newquay, Land's End, Lizard Pt.

France towns: Calais, Boulogne-sur-Mer, Dieppe, Le Havre, Rouen, Caen, Cherbourg, Évreux, Lisieux, Bayeux, Fécamp, Étaples, Le Tréport.

Isles of Scilly (on same scale): Tresco, St. Mary's

Counties: NORFOLK, SUFFOLK, ESSEX, KENT, EAST SUSSEX, WEST SUSSEX, SURREY, HAMPSHIRE, DORSET, SOMERSET, DEVON, CORNWALL, WILTSHIRE, BERKSHIRE, OXON, BUCKS, HERTS, CAMBRIDGE, GLOUCS, WORCESTER, WARWICK, SHROPSHIRE, HEREFORD, POWYS, CEREDIGION, PEMBROKESHIRE, CARMARTHENSHIRE, GLAMORGAN, WEST MIDLANDS, WEALD

ISLE OF WIGHT — Newport, Cowes, Ryde, Ventnor, The Needles

Dartmoor, Exmoor, Bodmin Moor, Mendip Hills, Cotswolds, Chilterns, North Downs, South Downs

Projection: Lambert's Conformal Conic

COPYRIGHT GEORGE PHILIP LTD.

East from Greenwich / West from Greenwich

Elevation legend: m / ft — 3000, 1500, 600, 300, 150, 100, 50, 0

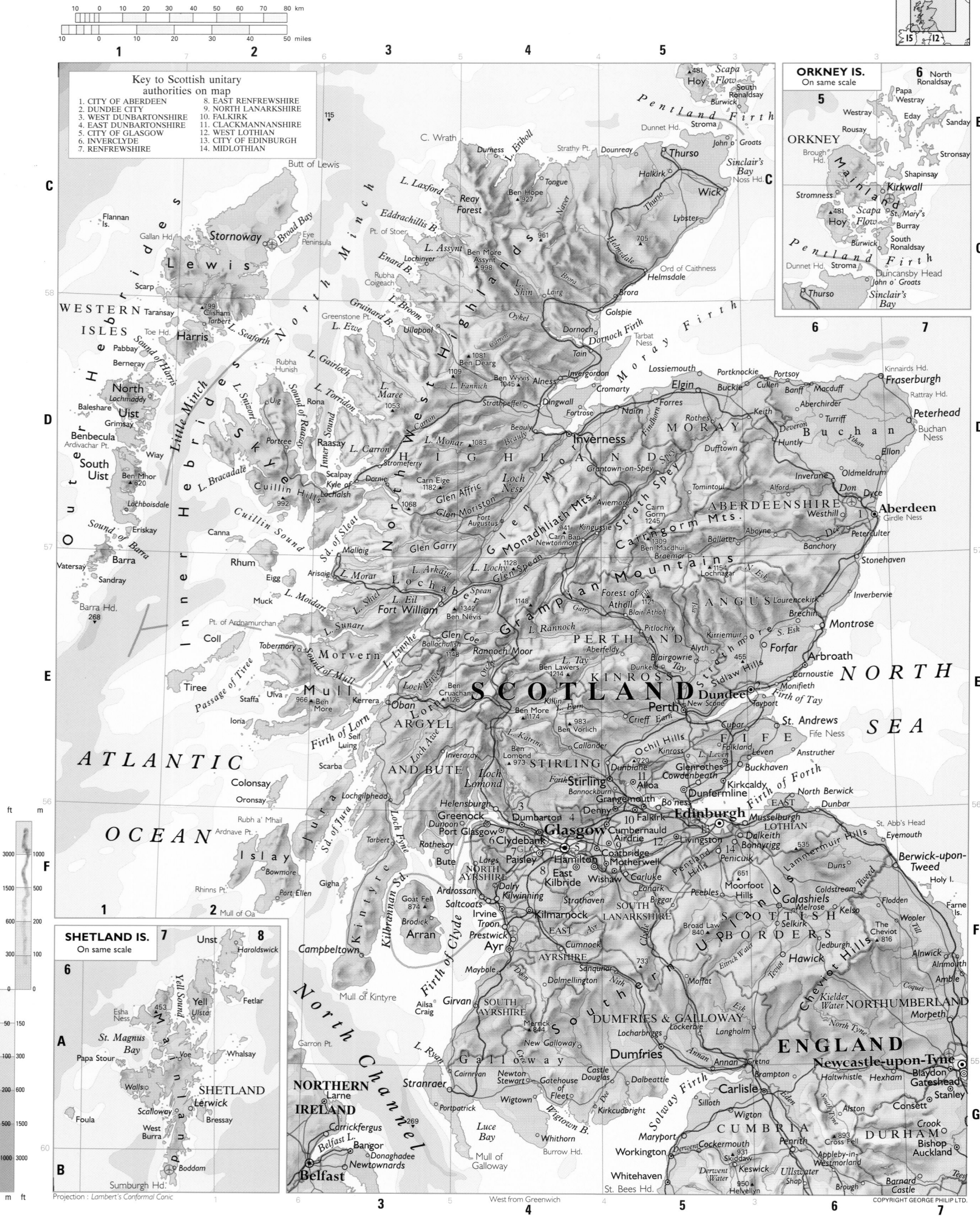

10 0 10 20 30 40 50 60 70 80 km
10 0 10 20 30 40 50 miles

**Key to Scottish unitary authorities on map**

1. CITY OF ABERDEEN
2. DUNDEE CITY
3. WEST DUNBARTONSHIRE
4. EAST DUNBARTONSHIRE
5. CITY OF GLASGOW
6. INVERCLYDE
7. RENFREWSHIRE
8. EAST RENFREWSHIRE
9. NORTH LANARKSHIRE
10. FALKIRK
11. CLACKMANNANSHIRE
12. WEST LOTHIAN
13. CITY OF EDINBURGH
14. MIDLOTHIAN

**ORKNEY IS.**
On same scale

ORKNEY

**SHETLAND IS.**
On same scale

SHETLAND

Projection : Lambert's Conformal Conic

West from Greenwich

COPYRIGHT GEORGE PHILIP LTD.

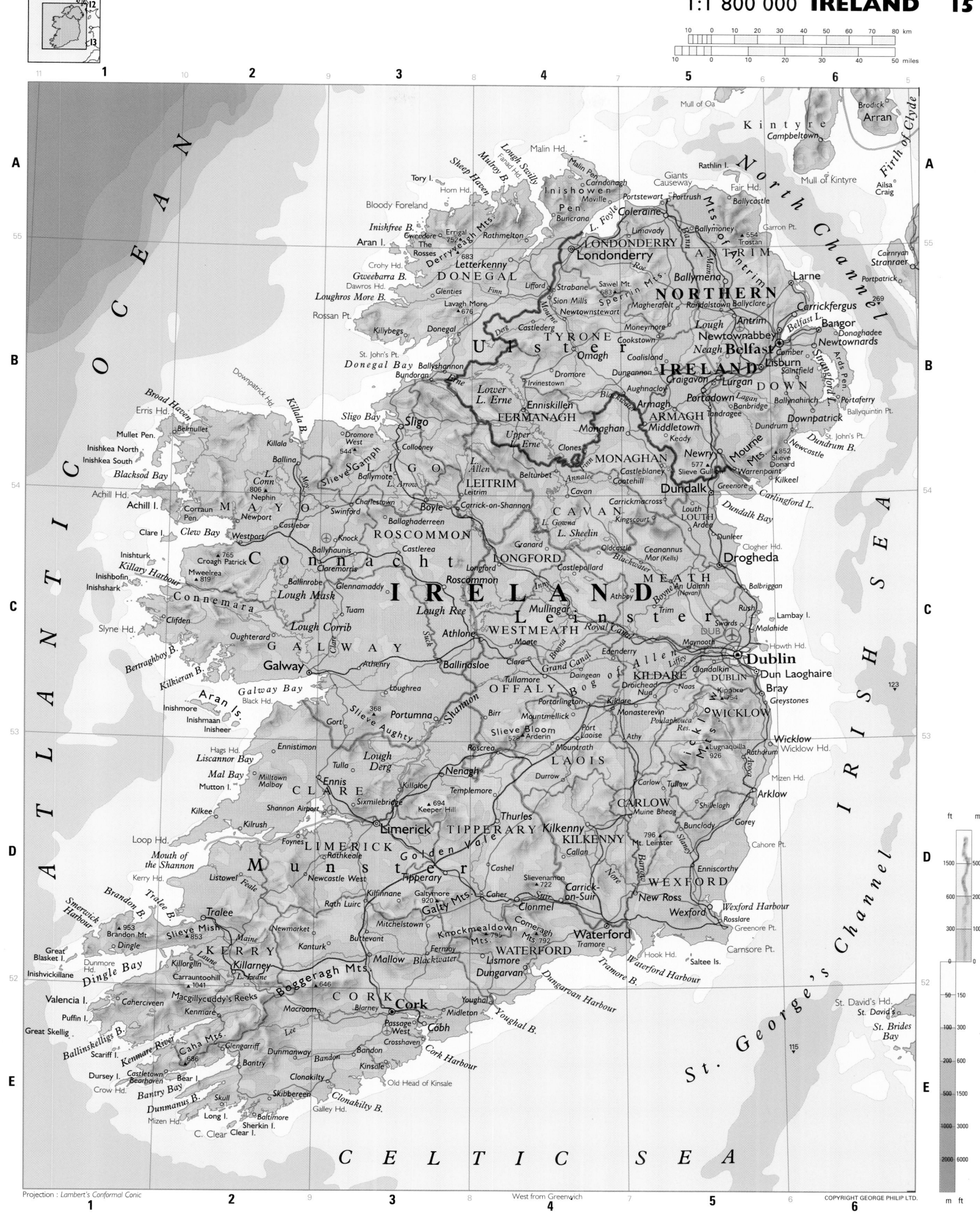

Projection : Lambert's Conformal Conic

West from Greenwich

Projection: Conical with two standard parallels

50   25   0   25   50   75   100   125   150   175 km
50        0        25        50        75        100   125 miles

ft   m
3000  1000
1500   500
600   200
0    0
50   150
100   300
200   600
500  1500
1000  3000
2000  6000
m   ft

**A T L A N T I C   O C E A N**

**NORWAY**

Askøy
Bergen
Osøyro
Leirvik
Stord
Bømlo
Haugesund
Kopervik
Åkrahamn
Bokn
Stavanger
Sandnes
Bryne
Nærbø

Shetland Is.
Yell
Unst
Fetlar
Foula
Mainland
Lerwick
Fair Isle

Orkney Is.
Westray
Sanday
Stronsay
Mainland
Kirkwall
Hoy
South Ronaldsay

**N O R T H   S E A**

Outer Hebrides
Lewis
Stornoway
St. Kilda
Harris
North Uist
Benbecula
South Uist
Barra

Inner Hebrides
Skye
Rhum
Eigg
Coll
Tiree
Mull
Tobermory
Colonsay
Jura
Islay

C. Wrath
Thurso
Wick
Helmsdale
Golspie
Lairg
North West Highlands
Ullapool
Tain
Dingwall
Invergordon
L. Ness
Inverness
Nairn
Elgin
Buckie
Banff
Fraserburgh
Peterhead
Huntly
Inverurie
Aberdeen
Stonehaven

Moray Firth
Pentland Firth

**S C O T L A N D**
Grampian Mts.
Aviemore
Fort William
Ben Nevis 1342
Oban
Dee
Ballater
Montrose
Arbroath
Forfar
Dundee
St. Andrews
Perth
Stirling
L. Lomond
Greenock
Paisley
East Kilbride
Glasgow
Hamilton
Kilmarnock
Irvine
Arran
Campbeltown
Ayr
Dunfermline
Kirkcaldy
Glenrothes
Edinburgh
Dunbar
Berwick-upon-Tweed

Southern Uplands
Galashiels
Jedburgh
Hawick
Cheviot Hills
Dumfries
Alnwick
Annan
Kirkcudbright
Stranraer
Girvan
Mull of Galloway

Firth of Clyde
North Channel

Malin Hd.
Buncrana
Aran I.
Letterkenny
Coleraine
Londonderry
Ballymena
Larne
Donegal
Lifford
Bangor
Lough Neagh
Antrim
**NORTHERN IRELAND**
Ulster
Omagh
Portadown
Belfast
Lurgan
Lisburn
Newry
Armagh
Enniskillen
Lower L. Erne
Clones
Castleblaney
Cavan
Leitrim
Dundalk
Drogheda

Workington
Whitehaven
Carlisle
Hexham
Newcastle-upon-Tyne
South Shields
Gateshead
Sunderland
Durham
Hartlepool
Redcar
Middlesbrough
Stockton-on-Tees
Darlington
Scarborough
Bridlington

Cumbrian Mts. 978
Pennines 893
Barrow-in-Furness
Lancaster
Harrogate
York
Beverley
Kingston upon Hull

Douglas
I. of Man

**UNITED KINGDOM**
**IRISH SEA**

**IRELAND**
Sligo
Ballina
Castlebar
Westport
Achill I.
Lough Mask
Connemara
Galway B.
Galway
Aran Is.
Ennis
Kilrush
Shannon
Tralee
Dingle
Listowel
Killarney
Macgillycuddy's Reeks 1041
Carrauntoohill
Valencia
Bantry
Kinsale
C. Clear
Mallow
Cork
Cobh
Kilkenny
Carlow
Athy
Port Laoise
Tullamore
Athlone
Ballinasloe
Roscommon
Longford
Mullingar
Lough Ree
Lough Corrib
Ceanannus Mor
Boyne
Cavan
Liffey
Dublin
Dun Laoghaire
Bray
Arklow
Wexford
Rosslare
Waterford
Carrick-on-Suir
Clonmel
Tipperary
Thurles
Nenagh
Limerick
Lough Derg
Birr

Holyhead
Anglesey
Bangor
Colwyn Bay
Conway
Snowdon 1085
Cambrian Mts.
Pwllheli
Cardigan Bay
Aberystwyth
**WALES**
Carmarthen
Llanelli
Swansea
Port Talbot
Neath
Merthyr Tydfil
Brecon 886
Rhondda
Cwmbran
Newport
Cardiff
Barry
Pembroke
Milford Haven
Haverfordwest
Fishguard
St. George's Channel

Blackpool
Preston
Blackburn
Burnley
Bolton
Halifax
Huddersfield
Leeds
Bradford
Barnsley
Wigan
Manchester
Oldham
Rotherham
Sheffield
Liverpool
Warrington
Chester
Crewe
Stockport
Chesterfield
Mansfield
Lincoln
Louth
Grimsby
Scunthorpe
Doncaster
The Wash
Boston
Skegness
Cromer

Wrexham
Stoke on Trent
Derby
Nottingham
Stafford
Telford
Shrewsbury
Welshpool
Wolverhampton
**BIRMINGHAM**
Redditch
Worcester
Hereford
**ENGLAND**
Nuneaton
Coventry
Leicester
Rugby
Royal Leamington Spa
Corby
Peterborough
Grantham
King's Lynn
Norwich
Great Yarmouth
Lowestoft
Thetford
Bury St. Edmunds
Ely
Cambridge
Ipswich
Felixstowe
Harwich
Colchester
Chelmsford
Northampton
Bedford
Milton Keynes
Stevenage
Luton
Harlow
Hemel Hempstead
Watford
Slough
Oxford
Cheltenham
Gloucester
Cotswold Hills
Cirencester
High Wycombe
London
Southend-on-Sea
Chatham
Maidstone
Margate
Canterbury
Dover
Folkestone
Ashford
Reigate
Guildford
Basingstoke
Newbury
Swindon
Bristol
Bath
Newport
Weston-super-Mare
Barnstaple
Exmoor
Taunton
Yeovil
Salisbury
Winchester
Southampton
Portsmouth
Isle of Wight
Newport
Fareham
Havant
Brighton
Worthing
Hastings
Eastbourne
Crawley
Str. of Dover
Bournemouth
Poole
Weymouth
Exmouth
Dartmoor 618
Exeter
Torbay
Bude
Newquay
Truro
St. Austell
Plymouth
Land's End
Penzance
Falmouth
Isles of Scilly

**CELTIC SEA**

**English Channel**
Bristol Channel

**NETHERLANDS**
Haarlem
's-Gravenhage (Den Haag)
Hoek van Holland
**ROTTERDAM**
Dordrecht
Den Helder
Texel
Alkmaar
Vlissingen
Zeebrugge
Oostende
Brugge
Gent
**BELGIUM**
**BRUSSEL (Bruxelles)**
Antwerpen
Mechelen
Tournai
Lille
Roubaix
Tourcoing
Lens
Béthune
Bruay-la-Buissière
Villeneuve d'Ascq
Valenciennes
Cambrai
St-Quentin

**FRANCE**
Calais
Gris-Nez
Boulogne-sur-Mer
Le Touquet-Paris-Plage
Dunkerque
Abbeville
Le Tréport
Dieppe
Fécamp
Amiens
Picardie
Pays de Caux
Le Havre
Bolbec
Rouen
Seine
Elbeuf
Lisieux
Caen
Bayeux
Trouville-sur-Mer
Cherbourg
Valognes
Cotentin
Pte. de Barfleur
C. de la Hague
Alderney
Guernsey
St. Peter Port
Sark
Jersey
St. Helier
Channel Is. (U.K.)

East from Greenwich
West from Greenwich
COPYRIGHT GEORGE PHILIP LTD.

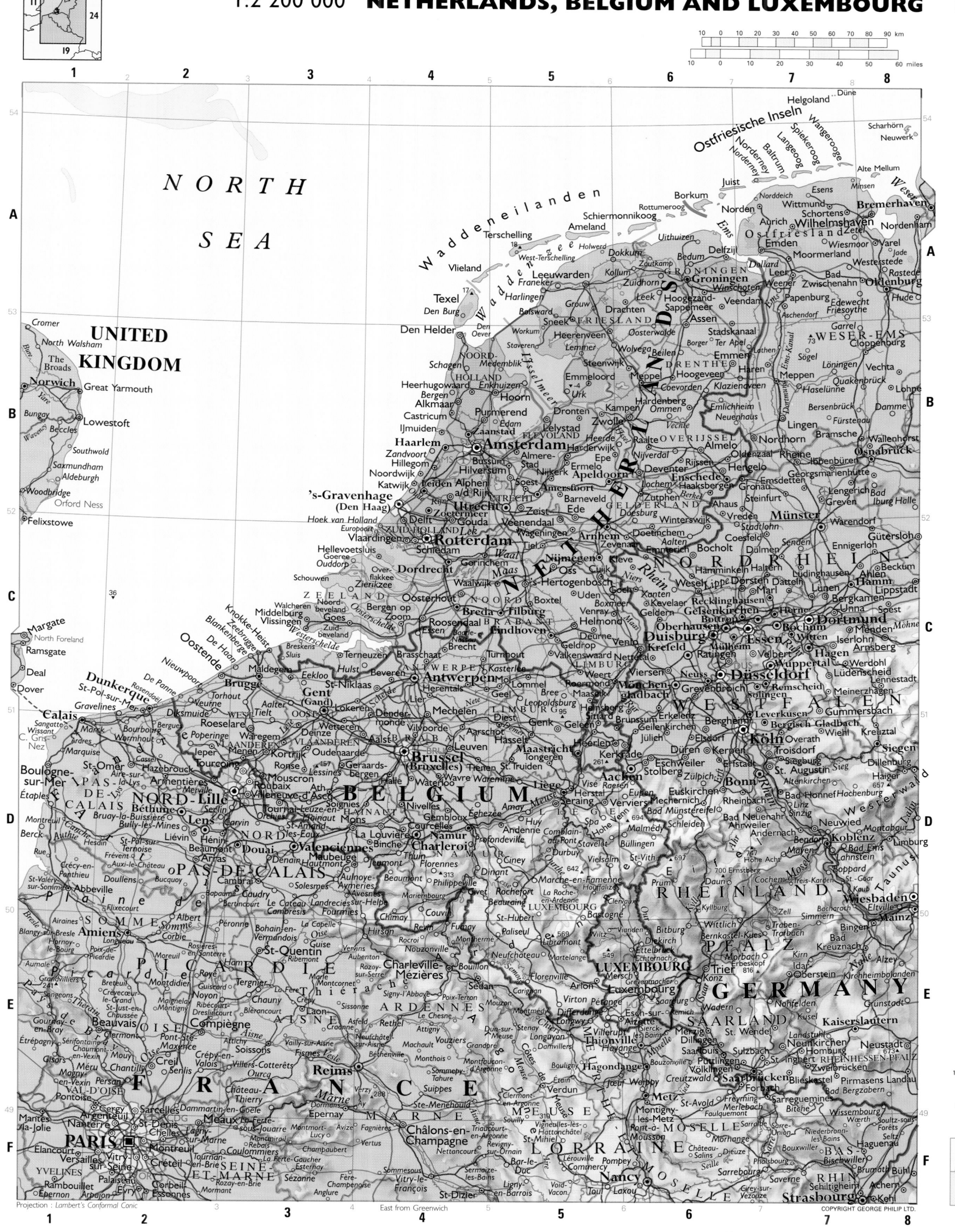

Projection : Lambert's Conformal Conic

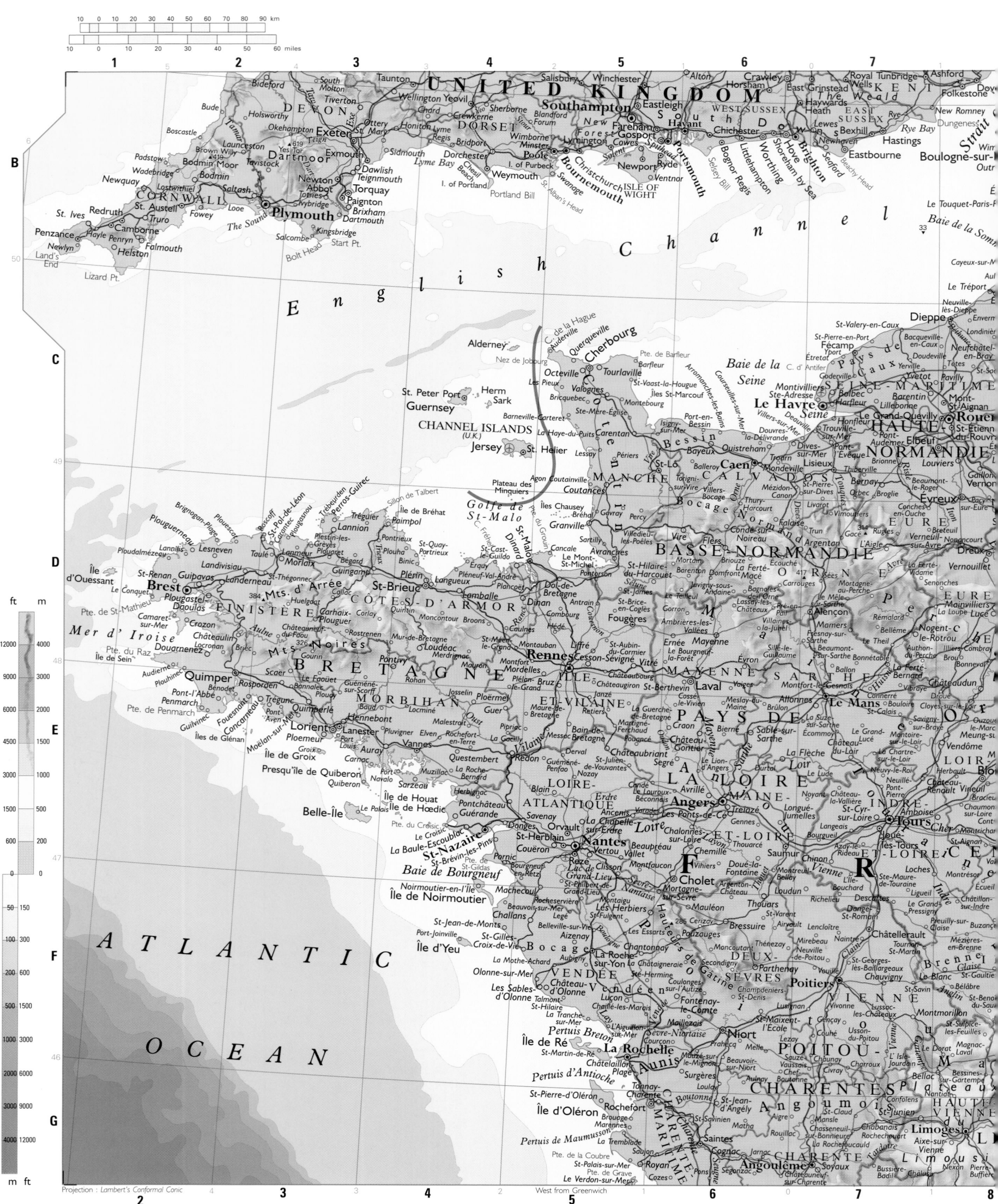

DÉPARTEMENTS IN THE PARIS AREA
1. Ville de Paris   3. Val-de-Marne
2. Seine-St-Denis   4. Hauts-de-Seine

Projection : Lambert's Conformal Conic

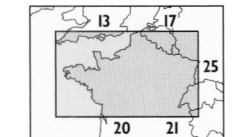

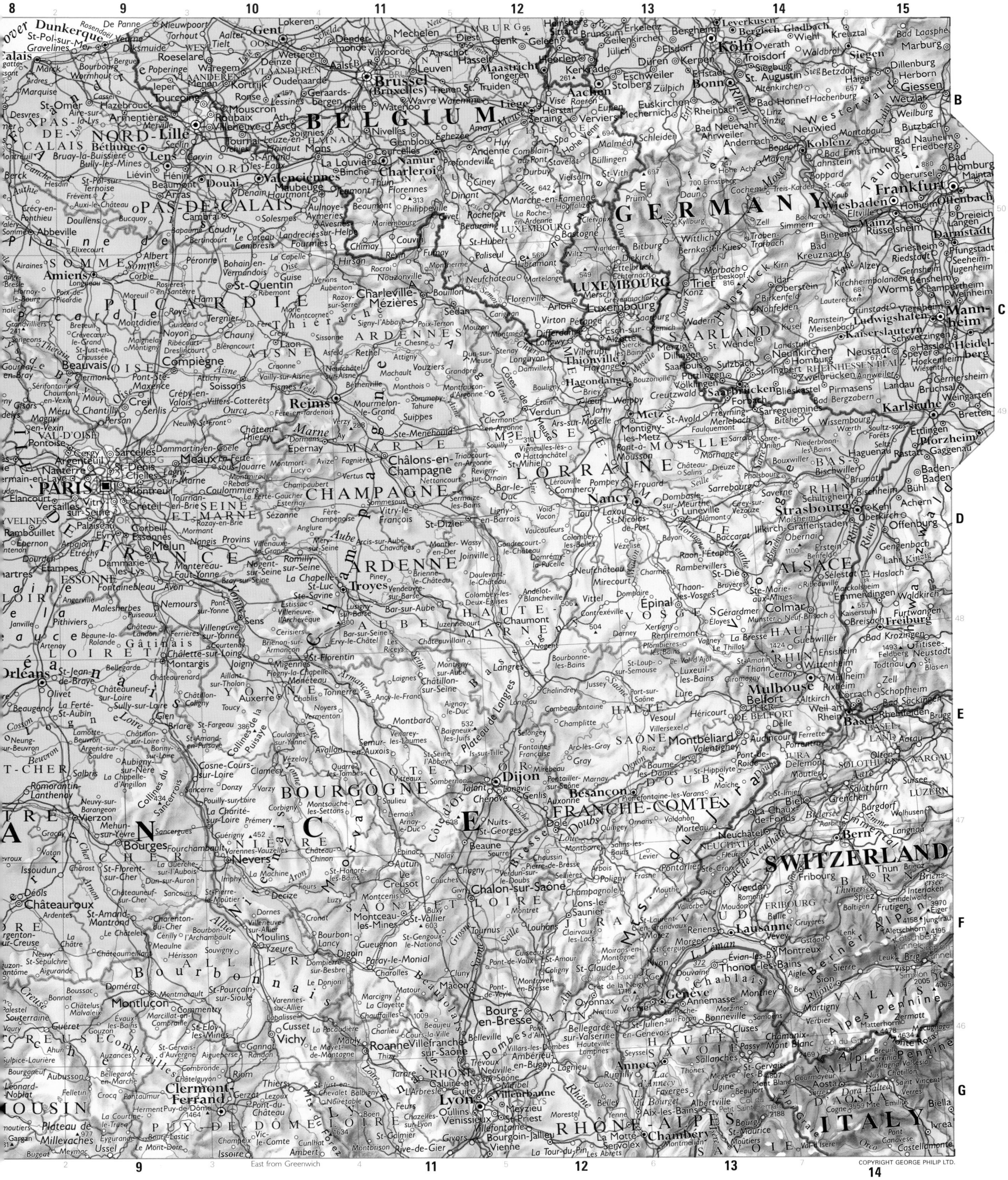

Underlined towns give their name to the
administrative area in which they stand.

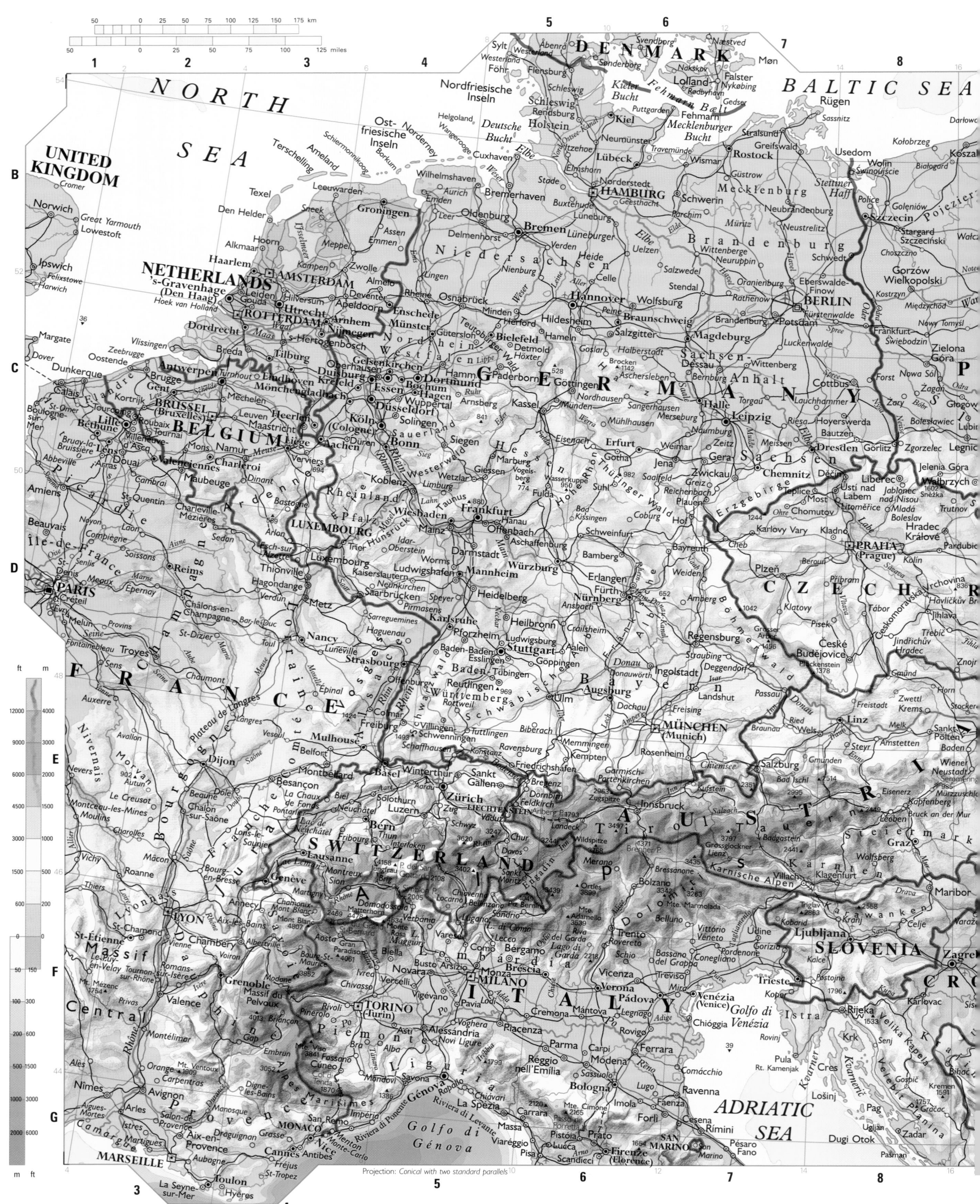

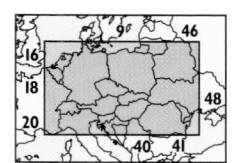

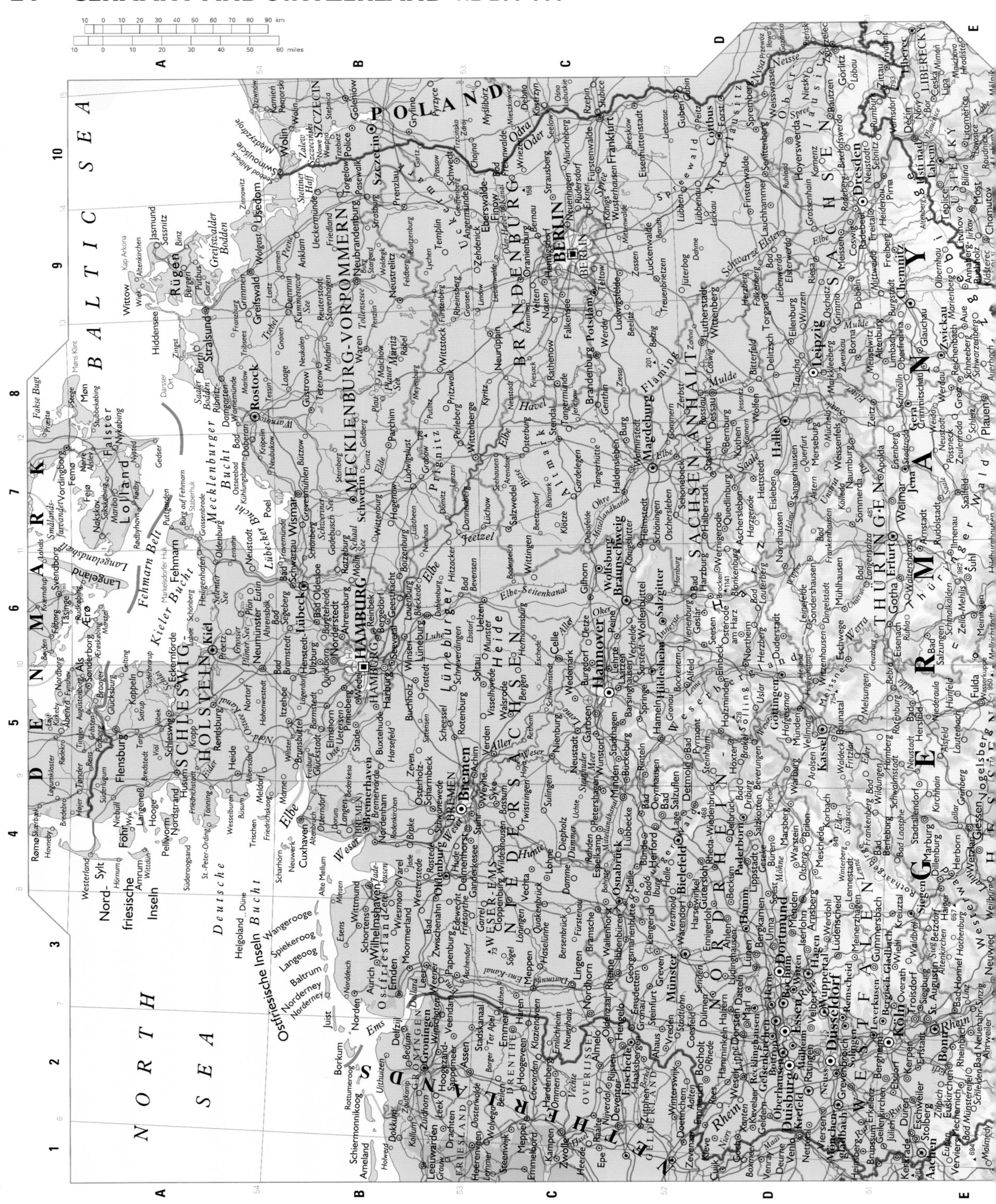

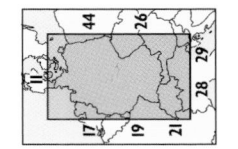

Underlined towns give their name to the administrative area in which they stand.

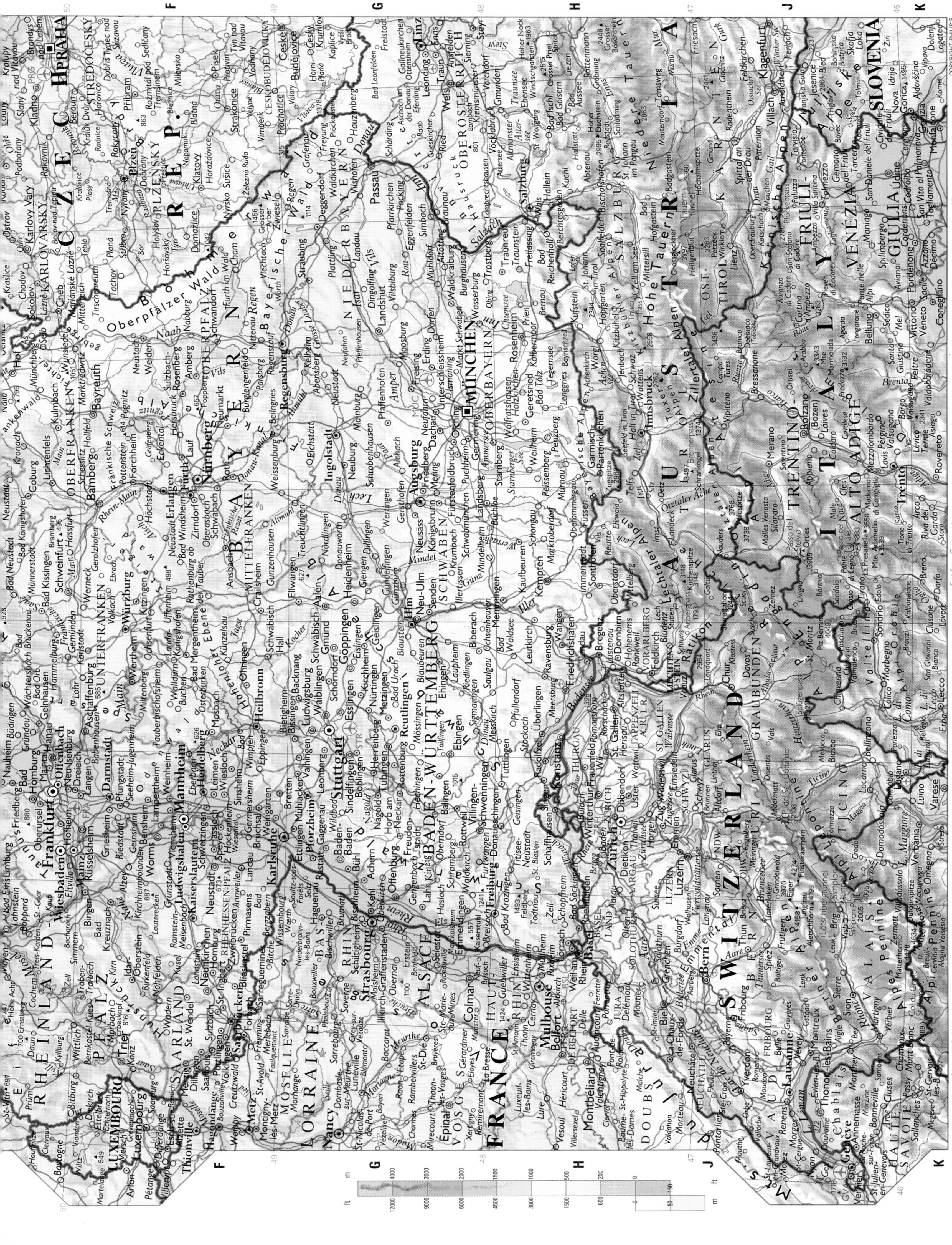

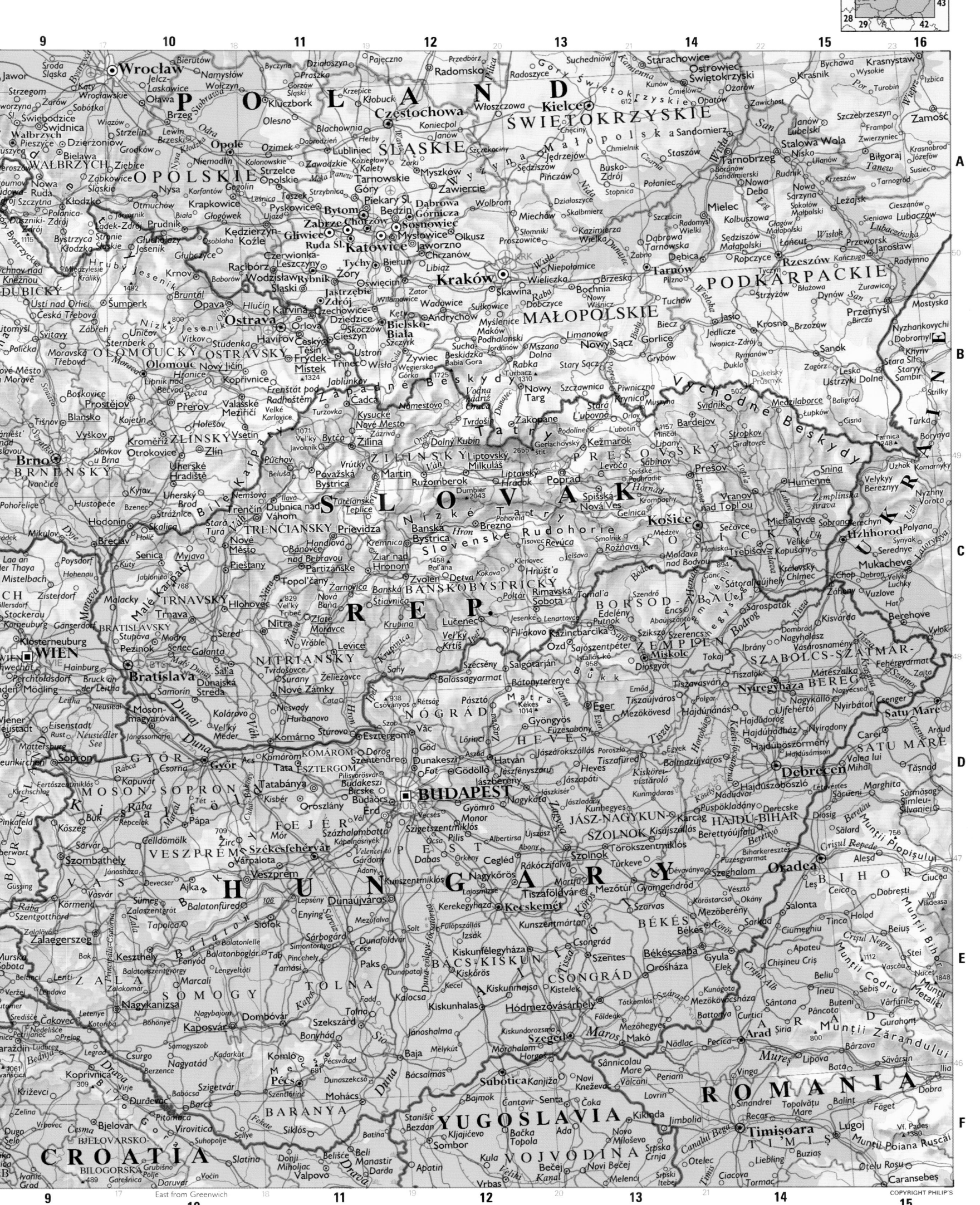

Underlined towns give their name to the
administrative area in which they stand.

East from Greenwich

COPYRIGHT PHILIP'S

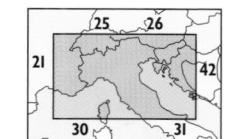

ministrative divisions in Croatia:

| | | |
|---|---|---|
| rodsko-Posavska | 4. Medimurska | 8. Virovitičko-Podravska |
| oprivničko-Križevačka | 6. Požeško-Slavonska | I0. Zagrebačka |
| rapinsko-Zagorska | 7. Varaždinska | |

- - - - - Inter-entity boundaries as agreed
at the 1995 Dayton Peace Agreement.

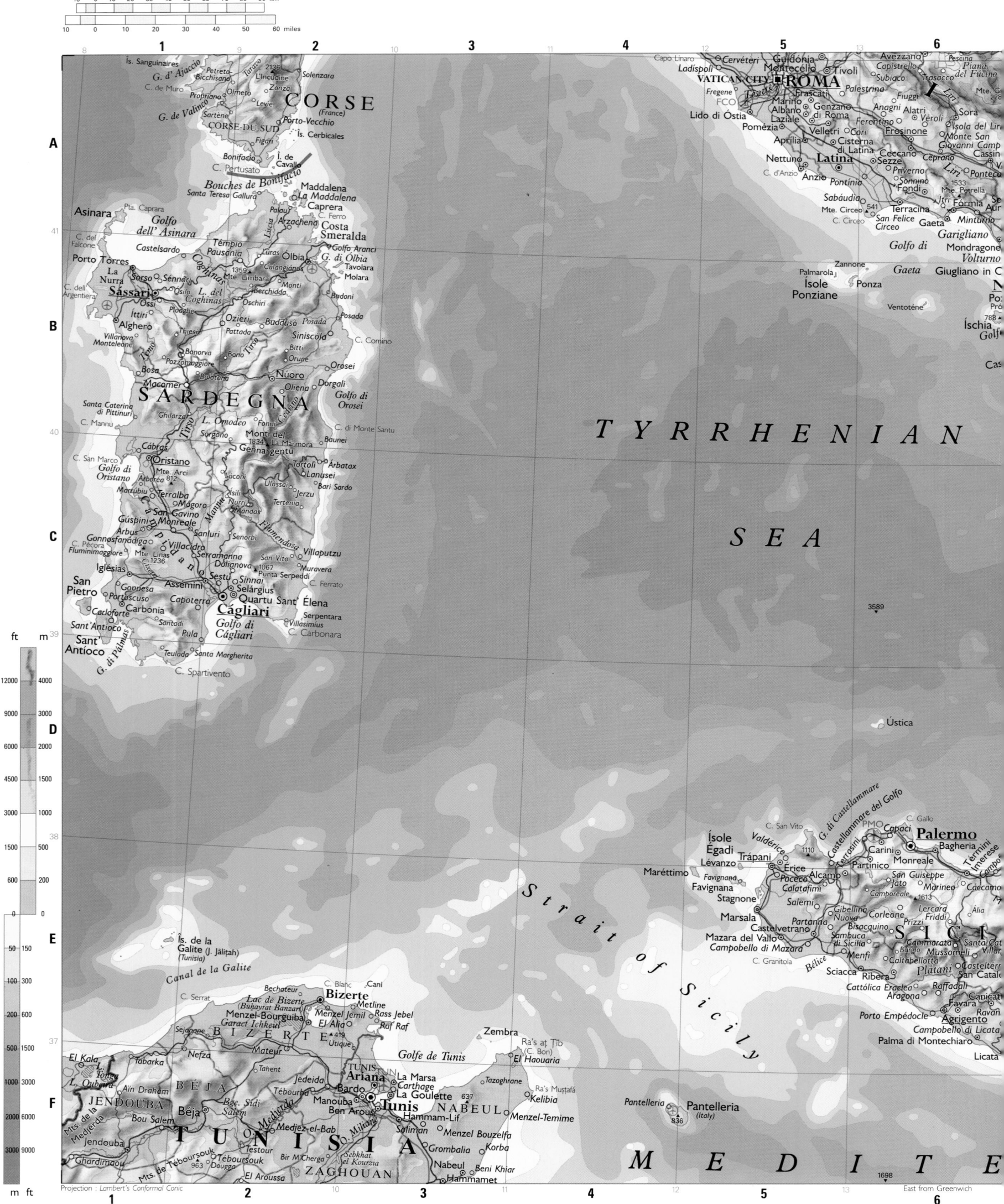

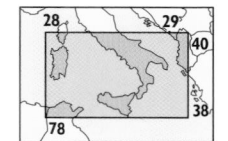

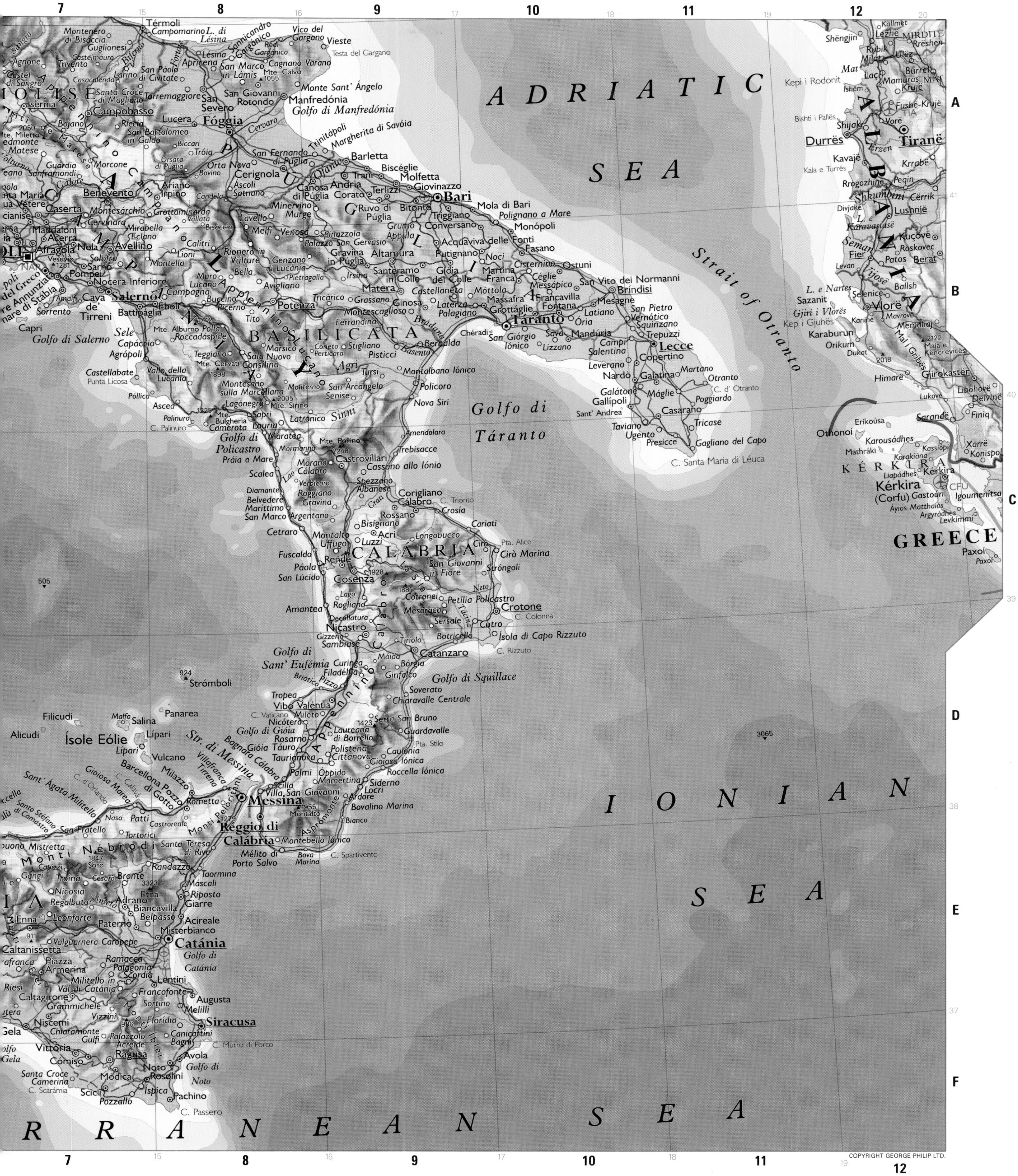


COPYRIGHT GEORGE PHILIP LTD.

Underlined towns give their name to the administrative area in which they stand.

# MEDITERRANEAN SEA

**SPAIN / ALGERIA**

## Spain

Valencia — VALENCIA — Golfo de Valencia
Costa Blanca
Alicante — Elche — Murcia — Cartagena
Almería — Granada — Costa del Sol
Albacete — CASTILLA-LA MANCHA — CIUDAD REAL
Sierra Nevada — Sierra de Segura — ANDALUCÍA
Islas — EIVISSA (IBIZA) — Formentera — Cabrera

Torrevieja, Orihuela, Lorca, Totana, Vera, Mojácar
Jumilla, Yecla, Villena, Elda, Novelda, Aspe
Denia, Gandía, Cullera, Sueca, Oliva, Benidorm, Calpe

## Algeria

ALGER (Algiers)
Blida — Médéa — MÉDÉA — Miliana — Khemis
Ech Cheliff — El Asnam — AÏN DEFLA — TISSEMSILT
Mostaganem — Relizane — RELIZANE — Mascara — MASCARA
Oran (Ouahran) — ORAN — Sidi-bel-Abbès — TLEMCEN (TÉMOUCHENT)
Tiaret — TIARET — DJELFA — Ksar Chellala

Cherchell, Ténès, Gouraya, Djidjelli, Mendès
Arzew, Golfe d'Arzew, C. Ferrat, Mers-el-Kébir

Nador — Melilla — Islas Chafarinas — Ghazaouet

Mediterranean Sea

2726   2850

Projection: Lambert's Conformal Conic

COPYRIGHT GEORGE PHILIP LTD.

East from Greenwich / West from Greenwich

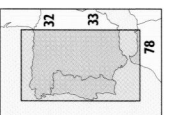

CASTILLA-LA MANCHA

CASTILLA-LA MANCHA

EXTREMADURA

CIUDAD REAL

ANDALUCÍA

CÓRDOBA

JAÉN

GRANADA

SEVILLA

HUELVA

CÁDIZ

MÁLAGA

ALMERÍA

Sierra de Segura

Sierra Nevada

Sierra Morena

Costa del Sol

Costa de la Luz

PORTUGAL

ALENTEJO

ALGARVE

ÉVORA

BEJA

SETÚBAL

Lisboa

Sevilla

Córdoba

Granada

Málaga

Almería

Cáceres

Badajoz

Jaén

Cádiz

Huelva

Marbella

Algeciras

Gibraltar (U.K.)

Tanger (Tangier)

Tétouan

Ceuta (Sp.)

Melilla

MOROCCO

MEDITERRANEAN SEA

ATLANTIC OCEAN

Golfo de Cádiz

Strait of Gibraltar

Alborán (Sp.)

Bahía de Setúbal

West from Greenwich

Projection: Lambert's Conformal Conic

COPYRIGHT GEORGE PHILIP LTD.

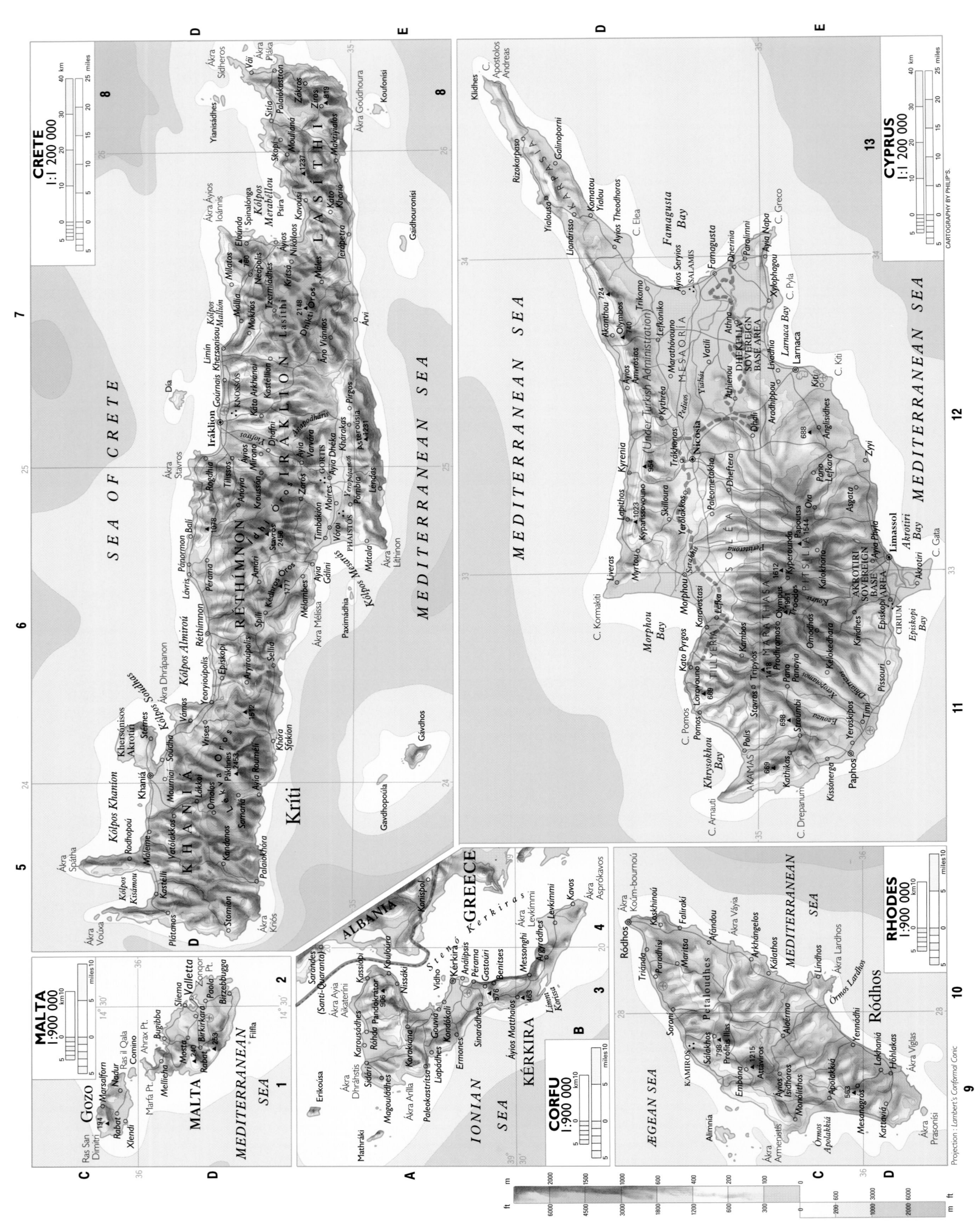

**CRETE** 1:1 200 000

**MALTA** 1:900 000

**CORFU** 1:900 000

**RHODES** 1:900 000

**CYPRUS** 1:1 200 000

CARTOGRAPHY BY PHILIP'S.

Projection: Lambert's Conformal Conic

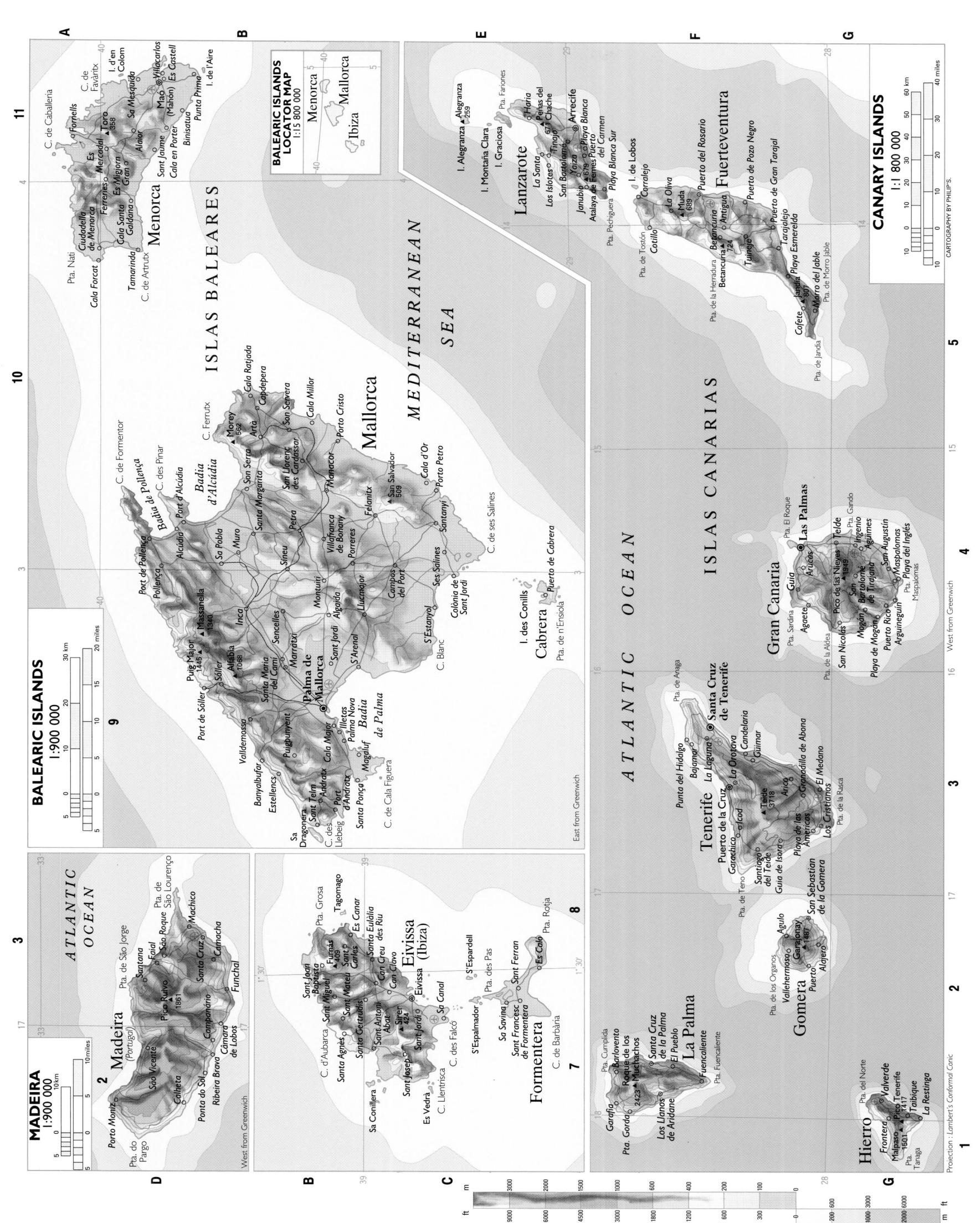

**MADEIRA**
1:900 000

**BALEARIC ISLANDS**
1:900 000

**BALEARIC ISLANDS LOCATOR MAP**
1:15 800 000

Menorca
Mallorca
Ibiza

**CANARY ISLANDS**
1:1 800 000

CARTOGRAPHY BY PHILIP'S

Madeira
(Portugal)

ATLANTIC OCEAN

Menorca

ISLAS BALEARES

MEDITERRANEAN SEA

Mallorca

Badia de Palma

Palma de Mallorca

Cabrera

Eivissa (Ibiza)

Formentera

ATLANTIC OCEAN

ISLAS CANARIAS

Lanzarote

Fuerteventura

Gran Canaria

Tenerife

La Palma

Gomera

Hierro

Projection: Lambert's Conformal Conic

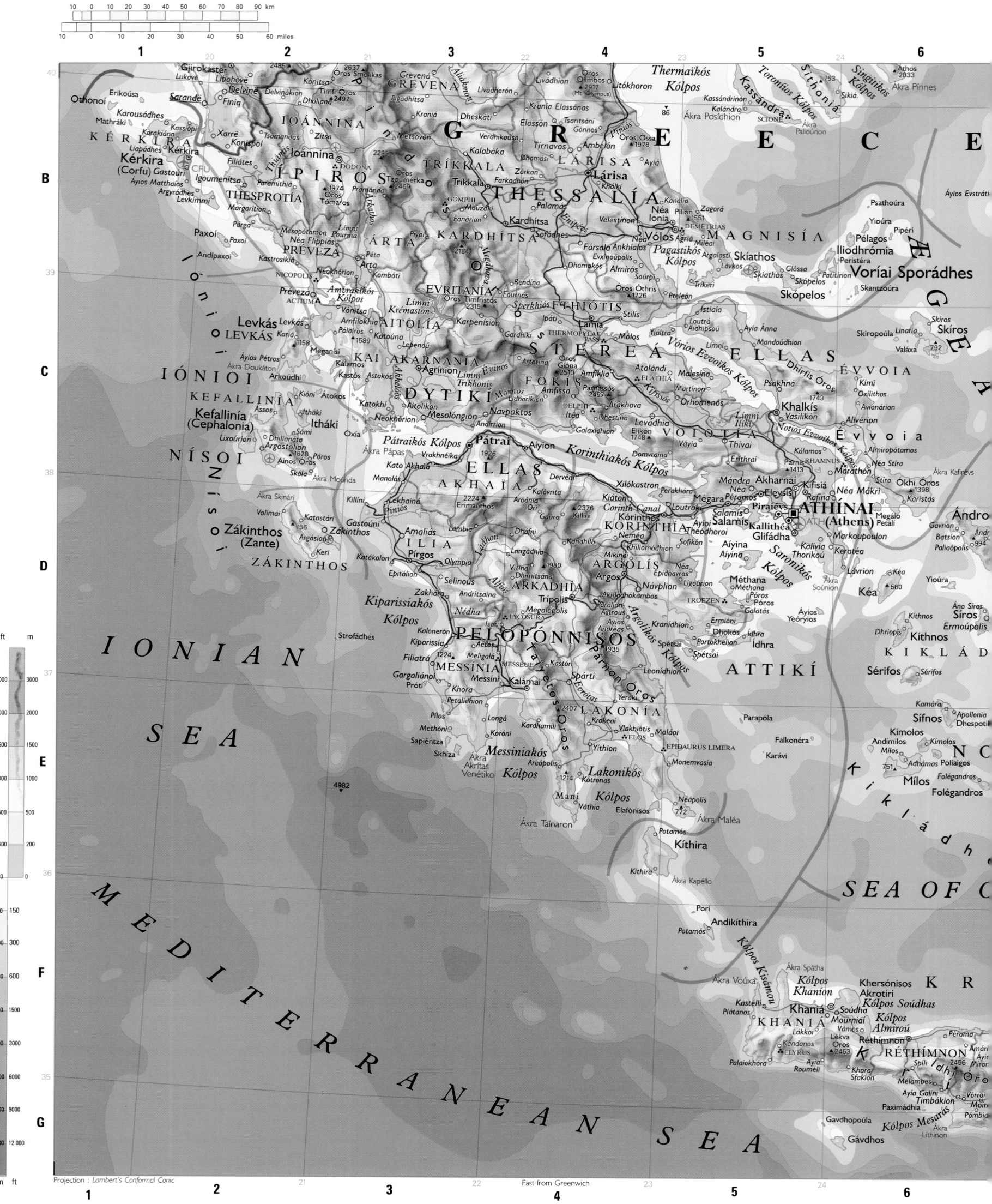

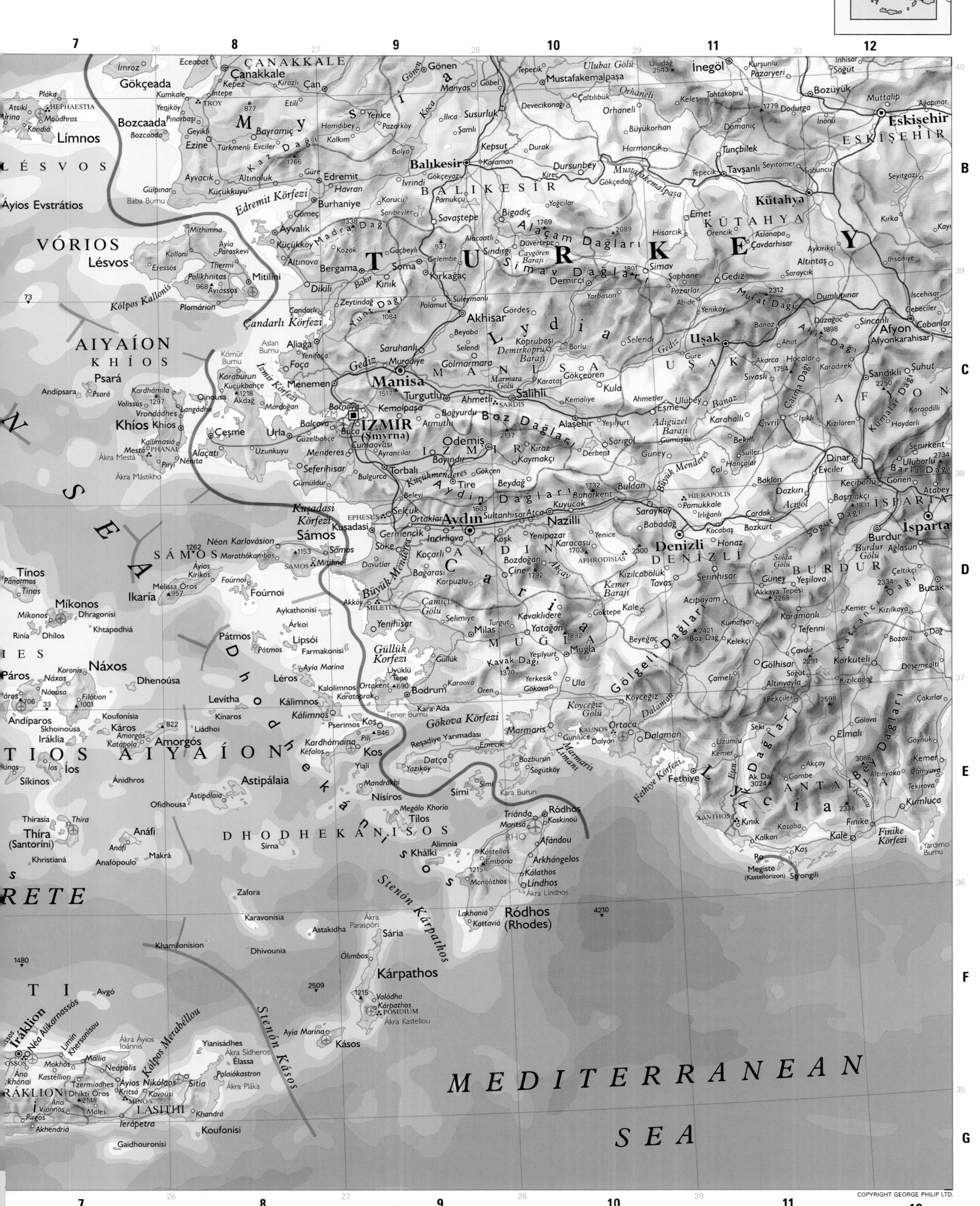

Projection : Lambert's Conformal Conic

East from Greenwich

- - - - - Inter-entity boundaries as agreed
at the 1995 Dayton Peace Agreement.

Underlined towns give their name to the
administrative area in which they stand.

COPYRIGHT GEORGE PHILIP LTD.

Administrative divisions in Croatia:
1. Brodsko-Posavska
2. Koprivničko-Križevačka
4. Međimurska
5. Osječko-Baranjska
6. Požeško-Slavonska
8. Virovitičko-Podravska
9. Vukovarsko-Srijemska

Inter-entity boundaries as agreed at the 1995 Dayton Peace Agreement.

Projection : Lambert's Conformal Conic

East from Greenwich

Underlined towns give their name to the
administrative area in which they stand.

COPYRIGHT GEORGE PHILIP LTD.

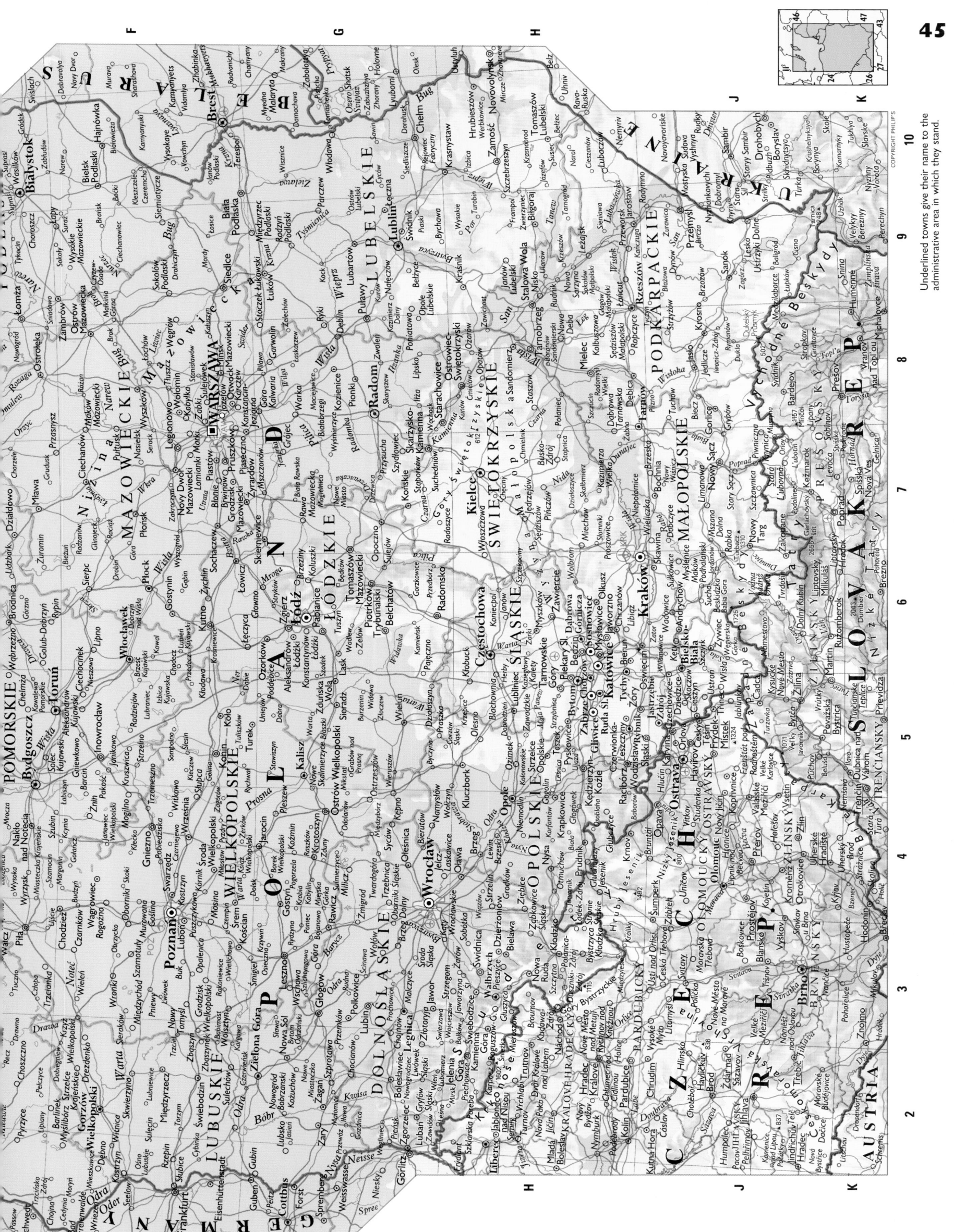

Underlined towns give their name to the
administrative area in which they stand.

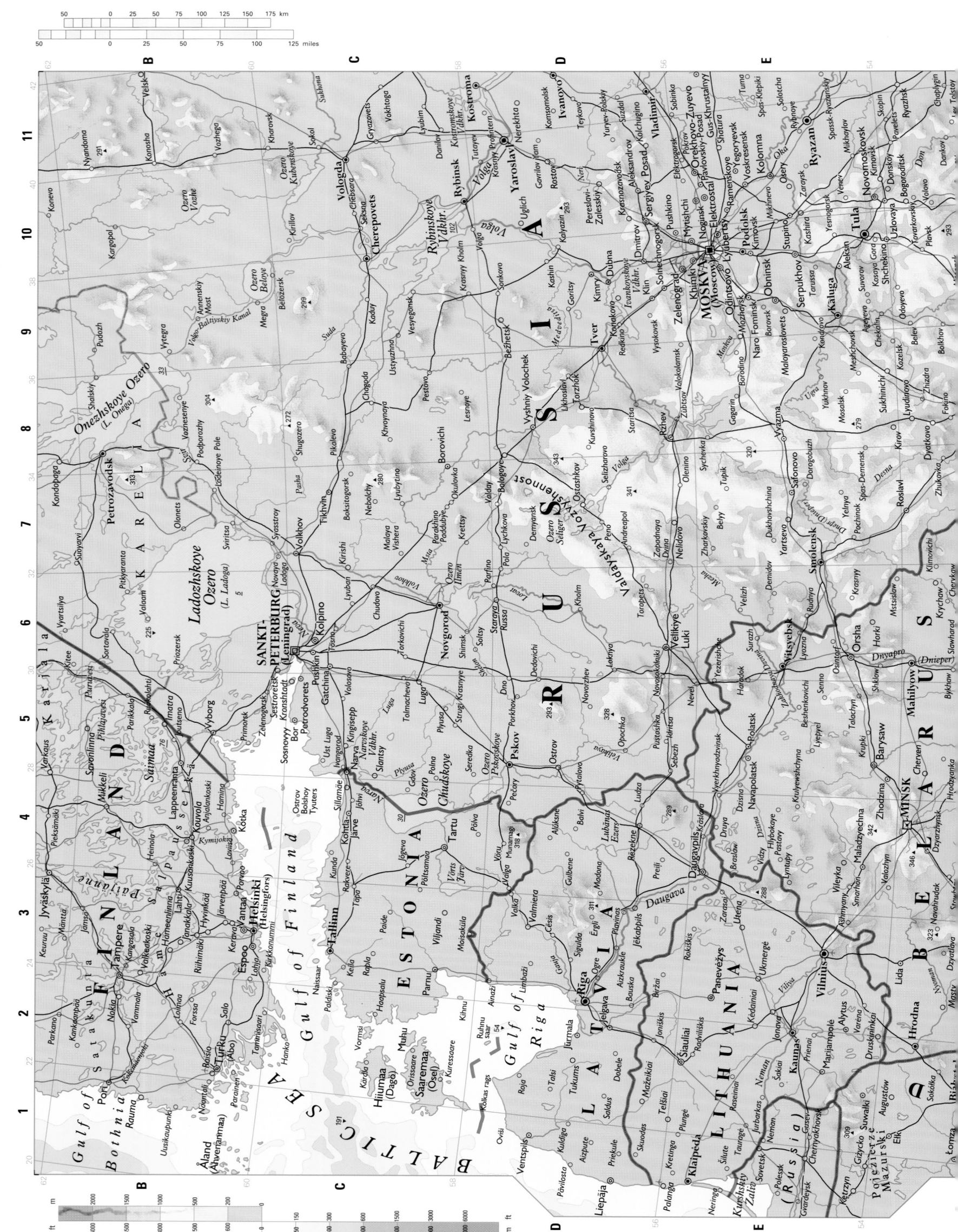

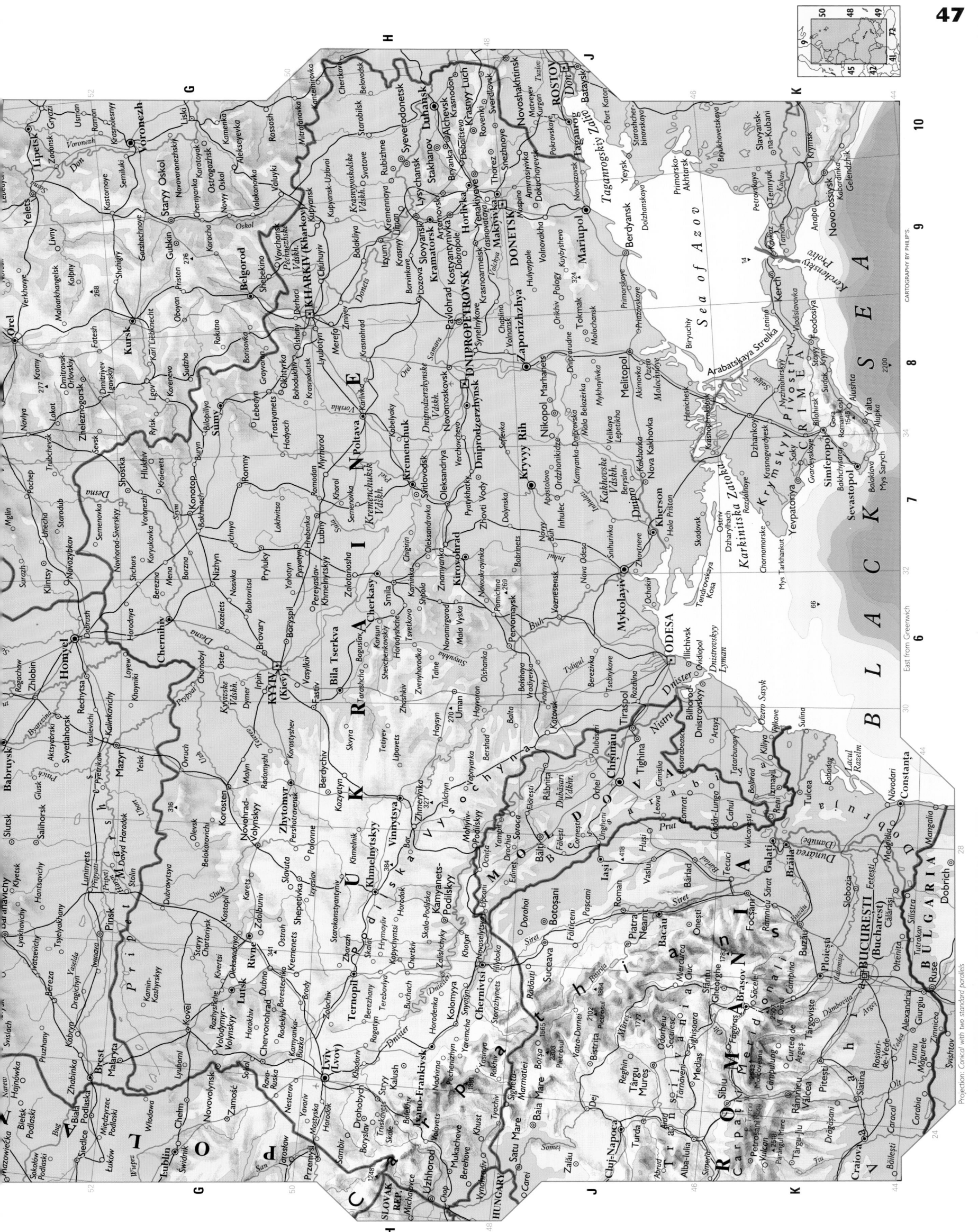

CRIMEA

Sea of Azov

BLACK SEA

Kerchenskiy Proliv

ROSTOV

Taganrog

Taganrogskiy Zaliv

Mariupol

Berdyansk

DONETSK

Luhansk

Novoshakhtinsk

Svedlovsk

KHARKIV (Kharkov)

Belgorod

Kursk

Voronezh

Orel

Lipetsk

Yelets

Sumy

POLTAVA

DNIPROPETROVSK

Zaporizhzhya

Melitopol

Simferopol

Sevastopol

Yalta

Feodosiya

Kerch

Kryvyy Rih

Nikopol

Kherson

Nova Kakhovka

Mykolayiv

ODESA

Kirovohrad

KYYIV (Kiev)

Chernihiv

Homyel

Babruysk

Pinsk

Brest

Lutsk

Rivne

Ternopil

Lviv (Lvov)

Ivano-Frankivsk

Khmelnytskyy

Vinnytsya

Zhytomyr

Bila Tserkva

Cherkasy

Kremenchuk

UKRAINE

MOLDOVA

Chişinău

Tiraspol

Tighina

Bălţi

ROMANIA

BUCUREŞTI (Bucharest)

Braşov

Galaţi

Braila

Ploieşti

Iaşi

Bacău

Suceava

Cluj-Napoca

Sibiu

Târgu Mures

BULGARIA

Ruse

Constanţa

SLOVAK REP.

HUNGARY

POLAND

Lublin

Dunărea (Danube)

Dnister

Carpaţii Meridionali

Transilvania

Dobrogea

Bessarabia

Bukovyna

Polissya

Pripet Marshes

CARTOGRAPHY BY PHILIP'S

Projection: Conical with two standard parallels

East from Greenwich

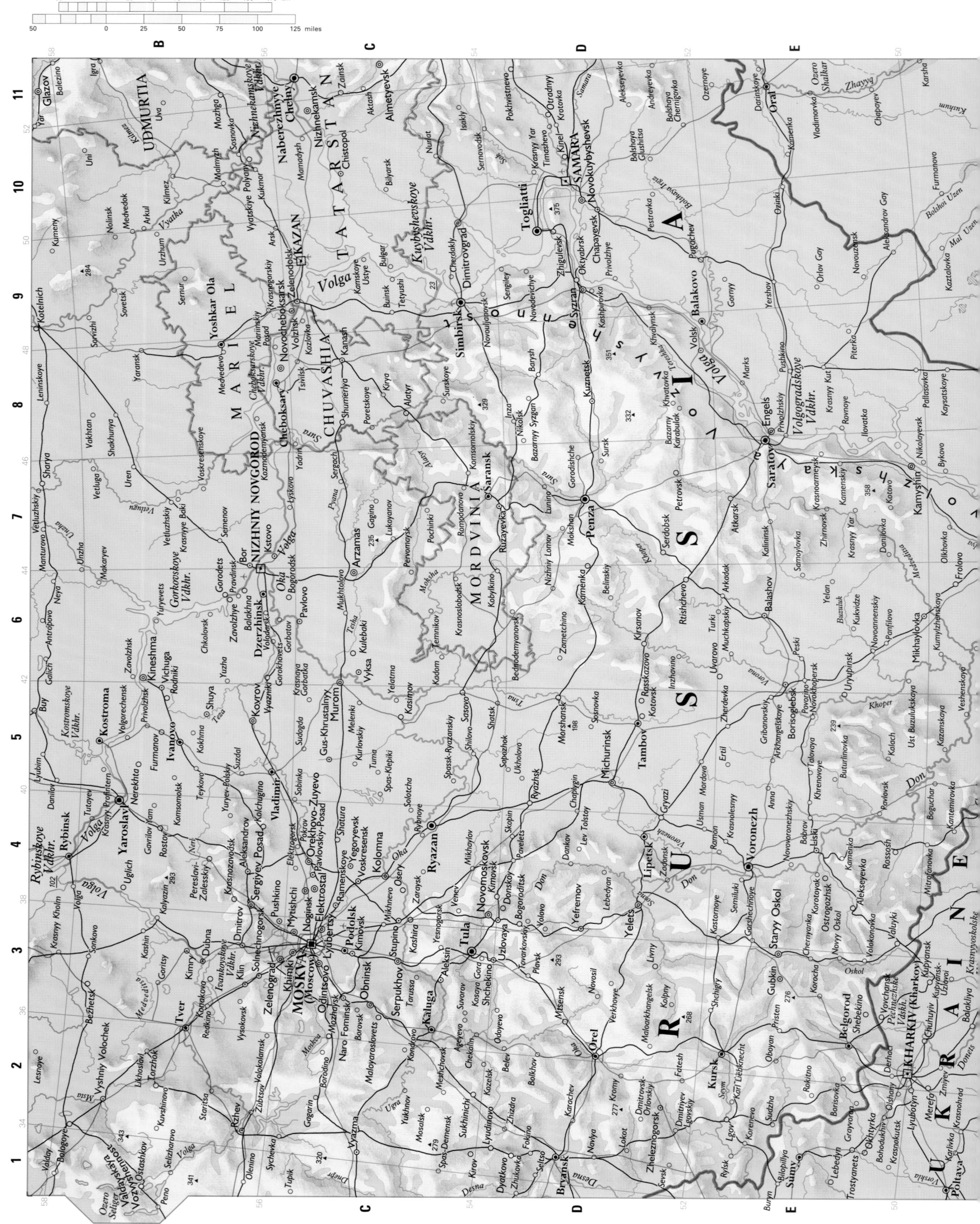

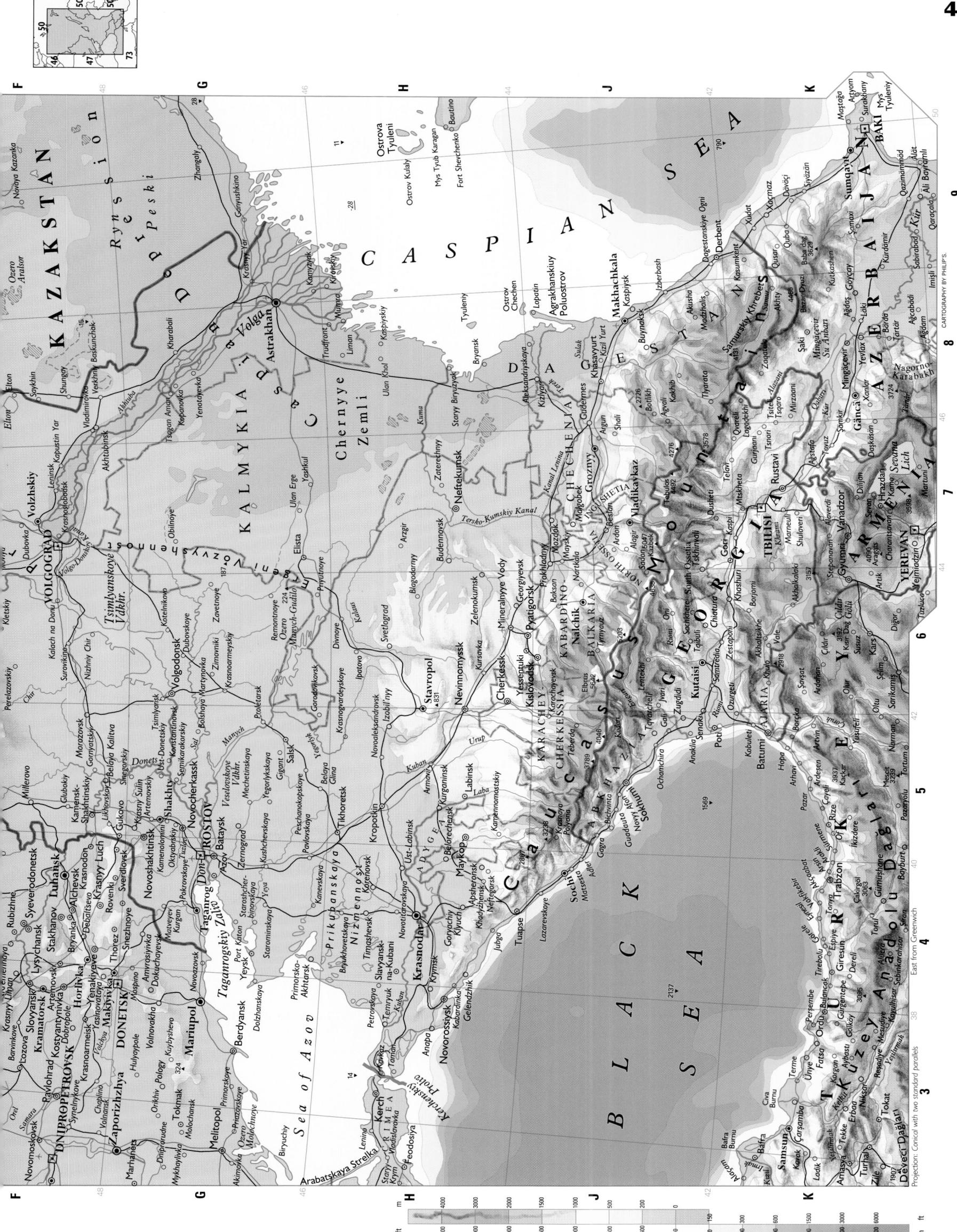

100  0  100  200  300  400  500  600  700  800 km
100  0  100  200  300  400  500 miles

| RUSSIA | |
|---|---|
| 1 | Adygea |
| 2 | Karachey-Cherkessia |
| 3 | Kabardino-Balkaria |
| 4 | North Ossetia |
| 5 | Ingushetia |
| 6 | Chechenia |
| 7 | Dagestan |
| 8 | Mordvinia |
| 9 | Chuvashia |
| 10 | Mari El |
| 11 | Tatarstan |
| 12 | Udmurtia |
| 13 | Khakassia |

**AZERBAIJAN**
14 Naxçivan

| GEORGIA | UKRAINE |
|---|---|
| 15 Ajaria | 17 Crimea |
| 16 Abkhazia | |

Projection: Conical Orthomorphic with two standard parallels

East from Greenwich

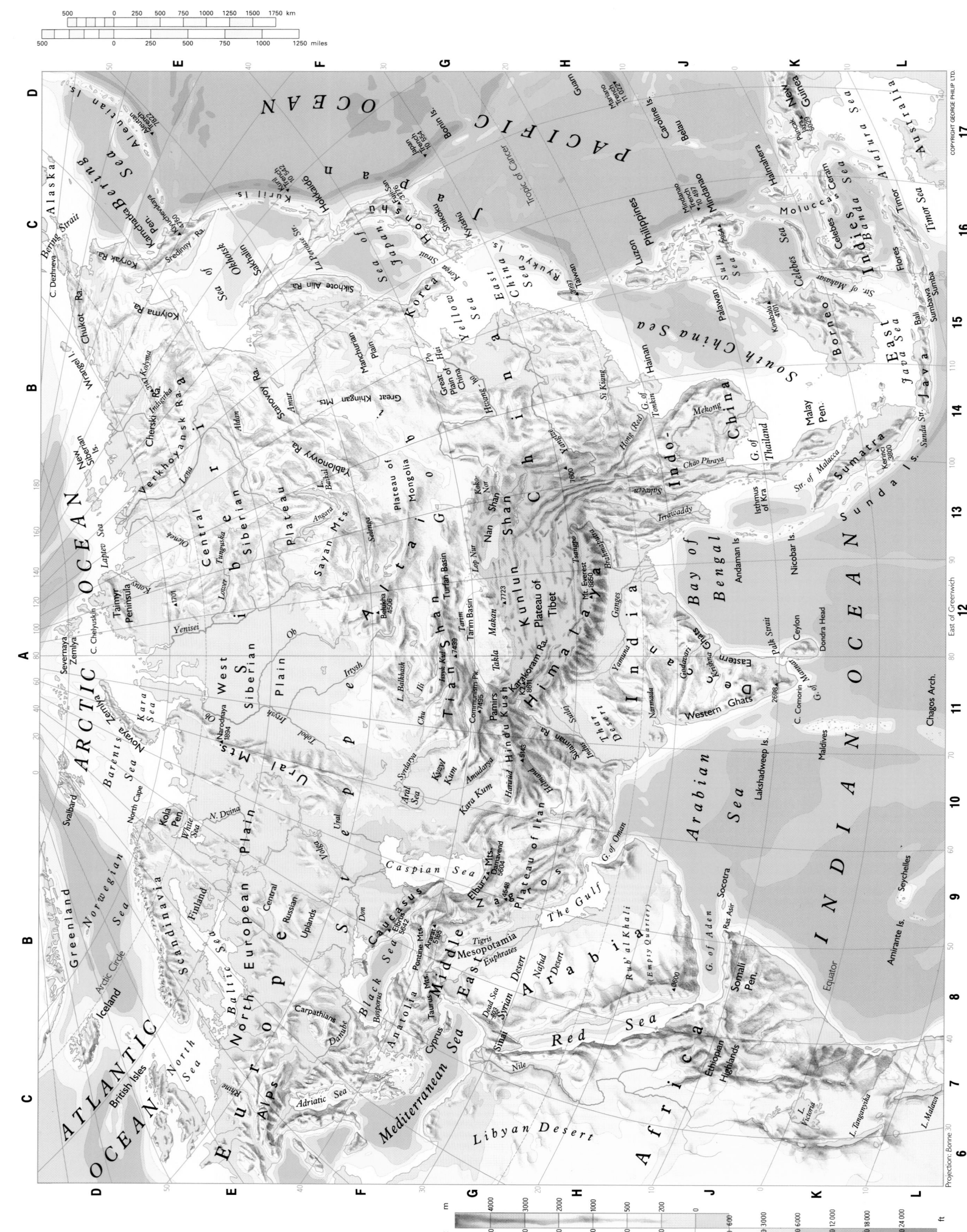

Projection: Bonne

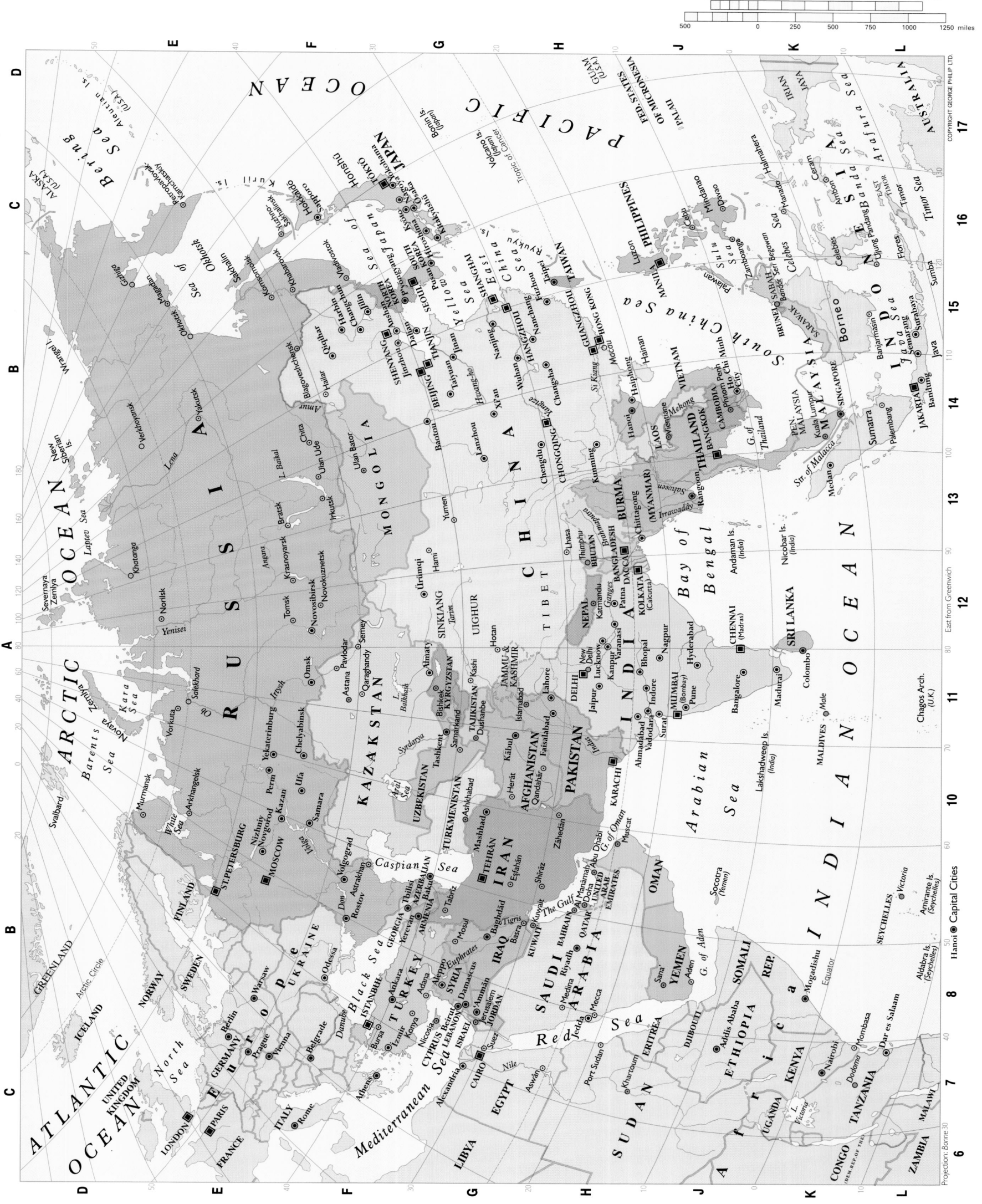

500  0  250  500  750  1000  1250  1500  1750 km
500  0  250  500  750  1000  1250 miles

PACIFIC OCEAN

GUAM (USA)
FEDERATED STATES OF MICRONESIA
PALAU
Bonin Is. (Japan)
Volcano Is. (Japan)
Tropic of Cancer

JAPAN
Sapporo
Hokkaido
TOKYO
Yokohama
Osaka
Nagoya
Honshu
Kyushu
Sea of Japan

Kurll Is.
Sakhalin
Petropavlovsk-Kamchatsky
Komsomolsk
Khabarovsk
Vladivostok
Yuzhno-Sakhalinsk

PHILIPPINES
Luzon
MANILA
Cebu
Mindanao
Davao
Palawan

Sulu Sea
Celebes Sea
BRUNEI
SABAH
SARAWAK
Bandar Seri Begawan
Kota Kinabalu
Borneo
Celebes
Manado
Halmahera
Ceram
Ambon
Banda Sea
EAST TIMOR
Timor
Timor Sea
Arafura Sea
AUSTRALIA
IRIAN JAYA
JAVA

INDONESIA
Ujung Pandang
Sumba
Flores
Bali
Java
Surabaya
Semarang
Bandung
JAKARTA
Banjarmasin
Palembang
Sumatra
Medan
SINGAPORE
Kuala Lumpur
MALAYSIA
Str. of Malacca
PEN. MALAYSIA
G. of Thailand

South China Sea
Hainan
Haiphong
Hanoi
VIETNAM
LAOS
Vientiane
CAMBODIA
Phnom Penh
Ho Chi Minh City
Mekong
THAILAND
BANGKOK

BURMA (MYANMAR)
Rangoon
Irrawaddy
Salween
Chittagong
Chiang
BANGLADESH
DACCA (DHAKA)
Bay of Bengal
Andaman Is. (India)
Nicobar Is. (India)
SRI LANKA
Colombo

TAIWAN
Taipei
Fuzhou
HONG KONG
GUANGZHOU
Nanchang
East China Sea
Ryukyu Is.
SHANGHAI
HANGZHOU
Wuhan
Changsha
Nanjing
Xian
Yangtze
CHONGQING
Chengdu
Kunming
CHINA
Lanzhou
Baotou
Hohhot
Taiyuan
Huang-ho
Zhengzhou
Jinan
Yellow Sea
TIANJIN
BEIJING
SHENYANG
Dalian
Harbin
Changchun
Jilin
SOUTH KOREA
SEOUL
Pyongyang
NORTH KOREA
Qingdao
Pusan

MONGOLIA
Ulan Bator
Ulan Ude
Irkutsk
Chita
L. Baikal
Bratsk
Krasnoyarsk
Angara
Novokuznetsk
Novosibirsk
Tomsk
Omsk
Semey
Pavlodar
Qaraghandy
Astana
Almaty

RUSSIA
Yenisei
Norilsk
Khatanga
Lena
Yakutsk
Verkhoyansk
Oymyakon
Amur
Blagoveshchensk
Chita
Severnaya Zemlya
New Siberian Is.
Wrangel I.

ARCTIC OCEAN

BERING Sea
ALASKA (USA)
Aleutian Is. (USA)

Sea of Okhotsk
Magadan

Novaya Zemlya
Kara Sea
Vorkuta
Salekhard
Yekaterinburg
Chelyabinsk
Perm
Ufa
Kazan
Samara
Irtysh
Volga

KAZAKSTAN
Aral Sea
L. Balkhash
Bishkek
KYRGYZSTAN
TAJIKISTAN
Dushanbe
Tashkent
UZBEKISTAN
Samarkand
TURKMENISTAN
Ashkhabad
Syrdarya

SINKIANG-UIGHUR
Ürümqi
Tarim
Hotan
Kashi
TIBET
Lhasa
Thimphu
BHUTAN
Brahmaputra
NEPAL
Katmandu
Ganges
Patna
KOLKATA (Calcutta)
Kanpur
Lucknow
Varanasi
New Delhi
DELHI
Jaipur
Ahmadabad
Vadodara
Surat
Indore
Bhopal
Nagpur
MUMBAI (Bombay)
Pune
Hyderabad
Bangalore
CHENNAI (Madras)
Madurai
INDIA

JAMMU & KASHMIR
Lahore
Islamabad
Faisalabad
PAKISTAN
Indus
KARACHI
Quetta
Qandahar
AFGHANISTAN
Kabul
Herat
Mashhad
Zahedan
IRAN
TEHRAN
Esfahan
Shiraz
Tabriz
Caspian Sea

MALDIVES
Male
Lakshadweep Is. (India)
Chagos Arch. (U.K.)

ARABIAN Sea
Muscat
OMAN
G. of Oman
Abu Dhabi
UNITED ARAB EMIRATES
Doha
QATAR
BAHRAIN
Manamah
The Gulf
Kuwait
KUWAIT
Basra
Tigris
Baghdad
IRAQ
Mosul
Euphrates

INDIAN OCEAN
Socotra (Yemen)
SEYCHELLES
Victoria
Amirante Is. (Seychelles)
Aldabra Is. (Seychelles)

East from Greenwich

AZERBAIJAN
Baku
ARMENIA
Yerevan
GEORGIA
Tbilisi
Rostov
Astrakhan
Volgograd
Don
ST. PETERSBURG
MOSCOW
Nizhniy Novgorod
Yaroslavl
FINLAND
Murmansk
Arkhangelsk
White Sea
Barents Sea
Svalbard

ATLANTIC OCEAN
GREENLAND
ICELAND
NORWAY
SWEDEN
Arctic Circle
UNITED KINGDOM
North Sea
LONDON
PARIS
FRANCE
GERMANY
Berlin
Prague
Warsaw
Vienna
ITALY
Rome
Belgrade
UKRAINE
Odessa
Danube
Black Sea
ROMANIA
Athens
Nicosia
CYPRUS
Bursa
Izmir
Konya
Ankara
ISTANBUL
TURKEY
Adana
Aleppo
SYRIA
Damascus
LEBANON
Beirut
ISRAEL
Jerusalem
JORDAN
Amman
Mediterranean Sea
Alexandria
CAIRO
EGYPT
Suez
Nile
Aswan
Port Sudan
Khartoum
SUDAN
LIBYA
Medina
Jedda
Mecca
SAUDI ARABIA
Riyadh
Red Sea
Sana
YEMEN
Aden
G. of Aden
DJIBOUTI
ERITREA
ETHIOPIA
Addis Ababa
SOMALI REP.
Mogadishu
KENYA
Nairobi
UGANDA
L. Victoria
TANZANIA
Dodoma
Dar es Salaam
Mombasa
CONGO (DEM. REP. OF THE CONGO)
ZAMBIA
MALAWI
Equator

A f r i c a

COPYRIGHT GEORGE PHILIP LTD.

Hanoi ⦿ Capital Cities

Projection Bonne 30

# JAPAN 1:4 400 000

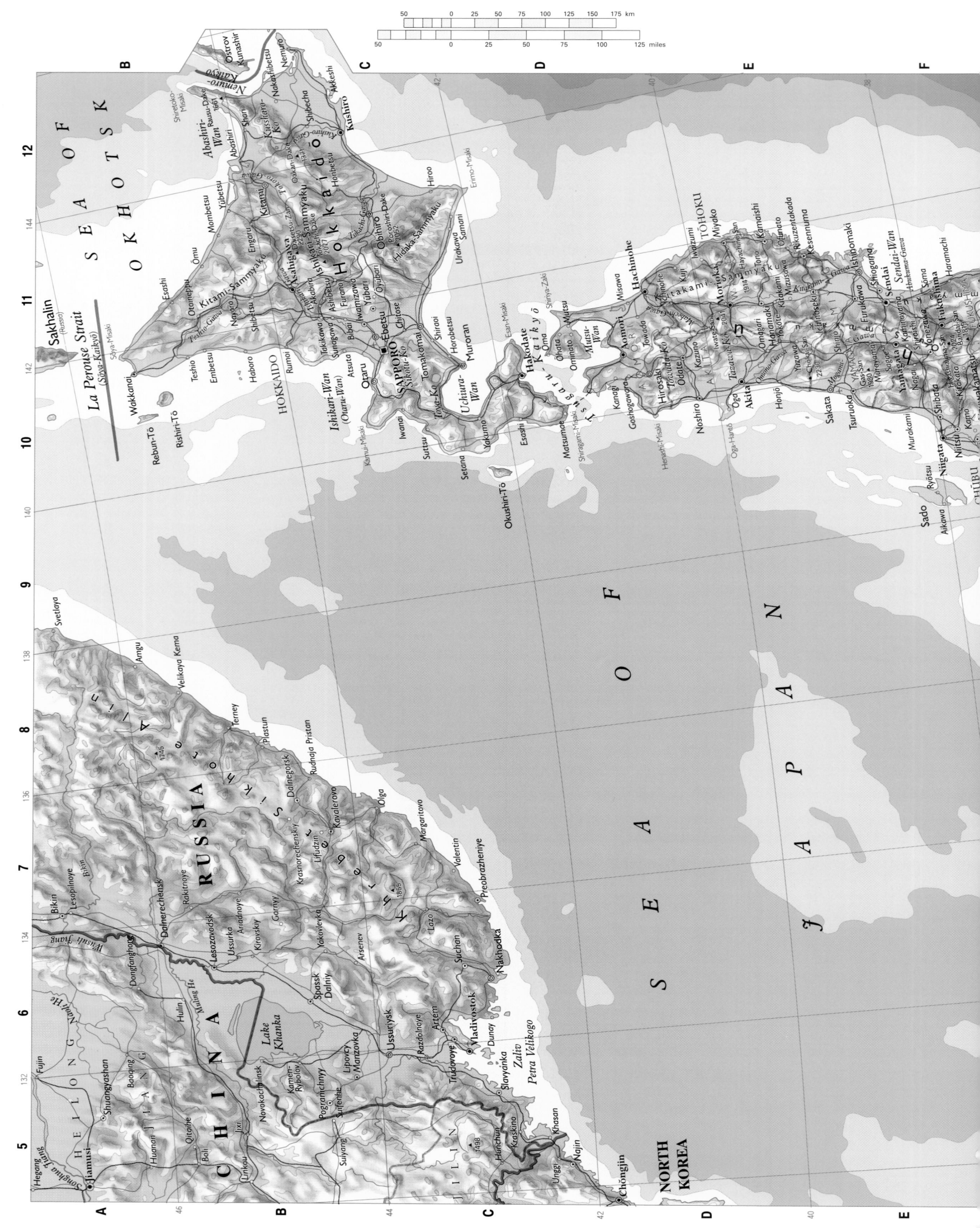

SEA OF OKHOTSK

Sakhalin (Russia)

La Perouse Strait (Sōya-Kaikyō)

Wakkanai

Rebun-Tō

Rishiri-Tō

HOKKAIDO

Kitami-Sammyaku

Asahigawa

Hokkaidō

Hidaka-Sammyaku

Abashiri-Wan

Abashiri

Nemuro-Kaikyō

Ostrov Kunashir (Russia)

Nakashibetsu

Nemuro

Akkeshi

Kushiro

Hiroo

Erimo-Misaki

SAPPORO

Ebetsu

Chitose

Muroran

Uchiura-Wan

Hakodate

Tsugaru-Kaikyō

Esan-Misaki

Okushiri-Tō

Setana

SEA OF JAPAN

RUSSIA

Svetlaya

Amgu

Velikaya Kema

Terney

Plastun

Rudnaja Pristan

Dalnegorsk

Kavalerovo

Olga

Margaritovo

Preobrazheniye

Valentin

Bikin

Lesopilnoye

Dalnerechensk

Rakitnoye

Arsenev

Suchan

Nakhodka

Spassk Dalniy

Ussuriysk

Artem

VLADIVOSTOK

Zaliv Petra Velikogo

CHINA

HEILONGJIANG

Songhua Jiang

Hegang

Fujin

Jiamusi

Boli

Suyang

JILIN

Hunchun

Kraskino

Khasan

Najin

NORTH KOREA

Chŏngjin

TOHOKU

Hachinohe

Ōu-Sammyaku

Morioka

Aomori

Mutsu-Wan

Hirosaki

Ōdate

Noshiro

Akita

Honjō

Sakata

Tsuruoka

Niigata

Sado

CHŪBU

Sendai-Wan

Sendai

Fukushima

Shiogama

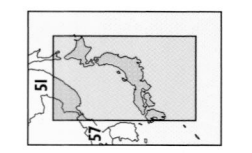

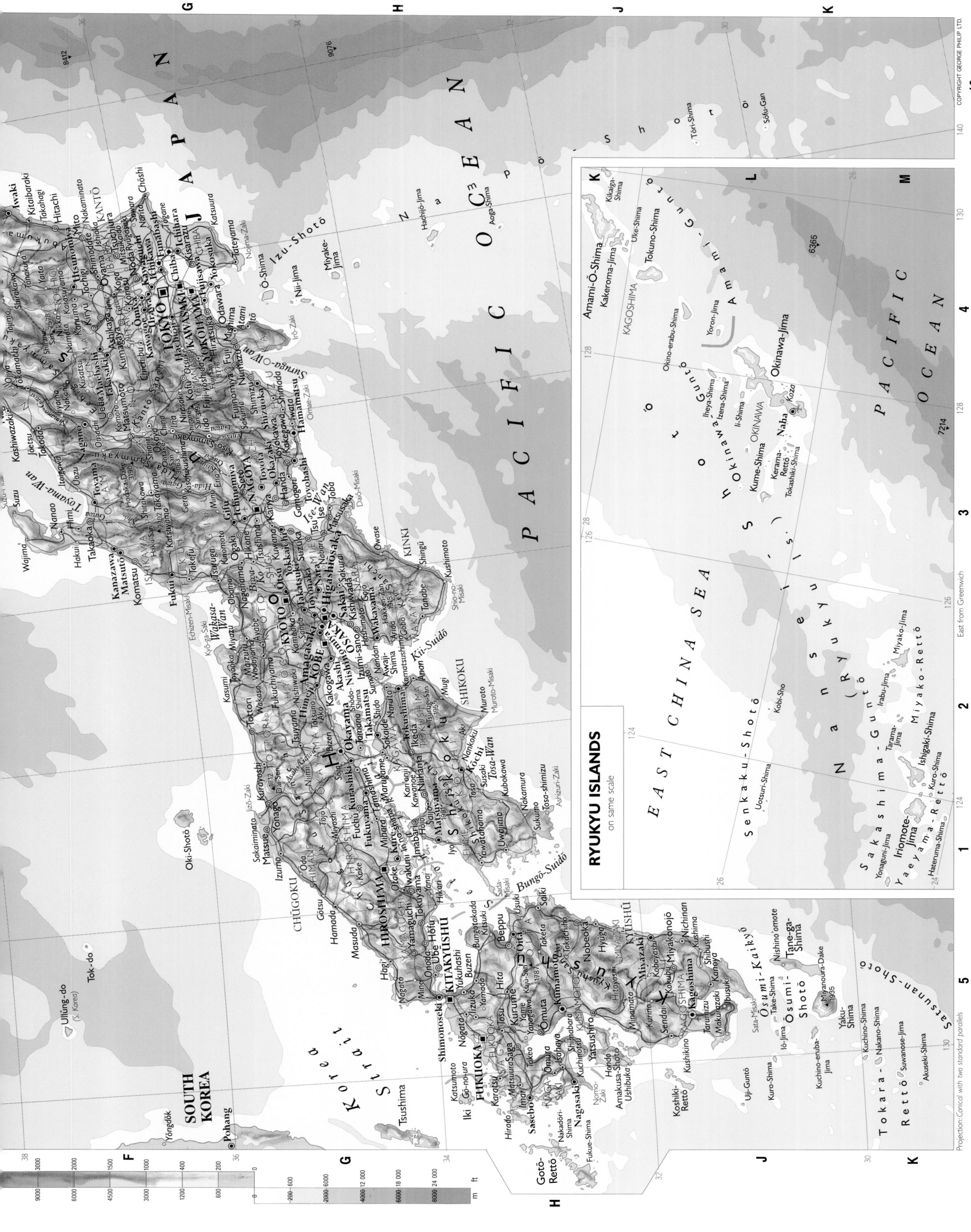

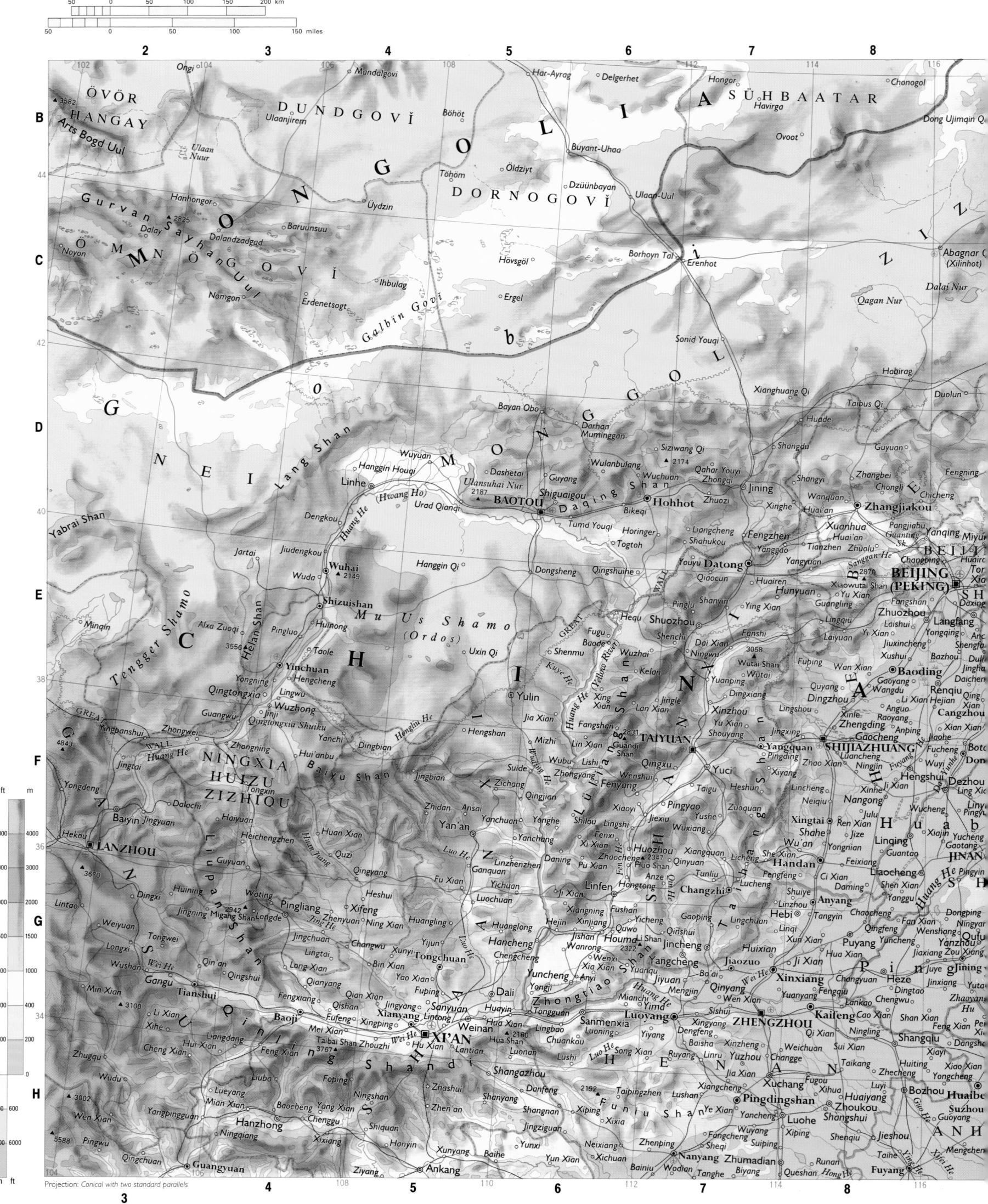

Projection: Conical with two standard parallels

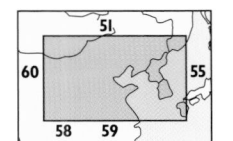

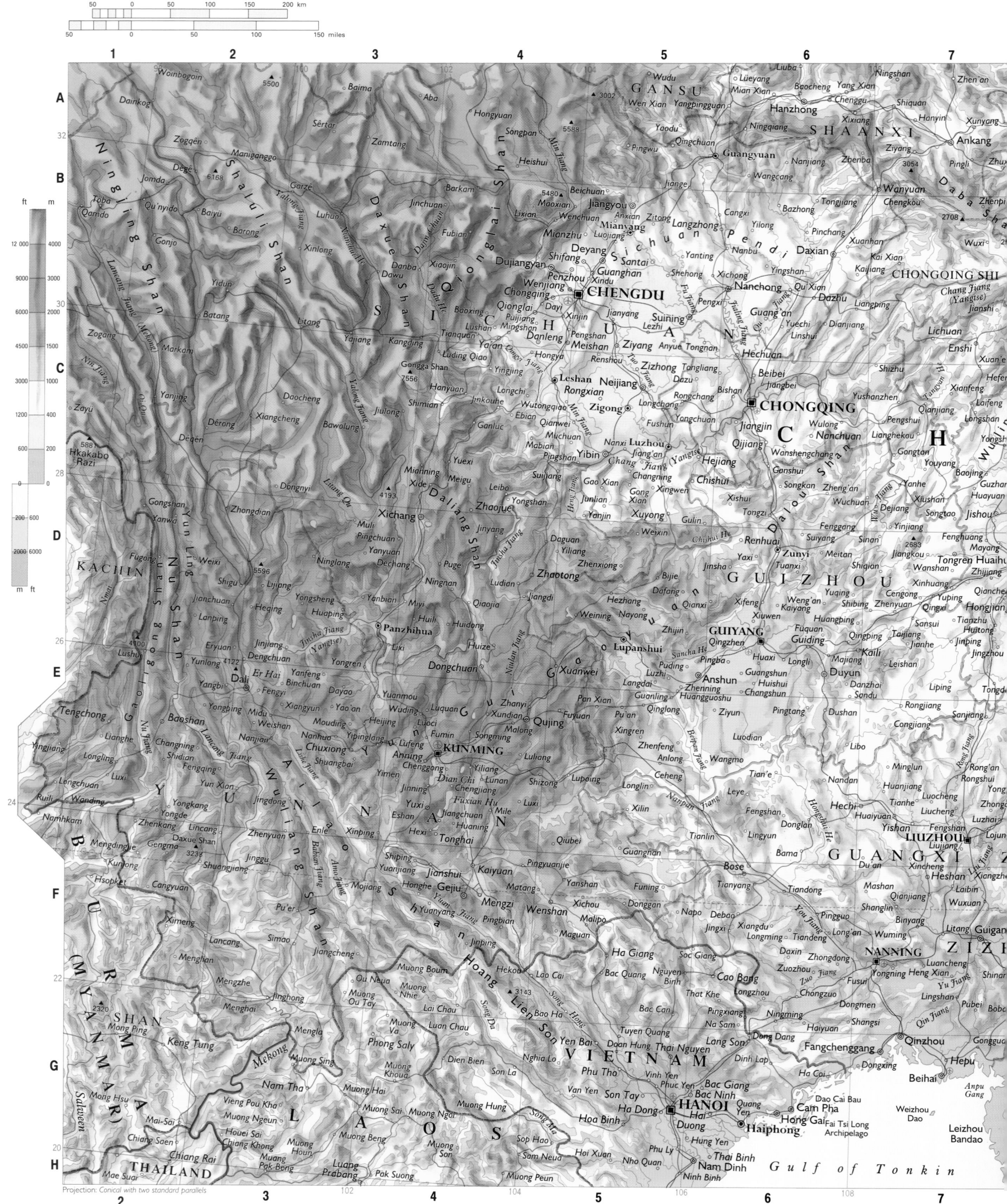

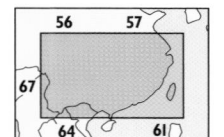

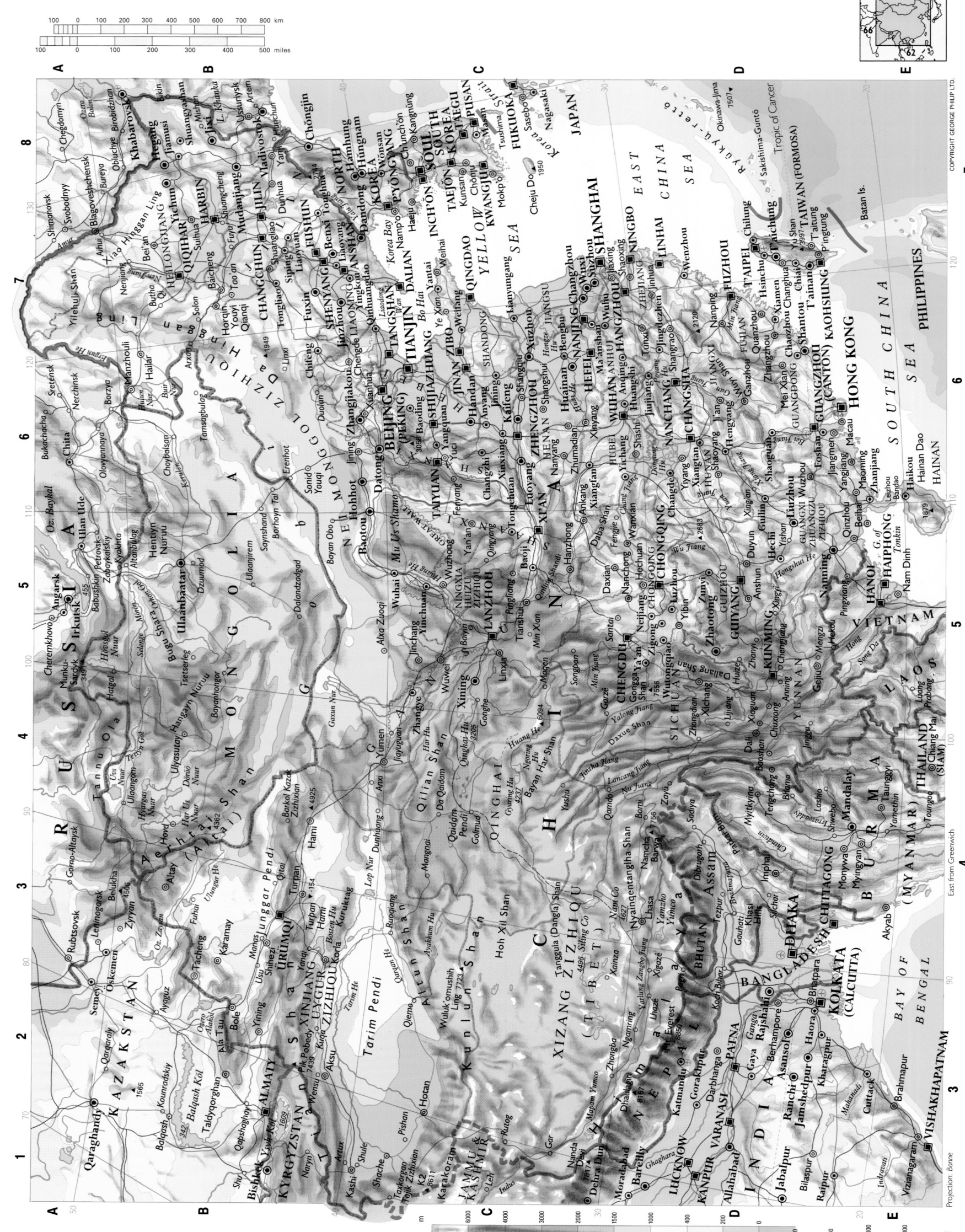

Projection: Borne

East from Greenwich

59
62 63

50 0 100 150 200 250 300 km
50 0 50 100 150 200 miles

**THE PHILIPPINES**

116 118 120 122 124 126 128

*Itbayat I.*
*Batan I.*

*Balintang Channel*

*Calayan I.* *Babuyan I.*

*Dalupiri I.* *Babuyan Islands* *Camiguin I.*
*Fuga I.*
*Babuyan Channel*
*Mayraira Pt.* *Claveria* *Santa Ana*
*Bacarra* *Bangui* *Aparri* *Gonzaga*
*San Nicolas* *Laoag* *Kabugao* *Gattaran*
*Batac* 2360 *Tuao* *Tuguegarao*
*Cabugao* *Bangued* *Tuao* *Mt. Cresta*
*Vigan* *Santa* *Cayayan* 1685
*Candon* *Maria* *Lubuagan* *Ilagan*
*Roxas* *Bontoc* *Santiago* *Palanan Pt.*
*Tagudin* *San Mateo* *Cordon* *Palanan*
*Balaoan* *Mt. Pulog* *Solana*
*San Fernando* 2929 *Bayombong* *Casiguran*
*Baguio* *Mt. Anacuao*
*Bolinao* *Rosario* 1852 *C. San Ildefonso*
*Aiaminos* *Dagupan*
*Lingayen* *San Manuel*

PACIFIC
OCEAN

SOUTH CHINA SEA

*Luzon*
PHILIPPINES

*Lingayen Gulf* *Bayambang* *San Jose* *Baler Bay*
*San Carlos* *Moncada* *Cuyapo* *Bale*
*Santa Cruz* *Camiling* *Victoria* *Baler*
*Masinloc* *Iba* 2037 *La* *Paz* *Gapan* *Dingalan*
*Concepcion* *Tarlac* *Cabanatuan*
*Mt. Pinatubo* 1780 *Angeles*
*San Antonio* *San Fernando*
*Olongapo* *Orani* *Malabon* *Polillo Is.*
*Bataan* *Caloocan* *Patnanongan I.*
*Manila Bay* *Quezon City* *Jomalig I.*
*Cavite* *MANILA* *Lamon Bay*
*Dasmariñas* *Pasay* *Santa Cruz* *Paracale*
*Tagaytay* *L. de Bay* *Lucban* *Labo* *Daet*
*Nasugbu* *San Pablo* *Atimonan* *Pandan*
*Balayan* *Lipa* *Lucena* *Calauag* *Viga*
*Lemery* *Batangas* *Lopez* *Catanduanes*
*Lubang Is.* *Lobo* *Tayabas Bay* *Catanauan* *Naga* *Iriga* *Virac*
*Verde I. Pass* *Boac* *Calabanga* *Nabua* *San Andres*
*C. Calavite* *Calapan* *Marinduque* *Tabaco* *Legazpi*
*Mamburao* *Victoria* *Burias I.* *Ligao* *Mayon Vol.* *Rapu Rapu I.*
*Mindoro* *Pinamalayan* *Donsol* *Sorsogon*
*Sablayan* *Mt. Baco* *Magallanes* *Gubat*
2487 *SIBUYAN* *Bulan*
*Bongabong* *Romblon* *Ticao I.* *Irosin* *San Bernardino Str.*
*San Jose* *Tablas I.* *Sibuyan I.* *Laoang*
*Roxas* *Odiongan* SEA *Aroroy* *Masbate* *Catarman* *Gamay* *Arteche*
*Ilin I.* *Mandaon* *Milagros* *Calbayog* *Oras*
*Busuanga I.* *Semirara Is.* *Masbate* *Taft*
*Culion I.* *Calamian Group* *Pandan* *Catbalogan* *Parang* *Samar*
*Kalibo* *Placer* *Catbalogan* *Borongan*
*Linapacan Str.* *Roxas* VISAYAN *Bilinan I.* *Caibiran* *Santa Rita* *General MacArthur*
*Linapacan I.* *Dao* *Pilar* SEA *Calubian* *Rita* *Borongan*
*Cuyo West Pass* *Tibiao* *Ajuy* *Sara* *Bantayan* *Carigara* *Basey* *Guiuan*
*Cuyo Is.* 2117 *Passi* *Palompon* *Leyte* *Tacloban*
*Taytay* *Bugasong* *Panay* *Cadiz* *Bogo* *Ormoc* *Dulag* *Homonhon I.*
*Cuyo* *San Jose* *Iloilo* *Sagay* *Tuburan* *Camotes Is.* *Abuyog*
*Cuyo East Pass* *Pototan* *Silay* *Danao* *Baybay*
*Palawan* *Dumaran I.* *Guimaras* *Victorias* *Camotes* *Sogod* *Leyte Gulf*
*San Carlos* *Mandaue* SEA *San Juan* 10 497
*Jordan* 2450 *Cebu* *Bato* *Dinagat I.*
*Hinigaran* *La* *Guihulngan* *Maasin* *Surigao Str.*
1593 *Binalbagan* *Carlota* *Carcar* *Panaon I.* *Siargao I.*
*Honda Bay* *Himamaylan* *Argao* *Bohol I.* *Surigao* *Placer*
*Irahuan* *Kabankalan* *Bais* *Tanon* *Bohol* *Bucas Grande I.*
*Puerto Princesa* *Sipalay* *Tanjay* *Oslob* *Tagbilaran* *Carrascal*
*Cagayan Is.* *Hinoba-an* *Dumaguete* *BOHOL* *L. Mainit* *Lahuza*
*Negros* *Bayawan* *Siquijor I.* 2012 *Tandag*
*Siaton* *Zamboanguita* *Cabadbaran* *Tago*
*Mt. Mantalingajan* *Camiguin I.* *Nasipit* *Marihatag*
2085 *Talisayan* *Butuan* *Bayugan* *Lianga*
*C. Buliluyan* SULU *Dipolog* *Dapitan* *SEA* *Balingasag* *Esperanza* *Talacogon* *Hinatuan*
*Bugsuk I.* *Alubijid* *Bislig*
*Balabac I.* SEA *Manukan* *Oroquieta* *Iligan Bay* *Opol* *Cagayan de Oro* *Cateel*
*Sindangan* *Ozamiz* *Iligan* 2938 *Malaybalay* *Baganga*
*Balabac Strait* *Labason* *Marawi City* *Bunawan*
*Balambangan* *Bangqi* *Kabasalan* *Malaig* *Tubod* *L. Lanao* *Tagum* *Pantukan* *Manay*
*Kudat* *Cagayan Sulu I.* *Pagadian* *Mindanao* *Panabo* *Mati*
*Langkon* *Siocon* *Margosatubig* *Malabang* 2815 *Davao*
*Tenghilan* *Suba Talan* *Sibuco* *Sibuguey Bay* *Illana* *Parang* *Midsayap* 2954 *Digos*
*Kota Belud* *Telok Labuk* *Zamboanga* *Bay* *Cotabato* *Pikit* *Mt. Apo* *Davao Gulf*
*Kota Kinabalu* *Moro Gulf* *Datu Piang* *Talayan* *San Isidro*
*G. Kinabalu* *Basilan Str.* *Kalamansig* *C. San Agustin*
*Papar* 4101 *Isabela* *Lebak* *Koronadal*
*Pilas Group* *Basilan I.* *Lamitan* *Malita*
*Sandakan* *Palimbang* 2083 *General Santos*
*Pangutaran Group* *Samales Group* *Kiamba* *Sarangani Bay*
SABAH *Turtle Is.* *Jolo* *Tinaca Pt.*
MALAYSIA *Jolo Group* *Sarangani Is.*
*Kuamut* *Silam* *Tg. Labian* *Parang* *Talipao*
*Tawi-tawi Group* *Tapul Group* *Siasi I.* *Pata I.* CELEBES
*Borneo* *Teluk Darvel* *Sibutu Group* *Semporna* *Sulu Archipelago* SEA

INDONESIA *Kep. Talaud*

ft m
9000 3000
6000 2000
4500 1500
3000 1000
1200 400
600 200
0 0
200 600
4000 12 000
8000 24 000
m ft

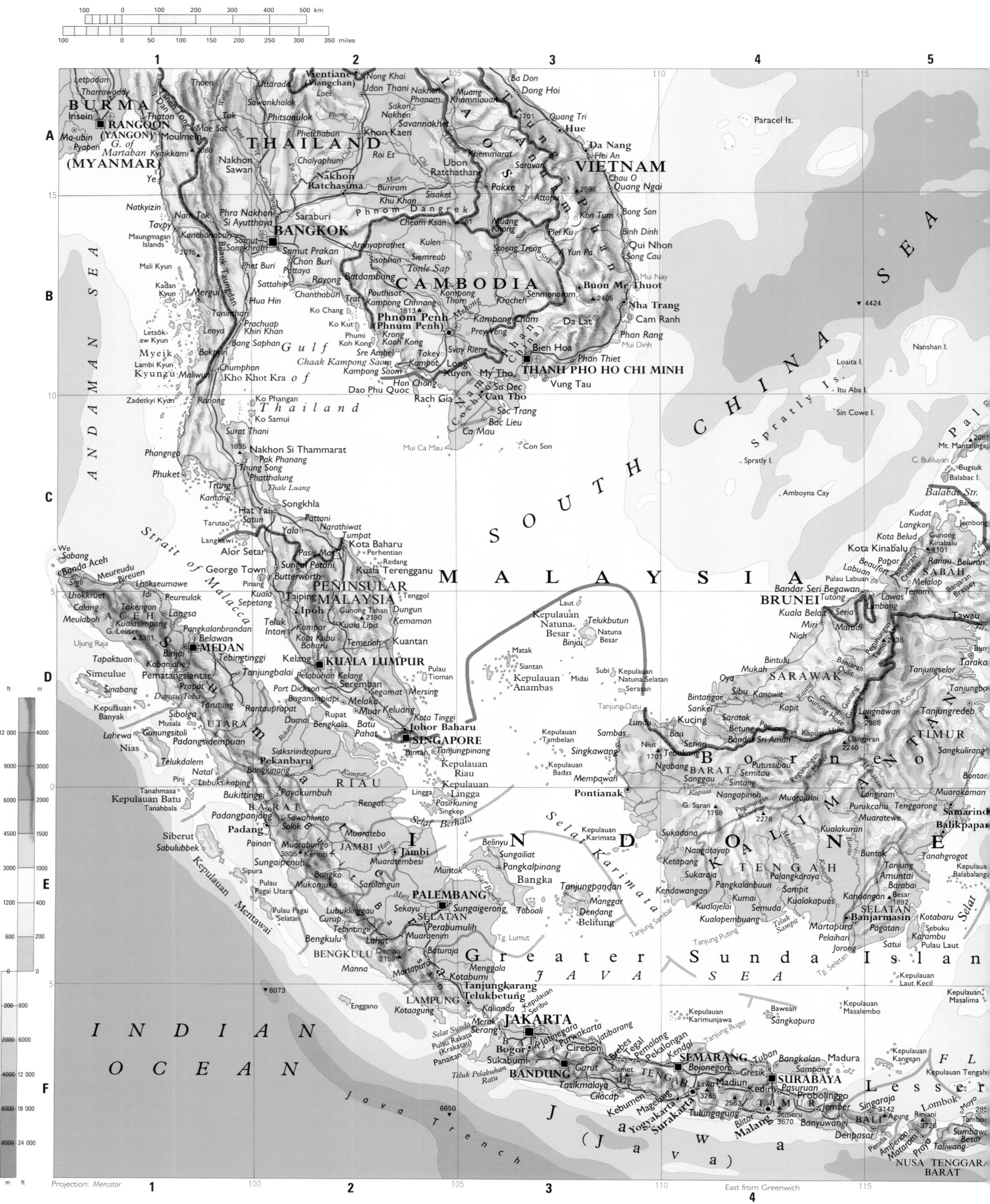

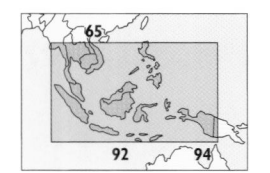

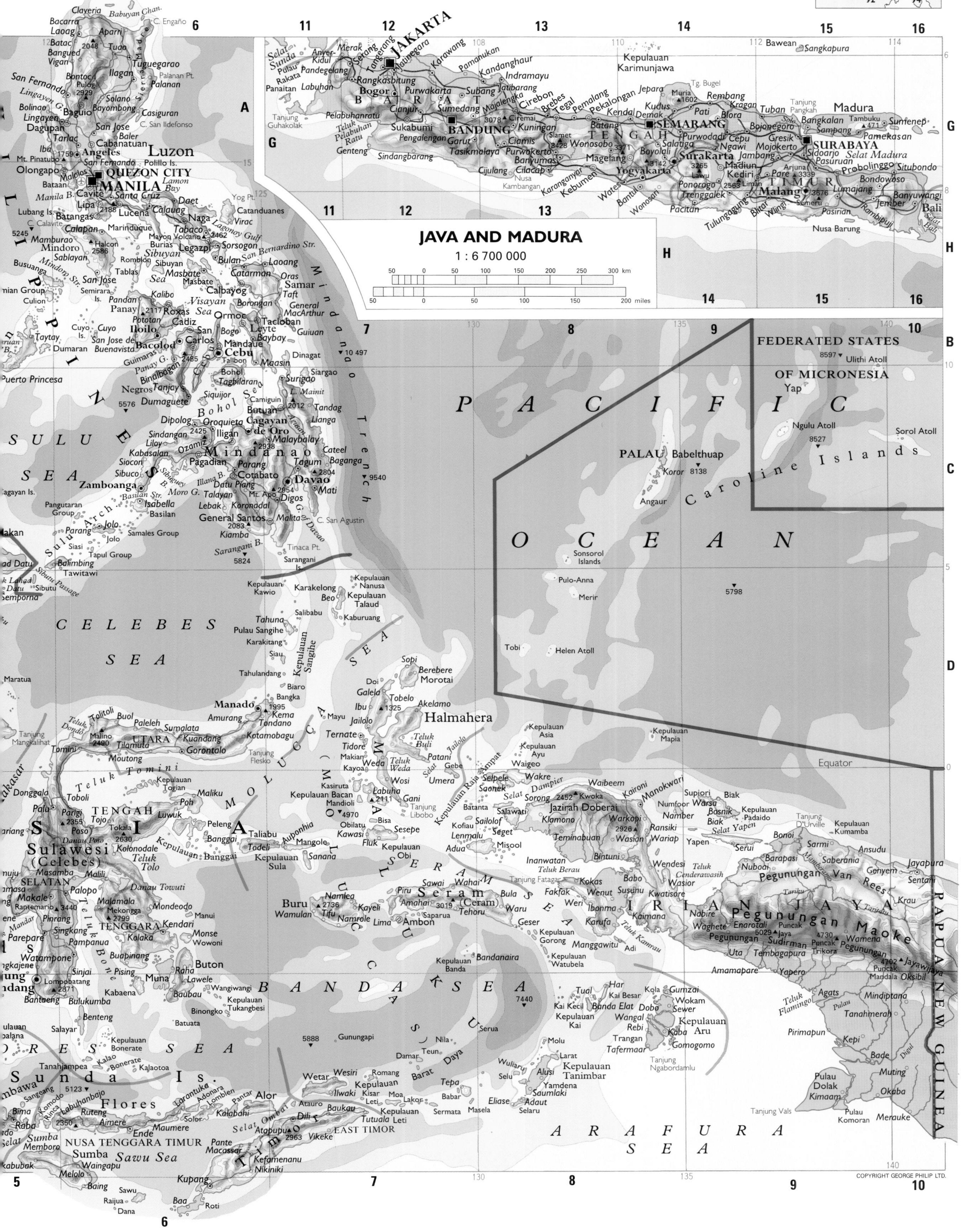

## JAVA AND MADURA

1 : 6 700 000

50  0  50  100  150  200  250  300 km
50  0  50  100  150  200 miles

PACIFIC

OCEAN

FEDERATED STATES
OF MICRONESIA
Yap

Ulithi Atoll
Ngulu Atoll
Sorol Atoll

PALAU  Babelthuap
Koror  Angaur

Caroline Islands

Sonsorol Islands
Pulo-Anna
Merir
Tobi  Helen Atoll

CELEBES
SEA

MOLUCCA SEA

Halmahera
Ternate
Tidore

Manado
Gorontalo

SULAWESI
(Celebes)
TENGAH
SELATAN
TENGGARA

Buru
Seram (Ceram)
Ambon

BANDA SEA

CERAM SEA

IRIAN JAYA
Pegunungan Van Rees
Pegunungan Maoke
Jayapura
Sentani

PAPUA NEW GUINEA

Flores
Sumba
Timor
EAST TIMOR
NUSA TENGGARA TIMUR
Kupang

Sawu Sea

ARAFURA
SEA

LUZON
MANILA
QUEZON CITY
Cebu
Mindanao
Davao
Zamboanga
General Santos

SULU
SEA

Bohol Sea

Mindanao Trench

COPYRIGHT GEORGE PHILIP LTD.

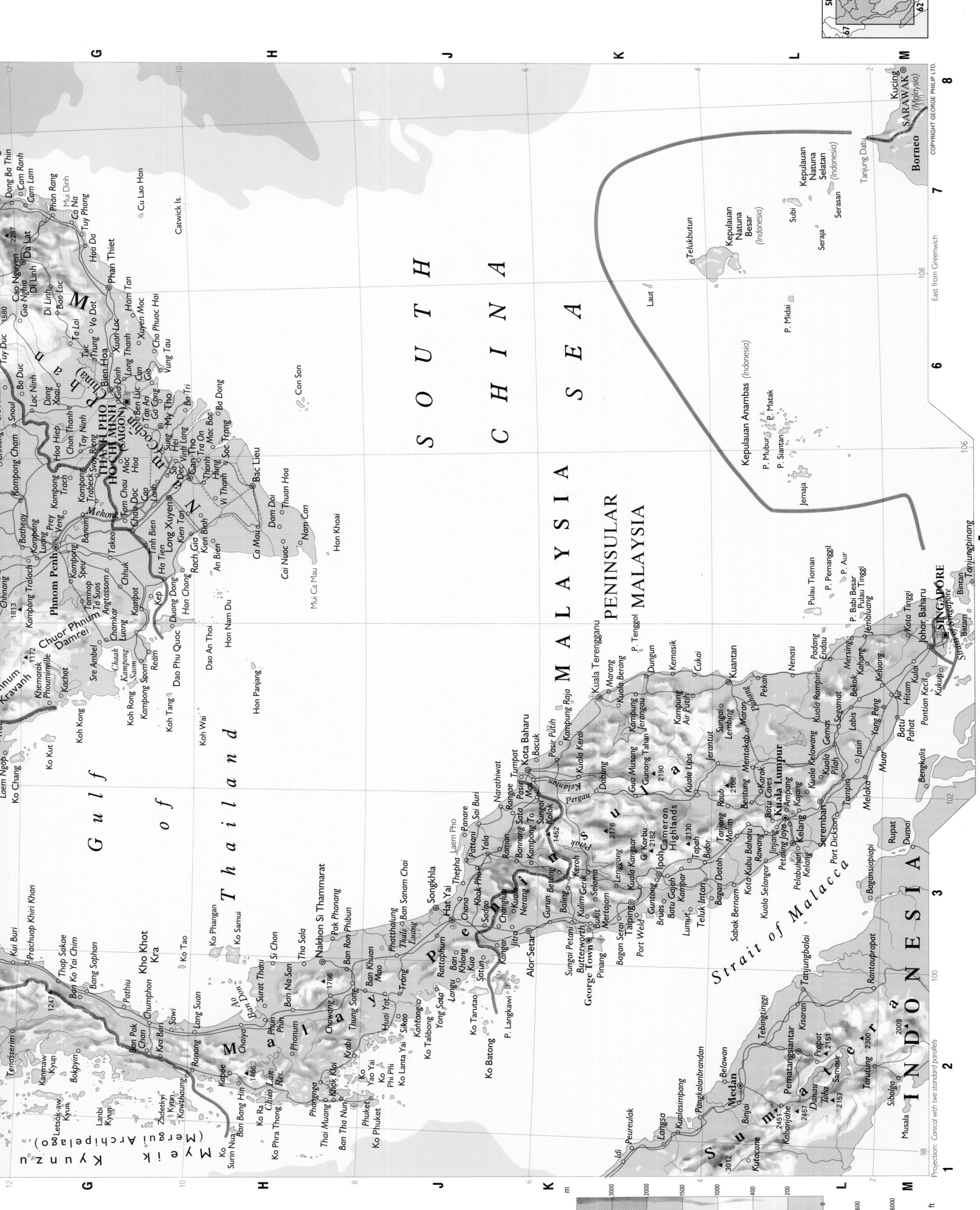

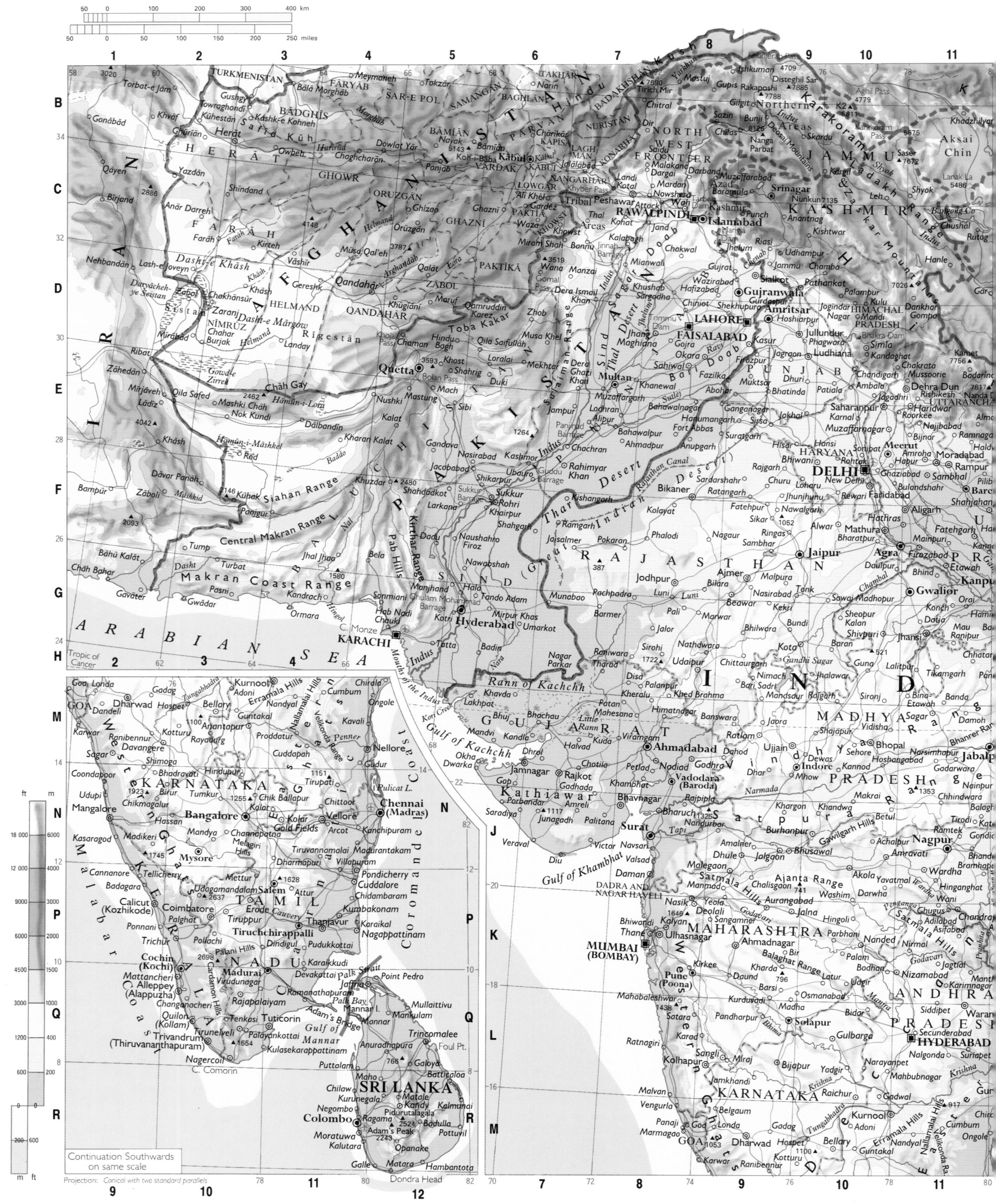

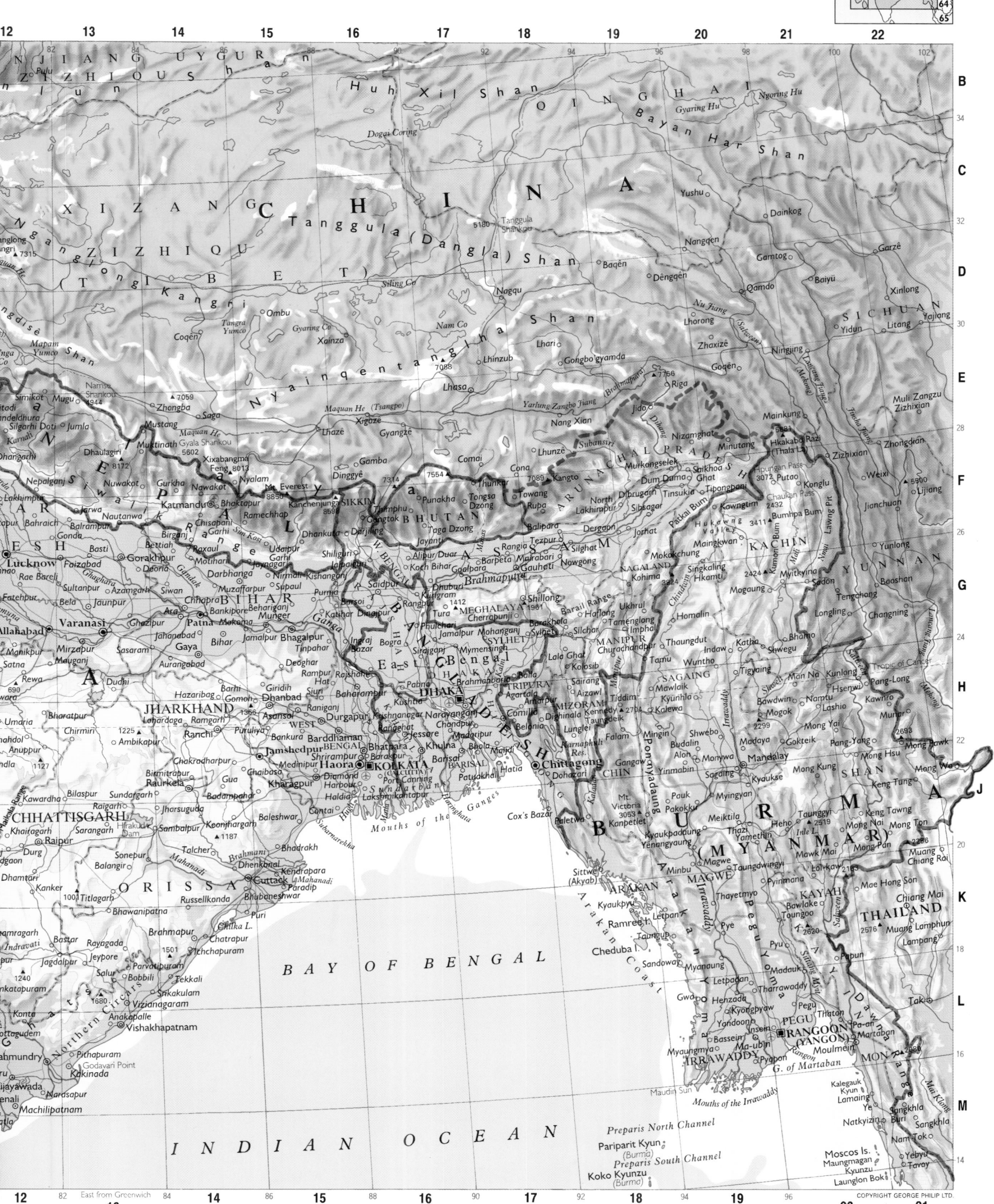

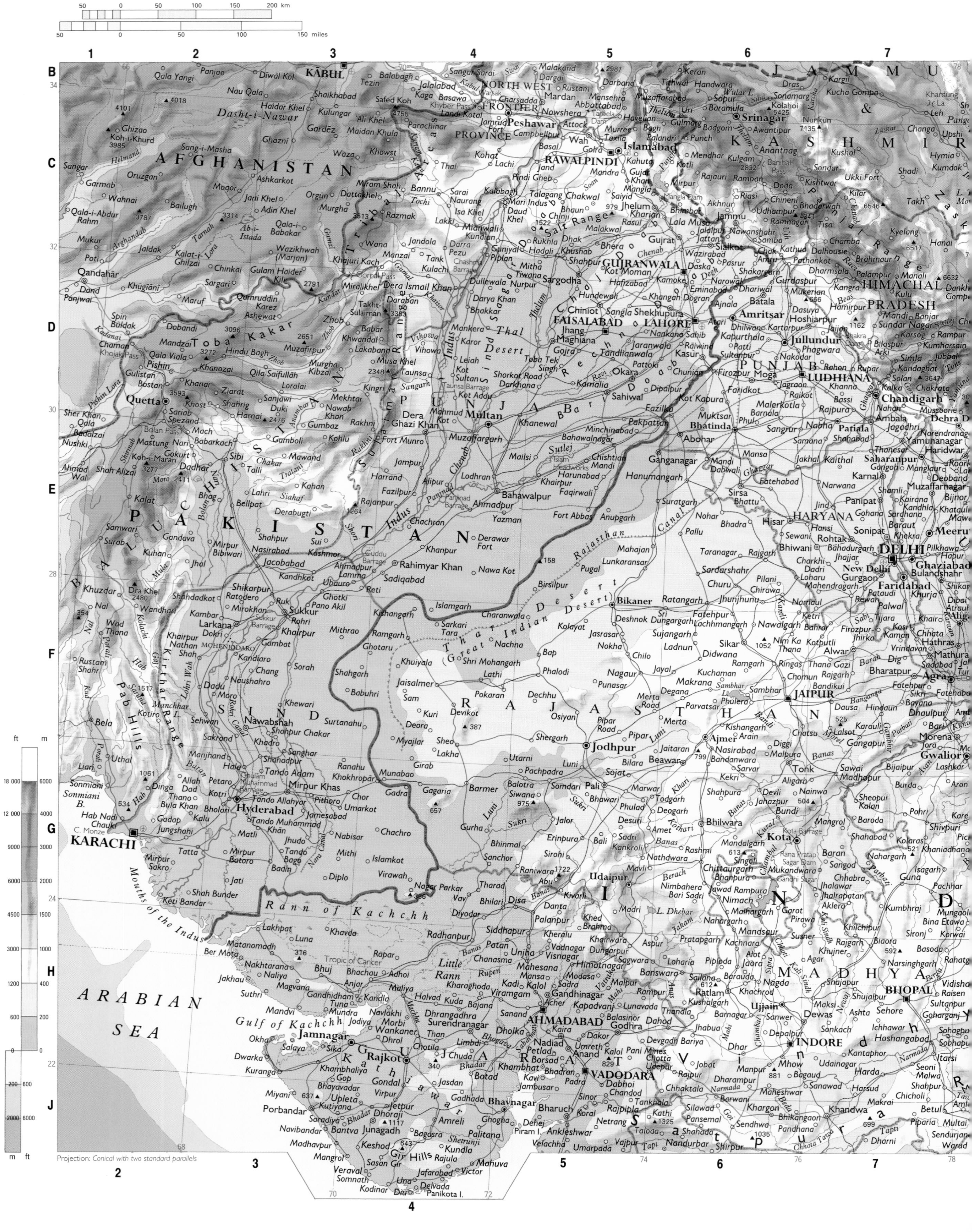

50  0  50  100  150  200 km
50  0  50  100  150 miles

**AFGHANISTAN**

**PAKISTAN**

**BALUCHISTAN**

**SIND**

**PUNJAB**

**RAJASTHAN**

(Great Indian Desert) Thar Desert

**HARYANA**

**DELHI**
New Delhi

**PUNJAB**

**HIMACHAL PRADESH**

**JAMMU & KASHMIR**

**MADHYA PRADESH**

**GUJARAT**

**ARABIAN SEA**

Gulf of Kachchh

Rann of Kachchh

Little Rann

Mouths of the Indus

Tropic of Cancer

KABUL
KARACHI
Quetta
Qandahar
Peshawar
Islamabad
RAWALPINDI
GUJRANWALA
FAISALABAD
LAHORE
Amritsar
LUDHIANA
Chandigarh
Srinagar
Jammu
Multan
Bahawalpur
Hyderabad
Sukkur
Bikaner
Jodhpur
Jaipur
Ajmer
Udaipur
Kota
Gwalior
Agra
Mathura
DELHI
Meerut
Faridabad
Ghaziabad
Bhopal
INDORE
AHMADABAD
VADODARA
Rajkot
Jamnagar
Bhavnagar
Junagadh
Porbandar
Bharuch

NORTH WEST FRONTIER PROVINCE
Khyber Pass

Dasht-i-Nawar

Toba Kakar

Salt Range

Kirthar Range

Pab Hills

Gir Hills

Kathiawar

Indus
Chenab
Sutlej
Narmada
Tapti

Projection: Conical with two standard parallels

ft  m
18 000  6000
12 000  4000
9000  3000
6000  2000
4500  1500
3000  1000
1200  400
600  200
0  0
200  600
2000  6000
m  ft

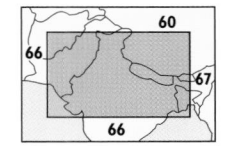

**JAMMU AND KASHMIR**

On same scale as Main Map

COPYRIGHT GEORGE PHILIP LTD.

East from Greenwich

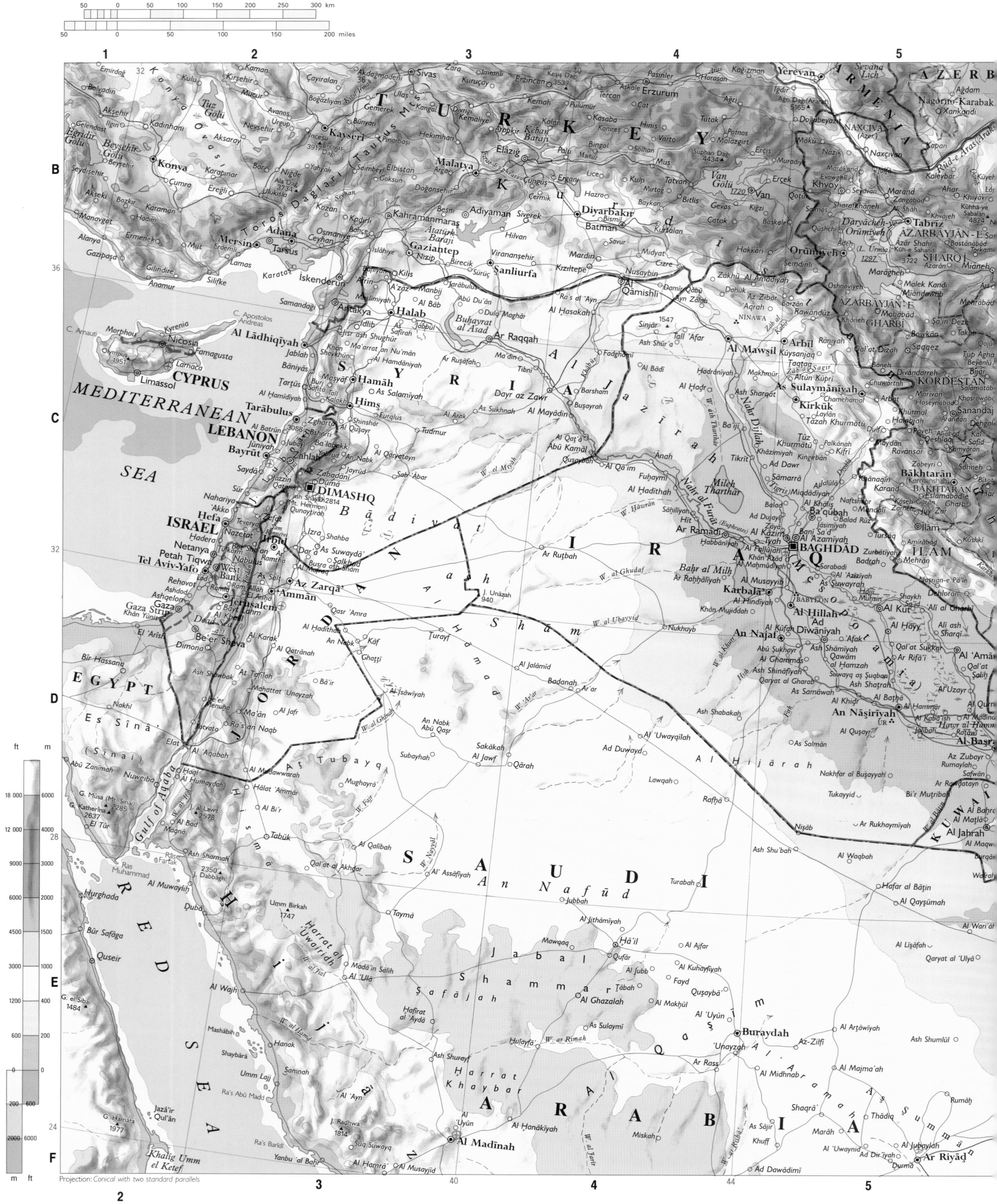

50 0 50 100 150 200 250 300 km
50 0 50 100 150 200 miles

**MEDITERRANEAN SEA**

**CYPRUS**
Nicosia
Limassol
Famagusta
Larnaca

**TURKEY**
Konya
Adana
Tarsus
Mersin
Kayseri
Malatya
Gaziantep
Şanlıurfa
Diyarbakır
Batman
Van
Van Gölü
Erzurum
Erzincan
Sivas

**ARMENIA**
Yerevan

**AZERBAIJAN**
Tabriz
ĀZARBĀYJĀN-E SHARQĪ

**SYRIA**
Halab
Ḥamāh
Ḥimṣ
DIMASHQ
Tarābulus
Ar Raqqah
Dayr az Zawr
Al Ḥasakah
Al Qāmishlī

**LEBANON**
Bayrūt
Saydā

**ISRAEL**
Hefa
Tel Aviv-Yafo
Jerusalem
Netanya
Nazaret
Gaza Strip
Gaza
West Bank

**JORDAN**
Amman
Az Zarqā'
Irbid
Ma'ān
Al 'Aqabah

**IRAQ**
BAGHDAD
Al Mawṣil
Arbīl
Kirkūk
As Sulaymānīyah
Karbalā'
An Najaf
Al Baṣrah
An Nāṣirīyah
Al Hillah
Samarra
Tikrīt

**IRAN**
Orūmīyeh
Bākhtarān
KORDESTĀN
ILĀM

**EGYPT**
Es Sînâ (Sinai)
G. Mûsa (Mt. Sinai) 2285
Katherîna 2637
Hurghada
Quseir
Bûr Safâga

**KUWAIT**
Al Jahrah

**SAUDI ARABIA**
Al Madīnah
Ar Riyāḍ
Buraydah
Tabūk
Ḥā'il
An Nafūd
Jabal Shammar
Harrat Khaybar
Hafar al Bāṭin

**RED SEA**
Gulf of Aqaba

Projection: Conical with two standard parallels

ft m
18 000 6000
12 000 4000
9000 3000
6000 2000
4500 1500
3000 1000
1200 400
600 200
0 0
200 600
2000 6000
m ft

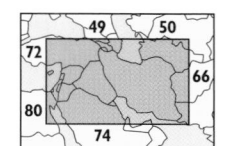

Division between Greeks and Turks in Cyprus; Turks to the North.

47 49
41 71
39
80 70

**CASPIAN SEA**

**RUSSIA**

**GEORGIA**

Caucasus Mountains

Sochi · Matsesta · Adler · Gagra · Bichvinta · Guadauta · Novyy Afon · Sokhumi · Ochamchira · Gali · Zugdidi · Anaklia · Senaki · Poti · Kobuleti · Batumi · ADJARIA · Hopa

Teberda · Elbrus 5642 · Tyrnyauz · KABARDINO-BALKARIA 5203 · Beslan · Groznyy · Argun · Shali · Khasavyurt · Kizil Yurt · Makhachkala · Kaspiysk · Izberbash · Buynaksk

Vladikavkaz · NORTH OSSETIA · INGUSHETIA · CHECHENIA · Botlikh · DAGESTAN · Derbent

Kutaisi · Tqibuli · Chiatura · Tskhinvali · SOUTH OSSETIA · Dusheti · Mtskheta · **TBILISI** · Rustavi · Gori · Kaspi · Telavi · Gurjaani · Lagodekhi · Zaqatala · Şäki · Kasumkent · Xudat · Xaçmaz · Qusar · Quba

**ARMENIA** · Gyumri · Vanadzor · **YEREVAN** · Yejmiadzin · Sevana Lich · Hrazdan · Martuni · Kamo · Ararat

**AZERBAIJAN** · **BAKI** · Sumqayıt · Maştağa · Artyom · Surakhany · Gäncä · Mingäçevir · Yevlax · Ağdam · Xankändi · NAXÇIVAN · Naxçivan · Kapan

**TURKEY** · Trabzon · Giresun · Erzurum · Erzincan · Elâzığ · Malatya · Diyarbakır · Batman · Siirt · Hakkâri · Van · Van Gölü 1720 · Kars · Ağrı · Bingöl Dağları · Güneydoğu Toroslar · Hakkâri Dağları · Şanlıurfa (Urfa) · Mardin · Nusaybin · Cizre · Zâkhū

Anadolu Dağları · Keban Barajı · Atatürk Barajı · Fırat (Euphrates) · Munzur Dağları

**IRAN** · Tabriz · Orūmīyeh (Urmia) · Daryācheh-ye Orūmīyeh (Lake Urmia) · Ardabīl · Rasht · Bandar-e Anzalī · Kūhhā-ye Talesh · Kūhhā-ye Sabalān 4824 · Marāgheh · Mīāneh · Zanjān · Mahābād · Saqqez · Sanandaj · Bākhtarān · Hamadān · Malāyer · Borūjerd · Khorramābād · Dezfūl · Shūsh · Andīmeshk

**IRAQ** · Al Mawşil (Mosul) · NĪNAWĀ · Arbīl · Kirkūk · As Sulaymānīyah · Tikrīt · Sāmarrā · **BAGHDĀD** · BABYLON · Al Hillah · Karbalā · An Najaf · An Nāşirīyah · Al Kūt · Al `Amārah · Al Hindīyah · Ad Dīwānīyah · Ba`qūbah · Khānaqīn

**SYRIA** · Ar Raqqah · Dayr az Zawr · Al Mayādīn · Abū Kamāl · Al Hasakah · Al Qāmishlī · Al Jazīrah (Mesopotamia) · Nahr al Furāt (Euphrates) · Nahr Dijlah (Tigris) · Bahret Assad · PALMYRA · Tudmur

East from Greenwich

ft m · 9000 3000 · 6000 · 4500 1500 · 3000 1000 · 1500 500 · 600 200 · 0 · 50 150 · 100 300 · 200 600 · 500 1500 · 1000 3000 · 2000 6000 · 3000 9000 · m ft

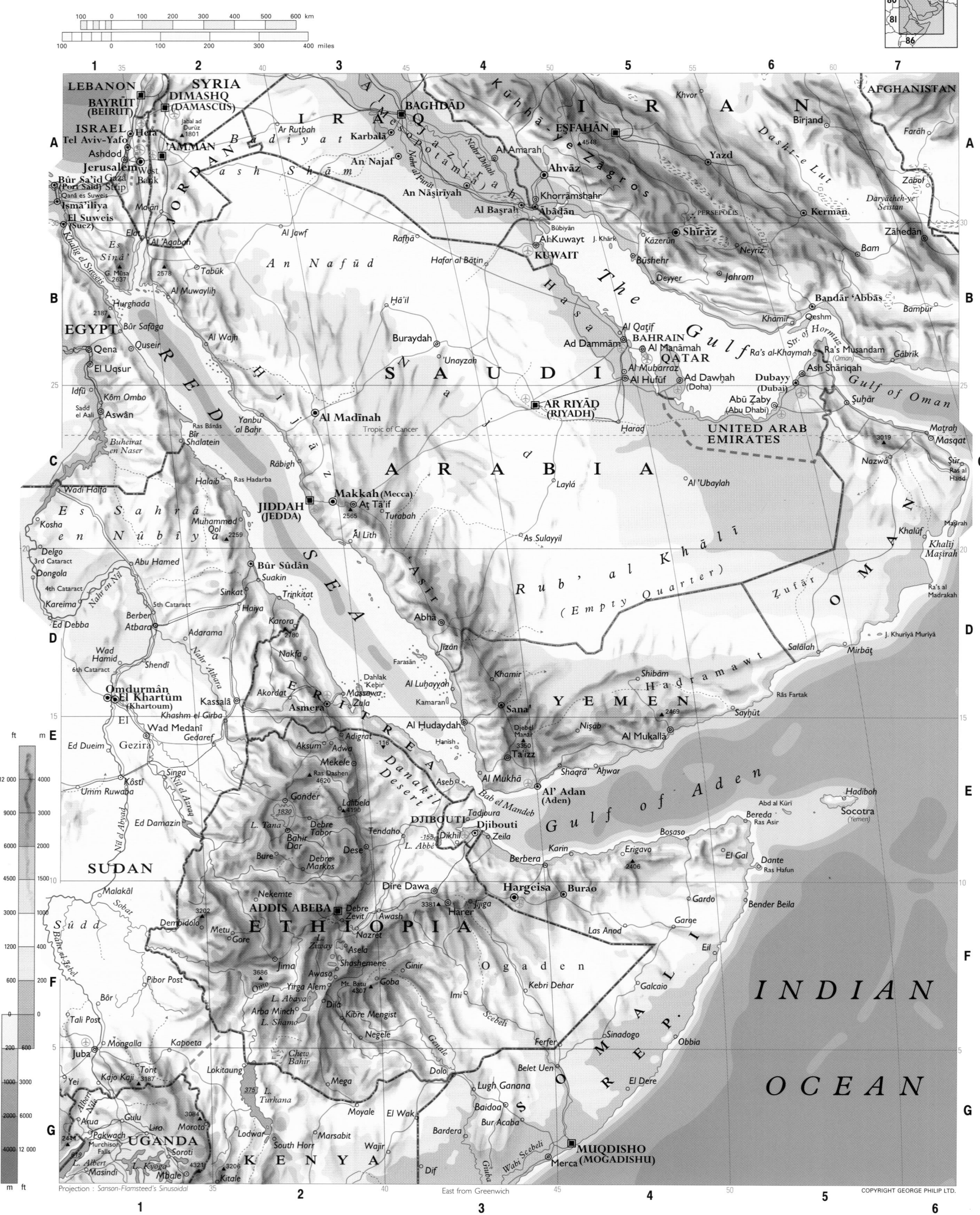

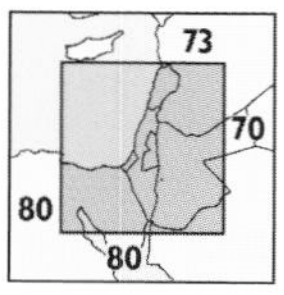

73
70
80
80

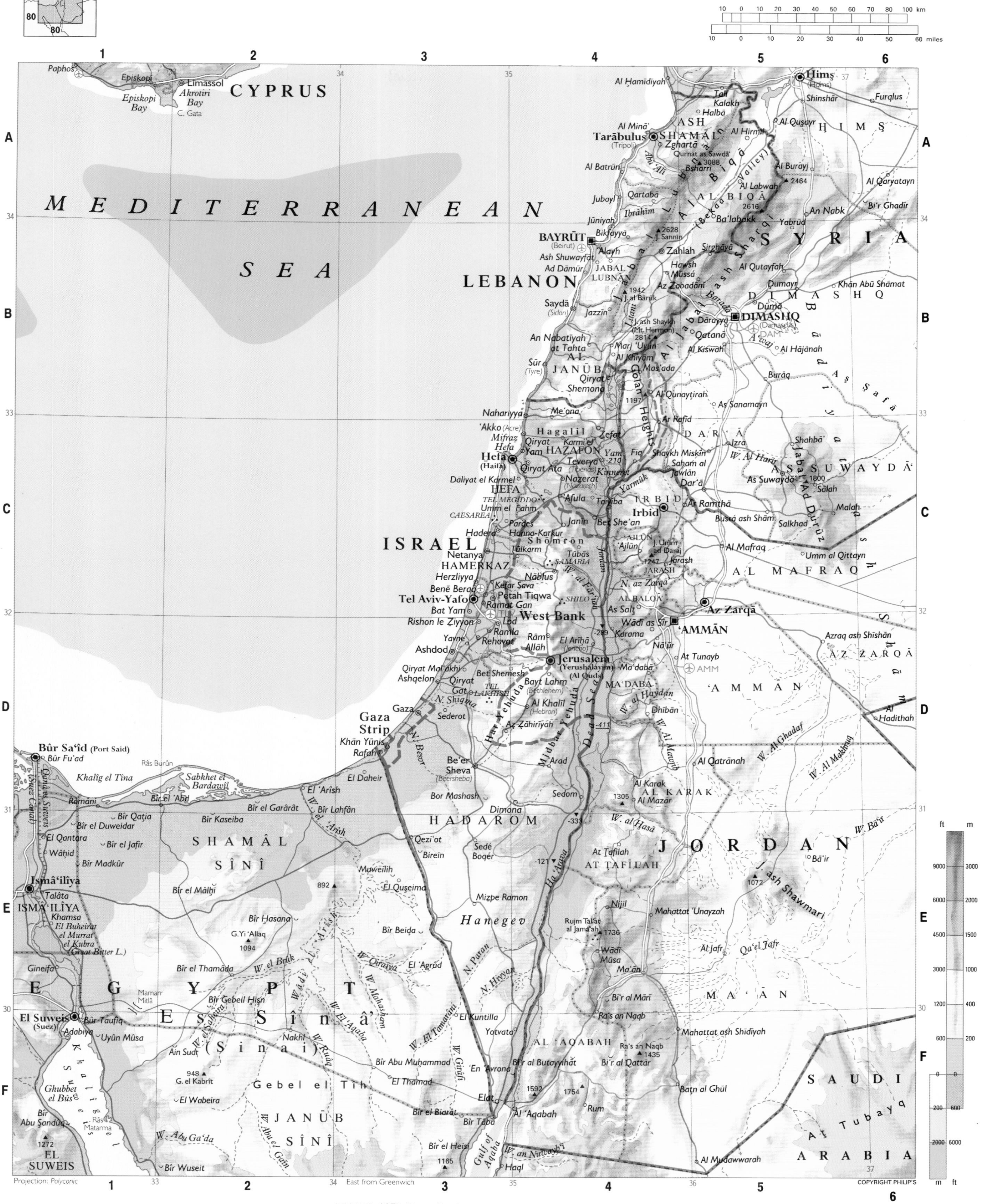

10 0 10 20 30 40 50 60 70 80 100 km
10 0 10 20 30 40 50 60 miles

**CYPRUS**

Paphos
Episkopi
Episkopi Bay
Limassol
Akrotiri Bay
C. Gata

34
35
37

Al Ḥamidīyah
Tall
Kalakh
Shinshār
Furqlus

Ḥims
(Homs)

*M E D I T E R R A N E A N*

ASH
SHAMÂL
Al Mīna'
Zgharta
Qurnat as Sawdā'
3088
Ḥalbā
Al Ḥirmil
Al Quṣayr
Al Qaryatayn

**Tarābulus**
(Tripoli)

*S E A*

Al Batrūn
Abu 'Ali
Bsharri
2616
Al Burayj
2464
Al Qaryatayn

Jubayl
Qarṭabā
Ibrāhīm
3088
Al Labwah
Al Qaryatayn

**HIMS**

Jūniyah
Bikfayyā
2628
J. Sannīn
Ba'labakk
Yabrūd
An Nabk
Bi'r Ghadīr

**BAYRŪT**
(Beirut)
'Alayh
Ash Shuwayfāt
Zaḥlah
Hawsh Mūssā
Sirghāyā
Az Zabadānī
Dumayr
Khān Abū Shāmat

**LEBANON**
Ad Dāmūr
JABAL
LUBNĀN
1942
J. al Bāruk
Az Zabadānī
Qaṭanā
A'waj
DIMASHQ

Saydā
(Sidon)
Jazzīn
Līṭānī
Mt. Hermon
2814
Marj 'Uyūn
Al Kiswah
Darayyā
Al Hājānah

**SYRIA**

An Nabaṭīyah at Tahtā
Al Khiyām
Golan Heights
Al Qutayfah
**DIMASHQ**
(Damascus)
DAM

AL
JANŪB
Sūr
(Tyre)
Qiryat Shemona
Maṣ'ada
1197
Al Qunayṭirah
As Sanamayn
Burāq

Nahariyya
Me'ona
Ḥagalil
Zefat
DAR'Ā
Ash Shaykh Miskīn
Izra
Shahbā
Aṣ Ṣafā

'Akko (Acre)
Mifraz Hefa
Qiryat Yam
Karmi'el
HAZAFON
Yami -210
Fiq
Ar Rafīd
W. Al Ḥarīr
Shahbā
AS SUWAYDĀ

**Ḥefa**
(Haifa)
Qiryat Ata
Teverya (Tiberias)
Kinneret
Sahm al Jawlān
Dar'ā
Ar Ramthā
As Suwaydā
1800
Ṣalāh

Dāliyat el Karmel
HEFA
Nazerat
(Nazareth)
Yarmūk
Irbid
Buṣrá ash Shām
Salkhad
Malaḥ

TEL MEGIDDO
Umm el Fahm
Afula
Ṭayiba
**IRBID**
Ar Ramthā
JABAL AD DURŪZ

CAESAREA
Hadera
Janīn
Bet She'an
'AJLŪN
Al Mafraq
Umm al Qittayn

Pardes
Hanna-Karkur
Shōmrōn
J. Umm ad Daraj
1247
Jarash
AL MAFRAQ

**ISRAEL**
Tūlkarm
SAMARIA
Tūbās
'Ajlūn
JARASH

Netanya
HAMERKAZ
Nāblus
N. az Zarqā
Az Zarqā

Herzliyya
Kefar Sava
SHILO
AL BALQĀ
**Az Zarqā**

Benē Beraq
Petaḥ Tiqwa
Ramat Gan
Wādī as Sīr
**'AMMĀN**
Azraq ash Shishān
AZ ZARQĀ

**Tel Aviv-Yafo**
Lod
**West Bank**
As Salt
Karama
Na'ūr
AMM

Bat Yam
Rishon le Ziyyon
Rām Allāh
El Arīḥa (Jericho)
289
At Tunayb

Yavne
Ramla
Rehovot
**Jerusalem**
(Yerushalayim)
(Al Quds)
Ma'daba
'AMMĀN

Ashdod
Ashqelon
Qiryat Mal'akhi
Bet Shemesh
Bayt Laḥm
(Bethlehem)
MA'DĀBĀ
W. al Haydān
Dhibān

Qiryat Gat
TEL LAKHISH
Al Khalīl
(Hebron)
Al Ḥadītha

**Gaza**
Gaza
Sederot
N. Shiqma
Az Ẓāhirīyah
Har Yehuda
Minṭaqat
Yehuda
Al Ḥadītha

**Gaza Strip**
Khān Yūnis
Rafaḥ
N. Besor
Be'er Sheva
(Beersheba)
Arad
W. al Mawjib
Al Qaṭrānah
W. Al Ghadaf

**Bûr Sa'îd** (Port Said)
Bûr Fu'ad
Râs Burûn
Sabkhet el Bardawîl
El 'Arîsh
El Daheir
Bor Mashash
Dimona
-333
1305
Al Mazar
AL KARAK
Sedom
W. al Ḥasā
W. Al Maʿujib
W. Bā'ir

Qantâ es Sueis
Ramâni
Bîr el 'Abd
Bîr el Garârât
**HADAROM**
Qezi'ot
Sedé Boqér
-121
JORDAN
Bā'ir

El Qantara
Bîr el Duweidar
Bîr el Jafir
Bîr Kaseiba
Bîr Lahfân
Muweilih
Mizpe Ramon
At Ṭafīlah
AT TAFĪLAH
1072
J. ash Shawmari

**Ismâ'îlîya**
Wâḥid
Bîr Madkûr
SHAMÂL SÎNÎ
892
El Quseima
**Hanegev**
Nijil
Mahattat 'Unayzah

ISMÂ'ÎLÎYA
Khamsa
El Buheirat el Murrat el Kubra
(Great Bitter L.)
Bîr Ḥasana
Bîr Beiḍa
Rujm Talat al Jamaʿah
1736
Al Jafr
Qa'el Jafr

Gineifa
Talâta
G.Yi 'Allaq
1094
W. el Bruk
W. Quraiya
El 'Agrûd
W. Mahasham
Wādī Mūsā
Ma'ān
MA'ĀN

**EGYPT**
Mamarr Mitlâ
Bîr Gebeil Hisn
W. El Sukhna
W. El Tamaryai
Bi'r al Mārī
Al Jafr

El Suweis
(Suez)
Bûr Taufîq
Adabiya
Uyûn Mûsa
Ain Sudr
Nakhl
W. Ruaq
El Kuntilla
Ra's an Naqb
Mahattat ash Shidīyah

Ghubbet el Bûs
Râs Matama
948
G. el Kabrît
Gebel el Tih
El Thamad
Bîr Abu Muḥammad
En Avrona
1435
Bi'r al Butayyiḥāt
Bi'r al Qaṭar

SÎNÎ
(Sinai)
El Wabeira
El Thamad
1592
1754
**SAUDI**

**EL SUWEIS**
1272
JANŪB SÎNÎ
W. Abu Ga'da
W. Abu el Gân
Bîr el Heisi
1165
Bîr el Biarât
Bîr Taba
Elat
Al 'Aqabah
Rum
Baṭn al Ghūl
AT TUBAYQ
**ARABIA**

Abu Ṣandûq
Bîr Wuseit
Gulf of Aqaba
W. an Nīṣwāni
Ḥaql
Al Mudawwarah

Projection: Polyconic
East from Greenwich
COPYRIGHT PHILIP'S

ft m
9000 3000
6000 2000
4500 1500
3000 1000
1200 400
600 200
0 0
200 600
2000 6000
m ft

**= = = 1974 Cease Fire Lines**

# 76 AFRICA : Physical 1:37 300 000

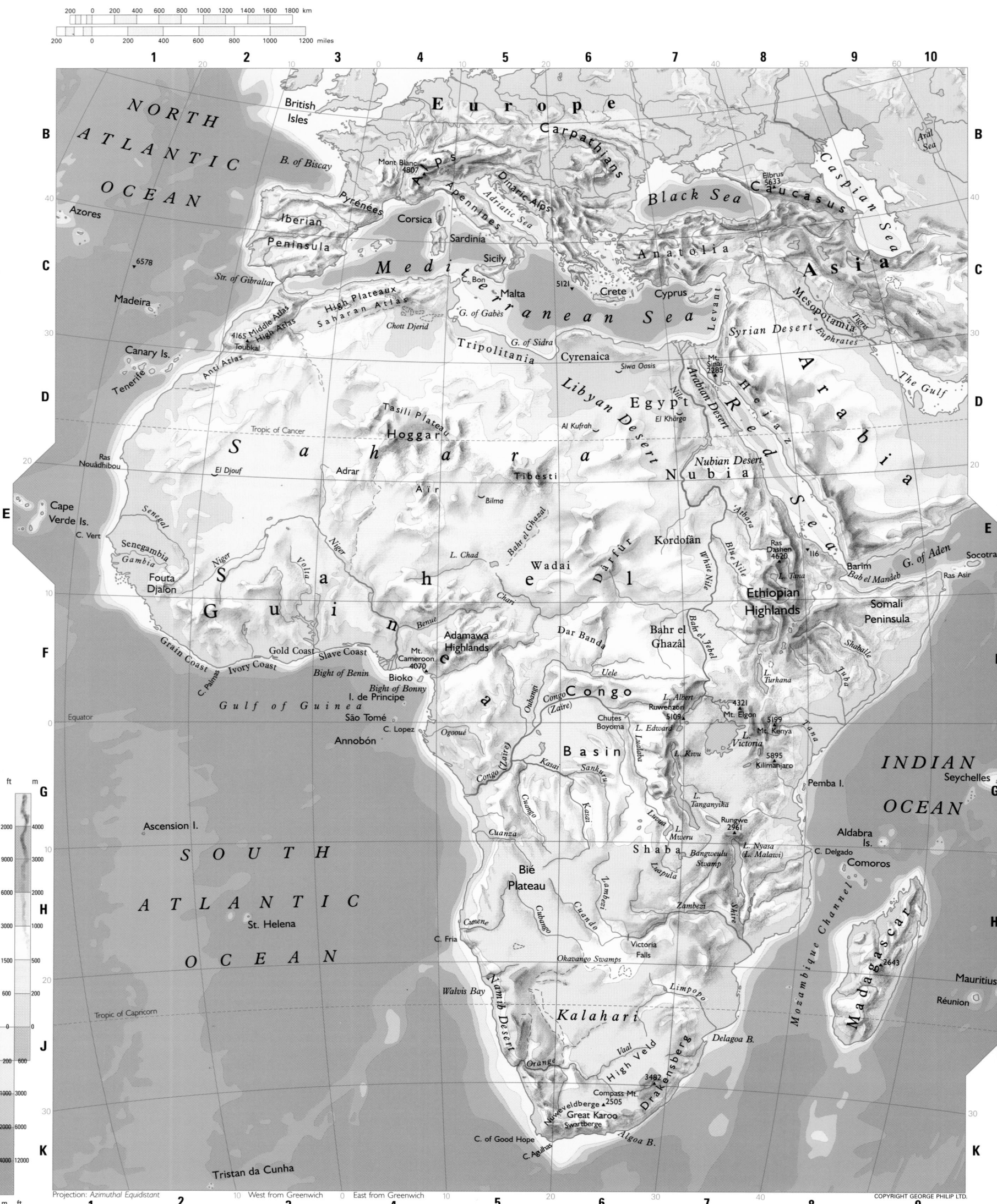

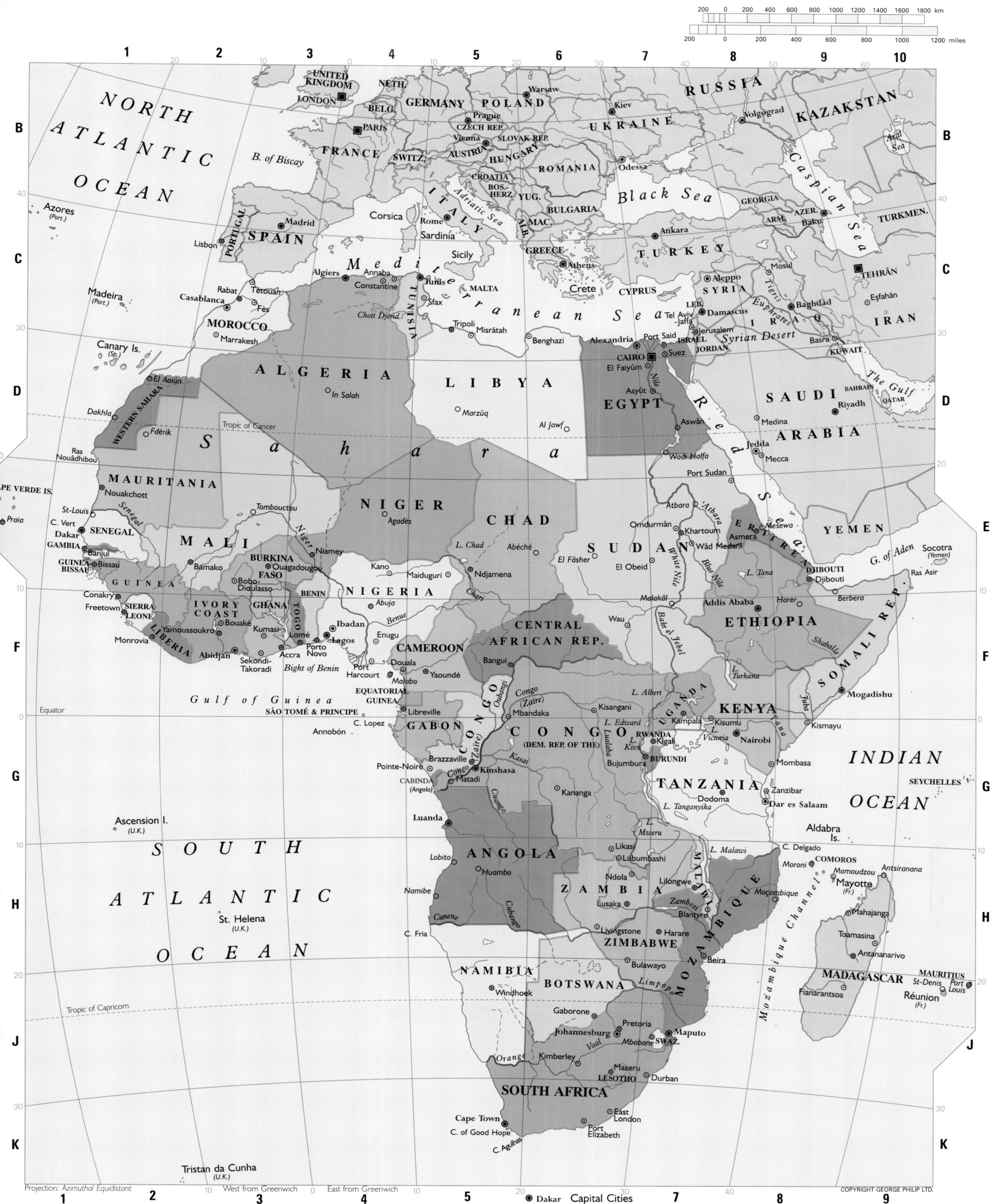

NORTH ATLANTIC OCEAN

UNITED KINGDOM
LONDON
NETH.
BELG.
FRANCE
GERMANY
POLAND
Warsaw
Prague
CZECH REP.
Vienna
SWITZ.
AUSTRIA
SLOVAK REP.
HUNGARY
CROATIA
BOS.-HERZ.
YUG.
ROMANIA
BULGARIA
Kiev
UKRAINE
Odessa
RUSSIA
Volgograd
KAZAKSTAN
Aral Sea

PARIS
B. of Biscay
Corsica
Rome
Sardinia
ITALY
Adriatic Sea
ALB.
MAC.
Black Sea
GEORGIA
ARM.
AZER.
Baku
TURKMEN.
Caspian Sea

Azores (Port.)
Madrid
Lisbon
PORTUGAL
SPAIN
Mediterranean Sea
Sicily
MALTA
Crete
GREECE
Athens
CYPRUS
TURKEY
Ankara
Aleppo
SYRIA
Mosul
Tigris
Baghdad
Euphrates
Eşfahān
TEHRĀN
IRAN

Madeira (Port.)
Rabat
Casablanca
Tétouan
Fès
MOROCCO
Marrakesh
Algiers
Annaba
Constantine
TUNISIA
Tunis
Sfax
Tripoli
Misrātah
Benghazi
Alexandria
Port Said
CAIRO
Suez
Tel Aviv-Jaffa
Damascus
LEB.
Jerusalem
ISRAEL
JORDAN
Syrian Desert
IRAQ
Basra
KUWAIT

Canary Is. (Sp.)
Dakhla
El Aaiún
WESTERN SAHARA
Fdérik
ALGERIA
In Salah
LIBYA
Marzūq
Al Jawf
EGYPT
El Faiyûm
Asyût
Nile
Aswân
Wadi Halfa
Medina
SAUDI ARABIA
Riyadh
BAHRAIN
QATAR
The Gulf

Ras Nouâdhibou
Tropic of Cancer
S  a  h  a  r  a
Port Sudan
Jedda
Mecca

CAPE VERDE IS.
Praia
St-Louis
C. Vert
Dakar
SENEGAL
GAMBIA
Banjul
GUINEA BISSAU
Bissau
Nouakchott
MAURITANIA
MALI
Senegal
Tombouctou
Niger
NIGER
Agadès
Niamey
CHAD
L. Chad
Abéché
Ndjamena
SUDAN
El Fâsher
El Obeid
Khartoum
Omdurmân
Atbara
Atbara
White Nile
Wâd Medani
Blue Nile
ERITREA
Mesewa
Asmera
L. Tana
Atbara

Conakry
Freetown
SIERRA LEONE
GUINEA
Bámako
BURKINA FASO
Ouagadougou
Bobo-Dioulasso
Kano
Maiduguri
Kano
YEMEN
G. of Aden
Socotra (Yemen)
Ras Asir
DJIBOUTI
Djibouti
Berbera

Monrovia
LIBERIA
Abidjan
IVORY COAST
Bouaké
GHANA
Kumasi
TOGO
BENIN
Porto Novo
NIGERIA
Abuja
Ibadan
Lagos
Enugu
Benue
CAMEROON
Douala
Yaoundé
Bangui
CENTRAL AFRICAN REP.
Wau
Malakâl
Bahr el Jebel
Addis Ababa
Harer
ETHIOPIA
Shabelle
SOMALI REP.

Yamoussoukro
Sekondi-Takoradi
Accra
Lomé
Bight of Benin
Port Harcourt
Malabo
EQUATORIAL GUINEA
SÃO TOMÉ & PRÍNCIPE
Libreville
GABON
CONGO
Ouhangi
Congo (Zaïre)
Mbandaka
Kisangani
CONGO (DEM. REP. OF THE)
L. Albert
UGANDA
L. Edward
Kampala
RWANDA
Kigali
L. Kivu
BURUNDI
Bujumbura
L. Victoria
Kisumu
KENYA
Nairobi
Kismayu
Mogadishu
Juba

Gulf of Guinea
C. Lopez
Annobón
Equator
Pointe-Noire
Brazzaville
Kinshasa
CABINDA (Angola)
Matadi
Kasai
Kananga
Luanda
Lualaba
L. Tanganyika
TANZANIA
Dodoma
Zanzibar
Dar es Salaam
Mombasa
INDIAN OCEAN
SEYCHELLES

Ascension I. (U.K.)
SOUTH ATLANTIC OCEAN
Lobito
Namibe
ANGOLA
Huambo
Cuanza
Cunene
Likasi
Lubumbashi
Kananga
L. Mweru
ZAMBIA
Ndola
Lusaka
L. Malawi
MALAWI
Lilongwe
C. Delgado
COMOROS
Moroni
Mamoudzou
Mayotte (Fr.)
Antsiranana
Mahajanga

St. Helena (U.K.)
C. Fria
Cubango
Livingstone
Harare
Zambezi
Blantyre
MOZAMBIQUE
Beira
Moçambique
Mozambique Channel
Toamasina
MADAGASCAR
Antananarivo
MAURITIUS
St-Denis
Port Louis
Réunion (Fr.)

Tropic of Capricorn
NAMIBIA
Windhoek
BOTSWANA
Gaborone
ZIMBABWE
Bulawayo
Limpopo
Fianarantsoa

Johannesburg
Pretoria
Maputo
SWAZ.
Mbabane
Vaal
Kimberley
Orange
LESOTHO
Maseru
Durban
SOUTH AFRICA
Cape Town
C. of Good Hope
East London
Port Elizabeth
C. Agulhas

Tristan da Cunha (U.K.)

100  0   100  200  300  400  500  600 km
100      0        100       200      300        400 miles

SPAIN
Cádiz · Málaga · Almería
Cabo de São Vicente
ALGER (Algiers) · Tizi-Ouzou · Bejaïa · Skikda · Annaba
Str. of Gibraltar · Ceuta (Sp.) · Al Hoceïma · Melilla (Sp.) · Nador · Ech Cheliff · Mostaganem · Blida · Sétif · Constantine
Tanger · Tétouan · Oujda · Oran · Mascara · Médéa · M'sila · Batna · Tébessa · Khenchela

ATLANTIC

Azores (Port.)

Ksar el Kebir · Ouezzane · Tlemcen · Chott ech Chergui · Aflou · Messad · Djelfa · Tazeur · Biskra · El Djem
Kenitra · Salé · Fès · Taza · Sidi-bel-Abbès · Tiaret · Chott el Hodna · Laghouat
Rabat · Meknès · Mecheria · El Bayadh · Touggourt · El Oued
OCEAN
Mohammedia · Khémisset · Moyen Atlas · Aïn-Sefra · Berriane · Ghardaïa
Porto Santo
CASABLANCA · Khouribga · Bouârfa · Figuig · Hassi Messaoud
El Jadida · Settat · Haut Atlas · Béchar · Ouargla
Madeira (Port.) · Funchal · Safi · Ras Beddouza · Beni Mellal · Abadla · El Goléa

MOROCCO · Marrakech · Essaouira · Er Rachidia · Maghreb
Dj. Toubkal 4165 · Ouarzazate · Grand Erg Occidental · Grand Erg Oriental
C. Rhir · Agadir · Taroudannt · Anti Atlas · 2359
Ifni · Goulimine · ALGERIA · Ohanet
Islas Canarias (Sp.) · Tan-tan · Kerzaz · Timimoun · Bordj Omar Driss
La Palma · Lanzarote · Arrecife
Santa Cruz de Tenerife · Las Palmas · Fuerteventura · Plateau du Tademaït · In Salah · Illizi
Gomera · 3718 · Gran Canaria · C. Juby · Tarfaya · Tindouf · Bordj Fly Ste. Marie · Arak · Tassili n'Ajjer
Hierro · Tenerife · El Aaiún · Smara · Zaouiet Reggâne · 2158 · Djanet
Bu Craa · Chegga · Ouallene

WESTERN · C. Bojador · Aïn Ben Tili · Erg Chech · Bordj-in-Eker · Ahaggar · Tahat 2918
SAHARA · Bir Mogreïn · Tamanrasset
Dakhla · Tropic of Cancer
Zouîrât · S · Taoudenni · Tanezrouft
Fdérik · El Djouf · Adrar des Iforas
Râs Nouâdhibou · Nouâdhibou · Atâr · Chinguetti · Tessalit · 598 · Arlit · Iférouane
Akjoujt · Adrar · Aïr 1900
Râs Timirist · MAURITANIA · Kidal · Agadez
Rachid · NIGER
Nouakchott · Tidjikja · In-Gall · Tanout
Aoukâr · Tombouctou · Niger · Bourem
St. Louis · Aleg · Kiffa · 'Ayoûn el 'Atroûs · Néma · Gao · Ansongo · Ménaka · SAHEL · Tahoua
Rosso · Kaédi · Homburi · Famalé · Niamey · Birni Nkonni · Zinder
Dagana · Sénégal · Sélibabi · Nara · Niger · Filingué · Maradi · Katsina
Mboro · Matam · Nioro du Sahel · Mopti · Dori · Dosso · Gusau · Gumel
C. Vert · Thiès · Tivaouane · Bakel · Kayes · Didiéni · Ségou · San · Tougan · Kaya · Niamey · Sokoto · Hadejia
DAKAR · Linguère · MALI · Diafarabé · BURKINA · Botou · Jega · Kano · Azare
Kaolack · SENEGAL · Bafoulabé · Kita · Ouagadougou · Birnin Kebbi · Funtua
Banjul · GAMBIA · Tambacounda · Koudougou · Fada-N'Gourma · Gaya · Kontagora · Zaria
Georgetown · Gambia · Satadougou · FASO · Kandi · Bena · Kaduna
Ziguinchor · GUINEA · Siguiri · Bobo-Dioulasso · Tumu · Dapaong · Shanga · NIGER · Bauchi
BISSAU · Fouta Djalon · Labé · Gaoual · Sikasso · Bawku · Mango · Natitingou · Bembéréke · Kainji Res. · Minna · Kafanchan · Shendam
Arq. dos Bijagós · Dalaba · Tingrela · Gaoua · Savelugu · Parakou · Abuja · Jos
GUINEA · Mamou · Dabola · Odienné · Korhogo · Bouna · Black Volta · Tamale · Sékodé · Shaki · Keffi · Lafia · Benue
C. Verga · Kindia · Faranah · Fabala · Boundiali · Ferkéssédougou · Kong · Salaga · Savalou · Ilorin · Bida · Baro · Makurdi · Wukari
Dubréka · SIERRA · Kissidougou · Koro · Ogbomosho · Offa · Lokoja
Conakry · LEONE · Kabala · 1948 · IVORY · Katiola · Berekum · Wenchi · Oyo · Oshogbo · Ikare · Owo · Enugu
Port Loko · Yonibana · Nzérékoré · Séguéla · Bouaké · Abengourou · L. Volta · GHANA · Ilesha · Ife · Akure · Benin City · Onitsha
Freetown · Bo · Kenema · Man · COAST · Kossou · Kumasi · Koforidua · IBADAN · Iwo · Ijebu-Ode · Sapele · Aba · Bafoussam
Sherbro I. · Bonthe · Ganta · Danané · Daloa · Yamoussoukro · Obuasi · Asamankese · Abeokuta · Warri · Uyo · Calabar · Kumba
Sulima · LIBERIA · Tapeta · Gagnoa · Adzopé · Tema · LAGOS · Enugu · Port Harcourt · Bamenda
Monrovia · Buchanan · Sassandra · Divo · Agboville · Accra · Lomé · Cotonou · Porto-Novo · Limbe · Mt. Cameroun 4070
Grain Coast · River Cess · Lakota · Koforidua · Slave Coast · Bight of Benin · Rey Malabo
Harper · San Pédro · Tabou · Ivory Coast · Sekondi-Takoradi · C. Three Points · Gold Coast · Bioko · Do
C. Palmas

West from Greenwich   East from Greenwich

Projection : Sanson-Flamsteed's Sinusoidal

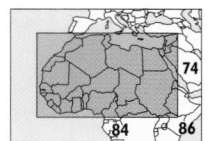

50 0 50 100 150 200 250 300 km

50 0 50 100 150 200 miles

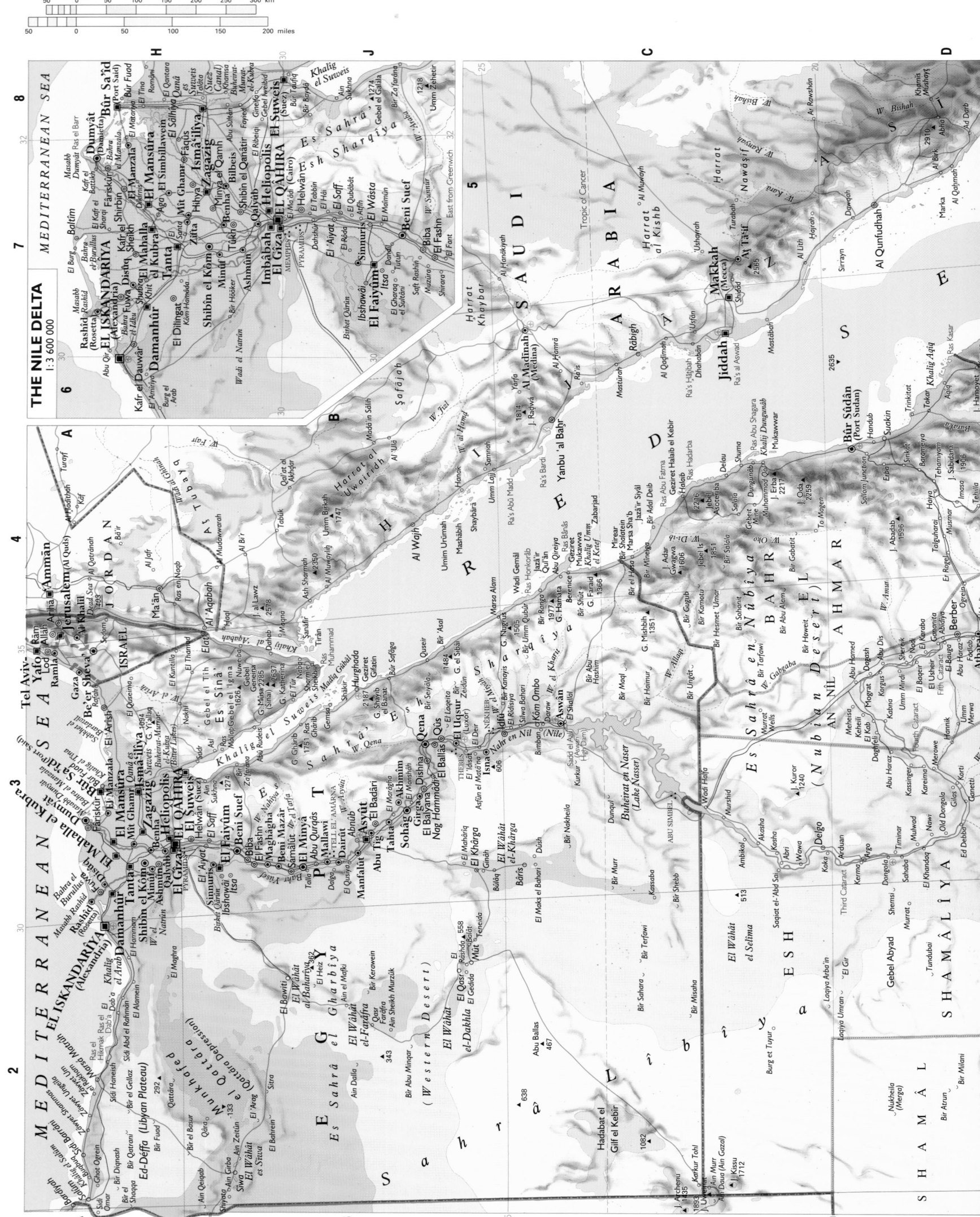

## THE NILE DELTA
### 1:3 600 000

MEDITERRANEAN SEA

Bûr Sa'îd (Port Said)
Dumyât
El Mansûra
Ismâ'ilîya
Zagazig
Heliopolis
EL QÂHIRA (Cairo)
Beni Suef
El Iskandarîya (Alexandria)
Rashîd (Rosetta)
Damanhûr
Tanta
El Mahalla el Kubra
Shibîn el Kôm
El Faiyûm

SAUDI ARABIA

Al Madînah (Medina)
Makkah (Mecca)
Jiddah
Bûr Sûdân (Port Sudan)

JORDAN
Ammân
Jerusalem (Al Quds)
ISRAEL
Tel Aviv
Gaza

Es Sahrâ' esh Sharqîya

Western Desert

Nubian Desert

Es Sahrâ' en Nûbîya

BAHR EL AHMAR

Khalîg el Suweis

Tropic of Cancer

Buheirat en Naser (Lake Nasser)

Aswân
El Uqsur (Luxor)
Qena
Asyût
El Minya
Sohâg
THEBES

EL WÂHÂT EL KHÂRGA

SHAMÂLÎYA

Sahrâ' Lîbîya

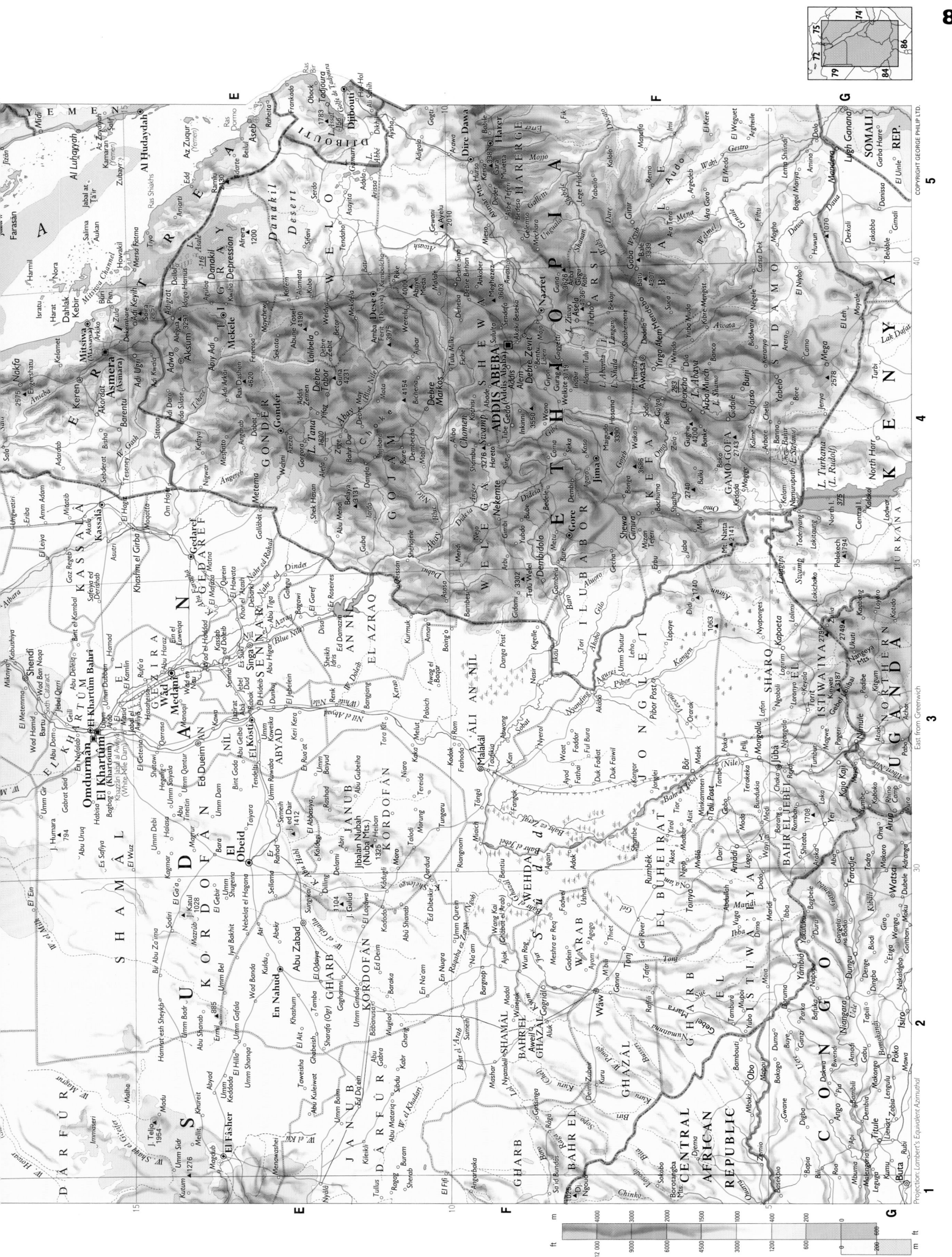

Projection: Lambert's Equivalent Azimuthal

East from Greenwich

50  0   50  100 150 200 250 300 km
50  0   50  100 150 200 miles

ATLANTIC

OCEAN

Projection : Lambert's Equivalent Azimuthal

West from Greenw

GULF

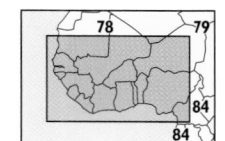

N. E.
NIGERIA
on same scale
as general map

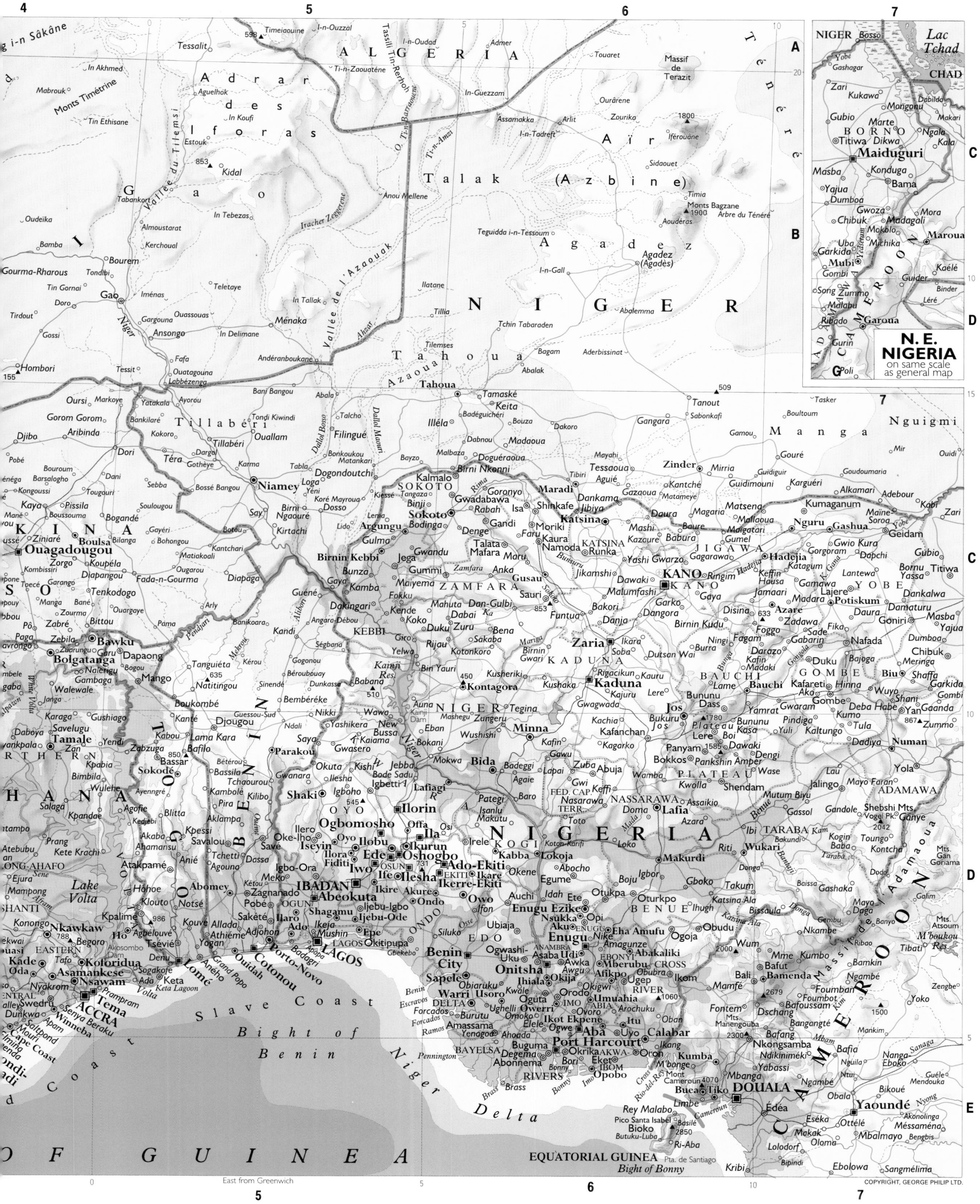

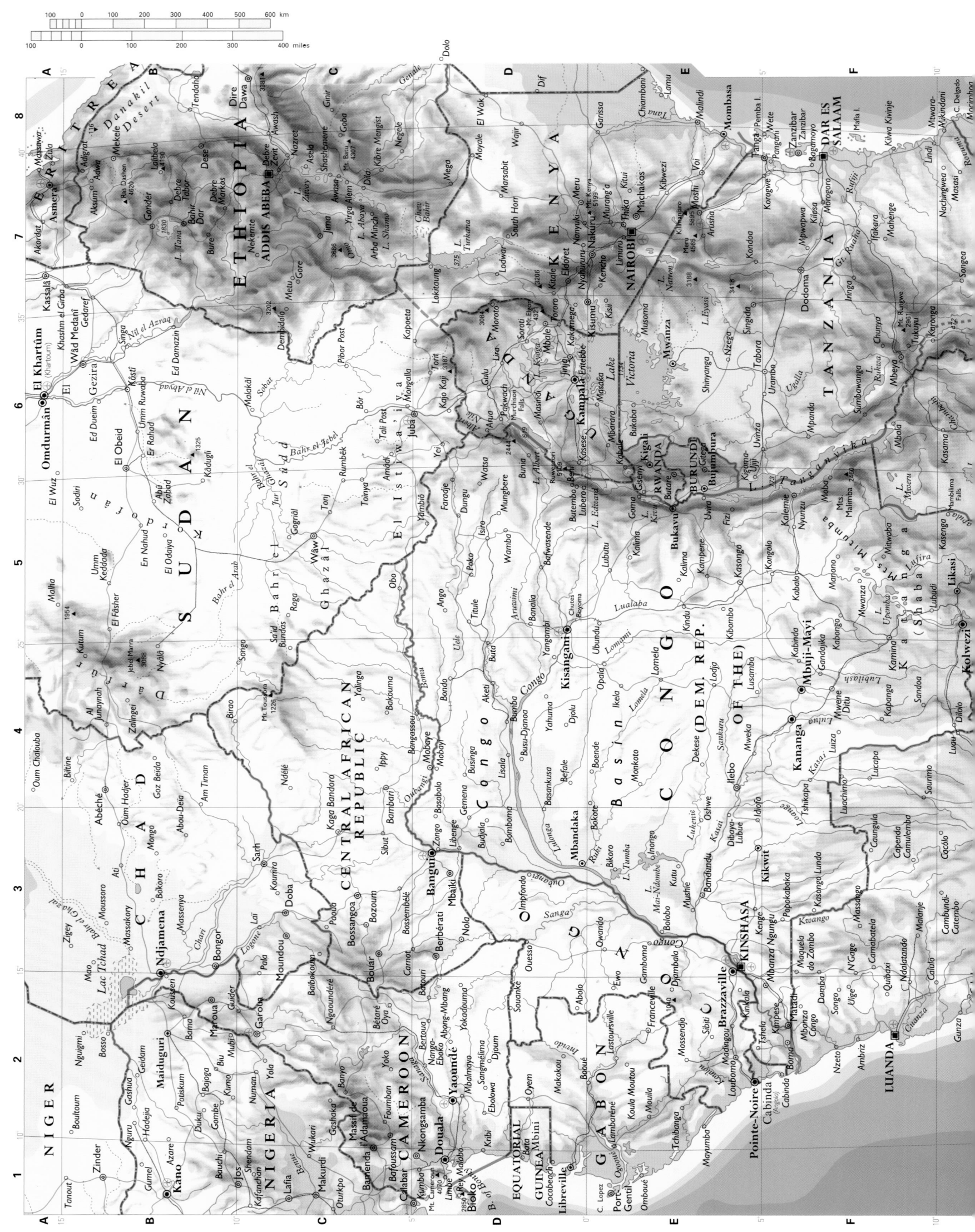

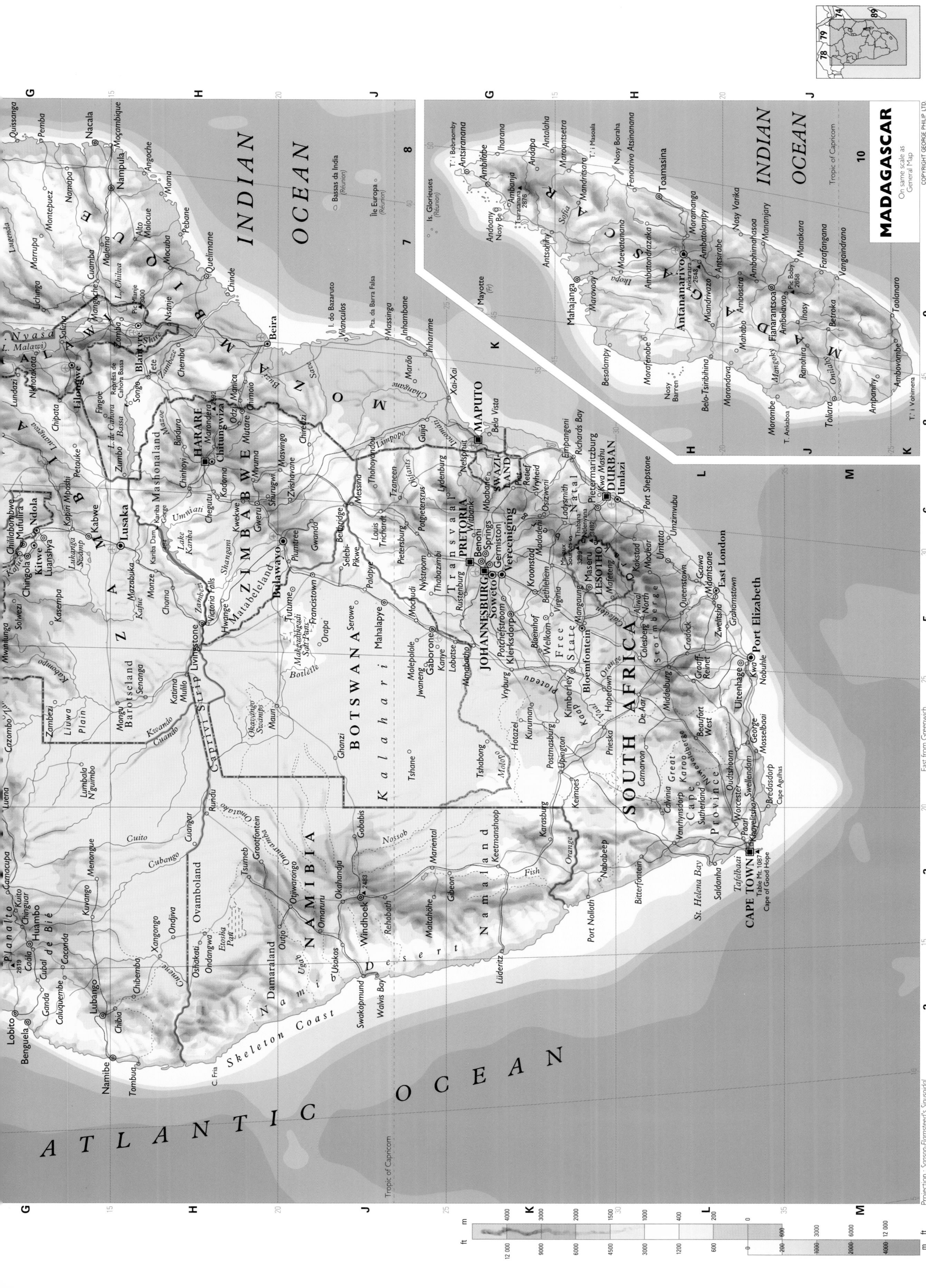

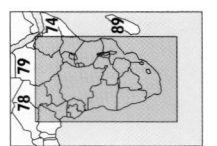

**MADAGASCAR**
On same scale as
General Map

COPYRIGHT GEORGE PHILIP LTD.

INDIAN OCEAN

INDIAN OCEAN

ATLANTIC OCEAN

Tropic of Capricorn

East from Greenwich

Projection Sanson-Flamsteed's Sinusoidal

*Madagascar inset labels:*
Bobraomby, Antsiranana, Iharana, Antalaha, T.¹ Masoala, Nosy Boraha, Ambilobe, Andapa, Maroantsetra, Nosy Bé, Ambanja, Tsaratanana 2876, Andoany, Nosy Varika, Andoany, Maromanga, Fenoarivo Atsinanana, Toamasina, Sofia, Mandritsara, Antsohihy, Miarinarivo, Maevatanana, Moramanga, Antananarivo, Ankarana, Ambatondrazaka, Ambatolampy, Mahajanga, Marovoay, Ihosy, Pic Boby 2658, Itaosy, Miandrivazo, Ambositra, Antsirabe, Fianarantsoa, Ambalavao, Manakara, Belo-Tsiribihina, Besalampy, Ambohimahasoa, Morafenobe, Nosy Barren, Morondava, Mahabo, Manja, Ranohira, Betroka, Farafangana, Ampanihy, Manambondro, Morombe, Mangoky, Onilahy, Vangaindrano, Toliara, Ankaboa, Ambovombe, T.¹ Vohimena, Taolanaro

*Main map labels (partial):*
Quissanga, Pemba, Nacala, Nampula, Moçambique, Montepuez, Napapa, Angoche, Mocuba, Moma, Lichinga, Alto Molocue, Marrupa, Pebane, Lugenda, Meluli, Cuamba, Mangoche, L. Chilwa, Pta. Maluane, Nsanje, Chinde, Quelimane, L. Nyasa (L. Malawi), Nkhotakota, Lilongwe, Zomba, Blantyre, Shire, Chembe, Mocuba, Tete, Represa de Cahora Bassa, Songo, Chemba, Beira, Zambezi, Vanduzi, I. do Bazaruto, Vilanculos, Pta. da Barra Falsa, I.le Europa (Réunion), Bassas da India (Réunion), Harare, Marondera, Chitungwiza, Mutare, Chimoio, Inhaminga, Sena, Marão, Chiredzi, Inhambane, Maxixe, Massinga, Chimanimani, Ruenya, Masvingo, Chivhu, Shurugwi, Inhambane, Gujā, Inhassoro, Maputo, Bela Vista, SWAZILAND, Mbabane, Piet Retief, Vryheid, Empangeni, Richards Bay, Durban, Umlazi, Port Shepstone, Pietermaritzburg, Ladysmith, Natal, Kwa Mashu, Harrismith, Umzimkulu, Kokstad, Umtata, Umtata, Port St Johns, East London, Queenstown, King William's Town, Grahamstown, Port Elizabeth, Uitenhage, Kwa Nobuhle, George, Mosselbaai, Oudtshoorn, Swellendam, Cape Agulhas, Cape Town, Table Mt 1087, Cape of Good Hope, Paarl, Worcester, Saldanha, St. Helena Bay, Bitterfontein, Port Nolloth, Vanrhynsdorp, Calvinia, Sutherland, Beaufort West, Graaff-Reinet, Middelburg, Cradock, Colesberg, De Aar, Carnarvon, Prieska, Kimberley, Bloemfontein, Welkom, Virginia, Bethlehem, Kroonstad, Vereeniging, Pretoria, Johannesburg, Soweto, Germiston, Benoni, Springs, Potchefstroom, Klerksdorp, Maseru, LESOTHO, Mafeteng, Vryburg, Kuruman, Postmasburg, Upington, Keimoes, Kenhardt, Karasburg, Lüderitz, Orange, Keetmanshoop, Mariental, Gibeon, Maltahöhe, Rehoboth, Windhoek, 2483, Okahandja, Gobabis, Nossob, Ghanzi, Tshane, Tshabong, Kalahari, BOTSWANA, Gaborone, Lobatse, Kanye, Jwaneng, Molepolole, Mahalapye, Serowe, Orapa, Mochudi, Selebi-Pikwe, Palapye, Francistown, Maun, Okavango Swamps, Rundu, Katima Mulilo, Caprivi Strip, Livingstone, Victoria Falls, Bulawayo, Matabeleland, ZIMBABWE, Plumtree, Gweru, Kwekwe, Kadoma, Chinhoyi, Bindura, Hwange, Gwanda, Beitbridge, Louis Trichardt, Messina, Pietersburg, Tzaneen, Thabazimbi, Nylstroom, Potgietersrus, Rustenburg, Mmabatho, ZAMBIA, Lusaka, Kabwe, Kafue, Kabwe, Kitwe, Ndola, Chingola, Mufulira, Luanshya, Chililabombwe, Kafue, Solwezi, Kasempa, Mwinilunga, Mongu, Barotseland, Liuwa Plain, Senanga, Zambezi, Lumbala N'guimbo, Luena, Luau, Cazombo, Kabompo, Lubango, Huambo, Planalto de Bié, Menongue, Cuito, Cubango, Cuangar, Omatako, Tsumeb, Grootfontein, Otavi, Otjiwarongo, Omaruru, Swakopmund, Walvis Bay, Skeleton Coast, Namib Desert, Namaqualand, Namibia, Damaraland, Ovamboland, Kunene, Namibe, Tombua, Benguela, Lobito, Ganda, Catumbela, Caconda, Cubal, Chibia, Caluquembe, Cangamba, Kuito, Chingar, C. Fria

ft m / 12 000 / 4000 / 9000 / 3000 / 6000 / 2000 / 4500 / 1500 / 3000 / 1000 / 1200 / 400 / 600 / 200 / 0 / 200 / 600 / 2000 / 6000 / 4000 / 12 000

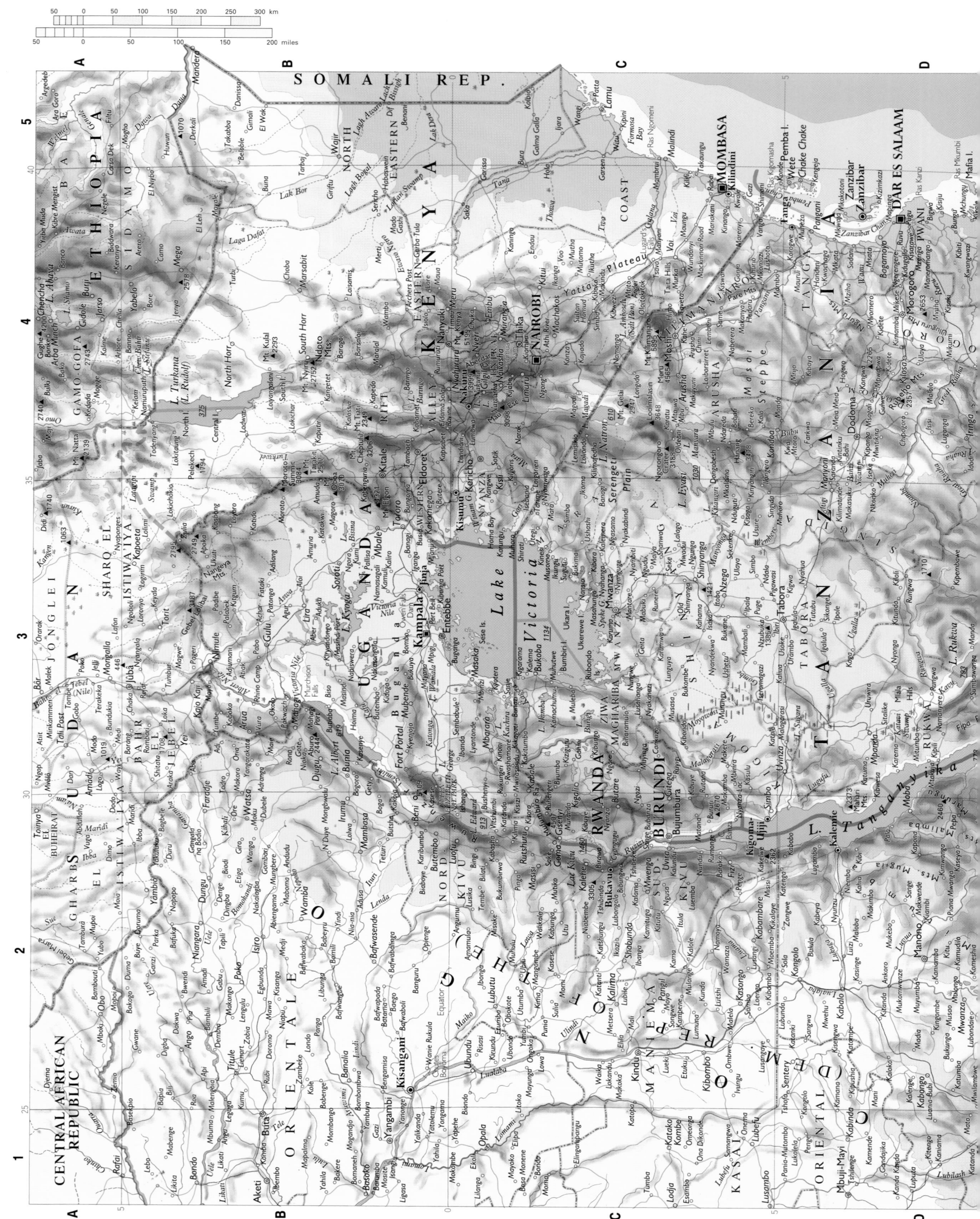

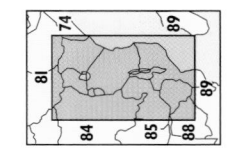

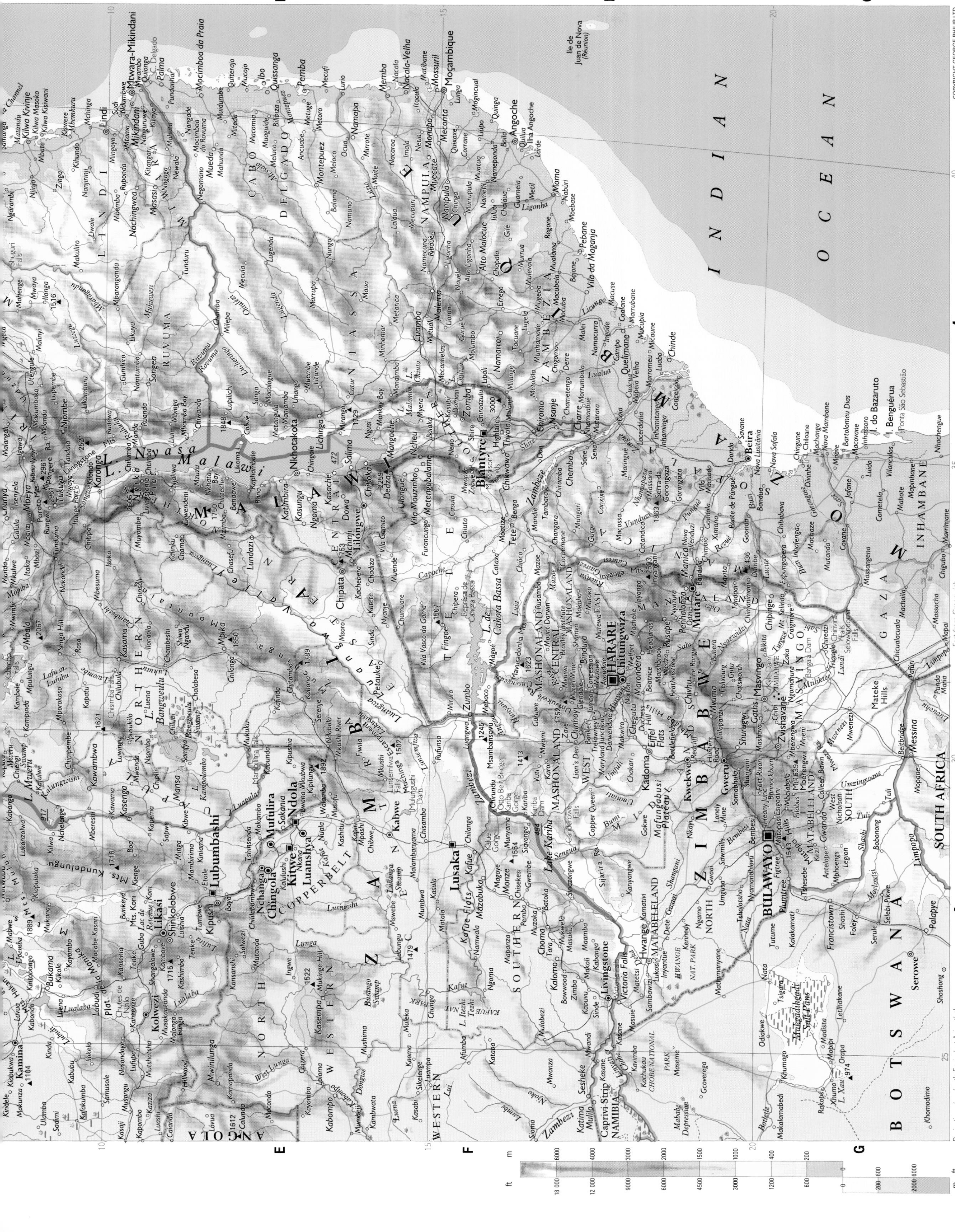

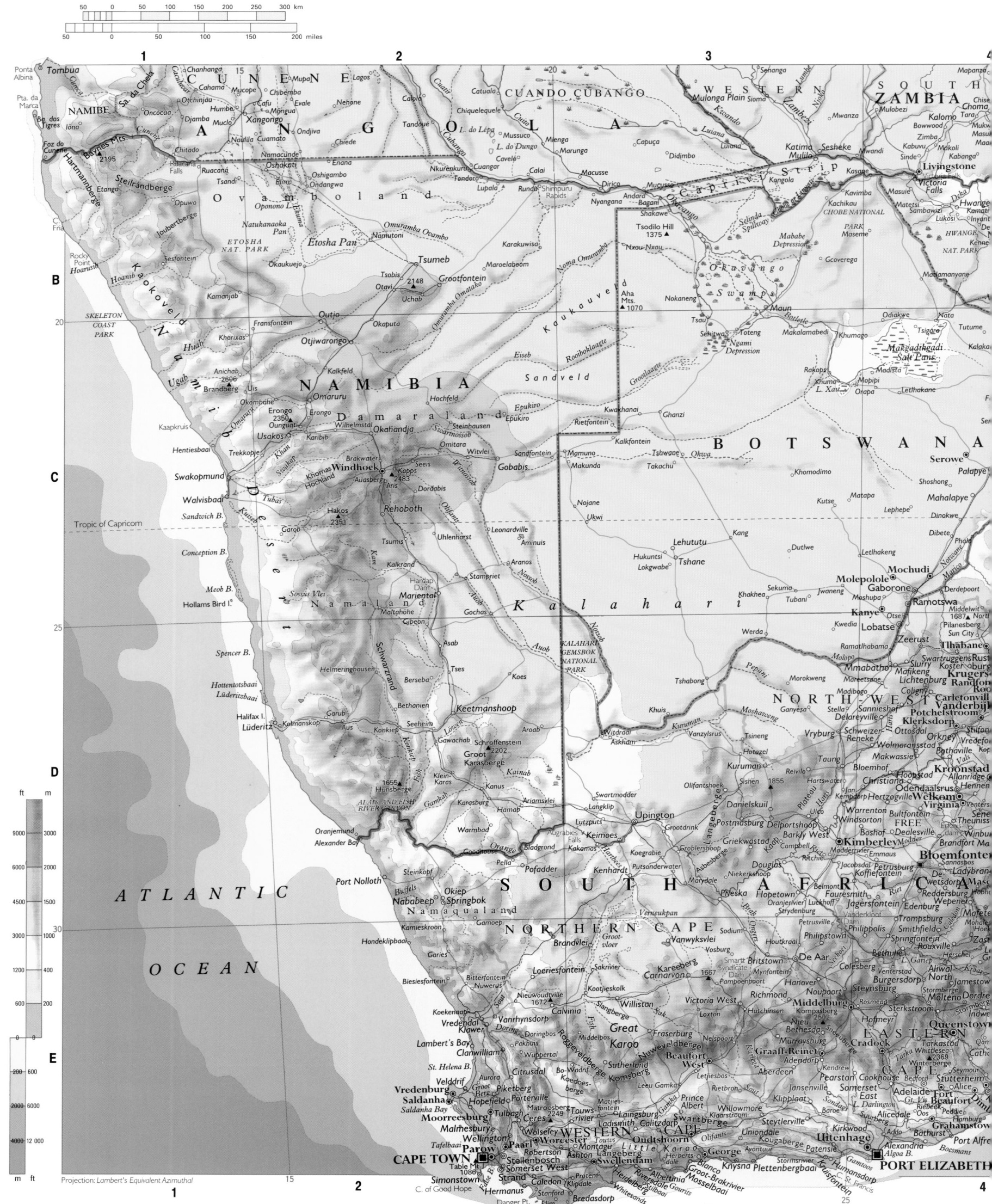

50  0  50  100  150  200  250  300 km
50  0  50  100  150  200 miles

**1**     **2**     **3**

Ponta
Albina
Tombua
Pta. da
Marca

**NAMIBE**
Bca. das
Tigres
Iona
Oncocua
Chananga
Cahama
Chibemba
Evale
Mupa N E
Lagos
Catula
Chiquelequele
**CUANDO CUBANGO**
Senanga
WESTERN
Mulonga Plain Sioma
Choma
Mapanza
Chitado
Ba. dos
Tigres
2195
Baynes Mts.
Steilrandberge
Hartmannberge
C. Fria
Ruacana
Falls
Namacunde
Oshakati
Enana
Tandoo
L. do Lépi
Cuito
Cubango
Mussoco
Caiundo
Dirico
Macusse
Luiana
Luiana
Kangola
Katima
Mulilo
Sesheke
Mwandi
Sinde
Mulobezi
Kalomo
**SOUTH**
**ZAMBIA**
Mazanza
Rocky
Point
Hoarusib
Kaokoveld
Otchinjau
Djamba
Muclo
Xangongo
Humbe
Mongua
Ondjiva
Nehone
Calola
Nkurenkuru
Cuangar
Calai
Shimpuru
Rapids
Nyangana
Andara
Bagani
Mucusso
Shakawe
Tsodilo Hill
1375
Okavango
Spillway
Selinda
Spillway
Mababe
Depression
CHOBE NATIONAL
PARK
Maseme
Kasane
Kazungula
Kachikau
Kavimba
Masuie
Matetsi
Matetsi
Sambwizi
Lukosi
HWANGE
NAT. PARK
Kenne
Livingstone
Victoria
Falls
Zimba
Kachuma
Wankie
Hwange

Ovamboland
Tsandi
Opuwo
Jouberberge
Oponona L.
Okahao
Ondangwa
Oshigambo
Lupala
Rundu
Caprivi Strip
Mwanza
Cgovereça
Maun
Nata
Tsigre
Tutume
Sesfontein
ETOSHA
NAT. PARK
Etosha Pan
Namutoni
Okaukuejo
Karakuwisa
Noma Omuramba
Nxau-Nxau
Aha Mts.
1070
Nokaneng
Okavango
Swamps
Bokote
Sehitwa
Toteng
Makalamabedi
Khumaga
Odiakwe

Kamanjab
Huab
Khorixas
Fransfontein
Outjo
Okaputa
Tsumeb
Tsobis
2148
Grootfontein
Otavi
Uchab
Omuramba Omatako
Koukauveld
Tsau
Ngami
Depression
L. Xau
Orapa
Letlhakane
Mopipi
Rakops
Madiba
Mokgadikgadi
Salt Pans
Kalala

20

**B**

SKELETON
COAST
PARK
Ugab
Anichab
2606
Brandberg
Uis
Omaruru
Erongo
2350
Ounguati
Karibib
**NAMIBIA**
Hochfeld
Eiseb
Sandveld
Rooiboklaagte
Groolaagte
Ghanzi
Rietfontein
**BOTSWANA**
Serowe
Palapye
Shoshong
Mahalapye
Kutse
Matapa
Lephepe
Dinokwe
Dibete
Phola

**C**

Kaapkruis
Hentiesbaai
Trekkopje
Usakos
Steinhausen
Omitara
Witvlei
Sandfontein
Mamuno
Makunda
Takachu
Okwa
Khomodimo
Damaraland
Wilhelmstal
Okahandja
Brakwater
Khomas
Hochland
Windhoek
Kapps
Seeis
Swarmossob
Epukiro
Epukiro
Kwakhanai
Kalkfontein
Tshwane
Mochudi
Molepolole
Gaborone
Ramotswa
Derdepoort
Swakopmund
Khan
Kapps
Aris
2483
Auasberge
Dordabis
Gobabis
Nojane
Ukwi
Kang
Khakhea
Tubani
Jwaneng
Moshupa
Kanye
Otse
Lobatse
Middelwit
1687
Pilanesberg
Sun City
Zeerust
Tlhabane
Walvisbaai
Rehoboth
Uhlenhorst
Leonardville
Aminuis
Aranos
Lehututu
Lokgwabe
Tshane
Hukuntsi
Letlhakeng
Sekuma
Kuke
Dutlwe
Werda
Molopo
Ramatlhabama
Mmabatho
Mafikeng
Lichtenburg
Coligny
Klerksdorp
Krugersdorp
Randfontein
Carletonville
Vanderbijl

Tropic of Capricorn
Sandwich B.
Hakos
2351
Tsumis
Tubas
Kuiseb
Garob
Rehoboth
Olifants
Dordabis
NORTH-WEST
Sannieshof
Delareyville
Stella
Schweizer-
Reneke
Ottosdal
Wolmaransstad
Orkney
Bothaville
Vredefort

Conception B.
Namaland
Hardap
Dam
Mariental
Maltahöhe
Gibeon
Gochas
Kalahari
Khuis
Tshabong
Morokweng
Madibogo
Vryburg
Taung
Hotazel
Kuruman
Reivilo
Makwassie
Bloemhof
Christiana
Hoopstad
Kroonstad
Allanridge
Hennen
Virginia
Welkom
Odendaalsrus

25

**D**

Spencer B.
Meob B.
Hollams Bird I.
Helmeringhausen
Schwarzrand
Tses
Bersaba
Asab
Koes
Auob
KALAHARI
GEMSBOK
NATIONAL
PARK
Nosob
Werda
Kalahari
Ganyeso
Tsineng
Vanzylsrus
Askham
Witdraai
Kuruman
Moshaweng
Kuruman
Olifantshoek
Sishen
1855
Postmasburg
Daniëlskuil
Delportshoop
Warrenton
Windsorton
Bultfontein
FREE
Theunissen
Brandfort
Winbu
Sannaspos

Halifax I.
Lüderitz
Kolmanskop
Aus
Garub
Konkiep
Bethanien
Seeheim
Gawachab
Schroffenstein
2202
Groot
Karasberge
Kainab
Aroab
Löwen
Upington
Keimoes
Kakamas
Kenhardt
Augrabies
Falls
Lutzputs
Groblershoop
Griekwastad
Campbell
Ritchie
Douglas
Modder
**Kimberley**
De-Aar
Belmont
Hopetown
Orange
Dealesville
Brandfort
**Bloemfontein**
Ladybrand

**E**

1665
Hunsberge
Klein
Karas
Kanus
Gumbab
Karasburg
Hamab
Ariamsvlei
Swartmodder
Langklip
Keimoes
Koegrabie
Putsonderwater
Prieska
Marydale
Niekerkshoop
Modderrivier
Koffiefontein
Jacobsdal
Petrusburg
Fauresmith
Jagersfontein
Edenburg
Wepener

ALAIN AND FISH
RIVER CANYON
Oranjemund
Alexander Bay
Warmbad
Goodhouse
Bladgrond
Pella
Pofadder
Kenhardt
Pella
**SOUTH**
Kenhardt
Vanwyksvlei
Brak
Strydenburg
Trompsburg
Smithfield
Springfontein
Rouxville
Zast

30

Port Nolloth
Steinkopf
Buffels
Nababeep
Okiep
Springbok
Namaqualand
Gamoep
Kamieskroon
NORTHERN CAPE
Brandvlei
Grootvloer
Verneukpan
Sodium
Houtkraal
Victoria West
Hanover
Noupoort
Colesberg
Venterstad
Steynsburg
Aliwal
North
Herschel
Dordre
**AFRICA**

ATLANTIC
OCEAN
Hondeklipbaai
Garies
Bitterfontein
Nuwerus
Nieuwoudtville
1672
Loeriesfontein
Sakrivier
Calvinia
Williston
Carnarvon
1667
Kareeberg
Pampoenpoort
Richmond
De Aar
Philipstown
Burgersdorp
Molteno
Stormberg
Sterkstroom
Queenstown

Koekenaap
Vredendal
Klawer
Vanrhynsdorp
Doringbos
Middelpos
Slangberge
Fraserburg
Nelspoort
Murraysburg
Aberdeen
Nieu
Bethesda
2369
Tarkastad
Cradock
Kendrew
Adendorp
Graaff-Reinet
Pearston
Cookhouse
Bedford
Hamburg

Lambert's Bay
Clanwilliam
Doring
Citrusdal
Great
Karoo
Rodgeveldberge
Komsberge
Nuweveldberge
Sutherland
Leeu Gamka
Beaufort
West
Willowmore
Somerset
East
Alicedale
**EASTERN**
Peddie

St. Helena B.
Velddrif
Aurora
Piketberg
Porterville
Wupperthal
Matjiesfontein
Laingsburg
Prince
Albert
Klipplaat
Baroe
Kougaberge
Uniondale
Kirkwood
Grahamstown
Bathurst

**Vredenburg**
**Saldanha**
Saldanha Bay
Hopefield
**Moorreesburg**
Malmesbury
Wellington
Tulbagh
Ceres
2249
Wolseley
Worcester
Tauws
Little
Karoo
Ladismith
Calitzdorp
Oudtshoorn
Swartberge
Langeberge
George
Knysna
Plettenbergbaai
Tsitsikamma
**Uitenhage**
Alexandria
Algoa B.
**PORT ELIZABETH**

**CAPE TOWN**
Parow
Stellenbosch
Somerset West
Strand
Table Mt.
1086
Paarl
Robertson
Ashton
Montagu
Swellendam
Heidelberg
Riversdale
Gourits
Mosselbaai
Groot-Brakrivier
Blanco
Albertinia
Boesmans
**CAPE**

Simonstown
C. of Good Hope
Hermanus
Caledon
Stanford
Klipdale
Bredasdorp
Protem
Riviersonderend
Heidelberg
Whitesands
WESTERN
Danger Pt.
Quoin Pt.
C. Agulhas

20

Projection: Lambert's Equivalent Azimuthal

ft  m
9000  3000
6000  2000
4500  1500
3000  1000
1200  400
600  200
0  0
200  600
2000  6000
4000  12 000
m  ft

**1**     **2**     **3**

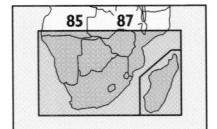

MADAGASCAR

On same scale as General Map

COPYRIGHT GEORGE PHILIP LTD.

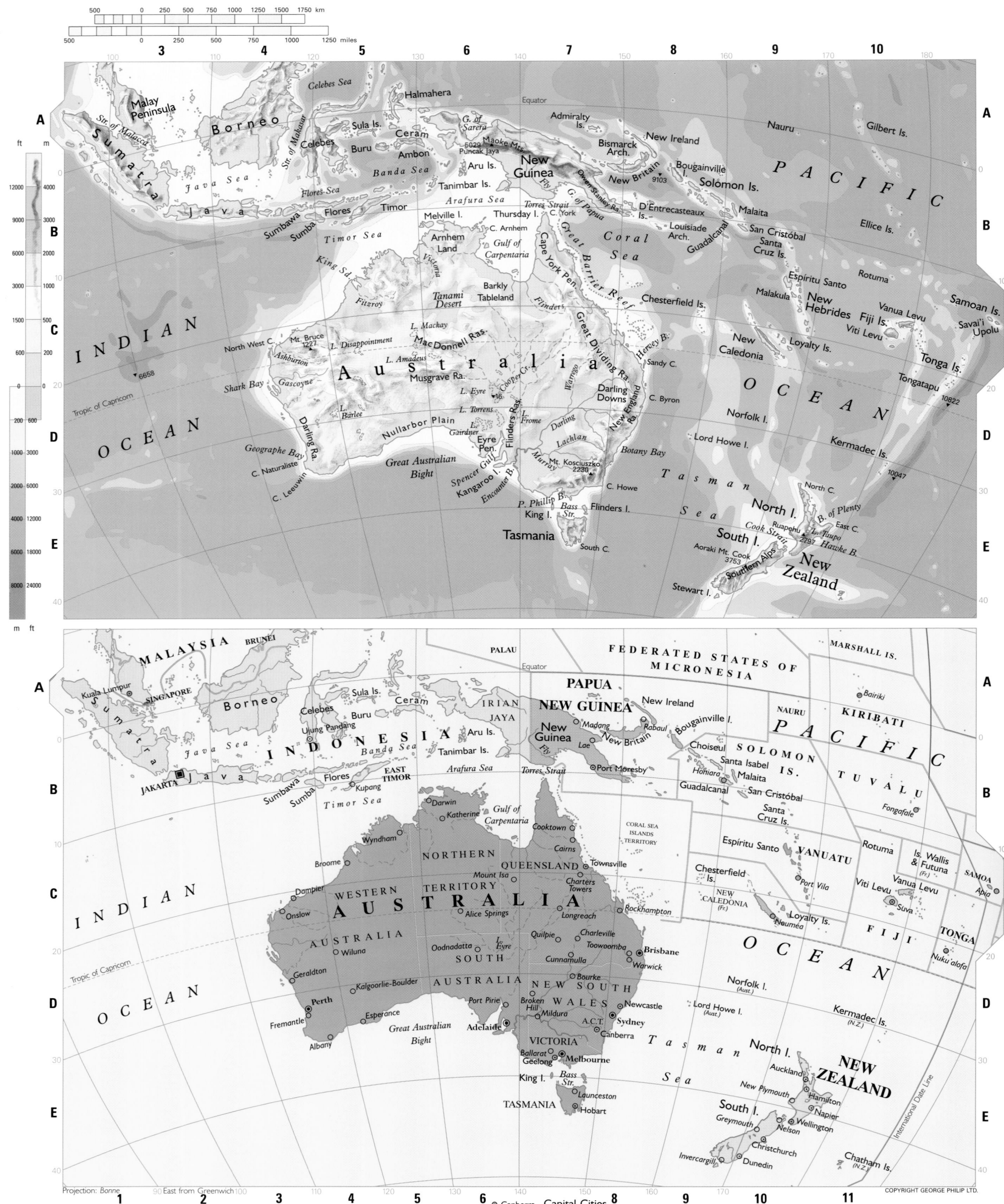

Projection: Bonne

90 East from Greenwich 100

⊙ Canberra  Capital Cities

COPYRIGHT GEORGE PHILIP LTD.

96
96 96 96
1

50 0 50 100 150 200 km
50 0 50 100 150 miles

PACIFIC

OCEAN

C. Reinga
C. Maria
van Diemen
North C.
Houhora Heads
Rangaunu B.
Doubtless B.
Mangonui
Whangaroa Harb.
Ahipara B.
Kaitaia
Tauroa Pt.
Okaihau
C. Brett
Raweae
Opua
B. of Islands
Hokianga Harbour
Kaikohe
Hikurangi
Donnelly's Crossing
Whangarei
Whangarei Harb.
Dargaville
Waipu
Bream Hd.
Bream B.
Little
Barrier I.
Great Barrier I.
Warkworth
C. Rodney
Cuvier I.
Kaipara Harbour
C. Colville
Helensville
Hauraki
Gulf
Coromandel
Takapuna
Devonport
Whitianga
Manukau
**AUCKLAND**
Papakura
Thames
Pukekohe
Waiuku
Mercer
Waihi
Mayor I.
Waikato
Huntly
Paeroa
Te Aroha
Tauranga Harb.
Morrinsville
Mount
Maunganui
Bay of Plenty
White I.
C. Runaway
**Hamilton**
Cambridge
Te Awamutu
Whakatane
Kawerau
East C.
Raglan
Putaruru
Rotorua
Taneatua
Opotiki
Raukumara Ra.
Hikurangi
Kawhia Harbour
Otorohanga
Tokoroa
L. Tarawera
Murupara
1753
Waipiro
North
Island
Te Kuiti
Kinleith
Motu
Mokau
Mokau
Wairakei
Ongarue
L. Taupo
Rangitaiki
Kaimanawa Mts.
Tarawera
Tolaga Bay
North Taranaki
Bight
Waitara
Turangi
Taumarunui
L. Waikaremoana
Ormond
**Gisborne**
**New Plymouth**
Whangamomona
Poverty Bay
Inglewood
Mt. Taranaki
(Mt. Egmont)
Ruapehu 2797
Nuhaka
Waikokopu
C. Egmont
2518
Stratford
Ohakune
Waiouru
Wairoa
Mahia Pen.
Opunake
Eltham
Raetihi
Bay
Kapuni
**Hawera**
Taihape
Ruahine
Ra.
View
Hawke Bay
Waverley
Mangaweka
Waioru
**Napier**
South Taranaki
Bight
Pateа
Morton
Hunterville
**Hastings**
**Wanganui**
Halcombe
Feilding
Waipawa
Bulls
**Palmerston**
Danneverke
Waipukurau
**North**
Foxton
Woodville
Shannon
Pahiatua
C. Turnagain
Levin
Otaki
Eketahuna

T A S M A N

S E A

C. Farewell
Golden
B.
D'Urville I.
Paraparaumu
Collingwood
Takaka
Tasman
B.
Kapiti I.
Masterton
Tasman
Mts.
Pelorus Sd.
Upper Hutt
Carterton
Karamea
Motueka
Havelock
Picton
Featherston
Greytown
Karamea
Bight
Nelson
Richmond
Wairarapa
Martinborough
Seddonville
Tadmor
Wakefield
Cook
Str.
Petone
Lower Hutt
Granity
Maruia Ra.
Wairau
**WELLINGTON**
Westport
Lyell
Murchison
Blenheim
Eastbourne
Seddon
Rotoroa
2885 Tapuaenuku
Ward
Reefton
Lewis Pass
2338
Spenser
Mts.
Kaikoura Ra.
Clarence
Blackball
Grey
Hanmer
Springs
Kaikoura
Runanga
Stillwater
L. Brunner
Jacksons
Culverden
Greymouth
Kumara
Hurunui
Waiau
Hokitika
Waikari
Waipara
Ross
Arthur's
Pass
Amberley
Rangiora
Oxford
Pegasus Bay
Coleridge
Springfield
South
Island
Abut Hd.
Whitecliffs
Waimakariri
New Brighton
Methven
Rakaia
Riccarton
**Christchurch**
Aoraki Mt. Cook
3753
Southern Alps
Rakaia
Southbridge
Lyttelton
Mount
Cook
Tekapo
Rangitata
Canterbury
Plains
L. Ellesmere
Little River
Banks Pen.
Jackson B.
Okuru
Haast
L.
Plains
Akaroa
Mt.
Aspiring
3027
Fairlie
Canterbury Bight
Westland Bight
L. Pukaki
Ohau
Temuka
Milford Sd.
Mt.
Earnslaw
2818
Wanaka L.
L.
Hawea
**Timaru**
St. Andrews
Sutherland Falls
Milford
Sound
Wanaka
Waitaki
Waimate
Bligh Sound
George Sound
Arrowtown
Cromwell
Kurow
Ngapara
Dunstan
Mts.
Tokarahi
Queenstown
Clyde
Kakanui
Mts.
**Oamaru**
Secretary I.
Te Anau
Kingston
Alexandra
Naseby
Maheno
Doubtful Sd.
L.
Wakatipu
Garvie
Mts.
Roxburgh
Hampden
Dunback
L.
Manapouri
Clutha
Waikouaiti
Palmerston
Resolution I.
Mossburn
Otago
Lawrence
Mosgiel
Port Chalmers
Dusky Sd.
Lumsden
Manapouri
Edievale
Kelso
Otago Harbour
Breaksea Sd.
Eyre
Mts.
Winton
Clinton
Saunders C.
Southland
Ohai
Nightcaps
Gore
Fairfield
**Dunedin**
Chatham
Inlet
Tuatapere
Hedgehope
Mataura
Balclutha
Clifden
Milton
Te Waewae B.
Orepuki
Riverton
Wyndham
Kaitangata
Nugget Pt.
Preservation
Inlet
**Invercargill**
Tokanui
Owaka
Foveaux Str.
Bluff
South Invercargill
Ruapuke I.
Halfmoon Bay
Stewart I.
Southwest C.
Port Pegasus

Projection : Conical with two standard parallels
East from Greenwich

**SAMOA ISLANDS**
1:10 700 000

SAMOA
AMERICAN
SAMOA
Savai'i
Apia
Upolu
Pago Pago
Tutuila
West from
Greenwich

Futuna
Wallis & Futuna (Fr.)
Niuafo'ou
(Tonga)
Thikombia
Labasa
Yasawa Group
Vanua Levu
Taveuni
Vanua Balavu
F I J I
Lautoka
Koro
Levuka
Ovalau
Nandi
1323
Viti Levu
Gau
Lau
Group
TONGA
(Friendly Is.)
Suva
Koro Sea
Lakeba
Vava'u
Moala
Kandavu
East from Greenwich
Vatoa
Tofua
Tongatapu
Nuku'alofa

**FIJI AND TONGA**
**ISLANDS**
1:10 700 000

50 0 50 100 150 200 km
50 0 50 100 150 miles

West from Greenwich

COPYRIGHT GEORGE PHILIP LTD.

ft m
9000 3000
6000 2000
3000 1000
1200 400
600 200
0
200 600
2000 6000
4000 12 000
6000 18 000
m ft

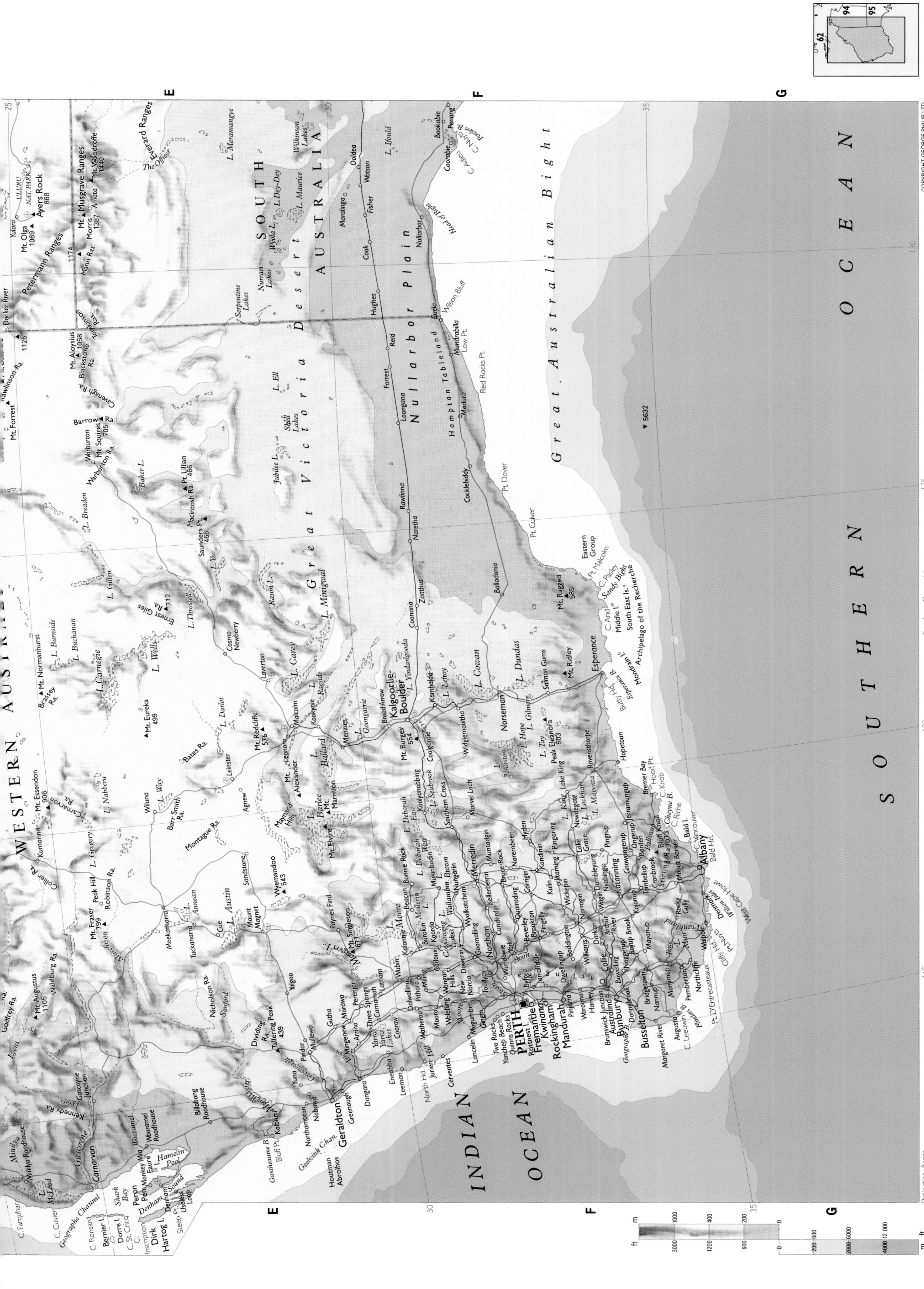

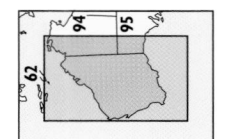

E F G

SOUTH AUSTRALIA

WESTERN AUSTRALIA

Great Victoria Desert

Nullarbor Plain

Hampton Tableland

Great Australian Bight

SOUTHERN OCEAN

INDIAN OCEAN

OCEAN

ULURU NAT. PARK
Ayers Rock 868
Mt. Olga 1069
Petermann Ranges
Musgrave Ranges
Mt. Woodroffe 1440
Mt. Morris 1387
Mann Ras.
Amata
L. Meramangye
L. Day-Dey
Wynda L.
L. Maurice
Wilkinson Lakes
Bookabie
Penong
C. Nuyts
Fowlers B.
Coombe
C. Adieu
Ooldea
Watson
Fisher
Cook
Maralinga
Hughes
Reid
Forrest
Loongana
Nurrari Lakes
Serpentine Lakes
L. Ifould
Wilson Bluff
Eucla
Mundrabilla
Low Pt.
Madura
Red Rocks Pt.
Cocklebiddy
Pt. Dover
Rawlinna
Naretha
Zanthus
Cundeelee
Coonana
Kitchener
Balladonia
Pt. Malcolm
Pt. Culver
Eastern Group
Middle I.
South East Is.
Archipelago of the Recherche
Mt. Ragged 585
C. Arid
C. Pasley
Sandy Bight
Esperance
Mondrain I.
Cape Le Grand
Hopetoun
Ravensthorpe
Bremer Bay
Hood Pt.
C. Knob
Bluff Knoll
C. Riche
C. Vancouver
Albany
Bald Hd.
Denmark
West Cape Howe
Wilson Inlet
Cliff Hd.
Pt. Nuyts
Pt. D'Entrecasteaux
C. Leeuwin
C. Naturaliste
Busselton
Bunbury
Australind
Mandurah
Rockingham
Kwinana
Fremantle
PERTH
Rottnest I.
Two Rocks
Yanchep Beach
Quinns Rocks
Lancelin
North Hd.
Jurien Hd.
Cervantes
Leeman
Dongara
Greenough
Geraldton
Northampton
Bluff Pt.
Kalbarri
Geelvink Chan.
Houtman Abrolhos
Hamelin Pool
Useless Loop
Denham
Steep Pt.
Dirk Hartog I.
Inscription Pt.
Peron Pen.
Monkey Mia
Faure I.
Shark Bay
Carnarvon
Point Cloates
Minilya Roadhouse
Bernier I.
Dorre I.
C. St. Cricq
C. Ronsard
C. Cuvier
C. Farquhar
Mardie
Gascoyne River
Mt. Augustus 1105
Godfrey Ra.
Kennedy Ra.
Collier Ra.
Robinson Ra.
Peak Hill
Mt. Fraser 799
Meekatharra
Cue
Mount Magnet
Sandstone
Yalgoo
Mullewa
Morawa
Perenjori
Mingenew
Three Springs
Carnamah
Coorow
Moora
New Norcia
Gingin
Mt. Essendon 906
Mt. Carnarvon Ra.
L. Carnegie
L. Breaden
L. Wells
L. Nabberu
Wiluna
L. Way
L. Violet
Leinster
Agnew
Bates Ra.
Montague Ra.
Mt. Eureka 499
L. Darlot
L. Miranda
Leonora
Laverton
L. Carey
L. Throssell
Cosmo Newbery
Rason L.
Raeside
Menzies
Kookynie
Malcolm
Broad Arrow
Kalgoorlie-Boulder
Coolgardie
Kambalda
Widgiemooltha
Norseman
Salmon Gums
Grass Patch
Mt. Burges 554
Mt. Redcliffe 576
Mt. Leonora
Bonnie Rock
Mukinbudin
Westonia
Southern Cross
Koolyanobbing
Marvel Loch
Hyden
Kondinin
Lake Grace
Newdegate
Lake King
L. Lefroy
L. Cowan
L. Dundas
L. Tay
L. Johnston
Peak Eleanora 503
Mt. Ridley
Mt. Hope
Mt. Gilmore
Ongerup
Gnowangerup
Borden
Jerramungup
Cranbrook
Mt. Barker
Kojonup
Tambellup
Katanning
Woodanilling
Wagin
Dumbleyung
Kukerin
Lake Dumbleyung
Nyabing
Pingrup
Darkan
Collie
Donnybrook
Boyup Brook
Bridgetown
Nannup
Manjimup
Pemberton
Northcliffe
Augusta
Margaret River
Wonnerup
Capel
Brunswick Junction
Harvey
Pinjarra
Dwellingup
Waroona
Boddington
Williams
Narrogin
Wickepin
Corrigin
Kulin
Kondinin
Wagin
Quairading
Brookton
Beverley
Pingelly
Cuballing
Wandering
Wongan Hills
Goomalling
Northam
Toodyay
York
Meckering
Cunderdin
Kellerberrin
Merredin
Tammin
Bruce Rock
Quairading
Corrigin
Narembeen
Muntadgin
Bullaring
Wyalkatchem
Dowerin
Koorda
Wialki
Beacon
L. Brown
Mollerin
Burakin
Dalwallinu
Kalannie
Wubin
Pithara
Latham
Coorow
Carnamah
L. Moore
Maynard Hills
Mt. Elvire
Yalgoo
Paynes Find
Dividing Peak
Tallering Peak 439
Nicholson Ra.
Sanford
Tuckanarra
Annean
L. Austin
Mount Farmer
Barr Smith Ra.
Ernest Giles Ra.
L. Gregory
Kumarina
L. Carey
Warburton
Barrow Ra.
Mt. Squires 705
Warburton Ra.
Baker L.
Pt. Lillian 466
Macintosh Ra.
Saunders Pt. 466
L. Yeo
Jubilee L.
Shell Lakes
L. Ell
Mt. Forrest
Mt. Blackstone 1058
Mt. Aloysius 1126
Cavenagh Ra.
Rawlinson Ra.
Blackstone Ra.
Docker River
The Officer
L. Minigwal
L. Yindarlgooda
Gunong
Gongarrie
Kookynie
Niagara
Gwalia
L. Ballard
Mt. Alexander
Mt. Burtee
Marmion
Wheneandoo 543
Mt. Deborah
L. Deborah East
L. Seabrook
Bullfinch
Koorda
Bencubbin
Mt. Jackson
Marmion

Projection: Bonne

East from Greenwich

COPYRIGHT GEORGE PHILIP LTD.

1 2 3 4 5

ft m
12 000 4000
6000 2000
3000 1200
1500 600
600 200
200 0
0
m ft

RUSSIA

MOSKVA • Yekaterinburg • Tomsk • Okhotsk • Sea of Okhotsk • Komandorskiye Ostrova (Russia) • Near Is. (U.S.A.) • Ber Se • Andrean

Volga • Astana (Aqmola) • Novosibirsk • Irkutsk • Chita • Blagoveshchensk • Sakhalin • Petropavlovsk -Kamchatskiy • Poluostrov Kamchatka • Aleuti • Aleutian Trench

KAZAKSTAN • Semey • Oz. Baykal • Khabarovsk • Kurilskiye Ostrova (Russia) • 7822

Aral Sea • Balqash Köl • Ulaanbaatar • Harbin • La Perouse Str. • Kuril Trench • 10,542 • Emperor Seamount Chain

Almaty • Ürümqi • Changchun • Sapporo • Vladivostok • Hakodate • Sea of Japan

Toshkent • KYRGYZSTAN • MONGOLIA • SHENYANG • Fuji-San 3776 • Sendai

TAJIKISTAN • BEIJING • TIANJIN • Taiyuan • Dalian • NORTH KOREA • SÕUL • Nagoya • TOKYO • Yokohama • JAPAN

AFGHANISTAN • CHINA • Lanzhou • Xi'an • Qingdao • SOUTH KOREA • Kyoto • Osaka • Shikoku • Kyushu • Japan Trench • 10,554 • Midway Is. (U.S.A.)

Kabul • Srinagar • Kunlun Shan • AIZANG • CHONGQING • Nanjing • Wuhan • SHANGHAI • Kitakyushu • Ogasawara Gunto (Japan) • Lisianski I. (U.S.A.)

PAKISTAN • Lhasa • HANGZHOU • East China Sea • South Honshu Ridge • Kazan-Retto (Japan)

Lahore • DELHI • Himalaya • Mt. Everest 8850 • Changsha • Fuzhou • Ryukyu-retto (Japan) • Minami-Tori-Shima (Japan)

Kanpur • NEPAL • Brahmaputra • Kunming • GUANGZHOU • Taipei • TAIWAN • Marcus Necker Ridge

Ganga • BANGLADESH • HONG KONG • Wake I. (U.S.A.) • International Dateline

INDIA • KOLKATA (Calcutta) • DHAKA • BURMA • Mandalay • Macau • Hainan • Hanoi • NORTHERN MARIANAS (U.S.A.) • P A

Hyderabad • Bay of Bengal • Rangoon • THAILAND • LAOS • Paracel Is. • C. Engano • Luzon • MANILA • Saipan • Mariana Trench

CHENNAI (Madras) • BANGKOK • CAMBODIA • Andaman Is. (India) • South China Sea • Mindoro • PHILIPPINES • GUAM (U.S.A.) • 11,022 • MARSHALL IS. • Bikini Atoll

SRI LANKA • Nicobar Is. (India) • Phnom Penh • Thanh Pho Ho Chi Minh • G. of Thailand • Palawan • Samar • 10,497 • Yap • Caroline Is. • Micronesia • Enewetak Atoll

Colombo • MALAYSIA • Sulu Sea • Mindanao • Koror • Truk • Dalap-Uliga-Darrit • Jaluit I.

Kuala Lumpur • PEN. MALAYSIA • BRUNEI • SABAH • Celebes Sea • 4101 • Mindanao Trench • PALAU • FEDERATED STATES OF MICRONESIA • Pohnpei • Palikir • Tarawa • Butaritari

SINGAPORE • Borneo • SARAWAK • Halmahera • Melan • NAURU • Banaba • Howland I. • Baker I.

Sumatera • INDONESIA • Sulawesi • Seram • Puncak Jaya 5029 • IRIAN JAYA • Admiralty Is. • Bismarck Arch. • New Ireland • PAPUA NEW GUINEA • Phoenix Is. • Abariring • Enderbu • O • KI

Palembang • Ujung Pandang • Buru • Banda Sea • 7440 • New Guinea • Rabaul • New Britain • Bougainville • Lae • SOLOMON IS. • Fongafale • TUVALU

Java Sea • JAKARTA • Jawa • Surabaya • Flores Sea • Flores • EAST TIMOR • Port Moresby • Honiara • Guadalcanal • Santa Cruz I. • 9165 • Tokelau (N.Z.)

Selat Sunda • Bali • Sumbawa • Sumba • Timor • Arafura Sea • Torres Strait • C. York • Rotuma • Is. Wallis & Futuna (Fr.) • SAM

Java Trench • Christmas I. (Austral.) • Sunda Islands • C. Arnhem • Darwin • Gulf of Carpentaria • Louisiade Arch. • Coral Sea • VANUATU • Espiritu Santo • Vanua Levu • Ap

Cocos Is. (Austral.) • Broome • Cairns • Is. Chesterfield • Port Vila • Viti Levu • Suva • FIJI • Nuku'alofa • TONG

INDIAN OCEAN • North West C. • Townsville • Mount Isa • AUSTRALIA • Alice Springs • Rockhampton • NEW CALEDONIA (Fr.) • Nouméa • Is. Loyauté • 7570 • 10,822 • Tonga Trench

Geraldton • L. Eyre • Brisbane • Norfolk I. (Austral.) • Kermadec Is. (N.Z.)

Perth • Great Australian Bight • Murray • Sydney • Canberra • Lord Howe I. (Austral.) • Kermadec Trench 10,047

Albany • Adelaide • Mt. Kosciuszko 2237 • Tasman Sea • NEW ZEALAND • Auckland

Nouvelle Amsterdam (Fr.) • I. St. Paul (Fr.) • Melbourne • Bass Str. • Cook Strait • Wellington

Mid-Indian Ridge • Kerguelen (Fr.) • Tasmania • Hobart • Aoraki Mt. Cook 3753 • Christchurch • Chatha

Is. Crozet (Fr.) • Dunedin • Bounty Is. (N.Z.)

Heard I. (Austral.) • Invercargill • Antipodes Is. (N.Z.)

Auckland Is. (N.Z.) • Campbell I. (N.Z.) • Macquarie I. (Austral.)

ft m / 12 000 4000 / 9000 3000 / 6000 2000 / 3000 1000 / 1500 500 / 600 200 / 0 0 / 200 600 / 1000 3000 / 2000 6000 / 4000 12 000 / 6000 18 000 / 8000 24 000 / m ft

Projection: Mollweide's Homolographic • East from Greenwich

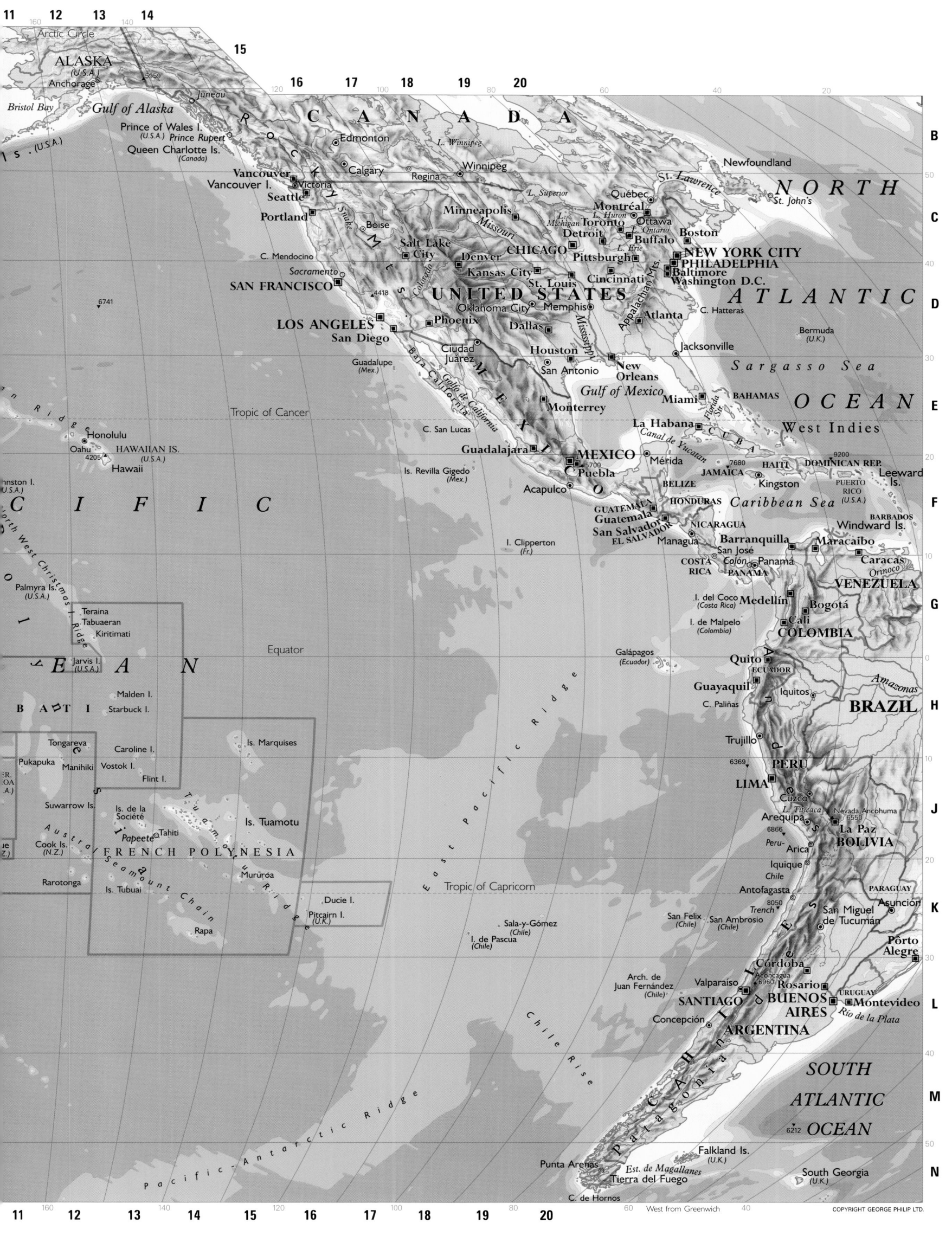

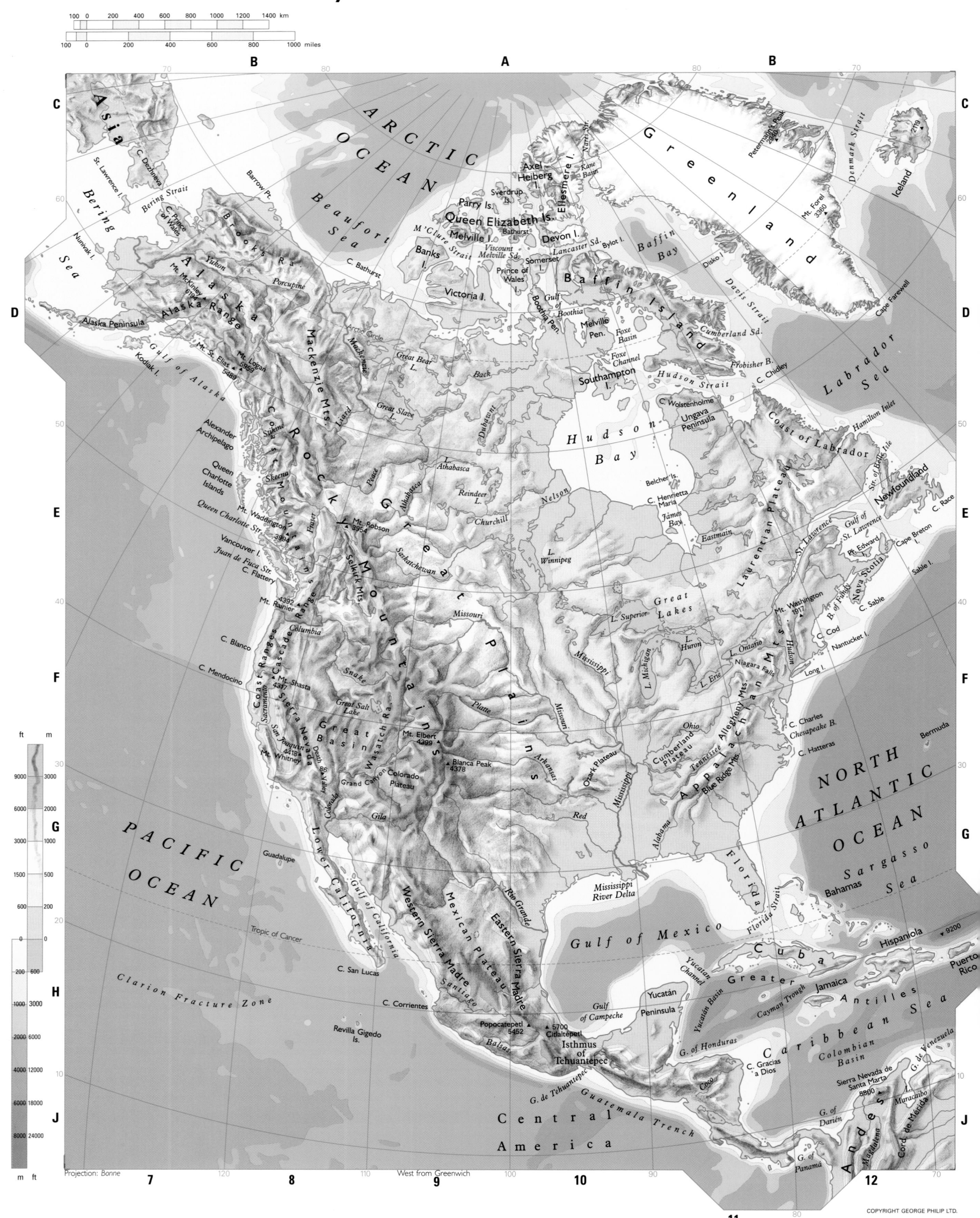

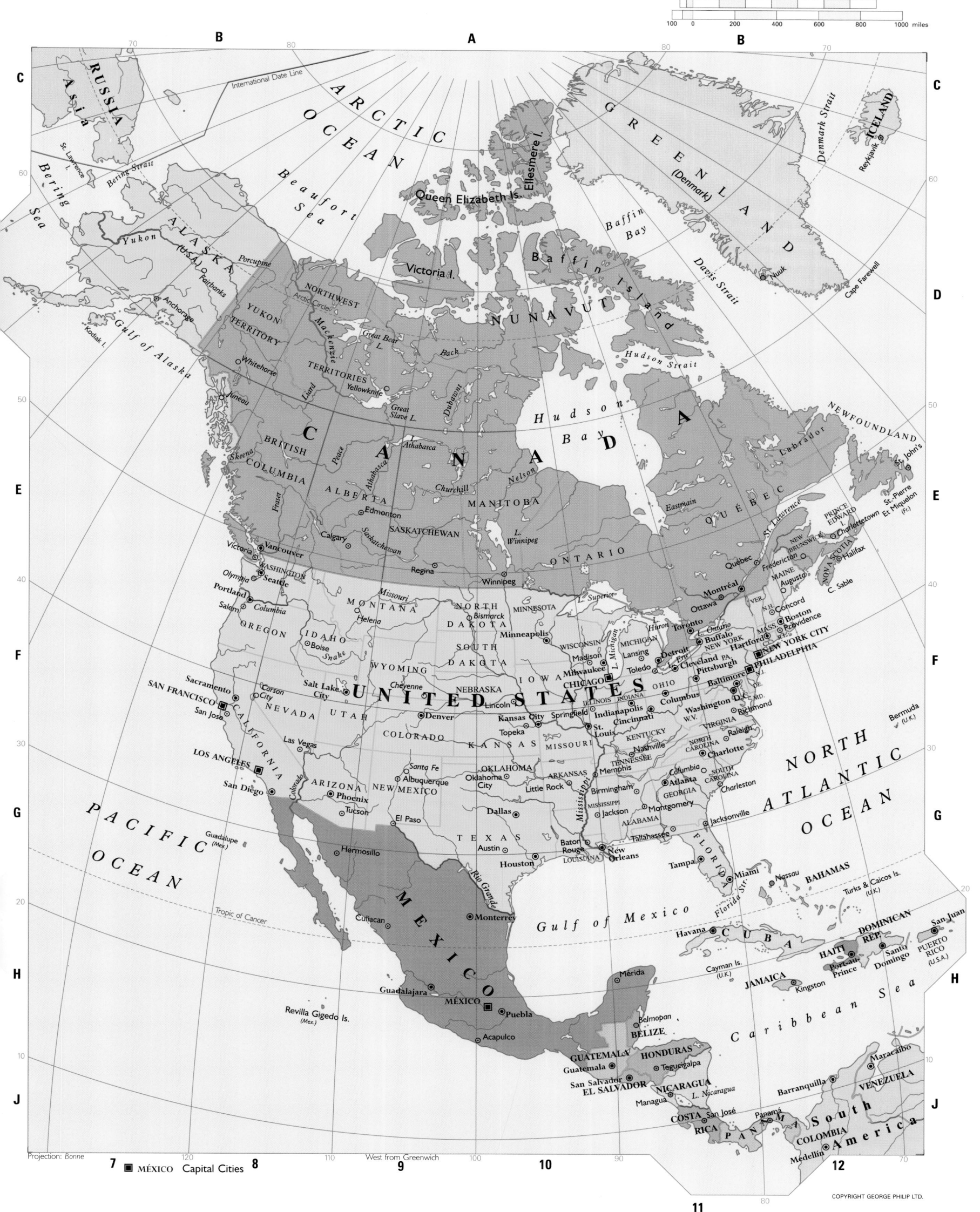

100  0  200  400  600  800  1000  1200  1400 km
100  0  200  400  600  800  1000 miles

7  ■ MÉXICO  Capital Cities  8

Projection: Bonne

COPYRIGHT GEORGE PHILIP LTD.

100 0 100 200 300 400 500 600 km
100 0 100 200 300 400 miles

**4** **5** **6** **7** **8** **9** **10**

PACIFIC

OCEAN

ALASKA
Anchorage
Cook Inlet
Kenai Seward
Soldotna Homer
Wasilla Palmer
Valdez
Cordova

Glennallen
Mt. Sanford 4949
Mt. Wrangell Mts. 4328
Mt. Lucania 5226
Mt. Logan 5959
Mt. St. Elias 5489

YUKON TERRITORY
Fairbanks
Delta Junction
Tok
Eagle
Dawson

Beaver Creek
Carmacks
Haines Junction
Mt. Fairweather 4663
Whitehorse
Skagway
Atlin
Teslin

Alexander
Archipelago
Chichagof I.
Sitka
Baranof I.
Admiralty I.
Juneau
Petersburg
Prince of Wales I.
Ketchikan
Stewart

NORTHWEST TERRITORIES

Old Crow
Fort McPherson
Tsiigehtchic
Inuvik
Tuktoyaktuk
Aklavik

Amundsen Gulf

Victoria Island

Banks Island

Prince Albert Pen.

McClintock Channel

Prince of Wales I.

Somerset I.

Boothia Peninsula

BRITISH COLUMBIA

ALBERTA

SASKATCHEWAN

MANITOBA

Edmonton
Calgary

VANCOUVER
Vancouver I.
Victoria
Nanaimo

WASHINGTON
SEATTLE
Olympia
Tacoma
Spokane

MONTANA

NORTH DAKOTA

SOUTH DAKOTA

NEBRASKA

UNITED STATES

MINNESOTA

Winnipeg

MINNEAPOLIS
ST. PAUL

Omaha

**ALASKA**
1:26 700 000

100 0 100 200 300 400 500 600 km
100 0 100 200 300 400 miles

CHUKCHI SEA

Barrow
Prudhoe Bay

Brooks Range

Point Hope
Kotzebue

ALASKA
(U.S.A.)

Fairbanks

Mt. McKinley 6194

Anchorage

RUSSIA

BERING SEA

PACIFIC OCEAN

GULF OF ALASKA

Aleutian Is.

Kodiak I.

Alexander Archipelago

Queen Charlotte Is.

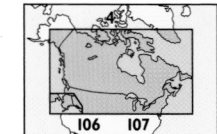

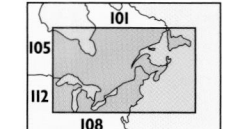

West from Greenwich

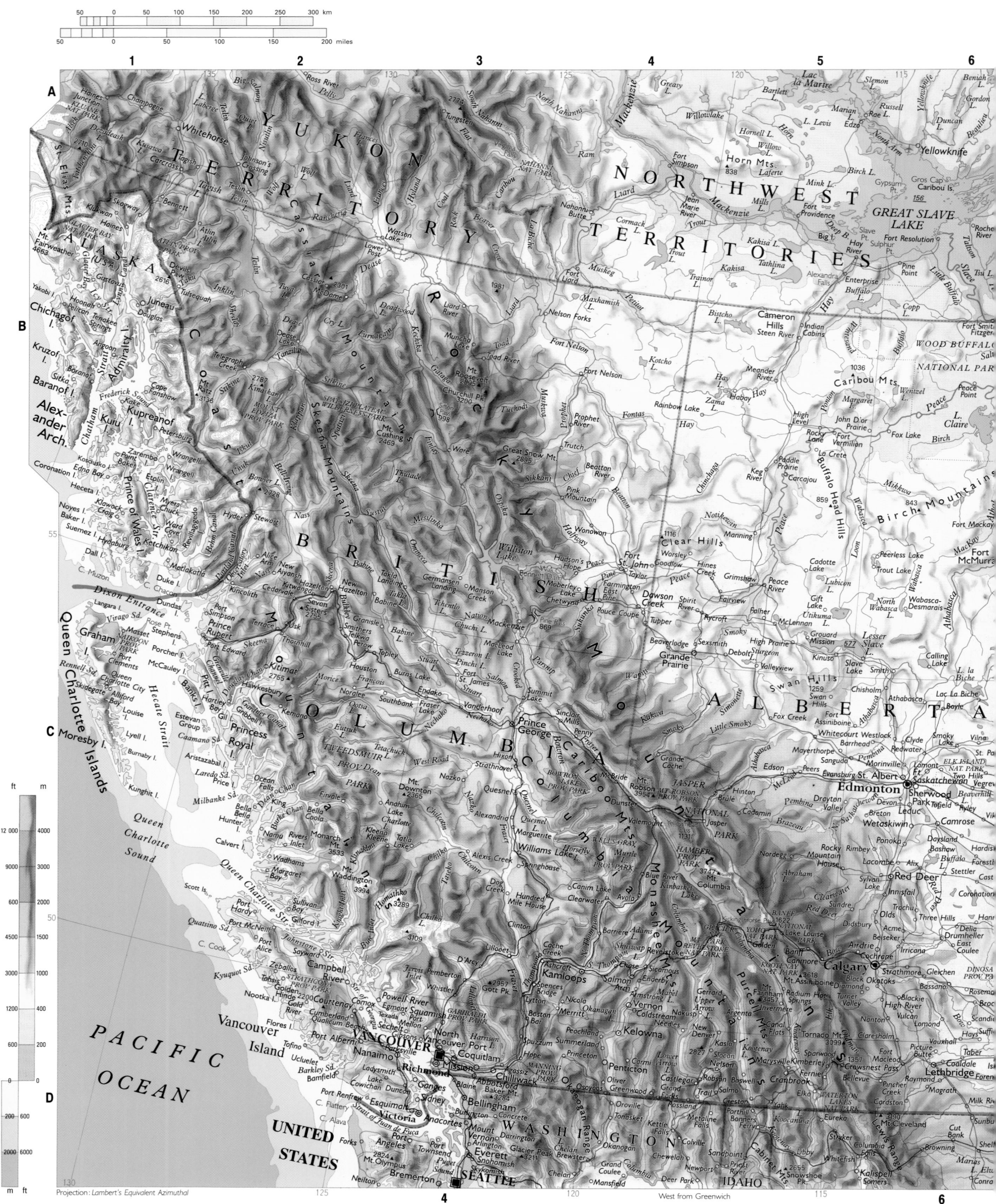

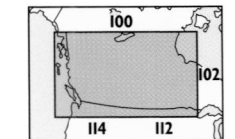

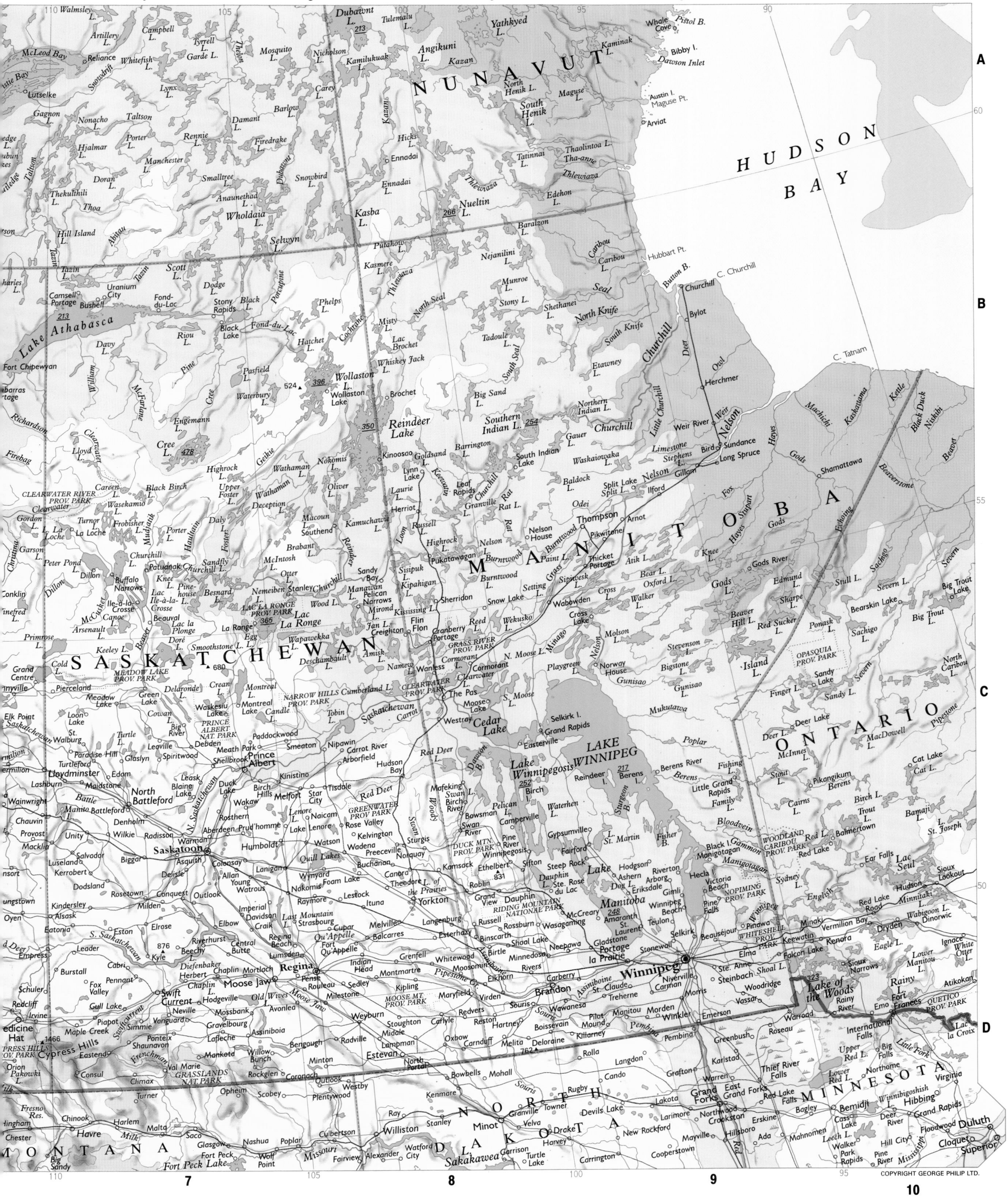

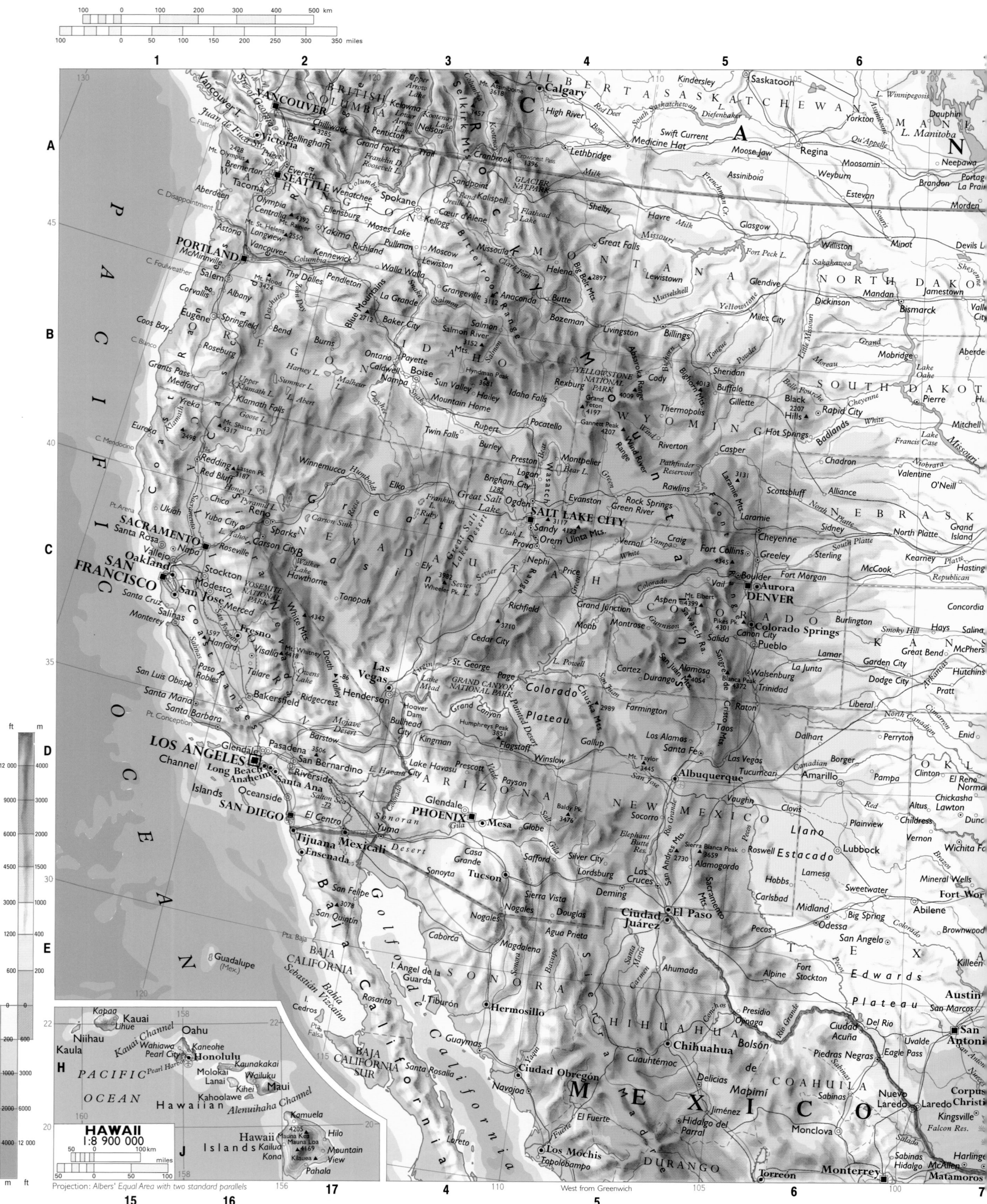

ft    m
12 000    4000
9000    3000
6000    2000
4500    1500
3000    1000
1200    400
600    200
0    0
200    600
1000    3000
2000    6000
4000    12 000
m    ft

**1**    **2**    **3**    **4**    **5**    **6**

130

**BRITISH COLUMBIA**
Vancouver I.
VANCOUVER
Victoria
Bellingham
C. Flattery

**WASHINGTON**
Everett
SEATTLE
Tacoma
Olympia
Centralia
Aberdeen

**PORTLAND**
McMinnville
Salem
Astoria
Vancouver

**OREGON**
Eugene
Springfield
Corvallis
Albany
Roseburg
Coos Bay
Grants Pass
Medford

**IDAHO**
Boise
Nampa
Caldwell

**MONTANA**
Helena
Great Falls
Butte
Bozeman
Billings

Calgary
High River
Lethbridge
Medicine Hat
Swift Current
Moose Jaw
Regina

**SASKATCHEWAN**
Saskatoon
Kindersley
Yorkton

**MAN.**
L. Winnipegosis
L. Manitoba

**NORTH DAKOTA**
Minot
Bismarck
Jamestown
Dickinson

**SOUTH DAKOTA**
Pierre
Rapid City
Mitchell

**WYOMING**
Casper
Cheyenne
Laramie
Cody

**NEVADA**
Reno
Carson City
Las Vegas
Henderson
Tonopah
Elko

**CALIFORNIA**
SACRAMENTO
SAN FRANCISCO
Oakland
San Jose
Fresno
Bakersfield
LOS ANGELES
Long Beach
Anaheim
San Diego

**UTAH**
SALT LAKE CITY
Ogden
Provo

**COLORADO**
DENVER
Aurora
Colorado Springs
Pueblo

**ARIZONA**
PHOENIX
Mesa
Tucson
Flagstaff

**NEW MEXICO**
Albuquerque
Santa Fe
Las Cruces

**NEBRASKA**
North Platte
Grand Island

**KANSAS**
Dodge City
Garden City

**OKLAHOMA**

**TEXAS**
El Paso
Austin
San Antonio

**MEXICO**
Tijuana
Mexicali
Ensenada
Hermosillo
Chihuahua
Ciudad Juárez
Ciudad Obregón
Los Mochis
Torreón
Monterrey
Matamoros

**BAJA CALIFORNIA**
**BAJA CALIFORNIA SUR**

**PACIFIC OCEAN**

**HAWAII**  1:8 900 000
Kauai
Niihau
Oahu
Honolulu
Pearl Harbor
Molokai
Lanai
Maui
Kahoolawe
Hawaii Islands
Hilo
Kona

Projection: Albers' Equal Area with two standard parallels

West from Greenwich

**15**    **16**    **17**    **4**    **5**    **6**    **7**

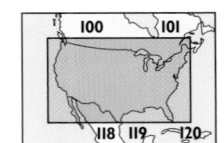

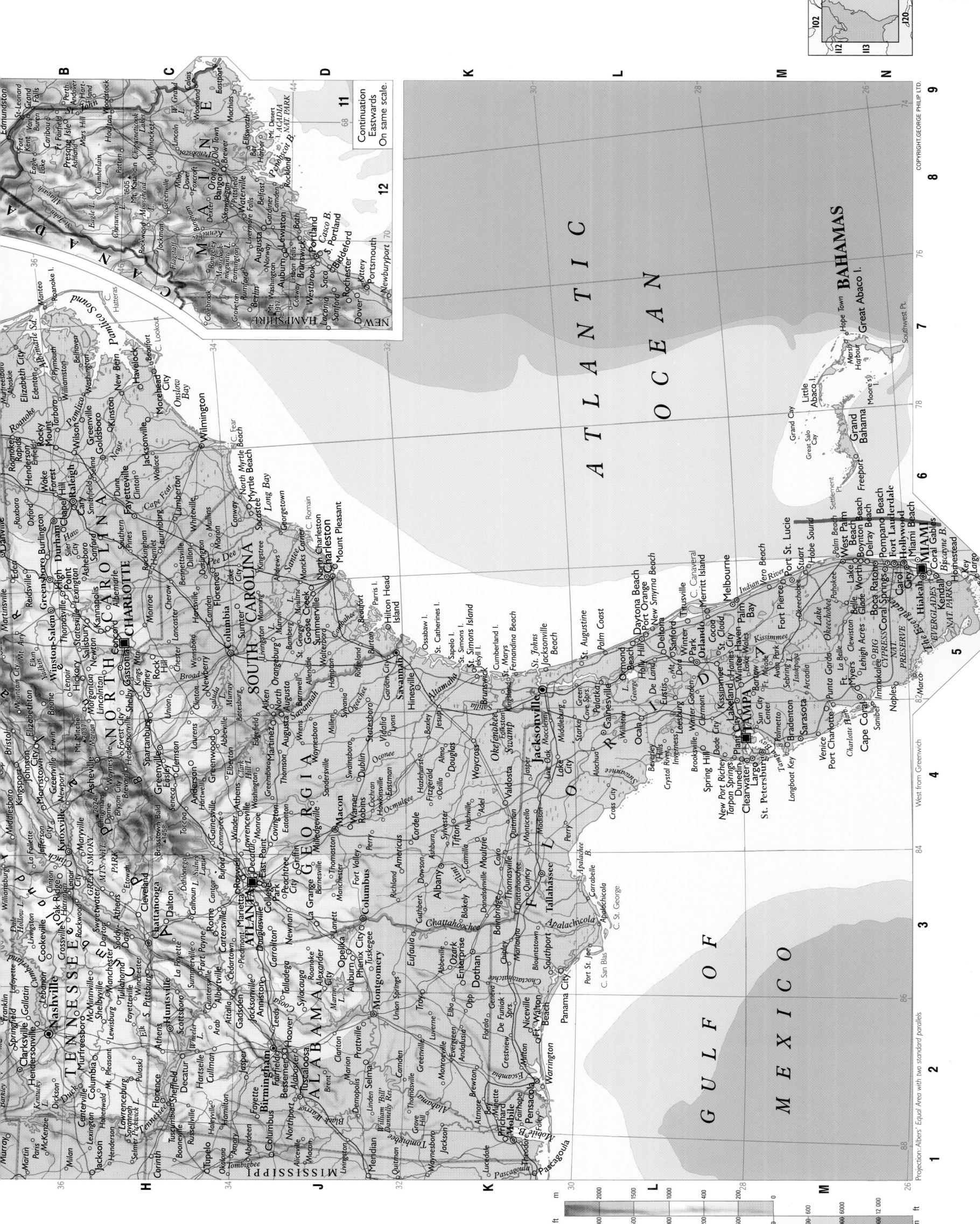

COPYRIGHT GEORGE PHILIP LTD.

102  120
112  113

B
C
D

11  Continuation
Eastwards
On same scale.
12

CANADA

MAINE

Edmundston
Fort
Kent
St-Léonard
York Grand
Falls
Buren
Perth-
Andover
Woodstock
Fredericton
Ft. Fairfield
Presque Isle
Ashland
Caribou
Limestone
Eastport
Calais
Lubec
Machias

Eagle L.
St. John
Houlton
St. Croix

Chamberlain
L. Chiputneticook Lakes
Old Town
Orono
Brewer
Bangor
Dover-
Foxcroft
Lincoln
Millinocket

Greenville
Dexter
Ellsworth
Mt. Desert I.
ACADIA
NAT. PARK
Penobscot B.

Mt. Katahdin
1605

Moosehead
L.

Rangeley
L.
Bingham
Skowhegan
Waterville
Belfast
Camden
Rockland

Flagstaff
L.

Rockwood

Jackman

Farmington
Pittsfield
Augusta
Gardiner
Bath

Livermore Falls
Norway
Auburn
Lewiston
Brunswick
Casco B.
S. Portland
Portland

MAINE
NEW HAMPSHIRE

Colebrook
Berlin
Mt. Washington
Conway
Laconia
Sanford
Biddeford

Groveton
Lisbon Falls
Saco

Washington
Westbrook
Dover
Rochester
Portsmouth
Kittery
Newburyport

44
68
70

ATLANTIC

OCEAN

BAHAMAS

Little
Abaco I.
Hope Town
Marsh
Harbour
Great Abaco I.
Moore's I.

Grand Cay
Great Sale
Cay
Grand
Bahama
Freeport
Settlement
Little
Abaco I.

Southwest Pt.

74
76
78

9
8
7
6

TENNESSEE
VIRGINIA
NORTH CAROLINA
SOUTH CAROLINA
GEORGIA
ALABAMA
MISSISSIPPI
FLORIDA

Murray
Paris
Milan
Martin
Jackson
Lexington
McKenzie
Aberdeen

Nashville
Clarksville
Gallatin
Springfield
Franklin
Lebanon
Murfreesboro
Columbia
Lawrenceburg
Pulaski

Cookeville
Crossville
Centerville
Hohenwald
Shelbyville
Manchester
Winchester
Tullahoma

Bristol
Kingsport
Johnson
City
Middlesboro
Williamsburg
Jefferson City
Morristown
Knoxville
Maryville
Sevierville

GREAT SMOKY
MTS. NAT.
PARK
Mt. Mitchell
2038

Boone
Lenoir
Hickory
Statesville
Salisbury
Kannapolis
CHARLOTTE
Concord
Gastonia
Shelby
Rock Hill

Asheville
Hendersonville
Brevard
Waynesville
Bryson City
Franklin

Mars Hill
Morganton
Lincolnton
Kings Mt.
Gaffney
Spartanburg
Greenville
Easley
Clemson
Anderson

Winston-Salem
Greensboro
High Point
Lexington
Thomasville
Albemarle
Monroe
Lancaster
Cheraw
Chester

Danville
Martinsville
Mt. Airy
Reidsville
Burlington
Durham
Chapel Hill
Raleigh
Sanford
Southern
Pines
Rockingham
Hamlet

Oxford
Roxboro
Henderson

Rocky
Mount
Wilson
Goldsboro
Dunn
Fayetteville
Clinton
Lumberton

Roanoke
Rapids
Enfield
Tarboro
Greenville
Kinston
New Bern
Jacksonville
Wallace

Murfreesboro
Ahoskie
Edenton
Washington
Havelock
Morehead
City
Beaufort
C. Lookout

Elizabeth City
Plymouth
Manteo
Roanoke I.
Nags Head
Pamlico
Sound
Hatteras
C. Hatteras

Albemarle Sd.
Belhaven

Whiteville
Wilmington
C. Fear
Southport
North Myrtle Beach
Myrtle Beach

Conway
Marion
Dillon
Darlington
Florence
Mullins
Long Bay

Sumter
Columbia
Camden
Hartsville
Bennettsville
Bishopville
Pee Dee

Newberry
Winnsboro

Rock Hill
Union
Laurens
Clinton
Greenwood
Abbeville

SOUTH CAROLINA
Saluda
Aiken
North Augusta
Augusta
Thomson
Martinez
Washington

Orangeburg
North Charleston
Summerville
Moncks Corner
Kingstree
Andrews
Georgetown
Winyah Bay
C. Romain

Charleston
Mount Pleasant

Elberton
Hartwell
Anderson
Seneca
Toccoa
Gainesville
Cornelia

Athens
Madison
Greensboro
Covington
Monroe
Lawrenceville
ATLANTA
Roswell
Marietta
Decatur
East Point
College Park
Peachtree
City

Dahlonega
Blue Ridge
Blairsville
Buford
Cleveland

Carrollton
Newnan
La Grange
West Point
Manchester
Griffin
Barnesville
Jonesboro

Columbus
Phenix City
Opelika
Auburn
Tuskegee
Alexander
City

Birmingham
Bessemer
Hoover
Gadsden
Anniston
Oxford
Talladega
Sylacauga
Pell City

Leeds
Pell City

Tuscaloosa
Northport
Brent
Clanton

Montgomery
Prattville
Wetumpka
Troy
Union Springs

Selma
Marion
Demopolis
Linden

Gadsden
Fort
Payne
Scottsboro
Guntersville
Albertville

Decatur
Huntsville
Athens
Hartselle
Cullman
Arab

Florence
Sheffield
Tuscumbia
Russellville
Moulton

Corinth
Booneville
Tupelo

Aliceville
Fayette
Jasper

Sheffield

MISSISSIPPI

Meridian
Waynesboro
Quitman
Lucedale

Hattiesburg

Laurel

Columbus
Aberdeen
Macon
Starkville
West Point

GEORGIA

Macon
Warner
Robins
Hawkinsville
Cochran
Eastman
Dublin
Sandersville
Milledgeville
Eatonton

Perry
Fort Valley
Americus
Cordele

Vidalia
Lyons
Swainsboro
Statesboro
Millen

Richland
Dawson
Cuthbert
Blakely

Albany
Sylvester
Tifton
Ashburn
Fitzgerald

Camilla
Moultrie
Adel
Nashville
Ocilla
Douglas

Bainbridge
Donaldsonville
Thomasville
Cairo
Quitman
Valdosta
Jasper

Waycross
Folkston
Okefenokee
Swamp

Hinesville
Jesup
Baxley
Reidsville
Alma

Savannah
Garden City
Port Wentworth
Ogeechee
Beaufort
Parris I.
Hilton Head
Island

Hardeeville
Ridgeland
Allendale
Barnwell
Bamberg
Walterboro

St. Simons Island
Jekyll I.
Brunswick
Darien
Altamaha

Ossabaw I.
St. Catherines I.
Sapelo I.

Fernandina
Beach
St. Marys
Cumberland I.

Jacksonville
St. Augustine
Palm Coast

Lake
City
Live Oak
Jasper
White
Springs

Gainesville
Starke
Middleburg
Green
Cove Spts.

Palatka
Ormond
Beach
Daytona Beach
Port Orange
New Smyrna Beach

DeLand
Deltona
Sanford
Titusville
Merritt Island
C. Canaveral

Cocoa
Melbourne
Palm Bay
Vero Beach
Sebastian
Indian River

Ocala
Eustis
Leesburg
Clermont
Winter
Garden
Orlando
Winter
Park
Kissimmee
St. Cloud

Dade
City
Zephyrhills
Plant
City
Lakeland
Haines City
Winter Haven
Lake Wales

Gainesville
Cross City
Chiefland
Williston
Inverness
Brooksville
Spring Hill

Crystal River

TAMPA
St. Petersburg
Clearwater
Dunedin
Tarpon Springs
New Port Richey
Largo
Longboat Key

Bradenton
Palmetto
Sarasota
Venice
Port Charlotte
Punta Gorda
Cape Coral
Sanibel
Ft. Myers

Avon Park
Sebring
Arcadia
Wauchula
Bartow
Sun City Center

Okeechobee
L.
Okeechobee
Clewiston
Belle
Glade
Pahokee

Fort Pierce
Port St. Lucie
Stuart
Hobe Sound
Palm Beach
West Palm
Beach
Lake
Worth
Belle Glade
Boynton Beach
Delray
Beach
Boca Raton
Pompano Beach
Fort Lauderdale
Hollywood

MIAMI
Miami Beach
Hialeah
Coral Gables
Kendall
Biscayne B.
Homestead
Key
Largo

BIG
CYPRESS
NAT.
PRESERVE
Immokalee
Naples
Marco I.
Lehigh Acres

La Belle

EVERGLADES
NAT. PARK
The Bend

FLORIDA

Tallahassee
Monticello
Perry
Madison
Apalachee B.

Marianna
Chattahoochee
Quincy

Chipley
Blountstown
Apalachicola
Port St. Joe
C. San Blas
Apalachicola
C. St. George

Panama City
Lynn Haven
Ft. Walton
Beach
Crestview
De Funiak
Springs

Pensacola
Ft. Barrancas
Milton
Warrington
Gulf Breeze

ALABAMA

Dothan
Ozark
Enterprise
Abbeville
Geneva
Opp
Elba
Andalusia

Brewton
Atmore
Flomaton

Mobile
Prichard
Theodore
Bayou La Batre
Mobile B.
Foley
Fairhope

Pascagoula

GULF OF

MEXICO

West from Greenwich

Projection: Albers' Equal Area with two standard parallels

30
84
86
88
82
28
26
32
34
36

A
H
X
Y
T
P
U
Z
F
R
O
G

9
8
7
6
5
4
3
2
1

K
L
M
N

H
J
K
L
M

ft
m
2000
1500
1000
400
200
0

6000
4500
3000
1200
600
0
200
2000
6000
12 000
m
ft

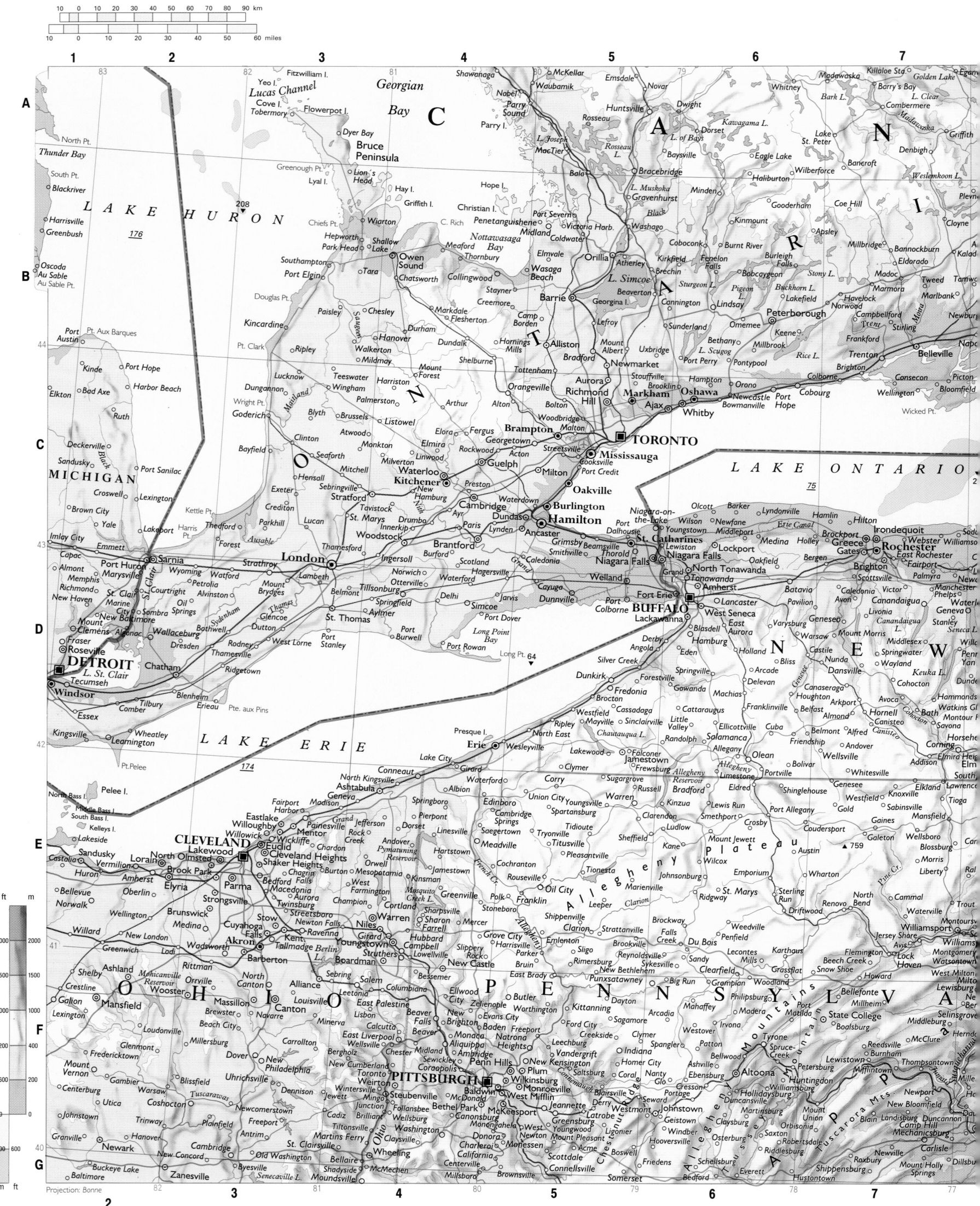

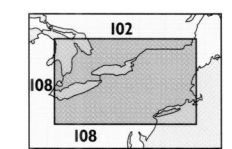

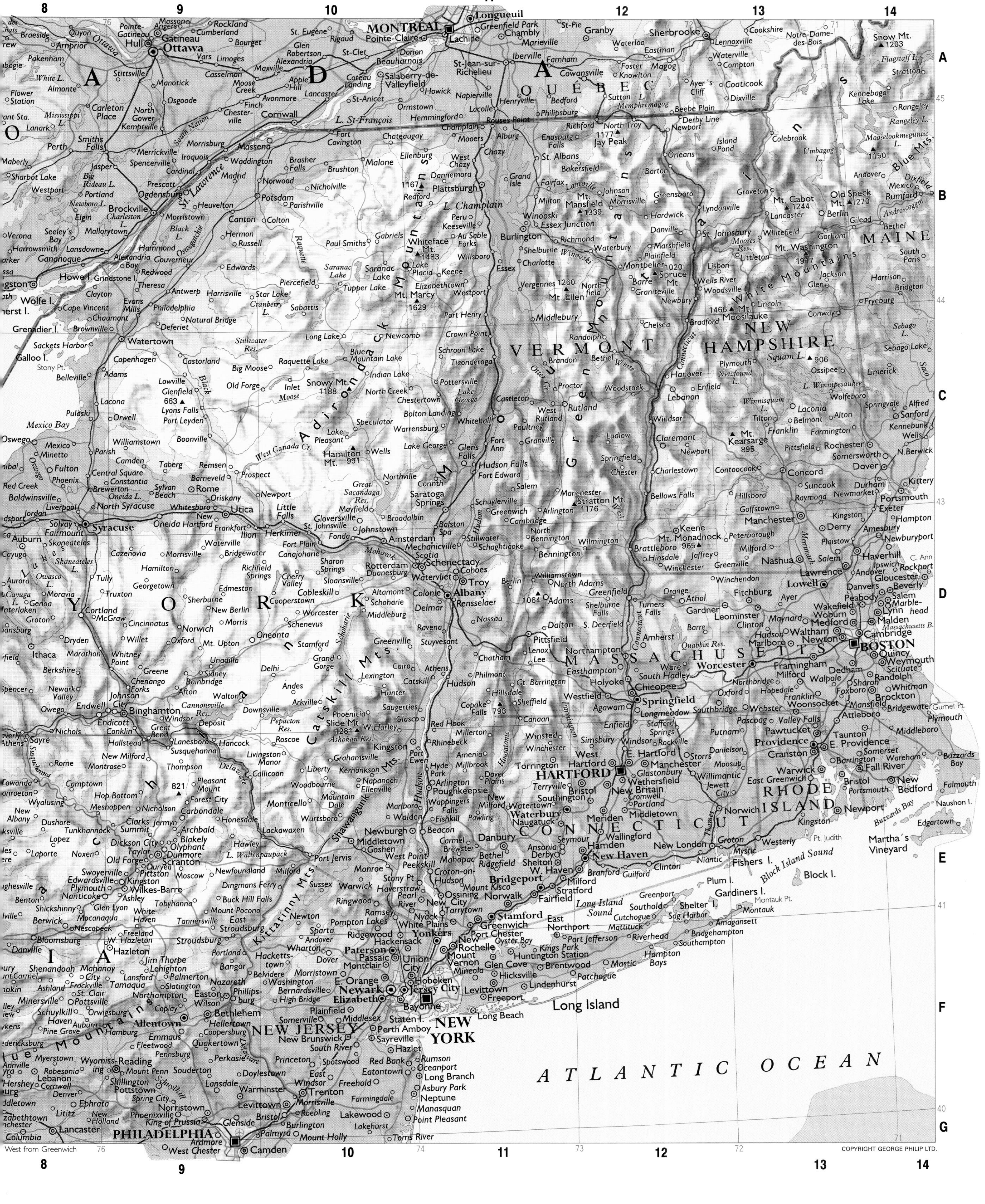

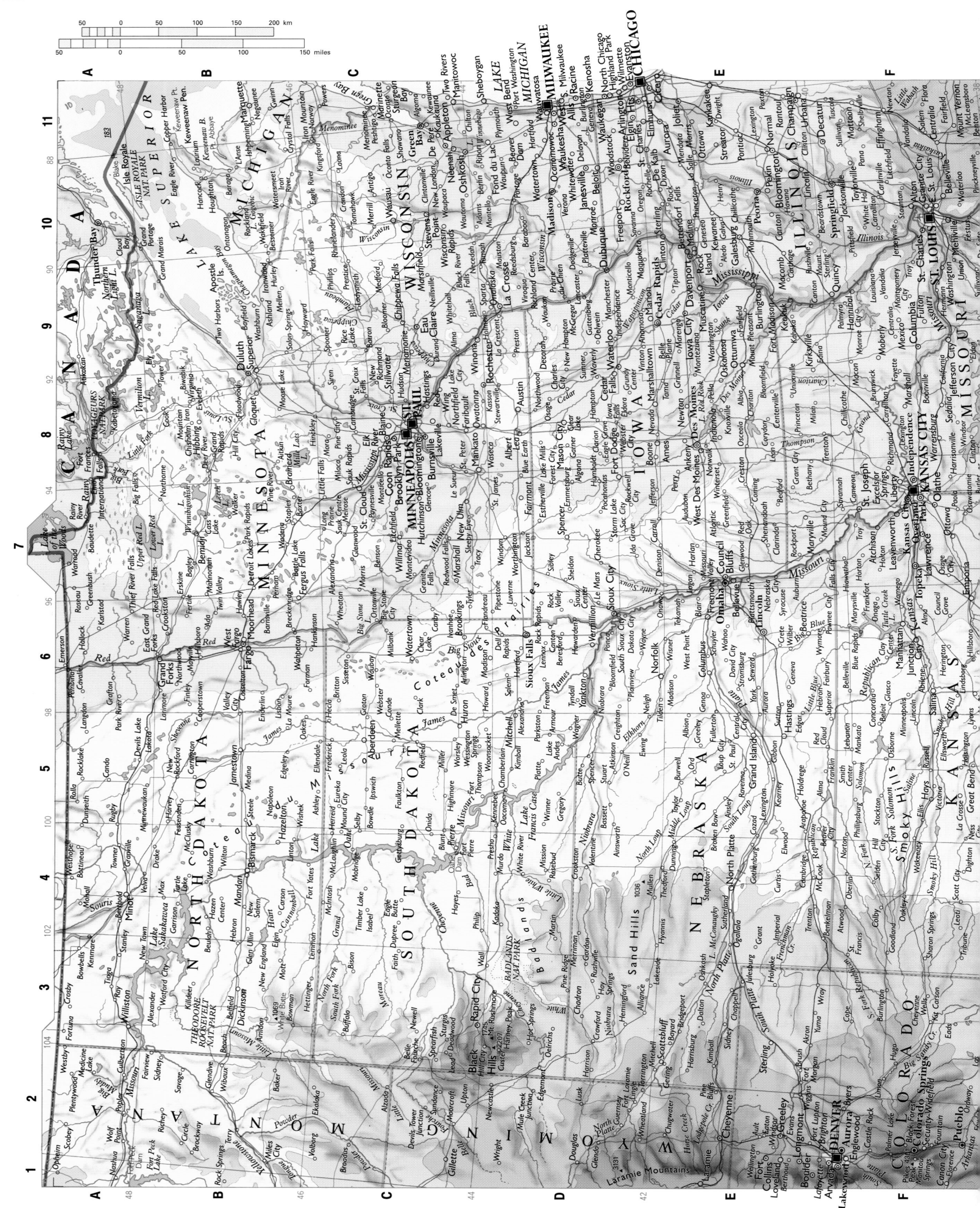

# Map (Texas, Oklahoma, Arkansas, Louisiana, Mississippi and surrounding states)

**States / Countries:** TENNESSEE · MISSISSIPPI · ARKANSAS · LOUISIANA · OKLAHOMA · TEXAS · NEW MEXICO · MEXICO · COAHUILA · CHIHUAHUA

**Major cities:** Memphis · New Orleans · Baton Rouge · Shreveport · Little Rock · Tulsa · Oklahoma City · Wichita · Dallas · Fort Worth · Arlington · Houston · Pasadena · San Antonio · Austin · Waco · Corpus Christi · Laredo · Nuevo Laredo · Galveston · Amarillo · Lubbock · Abilene · Odessa · Midland

**Physical features:** GULF OF MEXICO · Mississippi River · Red River · Arkansas R. · Rio Grande (Rio Bravo del Norte) · Edwards Plateau · Llano Estacado · Boston Mts. · Ouachita · Stockton Plateau · Balcones Escarpment · Sangre de Cristo Mts. · Guadalupe Mts. · Davis Mts. · Chisos Mts. · Laguna Madre · Padre I. · Matagorda I.

**Parks:** BIG BEND NATIONAL PARK · CARLSBAD CAVERNS NAT. PARK · GUADALUPE MTS. NAT. PARK

*Continuation Southwards on same scale* (inset)

West from Greenwich

Projection: Albers' Equal Area with two standard parallels

COPYRIGHT GEORGE PHILIP LTD.

Scale bars:
ft — 12 000 / 9000 / 6000 / 4500 / 3000 / 1500 / 600 / 200 / 0
m — 4000 / 3000 / 2000 / 1500 / 1000 / 600 / 400 / 200 / 0

50   0   50   100   150   200 km
50   0   50   100   150 miles

PACIFIC

OCEAN

BAJA CALIFORNIA

Golfo de California

SONORA

CHIHUAHUA

MEXICO

TEXAS

NEW MEXICO

ARIZONA

COLORADO

NEVADA

CALIFORNIA

Projection: Albers' Equal Area with two standard parallels

West from Greenwich

WESTERN WASHINGTON REGION
On same scale

NEVADA

ARIZONA

CALIFORNIA

BAJA CALIFORNIA

MEXICO

PACIFIC OCEAN

Mojave Desert

Sonoran Desert

Death Valley

Amargosa Range

Channel Islands

San Pedro Channel

Santa Barbara Channel

Gulf of Santa Catalina

Chocolate Mts.

San Bernardino Mts.

San Gabriel Mts.

Santa Monica Mts.

Tehachapi Mts.

San Rafael Mts.

Lake Mead

Lake Mohave

Lake Havasu

Salton Sea

Colorado River

LOS ANGELES

SAN DIEGO

Las Vegas

Bakersfield

Tijuana

Mexicali

Projection: Bonne

West from Greenwich

REFERENCE TO NUMBERS

1 Distrito Federal    5 México
2 Aguascalientes    6 Morelos
3 Guanajuato    7 Querétaro
4 Hidalgo    8 Tlaxcala

Projection: Bi-polar oblique Conical Orthomorphic

West from Greenwich

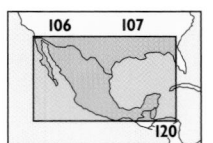

**GULF OF MEXICO**

**PACIFIC OCEAN**

**CARIBBEAN** (CARI...)

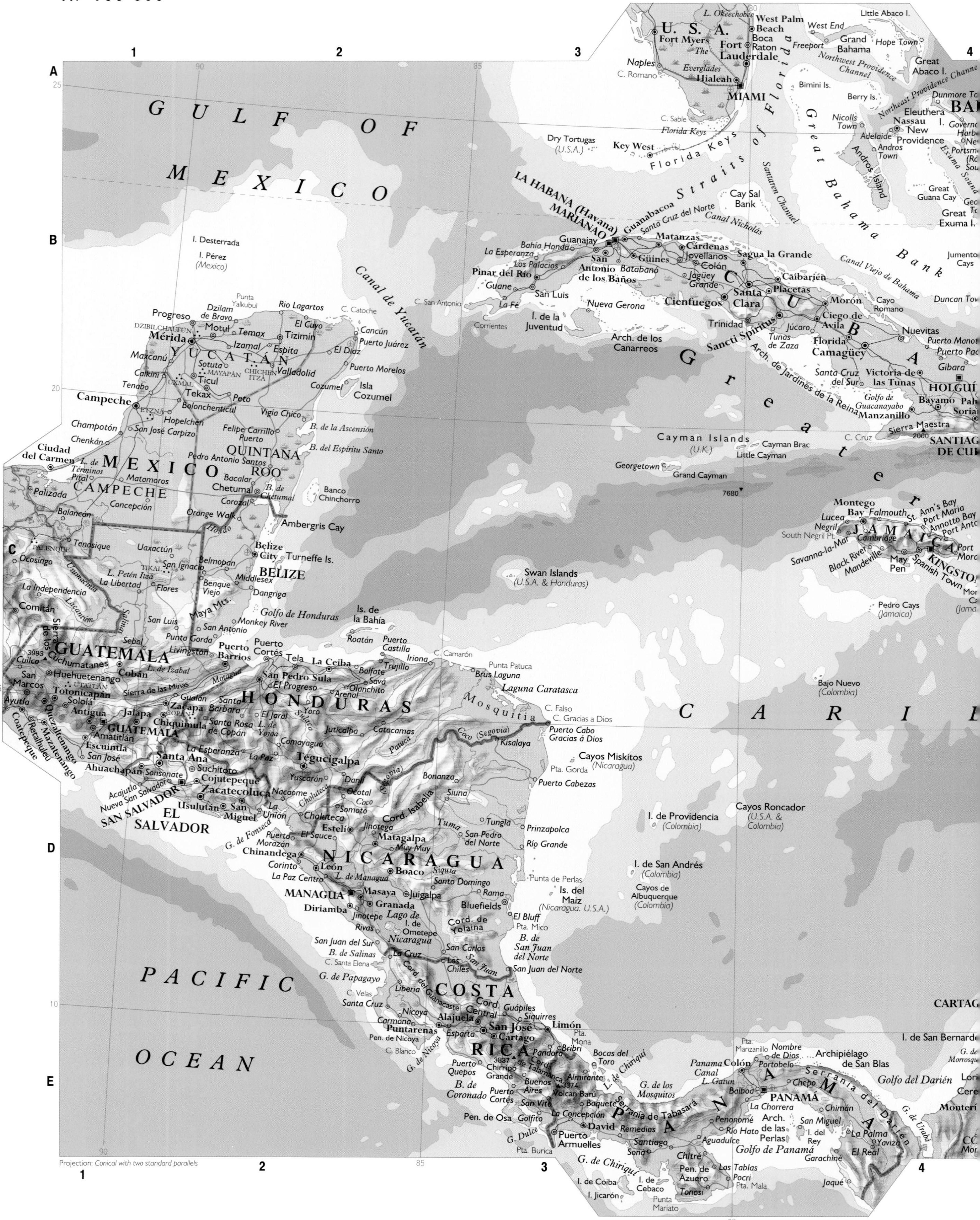

Projection: Conical with two standard parallels

U.S.A.

L. Okeechobee
West Palm Beach
Fort Myers
Boca Raton
Fort Lauderdale
Naples
C. Romano
Hialeah
MIAMI
The Everglades
C. Sable
Dry Tortugas (U.S.A.)
Key West
Florida Keys
West End
Freepot
Hope Town
Little Abaco I.
Grand Bahama
Great Abaco I.
Bimini Is.
Berry Is.
Nicolls Town
Adelaide
Nassau
New Providence
Eleuthera
Dunmore Town
Great Guana Cay
Great Exuma I.
Exuma Sound
Andros Island
Andros Town

Straits of Florida
Florida Keys
Great Bahama Bank
Northwest Providence Channel
Northeast Providence Channel
Santaren Channel
Cay Sal Bank
Canal Viejo de Bahama

LA HABANA (Havana)
MARIANAO
Guanabacoa
Bahía Honda
Guanajay
Matanzas
Santa Cruz del Norte
Canal Nicholas
La Esperanza
San Antonio de los Baños
Güines
Jovellanos
Colón
Sagua la Grande
Caibarién
Pinar del Río
Guane
Los Palacios
Batabanó
Jagüey Grande
Santa Clara
Placetas
Morón
Cayo Coco
Cayo Romano
La Fé
San Luis
Nueva Gerona
Cienfuegos
Ciego de Ávila
Nuevitas
Puerto Manatí
Puerto Padre
Corrientes
I. de la Juventud
Trinidad
Júcaro
Tunas de Zaza
Florida
Camagüey
Gibara
HOLGUÍN
C. San Antonio
Arch. de los Canarreos
Sancti Spíritus
Arch. de Jardines de la Reina
Santa Cruz del Sur
Golfo de Guacanayabo
Victoria de las Tunas
Bayamo
Manzanillo
Soria
CUBA
Sierra Maestra
C. Cruz
SANTIAGO DE CUBA

Cayman Islands (U.K.)
Cayman Brac
Little Cayman
Georgetown
Grand Cayman
7680

Swan Islands (U.S.A. & Honduras)

Montego Bay
Lucea
Negril
South Negril Pt.
St. Ann's Bay
Falmouth
Port Maria
Annotto Bay
Port Antonio
JAMAICA
Cambridge
Savanna-la-Mar
Black River
Mandeville
May Pen
Spanish Town
KINGSTON
Port Royal
Pedro Cays (Jamaica)
Bajo Nuevo (Colombia)

I. Desterrada
I. Pérez (Mexico)
Canal de Yucatán
Punta Yalkubul
Río Lagartos
C. Catoche
Progreso
Dzilam de Bravo
El Cuyo
Cancún
Puerto Juárez
DZIBILCHALTUN
Motul
Temax
Tizimín
El Díaz
MÉRIDA
Izamal
Maxcanú
Sotuta
MAYAPÁN
Ticul
CHICHEN ITZA
Puerto Morelos
Calkiní
UXMAL
Tekax
Valladolid
Cozumel
Isla Cozumel
Tenabo
Peto
YUCATÁN
Campeche
EDZNA
Bolonchenticul
Hopelchén
Felipe Carrillo Puerto
Vigía Chico
B. de la Ascensión
Champotón
Chenkán
QUINTANA ROO
B. del Espíritu Santo
Ciudad del Carmen
I. de Términos
Pital
Matamoros
Bacalar
Banco Chinchorro
Palizada
Concepción
Chetumal
Corozal
B. de Chetumal
MEXICO
CAMPECHE
Balancán
Orange Walk
Ambergris Cay
PALENQUE
Tenosique
Hondo
Belize City
Turneffe Is.
Ocosingo
Uaxactún
San Ignacio
Belmopan
Middlesex
La Independencia
L. Petén Itzá
TIKAL
Benque Viejo
BELIZE
Dangriga
Comitán
Lacantun
La Libertad
Flores
Maya Mts.
San Luis
Monkey River
Sebol
San Antonio
Golfo de Honduras
Is. de la Bahía
Cuilco
CUCHUMATANES
Cobán
Punta Gorda
Livingston
L. de Izabal
Puerto Barrios
Puerto Cortés
Tela
La Ceiba
Roatán
Puerto Castilla
Iriona
C. Camarón
GUATEMALA
Huehuetenango
San Marcos
Totonicapán
Sololá
Sierra de las Minas
San Pedro Sula
El Progreso
Trujillo
Balfate
Savá
Olanchito
Punta Patuca
Brus Laguna
Laguna Caratasca
Ayutla
Quezaltenango
Antigua
Jalapa
Zacapa
Santa Bárbara
Yoro
Arenal
HONDURAS
Mazatenango
Chiquimula
Santa Rosa de Copán
El Jaral
Yoro
Olancho
Mosquitia
Retalhuleu
Amatitlán
GUATEMALA
La Esperanza
La Paz
Juticalpa
Catacamas
Coco (Segovia)
C. Falso
C. Gracias a Dios
Coatepeque
Escuintla
Comayagua
Patuca
Puerto Cabo Gracias á Dios
San José
Ahuachapán
Sonsonate
Suchitoto
Cojutepeque
Tegucigalpa
Yuscarán
Danlí
Kisalaya
Acajutla
Nueva San Salvador
SAN SALVADOR
Zacatecoluca
La Unión
Nacaome
Choluteca
Ocotal
Coco
Somoto
Cayos Miskitos (Nicaragua)
Pta. Gorda
Usulután
San Miguel
Estelí
Jinotega
Tuma
Tungla
Puerto Cabezas
EL SALVADOR
G. de Fonseca
Puerto Morazán
El Sauce
Matagalpa
Muy Muy
San Pedro del Norte
Prinzapolca
I. de Providencia (Colombia)
Cayos Roncador (U.S.A. & Colombia)
Chinandega
Corinto
León
Boaco
Siquia
Santo Domingo
Río Grande
Punta de Perlas
La Paz Centro
Managua
L. de Managua
Rama
I. de San Andrés (Colombia)
MANAGUA
Masaya
Granada
Juigalpa
Bluefields
Is. del Maiz (Nicaragua, U.S.A.)
Cayos de Albuquerque (Colombia)
Diriamba
Jinotepe
NICARAGUA
El Bluff
Rivas
Lago de Nicaragua
Cord. de Yolaina
Pta. Mico
B. de San Juan del Norte
San Juan del Sur
I. de Ometepe
San Carlos
San Juan
B. de Salinas
La Cruz
Los Chiles
San Juan del Norte
C. Santa Elena
G. de Papagayo
Liberia
Cord. de Guanacaste
Cord. Central
Guápiles
Siquirres
Limón
Santa Cruz
Nicoya
Alajuela
San José
Cartago
Carmona
Puntarenas
Espárza
COSTA RICA
Bribri
Pta. Mona
Bocas del Toro
C. Velas
Pen. de Nicoya
Cord. de Talamanca
Pandora
Almirante
Nombre de Dios
Archipiélago de San Blas
C. Blanco
Buenos Aires
Cord.
Guápiles
Chiriquí Grande
Panamá Canal
Colón
Portobelo
Serranía de San Blas
Golfo del Darién
Puerto Quepos
Chirripó 3837
Volcán Barú 3374
Boquete
Serranía de Tabasara
G. de los Mosquitos
L. Gatun
Balboa
PANAMÁ
Chepo
B. de Coronado
Puerto Cortés
San Vito
La Concepción
David
Remedios
Penonomé
Río Hato
Santiago
La Chorrera
Chimán
San Miguel
El Real
La Palma
Yaviza
Pen. de Osa
Golfito
Puerto Armuelles
Pta. Burica
G. de Chiriquí
Chitré
Pen. de Azuero
Aguadulce
Las Tablas
Pocrí
Golfo de Panamá
Garachiné
I. de Coiba
I. de Cebaco
Tonosí
Punta Mala
Pta. Mariato
PANAMÁ
CARTAGENA

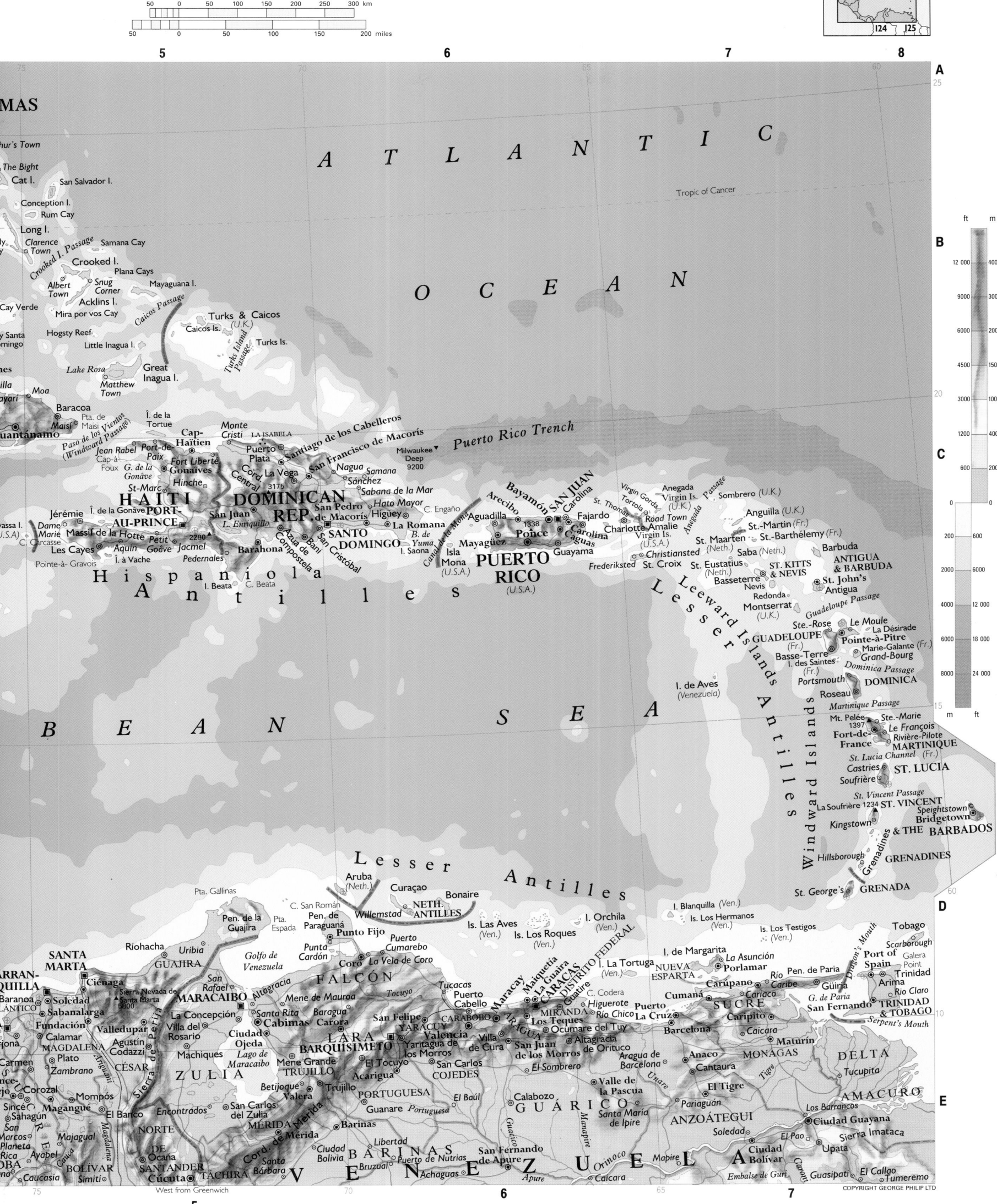

ft m

12 000
4000
9000
3000
6000
2000
4500
1500
3000
1000
1200
400
600
200
0 0
200 600
2000 6000
4000 12 000
6000 18 000
8000 24 000
m ft

50 0 50 100 150 200 250 300 km
50 0 50 100 150 200 miles

5 6 7 8

A

MAS

ATLANTIC

hur's Town
The Bight
Cat I.
San Salvador I.
Conception I.
Rum Cay
Long I.
Clarence Town
Samana Cay
Crooked I. Passage
Crooked I.
Plana Cays
Albert Town
Snug Corner
Mayaguana I.
Acklins I.
Mira por vos Cay
Cay Verde
Caicos Passage
Turks & Caicos (U.K.)
Hogsty Reef
Caicos Is.
Little Inagua I.
Turks Island
Turks Is.
Turks Passage
Lake Rosa
Great Inagua I.
Matthew Town

OCEAN

Tropic of Cancer

25

B

20

y Santa
omingo
nes
illa
ayari
Moa
Baracoa
Pta. de Maisi
uantánamo
Paso de los Vientos
(Windward Passage)
Cap-à-Foux
Jean Rabel
Port-de-Paix
Cap-Haïtien
Monte Cristi
LA ISABELA
Puerto Plata
Santiago de los Cabelleros
San Francisco de Macorís
Milwaukee Deep 9200
Puerto Rico Trench
C

Fort Liberté
St-Marc
Hinche
Gonaïves
G. de la Gonâve
Cord. Central
La Vega
Nagua
Samana
Sánchez
Sabana de la Mar
Hato Mayor
C. Engaño
Bayamón
SAN JUAN
Carolina
Anegada
Virgin Gorda
Tortola
St. Thomas
Anegada Passage
Sombrero (U.K.)
3175
Arecibo
Aguadilla
1338
Ponce
Fajardo
Virgin Is. (U.K.)
Road Town
Anguilla (U.K.)
St.-Martin (Fr.)
HAÏTI
DOMINICAN REP.
Î. de la Gonâve
San Juan
L. Enriquillo
Azua
La Romana
B. de Yuma
Higüey
Caguas
Carolina
Charlotte Amalie
Virgin Is. (U.S.A.)
St. Maarten (Neth.)
Saba (Neth.)
St.-Barthélemy (Fr.)
Jérémie
PORT-AU-PRINCE
2280
La Vega
San Cristóbal
SANTO DOMINGO
Mayagüez
Guayama
Christiansted
St. Croix
St. Eustatius (Neth.)
Redonda
Barbuda
ANTIGUA & BARBUDA
vassa I.
(U.S.A.)
e Marie
C. Carcasse
Massif de la Hotte
Petit Goâve
Jacmel
Barahona
Compostela
Isla Mona (U.S.A.)
Frederiksted
Basseterre
Nevis
ST. KITTS & NEVIS
St. John's
Antigua
Les Cayes
Aquin
Pointe-à- Gravois
Pedernales
I. Beata
C. Beata
PUERTO RICO (U.S.A.)
Montserrat (U.K.)
Ste.-Rose
Le Moule
La Désirade

Hispaniola

Antilles

Guadeloupe Passage
GUADELOUPE (Fr.)
Pointe-à-Pitre
Marie-Galante (Fr.)
Grand-Bourg
I. des Saintes (Fr.)
Basse-Terre
Dominica Passage
Portsmouth
DOMINICA
I. de Aves (Venezuela)
Roseau
Martinique Passage
Mt. Pelée 1397
Ste.-Marie
Fort-de-France
Le François
Rivière-Pilote
MARTINIQUE (Fr.)
St. Lucia Channel
Castries
Soufrière
ST. LUCIA
St. Vincent Passage
La Soufrière 1234
ST. VINCENT
Speightstown
Bridgetown
BARBADOS
Kingstown
& THE
Hillsborough
Grenadines
GRENADINES
St. George's
GRENADA

BEAN

SEA

Leeward Islands Lesser Antilles
Windward Islands Lesser Antilles

15

60

D

Lesser

Antilles

Pta. Gallinas
Pen. de la Guajira
Pta. Espada
C. San Román
Aruba (Neth.)
Curaçao
Willemstad
NETH. ANTILLES
Bonaire
Is. Las Aves (Ven.)
Is. Los Roques (Ven.)
I. Orchila (Ven.)
I. Blanquilla (Ven.)
Is. Los Hermanos (Ven.)
Is. Los Testigos (Ven.)
Tobago
Scarborough
Port of Spain
Galera Point

SANTA MARTA
Ríohacha
Uribia
GUAJIRA
Cienaga
Sierra Nevada de Santa Marta 5800
San Rafael
Pen. de Paraguaná
Punto Fijo
Golfo de Venezuela
Punta Cardón
Puerto Cumarebo
Coro
La Vela de Coro
Tucacas
Puerto Cabello
Maracay
Maiquetía
La Guaira
CARACAS
DISTRITO FEDERAL
I. La Tortuga (Ven.)
NUEVA ESPARTA
I. de Margarita
La Asunción
Porlamar
Río Caribe
Pen. de Paria
Güiria
G. de Paria
Trinidad
Arima
Río Claro
San Fernando
Serpent's Mouth
Dragon's Mouth

ARRAN-QUILLA
Baranoa
LÁNTICO
Soledad
Sabanalarga
San
Fundación
Calamar
Valledupar
Agustín Codazzi
CÉSAR
La Concepción
Villa del Rosario
Ciudad Ojeda
MARACAIBO
Santa Rita
Cabimas
Baragua
Carora
San Felipe
YARACUY
FALCÓN
Mene de Mauroa
Altagracia
Mene Grande
LARA
Valencia
CARABOBO
Villa de Cura
MIRANDA
ARAGUA
Los Teques
Río Chico
Ocumare del Tuy
Cúpira
Barcelona
Puerto La Cruz
Cumaná
Cariaco
Carúpano
SUCRE
Caripito
Caicara
Maturín
MONAGAS
DELTA
Tucupita
AMACURO
Los Barrancos

Lago de Maracaibo
Machiques
BARQUISIMETO
Yaritagua
Yaritagua de los Morros
San Carlos
El Tocuyo
Acarigua
San Juan de los Morros
Altagracia de Orituco
Anaco
Cantaura
El Tigre
Ciudad Guayana
Sierra Imataca

10

E

Fundación
MAGDALENA
Plato
Zambrano
Carmen
nce-
Rica
OBA
ABA
Corozal
Sincé
Sahagún
San Planeta
Majagual
Mompós
Magangué
El Banco
Encontrados
San Carlos del Zulia
ZULIA
Betijoque
Trujillo
Valera
TRUJILLO
Acarigua
PORTUGUESA
Guanare
San Fernando de Apure
Valle de la Pascua
GUÁRICO
Santa María de Ipire
Pariaguán
Soledad
El Pao
ANZOÁTEGUI
Ciudad Bolívar
Upata
El Callao
Tumeremo
Guasipati

Ayapel
Caucasia
BOLÍVAR
Simití
NORTE DE SANTANDER
Ocaña
Cúcuta
TACHIRA
Barinas
BARINAS
San
Santa Bárbara
Achaguas
VENEZUELA
Apure
Caicara
Embalse de Guri

Sierra de Perijá
MÉRIDA
Cord. de Mérida
Ciudad Bolivia
Libertad
San Fernando de Apure
Bruzual
Puerto de Nutrias
El Baúl
Calabozo
Manapire
Orinoco
Mapire
Guárico
Portuguesa

West from Greenwich
COPYRIGHT GEORGE PHILIP LTD

75 70 65 60
5 6 7

109
119
124 125

100 0 200 400 600 800 1000 1200 1400 km
100 0 200 400 600 800 1000 miles

Havana
BAHAMAS
Turks & Caicos Is.
(U.K.)
Tropic of Cancer
C U B A
Virgin Is.
(U.K.)
HAITI
DOMINICAN
REP.
San Juan
ANTIGUA &
BARBUDA
Port-au-
Prince
PUERTO
RICO
(U.S.A.)
ST. KITTS
& NEVIS
GUADELOUPE
(Fr.)
JAMAICA
Kingston
DOMINICA
MARTINIQUE
(Fr.)
MEXICO
Basse-Terre
Fort-de-France
Castries ST. LUCIA
ST. VINCENT
BARBADOS
GUATEMALA
BELIZE
C a r i b b e a n   S e a
Aruba
Curaçao
Kingstown Bridgetown
GRENADA St. George's
Guatemala
HONDURAS
San Salvador
EL SALVADOR
Tegucigalpa
NICARAGUA
GRENADA
Port of
Spain
TRINIDAD &
TOBAGO
Managua
Barranquilla
C. de
la Aguja
Maracaibo
Caracas
COSTA
San José
Cartagena
Bárquisimeto
RICA
G. of
Darién
Cúcuta
Valencia
Panamá
San Cristóbal
Orinoco
PANAMA
Medellín
Bucaramanga
VENEZUELA
Ciudad Guayana
Georgetown
Gulf of Panamá
Bogotá
Paramaribo
Cali
GUYANA
Cayenne
C. Orange
COLOMBIA
SURINAM
FRENCH
GUIANA
RORAIMA
Galapagos Is.
(Ecuador)
Quito
AMAPÁ
ECUADOR
Putumayo
Japurá
Equator
Guayaquil
Napo
Amazon
Marajó
I.
Belém
G. of Guayaquil
Iquitos
Manaus
Santarém
São Luís
Marañón
AMAZONAS
Amazon
Fortaleza
Chiclayo
Ucayali
Juruá
Madeira
PARÁ
C. de
São Roque
Trujillo
Purus
MARANHÃO
Teresina
CEARÁ
Natal
Chimbote
ACRE
Pôrto Velho
PIAUÍ
RIO G.
DO NORTE
PARAÍBA
PERU
Madre de Dios
RONDÔNIA
Tocantins
Campina Grande
PERNAMBUCO
Recife
Callao LIMA
B R A Z I L
Cuzco
Mamoré
MATO GROSSO
ALAGOAS
Maceió
L.
Titicaca
TOCANTINS
SERGIPE
Aracaju
Arequipa
La Paz
BOLIVIA
Cuiabá
GOIÁS
BAHÍA
Salvador
Cochabamba
Santa Cruz
DIS. FED Brasília
São Francisco
Sucre
Goiânia
Iquique
MATO GROSSO
DO SUL
MINAS GERAIS
ESPÍRITO
SANTO
Belo
Horizonte
Vitória
PACIFIC
Paraguay
Paraná
Ribeirão
Prêto
Juiz
de Fora
Campos
Antofagasta
PARAGUAY
Pilcomayo
SÃO PAULO
Campinas
R. DE J.
San Félix
(Chile)
San Ambrosio
(Chile)
Salta
Asunción
PARANÁ
SÃO
PAULO
Niterói
RIO DE
JANEIRO
San Miguel
de Tucumán
Resistencia
Corrientes
Curitiba
OCEAN
Salado
Uruguay
SANTA CATARINA
Córdoba
Santa Fe
Paraná
RIO GRANDE
DO SUL
Pelotas
Pôrto Alegre
Arch. de Juan Fernández
(Chile)
San Juan
Mendoza
Rosario
URUGUAY
Viña del Mar
Valparaíso
SANTIAGO
BUENOS AIRES
Montevideo
Talca
La Plata
Río de la Plata
Concepción
A R G E N T I N A
Bahía
Blanca
Mar del Plata
Valdivia
C H I L E
Colorado
Negro
Puerto Montt
Viedma
Chubut
Comodoro Rivadavia
Gulf of San Jorge
Gulf of Penas
West Falkland
FALKLAND IS.
(U.K.)
Stanley
East Falkland
Magellan's Str.
Punta Arenas
Tierra del Fuego
South Georgia
(U.K.)
C. Horn

N O R T H

A T L A N T I C

O C E A N

S O U T H

A T L A N T I C

O C E A N

Tropic of Capricorn

Projection: Lambert's Azimuthal Equal Area

■ LIMA Capital Cities

West from Greenwich

CARTOGRAPHY BY PHILIP'S.

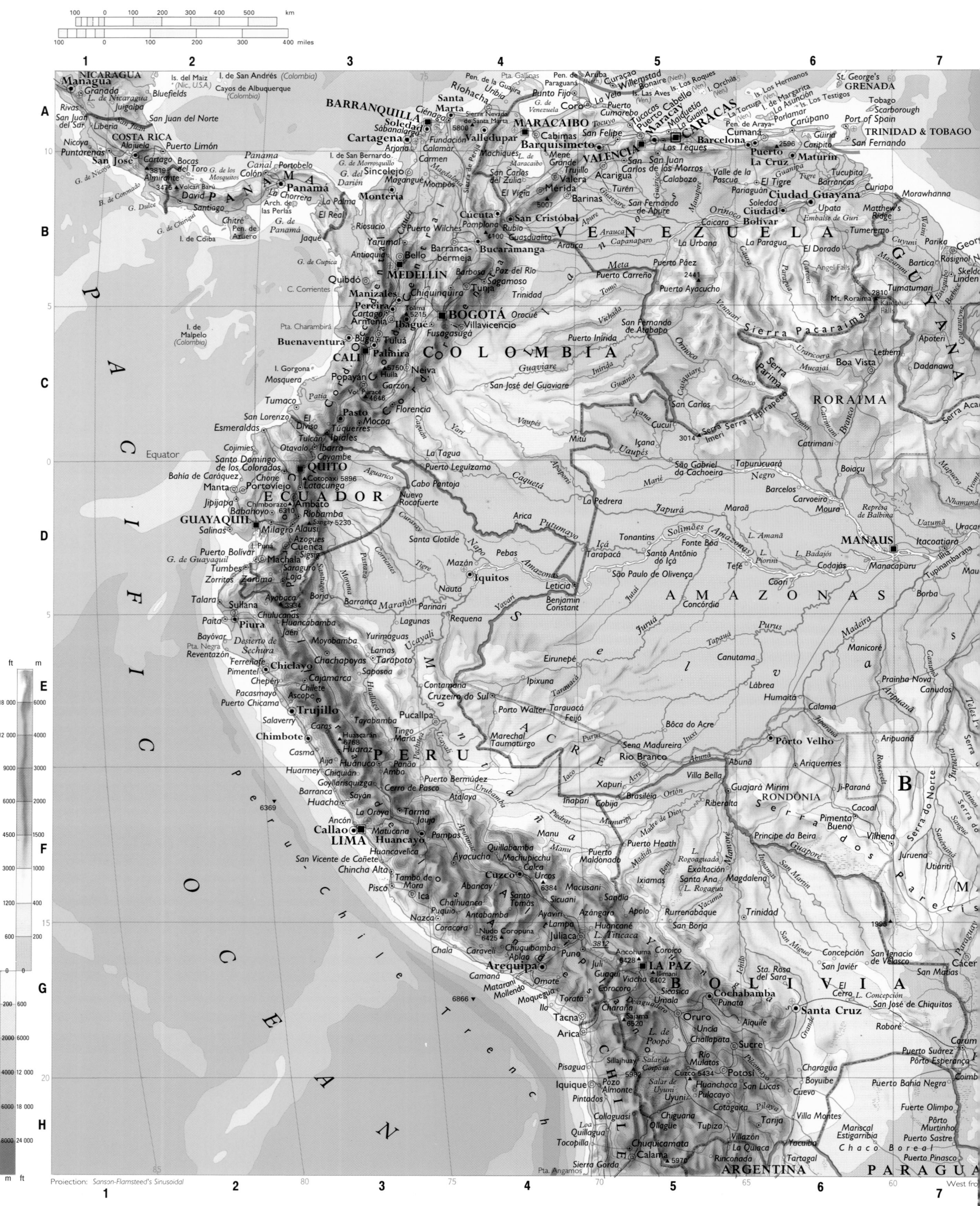

A T L A N T I C

O C E A N

Equator

São Paulo
(Braz.)

Fernando de Noronha
(Braz.)

Rocas

SURINAM
FRENCH
GUIANA

AMAPÁ

Serra Tumucumaque

Macapá

I. Caviana
I. Mexiana

I. de Maracá

Merirumã

Serra do Navio

C. Maguarinho

Chaves

I. de Soure

Afuá

Salinópolis

Curuçá

Vigia

Bragança

Viseu

Marajó

BELÉM

Castanhal

Abaetetuba

Cametá

Cururupu

B. de São Marcos

São Luís

Alcântara

Barreirinhas

Tutóia

Luís Correia

Camocim

Granja

Itapipoca

Caucaia

FORTALEZA

Cascavel

Sobral

Maranguape

Baturité

Aracati

Areia Branca

Macau

Ceará Mirim

C. de São Roque

Mossoró

RIO GRANDE
DO NORTE

Natal

Canguaretama

Mamanguape

Cabedelo

João Pessoa

PARAÍBA

Campina
Grande

Olinda

RECIFE

Jaboatão

Vitória de Santo Antão

Garanhuns

Palmares

Rio Largo

Arapiraca

Maceió

ALAGOAS

Penedo

Propriá

SERGIPE

Capela

Aracaju

São Cristóvão

Estância

OBIDOS

Santarém

Belterra

Aveiro

Brasília Legal

Itaituba

PARÁ

Altamira

Tucuruí

Represa de
Tucuruí

Marabá

Serra dos Carajás

Carajás

São João do
Araguaia

Tocantinópolis

Araguaína

Conceição do
Araguaia

Araguacema

MARANHÃO

Imperatriz

Barra
do Corda

Grajaú

Pôrto Franco

Estreito

Carolina

Riachão

Loreto

Balsas

Pedreiras

Caxias

Codó

Coroatá

Campo
Maior

Oiticica

Teresina

Crateús

Senador Pompeu

Quixadá

Ipu

Quixeramobim

Amarante

Valença
do Piauí

Floriano

Nova Iorque

Oeiras

Picos

Iguatu

Caicó

Currais
Novos

Cedro

Cajàzeiras

Sousa

Patos

Alagoa
Grande

Pombal

Crato

Juàzeiro
do Norte

Paulistana

Uruçuí

São João
do Piauí

Santa
Filomena

Novo Remanso

Caracol

Chapada do
Araripe

Ouricuri

Salgueiro

Pesqueira

PERNAMBUCO

Caruaru

Petrolina

Juàzeiro

São Francisco

Senhor do
Bonfim

Paulo Afonso

Palmeira
dos
Indios

Palmas

Pôrto Nacional

TOCANTINS

Peixe

Gurupi

Serra da Mangabeiras

Parnaguá

Parnaguá

Barra

Xique-Xique

Jacobina

Mundo
Novo

Queimadas

Serrinha

Feira de
Santana

Alagoinhas

Santo Amaro

SALVADOR

B. de Todos os Santos

Nazaré

Valença

Serra Geral de Goiás

BAHÍA

Taguatinga

Barreiras

Ibotirama

Bom Jesus
da Lápa

Serra do Sincorá

Castro
Alves

Cachoeira

Santa Isabel
do Morro

I. do Bananal

Santa Maria
da Vitória

São Domingos

Campos Belos

Paranã

Posse

Carinhanha

Caetité

Brumado

Condeúba

Jequié

Ubaitaba

Itabuna

Vitória da
Conquista

Ilhéus

Canavieiras

MATO GROSSO

Planalto do

MATO GROSSO
DO SUL

Santo Antonio

Barra do Garças

Rondonópolis

Goiás

Aruanã

Niquelândia

Uruaçu

Formosa

Taguatinga

DIST
FED

BRASÍLIA

Luziânia

Anápolis

Vianópolis

GOIÁS

Goiânia

Januária

São Francisco

Janaúba

Montes
Claros

Salinas

Araçuaí

Teófilo Otoni

Pedra Azul

Monte Azul

Jequitinhonha

Itamaraju

Prado

Caravelas

Nanuque

Belmonte

Pôrto Seguro

Mucuri

Vitória

Vila Velha

Cariacica

Conceição da Barra

São Mateus

Linhares

Colatina

Caratinga

Governador
Valadares

Nova
Venécia

Diamantina

Corinto

Ipatinga

MINAS GERAIS

Campo
Grande

Miranda

Aquidauana

Ribas do Rio
Pardo

Três Lagoas

Panorama

Dourados

Ponta Porã

Pedro Juan
Caballero

Paranaíba

Santa Fé do Sul

Rio Prêto

Andradina

Araçatuba

Penápolis

Presidente
Epitácio

Presidente
Prudente

Marília

Assis

Bauru

Jaú

Botucatu

Piracicaba

Limeira

Campinas

Uberlândia

Uberaba

Frutal

Prata

Araxá

Patrocínio

Patos de
Minas

Ibiá

Araguari

Ituiutaba

Catalão

Itumbiara

Rio Verde

Jataí

Quirinópolis

Alto Araguaia

Coxim

Morrinhos

Pirapora

Curvelo

Sête Lagoas

Sabará

Itabira

Ponte Nova

BELO HORIZONTE

Divinópolis

Nova
Lima

Ouro
Prêto

Conselheiro
Lafaiete

Barbacena

Juiz de Fora

Ubá

Cachoeiro de Itapemirim

Itaperuna

Campos

Cabo Frio

Três Rios

Nova Friburgo

Petrópolis

Niterói

RIO DE JANEIRO

Volta
Redonda

São
João
del Rei

Poços de
Caldas

Moji-Mirim

São Carlos

Catanduva

Lins

SÃO
PAULO

Ribeirão Prêto

Franca

Passos

Guaxupé

Igarapava

São José do
Rio Prêto

Paracatu

Ipameri

Pedro Afonso

Chapada das Mangabeiras

PIAUÍ

Paulo Afonso

Araguaína

Crixás

Formosa

Água Clara

COPYRIGHT GEORGE PHILIP LTD.

Trindade
(Braz.)

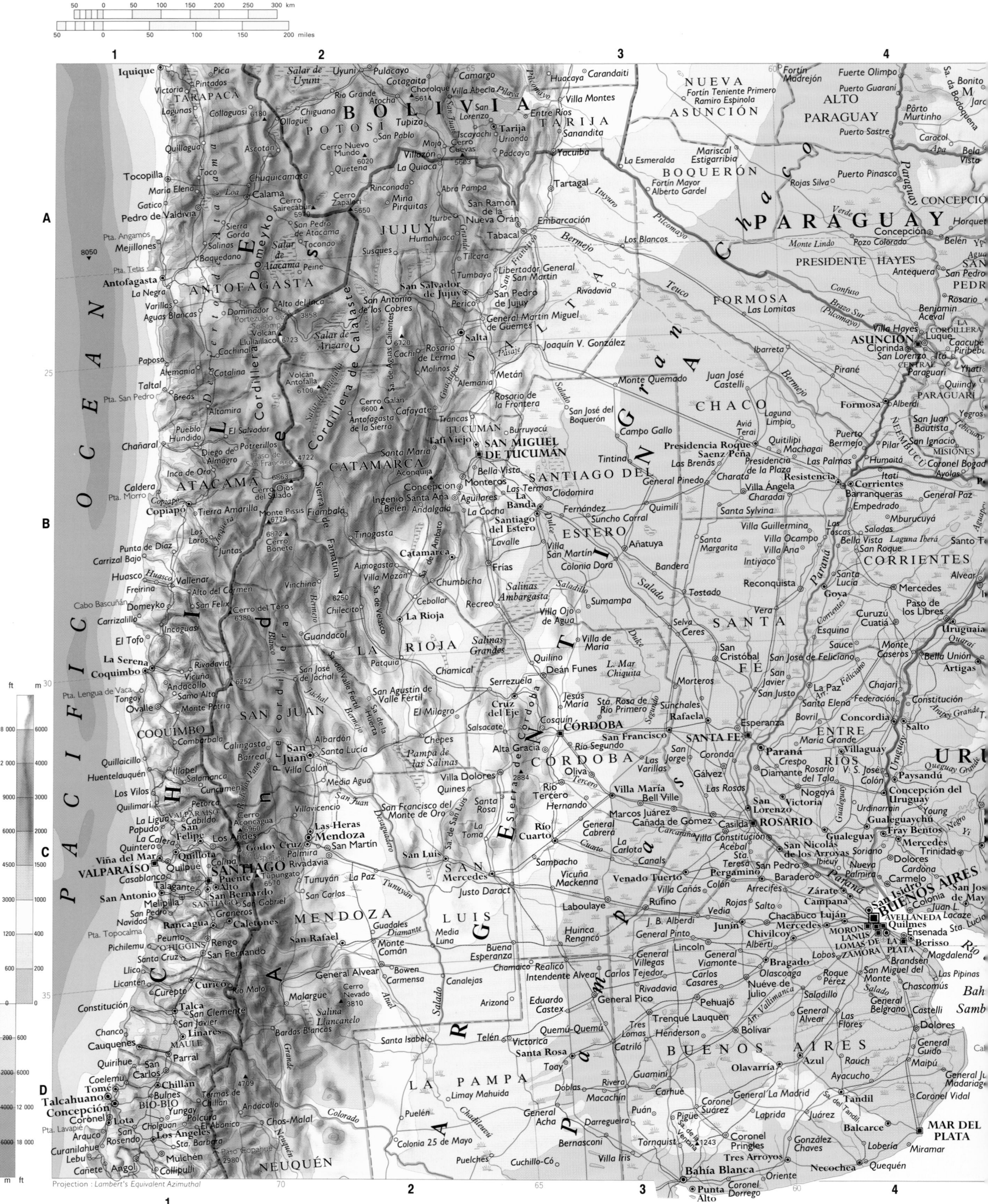

Projection : Lambert's Equivalent Azimuthal

**A T L A N T I C**

**O C E A N**

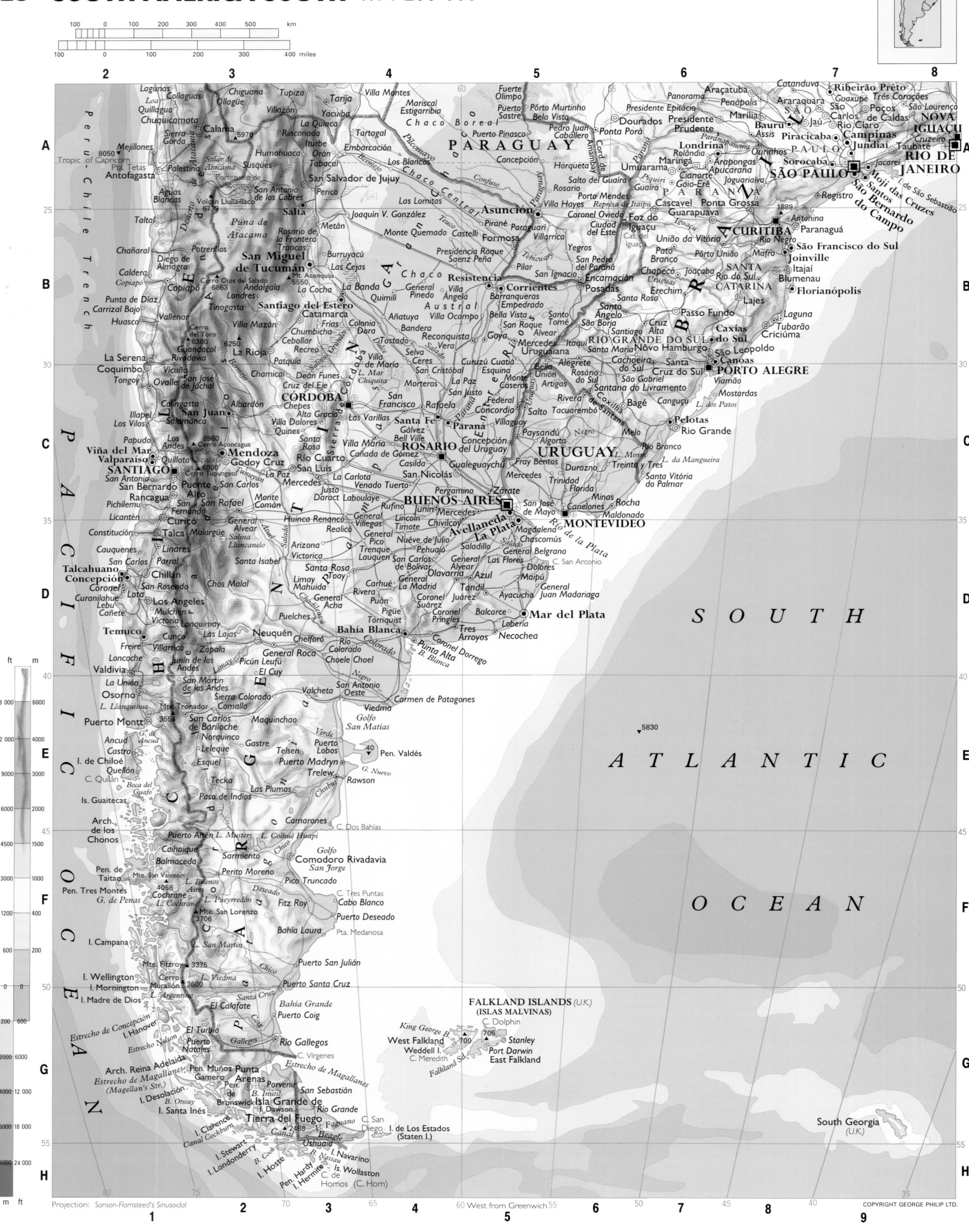

# INDEX

The index contains the names of all the principal places and features shown on the World Maps. Each name is followed by an additional entry in italics giving the country or region within which it is located. The alphabetical order of names composed of two or more words is governed primarily by the first word and then by the second. This is an example of the rule:

| | | |
|---|---|---|
| Mīr Kūh, *Iran* ............. | **71** | **E8** |
| Mīr Shahdād, *Iran* ......... | **71** | **E8** |
| Mira, *Italy* ................. | **29** | **C9** |
| Mira por vos Cay, *Bahamas* .. | **121** | **B5** |
| Miraj, *India* ............... | **66** | **79** |

Physical features composed of a proper name (Erie) and a description (Lake) are positioned alphabetically by the proper name. The description is positioned after the proper name and is usually abbreviated:

Erie, L., *N. Amer.* .......... **110 D4**

Where a description forms part of a settlement or administrative name however, it is always written in full and put in its true alphabetic position:

Mount Morris, *U.S.A.* ....... **110 D7**

Names beginning with M' and Mc are indexed as if they were spelled Mac. Names beginning St. are alphabetised under Saint, but Sankt, Sint, Sant', Santa and San are all spelt in full and are alphabetised accordingly. If the same place name occurs two or more times in the index and all are in the same country, each is followed by the name of the administrative subdivision in which it is located. The names are placed in the alphabetical order of the subdivisions. For example:

| | | |
|---|---|---|
| Jackson, *Ky., U.S.A.* ......... | **108** | **G4** |
| Jackson, *Mich., U.S.A.* ....... | **108** | **D3** |
| Jackson, *Minn., U.S.A.* ....... | **112** | **D7** |

The number in bold type which follows each name in the index refers to the number of the map page where that feature or place will be found. This is usually the largest scale at which the place or feature appears.

The letter and figure which are in bold type immediately after the page number give the grid square on the map page, within which the feature is situated. The letter represents the latitude and the figure the longitude.

In some cases the feature itself may fall within the specified square, while the name is outside. This is usually the case only with features which are larger than a grid square.

Rivers are indexed to their mouths or confluences, and carry the symbol → after their names. A solid square ■ follows the name of a country, while an open square □ refers to a first order administrative area.

## ABBREVIATIONS USED IN THE INDEX

*A.C.T.* – Australian Capital Territory
*A.R.* – Autonomous Region
*Afghan.* – Afghanistan
*Afr.* – Africa
*Ala.* – Alabama
*Alta.* – Alberta
*Amer.* – America(n)
*Arch.* – Archipelago
*Ariz.* – Arizona
*Ark.* – Arkansas
*Atl. Oc.* – Atlantic Ocean
*B.* – Baie, Bahía, Bay, Bucht, Bugt
*B.C.* – British Columbia
*Bangla.* – Bangladesh
*Barr.* – Barrage
*Bos.-H.* – Bosnia-Herzegovina
*C.* – Cabo, Cap, Cape, Coast
*C.A.R.* – Central African Republic
*C. Prov.* – Cape Province
*Calif.* – California
*Cat.* – Catarata
*Cent.* – Central
*Chan.* – Channel
*Colo.* – Colorado
*Conn.* – Connecticut
*Cord.* – Cordillera
*Cr.* – Creek
*Czech.* – Czech Republic
*D.C.* – District of Columbia
*Del.* – Delaware
*Dem.* – Democratic
*Dep.* – Dependency
*Des.* – Desert
*Dét.* – Détroit
*Dist.* – District
*Dj.* – Djebel
*Domin.* – Dominica
*Dom. Rep.* – Dominican Republic
*E.* – East
*E. Salv.* – El Salvador
*Eq. Guin.* – Equatorial Guinea
*Est.* – Estrecho
*Falk. Is.* – Falkland Is.
*Fd.* – Fjord
*Fla.* – Florida
*Fr.* – French
*G.* – Golfe, Golfo, Gulf, Guba, Gebel
*Ga.* – Georgia
*Gt.* – Great, Greater
*Guinea-Biss.* – Guinea-Bissau
*H.K.* – Hong Kong
*H.P.* – Himachal Pradesh
*Hants.* – Hampshire
*Harb.* – Harbor, Harbour
*Hd.* – Head
*Hts.* – Heights
*I.(s).* – Île, Ilha, Insel, Isla, Island, Isle
*Ill.* – Illinois
*Ind.* – Indiana
*Ind. Oc.* – Indian Ocean
*Ivory C.* – Ivory Coast
*J.* – Jabal, Jebel
*Jaz.* – Jazīrah
*Junc.* – Junction
*K.* – Kap, Kapp
*Kans.* – Kansas
*Kep.* – Kepulauan
*Ky.* – Kentucky
*L.* – Lac, Lacul, Lago, Lagoa, Lake, Limni, Loch, Lough
*La.* – Louisiana
*Ld.* – Land
*Liech.* – Liechtenstein
*Lux.* – Luxembourg
*Mad. P.* – Madhya Pradesh
*Madag.* – Madagascar
*Man.* – Manitoba
*Mass.* – Massachusetts
*Md.* – Maryland
*Me.* – Maine
*Medit. S.* – Mediterranean Sea
*Mich.* – Michigan
*Minn.* – Minnesota
*Miss.* – Mississippi
*Mo.* – Missouri
*Mont.* – Montana
*Mozam.* – Mozambique
*Mt.(s)* – Mont, Montaña, Mountain
*Mte.* – Monte
*Mti.* – Monti
*N.* – Nord, Norte, North, Northern, Nouveau
*N.B.* – New Brunswick
*N.C.* – North Carolina
*N. Cal.* – New Caledonia
*N. Dak.* – North Dakota
*N.H.* – New Hampshire
*N.I.* – North Island
*N.J.* – New Jersey
*N. Mex.* – New Mexico
*N.S.* – Nova Scotia
*N.S.W.* – New South Wales
*N.W.T.* – North West Territory
*N.Y.* – New York
*N.Z.* – New Zealand
*Nat.* – National
*Nebr.* – Nebraska
*Neths.* – Netherlands
*Nev.* – Nevada
*Nfld.* – Newfoundland
*Nic.* – Nicaragua
*O.* – Oued, Ouadi
*Occ.* – Occidentale
*Okla.* – Oklahoma
*Ont.* – Ontario
*Or.* – Orientale
*Oreg.* – Oregon
*Os.* – Ostrov
*Oz.* – Ozero
*P.* – Pass, Passo, Pasul, Pulau
*P.E.I.* – Prince Edward Island
*Pa.* – Pennsylvania
*Pac. Oc.* – Pacific Ocean
*Papua N.G.* – Papua New Guinea
*Pass.* – Passage
*Peg.* – Pegunungan
*Pen.* – Peninsula, Péninsule
*Phil.* – Philippines
*Pk.* – Peak
*Plat.* – Plateau
*Prov.* – Province, Provincial
*Pt.* – Point
*Pta.* – Ponta, Punta
*Pte.* – Pointe
*Qué.* – Québec
*Queens.* – Queensland
*R.* – Rio, River
*R.I.* – Rhode Island
*Ra.* – Range
*Raj.* – Rajasthan
*Recr.* – Recreational, Récréatif
*Reg.* – Region
*Rep.* – Republic
*Res.* – Reserve, Reservoir
*Rhld-Pfz.* – Rheinland-Pfalz
*S.* – South, Southern, Sur
*Si. Arabia* – Saudi Arabia
*S.C.* – South Carolina
*S. Dak.* – South Dakota
*S.I.* – South Island
*S. Leone* – Sierra Leone
*Sa.* – Serra, Sierra
*Sask.* – Saskatchewan
*Scot.* – Scotland
*Sd.* – Sound
*Sev.* – Severnaya
*Sib.* – Siberia
*Sprs.* – Springs
*St.* – Saint
*Sta.* – Santa
*Ste.* – Sainte
*Sto.* – Santo
*Str.* – Strait, Stretto
*Switz.* – Switzerland
*Tas.* – Tasmania
*Tenn.* – Tennessee
*Terr.* – Territory, Territoire
*Tex.* – Texas
*Tg.* – Tanjung
*Trin. & Tob.* – Trinidad & Tobago
*U.A.E.* – United Arab Emirates
*U.K.* – United Kingdom
*U.S.A.* – United States of America
*Ut. P.* – Uttar Pradesh
*Va.* – Virginia
*Vdkhr.* – Vodokhranilishche
*Vdskh.* – Vodoskhovyshche
*Vf.* – Vîrful
*Vic.* – Victoria
*Vol.* – Volcano
*Vt.* – Vermont
*W.* – Wadi, West
*W. Va.* – West Virginia
*Wall. & F. Is.* – Wallis and Futuna Is.
*Wash.* – Washington
*Wis.* – Wisconsin
*Wlkp.* – Wielkopolski
*Wyo.* – Wyoming
*Yorks.* – Yorkshire
*Yug.* – Yugoslavia

A Baña

# A


A Baña, Spain 34 C2
A Cañiza, Spain 34 C2
A Coruña, Spain 34 B2
A Estrada, Spain 34 C2
A Fonsagrada, Spain 34 B3
A Guarda, Spain 34 D2
A Gudiña, Spain 34 C3
A Rúa, Spain 34 C3
Aachen, Germany 24 E2
Aalborg = Ålborg, Denmark 11 G3
Aalen, Germany 25 G6
A'âli an Nîl □, Sudan 81 F3
Aalst, Belgium 17 D4
Aalten, Neths. 17 C6
Aalter, Belgium 17 C3
Äänekoski, Finland 9 E21
Aarau, Switz. 25 H4
Aarberg, Switz. 25 H3
Aare →, Switz. 25 H4
Aargau □, Switz. 25 H4
Aarhus = Århus, Denmark 11 H4
Aarschot, Belgium 17 D4
Aba, China 58 A3
Aba, Dem. Rep. of the Congo 86 B3
Aba, Nigeria 83 D6
Âbâ, Jazîrat, Sudan 81 E3
Abadab, J., Sudan 80 D4
Ābādān, Iran 71 D6
Abade, Ethiopia 81 F4
Ābādeh, Iran 71 D7
Abadin, Spain 34 B3
Abadla, Algeria 78 B5
Abaetetuba, Brazil 125 D9
Abagnar Qi, China 56 C9
Abai, Paraguay 127 B4
Abak, Nigeria 83 E6
Abakaliki, Nigeria 83 D6
Abakan, Russia 51 D10
Abala, Niger 83 C5
Abalak, Niger 83 B6
Abalemma, Niger 83 B6
Abana, Turkey 72 B6
Abancay, Peru 124 F4
Abano Terme, Italy 29 C8
Abarán, Spain 33 G3
Abariringa, Kiribati 96 H10
Abarqū, Iran 71 D7
Abashiri, Japan 54 B12
Abashiri-Wan, Japan 54 C12
Abaújszántó, Hungary 42 B6
Abava →, Latvia 44 A8
Ābay = Nîl el Azraq →, Sudan 81 D3
Abay, Kazakstan 50 E8
Abaya, L., Ethiopia 81 F4
Abaza, Russia 50 D9
Abbadia San Salvatore, Italy 29 F8
'Abbāsābād, Iran 71 C8
Abbay = Nîl el Azraq →, Sudan 81 D3
Abbaye, Pt., U.S.A. 108 B1
Abbé, L., Ethiopia 81 E5
Abbeville, France 19 B8
Abbeville, Ala., U.S.A. 109 K3
Abbeville, La., U.S.A. 113 L8
Abbeville, S.C., U.S.A. 109 H4
Abbiategrasso, Italy 28 C5
Abbot Ice Shelf, Antarctica 5 D16
Abbottabad, Pakistan 68 B5
Abd al Kūrī, Ind. Oc. 74 E5
Ābdar, Iran 71 D7
'Abdolābād, Iran 71 C8
Abdulpur, Bangla. 69 G13
Abéché, Chad 79 F10
Abejar, Spain 32 D2
Abekr, Sudan 81 E2
Abengourou, Ivory C. 82 D4
Abenójar, Spain 35 G6
Åbenrå, Denmark 11 J3
Abensberg, Germany 25 G7
Abeokuta, Nigeria 83 D5
Aber, Uganda 86 B3
Aberaeron, U.K. 13 E3
Aberayron = Aberaeron, U.K. 13 E3
Aberchirder, U.K. 14 D6
Abercorn = Mbala, Zambia 87 D3
Abercorn, Australia 95 D5
Aberdare, U.K. 13 F4
Aberdare Ra., Kenya 86 C4
Aberdeen, Australia 95 E5
Aberdeen, Canada 105 C7
Aberdeen, S. Africa 88 E3
Aberdeen, U.K. 14 D6
Aberdeen, Ala., U.S.A. 109 J1
Aberdeen, Idaho, U.S.A. 114 E7
Aberdeen, Md., U.S.A. 108 F7
Aberdeen, S. Dak., U.S.A. 112 C5
Aberdeen, Wash., U.S.A. 116 D3
Aberdeen, City of □, U.K. 14 D6
Aberdeenshire □, U.K. 14 D6
Aberdovey = Aberdyfi, U.K. 13 E3
Aberdyfi, U.K. 13 E3
Aberfeldy, U.K. 14 E5
Abergavenny, U.K. 13 F4
Abergele, U.K. 12 D4
Abernathy, U.S.A. 113 J4
Abert, L., U.S.A. 114 E3
Aberystwyth, U.K. 13 E3
Abhā, Si. Arabia 74 D3
Abhar, Iran 71 B6
Abhayapuri, India 69 F14
Abia □, Nigeria 83 D6
Abide, Turkey 39 C11
Abidiya, Sudan 80 D3
Abidjan, Ivory C. 82 D4
Abilene, Kans., U.S.A. 112 F6
Abilene, Tex., U.S.A. 113 J5
Abingdon, U.K. 13 F6
Abingdon, U.S.A. 109 G5
Abington Reef, Australia 94 B4
Abitau →, Canada 105 B7
Abitibi →, Canada 102 B3
Abitibi, L., Canada 102 C4
Abiy Adi, Ethiopia 81 E4
Abkhaz Republic = Abkhazia □, Georgia 49 J5
Abkhazia □, Georgia 49 J5
Abminga, Australia 95 D1
Abnûb, Egypt 80 B3
Åbo = Turku, Finland 9 F20
Abocho, Nigeria 83 D6
Abohar, India 68 D6
Aboisso, Ivory C. 82 D4
Abomey, Benin 83 D5
Abong-Mbang, Cameroon 84 D2
Abonnema, Nigeria 83 E6
Abony, Hungary 42 C5
Aboso, Ghana 82 D4
Abou-Deïa, Chad 79 F9
Aboyne, U.K. 14 D6
Abra Pampa, Argentina 126 A2
Abraham L., Canada 104 C5
Abrantes, Portugal 35 F2
Abreojos, Pta., Mexico 118 B2
Abri, Esh Shamâliya, Sudan 80 C3
Abri, Janub Kordofân, Sudan 81 E3
Abrud, Romania 42 D8
Abruzzo □, Italy 29 F10
Absaroka Range, U.S.A. 114 D9
Abtenau, Austria 26 D6
Abu, India 68 G5
Abū al Abyad, U.A.E. 71 E7
Abū al Khaṣīb, Iraq 71 D6
Abū 'Alī, Si. Arabia 71 E6
Abū 'Alī →, Lebanon 75 A4
Abu Ballas, Egypt 80 C2
Abu Deleiq, Sudan 81 D3
Abu Dhabi = Abū Ẓāby, U.A.E. 71 E7
Abu Dis, Sudan 80 D3
Abu Dom, Sudan 81 D3
Abū Du'ān, Syria 70 B3
Abu el Gairi, W. →, Egypt 75 F2
Abu Fatma, Ras, Sudan 80 C4
Abu Gabra, Sudan 81 E2
Abu Ga'da, W. →, Egypt 75 F1
Abu Gelba, Sudan 81 E3
Abu Gubeiha, Sudan 81 E3
Abu Habl, Khawr →, Sudan 81 E3
Abū Ḥadrīyah, Si. Arabia 71 E6
Abu Hamed, Sudan 80 D3
Abu Haraz, An Nîl el Azraq, Sudan 80 D3
Abu Haraz, El Gezira, Sudan 81 E3
Abu Haraz, Esh Shamâliya, Sudan 80 D3
Abu Higar, Sudan 81 E3
Abū Kamāl, Syria 70 C4
Abu Kuleiwat, Sudan 81 E2
Abū Madd, Ra's, Si. Arabia 70 E3
Abu Matariq, Sudan 81 E2
Abu Mendi, Ethiopia 81 E4
Abū Mūsā, U.A.E. 71 E7
Abū Qaṣr, Si. Arabia 70 D3
Abu Qir, Egypt 80 H7
Abu Qireiya, Egypt 80 C4
Abu Qurqâs, Egypt 80 B3
Abu Ṣafāt, W. →, Jordan 75 E5
Abu Shagara, Ras, Sudan 80 C4
Abu Shanab, Sudan 81 E2
Abu Simbel, Egypt 80 C3
Abū Şukhayr, Iraq 70 D5
Abu Sultân, Egypt 80 H8
Abu Tabari, Sudan 80 D2
Abu Tig, Egypt 80 B3
Abu Tiga, Sudan 81 E3
Abu Tineitin, Sudan 81 E3
Abu Uruq, Sudan 81 D3
Abu Zabad, Sudan 81 E2
Abū Ẓāby, U.A.E. 71 E7
Abū Zeydābād, Iran 71 C6
Abuja, Nigeria 83 D6
Abukuma-Gawa →, Japan 54 E10
Abukuma-Sammyaku, Japan 54 F10
Abunā, Brazil 124 E5
Abunā →, Brazil 124 E5
Abune Yosef, Ethiopia 81 E4
Aburo, Dem. Rep. of the Congo 86 B3
Abut Hd., N.Z. 91 K3
Abuye Meda, Ethiopia 81 E4
Abwong, Sudan 81 F3
Åby, Sweden 11 F10
Aby, Lagune, Ivory C. 82 D4
Abyad, Sudan 81 E2
Åbybro, Denmark 11 G3
Acadia National Park, U.S.A. 109 C11
Açailândia, Brazil 125 D9
Acajutla, El Salv. 120 D2
Acámbaro, Mexico 118 D4
Acanthus, Greece 40 F7
Acaponeta, Mexico 118 C3
Acapulco, Mexico 119 D5
Acarai, Serra, Brazil 124 C7
Acarigua, Venezuela 124 B5
Acatlán, Mexico 119 D5
Acayucan, Mexico 119 D6
Accéglio, Italy 28 D4
Accomac, U.S.A. 108 G8
Accous, France 20 E3
Accra, Ghana 83 D4
Accrington, U.K. 12 D5
Acebal, Argentina 126 C3
Aceh □, Indonesia 62 D1
Acerra, Italy 31 B7
Aceuchal, Spain 35 G4
Achalpur, India 66 J10
Acheng, China 57 B14
Achenkirch, Austria 26 D4
Achensee, Austria 26 D4
Acher, India 68 H5
Achern, Germany 25 G4
Achill Hd., Ireland 15 C1
Achill I., Ireland 15 C1
Achim, Germany 24 B5
Achinsk, Russia 51 D10
Acıgöl, Turkey 39 D11
Acıpayam, Turkey 39 D11
Acireale, Italy 31 E8
Ackerman, U.S.A. 113 J10
Acklins I., Bahamas 121 B5
Acme, Canada 104 C6
Acme, U.S.A. 110 F5
Aconcagua, Cerro, Argentina 126 C2
Aconquija, Mt., Argentina 126 B2
Açores, Is. dos = Azores, Atl. Oc. 78 A1
Acornhoek, S. Africa 89 C5
Acquapendente, Italy 29 F8
Acquasanta Terme, Italy 29 F10
Acquasparta, Italy 29 F9
Acquaviva delle Fonti, Italy 31 B9
Ácqui Terme, Italy 28 D5
Acraman, L., Australia 95 E2
Acre = 'Akko, Israel 75 C4
Acre □, Brazil 124 E4
Acre →, Brazil 124 E5
Acri, Italy 31 C9
Acs, Hungary 42 C3
Actium, Greece 38 C2
Acton, Canada 110 C4
Acuña, Mexico 118 B4
Ad Dammām, Si. Arabia 71 E6
Ad Dāmūr, Lebanon 75 B4
Ad Dawādimī, Si. Arabia 70 E5
Ad Dawḥah, Qatar 71 E6
Ad Dawr, Iraq 70 C4
Ad Dir'īyah, Si. Arabia 70 E5
Ad Dīwānīyah, Iraq 70 D5
Ad Dujayl, Iraq 70 C5
Ad Duwayd, Si. Arabia 70 D4
Ada, Ghana 83 D5
Ada, Serbia, Yug. 42 E5
Ada, Minn., U.S.A. 112 B6
Ada, Okla., U.S.A. 113 H6
Adabiya, Egypt 75 F1
Adair, C., Canada 101 A12
Adaja →, Spain 34 D6
Adak I., U.S.A. 100 C2
Adamaoua, Massif de l', Cameroon 83 D7
Adamawa □, Nigeria 83 D7
Adamawa Highlands = Adamaoua, Massif de l', Cameroon 83 D7
Adamello, Mte., Italy 28 B7
Adami Tulu, Ethiopia 81 F4
Adaminaby, Australia 95 F4
Adams, Mass., U.S.A. 111 D11
Adams, N.Y., U.S.A. 111 C8
Adams, Wis., U.S.A. 112 D10
Adam's Bridge, Sri Lanka 66 Q11
Adams L., Canada 104 C5
Adams Mt., U.S.A. 116 D5
Adam's Peak, Sri Lanka 66 R12
Adamuz, Spain 35 G6
Adana, Turkey 70 B2
Adanero, Spain 34 E6
Adapazarı = Sakarya, Turkey 72 B4
Adar Gwagwa, J., Sudan 80 C4
Adarama, Sudan 81 D3
Adare, C., Antarctica 5 D11
Adarte, Eritrea 81 E5
Adaut, Indonesia 63 F8
Adavale, Australia 95 D3
Adda →, Italy 28 C6
Addis Ababa = Addis Abeba, Ethiopia 81 F4
Addis Abeba, Ethiopia 81 F4
Addis Alem, Ethiopia 81 F4
Addis Zemen, Ethiopia 81 E4
Addison, U.S.A. 110 D7
Addo, S. Africa 88 E4
Adebour, Niger 83 C7
Ādeh, Iran 70 B5
Adel, U.S.A. 109 K4
Adelaide, Australia 95 E2
Adelaide, Bahamas 120 A4
Adelaide, S. Africa 88 E4
Adelaide I., Antarctica 5 C17
Adelaide Pen., Canada 100 B10
Adelaide River, Australia 92 B5
Adelanto, U.S.A. 117 L9
Adele I., Australia 92 C3
Adélie, Terre, Antarctica 5 C10
Adélie Land = Adélie, Terre, Antarctica 5 C10
Ademuz, Spain 32 E3
Aden = Al 'Adan, Yemen 74 E4
Aden, G. of, Asia 74 E4
Adendorp, S. Africa 88 E3
Aderbissinat, Niger 83 B6
Adh Dhayd, U.A.E. 71 E7
Adhoi, India 68 H4
Adi, Indonesia 63 E8
Adi Arkai, Ethiopia 81 E4
Adi Daro, Ethiopia 81 E4
Adi Keyih, Eritrea 81 E4
Adi Kwala, Eritrea 81 E4
Adi Ugri, Eritrea 81 E4
Adieu, C., Australia 93 F5
Adieu Pt., Australia 92 C3
Adigala, Ethiopia 81 E5
Adige →, Italy 29 C9
Adigrat, Ethiopia 81 E4
Adıgüzel Barajı, Turkey 39 C11
Adilabad, India 66 K11
Adilcevaz, Turkey 73 C10
Adirondack Mts., U.S.A. 111 C10
Adıyaman, Turkey 73 D8
Adjohon, Benin 83 D5
Adjud, Romania 43 D12
Adjumani, Uganda 86 B3
Adlavik Is., Canada 103 A8
Adler, Russia 49 J4
Admer, Algeria 83 A6
Admiralty G., Australia 92 B4
Admiralty I., U.S.A. 104 B2
Admiralty Is., Papua N. G. 96 H6
Ado, Nigeria 83 D5
Ado-Ekiti, Nigeria 83 D6
Adok, Sudan 81 F3
Adola, Ethiopia 81 E5
Adonara, Indonesia 63 F6
Adoni, India 66 M10
Adony, Hungary 42 C3
Adour →, France 20 E2
Adra, India 69 H12
Adra, Spain 35 J7
Adrano, Italy 31 E7
Adrar, Mauritania 78 D3
Adrar des Iforas, Algeria 78 C5
Ádria, Italy 29 C9
Adrian, Mich., U.S.A. 108 E3
Adrian, Tex., U.S.A. 113 H3
Adriatic Sea, Medit. S. 6 G9
Adua, Indonesia 63 E7
Adwa, Ethiopia 81 E4
Adygea □, Russia 49 H5
Adzhar Republic = Ajaria □, Georgia 49 K6
Adzopé, Ivory C. 82 D4
Ægean Sea, Medit. S. 39 C7
Aerhtai Shan, Mongolia 60 B4
Ærø, Denmark 11 K4
Ærøskøbing, Denmark 11 K4
Aëtós, Greece 38 D3
'Afak, Iraq 70 C5
Afándou, Greece 36 C10
Afghanistan ■, Asia 66 C4
Afikpo, Nigeria 83 D6
Aflou, Algeria 78 B6
Afragóla, Italy 31 B7
Afram →, Ghana 83 D4
Afrera, Ethiopia 81 E5
Africa 76 E6
'Afrīn, Syria 70 B3
Afşin, Turkey 72 C7
Afton, N.Y., U.S.A. 111 D9
Afton, Wyo., U.S.A. 114 E8
Afuá, Brazil 125 D8
'Afula, Israel 75 C4
Afyon, Turkey 39 C12
Afyon □, Turkey 39 C12
Afyonkarahisar = Afyon, Turkey 39 C12
Aga, Egypt 80 H7
Agadès = Agadez, Niger 83 B6
Agadez, Niger 83 B6
Agadir, Morocco 78 B4
Agaete, Canary Is. 37 F4
Agaie, Nigeria 83 D6
Again, Sudan 81 F2
Ağapınar, Turkey 39 B12
Agar, India 68 H7
Agaro, Ethiopia 81 F4
Agartala, India 67 H17
Agăş, Romania 43 D11
Agassiz, Canada 104 D4
Agats, Indonesia 63 F9
Agawam, U.S.A. 111 D12
Agbélouvé, Togo 83 D5
Agboville, Ivory C. 82 D4
Ağcabädi, Azerbaijan 49 K8
Ağdam, Azerbaijan 49 L8
Ağdaş, Azerbaijan 49 K8
Agde, France 20 E7
Agde, C. d', France 20 E7
Agdzhabedi = Ağcabädi, Azerbaijan 49 K8
Agen, France 20 D4
Agerbæk, Denmark 11 J2
Agersø, Denmark 11 J5
Ageyevo, Russia 46 E9
Āgh Kand, Iran 71 B6
Aghireşu, Romania 43 D8
Aginskoye, Russia 51 D12
Ağlasun, Turkey 39 D12
Agly →, France 20 F7
Agnew, Australia 93 E3
Agnibilékrou, Ivory C. 82 D4
Agnita, Romania 43 E9
Agnone, Italy 29 G11
Agofie, Ghana 83 D5
Agogna →, Italy 28 C5
Agogo, Sudan 81 F2
Agön, Sweden 10 C11
Agon Coutainville, France 18 C5
Ágordo, Italy 29 B9
Agori, India 69 G10
Agouna, Benin 83 D5
Agout →, France 20 E5
Agra, India 68 F7
Agrakhanskiy Poluostrov, Russia 49 J8
Agramunt, Spain 32 D6
Agreda, Spain 32 D3
Ağri, Turkey 73 C10
Agri →, Italy 31 B9
Ağrı Dağı, Turkey 70 B5
Ağri Karakose = Ağri, Turkey 73 C10
Agriá, Greece 38 B5
Agrigento, Italy 30 E6
Agrínion, Greece 38 C3
Agrópoli, Italy 31 B7
Ağstafa, Azerbaijan 49 K7
Agua Caliente, Baja Calif., Mexico 117 N10
Agua Caliente, Sinaloa, Mexico 118 B3
Agua Caliente Springs, U.S.A. 117 N10
Água Clara, Brazil 125 H8
Agua Hechicero, Mexico 117 N10
Agua Prieta, Mexico 118 A3
Aguadilla, Puerto Rico 121 C6
Aguadulce, Panama 120 E3
Aguanga, U.S.A. 117 M10
Aguanish, Canada 103 B7
Aguanus →, Canada 103 B7
Aguapey →, Argentina 126 B4
Aguaray Guazú →, Paraguay 126 A4
Aguarico →, Ecuador 124 D3
Aguas →, Spain 32 D4
Aguas Blancas, Chile 126 A2
Aguas Calientes, Sierra de, Argentina 126 B2
Aguascalientes, Mexico 118 C4
Aguascalientes □, Mexico 118 C4
Agudo, Spain 35 G6
Águeda, Portugal 34 E2
Agueda →, Spain 34 D4
Aguelhok, Mali 83 B5
Aguié, Niger 83 C6
Aguilafuente, Spain 34 D6
Aguilar, Spain 35 H6
Aguilar de Campóo, Spain 34 C6
Aguilares, Argentina 126 B2
Aguilas, Spain 33 H3
Agüimes, Canary Is. 37 G4
Aguja, C. de la, Colombia 122 B3
Agulaa, Ethiopia 81 E4
Agulhas, C., S. Africa 88 E3
Agulo, Canary Is. 37 F2
Agung, Indonesia 62 F5
Agur, Uganda 86 B3
Agusan →, Phil. 61 G6
Ağva, Turkey 41 E13
Agvali, Russia 49 J8
Aha Mts., Botswana 88 B3
Ahaggar, Algeria 78 D7
Ahamansu, Ghana 83 D5
Ahar, Iran 70 B5
Ahat, Turkey 39 C11
Ahaus, Germany 24 C2
Ahipara B., N.Z. 91 F4
Ahir Dağı, Turkey 39 C12
Ahiri, India 66 K12
Ahlat, Turkey 73 C10
Ahlen, Germany 24 D3
Ahmad Wal, Pakistan 68 E1
Ahmadabad, India 68 H5
Aḥmadābād, Khorāsān, Iran 71 C9
Aḥmadābād, Khorāsān, Iran 71 C8
Aḥmadī, Iran 71 E8
Ahmadnagar, India 66 K9
Ahmadpur, Pakistan 68 E4
Ahmadpur Lamma, Pakistan 68 E4
Ahmar, Ethiopia 81 F5
Ahmedabad = Ahmadabad, India 68 H5
Ahmednagar = Ahmadnagar, India 66 K9
Ahmetbey, Turkey 41 E11
Ahmetler, Turkey 39 C11
Ahmetli, Turkey 39 C9
Ahoada, Nigeria 83 D6
Ahome, Mexico 118 B3
Ahoskie, U.S.A. 109 G7
Ahr →, Germany 24 E3
Ahram, Iran 71 D6
Ahrax Pt., Malta 36 D1
Ahrensbök, Germany 24 A6
Ahrensburg, Germany 24 B6
Āhū, Iran 71 C6
Ahuachapán, El Salv. 120 D2
Ahun, France 19 F9
Åhus, Sweden 11 J8
Ahvāz, Iran 71 D6
Ahvenanmaa = Åland, Finland 9 F19
Aḥwar, Yemen 74 E4
Ahzar →, Mali 83 B5
Ai →, India 69 F14
Ai-Ais, Namibia 88 D2
Aichach, Germany 25 G7
Aichi □, Japan 55 G8
Aigle, Switz. 25 J2
Aignay-le-Duc, France 19 E11
Aigoual, Mt., France 20 D7
Aigre, France 20 C4
Aigua, Uruguay 127 C5
Aigueperse, France 19 F10
Aigues →, France 21 D8
Aigues-Mortes, France 21 E8
Aigues-Mortes, G. d', France 21 E8
Aiguilles, France 21 D10
Aiguillon, France 20 D4
Aigurande, France 19 F8
Aihui, China 60 A7
Aija, Peru 124 E3
Aikawa, Japan 54 E9
Aiken, U.S.A. 109 J5
Ailao Shan, China 58 F3
Aileron, Australia 94 C1
Aillant-sur-Tholon, France 19 E10
Aillik, Canada 103 A8
Ailsa Craig, U.K. 14 F3
'Ailūn, Jordan 75 C4
Aim, Russia 51 D14

**Aleşd**


Aimere, *Indonesia* 63 F6
Aimogasta, *Argentina* 126 B2
Ain □, *France* 19 F12
Ain →, *France* 21 C9
Aïn Ben Tili, *Mauritania* 78 C4
Ain Dalla, *Egypt* 80 B2
Ain el Mafki, *Egypt* 80 B2
Ain Girba, *Egypt* 80 B2
Ain Murr, *Sudan* 80 C2
Ain Qeiqab, *Egypt* 80 B1
Aïn Sefra, *Algeria* 78 B5
Ain Sheikh Murzûk, *Egypt* 80 B2
Ain Sudr, *Egypt* 75 F2
Ain Sukhna, *Egypt* 80 J8
Ain Zeitûn, *Egypt* 80 B2
Ainaži, *Latvia* 9 H21
Aínos Óros, *Greece* 38 C2
Ainsworth, *U.S.A.* 112 D5
Aiquile, *Bolivia* 124 G5
Aïr, *Niger* 83 B6
Air Force I., *Canada* 101 B12
Air Hitam, *Malaysia* 65 M4
Airaines, *France* 19 C8
Airdrie, *Canada* 104 C6
Airdrie, *U.K.* 14 F5
Aire →, *France* 19 C11
Aire →, *U.K.* 12 D7
Aire, I. de l', *Spain* 37 B11
Aire-sur-la-Lys, *France* 19 B9
Aire-sur-l'Adour, *France* 20 E3
Airlie Beach, *Australia* 94 C4
Airvault, *France* 18 F6
Aisch →, *Germany* 25 F6
Aisne □, *France* 19 C10
Aisne →, *France* 19 C9
Ait, *India* 69 G8
Aitana, Sierra de, *Spain* 33 G4
Aitkin, *U.S.A.* 112 B8
Aitolía Kai Akarnanía □, *Greece* 38 C3
Aitolikón, *Greece* 38 C3
Aiud, *Romania* 43 D8
Aix-en-Provence, *France* 21 E9
Aix-la-Chapelle = Aachen, *Germany* 24 E2
Aix-les-Bains, *France* 21 C9
Aixe-sur-Vienne, *France* 20 C5
Aíyina, *Greece* 38 D5
Aiyínion, *Greece* 40 F6
Aíyion, *Greece* 38 C4
Aizawl, *India* 67 H18
Aizenay, *France* 18 F5
Aizkraukle, *Latvia* 9 H21
Aizpute, *Latvia* 9 H19
Aizuwakamatsu, *Japan* 54 F9
Ajaccio, *France* 21 G12
Ajaccio, G. d', *France* 21 G12
Ajaigarh, *India* 69 G9
Ajalpan, *Mexico* 119 D5
Ajanta Ra., *India* 66 J9
Ajari Rep. = Ajaria □, *Georgia* 49 K6
Ajaria □, *Georgia* 49 K6
Ajax, *Canada* 110 C5
Ajdâbiyā, *Libya* 79 B10
Ajdovščina, *Slovenia* 29 C10
Ajibar, *Ethiopia* 81 E4
Ajka, *Hungary* 42 C2
'Ajmān, *U.A.E.* 71 E7
Ajmer, *India* 68 F6
Ajnala, *India* 68 D6
Ajo, *U.S.A.* 115 K7
Ajo, C. de, *Spain* 34 B7
Ajok, *Sudan* 81 F2
Ajuy, *Phil.* 61 F5
Ak Dağ, *Turkey* 39 E11
Ak Dağları, *Muğla, Turkey* 39 E11
Ak Dağları, *Sivas, Turkey* 72 C7
Akaba, *Togo* 83 D5
Akabira, *Japan* 54 C11
Akaki Beseka, *Ethiopia* 81 F4
Akala, *Sudan* 81 D4
Akamas □, *Cyprus* 36 D11
Akanthou, *Cyprus* 36 D12
Akarca, *Turkey* 39 C11
Akaroa, *N.Z.* 91 K4
Akasha, *Sudan* 80 C3
Akashi, *Japan* 55 G7
Akbarpur, *Bihar, India* 69 G10
Akbarpur, *Ut. P., India* 69 F10
Akçaabat, *Turkey* 73 B8
Akçadağ, *Turkey* 72 C7
Akçakale, *Turkey* 73 D8
Akçakoca, *Turkey* 72 B4
Akçaova, *Turkey* 41 E13
Akçay, *Turkey* 39 E11
Akçay →, *Turkey* 39 D10
Akdağ, *Turkey* 39 C8
Akdağmadeni, *Turkey* 72 C6
Akelamo, *Indonesia* 63 D7
Åkers styckebruk, *Sweden* 10 E11
Åkersberga, *Sweden* 10 E12
Aketi, *Dem. Rep. of the Congo* 84 D4
Akhaïa □, *Greece* 38 C3
Akhalkalaki, *Georgia* 49 K6
Akhaltsikhe, *Georgia* 49 K6
Akharnaí, *Greece* 38 C5
Akhelóös →, *Greece* 38 C3
Akhendriá, *Greece* 39 G7
Akhisar, *Turkey* 39 C9
Akhladhókambos, *Greece* 38 D4
Akhmîm, *Egypt* 80 B3
Akhnur, *India* 69 C6
Akhtopol, *Bulgaria* 41 D11
Akhtuba →, *Russia* 49 G8
Akhtubinsk, *Russia* 49 F8
Akhty, *Russia* 49 K8
Akhtyrka = Okhtyrka, *Ukraine* 47 G8
Aki, *Japan* 55 H6
Akimiski I., *Canada* 102 B3
Akimovka, *Ukraine* 47 J8
Åkirkeby, *Denmark* 11 J8
Akita, *Japan* 54 E10
Akita □, *Japan* 54 E10
Akjoujt, *Mauritania* 82 B2
Akka, *Mali* 82 B4
Akkaya Tepesi, *Turkey* 39 D11
Akkeshi, *Japan* 54 C12
'Akko, *Israel* 75 C4
Akköy, *Turkey* 39 D9
Aklampa, *Benin* 83 D5
Aklavik, *Canada* 100 B6
Aklera, *India* 68 G7
Akmenė, *Lithuania* 44 B9
Akmenrags, *Latvia* 44 B8
Akmolinsk = Astana, *Kazakstan* 50 D8
Akmonte = Almonte, *Spain* 35 H4
Akō, *Japan* 55 G7
Ako, *Nigeria* 83 C7
Akôbô, *Sudan* 81 F3
Akobo →, *Ethiopia* 81 F3
Akola, *India* 66 J10
Akonolinga, *Cameroon* 83 E7
Akor, *Mali* 82 C3
Akordat, *Eritrea* 81 D4
Akosombo Dam, *Ghana* 83 D5
Akot, *Sudan* 81 F3
Akoupé, *Ivory C.* 82 D4
Akpatok I., *Canada* 101 B13
Åkrahamn, *Norway* 9 G11
Akranes, *Iceland* 8 D2
Akreïjit, *Mauritania* 82 B3
Akrítas Venétiko, Ákra, *Greece* 38 E3
Akron, *Colo., U.S.A.* 112 E3
Akron, *Ohio, U.S.A.* 110 E3
Akrotiri, *Cyprus* 36 E11
Akrotíri, Ákra, *Greece* 41 F9
Akrotiri Bay, *Cyprus* 36 E12
Aksai Chin, *India* 69 B8
Aksaray, *Turkey* 70 B2
Aksay, *Kazakstan* 50 D6
Akşehir, *Turkey* 70 B1
Akşehir Gölü, *Turkey* 72 C4
Akstafa = Ağstafa, *Azerbaijan* 49 K7
Aksu, *China* 60 B3
Aksu →, *Turkey* 72 D4
Aksum, *Ethiopia* 81 E4
Aktash, *Russia* 48 C11
Aktogay, *Kazakstan* 50 E8
Aktsyabrski, *Belarus* 47 F5
Aktyubinsk = Aqtöbe, *Kazakstan* 50 D6
Aku, *Nigeria* 83 D6
Akure, *Nigeria* 83 D6
Akureyri, *Iceland* 8 D4
Akuseki-Shima, *Japan* 55 K4
Akusha, *Russia* 49 J8
Akwa-Ibom □, *Nigeria* 83 E6
Akyab = Sittwe, *Burma* 67 J18
Akyazı, *Turkey* 72 B4
Al 'Adan, *Yemen* 74 E4
Al Aḥsā = Hasa □, *Si. Arabia* 71 E6
Al Ajfar, *Si. Arabia* 70 E4
Al Amādīyah, *Iraq* 70 B4
Al 'Amārah, *Iraq* 70 D5
Al 'Aqabah, *Jordan* 75 F4
Al Arak, *Syria* 70 C3
Al 'Aramah, *Si. Arabia* 70 E5
Al Artāwīyah, *Si. Arabia* 70 E5
Al 'Āşimah = 'Ammān □, *Jordan* 75 D5
Al 'Assāfīyah, *Si. Arabia* 70 D3
Al 'Ayn, *Oman* 71 E7
Al 'Ayn, *Si. Arabia* 70 E3
Al 'Azamīyah, *Iraq* 70 C5
Al 'Azīzīyah, *Iraq* 70 C5
Al Bāb, *Syria* 70 B3
Al Bad', *Si. Arabia* 70 D2
Al Bādī, *Iraq* 70 C4
Al Baḥrah, *Kuwait* 70 D5
Al Baḥral Mayyit = Dead Sea, *Asia* 75 D4
Al Balqā' □, *Jordan* 75 C4
Al Bārūk, J., *Lebanon* 75 B4
Al Başrah, *Iraq* 70 D5
Al Baṭḥā, *Iraq* 70 D5
Al Batrūn, *Lebanon* 75 A4
Al Bayḍā, *Libya* 79 B10
Al Biqā, *Lebanon* 75 A5
Al Bi'r, *Si. Arabia* 70 D3
Al Burayj, *Syria* 75 A5
Al Faḍilī, *Si. Arabia* 71 E6
Al Fallūjah, *Iraq* 70 C4
Al Fāw, *Iraq* 71 D6
Al Fujayrah, *U.A.E.* 71 E8
Al Ghadaf, W. →, *Jordan* 75 D5
Al Ghammās, *Iraq* 70 D5
Al Ghazālah, *Si. Arabia* 70 E4
Al Ḥadīthah, *Iraq* 70 C4
Al Ḥadīthah, *Si. Arabia* 75 D6
Al Ḥaḍr, *Iraq* 70 C4
Al Ḥājānah, *Syria* 75 B5
Al Hajar al Gharbi, *Oman* 71 E8
Al Hāmad, *Si. Arabia* 70 D3
Al Hamdānīyah, *Syria* 70 C3
Al Ḥamīdīyah, *Syria* 75 A4
Al Ḥammār, *Iraq* 70 D5
Al Ḥamrā', *Si. Arabia* 70 E3
Al Ḥanākīyah, *Si. Arabia* 70 E4
Al Harīr, W. →, *Syria* 75 C4
Al Ḥasā, W. →, *Jordan* 75 D4
Al Ḥasakah, *Syria* 70 B4
Al Ḥaydān, W. →, *Jordan* 75 D4
Al Ḥayy, *Iraq* 70 C5
Al Ḥijarah, *Asia* 70 D4
Al Ḥillah, *Iraq* 70 C5
Al Ḥillah, *Si. Arabia* 74 B4
Al Hindīyah, *Iraq* 70 C5
Al Hirmil, *Lebanon* 75 A5
Al Hoceïma, *Morocco* 78 A5
Al Ḥudaydah, *Yemen* 74 E3
Al Hufūf, *Si. Arabia* 71 E6
Al Ḥumayḍah, *Si. Arabia* 70 D2
Al Ḥunayy, *Si. Arabia* 71 E6
Al Īsāwīyah, *Si. Arabia* 70 D3
Al Jafr, *Jordan* 75 E5
Al Jāfūrah, *Si. Arabia* 71 E7
Al Jaghbūb, *Libya* 79 C10
Al Jahrah, *Kuwait* 70 D5
Al Jalāmīd, *Si. Arabia* 70 D3
Al Jamalīyah, *Qatar* 71 E6
Al Janūb □, *Lebanon* 75 B4
Al Jawf, *Libya* 79 D10
Al Jawf, *Si. Arabia* 70 D3
Al Jazirah, *Iraq* 70 C5
Al Jithāmīyah, *Si. Arabia* 70 E4
Al Jubayl, *Si. Arabia* 71 E6
Al Jubaylah, *Si. Arabia* 70 E5
Al Jubb, *Si. Arabia* 70 E4
Al Junaynah, *Sudan* 79 F10
Al Kabā'ish, *Iraq* 70 D5
Al Karak, *Jordan* 75 D4
Al Karak □, *Jordan* 75 E5
Al Kāzim Tyah, *Iraq* 70 C5
Al Khābūra, *Oman* 71 F8
Al Khafji, *Si. Arabia* 71 E6
Al Khalīl, *West Bank* 75 D4
Al Khāliş, *Iraq* 70 C5
Al Kharsānīyah, *Si. Arabia* 71 E6
Al Khaşab, *Oman* 71 E8
Al Khawr, *Qatar* 71 E6
Al Khiḍr, *Iraq* 70 D5
Al Khiyām, *Lebanon* 75 B4
Al Kiswah, *Syria* 75 B5
Al Kūfah, *Iraq* 70 C5
Al Kufrah, *Libya* 79 D10
Al Kuhayfīyah, *Si. Arabia* 70 E4
Al Kūt, *Iraq* 70 C5
Al Kuwayt, *Kuwait* 70 D5
Al Labwah, *Lebanon* 75 A5
Al Lādhiqīyah, *Syria* 70 C2
Al Līth, *Si. Arabia* 74 C3
Al Liwā', *Oman* 71 E8
Al Luḥayyah, *Yemen* 74 D3
Al Madīnah, *Iraq* 70 D5
Al Madīnah, *Si. Arabia* 70 E3
Al Mafraq, *Jordan* 75 C5
Al Maḥmūdīyah, *Iraq* 70 C5
Al Majma'ah, *Si. Arabia* 70 E5
Al Makhruq, W. →, *Jordan* 75 D6
Al Makḥūl, *Si. Arabia* 70 E4
Al Manāmah, *Bahrain* 71 E6
Al Maqwa', *Kuwait* 70 D5
Al Marj, *Libya* 79 B10
Al Maṭlā, *Kuwait* 70 D5
Al Mawjib, W. →, *Jordan* 75 D4
Al Mawşil, *Iraq* 70 B4
Al Mayādin, *Syria* 70 C4
Al Mazār, *Jordan* 75 D4
Al Midhnab, *Si. Arabia* 70 E5
Al Minā', *Lebanon* 75 A4
Al Miqdādīyah, *Iraq* 70 C5
Al Mubarraz, *Si. Arabia* 71 E6
Al Mudawwarah, *Jordan* 75 F5
Al Mughayrā', *U.A.E.* 71 E7
Al Muḥarraq, *Bahrain* 71 E6
Al Mukallā, *Yemen* 74 E4
Al Mukhā, *Yemen* 74 E3
Al Musayjīd, *Si. Arabia* 70 E3
Al Musayyib, *Iraq* 70 C5
Al Muwayh, *Si. Arabia* 80 C5
Al Muwayliḥ, *Si. Arabia* 70 E2
Al Owuho = Otukpa, *Nigeria* 83 D6
Al Qā'im, *Iraq* 70 C4
Al Qalībah, *Si. Arabia* 70 D3
Al Qāmishlī, *Syria* 70 B4
Al Qaryatayn, *Syria* 75 A6
Al Qaşīm, *Si. Arabia* 70 E4
Al Qaṭ'ā, *Syria* 70 C4
Al Qaṭīf, *Si. Arabia* 71 E6
Al Qatrānah, *Jordan* 75 D5
Al Qaṭrūn, *Libya* 79 D9
Al Qayşūmah, *Si. Arabia* 70 D5
Al Quds = Jerusalem, *Israel* 75 D4
Al Qunayṭirah, *Syria* 75 C4
Al Qunfudhah, *Si. Arabia* 80 D5
Al Qurnah, *Iraq* 70 D5
Al Quşayr, *Iraq* 70 D5
Al Quşayr, *Syria* 75 A5
Al Qutayfah, *Syria* 75 B5
Al 'Ubaylah, *Si. Arabia* 74 C5
Al 'Uḍaylīyah, *Si. Arabia* 71 E6
Al 'Ulā, *Si. Arabia* 70 E3
Al 'Uqayr, *Si. Arabia* 71 E6
Al 'Uwaynid, *Si. Arabia* 70 E5
Al 'Uwayqīlah, *Si. Arabia* 70 D4
Al 'Uyūn, *Ḥijāz, Si. Arabia* 70 E3
Al 'Uyūn, *Najd, Si. Arabia* 70 E4
Al 'Uzayr, *Iraq* 70 D5
Al Wajh, *Si. Arabia* 70 E3
Al Wakrah, *Qatar* 71 E6
Al Waqbah, *Si. Arabia* 70 D5
Al Wari'āh, *Si. Arabia* 70 E5
Ala, *Italy* 28 C8
Ala Dağ, *Turkey* 70 B2
Ala Dağları, *Turkey* 73 C10
Alabama □, *U.S.A.* 109 J2
Alabama →, *U.S.A.* 109 K2
Alabaster, *U.S.A.* 109 J2
Alaca, *Turkey* 72 B6
Alacaatlı, *Turkey* 39 B10
Alaçam, *Turkey* 72 B6
Alaçam Dağları, *Turkey* 39 B10
Alaçatı, *Turkey* 39 C8
Alachua, *U.S.A.* 109 L4
Alaejos, *Spain* 34 D5
Alaérma, *Greece* 36 C9
Alagir, *Russia* 49 J7
Alagna Valsésia, *Italy* 28 C4
Alagoa Grande, *Brazil* 125 E11
Alagoas □, *Brazil* 125 E11
Alagoinhas, *Brazil* 125 F11
Alagón, *Spain* 32 D3
Alagón →, *Spain* 34 F4
Alaior, *Spain* 37 B11
Alajero, *Canary Is.* 37 F2
Alajuela, *Costa Rica* 120 D3
Alakamisy, *Madag.* 89 C8
Alaknanda →, *India* 69 D8
Alakol, Ozero, *Kazakstan* 60 B3
Alamarvdasht, *Iran* 71 E7
Alamata, *Ethiopia* 81 E4
Alameda, *Calif., U.S.A.* 116 H4
Alameda, *N. Mex., U.S.A.* 115 J10
Alaminos, *Phil.* 61 C3
Alamo, *U.S.A.* 117 J11
Alamo Crossing, *U.S.A.* 117 L13
Alamogordo, *U.S.A.* 115 K11
Alamos, *Mexico* 118 B3
Alamosa, *U.S.A.* 115 H11
Åland, *Finland* 9 F19
Alandroal, *Portugal* 35 G3
Ålands hav, *Sweden* 9 F18
Alange, Presa de, *Spain* 35 G4
Alania = North Ossetia □, *Russia* 49 J7
Alanís, *Spain* 35 G5
Alanya, *Turkey* 70 B1
Alaotra, Farihin', *Madag.* 89 B8
Alapayevsk, *Russia* 50 D7
Alappuzha = Alleppey, *India* 66 Q10
Alar del Rey, *Spain* 34 C6
Alaraz, *Spain* 34 E5
Alarcón, Embalse de, *Spain* 32 F2
Alarobia-Vohiposa, *Madag.* 89 C8
Alaşehir, *Turkey* 39 C10
Alaska □, *U.S.A.* 100 B5
Alaska, G. of, *Pac. Oc.* 100 C5
Alaska Peninsula, *U.S.A.* 100 C4
Alaska Range, *U.S.A.* 100 B4
Alássio, *Italy* 28 E5
Älät, *Azerbaijan* 49 L9
Alatri, *Italy* 29 G10
Alatyr, *Russia* 48 C8
Alatyr →, *Russia* 48 C8
Alausi, *Ecuador* 124 D3
Álava □, *Spain* 32 C2
Alava, C., *U.S.A.* 114 B1
Alaverdi, *Armenia* 49 K7
Alavus, *Finland* 9 E20
Alawoona, *Australia* 95 E3
'Alayh, *Lebanon* 75 B4
Alazani →, *Azerbaijan* 49 K8
Alba, *Italy* 28 D5
Alba □, *Romania* 43 D8
Alba Adriática, *Italy* 29 F10
Alba de Tormes, *Spain* 34 E5
Alba-Iulia, *Romania* 43 D8
Albac, *Romania* 42 D7
Albacete, *Spain* 33 F3
Albacete □, *Spain* 33 G3
Albacutya, L., *Australia* 95 F3
Ålbæk, *Denmark* 11 G4
Ålbæk Bugt, *Denmark* 11 G4
Albaida, *Spain* 33 G4
Albalate de las Nogueras, *Spain* 32 E2
Albalate del Arzobispo, *Spain* 32 D4
Alban, *France* 20 E6
Albanel, L., *Canada* 102 B5
Albania ■, *Europe* 40 E4
Albano Laziale, *Italy* 29 G9
Albany, *Australia* 93 G2
Albany, *Ga., U.S.A.* 109 K3
Albany, *N.Y., U.S.A.* 111 D11
Albany, *Oreg., U.S.A.* 114 D2
Albany, *Tex., U.S.A.* 113 J5
Albany →, *Canada* 102 B3
Albardón, *Argentina* 126 C2
Albarracín, *Spain* 32 E3
Albarracín, Sierra de, *Spain* 32 E3
Albatera, *Spain* 33 G4
Albatross B., *Australia* 94 A3
Albegna →, *Italy* 29 F8
Albemarle, *U.S.A.* 109 H5
Albemarle Sd., *U.S.A.* 109 H7
Albenga, *Italy* 28 D5
Alberche →, *Spain* 34 F6
Alberdi, *Paraguay* 126 B4
Alberes, Mts., *France* 20 F6
Ålberga, *Sweden* 11 F10
Albersdorf, *Germany* 24 A5
Albert, *France* 19 C9
Albert, L., *Africa* 86 B3
Albert, L., *Australia* 95 F2
Albert Edward Ra., *Australia* 92 C4
Albert Lea, *U.S.A.* 112 D8
Albert Nile →, *Uganda* 86 B3
Albert Town, *Bahamas* 121 B5
Alberta □, *Canada* 104 C6
Alberti, *Argentina* 126 D3
Albertinia, *S. Africa* 88 E3
Albertirsa, *Hungary* 42 C4
Alberton, *Canada* 103 C7
Albertville = Kalemie, *Dem. Rep. of the Congo* 86 D2
Albertville, *France* 21 C10
Albertville, *U.S.A.* 109 H2
Albi, *France* 20 E6
Albia, *U.S.A.* 112 E8
Albina, *Surinam* 125 B8
Albina, Ponta, *Angola* 88 B1
Albino, *Italy* 28 C6
Albion, *Mich., U.S.A.* 108 D3
Albion, *Nebr., U.S.A.* 112 E6
Albion, *Pa., U.S.A.* 110 E4
Albocácer, *Spain* 32 E5
Albolote, *Spain* 35 H7
Alborán, *Medit. S.* 35 K7
Alborea, *Spain* 33 F3
Ålborg, *Denmark* 11 G3
Ålborg Bugt, *Denmark* 11 H4
Alborz, Reshteh-ye Kūhhā-ye, *Iran* 71 C7
Albox, *Spain* 33 H2
Albufeira, *Portugal* 35 H2
Albula →, *Switz.* 25 J5
Albuñol, *Spain* 35 J7
Albuquerque, *U.S.A.* 115 J10
Albuquerque, Cayos de, *Caribbean* 120 D3
Alburg, *U.S.A.* 111 B11
Alburno, Mte., *Italy* 31 B8
Alburquerque, *Spain* 35 F4
Albury = Albury-Wodonga, *Australia* 95 F4
Albury-Wodonga, *Australia* 95 F4
Alcácer do Sal, *Portugal* 35 G2
Alcáçovas, *Portugal* 35 G2
Alcalá de Chivert, *Spain* 32 E5
Alcalá de Guadaira, *Spain* 35 H5
Alcalá de Henares, *Spain* 34 E7
Alcalá de los Gazules, *Spain* 35 J5
Alcalá del Júcar, *Spain* 33 F3
Alcalá del Río, *Spain* 35 H5
Alcalá del Valle, *Spain* 35 J5
Alcalá la Real, *Spain* 35 H7
Álcamo, *Italy* 30 E5
Alcanadre, *Spain* 32 C2
Alcanadre →, *Spain* 32 D4
Alcanar, *Spain* 32 E5
Alcanede, *Portugal* 35 F2
Alcanena, *Portugal* 35 F2
Alcañices, *Spain* 34 D4
Alcañiz, *Spain* 32 D4
Alcântara, *Brazil* 125 D10
Alcántara, *Spain* 34 F4
Alcántara, Embalse de, *Spain* 34 F4
Alcantarilla, *Spain* 33 H3
Alcaracejos, *Spain* 35 G6
Alcaraz, *Spain* 33 G2
Alcaraz, Sierra de, *Spain* 33 G2
Alcaudete, *Spain* 35 H6
Alcázar de San Juan, *Spain* 35 F7
Alchevsk, *Ukraine* 47 H10
Alcira = Alzira, *Spain* 33 F4
Alcobaça, *Portugal* 35 F2
Alcobendas, *Spain* 34 E7
Alcolea del Pinar, *Spain* 32 D2
Alcora, *Spain* 32 E4
Alcorcón, *Spain* 34 E7
Alcoutim, *Portugal* 35 H3
Alcova, *U.S.A.* 114 E10
Alcoy, *Spain* 33 G4
Alcubierre, Sierra de, *Spain* 32 D4
Alcublas, *Spain* 32 F4
Alcúdia, *Spain* 37 B10
Alcúdia, B. d', *Spain* 37 B10
Alcudia, Sierra de la, *Spain* 35 G6
Aldabra Is., *Seychelles* 77 G8
Aldama, *Mexico* 119 C5
Aldan, *Russia* 51 D13
Aldan →, *Russia* 51 C13
Aldea, Pta. de la, *Canary Is.* 37 G4
Aldeburgh, *U.K.* 13 E9
Alder Pk., *U.S.A.* 116 K5
Alderney, *U.K.* 13 H5
Aldershot, *U.K.* 13 F7
Åled, *Sweden* 11 H6
Aledo, *U.S.A.* 112 E9
Alefa, *Ethiopia* 81 E4
Aleg, *Mauritania* 82 B2
Alegranza, *Canary Is.* 37 E6
Alegranza, I., *Canary Is.* 37 E6
Alegre, *Brazil* 127 A7
Alegrete, *Brazil* 127 B4
Aleisk, *Russia* 50 D9
Aleksandriya = Oleksandriya, *Kirovohrad, Ukraine* 47 H7
Aleksandriya = Oleksandriya, *Rivne, Ukraine* 47 G4
Aleksandriyskaya, *Russia* 49 J8
Aleksandrov, *Russia* 46 D10
Aleksandrov Gay, *Russia* 48 E9
Aleksandrovac, *Serbia, Yug.* 40 C5
Aleksandrovac, *Serbia, Yug.* 40 B5
Aleksandrovka = Oleksandrovka, *Ukraine* 47 H7
Aleksandrovo, *Bulgaria* 41 C8
Aleksandrovsk-Sakhalinskiy, *Russia* 51 D15
Aleksandrów Kujawski, *Poland* 45 F5
Aleksandrów Łódźki, *Poland* 45 G6
Alekseyevka, *Samara, Russia* 48 D10
Alekseyevka, *Voronezh, Russia* 47 G10
Aleksin, *Russia* 46 E9
Aleksinac, *Serbia, Yug.* 40 C5
Além Paraíba, *Brazil* 127 A7
Alemania, *Argentina* 126 B2
Alemania, *Chile* 126 B2
Alençon, *France* 18 D7
Alenquer, *Brazil* 125 D8
Alenuihaha Channel, *U.S.A.* 106 H17
Alépé, *Ivory C.* 82 D4
Aleppo = Ḥalab, *Syria* 70 B3
Aléria, *France* 21 F13
Alès, *France* 21 D8
Aleşd, *Romania* 42 C7

Aragona


Amurang, *Indonesia* 63 D6
Amurrio, *Spain* 32 B1
Amursk, *Russia* 51 D14
Amusco, *Spain* 34 C6
Amvrakikós Kólpos, *Greece* 38 C2
Amvrosiyivka, *Ukraine* 47 J10
Amyderya = Amudarya →, *Uzbekistan* 50 E6
An Bien, *Vietnam* 65 H5
An Hoa, *Vietnam* 64 E7
An Nabatīyah at Tahta, *Lebanon* 75 B4
An Nabk, *Si. Arabia* 70 D3
An Nabk, *Syria* 75 A5
An Nafūd, *Si. Arabia* 70 D4
An Najaf, *Iraq* 70 C5
An Nāṣirīyah, *Iraq* 70 D5
An Nhon, *Vietnam* 64 F7
An Nîl □, *Sudan* 80 D3
An Nîl el Abyad □, *Sudan* 81 E3
An Nîl el Azraq □, *Sudan* 81 E3
An Nu'ayrīyah, *Si. Arabia* 71 E6
An Nu'mānīyah, *Iraq* 73 F11
An Nuwayb'ī, W. →, *Si. Arabia* 75 F3
An Thoi, Dao, *Vietnam* 65 H4
An Uaimh, *Ireland* 15 C5
Anabar →, *Russia* 51 B12
'Anabtā, *West Bank* 75 C4
Anaconda, *U.S.A.* 114 C7
Anacortes, *U.S.A.* 116 B4
Anacuao, Mt., *Phil.* 61 C4
Anadarko, *U.S.A.* 113 H5
Anadia, *Portugal* 34 E2
Anadolu, *Turkey* 72 C5
Anadyr, *Russia* 51 C18
Anadyr →, *Russia* 51 C18
Anadyrskiy Zaliv, *Russia* 51 C19
Anáfi, *Greece* 39 E7
Anafópoulo, *Greece* 39 E7
Anaga, Pta. de, *Canary Is.* 37 F3
Anagni, *Italy* 29 G10
'Ānah, *Iraq* 70 C4
Anaheim, *U.S.A.* 117 M9
Anahim Lake, *Canada* 104 C3
Anáhuac, *Mexico* 118 B4
Anakapalle, *India* 67 L13
Anakie, *Australia* 94 C4
Anaklia, *Georgia* 49 J5
Analalava, *Madag.* 89 A8
Analavoka, *Madag.* 89 C8
Análipsis, *Greece* 36 A3
Anambar →, *Pakistan* 68 D3
Anambas, Kepulauan, *Indonesia* 65 L6
Anambas Is. = Anambas, Kepulauan, *Indonesia* 65 L6
Anambra □, *Nigeria* 83 D6
Anamosa, *U.S.A.* 112 D9
Anamur, *Turkey* 70 B2
Anamur Burnu, *Turkey* 72 D5
Anan, *Japan* 55 H7
Anand, *India* 68 H5
Anánes, *Greece* 38 E6
Anantnag, *India* 69 C6
Ananyiv, *Ukraine* 47 J5
Anapa, *Russia* 47 K9
Anapodháris →, *Greece* 36 E7
Anápolis, *Brazil* 125 G9
Anapu →, *Brazil* 125 D8
Anār, *Iran* 71 D7
Anārak, *Iran* 71 C7
Anarisfjällen, *Sweden* 10 A7
Anas →, *India* 68 H5
Anatolia = Anadolu, *Turkey* 72 C5
Anatsogno, *Madag.* 89 C7
Añatuya, *Argentina* 126 B3
Anaunethad L., *Canada* 105 A8
Anbyŏn, *N. Korea* 57 E14
Ancares, Sierra de, *Spain* 34 C4
Ancaster, *Canada* 110 C5
Ancenis, *France* 18 E5
Anchor Bay, *U.S.A.* 116 G3
Anchorage, *U.S.A.* 100 B5
Anci, *China* 56 E9
Ancohuma, Nevada, *Bolivia* 122 E4
Ancón, *Peru* 124 F3
Ancona, *Italy* 29 E10
Ancud, *Chile* 128 E2
Ancud, G. de, *Chile* 128 E2
Ancy-le-Franc, *France* 19 E11
Andacollo, *Argentina* 126 D1
Andacollo, *Chile* 126 C1
Andaingo, *Madag.* 89 B8
Andalgalá, *Argentina* 126 B2
Åndalsnes, *Norway* 9 E12
Andalucía □, *Spain* 35 H6
Andalusia = Andalucía □, *Spain* 35 H6
Andalusia, *U.S.A.* 109 K2
Andaman Is., *Ind. Oc.* 52 H13
Andaman Sea, *Ind. Oc.* 62 B1
Andamooka Opal Fields, *Australia* 95 E2
Andapa, *Madag.* 89 A8
Andara, *Namibia* 88 B3
Andelot-Blancheville, *France* 19 D12
Andenes, *Norway* 8 B17
Andenne, *Belgium* 17 D5
Andéranboukane, *Mali* 83 B5
Andermatt, *Switz.* 25 J4
Andernach, *Germany* 24 E3
Andernos-les-Bains, *France* 20 D2
Anderslöv, *Sweden* 11 J7
Anderson, *Alaska, U.S.A.* 100 B5
Anderson, *Calif., U.S.A.* 114 F2
Anderson, *Ind., U.S.A.* 108 E3
Anderson, *Mo., U.S.A.* 113 G7
Anderson, *S.C., U.S.A.* 109 H4
Anderson →, *Canada* 100 B7
Anderstorp, *Sweden* 11 G7
Andes, *U.S.A.* 111 D10
Andes, Cord. de los, *S. Amer.* 122 F4
Andfjorden, *Norway* 8 B17
Andhra Pradesh □, *India* 66 L11
Andijon, *Uzbekistan* 50 E8
Andikíthira, *Greece* 38 F5
Andilamena, *Madag.* 89 B8
Andīmeshk, *Iran* 71 C6
Andímilos, *Greece* 38 E6
Andíparos, *Greece* 39 D7
Andípaxoi, *Greece* 38 B2
Andípsara, *Greece* 39 C7
Andírrion, *Greece* 38 C3
Andizhan = Andijon, *Uzbekistan* 50 E8
Andoain, *Spain* 32 B2
Andoany, *Madag.* 89 A8
Andong, *S. Korea* 57 F15
Andongwei, *China* 57 G10
Andoom, *Australia* 94 A3
Andorra, *Spain* 32 E4
Andorra ■, *Europe* 20 F5
Andorra La Vella, *Andorra* 20 F5
Andover, *U.K.* 13 F6
Andover, *Maine, U.S.A.* 111 B14
Andover, *Mass., U.S.A.* 111 D13
Andover, *N.J., U.S.A.* 111 F10
Andover, *N.Y., U.S.A.* 110 D7
Andover, *Ohio, U.S.A.* 110 E4
Andøya, *Norway* 8 B16
Andradina, *Brazil* 125 H8
Andrahary, Mt., *Madag.* 89 A8
Andramasina, *Madag.* 89 B8
Andranopasy, *Madag.* 89 C7
Andranovory, *Madag.* 89 C7
Andratx, *Spain* 37 B9
Andreanof Is., *U.S.A.* 100 C2
Andreapol, *Russia* 46 D7
Andrews, *S.C., U.S.A.* 109 J6
Andrews, *Tex., U.S.A.* 113 J3
Andreyevka, *Russia* 48 D10
Ándria, *Italy* 31 A9
Andriamena, *Madag.* 89 B8
Andriandampy, *Madag.* 89 C8
Andriba, *Madag.* 89 B8
Andrijevica, *Montenegro, Yug.* 40 D3
Andrítsaina, *Greece* 38 D3
Androka, *Madag.* 89 C7
Andropov = Rybinsk, *Russia* 46 C10
Ándros, *Greece* 38 D6
Andros I., *Bahamas* 120 B4
Andros Town, *Bahamas* 120 B4
Androscoggin →, *U.S.A.* 111 C14
Andrychów, *Poland* 45 J6
Andselv, *Norway* 8 B18
Andújar, *Spain* 35 G6
Andulo, *Angola* 84 G3
Aneby, *Sweden* 11 G8
Anegada I., *U.S. Virgin Is.* 121 C7
Anegada Passage, *W. Indies* 121 C7
Aného, *Togo* 83 D5
Anenni-Noi, *Moldova* 43 D14
Aneto, Pico de, *Spain* 32 C5
Anfu, *China* 59 D10
Ang Thong, *Thailand* 64 E3
Angamos, Punta, *Chile* 126 A1
Angara →, *Russia* 51 D10
Angara-Débou, *Benin* 83 C5
Angarab, *Ethiopia* 81 E4
Angarbaka, *Sudan* 81 F1
Angarsk, *Russia* 51 D11
Angas Hills, *Australia* 92 D4
Angaston, *Australia* 95 E2
Angaur I., *Pac. Oc.* 63 C8
Ånge, *Sweden* 10 B9
Ángel, Salto = Angel Falls, *Venezuela* 124 B6
Ángel de la Guarda, I., *Mexico* 118 B2
Angel Falls, *Venezuela* 124 B6
Angeles, *Phil.* 61 D4
Ängelholm, *Sweden* 11 H6
Angels Camp, *U.S.A.* 116 G6
Ängelsberg, *Sweden* 10 E10
Anger →, *Ethiopia* 81 F4
Angereb →, *Ethiopia* 81 E4
Ångermanälven →, *Sweden* 10 B11
Ångermanland, *Sweden* 8 E18
Angermünde, *Germany* 24 B9
Angers, *Canada* 111 A9
Angers, *France* 18 E6
Angerville, *France* 19 D9
Ängesån →, *Sweden* 8 C20
Angikuni L., *Canada* 105 A9
Angkor, *Cambodia* 64 F4
Anglès, *Spain* 32 D7
Anglesey, Isle of □, *U.K.* 12 D3
Anglet, *France* 20 E2
Angleton, *U.S.A.* 113 L7
Anglin →, *France* 20 B4
Anglisidhes, *Cyprus* 36 E12
Anglure, *France* 19 D10
Angmagssalik = Tasiilaq, *Greenland* 4 C6
Ango, *Dem. Rep. of the Congo* 86 B2
Angoche, *Mozam.* 87 F4
Angoche, I., *Mozam.* 87 F4
Angol, *Chile* 126 D1
Angola, *Ind., U.S.A.* 108 E3
Angola, *N.Y., U.S.A.* 110 D5
Angola ■, *Africa* 85 G3
Angoulême, *France* 20 C4
Angoumois, *France* 20 C4
Angra dos Reis, *Brazil* 127 A7
Angren, *Uzbekistan* 50 E8
Angtassom, *Cambodia* 65 G5
Angu, *Dem. Rep. of the Congo* 86 B1
Anguang, *China* 57 B12
Anguilla ■, *W. Indies* 121 C7
Anguo, *China* 56 E8
Angurugu, *Australia* 94 A2
Angus □, *U.K.* 14 E6
Angwa →, *Zimbabwe* 89 B5
Anhanduí →, *Brazil* 127 A5
Anholt, *Denmark* 11 H5
Anhua, *China* 59 C8
Anhui □, *China* 59 B11
Anhwei = Anhui □, *China* 59 B11
Anichab, *Namibia* 88 C1
Ánidhros, *Greece* 39 E7
Anié, *Togo* 83 D5
Animas →, *U.S.A.* 115 H9
Anina, *Romania* 42 E6
Aninoasa, *Romania* 43 F9
Anivorano, *Madag.* 89 B8
Anjalankoski, *Finland* 9 F22
Anjar, *India* 68 H4
Anji, *China* 59 B12
Anjou, *France* 18 E6
Anjozorobe, *Madag.* 89 B8
Anju, *N. Korea* 57 E13
Anka, *Nigeria* 83 C6
Ankaboa, Tanjona, *Madag.* 89 C7
Ankang, *China* 56 H5
Ankara, *Turkey* 72 C5
Ankaramena, *Madag.* 89 C8
Ankaratra, *Madag.* 85 H9
Ankarsrum, *Sweden* 11 G10
Ankasakasa, *Madag.* 89 B7
Ankavandra, *Madag.* 89 B8
Ankazoabo, *Madag.* 89 C7
Ankazobe, *Madag.* 89 B8
Ankeny, *U.S.A.* 112 E8
Ankilimalinika, *Madag.* 89 C7
Ankilizato, *Madag.* 89 C8
Ankisabe, *Madag.* 89 B8
Anklam, *Germany* 24 B9
Ankober, *Ethiopia* 81 F4
Ankoro, *Dem. Rep. of the Congo* 86 D2
Ankororoka, *Madag.* 89 D8
Anlong, *China* 58 E5
Anlu, *China* 59 B9
Anmyŏn-do, *S. Korea* 57 F14
Ånn, *Sweden* 10 A6
Ann, C., *U.S.A.* 111 D14
Ann Arbor, *U.S.A.* 108 D4
Anna, *Russia* 48 E5
Anna, *U.S.A.* 113 G10
Annaba, *Algeria* 78 A7
Annaberg-Buchholz, *Germany* 24 E9
Annalee →, *Ireland* 15 B4
Annam, *Vietnam* 64 E7
Annamitique, Chaîne, *Asia* 64 D6
Annan, *U.K.* 14 G5
Annan →, *U.K.* 14 G5
Annapolis, *U.S.A.* 108 F7
Annapolis Royal, *Canada* 103 D6
Annapurna, *Nepal* 69 E10
Annean, L., *Australia* 93 E2
Anneberg, *Sweden* 11 G8
Annecy, *France* 21 C10
Annecy, Lac d', *France* 21 C10
Annemasse, *France* 19 F13
Annenskiy Most, *Russia* 46 B9
Anning, *China* 58 E4
Anniston, *U.S.A.* 109 J3
Annobón, *Atl. Oc.* 77 G4
Annonay, *France* 21 C8
Annot, *France* 21 E10
Annotto Bay, *Jamaica* 120 C4
Ånnsjön, *Sweden* 10 A6
Annville, *U.S.A.* 111 F8
Annweiler, *Germany* 25 F3
Áno Arkhánai, *Greece* 39 F7
Áno Porróia, *Greece* 40 E7
Áno Síros, *Greece* 38 D6
Áno Viánnos, *Greece* 36 D7
Anorotsangana, *Madag.* 89 A8
Anosibe, *Madag.* 89 B8
Anou Mellene, *Mali* 83 B5
Anoumaba, *Ivory C.* 82 D4
Anóyia, *Greece* 36 D6
Anping, *Hebei, China* 56 E8
Anping, *Liaoning, China* 57 D12
Anpu Gang, *China* 58 G7
Anqing, *China* 59 B11
Anqiu, *China* 57 F10
Anren, *China* 59 D9
Ansager, *Denmark* 11 J2
Ansai, *China* 56 F5
Ansbach, *Germany* 25 F6
Anseba →, *Eritrea* 81 D4
Ansfelden, *Austria* 26 C7
Anshan, *China* 57 D12
Anshun, *China* 58 D5
Ansião, *Portugal* 34 F2
Ansley, *U.S.A.* 112 E5
Ansó, *Spain* 32 C4
Ansoain, *Spain* 32 C3
Anson, *U.S.A.* 113 J5
Anson B., *Australia* 92 B5
Ansongo, *Mali* 83 B5
Ansonia, *U.S.A.* 111 E11
Anstruther, *U.K.* 14 E6
Ansudu, *Indonesia* 63 E9
Antabamba, *Peru* 124 F4
Antakya, *Turkey* 70 B3
Antalaha, *Madag.* 89 A9
Antalya, *Turkey* 72 D4
Antalya □, *Turkey* 39 E12
Antalya Körfezi, *Turkey* 72 D4
Antambohobe, *Madag.* 89 C8
Antanambao-Manampotsy, *Madag.* 89 B8
Antanambe, *Madag.* 89 B8
Antananarivo, *Madag.* 89 B8
Antananarivo □, *Madag.* 89 B8
Antanifotsy, *Madag.* 89 B8
Antanimbaribe, *Madag.* 89 C7
Antanimora, *Madag.* 89 C8
Antarctic Pen., *Antarctica* 5 C18
Antarctica 5 E3
Antelope, *Zimbabwe* 87 G2
Antequera, *Paraguay* 126 A4
Antequera, *Spain* 35 H6
Antero, Mt., *U.S.A.* 115 G10
Antevamena, *Madag.* 89 C7
Anthemoús, *Greece* 40 F7
Anthony, *Kans., U.S.A.* 113 G5
Anthony, *N. Mex., U.S.A.* 115 K10
Anti Atlas, *Morocco* 78 C4
Anti-Lebanon = Ash Sharqi, Al Jabal, *Lebanon* 75 B5
Antibes, *France* 21 E11
Antibes, C. d', *France* 21 E11
Anticosti, Î. d', *Canada* 103 C7
Antifer, C. d', *France* 18 C7
Antigo, *U.S.A.* 112 C10
Antigonish, *Canada* 103 C7
Antigua, *Canary Is.* 37 F5
Antigua, *W. Indies* 121 C7
Antigua & Barbuda ■, *W. Indies* 121 C7
Antigua Guatemala, *Guatemala* 120 D1
Antilla, *Cuba* 120 B4
Antilles = West Indies, *Cent. Amer.* 121 D7
Antioch, *U.S.A.* 116 G5
Antioche, Pertuis d', *France* 20 B2
Antioquia, *Colombia* 124 B3
Antipodes Is., *Pac. Oc.* 96 M9
Antlers, *U.S.A.* 113 H7
Antoetra, *Madag.* 89 C8
Antofagasta, *Chile* 126 A1
Antofagasta □, *Chile* 126 A2
Antofagasta de la Sierra, *Argentina* 126 B2
Antofalla, *Argentina* 126 B2
Antofalla, Salar de, *Argentina* 126 B2
Anton, *U.S.A.* 113 J3
Antongila, Helodrano, *Madag.* 89 B8
Antonibé, *Madag.* 89 B8
Antonibé, Presqu'île d', *Madag.* 89 A8
Antonina, *Brazil* 127 B6
Antrain, *France* 18 D5
Antrim, *U.K.* 15 B5
Antrim, *U.S.A.* 110 F3
Antrim □, *U.K.* 15 B5
Antrim, Mts. of, *U.K.* 15 A5
Antrim Plateau, *Australia* 92 C4
Antrodoco, *Italy* 29 F10
Antropovo, *Russia* 48 A6
Antsakabary, *Madag.* 89 B8
Antsalova, *Madag.* 89 B7
Antsenavolo, *Madag.* 89 C8
Antsiafabositra, *Madag.* 89 B8
Antsirabe, *Antananarivo, Madag.* 89 B8
Antsirabe, *Antsiranana, Madag.* 89 A8
Antsirabe, *Mahajanga, Madag.* 89 B8
Antsiranana, *Madag.* 89 A8
Antsiranana □, *Madag.* 89 A8
Antsohihy, *Madag.* 89 A8
Antsohimbondrona Seranana, *Madag.* 89 A8
Antu, *China* 57 C15
Antwerp = Antwerpen, *Belgium* 17 C4
Antwerp, *U.S.A.* 111 B9
Antwerpen, *Belgium* 17 C4
Antwerpen □, *Belgium* 17 C4
Anupgarh, *India* 68 E5
Anuppur, *India* 69 H9
Anuradhapura, *Sri Lanka* 66 Q12
Anveh, *Iran* 71 E7
Anvers = Antwerpen, *Belgium* 17 C4
Anvers I., *Antarctica* 5 C17
Anwen, *China* 59 C13
Anxi, *Fujian, China* 59 E12
Anxi, *Gansu, China* 60 B4
Anxian, *China* 58 B5
Anxiang, *China* 59 C9
Anxious B., *Australia* 95 E1
Anyama, *Ivory C.* 82 D4
Anyang, *China* 56 F8
Anyer-Kidul, *Indonesia* 63 G11
Anyi, *Jiangxi, China* 59 C10
Anyi, *Shanxi, China* 56 G6
Anyuan, *China* 59 E10
Anyue, *China* 58 B5
Anza, *U.S.A.* 117 M10
Anze, *China* 56 F7
Anzhero-Sudzhensk, *Russia* 50 D9
Ánzio, *Italy* 30 A5
Aoga-Shima, *Japan* 55 H9
Aoiz, *Spain* 32 C3
Aomen = Macau □, *China* 59 F9
Aomori, *Japan* 54 D10
Aomori □, *Japan* 54 D10
Aonla, *India* 69 E8
Aoraki Mount Cook, *N.Z.* 91 K3
Aosta, *Italy* 28 C4
Aoudéras, *Niger* 83 B6
Aoukâr, *Mauritania* 82 B3
Apa →, *S. Amer.* 126 A4
Apache, *U.S.A.* 113 H5
Apache Junction, *U.S.A.* 115 K8
Apalachee B., *U.S.A.* 109 L4
Apalachicola, *U.S.A.* 109 L3
Apalachicola →, *U.S.A.* 109 L3
Apam, *Ghana* 83 D4
Apapa, *Nigeria* 83 D5
Apaporis →, *Colombia* 124 D5
Aparri, *Phil.* 61 B4
Apateu, *Romania* 42 D6
Apatin, *Serbia, Yug.* 42 E4
Apatity, *Russia* 50 C4
Apatzingán, *Mexico* 118 D4
Apeldoorn, *Neths.* 17 B5
Apen, *Germany* 24 B3
Apennines = Appennini, *Italy* 28 E7
Aphrodisias, *Turkey* 39 D10
Apia, *Samoa* 91 A13
Apiacás, Serra dos, *Brazil* 124 E7
Apies →, *S. Africa* 89 D4
Apizaco, *Mexico* 119 D5
Aplao, *Peru* 124 G4
Apo, Mt., *Phil.* 63 C7
Apolakkiá, *Greece* 36 C9
Apolakkiá, Órmos, *Greece* 36 C9
Apolda, *Germany* 24 D7
Apollonia, *Greece* 38 E6
Apolo, *Bolivia* 124 F5
Aporé →, *Brazil* 125 G8
Apostle Is., *U.S.A.* 112 B9
Apóstoles, *Argentina* 127 B4
Apostolos Andreas, C., *Cyprus* 36 D13
Apostolovo, *Ukraine* 47 J7
Apoteri, *Guyana* 124 C7
Appalachian Mts., *U.S.A.* 108 G6
Äppelbo, *Sweden* 10 D8
Appennini, *Italy* 28 E7
Appennino Ligure, *Italy* 28 D6
Appenzell-Ausser Rhoden □, *Switz.* 25 H5
Appenzell-Inner Rhoden □, *Switz.* 25 H5
Appiano, *Italy* 29 B8
Apple Hill, *Canada* 111 A10
Apple Valley, *U.S.A.* 117 L9
Appleby-in-Westmorland, *U.K.* 12 C5
Appleton, *U.S.A.* 108 C1
Approuague →, *Fr. Guiana* 125 C8
Apricena, *Italy* 29 G12
Aprília, *Italy* 30 A5
Apsheronsk, *Russia* 49 H4
Apsley, *Canada* 110 B6
Apt, *France* 21 E9
Apuane, Alpi, *Italy* 28 D7
Apucarana, *Brazil* 127 A5
Apulia = Púglia □, *Italy* 31 A9
Apure →, *Venezuela* 124 B5
Apurimac →, *Peru* 124 F4
Apuseni, Munţii, *Romania* 42 D7
Āqā Jarī, *Iran* 71 D6
Aqaba = Al 'Aqabah, *Jordan* 75 F4
Aqaba, G. of, *Red Sea* 70 D2
'Aqabah, Khalīj al = Aqaba, G. of, *Red Sea* 70 D2
'Aqdā, *Iran* 71 C7
Aqīq, *Sudan* 80 D4
Aqīq, Khalīg, *Sudan* 80 D4
Aqmola = Astana, *Kazakstan* 50 D8
'Aqrah, *Iraq* 70 B4
Aqtaū, *Kazakstan* 50 E6
Aqtöbe, *Kazakstan* 50 D6
Aquidauana, *Brazil* 125 H7
Aquiles Serdán, *Mexico* 118 B3
Aquin, *Haiti* 121 C5
Aquitaine □, *France* 20 D3
Aqviligjuaq = Pelly Bay, *Canada* 101 B11
Ar Rachidiya = Er Rachidia, *Morocco* 78 B5
Ar Rafīd, *Syria* 75 C4
Ar Raḥḥālīyah, *Iraq* 70 C4
Ar Ramādī, *Iraq* 70 C4
Ar Ramthā, *Jordan* 75 C5
Ar Raqqah, *Syria* 70 C3
Ar Rass, *Si. Arabia* 70 E4
Ar Rawshān, *Si. Arabia* 80 C5
Ar Rifā'ī, *Iraq* 70 D5
Ar Riyāḍ, *Si. Arabia* 70 E5
Ar Ru'ays, *Qatar* 71 E6
Ar Rukhaymīyah, *Iraq* 70 D5
Ar Ruṣāfah, *Syria* 70 C3
Ar Ruṭbah, *Iraq* 70 C4
Ara, *India* 69 G11
Ara Goro, *Ethiopia* 81 F5
Ara Tera, *Ethiopia* 81 F5
Arab, *U.S.A.* 109 H2
'Arab, Bahr el →, *Sudan* 81 F2
Arab, Khalîg el, *Egypt* 80 A2
Arab, Shatt al →, *Asia* 71 D6
'Araba, W. →, *Egypt* 80 J8
'Arabābād, *Iran* 71 C8
Araban, *Turkey* 72 D7
Arabatskaya Strelka, *Ukraine* 47 K8
Arabba, *Italy* 29 B8
Arabia, *Asia* 52 G8
Arabian Desert = Es Sahrâ' Esh Sharqîya, *Egypt* 80 B3
Arabian Gulf = Gulf, The, *Asia* 71 E6
Arabian Sea, *Ind. Oc.* 52 H10
Araç, *Turkey* 72 B5
Aracaju, *Brazil* 125 F11
Aracati, *Brazil* 125 D11
Araçatuba, *Brazil* 127 A5
Aracena, *Spain* 35 H4
Aracena, Sierra de, *Spain* 35 H4
Aračinovo, *Macedonia* 40 D5
Araçuaí, *Brazil* 125 G10
'Arad, *Israel* 75 D4
Arad, *Romania* 42 D6
Arad □, *Romania* 42 D6
Arādān, *Iran* 71 C7
Aradhippou, *Cyprus* 36 E12
Arafura Sea, *E. Indies* 52 K17
Aragats, *Armenia* 49 K7
Aragón □, *Spain* 32 D4
Aragón →, *Spain* 32 C3
Aragona, *Italy* 30 E6

Araguacema


Araguacema, Brazil 125 E9
Araguaia →, Brazil 122 D6
Araguaína, Brazil 125 E9
Araguari, Brazil 125 G9
Araguari →, Brazil 125 C9
Arain, India 68 F6
Arak, Algeria 78 C6
Arāk, Iran 71 C6
Araka, Sudan 81 G3
Arakan Coast, Burma 67 K19
Arakan Yoma, Burma 67 K19
Arákhova, Greece 38 C4
Arakli, Turkey 73 B8
Araks = Aras, Rūd-e →, Asia 49 K9
Aral, Kazakstan 50 E7
Aral Sea, Asia 50 E7
Aral Tengizi = Aral Sea, Asia 50 E7
Aralsk = Aral, Kazakstan 50 E7
Aralskoye More = Aral Sea, Asia 50 E7
Aralsor, Ozero, Kazakstan 49 F9
Aramac, Australia 94 C4
Aran I., Ireland 15 A3
Aran Is., Ireland 15 C2
Aranda de Duero, Spain 34 D7
Arandān, Iran 70 C5
Aranđelovac, Serbia, Yug. 40 B4
Aranjuez, Spain 34 E7
Aranos, Namibia 88 C2
Aransas Pass, U.S.A. 113 M6
Aranyaprathet, Thailand 64 F4
Araouane, Mali 82 B4
Arapahoe, U.S.A. 112 E5
Arapey Grande →, Uruguay 126 C4
Arapgir, Turkey 70 B3
Arapiraca, Brazil 125 E11
Arapongas, Brazil 127 A5
Ar'ar, Si. Arabia 70 D4
Araranguá, Brazil 127 B6
Araraquara, Brazil 125 H9
Ararás, Serra das, Brazil 127 B5
Ararat, Armenia 73 C11
Ararat, Australia 95 F3
Ararat, Mt. = Ağrı Dağı, Turkey 70 B5
Araria, India 69 F12
Araripe, Chapada do, Brazil 125 E11
Araruama, L. de, Brazil 127 A7
Aras, Rūd-e →, Asia 49 K9
Aratāne, Mauritania 82 B3
Arauca, Colombia 124 B4
Arauca →, Venezuela 124 B5
Arauco, Chile 126 D1
Arawa, Ethiopia 81 F5
Araxá, Brazil 125 G9
Araya, Pen. de, Venezuela 124 A6
Arba Gugu, Ethiopia 81 F5
Arba Minch, Ethiopia 81 F4
Arbat, Iraq 70 C5
Árbatax, Italy 30 C2
Arbi, Ethiopia 81 F4
Arbīl, Iraq 70 B5
Arboga, Sweden 10 E9
Arbois, France 19 F12
Arbore, Ethiopia 81 F4
Arboréa, Italy 30 C1
Arborfield, Canada 105 C8
Arborg, Canada 105 C9
Arbre du Ténéré, Niger 83 B7
Arbroath, U.K. 14 E6
Arbuckle, U.S.A. 116 F4
Arbus, Italy 30 C1
Arc →, France 21 C10
Arc-lès-Gray, France 19 E12
Arcachon, France 20 D2
Arcachon, Bassin d', France 20 D2
Arcade, Calif., U.S.A. 117 L8
Arcade, N.Y., U.S.A. 110 D6
Arcadia, Fla., U.S.A. 109 M5
Arcadia, La., U.S.A. 113 J8
Arcadia, Pa., U.S.A. 110 F6
Arcata, U.S.A. 114 F1
Arcévia, Italy 29 E9
Archangel = Arkhangelsk, Russia 50 C5
Archar, Bulgaria 40 C6
Archbald, U.S.A. 111 E9
Archena, Spain 33 G3
Archer →, Australia 94 A3
Archer B., Australia 94 A3
Archers Post, Kenya 86 B4
Arches National Park, U.S.A. 115 G9
Archidona, Spain 35 H6
Arci, Mte., Italy 30 C1
Arcidosso, Italy 29 F8
Arcis-sur-Aube, France 19 D11
Arckaringa Cr. →, Australia 95 D2
Arco, Italy 28 C7
Arco, U.S.A. 114 E7
Arcos = Arcos de Jalón, Spain 32 D2
Arcos de Jalón, Spain 32 D2
Arcos de la Frontera, Spain 35 J5
Arcos de Valdevez, Portugal 34 D2
Arcot, India 66 N11
Arcozelo, Portugal 34 E3
Arctic Bay, Canada 101 A11
Arctic Ocean, Arctic 4 B18
Arctic Red River = Tsiigehtchic, Canada 100 B6
Arda →, Bulgaria 41 E10
Arda →, Italy 28 C7
Ardabīl, Iran 71 B6
Ardahan, Turkey 73 B10
Ardakān = Sepīdān, Iran 71 D7
Ardakān, Iran 71 C7
Ardala, Sweden 11 F7
Ardales, Spain 35 J6
Ardèche □, France 21 D8
Ardèche →, France 21 D8
Ardee, Ireland 15 C5
Arden, Canada 110 B8
Arden, Denmark 11 H3
Arden, Calif., U.S.A. 116 G5
Arden, Nev., U.S.A. 117 J11
Ardenne, Belgium 6 F7
Ardennes = Ardenne, Belgium 6 F7
Ardennes □, France 19 C11
Ardentes, France 19 F8
Arderin, Ireland 15 C4
Ardeşen, Turkey 73 B9
Ardestān, Iran 71 C7
Árdhas →, Greece 41 E10
Ardhéa, Greece 40 F6
Ardila →, Portugal 35 G3
Ardino, Bulgaria 41 E9
Ardivachar Pt., U.K. 14 D1
Ardlethan, Australia 95 E4
Ardmore, Okla., U.S.A. 113 H6
Ardmore, Pa., U.S.A. 111 G9
Ardnamurchan, Pt. of, U.K. 14 E2
Ardnave Pt., U.K. 14 F2
Ardon, Russia 49 J7
Ardore, Italy 31 D9
Ardres, France 19 B8
Ardrossan, Australia 95 E2
Ardrossan, U.K. 14 F4
Ards Pen., U.K. 15 B6
Arduan, Sudan 80 D3
Ardud, Romania 42 C7
Åre, Sweden 10 A7
Arecibo, Puerto Rico 121 C6
Areia Branca, Brazil 125 E11
Arena, Pt., U.S.A. 116 G3
Arenal, Honduras 120 C2
Arenas = Las Arenas, Spain 34 B6
Arenas de San Pedro, Spain 34 E5
Arendal, Norway 9 G13
Arendsee, Germany 24 C7
Arenys de Mar, Spain 32 D7
Arenzano, Italy 28 D5
Areópolis, Greece 38 E4
Arequipa, Peru 124 G4
Arero, Ethiopia 81 G4
Arès, France 20 D2
Arévalo, Spain 34 D6
Arezzo, Italy 29 E8
Arga, Turkey 70 B3
Arga →, Spain 32 C3
Argalastí, Greece 38 B5
Argamasilla de Alba, Spain 35 F7
Argamasilla de Calatrava, Spain 35 G6
Arganda, Spain 34 E7
Arganil, Portugal 34 E2
Argedeb, Ethiopia 81 F5
Argelès-Gazost, France 20 E3
Argelès-sur-Mer, France 20 F7
Argens →, France 21 E10
Argent-sur-Sauldre, France 19 E9
Argenta, Canada 104 C5
Argenta, Italy 29 D8
Argentan, France 18 D6
Argentário, Mte., Italy 29 F8
Argentat, France 20 C5
Argentera, Italy 28 D4
Argenteuil, France 19 D9
Argentia, Canada 103 C9
Argentiera, C. dell', Italy 30 B1
Argentina ■, S. Amer. 128 D3
Argentina Is., Antarctica 5 C17
Argentino, L., Argentina 128 G2
Argenton-Château, France 18 F6
Argenton-sur-Creuse, France 19 F8
Argeş □, Romania 43 F9
Argeş →, Romania 43 F11
Arghandab →, Afghan. 68 D1
Argheile, Ethiopia 81 F5
Argo, Sudan 80 D3
Argolikós Kólpos, Greece 38 D4
Argolís □, Greece 38 D4
Argonne, France 19 C12
Árgos, Greece 38 D4
Árgos Orestikón, Greece 40 F5
Argostólion, Greece 38 C2
Arguedas, Spain 32 C3
Arguello, Pt., U.S.A. 117 L6
Arguineguín, Canary Is. 37 G4
Argun, Russia 49 J7
Argun →, Russia 51 D13
Argungu, Nigeria 83 C5
Argus Pk., U.S.A. 117 K9
Argyle, L., Australia 92 C4
Argyll & Bute □, U.K. 14 E3
Arhavi, Turkey 73 B9
Århus, Denmark 11 H4
Århus Amtskommune □, Denmark 11 H4
Ariadnoye, Russia 54 B7
Ariamsvlei, Namibia 88 D2
Ariano Irpino, Italy 31 A8
Aribinda, Burkina Faso 83 C4
Arica, Chile 124 G4
Arica, Colombia 124 D4
Arico, Canary Is. 37 F3
Arid, C., Australia 93 F3
Arida, Japan 55 G7
Ariège □, France 20 F5
Ariège →, France 20 E5
Arieş →, Romania 43 D8
Arihā, Israel 80 A4
Arilje, Serbia, Yug. 40 C4
Arílla, Ákra, Greece 36 A3
Arima, Trin. & Tob. 121 D7
Arinos →, Brazil 122 E5
Ario de Rosales, Mexico 118 D4
Ariogala, Lithuania 44 C10
Aripuanã, Brazil 124 E6
Aripuanã →, Brazil 122 D4
Ariquemes, Brazil 124 E6
Arisaig, U.K. 14 E3
Arîsh, W. el →, Egypt 80 A3
Arissa, Ethiopia 81 E5
Aristazabal I., Canada 104 C3
Arivonimamo, Madag. 89 B8
Ariza, Spain 32 D2
Arizaro, Salar de, Argentina 126 A2
Arizona, Argentina 126 D2
Arizona □, U.S.A. 115 J8
Arizpe, Mexico 118 A2
Årjäng, Sweden 10 E6
Arjeplog, Sweden 8 D18
Arjona, Colombia 124 A3
Arjona, Spain 35 H6
Arjuna, Indonesia 63 G15
Arka, Russia 51 C15
Arkadak, Russia 48 E6
Arkadelphia, U.S.A. 113 H8
Arkadhía □, Greece 38 D4
Arkaig, L., U.K. 14 E3
Arkalyk = Arqalyk, Kazakstan 50 D7
Arkansas □, U.S.A. 113 H8
Arkansas →, U.S.A. 113 J9
Arkansas City, U.S.A. 113 G6
Arkaroola, Australia 95 E2
Árkathos →, Greece 38 B3
Arkhángelos, Greece 36 C10
Arkhangelsk, Russia 50 C5
Arkhangelskoye, Russia 48 E5
Arki, India 68 D7
Arkiko, Eritrea 81 D4
Arklow, Ireland 15 D5
Árkoi, Greece 39 D8
Arkona, Kap, Germany 24 A9
Arkösund, Sweden 11 F10
Arkoúdhi, Greece 38 C2
Arkport, U.S.A. 110 D7
Arkticheskiy, Mys, Russia 51 A10
Arkul, Russia 48 B10
Arkville, U.S.A. 111 D10
Ärla, Sweden 10 E10
Arlanza →, Spain 34 C6
Arlanzón →, Spain 34 C6
Arlbergpass, Austria 26 D3
Arles, France 21 E8
Arlington, S. Africa 89 D4
Arlington, N.Y., U.S.A. 111 E11
Arlington, Oreg., U.S.A. 114 D3
Arlington, S. Dak., U.S.A. 112 C6
Arlington, Tex., U.S.A. 113 J6
Arlington, Va., U.S.A. 108 F7
Arlington, Vt., U.S.A. 111 C11
Arlington, Wash., U.S.A. 116 B4
Arlington Heights, U.S.A. 108 D2
Arlit, Niger 78 E7
Arlon, Belgium 17 E5
Arltunga, Australia 94 C1
Arly, Burkina Faso 83 C5
Armagh, U.K. 15 B5
Armagh □, U.K. 15 B5
Armagnac, France 20 E4
Armançon →, France 19 E10
Armavir, Russia 49 H5
Armenia, Colombia 124 C3
Armenia ■, Asia 49 K7
Armeniş, Romania 42 E7
Armenistís, Ákra, Greece 36 C9
Armentières, France 19 B9
Armidale, Australia 95 E5
Armilla, Spain 35 H7
Armour, U.S.A. 112 D5
Armstrong, B.C., Canada 104 C5
Armstrong, Ont., Canada 102 B2
Armutlu, Bursa, Turkey 41 F12
Armutlu, İzmir, Turkey 39 C9
Arnaía, Greece 40 F7
Arnarfjörður, Iceland 8 D2
Arnaud →, Canada 101 B12
Arnauti, C., Cyprus 36 D11
Arnay-le-Duc, France 19 E11
Arnedillo, Spain 32 C2
Arnedo, Spain 32 C2
Arnett, U.S.A. 113 G5
Arnhem, Neths. 17 C5
Arnhem, C., Australia 94 A2
Arnhem B., Australia 94 A2
Arnhem Land, Australia 94 A1
Árnissa, Greece 40 F5
Arno →, Italy 28 E7
Arno Bay, Australia 95 E2
Arnold, U.K. 12 D6
Arnold, U.S.A. 116 G6
Arnoldstein, Austria 26 E6
Arnon →, France 19 E9
Arnot, Canada 105 B9
Arnøy, Norway 8 A19
Arnprior, Canada 102 C4
Arnsberg, Germany 24 D4
Arnstadt, Germany 24 E6
Aroab, Namibia 88 D2
Aroánia Óri, Greece 38 D4
Aroche, Spain 35 H4
Arochuku, Nigeria 83 D6
Arolsen, Germany 24 D5
Aron, India 68 G6
Aron →, France 19 F10
Arona, Italy 28 C5
Aroroy, Phil. 61 E5
Arosa, Ría de, Spain 34 C2
Arpajon, France 19 D9
Arpajon-sur-Cère, France 20 D6
Arpaşu de Jos, Romania 43 E9
Arqalyk, Kazakstan 50 D7
Arrah = Ara, India 69 G11
Arrah, Ivory C. 82 D4
Arraiolos, Portugal 35 G3
Arran, U.K. 14 F3
Arras, France 19 B9
Arrasate, Spain 32 B2
Arrats →, France 20 D4
Arreau, France 20 F4
Arrecife, Canary Is. 37 F6
Arrecifes, Argentina 126 C3
Arrée, Mts. d', France 18 D3
Arresø, Denmark 11 J6
Arriaga, Chiapas, Mexico 119 D6
Arriaga, San Luis Potosí, Mexico 118 C4
Arrilalah, Australia 94 C3
Arrino, Australia 93 E2
Arriondas, Spain 34 B5
Arromanches-les-Bains, France 18 C6
Arronches, Portugal 35 F3
Arros →, France 20 E3
Arrow, L., Ireland 15 B3
Arrowhead, L., U.S.A. 117 L9
Arrowtown, N.Z. 91 L2
Arroyo de la Luz, Spain 35 F4
Arroyo Grande, U.S.A. 117 K6
Års, Denmark 11 H3
Ars, Iran 70 B5
Ars-sur-Moselle, France 19 C13
Arsenault L., Canada 105 B7
Arsenev, Russia 54 B6
Arsi □, Ethiopia 81 F4
Arsiero, Italy 29 C8
Arsin, Turkey 73 B8
Arsk, Russia 48 B9
Årsunda, Sweden 10 D10
Árta, Greece 38 B3
Artà, Spain 37 B10
Árta □, Greece 38 B3
Arteaga, Mexico 118 D4
Arteche, Phil. 61 E6
Arteijo = Arteixo, Spain 34 B2
Arteixo, Spain 34 B2
Artem = Artyom, Azerbaijan 49 K10
Artem, Russia 54 C6
Artemovsk, Russia 51 D10
Artemovsk, Ukraine 47 H9
Artemovskiy, Russia 49 G5
Artenay, France 19 D8
Artern, Germany 24 D7
Artesa de Segre, Spain 32 D6
Artesia = Mosomane, Botswana 88 C4
Artesia, U.S.A. 113 J2
Arthington, Liberia 82 D2
Arthur, Canada 110 C4
Arthur →, Australia 94 G3
Arthur Cr. →, Australia 94 C2
Arthur Pt., Australia 94 C5
Arthur River, Australia 93 F2
Arthur's Pass, N.Z. 91 K3
Arthur's Town, Bahamas 121 B4
Artigas, Uruguay 126 C4
Artik, Armenia 49 K6
Artillery L., Canada 105 A7
Artois, France 19 B9
Artotína, Greece 38 C4
Artrutx, C. de, Spain 37 B10
Artsyz, Ukraine 47 J5
Artvin, Turkey 73 B9
Artyom, Azerbaijan 49 K10
Aru, Kepulauan, Indonesia 63 F8
Aru Is. = Aru, Kepulauan, Indonesia 63 F8
Arua, Uganda 86 B3
Aruanã, Brazil 125 F8
Aruba ■, W. Indies 121 D6
Arucas, Canary Is. 37 F4
Arudy, France 20 E3
Arun →, Nepal 69 F12
Arun →, U.K. 13 G7
Arunachal Pradesh □, India 67 F19
Arusha, Tanzania 86 C4
Arusha □, Tanzania 86 C4
Arusha Chini, Tanzania 86 C4
Aruwimi →, Dem. Rep. of the Congo 86 B1
Arvada, Colo., U.S.A. 112 F2
Arvada, Wyo., U.S.A. 114 D10
Arve →, France 19 F13
Árvi, Greece 36 E7
Arviat, Canada 105 A10
Arvidsjaur, Sweden 8 D18
Arvika, Sweden 10 E6
Arvin, U.S.A. 117 K8
Arwal, India 69 G11
Arxan, China 60 B6
Åryd, Sweden 11 H8
Aryirádhes, Greece 36 B3
Aryiroúpolis, Greece 36 D6
Arys, Kazakstan 50 E7
Arzachena, Italy 30 A2
Arzamas, Russia 48 C6
Arzgir, Russia 49 H7
Arzignano, Italy 29 C8
Arzúa, Spain 34 C2
Aš, Czech Rep. 26 A5
Ås, Sweden 10 A8
As Pontes de García Rodríguez, Spain 34 B3
Aş Şafā, Syria 75 B6
As Saffānīyah, Si. Arabia 71 E6
As Safīrah, Syria 70 B3
Aş Şahm, Oman 71 E8
As Sājir, Si. Arabia 70 E5
As Salamīyah, Syria 70 C3
As Salmān, Iraq 70 D5
As Salţ, Jordan 75 C4
As Sal'w'a, Qatar 71 E6
As Samāwah, Iraq 70 D5
As Sanamayn, Syria 75 B5
As Sohar = Şuḩār, Oman 71 E8
As Sukhnah, Syria 70 C3
As Sulaymānīyah, Iraq 70 C5
As Sulaymī, Si. Arabia 70 E4
As Sulayyil, Si. Arabia 74 C4
As Summān, Si. Arabia 70 E5
As Suwaydā', Syria 75 C5
As Suwaydā' □, Syria 75 C5
As Suwayq, Oman 71 F8
As Şuwayrah, Iraq 70 C5
Åsa, Sweden 11 G6
Asab, Namibia 88 D2
Asaba, Nigeria 83 D6
Asad, Buḩayrat al, Syria 70 C3
Asadābād, Iran 73 E13
Asafo, Ghana 82 D4
Asahi-Gawa →, Japan 55 G6
Asahigawa, Japan 54 C11
Asale, L., Ethiopia 81 E5
Asamankese, Ghana 83 D4
Asan →, India 69 F8
Asansol, India 69 H12
Åsarna, Sweden 10 B8
Asayita, Ethiopia 81 E5
Asbe Teferi, Ethiopia 81 F5
Asbesberge, S. Africa 88 D3
Asbestos, Canada 103 C5
Asbury Park, U.S.A. 111 F10
Ascea, Italy 31 B8
Ascensión, Mexico 118 A3
Ascensión, B. de la, Mexico 119 D7
Ascension I., Atl. Oc. 77 G2
Aschach an der Donau, Austria 26 C7
Aschaffenburg, Germany 25 F5
Aschendorf, Germany 24 B3
Aschersleben, Germany 24 D7
Asciano, Italy 29 E8
Áscoli Piceno, Italy 29 F10
Áscoli Satriano, Italy 31 A8
Ascope, Peru 124 E3
Ascotán, Chile 126 A2
Aseb, Eritrea 81 E5
Åseda, Sweden 11 G9
Asela, Ethiopia 81 F4
Åsen, Sweden 10 C7
Asenovgrad, Bulgaria 41 D8
Aserradero, Mexico 118 C3
Asfeld, France 19 C11
Asfûn el Matâ'na, Egypt 80 B3
Asgata, Cyprus 36 E12
Ash Fork, U.S.A. 115 J7
Ash Grove, U.S.A. 113 G8
Ash Shabakah, Iraq 70 D4
Ash Shamāl □, Lebanon 75 A5
Ash Shāmīyah, Iraq 70 D5
Ash Shāriqah, U.A.E. 71 E7
Ash Sharmah, Si. Arabia 70 D2
Ash Sharqāt, Iraq 70 C4
Ash Sharqi, Al Jabal, Lebanon 75 B5
Ash Shaţrah, Iraq 70 D5
Ash Shawbak, Jordan 70 D2
Ash Shawmari, J., Jordan 75 E5
Ash Shināfīyah, Iraq 70 D5
Ash Shu'bah, Si. Arabia 70 D5
Ash Shumlūl, Si. Arabia 70 E5
Ash Shūr'a, Iraq 70 C4
Ash Shurayf, Si. Arabia 70 E3
Ash Shuwayfāt, Lebanon 75 B4
Ashanti □, Ghana 83 D4
Ashau, Vietnam 64 D6
Ashbourne, U.K. 12 D6
Ashburn, U.S.A. 109 K4
Ashburton, N.Z. 91 K3
Ashburton →, Australia 92 D1
Ashcroft, Canada 104 C4
Ashdod, Israel 75 D3
Ashdown, U.S.A. 113 J7
Asheboro, U.S.A. 109 H6
Ashern, Canada 105 C9
Asherton, U.S.A. 113 L5
Asheville, U.S.A. 109 H4
Ashewat, Pakistan 68 D3
Asheweig →, Canada 102 B2
Ashford, Australia 95 D5
Ashford, U.K. 13 F8
Ashgabat, Turkmenistan 50 F6
Ashibetsu, Japan 54 C11
Ashikaga, Japan 55 F9
Ashington, U.K. 12 B6
Ashizuri-Zaki, Japan 55 H6
Ashkarkot, Afghan. 68 C2
Ashkhabad = Ashgabat, Turkmenistan 50 F6
Āshkhāneh, Iran 71 B8
Ashland, Kans., U.S.A. 113 G5
Ashland, Ky., U.S.A. 108 F4
Ashland, Mont., U.S.A. 114 D10
Ashland, Ohio, U.S.A. 110 F2
Ashland, Oreg., U.S.A. 114 E2
Ashland, Pa., U.S.A. 111 F8
Ashland, Va., U.S.A. 108 G7
Ashland, Wis., U.S.A. 112 B9
Ashley, N. Dak., U.S.A. 112 B5
Ashley, Pa., U.S.A. 111 E9
Ashmore Reef, Australia 92 B3
Ashmûn, Egypt 80 H7
Ashmyany, Belarus 9 J21
Ashokan Reservoir, U.S.A. 111 E10
Ashqelon, Israel 75 D3
Ashta, India 68 H7
Ashtabula, U.S.A. 110 E4
Ashton, S. Africa 88 E3
Ashton, U.S.A. 114 D8
Ashuanipi, L., Canada 103 B6
Ashville, U.S.A. 110 F6
'Āṣī →, Asia 72 D6

Băbeni


Asia 52 E11
Asia, Kepulauan, Indonesia 63 D8
Āsīā Bak, Iran 71 C6
Asiago, Italy 29 C8
Asifabad, India 66 K11
Asinara, Italy 30 A1
Asinara, G. dell', Italy 30 A1
Asino, Russia 50 D9
Asipovichy, Belarus 46 F5
'Asīr □, Si. Arabia 74 D3
Asir, Ras, Somali Rep. 74 E5
Aşkale, Turkey 73 C9
Askersund, Sweden 11 F8
Askham, S. Africa 88 D3
Askim, Norway 9 G14
Askja, Iceland 8 D5
Askøy, Norway 9 F11
Asl, Egypt 80 B3
Aslan Burnu, Turkey 39 C8
Aslanapa, Turkey 39 B11
Asmara = Asmera, Eritrea 81 D4
Asmera, Eritrea 81 D4
Asnæs, Denmark 11 J4
Åsnen, Sweden 11 H8
Asola, Italy 28 C7
Asosa, Ethiopia 81 E3
Asoteriba, Jebel, Sudan 80 C4
Aspe, Spain 33 G4
Aspen, U.S.A. 115 G10
Aspendos, Turkey 72 D4
Aspermont, U.S.A. 113 J4
Aspet, France 20 E4
Aspiring, Mt., N.Z. 91 L2
Aspres-sur-Buëch, France 21 D9
Asprókavos, Ákra, Greece 36 B4
Aspromonte, Italy 31 D9
Aspur, India 68 H6
Asquith, Canada 105 C7
Assâba, Massif de l', Mauritania 82 B2
Assaikio, Nigeria 83 D6
Assal, L., Djibouti 81 E5
Assam □, India 67 G18
Assamakka, Niger 83 B6
Asse, Belgium 17 D4
Assémini, Italy 30 C1
Assen, Neths. 17 A6
Assens, Denmark 11 J3
Assini, Ivory C. 82 D4
Assiniboia, Canada 105 D7
Assiniboine →, Canada 105 D9
Assiniboine, Mt., Canada 104 C5
Assis, Brazil 127 A5
Assisi, Italy 29 E9
Ássos, Greece 38 C2
Assynt, L., U.K. 14 C3
Astaffort, France 20 D4
Astakidha, Greece 39 F8
Astakós, Greece 38 C3
Astana, Kazakstan 50 D8
Āstāneh, Iran 71 B6
Astara, Azerbaijan 71 B6
Āstārā, Iran 73 C13
Asteroúsia, Greece 36 E7
Asti, Italy 28 D5
Astipálaia, Greece 39 E8
Astorga, Spain 34 C4
Astoria, U.S.A. 116 D3
Åstorp, Sweden 11 H6
Astrakhan, Russia 49 G9
Astudillo, Spain 34 C6
Asturias □, Spain 34 B5
Asunción, Paraguay 126 B4
Asunción Nochixtlán, Mexico 119 D5
Åsunden, Sweden 11 F9
Asutri, Sudan 81 D4
Aswa →, Uganda 86 B3
Aswad, Ra's al, Si. Arabia 80 C4
Aswân, Egypt 80 C3
Aswân High Dam = Sadd el Aali, Egypt 80 C3
Asyût, Egypt 80 B3
Asyûti, Wadi →, Egypt 80 B3
Aszód, Hungary 42 C4
At Ţafīlah, Jordan 75 E4
At Tā'if, Si. Arabia 74 C3
Aţ Ţirāq, Si. Arabia 70 E5
Aţ Tubayq, Si. Arabia 70 D3
Atabey, Turkey 39 D12
Atacama □, Chile 126 B2
Atacama, Desierto de, Chile 126 A2
Atacama, Salar de, Chile 126 A2
Atakpamé, Togo 83 D5
Atalándi, Greece 38 C4
Atalaya, Peru 124 F4
Atalaya de Femes, Canary Is. 37 F6
Atami, Japan 55 G9
Atapupu, Indonesia 63 F6
Atâr, Mauritania 78 D3
Atarfe, Spain 35 H7
Atari, Pakistan 68 D6
Atascadero, U.S.A. 116 K6
Atasu, Kazakstan 50 E8
Atatürk Barajı, Turkey 73 D8
Atauro, Indonesia 63 F7
'Atbara, Sudan 80 D3
'Atbara, Nahr →, Sudan 80 D3
Atbasar, Kazakstan 50 D7
Atça, Turkey 39 D10
Atchafalaya B., U.S.A. 113 L9
Atchison, U.S.A. 112 F7
Atebubu, Ghana 83 D4
Ateca, Spain 32 D3
Aterno →, Italy 29 F10
Āteshān, Iran 71 C7
Atesine, Alpi, Italy 29 B8
Atessa, Italy 29 F11
Atfîh, Egypt 80 J7
Ath, Belgium 17 D3
Athabasca, Canada 104 C6
Athabasca →, Canada 105 B6
Athabasca, L., Canada 105 B7
Athboy, Ireland 15 C5
Athenry, Ireland 15 C3
Athens = Athínai, Greece 38 D5
Athens, Ala., U.S.A. 109 H2
Athens, Ga., U.S.A. 109 J4
Athens, N.Y., U.S.A. 111 D11
Athens, Ohio, U.S.A. 108 F4
Athens, Pa., U.S.A. 111 E8
Athens, Tenn., U.S.A. 109 H3
Athens, Tex., U.S.A. 113 J7
Atherley, Canada 110 B5
Atherton, Australia 94 B4
Athiéme, Benin 83 D5
Athienou, Cyprus 36 D12
Athínai, Greece 38 D5
Athlone, Ireland 15 C4
Athna, Cyprus 36 D12
Athol, U.S.A. 111 D12
Atholl, Forest of, U.K. 14 E5
Atholville, Canada 103 C6
Áthos, Greece 41 F8
Athy, Ireland 15 C5
Ati, Chad 79 F9
Ati, Sudan 81 E2
Atiak, Uganda 86 B3
Atienza, Spain 32 D2
Atiit, Sudan 81 F3
Atik L., Canada 105 B9
Atikameg →, Canada 102 B3
Atikokan, Canada 102 C1
Atikonak L., Canada 103 B7
Atimonan, Phil. 61 E4
Atka, Russia 51 C16
Atka I., U.S.A. 100 C2
Atkarsk, Russia 48 E7
Atkinson, U.S.A. 112 D5
Atlanta, Ga., U.S.A. 109 J3
Atlanta, Tex., U.S.A. 113 J7
Atlantic, U.S.A. 112 E7
Atlantic City, U.S.A. 108 F8
Atlantic Ocean 2 E9
Atlas Mts. = Haut Atlas, Morocco 78 B4
Atlin, Canada 104 B2
Atlin, L., Canada 104 B2
Atlin Prov. Park, Canada 104 B2
Atmore, U.S.A. 109 K2
Atoka, U.S.A. 113 H6
Átokos, Greece 38 C2
Atolia, U.S.A. 117 K9
Atrai →, Bangla. 69 G13
Atrak = Atrek →, Turkmenistan 71 B8
Ätran, Sweden 11 G6
Ätran →, Sweden 11 H6
Atrauli, India 68 E8
Atrek →, Turkmenistan 71 B8
Atri, Italy 29 F10
Atsikí, Greece 39 B7
Atsoum, Mts., Cameroon 83 D7
Atsuta, Japan 54 C10
Attalla, U.S.A. 109 H2
Attapu, Laos 64 E6
Attáviros, Greece 36 C9
Attawapiskat, Canada 102 B3
Attawapiskat →, Canada 102 B3
Attawapiskat L., Canada 102 B2
Attersee, Austria 26 D6
Attica, Ind., U.S.A. 108 E2
Attica, Ohio, U.S.A. 110 E2
Attichy, France 19 C10
Attigny, France 19 C11
Attika = Attikí □, Greece 38 D5
Attikamagen L., Canada 103 B6
Attikí □, Greece 38 D5
Attleboro, U.S.A. 111 E13
Attock, Pakistan 68 C5
Attopeu = Attapu, Laos 64 E6
Attu I., U.S.A. 100 C1
Attur, India 66 P11
Atuel →, Argentina 126 D2
Åtvidaberg, Sweden 11 F10
Atwater, U.S.A. 116 H6
Atwood, Canada 110 C3
Atwood, U.S.A. 112 F4
Atyraū, Kazakstan 50 E6
Au Sable, U.S.A. 110 B1
Au Sable →, U.S.A. 108 C4
Au Sable Forks, U.S.A. 111 B11
Au Sable Pt., U.S.A. 110 B1
Aubagne, France 21 E9
Aubarca, C. d', Spain 37 B7
Aube □, France 19 D11
Aube →, France 19 D10
Aubenas, France 21 D8
Aubenton, France 19 C11
Auberry, U.S.A. 116 H7
Aubigny-sur-Nère, France 19 E9
Aubin, France 20 D6
Aubrac, Mts. d', France 20 D7
Auburn, Ala., U.S.A. 109 J3
Auburn, Calif., U.S.A. 116 G5
Auburn, Ind., U.S.A. 108 E3
Auburn, Maine, U.S.A. 109 C10
Auburn, N.Y., U.S.A. 111 D8
Auburn, Nebr., U.S.A. 112 E7
Auburn, Pa., U.S.A. 111 F8
Auburn, Wash., U.S.A. 116 C4
Auburn Ra., Australia 95 D5
Auburndale, U.S.A. 109 L5
Aubusson, France 20 C6
Auce, Latvia 44 B9
Auch, France 20 E4
Auchi, Nigeria 83 D6
Auckland, N.Z. 91 G5
Auckland Is., Pac. Oc. 96 N8
Aude □, France 20 E6
Aude →, France 20 E7
Auden, Canada 102 B2
Auderville, France 18 C5
Audierne, France 18 D2
Audincourt, France 19 E13
Audo, Ethiopia 81 F5
Audubon, U.S.A. 112 E7
Aue, Germany 24 E8
Auerbach, Germany 24 E8
Augathella, Australia 95 D4
Aughnacloy, U.K. 15 B5
Augrabies Falls, S. Africa 88 D3
Augsburg, Germany 25 G6
Augusta, Australia 93 F2
Augusta, Italy 31 E8
Augusta, Ark., U.S.A. 113 H9
Augusta, Ga., U.S.A. 109 J5
Augusta, Kans., U.S.A. 113 G6
Augusta, Maine, U.S.A. 101 D13
Augusta, Mont., U.S.A. 114 C7
Augustenborg, Denmark 11 K3
Augustów, Poland 44 E9
Augustus, Mt., Australia 93 D2
Augustus I., Australia 92 C3
Aukan, Eritrea 81 D5
Aukum, U.S.A. 116 G6
Auld, L., Australia 92 D3
Aulla, Italy 28 D6
Aulnay, France 20 B3
Aulne →, France 18 D2
Aulnoye-Aymeries, France 19 B10
Ault, France 18 B8
Ault, U.S.A. 112 E2
Aulus-les-Bains, France 20 F5
Aumale, France 19 C8
Aumont-Aubrac, France 20 D7
Auna, Nigeria 83 C5
Auning, Denmark 11 H4
Aunis, France 20 B3
Auponhia, Indonesia 63 E7
Aups, France 21 E10
Aur, Pulau, Malaysia 65 L5
Auraiya, India 69 F8
Aurangabad, Bihar, India 69 G11
Aurangabad, Maharashtra, India 66 K9
Auray, France 18 E4
Aurich, Germany 24 B3
Aurillac, France 20 D6
Auronzo di Cadore, Italy 29 B9
Aurora, Canada 110 C5
Aurora, S. Africa 88 E2
Aurora, Colo., U.S.A. 112 F2
Aurora, Ill., U.S.A. 108 E1
Aurora, Mo., U.S.A. 113 G8
Aurora, N.Y., U.S.A. 111 D8
Aurora, Nebr., U.S.A. 112 E6
Aurora, Ohio, U.S.A. 110 E3
Aurukun, Australia 94 A3
Aus, Namibia 88 D2
Ausable →, Canada 110 C3
Auschwitz = Oświęcim, Poland 45 H6
Austerlitz = Slavkov u Brna, Czech Rep. 27 B9
Austin, Minn., U.S.A. 112 D8
Austin, Nev., U.S.A. 114 G5
Austin, Pa., U.S.A. 110 E6
Austin, Tex., U.S.A. 113 K6
Austin, L., Australia 93 E2
Austin I., Canada 105 A10
Austra, Norway 8 D14
Austral Is. = Tubuai Is., Pac. Oc. 97 K13
Austral Seamount Chain, Pac. Oc. 97 K13
Australia ■, Oceania 96 K5
Australian Capital Territory □, Australia 95 F4
Australind, Australia 93 F2
Austria ■, Europe 26 E7
Austvågøy, Norway 8 B16
Auterive, France 20 E5
Authie →, France 19 B8
Authon-du-Perche, France 18 D7
Autlán, Mexico 118 D4
Autun, France 19 F11
Auvergne, France 20 C7
Auvergne, Mts. d', France 20 C6
Auvézère →, France 20 C4
Auxerre, France 19 E10
Auxi-le-Château, France 19 B9
Auxonne, France 19 E12
Auzances, France 19 F9
Ava, U.S.A. 113 G8
Avallon, France 19 E10
Avalon, U.S.A. 117 M8
Avalon Pen., Canada 103 C9
Avanos, Turkey 70 B2
Avaré, Brazil 127 A6
Ávas, Greece 41 F9
Avawatz Mts., U.S.A. 117 K10
Avdan Dağı, Turkey 41 F13
Aveiro, Brazil 125 D7
Aveiro, Portugal 34 E2
Aveiro □, Portugal 34 E2
Āvej, Iran 71 C6
Avellaneda, Argentina 126 C4
Avellino, Italy 31 B7
Avenal, U.S.A. 116 K6
Aversa, Italy 31 B7
Avery, U.S.A. 114 C6
Aves, Is. las, Venezuela 121 D6
Avesnes-sur-Helpe, France 19 B10
Avesta, Sweden 10 D10
Aveyron □, France 20 D6
Aveyron →, France 20 D5
Avezzano, Italy 29 F10
Avgó, Greece 39 F7
Aviá Terai, Argentina 126 B3
Aviano, Italy 29 B9
Aviemore, U.K. 14 D5
Avigliana, Italy 28 C4
Avigliano, Italy 31 B8
Avignon, France 21 E8
Ávila, Spain 34 E6
Ávila □, Spain 34 E6
Ávila, Sierra de, Spain 34 E5
Avila Beach, U.S.A. 117 K6
Avilés, Spain 34 B5
Avintes, Portugal 34 D2
Avionárion, Greece 38 C6
Avis, Portugal 35 F3
Avis, U.S.A. 110 E7
Avísio →, Italy 28 B8
Aviz = Avis, Portugal 35 F3
Avize, France 19 D11
Avlum, Denmark 11 H2
Avoca, U.S.A. 110 D7
Avoca →, Australia 95 F3
Avoca →, Ireland 15 D5
Avola, Canada 104 C5
Avola, Italy 31 F8
Avon, U.S.A. 110 D7
Avon →, Australia 93 F2
Avon →, Bristol, U.K. 13 F5
Avon →, Dorset, U.K. 13 G6
Avon →, Warks., U.K. 13 E5
Avon Park, U.S.A. 109 M5
Avondale, Zimbabwe 87 F3
Avonlea, Canada 105 D8
Avonmore, Canada 111 A10
Avramov, Bulgaria 41 D10
Avranches, France 18 D5
Avre →, France 18 D8
Avrig, Romania 43 E9
Avrillé, France 18 E6
Avtovac, Bos.-H. 40 C2
Awag el Baqar, Sudan 81 E3
A'waj →, Syria 75 B5
Awaji-Shima, Japan 55 G7
'Awālī, Bahrain 71 E6
Awantipur, India 69 C6
Awasa, Ethiopia 81 F4
Awasa, L., Ethiopia 81 F4
Awash, Ethiopia 81 F5
Awash →, Ethiopia 81 E5
Awaso, Ghana 82 D4
Awatere →, N.Z. 91 J5
Awbārī, Libya 79 C8
Awe, L., U.K. 14 E3
Aweil, Sudan 81 F2
Awgu, Nigeria 83 D6
Awjilah, Libya 79 C10
Awka, Nigeria 83 D6
Ax-les-Thermes, France 20 F5
Axat, France 20 F6
Axe →, U.K. 13 F5
Axel Heiberg I., Canada 4 B3
Axim, Ghana 82 E4
Axintele, Romania 43 F11
Axiós →, Greece 40 F6
Axminster, U.K. 13 G4
Axvall, Sweden 11 F7
Ay, France 19 C11
Ayabaca, Peru 124 D3
Ayabe, Japan 55 G7
Ayacucho, Argentina 126 D4
Ayacucho, Peru 124 F4
Ayaguz, Kazakstan 50 E9
Ayamé, Ivory C. 82 D4
Ayamonte, Spain 35 H3
Ayan, Russia 51 D14
Ayancık, Turkey 72 B6
Ayas, Turkey 72 B5
Ayaviri, Peru 124 F4
Aybastı, Turkey 72 B7
Aydın, Turkey 72 D2
Aydin □, Turkey 39 D9
Aydin Dağları, Turkey 39 D10
Ayelu, Ethiopia 81 E5
Ayenngré, Togo 83 D5
Ayer, U.S.A. 111 D13
Ayerbe, Spain 32 C4
Ayer's Cliff, Canada 111 A12
Ayers Rock, Australia 93 E5
Ayiá, Greece 38 B4
Ayia Aikateríni, Ákra, Greece 36 A3
Ayía Ánna, Greece 38 C5
Ayía Dhéka, Greece 36 D6
Ayia Gálini, Greece 36 D6
Ayía Marína, Kásos, Greece 39 F8
Ayía Marína, Léros, Greece 39 D8
Ayia Napa, Cyprus 36 E13
Ayía Paraskeví, Greece 39 B8
Ayia Phyla, Cyprus 36 E12
Ayía Rouméli, Greece 38 F5
Ayía Varvára, Greece 36 D7
Ayiássos, Greece 39 B8
Ayioi Theódhoroi, Greece 38 D5
Áyion Óros □, Greece 41 F8
Áyios Amvrósios, Cyprus 36 D12
Áyios Andréas, Greece 38 D4
Áyios Evstrátios, Greece 38 B6
Áyios Ioánnis, Ákra, Greece 36 D7
Áyios Isidhoros, Greece 36 C9
Áyios Kiríkos, Greece 39 D8
Áyios Matthaíos, Greece 36 B3
Áyios Mírono, Greece 39 F7
Áyios Nikólaos, Greece 36 D7
Áyios Pétros, Greece 38 C2
Áyios Seryios, Cyprus 36 D12
Áyios Theodhoros, Cyprus 36 D13
Áyios Yeóryios, Greece 38 D5
Aykathonisi, Greece 39 D8
Aykirikçi, Turkey 39 B12
Aylesbury, U.K. 13 F7
Aylmer, Canada 110 D4
Aylmer, L., Canada 100 B8
'Ayn, Wādī al, Oman 71 F7
Ayn Dār, Si. Arabia 71 E7
Ayn Zālah, Iraq 70 B4
Ayna, Spain 33 G2
Ayod, Sudan 81 F3
Ayolas, Paraguay 126 B4
Ayom, Sudan 81 F2
Ayon, Ostrov, Russia 51 C17
Ayora, Spain 33 F3
Ayorou, Niger 83 C5
'Ayoûn el 'Atroûs, Mauritania 82 B3
Ayr, Australia 94 B4
Ayr, Canada 110 C4
Ayr, U.K. 14 F4
Ayr →, U.K. 14 F4
Ayrancı, Turkey 72 D5
Ayrancılar, Turkey 39 C9
Ayre, Pt. of, U.K. 12 C3
Aysha, Ethiopia 81 E5
Ayton, Australia 94 B4
Aytos, Bulgaria 41 D11
Aytoska Planina, Bulgaria 41 D11
Ayu, Kepulauan, Indonesia 63 D8
Ayutla, Guatemala 120 D1
Ayutla, Mexico 119 D5
Ayvacık, Turkey 72 C2
Ayvalık, Turkey 39 B8
Az Zabadānī, Syria 75 B5
Az Zāhirīyah, West Bank 75 D3
Az Zahrān, Si. Arabia 71 E6
Az Zarqā, Jordan 75 C5
Az Zarqā', U.A.E. 71 E7
Az Zībār, Iraq 70 B5
Az Zilfī, Si. Arabia 70 E5
Az Zubayr, Iraq 70 D5
Az Zuqur, Yemen 81 E5
Azambuja, Portugal 35 F2
Azamgarh, India 69 F10
Azangaro, Peru 124 F4
Azaoua, Niger 83 B5
Azaouad, Mali 82 B4
Azaouak, Vallée de l', Mali 83 B5
Āzār Shahr, Iran 70 B5
Azara, Nigeria 83 D6
Azarān, Iran 70 B5
Azärbayjan = Azerbaijan ■, Asia 49 K9
Āzarbāyjān-e Gharbī □, Iran 70 B5
Āzarbāyjān-e Sharqī □, Iran 70 B5
Azare, Nigeria 83 C7
Azay-le-Rideau, France 18 E7
A'zāz, Syria 70 B3
Azbine = Aïr, Niger 83 B6
Azerbaijan ■, Asia 49 K9
Azerbaijchan = Azerbaijan ■, Asia 49 K9
Azezo, Ethiopia 81 E4
Azimganj, India 69 G13
Aznalcóllar, Spain 35 H4
Azogues, Ecuador 124 D3
Azores, Atl. Oc. 78 A1
Azov, Russia 49 G4
Azov, Sea of, Europe 47 J9
Azovskoye More = Azov, Sea of, Europe 47 J9
Azpeitia, Spain 32 B2
Azraq ash Shīshān, Jordan 75 D5
Aztec, U.S.A. 115 H10
Azúa de Compostela, Dom. Rep. 121 C5
Azuaga, Spain 35 G5
Azuara, Spain 32 D4
Azuer →, Spain 35 F7
Azuero, Pen. de, Panama 120 E3
Azuga, Romania 43 E10
Azul, Argentina 126 D4
Azusa, U.S.A. 117 L9
Azzano Décimo, Italy 29 C9


# B


Ba Don, Vietnam 64 D6
Ba Dong, Vietnam 65 H6
Ba Ngoi = Cam Lam, Vietnam 65 G7
Ba Tri, Vietnam 65 G6
Ba Xian = Bazhou, China 56 E9
Baa, Indonesia 63 F6
Baamonde, Spain 34 B3
Baarle-Nassau, Belgium 17 C4
Bab el Mandeb, Red Sea 74 E3
Baba, Bulgaria 40 D7
Bābā, Koh-i-, Afghan. 66 B5
Baba Burnu, Turkey 39 B8
Baba dag, Azerbaijan 49 K9
Bābā Kalū, Iran 71 D6
Babadag, Romania 43 F13
Babadağ, Turkey 39 D10
Babadayhan, Turkmenistan 50 F7
Babaeski, Turkey 41 E11
Babahoyo, Ecuador 124 D3
Babai = Sarju →, India 69 F9
Babana, Nigeria 83 C5
Babanusa, Sudan 81 E2
Babar, Indonesia 63 F7
Babar, Pakistan 68 D3
Babarkach, Pakistan 68 E3
Babayevo, Russia 46 C8
Babb, U.S.A. 114 B7
Babelthuap, Pac. Oc. 63 C8
Babenhausen, Germany 25 F4
Băbeni, Romania 43 F9

Baberu


Baberu, India 69 G9
Babi Besar, Pulau, Malaysia 65 L4
Babia Gora, Europe 45 J6
Babian Jiang →, China 58 F3
Babile, Ethiopia 81 F5
Babimost, Poland 45 F2
Babinda, Australia 94 B4
Babine, Canada 104 B3
Babine →, Canada 104 B3
Babine L., Canada 104 C3
Babo, Indonesia 63 E8
Babócsa, Hungary 42 D2
Bābol, Iran 71 B7
Bābol Sar, Iran 71 B7
Baborów, Poland 45 H5
Babruysk, Belarus 47 F5
Babuhri, India 68 F3
Babuna, Macedonia 40 E5
Babura, Nigeria 83 C6
Babusar Pass, Pakistan 69 B5
Babushkin, Russia 60 A5
Babušnica, Serbia, Yug. 40 C6
Babuyan Chan., Phil. 61 B4
Babylon, Iraq 70 C5
Bač, Serbia, Yug. 42 E4
Bâc →, Moldova 43 D14
Bac Can, Vietnam 58 F5
Bac Giang, Vietnam 58 G6
Bac Lieu, Vietnam 65 H5
Bac Ninh, Vietnam 58 G6
Bac Phan, Vietnam 64 B5
Bac Quang, Vietnam 58 F5
Bacabal, Brazil 125 D10
Bacalar, Mexico 119 D7
Bacan, Kepulauan, Indonesia 63 E7
Bacarra, Phil. 61 B4
Bacău, Romania 43 D11
Bacău □, Romania 43 D11
Baccarat, France 19 D13
Bacerac, Mexico 118 A3
Băceşti, Romania 43 D12
Bach Long Vi, Dao, Vietnam 64 B6
Bacharach, Germany 25 E3
Bachelina, Russia 50 D7
Bachhwara, India 69 G11
Bachuma, Ethiopia 81 F4
Bačina, Serbia, Yug. 40 C5
Back →, Canada 100 B9
Bačka Palanka, Serbia, Yug. 42 E4
Bačka Topola, Serbia, Yug. 42 E4
Bäckebo, Sweden 11 H10
Bäckefors, Sweden 11 F6
Bäckhammar, Sweden 10 E8
Bački Petrovac, Serbia, Yug. 42 E4
Backnang, Germany 25 G5
Baco, Mt., Phil. 61 E4
Bacolod, Phil. 61 F5
Bacqueville-en-Caux, France 18 C8
Bács-Kiskun □, Hungary 42 D4
Bácsalmás, Hungary 42 D4
Bacuag = Placer, Phil. 61 G6
Bacuk, Malaysia 65 J4
Bād, Iran 71 C7
Bad →, U.S.A. 112 C4
Bad Aussee, Austria 26 D6
Bad Axe, U.S.A. 110 C2
Bad Bergzabern, Germany 25 F3
Bad Berleburg, Germany 24 D4
Bad Bevensen, Germany 24 B6
Bad Bramstedt, Germany 24 B5
Bad Brückenau, Germany 25 E5
Bad Doberan, Germany 24 A7
Bad Driburg, Germany 24 D5
Bad Ems, Germany 25 E3
Bad Frankenhausen, Germany 24 D7
Bad Freienwalde, Germany 24 C10
Bad Goisern, Austria 26 D6
Bad Harzburg, Germany 24 D6
Bad Hersfeld, Germany 24 E5
Bad Hofgastein, Austria 26 D6
Bad Homburg, Germany 25 E4
Bad Honnef, Germany 24 E3
Bad Iburg, Germany 24 C4
Bad Ischl, Austria 26 D6
Bad Kissingen, Germany 25 E6
Bad Königshofen, Germany 25 E6
Bad Kreuznach, Germany 25 F3
Bad Krozingen, Germany 25 H3
Bad Laasphe, Germany 24 E4
Bad Lands, U.S.A. 112 D3
Bad Langensalza, Germany 24 D6
Bad Lauterberg, Germany 24 D6
Bad Leonfelden, Austria 26 C7
Bad Liebenwerda, Germany 24 D9
Bad Mergentheim, Germany 25 F5
Bad Münstereifel, Germany 24 E2
Bad Nauheim, Germany 25 E4
Bad Neuenahr-Ahrweiler, Germany 24 E3
Bad Neustadt, Germany 25 E6
Bad Oeynhausen, Germany 24 C4
Bad Oldesloe, Germany 24 B6
Bad Orb, Germany 25 E5
Bad Pyrmont, Germany 24 D5
Bad Reichenhall, Germany 25 H8
Bad Säckingen, Germany 25 H3
Bad Salzuflen, Germany 24 C4
Bad Salzungen, Germany 24 E6
Bad Schwartau, Germany 24 B6
Bad Segeberg, Germany 24 B6
Bad St. Leonhard, Austria 26 E7
Bad Tölz, Germany 25 H7
Bad Urach, Germany 25 G5
Bad Vöslau, Austria 27 D9
Bad Waldsee, Germany 25 H5
Bad Wildungen, Germany 24 D5
Bad Wimpfen, Germany 25 F5
Bad Windsheim, Germany 25 F6
Bad Zwischenahn, Germany 24 B4
Bada Barabil, India 69 H11
Badagara, India 66 P9
Badagri, Nigeria 83 D5
Badajós, L., Brazil 124 D6
Badajoz, Spain 35 G4
Badajoz □, Spain 35 G4
Badakhshān □, Afghan. 66 A7
Badalona, Spain 32 D7
Badalzai, Afghan. 68 E1
Badampahar, India 67 H15
Badanah, Si. Arabia 70 D4
Badarinath, India 69 D8
Badas, Kepulauan, Indonesia 62 D3
Baddo →, Pakistan 66 F4
Bade, Indonesia 63 F9
Badeggi, Nigeria 83 D6
Badéguichéri, Niger 83 C6
Baden, Austria 27 C9
Baden, Switz. 25 H4
Baden, U.S.A. 110 F4
Baden-Baden, Germany 25 G4
Baden-Württemberg □, Germany 25 G4
Badgastein, Austria 26 D6
Badger, Canada 103 C8
Badger, U.S.A. 116 J7
Bādghīs □, Afghan. 66 B3
Badgom, India 69 B6
Badia Polèsine, Italy 29 C8
Badin, Pakistan 68 G3
Badlands National Park, U.S.A. 112 D3
Badogo, Mali 82 C3
Badoumbé, Mali 82 C2
Badrah, Iraq 70 C5
Badrinath, India 69 D8
Badulla, Sri Lanka 66 R12
Baena, Spain 35 H6
Baeza, Spain 35 H7
Bafang, Cameroon 83 D7
Bafatá, Guinea-Biss. 82 C2
Baffin B., Canada 101 A13
Baffin I., Canada 101 B12
Bafia, Cameroon 83 E7
Bafilo, Togo 83 D5
Bafing →, Mali 82 C2
Bafliyūn, Syria 70 B3
Bafoulabé, Mali 82 C2
Bafoussam, Cameroon 83 D7
Bāfq, Iran 71 D7
Bafra, Turkey 72 B6
Bafra Burnu, Turkey 72 B7
Bāft, Iran 71 D8
Bafut, Cameroon 83 D7
Bafwasende, Dem. Rep. of the Congo 86 B2
Bagam, Niger 83 B6
Bagamoyo, Tanzania 86 D4
Bagan Datoh, Malaysia 65 L3
Bagan Serai, Malaysia 65 K3
Baganga, Phil. 61 H7
Bagani, Namibia 88 B3
Bagansiapiapi, Indonesia 62 D2
Bagasra, India 68 J4
Bagaud, India 68 H6
Bagawi, Sudan 81 E3
Bagbag, Sudan 81 D3
Bagdad, U.S.A. 117 L11
Bagdarin, Russia 51 D12
Bagé, Brazil 127 C5
Bagenalstown = Muine Bheag, Ireland 15 D5
Baggs, U.S.A. 114 F10
Bagh, Pakistan 69 C5
Baghain →, India 69 G9
Baghdād, Iraq 70 C5
Bagheria, Italy 30 D6
Baghlān, Afghan. 66 A6
Baghlān □, Afghan. 66 B6
Bagley, U.S.A. 112 B7
Bagnara Cálabra, Italy 31 D8
Bagnasco, Italy 28 D5
Bagnères-de-Bigorre, France 20 E4
Bagnères-de-Luchon, France 20 F4
Bagni di Lucca, Italy 28 D7
Bagno di Romagna, Italy 29 E8
Bagnoles-de-l'Orne, France 18 D6
Bagnols-sur-Cèze, France 21 D8
Bagnorégio, Italy 29 F9
Bago = Pegu, Burma 67 L20
Bagodar, India 69 G11
Bagrationovsk, Russia 9 J19
Bagrdan, Serbia, Yug. 40 B5
Baguio, Phil. 61 C4
Bağyurdu, Turkey 39 C9
Bagzane, Monts, Niger 83 B6
Bah, India 69 F8
Bahabón de Esgueva, Spain 34 D7
Bahadurganj, India 69 F12
Bahadurgarh, India 68 E7
Bahama, Canal Viejo de, W. Indies 120 B4
Bahamas ■, N. Amer. 121 B5
Bahār, Iran 73 E13
Baharampur, India 69 G13
Baharîya, El Wâhât al, Egypt 80 B2
Bahawalnagar, Pakistan 68 E5
Bahawalpur, Pakistan 68 E4
Bahçe, Turkey 72 D7
Bahçecik, Turkey 41 F13
Baheri, India 69 E8
Bahgul →, India 69 F8
Bahi, Tanzania 86 D4
Bahi Swamp, Tanzania 86 D4
Bahía = Salvador, Brazil 125 F11
Bahía □, Brazil 125 F10
Bahía, Is. de la, Honduras 120 C2
Bahía Blanca, Argentina 126 D3
Bahía de Caráquez, Ecuador 124 D2
Bahía Honda, Cuba 120 B3
Bahía Laura, Argentina 128 F3
Bahía Negra, Paraguay 124 H7
Bahir Dar, Ethiopia 81 E4
Bahmanzād, Iran 71 D6
Bahr el Ahmar □, Sudan 80 D4
Bahr el Ghazâl □, Sudan 81 F2
Bahr el Jabal □, Sudan 81 G3
Bahr Yûsef →, Egypt 80 B3
Bahraich, India 69 F9
Bahrain ■, Asia 71 E6
Bahror, India 68 F7
Bāhū Kalāt, Iran 71 E9
Bai, Mali 82 C4
Bai Bung, Mui = Ca Mau, Mui, Vietnam 65 H5
Bai Duc, Vietnam 64 C5
Bai Thuong, Vietnam 64 C5
Baia de Aramă, Romania 42 E7
Baia Mare, Romania 43 C8
Baia-Sprie, Romania 43 C8
Baião, Brazil 125 D9
Baïbokoum, Chad 79 G9
Baicheng, China 57 B12
Băicoi, Romania 43 E10
Baidoa, Somali Rep. 74 G3
Baie Comeau, Canada 103 C6
Baie-St-Paul, Canada 103 C5
Baie Trinité, Canada 103 C6
Baie Verte, Canada 103 C8
Baignes-Ste-Radegonde, France 20 C3
Baigneux-les-Juifs, France 19 E11
Baihar, India 69 H9
Baihe, China 56 H6
Ba'ījī, Iraq 70 C4
Baijnath, India 69 E8
Baikal, L. = Baykal, Oz., Russia 51 D11
Baikunthpur, India 69 H10
Baile Atha Cliath = Dublin, Ireland 15 C5
Băile Govora, Romania 43 E9
Băile Herculane, Romania 42 F7
Băile Olăneşti, Romania 43 E9
Băile Tuşnad, Romania 43 D10
Bailén, Spain 35 G7
Băileşti, Romania 43 F8
Baima, China 58 A3
Bain-de-Bretagne, France 18 E5
Bainbridge, Ga., U.S.A. 109 K3
Bainbridge, N.Y., U.S.A. 111 D9
Baing, Indonesia 63 F6
Bainiu, China 56 H7
Baiona, Spain 34 C2
Bā'ir, Jordan 75 E5
Bairin Youqi, China 57 C10
Bairin Zuoqi, China 57 C10
Bairnsdale, Australia 95 F4
Bais, Phil. 61 G5
Baisha, China 56 G7
Baissa, Nigeria 83 D7
Baitadi, Nepal 69 E9
Baiyin, China 56 F3
Baiyü, China 58 B2
Baiyu Shan, China 56 F4
Baiyuda, Sudan 80 D3
Baj Baj, India 69 H13
Baja, Hungary 42 D3
Baja, Pta., Mexico 118 B1
Baja California, Mexico 118 A1
Baja California □, Mexico 118 B2
Baja California Sur □, Mexico 118 B2
Bajag, India 69 H9
Bajamar, Canary Is. 37 F3
Bajana, India 68 H4
Bājgīrān, Iran 71 B8
Bajimba, Mt., Australia 95 D5
Bajina Bašta, Serbia, Yug. 40 C3
Bajmok, Serbia, Yug. 42 E4
Bajo Nuevo, Caribbean 120 C4
Bajoga, Nigeria 83 C7
Bajool, Australia 94 C5
Bak, Hungary 42 D1
Bakar, Croatia 29 C11
Bakel, Senegal 82 C2
Baker, Calif., U.S.A. 117 K10
Baker, Mont., U.S.A. 112 B2
Baker, L., Canada 100 B10
Baker City, U.S.A. 114 D5
Baker I., Pac. Oc. 96 G10
Baker I., U.S.A. 104 B2
Baker L., Australia 93 E4
Baker Lake, Canada 100 B10
Baker Mt., U.S.A. 114 B3
Bakers Creek, Australia 94 C4
Baker's Dozen Is., Canada 102 A4
Bakersfield, Calif., U.S.A. 117 K8
Bakersfield, Vt., U.S.A. 111 B12
Bakhchysaray, Ukraine 47 K7
Bakhmach, Ukraine 47 G7
Bākhtarān, Iran 70 C5
Bākhtarān □, Iran 70 C5
Bakı, Azerbaijan 49 K9
Bakır →, Turkey 39 C9
Bakırdaği, Turkey 72 C6
Bakkafjörður, Iceland 8 C6
Baklan, Turkey 39 C11
Bako, Ethiopia 81 F4
Bako, Ivory C. 82 D3
Bakony, Hungary 42 C2
Bakony Forest = Bakony, Hungary 42 C2
Bakori, Nigeria 83 C6
Bakouma, C.A.R. 84 C4
Baksan, Russia 49 J6
Bakswaho, India 69 G8
Baku = Bakı, Azerbaijan 49 K9
Bakundi, Nigeria 83 D7
Bakutis Coast, Antarctica 5 D15
Baky = Bakı, Azerbaijan 49 K9
Bala, Canada 110 A5
Bala, Senegal 82 C2
Bâlâ, Turkey 72 C5
Bala, U.K. 12 E4
Bala, L., U.K. 12 E4
Balabac I., Phil. 62 C5
Balabac Str., E. Indies 62 C5
Balabagh, Afghan. 68 B4
Ba'labakk, Lebanon 75 B5
Balabalangan, Kepulauan, Indonesia 62 E5
Bălăciţa, Romania 43 F8
Balad, Iraq 70 C5
Balad Rūz, Iraq 70 C5
Bālādeh, Fārs, Iran 71 D6
Bālādeh, Māzandaran, Iran 71 B6
Balaghat, India 66 J12
Balaghat Ra., India 66 K10
Balaguer, Spain 32 D5
Balakhna, Russia 48 B6
Balaklava, Ukraine 47 K7
Balakliya, Ukraine 47 H9
Balakovo, Russia 48 D8
Balamau, India 69 F9
Bălan, Romania 43 D10
Balancán, Mexico 119 D6
Balashov, Russia 48 E6
Balasinor, India 68 H5
Balasore = Baleshwar, India 67 J15
Balassagyarmat, Hungary 42 B4
Balât, Egypt 80 B2
Balaton, Hungary 42 D2
Balatonboglár, Hungary 42 D2
Balatonfüred, Hungary 42 D2
Balatonszentgyörgy, Hungary 42 D2
Balayan, Phil. 61 E4
Balazote, Spain 33 G2
Balbieriškis, Lithuania 44 D10
Balbigny, France 21 C8
Balbina, Reprêsa de, Brazil 124 D7
Balboa, Panama 120 E4
Balbriggan, Ireland 15 C5
Balcarce, Argentina 126 D4
Balcarres, Canada 105 C8
Bălceşti, Romania 43 F8
Balchik, Bulgaria 41 C12
Balclutha, N.Z. 91 M2
Balcones Escarpment, U.S.A. 113 L5
Balçova, Turkey 39 C9
Bald Hd., Australia 93 G2
Bald I., Australia 93 F2
Bald Knob, U.S.A. 113 H9
Baldock L., Canada 105 B9
Baldwin, Mich., U.S.A. 108 D3
Baldwin, Pa., U.S.A. 110 F5
Baldwinsville, U.S.A. 111 C8
Baldy Mt., U.S.A. 114 B9
Baldy Peak, U.S.A. 115 K9
Bale, Croatia 29 C10
Bale, Ethiopia 81 F5
Bale □, Ethiopia 81 F5
Baleares, Is., Spain 37 B10
Balearic Is. = Baleares, Is., Spain 37 B10
Baleine = Whale →, Canada 103 A6
Băleni, Romania 43 E12
Baler, Phil. 61 D4
Baler Bay, Phil. 61 D4
Baleshare, U.K. 14 D1
Baleshwar, India 67 J15
Balezino, Russia 48 B11
Balfate, Honduras 120 C2
Bali, Cameroon 83 D7
Balí, Greece 36 D6
Bali, India 68 G5
Bali, Indonesia 62 F4
Bali □, Indonesia 62 F5
Bali, Selat, Indonesia 63 H16
Balia, S. Leone 82 D2
Baliapal, India 69 J12
Baligród, Poland 45 J9
Balikeşir, Turkey 39 B9
Balikeşir □, Turkey 39 B9
Balıklıçeşme, Turkey 41 F11
Balikpapan, Indonesia 62 E5
Balimbing, Phil. 63 C5
Baling, Malaysia 65 K3
Balingen, Germany 25 G4
Balinţ, Romania 42 E6
Balintang Channel, Phil. 61 B4
Balipara, India 67 F18
Balkan Mts. = Stara Planina, Bulgaria 40 C7
Balkhash = Balqash, Kazakstan 50 E8
Balkhash, Ozero = Balqash Köl, Kazakstan 50 E8
Balla, Bangla. 67 G17
Ballachulish, U.K. 14 E3
Balladonia, Australia 93 F3
Ballaghaderreen, Ireland 15 C3
Ballarat, Australia 95 F3
Ballard, L., Australia 93 E3
Ballater, U.K. 14 D5
Ballé, Mali 82 B3
Ballenas, Canal de, Mexico 118 B2
Balleny Is., Antarctica 5 C11
Balleroy, France 18 C6
Ballerup, Denmark 11 J6
Ballı, Turkey 41 F11
Ballia, India 69 G11
Ballina, Australia 95 D5
Ballina, Ireland 15 B2
Ballinasloe, Ireland 15 C3
Ballinger, U.S.A. 113 K5
Ballinrobe, Ireland 15 C2
Ballinskelligs B., Ireland 15 E1
Ballon, France 18 D7
Ballsh, Albania 40 F3
Ballston Spa, U.S.A. 111 D11
Ballycastle, U.K. 15 A5
Ballyclare, U.K. 15 B5
Ballyhaunis, Ireland 15 C3
Ballymena, U.K. 15 B5
Ballymoney, U.K. 15 A5
Ballymote, Ireland 15 B3
Ballynahinch, U.K. 15 B6
Ballyquintin Pt., U.K. 15 B6
Ballyshannon, Ireland 15 B3
Balmaceda, Chile 128 F2
Balmaseda, Spain 32 B1
Balmazújváros, Hungary 42 C6
Balmertown, Canada 105 C10
Balmoral, Australia 95 F3
Balmorhea, U.S.A. 113 K3
Balonne →, Australia 95 D4
Balotra, India 68 G5
Balqash, Kazakstan 50 E8
Balqash Köl, Kazakstan 50 E8
Balrampur, India 69 F10
Balranald, Australia 95 E3
Balş, Romania 43 F9
Balsas, Mexico 119 D5
Balsas →, Brazil 125 E9
Balsas →, Mexico 118 D4
Bålsta, Sweden 10 E11
Balston Spa, U.S.A. 111 D11
Balta, Romania 42 F7
Balta, Ukraine 47 H5
Baltanás, Spain 34 D6
Bălţi, Moldova 43 C12
Baltic Sea, Europe 9 H18
Baltîm, Egypt 80 H7
Baltimore, Ireland 15 E2
Baltimore, Md., U.S.A. 108 F7
Baltimore, Ohio, U.S.A. 110 G2
Baltit, Pakistan 69 A6
Baltiysk, Russia 9 J18
Baltrum, Germany 24 B3
Baluchistan □, Pakistan 66 F4
Balurghat, India 69 G13
Balvi, Latvia 9 H22
Balya, Turkey 39 B9
Bam, Iran 71 D8
Bama, China 58 E6
Bama, Nigeria 83 C7
Bamaga, Australia 94 A3
Bamaji L., Canada 102 B1
Bamako, Mali 82 C3
Bamba, Mali 83 B4
Bambara Maoundé, Mali 82 B4
Bambari, C.A.R. 84 C4
Bambaroo, Australia 94 B4
Bambaya, Guinea 82 D2
Bamberg, Germany 25 F6
Bamberg, U.S.A. 109 J5
Bambesi, Ethiopia 81 F3
Bambey, Senegal 82 C1
Bambili, Dem. Rep. of the Congo 86 B2
Bamboi, Ghana 82 D4
Bamenda, Cameroon 83 D7
Bamfield, Canada 104 D3
Bāmīān □, Afghan. 66 B5
Bamiancheng, China 57 C13
Bamkin, Cameroon 83 D7
Bampūr, Iran 71 E9
Ban, Burkina Faso 82 C4
Ban Ban, Laos 64 C4
Ban Bang Hin, Thailand 65 H2
Ban Chiang Klang, Thailand 64 C3
Ban Chik, Laos 64 D4
Ban Choho, Thailand 64 E4
Ban Dan Lan Hoi, Thailand 64 D2
Ban Don = Surat Thani, Thailand 65 H2
Ban Don, Vietnam 64 F6
Ban Don, Ao →, Thailand 65 H2
Ban Dong, Thailand 64 C3
Ban Hong, Thailand 64 C2
Ban Kaeng, Thailand 64 D3
Ban Kantang, Thailand 65 J2
Ban Keun, Laos 64 C4
Ban Khai, Thailand 64 F3
Ban Kheun, Laos 64 B3
Ban Khlong Kua, Thailand 65 J3
Ban Khuan Mao, Thailand 65 J2
Ban Ko Yai Chim, Thailand 65 G2
Ban Kok, Thailand 64 D4
Ban Laem, Thailand 64 F2
Ban Lao Ngam, Laos 64 E6
Ban Le Kathe, Thailand 64 E2
Ban Mae Chedi, Thailand 64 C2
Ban Mae Laeng, Thailand 64 B2
Ban Mae Sariang, Thailand 64 C1
Ban Mê Thuôt = Buon Ma Thuot, Vietnam 64 F7
Ban Mi, Thailand 64 E3
Ban Muong Mo, Laos 64 C4
Ban Na Mo, Laos 64 D5
Ban Na San, Thailand 65 H2
Ban Na Tong, Laos 64 B3
Ban Nam Bac, Laos 64 B4
Ban Nam Ma, Laos 64 A3
Ban Ngang, Laos 64 E6
Ban Nong Bok, Laos 64 D5
Ban Nong Boua, Laos 64 E6
Ban Nong Pling, Thailand 64 E3
Ban Pak Chan, Thailand 65 G2
Ban Phai, Thailand 64 D4
Ban Pong, Thailand 64 F2
Ban Ron Phibun, Thailand 65 H2

Batavia


Ban Sanam Chai, *Thailand* 65 J3
Ban Sangkha, *Thailand* 64 E4
Ban Tak, *Thailand* 64 D2
Ban Tako, *Thailand* 64 E4
Ban Tha Dua, *Thailand* 64 D2
Ban Tha Li, *Thailand* 64 D3
Ban Tha Nun, *Thailand* 65 H2
Ban Thahine, *Laos* 64 E5
Ban Xien Kok, *Laos* 64 B3
Ban Yen Nhan, *Vietnam* 64 B6
Banaba, *Kiribati* 96 H8
Banalia, *Dem. Rep. of the Congo* 86 B2
Banam, *Cambodia* 65 G5
Banamba, *Mali* 82 C3
Banana Is., *S. Leone* 82 D2
Bananal, I. do, *Brazil* 125 F8
Banaras = Varanasi, *India* 69 G10
Banas →, *Gujarat, India* 68 H4
Banas →, *Mad. P., India* 69 G9
Bânâs, Ras, *Egypt* 80 C4
Banaz, *Turkey* 39 C11
Banaz →, *Turkey* 39 C11
Banbridge, *U.K.* 15 B5
Banbury, *U.K.* 13 E6
Banchory, *U.K.* 14 D6
Banco, *Ethiopia* 81 F4
Bancroft, *Canada* 102 C4
Band, *Romania* 43 D9
Band Bonī, *Iran* 71 E8
Band Qīr, *Iran* 71 D6
Banda, *Mad. P., India* 69 G8
Banda, *Ut. P., India* 69 G9
Banda, Kepulauan, *Indonesia* 63 E7
Banda Aceh, *Indonesia* 62 C1
Banda Banda, Mt., *Australia* 95 E5
Banda Elat, *Indonesia* 63 F8
Banda Is. = Banda, Kepulauan, *Indonesia* 63 E7
Banda Sea, *Indonesia* 63 F7
Bandai-San, *Japan* 54 F10
Bandama →, *Ivory C.* 82 D3
Bandama Blanc →, *Ivory C.* 82 D3
Bandama Rouge →, *Ivory C.* 82 D4
Bandān, *Iran* 71 D9
Bandanaira, *Indonesia* 63 E7
Bandanwara, *India* 68 F6
Bandar = Machilipatnam, *India* 67 L12
Bandār 'Abbās, *Iran* 71 E8
Bandar-e Anzalī, *Iran* 71 B6
Bandar-e Bushehr = Būshehr, *Iran* 71 D6
Bandar-e Chārak, *Iran* 71 E7
Bandar-e Deylam, *Iran* 71 D6
Bandar-e Khomeynı, *Iran* 71 D6
Bandar-e Lengeh, *Iran* 71 E7
Bandar-e Maqām, *Iran* 71 E7
Bandar-e Ma'shur, *Iran* 71 D6
Bandar-e Rīg, *Iran* 71 D6
Bandar-e Torkeman, *Iran* 71 B7
Bandar Maharani = Muar, *Malaysia* 65 L4
Bandar Penggaram = Batu Pahat, *Malaysia* 65 M4
Bandar Seri Begawan, *Brunei* 62 C4
Bandar Sri Aman, *Malaysia* 62 D4
Bandawe, *Malawi* 87 E3
Bande, *Spain* 34 C3
Bandeira, Pico da, *Brazil* 127 A7
Bandera, *Argentina* 126 B3
Banderas, B. de, *Mexico* 118 C3
Bandhogarh, *India* 69 H9
Bandi →, *India* 68 F6
Bandiagara, *Mali* 82 C4
Bandikui, *India* 68 F7
Bandırma, *Turkey* 41 F11
Bandol, *France* 21 E9
Bandon, *Ireland* 15 E3
Bandon →, *Ireland* 15 E3
Bandula, *Mozam.* 87 F3
Bandundu, *Dem. Rep. of the Congo* 84 E3
Bandung, *Indonesia* 62 F3
Bané, *Burkina Faso* 83 C4
Băneasa, *Romania* 43 E12
Bāneh, *Iran* 70 C5
Bañeres, *Spain* 33 G4
Banes, *Cuba* 121 B4
Banff, *Canada* 104 C5
Banff, *U.K.* 14 D6
Banff Nat. Park, *Canada* 104 C5
Banfora, *Burkina Faso* 82 C4
Bang Fai →, *Laos* 64 D5
Bang Hieng →, *Laos* 64 D5
Bang Krathum, *Thailand* 64 D3
Bang Lamung, *Thailand* 64 F3
Bang Mun Nak, *Thailand* 64 D3
Bang Pa In, *Thailand* 64 E3
Bang Rakam, *Thailand* 64 D3
Bang Saphan, *Thailand* 65 G2
Bangaduni I., *India* 69 J13
Bangala Dam, *Zimbabwe* 87 G3
Bangalore, *India* 66 N10
Banganga →, *India* 68 F6
Bangangté, *Cameroon* 83 D7
Bangaon, *India* 69 H13
Bangassou, *C.A.R.* 84 D4
Banggai, *Indonesia* 63 E6
Banggai, Kepulauan, *Indonesia* 63 E6
Banggai Arch. = Banggai, Kepulauan, *Indonesia* 63 E6
Banggi, *Malaysia* 62 C5
Banghāzī, *Libya* 79 B10
Bangjang, *Sudan* 81 E3
Bangka, *Sulawesi, Indonesia* 63 D7
Bangka, *Sumatera, Indonesia* 62 E3
Bangka, Selat, *Indonesia* 62 E3
Bangkalan, *Indonesia* 63 G15
Bangkinang, *Indonesia* 62 D2
Bangko, *Indonesia* 62 E2
Bangkok, *Thailand* 64 F3
Bangladesh ■, *Asia* 67 H17
Bangolo, *Ivory C.* 82 D3
Bangong Co, *India* 69 B8
Bangor, *Down, U.K.* 15 B6
Bangor, *Gwynedd, U.K.* 12 D3
Bangor, *Maine, U.S.A.* 101 D13
Bangor, *Pa., U.S.A.* 111 F9
Bangued, *Phil.* 61 C4
Bangui, *C.A.R.* 84 D3
Bangui, *Phil.* 61 B4
Banguru, *Dem. Rep. of the Congo* 86 B2
Bangweulu, L., *Zambia* 87 E3
Bangweulu Swamp, *Zambia* 87 E3
Bani, *Dom. Rep.* 121 C5
Bani →, *Mali* 82 C4
Bani Bangou, *Niger* 83 B5
Banī Sa'd, *Iraq* 70 C5
Bania, *Ivory C.* 82 D4
Banihal Pass, *India* 69 C6
Banikoara, *Benin* 83 C5
Bāniyās, *Syria* 70 C3
Banja Luka, *Bos.-H.* 42 F2
Banjar, *India* 68 D7
Banjar →, *India* 69 H9
Banjarmasin, *Indonesia* 62 E4
Banjul, *Gambia* 82 C1
Banka, *India* 69 G12
Bankas, *Mali* 82 C4
Bankeryd, *Sweden* 11 G8
Banket, *Zimbabwe* 87 F3
Bankilaré, *Niger* 83 C5
Bankipore, *India* 67 G14
Banks I., *B.C., Canada* 104 C3
Banks I., *N.W.T., Canada* 100 A7
Banks Pen., *N.Z.* 91 K4
Banks Str., *Australia* 94 G4
Bankura, *India* 69 H12
Bankya, *Bulgaria* 40 D7
Banmankhi, *India* 69 G12
Bann →, *Arm., U.K.* 15 B5
Bann →, *L'derry., U.K.* 15 A5
Bannalec, *France* 18 E3
Bannang Sata, *Thailand* 65 J3
Banning, *U.S.A.* 117 M10
Banningville = Bandundu, *Dem. Rep. of the Congo* 84 E3
Banno, *Ethiopia* 81 G4
Bannockburn, *Canada* 110 B7
Bannockburn, *U.K.* 14 E5
Bannockburn, *Zimbabwe* 87 G2
Bannu, *Pakistan* 66 C7
Bano, *India* 69 H11
Bañolas = Banyoles, *Spain* 32 C7
Banon, *France* 21 D9
Baños de la Encina, *Spain* 35 G7
Baños de Molgas, *Spain* 34 C3
Bánovce nad Bebravou, *Slovak Rep.* 27 C11
Banovići, *Bos.-H.* 42 F3
Bansgaon, *India* 69 F10
Banská Bystrica, *Slovak Rep.* 27 C12
Banská Štiavnica, *Slovak Rep.* 27 C11
Bansko, *Bulgaria* 40 E7
Banskobystrický □, *Slovak Rep.* 27 C12
Banswara, *India* 68 H6
Bantaeng, *Indonesia* 63 F5
Bantaji, *Nigeria* 83 D7
Bantayan, *Phil.* 61 F5
Bantry, *Ireland* 15 E2
Bantry B., *Ireland* 15 E2
Bantul, *Indonesia* 63 G14
Bantva, *India* 68 J4
Banya, *Bulgaria* 41 D8
Banyak, Kepulauan, *Indonesia* 62 D1
Banyalbufar, *Spain* 37 B9
Banyo, *Cameroon* 83 D7
Banyoles, *Spain* 32 C7
Banyuls-sur-Mer, *France* 20 F7
Banyumas, *Indonesia* 63 G13
Banyuwangi, *Indonesia* 63 H16
Banzare Coast, *Antarctica* 5 C9
Banzyville = Mobayi, *Dem. Rep. of the Congo* 84 D4
Bao Ha, *Vietnam* 58 F5
Bao Lac, *Vietnam* 64 A5
Bao Loc, *Vietnam* 65 G6
Bao'an = Shenzhen, *China* 59 F10
Baocheng, *China* 56 H4
Baode, *China* 56 E6
Baodi, *China* 57 E9
Baoding, *China* 56 E8
Baoji, *China* 56 G4
Baojing, *China* 58 C7
Baokang, *China* 59 B8
Baoshan, *Shanghai, China* 59 B13
Baoshan, *Yunnan, China* 58 E2
Baotou, *China* 56 D6
Baoxing, *China* 58 B4
Baoying, *China* 57 H10
Bap, *India* 68 F5
Bapatla, *India* 67 M12
Bapaume, *France* 19 B9
Bāqerābād, *Iran* 71 C6
Ba'qūbah, *Iraq* 70 C5
Baquedano, *Chile* 126 A2
Bar, *Montenegro, Yug.* 40 D3
Bar, *Ukraine* 47 H4
Bar Bigha, *India* 69 G11
Bar Harbor, *U.S.A.* 109 C11
Bar-le-Duc, *France* 19 D12
Bar-sur-Aube, *France* 19 D11
Bar-sur-Seine, *France* 19 D11
Bara, *India* 69 G9
Bâra, *Romania* 43 C12
Bara Banki, *India* 69 F9
Barabai, *Indonesia* 62 E5
Baraboo, *U.S.A.* 112 D10
Baracoa, *Cuba* 121 B5
Baradā →, *Syria* 75 B5
Baradero, *Argentina* 126 C4
Baraga, *U.S.A.* 112 B10
Bărăganul, *Romania* 43 F12
Barah →, *India* 68 F6
Barahona, *Dom. Rep.* 121 C5
Barahona, *Spain* 32 D2
Barail Range, *India* 67 G18
Baraka, *Sudan* 81 E2
Baraka →, *Sudan* 80 D4
Barakaldo, *Spain* 32 B2
Barakar →, *India* 69 G12
Barakhola, *India* 67 G18
Barakot, *India* 69 J11
Barakpur, *India* 69 H13
Baralaba, *Australia* 94 C4
Baralla, *Spain* 34 C3
Baralzon L., *Canada* 105 B9
Barameiya, *Sudan* 80 D4
Baramula, *India* 69 B6
Baran, *India* 68 G7
Baran →, *Pakistan* 68 G3
Barañain, *Spain* 32 C3
Baranavichy, *Belarus* 47 F4
Barani, *Burkina Faso* 82 C4
Baranof, *U.S.A.* 104 B2
Baranof I., *U.S.A.* 100 C6
Baranów Sandomierski, *Poland* 45 H8
Baranya □, *Hungary* 42 E3
Baraolt, *Romania* 43 D10
Barapasi, *Indonesia* 63 E9
Barasat, *India* 69 H13
Barat Daya, Kepulauan, *Indonesia* 63 F7
Barataria B., *U.S.A.* 113 L10
Barauda, *India* 68 H6
Baraut, *India* 68 E7
Barbacena, *Brazil* 127 A7
Barbados ■, *W. Indies* 121 D8
Barban, *Croatia* 29 C11
Barbària, C. de, *Spain* 37 C7
Barbaros, *Turkey* 41 F11
Barbastro, *Spain* 32 C5
Barbate = Barbate de Franco, *Spain* 35 J5
Barbate de Franco, *Spain* 35 J5
Barberino di Mugello, *Italy* 29 E8
Barberton, *S. Africa* 89 D5
Barberton, *U.S.A.* 110 E3
Barbezieux-St-Hilaire, *France* 20 C3
Barbosa, *Colombia* 124 B4
Barbourville, *U.S.A.* 109 G4
Barbuda, *W. Indies* 121 C7
Bârca, *Romania* 43 G8
Barcaldine, *Australia* 94 C4
Barcarrota, *Spain* 35 G4
Barcellona Pozzo di Gotto, *Italy* 31 D8
Barcelona, *Spain* 32 D7
Barcelona, *Venezuela* 124 A6
Barcelona □, *Spain* 32 D7
Barcelonette, *France* 21 D10
Barcelos, *Brazil* 124 D6
Barcin, *Poland* 45 F4
Barclayville, *Liberia* 82 E3
Barcoo →, *Australia* 94 D3
Barcs, *Hungary* 42 E2
Barczewo, *Poland* 44 E7
Bärdä, *Azerbaijan* 49 K8
Bardaï, *Chad* 79 D9
Bardas Blancas, *Argentina* 126 D2
Barddhaman, *India* 69 H12
Bardejov, *Slovak Rep.* 27 B14
Bardera, *Somali Rep.* 74 G3
Bardi, *Italy* 28 D6
Bardīyah, *Libya* 79 B10
Bardolino, *Italy* 28 C7
Bardonécchia, *Italy* 28 C3
Bardsey I., *U.K.* 12 E3
Bardstown, *U.S.A.* 108 G3
Bareilly, *India* 69 E8
Barela, *India* 69 H9
Barentin, *France* 18 C7
Barenton, *France* 18 D6
Barents Sea, *Arctic* 4 B9
Barentu, *Eritrea* 81 D4
Barfleur, *France* 18 C5
Barfleur, Pte. de, *France* 18 C5
Barga, *Italy* 28 D7
Bargara, *Australia* 94 C5
Bargas, *Spain* 34 F6
Bârgăului Bistriţa, *Romania* 43 C9
Barge, *Italy* 28 D4
Bargnop, *Sudan* 81 F2
Bargteheide, *Germany* 24 B6
Barguzin, *Russia* 51 D11
Barh, *India* 69 G11
Barhaj, *India* 69 F10
Barharwa, *India* 69 G12
Barhi, *India* 69 G11
Bari, *India* 68 F7
Bari, *Italy* 31 A9
Bari Doab, *Pakistan* 68 D5
Bari Sadri, *India* 68 G6
Bari Sardo, *Italy* 30 C2
Barīdī, Ra's, *Si. Arabia* 70 E3
Barīm, *Yemen* 76 E8
Barinas, *Venezuela* 124 B4
Baring, C., *Canada* 100 B8
Baringo, *Kenya* 86 B4
Baringo, L., *Kenya* 86 B4
Bârîs, *Egypt* 80 C3
Barisal, *Bangla.* 67 H17
Barisal □, *Bangla.* 67 H17
Barisan, Bukit, *Indonesia* 62 E2
Barito →, *Indonesia* 62 E4
Barjac, *France* 21 D8
Barjols, *France* 21 E10
Bark L., *Canada* 110 A7
Barka = Baraka →, *Sudan* 80 D4
Barkakana, *India* 69 H11
Barkam, *China* 58 B4
Barker, *U.S.A.* 110 C6
Barkley, L., *U.S.A.* 109 G2
Barkley Sound, *Canada* 104 D3
Barkly East, *S. Africa* 88 E4
Barkly Roadhouse, *Australia* 94 B2
Barkly Tableland, *Australia* 94 B2
Barkly West, *S. Africa* 88 D3
Barkol, Wadi →, *Sudan* 80 D3
Barla Dağı, *Turkey* 39 C12
Bârlad, *Romania* 43 D12
Bârlad →, *Romania* 43 E12
Barlee, L., *Australia* 93 E2
Barlee, Mt., *Australia* 93 D4
Barletta, *Italy* 31 A9
Barlinek, *Poland* 45 F2
Barlovento, *Canary Is.* 37 F2
Barlow L., *Canada* 105 A8
Barmedman, *Australia* 95 E4
Barmer, *India* 68 G4
Barmera, *Australia* 95 E3
Barmouth, *U.K.* 12 E3
Barmstedt, *Germany* 24 B5
Barna →, *India* 69 G10
Barnagar, *India* 68 H6
Barnala, *India* 68 D6
Barnard Castle, *U.K.* 12 C6
Barnaul, *Russia* 50 D9
Barnesville, *U.S.A.* 109 J3
Barnet □, *U.K.* 13 F7
Barneveld, *Neths.* 17 B5
Barneveld, *U.S.A.* 111 C9
Barneville-Cartevert, *France* 18 C5
Barnhart, *U.S.A.* 113 K4
Barnsley, *U.K.* 12 D6
Barnstaple, *U.K.* 13 F3
Barnstaple Bay = Bideford Bay, *U.K.* 13 F3
Barnsville, *U.S.A.* 112 B6
Barnwell, *U.S.A.* 109 J5
Baro, *Nigeria* 83 D6
Baro →, *Ethiopia* 81 F3
Baroda = Vadodara, *India* 68 H5
Baroda, *India* 68 G7
Baroe, *S. Africa* 88 E3
Baron Ra., *Australia* 92 D4
Barong, *China* 58 B2
Barotseland, *Zambia* 85 H4
Barouéli, *Mali* 82 C3
Barpeta, *India* 67 F17
Barques, Pt. Aux, *U.S.A.* 110 B2
Barquísimeto, *Venezuela* 124 A5
Barr, Ras el, *Egypt* 80 H7
Barr Smith Range, *Australia* 93 E3
Barra, *Brazil* 125 F10
Barra, *U.K.* 14 E1
Barra, Sd. of, *U.K.* 14 D1
Barra de Navidad, *Mexico* 118 D4
Barra do Corda, *Brazil* 125 E9
Barra do Piraí, *Brazil* 127 A7
Barra Falsa, Pta. da, *Mozam.* 89 C6
Barra Hd., *U.K.* 14 E1
Barra Mansa, *Brazil* 127 A7
Barraba, *Australia* 95 E5
Barrackpur = Barakpur, *India* 69 H13
Barradale Roadhouse, *Australia* 92 D1
Barrafranca, *Italy* 31 E7
Barraigh = Barra, *U.K.* 14 E1
Barranca, *Lima, Peru* 124 F3
Barranca, *Loreto, Peru* 124 D3
Barrancabermeja, *Colombia* 124 B4
Barrancas, *Venezuela* 124 B6
Barrancos, *Portugal* 35 G4
Barranqueras, *Argentina* 126 B4
Barranquilla, *Colombia* 124 A4
Barraute, *Canada* 102 C4
Barre, *Mass., U.S.A.* 111 D12
Barre, *Vt., U.S.A.* 111 B12
Barreal, *Argentina* 126 C2
Barreiras, *Brazil* 125 F10
Barreirinhas, *Brazil* 125 D10
Barreiro, *Portugal* 35 G1
Barrême, *France* 21 E10
Barren, Nosy, *Madag.* 89 B7
Barretos, *Brazil* 125 H9
Barrhead, *Canada* 104 C6
Barrie, *Canada* 102 D4
Barrier Ra., *Australia* 95 E3
Barrière, *Canada* 104 C4
Barrington, *U.S.A.* 111 E13
Barrington L., *Canada* 105 B8
Barrington Tops, *Australia* 95 E5
Barringun, *Australia* 95 D4
Barro do Garças, *Brazil* 125 G8
Barron, *U.S.A.* 112 C9
Barrow, *U.S.A.* 100 A4
Barrow →, *Ireland* 15 D5
Barrow, Pt., *U.S.A.* 98 B4
Barrow Creek, *Australia* 94 C1
Barrow I., *Australia* 92 D2
Barrow-in-Furness, *U.K.* 12 C4
Barrow Pt., *Australia* 94 A3
Barrow Ra., *Australia* 93 E4
Barrow Str., *Canada* 4 B3
Barruecopardo, *Spain* 34 D4
Barruelo de Santullán, *Spain* 34 C6
Barry, *U.K.* 13 F4
Barry's Bay, *Canada* 102 C4
Barsalogho, *Burkina Faso* 83 C4
Barsat, *Pakistan* 69 A5
Barsham, *Syria* 70 C4
Barsi, *India* 66 K9
Barsinghausen, *Germany* 24 C5
Barsoi, *India* 67 G15
Barstow, *U.S.A.* 117 L9
Barth, *Germany* 24 A8
Barthélemy, Col, *Vietnam* 64 C5
Bartica, *Guyana* 124 B7
Bartin, *Turkey* 72 B5
Bartlesville, *U.S.A.* 113 G7
Bartlett, *U.S.A.* 116 J8
Bartlett, L., *Canada* 104 A5
Bartolomeu Dias, *Mozam.* 87 G4
Barton, *U.S.A.* 111 B12
Barton upon Humber, *U.K.* 12 D7
Bartoszyce, *Poland* 44 D7
Bartow, *U.S.A.* 109 M5
Barú, Volcan, *Panama* 120 E3
Barumba, *Dem. Rep. of the Congo* 86 B1
Baruth, *Germany* 24 C9
Baruunsuu, *Mongolia* 56 C3
Barvinkove, *Ukraine* 47 H9
Barwani, *India* 68 H6
Barwice, *Poland* 44 E3
Barycz →, *Poland* 45 G3
Barysaw, *Belarus* 46 E5
Barysh, *Russia* 48 D8
Barzān, *Iraq* 70 B5
Bârzava, *Romania* 42 D6
Bas-Rhin □, *France* 19 D14
Bašaid, *Serbia, Yug.* 42 E5
Bāsa'idū, *Iran* 71 E7
Basal, *Pakistan* 68 C5
Basankusa, *Dem. Rep. of the Congo* 84 D3
Basarabeasca, *Moldova* 43 D13
Basarabi, *Romania* 43 F13
Basauri, *Spain* 32 B2
Basawa, *Afghan.* 68 B4
Bascuñán, C., *Chile* 126 B1
Basel, *Switz.* 25 H3
Basel-Landschaft □, *Switz.* 25 H3
Basento →, *Italy* 31 B9
Bashākerd, Kūhhā-ye, *Iran* 71 E8
Bashaw, *Canada* 104 C6
Bāshī, *Iran* 71 D6
Bashkir Republic = Bashkortostan □, *Russia* 50 D6
Bashkortostan □, *Russia* 50 D6
Basibasy, *Madag.* 89 C7
Basilan I., *Phil.* 61 H5
Basilan Str., *Phil.* 61 H5
Basildon, *U.K.* 13 F8
Basile, *Eq. Guin.* 83 E6
Basilicata □, *Italy* 31 B9
Basim = Washim, *India* 66 J10
Basin, *U.S.A.* 114 D9
Basingstoke, *U.K.* 13 F6
Baška, *Croatia* 29 D11
Başkale, *Turkey* 73 C10
Baskatong, Rés., *Canada* 102 C4
Basle = Basel, *Switz.* 25 H3
Başmakçı, *Turkey* 39 D12
Basoda, *India* 68 H7
Basoka, *Dem. Rep. of the Congo* 86 B1
Basque, Pays, *France* 20 E2
Basque Provinces = País Vasco □, *Spain* 32 C2
Basra = Al Başrah, *Iraq* 70 D5
Bass Str., *Australia* 94 F4
Bassano, *Canada* 104 C6
Bassano del Grappa, *Italy* 29 C8
Bassar, *Togo* 83 D5
Bassas da India, *Ind. Oc.* 85 J7
Basse-Normandie □, *France* 18 D6
Basse Santa-Su, *Gambia* 82 C2
Basse-Terre, *Guadeloupe* 121 C7
Bassein, *Burma* 67 L19
Basseterre, *St. Kitts & Nevis* 121 C7
Bassett, *U.S.A.* 112 D5
Bassi, *India* 68 D7
Bassigny, *France* 19 E12
Bassikounou, *Mauritania* 82 B3
Bassila, *Benin* 83 D5
Bassum, *Germany* 24 C4
Båstad, *Sweden* 11 H6
Bastak, *Iran* 71 E7
Baştām, *Iran* 71 B7
Bastar, *India* 67 K12
Bastelica, *France* 21 F13
Basti, *India* 69 F10
Bastia, *France* 21 F13
Bastogne, *Belgium* 17 D5
Bastrop, *La., U.S.A.* 113 J9
Bastrop, *Tex., U.S.A.* 113 K6
Bat Yam, *Israel* 75 C3
Bata, *Eq. Guin.* 84 D1
Bata, *Romania* 42 D7
Bataan □, *Phil.* 61 D4
Batabanó, *Cuba* 120 B3
Batabanó, G. de, *Cuba* 120 B3
Batac, *Phil.* 61 B4
Batagai, *Russia* 51 C14
Batajnica, *Serbia, Yug.* 40 B4
Batak, *Bulgaria* 41 E8
Batala, *India* 68 D6
Batalha, *Portugal* 34 F2
Batama, *Dem. Rep. of the Congo* 86 B2
Batamay, *Russia* 51 C13
Batang, *China* 58 B2
Batang, *Indonesia* 63 G13
Batangas, *Phil.* 61 E4
Batanta, *Indonesia* 63 E8
Batatais, *Brazil* 127 A6
Batavia, *U.S.A.* 110 D6

Bataysk


Bataysk, Russia 47 J10
Batchelor, Australia 92 B5
Batdambang, Cambodia 64 F4
Batemans B., Australia 95 F5
Batemans Bay, Australia 95 F5
Bates Ra., Australia 93 E3
Batesburg-Leesville, U.S.A. 109 J5
Batesville, Ark., U.S.A. 113 H9
Batesville, Miss., U.S.A. 113 H10
Batesville, Tex., U.S.A. 113 L5
Bath, Canada 111 B8
Bath, U.K. 13 F5
Bath, Maine, U.S.A. 109 D11
Bath, N.Y., U.S.A. 110 D7
Bath & North East Somerset □, U.K. 13 F5
Batheay, Cambodia 65 G5
Bathurst = Banjul, Gambia 82 C1
Bathurst, Australia 95 E4
Bathurst, Canada 103 C6
Bathurst, S. Africa 88 E4
Bathurst, C., Canada 100 A7
Bathurst B., Australia 94 A3
Bathurst Harb., Australia 94 G4
Bathurst I., Australia 92 B5
Bathurst I., Canada 4 B2
Bathurst Inlet, Canada 100 B9
Bati, Ethiopia 81 E5
Batie, Burkina Faso 82 D4
Batlow, Australia 95 F4
Batman, Turkey 70 B4
Baṭn al Ghūl, Jordan 75 F4
Batna, Algeria 78 A7
Batobato = San Isidro, Phil. 61 H7
Batočina, Serbia, Yug. 40 B5
Batoka, Zambia 87 F2
Baton Rouge, U.S.A. 113 K9
Batong, Ko, Thailand 65 J2
Bátonyterenye, Hungary 42 C4
Batopilas, Mexico 118 B3
Batouri, Cameroon 84 D2
Båtsfjord, Norway 8 A23
Battambang = Batdambang, Cambodia 64 F4
Batticaloa, Sri Lanka 66 R12
Battipáglia, Italy 31 B7
Battle, U.K. 13 G8
Battle →, Canada 105 C7
Battle Creek, U.S.A. 108 D3
Battle Ground, U.S.A. 116 E4
Battle Harbour, Canada 103 B8
Battle Lake, U.S.A. 112 B7
Battle Mountain, U.S.A. 114 F5
Battlefields, Zimbabwe 87 F2
Battleford, Canada 105 C7
Battonya, Hungary 42 D6
Batu, Ethiopia 81 F4
Batu, Kepulauan, Indonesia 62 E1
Batu Caves, Malaysia 65 L3
Batu Gajah, Malaysia 65 K3
Batu Is. = Batu, Kepulauan, Indonesia 62 E1
Batu Pahat, Malaysia 65 M4
Batuata, Indonesia 63 F6
Batumi, Georgia 49 K5
Baturaja, Indonesia 62 E2
Baturité, Brazil 125 D11
Bau, Malaysia 62 D4
Baubau, Indonesia 63 F6
Bauchi, Nigeria 83 C6
Bauchi □, Nigeria 83 C7
Baud, France 18 E3
Baudette, U.S.A. 112 A7
Bauer, C., Australia 95 E1
Bauhinia, Australia 94 C4
Baukau, E. Timor 63 F7
Bauld, C., Canada 101 C14
Baume-les-Dames, France 19 E13
Baunatal, Germany 24 D5
Baunei, Italy 30 B2
Baure, Nigeria 83 C6
Bauru, Brazil 127 A6
Bausi, India 69 G12
Bauska, Latvia 9 H21
Bautino, Kazakstan 49 H10
Bautzen, Germany 24 D10
Bauya, S. Leone 82 D2
Bavānāt, Iran 71 D7
Bavanište, Serbia, Yug. 42 F5
Bavaria = Bayern □, Germany 25 G7
Båven, Sweden 10 E10
Bavispe →, Mexico 118 B3
Bawdwin, Burma 67 H20
Bawean, Indonesia 62 F4
Bawku, Ghana 83 C4
Bawlake, Burma 67 K20
Bawolung, China 58 C3
Baxley, U.S.A. 109 K4
Baxoi, China 58 B1
Baxter, U.S.A. 112 B7
Baxter Springs, U.S.A. 113 G7
Bay, L. de, Phil. 61 D4
Bay City, Mich., U.S.A. 108 D4
Bay City, Tex., U.S.A. 113 L7
Bay Minette, U.S.A. 109 K2
Bay Roberts, Canada 103 C9
Bay St. Louis, U.S.A. 113 K10
Bay Springs, U.S.A. 113 K10
Bay View, N.Z. 91 H6
Baya, Dem. Rep. of the Congo 87 E2
Bayamo, Cuba 120 B4
Bayamón, Puerto Rico 121 C6
Bayan Har Shan, China 60 C4
Bayan Hot = Alxa Zuoqi, China 56 E3
Bayan Obo, China 56 D5
Bayan-Ovoo = Erdenetsogt, Mongolia 56 C4
Bayana, India 68 F7
Bayanaūyl, Kazakstan 50 D8
Bayandalay, Mongolia 56 C2
Bayanhongor, Mongolia 60 B5
Bayard, N. Mex., U.S.A. 115 K9
Bayard, Nebr., U.S.A. 112 E3
Bayawan, Phil. 61 G5
Baybay, Phil. 61 F6
Bayburt, Turkey 73 B9
Bayelsa □, Nigeria 83 E6
Bayerische Alpen, Germany 25 H7
Bayerischer Wald, Germany 25 G8
Bayern □, Germany 25 G7
Bayeux, France 18 C6
Bayfield, Canada 110 C3
Bayfield, U.S.A. 112 B9
Bayındır, Turkey 39 C9
Baykal, Oz., Russia 51 D11
Baykan, Turkey 70 B4
Baykonur = Bayqongyr, Kazakstan 50 E7
Baynes Mts., Namibia 88 B1
Bayombong, Phil. 61 C4
Bayon, France 19 D13
Bayona = Baiona, Spain 34 C2
Bayonne, France 20 E2
Bayonne, U.S.A. 111 F10
Bayovar, Peru 124 E2
Bayqongyr, Kazakstan 50 E7
Bayram-Ali = Bayramaly, Turkmenistan 50 F7
Bayramaly, Turkmenistan 50 F7
Bayramiç, Turkey 39 B8
Bayreuth, Germany 25 F7
Bayrischzell, Germany 25 H8
Bayrūt, Lebanon 75 B4
Bays, L. of, Canada 110 A5
Baysville, Canada 110 A5
Bayt Lahm, West Bank 75 D4
Baytown, U.S.A. 113 L7
Bayzo, Niger 83 C5
Baza, Spain 35 H8
Bazar Dyuzi, Russia 49 K8
Bazardüzü = Bazar Dyuzi, Russia 49 K8
Bazarny Karabulak, Russia 48 D8
Bazarnyy Syzgan, Russia 48 D8
Bazaruto, I. do, Mozam. 89 C6
Bazas, France 20 D3
Bazhong, China 58 B6
Bazhou, China 56 E9
Bazmān, Kūh-e, Iran 71 D9
Beach, U.S.A. 112 B3
Beach City, U.S.A. 110 F3
Beachport, Australia 95 F3
Beachy Hd., U.K. 13 G8
Beacon, Australia 93 F2
Beacon, U.S.A. 111 E11
Beaconsfield, Australia 94 G4
Beagle, Canal, S. Amer. 122 J4
Beagle Bay, Australia 92 C3
Bealanana, Madag. 89 A8
Beals Cr. →, U.S.A. 113 J4
Beamsville, Canada 110 C5
Bear →, Calif., U.S.A. 116 G5
Bear →, Utah, U.S.A. 106 B4
Béar, C., France 20 F7
Bear I., Ireland 15 E2
Bear L., Canada 105 B9
Bear L., U.S.A. 114 F8
Beardmore, Canada 102 C2
Beardmore Glacier, Antarctica 5 E11
Beardstown, U.S.A. 112 F9
Bearma →, India 69 G8
Béarn, France 20 E3
Bearpaw Mts., U.S.A. 114 B9
Bearskin Lake, Canada 102 B1
Beas →, India 68 D6
Beas de Segura, Spain 35 G8
Beasain, Spain 32 B2
Beata, C., Dom. Rep. 121 C5
Beata, I., Dom. Rep. 121 C5
Beatrice, U.S.A. 112 E6
Beatrice, Zimbabwe 87 F3
Beatrice, C., Australia 94 A2
Beatton →, Canada 104 B4
Beatton River, Canada 104 B4
Beatty, U.S.A. 116 J10
Beaucaire, France 21 E8
Beauce, Plaine de la, France 19 D8
Beauceville, Canada 103 C5
Beaudesert, Australia 95 D5
Beaufort, France 21 C10
Beaufort, Malaysia 62 C5
Beaufort, N.C., U.S.A. 109 H7
Beaufort, S.C., U.S.A. 109 J5
Beaufort Sea, Arctic 4 B1
Beaufort West, S. Africa 88 E3
Beaugency, France 19 E8
Beauharnois, Canada 111 A11
Beaujeu, France 19 F11
Beaujolais, France 19 F11
Beaulieu →, Canada 104 A6
Beaulieu-sur-Dordogne, France 20 D5
Beaulieu-sur-Mer, France 21 E11
Beauly, U.K. 14 D4
Beauly →, U.K. 14 D4
Beaumaris, U.K. 12 D3
Beaumont, Belgium 17 D4
Beaumont, France 20 D4
Beaumont, U.S.A. 113 K7
Beaumont-de-Lomagne, France 20 E5
Beaumont-le-Roger, France 18 C7
Beaumont-sur-Sarthe, France 18 D7
Beaune, France 19 E11
Beaune-la-Rolande, France 19 D9
Beaupré, Canada 103 C5
Beaupréau, France 18 E6
Beauraing, Belgium 17 D4
Beaurepaire, France 21 C9
Beauséjour, Canada 105 C9
Beauvais, France 19 C9
Beauval, Canada 105 B7
Beauvoir-sur-Mer, France 18 F4
Beauvoir-sur-Niort, France 20 B3
Beaver, Okla., U.S.A. 113 G4
Beaver, Pa., U.S.A. 110 F4
Beaver, Utah, U.S.A. 115 G7
Beaver →, B.C., Canada 104 B4
Beaver →, Ont., Canada 102 A2
Beaver →, Sask., Canada 105 B7
Beaver →, U.S.A. 113 G5
Beaver City, U.S.A. 112 E5
Beaver Creek, Canada 100 B5
Beaver Dam, U.S.A. 112 D10
Beaver Falls, U.S.A. 110 F4
Beaver Hill L., Canada 105 C10
Beaver I., U.S.A. 108 C3
Beaverhill L., Canada 104 C6
Beaverlodge, Canada 104 B5
Beaverstone →, Canada 102 B2
Beaverton, Canada 110 B5
Beaverton, U.S.A. 116 E4
Beawar, India 68 F6
Bebedouro, Brazil 127 A6
Beboa, Madag. 89 B7
Bebra, Germany 24 E5
Beccles, U.K. 13 E9
Bečej, Serbia, Yug. 42 E5
Beceni, Romania 43 E11
Becerreá, Spain 34 C3
Béchar, Algeria 78 B5
Bechyně, Czech Rep. 26 B7
Beckley, U.S.A. 108 G5
Beckum, Germany 24 D4
Beclean, Romania 43 C9
Bečov nad Teplou, Czech Rep. 26 A5
Bečva →, Czech Rep. 27 B10
Bédar, Spain 33 H3
Bédarieux, France 20 E7
Beddouza, Ras, Morocco 78 B4
Bedele, Ethiopia 81 F4
Bederkesa, Germany 24 B4
Bedeso, Ethiopia 81 F5
Bedford, Canada 111 A12
Bedford, S. Africa 88 E4
Bedford, U.K. 13 E7
Bedford, Ind., U.S.A. 108 F2
Bedford, Iowa, U.S.A. 112 E7
Bedford, Ohio, U.S.A. 110 E3
Bedford, Pa., U.S.A. 110 F6
Bedford, Va., U.S.A. 108 G6
Bedford, C., Australia 94 B4
Bedfordshire □, U.K. 13 E7
Będków, Poland 45 G6
Bednja →, Croatia 29 B13
Bednodemyanovsk, Russia 48 D6
Bedónia, Italy 28 D6
Bedourie, Australia 94 C2
Bedum, Neths. 17 A6
Będzin, Poland 45 H6
Beebe Plain, Canada 111 A12
Beech Creek, U.S.A. 110 E7
Beelitz, Germany 24 C8
Beenleigh, Australia 95 D5
Be'er Menuḥa, Israel 70 D2
Be'er Sheva, Israel 75 D3
Beersheba = Be'er Sheva, Israel 75 D3
Beeskow, Germany 24 C10
Beestekraal, S. Africa 89 D4
Beeston, U.K. 12 E6
Beetzendorf, Germany 24 C7
Beeville, U.S.A. 113 L6
Befale, Dem. Rep. of the Congo 84 D4
Befandriana, Mahajanga, Madag. 89 B8
Befandriana, Toliara, Madag. 89 C7
Befasy, Madag. 89 C7
Befotaka, Antsiranana, Madag. 89 A8
Befotaka, Fianarantsoa, Madag. 89 C8
Bega, Australia 95 F4
Bega, Canalul, Romania 42 E5
Bégard, France 18 D3
Beğendik, Turkey 41 F10
Begoro, Ghana 83 D4
Begusarai, India 69 G12
Behābād, Iran 71 C8
Behala, India 69 H13
Behara, Madag. 89 C8
Behbehān, Iran 71 D6
Behm Canal, U.S.A. 104 B2
Behshahr, Iran 71 B7
Bei Jiang →, China 59 F9
Bei'an, China 60 B7
Beibei, China 58 C6
Beichuan, China 58 B5
Beihai, China 58 G7
Beijing, China 56 E9
Beijing □, China 56 E9
Beilen, Neths. 17 B6
Beiliu, China 59 F8
Beilngries, Germany 25 F7
Beilpajah, Australia 95 E3
Beilul, Eritrea 81 E5
Beinn na Faoghla = Benbecula, U.K. 14 D1
Beipan Jiang, China 58 E5
Beipiao, China 57 D11
Beira, Mozam. 87 F3
Beirut = Bayrūt, Lebanon 75 B4
Beiseker, Canada 104 C6
Beitaolaizhao, China 57 B13
Beitbridge, Zimbabwe 87 G3
Beiuş, Romania 42 D7
Beizhen = Binzhou, China 57 F10
Beizhen, China 57 D11
Beizhengzhen, China 57 B12
Beja, Portugal 35 G3
Béja, Tunisia 79 A7
Beja □, Portugal 35 H3
Bejaïa, Algeria 78 A7
Béjar, Spain 34 E5
Bejestān, Iran 71 C8
Bekçiler, Turkey 39 E11
Békés, Hungary 42 D6
Békés □, Hungary 42 D6
Békéscsaba, Hungary 42 D6
Bekilli, Turkey 39 C11
Bekily, Madag. 89 C8
Bekisopa, Madag. 89 C8
Bekitro, Madag. 89 C8
Bekodoka, Madag. 89 B8
Bekoji, Ethiopia 81 F4
Bekok, Malaysia 65 L4
Bekopaka, Madag. 89 B7
Bekwai, Ghana 83 D4
Bela, India 69 G10
Bela, Pakistan 68 F2
Bela Crkva, Serbia, Yug. 42 F6
Bela Palanka, Serbia, Yug. 40 C6
Bela Vista, Brazil 126 A4
Bela Vista, Mozam. 89 D5
Bélâbre, France 20 B5
Belalcázar, Spain 35 G5
Belan →, India 69 G9
Belanovica, Serbia, Yug. 40 B4
Belarus ■, Europe 46 F4
Belau = Palau ■, Pac. Oc. 52 J17
Belavenona, Madag. 89 C8
Belawan, Indonesia 62 D1
Belaya, Ethiopia 81 E4
Belaya Glina, Russia 49 G5
Belaya Kalitva, Russia 49 F5
Belaya Tserkov = Bila Tserkva, Ukraine 47 H6
Belceşti, Romania 43 C12
Bełchatów, Poland 45 G6
Belcher Is., Canada 102 A3
Belchite, Spain 32 D4
Belden, U.S.A. 116 E5
Belém, Brazil 125 D9
Belén, Argentina 126 B2
Belén, Paraguay 126 A4
Belen, U.S.A. 115 J10
Belene, Bulgaria 41 C9
Beleni, Turkey 72 D7
Bélesta, France 20 F5
Belet Uen, Somali Rep. 74 G4
Belev, Russia 46 F9
Belevi, Turkey 39 C9
Belfair, U.S.A. 116 C4
Belfast, S. Africa 89 D5
Belfast, U.K. 15 B6
Belfast, Maine, U.S.A. 109 C11
Belfast, N.Y., U.S.A. 110 D6
Belfast L., U.K. 15 B6
Belfield, U.S.A. 112 B3
Belfort, France 19 E13
Belfort, Territoire de □, France 19 E13
Belfry, U.S.A. 114 D9
Belgaum, India 66 M9
Belgioioso, Italy 28 C6
Belgium ■, Europe 17 D4
Belgodère, France 21 F13
Belgorod, Russia 47 G9
Belgorod-Dnestrovskiy = Bilhorod-Dnistrovskyy, Ukraine 47 J6
Belgrade = Beograd, Serbia, Yug. 40 B4
Belgrade, U.S.A. 114 D8
Belhaven, U.S.A. 109 H7
Beli Drim →, Europe 40 D4
Beli Manastir, Croatia 42 E3
Beli Timok →, Serbia, Yug. 40 C6
Bélice →, Italy 30 E5
Belinskiy, Russia 48 D6
Belinyu, Indonesia 62 E3
Beliton Is. = Belitung, Indonesia 62 E3
Belitung, Indonesia 62 E3
Beliu, Romania 42 D6
Belize ■, Cent. Amer. 119 D7
Belize City, Belize 119 D7
Beljakovci, Macedonia 40 D5
Beljanica, Serbia, Yug. 40 B5
Belkovskiy, Ostrov, Russia 51 B14
Bell →, Canada 102 C4
Bell I., Canada 103 B8
Bell-Irving →, Canada 104 B3
Bell Peninsula, Canada 101 B11
Bell Ville, Argentina 126 C3
Bella, Italy 31 B8
Bella Bella, Canada 104 C3
Bella Coola, Canada 104 C3
Bella Unión, Uruguay 126 C4
Bella Vista, Corrientes, Argentina 126 B4
Bella Vista, Tucuman, Argentina 126 B2
Bellac, France 20 B5
Bellágio, Italy 28 C6
Bellaire, U.S.A. 110 F4
Bellária, Italy 29 D9
Bellary, India 66 M10
Bellata, Australia 95 D4
Belle-Chasse, U.S.A. 113 L10
Belle Fourche, U.S.A. 112 C3
Belle Fourche →, U.S.A. 112 C3
Belle Glade, U.S.A. 109 M5
Belle-Île, France 18 E3
Belle Isle, Canada 103 B8
Belle Isle, Str. of, Canada 103 B8
Belle Plaine, U.S.A. 112 E8
Belle Yella, Liberia 82 D3
Belledonne, France 21 C10
Bellefontaine, U.S.A. 108 E4
Bellefonte, U.S.A. 110 F7
Bellegarde, France 19 E9
Bellegarde-en-Marche, France 20 C6
Bellegarde-sur-Valserine, France 19 F12
Bellême, France 18 D7
Belleoram, Canada 103 C8
Belleville, Canada 102 D4
Belleville, France 19 F11
Belleville, Ill., U.S.A. 112 F10
Belleville, Kans., U.S.A. 112 F6
Belleville, N.Y., U.S.A. 111 C8
Belleville-sur-Vie, France 18 F5
Bellevue, Canada 104 D6
Bellevue, Idaho, U.S.A. 114 E6
Bellevue, Nebr., U.S.A. 112 E7
Bellevue, Ohio, U.S.A. 110 E2
Bellevue, Wash., U.S.A. 116 C4
Belley, France 21 C9
Bellin = Kangirsuk, Canada 101 B13
Bellinge, Denmark 11 J4
Bellingen, Australia 95 E5
Bellingham, U.S.A. 100 D7
Bellingshausen Sea, Antarctica 5 C17
Bellinzona, Switz. 25 J5
Bello, Colombia 124 B3
Bellows Falls, U.S.A. 111 C12
Bellpat, Pakistan 68 E3
Bellpuig d'Urgell, Spain 32 D6
Belluno, Italy 29 B9
Bellwood, U.S.A. 110 F6
Bélmez, Spain 35 G5
Belmont, Canada 110 D3
Belmont, S. Africa 88 D3
Belmont, U.S.A. 110 D6
Belmonte, Brazil 125 G11
Belmonte, Portugal 34 E3
Belmonte, Spain 33 F2
Belmopan, Belize 119 D7
Belmullet, Ireland 15 B2
Belo Horizonte, Brazil 125 G10
Belo-sur-Mer, Madag. 89 C7
Belo-Tsiribihina, Madag. 89 B7
Belogorsk = Bilohirsk, Ukraine 47 K8
Belogorsk, Russia 51 D13
Belogradchik, Bulgaria 40 C6
Belogradets, Bulgaria 41 C11
Beloha, Madag. 89 D8
Beloit, Kans., U.S.A. 112 F5
Beloit, Wis., U.S.A. 112 D10
Belokorovichi, Ukraine 47 G5
Belomorsk, Russia 50 C4
Belonia, India 67 H17
Belopolye = Bilopillya, Ukraine 47 G8
Belorechensk, Russia 49 H4
Belorussia = Belarus ■, Europe 46 F4
Beloslav, Bulgaria 41 C11
Belovo, Bulgaria 41 D8
Belovo, Russia 50 D9
Belovodsk, Ukraine 47 H10
Beloye, Ozero, Russia 46 B9
Beloye More, Russia 50 C4
Belozem, Bulgaria 41 D9
Belozersk, Russia 46 B9
Belpasso, Italy 31 E7
Belpre, U.S.A. 108 F5
Belrain, India 69 E9
Belt, U.S.A. 114 C8
Beltana, Australia 95 E2
Belterra, Brazil 125 D8
Beltinci, Slovenia 29 B13
Belton, U.S.A. 113 K6
Belton L., U.S.A. 113 K6
Beltsy = Bălţi, Moldova 43 C12
Belturbet, Ireland 15 B4
Belukha, Russia 50 E9
Beluran, Malaysia 62 C5
Beluša, Slovak Rep. 27 B11
Belušić, Serbia, Yug. 40 C5
Belvedere Maríttimo, Italy 31 C8
Belvès, France 20 D5
Belvidere, Ill., U.S.A. 112 D10
Belvidere, N.J., U.S.A. 111 F9
Belvis de la Jara, Spain 34 F6
Belyando →, Australia 94 C4
Belyy, Russia 46 E7
Belyy, Ostrov, Russia 50 B8
Belyy Yar, Russia 50 D9
Bełżec, Poland 45 H10
Belzig, Germany 24 C8
Belzoni, U.S.A. 113 J9
Bełżyce, Poland 45 G9
Bemaraha, Lembalemban' i, Madag. 89 B7
Bemarivo, Madag. 89 C7
Bemarivo →, Antsiranana, Madag. 89 A9
Bemarivo →, Mahajanga, Madag. 89 B8
Bemavo, Madag. 89 C8
Bembéréke, Benin 83 C5
Bembesi, Zimbabwe 87 G2
Bembesi →, Zimbabwe 87 F2
Bembézar →, Spain 35 H5
Bembibre, Spain 34 C4
Bemetara, India 69 J9
Bemidji, U.S.A. 112 B7
Bemolanga, Madag. 89 B8
Ben, Iran 71 C6
Ben Cruachan, U.K. 14 E3
Ben Dearg, U.K. 14 D4
Ben Hope, U.K. 14 C4
Ben Lawers, U.K. 14 E4
Ben Lomond, N.S.W., Australia 95 E5

**Bilciureşti**


Ben Lomond, *Tas., Australia* 94 G4
Ben Lomond, *U.K.* 14 E4
Ben Luc, *Vietnam* 65 G6
Ben Macdhui, *U.K.* 14 D5
Ben Mhor, *U.K.* 14 D1
Ben More, *Arg. & Bute, U.K.* 14 E2
Ben More, *Stirl., U.K.* 14 E4
Ben More Assynt, *U.K.* 14 C4
Ben Nevis, *U.K.* 14 E3
Ben Quang, *Vietnam* 64 D6
Ben Vorlich, *U.K.* 14 E4
Ben Wyvis, *U.K.* 14 D4
Bena, *Nigeria* 83 C6
Benāb, *Iran* 73 D12
Benalla, *Australia* 95 F4
Benalmádena, *Spain* 35 J6
Benares = Varanasi, *India* 69 G10
Bénat, C., *France* 21 E10
Benavente, *Portugal* 35 G2
Benavente, *Spain* 34 C5
Benavides, *U.S.A.* 113 M5
Benavides de Órbigo, *Spain* 34 C5
Benbecula, *U.K.* 14 D1
Benbonyathe, *Australia* 95 E2
Bend, *U.S.A.* 114 D3
Bender Beila, *Somali Rep.* 74 F5
Bendery = Tighina, *Moldova* 43 D14
Bendigo, *Australia* 95 F3
Bendorf, *Germany* 24 E3
Benē Beraq, *Israel* 75 C3
Bénéna, *Mali* 82 C4
Benenitra, *Madag.* 89 C8
Benešov, *Czech Rep.* 26 B7
Benevento, *Italy* 31 A7
Benfeld, *France* 19 D14
Benga, *Mozam.* 87 F3
Bengal, Bay of, *Ind. Oc.* 67 M17
Bengbis, *Cameroon* 83 E7
Bengbu, *China* 57 H9
Benghazi = Banghāzī, *Libya* 79 B10
Bengkalis, *Indonesia* 62 D2
Bengkulu, *Indonesia* 62 E2
Bengkulu □, *Indonesia* 62 E2
Bengough, *Canada* 105 D7
Bengtsfors, *Sweden* 10 E6
Benguela, *Angola* 85 G2
Benguérua, I., *Mozam.* 89 C6
Benha, *Egypt* 80 H7
Beni, *Dem. Rep. of the Congo* 86 B2
Beni →, *Bolivia* 124 F5
Beni Mazâr, *Egypt* 80 B3
Beni Mellal, *Morocco* 78 B4
Beni Suef, *Egypt* 80 J7
Beniah L., *Canada* 104 A6
Benicarló, *Spain* 32 E5
Benicàssim, *Spain* 32 E5
Benicia, *U.S.A.* 116 G4
Benidorm, *Spain* 33 G4
Benin ■, *Africa* 83 D5
Benin →, *Nigeria* 83 D6
Benin, Bight of, *W. Afr.* 83 E5
Benin City, *Nigeria* 83 D6
Benisa, *Spain* 33 G5
Benitses, *Greece* 36 A3
Benjamin Aceval, *Paraguay* 126 A4
Benjamin Constant, *Brazil* 124 D4
Benjamin Hill, *Mexico* 118 A2
Benkelman, *U.S.A.* 112 E4
Benkovac, *Croatia* 29 D12
Bennett, *Canada* 104 B2
Bennett, L., *Australia* 92 D5
Bennetta, Ostrov, *Russia* 5 B15
Bennettsville, *U.S.A.* 109 H6
Bennichchāb, *Mauritania* 82 B1
Bennington, *N.H., U.S.A.* 111 D11
Bennington, *Vt., U.S.A.* 111 D11
Bénodet, *France* 18 E2
Benoni, *S. Africa* 89 D4
Benque Viejo, *Belize* 119 D7
Bensheim, *Germany* 25 F4
Benson, *Ariz., U.S.A.* 115 L8
Benson, *Minn., U.S.A.* 112 C7
Bent, *Iran* 71 E8
Benteng, *Indonesia* 63 F6
Bentinck I., *Australia* 94 B2
Bentiu, *Sudan* 81 F2
Bento Gonçalves, *Brazil* 127 B5
Benton, *Ark., U.S.A.* 113 H8
Benton, *Calif., U.S.A.* 116 H8
Benton, *Ill., U.S.A.* 112 G10
Benton, *Pa., U.S.A.* 111 E8
Benton Harbor, *U.S.A.* 108 D2
Bentonville, *U.S.A.* 113 G7
Bentu Liben, *Ethiopia* 81 F4
Bentung, *Malaysia* 65 L3
Benue □, *Nigeria* 83 D6
Benue →, *Nigeria* 83 D6
Benxi, *China* 57 D12
Beo, *Indonesia* 63 D7
Beograd, *Serbia, Yug.* 40 B4
Beoumi, *Ivory C.* 82 D3
Bepan Jiang →, *China* 58 E6
Beppu, *Japan* 55 H5
Beqaa Valley = Al Biqā, *Lebanon* 75 A5
Ber Mota, *India* 68 H3
Berach →, *India* 68 G6
Beraketa, *Madag.* 89 C7
Berane, *Montenegro, Yug.* 40 D3
Berat, *Albania* 40 F3
Berau, Teluk, *Indonesia* 63 E8
Beravina, *Madag.* 89 B8
Berber, *Sudan* 80 D3
Berbera, *Somali Rep.* 74 E4
Berbérati, *C.A.R.* 84 D3
Berbice →, *Guyana* 124 B7
Berceto, *Italy* 28 D6
Berchidda, *Italy* 30 B2
Berchtesgaden, *Germany* 25 H8
Berck, *France* 19 B8
Berdichev = Berdychiv, *Ukraine* 47 H5
Berdsk, *Russia* 50 D9
Berdyansk, *Ukraine* 47 J9
Berdychiv, *Ukraine* 47 H5
Berea, *U.S.A.* 108 G3
Berebere, *Indonesia* 63 D7
Bereda, *Somali Rep.* 74 E5
Berehove, *Ukraine* 47 H2
Berekum, *Ghana* 82 D4
Berenice, *Egypt* 80 C4
Berens →, *Canada* 105 C9
Berens I., *Canada* 105 C9
Berens River, *Canada* 105 C9
Beresford, *U.S.A.* 112 D6
Berestechko, *Ukraine* 47 G3
Bereşti, *Romania* 43 D12
Beretău →, *Romania* 42 C6
Berettyó →, *Hungary* 42 D6
Berettyóújfalu, *Hungary* 42 C6
Berevo, *Mahajanga, Madag.* 89 B7
Berevo, *Toliara, Madag.* 89 B7
Bereza = Byaroza, *Belarus* 47 F3
Berezhany, *Ukraine* 47 H3
Berezina = Byarezina →, *Belarus* 47 F6
Berezivka, *Ukraine* 47 J6
Berezna, *Ukraine* 47 G6
Berezniki, *Russia* 50 C5
Berezniki, *Russia* 50 D6
Berezovo, *Russia* 50 C7
Berga, *Spain* 32 C6
Berga, *Sweden* 11 G10
Bergama, *Turkey* 39 B9
Bérgamo, *Italy* 28 C6
Bergara, *Spain* 32 B2
Bergby, *Sweden* 10 D11
Bergedorf, *Germany* 24 B6
Bergeforsen, *Sweden* 10 B11
Bergen, *Mecklenburg-Vorpommern, Germany* 24 A9
Bergen, *Niedersachsen, Germany* 24 C5
Bergen, *Neths.* 17 B4
Bergen, *Norway* 9 F11
Bergen, *U.S.A.* 110 C7
Bergen op Zoom, *Neths.* 17 C4
Bergerac, *France* 20 D4
Bergheim, *Germany* 24 E2
Bergholz, *U.S.A.* 110 F4
Bergisch Gladbach, *Germany* 17 D7
Bergkamen, *Germany* 24 D3
Bergkvara, *Sweden* 11 H10
Bergshamra, *Sweden* 10 E12
Bergsjö, *Sweden* 10 C11
Bergues, *France* 19 B9
Bergviken, *Sweden* 10 C10
Bergville, *S. Africa* 89 D4
Berhala, Selat, *Indonesia* 62 E2
Berhampore = Baharampur, *India* 69 G13
Berhampur = Brahmapur, *India* 67 K14
Berheci →, *Romania* 43 E12
Bering Sea, *Pac. Oc.* 100 C1
Bering Strait, *Pac. Oc.* 100 B3
Beringovskiy, *Russia* 51 C18
Berisso, *Argentina* 126 C4
Berja, *Spain* 35 J8
Berkeley, *U.S.A.* 116 H4
Berkner I., *Antarctica* 5 D18
Berkovitsa, *Bulgaria* 40 C7
Berkshire, *U.S.A.* 111 D8
Berkshire Downs, *U.K.* 13 F6
Berlanga, *Spain* 35 G5
Berlenga, I., *Portugal* 35 F1
Berlin, *Germany* 24 C9
Berlin, *Md., U.S.A.* 108 F8
Berlin, *N.H., U.S.A.* 111 B13
Berlin, *N.Y., U.S.A.* 111 D11
Berlin, *Wis., U.S.A.* 108 D1
Berlin □, *Germany* 24 C9
Berlin L., *U.S.A.* 110 E4
Bermeja, Sierra, *Spain* 35 J5
Bermejo →, *Formosa, Argentina* 126 B4
Bermejo →, *San Juan, Argentina* 126 C2
Bermen, L., *Canada* 103 B6
Bermeo, *Spain* 32 B2
Bermillo de Sayago, *Spain* 34 D4
Bermuda ■, *Atl. Oc.* 98 F13
Bern, *Switz.* 25 J3
Bern □, *Switz.* 25 J3
Bernalda, *Italy* 31 B9
Bernalillo, *U.S.A.* 115 J10
Bernardo de Irigoyen, *Argentina* 127 B5
Bernardo O'Higgins □, *Chile* 126 C1
Bernardsville, *U.S.A.* 111 F10
Bernasconi, *Argentina* 126 D3
Bernau, *Bayern, Germany* 25 H8
Bernau, *Brandenburg, Germany* 24 C9
Bernay, *France* 18 C7
Bernburg, *Germany* 24 D7
Berndorf, *Austria* 26 D9
Berne = Bern, *Switz.* 25 J3
Berne = Bern □, *Switz.* 25 J3
Berner Alpen, *Switz.* 25 J3
Berneray, *U.K.* 14 D1
Bernier I., *Australia* 93 D1
Bernina, Piz, *Switz.* 25 J5
Bernkastel-Kues, *Germany* 25 F3
Beroroha, *Madag.* 89 C8
Béroubouay, *Benin* 83 C5
Beroun, *Czech Rep.* 26 B7
Berounka →, *Czech Rep.* 26 B7
Berovo, *Macedonia* 40 E6
Berre, Étang de, *France* 21 E9
Berre-l'Étang, *France* 21 E9
Berri, *Australia* 95 E3
Berriane, *Algeria* 78 B6
Berry, *Australia* 95 E5
Berry, *France* 19 F8
Berry Is., *Bahamas* 120 A4
Berryessa L., *U.S.A.* 116 G4
Berryville, *U.S.A.* 113 G8
Berseba, *Namibia* 88 D2
Bersenbrück, *Germany* 24 C3
Bershad, *Ukraine* 47 H5
Berthold, *U.S.A.* 112 A4
Berthoud, *U.S.A.* 112 E2
Bertincourt, *France* 19 B9
Bertoua, *Cameroon* 84 D2
Bertraghboy B., *Ireland* 15 C2
Berwick, *U.S.A.* 111 E8
Berwick-upon-Tweed, *U.K.* 12 B6
Berwyn Mts., *U.K.* 12 E4
Beryslav, *Ukraine* 47 J7
Berzasca, *Romania* 42 F6
Berzence, *Hungary* 42 D2
Besal, *Pakistan* 69 B5
Besalampy, *Madag.* 89 B7
Besançon, *France* 19 E13
Besar, *Indonesia* 62 E5
Beshenkovichi, *Belarus* 46 E5
Beška, *Serbia, Yug.* 42 E5
Beslan, *Russia* 49 J7
Besna Kobila, *Serbia, Yug.* 40 D6
Besnard L., *Canada* 105 B7
Besni, *Turkey* 70 B3
Besor, N. →, *Egypt* 75 D3
Bessarabiya, *Moldova* 47 J5
Bessarabka = Basarabeasca, *Moldova* 43 D13
Bessèges, *France* 21 D8
Bessemer, *Ala., U.S.A.* 109 J2
Bessemer, *Mich., U.S.A.* 112 B9
Bessemer, *Pa., U.S.A.* 110 F4
Bessin, *France* 18 C6
Bessines-sur-Gartempe, *France* 20 B5
Beswick, *Australia* 92 B5
Bet She'an, *Israel* 75 C4
Bet Shemesh, *Israel* 75 D4
Betafo, *Madag.* 89 B8
Betancuria, *Canary Is.* 37 F5
Betanzos, *Spain* 34 B2
Bétaré Oya, *Cameroon* 84 C2
Betatao, *Madag.* 89 B8
Bétera, *Spain* 33 F4
Bétérou, *Benin* 83 D5
Bethal, *S. Africa* 89 D4
Bethanien, *Namibia* 88 D2
Bethany, *Canada* 110 B6
Bethany, *U.S.A.* 112 E7
Bethel, *Alaska, U.S.A.* 100 B3
Bethel, *Conn., U.S.A.* 111 E11
Bethel, *Maine, U.S.A.* 111 B14
Bethel, *Vt., U.S.A.* 111 C12
Bethel Park, *U.S.A.* 110 F4
Béthenville, *France* 19 C11
Bethlehem = Bayt Lahm, *West Bank* 75 D4
Bethlehem, *S. Africa* 89 D4
Bethlehem, *U.S.A.* 111 F9
Bethulie, *S. Africa* 88 E4
Béthune, *France* 19 B9
Béthune →, *France* 18 C8
Betioky, *Madag.* 89 C7
Betong, *Thailand* 65 K3
Betoota, *Australia* 94 D3
Betor, *Ethiopia* 81 E4
Betroka, *Madag.* 89 C8
Betsiamites, *Canada* 103 C6
Betsiamites →, *Canada* 103 C6
Betsiboka →, *Madag.* 89 B8
Bettendorf, *U.S.A.* 112 E9
Bettiah, *India* 69 F11
Bettna, *Sweden* 11 F10
Béttola, *Italy* 28 D6
Betul, *India* 66 J10
Betung, *Malaysia* 62 D4
Betws-y-Coed, *U.K.* 12 D4
Betxi, *Spain* 32 F4
Betzdorf, *Germany* 24 E3
Beuil, *France* 21 D10
Beulah, *Mich., U.S.A.* 108 C2
Beulah, *N. Dak., U.S.A.* 112 B4
Beuvron →, *France* 18 E8
Beveren, *Belgium* 17 C4
Beverley, *Australia* 93 F2
Beverley, *U.K.* 12 D7
Beverley Hills, *U.S.A.* 109 L4
Beverly, *U.S.A.* 111 D14
Beverly Hills, *U.S.A.* 117 L8
Beverungen, *Germany* 24 D5
Bevoalavo, *Madag.* 89 D7
Bewas →, *India* 69 H8
Bex, *Switz.* 25 J3
Bexhill, *U.K.* 13 G8
Bey Dağları, *Turkey* 39 E12
Beyānlū, *Iran* 70 C5
Beyazköy, *Turkey* 41 E11
Beyçayırı, *Turkey* 41 F10
Beydağ, *Turkey* 39 C10
Beyeğaç, *Turkey* 39 D10
Beyin, *Ghana* 82 D4
Beykoz, *Turkey* 41 E13
Beyla, *Guinea* 82 D3
Beynat, *France* 20 C5
Beyneu, *Kazakstan* 50 E6
Beyoba, *Turkey* 39 C9
Beyoğlu, *Turkey* 41 E12
Beypazarı, *Turkey* 72 B4
Beyşehir, *Turkey* 72 D4
Beyşehir Gölü, *Turkey* 70 B1
Beytüşşebap, *Turkey* 73 D10
Bezdan, *Serbia, Yug.* 42 E3
Bezhetsk, *Russia* 46 D9
Béziers, *France* 20 E7
Bezwada = Vijayawada, *India* 67 L12
Bhabua, *India* 69 G10
Bhachau, *India* 66 H7
Bhadar →, *Gujarat, India* 68 H5
Bhadar →, *Gujarat, India* 68 J3
Bhadarwah, *India* 69 C6
Bhadohi, *India* 69 G10
Bhadra, *India* 68 E6
Bhadrakh, *India* 67 J15
Bhadran, *India* 68 H5
Bhadravati, *India* 66 N9
Bhag, *Pakistan* 68 E2
Bhagalpur, *India* 69 G12
Bhagirathi →, *Ut. P., India* 69 D8
Bhagirathi →, *W. Bengal, India* 69 H13
Bhakkar, *Pakistan* 68 D4
Bhakra Dam, *India* 68 D7
Bhamo, *Burma* 67 G20
Bhandara, *India* 66 J11
Bhanpura, *India* 68 G6
Bhanrer Ra., *India* 68 H8
Bhaptiahi, *India* 69 F12
Bharat = India ■, *Asia* 66 K11
Bharatpur, *Mad. P., India* 69 H9
Bharatpur, *Raj., India* 68 F7
Bharno, *India* 69 H11
Bhatinda, *India* 68 D6
Bhatpara, *India* 69 H13
Bhattu, *India* 68 E6
Bhaun, *Pakistan* 68 C5
Bhaunagar = Bhavnagar, *India* 66 J8
Bhavnagar, *India* 66 J8
Bhawari, *India* 68 G5
Bhayavadar, *India* 68 J4
Bhera, *Pakistan* 68 C5
Bhikangaon, *India* 68 J6
Bhilsa = Vidisha, *India* 68 H7
Bhilwara, *India* 68 G6
Bhima →, *India* 66 L10
Bhimbar, *Pakistan* 69 C6
Bhind, *India* 69 F8
Bhinga, *India* 69 F9
Bhinmal, *India* 68 G5
Bhiwandi, *India* 66 K8
Bhiwani, *India* 68 E7
Bhogava →, *India* 68 H5
Bhola, *Bangla.* 67 H17
Bholari, *Pakistan* 68 G3
Bhopal, *India* 68 H7
Bhubaneshwar, *India* 67 J14
Bhuj, *India* 68 H3
Bhusaval, *India* 66 J9
Bhutan ■, *Asia* 67 F17
Biafra, B. of = Bonny, Bight of, *Africa* 83 E6
Biak, *Indonesia* 63 E9
Biała, *Poland* 45 H4
Biała →, *Poland* 45 H7
Biała Piska, *Poland* 44 E9
Biała Podlaska, *Poland* 45 F10
Biała Rawska, *Poland* 45 G7
Białobrzegi, *Poland* 45 G7
Białogard, *Poland* 44 D2
Białowieża, *Poland* 45 F10
Biały Bór, *Poland* 44 E3
Białystok, *Poland* 45 E10
Biancavilla, *Italy* 31 E7
Bianco, *Italy* 31 D9
Biankouma, *Ivory C.* 82 D3
Biaora, *India* 68 H7
Bīārjmand, *Iran* 71 B7
Biaro, *Indonesia* 63 D7
Biarritz, *France* 20 E2
Biasca, *Switz.* 25 J4
Biba, *Egypt* 80 J7
Bibai, *Japan* 54 C10
Bibbiena, *Italy* 29 E8
Bibby I., *Canada* 105 A10
Bibel →, *Spain* 34 C3
Biberach, *Germany* 25 G5
Bibiani, *Ghana* 82 D4
Bibungwa, *Dem. Rep. of the Congo* 86 C2
Bic, *Canada* 103 C6
Bicaj, *Albania* 40 E4
Bicaz, *Romania* 43 D11
Bicazu Ardelean, *Romania* 43 D10
Bíccari, *Italy* 31 A8
Bicester, *U.K.* 13 F6
Bichena, *Ethiopia* 81 E4
Bicheno, *Australia* 94 G4
Bichia, *India* 69 H9
Bichvinta, *Georgia* 49 J5
Bickerton I., *Australia* 94 A2
Bicske, *Hungary* 42 C3
Bida, *Nigeria* 83 D6
Bidar, *India* 66 L10
Biddeford, *U.S.A.* 109 D10
Biddwara, *Ethiopia* 81 F4
Bideford, *U.K.* 13 F3
Bideford Bay, *U.K.* 13 F3
Bidhuna, *India* 69 F8
Bidor, *Malaysia* 65 K3
Bie, *Sweden* 10 E10
Bié, Planalto de, *Angola* 85 G3
Bieber, *U.S.A.* 114 F3
Biebrza →, *Poland* 45 E9
Biecz, *Poland* 45 J8
Biel, *Switz.* 25 H3
Bielawa, *Poland* 45 H3
Bielefeld, *Germany* 24 C4
Bielersee, *Switz.* 25 H3
Biella, *Italy* 28 C5
Bielsk Podlaski, *Poland* 45 F10
Bielsko-Biała, *Poland* 45 J6
Bien Hoa, *Vietnam* 65 G6
Bienne = Biel, *Switz.* 25 H3
Bienvenida, *Spain* 35 G4
Bienville, L., *Canada* 102 A5
Bierné, *France* 18 E6
Bierun, *Poland* 45 H6
Bierutów, *Poland* 45 G4
Biescas, *Spain* 32 C4
Biese →, *Germany* 24 C7
Biesiesfontein, *S. Africa* 88 E2
Bietigheim-Bissingen, *Germany* 25 G5
Bieżuń, *Poland* 45 F6
Biferno →, *Italy* 29 G12
Big →, *Canada* 103 B8
Big B., *Canada* 103 A7
Big Bear City, *U.S.A.* 117 L10
Big Bear Lake, *U.S.A.* 117 L10
Big Belt Mts., *U.S.A.* 114 C8
Big Bend, *Swaziland* 89 D5
Big Bend National Park, *U.S.A.* 113 L3
Big Black →, *U.S.A.* 113 K9
Big Blue →, *U.S.A.* 112 F6
Big Creek, *U.S.A.* 116 H7
Big Cypress National Preserve, *U.S.A.* 109 M5
Big Cypress Swamp, *U.S.A.* 109 M5
Big Falls, *U.S.A.* 112 A8
Big Fork →, *U.S.A.* 112 A8
Big Horn Mts. = Bighorn Mts., *U.S.A.* 114 D10
Big I., *Canada* 104 A5
Big Lake, *U.S.A.* 113 K4
Big Moose, *U.S.A.* 111 C10
Big Muddy Cr. →, *U.S.A.* 112 A2
Big Pine, *U.S.A.* 116 H8
Big Piney, *U.S.A.* 114 E8
Big Rapids, *U.S.A.* 108 D3
Big Rideau L., *Canada* 111 B8
Big River, *Canada* 105 C7
Big Run, *U.S.A.* 110 F6
Big Sable Pt., *U.S.A.* 108 C2
Big Salmon →, *Canada* 104 A2
Big Sand L., *Canada* 105 B9
Big Sandy, *U.S.A.* 114 B8
Big Sandy →, *U.S.A.* 108 F4
Big Sandy Cr. →, *U.S.A.* 112 F3
Big Sioux →, *U.S.A.* 112 D6
Big Spring, *U.S.A.* 113 J4
Big Stone City, *U.S.A.* 112 C6
Big Stone Gap, *U.S.A.* 109 G4
Big Stone L., *U.S.A.* 112 C6
Big Sur, *U.S.A.* 116 J5
Big Timber, *U.S.A.* 114 D9
Big Trout L., *Canada* 102 B2
Big Trout Lake, *Canada* 102 B2
Biğa, *Turkey* 41 F11
Biga →, *Turkey* 41 F11
Bigadiç, *Turkey* 39 B10
Biganos, *France* 20 D3
Biggar, *Canada* 105 C7
Biggar, *U.K.* 14 F5
Bigge I., *Australia* 92 B4
Biggenden, *Australia* 95 D5
Biggleswade, *U.K.* 13 E7
Biggs, *U.S.A.* 116 F5
Bighorn, *U.S.A.* 114 C10
Bighorn →, *U.S.A.* 114 C10
Bighorn L., *U.S.A.* 114 D9
Bighorn Mts., *U.S.A.* 114 D10
Bignona, *Senegal* 82 C1
Bigorre, *France* 20 E4
Bigstone L., *Canada* 105 C9
Biguglia, Étang de, *France* 21 F13
Bigwa, *Tanzania* 86 D4
Bihać, *Bos.-H.* 29 D12
Bihar, *India* 69 G11
Bihar □, *India* 69 G12
Biharamulo, *Tanzania* 86 C3
Bihariganj, *India* 69 G12
Biharkeresztes, *Hungary* 42 C6
Bihor □, *Romania* 42 D7
Bihor, Munţii, *Romania* 42 D7
Bijagós, Arquipélago dos, *Guinea-Biss.* 82 C1
Bijaipur, *India* 68 F7
Bijapur, *Karnataka, India* 66 L9
Bijapur, *Mad. P., India* 67 K12
Bījār, *Iran* 70 C5
Bijawar, *India* 69 G8
Bijeljina, *Bos.-H.* 42 F4
Bijelo Polje, *Montenegro, Yug.* 40 C3
Bijie, *China* 58 D5
Bijnor, *India* 68 E8
Bikaner, *India* 68 E5
Bikapur, *India* 69 F10
Bikeqi, *China* 56 D6
Bikfayyā, *Lebanon* 75 B4
Bikin, *Russia* 51 E14
Bikin →, *Russia* 54 A7
Bikini Atoll, *Marshall Is.* 96 F8
Bikita, *Zimbabwe* 89 C5
Bikoué, *Cameroon* 83 E7
Bila Tserkva, *Ukraine* 47 H6
Bilanga, *Burkina Faso* 83 C4
Bilara, *India* 68 F5
Bilaspur, *Mad. P., India* 69 H10
Bilaspur, *Punjab, India* 68 D7
Biläsuvar, *Azerbaijan* 73 C13
Bilauk Taungdan, *Thailand* 64 F2
Bilbao, *Spain* 32 B2
Bilbeis, *Egypt* 80 H7
Bilbo = Bilbao, *Spain* 32 B2
Bilbor, *Romania* 43 C10
Bilciureşti, *Romania* 43 F10

Bíldudalur


Bíldudalur, Iceland 8 D2
Bílé Karpaty, Europe 27 B11
Bileća, Bos.-H. 40 D2
Bilecik, Turkey 72 B4
Biłgoraj, Poland 45 H9
Bilgram, India 69 F9
Bilhaur, India 69 F9
Bilhorod-Dnistrovskyy, Ukraine 47 J6
Bilibino, Russia 51 C17
Bilibiza, Mozam. 87 E5
Bilisht, Albania 40 F5
Billabalong Roadhouse, Australia 93 E2
Billdal, Sweden 11 G5
Billiluna, Australia 92 C4
Billings, U.S.A. 114 D9
Billiton Is. = Belitung, Indonesia 62 E3
Billsta, Sweden 10 A12
Billund, Denmark 11 J3
Bilma, Niger 79 E8
Bilo Gora, Croatia 42 E2
Biloela, Australia 94 C5
Bilohirsk, Ukraine 47 K8
Bilopillya, Ukraine 47 G8
Biloxi, U.S.A. 113 K10
Bilpa Morea Claypan, Australia 94 D3
Biltine, Chad 79 F10
Bilyarsk, Russia 48 C10
Bima, Indonesia 63 F5
Bimban, Egypt 80 C3
Bimbila, Ghana 83 D5
Bimini Is., Bahamas 120 A4
Bin Xian, Heilongjiang, China 57 B14
Bin Xian, Shaanxi, China 56 G5
Bin Yauri, Nigeria 83 C5
Bina-Etawah, India 68 G8
Bināb, Iran 71 B6
Binalbagan, Phil. 61 F5
Binalong, Australia 95 E4
Bīnālūd, Kūh-e, Iran 71 B8
Binatang = Bintangor, Malaysia 62 D4
Binche, Belgium 17 D4
Binchuan, China 58 E3
Binder, Chad 83 D7
Bindki, India 69 F9
Bindslev, Denmark 11 G4
Bindura, Zimbabwe 87 F3
Binefar, Spain 32 D5
Bingara, Australia 95 D5
Bingen, Germany 25 F3
Bingerville, Ivory C. 82 D4
Bingham, U.S.A. 109 C11
Binghamton, U.S.A. 111 D9
Bingöl, Turkey 70 B4
Bingöl Dağları, Turkey 73 C9
Bingsjö, Sweden 10 C9
Binh Dinh = An Nhon, Vietnam 64 F7
Binh Khe, Vietnam 64 F7
Binh Son, Vietnam 64 E7
Binhai, China 57 G10
Binic, France 18 D4
Binisatua, Spain 37 B11
Binjai, Indonesia 62 D3
Binji, Nigeria 83 C5
Binnaway, Australia 95 E4
Binongko, Indonesia 63 F6
Binscarth, Canada 105 C8
Bint Goda, Sudan 81 E3
Bintan, Indonesia 62 D2
Bintangor, Malaysia 62 D4
Bintulu, Malaysia 62 D4
Bintuni, Indonesia 63 E8
Binyang, China 58 F7
Binz, Germany 24 A9
Binzert = Bizerte, Tunisia 79 A7
Binzhou, China 57 F10
Bío Bío □, Chile 126 D1
Biograd na Moru, Croatia 29 E12
Bioko, Eq. Guin. 83 E6
Biokovo, Croatia 29 E14
Bipindi, Cameroon 83 E7
Bir, India 66 K9
Bir, Ras, Djibouti 81 E5
Bîr Abu Hashim, Egypt 80 C3
Bîr Abu Minqar, Egypt 80 B2
Bîr Abu Muḩammad, Egypt 75 F3
Bi'r ad Dabbāghāt, Jordan 75 E4
Bîr Adal Deib, Sudan 80 C4
Bi'r al Butayyihāt, Jordan 75 F4
Bi'r al Mārī, Jordan 75 E4
Bi'r al Qattār, Jordan 75 F4
Bîr 'Asal, Egypt 80 B3
Bîr Atrun, Sudan 80 D2
Bîr Beiḍa, Egypt 75 E3
Bîr Diqnash, Egypt 80 A2
Bîr el 'Abd, Egypt 75 D2
Bîr el Basur, Egypt 80 B2
Bîr el Biarât, Egypt 75 F3
Bîr el Duweidar, Egypt 75 E1
Bîr el Garârât, Egypt 75 D2
Bîr el Gellaz, Egypt 80 A2
Bîr el Heisi, Egypt 75 F3
Bîr el Jafir, Egypt 75 E1
Bîr el Mâlḥi, Egypt 75 E2
Bîr el Shaqqa, Egypt 80 A2
Bîr el Thamâda, Egypt 75 E2
Bîr Fuad, Egypt 80 A2
Bîr Gebeil Ḥiṣn, Egypt 75 E2
Bi'r Ghadīr, Syria 75 A6
Bîr Haimur, Egypt 80 C3
Bîr Ḥasana, Egypt 75 E2
Bîr Hööker, Egypt 80 H7
Bîr Kanayis, Egypt 80 C3
Bîr Kaseiba, Egypt 75 E2
Bîr Kerawein, Egypt 80 B2
Bîr Lahfân, Egypt 75 E2
Bîr Madkûr, Egypt 75 E1
Bîr Maql, Egypt 80 C3
Bîr Mîneiga, Sudan 80 C4
Bîr Misaha, Egypt 80 C2
Bîr Mogreïn, Mauritania 78 C3
Bîr Murr, Egypt 80 C3
Bi'r Muţribah, Kuwait 70 D5
Bîr Nakheila, Egypt 80 C3
Bîr Qaţia, Egypt 75 E1
Bîr Qatrani, Egypt 80 A2
Bîr Ranga, Egypt 80 C4
Bîr Sahara, Egypt 80 C2
Bîr Seiyâla, Egypt 80 B3
Bîr Shalatein, Egypt 80 C4
Bîr Shebb, Egypt 80 C2
Bîr Shût, Egypt 80 C4
Bîr Terfawi, Egypt 80 C2
Bîr Umm Qubûr, Egypt 80 C3
Bîr Ungât, Egypt 80 C3
Bîr Za'farâna, Egypt 80 J8
Bîr Zeidûn, Egypt 80 B3
Biramféro, Guinea 82 C3
Biratnagar, Nepal 69 F12
Birawa, Dem. Rep. of the Congo 86 C2
Birch →, Canada 104 B6
Birch Hills, Canada 105 C7
Birch I., Canada 105 C9
Birch L., N.W.T., Canada 104 A5
Birch L., Ont., Canada 102 B1
Birch Mts., Canada 104 B6
Birch River, Canada 105 C8
Birchip, Australia 95 F3
Birchiş, Romania 42 E7
Bird, Canada 105 B10
Bird I. = Las Aves, Is., W. Indies 121 C7
Birdsville, Australia 94 D2
Birdum Cr. →, Australia 92 C5
Birecik, Turkey 70 B3
Birein, Israel 75 E3
Bireuen, Indonesia 62 C1
Biri →, Sudan 81 F2
Birifo, Gambia 82 C2
Birigui, Brazil 127 A5
Birjand, Iran 71 C8
Birkenfeld, Germany 25 F3
Birkenhead, U.K. 12 D4
Birkerød, Denmark 11 J6
Birket Qârûn, Egypt 80 J7
Birkfeld, Austria 26 D8
Bîrlad = Bârlad, Romania 43 D12
Birmingham, U.K. 13 E6
Birmingham, U.S.A. 109 J2
Birmitrapur, India 67 H14
Birni Ngaouré, Niger 83 C5
Birni Nkonni, Niger 83 C6
Birnin Gwari, Nigeria 83 C6
Birnin Kebbi, Nigeria 83 C5
Birnin Kudu, Nigeria 83 C6
Birobidzhan, Russia 51 E14
Birr, Ireland 15 C4
Birrie →, Australia 95 D4
Birsilpur, India 68 E5
Birsk, Russia 50 D6
Birštonas, Lithuania 44 D11
Birtle, Canada 105 C8
Birur, India 66 N9
Biryuchiy, Ukraine 47 J8
Biržai, Lithuania 9 H21
Birzebbugga, Malta 36 D2
Bisa, Indonesia 63 E7
Bisáccia, Italy 31 A8
Bisacquino, Italy 30 E6
Bisalpur, India 69 E8
Bisbee, U.S.A. 115 L9
Biscarrosse, France 20 D2
Biscarrosse et de Parentis, Étang de, France 20 D2
Biscay, B. of, Atl. Oc. 6 F5
Biscayne B., U.S.A. 109 N5
Biscéglie, Italy 31 A9
Bischheim, France 19 D14
Bischofshofen, Austria 26 D6
Bischofswerda, Germany 24 D10
Bischwiller, France 19 D14
Biscoe Bay, Antarctica 5 D13
Biscoe Is., Antarctica 5 C17
Biscostasing, Canada 102 C3
Biševo, Croatia 29 F13
Bisha, Eritrea 81 D4
Bishah, W. →, Si. Arabia 80 C5
Bishan, China 58 C6
Bishkek, Kyrgyzstan 50 E8
Bishnupur, India 69 H12
Bisho, S. Africa 89 E4
Bishop, Calif., U.S.A. 116 H8
Bishop, Tex., U.S.A. 113 M6
Bishop Auckland, U.K. 12 C6
Bishop's Falls, Canada 103 C8
Bishop's Stortford, U.K. 13 F8
Bisignano, Italy 31 C9
Bisina, L., Uganda 86 B3
Biskra, Algeria 78 B7
Biskupiec, Poland 44 E7
Bismarck, U.S.A. 112 B4
Bismarck Arch., Papua N. G. 96 H7
Bismark, Germany 24 C7
Bismil, Turkey 73 D9
Biso, Uganda 86 B3
Bison, U.S.A. 112 C3
Bīsotūn, Iran 70 C5
Bispgården, Sweden 10 A10
Bissagos = Bijagós, Arquipélago dos, Guinea-Biss. 82 C1
Bissau, Guinea-Biss. 82 C1
Bissaula, Nigeria 83 D7
Bissikrima, Guinea 82 C2
Bissorã, Guinea-Biss. 82 C1
Bistcho L., Canada 104 B5
Bistreţ, Romania 43 G8
Bistrica = Ilirska-Bistrica, Slovenia 29 C11
Bistriţa, Romania 43 C9
Bistriţa →, Romania 43 D11
Bistriţa Năsăud □, Romania 43 C9
Bistriţei, Munţii, Romania 43 C10
Biswan, India 69 F9
Bisztynek, Poland 44 D7
Bitburg, Germany 25 F2
Bitche, France 19 C14
Bithynia, Turkey 72 B4
Bitlis, Turkey 70 B4
Bitola, Macedonia 40 E5
Bitolj = Bitola, Macedonia 40 E5
Bitonto, Italy 31 A9
Bitter Creek, U.S.A. 114 F9
Bitter L. = Buheirat-Murrat-el-Kubra, Egypt 80 H8
Bitterfeld, Germany 24 D8
Bitterfontein, S. Africa 88 E2
Bitterroot →, U.S.A. 114 C6
Bitterroot Range, U.S.A. 114 D6
Bitterwater, U.S.A. 116 J6
Bitti, Italy 30 B2
Bittou, Burkina Faso 83 C4
Biu, Nigeria 83 C7
Bivolari, Romania 43 C12
Bivolu, Vf., Romania 43 C10
Biwa-Ko, Japan 55 G8
Biwabik, U.S.A. 112 B8
Bixad, Romania 43 C8
Bixby, U.S.A. 113 H7
Biyang, China 56 H7
Biysk, Russia 50 D9
Bizana, S. Africa 89 E4
Bizen, Japan 55 G7
Bizerte, Tunisia 79 A7
Bjargtangar, Iceland 8 D1
Bjärnum, Sweden 11 H7
Bjästa, Sweden 10 A12
Bjelasica, Montenegro, Yug. 40 D3
Bjelašnica, Bos.-H. 42 G3
Bjelovar, Croatia 29 C13
Bjerringbro, Denmark 11 H3
Björbo, Sweden 10 D8
Björklinge, Sweden 10 D11
Björneborg, Sweden 10 E8
Bjørnevatn, Norway 8 B23
Bjørnøya, Arctic 4 B8
Bjursås, Sweden 10 D9
Bjuv, Sweden 11 H6
Bla, Mali 82 C3
Blace, Serbia, Yug. 40 C5
Blachownia, Poland 45 H5
Black = Da →, Vietnam 58 G5
Black →, Canada 110 B5
Black →, Ariz., U.S.A. 115 K8
Black →, Ark., U.S.A. 113 H9
Black →, Mich., U.S.A. 110 D2
Black →, N.Y., U.S.A. 111 C8
Black →, Wis., U.S.A. 112 D9
Black Bay Pen., Canada 102 C2
Black Birch L., Canada 105 B7
Black Diamond, Canada 104 C6
Black Duck →, Canada 102 A2
Black Forest = Schwarzwald, Germany 25 G4
Black Forest, U.S.A. 112 F2
Black Hd., Ireland 15 C2
Black Hills, U.S.A. 112 D3
Black I., Canada 105 C9
Black L., Canada 105 B7
Black L., Mich., U.S.A. 108 C3
Black L., N.Y., U.S.A. 111 B9
Black Lake, Canada 105 B7
Black Mesa, U.S.A. 113 G3
Black Mt. = Mynydd Du, U.K. 13 F4
Black Mts., U.K. 13 F4
Black Range, U.S.A. 115 K10
Black River, Jamaica 120 C4
Black River Falls, U.S.A. 112 C9
Black Sea, Eurasia 6 G12
Black Tickle, Canada 103 B8
Black Volta →, Africa 82 D4
Black Warrior →, U.S.A. 109 J2
Blackall, Australia 94 C4
Blackball, N.Z. 91 K3
Blackbull, Australia 94 B3
Blackburn, U.K. 12 D5
Blackburn with Darwen □, U.K. 12 D5
Blackfoot, U.S.A. 114 E7
Blackfoot →, U.S.A. 114 C7
Blackfoot River Reservoir, U.S.A. 114 E8
Blackpool, U.K. 12 D4
Blackpool □, U.K. 12 D4
Blackriver, U.S.A. 110 B1
Blacks Harbour, Canada 103 C6
Blacksburg, U.S.A. 108 G5
Blacksod B., Ireland 15 B1
Blackstone, U.S.A. 108 G7
Blackstone Ra., Australia 93 E4
Blackwater, Australia 94 C4
Blackwater →, Meath, Ireland 15 C4
Blackwater →, Waterford, Ireland 15 D4
Blackwater →, U.K. 15 B5
Blackwell, U.S.A. 113 G6
Blackwells Corner, U.S.A. 117 K7
Blaenau Ffestiniog, U.K. 12 E4
Blaenau Gwent □, U.K. 13 F4
Blagaj, Bos.-H. 40 C1
Blagnac, France 20 E5
Blagodarnoye = Blagodarnyy, Russia 49 H6
Blagodarnyy, Russia 49 H6
Blagoevgrad, Bulgaria 40 D7
Blagoveshchensk, Russia 51 D13
Blain, France 18 E5
Blain, U.S.A. 110 F7
Blaine, Minn., U.S.A. 112 C8
Blaine, Wash., U.S.A. 116 B4
Blaine Lake, Canada 105 C7
Blair, U.S.A. 112 E6
Blair Athol, Australia 94 C4
Blair Atholl, U.K. 14 E5
Blairgowrie, U.K. 14 E5
Blairsden, U.S.A. 116 F6
Blairsville, U.S.A. 110 F5
Blaj, Romania 43 D8
Blake Pt., U.S.A. 112 A10
Blakely, Ga., U.S.A. 109 K3
Blakely, Pa., U.S.A. 111 E9
Blâmont, France 19 D13
Blanc, C., Spain 37 B9
Blanc, Mont, Alps 21 C10
Blanc-Sablon, Canada 103 B8
Blanca, B., Argentina 122 G4
Blanca Peak, U.S.A. 115 H11
Blanche, C., Australia 95 E1
Blanche, L., S. Austral., Australia 95 D2
Blanche, L., W. Austral., Australia 92 D3
Blanco, S. Africa 88 E3
Blanco, U.S.A. 113 K5
Blanco →, Argentina 126 C2
Blanco, C., Costa Rica 120 E2
Blanco, C., U.S.A. 114 E1
Blanda →, Iceland 8 D3
Blandford Forum, U.K. 13 G5
Blanding, U.S.A. 115 H9
Blanes, Spain 32 D7
Blangy-sur-Bresle, France 19 C8
Blanice →, Czech Rep. 26 B7
Blankaholm, Sweden 11 G10
Blankenberge, Belgium 17 C3
Blankenburg, Germany 24 D6
Blanquefort, France 20 D3
Blanquilla, I., Venezuela 121 D7
Blanquillo, Uruguay 127 C4
Blansko, Czech Rep. 27 B9
Blantyre, Malawi 87 F4
Blarney, Ireland 15 E3
Blasdell, U.S.A. 110 D6
Błaszki, Poland 45 G5
Blatná, Czech Rep. 26 B6
Blato, Croatia 29 F13
Blaubeuren, Germany 25 G5
Blaustein, Germany 25 G5
Blåvands Huk, Denmark 11 J2
Blaydon, U.K. 12 C6
Blaye, France 20 C3
Blaye-les-Mines, France 20 D6
Blayney, Australia 95 E4
Blaze, Pt., Australia 92 B5
Błażowa, Poland 45 J9
Bleckede, Germany 24 B6
Bled, Slovenia 29 B11
Bleiburg, Austria 26 E7
Blejeşti, Romania 43 F10
Blekinge, Sweden 9 H16
Blekinge län □, Sweden 11 H9
Blenheim, Canada 110 D3
Blenheim, N.Z. 91 J4
Bléone →, France 21 D10
Blérancourt, France 19 C10
Bletchley, U.K. 13 F7
Blida, Algeria 78 A6
Blidö, Sweden 10 E12
Blidsberg, Sweden 11 G7
Blieskastel, Germany 25 F3
Bligh Sound, N.Z. 91 L1
Blind River, Canada 102 C3
Blinisht, Albania 40 E3
Bliss, Idaho, U.S.A. 114 E6
Bliss, N.Y., U.S.A. 110 D6
Blissfield, U.S.A. 110 F3
Blitar, Indonesia 63 H15
Blitta, Togo 83 D5
Block I., U.S.A. 111 E13
Block Island Sd., U.S.A. 111 E13
Blodgett Iceberg Tongue, Antarctica 5 C9
Bloemfontein, S. Africa 88 D4
Bloemhof, S. Africa 88 D4
Blois, France 18 E8
Blomskog, Sweden 10 E6
Blomstermåla, Sweden 11 H10
Blönduós, Iceland 8 D3
Błonie, Poland 45 F7
Bloodvein →, Canada 105 C9
Bloody Foreland, Ireland 15 A3
Bloomer, U.S.A. 112 C9
Bloomfield, Canada 110 C7
Bloomfield, Iowa, U.S.A. 112 E8
Bloomfield, N. Mex., U.S.A. 115 H10
Bloomfield, Nebr., U.S.A. 112 D6
Bloomington, Ill., U.S.A. 112 E10
Bloomington, Ind., U.S.A. 108 F2
Bloomington, Minn., U.S.A. 112 C8
Bloomsburg, U.S.A. 111 F8
Blora, Indonesia 63 G14
Blossburg, U.S.A. 110 E7
Blouberg, S. Africa 89 C4
Blountstown, U.S.A. 109 K3
Bludenz, Austria 26 D2
Blue Earth, U.S.A. 112 D8
Blue Mesa Reservoir, U.S.A. 115 G10
Blue Mountain Lake, U.S.A. 111 C10
Blue Mts., Maine, U.S.A. 111 B14
Blue Mts., Oreg., U.S.A. 114 D4
Blue Mts., Pa., U.S.A. 111 F8
Blue Mud B., Australia 94 A2
Blue Nile = Nîl el Azraq →, Sudan 81 D3
Blue Rapids, U.S.A. 112 F6
Blue Ridge Mts., U.S.A. 109 G5
Blue River, Canada 104 C5
Bluefield, U.S.A. 108 G5
Bluefields, Nic. 120 D3
Bluff, Australia 94 C4
Bluff, N.Z. 91 M2
Bluff, U.S.A. 115 H9
Bluff Knoll, Australia 93 F2
Bluff Pt., Australia 93 E1
Bluffton, U.S.A. 108 E3
Blumenau, Brazil 127 B6
Blunt, U.S.A. 112 C5
Bly, U.S.A. 114 E3
Blyth, Canada 110 C3
Blyth, U.K. 12 B6
Blythe, U.S.A. 117 M12
Blytheville, U.S.A. 113 H10
Bo, S. Leone 82 D2
Bo Duc, Vietnam 65 G6
Bo Hai, China 57 E10
Bo Xian = Bozhou, China 56 H8
Boa Vista, Brazil 124 C6
Boac, Phil. 61 E4
Boaco, Nic. 120 D2
Bo'ai, China 56 G7
Boal, Spain 34 B4
Boalsburg, U.S.A. 110 F7
Boane, Mozam. 89 D5
Boardman, U.S.A. 110 E4
Bobadah, Australia 95 E4
Bobai, China 58 F7
Bobbili, India 67 K13
Bóbbio, Italy 28 D6
Bobcaygeon, Canada 102 D4
Böblingen, Germany 25 G5
Bobo-Dioulasso, Burkina Faso 82 C4
Bobolice, Poland 44 E3
Boboshevo, Bulgaria 40 D7
Bobov Dol, Bulgaria 40 D6
Bóbr →, Poland 45 F2
Bobraomby, Tanjon' i, Madag. 89 A8
Bobrinets, Ukraine 47 H7
Bobrov, Russia 48 E5
Bobrovitsa, Ukraine 47 G6
Bobruysk = Babruysk, Belarus 47 F5
Boby, Pic, Madag. 85 J9
Bôca do Acre, Brazil 124 E5
Boca Raton, U.S.A. 109 M5
Bocanda, Ivory C. 82 D4
Bocas del Toro, Panama 120 E3
Boceguillas, Spain 34 D7
Bochnia, Poland 45 J7
Bocholt, Germany 24 D2
Bochum, Germany 24 D3
Bockenem, Germany 24 C6
Boćki, Poland 45 F10
Bocognano, France 21 F13
Bocoyna, Mexico 118 B3
Bocşa, Romania 42 E6
Boda, Dalarnas, Sweden 10 C9
Böda, Kalmar, Sweden 11 G11
Boda, Västernorrland, Sweden 10 B10
Bodafors, Sweden 11 G8
Bodaybo, Russia 51 D12
Boddam, U.K. 14 B7
Boddington, Australia 93 F2
Bode Sadu, Nigeria 83 D5
Bodega Bay, U.S.A. 116 G3
Boden, Sweden 8 D19
Bodensee, Europe 25 H5
Bodenteich, Germany 24 C6
Bodhan, India 66 K10
Bodinga, Nigeria 83 C6
Bodmin, U.K. 13 G3
Bodmin Moor, U.K. 13 G3
Bodø, Norway 8 C16
Bodrog →, Hungary 42 B6
Bodrum, Turkey 39 D9
Bódva →, Hungary 42 B5
Boën, France 21 C8
Boende, Dem. Rep. of the Congo 84 E4
Boerne, U.S.A. 113 L5
Boesmans →, S. Africa 88 E4
Boffa, Guinea 82 C2
Bogalusa, U.S.A. 113 K10
Bogan →, Australia 95 D4
Bogan Gate, Australia 95 E4
Bogandé, Burkina Faso 83 C4
Bogantungan, Australia 94 C4
Bogata, U.S.A. 113 J7
Bogatić, Serbia, Yug. 40 B3
Boğazkale, Turkey 72 B6
Boğazlıyan, Turkey 72 C6
Bogen, Sweden 10 D6
Bogense, Denmark 11 J4
Bogetići, Montenegro, Yug. 40 D2
Boggabilla, Australia 95 D5
Boggabri, Australia 95 E5
Boggeragh Mts., Ireland 15 D3
Boglan = Solhan, Turkey 70 B4
Bognor Regis, U.K. 13 G7
Bogo, Phil. 61 F6
Bogodukhov = Bohodukhiv, Ukraine 47 G8
Bogol Manya, Ethiopia 81 G5
Bogong, Mt., Australia 95 F4
Bogor, Indonesia 62 F3
Bogoroditsk, Russia 46 F10
Bogorodsk, Russia 48 B6
Bogoso, Ghana 82 D4
Bogotá, Colombia 124 C4
Bogotol, Russia 50 D9
Bogou, Togo 83 C5

# Braga


Braga, *Portugal* 34 D2
Braga □, *Portugal* 34 D2
Bragadiru, *Romania* 43 G10
Bragado, *Argentina* 126 D3
Bragança, *Brazil* 125 D9
Bragança, *Portugal* 34 D4
Bragança □, *Portugal* 34 D4
Bragança Paulista, *Brazil* 127 A6
Brahmanbaria, *Bangla.* 67 H17
Brahmani →, *India* 67 J15
Brahmapur, *India* 67 K14
Brahmaputra →, *India* 69 H13
Braich-y-pwll, *U.K.* 12 E3
Braidwood, *Australia* 95 F4
Brăila, *Romania* 43 E12
Brăila □, *Romania* 43 E12
Brainerd, *U.S.A.* 112 B7
Braintree, *U.K.* 13 F8
Braintree, *U.S.A.* 111 D14
Brak →, *S. Africa* 88 D3
Brake, *Germany* 24 B4
Brakel, *Germany* 24 D5
Bräkne-Hoby, *Sweden* 11 H9
Brakwater, *Namibia* 88 C2
Brålanda, *Sweden* 11 F6
Bramberg, *Germany* 25 E6
Bramdrupdam, *Denmark* 11 J3
Bramming, *Denmark* 11 J2
Brämön, *Sweden* 10 B11
Brampton, *Canada* 102 D4
Brampton, *U.K.* 12 C5
Bramsche, *Germany* 24 C3
Branco →, *Brazil* 122 D4
Brandberg, *Namibia* 88 B2
Brande, *Denmark* 11 J3
Brandenburg = Neubrandenburg, *Germany* 24 B9
Brandenburg, *Germany* 24 C8
Brandenburg □, *Germany* 24 C9
Brandfort, *S. Africa* 88 D4
Brando, *France* 21 F13
Brandon, *Canada* 105 D9
Brandon, *U.S.A.* 111 C11
Brandon B., *Ireland* 15 D1
Brandon Mt., *Ireland* 15 D1
Brandsen, *Argentina* 126 D4
Brandvlei, *S. Africa* 88 E3
Brandýs nad Labem, *Czech Rep.* 26 A7
Brănești, *Romania* 43 F11
Branford, *U.S.A.* 111 E12
Braniewo, *Poland* 44 D6
Bransfield Str., *Antarctica* 5 C18
Brańsk, *Poland* 45 F9
Branson, *U.S.A.* 113 G8
Brantford, *Canada* 102 D3
Brantôme, *France* 20 C4
Branzi, *Italy* 28 B6
Bras d'Or L., *Canada* 103 C7
Brasher Falls, *U.S.A.* 111 B10
Brasil, Planalto, *Brazil* 122 E6
Brasiléia, *Brazil* 124 F5
Brasília, *Brazil* 125 G9
Brasília Legal, *Brazil* 125 D7
Braslaw, *Belarus* 9 J22
Braslovče, *Slovenia* 29 B12
Brașov, *Romania* 43 E10
Brașov □, *Romania* 43 E10
Brass, *Nigeria* 83 E6
Brass →, *Nigeria* 83 E6
Brassac-les-Mines, *France* 20 C7
Brasschaat, *Belgium* 17 C4
Brassey, Banjaran, *Malaysia* 62 D5
Brassey Ra., *Australia* 93 E3
Brasstown Bald, *U.S.A.* 109 H4
Brastad, *Sweden* 11 F5
Brastavățu, *Romania* 43 G9
Bratan = Morozov, *Bulgaria* 41 D9
Brateș, *Romania* 43 E11
Bratislava, *Slovak Rep.* 27 C10
Bratislavský □, *Slovak Rep.* 27 C10
Bratsigovo, *Bulgaria* 41 D8
Bratsk, *Russia* 51 D11
Brattleboro, *U.S.A.* 111 D12
Bratunac, *Bos.-H.* 42 F4
Braunau, *Austria* 26 C6
Braunschweig, *Germany* 24 C6
Braunton, *U.K.* 13 F3
Bravicea, *Moldova* 43 C13
Bråviken, *Sweden* 11 F10
Bravo del Norte, Rio = Grande, Rio →, *U.S.A.* 113 N6
Brawley, *U.S.A.* 117 N11
Bray, *Ireland* 15 C5
Bray, Mt., *Australia* 94 A1
Bray-sur-Seine, *France* 19 D10
Brazeau →, *Canada* 104 C5
Brazil, *U.S.A.* 108 F2
Brazil ■, *S. Amer.* 125 F9
Brazilian Highlands = Brasil, Planalto, *Brazil* 122 E6
Brazo Sur →, *S. Amer.* 126 B4
Brazos →, *U.S.A.* 113 L7
Brazzaville, *Congo* 84 E3
Brčko, *Bos.-H.* 42 F3
Brda →, *Poland* 45 E5
Brdy, *Czech Rep.* 26 B6
Breaden, L., *Australia* 93 E4
Breaksea Sd., *N.Z.* 91 L1
Bream B., *N.Z.* 91 F5
Bream Hd., *N.Z.* 91 F5
Breas, *Chile* 126 B1
Breaza, *Romania* 43 E10
Brebes, *Indonesia* 63 G13
Brechin, *Canada* 110 B5
Brechin, *U.K.* 14 E6
Brecht, *Belgium* 17 C4
Breckenridge, *Colo., U.S.A.* 114 G10
Breckenridge, *Minn., U.S.A.* 112 B6
Breckenridge, *Tex., U.S.A.* 113 J5
Breckland, *U.K.* 13 E8
Břeclav, *Czech Rep.* 27 C9
Brecon, *U.K.* 13 F4
Brecon Beacons, *U.K.* 13 F4
Breda, *Neths.* 17 C4
Bredaryd, *Sweden* 11 G7
Bredasdorp, *S. Africa* 88 E3
Bredebro, *Denmark* 11 J2
Bredstedt, *Germany* 24 A4
Bree, *Belgium* 17 C5
Bregalnica →, *Macedonia* 40 E6
Bregenz, *Austria* 26 D2
Bregovo, *Bulgaria* 40 B6
Bréhal, *France* 18 D5
Bréhat, Î. de, *France* 18 D4
Breiðafjörður, *Iceland* 8 D2
Breil-sur-Roya, *France* 21 E11
Breisach, *Germany* 25 G3
Brejo, *Brazil* 125 D10
Bremen, *Germany* 24 B4
Bremen □, *Germany* 24 B4
Bremer Bay, *Australia* 93 F2
Bremer I., *Australia* 94 A2
Bremerhaven, *Germany* 24 B4
Bremerton, *U.S.A.* 116 C4
Bremervörde, *Germany* 24 B5
Brenes, *Spain* 35 H5
Brenham, *U.S.A.* 113 K6
Brenne, *France* 20 B5
Brennerpass, *Austria* 26 D4
Breno, *Italy* 28 C7
Brent, *U.S.A.* 109 J2
Brenta →, *Italy* 29 C9
Brentwood, *U.K.* 13 F8
Brentwood, *Calif., U.S.A.* 116 H5
Brentwood, *N.Y., U.S.A.* 111 F11
Bréscia, *Italy* 28 C7
Breskens, *Neths.* 17 C3
Breslau = Wrocław, *Poland* 45 G4
Bresle →, *France* 18 B8
Bressanone, *Italy* 29 B8
Bressay, *U.K.* 14 A7
Bresse, *France* 19 F12
Bressuire, *France* 18 F6
Brest, *Belarus* 47 F2
Brest, *France* 18 D2
Brest-Litovsk = Brest, *Belarus* 47 F2
Bretagne, *France* 18 D3
Bretçu, *Romania* 43 D11
Bretenoux, *France* 20 D5
Breteuil, *Eure, France* 18 D7
Breteuil, *Oise, France* 19 C9
Breton, *Canada* 104 C6
Breton, Pertuis, *France* 20 B2
Breton Sd., *U.S.A.* 113 L10
Brett, C., *N.Z.* 91 F5
Bretten, *Germany* 25 F4
Breuil-Cervínia, *Italy* 28 C4
Brevard, *U.S.A.* 109 H4
Breves, *Brazil* 125 D8
Brewarrina, *Australia* 95 E4
Brewer, *U.S.A.* 109 C11
Brewer, Mt., *U.S.A.* 116 J8
Brewerville, *Liberia* 82 D2
Brewster, *N.Y., U.S.A.* 111 E11
Brewster, *Ohio, U.S.A.* 110 F3
Brewster, *Wash., U.S.A.* 114 B4
Brewster, Kap = Kangikajik, *Greenland* 4 B6
Brewton, *U.S.A.* 109 K2
Breyten, *S. Africa* 89 D5
Breza, *Bos.-H.* 42 F3
Brezhnev = Naberezhnyye Chelny, *Russia* 48 C11
Brežice, *Slovenia* 29 C12
Březnice, *Czech Rep.* 26 B6
Breznik, *Bulgaria* 40 D6
Brezno, *Slovak Rep.* 27 C12
Brezoi, *Romania* 43 E9
Brezovica, *Kosovo, Yug.* 40 D5
Brezovo, *Bulgaria* 41 D9
Briançon, *France* 21 D10
Briare, *France* 19 E9
Briático, *Italy* 31 D9
Bribie I., *Australia* 95 D5
Bribri, *Costa Rica* 120 E3
Briceni, *Moldova* 43 B12
Bricquebec, *France* 18 C5
Bridgehampton, *U.S.A.* 111 F12
Bridgend, *U.K.* 13 F4
Bridgend □, *U.K.* 13 F4
Bridgeport, *Calif., U.S.A.* 116 G7
Bridgeport, *Conn., U.S.A.* 111 E11
Bridgeport, *Nebr., U.S.A.* 112 E3
Bridgeport, *Tex., U.S.A.* 113 J6
Bridger, *U.S.A.* 114 D9
Bridgeton, *U.S.A.* 108 F8
Bridgetown, *Australia* 93 F2
Bridgetown, *Barbados* 121 D8
Bridgetown, *Canada* 103 D6
Bridgewater, *Canada* 103 D7
Bridgewater, *Mass., U.S.A.* 111 E14
Bridgewater, *N.Y., U.S.A.* 111 D9
Bridgewater, C., *Australia* 95 F3
Bridgewater-Gagebrook, *Australia* 94 G4
Bridgnorth, *U.K.* 13 E5
Bridgton, *U.S.A.* 111 B14
Bridgwater, *U.K.* 13 F5
Bridgwater B., *U.K.* 13 F4
Bridlington, *U.K.* 12 C7
Bridlington B., *U.K.* 12 C7
Bridport, *Australia* 94 G4
Bridport, *U.K.* 13 G5
Briec, *France* 18 D2
Brienne-le-Château, *France* 19 D11
Brienon-sur-Armançon, *France* 19 E10
Brienz, *Switz.* 25 J4
Brienzersee, *Switz.* 25 J3
Brig, *Switz.* 25 J3
Brigg, *U.K.* 12 D7
Brigham City, *U.S.A.* 114 F7
Bright, *Australia* 95 F4
Brighton, *Australia* 95 F2
Brighton, *Canada* 110 B7
Brighton, *U.K.* 13 G7
Brighton, *Colo., U.S.A.* 112 F2
Brighton, *N.Y., U.S.A.* 110 C7
Brignogan-Plage, *France* 18 D2
Brignoles, *France* 21 E10
Brihuega, *Spain* 32 E2
Brikama, *Gambia* 82 C1
Brilliant, *U.S.A.* 110 F4
Brilon, *Germany* 24 D4
Bríndisi, *Italy* 31 B10
Brinje, *Croatia* 29 D12
Brinkley, *U.S.A.* 113 H9
Brinnon, *U.S.A.* 116 C4
Brion, I., *Canada* 103 C7
Brionne, *France* 18 C7
Brionski, *Croatia* 29 D10
Brioude, *France* 20 C7
Briouze, *France* 18 D6
Brisbane, *Australia* 95 D5
Brisbane →, *Australia* 95 D5
Brisighella, *Italy* 29 D8
Bristol, *U.K.* 13 F5
Bristol, *Conn., U.S.A.* 111 E12
Bristol, *Pa., U.S.A.* 111 F10
Bristol, *R.I., U.S.A.* 111 E13
Bristol, *Tenn., U.S.A.* 109 G4
Bristol, City of □, *U.K.* 13 F5
Bristol B., *U.S.A.* 100 C4
Bristol Channel, *U.K.* 13 F3
Bristol I., *Antarctica* 5 B1
Bristol L., *U.S.A.* 115 J5
Bristow, *U.S.A.* 113 H6
Britain = Great Britain, *Europe* 6 E5
British Columbia □, *Canada* 104 C3
British Indian Ocean Terr. = Chagos Arch., *Ind. Oc.* 52 K11
British Isles, *Europe* 6 E5
Brits, *S. Africa* 89 D4
Britstown, *S. Africa* 88 E3
Britt, *Canada* 102 C3
Brittany = Bretagne, *France* 18 D3
Britton, *U.S.A.* 112 C6
Brive-la-Gaillarde, *France* 20 C5
Briviesca, *Spain* 34 C7
Brixen = Bressanone, *Italy* 29 B8
Brixham, *U.K.* 13 G4
Brnaze, *Croatia* 29 E13
Brnenský □, *Czech Rep.* 27 B9
Brno, *Czech Rep.* 27 B9
Broad →, *U.S.A.* 109 J5
Broad Arrow, *Australia* 93 F3
Broad B., *U.K.* 14 C2
Broad Haven, *Ireland* 15 B2
Broad Law, *U.K.* 14 F5
Broad Sd., *Australia* 94 C4
Broadalbin, *U.S.A.* 111 C10
Broadback →, *Canada* 102 B4
Broadhurst Ra., *Australia* 92 D3
Broads, The, *U.K.* 12 E9
Broadus, *U.S.A.* 112 C2
Broager, *Denmark* 11 K3
Broby, *Sweden* 11 H8
Brocēni, *Latvia* 44 B9
Brochet, *Canada* 105 B8
Brochet, L., *Canada* 105 B8
Brocken, *Germany* 24 D6
Brockport, *U.S.A.* 110 C7
Brockton, *U.S.A.* 111 D13
Brockville, *Canada* 102 D4
Brockway, *Mont., U.S.A.* 112 B2
Brockway, *Pa., U.S.A.* 110 E6
Brocton, *U.S.A.* 110 D5
Brod, *Macedonia* 40 E5
Brodarevo, *Serbia, Yug.* 40 C3
Brodeur Pen., *Canada* 101 A11
Brodhead, Mt., *U.S.A.* 110 E7
Brodick, *U.K.* 14 F3
Brodnica, *Poland* 45 E6
Brody, *Ukraine* 47 G3
Brogan, *U.S.A.* 114 D5
Broglie, *France* 18 C7
Brok, *Poland* 45 F8
Broken Arrow, *U.S.A.* 113 G7
Broken Bow, *Nebr., U.S.A.* 112 E5
Broken Bow, *Okla., U.S.A.* 113 H7
Broken Bow Lake, *U.S.A.* 113 H7
Broken Hill = Kabwe, *Zambia* 87 E2
Broken Hill, *Australia* 95 E3
Brokind, *Sweden* 11 F9
Bromley □, *U.K.* 13 F8
Bromölla, *Sweden* 11 H8
Bromsgrove, *U.K.* 13 E5
Brønderslev, *Denmark* 11 G3
Brong-Ahafo □, *Ghana* 82 D4
Broni, *Italy* 28 C6
Bronkhorstspruit, *S. Africa* 89 D4
Brønnøysund, *Norway* 8 D15
Bronte, *Italy* 31 E7
Brook Park, *U.S.A.* 110 E4
Brookhaven, *U.S.A.* 113 K9
Brookings, *Oreg., U.S.A.* 114 E1
Brookings, *S. Dak., U.S.A.* 112 C6
Brooklin, *Canada* 110 C6
Brooklyn Park, *U.S.A.* 112 C8
Brooks, *Canada* 104 C6
Brooks Range, *U.S.A.* 100 B5
Brooksville, *U.S.A.* 109 L4
Brookton, *Australia* 93 F2
Brookville, *U.S.A.* 110 E5
Broom, L., *U.K.* 14 D3
Broome, *Australia* 92 C3
Broons, *France* 18 D4
Brora, *U.K.* 14 C5
Brora →, *U.K.* 14 C5
Brørup, *Denmark* 11 J2
Brösarp, *Sweden* 11 J8
Brosna →, *Ireland* 15 C4
Broșteni, *Mehedinți, Romania* 42 F7
Broșteni, *Suceava, Romania* 43 C10
Brothers, *U.S.A.* 114 E3
Brou, *France* 18 D8
Brouage, *France* 20 C2
Brough, *U.K.* 12 C5
Brough Hd., *U.K.* 14 B5
Broughton Island = Qikiqtarjuaq, *Canada* 101 B13
Broumov, *Czech Rep.* 27 A9
Brovary, *Ukraine* 47 G6
Brovst, *Denmark* 11 G3
Brown, L., *Australia* 93 F2
Brown, Pt., *Australia* 95 E1
Brown City, *U.S.A.* 110 C2
Brown Willy, *U.K.* 13 G3
Brownfield, *U.S.A.* 113 J3
Browning, *U.S.A.* 114 B7
Brownsville, *Oreg., U.S.A.* 114 D2
Brownsville, *Pa., U.S.A.* 110 F5
Brownsville, *Tenn., U.S.A.* 113 H10
Brownsville, *Tex., U.S.A.* 113 N6
Brownville, *U.S.A.* 111 C9
Brownwood, *U.S.A.* 113 K5
Browse I., *Australia* 92 B3
Bruas, *Malaysia* 65 K3
Bruay-la-Buissière, *France* 19 B9
Bruce, Mt., *Australia* 92 D2
Bruce Pen., *Canada* 110 B3
Bruce Rock, *Australia* 93 F2
Bruche →, *France* 19 D14
Bruchsal, *Germany* 25 F4
Bruck an der Leitha, *Austria* 27 C9
Bruck an der Mur, *Austria* 26 D8
Brue →, *U.K.* 13 F5
Bruges = Brugge, *Belgium* 17 C3
Brugg, *Switz.* 25 H4
Brugge, *Belgium* 17 C3
Bruin, *U.S.A.* 110 E5
Brûlé, *Canada* 104 C5
Brûlon, *France* 18 E6
Brumado, *Brazil* 125 F10
Brumath, *France* 19 D14
Brumunddal, *Norway* 9 F14
Bruneau, *U.S.A.* 114 E6
Bruneau →, *U.S.A.* 114 E6
Bruneck = Brunico, *Italy* 29 B8
Brunei = Bandar Seri Begawan, *Brunei* 62 C4
Brunei ■, *Asia* 62 D4
Brunflo, *Sweden* 10 A8
Brunico, *Italy* 29 B8
Brunna, *Sweden* 10 E11
Brunnen, *Switz.* 25 J4
Brunner, L., *N.Z.* 91 K3
Brunsbüttel, *Germany* 24 B5
Brunssum, *Neths.* 17 D5
Brunswick = Braunschweig, *Germany* 24 C6
Brunswick, *Ga., U.S.A.* 109 K5
Brunswick, *Maine, U.S.A.* 109 D11
Brunswick, *Md., U.S.A.* 108 F7
Brunswick, *Mo., U.S.A.* 112 F8
Brunswick, *Ohio, U.S.A.* 110 E3
Brunswick, Pen. de, *Chile* 128 G2
Brunswick B., *Australia* 92 C3
Brunswick Junction, *Australia* 93 F2
Bruntál, *Czech Rep.* 27 B10
Bruny I., *Australia* 94 G4
Brus Laguna, *Honduras* 120 C3
Brusartsi, *Bulgaria* 40 C7
Brush, *U.S.A.* 112 E3
Brushton, *U.S.A.* 111 B10
Brusio, *Switz.* 25 J6
Brusque, *Brazil* 127 B6
Brussel, *Belgium* 17 D4
Brussels = Brussel, *Belgium* 17 D4
Brussels, *Canada* 110 C3
Brusy, *Poland* 44 E4
Bruthen, *Australia* 95 F4
Bruxelles = Brussel, *Belgium* 17 D4
Bruyères, *France* 19 D13
Bruz, *France* 18 D5
Brwinów, *Poland* 45 F7
Bryagovo, *Bulgaria* 41 E9
Bryan, *Ohio, U.S.A.* 108 E3
Bryan, *Tex., U.S.A.* 113 K6
Bryan, Mt., *Australia* 95 E2
Bryanka, *Ukraine* 47 H10
Bryansk, *Bryansk, Russia* 47 F8
Bryansk, *Dagestan, Russia* 49 H8
Bryanskoye = Bryansk, *Russia* 49 H8
Bryce Canyon National Park, *U.S.A.* 115 H7
Bryne, *Norway* 9 G11
Bryson City, *U.S.A.* 109 H4
Bryukhovetskaya, *Russia* 47 K10
Brza Palanka, *Serbia, Yug.* 40 B6
Brzeg, *Poland* 45 H4
Brzeg Dolny, *Poland* 45 G3
Brześć Kujawski, *Poland* 45 F5
Brzesko, *Poland* 45 J7
Brzeziny, *Poland* 45 G6
Brzozów, *Poland* 45 J9
Bsharri, *Lebanon* 75 A5
Bū Baqarah, *U.A.E.* 71 E8
Bu Craa, *W. Sahara* 78 C3
Bū Ḩasā, *U.A.E.* 71 F7
Bua, *Sweden* 11 G6
Bua Yai, *Thailand* 64 E4
Buapinang, *Indonesia* 63 E6
Buba, *Guinea-Biss.* 82 C2
Bubanza, *Burundi* 86 C2
Bubaque, *Guinea-Biss.* 82 C1
Bube, *Ethiopia* 81 F4
Būbiyān, *Kuwait* 71 D6
Buca, *Turkey* 39 C9
Bucak, *Turkey* 39 D12
Bucaramanga, *Colombia* 124 B4
Bucas Grande I., *Phil.* 61 G6
Bucasia, *Australia* 94 C4
Buccaneer Arch., *Australia* 92 C3
Buccino, *Italy* 31 B8
Bucecea, *Romania* 43 C11
Buchach, *Ukraine* 47 H3
Buchan, *U.K.* 14 D6
Buchan Ness, *U.K.* 14 D7
Buchanan, *Canada* 105 C8
Buchanan, *Liberia* 82 D2
Buchanan, L., *Queens., Australia* 94 C4
Buchanan, L., *W. Austral., Australia* 93 E3
Buchanan, L., *U.S.A.* 113 K5
Buchanan Cr. →, *Australia* 94 B2
Buchans, *Canada* 103 C8
Bucharest = București, *Romania* 43 F11
Buchen, *Germany* 25 F5
Buchholz, *Germany* 24 B5
Buchloe, *Germany* 25 G6
Buchon, Pt., *U.S.A.* 116 K6
Buciumi, *Romania* 42 C8
Buck Hill Falls, *U.S.A.* 111 E9
Bückeburg, *Germany* 24 C5
Buckeye, *U.S.A.* 115 K7
Buckeye Lake, *U.S.A.* 110 G2
Buckhannon, *U.S.A.* 108 F5
Buckhaven, *U.K.* 14 E5
Buckhorn L., *Canada* 110 B6
Buckie, *U.K.* 14 D6
Buckingham, *Canada* 102 C4
Buckingham, *U.K.* 13 F7
Buckingham B., *Australia* 94 A2
Buckinghamshire □, *U.K.* 13 F7
Buckle Hd., *Australia* 92 B4
Buckleboo, *Australia* 95 E2
Buckley, *U.K.* 12 D4
Buckley →, *Australia* 94 C2
Bucklin, *U.S.A.* 113 G5
Bucks L., *U.S.A.* 116 F5
Bucquoy, *France* 19 B9
Buctouche, *Canada* 103 C7
București, *Romania* 43 F11
Bucyrus, *U.S.A.* 108 E4
Budacu, Vf., *Romania* 43 C10
Budalin, *Burma* 67 H19
Budaörs, *Hungary* 42 C3
Budapest, *Hungary* 42 C4
Budapest □, *Hungary* 42 C4
Budaun, *India* 69 E8
Budd Coast, *Antarctica* 5 C8
Buddusò, *Italy* 30 B2
Bude, *U.K.* 13 G3
Budennovsk, *Russia* 49 H7
Budești, *Romania* 43 F11
Budge Budge = Baj Baj, *India* 69 H13
Budgewoi, *Australia* 95 E5
Budia, *Spain* 32 E2
Büdingen, *Germany* 25 E5
Budjala, *Dem. Rep. of the Congo* 84 D3
Budoni, *Italy* 30 B2
Búdrio, *Italy* 29 D8
Budva, *Montenegro, Yug.* 40 D2
Budzyń, *Poland* 45 F3
Buea, *Cameroon* 83 E6
Buellton, *U.S.A.* 117 L6
Buena Esperanza, *Argentina* 126 C2
Buena Park, *U.S.A.* 117 M9
Buena Vista, *Colo., U.S.A.* 115 G10
Buena Vista, *Va., U.S.A.* 108 G6
Buena Vista Lake Bed, *U.S.A.* 117 K7
Buenaventura, *Colombia* 124 C3
Buenaventura, *Mexico* 118 B3
Buendía, Embalse de, *Spain* 32 E2
Buenos Aires, *Argentina* 126 C4
Buenos Aires, *Costa Rica* 120 E3
Buenos Aires □, *Argentina* 126 D4
Buenos Aires, L., *Chile* 128 F2
Buffalo, *Mo., U.S.A.* 113 G8
Buffalo, *N.Y., U.S.A.* 110 D6
Buffalo, *Okla., U.S.A.* 113 G5
Buffalo, *S. Dak., U.S.A.* 112 C3
Buffalo, *Wyo., U.S.A.* 114 D10
Buffalo →, *Canada* 104 A5
Buffalo →, *S. Africa* 89 D5
Buffalo Head Hills, *Canada* 104 B5
Buffalo L., *Alta., Canada* 104 C6
Buffalo L., *N.W.T., Canada* 104 A5
Buffalo Narrows, *Canada* 105 B7
Buffels →, *S. Africa* 88 D2
Buford, *U.S.A.* 109 H4
Bug = Buh →, *Ukraine* 47 J6
Bug →, *Poland* 45 F8
Buga, *Colombia* 124 C3
Buganda, *Uganda* 86 C3
Buganga, *Uganda* 86 C3
Bugasong, *Phil.* 61 F5
Bugeat, *France* 20 C5
Bugel, Tanjung, *Indonesia* 63 G14
Bugibba, *Malta* 36 D1
Bugojno, *Bos.-H.* 42 F2
Bugsuk, *Phil.* 62 C5
Buguma, *Nigeria* 83 E6
Bugun Shara, *Mongolia* 60 B5
Buguruslan, *Russia* 50 D6

Clairton


Cheyenne, *Okla., U.S.A.* 113 H5
Cheyenne, *Wyo., U.S.A.* 112 E2
Cheyenne →, *U.S.A.* 112 C4
Cheyenne Wells, *U.S.A.* 112 F3
Cheyne B., *Australia* 93 F2
Chhabra, *India* 68 G7
Chhaktala, *India* 68 H6
Chhapra, *India* 69 G11
Chhata, *India* 68 F7
Chhatarpur, *Bihar, India* 69 G11
Chhatarpur, *Mad. P., India* 69 G8
Chhattisgarh □, *India* 69 J10
Chhep, *Cambodia* 64 F5
Chhindwara, *Mad. P., India* 69 H8
Chhindwara, *Mad. P., India* 69 H8
Chhlong, *Cambodia* 65 F5
Chhota Tawa →, *India* 68 H7
Chhoti Kali Sindh →, *India* 68 G6
Chhuikhadan, *India* 69 J9
Chhuk, *Cambodia* 65 G5
Chi →, *Thailand* 64 E5
Chiai, *Taiwan* 59 F13
Chiali, *Taiwan* 59 F13
Chiamboni, *Somali Rep.* 84 E8
Chiamussu = Jiamusi, *China* 60 B8
Chianciano Terme, *Italy* 29 E8
Chiang Dao, *Thailand* 64 C2
Chiang Kham, *Thailand* 64 C3
Chiang Khan, *Thailand* 64 D3
Chiang Khong, *Thailand* 58 G3
Chiang Mai, *Thailand* 64 C2
Chiang Rai, *Thailand* 58 H2
Chiang Saen, *Thailand* 58 G3
Chiapa →, *Mexico* 119 D6
Chiapa de Corzo, *Mexico* 119 D6
Chiapas □, *Mexico* 119 D6
Chiaramonte Gulfi, *Italy* 31 E7
Chiaravalle, *Italy* 29 E10
Chiaravalle Centrale, *Italy* 31 D9
Chiari, *Italy* 28 C6
Chiatura, *Georgia* 49 J6
Chiautla, *Mexico* 119 D5
Chiávari, *Italy* 28 D6
Chiavenna, *Italy* 28 B6
Chiba, *Japan* 55 G10
Chiba □, *Japan* 55 G10
Chibabava, *Mozam.* 89 C5
Chibemba, *Cunene, Angola* 85 H2
Chibemba, *Huila, Angola* 88 B2
Chibi, *Zimbabwe* 89 C5
Chibia, *Angola* 85 H2
Chibougamau, *Canada* 102 C5
Chibougamau, L., *Canada* 102 C5
Chibuk, *Nigeria* 83 C7
Chibuto, *Mozam.* 89 C5
Chic-Chocs, Mts., *Canada* 103 C6
Chicacole = Srikakulam, *India* 67 K13
Chicago, *U.S.A.* 108 E2
Chicago Heights, *U.S.A.* 108 E2
Chichagof I., *U.S.A.* 100 C6
Chichén-Itzá, *Mexico* 119 C7
Chicheng, *China* 56 D8
Chichester, *U.K.* 13 G7
Chichester Ra., *Australia* 92 D2
Ch'ich'ihaerh = Qiqihar, *China* 51 E13
Chicholi, *India* 68 H8
Chickasha, *U.S.A.* 113 H6
Chiclana de la Frontera, *Spain* 35 J4
Chiclayo, *Peru* 124 E3
Chico, *U.S.A.* 116 F5
Chico →, *Chubut, Argentina* 128 E3
Chico →, *Santa Cruz, Argentina* 128 G3
Chicomo, *Mozam.* 89 C5
Chicontepec, *Mexico* 119 C5
Chicopee, *U.S.A.* 111 D12
Chicoutimi, *Canada* 103 C5
Chicualacuala, *Mozam.* 89 C5
Chidambaram, *India* 66 P11
Chidenguele, *Mozam.* 89 C5
Chidley, C., *Canada* 101 B13
Chiducuane, *Mozam.* 89 C5
Chiede, *Angola* 88 B2
Chiefs Pt., *Canada* 110 B3
Chiem Hoa, *Vietnam* 64 A5
Chiemsee, *Germany* 25 H8
Chiengi, *Zambia* 87 D2
Chiengmai = Chiang Mai, *Thailand* 64 C2
Chienti →, *Italy* 29 E10
Chieri, *Italy* 28 C4
Chiers →, *France* 19 C11
Chiesa in Valmalenco, *Italy* 28 B6
Chiese →, *Italy* 28 C7
Chieti, *Italy* 29 F11
Chifeng, *China* 57 C10
Chigirin, *Ukraine* 47 H7
Chignecto B., *Canada* 103 C7
Chiguana, *Bolivia* 126 A2
Chigwell, *U.K.* 13 F8
Chiha-ri, *N. Korea* 57 E14
Chihli, G. of = Bo Hai, *China* 57 E10
Chihuahua, *Mexico* 118 B3
Chihuahua □, *Mexico* 118 B3
Chiili = Shīeli, *Kazakstan* 50 E7
Chik Bollapur, *India* 66 N10
Chikmagalur, *India* 66 N9
Chikwawa, *Malawi* 87 F3
Chilac, *Mexico* 119 D5
Chilam Chavki, *Pakistan* 69 B6
Chilanga, *Zambia* 87 F2
Chilapa, *Mexico* 119 D5
Chilas, *Pakistan* 69 B6
Chilaw, *Sri Lanka* 66 R11
Chilcotin →, *Canada* 104 C4
Childers, *Australia* 95 D5
Childress, *U.S.A.* 113 H4
Chile ■, *S. Amer.* 128 D2
Chile Rise, *Pac. Oc.* 97 L18
Chilecito, *Argentina* 126 B2
Chilete, *Peru* 124 E3
Chilia, Braţul →, *Romania* 43 E14
Chililabombwe, *Zambia* 87 E2
Chilin = Jilin, *China* 57 C14
Chilka L., *India* 67 K14
Chilko →, *Canada* 104 C4
Chilko L., *Canada* 104 C4
Chillagoe, *Australia* 94 B3
Chillán, *Chile* 126 D1
Chillicothe, *Ill., U.S.A.* 112 E10
Chillicothe, *Mo., U.S.A.* 112 F8
Chillicothe, *Ohio, U.S.A.* 108 F4
Chilliwack, *Canada* 104 D4
Chilo, *India* 68 F5
Chiloane, I., *Mozam.* 89 C5
Chiloé, I. de, *Chile* 122 H3
Chilpancingo, *Mexico* 119 D5
Chiltern Hills, *U.K.* 13 F7
Chilton, *U.S.A.* 108 C1
Chilubi, *Zambia* 87 E2
Chilubula, *Zambia* 87 E3
Chilumba, *Malawi* 87 E3
Chilung, *Taiwan* 59 E13
Chilwa, L., *Malawi* 87 F4
Chimaltitán, *Mexico* 118 C4
Chimán, *Panama* 120 E4
Chimanimani, *Zimbabwe* 89 B5
Chimay, *Belgium* 17 D4
Chimayo, *U.S.A.* 115 H11
Chimbay, *Uzbekistan* 50 E6
Chimborazo, *Ecuador* 122 D3
Chimbote, *Peru* 124 E3
Chimkent = Shymkent, *Kazakstan* 50 E7
Chimoio, *Mozam.* 87 F3
Chimpembe, *Zambia* 87 D2
Chin □, *Burma* 67 J18
Chin Ling Shan = Qinling Shandi, *China* 56 H5
China, *Mexico* 119 B5
China ■, *Asia* 60 D6
China Lake, *U.S.A.* 117 K9
Chinan = Jinan, *China* 56 F9
Chinandega, *Nic.* 120 D2
Chinati Peak, *U.S.A.* 113 L2
Chincha Alta, *Peru* 122 E3
Chinchaga →, *Canada* 104 B5
Chinchilla, *Australia* 95 D5
Chinchilla de Monte Aragón, *Spain* 33 G3
Chinchorro, Banco, *Mexico* 119 D7
Chinchou = Jinzhou, *China* 57 D11
Chincoteague, *U.S.A.* 108 G8
Chinde, *Mozam.* 87 F4
Chindo, *S. Korea* 57 G14
Chindwin →, *Burma* 67 J19
Chineni, *India* 69 C6
Chinga, *Mozam.* 87 F4
Chingola, *Zambia* 87 E2
Chingole, *Malawi* 87 E3
Ch'ingtao = Qingdao, *China* 57 F11
Chinguetti, *Mauritania* 78 D3
Chingune, *Mozam.* 89 C5
Chinhae, *S. Korea* 57 G15
Chinhanguanine, *Mozam.* 89 D5
Chinhoyi, *Zimbabwe* 87 F3
Chini, *India* 68 D8
Chiniot, *Pakistan* 68 D5
Chínipas, *Mexico* 118 B3
Chinji, *Pakistan* 68 C5
Chinju, *S. Korea* 57 G15
Chinle, *U.S.A.* 115 H9
Chinmen, *Taiwan* 59 E13
Chinmen Tao, *Taiwan* 59 E12
Chinnampo = Namp'o, *N. Korea* 57 E13
Chino, *Japan* 55 G9
Chino, *U.S.A.* 117 L9
Chino Valley, *U.S.A.* 115 J7
Chinon, *France* 18 E7
Chinook, *U.S.A.* 114 B9
Chinsali, *Zambia* 87 E3
Chióggia, *Italy* 29 C9
Chíos = Khíos, *Greece* 39 C8
Chipata, *Zambia* 87 E3
Chiperceni, *Moldova* 43 C13
Chipinge, *Zimbabwe* 87 G3
Chipiona, *Spain* 35 J4
Chipley, *U.S.A.* 109 K3
Chipman, *Canada* 103 C6
Chipoka, *Malawi* 87 E3
Chippenham, *U.K.* 13 F5
Chippewa →, *U.S.A.* 112 C8
Chippewa Falls, *U.S.A.* 112 C9
Chipping Norton, *U.K.* 13 F6
Chiprovtsi, *Bulgaria* 40 C6
Chiputneticook Lakes, *U.S.A.* 109 C11
Chiquián, *Peru* 124 F3
Chiquimula, *Guatemala* 120 D2
Chiquinquira, *Colombia* 124 B4
Chir →, *Russia* 49 F6
Chirala, *India* 66 M12
Chiramba, *Mozam.* 87 F3
Chirawa, *India* 68 E6
Chirchiq, *Uzbekistan* 50 E7
Chiredzi, *Zimbabwe* 89 C5
Chiricahua Peak, *U.S.A.* 115 L9
Chiriquí, G. de, *Panama* 120 E3
Chiriquí, L. de, *Panama* 120 E3
Chirivira Falls, *Zimbabwe* 87 G3
Chirmiri, *India* 67 H13
Chirnogi, *Romania* 43 F11
Chirpan, *Bulgaria* 41 D9
Chirripó Grande, Cerro, *Costa Rica* 120 E3
Chirundu, *Zimbabwe* 89 B4
Chisamba, *Zambia* 87 E2
Chisapani Garhi, *Nepal* 67 F14
Chisasibi, *Canada* 102 B4
Ch'ishan, *Taiwan* 59 F13
Chisholm, *Canada* 104 C6
Chisholm, *U.S.A.* 112 B8
Chishtian Mandi, *Pakistan* 68 E5
Chishui, *China* 58 C5
Chishui He →, *China* 58 C5
Chisimaio, *Somali Rep.* 77 G8
Chisimba Falls, *Zambia* 87 E3
Chişinău, *Moldova* 43 C13
Chişineu Criş, *Romania* 42 D6
Chisone →, *Italy* 28 D4
Chisos Mts., *U.S.A.* 113 L3
Chistopol, *Russia* 48 C10
Chita, *Russia* 51 D12
Chitipa, *Malawi* 87 D3
Chitose, *Japan* 54 C10
Chitral, *Pakistan* 66 B7
Chitré, *Panama* 120 E3
Chittagong, *Bangla.* 67 H17
Chittagong □, *Bangla.* 67 G17
Chittaurgarh, *India* 68 G6
Chittoor, *India* 66 N11
Chitungwiza, *Zimbabwe* 87 F3
Chiusi, *Italy* 29 E8
Chiva, *Spain* 33 F4
Chivasso, *Italy* 28 C4
Chivhu, *Zimbabwe* 87 F3
Chivilcoy, *Argentina* 126 C4
Chiwanda, *Tanzania* 87 E3
Chixi, *China* 59 G9
Chizera, *Zambia* 87 E2
Chkalov = Orenburg, *Russia* 50 D6
Chkolovsk, *Russia* 48 B6
Chloride, *U.S.A.* 117 K12
Chlumec nad Cidlinou, *Czech Rep.* 26 A8
Chmielnik, *Poland* 45 H7
Cho Bo, *Vietnam* 58 G5
Cho-do, *N. Korea* 57 E13
Cho Phuoc Hai, *Vietnam* 65 G6
Choba, *Kenya* 86 B4
Chobe National Park, *Botswana* 88 B4
Choch'iwŏn, *S. Korea* 57 F14
Chocianów, *Poland* 45 G2
Chociwel, *Poland* 44 E2
Chocolate Mts., *U.S.A.* 117 M11
Choctawhatchee →, *U.S.A.* 109 K3
Chodecz, *Poland* 45 F6
Chodov, *Czech Rep.* 26 A5
Chodziez, *Poland* 45 F3
Choele Choel, *Argentina* 128 D3
Choix, *Mexico* 118 B3
Chojna, *Poland* 45 F1
Chojnice, *Poland* 44 E4
Chojnów, *Poland* 45 G2
Chōkai-San, *Japan* 54 E10
Choke, *Ethiopia* 81 E4
Choke Canyon L., *U.S.A.* 113 L5
Chokurdakh, *Russia* 51 B15
Cholame, *U.S.A.* 116 K6
Cholet, *France* 18 E6
Cholguan, *Chile* 126 D1
Choluteca, *Honduras* 120 D2
Choluteca →, *Honduras* 120 D2
Chom Bung, *Thailand* 64 F2
Chom Thong, *Thailand* 64 C2
Choma, *Zambia* 87 F2
Chomen Swamp, *Ethiopia* 81 F4
Chomun, *India* 68 F6
Chomutov, *Czech Rep.* 26 A6
Chon Buri, *Thailand* 64 F3
Chon Thanh, *Vietnam* 65 G6
Ch'onan, *S. Korea* 57 F14
Chone, *Ecuador* 124 D3
Chong Kai, *Cambodia* 64 F4
Chong Mek, *Thailand* 64 E5
Chongde, *China* 59 B13
Chŏngdo, *S. Korea* 57 G15
Chŏngha, *S. Korea* 57 F15
Chŏngjin, *N. Korea* 57 D15
Chŏngjiu, *S. Korea* 57 F14
Chŏngju, *N. Korea* 57 E13
Chongli, *China* 56 D8
Chongming, *China* 59 B13
Chongming Dao, *China* 59 B13
Chongqing, *Chongqing, China* 58 C6
Chongqing, *Sichuan, China* 58 B4
Chongqing Shi □, *China* 58 C6
Chongren, *China* 59 D11
Chonguene, *Mozam.* 89 C5
Chongŭp, *S. Korea* 57 G14
Chongyi, *China* 59 E10
Chongzuo, *China* 58 F6
Chŏnju, *S. Korea* 57 G14
Chonos, Arch. de los, *Chile* 122 H3
Chop, *Ukraine* 47 H2
Chopim →, *Brazil* 127 B5
Chor, *Pakistan* 68 G3
Chorbat La, *India* 69 B7
Chorley, *U.K.* 12 D5
Chornobyl, *Ukraine* 47 G6
Chornomorske, *Ukraine* 47 K7
Chorolque, Cerro, *Bolivia* 126 A2
Choroszcz, *Poland* 45 E9
Chorregon, *Australia* 94 C3
Chortkiv, *Ukraine* 47 H3
Ch'ŏrwon, *S. Korea* 57 E14
Chorzele, *Poland* 45 E7
Chorzów, *Poland* 45 H5
Chos-Malal, *Argentina* 126 D1
Ch'osan, *N. Korea* 57 D13
Choszczno, *Poland* 45 E2
Choteau, *U.S.A.* 114 C7
Chotěboř, *Czech Rep.* 26 B8
Chotila, *India* 68 H4
Chotta Udepur, *India* 68 H6
Chowchilla, *U.S.A.* 116 H6
Choybalsan, *Mongolia* 60 B6
Christchurch, *N.Z.* 91 K4
Christchurch, *U.K.* 13 G6
Christian I., *Canada* 110 B4
Christiana, *S. Africa* 88 D4
Christiansfeld, *Denmark* 11 J3
Christiansted, *U.S. Virgin Is.* 121 C7
Christie B., *Canada* 105 A6
Christina →, *Canada* 105 B6
Christmas Cr. →, *Australia* 92 C4
Christmas I. = Kiritimati, *Kiribati* 97 G12
Christmas I., *Ind. Oc.* 96 J2
Christopher L., *Australia* 93 D4
Chrudim, *Czech Rep.* 26 B8
Chrzanów, *Poland* 45 H6
Chtimba, *Malawi* 87 E3
Chu = Shū, *Kazakstan* 50 E8
Chu →, *Vietnam* 64 C5
Chu Lai, *Vietnam* 64 E7
Ch'uanchou = Quanzhou, *China* 59 E12
Chuankou, *China* 56 G6
Chubbuck, *U.S.A.* 114 E7
Chūbu □, *Japan* 55 F8
Chubut →, *Argentina* 122 H4
Chuchi L., *Canada* 104 B4
Chuda, *India* 68 H4
Chudovo, *Russia* 46 C6
Chudskoye, Ozero, *Russia* 9 G22
Chūgoku □, *Japan* 55 G6
Chūgoku-Sanchi, *Japan* 55 G6
Chuguyev = Chuhuyiv, *Ukraine* 47 H9
Chugwater, *U.S.A.* 112 E2
Chuhuyiv, *Ukraine* 47 H9
Chukchi Sea, *Russia* 51 C19
Chukotskoye Nagorye, *Russia* 51 C18
Chula Vista, *U.S.A.* 117 N9
Chulucanas, *Peru* 124 E2
Chulym →, *Russia* 50 D9
Chum Phae, *Thailand* 64 D4
Chum Saeng, *Thailand* 64 E3
Chumar, *India* 69 C8
Chumbicha, *Argentina* 126 B2
Chumerna, *Bulgaria* 41 D9
Chumikan, *Russia* 51 D14
Chumphon, *Thailand* 65 G2
Chumuare, *Mozam.* 87 E3
Chumunjin, *S. Korea* 57 F15
Chuna →, *Russia* 51 D10
Chun'an, *China* 59 C12
Ch'unch'ŏn, *S. Korea* 57 F14
Chunchura, *India* 69 H13
Chunga, *Zambia* 87 F2
Chunggang-ŭp, *N. Korea* 57 D14
Chunghwa, *N. Korea* 57 E13
Ch'ungju, *S. Korea* 57 F14
Chungking = Chongqing, *China* 58 C6
Chungli, *Taiwan* 59 E13
Ch'ungmu, *S. Korea* 57 G15
Chungt'iaoshan = Zhongtiao Shan, *China* 56 G6
Chungyang Shanmo, *Taiwan* 59 F13
Chunian, *Pakistan* 68 D6
Chunya, *Tanzania* 87 D3
Chunyang, *China* 57 C15
Chuquibamba, *Peru* 124 G4
Chuquicamata, *Chile* 126 A2
Chur, *Switz.* 25 J5
Churachandpur, *India* 67 G18
Churchill, *Canada* 105 B10
Churchill →, *Man., Canada* 105 B10
Churchill →, *Nfld., Canada* 103 B7
Churchill, C., *Canada* 105 B10
Churchill Falls, *Canada* 103 B7
Churchill L., *Canada* 105 B7
Churchill Pk., *Canada* 104 B3
Churki, *India* 69 H10
Churu, *India* 68 E6
Churún Merú = Angel Falls, *Venezuela* 124 B6
Chushal, *India* 69 C8
Chuska Mts., *U.S.A.* 115 H9
Chusovoy, *Russia* 50 D6
Chute-aux-Outardes, *Canada* 103 C6
Chuuronjang, *N. Korea* 57 D15
Chuvash Republic = Chuvashia □, *Russia* 48 C8
Chuvashia □, *Russia* 48 C8
Chuwārtah, *Iraq* 70 C5
Chuxiong, *China* 58 E3
Chūy = Shū →, *Kazakstan* 52 E10
Chuy, *Uruguay* 127 C5
Chuzhou, *China* 59 A12
Ci Xian, *China* 56 F8
Ciacova, *Romania* 42 E6
Ciadâr-Lunga, *Moldova* 43 D13
Ciamis, *Indonesia* 63 G13
Cianjur, *Indonesia* 63 G12
Cianorte, *Brazil* 127 A5
Cibola, *U.S.A.* 117 M12
Cicero, *U.S.A.* 108 E2
Cidacos →, *Spain* 32 C3
Cide, *Turkey* 72 B5
Ciechanów, *Poland* 45 F7
Ciechanowiec, *Poland* 45 F9
Ciechocinek, *Poland* 45 F5
Ciego de Avila, *Cuba* 120 B4
Ciénaga, *Colombia* 124 A4
Cienfuegos, *Cuba* 120 B3
Cierp, *France* 20 F4
Cíes, Is., *Spain* 34 C2
Cieszanów, *Poland* 45 H10
Cieszyn, *Poland* 45 J5
Cieza, *Spain* 33 G3
Çifteler, *Turkey* 72 C4
Cifuentes, *Spain* 32 E2
Cihanbeyli, *Turkey* 72 C5
Cihuatlán, *Mexico* 118 D4
Cijara, Embalse de, *Spain* 35 F6
Cijulang, *Indonesia* 63 G13
Cilacap, *Indonesia* 63 G13
Çıldır, *Turkey* 73 B10
Çıldır Gölü, *Turkey* 73 B10
Cili, *China* 59 C8
Cilibia, *Romania* 43 E12
Cilicia, *Turkey* 72 D5
Cill Chainnigh = Kilkenny, *Ireland* 15 D4
Cilo Dağı, *Turkey* 73 D10
Cima, *U.S.A.* 117 K11
Cimarron, *Kans., U.S.A.* 113 G4
Cimarron, *N. Mex., U.S.A.* 113 G2
Cimarron →, *U.S.A.* 113 G6
Cimişlia, *Moldova* 43 D13
Cimone, Mte., *Italy* 28 D7
Çınar, *Turkey* 73 D9
Çınarcık, *Turkey* 41 F13
Cinca →, *Spain* 32 D5
Cincar, *Bos.-H.* 42 G2
Cincinnati, *U.S.A.* 108 F3
Cincinnatus, *U.S.A.* 111 D9
Çine, *Turkey* 39 D10
Ciney, *Belgium* 17 D5
Cíngoli, *Italy* 29 E10
Cinigiano, *Italy* 29 F8
Cinto, Mte., *France* 21 F12
Cintruénigo, *Spain* 32 C3
Ciocile, *Romania* 43 F12
Ciolăneşti din Deal, *Romania* 43 F10
Ciorani, *Romania* 43 F11
Čiovo, *Croatia* 29 E13
Circeo, Mte., *Italy* 30 A6
Çirçir, *Turkey* 72 C7
Circle, *Alaska, U.S.A.* 100 B5
Circle, *Mont., U.S.A.* 112 B2
Circleville, *U.S.A.* 108 F4
Cirebon, *Indonesia* 62 F3
Ciremai, *Indonesia* 63 G13
Cirencester, *U.K.* 13 F6
Cireşu, *Romania* 42 F7
Cirey-sur-Vezouze, *France* 19 D13
Ciriè, *Italy* 28 C4
Cirium, *Cyprus* 36 E11
Cirò, *Italy* 31 C10
Cirò Marina, *Italy* 31 C10
Ciron →, *France* 20 D3
Cisco, *U.S.A.* 113 J5
Cislău, *Romania* 43 E11
Cisna, *Poland* 45 J9
Cisnădie, *Romania* 43 E9
Cisterna di Latina, *Italy* 30 A5
Cisternino, *Italy* 31 B10
Cistierna, *Spain* 34 C5
Citeli-Ckaro = Tsiteli-Tsqaro, *Georgia* 49 K8
Citlaltépetl, *Mexico* 119 D5
Citrus Heights, *U.S.A.* 116 G5
Citrusdal, *S. Africa* 88 E2
Città della Pieve, *Italy* 29 F9
Città di Castello, *Italy* 29 E9
Città Sant' Angelo, *Italy* 29 F11
Cittadella, *Italy* 29 C8
Cittaducale, *Italy* 29 F9
Cittanova, *Italy* 31 D9
Ciuc, Munţii, *Romania* 43 D11
Ciucaş, Vf., *Romania* 43 E10
Ciucea, *Romania* 42 D7
Ciuciulea, *Moldova* 43 C12
Ciuciuleni, *Moldova* 43 C13
Ciudad Altamirano, *Mexico* 118 D4
Ciudad Bolívar, *Venezuela* 124 B6
Ciudad Camargo, *Mexico* 118 B3
Ciudad de Valles, *Mexico* 119 C5
Ciudad del Carmen, *Mexico* 119 D6
Ciudad del Este, *Paraguay* 127 B5
Ciudad Delicias = Delicias, *Mexico* 118 B3
Ciudad Guayana, *Venezuela* 124 B6
Ciudad Guerrero, *Mexico* 118 B3
Ciudad Guzmán, *Mexico* 118 D4
Ciudad Juárez, *Mexico* 118 A3
Ciudad Madero, *Mexico* 119 C5
Ciudad Mante, *Mexico* 119 C5
Ciudad Obregón, *Mexico* 118 B3
Ciudad Real, *Spain* 35 G7
Ciudad Real □, *Spain* 35 G7
Ciudad Rodrigo, *Spain* 34 E4
Ciudad Trujillo = Santo Domingo, *Dom. Rep.* 121 C6
Ciudad Victoria, *Mexico* 119 C5
Ciudadela, *Spain* 37 B10
Ciulniţa, *Romania* 43 F12
Ciumeghiu, *Romania* 42 D6
Ciuperceni, *Romania* 42 F8
Civa Burnu, *Turkey* 72 B7
Cividale del Friuli, *Italy* 29 B10
Civita Castellana, *Italy* 29 F9
Civitanova Marche, *Italy* 29 E10
Civitavécchia, *Italy* 29 F8
Civray, *France* 20 B4
Çivril, *Turkey* 39 C11
Cixerri →, *Italy* 30 C1
Cixi, *China* 59 B13
Cizre, *Turkey* 70 B4
Cizur Mayor, *Spain* 32 C3
Clackmannanshire □, *U.K.* 14 E5
Clacton-on-Sea, *U.K.* 13 F9
Clain →, *France* 18 F7
Claire, L., *Canada* 104 B6
Clairton, *U.S.A.* 110 F5

Cuamba


Conselheiro Lafaiete, *Brazil* 127 A7
Conselve, *Italy* 29 C8
Consett, *U.K.* 12 C6
Consort, *Canada* 105 C6
Constance = Konstanz, *Germany* 25 H5
Constance, L. = Bodensee, *Europe* 25 H5
Constanţa, *Romania* 43 F13
Constanţa □, *Romania* 43 F13
Constantia, *U.S.A.* 111 C8
Constantina, *Spain* 35 H5
Constantine, *Algeria* 78 A7
Constitución, *Chile* 126 D1
Constitución, *Uruguay* 126 C4
Consuegra, *Spain* 35 F7
Consul, *Canada* 105 D7
Contact, *U.S.A.* 114 F6
Contai, *India* 69 J12
Contamana, *Peru* 124 E4
Contarina, *Italy* 29 C9
Contas →, *Brazil* 125 F11
Contes, *France* 21 E11
Contoocook, *U.S.A.* 111 C13
Contra Costa, *Mozam.* 89 D5
Contres, *France* 18 E8
Contrexéville, *France* 19 D12
Contwoyto L., *Canada* 100 B8
Conversano, *Italy* 31 B10
Conway = Conwy, *U.K.* 12 D4
Conway = Conwy →, *U.K.* 12 D4
Conway, *Ark., U.S.A.* 113 H8
Conway, *N.H., U.S.A.* 111 C13
Conway, *S.C., U.S.A.* 109 J6
Conway, L., *Australia* 95 D2
Conwy, *U.K.* 12 D4
Conwy □, *U.K.* 12 D4
Conwy →, *U.K.* 12 D4
Coober Pedy, *Australia* 95 D1
Cooch Behar = Koch Bihar, *India* 67 F16
Cooinda, *Australia* 92 B5
Cook, *Australia* 93 F5
Cook, *U.S.A.* 112 B8
Cook, B., *Chile* 128 H3
Cook, C., *Canada* 104 C3
Cook, Mt. = Aoraki Mount Cook, *N.Z.* 91 K3
Cook Inlet, *U.S.A.* 100 C4
Cook Is., *Pac. Oc.* 97 J12
Cook Strait, *N.Z.* 91 J5
Cookeville, *U.S.A.* 109 G3
Cookhouse, *S. Africa* 88 E4
Cookshire, *Canada* 111 A13
Cookstown, *U.K.* 15 B5
Cooksville, *Canada* 110 C5
Cooktown, *Australia* 94 B4
Coolabah, *Australia* 95 E4
Cooladdi, *Australia* 95 D4
Coolah, *Australia* 95 E4
Coolamon, *Australia* 95 E4
Coolgardie, *Australia* 93 F3
Coolidge, *U.S.A.* 115 K8
Coolidge Dam, *U.S.A.* 115 K8
Cooma, *Australia* 95 F4
Coon Rapids, *U.S.A.* 112 C8
Coonabarabran, *Australia* 95 E4
Coonamble, *Australia* 95 E4
Coonana, *Australia* 93 F3
Coondapoor, *India* 66 N9
Cooninie, L., *Australia* 95 D2
Cooper, *U.S.A.* 113 J7
Cooper Cr. →, *Australia* 95 D2
Cooperstown, *N. Dak., U.S.A.* 112 B5
Cooperstown, *N.Y., U.S.A.* 111 D10
Coorabie, *Australia* 93 F5
Coorong, The, *Australia* 95 F2
Coorow, *Australia* 93 E2
Cooroy, *Australia* 95 D5
Coos Bay, *U.S.A.* 114 E1
Coosa →, *U.S.A.* 109 J2
Cootamundra, *Australia* 95 E4
Cootehill, *Ireland* 15 B4
Copahue Paso, *Argentina* 126 D1
Copainalá, *Mexico* 119 D6
Copake Falls, *U.S.A.* 111 D11
Copalnic Mănăştur, *Romania* 43 C8
Copán, *Honduras* 120 D2
Cope, *U.S.A.* 112 F3
Cope, C., *Spain* 33 H3
Copenhagen = København, *Denmark* 11 J6
Copenhagen, *U.S.A.* 111 C9
Copertino, *Italy* 31 B11
Copiapó, *Chile* 126 B1
Copiapó →, *Chile* 126 B1
Coplay, *U.S.A.* 111 F9
Copp L., *Canada* 104 A6
Copparo, *Italy* 29 D8
Coppename →, *Surinam* 125 B7
Copper Harbor, *U.S.A.* 108 B2
Copper Queen, *Zimbabwe* 87 F2
Copperas Cove, *U.S.A.* 113 K6
Copperbelt □, *Zambia* 87 E2
Coppermine = Kugluktuk, *Canada* 100 B8
Coppermine →, *Canada* 100 B8
Copperopolis, *U.S.A.* 116 H6
Copşa Mică, *Romania* 43 D9
Coquet →, *U.K.* 12 B6
Coquille, *U.S.A.* 114 E1
Coquimbo, *Chile* 126 C1
Coquimbo □, *Chile* 126 C1
Corabia, *Romania* 43 G9
Coracora, *Peru* 124 G4
Coraki, *Australia* 95 D5
Coral, *U.S.A.* 110 F5
Coral Gables, *U.S.A.* 109 N5
Coral Harbour = Salliq, *Canada* 101 B11
Coral Sea, *Pac. Oc.* 96 J7
Coral Springs, *U.S.A.* 109 M5
Coraopolis, *U.S.A.* 110 F4
Corato, *Italy* 31 A9
Corbeil-Essonnes, *France* 19 D9
Corbie, *France* 19 C9
Corbières, *France* 20 F6
Corbigny, *France* 19 E10
Corbin, *U.S.A.* 108 G3
Corbones →, *Spain* 35 H5
Corbu, *Romania* 43 F13
Corby, *U.K.* 13 E7
Corcaigh = Cork, *Ireland* 15 E3
Corcoran, *U.S.A.* 116 J7
Cordele, *U.S.A.* 109 K4
Cordell, *U.S.A.* 113 H5
Cordenòns, *Italy* 29 C9
Cordes, *France* 20 D5
Córdoba, *Argentina* 126 C3
Córdoba, *Mexico* 119 D5
Córdoba, *Spain* 35 H6
Córdoba □, *Argentina* 126 C3
Córdoba □, *Spain* 35 G6
Córdoba, Sierra de, *Argentina* 126 C3
Cordon, *Phil.* 61 C4
Cordova, *U.S.A.* 100 B5
Corella, *Spain* 32 C3
Corella →, *Australia* 94 B3
Corfield, *Australia* 94 C3
Corfu = Kérkira, *Greece* 36 A3
Corfu, Str. of, *Greece* 36 A4
Corgo = O Corgo, *Spain* 34 C3
Cori, *Italy* 30 A5
Coria, *Spain* 34 F4
Coria del Río, *Spain* 35 H4
Corigliano Cálabro, *Italy* 31 C9
Coringa Is., *Australia* 94 B4
Corinth = Kórinthos, *Greece* 38 D4
Corinth, *Miss., U.S.A.* 109 H1
Corinth, *N.Y., U.S.A.* 111 C11
Corinth, G. of = Korinthiakós Kólpos, *Greece* 38 C4
Corinth Canal, *Greece* 38 D4
Corinto, *Brazil* 125 G10
Corinto, *Nic.* 120 D2
Cork, *Ireland* 15 E3
Cork □, *Ireland* 15 E3
Cork Harbour, *Ireland* 15 E3
Corlay, *France* 18 D3
Corleone, *Italy* 30 E6
Corleto Perticara, *Italy* 31 B9
Çorlu, *Turkey* 41 E11
Cormack L., *Canada* 104 A4
Cormòns, *Italy* 29 C10
Cormorant, *Canada* 105 C8
Cormorant L., *Canada* 105 C8
Corn Is. = Maiz, Is. del, *Nic.* 120 D3
Cornélio Procópio, *Brazil* 127 A5
Corner Brook, *Canada* 103 C8
Corneşti, *Moldova* 43 C13
Corníglio, *Italy* 28 D7
Corning, *Ark., U.S.A.* 113 G9
Corning, *Calif., U.S.A.* 114 G2
Corning, *Iowa, U.S.A.* 112 E7
Corning, *N.Y., U.S.A.* 110 D7
Corno Grande, *Italy* 29 F10
Cornwall, *Canada* 102 C5
Cornwall, *U.S.A.* 111 F8
Cornwall □, *U.K.* 13 G3
Corny Pt., *Australia* 95 E2
Coro, *Venezuela* 124 A5
Coroatá, *Brazil* 125 D10
Corocoro, *Bolivia* 124 G5
Coroico, *Bolivia* 124 G5
Coromandel, *N.Z.* 91 G5
Coromandel Coast, *India* 66 N12
Corona, *Calif., U.S.A.* 117 M9
Corona, *N. Mex., U.S.A.* 115 J11
Coronach, *Canada* 105 D7
Coronado, *U.S.A.* 117 N9
Coronado, B. de, *Costa Rica* 120 E3
Coronados, Is. los, *U.S.A.* 117 N9
Coronation, *Canada* 104 C6
Coronation Gulf, *Canada* 100 B8
Coronation I., *Antarctica* 5 C18
Coronation Is., *Australia* 92 B3
Coronda, *Argentina* 126 C3
Coronel, *Chile* 126 D1
Coronel Bogado, *Paraguay* 126 B4
Coronel Dorrego, *Argentina* 126 D3
Coronel Oviedo, *Paraguay* 126 B4
Coronel Pringles, *Argentina* 126 D3
Coronel Suárez, *Argentina* 126 D3
Coronel Vidal, *Argentina* 126 D4
Coropuna, Nevado, *Peru* 124 G4
Çorovodë, *Albania* 40 F4
Corowa, *Australia* 95 F4
Corozal, *Belize* 119 D7
Corps, *France* 21 D9
Corpus, *Argentina* 127 B4
Corpus Christi, *U.S.A.* 113 M6
Corpus Christi, L., *U.S.A.* 113 L6
Corral de Almaguer, *Spain* 34 F7
Corralejo, *Canary Is.* 37 F6
Corraun Pen., *Ireland* 15 C2
Corréggio, *Italy* 28 D7
Correntes, C. das, *Mozam.* 89 C6
Corrèze □, *France* 20 C5
Corrèze →, *France* 20 C5
Corrib, L., *Ireland* 15 C2
Corridónia, *Italy* 29 E10
Corrientes, *Argentina* 126 B4
Corrientes □, *Argentina* 126 B4
Corrientes →, *Argentina* 126 C4
Corrientes →, *Peru* 124 D4
Corrientes, C., *Colombia* 124 B3
Corrientes, C., *Cuba* 120 B3
Corrientes, C., *Mexico* 118 C3
Corrigan, *U.S.A.* 113 K7
Corrigin, *Australia* 93 F2
Corry, *U.S.A.* 110 E5
Corse, *France* 21 G13
Corse, C., *France* 21 E13
Corse-du-Sud □, *France* 21 G13
Corsica = Corse, *France* 21 G13
Corsicana, *U.S.A.* 113 J6
Corte, *France* 21 F13
Corte Pinto, *Portugal* 35 H3
Cortegana, *Spain* 35 H4
Cortez, *U.S.A.* 115 H9
Cortina d'Ampezzo, *Italy* 29 B9
Cortland, *N.Y., U.S.A.* 111 D8
Cortland, *Ohio, U.S.A.* 110 E4
Cortona, *Italy* 29 E8
Corubal →, *Guinea-Biss.* 82 C2
Coruche, *Portugal* 35 G2
Çoruh →, *Turkey* 49 K5
Çorum, *Turkey* 72 B6
Corumbá, *Brazil* 124 G7
Corund, *Romania* 43 D10
Corunna = A Coruña, *Spain* 34 B2
Corvallis, *U.S.A.* 114 D2
Corvette, L. de la, *Canada* 102 B5
Corydon, *U.S.A.* 112 E8
Cosalá, *Mexico* 118 C3
Cosamaloapan, *Mexico* 119 D5
Cosenza, *Italy* 31 C9
Coşereni, *Romania* 43 F11
Coshocton, *U.S.A.* 110 F3
Cosmo Newberry, *Australia* 93 E3
Cosne-Cours-sur-Loire, *France* 19 E9
Coso Junction, *U.S.A.* 117 J9
Coso Pk., *U.S.A.* 117 J9
Cospeito, *Spain* 34 B3
Cosquín, *Argentina* 126 C3
Cossato, *Italy* 28 C5
Cossé-le-Vivien, *France* 18 E6
Cosson →, *France* 18 E8
Costa Blanca, *Spain* 33 G4
Costa Brava, *Spain* 32 D8
Costa del Sol, *Spain* 35 J6
Costa Dorada, *Spain* 32 D6
Costa Mesa, *U.S.A.* 117 M9
Costa Rica ■, *Cent. Amer.* 120 E3
Costa Smeralda, *Italy* 30 A2
Costeşti, *Romania* 43 F9
Costigliole d'Asti, *Italy* 28 D5
Cosumnes →, *U.S.A.* 116 G5
Coswig, *Sachsen, Germany* 24 D9
Coswig, *Sachsen-Anhalt, Germany* 24 D8
Cotabato, *Phil.* 61 H6
Cotagaita, *Bolivia* 126 A2
Côte d'Azur, *France* 21 E11
Côte-d'Ivoire = Ivory Coast ■, *Africa* 82 D4
Côte d'Or, *France* 19 E11
Côte-d'Or □, *France* 19 E11
Coteau des Prairies, *U.S.A.* 112 C6
Coteau du Missouri, *U.S.A.* 112 B4
Coteau Landing, *Canada* 111 A10
Cotentin, *France* 18 C5
Côtes-d'Armor □, *France* 18 D4
Côtes de Meuse, *France* 19 C12
Côtes-du-Nord = Côtes-d'Armor □, *France* 18 D4
Cotiella, *Spain* 32 C5
Cotillo, *Canary Is.* 37 F5
Cotiujeni, *Moldova* 43 C13
Cotonou, *Benin* 83 D5
Cotopaxi, *Ecuador* 122 D3
Cotronei, *Italy* 31 C9
Cotswold Hills, *U.K.* 13 F5
Cottage Grove, *U.S.A.* 114 E2
Cottbus, *Germany* 24 D10
Cottonwood, *U.S.A.* 115 J7
Cotulla, *U.S.A.* 113 L5
Coubre, Pte. de la, *France* 20 C2
Couches, *France* 19 F11
Couço, *Portugal* 35 G2
Coudersport, *U.S.A.* 110 E6
Couedic, C. du, *Australia* 95 F2
Couëron, *France* 18 E5
Couesnon →, *France* 18 D5
Couhé, *France* 20 B4
Coulanges-sur-Yonne, *France* 19 E10
Coulee City, *U.S.A.* 114 C4
Coulman I., *Antarctica* 5 D11
Coulommiers, *France* 19 D10
Coulon →, *France* 21 E9
Coulonge →, *Canada* 102 C4
Coulonges-sur-l'Autize, *France* 20 B3
Coulounieix-Chamiers, *France* 20 C4
Coulterville, *U.S.A.* 116 H6
Council, *U.S.A.* 114 D5
Council Bluffs, *U.S.A.* 112 E7
Council Grove, *U.S.A.* 112 F6
Coupeville, *U.S.A.* 116 B4
Courantyne →, *S. Amer.* 122 C5
Courcelles, *Belgium* 17 D4
Courçon, *France* 20 B3
Courmayeur, *Italy* 28 C3
Couronne, C., *France* 21 E9
Cours-la-Ville, *France* 19 F11
Coursan, *France* 20 E7
Courseulles-sur-Mer, *France* 18 C6
Courtenay, *Canada* 104 D4
Courtenay, *France* 19 D10
Courtland, *U.S.A.* 116 G5
Courtrai = Kortrijk, *Belgium* 17 D3
Courtright, *Canada* 110 D2
Coushatta, *U.S.A.* 113 J8
Coutances, *France* 18 C5
Coutras, *France* 20 C3
Coutts Crossing, *Australia* 95 D5
Couvin, *Belgium* 17 D4
Covarrubias, *Spain* 34 C7
Covasna, *Romania* 43 E11
Covasna □, *Romania* 43 E10
Cove I., *Canada* 110 A3
Coventry, *U.K.* 13 E6
Covilhã, *Portugal* 34 E3
Covington, *Ga., U.S.A.* 109 J4
Covington, *Ky., U.S.A.* 108 F3
Covington, *Okla., U.S.A.* 113 G6
Covington, *Tenn., U.S.A.* 113 H10
Covington, *Va., U.S.A.* 108 G5
Cowal, L., *Australia* 95 E4
Cowan, L., *Australia* 93 F3
Cowan L., *Canada* 105 C7
Cowangie, *Australia* 95 F3
Cowansville, *Canada* 102 C5
Coward Springs, *Australia* 95 D2
Cowcowing Lakes, *Australia* 93 F2
Cowdenbeath, *U.K.* 14 E5
Cowell, *Australia* 95 E2
Cowes, *U.K.* 13 G6
Cowichan L., *Canada* 116 B2
Cowlitz →, *U.S.A.* 116 D4
Cowra, *Australia* 95 E4
Cox, *Spain* 33 G4
Coxilha Grande, *Brazil* 127 B5
Coxim, *Brazil* 125 G8
Cox's Bazar, *Bangla.* 67 J17
Coyote Wells, *U.S.A.* 117 N11
Coyuca de Benítez, *Mexico* 119 D4
Coyuca de Catalan, *Mexico* 118 D4
Cozad, *U.S.A.* 112 E5
Cozes, *France* 20 C3
Cozumel, *Mexico* 119 C7
Cozumel, Isla, *Mexico* 119 C7
Cracow = Kraków, *Poland* 45 H6
Cracow, *Australia* 95 D5
Cradock, *Australia* 95 E2
Cradock, *S. Africa* 88 E4
Craig, *U.S.A.* 114 F10
Craigavon, *U.K.* 15 B5
Craigmore, *Zimbabwe* 87 G3
Craik, *Canada* 105 C7
Crailsheim, *Germany* 25 F6
Craiova, *Romania* 43 F8
Cramsie, *Australia* 94 C3
Cranberry L., *U.S.A.* 111 B10
Cranberry Portage, *Canada* 105 C8
Cranbrook, *Australia* 93 F2
Cranbrook, *Canada* 104 D5
Crandon, *U.S.A.* 112 C10
Crane, *Oreg., U.S.A.* 114 E4
Crane, *Tex., U.S.A.* 113 K3
Cranston, *U.S.A.* 111 E13
Craon, *France* 18 E6
Craonne, *France* 19 C10
Craponne-sur-Arzon, *France* 20 C7
Crasna, *Romania* 43 D12
Crasna →, *Romania* 42 C7
Crasnei, Munţii, *Romania* 43 C8
Crater L., *U.S.A.* 114 E2
Crater Lake National Park, *U.S.A.* 114 E2
Crateús, *Brazil* 125 E10
Crati →, *Italy* 31 C9
Crato, *Brazil* 125 E11
Crato, *Portugal* 35 F3
Craven, L., *Canada* 102 B4
Crawford, *U.S.A.* 112 D3
Crawfordsville, *U.S.A.* 108 E2
Crawley, *U.K.* 13 F7
Crazy Mts., *U.S.A.* 114 C8
Crean L., *Canada* 105 C7
Crécy-en-Ponthieu, *France* 19 B8
Crediton, *Canada* 110 C3
Cree →, *Canada* 105 B7
Cree →, *U.K.* 14 G4
Cree L., *Canada* 105 B7
Creede, *U.S.A.* 115 H10
Creekside, *U.S.A.* 110 F5
Creel, *Mexico* 118 B3
Creemore, *Canada* 110 B4
Creighton, *Canada* 105 C8
Creighton, *U.S.A.* 112 D6
Creil, *France* 19 C9
Crema, *Italy* 28 C6
Cremona, *Italy* 28 C7
Crepaja, *Serbia, Yug.* 42 E5
Crépy, *France* 19 C10
Crépy-en-Valois, *France* 19 C9
Cres, *Croatia* 29 D11
Crescent City, *U.S.A.* 114 F1
Crescentino, *Italy* 28 C5
Crespo, *Argentina* 126 C3
Cresson, *U.S.A.* 110 F6
Crest, *France* 21 D9
Cresta, Mt., *Phil.* 61 C5
Crestline, *Calif., U.S.A.* 117 L9
Crestline, *Ohio, U.S.A.* 110 F2
Creston, *Canada* 104 D5
Creston, *Calif., U.S.A.* 116 K6
Creston, *Iowa, U.S.A.* 112 E7
Crestview, *Calif., U.S.A.* 116 H8
Crestview, *Fla., U.S.A.* 109 K2
Crêt de la Neige, *France* 19 F12
Crete = Kríti, *Greece* 36 D7
Crete, *U.S.A.* 112 E6
Crete, Sea of, *Greece* 39 E7
Créteil, *France* 19 D9
Creus, C. de, *Spain* 32 C8
Creuse □, *France* 19 F9
Creuse →, *France* 20 B4
Creutzwald, *France* 19 C13
Creuzburg, *Germany* 24 D6
Crèvecœur-le-Grand, *France* 19 C9
Crevillente, *Spain* 33 G4
Crewe, *U.K.* 12 D5
Crewkerne, *U.K.* 13 G5
Criciúma, *Brazil* 127 B6
Cricova, *Moldova* 43 C13
Crieff, *U.K.* 14 E5
Crikvenica, *Croatia* 29 C11
Crimea □, *Ukraine* 47 K8
Crimean Pen. = Krymskyy Pivostriv, *Ukraine* 47 K8
Crimmitschau, *Germany* 24 E8
Cristuru Secuiesc, *Romania* 43 D10
Crişul Alb →, *Romania* 42 D6
Crişul Negru →, *Romania* 42 D6
Crişul Repede →, *Romania* 42 D5
Criuleni, *Moldova* 43 C14
Crivitz, *Germany* 24 B7
Crna →, *Macedonia* 40 E5
Crna Gora = Montenegro □, *Yugoslavia* 40 D3
Crna Gora, *Macedonia* 40 D5
Crna Reka = Crna →, *Macedonia* 40 E5
Crna Trava, *Serbia, Yug.* 40 D6
Crni Drim →, *Macedonia* 40 E4
Crni Timok →, *Serbia, Yug.* 40 C6
Crnoljeva Planina, *Kosovo, Yug.* 40 D5
Črnomelj, *Slovenia* 29 C12
Croagh Patrick, *Ireland* 15 C2
Croatia ■, *Europe* 29 C13
Crocker, Banjaran, *Malaysia* 62 C5
Crockett, *U.S.A.* 113 K7
Crocodile = Krokodil →, *Mozam.* 89 D5
Crocodile Is., *Australia* 94 A1
Crocq, *France* 20 C6
Crodo, *Italy* 28 B5
Crohy Hd., *Ireland* 15 B3
Croisette, C., *France* 21 E9
Croisic, Pte. du, *France* 18 E4
Croix, L. La, *Canada* 102 C1
Croker, C., *Australia* 92 B5
Croker, C., *Canada* 110 B4
Croker I., *Australia* 92 B5
Cromarty, *U.K.* 14 D4
Cromer, *U.K.* 12 E9
Cromwell, *N.Z.* 91 L2
Cromwell, *U.S.A.* 111 E12
Cronat, *France* 19 F10
Crook, *U.K.* 12 C6
Crooked →, *Canada* 104 C4
Crooked →, *U.S.A.* 114 D3
Crooked I., *Bahamas* 121 B5
Crooked Island Passage, *Bahamas* 121 B5
Crookston, *Minn., U.S.A.* 112 B6
Crookston, *Nebr., U.S.A.* 112 D4
Crookwell, *Australia* 95 E4
Crosby, *U.K.* 12 D4
Crosby, *N. Dak., U.S.A.* 112 A3
Crosby, *Pa., U.S.A.* 110 E6
Crosbyton, *U.S.A.* 113 J4
Crosía, *Italy* 31 C9
Cross →, *Nigeria* 83 E6
Cross City, *U.S.A.* 109 L4
Cross Fell, *U.K.* 12 C5
Cross L., *Canada* 105 C9
Cross Lake, *Canada* 105 C9
Cross River □, *Nigeria* 83 D6
Cross Sound, *U.S.A.* 100 C6
Crossett, *U.S.A.* 113 J9
Crosshaven, *Ireland* 15 E3
Crossville, *U.S.A.* 109 G3
Croswell, *U.S.A.* 110 C2
Croton-on-Hudson, *U.S.A.* 111 E11
Crotone, *Italy* 31 C10
Crow →, *Canada* 104 B4
Crow Agency, *U.S.A.* 114 D10
Crow Hd., *Ireland* 15 E1
Crowell, *U.S.A.* 113 J5
Crowley, *U.S.A.* 113 K8
Crowley, L., *U.S.A.* 116 H8
Crown Point, *Ind., U.S.A.* 108 E2
Crown Point, *N.Y., U.S.A.* 111 C11
Crownpoint, *U.S.A.* 115 J9
Crows Landing, *U.S.A.* 116 H5
Crows Nest, *Australia* 95 D5
Crowsnest Pass, *Canada* 104 D6
Croydon, *Australia* 94 B3
Croydon □, *U.K.* 13 F7
Crozet, Is., *Ind. Oc.* 3 G12
Crozon, *France* 18 D2
Cruz, C., *Cuba* 120 C4
Cruz Alta, *Brazil* 127 B5
Cruz de Incio, *Spain* 34 C3
Cruz del Eje, *Argentina* 126 C3
Cruzeiro, *Brazil* 127 A7
Cruzeiro do Oeste, *Brazil* 127 A5
Cruzeiro do Sul, *Brazil* 124 E4
Cry L., *Canada* 104 B3
Crystal Bay, *U.S.A.* 116 F7
Crystal Brook, *Australia* 95 E2
Crystal City, *U.S.A.* 113 L5
Crystal Falls, *U.S.A.* 108 B1
Crystal River, *U.S.A.* 109 L4
Crystal Springs, *U.S.A.* 113 K9
Csenger, *Hungary* 42 C7
Csongrád, *Hungary* 42 D5
Csongrád □, *Hungary* 42 D5
Csorna, *Hungary* 42 C2
Csurgo, *Hungary* 42 D2
Cu Lao Hon, *Vietnam* 65 G7
Cua Rao, *Vietnam* 64 C5
Cuácua →, *Mozam.* 87 F4
Cuamato, *Angola* 88 B2
Cuamba, *Mozam.* 87 E4

Diala


Diala, *Mali* 82 C3
Dialakoro, *Mali* 82 C3
Dialakoto, *Senegal* 82 C2
Diallassagou, *Mali* 82 C4
Diamante, *Argentina* 126 C3
Diamante, *Italy* 31 C8
Diamante →, *Argentina* 126 C2
Diamantina, *Brazil* 125 G10
Diamantina →, *Australia* 95 D2
Diamantino, *Brazil* 125 F7
Diamond Bar, *U.S.A.* 117 L9
Diamond Harbour, *India* 69 H13
Diamond Is., *Australia* 94 B5
Diamond Mts., *U.S.A.* 114 G6
Diamond Springs, *U.S.A.* 116 G6
Dian Chi, *China* 58 E4
Dianalund, *Denmark* 11 J5
Dianbai, *China* 59 G8
Diancheng, *China* 59 G8
Dianjiang, *China* 58 B6
Diano Marina, *Italy* 28 E5
Dianra, *Ivory C.* 82 D3
Diapaga, *Burkina Faso* 83 C5
Diapangou, *Burkina Faso* 83 C5
Diariguila, *Guinea* 82 C2
Dībā, *Oman* 71 E8
Dibai, *India* 68 E8
Dibaya-Lubue, *Dem. Rep. of the Congo* 84 E3
Dibete, *Botswana* 88 C4
Dibrugarh, *India* 67 F19
Dickens, *U.S.A.* 113 J4
Dickinson, *U.S.A.* 112 B3
Dickson = Dikson, *Russia* 50 B9
Dickson, *U.S.A.* 109 G2
Dickson City, *U.S.A.* 111 E9
Dicle Nehri →, *Turkey* 73 D9
Dicomano, *Italy* 29 E8
Didesa, W. →, *Ethiopia* 81 E4
Didi, *Sudan* 81 F3
Didiéni, *Mali* 82 C3
Didsbury, *Canada* 104 C6
Didwana, *India* 68 F6
Die, *France* 21 D9
Diébougou, *Burkina Faso* 82 C4
Diecke, *Guinea* 82 D3
Diefenbaker, L., *Canada* 105 C7
Diego de Almagro, *Chile* 126 B1
Diego Garcia, *Ind. Oc.* 3 E13
Diekirch, *Lux.* 17 E6
Diéma, *Mali* 82 C3
Diembéring, *Senegal* 82 C1
Dien Ban, *Vietnam* 64 E7
Dien Bien, *Vietnam* 58 G4
Dien Khanh, *Vietnam* 65 F7
Diepholz, *Germany* 24 C4
Dieppe, *France* 18 C8
Dierks, *U.S.A.* 113 H8
Diest, *Belgium* 17 D5
Dietikon, *Switz.* 25 H4
Dieulefit, *France* 21 D9
Dieuze, *France* 19 D13
Dif, *Somali Rep.* 74 G3
Differdange, *Lux.* 17 E5
Dig, *India* 68 F7
Digba, *Dem. Rep. of the Congo* 86 B2
Digby, *Canada* 103 D6
Diggi, *India* 68 F6
Dighinala, *Bangla.* 67 H18
Dighton, *U.S.A.* 112 F4
Digna, *Mali* 82 C3
Digne-les-Bains, *France* 21 D10
Digoin, *France* 19 F11
Digor, *Turkey* 73 B10
Digos, *Phil.* 61 H6
Digranes, *Iceland* 8 C6
Digul →, *Indonesia* 63 F9
Dihang →, *India* 67 F19
Dijlah, Nahr →, *Asia* 70 D5
Dijon, *France* 19 E12
Dikhil, *Djibouti* 81 E5
Dikili, *Turkey* 39 B8
Dikirnis, *Egypt* 80 H7
Dikkil = Dikhil, *Djibouti* 81 E5
Dikodougou, *Ivory C.* 82 D3
Diksmuide, *Belgium* 17 C2
Dikson, *Russia* 50 B9
Dikwa, *Nigeria* 83 C7
Dila, *Ethiopia* 81 F4
Dili, *E. Timor* 63 F7
Dilijan, *Armenia* 49 K7
Dilizhan = Dilijan, *Armenia* 49 K7
Dilj, *Croatia* 42 E3
Dillenburg, *Germany* 24 E4
Dilley, *U.S.A.* 113 L5
Dilling, *Sudan* 81 E2
Dillingen, *Bayern, Germany* 25 G6
Dillingen, *Saarland, Germany* 25 F2
Dillingham, *U.S.A.* 100 C4
Dillon, *Canada* 105 B7
Dillon, *Mont., U.S.A.* 114 D7
Dillon, *S.C., U.S.A.* 109 H6
Dillon →, *Canada* 105 B7
Dillsburg, *U.S.A.* 110 F7
Dilly, *Mali* 82 C3
Dilolo, *Dem. Rep. of the Congo* 84 G4
Dimas, *Mexico* 118 C3
Dimashq, *Syria* 75 B5
Dimashq □, *Syria* 75 B5
Dimbaza, *S. Africa* 89 E4
Dimbokro, *Ivory C.* 82 D4
Dimboola, *Australia* 95 F3
Dîmbovița = Dâmbovița →, *Romania* 43 F11
Dimbulah, *Australia* 94 B4
Dimitrovgrad, *Bulgaria* 41 D9
Dimitrovgrad, *Russia* 48 C9
Dimitrovgrad, *Serbia, Yug.* 40 C6
Dimitrovo = Pernik, *Bulgaria* 40 D7
Dimmitt, *U.S.A.* 113 H3
Dimo, *Sudan* 81 F2
Dimona, *Israel* 75 D4
Dimovo, *Bulgaria* 40 C6
Dinagat, *Phil.* 61 F6
Dinajpur, *Bangla.* 67 G16
Dinan, *France* 18 D4
Dīnān Āb, *Iran* 71 C8
Dinant, *Belgium* 17 D4
Dinapur, *India* 69 G11
Dinar, *Turkey* 39 C12
Dīnār, Kūh-e, *Iran* 71 D6
Dinara Planina, *Croatia* 29 D13
Dinard, *France* 18 D4
Dinaric Alps = Dinara Planina, *Croatia* 29 D13
Dindanko, *Mali* 82 C3
Dinder, Nahr ed →, *Sudan* 81 E3
Dindigul, *India* 66 P11
Dindori, *India* 69 H9
Ding Xian = Dingzhou, *China* 56 E8
Dinga, *Pakistan* 68 G2
Dingalan, *Phil.* 61 D4
Dingbian, *China* 56 F4
Dingelstädt, *Germany* 24 D6
Dingle, *Ireland* 15 D1
Dingle, *Sweden* 11 F5
Dingle B., *Ireland* 15 D1
Dingmans Ferry, *U.S.A.* 111 E10
Dingnan, *China* 59 E10
Dingo, *Australia* 94 C4
Dingolfing, *Germany* 25 G8
Dingtao, *China* 56 G8
Dinguira, *Mali* 82 C2
Dinguiraye, *Guinea* 82 C2
Dingwall, *U.K.* 14 D4
Dingxi, *China* 56 G3
Dingxiang, *China* 56 E7
Dingyuan, *China* 59 A11
Dingzhou, *China* 56 E8
Dinh, Mui, *Vietnam* 65 G7
Dinh Lap, *Vietnam* 58 G6
Dinokwe, *Botswana* 88 C4
Dinorwic, *Canada* 105 D10
Dinosaur National Monument, *U.S.A.* 114 F9
Dinosaur Prov. Park, *Canada* 104 C6
Dinuba, *U.S.A.* 116 J7
Diö, *Sweden* 11 H8
Dioïla, *Mali* 82 C3
Dioka, *Mali* 82 C2
Diongoï, *Mali* 82 C3
Diósgyör, *Hungary* 42 B5
Diosig, *Romania* 42 C7
Diougani, *Mali* 82 C4
Diouloulou, *Senegal* 82 C1
Dioura, *Mali* 82 C3
Diourbel, *Senegal* 82 C1
Dipalpur, *Pakistan* 68 D5
Diplo, *Pakistan* 68 G3
Dipolog, *Phil.* 61 G5
Dir, *Pakistan* 66 B7
Diré, *Mali* 82 B4
Dire Dawa, *Ethiopia* 81 F5
Diriamba, *Nic.* 120 D2
Dirk Hartog I., *Australia* 93 E1
Dirranbandi, *Australia* 95 D4
Disa, *India* 68 G5
Disa, *Sudan* 81 E3
Disappointment, C., *U.S.A.* 114 C2
Disappointment, L., *Australia* 92 D3
Disaster B., *Australia* 95 F4
Discovery B., *Australia* 95 F3
Disentis Muster, *Switz.* 25 J4
Dishna, *Egypt* 80 B3
Disina, *Nigeria* 83 C6
Disko = Qeqertarsuaq, *Greenland* 101 B5
Disko Bugt, *Greenland* 4 C5
Disna = Dzisna →, *Belarus* 46 E5
Diss, *U.K.* 13 E9
Disteghil Sar, *Pakistan* 69 A6
Distrito Federal □, *Brazil* 125 G9
Distrito Federal □, *Mexico* 119 D5
Disûq, *Egypt* 80 H7
Diu, *India* 68 J4
Dīvāndarreh, *Iran* 70 C5
Dives →, *France* 18 C6
Dives-sur-Mer, *France* 18 C6
Divichi = Däväçi, *Azerbaijan* 49 K9
Divide, *U.S.A.* 114 D7
Dividing Ra., *Australia* 93 E2
Divinópolis, *Brazil* 125 H10
Divjake, *Albania* 40 F3
Divnoye, *Russia* 49 H6
Divo, *Ivory C.* 82 D3
Divriği, *Turkey* 73 C8
Dīwāl Kol, *Afghan.* 68 B2
Dixie Mt., *U.S.A.* 116 F6
Dixon, *Calif., U.S.A.* 116 G5
Dixon, *Ill., U.S.A.* 112 E10
Dixon Entrance, *U.S.A.* 100 C6
Dixville, *Canada* 111 A13
Diyadin, *Turkey* 73 C10
Diyālā →, *Iraq* 70 C5
Diyarbakır, *Turkey* 70 B4
Diyodar, *India* 68 G4
Djakarta = Jakarta, *Indonesia* 62 F3
Djamba, *Angola* 88 B1
Djambala, *Congo* 84 E2
Djanet, *Algeria* 78 D7
Djawa = Jawa, *Indonesia* 62 F3
Djelfa, *Algeria* 78 B6
Djema, *C.A.R.* 86 A2
Djenné, *Mali* 82 C4
Djerba, I. de, *Tunisia* 79 B8
Djerid, Chott, *Tunisia* 78 B7
Djibo, *Burkina Faso* 83 C4
Djibouti, *Djibouti* 81 E5
Djibouti ■, *Africa* 81 E5
Djolu, *Dem. Rep. of the Congo* 84 D4
Djougou, *Benin* 83 D5
Djoum, *Cameroon* 84 D2
Djourab, Erg du, *Chad* 79 E9
Djugu, *Dem. Rep. of the Congo* 86 B3
Djúpivogur, *Iceland* 8 D6
Djurås, *Sweden* 10 D9
Djursland, *Denmark* 11 H4
Dmitriya Lapteva, Proliv, *Russia* 51 B15
Dmitriyev Lgovskiy, *Russia* 47 F8
Dmitrov, *Russia* 46 D9
Dmitrovsk-Orlovskiy, *Russia* 47 F8
Dnepr → = Dnipro →, *Ukraine* 47 J7
Dneprodzerzhinsk = Dniprodzerzhynsk, *Ukraine* 47 H8
Dneprodzerzhinskoye Vdkhr. = Dniprodzerzhynske Vdskh., *Ukraine* 47 H8
Dnepropetrovsk = Dnipropetrovsk, *Ukraine* 47 H8
Dneprorudnoye = Dniprorudne, *Ukraine* 47 J8
Dnestr → = Dnister →, *Europe* 47 J6
Dnestrovski = Belgorod, *Russia* 47 G9
Dnieper = Dnipro →, *Ukraine* 47 J7
Dniester = Dnister →, *Europe* 47 J6
Dnipro →, *Ukraine* 47 J7
Dniprodzerzhynsk, *Ukraine* 47 H8
Dniprodzerzhynske Vdskh., *Ukraine* 47 H8
Dnipropetrovsk, *Ukraine* 47 H8
Dniprorudne, *Ukraine* 47 J8
Dnister →, *Europe* 47 J6
Dnistrovskyy Lyman, *Ukraine* 47 J6
Dno, *Russia* 46 D5
Dnyapro = Dnipro →, *Ukraine* 47 J7
Doaktown, *Canada* 103 C6
Doan Hung, *Vietnam* 58 G5
Doany, *Madag.* 89 A8
Doba, *Chad* 79 G9
Dobandi, *Pakistan* 68 D2
Dobbiaco, *Italy* 29 B9
Dobbyn, *Australia* 94 B3
Dobczyce, *Poland* 45 J7
Dobele, *Latvia* 9 H20
Dobele □, *Latvia* 44 B10
Döbeln, *Germany* 24 D9
Doberai, Jazirah, *Indonesia* 63 E8
Dobiegniew, *Poland* 45 F2
Doblas, *Argentina* 126 D3
Dobo, *Indonesia* 63 F8
Doboj, *Bos.-H.* 42 F3
Dobra, *Wielkopolskie, Poland* 45 G5
Dobra, *Zachodnio-Pomorskie, Poland* 44 E2
Dobra, *Dîmbovita, Romania* 43 F10
Dobra, *Hunedoara, Romania* 42 E7
Dobre Miasto, *Poland* 44 E7
Dobreşti, *Romania* 42 D7
Dobrich, *Bulgaria* 41 C11
Dobrinishta, *Bulgaria* 40 E7
Dobříš, *Czech Rep.* 26 B7
Dobrodzień, *Poland* 45 H5
Dobropole, *Ukraine* 47 H9
Dobruja, *Europe* 43 F13
Dobrush, *Belarus* 47 F6
Dobrzany, *Poland* 44 E2
Dobrzyń nad Wisłą, *Poland* 45 F6
Doc, Mui, *Vietnam* 64 D6
Docker River, *Australia* 93 D4
Docksta, *Sweden* 10 A12
Doctor Arroyo, *Mexico* 118 C4
Doda, *India* 69 C6
Doda, L., *Canada* 102 C4
Dodecanese = Dhodhekánisos, *Greece* 39 E8
Dodge City, *U.S.A.* 113 G5
Dodge L., *Canada* 105 B7
Dodgeville, *U.S.A.* 112 D9
Dodo, *Cameroon* 83 D7
Dodo, *Sudan* 81 F2
Dodola, *Ethiopia* 81 F4
Dodoma, *Tanzania* 86 D4
Dodoma □, *Tanzania* 86 D4
Dodona, *Greece* 38 B2
Dodsland, *Canada* 105 C7
Dodson, *U.S.A.* 114 B9
Dodurga, *Turkey* 39 B11
Doesburg, *Neths.* 17 B6
Doetinchem, *Neths.* 17 C6
Dog Creek, *Canada* 104 C4
Dog L., *Man., Canada* 105 C9
Dog L., *Ont., Canada* 102 C2
Doğanşehir, *Turkey* 72 C7
Dogliani, *Italy* 28 D4
Dogondoutchi, *Niger* 83 C5
Dogran, *Pakistan* 68 D5
Doğubayazıt, *Turkey* 70 B5
Doguéraoua, *Niger* 83 C6
Doha = Ad Dawḩah, *Qatar* 71 E6
Dohazari, *Bangla.* 67 H18
Dohrighat, *India* 69 F10
Doi, *Indonesia* 63 D7
Doi Luang, *Thailand* 64 C3
Doi Saket, *Thailand* 64 C2
Dois Irmãos, Sa., *Brazil* 125 E10
Dojransko Jezero, *Macedonia* 40 E6
Dokkum, *Neths.* 17 A5
Dokri, *Pakistan* 68 F3
Dokuchayevsk, *Ukraine* 47 J9
Dol-de-Bretagne, *France* 18 D5
Dolac, *Kosovo, Yug.* 40 D4
Dolak, Pulau, *Indonesia* 63 F9
Dolbeau, *Canada* 103 C5
Dole, *France* 19 E12
Doleib, Wadi →, *Sudan* 81 E3
Dolenji Logatec, *Slovenia* 29 C11
Dolgellau, *U.K.* 12 E4
Dolgelley = Dolgellau, *U.K.* 12 E4
Dolhasca, *Romania* 43 C11
Dolianova, *Italy* 30 C2
Dolinskaya = Dolynska, *Ukraine* 47 H7
Dolj □, *Romania* 43 F8
Dollard, *Neths.* 17 A7
Dolna Banya, *Bulgaria* 40 D7
Dolni Chiflik, *Bulgaria* 41 D11
Dolni Dŭbnik, *Bulgaria* 41 C8
Dolnośląskie □, *Poland* 45 G3
Dolný Kubín, *Slovak Rep.* 27 B12
Dolo, *Ethiopia* 81 G5
Dolo, *Italy* 29 C9
Dolomites = Dolomiti, *Italy* 29 B8
Dolomiti, *Italy* 29 B8
Dolores, *Argentina* 126 D4
Dolores, *Uruguay* 126 C4
Dolores, *U.S.A.* 115 H9
Dolores →, *U.S.A.* 115 G9
Dolovo, *Serbia, Yug.* 42 F5
Dolphin, C., *Falk. Is.* 128 G5
Dolphin and Union Str., *Canada* 100 B8
Dolsk, *Poland* 45 G4
Dolynska, *Ukraine* 47 H7
Dolzhanskaya, *Russia* 47 J9
Dom Pedrito, *Brazil* 127 C5
Doma, *Nigeria* 83 D6
Domaniç, *Turkey* 39 B11
Domariaganj →, *India* 69 F10
Domasi, *Malawi* 87 F4
Domažlice, *Czech Rep.* 26 B5
Dombarovskiy, *Russia* 50 D6
Dombås, *Norway* 9 E13
Dombasle-sur-Meurthe, *France* 19 D13
Dombes, *France* 21 C9
Dombóvár, *Hungary* 42 D3
Dombrád, *Hungary* 42 B6
Domel I. = Letsôk-aw Kyun, *Burma* 65 G2
Domérat, *France* 19 F9
Domeyko, *Chile* 126 B1
Domeyko, Cordillera, *Chile* 126 A2
Domfront, *France* 18 D6
Dominador, *Chile* 126 A2
Dominica ■, *W. Indies* 121 C7
Dominica Passage, *W. Indies* 121 C7
Dominican Rep. ■, *W. Indies* 121 C5
Dömitz, *Germany* 24 B7
Domme, *France* 20 D5
Domneşti, *Romania* 43 E9
Domodóssola, *Italy* 28 B5
Dompaire, *France* 19 D13
Dompierre-sur-Besbre, *France* 19 F10
Dompim, *Ghana* 82 D4
Domrémy-la-Pucelle, *France* 19 D12
Domville, Mt., *Australia* 95 D5
Domvraína, *Greece* 38 C4
Domžale, *Slovenia* 29 B11
Don →, *Russia* 47 J10
Don →, *Aberds., U.K.* 14 D6
Don →, *S. Yorks., U.K.* 12 D7
Don, C., *Australia* 92 B5
Don Benito, *Spain* 35 G5
Dona Ana = Nhamaabué, *Mozam.* 87 F4
Doña Mencía, *Spain* 35 H6
Donaghadee, *U.K.* 15 B6
Donald, *Australia* 95 F3
Donaldsonville, *U.S.A.* 113 K9
Donalsonville, *U.S.A.* 109 K3
Donau = Dunărea →, *Europe* 43 E14
Donau →, *Austria* 17 D3
Donaueschingen, *Germany* 25 H4
Donauwörth, *Germany* 25 G6
Doncaster, *U.K.* 12 D6
Dondo, *Mozam.* 87 F3
Dondo, Teluk, *Indonesia* 63 D6
Dondra Head, *Sri Lanka* 66 S12
Donduşeni, *Moldova* 43 B12
Donegal, *Ireland* 15 B3
Donegal □, *Ireland* 15 B4
Donegal B., *Ireland* 15 B3
Donets →, *Russia* 49 G5
Donetsk, *Ukraine* 47 J9
Dong Ba Thin, *Vietnam* 65 F7
Dong Dang, *Vietnam* 58 G6
Dong Giam, *Vietnam* 64 C5
Dong Ha, *Vietnam* 64 D6
Dong Hene, *Laos* 64 D5
Dong Hoi, *Vietnam* 64 D6
Dong Jiang →, *China* 59 F10
Dong Khe, *Vietnam* 64 A6
Dong Ujimqin Qi, *China* 56 B9
Dong Van, *Vietnam* 64 A5
Dong Xoai, *Vietnam* 65 G6
Donga, *Nigeria* 83 D7
Donga →, *Nigeria* 83 D7
Dong'an, *China* 59 D8
Dongara, *Australia* 93 E1
Dongbei, *China* 57 D13
Dongchuan, *China* 58 D4
Donges, *France* 18 E4
Dongfang, *China* 64 C7
Dongfeng, *China* 57 C13
Donggala, *Indonesia* 63 E5
Donggan, *China* 58 F5
Donggou, *China* 57 E13
Dongguan, *China* 59 F9
Dongguang, *China* 56 F9
Donghai Dao, *China* 59 G8
Dongjingcheng, *China* 57 B15
Dongkou, *China* 59 D8
Donglan, *China* 58 E6
Dongliu, *China* 59 B11
Dongmen, *China* 58 F6
Dongning, *China* 57 B16
Dongnyi, *China* 58 C3
Dongola, *Sudan* 80 D3
Dongping, *China* 56 G9
Dongshan, *China* 59 F11
Dongsheng, *China* 56 E6
Dongtai, *China* 57 H11
Dongting Hu, *China* 59 C9
Dongtou, *China* 59 D13
Dongxiang, *China* 59 C11
Dongxing, *China* 58 G7
Dongyang, *China* 59 C13
Dongzhi, *China* 59 B11
Donington, C., *Australia* 95 E2
Doniphan, *U.S.A.* 113 G9
Donja Stubica, *Croatia* 29 C12
Donji Dušnik, *Serbia, Yug.* 40 C6
Donji Miholjac, *Croatia* 42 E3
Donji Milanovac, *Serbia, Yug.* 40 B6
Donji Vakuf, *Bos.-H.* 42 F2
Dønna, *Norway* 8 C15
Donna, *U.S.A.* 113 M5
Donnaconna, *Canada* 103 C5
Donnelly's Crossing, *N.Z.* 91 F4
Donnybrook, *Australia* 93 F2
Donnybrook, *S. Africa* 89 D4
Donora, *U.S.A.* 110 F5
Donostia = Donostia-San Sebastián, *Spain* 32 B3
Donostia-San Sebastián, *Spain* 32 B3
Donskoy, *Russia* 46 F10
Donsol, *Phil.* 61 E5
Donzère, *France* 21 D8
Donzy, *France* 19 E10
Doon →, *U.K.* 14 F4
Dora, L., *Australia* 92 D3
Dora Báltea →, *Italy* 28 C5
Dora Ripária →, *Italy* 28 C4
Doran L., *Canada* 105 A7
Dorchester, *U.K.* 13 G5
Dorchester, C., *Canada* 101 B12
Dordabis, *Namibia* 88 C2
Dordogne □, *France* 20 C4
Dordogne →, *France* 20 C3
Dordrecht, *Neths.* 17 C4
Dordrecht, *S. Africa* 88 E4
Dore →, *France* 20 C7
Dore, Mts., *France* 20 C6
Doré L., *Canada* 105 C7
Doré Lake, *Canada* 105 C7
Dorfen, *Germany* 25 G8
Dorgali, *Italy* 30 B2
Dori, *Burkina Faso* 83 C4
Doring →, *S. Africa* 88 E2
Doringbos, *S. Africa* 88 E2
Dorion, *Canada* 111 A10
Dormaa-Ahenkro, *Ghana* 82 D4
Dormans, *France* 19 C10
Dormo, Ras, *Eritrea* 81 E5
Dornbirn, *Austria* 26 D2
Dornes, *France* 19 F10
Dorneşti, *Romania* 43 C11
Dornie, *U.K.* 14 D3
Dornoch, *U.K.* 14 D4
Dornoch Firth, *U.K.* 14 D4
Dornogovĭ □, *Mongolia* 56 C6
Doro, *Mali* 83 B4
Dorog, *Hungary* 42 C3
Dorogobuzh, *Russia* 46 E7
Dorohoi, *Romania* 43 C11
Döröö Nuur, *Mongolia* 60 B4
Dorr, *Iran* 71 C6
Dorre I., *Australia* 93 E1
Dorrigo, *Australia* 95 E5
Dorris, *U.S.A.* 114 F3
Dorset, *Canada* 110 A6
Dorset, *U.S.A.* 110 E4
Dorset □, *U.K.* 13 G5
Dorsten, *Germany* 24 D2
Dortmund, *Germany* 24 D3
Dortmund-Ems-Kanal →, *Germany* 24 D3
Dörtyol, *Turkey* 72 D7
Dorum, *Germany* 24 B4
Doruma, *Dem. Rep. of the Congo* 86 B2
Dorūneh, *Iran* 71 C8
Dos Bahías, C., *Argentina* 128 E3
Dos Hermanas, *Spain* 35 H5
Dos Palos, *U.S.A.* 116 J6
Döşemealtı, *Turkey* 39 D12
Dosso, *Niger* 83 C5
Dothan, *U.S.A.* 109 K3
Doty, *U.S.A.* 116 D3
Douai, *France* 19 B10
Douako, *Guinea* 82 D2
Douala, *Cameroon* 83 E6
Douarnenez, *France* 18 D2
Doubabougou, *Mali* 82 C3
Double Island Pt., *Australia* 95 D5
Double Mountain Fork →, *U.S.A.* 113 J4
Doubrava →, *Czech Rep.* 26 A8
Doubs □, *France* 19 E13
Doubs →, *France* 19 F12
Doubtful Sd., *N.Z.* 91 L1
Doubtless B., *N.Z.* 91 F4
Doudeville, *France* 18 C7
Doué-la-Fontaine, *France* 18 E6
Douentza, *Mali* 82 C4
Douglas, *S. Africa* 88 D3
Douglas, *U.K.* 12 C3
Douglas, *Ariz., U.S.A.* 115 L9

**East Stroudsburg**


East Stroudsburg, U.S.A. 111 E9
East Sussex □, U.K. 13 G8
East Tawas, U.S.A. 108 C4
East Timor ■, Asia 63 F7
East Toorale, Australia 95 E4
East Walker →, U.S.A. 116 G7
East Windsor, U.S.A. 111 F10
Eastbourne, N.Z. 91 J5
Eastbourne, U.K. 13 G8
Eastend, Canada 105 D7
Easter I. = Pascua, I. de, Pac. Oc. 97 K17
Eastern □, Ghana 83 D4
Eastern □, Kenya 86 C4
Eastern Cape □, S. Africa 88 E4
Eastern Cr. →, Australia 94 C3
Eastern Ghats, India 66 N11
Eastern Group = Lau Group, Fiji 91 C9
Eastern Group, Australia 93 F3
Eastern Province □, S. Leone 82 D2
Eastern Transvaal = Mpumalanga □, S. Africa 89 B5
Easterville, Canada 105 C9
Easthampton, U.S.A. 111 D12
Eastlake, U.S.A. 110 E3
Eastland, U.S.A. 113 J5
Eastleigh, U.K. 13 G6
Eastmain, Canada 102 B4
Eastmain →, Canada 102 B4
Eastman, Canada 111 A12
Eastman, U.S.A. 109 J4
Easton, Md., U.S.A. 108 F7
Easton, Pa., U.S.A. 111 F9
Easton, Wash., U.S.A. 116 C5
Eastpointe, U.S.A. 110 D2
Eastport, U.S.A. 109 C12
Eastsound, U.S.A. 116 B4
Eaton, U.S.A. 112 E2
Eatonia, Canada 105 C7
Eatonton, U.S.A. 109 J4
Eatontown, U.S.A. 111 F10
Eatonville, U.S.A. 116 D4
Eau Claire, U.S.A. 112 C9
Eau Claire, L. à l', Canada 102 A5
Eauze, France 20 E4
Eban, Nigeria 83 D5
Ebbw Vale, U.K. 13 F4
Ebeltoft, Denmark 11 H4
Ebeltoft Vig, Denmark 11 H4
Ebensburg, U.S.A. 110 F6
Ebensee, Austria 26 D6
Eber Gölü, Turkey 72 C4
Eberbach, Germany 25 F4
Eberswalde-Finow, Germany 24 C9
Ebetsu, Japan 54 C10
Ebian, China 58 C4
Ebingen, Germany 25 G5
Éboli, Italy 31 B8
Ebolowa, Cameroon 83 E7
Ebonyi □, Nigeria 83 D6
Ebrach, Germany 25 F6
Ébrié, Lagune, Ivory C. 82 D4
Ebro →, Spain 32 E5
Ebro, Embalse del, Spain 34 C7
Ebstorf, Germany 24 B6
Eceabat, Turkey 41 F10
Ech Cheliff, Algeria 78 A6
Echigo-Sammyaku, Japan 55 F9
Échirolles, France 21 C9
Echizen-Misaki, Japan 55 G7
Echmiadzin = Yejmiadzin, Armenia 49 K7
Echo Bay, N.W.T., Canada 100 B8
Echo Bay, Ont., Canada 102 C3
Echoing →, Canada 102 B1
Echternach, Lux. 17 E6
Echuca, Australia 95 F3
Ecija, Spain 35 H5
Eckental, Germany 25 F7
Eckernförde, Germany 24 A5
Eclipse Is., Australia 92 B4
Eclipse Sd., Canada 101 A11
Écommoy, France 18 E7
Écouché, France 18 D6
Ecuador ■, S. Amer. 124 D3
Écueillé, France 18 E8
Ed, Sweden 11 F5
Ed Dabbura, Sudan 80 D3
Ed Da'ein, Sudan 81 E2
Ed Damazin, Sudan 79 F12
Ed Dâmer, Sudan 80 D3
Ed Debba, Sudan 80 D3
Ed-Déffa, Egypt 80 A2
Ed Deim, Sudan 81 E2
Ed Dueim, Sudan 81 E3
Edam, Canada 105 C7
Edam, Neths. 17 B5
Edane, Sweden 10 E6
Eday, U.K. 14 B6
Edd, Eritrea 81 E5
Eddrachillis B., U.K. 14 C3
Eddystone Pt., Australia 94 G4
Ede, Neths. 17 B5
Ede, Nigeria 83 D5
Edéa, Cameroon 83 E7
Edebäck, Sweden 10 D7
Edehon L., Canada 105 A9
Edelény, Hungary 42 B5
Eden, Australia 95 F4
Eden, N.C., U.S.A. 109 G6
Eden, N.Y., U.S.A. 110 D6
Eden, Tex., U.S.A. 113 K5
Eden →, U.K. 12 C4
Edenburg, S. Africa 88 D4
Edendale, S. Africa 89 D5
Edenderry, Ireland 15 C4
Edenton, U.S.A. 109 G7
Edenville, S. Africa 89 D4
Eder →, Germany 24 D5
Eder-Stausee, Germany 24 D4
Edewecht, Germany 24 B3
Edgar, U.S.A. 112 E6
Edgartown, U.S.A. 111 E14
Edge Hill, U.K. 13 E6
Edgefield, U.S.A. 109 J5
Edgeley, U.S.A. 112 B5
Edgemont, U.S.A. 112 D3
Edgeøya, Svalbard 4 B9
Édhessa, Greece 40 F6
Edievale, N.Z. 91 L2
Edina, Liberia 82 D2
Edina, U.S.A. 112 E8
Edinboro, U.S.A. 110 E4
Edinburg, U.S.A. 113 M5
Edinburgh, U.K. 14 F5
Edinburgh, City of □, U.K. 14 F5
Edineţ, Moldova 43 B12
Edirne, Turkey 41 E10
Edirne □, Turkey 41 E10
Edison, U.S.A. 116 B4
Edithburgh, Australia 95 F2
Edmeston, U.S.A. 111 D9
Edmond, U.S.A. 113 H6
Edmonds, U.S.A. 116 C4
Edmonton, Australia 94 B4
Edmonton, Canada 104 C6
Edmund L., Canada 102 B1
Edmundston, Canada 103 C6
Edna, U.S.A. 113 L6
Edo □, Nigeria 83 D6
Edolo, Italy 28 B7
Edremit, Turkey 39 B9
Edremit Körfezi, Turkey 39 B8
Edsbro, Sweden 10 E12
Edsbyn, Sweden 10 C9
Edson, Canada 104 C5
Eduardo Castex, Argentina 126 D3
Edward →, Australia 95 F3
Edward, L., Africa 86 C2
Edward River, Australia 94 A3
Edward VII Land, Antarctica 5 E13
Edwards, Calif., U.S.A. 117 L9
Edwards, N.Y., U.S.A. 111 B9
Edwards Air Force Base, U.S.A. 117 L9
Edwards Plateau, U.S.A. 113 K4
Edwardsville, U.S.A. 111 E9
Edzo, Canada 104 A5
Eeklo, Belgium 17 C3
Eferding, Austria 26 C7
Effingham, U.S.A. 108 F1
Eforie, Romania 43 F13
Ega →, Spain 32 C3
Égadi, Ísole, Italy 30 E5
Egan Range, U.S.A. 114 G6
Eganville, Canada 102 C4
Eger = Cheb, Czech Rep. 26 A5
Eger, Hungary 42 C5
Eger →, Hungary 42 C5
Egersund, Norway 9 G12
Egg L., Canada 105 B7
Eggenburg, Austria 26 C8
Eggenfelden, Germany 25 G8
Éghezée, Belgium 17 D4
Égletons, France 20 C6
Egmont, Canada 104 D4
Egmont, C., N.Z. 91 H4
Egmont, Mt. = Taranaki, Mt., N.Z. 91 H5
Egra, India 69 J12
Eğridir, Turkey 72 D4
Eğridir Gölü, Turkey 70 B1
Egtved, Denmark 11 J3
Egume, Nigeria 83 D6
Éguzon-Chantôme, France 19 F8
Egvekinot, Russia 51 C19
Egyek, Hungary 42 C5
Egypt ■, Africa 80 B3
Eha Amufu, Nigeria 83 D6
Ehime □, Japan 55 H6
Ehingen, Germany 25 G5
Ehrenberg, U.S.A. 117 M12
Ehrwald, Austria 26 D3
Eibar, Spain 32 B2
Eichstätt, Germany 25 G7
Eider →, Germany 24 A4
Eidsvold, Australia 95 D5
Eidsvoll, Norway 9 F14
Eifel, Germany 25 E2
Eiffel Flats, Zimbabwe 87 F3
Eiger, Switz. 28 B5
Eigg, U.K. 14 E2
Eighty Mile Beach, Australia 92 C3
Eil, Somali Rep. 74 F4
Eil, L., U.K. 14 E3
Eildon, L., Australia 95 F4
Eilenburg, Germany 24 D8
Ein el Luweiqa, Sudan 81 E3
Einasleigh, Australia 94 B3
Einasleigh →, Australia 94 B3
Einbeck, Germany 24 D5
Eindhoven, Neths. 17 C5
Einsiedeln, Switz. 25 H4
Eire = Ireland ■, Europe 15 C4
Eiríksjökull, Iceland 8 D3
Eirunepé, Brazil 124 E5
Eiseb →, Namibia 88 C2
Eisenach, Germany 24 E6
Eisenberg, Germany 24 E7
Eisenerz, Austria 26 D7
Eisenhüttenstadt, Germany 24 C10
Eisenkappel, Austria 26 E7
Eisenstadt, Austria 27 D9
Eisfeld, Germany 25 E6
Eisleben, Germany 24 D7
Eislingen, Germany 25 G5
Eivissa, Spain 37 C7
Eixe, Serra do, Spain 34 C4
Ejea de los Caballeros, Spain 32 C3
Ejeda, Madag. 89 C7
Ejura, Ghana 83 D4
Ejutla, Mexico 119 D5
Ekalaka, U.S.A. 112 C2
Ekenässjön, Sweden 11 G9
Ekerö, Sweden 10 E11
Eket, Nigeria 83 E6
Eketahuna, N.Z. 91 J5
Ekhínos, Greece 41 E9
Ekibastuz, Kazakstan 50 D8
Ekiti □, Nigeria 83 D6
Ekoli, Dem. Rep. of the Congo 86 C1
Ekoln, Sweden 10 E11
Ekshärad, Sweden 10 D7
Eksjö, Sweden 11 G8
Ekuma →, Namibia 88 B2
Ekwan →, Canada 102 B3
Ekwan Pt., Canada 102 B3
El Aaiún, W. Sahara 78 C3
El Abanico, Chile 126 D1
El Abbasiya, Sudan 81 E3
El 'Agrûd, Egypt 75 E3
El Ait, Sudan 81 E2
El 'Aiyat, Egypt 80 J7
El Alamein, Egypt 80 A2
El 'Aqaba, W. →, Egypt 75 E2
El 'Arag, Egypt 80 B2
El Arahal, Spain 35 H5
El Arīḥā, West Bank 75 D4
El 'Arîsh, Egypt 75 D2
El 'Arîsh, W. →, Egypt 75 D2
El Asnam = Ech Cheliff, Algeria 78 A6
El Astillero, Spain 34 B7
El Badâri, Egypt 80 B3
El Bahrein, Egypt 80 B2
El Ballâs, Egypt 80 B3
El Balyana, Egypt 80 B3
El Baqeir, Sudan 80 D3
El Barco de Ávila, Spain 34 E5
El Barco de Valdeorras = O Barco, Spain 34 C4
El Bauga, Sudan 80 D3
El Bawiti, Egypt 80 B2
El Bayadh, Algeria 78 B6
El Bierzo, Spain 34 C4
El Bluff, Nic. 120 D3
El Bonillo, Spain 33 G2
El Brûk, W. →, Egypt 75 E2
El Buheirat □, Sudan 81 F3
El Burgo de Osma, Spain 32 D1
El Cajon, U.S.A. 117 N10
El Campo, U.S.A. 113 L6
El Centro, U.S.A. 117 N11
El Cerro, Bolivia 124 G6
El Cerro de Andévalo, Spain 35 H4
El Compadre, Mexico 117 N10
El Coronil, Spain 35 H5
El Cuy, Argentina 128 D3
El Cuyo, Mexico 119 C7
El Dab'a, Egypt 80 H6
El Daheir, Egypt 75 D3
El Dátil, Mexico 118 B2
El Deir, Egypt 80 B3
El Dere, Somali Rep. 74 G4
El Descanso, Mexico 117 N10
El Desemboque, Mexico 118 A2
El Dilingat, Egypt 80 H7
El Diviso, Colombia 124 C3
El Djouf, Mauritania 78 D4
El Dorado, Ark., U.S.A. 113 J8
El Dorado, Kans., U.S.A. 113 G6
El Dorado, Venezuela 124 B6
El 'Ein, Sudan 81 D2
El Ejido, Spain 35 J8
El Escorial, Spain 34 E6
El Espinar, Spain 34 D6
El Faiyûm, Egypt 80 J7
El Fâsher, Sudan 81 E2
El Fashn, Egypt 80 J7
El Ferrol = Ferrol, Spain 34 B2
El Fifi, Sudan 81 E2
El Fuerte, Mexico 118 B3
El Ga'a, Sudan 81 E2
El Gal, Somali Rep. 74 E5
El Garef, Sudan 81 E3
El Gebir, Sudan 81 E2
El Gedida, Egypt 80 B2
El Geneina = Al Junaynah, Sudan 79 F10
El Geteina, Sudan 81 E3
El Gezira □, Sudan 81 E3
El Gir, Sudan 80 D2
El Gîza, Egypt 80 J7
El Goléa, Algeria 78 B6
El Grau, Spain 33 G4
El Hagiz, Sudan 81 D4
El Hâi, Egypt 80 J7
El Hammam, Egypt 80 A2
El Hawata, Sudan 81 E3
El Heiz, Egypt 80 B2
El Hideib, Sudan 81 E3
El Hilla, Sudan 81 E2
El 'Idisât, Egypt 80 B3
El Iskandarîya, Egypt 80 H7
El Istiwa'iya, Sudan 79 G11
El Jadida, Morocco 78 B4
El Jardal, Honduras 120 D2
El Jebelein, Sudan 81 E3
El Kab, Sudan 80 D3
El Kabrît, G., Egypt 75 F2
El Kafr el Sharqi, Egypt 80 H7
El Kamlin, Sudan 81 D3
El Karaba, Sudan 80 D3
El Kere, Ethiopia 81 F5
El Khandaq, Sudan 80 D3
El Khârga, Egypt 80 B3
El Khartûm, Sudan 81 D3
El Khartûm □, Sudan 81 D3
El Khartûm Bahrî, Sudan 81 D3
El Kuntilla, Egypt 75 E3
El Laqâwa, Sudan 81 E2
El Laqeita, Egypt 80 B3
El Leh, Ethiopia 81 G4
El Leiya, Sudan 81 D4
El Maestrazgo, Spain 32 E4
El Mafâza, Sudan 81 E3
El Maghra, Egypt 80 A2
El Mahalla el Kubra, Egypt 80 H7
El Mahârîq, Egypt 80 B3
El Maîmûn, Egypt 80 J7
El Maks el Bahari, Egypt 80 C3
El Manshâh, Egypt 80 B3
El Mansûra, Egypt 80 H7
El Manzala, Egypt 80 H7
El Marâgha, Egypt 80 B3
El Masid, Sudan 81 D3
El Masnou, Spain 32 D7
El Matariya, Egypt 80 H8
El Meda, Ethiopia 81 F5
El Medano, Canary Is. 37 F3
El Metemma, Sudan 81 D3
El Milagro, Argentina 126 C2
El Minyâ, Egypt 80 B3
El Monte, U.S.A. 117 L8
El Montseny, Spain 32 D7
El Mreyye, Mauritania 82 B3
El Niybo, Ethiopia 81 G4
El Obeid, Sudan 81 E3
El Odaiya, Sudan 81 E2
El Oro, Mexico 119 D4
El Oued, Algeria 78 B7
El Palmito, Presa, Mexico 118 B3
El Paso, U.S.A. 115 L10
El Paso Robles, U.S.A. 116 K6
El Pedernoso, Spain 33 F2
El Pedroso, Spain 35 H5
El Pobo de Dueñas, Spain 32 E3
El Portal, U.S.A. 116 H7
El Porvenir, Mexico 118 A3
El Prat de Llobregat, Spain 32 D7
El Progreso, Honduras 120 C2
El Pueblito, Mexico 118 B3
El Pueblo, Canary Is. 37 F2
El Puente del Arzobispo, Spain 34 F5
El Puerto de Santa María, Spain 35 J4
El Qâhira, Egypt 80 H7
El Qantara, Egypt 75 E1
El Qasr, Egypt 80 B2
El Qubâbât, Egypt 80 J7
El Quseima, Egypt 75 E3
El Qusîya, Egypt 80 B3
El Râshda, Egypt 80 B2
El Real, Panama 124 B3
El Reno, U.S.A. 113 H6
El Rîdisiya, Egypt 80 C3
El Rio, U.S.A. 117 L7
El Ronquillo, Spain 35 H4
El Roque, Pta., Canary Is. 37 F4
El Rosarito, Mexico 118 B2
El Rubio, Spain 35 H5
El Saff, Egypt 80 J7
El Saheira, W. →, Egypt 75 E2
El Salto, Mexico 118 C3
El Salvador ■, Cent. Amer. 120 D2
El Sauce, Nic. 120 D2
El Saucejo, Spain 35 H5
El Shallal, Egypt 80 C3
El Simbillawein, Egypt 80 H7
El Sueco, Mexico 118 B3
El Suweis, Egypt 80 J8
El Tabbîn, Egypt 80 J7
El Tamarâni, W. →, Egypt 75 E3
El Thamad, Egypt 75 F3
El Tigre, Venezuela 124 B6
El Tîh, Gebal, Egypt 75 F2
El Tîna, Egypt 80 H8
El Tîna, Khalîg, Egypt 75 D1
El Tofo, Chile 126 B1
El Tránsito, Chile 126 B1
El Tûr, Egypt 70 D2
El Turbio, Argentina 128 G2
El Uqsur, Egypt 80 B3
El Venado, Mexico 118 C4
El Vendrell, Spain 32 D6
El Vergel, Mexico 118 B3
El Vigía, Venezuela 124 B4
El Viso del Alcor, Spain 35 H5
El Wabeira, Egypt 75 F2
El Wak, Kenya 86 B5
El Waqf, Egypt 80 B3
El Weguet, Ethiopia 81 F5
El Wuz, Sudan 81 D3
Elafónisos, Greece 38 E4
Élancourt, France 19 D8
Élassa, Greece 39 F8
Elassón, Greece 38 B4
Elat, Israel 75 F3
Eláthia, Greece 38 C4
Elâzığ, Turkey 70 B3
Elba, Italy 28 F7
Elba, U.S.A. 109 K2
Elbasan, Albania 40 E4
Elbe, U.S.A. 116 D4
Elbe →, Europe 24 B4
Elbe-Seitenkanal, Germany 24 C6
Elbert, Mt., U.S.A. 115 G10
Elberton, U.S.A. 109 H4
Elbeuf, France 18 C8
Elbidtan, Turkey 70 B3
Elbing = Elbląg, Poland 44 D6
Elbistan, Turkey 72 C7
Elbląg, Poland 44 D6
Elbow, Canada 105 C7
Elbrus, Asia 49 J6
Elburz Mts. = Alborz, Reshteh-ye Kūhhā-ye, Iran 71 C7
Elche, Spain 33 G4
Elche de la Sierra, Spain 33 G2
Elcho I., Australia 94 A2
Elda, Spain 33 G4
Elde →, Germany 24 B7
Eldon, Mo., U.S.A. 112 F8
Eldon, Wash., U.S.A. 116 C3
Eldora, U.S.A. 112 D8
Eldorado, Argentina 127 B5
Eldorado, Canada 110 B7
Eldorado, Mexico 118 C3
Eldorado, Ill., U.S.A. 108 G1
Eldorado, Tex., U.S.A. 113 K4
Eldorado Springs, U.S.A. 113 G8
Eldoret, Kenya 86 B4
Eldred, U.S.A. 110 E6
Elea, C., Cyprus 36 D13
Eleanora, Pk., Australia 93 F3
Elefantes →, Mozam. 89 C5
Elektrogorsk, Russia 46 E10
Elektrostal, Russia 46 E10
Elele, Nigeria 83 D6
Elena, Bulgaria 41 D9
Elephant Butte Reservoir, U.S.A. 115 K10
Elephant I., Antarctica 5 C18
Eleshnitsa, Bulgaria 40 E7
Eleşkirt, Turkey 73 C10
Eleuthera, Bahamas 120 B4
Elevsís, Greece 38 C5
Elevtheroúpolis, Greece 41 F8
Elgin, Canada 111 B8
Elgin, U.K. 14 D5
Elgin, Ill., U.S.A. 108 D1
Elgin, N. Dak., U.S.A. 112 B4
Elgin, Oreg., U.S.A. 114 D5
Elgin, Tex., U.S.A. 113 K6
Elgoibar, Spain 32 B2
Elgon, Mt., Africa 86 B3
Eliase, Indonesia 63 F8
Elikón, Greece 38 C4
Elim, Namibia 88 B2
Elim, S. Africa 88 E2
Elin Pelin, Bulgaria 40 D7
Elista, Russia 49 G7
Elizabeth, Australia 95 E2
Elizabeth, N.J., U.S.A. 111 F10
Elizabeth, N.J., U.S.A. 111 F10
Elizabeth City, U.S.A. 109 G7
Elizabethton, U.S.A. 109 G4
Elizabethtown, Ky., U.S.A. 108 G3
Elizabethtown, N.Y., U.S.A. 111 B11
Elizabethtown, Pa., U.S.A. 111 F8
Elizondo, Spain 32 B3
Ełk, Poland 44 E9
Elk →, Canada 104 C5
Ełk →, Poland 44 E9
Elk →, U.S.A. 109 H2
Elk City, U.S.A. 113 H5
Elk Creek, U.S.A. 116 F4
Elk Grove, U.S.A. 116 G5
Elk Island Nat. Park, Canada 104 C6
Elk Lake, Canada 102 C3
Elk Point, Canada 105 C6
Elk River, Idaho, U.S.A. 114 C5
Elk River, Minn., U.S.A. 112 C8
Elkedra →, Australia 94 C2
Elkhart, Ind., U.S.A. 108 E3
Elkhart, Kans., U.S.A. 113 G4
Elkhorn, Canada 105 D8
Elkhorn →, U.S.A. 112 E6
Elkhovo, Bulgaria 41 D10
Elkin, U.S.A. 109 G5
Elkins, U.S.A. 108 F6
Elkland, U.S.A. 110 E7
Elko, Canada 104 D5
Elko, U.S.A. 114 F6
Elkton, U.S.A. 110 C1
Ell, L., Australia 93 E4
Ellef Ringnes I., Canada 4 B2
Ellen, Mt., U.S.A. 111 B12
Ellenburg, U.S.A. 111 B11
Ellendale, U.S.A. 112 B5
Ellensburg, U.S.A. 114 C3
Ellenville, U.S.A. 111 E10
Ellery, Mt., Australia 95 F4
Ellesmere, L., N.Z. 91 M4
Ellesmere I., Canada 4 B4
Ellesmere Port, U.K. 12 D5
Ellice Is. = Tuvalu ■, Pac. Oc. 96 H9
Ellicottville, U.S.A. 110 D6
Elliot, Australia 94 B1
Elliot, S. Africa 89 E4
Elliot Lake, Canada 102 C3
Elliotdale = Xhora, S. Africa 89 E4
Ellis, U.S.A. 112 F5
Elliston, Australia 95 E1
Ellisville, U.S.A. 113 K10
Ellon, U.K. 14 D6
Ellore = Eluru, India 67 L12
Ellsworth, Kans., U.S.A. 112 F5
Ellsworth, Maine, U.S.A. 109 C11
Ellsworth Land, Antarctica 5 D16
Ellsworth Mts., Antarctica 5 D16
Ellwangen, Germany 25 G6
Ellwood City, U.S.A. 110 F4
Elm, Switz. 25 J5
Elma, Canada 105 D9
Elma, U.S.A. 116 D3
Elmadağ, Turkey 72 C5

Evergreen


Evergreen, *Mont., U.S.A.* 114 B6
Everöd, *Sweden* 11 J8
Evertsberg, *Sweden* 10 C7
Evesham, *U.K.* 13 E6
Évian-les-Bains, *France* 19 F13
Évinos →, *Greece* 38 C3
Évisa, *France* 21 F12
Evje, *Norway* 9 G12
Évora, *Portugal* 35 G3
Évora □, *Portugal* 35 G3
Evowghlī, *Iran* 70 B5
Évreux, *France* 18 C8
Evritanía □, *Greece* 38 B3
Évron, *France* 18 D6
Évros □, *Greece* 41 E10
Évros →, *Greece* 72 B2
Evrótas →, *Greece* 38 E4
Évry, *France* 19 D9
Évvoia, *Greece* 38 C6
Évvoia □, *Greece* 38 C5
Evxinoúpolis, *Greece* 38 B4
Ewe, L., *U.K.* 14 D3
Ewing, *U.S.A.* 112 D5
Ewo, *Congo* 84 E2
Exaltación, *Bolivia* 124 F5
Excelsior Springs, *U.S.A.* 112 F7
Excideuil, *France* 20 C5
Exe →, *U.K.* 13 G4
Exeter, *Canada* 110 C3
Exeter, *U.K.* 13 G4
Exeter, *Calif., U.S.A.* 116 J7
Exeter, *N.H., U.S.A.* 111 D14
Exmoor, *U.K.* 13 F4
Exmouth, *Australia* 92 D1
Exmouth, *U.K.* 13 G4
Exmouth G., *Australia* 92 D1
Expedition Ra., *Australia* 94 C4
Extremadura □, *Spain* 35 F4
Exuma Sound, *Bahamas* 120 B4
Eyasi, L., *Tanzania* 86 C4
Eye Pen., *U.K.* 14 C2
Eyemouth, *U.K.* 14 F6
Eygurande, *France* 19 G9
Eyjafjörður, *Iceland* 8 C4
Eymet, *France* 20 D4
Eymoutiers, *France* 20 C5
Eynesil, *Turkey* 73 B8
Eyre (North), L., *Australia* 95 D2
Eyre (South), L., *Australia* 95 D2
Eyre Mts., *N.Z.* 91 L2
Eyre Pen., *Australia* 95 E2
Eysturoy, *Færoe Is.* 8 E9
Eyvānkī, *Iran* 71 C6
Ez Zeidab, *Sudan* 80 D3
Ezcaray, *Spain* 32 C1
Ežerėlis, *Lithuania* 44 D10
Ezhou, *China* 59 B10
Ezine, *Turkey* 39 B8
Ezouza →, *Cyprus* 36 E11


# F


F.Y.R.O.M. = Macedonia ■, *Europe* 40 E5
Fabala, *Guinea* 82 D3
Fabens, *U.S.A.* 115 L10
Fabero, *Spain* 34 C4
Fåborg, *Denmark* 11 J4
Fabriano, *Italy* 29 E9
Făcăeni, *Romania* 43 F12
Fachi, *Niger* 79 E8
Fada, *Chad* 79 E10
Fada-n-Gourma, *Burkina Faso* 83 C5
Fadd, *Hungary* 42 D3
Faddeyevskiy, Ostrov, *Russia* 51 B15
Faddor, *Sudan* 81 F3
Fadghāmī, *Syria* 70 C4
Fadlab, *Sudan* 80 D3
Faenza, *Italy* 29 D8
Færoe Is. = Føroyar, *Atl. Oc.* 8 F9
Fafa, *Mali* 83 B5
Fafe, *Portugal* 34 D2
Fagam, *Nigeria* 83 C7
Făgăras, *Romania* 43 E9
Făgăras, Munţii, *Romania* 43 E9
Fågelmara, *Sweden* 11 H9
Fagerhult, *Sweden* 11 G9
Fagersta, *Sweden* 10 D9
Făget, *Romania* 42 E7
Făget, Munţii, *Romania* 43 C8
Fagnano, L., *Argentina* 128 G3
Fagnières, *France* 19 D11
Faguibine, L., *Mali* 82 B4
Fahlīān, *Iran* 71 D6
Fahraj, *Kermān, Iran* 71 D8
Fahraj, *Yazd, Iran* 71 D7
Fai Tsi Long Archipelago, *Vietnam* 58 G6
Faial, *Madeira* 37 D3
Fair Haven, *U.S.A.* 108 D9
Fair Hd., *U.K.* 15 A5
Fair Oaks, *U.S.A.* 116 G5
Fairbanks, *U.S.A.* 100 B5
Fairbury, *U.S.A.* 112 E6
Fairfax, *U.S.A.* 111 B11
Fairfield, *Ala., U.S.A.* 109 J2
Fairfield, *Calif., U.S.A.* 116 G4
Fairfield, *Conn., U.S.A.* 111 E11
Fairfield, *Idaho, U.S.A.* 114 E6
Fairfield, *Ill., U.S.A.* 108 F1
Fairfield, *Iowa, U.S.A.* 112 E9
Fairfield, *Tex., U.S.A.* 113 K7
Fairford, *Canada* 105 C9
Fairhope, *U.S.A.* 109 K2
Fairlie, *N.Z.* 91 L3
Fairmead, *U.S.A.* 116 H6
Fairmont, *Minn., U.S.A.* 112 D7
Fairmont, *W. Va., U.S.A.* 108 F5
Fairmount, *Calif., U.S.A.* 117 L8
Fairmount, *N.Y., U.S.A.* 111 C8
Fairplay, *U.S.A.* 115 G11
Fairport, *U.S.A.* 110 C7
Fairport Harbor, *U.S.A.* 110 E3
Fairview, *Canada* 104 B5
Fairview, *Mont., U.S.A.* 112 B2
Fairview, *Okla., U.S.A.* 113 G5
Fairweather, Mt., *U.S.A.* 104 B1
Faisalabad, *Pakistan* 68 D5
Faith, *U.S.A.* 112 C3
Faizabad, *India* 69 F10
Fajardo, *Puerto Rico* 121 C6
Fajr, W. →, *Si. Arabia* 70 D3
Fakenham, *U.K.* 12 E8
Fåker, *Sweden* 10 A8
Fakfak, *Indonesia* 63 E8
Fakiya, *Bulgaria* 41 D11
Fakobli, *Ivory C.* 82 D3
Fakse, *Denmark* 11 J6
Fakse Bugt, *Denmark* 11 J6
Fakse Ladeplads, *Denmark* 11 J6
Faku, *China* 57 C12
Falaba, *S. Leone* 82 D2
Falaise, *France* 18 D6
Falaise, Mui, *Vietnam* 64 C5
Falakrón Óros, *Greece* 40 E7
Falam, *Burma* 67 H18
Falces, *Spain* 32 C3
Fălciu, *Romania* 43 D13
Falcó, C. des, *Spain* 37 C7
Falcón, Presa, *Mexico* 119 B5
Falcon Lake, *Canada* 105 D9
Falcon Reservoir, *U.S.A.* 113 M5
Falconara Marittima, *Italy* 29 E10
Falcone, C. del, *Italy* 30 B1
Falconer, *U.S.A.* 110 D5
Faléa, *Mali* 82 C2
Falémé →, *Senegal* 82 C2
Falerum, *Sweden* 11 F10
Faleshty = Făleşti, *Moldova* 43 C12
Făleşti, *Moldova* 43 C12
Falfurrias, *U.S.A.* 113 M5
Falher, *Canada* 104 B5
Falirakí, *Greece* 36 C10
Falkenberg, *Germany* 24 D9
Falkenberg, *Sweden* 11 H6
Falkensee, *Germany* 24 C9
Falkirk, *U.K.* 14 F5
Falkirk □, *U.K.* 14 F5
Falkland, *U.K.* 14 E5
Falkland Is. □, *Atl. Oc.* 128 G5
Falkland Sd., *Falk. Is.* 128 G5
Falkonéra, *Greece* 38 E5
Falköping, *Sweden* 11 F7
Fall River, *U.S.A.* 111 E13
Fallbrook, *U.S.A.* 117 M9
Fallon, *U.S.A.* 114 G4
Falls City, *U.S.A.* 112 E7
Falls Creek, *U.S.A.* 110 E6
Falmouth, *Jamaica* 120 C4
Falmouth, *U.K.* 13 G2
Falmouth, *U.S.A.* 111 E14
Falsa, Pta., *Mexico* 118 B1
False B., *S. Africa* 88 E2
Falso, C., *Honduras* 120 C3
Falster, *Denmark* 11 K5
Falsterbo, *Sweden* 9 J15
Fălticeni, *Romania* 43 C11
Falun, *Sweden* 10 D9
Famagusta, *Cyprus* 36 D12
Famagusta Bay, *Cyprus* 36 D13
Famalé, *Niger* 78 F6
Famatina, Sierra de, *Argentina* 126 B2
Family L., *Canada* 105 C9
Famoso, *U.S.A.* 117 K7
Fan Xian, *China* 56 G8
Fana, *Mali* 82 C3
Fanad Hd., *Ireland* 15 A4
Fanárion, *Greece* 38 B3
Fandriana, *Madag.* 89 C8
Fang, *Thailand* 58 H2
Fang Xian, *China* 59 A8
Fangaga, *Sudan* 80 D4
Fangak, *Sudan* 81 F3
Fangchang, *China* 59 B12
Fangcheng, *China* 56 H7
Fangchenggang, *China* 58 G7
Fangliao, *Taiwan* 59 F13
Fangshan, *China* 56 E6
Fangzi, *China* 57 F10
Fani i Madh →, *Albania* 40 E4
Fanjakana, *Madag.* 89 C8
Fanjiatun, *China* 57 C13
Fannich, L., *U.K.* 14 D4
Fannūj, *Iran* 71 E8
Fanø, *Denmark* 11 J2
Fano, *Italy* 29 E10
Fanshi, *China* 56 E7
Fao = Al Fāw, *Iraq* 71 D6
Faqirwali, *Pakistan* 68 E5
Fâqûs, *Egypt* 80 H7
Fara in Sabina, *Italy* 29 F9
Faradje, *Dem. Rep. of the Congo* 86 B2
Farafangana, *Madag.* 89 C8
Farâfra, El Wâhât el-, *Egypt* 80 B2
Farāh, *Afghan.* 66 C3
Farāh □, *Afghan.* 66 C3
Farahalana, *Madag.* 89 A9
Faraid, Gebel, *Egypt* 80 C4
Farako, *Ivory C.* 82 D4
Faramana, *Burkina Faso* 82 C4
Faranah, *Guinea* 82 C2
Farasān, Jazā'ir, *Si. Arabia* 74 D3
Farasan Is. = Farasān, Jazā'ir, *Si. Arabia* 74 D3
Faratsiho, *Madag.* 89 B8
Fardes →, *Spain* 35 H7
Fareham, *U.K.* 13 G6
Farewell, C., *N.Z.* 91 J4
Farewell C. = Nunap Isua, *Greenland* 101 C15
Färgelanda, *Sweden* 11 F5
Farghona, *Uzbekistan* 50 E8
Fargo, *U.S.A.* 112 B6
Fār'iah, W. al →, *West Bank* 75 C4
Faribault, *U.S.A.* 112 C8
Faridabad, *India* 68 E6
Faridkot, *India* 68 D6
Faridpur, *Bangla.* 69 H13
Faridpur, *India* 69 E8
Färila, *Sweden* 10 C9
Farim, *Guinea-Biss.* 82 C1
Farīmān, *Iran* 71 C8
Farina, *Australia* 95 E2
Fariones, Pta., *Canary Is.* 37 E6
Fâriskûr, *Egypt* 80 H7
Färjestaden, *Sweden* 11 H10
Farkadhón, *Greece* 38 B4
Farmakonisi, *Greece* 39 D9
Farmerville, *U.S.A.* 113 J8
Farmingdale, *U.S.A.* 111 F10
Farmington, *Canada* 104 B4
Farmington, *Calif., U.S.A.* 116 H6
Farmington, *Maine, U.S.A.* 109 C10
Farmington, *Mo., U.S.A.* 113 G9
Farmington, *N.H., U.S.A.* 111 C13
Farmington, *N. Mex., U.S.A.* 115 H9
Farmington, *Utah, U.S.A.* 114 F8
Farmington →, *U.S.A.* 111 E12
Farmville, *U.S.A.* 108 G6
Färnäs, *Sweden* 10 D8
Farne Is., *U.K.* 12 B6
Farnham, *Canada* 111 A12
Farnham, Mt., *Canada* 104 C5
Faro, *Brazil* 125 D7
Faro, *Canada* 100 B6
Faro, *Portugal* 35 H3
Fårö, *Sweden* 9 H18
Faro □, *Portugal* 35 H2
Fårösund, *Sweden* 11 G13
Farquhar, C., *Australia* 93 D1
Farrars Cr. →, *Australia* 94 D3
Farrāshband, *Iran* 71 D7
Farrell, *U.S.A.* 110 E4
Farrokhī, *Iran* 71 C8
Farruch, C. = Ferrutx, C., *Spain* 37 B10
Fārs □, *Iran* 71 D7
Fársala, *Greece* 38 B4
Farsø, *Denmark* 11 H3
Farson, *U.S.A.* 114 E9
Farsund, *Norway* 9 G12
Fartak, Râs, *Si. Arabia* 70 D2
Fartak, Ra's, *Yemen* 74 D5
Fărţăneşti, *Romania* 43 E12
Fartura, Serra da, *Brazil* 127 B5
Faru, *Nigeria* 83 C6
Farūj, *Iran* 71 B8
Fårup, *Denmark* 11 H3
Farvel, Kap = Nunap Isua, *Greenland* 101 C15
Farwell, *U.S.A.* 113 H3
Fāryāb □, *Afghan.* 66 B4
Fasā, *Iran* 71 D7
Fasano, *Italy* 31 B10
Fashoda, *Sudan* 81 F3
Fassa, *Mali* 82 C3
Fastiv, *Ukraine* 47 G5
Fastov = Fastiv, *Ukraine* 47 G5
Fatagar, Tanjung, *Indonesia* 63 E8
Fatehabad, *Haryana, India* 68 E6
Fatehabad, *Ut. P., India* 68 F8
Fatehgarh, *India* 69 F8
Fatehpur, *Bihar, India* 69 G11
Fatehpur, *Raj., India* 68 F6
Fatehpur, *Ut. P., India* 69 G9
Fatehpur, *Ut. P., India* 69 F9
Fatehpur Sikri, *India* 68 F6
Fatesh, *Russia* 47 F8
Fathai, *Sudan* 81 F3
Fatick, *Senegal* 82 C1
Fatima, *Canada* 103 C7
Fátima, *Portugal* 35 F2
Fatoya, *Guinea* 82 C3
Fatsa, *Turkey* 72 B7
Faucille, Col de la, *France* 19 F13
Faulkton, *U.S.A.* 112 C5
Faulquemont, *France* 19 C13
Faure I., *Australia* 93 E1
Făurei, *Romania* 43 E12
Fauresmith, *S. Africa* 88 D4
Fauske, *Norway* 8 C16
Favara, *Italy* 30 E6
Faváritx, C. de, *Spain* 37 B11
Faverges, *France* 21 C10
Favignana, *Italy* 30 E5
Favignana, I., *Italy* 30 E5
Fawcett, Pt., *Australia* 92 B5
Fawn →, *Canada* 102 A2
Fawnskin, *U.S.A.* 117 L10
Faxaflói, *Iceland* 8 D2
Faxälven →, *Sweden* 10 A10
Faya-Largeau, *Chad* 79 E9
Fayd, *Si. Arabia* 70 E4
Fayence, *France* 21 E10
Fayette, *Ala., U.S.A.* 109 J2
Fayette, *Mo., U.S.A.* 112 F8
Fayetteville, *Ark., U.S.A.* 113 G7
Fayetteville, *N.C., U.S.A.* 109 H6
Fayetteville, *Tenn., U.S.A.* 109 H2
Fayied, *Egypt* 80 H8
Fayón, *Spain* 32 D5
Fazilka, *India* 68 D6
Fazilpur, *Pakistan* 68 E4
Fdérik, *Mauritania* 78 D3
Feale →, *Ireland* 15 D2
Fear, C., *U.S.A.* 109 J7
Feather →, *U.S.A.* 114 G3
Feather Falls, *U.S.A.* 116 F5
Featherston, *N.Z.* 91 J5
Featherstone, *Zimbabwe* 87 F3
Fécamp, *France* 18 C7
Fedala = Mohammedia, *Morocco* 78 B4
Federación, *Argentina* 126 C4
Féderal, *Argentina* 128 C5
Federal Capital Terr. □, *Nigeria* 83 D6
Federal Way, *U.S.A.* 116 C4
Fedeshkūh, *Iran* 71 D7
Fehérgyarmat, *Hungary* 42 C7
Fehmarn, *Germany* 24 A7
Fehmarn Bælt, *Europe* 11 K5
Fehmarn Belt = Fehmarn Bælt, *Europe* 11 K5
Fei Xian, *China* 57 G9
Feijó, *Brazil* 124 E4
Feilding, *N.Z.* 91 J5
Feira de Santana, *Brazil* 125 F11
Feixi, *China* 59 B11
Feixiang, *China* 56 F8
Fejér □, *Hungary* 42 C3
Fejø, *Denmark* 11 K5
Feke, *Turkey* 72 D6
Fekete →, *Hungary* 42 E3
Felanitx, *Spain* 37 B10
Feldbach, *Austria* 26 E8
Feldberg, *Baden-W., Germany* 25 H3
Feldberg, *Mecklenburg-Vorpommern, Germany* 24 B9
Feldkirch, *Austria* 26 D2
Feldkirchen, *Austria* 26 E7
Felipe Carrillo Puerto, *Mexico* 119 D7
Felixburg, *Zimbabwe* 89 B5
Felixstowe, *U.K.* 13 F9
Felletin, *France* 20 C6
Fellingsbro, *Sweden* 10 E9
Felton, *U.S.A.* 116 H4
Feltre, *Italy* 29 B8
Femer Bælt = Fehmarn Bælt, *Europe* 11 K5
Femø, *Denmark* 11 K5
Femunden, *Norway* 9 E14
Fen He →, *China* 56 G6
Fene, *Spain* 34 B2
Fenelon Falls, *Canada* 110 B6
Fener Burnu, *Turkey* 39 E9
Feneroa, *Ethiopia* 81 E4
Feng Xian, *Jiangsu, China* 56 G9
Feng Xian, *Shaanxi, China* 56 H4
Fengári, *Greece* 41 F9
Fengcheng, *Jiangxi, China* 59 C10
Fengcheng, *Liaoning, China* 57 D13
Fengfeng, *China* 56 F8
Fenggang, *China* 58 D6
Fenghua, *China* 59 C13
Fenghuang, *China* 58 D7
Fengkai, *China* 59 F8
Fengkang, *Taiwan* 59 F13
Fengle, *China* 59 B9
Fenglin, *Taiwan* 59 F13
Fengning, *China* 56 D9
Fengqing, *China* 58 E2
Fengqiu, *China* 56 G8
Fengrun, *China* 57 E10
Fengshan, *Guangxi Zhuangzu, China* 58 E7
Fengshan, *Guangxi Zhuangzu, China* 58 E6
Fengshan, *Taiwan* 59 F13
Fengshun, *China* 59 F11
Fengtai, *Anhui, China* 59 A11
Fengtai, *Beijing, China* 56 E9
Fengxian, *China* 59 B13
Fengxiang, *China* 56 G4
Fengxin, *China* 59 C10
Fengyang, *China* 57 H9
Fengyi, *China* 58 E3
Fengyüan, *Taiwan* 59 E13
Fengzhen, *China* 56 D7
Feno, C. de, *France* 21 G12
Fenoarivo, *Fianarantsoa, Madag.* 89 C8
Fenoarivo, *Fianarantsoa, Madag.* 89 C8
Fenoarivo Afovoany, *Madag.* 89 B8
Fenoarivo Atsinanana, *Madag.* 89 B8
Fens, The, *U.K.* 12 E7
Fensmark, *Denmark* 11 J5
Fenton, *U.S.A.* 108 D4
Fenxi, *China* 56 F6
Fenyang, *China* 56 F6
Fenyi, *China* 59 D10
Feodosiya, *Ukraine* 47 K8
Ferdows, *Iran* 71 C8
Fère-Champenoise, *France* 19 D10
Fère-en-Tardenois, *France* 19 C10
Ferentino, *Italy* 29 G10
Ferfer, *Somali Rep.* 74 F4
Fergana = Farghona, *Uzbekistan* 50 E8
Fergus, *Canada* 110 C4
Fergus Falls, *U.S.A.* 112 B6
Feričanci, *Croatia* 42 E2
Ferkéssédougou, *Ivory C.* 82 D3
Ferlach, *Austria* 26 E7
Ferland, *Canada* 102 B2
Ferlo, Vallée du, *Senegal* 82 B2
Fermanagh □, *U.K.* 15 B4
Fermo, *Italy* 29 E10
Fermont, *Canada* 103 B6
Fermoselle, *Spain* 34 D4
Fermoy, *Ireland* 15 D3
Fernán Nuñéz, *Spain* 35 H6
Fernández, *Argentina* 126 B3
Fernandina Beach, *U.S.A.* 109 K5
Fernando de Noronha, *Brazil* 125 D12
Fernando Póo = Bioko, *Eq. Guin.* 83 E6
Ferndale, *U.S.A.* 116 B4
Fernie, *Canada* 104 D5
Fernlees, *Australia* 94 C4
Fernley, *U.S.A.* 114 G4
Ferozepore = Firozpur, *India* 68 D6
Férrai, *Greece* 41 F10
Ferrandina, *Italy* 31 B9
Ferrara, *Italy* 29 D8
Ferrato, C., *Italy* 30 C2
Ferreira do Alentejo, *Portugal* 35 G2
Ferreñafe, *Peru* 124 E3
Ferrerías, *Spain* 37 B11
Ferret, C., *France* 20 D2
Ferrette, *France* 19 E14
Ferriday, *U.S.A.* 113 K9
Ferriere, *Italy* 28 D6
Ferrières, *France* 19 D9
Ferro, Capo, *Italy* 30 A2
Ferrol, *Spain* 34 B2
Ferron, *U.S.A.* 115 G8
Ferrutx, C., *Spain* 37 B10
Ferryland, *Canada* 103 C9
Fertile, *U.S.A.* 112 B6
Fertőszentmiklós, *Hungary* 42 C1
Fès, *Morocco* 78 B5
Fessenden, *U.S.A.* 112 B5
Festus, *U.S.A.* 112 F9
Feté Bowé, *Senegal* 82 C2
Feteşti, *Romania* 43 F12
Fethiye, *Turkey* 39 E11
Fethiye Körfezi, *Turkey* 39 E10
Fetlar, *U.K.* 14 A8
Feuilles →, *Canada* 101 C12
Feurs, *France* 21 C8
Fez = Fès, *Morocco* 78 B5
Fezzan, *Libya* 79 C8
Fiambalá, *Argentina* 126 B2
Fianarantsoa, *Madag.* 89 C8
Fianarantsoa □, *Madag.* 89 B8
Fiche, *Ethiopia* 81 F4
Fichtelgebirge, *Germany* 25 E7
Ficksburg, *S. Africa* 89 D4
Fidenza, *Italy* 28 D7
Fiditi, *Nigeria* 83 D5
Field →, *Australia* 94 C2
Field I., *Australia* 92 B5
Fieni, *Romania* 43 E10
Fier, *Albania* 40 F3
Fierzë, *Albania* 40 D4
Fife □, *U.K.* 14 E5
Fife Ness, *U.K.* 14 E6
Fifth Cataract, *Sudan* 80 D3
Figari, *France* 21 G13
Figeac, *France* 20 D6
Figeholm, *Sweden* 11 G10
Figline Valdarno, *Italy* 29 E8
Figtree, *Zimbabwe* 87 G2
Figueira Castelo Rodrigo, *Portugal* 34 E4
Figueira da Foz, *Portugal* 34 E2
Figueiró dos Vinhos, *Portugal* 34 F2
Figueres, *Spain* 32 C7
Figuig, *Morocco* 78 B5
Fihaonana, *Madag.* 89 B8
Fiherenana, *Madag.* 89 B8
Fiherenana →, *Madag.* 89 C7
Fiji ■, *Pac. Oc.* 91 C8
Fik, *Ethiopia* 81 F5
Fika, *Nigeria* 83 C7
Filabres, Sierra de los, *Spain* 35 H8
Filabusi, *Zimbabwe* 89 C4
Filadélfia, *Italy* 31 D9
Fil'akovo, *Slovak Rep.* 27 C12
Filey, *U.K.* 12 C7
Filey B., *U.K.* 12 C7
Filfla, *Malta* 36 D1
Filiaşi, *Romania* 43 F8
Filiátes, *Greece* 38 B2
Filiatrá, *Greece* 38 D3
Filicudi, *Italy* 31 D7
Filingué, *Niger* 83 C5
Filiourí →, *Greece* 41 E9
Filipstad, *Sweden* 10 E8
Filisur, *Switz.* 25 J5
Fillmore, *Calif., U.S.A.* 117 L8
Fillmore, *Utah, U.S.A.* 115 G7
Filótion, *Greece* 39 D7
Filottrano, *Italy* 29 E10
Filtu, *Ethiopia* 81 F5
Finale Emília, *Italy* 29 D8
Finale Lígure, *Italy* 28 D5
Fiñana, *Spain* 35 H8
Finch, *Canada* 111 A9
Findhorn →, *U.K.* 14 D5
Findlay, *U.S.A.* 108 E4
Finger L., *Canada* 102 B1
Finger Lakes, *U.S.A.* 111 D8
Fíngoè, *Mozam.* 87 E3
Finike, *Turkey* 39 E12
Finike Körfezi, *Turkey* 39 E12
Finiq, *Albania* 40 G4
Finistère □, *France* 18 D3
Finisterre = Fisterra, *Spain* 34 C1
Finisterre, C. = Fisterra, C., *Spain* 34 C1
Finke, *Australia* 94 D1
Finland ■, *Europe* 8 E22
Finland, G. of, *Europe* 9 G21
Finlay →, *Canada* 104 B3

# Fremont



Fremont, *Calif., U.S.A.* 116 H4
Fremont, *Mich., U.S.A.* 108 D3
Fremont, *Nebr., U.S.A.* 112 E6
Fremont, *Ohio, U.S.A.* 108 E4
Fremont →, *U.S.A.* 115 G8
French Camp, *U.S.A.* 116 H5
French Creek →, *U.S.A.* 110 E5
French Guiana ■, *S. Amer.* 125 C8
French Polynesia ■, *Pac. Oc.* 97 K13
Frenchman Cr. →, *N. Amer.* 114 B10
Frenchman Cr. →, *U.S.A.* 112 E4
Frenštát pod Radhoštěm, *Czech Rep.* 27 B11
Fresco, *Ivory C.* 82 D3
Fresco →, *Brazil* 125 E8
Freshfield, C., *Antarctica* 5 C10
Fresnay-sur-Sarthe, *France* 18 D7
Fresnillo, *Mexico* 118 C4
Fresno, *U.S.A.* 116 J7
Fresno Alhandiga, *Spain* 34 E5
Fresno Reservoir, *U.S.A.* 114 B9
Freudenstadt, *Germany* 25 G4
Frévent, *France* 19 B9
Frew →, *Australia* 94 C2
Frewsburg, *U.S.A.* 110 D5
Freycinet Pen., *Australia* 94 G4
Freyming-Merlebach, *France* 19 C13
Freyung, *Germany* 25 G9
Fria, *Guinea* 82 C2
Fria, C., *Namibia* 88 B1
Friant, *U.S.A.* 116 J7
Frías, *Argentina* 126 B2
Fribourg, *Switz.* 25 J3
Fribourg □, *Switz.* 25 J3
Fridafors, *Sweden* 11 H8
Friday Harbor, *U.S.A.* 116 B3
Friedberg, *Bayern, Germany* 25 G6
Friedberg, *Hessen, Germany* 25 E4
Friedens, *U.S.A.* 110 F6
Friedland, *Germany* 24 B9
Friedrichshafen, *Germany* 25 H5
Friedrichskoog, *Germany* 24 A4
Friedrichstadt, *Germany* 24 A5
Friendly Is. = Tonga ■, *Pac. Oc.* 91 D11
Friendship, *U.S.A.* 110 D6
Friesach, *Austria* 26 E7
Friesack, *Germany* 24 C8
Friesland □, *Neths.* 17 A5
Friesoythe, *Germany* 24 B3
Friggesund, *Sweden* 10 C10
Frillesås, *Sweden* 11 G6
Frinnaryd, *Sweden* 11 G8
Frio →, *U.S.A.* 113 L5
Frio, C., *Brazil* 122 F6
Friol, *Spain* 34 B3
Friona, *U.S.A.* 113 H3
Fristad, *Sweden* 11 G6
Fritch, *U.S.A.* 113 H4
Fritsla, *Sweden* 11 G6
Fritzlar, *Germany* 24 D5
Friuli-Venézia Giulia □, *Italy* 29 B9
Frobisher B., *Canada* 101 B13
Frobisher Bay = Iqaluit, *Canada* 101 B13
Frobisher L., *Canada* 105 B7
Frohavet, *Norway* 8 E13
Frohnleiten, *Austria* 26 D8
Frolovo, *Russia* 48 F6
Frombork, *Poland* 44 D6
Frome, *U.K.* 13 F5
Frome →, *U.K.* 13 G5
Frome, L., *Australia* 95 E2
Frómista, *Spain* 34 C6
Front Range, *U.S.A.* 106 C5
Front Royal, *U.S.A.* 108 F6
Fronteira, *Portugal* 35 F3
Frontera, *Canary Is.* 37 G2
Frontera, *Mexico* 119 D6
Fronteras, *Mexico* 118 A3
Frontignan, *France* 20 E7
Frosinone, *Italy* 30 A6
Frostburg, *U.S.A.* 108 F6
Frostisen, *Norway* 8 B17
Frouard, *France* 19 D13
Frövi, *Sweden* 10 E9
Frøya, *Norway* 8 E13
Frumoasa, *Romania* 43 D10
Frunze = Bishkek, *Kyrgyzstan* 50 E8
Fruška Gora, *Serbia, Yug.* 42 E4
Frutal, *Brazil* 125 H9
Frutigen, *Switz.* 25 J3
Frýdek-Místek, *Czech Rep.* 27 B11
Frýdlant, *Czech Rep.* 26 A8
Fryeburg, *U.S.A.* 111 B14
Fryvaldov = Jeseník, *Czech Rep.* 27 A10
Fthiótis □, *Greece* 38 C4
Fu Jiang →, *China* 58 C6
Fu Xian = Wafangdian, *China* 57 E11
Fu Xian, *China* 56 G5
Fu'an, *China* 59 D12
Fubian, *China* 58 B4
Fucécchio, *Italy* 28 E7
Fucheng, *China* 56 F9
Fuchou = Fuzhou, *China* 59 D12
Fuchū, *Japan* 55 G6
Fuchuan, *China* 59 E8
Fuchun Jiang →, *China* 59 B13
Fúcino, Piana del, *Italy* 29 F10
Fuding, *China* 59 D13
Fuencaliente, *Canary Is.* 37 F2
Fuencaliente, *Spain* 35 G6
Fuencaliente, Pta., *Canary Is.* 37 F2
Fuengirola, *Spain* 35 J6
Fuenlabrada, *Spain* 34 E7
Fuensalida, *Spain* 34 E6
Fuente-Álamo, *Spain* 33 G3
Fuente-Álamo de Murcia, *Spain* 33 H3
Fuente de Cantos, *Spain* 35 G4
Fuente del Maestre, *Spain* 35 G4
Fuente el Fresno, *Spain* 35 F7
Fuente Obejuna, *Spain* 35 G5
Fuente Palmera, *Spain* 35 H5
Fuentes de Andalucía, *Spain* 35 H5
Fuentes de Ebro, *Spain* 32 D4
Fuentes de León, *Spain* 35 G4
Fuentes de Oñoro, *Spain* 34 E4
Fuentesaúco, *Spain* 34 D5
Fuerte →, *Mexico* 118 B3
Fuerte Olimpo, *Paraguay* 126 A4
Fuerteventura, *Canary Is.* 37 F6
Fufeng, *China* 56 G5
Fuga I., *Phil.* 61 B4
Fugong, *China* 58 D2
Fugou, *China* 56 G8
Fugu, *China* 56 E6
Fuhai, *China* 60 B3
Fuḩaymī, *Iraq* 70 C4
Fuji, *Japan* 55 G9
Fuji-San, *Japan* 55 G9
Fuji-Yoshida, *Japan* 55 G9
Fujian □, *China* 59 E12
Fujinomiya, *Japan* 55 G9
Fujisawa, *Japan* 55 G9
Fujiyama, Mt. = Fuji-San, *Japan* 55 G9
Fukien = Fujian □, *China* 59 E12
Fukuchiyama, *Japan* 55 G7
Fukue-Shima, *Japan* 55 H4
Fukui, *Japan* 55 F8
Fukui □, *Japan* 55 G8
Fukuoka, *Japan* 55 H5
Fukuoka □, *Japan* 55 H5
Fukushima, *Japan* 54 F10
Fukushima □, *Japan* 54 F10
Fukuyama, *Japan* 55 G6
Fulacunda, *Guinea-Biss.* 82 C1
Fulda, *Germany* 24 E5
Fulda →, *Germany* 24 D5
Fulford Harbour, *Canada* 116 B3
Fuliang, *China* 59 C11
Fullerton, *Calif., U.S.A.* 117 M9
Fullerton, *Nebr., U.S.A.* 112 E6
Fulongquan, *China* 57 B13
Fülöpszállás, *Hungary* 42 D4
Fulton, *Mo., U.S.A.* 112 F9
Fulton, *N.Y., U.S.A.* 111 C8
Fuluälven →, *Sweden* 10 C7
Fulufjället, *Sweden* 10 C6
Fumay, *France* 19 C11
Fumel, *France* 20 D4
Fumin, *China* 58 E4
Funabashi, *Japan* 55 G10
Funafuti = Fongafale, *Tuvalu* 96 H9
Funäsdalen, *Sweden* 10 B6
Funchal, *Madeira* 37 D3
Fundación, *Colombia* 124 A4
Fundão, *Portugal* 34 E3
Fundu Moldovei, *Romania* 43 C10
Fundulea, *Romania* 43 F11
Fundy, B. of, *Canada* 103 D6
Funhalouro, *Mozam.* 89 C5
Funing, *Hebei, China* 57 E10
Funing, *Jiangsu, China* 57 H10
Funing, *Yunnan, China* 58 F5
Funiu Shan, *China* 56 H7
Funsi, *Ghana* 82 C4
Funtua, *Nigeria* 83 C6
Fuping, *Hebei, China* 56 E8
Fuping, *Shaanxi, China* 56 G5
Fuqing, *China* 59 E12
Fuquan, *China* 58 D6
Furano, *Japan* 54 C11
Furāt, Nahr al →, *Asia* 70 D5
Fürg, *Iran* 71 D7
Furmanov, *Russia* 48 B5
Furmanovo, *Kazakstan* 48 F9
Furnás, *Spain* 37 B8
Furnas, Reprêsa de, *Brazil* 127 A6
Furneaux Group, *Australia* 94 G4
Furqlus, *Syria* 75 A6
Fürstenau, *Germany* 24 C3
Fürstenberg, *Germany* 24 B9
Fürstenfeld, *Austria* 26 D9
Fürstenfeldbruck, *Germany* 25 G7
Fürstenwalde, *Germany* 24 C10
Fürth, *Germany* 25 F6
Furth im Wald, *Germany* 25 F8
Furtwangen, *Germany* 25 G4
Furudal, *Sweden* 10 C9
Furukawa, *Japan* 54 E10
Furulund, *Sweden* 11 J7
Fury and Hecla Str., *Canada* 101 B11
Fusagasuga, *Colombia* 124 C4
Fuscaldo, *Italy* 31 C9
Fushan, *Shandong, China* 57 F11
Fushan, *Shanxi, China* 56 G6
Fushë Arrëz, *Albania* 40 D4
Fushë-Krujë, *Albania* 40 E3
Fushun, *Liaoning, China* 57 D12
Fushun, *Sichuan, China* 58 C5
Fusong, *China* 57 C14
Füssen, *Germany* 25 H6
Fusui, *China* 58 F6
Futog, *Yugoslavia* 42 E4
Futuna, *Wall. & F. Is.* 91 B8
Fuwa, *Egypt* 80 H7
Fuxian Hu, *China* 58 E4
Fuxin, *China* 57 C11
Fuyang, *Anhui, China* 56 H8
Fuyang, *Zhejiang, China* 59 B12
Fuyang He →, *China* 56 E9
Fuying Dao, *China* 59 D13
Fuyu, *China* 57 B13
Fuyuan, *China* 58 E5
Füzesgyarmat, *Hungary* 42 C6
Fuzhou, *China* 59 D12
Fylde, *U.K.* 12 D5
Fyn, *Denmark* 11 J4
Fyne, L., *U.K.* 14 F3
Fyns Amtskommune □, *Denmark* 11 J4
Fynshav, *Denmark* 11 K3


# G


Ga, *Ghana* 82 D4
Gaanda, *Nigeria* 83 C7
Gabarin, *Nigeria* 83 C7
Gabas →, *France* 20 E3
Gabela, *Angola* 84 G2
Gabès, *Tunisia* 79 B8
Gabès, G. de, *Tunisia* 79 B8
Gabgaba, W. →, *Egypt* 80 C3
Gąbin, *Poland* 45 F6
Gabon ■, *Africa* 84 E2
Gaborone, *Botswana* 88 C4
Gabriels, *U.S.A.* 111 B10
Gābrīk, *Iran* 71 E8
Gabrovo, *Bulgaria* 41 D9
Gacé, *France* 18 D7
Gāch Sār, *Iran* 71 B6
Gachsārān, *Iran* 71 D6
Gacko, *Bos.-H.* 40 C2
Gadag, *India* 66 M9
Gadamai, *Sudan* 81 D4
Gadap, *Pakistan* 68 G2
Gadarwara, *India* 69 H8
Gadebusch, *Germany* 24 B7
Gadein, *Sudan* 81 F2
Gadhada, *India* 68 J4
Gádor, Sierra de, *Spain* 35 J8
Gadra, *Pakistan* 68 G4
Gadsden, *U.S.A.* 109 H3
Gadwal, *India* 66 L10
Gadyach = Hadyach, *Ukraine* 47 G8
Găeşti, *Romania* 43 F10
Gaeta, *Italy* 30 A6
Gaeta, G. di, *Italy* 30 A6
Gaffney, *U.S.A.* 109 H5
Gafsa, *Tunisia* 78 B7
Gagarawa, *Nigeria* 83 C6
Gagaria, *India* 68 G4
Gagarin, *Russia* 46 E8
Gaggenau, *Germany* 25 G4
Gaghamni, *Sudan* 81 E2
Gagino, *Russia* 48 C7
Gagliano del Capo, *Italy* 31 C11
Gagnef, *Sweden* 10 D9
Gagnoa, *Ivory C.* 82 D3
Gagnon, *Canada* 103 B6
Gagnon, L., *Canada* 105 A6
Gagra, *Georgia* 49 J5
Gahini, *Rwanda* 86 C3
Gahmar, *India* 69 G10
Gai Xian = Gaizhou, *China* 57 D12
Gaïdhouronísi, *Greece* 36 E7
Gail, *U.S.A.* 113 J4
Gail →, *Austria* 26 E6
Gaillac, *France* 20 E5
Gaillimh = Galway, *Ireland* 15 C2
Gaillon, *France* 18 C8
Gaines, *U.S.A.* 110 E7
Gainesville, *Fla., U.S.A.* 109 L4
Gainesville, *Ga., U.S.A.* 109 H4
Gainesville, *Mo., U.S.A.* 113 G8
Gainesville, *Tex., U.S.A.* 113 J6
Gainsborough, *U.K.* 12 D7
Gairdner, L., *Australia* 95 E2
Gairloch, L., *U.K.* 14 D3
Gaizhou, *China* 57 D12
Gaj, *Croatia* 42 E2
Gaj →, *Pakistan* 68 F2
Gakuch, *Pakistan* 69 A5
Galala, Gebel el, *Egypt* 80 J8
Galán, Cerro, *Argentina* 126 B2
Galana →, *Kenya* 86 C5
Galanta, *Slovak Rep.* 27 C10
Galapagar, *Spain* 34 E7
Galápagos, *Pac. Oc.* 122 D1
Galashiels, *U.K.* 14 F6
Galatás, *Greece* 38 D5
Galaţi, *Romania* 43 E13
Galaţi □, *Romania* 43 E12
Galatia, *Turkey* 72 C5
Galatina, *Italy* 31 B11
Galátone, *Italy* 31 B11
Galax, *U.S.A.* 109 G5
Galaxídhion, *Greece* 38 C4
Galcaio, *Somali Rep.* 74 F4
Galdhøpiggen, *Norway* 9 F12
Galeana, *Chihuahua, Mexico* 118 A3
Galeana, *Nuevo León, Mexico* 118 A3
Galegu, *Sudan* 81 E4
Galela, *Indonesia* 63 D7
Galena, *U.S.A.* 100 B4
Galera, *Spain* 33 H2
Galera Pt., *Trin. & Tob.* 121 D7
Galesburg, *U.S.A.* 112 E9
Galeton, *U.S.A.* 110 E7
Galga, *Ethiopia* 81 F4
Gali, *Georgia* 49 J5
Galicea Mare, *Romania* 43 F8
Galich, *Russia* 48 A6
Galiche, *Bulgaria* 40 C7
Galicia □, *Spain* 34 C3
Galilee = Hagalil, *Israel* 75 C4
Galilee, L., *Australia* 94 C4
Galilee, Sea of = Yam Kinneret, *Israel* 75 C4
Galim, *Cameroon* 83 D7
Galinoporni, *Cyprus* 36 D13
Galion, *U.S.A.* 110 F2
Galiuro Mts., *U.S.A.* 115 K8
Galiwinku, *Australia* 94 A2
Gallabat, *Sudan* 81 E4
Gallan Hd., *U.K.* 14 C1
Gallarate, *Italy* 28 C5
Gallatin, *U.S.A.* 109 G2
Galle, *Sri Lanka* 66 R12
Gállego →, *Spain* 32 D4
Gallegos →, *Argentina* 128 G3
Galletti →, *Ethiopia* 81 F5
Galley Hd., *Ireland* 15 E3
Galliate, *Italy* 28 C5
Gallinas, Pta., *Colombia* 124 A4
Gallipoli = Gelibolu, *Turkey* 41 F10
Gallípoli, *Italy* 31 B10
Gallipolis, *U.S.A.* 108 F4
Gällivare, *Sweden* 8 C19
Gallneukirchen, *Austria* 26 C7
Gällö, *Sweden* 10 B9
Gallo, C., *Italy* 30 D6
Gallocanta, L. de, *Spain* 32 E3
Galloo I., *U.S.A.* 111 C8
Galloway, *U.K.* 14 F4
Galloway, Mull of, *U.K.* 14 G4
Gallup, *U.S.A.* 115 J9
Gallur, *Spain* 32 D3
Galoya, *Sri Lanka* 66 Q12
Galt, *U.S.A.* 116 G5
Galten, *Denmark* 11 H3
Galtür, *Austria* 26 E3
Galty Mts., *Ireland* 15 D3
Galtymore, *Ireland* 15 D3
Galva, *U.S.A.* 112 E9
Galve de Sorbe, *Spain* 32 D1
Galveston, *U.S.A.* 113 L7
Galveston B., *U.S.A.* 113 L7
Gálvez, *Argentina* 126 C3
Galway, *Ireland* 15 C2
Galway □, *Ireland* 15 C2
Galway B., *Ireland* 15 C2
Gam →, *Vietnam* 64 B5
Gamagōri, *Japan* 55 G8
Gamari, L., *Ethiopia* 81 E5
Gamawa, *Nigeria* 83 C7
Gamay, *Phil.* 61 E6
Gambaga, *Ghana* 83 C4
Gambat, *Pakistan* 68 F3
Gambela, *Ethiopia* 81 F3
Gambhir →, *India* 68 F6
Gambia ■, *W. Afr.* 82 C1
Gambia →, *W. Afr.* 82 C1
Gambier, *U.S.A.* 110 F2
Gambier, C., *Australia* 92 B5
Gambier Is., *Australia* 95 F2
Gambo, *Canada* 103 C9
Gamboli, *Pakistan* 68 E3
Gamboma, *Congo* 84 E3
Gamka →, *S. Africa* 88 E3
Gamkab →, *Namibia* 88 D2
Gamla Uppsala, *Sweden* 10 E11
Gamlakarleby = Kokkola, *Finland* 8 E20
Gamleby, *Sweden* 11 G10
Gammon →, *Canada* 105 C9
Gamo-Gofa □, *Ethiopia* 81 F4
Gamou, *Niger* 83 C6
Gamtoos →, *S. Africa* 88 E4
Gan, *France* 20 E3
Gan Goriama, Mts., *Cameroon* 83 D7
Gan Jiang →, *China* 59 C11
Ganado, *U.S.A.* 115 J9
Gananita, *Sudan* 80 D3
Gananoque, *Canada* 102 D4
Ganāveh, *Iran* 71 D6
Gäncä, *Azerbaijan* 49 K8
Gancheng, *China* 64 C7
Gand = Gent, *Belgium* 17 C3
Ganda, *Angola* 85 G2
Gandajika, *Dem. Rep. of the Congo* 84 F4
Gandak →, *India* 69 G11
Gandava, *Pakistan* 68 E2
Gander, *Canada* 103 C9
Gander L., *Canada* 103 C9
Ganderkesee, *Germany* 24 B4
Ganderowe Falls, *Zimbabwe* 87 F2
Gandesa, *Spain* 32 D5
Gandhi Sagar, *India* 68 G6
Gandhinagar, *India* 68 H5
Gandi, *Nigeria* 83 C6
Gandía, *Spain* 33 G4
Gandino, *Italy* 28 C6
Gando, Pta., *Canary Is.* 37 G4
Gandole, *Nigeria* 83 D7
Gâneb, *Mauritania* 82 B2
Ganedidalem = Gani, *Indonesia* 63 E7
Ganetti, *Sudan* 80 D3
Ganga →, *India* 69 H14
Ganga Sagar, *India* 69 J13
Gangafani, *Mali* 82 C4
Gangan →, *India* 69 E8
Ganganagar, *India* 68 E5
Gangapur, *India* 68 F7
Gangara, *Niger* 83 C6
Gangaw, *Burma* 67 H19
Gangdisê Shan, *China* 67 D12
Ganges = Ganga →, *India* 69 H14
Ganges, *Canada* 104 D4
Ganges, *France* 20 E7
Ganges, Mouths of the, *India* 69 J14
Gånghester, *Sweden* 11 G7
Gangi, *Italy* 31 E7
Gângiova, *Romania* 43 G8
Gangoh, *India* 68 E7
Gangroti, *India* 69 D8
Gangtok, *India* 67 F16
Gangu, *China* 56 G3
Gangyao, *China* 57 B14
Gani, *Indonesia* 63 E7
Ganj, *India* 69 F8
Ganluc, *China* 58 C4
Gannat, *France* 19 F10
Gannett Peak, *U.S.A.* 114 E9
Ganquan, *China* 56 F5
Gänserdorf, *Austria* 27 C9
Ganshui, *China* 58 C6
Gansu □, *China* 56 G3
Ganta, *Liberia* 82 D3
Gantheaume, C., *Australia* 95 F2
Gantheaume B., *Australia* 93 E1
Gantsevichi = Hantsavichy, *Belarus* 47 F4
Ganye, *Nigeria* 83 D7
Ganyem = Genyem, *Indonesia* 63 E10
Ganyu, *China* 57 G10
Ganyushkino, *Kazakstan* 49 G9
Ganzhou, *China* 59 E10
Gao, *Mali* 83 B4
Gao Xian, *China* 58 C5
Gao'an, *China* 59 C10
Gaochun, *China* 59 B12
Gaohe, *China* 59 F9
Gaohebu, *China* 59 B11
Gaokeng, *China* 59 D9
Gaolan Dao, *China* 59 G9
Gaoligong Shan, *China* 58 E2
Gaomi, *China* 57 F10
Gaoming, *China* 59 F9
Gaoping, *China* 56 G7
Gaotang, *China* 56 F9
Gaoua, *Burkina Faso* 82 C4
Gaoual, *Guinea* 82 C2
Gaoxiong = Kaohsiung, *Taiwan* 59 F13
Gaoyang, *China* 56 E8
Gaoyao, *China* 59 F9
Gaoyou, *China* 59 A12
Gaoyou Hu, *China* 57 H10
Gaoyuan, *China* 57 F9
Gaozhou, *China* 59 G8
Gap, *France* 21 D10
Gapan, *Phil.* 61 D4
Gapat →, *India* 69 G10
Gapuwiyak, *Australia* 94 A2
Gar, *China* 60 C2
Garabogazköl Aylagy, *Turkmenistan* 50 E6
Garachico, *Canary Is.* 37 F3
Garachiné, *Panama* 120 E4
Garafia, *Canary Is.* 37 F2
Garah, *Australia* 95 D4
Garajonay, *Canary Is.* 37 F2
Garango, *Burkina Faso* 83 C4
Garanhuns, *Brazil* 125 E11
Garautha, *India* 69 G8
Garawe, *Liberia* 82 E3
Garba Tula, *Kenya* 86 B4
Garberville, *U.S.A.* 114 F2
Garbiyang, *India* 69 D9
Garbsen, *Germany* 24 C5
Gard □, *France* 21 D8
Gard →, *France* 21 E8
Garda, L. di, *Italy* 28 C7
Gardanne, *France* 21 E9
Gårdby, *Sweden* 11 H10
Garde L., *Canada* 105 A7
Gardelegen, *Germany* 24 C7
Garden City, *Ga., U.S.A.* 109 J5
Garden City, *Kans., U.S.A.* 113 G4
Garden City, *Tex., U.S.A.* 113 K4
Garden Grove, *U.S.A.* 117 M9
Gardēz, *Afghan.* 68 C3
Gardhíki, *Greece* 38 C3
Gardiner, *Maine, U.S.A.* 109 C11
Gardiner, *Mont., U.S.A.* 114 D8
Gardiners I., *U.S.A.* 111 E12
Gardner, *U.S.A.* 111 D13
Gardner Canal, *Canada* 104 C3
Gardnerville, *U.S.A.* 116 G7
Gardno, Jezioro, *Poland* 44 D4
Gardo, *Somali Rep.* 74 F4
Gardone Val Trómpia, *Italy* 28 C7
Gárdony, *Hungary* 42 C3
Garešnica, *Croatia* 29 C13
Garéssio, *Italy* 28 D5
Garey, *U.S.A.* 117 L6
Garfield, *U.S.A.* 114 C5
Garforth, *U.K.* 12 D6
Gargaliánoi, *Greece* 38 D3
Gargan, Mt., *France* 20 C5
Gargouna, *Mali* 83 B5
Gargždai, *Lithuania* 44 C8
Garibaldi Prov. Park, *Canada* 104 D4
Gariep, L., *S. Africa* 88 E4
Garies, *S. Africa* 88 E2
Garigliano →, *Italy* 30 A6
Garissa, *Kenya* 86 C4
Garkida, *Nigeria* 83 C7
Garko, *Nigeria* 83 C6
Garland, *Tex., U.S.A.* 113 J6
Garland, *Utah, U.S.A.* 114 F7
Garlasco, *Italy* 28 C5
Garliava, *Lithuania* 44 D10
Garlin, *France* 20 E3
Garm, *Tajikistan* 50 F8
Garmāb, *Iran* 71 C8
Garmisch-Partenkirchen, *Germany* 25 H7
Garmo, Qullai = Kommunizma, Pik, *Tajikistan* 50 F8
Garmsār, *Iran* 71 C7
Garner, *U.S.A.* 112 D8
Garnett, *U.S.A.* 112 F7

## Guardamar del Segura



*Somali Rep.* 74 **E5**
Guardamar del Segura, *Spain* 33 **G4**
Guardavalle, *Italy* 31 **D9**
Guárdia Sanframondi, *Italy* 31 **A7**
Guardiagrele, *Italy* 29 **F11**
Guardo, *Spain* 34 **C6**
Guareña, *Spain* 35 **G4**
Guareña →, *Spain* 34 **D5**
Guárico □, *Venezuela* 124 **B5**
Guarujá, *Brazil* 127 **A6**
Guarus, *Brazil* 127 **A7**
Guasave, *Mexico* 118 **B3**
Guasdualito, *Venezuela* 124 **B4**
Guastalla, *Italy* 28 **D7**
Guatemala, *Guatemala* 120 **D1**
Guatemala ■, *Cent. Amer.* 120 **C1**
Guaviare →, *Colombia* 122 **C4**
Guaxupé, *Brazil* 127 **A6**
Guayama, *Puerto Rico* 121 **C6**
Guayaquil, *Ecuador* 124 **D3**
Guayaquil, G. de, *Ecuador* 122 **D2**
Guaymas, *Mexico* 118 **B2**
Guba, *Dem. Rep. of the Congo* 87 **E2**
Guba, *Ethiopia* 81 **E4**
Gûbâl, Madîq, *Egypt* 80 **B3**
Gubat, *Phil.* 61 **E6**
Gúbbio, *Italy* 29 **E9**
Guben, *Germany* 24 **D10**
Gubin, *Poland* 45 **G1**
Gubio, *Nigeria* 83 **C7**
Gubkin, *Russia* 47 **G9**
Guča, *Serbia, Yug.* 40 **C4**
Gucheng, *China* 59 **A8**
Gudata = Guadauta, *Georgia* 49 **J5**
Gudbrandsdalen, *Norway* 9 **F14**
Guddu Barrage, *Pakistan* 66 **E6**
Gudenå →, *Denmark* 11 **H4**
Gudermes, *Russia* 49 **J8**
Gudhjem, *Denmark* 11 **J8**
Gudur, *India* 66 **M11**
Guebwiller, *France* 19 **E14**
Guecho = Getxo, *Spain* 32 **B2**
Guékédou, *Guinea* 82 **D2**
Guéle Mendouka, *Cameroon* 83 **E7**
Guelph, *Canada* 102 **D3**
Guéméné-Penfao, *France* 18 **E5**
Guéméné-sur-Scorff, *France* 18 **D3**
Guéné, *Benin* 83 **C5**
Guer, *France* 18 **E4**
Guérande, *France* 18 **E4**
Guéret, *France* 19 **F8**
Guérigny, *France* 19 **E10**
Guerneville, *U.S.A.* 116 **G4**
Guernica = Gernika-Lumo, *Spain* 32 **B2**
Guernsey, *U.K.* 13 **H5**
Guernsey, *U.S.A.* 112 **D2**
Guerrero □, *Mexico* 119 **D5**
Guessou-Sud, *Benin* 83 **C5**
Gueugnon, *France* 19 **F11**
Guéyo, *Ivory C.* 82 **D3**
Gughe, *Ethiopia* 81 **F4**
Gügher, *Iran* 71 **D8**
Guglionesi, *Italy* 29 **G11**
Guhakolak, Tanjung, *Indonesia* 63 **G11**
Gui Jiang →, *China* 59 **F8**
Guia, *Canary Is.* 37 **F4**
Guia de Isora, *Canary Is.* 37 **F3**
Guia Lopes da Laguna, *Brazil* 127 **A4**
Guiana, *S. Amer.* 122 **C4**
Guibéroua, *Ivory C.* 82 **D3**
Guichi, *China* 59 **B11**
Guider, *Cameroon* 83 **D7**
Guidiguir, *Niger* 83 **C6**
Guidimouni, *Niger* 83 **C6**
Guiding, *China* 58 **D6**
Guidong, *China* 59 **D9**
Guidónia-Montecélio, *Italy* 29 **F9**
Guiers, L. de, *Senegal* 82 **B1**
Guigang, *China* 58 **F7**
Guiglo, *Ivory C.* 82 **D3**
Guihulñgan, *Phil.* 61 **F5**
Guijá, *Mozam.* 89 **C5**
Guijuelo, *Spain* 34 **E5**
Guildford, *U.K.* 13 **F7**
Guilford, *U.S.A.* 111 **E12**
Guilin, *China* 59 **E8**
Guillaume-Delisle L., *Canada* 102 **A4**
Guillaumes, *France* 21 **D10**
Guillestre, *France* 21 **D10**
Guilvinec, *France* 18 **E2**
Güimar, *Canary Is.* 37 **F3**
Guimarães, *Portugal* 34 **D2**
Guimaras □, *Phil.* 61 **F5**
Guinda, *U.S.A.* 116 **G4**
Guinea, *Africa* 76 **F4**
Guinea ■, *W. Afr.* 82 **C2**
Guinea, Gulf of, *Atl. Oc.* 83 **E5**
Guinea-Bissau ■, *Africa* 82 **C2**
Güines, *Cuba* 120 **B3**
Guingamp, *France* 18 **D3**
Guinguinéo, *Senegal* 82 **C1**
Guipavas, *France* 18 **D2**
Guiping, *China* 59 **F8**
Guipúzcoa □, *Spain* 32 **B2**
Guir, *Mali* 82 **B4**
Guirel, *Mauritania* 82 **B3**
Güiria, *Venezuela* 124 **A6**
Guiscard, *France* 19 **C10**
Guise, *France* 19 **C10**
Guitiriz, *Spain* 34 **B3**
Guitri, *Ivory C.* 82 **D3**
Guiuan, *Phil.* 61 **F6**
Guixi, *China* 59 **C11**
Guiyang, *Guizhou, China* 58 **D6**
Guiyang, *Hunan, China* 59 **E9**
Guizhou □, *China* 58 **D6**
Gujan-Mestras, *France* 20 **D2**
Gujar Khan, *Pakistan* 68 **C5**
Gujarat □, *India* 68 **H4**
Gujiang, *China* 59 **D10**
Gujranwala, *Pakistan* 68 **C6**
Gujrat, *Pakistan* 68 **C6**
Gukovo, *Russia* 49 **F5**
Gulbarga, *India* 66 **L10**
Gulbene, *Latvia* 9 **H22**
Gulf, The, *Asia* 71 **E6**
Gulfport, *U.S.A.* 113 **K10**
Gulgong, *Australia* 95 **E4**
Gulin, *China* 58 **C5**
Gulistan, *Pakistan* 68 **D2**
Gull Lake, *Canada* 105 **C7**
Gullbrandstorp, *Sweden* 11 **H6**
Gullspång, *Sweden* 11 **F8**
Güllük, *Turkey* 39 **D9**
Güllük Korfezi, *Turkey* 39 **D9**
Gulma, *Nigeria* 83 **C5**
Gulmarg, *India* 69 **B6**
Gülnar, *Turkey* 72 **D5**
Gülpınar, *Turkey* 39 **B8**
Gülşehir, *Turkey* 72 **C6**
Gulshad, *Kazakstan* 50 **E8**
Gulu, *Uganda* 86 **B3**
Gŭlŭbovo, *Bulgaria* 41 **D9**
Gulud, J., *Sudan* 81 **E2**
Gulwe, *Tanzania* 86 **D4**
Gulyaypole = Hulyaypole, *Ukraine* 47 **J9**
Gumal →, *Pakistan* 68 **D4**
Gumbaz, *Pakistan* 68 **D3**
Gumel, *Nigeria* 83 **C6**
Gumiel de Hizán, *Spain* 34 **D7**
Gumla, *India* 69 **H11**
Gumlu, *Australia* 94 **B4**
Gumma □, *Japan* 55 **F9**
Gummersbach, *Germany* 24 **D3**
Gummi, *Nigeria* 83 **C6**
Gümüldür, *Turkey* 39 **C9**
Gümüşçay, *Turkey* 41 **F11**
Gümüşhaciköy, *Turkey* 72 **B6**
Gümüşhane, *Turkey* 73 **B8**
Gümüşsu, *Turkey* 39 **C11**
Gumzai, *Indonesia* 63 **F8**
Guna, *Ethiopia* 81 **F4**
Guna, *India* 68 **G7**
Gundelfingen, *Germany* 25 **G6**
Güney, *Burdur, Turkey* 39 **D11**
Güney, *Denizli, Turkey* 39 **C11**
Güneydoğu Toroslar, *Turkey* 73 **C9**
Gunisao →, *Canada* 105 **C9**
Gunisao L., *Canada* 105 **C9**
Gunjyal, *Pakistan* 68 **C4**
Günlüce, *Turkey* 39 **E10**
Gunnarskog, *Sweden* 10 **E6**
Gunnbjørn Fjeld, *Greenland* 4 **C6**
Gunnebo, *Sweden* 11 **G10**
Gunnedah, *Australia* 95 **E5**
Gunnewin, *Australia* 95 **D4**
Gunningbar Cr. →, *Australia* 95 **E4**
Gunnison, *Colo., U.S.A.* 115 **G10**
Gunnison, *Utah, U.S.A.* 114 **G8**
Gunnison →, *U.S.A.* 115 **G9**
Gunpowder, *Australia* 94 **B2**
Guntakal, *India* 66 **M10**
Guntersville, *U.S.A.* 109 **H2**
Guntong, *Malaysia* 65 **K3**
Guntur, *India* 67 **L12**
Gunungapi, *Indonesia* 63 **F7**
Gunungsitoli, *Indonesia* 62 **D1**
Günz →, *Germany* 25 **G6**
Gunza, *Angola* 84 **G2**
Günzburg, *Germany* 25 **G6**
Gunzenhausen, *Germany* 25 **F6**
Guo He →, *China* 57 **H9**
Guoyang, *China* 56 **H9**
Gupis, *Pakistan* 69 **A5**
Gura Humorului, *Romania* 43 **C10**
Gura-Teghii, *Romania* 43 **E11**
Gurag, *Ethiopia* 81 **F4**
Gurahonț, *Romania* 42 **D7**
Gurdaspur, *India* 68 **C6**
Gurdon, *U.S.A.* 113 **J8**
Güre, *Balıkesir, Turkey* 39 **B8**
Güre, *Uşak, Turkey* 39 **C11**
Gurgaon, *India* 68 **E7**
Gürgentepe, *Turkey* 72 **B7**
Gurghiu, Munții, *Romania* 43 **D10**
Gurgueia →, *Brazil* 125 **E10**
Gurha, *India* 68 **G4**
Guri, Embalse de, *Venezuela* 124 **B6**
Gurin, *Nigeria* 83 **D7**
Gurjaani, *Georgia* 49 **K7**
Gurk →, *Austria* 26 **E7**
Gurkha, *Nepal* 69 **E11**
Gurley, *Australia* 95 **D4**
Gurnet Point, *U.S.A.* 111 **D14**
Gürpınar, *Ist., Turkey* 41 **F12**
Gürpınar, *Van, Turkey* 73 **C10**
Gürsu, *Turkey* 41 **F13**
Gurué, *Mozam.* 87 **F4**
Gurun, *Malaysia* 65 **K3**
Gürün, *Turkey* 72 **C7**
Gurupá, *Brazil* 125 **D8**
Gurupá, I. Grande de, *Brazil* 125 **D8**
Gurupi, *Brazil* 125 **F9**
Gurupi →, *Brazil* 125 **D9**
Guruwe, *Zimbabwe* 89 **B5**
Guryev = Atyraū, *Kazakstan* 50 **E6**
Gus-Khrustalnyy, *Russia* 48 **C5**
Gusau, *Nigeria* 83 **C6**
Gusev, *Russia* 9 **J20**
Gushan, *China* 57 **E12**
Gushgy, *Turkmenistan* 50 **F7**
Gushi, *China* 59 **A10**
Gushiago, *Ghana* 83 **D4**
Gusinje, *Montenegro, Yug.* 40 **D3**
Gusinoozersk, *Russia* 51 **D11**
Gúspini, *Italy* 30 **C1**
Güssing, *Austria* 27 **D9**
Gustavsberg, *Sweden* 10 **E12**
Gustavus, *U.S.A.* 104 **B1**
Gustine, *U.S.A.* 116 **H6**
Güstrow, *Germany* 24 **B8**
Gusum, *Sweden* 11 **F10**
Guta = Kolárovo, *Slovak Rep.* 27 **D10**
Gütersloh, *Germany* 24 **D4**
Gutha, *Australia* 93 **E2**
Guthalungra, *Australia* 94 **B4**
Guthrie, *Okla., U.S.A.* 113 **H6**
Guthrie, *Tex., U.S.A.* 113 **J4**
Gutian, *China* 59 **D12**
Guttenberg, *U.S.A.* 112 **D9**
Gutu, *Zimbabwe* 89 **B5**
Guyana ■, *S. Amer.* 124 **C7**
Guyane française = French Guiana ■, *S. Amer.* 125 **C8**
Guyang, *China* 56 **D6**
Guyenne, *France* 20 **D4**
Guymon, *U.S.A.* 113 **G4**
Guyra, *Australia* 95 **E5**
Guyuan, *Hebei, China* 56 **D8**
Guyuan, *Ningxia Huizu, China* 56 **G4**
Güzelbahçe, *Turkey* 39 **C8**
Guzhang, *China* 58 **C7**
Guzhen, *China* 57 **H9**
Guzmán, L. de, *Mexico* 118 **A3**
Gvardeysk, *Russia* 9 **J19**
Gvardeyskoye, *Ukraine* 47 **K8**
Gwa, *Burma* 67 **L19**
Gwaai, *Zimbabwe* 87 **F2**
Gwabegar, *Australia* 95 **E4**
Gwadabawa, *Nigeria* 83 **C6**
Gwādar, *Pakistan* 66 **G3**
Gwagwada, *Nigeria* 83 **C6**
Gwalior, *India* 68 **F8**
Gwanara, *Nigeria* 83 **D5**
Gwanda, *Zimbabwe* 87 **G2**
Gwandu, *Nigeria* 83 **C5**
Gwane, *Dem. Rep. of the Congo* 86 **B2**
Gwaram, *Nigeria* 83 **C7**
Gwarzo, *Nigeria* 83 **C6**
Gwasero, *Nigeria* 83 **D5**
Gwda →, *Poland* 45 **E3**
Gweebarra B., *Ireland* 15 **B3**
Gweedore, *Ireland* 15 **A3**
Gweru, *Zimbabwe* 87 **F2**
Gwi, *Nigeria* 83 **D6**
Gwinn, *U.S.A.* 108 **B2**
Gwio Kura, *Nigeria* 83 **C7**
Gwoza, *Nigeria* 83 **C7**
Gwydir →, *Australia* 95 **D4**
Gwynedd □, *U.K.* 12 **E3**
Gyandzha = Gäncä, *Azerbaijan* 49 **K8**
Gyaring Hu, *China* 60 **C4**
Gydanskiy Poluostrov, *Russia* 50 **C8**
Gympie, *Australia* 95 **D5**
Gyomaendrőd, *Hungary* 42 **D5**
Gyöngyös, *Hungary* 42 **C4**
Győr, *Hungary* 42 **C2**
Győr-Moson-Sopron □, *Hungary* 42 **C2**
Gypsum Pt., *Canada* 104 **A6**
Gypsumville, *Canada* 105 **C9**
Gyueshevo, *Bulgaria* 40 **D6**
Gyula, *Hungary* 42 **D6**
Gyumri, *Armenia* 49 **K6**
Gyzylarbat, *Turkmenistan* 50 **F6**
Gyzyletrek, *Turkmenistan* 71 **B7**
Gzhatsk = Gagarin, *Russia* 46 **E8**


# H


Ha 'Arava →, *Israel* 75 **E4**
Ha Coi, *Vietnam* 58 **G6**
Ha Dong, *Vietnam* 58 **G5**
Ha Giang, *Vietnam* 58 **F5**
Ha Tien, *Vietnam* 65 **G5**
Ha Tinh, *Vietnam* 64 **C5**
Ha Trung, *Vietnam* 64 **C5**
Haaksbergen, *Neths.* 17 **B6**
Haapsalu, *Estonia* 9 **G20**
Haarlem, *Neths.* 17 **B4**
Haast →, *N.Z.* 91 **K2**
Haast Bluff, *Australia* 92 **D5**
Hab →, *Pakistan* 68 **G3**
Hab Nadi Chauki, *Pakistan* 68 **G2**
Habaswein, *Kenya* 86 **B4**
Habay, *Canada* 104 **B5**
Ḥabbānīyah, *Iraq* 70 **C4**
Ḥabbānīyah, Hawr al, *Iraq* 73 **F10**
Habo, *Sweden* 11 **G8**
Haboro, *Japan* 54 **B10**
Ḥabshān, *U.A.E.* 71 **F7**
Hachenburg, *Germany* 24 **E3**
Hachijō-Jima, *Japan* 55 **H9**
Hachinohe, *Japan* 54 **D10**
Hachiōji, *Japan* 55 **G9**
Hachŏn, *N. Korea* 57 **D15**
Hacıbektaş, *Turkey* 72 **C6**
Hacılar, *Turkey* 72 **C6**
Hackås, *Sweden* 10 **B8**
Hackensack, *U.S.A.* 111 **F10**
Hackettstown, *U.S.A.* 111 **F10**
Hadali, *Pakistan* 68 **C5**
Hadarba, Ras, *Sudan* 80 **C4**
Hadarom □, *Israel* 75 **E4**
Hadd, Ra's al, *Oman* 74 **C6**
Hadejia, *Nigeria* 83 **C7**
Hadejia →, *Nigeria* 83 **C7**
Ḥadera, *Israel* 75 **C3**
Ḥadera, N. →, *Israel* 75 **C3**
Haderslev, *Denmark* 11 **J3**
Hadhramaut = Ḥaḍramawt, *Yemen* 74 **D4**
Hadibu, *Yemen* 74 **E5**
Hadım, *Turkey* 72 **D5**
Hadong, *S. Korea* 57 **G14**
Ḥaḍramawt, *Yemen* 74 **D4**
Ḥadrānīyah, *Iraq* 70 **C4**
Hadrian's Wall, *U.K.* 12 **B5**
Hadsten, *Denmark* 11 **H4**
Hadsund, *Denmark* 11 **H4**
Hadyach, *Ukraine* 47 **G8**
Haeju, *N. Korea* 57 **E13**
Haenam, *S. Korea* 57 **G14**
Haenertsburg, *S. Africa* 89 **C4**
Haerhpin = Harbin, *China* 57 **B14**
Hafar al Bāṭin, *Si. Arabia* 70 **D5**
Hafik, *Turkey* 72 **C7**
Ḥafīrat al 'Aydā, *Si. Arabia* 70 **E3**
Ḥafit, *Oman* 71 **F7**
Hafizabad, *Pakistan* 68 **C5**
Haflong, *India* 67 **G18**
Hafnarfjörður, *Iceland* 8 **D3**
Haft Gel, *Iran* 71 **D6**
Hafun, Ras, *Somali Rep.* 74 **E5**
Hagalil, *Israel* 75 **C4**
Hagby, *Sweden* 11 **H10**
Hagen, *Germany* 24 **D3**
Hagenow, *Germany* 24 **B7**
Hagerman, *U.S.A.* 113 **J2**
Hagerstown, *U.S.A.* 108 **F7**
Hagersville, *Canada* 110 **D4**
Hagetmau, *France* 20 **E3**
Hagfors, *Sweden* 10 **D7**
Hagi, *Japan* 55 **G5**
Hagolan, *Syria* 75 **C4**
Hagondange, *France* 19 **C13**
Hags Hd., *Ireland* 15 **D2**
Hague, C. de la, *France* 18 **C5**
Hague, The = 's-Gravenhage, *Neths.* 17 **B4**
Haguenau, *France* 19 **D14**
Hai Duong, *Vietnam* 58 **G6**
Hai'an, *Guangdong, China* 59 **G8**
Hai'an, *Jiangsu, China* 59 **A13**
Haicheng, *Fujian, China* 59 **E11**
Haicheng, *Liaoning, China* 57 **D12**
Haidar Khel, *Afghan.* 68 **C3**
Haidargarh, *India* 69 **F9**
Haifa = Ḥefa, *Israel* 75 **C4**
Haifeng, *China* 59 **F10**
Haiger, *Germany* 24 **E4**
Haikou, *China* 60 **D6**
Ḥā'il, *Si. Arabia* 70 **E4**
Hailar, *China* 60 **B6**
Hailey, *U.S.A.* 114 **E6**
Haileybury, *Canada* 102 **C4**
Hailin, *China* 57 **B15**
Hailing Dao, *China* 59 **G8**
Hailong, *China* 57 **C13**
Hailuoto, *Finland* 8 **D21**
Haimen, *Guangdong, China* 59 **F11**
Haimen, *Jiangsu, China* 59 **B13**
Hainan □, *China* 60 **E5**
Hainaut □, *Belgium* 17 **D4**
Hainburg, *Austria* 27 **C9**
Haines, *Alaska, U.S.A.* 104 **B1**
Haines, *Oreg., U.S.A.* 114 **D5**
Haines City, *U.S.A.* 109 **L5**
Haines Junction, *Canada* 104 **A1**
Hainfeld, *Austria* 26 **C8**
Haining, *China* 59 **B13**
Haiphong, *Vietnam* 58 **G6**
Haitan Dao, *China* 59 **E12**
Haiti ■, *W. Indies* 121 **C5**
Haiya, *Sudan* 80 **D4**
Haiyan, *China* 59 **B13**
Haiyang, *China* 57 **F11**
Haiyuan, *Guangxi Zhuangzu, China* 58 **F6**
Haiyuan, *Ningxia Huizu, China* 56 **F3**
Haizhou, *China* 57 **G10**
Haizhou Wan, *China* 57 **G10**
Hajdú-Bihar □, *Hungary* 42 **C6**
Hajdúböszörmény, *Hungary* 42 **C6**
Hajdúdorog, *Hungary* 42 **C6**
Hajdúhadház, *Hungary* 42 **C6**
Hajdúnánás, *Hungary* 42 **C6**
Hajdúsámson, *Hungary* 42 **C6**
Hajdúszoboszló, *Hungary* 42 **C6**
Hajipur, *India* 69 **G11**
Ḥājjī Muḥsin, *Iraq* 70 **C5**
Ḥājjīābād, *Iran* 71 **D7**
Ḥājjīābād-e Zarrīn, *Iran* 71 **C7**
Hajnówka, *Poland* 45 **F10**
Hakansson, Mts., *Dem. Rep. of the Congo* 87 **D2**
Hakkâri, *Turkey* 70 **B4**
Hakkâri Dağları, *Turkey* 73 **C10**
Hakken-Zan, *Japan* 55 **G7**
Hakodate, *Japan* 54 **D10**
Hakos, *Namibia* 88 **C2**
Håksberg, *Sweden* 10 **D9**
Haku-San, *Japan* 55 **F8**
Hakui, *Japan* 55 **F8**
Hala, *Pakistan* 66 **G6**
Ḥalab, *Syria* 70 **B3**
Ḥalabjah, *Iraq* 70 **C5**
Halaib, *Sudan* 80 **C4**
Halasa, *Sudan* 81 **E3**
Hālat 'Ammār, *Si. Arabia* 70 **D3**
Halbā, *Lebanon* 75 **A5**
Halberstadt, *Germany* 24 **D7**
Halcombe, *N.Z.* 91 **J5**
Halcon, *Phil.* 63 **B6**
Halden, *Norway* 9 **G14**
Haldensleben, *Germany* 24 **C7**
Haldia, *India* 67 **H16**
Haldwani, *India* 69 **E8**
Hale →, *Australia* 94 **C2**
Halesowen, *U.K.* 13 **E5**
Haleyville, *U.S.A.* 109 **H2**
Half Assini, *Ghana* 82 **D4**
Halfmoon Bay, *N.Z.* 91 **M2**
Halfway →, *Canada* 104 **B4**
Halia, *India* 69 **G10**
Haliburton, *Canada* 102 **C4**
Halifax, *Australia* 94 **B4**
Halifax, *Canada* 103 **D7**
Halifax, *U.K.* 12 **D6**
Halifax, *U.S.A.* 110 **F8**
Halifax B., *Australia* 94 **B4**
Halifax I., *Namibia* 88 **D2**
Halīl →, *Iran* 71 **E8**
Halkirk, *U.K.* 14 **C5**
Hall Beach = Sanirajak, *Canada* 101 **B11**
Hall in Tirol, *Austria* 26 **D4**
Hall Pen., *Canada* 101 **B13**
Hall Pt., *Australia* 92 **C3**
Hallabro, *Sweden* 11 **H9**
Halland, *Sweden* 9 **H15**
Hallands län □, *Sweden* 11 **H6**
Hallands Väderö, *Sweden* 11 **H6**
Hallandsås, *Sweden* 11 **H7**
Hällbybrunn, *Sweden* 10 **E10**
Halle, *Belgium* 17 **D4**
Halle, *Nordrhein-Westfalen, Germany* 24 **C4**
Halle, *Sachsen-Anhalt, Germany* 24 **D7**
Hällefors, *Sweden* 10 **E8**
Hälleforsnäs, *Sweden* 10 **E10**
Hallein, *Austria* 26 **D6**
Hällekis, *Sweden* 11 **F7**
Hallen, *Sweden* 10 **A8**
Hallett, *Australia* 95 **E2**
Hallettsville, *U.S.A.* 113 **L6**
Hallim, *S. Korea* 57 **H14**
Hallingdalselvi →, *Norway* 9 **F13**
Hallock, *U.S.A.* 112 **A6**
Halls Creek, *Australia* 92 **C4**
Hallsberg, *Sweden* 10 **E9**
Hallstahammar, *Sweden* 10 **E10**
Hallstatt, *Austria* 26 **D6**
Hallstavik, *Sweden* 10 **D12**
Hallstead, *U.S.A.* 111 **E9**
Halmahera, *Indonesia* 63 **D7**
Halmeu, *Romania* 42 **C8**
Halmstad, *Sweden* 11 **H6**
Hals, *Denmark* 11 **H4**
Hälsingborg = Helsingborg, *Sweden* 11 **H6**
Hälsingland, *Sweden* 10 **C10**
Halstead, *U.K.* 13 **F8**
Haltern, *Germany* 24 **D3**
Halti, *Finland* 8 **B19**
Halton □, *U.K.* 12 **D5**
Haltwhistle, *U.K.* 12 **C5**
Ḥalul, *Qatar* 71 **E7**
Ḥalvad, *India* 68 **H4**
Ḥalvān, *Iran* 71 **C8**
Ham, *France* 19 **C10**
Ham Tan, *Vietnam* 65 **G6**
Ham Yen, *Vietnam* 64 **A5**
Hamab, *Namibia* 88 **D2**
Hamad, *Sudan* 81 **D3**
Hamada, *Japan* 55 **G6**
Hamadān, *Iran* 71 **C6**
Hamadān □, *Iran* 71 **C6**
Hamāh, *Syria* 70 **C3**
Hamamatsu, *Japan* 55 **G8**
Hamar, *Norway* 9 **F14**
Hamâta, Gebel, *Egypt* 70 **E2**
Hambantota, *Sri Lanka* 66 **R12**
Hamber Prov. Park, *Canada* 104 **C5**
Hamburg, *Germany* 24 **B5**
Hamburg, *Ark., U.S.A.* 113 **J9**
Hamburg, *N.Y., U.S.A.* 110 **D6**
Hamburg, *Pa., U.S.A.* 111 **F9**
Hamburg □, *Germany* 24 **B5**
Ḥamḍ, W. al →, *Si. Arabia* 70 **E3**
Hamden, *U.S.A.* 111 **E12**
Hamdibey, *Turkey* 39 **B9**
Häme, *Finland* 9 **F20**
Hämeenlinna, *Finland* 9 **F21**
Hamélé, *Ghana* 82 **C4**
Hamelin Pool, *Australia* 93 **E1**
Hameln, *Germany* 24 **C5**
Hamerkaz □, *Israel* 75 **C3**
Hamersley Ra., *Australia* 92 **D2**
Hamhung, *N. Korea* 57 **E14**
Hami, *China* 60 **B4**
Hamilton, *Australia* 95 **F3**
Hamilton, *Canada* 102 **D4**
Hamilton, *N.Z.* 91 **G5**
Hamilton, *U.K.* 14 **F4**
Hamilton, *Ala., U.S.A.* 109 **H1**
Hamilton, *Mont., U.S.A.* 114 **C6**
Hamilton, *N.Y., U.S.A.* 111 **D9**
Hamilton, *Ohio, U.S.A.* 108 **F3**
Hamilton, *Tex., U.S.A.* 113 **K5**
Hamilton →, *Australia* 94 **C2**
Hamilton City, *U.S.A.* 116 **F4**
Hamilton Inlet, *Canada* 103 **B8**
Hamilton Mt., *U.S.A.* 111 **C10**
Hamina, *Finland* 9 **F22**
Hamirpur, *H.P., India* 68 **D7**
Hamirpur, *Ut. P., India* 69 **G9**
Hamitabat, *Turkey* 41 **E11**
Hamlet, *U.S.A.* 109 **H6**
Hamley Bridge, *Australia* 95 **E2**
Hamlin = Hameln, *Germany* 24 **C5**

**Heng Xian**


Hamlin, *N.Y., U.S.A.* 110 C7
Hamlin, *Tex., U.S.A.* 113 J4
Hamm, *Germany* 24 D3
Ḩammār, Hawr al, *Iraq* 70 D5
Hammarstrand, *Sweden* 10 A10
Hammelburg, *Germany* 25 E5
Hammeren, *Denmark* 11 J8
Hammerfest, *Norway* 8 A20
Hammerum, *Denmark* 11 H3
Hamminkeln, *Germany* 24 D2
Hammond, *Ind., U.S.A.* 108 E2
Hammond, *La., U.S.A.* 113 K9
Hammond, *N.Y., U.S.A.* 111 B9
Hammondsport, *U.S.A.* 110 D7
Hammonton, *U.S.A.* 108 F8
Hamneda, *Sweden* 11 H7
Hamoyet, Jebel, *Sudan* 80 D4
Hampden, *N.Z.* 91 L3
Hampshire □, *U.K.* 13 F6
Hampshire Downs, *U.K.* 13 F6
Hampton, *N.B., Canada* 103 C6
Hampton, *Ont., Canada* 110 C6
Hampton, *Ark., U.S.A.* 113 J8
Hampton, *Iowa, U.S.A.* 112 D8
Hampton, *N.H., U.S.A.* 111 D14
Hampton, *S.C., U.S.A.* 109 J5
Hampton, *Va., U.S.A.* 108 G7
Hampton Bays, *U.S.A.* 111 F12
Hampton Tableland, *Australia* 93 F4
Hamra, *Sweden* 10 C8
Hamrat esh Sheykh, *Sudan* 81 E2
Hamur, *Turkey* 73 C10
Hamyang, *S. Korea* 57 G14
Han Jiang →, *China* 59 F11
Han Shui, *China* 58 A7
Han Shui →, *China* 59 B10
Hanak, *Si. Arabia* 70 E3
Hanamaki, *Japan* 54 E10
Hanang, *Tanzania* 86 C4
Hanau, *Germany* 25 E4
Hanbogd = Ihbulag, *Mongolia* 56 C4
Hançalar, *Turkey* 39 C11
Hânceşti, *Moldova* 43 D13
Hancheng, *China* 56 G6
Hanchuan, *China* 59 B9
Hancock, *Mich., U.S.A.* 112 B10
Hancock, *N.Y., U.S.A.* 111 E9
Handa, *Japan* 55 G8
Handan, *China* 56 F8
Handeni, *Tanzania* 86 D4
Handlová, *Slovak Rep.* 27 C11
Handub, *Sudan* 80 D4
Handwara, *India* 69 B6
Hanegev, *Israel* 75 E4
Hanford, *U.S.A.* 116 J7
Hang Chat, *Thailand* 64 C2
Hang Dong, *Thailand* 64 C2
Hangang →, *S. Korea* 57 F14
Hangayn Nuruu, *Mongolia* 60 B4
Hangchou = Hangzhou, *China* 59 B13
Hanggin Houqi, *China* 56 D4
Hanggin Qi, *China* 56 E5
Hangu, *China* 57 E9
Hangzhou, *China* 59 B13
Hangzhou Wan, *China* 59 B13
Hanhongor, *Mongolia* 56 C3
Ḩanīdh, *Si. Arabia* 71 E6
Ḩanīsh, *Yemen* 74 E3
Haniska, *Slovak Rep.* 27 C14
Hanjiang, *China* 59 E12
Hankinson, *U.S.A.* 112 B6
Hanko, *Finland* 9 G20
Hankou, *China* 59 B10
Hanksville, *U.S.A.* 115 G8
Hanle, *India* 69 C8
Hanmer Springs, *N.Z.* 91 K4
Hann →, *Australia* 92 C4
Hann, Mt., *Australia* 92 C4
Hanna, *Canada* 104 C6
Hanna, *U.S.A.* 114 F10
Hannah B., *Canada* 102 B4
Hannibal, *Mo., U.S.A.* 112 F9
Hannibal, *N.Y., U.S.A.* 111 C8
Hannik, *Sudan* 80 D3
Hannover, *Germany* 24 C5
Hanö, *Sweden* 11 H8
Hanöbukten, *Sweden* 11 J8
Hanoi, *Vietnam* 58 G5
Hanover = Hannover, *Germany* 24 C5
Hanover, *Canada* 102 D3
Hanover, *S. Africa* 88 E3
Hanover, *N.H., U.S.A.* 111 C12
Hanover, *Ohio, U.S.A.* 110 F2
Hanover, *Pa., U.S.A.* 108 F7
Hanover, I., *Chile* 128 G2
Hansdiha, *India* 69 G12
Hanshou, *China* 59 C8
Hansi, *India* 68 E6
Hanson, L., *Australia* 95 E2
Hanstholm, *Denmark* 11 G2
Hantsavichy, *Belarus* 47 F4
Hanumangarh, *India* 68 E6
Hanyin, *China* 58 A7
Hanyuan, *China* 58 C4
Hanzhong, *China* 56 H4
Hanzhuang, *China* 57 G9
Haora, *India* 69 H13
Haoxue, *China* 59 B9
Haparanda, *Sweden* 8 D21
Happy, *U.S.A.* 113 H4
Happy Camp, *U.S.A.* 114 F2
Happy Valley-Goose Bay, *Canada* 103 B7
Hapsu, *N. Korea* 57 D15
Hapur, *India* 68 E7
Ḩaql, *Si. Arabia* 75 F3
Har, *Indonesia* 63 F8
Har-Ayrag, *Mongolia* 56 B5
Har Hu, *China* 60 C4
Har Us Nuur, *Mongolia* 60 B4
Har Yehuda, *Israel* 75 D3
Ḩaraḑ, *Si. Arabia* 74 C4
Haradok, *Belarus* 46 E6
Häradsbäck, *Sweden* 11 H8
Haranomachi, *Japan* 54 F10
Harare, *Zimbabwe* 87 F3
Harat, *Eritrea* 81 D4
Harbin, *China* 57 B14
Harbiye, *Turkey* 72 D7
Harbo, *Sweden* 10 D11
Harboør, *Denmark* 11 H2
Harbor Beach, *U.S.A.* 110 C2
Harbour Breton, *Canada* 103 C8
Harbour Deep, *Canada* 103 B8
Harburg, *Germany* 24 B5
Hårby, *Denmark* 11 J4
Harda, *India* 68 H7
Hardangerfjorden, *Norway* 9 F12
Hardangervidda, *Norway* 9 F12
Hardap Dam, *Namibia* 88 C2
Hardenberg, *Neths.* 17 B6
Harderwijk, *Neths.* 17 B5
Hardey →, *Australia* 92 D2
Hardin, *U.S.A.* 114 D10
Harding, *S. Africa* 89 E4
Harding Ra., *Australia* 92 C3
Hardisty, *Canada* 104 C6
Hardoi, *India* 69 F9
Hardwar = Haridwar, *India* 68 E8
Hardwick, *U.S.A.* 111 B12
Hardy, Pen., *Chile* 128 H3
Hare B., *Canada* 103 B8
Hareid, *Norway* 9 E12
Haren, *Germany* 24 C3
Harer, *Ethiopia* 81 F5
Harerge □, *Ethiopia* 81 F5
Hareto, *Ethiopia* 81 F4
Harfleur, *France* 18 C7
Hargeisa, *Somali Rep.* 74 F3
Harghita □, *Romania* 43 D10
Harghita, Munţii, *Romania* 43 D10
Hargshamn, *Sweden* 10 D12
Hari →, *Indonesia* 62 E2
Haria, *Canary Is.* 37 E6
Haridwar, *India* 68 E8
Harim, Jabal al, *Oman* 71 E8
Haringhata →, *Bangla.* 67 J16
Harīrūd →, *Asia* 66 A2
Härjedalen, *Sweden* 10 B7
Harlan, *Iowa, U.S.A.* 112 E7
Harlan, *Ky., U.S.A.* 109 G4
Hârlău, *Romania* 43 C11
Harlech, *U.K.* 12 E3
Harlem, *U.S.A.* 114 B9
Hårlev, *Denmark* 11 J6
Harlingen, *Neths.* 17 A5
Harlingen, *U.S.A.* 113 M6
Harlow, *U.K.* 13 F8
Harlowton, *U.S.A.* 114 C9
Harmancık, *Turkey* 39 B11
Harmånger, *Sweden* 10 C11
Harmil, *Eritrea* 81 D5
Harnai, *Pakistan* 68 D2
Harney Basin, *U.S.A.* 114 E4
Harney L., *U.S.A.* 114 E4
Harney Peak, *U.S.A.* 112 D3
Härnön, *Sweden* 10 B12
Härnösand, *Sweden* 10 B11
Haro, *Spain* 32 C2
Haroldswick, *U.K.* 14 A8
Harp L., *Canada* 103 A7
Harper, *Liberia* 82 E3
Harplinge, *Sweden* 11 H6
Harr, *Mauritania* 82 B2
Harrai, *India* 69 H8
Harrand, *Pakistan* 68 E4
Ḩarrat Khaybar, *Si. Arabia* 80 B5
Ḩarrat Nawāşīf, *Si. Arabia* 80 C5
Harricana →, *Canada* 102 B4
Harriman, *U.S.A.* 109 H3
Harrington Harbour, *Canada* 103 B8
Harris, *U.K.* 14 D2
Harris, Sd. of, *U.K.* 14 D1
Harris L., *Australia* 95 E2
Harris Pt., *Canada* 110 C2
Harrisburg, *Ill., U.S.A.* 113 G10
Harrisburg, *Nebr., U.S.A.* 112 E3
Harrisburg, *Pa., U.S.A.* 110 F8
Harrismith, *S. Africa* 89 D4
Harrison, *Ark., U.S.A.* 113 G8
Harrison, *Maine, U.S.A.* 111 B14
Harrison, *Nebr., U.S.A.* 112 D3
Harrison, C., *Canada* 103 B8
Harrison L., *Canada* 104 D4
Harrisonburg, *U.S.A.* 108 F6
Harrisonville, *U.S.A.* 112 F7
Harriston, *Canada* 110 C4
Harrisville, *Mich., U.S.A.* 110 B1
Harrisville, *N.Y., U.S.A.* 111 B9
Harrisville, *Pa., U.S.A.* 110 E5
Harrodsburg, *U.S.A.* 108 G3
Harrogate, *U.K.* 12 C6
Harrow □, *U.K.* 13 F7
Harrowsmith, *Canada* 111 B8
Harry S. Truman Reservoir, *U.S.A.* 112 F7
Harsefeld, *Germany* 24 B5
Harsewinkel, *Germany* 24 D4
Harsīn, *Iran* 70 C5
Hârşova, *Romania* 43 F12
Harstad, *Norway* 8 B17
Harsud, *India* 68 H7
Hart, *U.S.A.* 108 D2
Hart, L., *Australia* 95 E2
Hartbees →, *S. Africa* 88 D3
Hartberg, *Austria* 26 D8
Hartford, *Conn., U.S.A.* 111 E12
Hartford, *Ky., U.S.A.* 108 G2
Hartford, *S. Dak., U.S.A.* 112 D6
Hartford, *Wis., U.S.A.* 112 D10
Hartford City, *U.S.A.* 108 E3
Hartland, *Canada* 103 C6
Hartland Pt., *U.K.* 13 F3
Hartlepool, *U.K.* 12 C6
Hartlepool □, *U.K.* 12 C6
Hartley Bay, *Canada* 104 C3
Hartmannberge, *Namibia* 88 B1
Hartney, *Canada* 105 D8
Hârtop, *Moldova* 43 D13
Harts →, *S. Africa* 88 D3
Hartselle, *U.S.A.* 109 H2
Hartshorne, *U.S.A.* 113 H7
Hartstown, *U.S.A.* 110 E4
Hartsville, *U.S.A.* 109 H5
Hartswater, *S. Africa* 88 D3
Hartwell, *U.S.A.* 109 H4
Harunabad, *Pakistan* 68 E5
Harvand, *Iran* 71 D7
Harvey, *Australia* 93 F2
Harvey, *Ill., U.S.A.* 108 E2
Harvey, *N. Dak., U.S.A.* 112 B5
Harwich, *U.K.* 13 F9
Haryana □, *India* 68 E7
Haryn →, *Belarus* 47 F4
Harz, *Germany* 24 D6
Harzgerode, *Germany* 24 D7
Hasa □, *Si. Arabia* 71 E6
Hasaheisa, *Sudan* 81 E3
Ḩasanābād, *Iran* 71 C7
Hasdo →, *India* 69 J10
Haselünne, *Germany* 24 C3
Hashimoto, *Japan* 55 G7
Hashtjerd, *Iran* 71 C6
Haskell, *U.S.A.* 113 J5
Hasköy, *Turkey* 41 E10
Haslach, *Germany* 25 G4
Hasle, *Denmark* 11 J8
Haslemere, *U.K.* 13 F7
Haslev, *Denmark* 11 J5
Hasparren, *France* 20 E2
Hassa, *Turkey* 72 D7
Hassela, *Sweden* 10 B10
Hasselt, *Belgium* 17 D5
Hassfurt, *Germany* 25 E6
Hassi Messaoud, *Algeria* 78 B7
Hässleholm, *Sweden* 11 H7
Hassloch, *Germany* 25 F4
Hästholmen, *Sweden* 11 F8
Hastings, *N.Z.* 91 H6
Hastings, *U.K.* 13 G8
Hastings, *Mich., U.S.A.* 108 D3
Hastings, *Minn., U.S.A.* 112 C8
Hastings, *Nebr., U.S.A.* 112 E5
Hastings Ra., *Australia* 95 E5
Hästveda, *Sweden* 11 H7
Hat Yai, *Thailand* 65 J3
Hatanbulag = Ergel, *Mongolia* 56 C5
Hatay = Antalya, *Turkey* 72 D4
Hatch, *U.S.A.* 115 K10
Hatchet L., *Canada* 105 B8
Haţeg, *Romania* 42 E7
Hateruma-Shima, *Japan* 55 M1
Hatfield P.O., *Australia* 95 E3
Hatgal, *Mongolia* 60 A5
Hathras, *India* 68 F8
Hatia, *Bangla.* 67 H17
Ḩāţibah, Ra's, *Si. Arabia* 80 C4
Hato Mayor, *Dom. Rep.* 121 C6
Hatta, *India* 69 G8
Hattah, *Australia* 95 E3
Hatteras, C., *U.S.A.* 109 H8
Hattiesburg, *U.S.A.* 113 K10
Hatvan, *Hungary* 42 C4
Hau Bon = Cheo Reo, *Vietnam* 62 B3
Hau Duc, *Vietnam* 64 E7
Haugesund, *Norway* 9 G11
Haukipudas, *Finland* 8 D21
Haultain →, *Canada* 105 B7
Hauraki G., *N.Z.* 91 G5
Hausruck, *Austria* 26 C6
Haut Atlas, *Morocco* 78 B4
Haut-Rhin □, *France* 19 E14
Haut-Zaïre = Orientale □, *Dem. Rep. of the Congo* 86 B2
Haute-Corse □, *France* 21 F13
Haute-Garonne □, *France* 20 E5
Haute-Loire □, *France* 20 C7
Haute-Marne □, *France* 19 D12
Haute-Normandie □, *France* 18 C7
Haute-Saône □, *France* 19 E13
Haute-Savoie □, *France* 21 C10
Haute-Vienne □, *France* 20 C5
Hautes-Alpes □, *France* 21 D10
Hautes Fagnes = Hohe Venn, *Belgium* 17 D6
Hautes-Pyrénées □, *France* 20 F4
Hauteville-Lompnès, *France* 21 C9
Hautmont, *France* 19 B10
Hauts-de-Seine □, *France* 19 D9
Hauts Plateaux, *Algeria* 76 C4
Hauzenberg, *Germany* 25 G9
Havana = La Habana, *Cuba* 120 B3
Havana, *U.S.A.* 112 E9
Havant, *U.K.* 13 G7
Havârna, *Romania* 43 B11
Havasu, L., *U.S.A.* 117 L12
Havdhem, *Sweden* 11 G12
Havel →, *Germany* 24 C8
Havelian, *Pakistan* 68 B5
Havelock, *Canada* 102 D4
Havelock, *N.Z.* 91 J4
Havelock, *U.S.A.* 109 H7
Haverfordwest, *U.K.* 13 F3
Haverhill, *U.S.A.* 111 D13
Haverstraw, *U.S.A.* 111 E11
Håverud, *Sweden* 11 F6
Havirga, *Mongolia* 56 B7
Havířov, *Czech Rep.* 27 B11
Havlíčkův Brod, *Czech Rep.* 26 B8
Havneby, *Denmark* 11 J2
Havran, *Turkey* 39 B9
Havre, *U.S.A.* 114 B9
Havre-Aubert, *Canada* 103 C7
Havre-St.-Pierre, *Canada* 103 B7
Havsa, *Turkey* 41 E10
Havza, *Turkey* 72 B6
Haw →, *U.S.A.* 109 H6
Hawaii □, *U.S.A.* 106 H16
Hawaii I., *Pac. Oc.* 106 J17
Hawaiian Is., *Pac. Oc.* 106 H17
Hawaiian Ridge, *Pac. Oc.* 97 E11
Hawarden, *U.S.A.* 112 D6
Hawea, L., *N.Z.* 91 L2
Hawera, *N.Z.* 91 H5
Hawick, *U.K.* 14 F6
Hawk Junction, *Canada* 102 C3
Hawke B., *N.Z.* 91 H6
Hawker, *Australia* 95 E2
Hawkesbury, *Canada* 102 C5
Hawkesbury I., *Canada* 104 C3
Hawkesbury Pt., *Australia* 94 A1
Hawkinsville, *U.S.A.* 109 J4
Hawley, *Minn., U.S.A.* 112 B6
Hawley, *Pa., U.S.A.* 111 E9
Ḩawrān, W. →, *Iraq* 70 C4
Hawsh Müssá, *Lebanon* 75 B4
Hawthorne, *U.S.A.* 114 G4
Hay, *Australia* 95 E3
Hay →, *Australia* 94 C2
Hay →, *Canada* 104 A5
Hay, C., *Australia* 92 B4
Hay I., *Canada* 110 B4
Hay L., *Canada* 104 B5
Hay-on-Wye, *U.K.* 13 E4
Hay River, *Canada* 104 A5
Hay Springs, *U.S.A.* 112 D3
Haya = Tehoru, *Indonesia* 63 E7
Hayachine-San, *Japan* 54 E10
Hayange, *France* 19 C13
Haydarlı, *Turkey* 39 C12
Hayden, *U.S.A.* 114 F10
Haydon, *Australia* 94 B3
Hayes, *U.S.A.* 112 C4
Hayes →, *Canada* 102 A1
Hayes Creek, *Australia* 92 B5
Hayle, *U.K.* 13 G2
Hayling I., *U.K.* 13 G7
Haymana, *Turkey* 72 C5
Hayrabolu, *Turkey* 41 E11
Hays, *Canada* 104 C6
Hays, *U.S.A.* 112 F5
Haysyn, *Ukraine* 47 H5
Hayvoron, *Ukraine* 47 H5
Hayward, *Calif., U.S.A.* 116 H4
Hayward, *Wis., U.S.A.* 112 B9
Haywards Heath, *U.K.* 13 G7
Hazafon □, *Israel* 75 C4
Hazārān, Kūh-e, *Iran* 71 D8
Hazard, *U.S.A.* 108 G4
Hazaribag, *India* 69 H11
Hazaribag Road, *India* 69 G11
Hazebrouck, *France* 19 B9
Hazelton, *Canada* 104 B3
Hazelton, *U.S.A.* 112 B4
Hazen, *U.S.A.* 112 B4
Hazlehurst, *Ga., U.S.A.* 109 K4
Hazlehurst, *Miss., U.S.A.* 113 K9
Hazlet, *U.S.A.* 111 F10
Hazleton, *U.S.A.* 111 F9
Hazlett, L., *Australia* 92 D4
Hazro, *Turkey* 70 B4
He Xian, *Anhui, China* 59 B12
He Xian, *Guangxi Zhuangzu, China* 59 E8
Head of Bight, *Australia* 93 F5
Headlands, *Zimbabwe* 87 F3
Healdsburg, *U.S.A.* 116 G4
Healdton, *U.S.A.* 113 H6
Healesville, *Australia* 95 F4
Heany Junction, *Zimbabwe* 89 C4
Heard I., *Ind. Oc.* 3 G13
Hearne, *U.S.A.* 113 K6
Hearst, *Canada* 102 C3
Heart →, *U.S.A.* 112 B4
Heart's Content, *Canada* 103 C9
Heath Pt., *Canada* 103 C7
Heavener, *U.S.A.* 113 H7
Hebbronville, *U.S.A.* 113 M5
Hebei □, *China* 56 E9
Hebel, *Australia* 95 D4
Heber, *U.S.A.* 117 N11
Heber City, *U.S.A.* 114 F8
Heber Springs, *U.S.A.* 113 H9
Hebert, *Canada* 105 C7
Hebgen L., *U.S.A.* 114 D8
Hebi, *China* 56 G8
Hebrides, *U.K.* 6 D4
Hebrides, Sea of the, *U.K.* 14 D2
Hebron = Al Khalīl, *West Bank* 75 D4
Hebron, *Canada* 101 C13
Hebron, *N. Dak., U.S.A.* 112 B3
Hebron, *Nebr., U.S.A.* 112 E6
Heby, *Sweden* 10 E10
Hecate Str., *Canada* 104 C2
Heceta I., *U.S.A.* 104 B2
Hechi, *China* 58 E7
Hechingen, *Germany* 25 G4
Hechuan, *China* 58 B6
Hecla, *U.S.A.* 112 C5
Hecla I., *Canada* 105 C9
Hédé, *France* 18 D5
Hede, *Sweden* 10 B7
Hedemora, *Sweden* 10 D9
Hedensted, *Denmark* 11 J3
Hedesunda, *Sweden* 10 D10
Heerde, *Neths.* 17 B6
Heerenveen, *Neths.* 17 B5
Heerhugowaard, *Neths.* 17 B4
Heerlen, *Neths.* 17 D5
Ḩefa, *Israel* 75 C4
Ḩefa □, *Israel* 75 C4
Hefei, *China* 59 B11
Hefeng, *China* 59 C8
Hegalig, *Sudan* 81 E3
Hegang, *China* 60 B8
Heiban, *Sudan* 81 E3
Heichengzhen, *China* 56 F4
Heide, *Germany* 24 A5
Heidelberg, *Germany* 25 F4
Heidelberg, *S. Africa* 88 E3
Heidenau, *Germany* 24 E9
Heidenheim, *Germany* 25 G6
Heijing, *China* 58 E3
Heilbad Heiligenstadt, *Germany* 24 D6
Heilbron, *S. Africa* 89 D4
Heilbronn, *Germany* 25 F5
Heiligenblut, *Austria* 26 D5
Heiligenhafen, *Germany* 24 A6
Heilongjiang □, *China* 60 B7
Heilunkiang = Heilongjiang □, *China* 60 B7
Heimaey, *Iceland* 8 E3
Heinola, *Finland* 9 F22
Heinsberg, *Germany* 24 D2
Heinze Kyun, *Burma* 64 E1
Heishan, *China* 57 D12
Heishui, *Liaoning, China* 57 C10
Heishui, *Sichuan, China* 58 A4
Hejaz = Ḩijāz □, *Si. Arabia* 70 E3
Hejian, *China* 56 E9
Hejiang, *China* 58 C5
Hejin, *China* 56 G6
Hekımhan, *Turkey* 70 B3
Hekla, *Iceland* 8 E4
Hekou, *Guangdong, China* 59 F9
Hekou, *Yunnan, China* 58 F4
Hel, *Poland* 44 D5
Helagsfjället, *Sweden* 10 B6
Helan Shan, *China* 56 E3
Helechosa, *Spain* 35 F6
Helen Atoll, *Pac. Oc.* 63 D8
Helena, *Ark., U.S.A.* 113 H9
Helena, *Mont., U.S.A.* 114 C7
Helendale, *U.S.A.* 117 L9
Helensburgh, *U.K.* 14 E4
Helensville, *N.Z.* 91 G5
Helenvale, *Australia* 94 B4
Helgasjön, *Sweden* 11 H8
Helgeland, *Norway* 8 C15
Helgoland, *Germany* 24 A3
Heligoland = Helgoland, *Germany* 24 A3
Heligoland B. = Deutsche Bucht, *Germany* 24 A4
Heliopolis, *Egypt* 80 H7
Hella, *Iceland* 8 E3
Hellertown, *U.S.A.* 111 F9
Hellespont = Çanakkale Boğazı, *Turkey* 41 F10
Hellevoetsluis, *Neths.* 17 C4
Hellín, *Spain* 33 G3
Helmand □, *Afghan.* 66 D4
Helmand →, *Afghan.* 66 D2
Helme →, *Germany* 24 D7
Helmeringhausen, *Namibia* 88 D2
Helmond, *Neths.* 17 C5
Helmsdale, *U.K.* 14 C5
Helmsdale →, *U.K.* 14 C5
Helmstedt, *Germany* 24 C7
Helong, *China* 57 C15
Helper, *U.S.A.* 114 G8
Helsingborg, *Sweden* 11 H6
Helsinge, *Denmark* 11 H6
Helsingfors = Helsinki, *Finland* 9 F21
Helsingør, *Denmark* 11 H6
Helsinki, *Finland* 9 F21
Helska, Mierzeja, *Poland* 44 D5
Helston, *U.K.* 13 G2
Helvellyn, *U.K.* 12 C4
Helwân, *Egypt* 80 J7
Hemel Hempstead, *U.K.* 13 F7
Hemet, *U.S.A.* 117 M10
Hemingford, *U.S.A.* 112 D3
Hemmingford, *Canada* 111 A11
Hempstead, *U.S.A.* 113 K6
Hemse, *Sweden* 11 G12
Hemsön, *Sweden* 10 B12
Henån, *Sweden* 11 F5
Henan □, *China* 56 H8
Henares →, *Spain* 34 E7
Henashi-Misaki, *Japan* 54 D9
Hendaye, *France* 20 E2
Hendek, *Turkey* 72 B4
Henderson, *Argentina* 126 D3
Henderson, *Ky., U.S.A.* 108 G2
Henderson, *N.C., U.S.A.* 109 G6
Henderson, *Nev., U.S.A.* 117 J12
Henderson, *Tenn., U.S.A.* 109 H1
Henderson, *Tex., U.S.A.* 113 J7
Hendersonville, *N.C., U.S.A.* 109 H4
Hendersonville, *Tenn., U.S.A.* 109 G2
Hendījān, *Iran* 71 D6
Hendorābī, *Iran* 71 E7
Heng Jiang, *China* 58 C5
Heng Xian, *China* 58 F7

Jessnitz


Island Lagoon, Australia 95 E2
Island Pond, U.S.A. 111 B13
Islands, B. of, Canada 103 C8
Islands, B. of, N.Z. 91 F5
Islay, U.K. 14 F2
Isle →, France 20 D3
Isle aux Morts, Canada 103 C8
Isle of Wight □, U.K. 13 G6
Isle Royale, U.S.A. 112 B10
Isle Royale National Park, U.S.A. 112 B10
Isleton, U.S.A. 116 G5
Ismail = Izmayil, Ukraine 47 K5
Ismâ'ilîya, Egypt 80 H8
Ismaning, Germany 25 G7
Isna, Egypt 80 B3
Isoanala, Madag. 89 C8
Isogstalo, India 69 B8
Ísola del Liri, Italy 29 G10
Ísola della Scala, Italy 28 C7
Ísola di Capo Rizzuto, Italy 31 D10
Isparta, Turkey 39 D12
Isperikh, Bulgaria 41 C10
Íspica, Italy 31 F7
Israel ■, Asia 75 D3
Isratu, Eritrea 81 D4
Issia, Ivory C. 82 D3
Issoire, France 20 C7
Issoudun, France 19 F8
Issyk-Kul, Ozero = Ysyk-Köl, Kyrgyzstan 50 E8
Ist, Croatia 29 D11
Istállós-kő, Hungary 42 B5
İstanbul, Turkey 41 E12
İstanbul □, Turkey 41 E12
İstanbul Boğazı, Turkey 41 E13
Istiaía, Greece 38 C5
Istok, Kosovo, Yug. 40 D4
Istokpoga, L., U.S.A. 109 M5
Istra, Croatia 29 C10
Istres, France 21 E8
Istria = Istra, Croatia 29 C10
Itá, Paraguay 126 B4
Itaberaba, Brazil 125 F10
Itabira, Brazil 125 G10
Itabirito, Brazil 127 A7
Itabuna, Brazil 125 F11
Itacaunas →, Brazil 125 E9
Itacoatiara, Brazil 124 D7
Itaipú, Reprêsa de, Brazil 127 B5
Itaituba, Brazil 125 D7
Itajaí, Brazil 127 B6
Itajubá, Brazil 127 A6
Itaka, Tanzania 87 D3
Italy ■, Europe 7 G8
Itamaraju, Brazil 125 G11
Itampolo, Madag. 89 C7
Itandrano, Madag. 89 C8
Itapecuru-Mirim, Brazil 125 D10
Itaperuna, Brazil 127 A7
Itapetininga, Brazil 127 A6
Itapeva, Brazil 127 A6
Itapicuru →, Bahia, Brazil 125 F11
Itapicuru →, Maranhão, Brazil 125 D10
Itapipoca, Brazil 125 D11
Itapuá □, Paraguay 127 B4
Itaquari, Brazil 127 A7
Itaquí, Brazil 126 B4
Itararé, Brazil 127 A6
Itarsi, India 68 H7
Itatí, Argentina 126 B4
Itbayat, Phil. 61 A4
Itchen →, U.K. 13 G6
Itéa, Greece 38 C4
Itezhi Tezhi, L., Zambia 87 F2
Ithaca = Itháki, Greece 38 C2
Ithaca, U.S.A. 111 D8
Itháki, Greece 38 C2
Itiquira →, Brazil 125 G7
Itō, Japan 55 G9
Itoigawa, Japan 55 F8
Iton →, France 18 C8
Itonamas →, Bolivia 124 F6
Itri, Italy 30 A6
Itsa, Egypt 80 J7
Íttiri, Italy 30 B1
Ittoqqortoormiit, Greenland 4 B6
Itu, Brazil 127 A6
Itu, Nigeria 83 D6
Itu Aba I., S. China Sea 62 B4
Ituiutaba, Brazil 125 G9
Itumbiara, Brazil 125 G9
Ituna, Canada 105 C8
Itunge Port, Tanzania 87 D3
Iturbe, Argentina 126 A2
Ituri →, Dem. Rep. of the Congo 86 B2
Iturup, Ostrov, Russia 51 E15
Ituxi →, Brazil 124 E6
Ituyuro →, Argentina 126 A3
Itzehoe, Germany 24 B5
Ivahona, Madag. 89 C8
Ivaí →, Brazil 127 A5
Ivalo, Finland 8 B22
Ivalojoki →, Finland 8 B22
Ivanava, Belarus 47 F3
Ivančice, Czech Rep. 27 B9
Ivăneşti, Romania 43 D12
Ivangorod, Russia 46 C5
Ivanhoe, Australia 95 E3
Ivanhoe, Calif., U.S.A. 116 J7
Ivanhoe, Minn., U.S.A. 112 C6
Ivanić Grad, Croatia 29 C13
Ivanjica, Serbia, Yug. 40 C4
Ivanjska, Bos.-H. 42 F2
Ivankoyskoye Vdkhr., Russia 46 D9
Ivano-Frankivsk, Ukraine 47 H3
Ivano-Frankovsk = Ivano-Frankivsk, Ukraine 47 H3
Ivanovo = Ivanava, Belarus 47 F3
Ivanovo, Russia 46 D11
Ivanšćica, Croatia 29 B13
Ivato, Madag. 89 C8
Ivatsevichy, Belarus 47 F3
Ivaylovgrad, Bulgaria 41 E10
Ivinheima →, Brazil 127 A5
Ivinhema, Brazil 127 A5
Ivohibe, Madag. 89 C8
Ivory Coast, W. Afr. 82 E4
Ivory Coast ■, Africa 82 D4
Ivösjön, Sweden 11 H8
Ivrea, Italy 28 C4
İvrindi, Turkey 39 B9
Ivujivik, Canada 101 B12
Ivybridge, U.K. 13 G4
Iwaizumi, Japan 54 E10
Iwaki, Japan 55 F10
Iwakuni, Japan 55 G6
Iwamizawa, Japan 54 C10
Iwanai, Japan 54 C10
Iwata, Japan 55 G8
Iwate □, Japan 54 E10
Iwate-San, Japan 54 E10
Iwo, Nigeria 83 D5
Iwonicz-Zdrój, Poland 45 J8
Ixiamas, Bolivia 124 F5
Ixopo, S. Africa 89 E5
Ixtepec, Mexico 119 D5
Ixtlán del Río, Mexico 118 C4
Iyal Bakhit, Sudan 81 E2
Iyo, Japan 55 H6
Izabal, L. de, Guatemala 120 C2
Izamal, Mexico 119 C7
Izberbash, Russia 49 J8
Izbica, Poland 45 H10
Izbica Kujawska, Poland 45 F5
Izbiceni, Romania 43 G9
Izena-Shima, Japan 55 L3
Izgrev, Bulgaria 41 C10
Izhevsk, Russia 50 D6
Izmayil, Ukraine 47 K5
İzmir, Turkey 39 C9
İzmir □, Turkey 39 C9
İzmir Körfezi, Turkey 39 C8
İzmit = Kocaeli, Turkey 41 F13
Iznájar, Spain 35 H6
Iznalloz, Spain 35 H7
İznik, Turkey 72 B3
İznik Gölü, Turkey 41 F13
Izobil'nyy, Russia 49 H5
Izola, Slovenia 29 C10
Izra, Syria 75 C5
Iztochni Rodopi, Bulgaria 41 E9
Izu-Shotō, Japan 55 G10
Izúcar de Matamoros, Mexico 119 D5
Izumi-Sano, Japan 55 G7
Izumo, Japan 55 G6
Izyaslav, Ukraine 47 G4
Izyum, Ukraine 47 H9


# J


Jaba, Ethiopia 81 F4
Jabal at Tā'ir, Red Sea 81 D5
Jabalón →, Spain 35 G6
Jabalpur, India 69 H8
Jabbūl, Syria 70 B3
Jabiru, Australia 92 B5
Jablah, Syria 70 C3
Jablanac, Croatia 29 D11
Jablanica, Bos.-H. 42 G2
Jablonec nad Nisou, Czech Rep. 26 A8
Jablonica, Slovak Rep. 27 C10
Jabłonowo Pomorskie, Poland 44 E6
Jablunkov, Czech Rep. 27 B11
Jaboatão, Brazil 125 E11
Jaboticabal, Brazil 127 A6
Jabukovac, Serbia, Yug. 40 B6
Jaca, Spain 32 C4
Jacareí, Brazil 127 A6
Jacarèzinho, Brazil 127 A6
Jackman, U.S.A. 109 C10
Jacksboro, U.S.A. 113 J5
Jackson, Ala., U.S.A. 109 K2
Jackson, Calif., U.S.A. 116 G6
Jackson, Ky., U.S.A. 108 G4
Jackson, Mich., U.S.A. 108 D3
Jackson, Minn., U.S.A. 112 D7
Jackson, Miss., U.S.A. 113 J9
Jackson, Mo., U.S.A. 113 G10
Jackson, N.H., U.S.A. 111 B13
Jackson, Ohio, U.S.A. 108 F4
Jackson, Tenn., U.S.A. 109 H1
Jackson, Wyo., U.S.A. 114 E8
Jackson B., N.Z. 91 K2
Jackson L., U.S.A. 114 E8
Jacksons, N.Z. 91 K3
Jackson's Arm, Canada 103 C8
Jacksonville, Ala., U.S.A. 109 J3
Jacksonville, Ark., U.S.A. 113 H8
Jacksonville, Calif., U.S.A. 116 H6
Jacksonville, Fla., U.S.A. 109 K5
Jacksonville, Ill., U.S.A. 112 F9
Jacksonville, N.C., U.S.A. 109 H7
Jacksonville, Tex., U.S.A. 113 K7
Jacksonville Beach, U.S.A. 109 K5
Jacmel, Haiti 121 C5
Jacob Lake, U.S.A. 115 H7
Jacobabad, Pakistan 68 E3
Jacobina, Brazil 125 F10
Jacques Cartier, Dét. de, Canada 103 C7
Jacques Cartier, Mt., Canada 103 C6
Jacques Cartier, Parc Prov., Canada 103 C5
Jacqueville, Ivory C. 82 D4
Jacuí →, Brazil 127 C5
Jacumba, U.S.A. 117 N10
Jacundá →, Brazil 125 D8
Jade, Germany 24 B4
Jadebusen, Germany 24 B4
Jadotville = Likasi, Dem. Rep. of the Congo 87 E2
Jadovnik, Serbia, Yug. 40 C3
Jadraque, Spain 32 E2
Jaén, Peru 124 E3
Jaén, Spain 35 H7
Jaén □, Spain 35 H7
Jafarabad, India 68 J4
Jaffa = Tel Aviv-Yafo, Israel 75 C3
Jaffa, C., Australia 95 F2
Jaffna, Sri Lanka 66 Q12
Jaffrey, U.S.A. 111 D12
Jagadhri, India 68 D7
Jagadishpur, India 69 G11
Jagdalpur, India 67 K13
Jagersfontein, S. Africa 88 D4
Jaghīn →, Iran 71 E8
Jagodina, Serbia, Yug. 40 B5
Jagraon, India 66 D9
Jagst →, Germany 25 F5
Jagtial, India 66 K11
Jaguariaíva, Brazil 127 A6
Jaguaribe →, Brazil 125 D11
Jagüey Grande, Cuba 120 B3
Jahanabad, India 69 G11
Jahazpur, India 68 G6
Jahrom, Iran 71 D7
Jaijon, India 68 D7
Jailolo, Indonesia 63 D7
Jailolo, Selat, Indonesia 63 D7
Jaipur, India 68 F6
Jais, India 69 F9
Jaisalmer, India 68 F4
Jaisinghnagar, India 69 H8
Jaitaran, India 68 F5
Jaithari, India 69 H8
Jājarm, Iran 71 B8
Jajce, Bos.-H. 42 F2
Jakam →, India 68 H6
Jakarta, Indonesia 62 F3
Jakhal, India 68 E6
Jakhau, India 68 H3
Jakobstad = Pietarsaari, Finland 8 E20
Jakupica, Macedonia 40 E5
Jal, U.S.A. 113 J3
Jalālābād, Afghan. 68 B4
Jalalabad, India 69 F8
Jalalpur Jattan, Pakistan 68 C6
Jalama, U.S.A. 117 L6
Jalapa, Guatemala 120 D2
Jalapa Enríquez, Mexico 119 D5
Jalasjärvi, Finland 9 E20
Jalaun, India 69 F8
Jaldhaka →, Bangla. 69 F13
Jalesar, India 68 F8
Jaleswar, Nepal 69 F11
Jalgaon, India 66 J9
Jalībah, Iraq 70 D5
Jalingo, Nigeria 83 D7
Jalisco □, Mexico 118 D4
Jalkot, Pakistan 69 B5
Jallas →, Spain 34 C1
Jalna, India 66 K9
Jalón →, Spain 32 D3
Jalor, India 68 G5
Jalpa, Mexico 118 C4
Jalpaiguri, India 67 F16
Jaluit I., Marshall Is. 96 G8
Jalūlā, Iraq 70 C5
Jamaari, Nigeria 83 C6
Jamaica ■, W. Indies 120 C4
Jamalpur, Bangla. 67 G16
Jamalpur, India 69 G12
Jamalpurganj, India 69 H13
Jamanxim →, Brazil 125 D7
Jambi, Indonesia 62 E2
Jambi □, Indonesia 62 E2
Jambusar, India 68 H5
James →, S. Dak., U.S.A. 112 D6
James →, Va., U.S.A. 108 G7
James B., Canada 102 B3
James Ranges, Australia 92 D5
James Ross I., Antarctica 5 C18
Jamesabad, Pakistan 68 G3
Jamestown, Australia 95 E2
Jamestown, S. Africa 88 E4
Jamestown, N. Dak., U.S.A. 112 B5
Jamestown, N.Y., U.S.A. 110 D5
Jamestown, Pa., U.S.A. 110 E4
Jamīlābād, Iran 71 C6
Jamiltepec, Mexico 119 D5
Jamira →, India 69 J13
Jämjö, Sweden 11 H9
Jamkhandi, India 66 L9
Jammerbugt, Denmark 11 G3
Jammu, India 68 C6
Jammu & Kashmir □, India 69 B7
Jamnagar, India 68 H4
Jamni →, India 69 G8
Jampur, Pakistan 68 E4
Jamrud, Pakistan 68 C4
Jämsä, Finland 9 F21
Jamshedpur, India 69 H12
Jamtara, India 69 H12
Jämtland, Sweden 8 E15
Jämtlands län □, Sweden 10 B7
Jan L., Canada 105 C8
Jan Mayen, Arctic 4 B7
Janakkala, Finland 9 F21
Janaúba, Brazil 125 G10
Jand, Pakistan 68 C5
Jandaq, Iran 71 C7
Jandia, Canary Is. 37 F5
Jandia, Pta. de, Canary Is. 37 F5
Jandola, Pakistan 68 C4
Jandowae, Australia 95 D5
Jándula →, Spain 35 G6
Janesville, U.S.A. 112 D10
Janga, Ghana 83 C4
Jangamo, Mozam. 89 C6
Janghai, India 69 G10
Janikowo, Poland 45 F5
Janīn, West Bank 75 C4
Janinà = Ioánnina □, Greece 38 B2
Janja, Bos.-H. 42 F4
Janjevo, Kosovo, Yug. 40 D5
Janjgir, India 69 J10
Janjina, Croatia 29 F14
Janjina, Madag. 89 C8
Janos, Mexico 118 A3
Jánoshalma, Hungary 42 D4
Jánosháza, Hungary 42 C2
Jánossomorja, Hungary 42 C2
Janów, Poland 45 H6
Janów Lubelski, Poland 45 H9
Janów Podlaski, Poland 45 F10
Janowiec Wielkopolski, Poland 45 F4
Januária, Brazil 125 G10
Janub Dârfûr □, Sudan 81 E2
Janub Kordofân □, Sudan 81 E3
Janûb Sînî □, Egypt 75 F2
Janubio, Canary Is. 37 F6
Janville, France 19 D8
Janzé, France 18 E5
Jaora, India 68 H6
Japan ■, Asia 55 G8
Japan, Sea of, Asia 54 E7
Japan Trench, Pac. Oc. 52 F18
Japen = Yapen, Indonesia 63 E9
Japla, India 69 G11
Japurá →, Brazil 122 D4
Jaquarão, Brazil 127 C5
Jaqué, Panama 120 E4
Jarābulus, Syria 70 B3
Jaraicejo, Spain 35 F5
Jaraíz de la Vera, Spain 34 E5
Jarama →, Spain 34 E7
Jaramānah, Syria 72 F7
Jarandilla, Spain 34 E5
Jaranwala, Pakistan 68 D5
Jarash, Jordan 75 C4
Järbo, Sweden 10 D10
Jardim, Brazil 126 A4
Jardín →, Spain 33 G2
Jardines de la Reina, Arch. de los, Cuba 120 B4
Jargalang, China 57 C12
Jargalant = Hovd, Mongolia 60 B4
Jari →, Brazil 125 D8
Jarīr, W. al →, Si. Arabia 70 E4
Järlåsa, Sweden 10 E11
Jarmen, Germany 24 B9
Järna, Dalarnas, Sweden 10 D8
Järna, Stockholm, Sweden 10 E11
Jarnac, France 20 C3
Jarny, France 19 C12
Jarocin, Poland 45 G4
Jaroměř, Czech Rep. 26 A8
Jarosław, Poland 45 H9
Järpås, Sweden 11 F6
Järpen, Sweden 10 A7
Jarrahdale, Australia 93 F2
Jarrahi →, Iran 71 D6
Jarres, Plaine des, Laos 64 C4
Jarso, Ethiopia 81 F4
Jartai, China 56 E3
Jarud Qi, China 57 B11
Järvenpää, Finland 9 F21
Jarvis, Canada 110 D4
Jarvis I., Pac. Oc. 97 H12
Jarvorník, Czech Rep. 27 A10
Järvsö, Sweden 10 C10
Jarwa, India 69 F10
Jaša Tomić, Serbia, Yug. 42 E5
Jasdan, India 68 H4
Jashpurnagar, India 69 H11
Jasidih, India 69 G12
Jasień, Poland 45 G2
Jāsimīyah, Iraq 70 C5
Jasin, Malaysia 65 L4
Jāsk, Iran 71 E8
Jasło, Poland 45 J8
Jasmund, Germany 24 A9
Jaso, India 69 G9
Jasper, Alta., Canada 104 C5
Jasper, Ont., Canada 111 B9
Jasper, Ala., U.S.A. 109 J2
Jasper, Fla., U.S.A. 109 K4
Jasper, Ind., U.S.A. 108 F2
Jasper, Tex., U.S.A. 113 K8
Jasper Nat. Park, Canada 104 C5
Jasrasar, India 68 F5
Jastarnia, Poland 44 D5
Jastrebarsko, Croatia 29 C12
Jastrowie, Poland 44 E3
Jastrzębie Zdrój, Poland 45 J5
Jász-Nagykun-Szolnok □, Hungary 42 C5
Jászapáti, Hungary 42 C5
Jászárokszállás, Hungary 42 C4
Jászberény, Hungary 42 C4
Jászkisér, Hungary 42 C5
Jászladány, Hungary 42 C5
Jataí, Brazil 125 G8
Jati, Pakistan 68 G3
Jatibarang, Indonesia 63 G13
Jatinegara, Indonesia 63 G12
Játiva = Xátiva, Spain 33 G4
Jättendal, Sweden 10 C11
Jaú, Brazil 127 A6
Jauja, Peru 124 F3
Jaunpur, India 69 G10
Java = Jawa, Indonesia 62 F3
Java Barat □, Indonesia 63 G12
Java Sea, Indonesia 62 E3
Java Tengah □, Indonesia 63 G14
Java Timur □, Indonesia 63 G15
Java Trench, Ind. Oc. 62 F3
Javalambre, Sa. de, Spain 32 E4
Jávea, Spain 33 G5
Javhlant = Ulyasutay, Mongolia 60 B4
Jawa, Indonesia 62 F3
Jawad, India 68 G6
Jawor, Poland 45 G3
Jaworzno, Poland 45 H6
Jaworzyna Śląska, Poland 45 H3
Jay Peak, U.S.A. 111 B12
Jaya, Puncak, Indonesia 63 E9
Jayanti, India 67 F16
Jayapura, Indonesia 63 E10
Jayawijaya, Pegunungan, Indonesia 63 E9
Jaynagar, India 67 F15
Jayrūd, Syria 70 C3
Jayton, U.S.A. 113 J4
Jāz Mūrīān, Hāmūn-e, Iran 71 E8
Jazīreh-ye Shīf, Iran 71 D6
Jazminal, Mexico 118 C4
Jazzīn, Lebanon 75 B4
Jean, U.S.A. 117 K11
Jean Marie River, Canada 104 A4
Jean Rabel, Haiti 121 C5
Jeanerette, U.S.A. 113 L9
Jeanette, Ostrov = Zhannetty, Ostrov, Russia 51 B16
Jeannette, U.S.A. 110 F5
Jebāl Bārez, Kūh-e, Iran 71 D8
Jebba, Nigeria 83 D5
Jebel, Bahr el →, Sudan 81 F3
Jebel Dud, Sudan 81 E3
Jebel Qerri, Sudan 81 D3
Jedburgh, U.K. 14 F6
Jedda = Jiddah, Si. Arabia 74 C2
Jeddore L., Canada 103 C8
Jedlicze, Poland 45 J8
Jędrzejów, Poland 45 H7
Jedwabne, Poland 45 E9
Jeetzel →, Germany 24 B7
Jefferson, Iowa, U.S.A. 112 D7
Jefferson, Ohio, U.S.A. 110 E4
Jefferson, Tex., U.S.A. 113 J7
Jefferson, Mt., Nev., U.S.A. 114 G5
Jefferson, Mt., Oreg., U.S.A. 114 D3
Jefferson City, Mo., U.S.A. 112 F8
Jefferson City, Tenn., U.S.A. 109 G4
Jeffersontown, U.S.A. 108 F3
Jeffersonville, U.S.A. 108 F3
Jeffrey City, U.S.A. 114 E10
Jega, Nigeria 83 C5
Jēkabpils, Latvia 9 H21
Jekyll I., U.S.A. 109 K5
Jelcz-Laskowice, Poland 45 G4
Jelenia Góra, Poland 45 H2
Jelgava, Latvia 9 H20
Jelgava □, Latvia 44 B10
Jelica, Serbia, Yug. 40 C4
Jelli, Sudan 81 F3
Jelšava, Slovak Rep. 27 C13
Jemaja, Indonesia 65 L5
Jemaluang, Malaysia 65 L4
Jember, Indonesia 63 H15
Jembongan, Malaysia 62 C5
Jena, Germany 24 E7
Jena, U.S.A. 113 K8
Jenbach, Austria 26 D4
Jenkins, U.S.A. 108 G4
Jenner, U.S.A. 116 G3
Jennings, U.S.A. 113 K8
Jepara, Indonesia 63 G14
Jeparit, Australia 95 F3
Jequié, Brazil 125 F10
Jequitinhonha, Brazil 125 G10
Jequitinhonha →, Brazil 125 G11
Jerantut, Malaysia 65 L4
Jérémie, Haiti 121 C5
Jerez, Punta, Mexico 119 C5
Jerez de García Salinas, Mexico 118 C4
Jerez de la Frontera, Spain 35 J4
Jerez de los Caballeros, Spain 35 G4
Jericho = El Arīḥā, West Bank 75 D4
Jericho, Australia 94 C4
Jerichow, Germany 24 C8
Jerid, Chott = Djerid, Chott, Tunisia 78 B7
Jerilderie, Australia 95 F4
Jermyn, U.S.A. 111 E9
Jerome, U.S.A. 114 E6
Jerramungup, Australia 93 F2
Jersey, U.K. 13 H5
Jersey City, U.S.A. 111 F10
Jersey Shore, U.S.A. 110 E7
Jerseyville, U.S.A. 112 F9
Jerusalem, Israel 75 D4
Jervis B., Australia 95 F5
Jervis Inlet, Canada 104 C4
Jerzu, Italy 30 C2
Jesenice, Slovenia 29 B11
Jeseník, Czech Rep. 27 A10
Jesenké, Slovak Rep. 27 C13
Jesi = Iesi, Italy 29 E10
Jesselton = Kota Kinabalu, Malaysia 62 C5
Jessnitz, Germany 24 D8

Kingwood

Kingwood, U.S.A. 113 K7
Kınık, Antalya, Turkey 39 E11
Kınık, İzmir, Turkey 39 B9
Kinistino, Canada 105 C7
Kinkala, Congo 84 E2
Kinki □, Japan 55 H8
Kinleith, N.Z. 91 H5
Kinmount, Canada 110 B6
Kinna, Sweden 11 G6
Kinnairds Hd., U.K. 14 D6
Kinnared, Sweden 11 G7
Kinnarodden, Norway 6 A11
Kinnarp, Sweden 11 F7
Kinneviken, Sweden 11 F7
Kinngait = Cape Dorset, Canada 101 B12
Kino, Mexico 118 B2
Kinoje →, Canada 102 B3
Kinomoto, Japan 55 G8
Kinoni, Uganda 86 C3
Kinoosao, Canada 105 B8
Kinross, U.K. 14 E5
Kinsale, Ireland 15 E3
Kinsale, Old Hd. of, Ireland 15 E3
Kinsha = Chang Jiang →, China 59 B13
Kinshasa, Dem. Rep. of the Congo 84 E3
Kinsley, U.S.A. 113 G5
Kinsman, U.S.A. 110 E4
Kinston, U.S.A. 109 H7
Kintampo, Ghana 83 D4
Kintore Ra., Australia 92 D4
Kintyre, U.K. 14 F3
Kintyre, Mull of, U.K. 14 F3
Kinushseo →, Canada 102 A3
Kinuso, Canada 104 B5
Kinyangiri, Tanzania 86 C3
Kinyeti, Sudan 81 G3
Kinzig →, Germany 25 G3
Kinzua, U.S.A. 110 E6
Kinzua Dam, U.S.A. 110 E6
Kióni, Greece 38 C2
Kiosk, Canada 102 C4
Kiowa, Kans., U.S.A. 113 G5
Kiowa, Okla., U.S.A. 113 H7
Kipahigan L., Canada 105 B8
Kipanga, Tanzania 86 D4
Kiparissía, Greece 38 D3
Kiparissiakós Kólpos, Greece 38 D3
Kipawa, L., Canada 102 C4
Kipembawe, Tanzania 86 D3
Kipengere Ra., Tanzania 87 D3
Kipili, Tanzania 86 D3
Kipini, Kenya 86 C5
Kipling, Canada 105 C8
Kippure, Ireland 15 C5
Kipushi, Dem. Rep. of the Congo 87 E2
Kirane, Mali 82 B2
Kiranomena, Madag. 89 B8
Kiraz, Turkey 39 C10
Kirazlı, Turkey 41 F10
Kirchhain, Germany 24 E4
Kirchheim, Germany 25 G5
Kirchheimbolanden, Germany 25 F3
Kirchschlag, Austria 27 D9
Kireç, Turkey 39 B10
Kirensk, Russia 51 D11
Kirghizia = Kyrgyzstan ■, Asia 50 E8
Kirghizstan = Kyrgyzstan ■, Asia 50 E8
Kiribati ■, Pac. Oc. 96 H10
Kırıkhan, Turkey 72 D7
Kırıkkale, Turkey 72 C5
Kirillov, Russia 46 C10
Kirin = Jilin, China 57 C14
Kirishi, Russia 46 C7
Kiritimati, Kiribati 97 G12
Kırka, Turkey 39 B12
Kırkağaç, Turkey 39 B9
Kirkby, U.K. 12 D5
Kirkby Lonsdale, U.K. 12 C5
Kirkcaldy, U.K. 14 E5
Kirkcudbright, U.K. 14 G4
Kirkee, India 66 K8
Kirkenes, Norway 8 B23
Kirkfield, Canada 110 B6
Kirkjubæjarklaustur, Iceland 8 E4
Kirkkonummi, Finland 9 F21
Kirkland Lake, Canada 102 C3
Kırklareli, Turkey 41 E11
Kırklareli □, Turkey 41 E11
Kirksville, U.S.A. 112 E8
Kirkūk, Iraq 70 C5
Kirkwall, U.K. 14 C6
Kirkwood, S. Africa 88 E4
Kirn, Germany 25 F3
Kirov, Kaluga, Russia 46 E8
Kirov, Kirov, Russia 50 D5
Kirovabad = Gäncä, Azerbaijan 49 K8
Kirovakan = Vanadzor, Armenia 49 K7
Kirovograd = Kirovohrad, Ukraine 47 H7
Kirovohrad, Ukraine 47 H7
Kirovsk = Babadayhan, Turkmenistan 50 F7
Kirovskiy, Astrakhan, Russia 49 H9
Kirovskiy, Kamchatka, Russia 51 D16
Kirovskiy, Primorsk, Russia 54 B6
Kirriemuir, U.K. 14 E5
Kirsanov, Russia 48 D6
Kırşehir, Turkey 70 B2
Kirtachi, Niger 83 C5
Kirthar Range, Pakistan 68 F2
Kirtland, U.S.A. 115 H9
Kiruna, Sweden 8 C19
Kirundu, Dem. Rep. of the Congo 86 C2
Kirya, Russia 48 C8
Kiryū, Japan 55 F9
Kisa, Sweden 11 G9
Kisaga, Tanzania 86 C3
Kisalaya, Nic. 120 D3
Kisalföld, Hungary 42 C2
Kisámou, Kólpos, Greece 36 D5
Kisanga, Dem. Rep. of the Congo 86 B2
Kisangani, Dem. Rep. of the Congo 86 B2
Kisar, Indonesia 63 F7
Kisarawe, Tanzania 86 D4
Kisarazu, Japan 55 G9
Kisbér, Hungary 42 C3
Kishanganga →, Pakistan 69 B5
Kishanganj, India 69 F13
Kishangarh, Raj., India 68 F6
Kishangarh, Raj., India 68 F4
Kishi, Nigeria 83 D5
Kishinev = Chişinău, Moldova 43 C13
Kishiwada, Japan 55 G7
Kishtwar, India 69 C6
Kisielice, Poland 44 E6
Kisii, Kenya 86 C3
Kisiju, Tanzania 86 D4
Kisir, Turkey 73 B10
Kisizi, Uganda 86 C2
Kiskomárom = Zalakomár, Hungary 42 D2
Kiskőrei-víztároló, Hungary 42 C5
Kiskőrös, Hungary 42 D4
Kiskundorozsma, Hungary 42 D5
Kiskunfélegyháza, Hungary 42 D4
Kiskunhalas, Hungary 42 D4
Kiskunmajsa, Hungary 42 D4
Kislovodsk, Russia 49 J6
Kismayu = Chisimaio, Somali Rep. 77 G8
Kiso-Gawa →, Japan 55 G8
Kiso-Sammyaku, Japan 55 G8
Kisofukushima, Japan 55 G8
Kisoro, Uganda 86 C2
Kissidougou, Guinea 82 D2
Kissimmee, U.S.A. 109 L5
Kissimmee →, U.S.A. 109 M5
Kississing L., Canada 105 B8
Kissónerga, Cyprus 36 E11
Kissu, J., Sudan 80 C2
Kistanje, Croatia 29 E12
Kisújszállás, Hungary 42 C5
Kisumu, Kenya 86 C3
Kisvárda, Hungary 42 B7
Kiswani, Tanzania 86 C4
Kiswere, Tanzania 87 D4
Kit Carson, U.S.A. 112 F3
Kita, Mali 82 C3
Kitaibaraki, Japan 55 F10
Kitakami, Japan 54 E10
Kitakami-Gawa →, Japan 54 E10
Kitakami-Sammyaku, Japan 54 E10
Kitakata, Japan 54 F9
Kitakyūshū, Japan 55 H5
Kitale, Kenya 86 B4
Kitami, Japan 54 C11
Kitami-Sammyaku, Japan 54 B11
Kitangiri, L., Tanzania 86 C3
Kitaya, Tanzania 87 E5
Kitchener, Canada 102 D3
Kitee, Finland 46 A6
Kitega = Gitega, Burundi 86 C2
Kitengo, Dem. Rep. of the Congo 86 D1
Kitgum, Uganda 86 B3
Kíthira, Greece 38 E5
Kíthnos, Greece 38 D6
Kiti, Cyprus 36 E12
Kiti, C., Cyprus 36 E12
Kitimat, Canada 104 C3
Kitinen →, Finland 8 C22
Kitiyab, Sudan 81 D3
Kítros, Greece 40 F6
Kitsuki, Japan 55 H5
Kittakittaooloo, L., Australia 95 D2
Kittanning, U.S.A. 110 F5
Kittatinny Mts., U.S.A. 111 F10
Kittery, U.S.A. 109 D10
Kittilä, Finland 8 C21
Kitui, Kenya 86 C4
Kitwanga, Canada 104 B3
Kitwe, Zambia 87 E2
Kitzbühel, Austria 26 D5
Kitzbühler Alpen, Austria 26 D5
Kitzingen, Germany 25 F6
Kivarli, India 68 G5
Kivertsi, Ukraine 47 G3
Kividhes, Cyprus 36 E11
Kivik, Sweden 11 J8
Kivotós, Greece 40 F5
Kivu, L., Dem. Rep. of the Congo 86 C2
Kiyev = Kyyiv, Ukraine 47 G6
Kiyevskoye Vdkhr. = Kyyivske Vdskh., Ukraine 47 G6
Kıyıköy, Turkey 41 E12
Kiziguru, Rwanda 86 C3
Kızıl Adalar, Turkey 41 F13
Kızıl Irmak →, Turkey 72 B6
Kizil Jilga, India 69 B8
Kizil Yurt, Russia 49 J8
Kızılcabölük, Turkey 39 D11
Kızılcadağ, Turkey 39 D11
Kızılcahamam, Turkey 72 B5
Kızılhisar, Turkey 72 D3
Kızılırmak, Turkey 72 B5
Kızılkaya, Turkey 39 D12
Kızılören, Turkey 39 C12
Kızıltepe, Turkey 70 B4
Kizimkazi, Tanzania 86 D4
Kizlyar, Russia 49 J8
Kizyl-Arvat = Gyzylarbat, Turkmenistan 50 F6
Kjellerup, Denmark 11 H3
Kjölur, Iceland 8 D4
Kladanj, Bos.-H. 42 F3
Kladnica, Serbia, Yug. 40 C4
Kladno, Czech Rep. 26 A7
Kladovo, Serbia, Yug. 40 B6
Klaeng, Thailand 64 F3
Klagenfurt, Austria 26 E7
Klaipėda, Lithuania 9 J19
Klaipėda □, Lithuania 44 C8
Klaksvík, Færoe Is. 8 E9
Klamath →, U.S.A. 114 F1
Klamath Falls, U.S.A. 114 E3
Klamath Mts., U.S.A. 114 F2
Klamono, Indonesia 63 E8
Klanjec, Croatia 29 B12
Klappan →, Canada 104 B3
Klarälven →, Sweden 10 E7
Klässbol, Sweden 10 E6
Klatovy, Czech Rep. 26 B6
Klawer, S. Africa 88 E2
Klazienaveen, Neths. 17 B6
Klé, Mali 82 C3
Klecko, Poland 45 F4
Kleczew, Poland 45 F5
Kleena Kleene, Canada 104 C4
Klein-Karas, Namibia 88 D2
Klekovača, Bos.-H. 29 D13
Klenoec, Macedonia 40 E4
Klenovec, Slovak Rep. 27 C12
Klerksdorp, S. Africa 88 D4
Kleszczele, Poland 45 F10
Kletnya, Russia 46 F7
Kletsk = Klyetsk, Belarus 47 F4
Kletskiy, Russia 49 F6
Kleve, Germany 24 D2
Klickitat, U.S.A. 114 D3
Klickitat →, U.S.A. 116 E5
Klidhes, Cyprus 36 D13
Klimovichi, Belarus 46 F6
Klin, Russia 46 D9
Klina, Kosovo, Yug. 40 D4
Klinaklini →, Canada 104 C3
Klintehamn, Sweden 11 G12
Klintsy, Russia 47 F7
Klip →, S. Africa 89 D4
Klipdale, S. Africa 88 E2
Klippan, Sweden 11 H7
Klipplaat, S. Africa 88 E3
Klisura, Bulgaria 41 D8
Kljajićevo, Serbia, Yug. 42 E4
Ključ, Bos.-H. 29 D13
Kłobuck, Poland 45 H5
Klockestrand, Sweden 10 B11
Kłodawa, Poland 45 F5
Kłodzko, Poland 45 H3
Klos, Albania 40 E4
Klosterneuburg, Austria 27 C9
Klosters, Switz. 25 J5
Klötze, Germany 24 C7
Klouto, Togo 83 D5
Kluane L., Canada 100 B6
Kluane Nat. Park, Canada 104 A1
Kluczbork, Poland 45 H5
Klukwan, U.S.A. 104 B1
Klyetsk, Belarus 47 F4
Klyuchevskaya, Gora, Russia 51 D17
Knäred, Sweden 11 H7
Knaresborough, U.K. 12 C6
Knee L., Man., Canada 102 A1
Knee L., Sask., Canada 105 B7
Knezha, Bulgaria 41 C8
Knić, Serbia, Yug. 40 C4
Knight Inlet, Canada 104 C3
Knighton, U.K. 13 E4
Knights Ferry, U.S.A. 116 H6
Knights Landing, U.S.A. 116 G5
Knin, Croatia 29 D13
Knislinge, Sweden 11 H8
Knittelfeld, Austria 26 D7
Knivsta, Sweden 10 E11
Knjaževac, Serbia, Yug. 40 C6
Knob, C., Australia 93 F2
Knock, Ireland 15 C3
Knockmealdown Mts., Ireland 15 D4
Knokke-Heist, Belgium 17 C3
Knossós, Greece 36 D7
Knowlton, Canada 111 A12
Knox, U.S.A. 108 E2
Knox Coast, Antarctica 5 C8
Knoxville, Iowa, U.S.A. 112 E8
Knoxville, Pa., U.S.A. 110 E7
Knoxville, Tenn., U.S.A. 109 H4
Knysna, S. Africa 88 E3
Knyszyn, Poland 44 E9
Ko Kha, Thailand 64 C2
Koartac = Quaqtaq, Canada 101 B13
Koba, Indonesia 63 F8
Kobarid, Slovenia 29 B10
Kobayashi, Japan 55 J5
Kobdo = Hovd, Mongolia 60 B4
Kōbe, Japan 55 G7
Kobelyaky, Ukraine 47 H8
København, Denmark 11 J6
Københavns Amtskommune □, Denmark 11 J6
Kobenni, Mauritania 82 B3
Kōbi-Sho, Japan 55 M1
Koblenz, Germany 25 E3
Kobo, Ethiopia 81 E4
Kobryn, Belarus 47 F3
Kobuleti, Georgia 49 K5
Kobylin, Poland 45 G4
Kobyłka, Poland 45 F8
Kobylkino, Russia 48 C6
Koca →, Turkey 41 F11
Kocabaş, Turkey 39 D11
Kocaeli, Turkey 41 F13
Kocaeli □, Turkey 41 F13
Kočane, Serbia, Yug. 40 C5
Kočani, Macedonia 40 E6
Koçarlı, Turkey 39 D9
Koceljevo, Serbia, Yug. 40 B3
Kočevje, Slovenia 29 C11
Koch Bihar, India 67 F16
Kochang, S. Korea 57 G14
Kochas, India 69 G10
Kocher →, Germany 25 F5
Kochi = Cochin, India 66 Q10
Kōchi, Japan 55 H6
Kōchi □, Japan 55 H6
Kochiu = Gejiu, China 58 F4
Kock, Poland 45 G9
Kodarma, India 69 G11
Kode, Sweden 11 G5
Kodiak, U.S.A. 100 C4
Kodiak I., U.S.A. 100 C4
Kodinar, India 68 J4
Kodok, Sudan 81 F3
Kodori →, Georgia 49 J5
Koedoesberge, S. Africa 88 E3
Koes, Namibia 88 D2
Kofçaz, Turkey 41 E11
Koffiefontein, S. Africa 88 D4
Kofiau, Indonesia 63 E7
Köflach, Austria 26 D8
Koforidua, Ghana 83 D4
Kōfu, Japan 55 G9
Koga, Japan 55 F9
Kogaluk →, Canada 103 A7
Køge, Denmark 11 J6
Køge Bugt, Denmark 11 J6
Kogi □, Nigeria 83 D6
Kogin Baba, Nigeria 83 D7
Koh-i-Khurd, Afghan. 68 C1
Koh-i-Maran, Pakistan 68 E2
Kohat, Pakistan 68 C4
Kohima, India 67 G19
Kohkīlūyeh va Būyer Aḥmadi □, Iran 71 D6
Kohler Ra., Antarctica 5 D15
Kohlu, Pakistan 68 E3
Kohtla-Järve, Estonia 9 G22
Koillismaa, Finland 8 D23
Koin-dong, N. Korea 57 D14
Koinare, Bulgaria 41 C8
Koindu, S. Leone 82 D2
Kojetín, Czech Rep. 27 B10
Kojō, N. Korea 57 E14
Kojonup, Australia 93 F2
Kojūr, Iran 71 B6
Koka, Sudan 80 C3
Kokand = Qūqon, Uzbekistan 50 E8
Kokas, Indonesia 63 E8
Kokava, Slovak Rep. 27 C12
Kokchetav = Kökshetaū, Kazakstan 50 D7
Kokemäenjoki →, Finland 9 F19
Kokhma, Russia 48 B5
Koki, Senegal 82 B1
Kokkola, Finland 8 E20
Koko, Nigeria 83 C5
Koko Kyunzu, Burma 67 M18
Kokolopozo, Ivory C. 82 D3
Kokomo, U.S.A. 108 E2
Kokoro, Niger 83 C5
Koksan, N. Korea 57 E14
Kökshetaū, Kazakstan 50 D7
Koksoak →, Canada 101 C13
Kokstad, S. Africa 89 E4
Kokubu, Japan 55 J5
Kola, Indonesia 63 F8
Kola Pen. = Kolskiy Poluostrov, Russia 50 C4
Kolachi →, Pakistan 68 F2
Kolahoi, India 69 B6
Kolahun, Liberia 82 D2
Kolaka, Indonesia 63 E6
Kolar, India 66 N11
Kolar Gold Fields, India 66 N11
Kolaras, India 68 G6
Kolari, Finland 8 C20
Kolárovo, Slovak Rep. 27 D10
Kolašin, Montenegro, Yug. 40 D3
Kolayat, India 66 F8
Kolbäck, Sweden 10 E10
Kolbäcksån →, Sweden 10 E10
Kolbermoor, Germany 25 H8
Kolbuszowa, Poland 45 H8
Kolchugino = Leninsk-Kuznetskiy, Russia 50 D9
Kolchugino, Russia 46 D10
Kolda, Senegal 82 C2
Koldegi, Sudan 81 E3
Kolding, Denmark 11 J3
Kolepom = Dolak, Pulau, Indonesia 63 F9
Kolguyev, Ostrov, Russia 50 C5
Kolhapur, India 66 L9
Kolia, Ivory C. 82 D3
Kolín, Czech Rep. 26 A8
Kolind, Denmark 11 H4
Kolkas rags, Latvia 9 H20
Kolkata, India 69 H13
Kollam = Quilon, India 66 Q10
Kölleda, Germany 24 D7
Kollum, Neths. 17 A6
Kolmanskop, Namibia 88 D2
Köln, Germany 24 E2
Kolno, Poland 44 E8
Koło, Poland 45 F5
Kołobrzeg, Poland 44 D2
Kolokani, Mali 82 C3
Koloko, Burkina Faso 82 C3
Kololo, Ethiopia 81 F5
Kolomna, Russia 46 E10
Kolomyya, Ukraine 47 H3
Kolondiéba, Mali 82 C3
Kolonodale, Indonesia 63 E6
Kolonowskie, Poland 45 H5
Kolosib, India 67 G18
Kolpashevo, Russia 50 D9
Kolpino, Russia 46 C6
Kolpny, Russia 47 F9
Kolskiy Poluostrov, Russia 50 C4
Kolsva, Sweden 10 E9
Kolubara →, Serbia, Yug. 40 B4
Koluszki, Poland 45 G6
Kolwezi, Dem. Rep. of the Congo 87 E2
Kolyma →, Russia 51 C17
Kolymskoye Nagorye, Russia 51 C16
Kôm Hamâda, Egypt 80 H7
Kôm Ombo, Egypt 80 C3
Komadugu Gana →, Nigeria 83 C7
Komandorskiye Is. = Komandorskiye Ostrova, Russia 51 D17
Komandorskiye Ostrova, Russia 51 D17
Komárno, Slovak Rep. 27 D11
Komárom, Hungary 42 C3
Komárom-Esztergom □, Hungary 42 C3
Komatipoort, S. Africa 89 D5
Komatou Yialou, Cyprus 36 D13
Komatsu, Japan 55 F8
Komatsushima, Japan 55 H7
Kombissiri, Burkina Faso 83 C4
Kombori, Burkina Faso 82 C4
Kombóti, Greece 38 B3
Komen, Slovenia 29 C10
Komenda, Ghana 83 D4
Komi □, Russia 50 C6
Komiža, Croatia 29 E13
Komló, Hungary 42 D3
Kommunarsk = Alchevsk, Ukraine 47 H10
Kommunizma, Pik, Tajikistan 50 F8
Komodo, Indonesia 63 F5
Komoé →, Ivory C. 82 D4
Komoran, Pulau, Indonesia 63 F9
Komoro, Japan 55 F9
Komotini, Greece 41 E9
Komovi, Montenegro, Yug. 40 D3
Kompasberg, S. Africa 88 E3
Kompong Bang, Cambodia 65 F5
Kompong Cham, Cambodia 65 F5
Kompong Chhnang = Kampang Chhnang, Cambodia 65 F5
Kompong Chikreng, Cambodia 64 F5
Kompong Kleang, Cambodia 64 F5
Kompong Luong, Cambodia 65 G5
Kompong Pranak, Cambodia 64 F5
Kompong Som = Kampong Saom, Cambodia 65 G4
Kompong Som, Chhung = Kampong Saom, Chaak, Cambodia 65 G4
Kompong Speu, Cambodia 65 G5
Kompong Sralao, Cambodia 64 E5
Kompong Thom, Cambodia 64 F5
Kompong Trabeck, Cambodia 64 F5
Kompong Trabeck, Cambodia 65 G5
Kompong Trach, Cambodia 65 G5
Kompong Tralach, Cambodia 65 G5
Komrat = Comrat, Moldova 43 D13
Komsberg, S. Africa 88 E3
Komsomolets, Ostrov, Russia 51 A10
Komsomolsk, Amur, Russia 51 D14
Komsomolsk, Ivanovo, Russia 46 D11
Komsomolskiy, Russia 48 C7
Kömür Burnu, Turkey 39 C8
Kon Tum, Vietnam 64 E7
Kon Tum, Plateau du, Vietnam 64 E7
Kona, Mali 82 C4
Konakovo, Russia 46 D9
Konarhā □, Afghan. 66 B7
Konārī, Iran 71 D6
Konch, India 69 G8
Konde, Tanzania 86 C4
Kondiá, Greece 39 B7
Kondinin, Australia 93 F2
Kondoa, Tanzania 86 C4
Kondókali, Greece 36 A3
Kondopaga, Russia 46 A8
Kondratyevo, Russia 51 D10
Kondrovo, Russia 46 E8
Konduga, Nigeria 83 C7
Köneürgench, Turkmenistan 50 E6
Konevo, Russia 46 A10
Kong = Khong →, Cambodia 64 F5
Kong, Ivory C. 82 D4
Kong, Koh, Cambodia 65 G4
Kong Christian IX Land, Greenland 4 C6
Kong Christian X Land, Greenland 4 B6
Kong Frederik IX Land, Greenland 4 C5
Kong Frederik VI Kyst, Greenland 4 C5
Kong Frederik VIII Land, Greenland 4 B6
Kong Oscar Fjord, Greenland 4 B6
Kongeå →, Denmark 11 J2
Kongerslev, Denmark 11 H4
Kongju, S. Korea 57 F14
Konglu, Burma 67 F20
Kongola, Namibia 88 B3

Kongolo, *Kasai-Or., Dem. Rep. of the Congo* 86 D1
Kongolo, *Katanga, Dem. Rep. of the Congo* 86 D2
Kongor, *Sudan* 81 F3
Kongoussi, *Burkina Faso* 83 C4
Kongsberg, *Norway* 9 G13
Kongsvinger, *Norway* 9 F15
Kongwa, *Tanzania* 86 D4
Koni, *Dem. Rep. of the Congo* 87 E2
Koni, Mts., *Dem. Rep. of the Congo* 87 E2
Koniakari, *Mali* 82 C2
Koniecpol, *Poland* 45 H6
Königs Wusterhausen, *Germany* 24 C9
Königsberg = Kaliningrad, *Russia* 9 J19
Königsbrunn, *Germany* 25 G6
Königslutter, *Germany* 24 C6
Konin, *Poland* 45 F5
Konispol, *Albania* 40 G4
Kónitsa, *Greece* 38 A2
Konjic, *Bos.-H.* 42 G2
Konkiep, *Namibia* 88 D2
Konkouré →, *Guinea* 82 D2
Könnern, *Germany* 24 D7
Kono, *S. Leone* 82 D2
Konongo, *Ghana* 83 D4
Konosha, *Russia* 46 B11
Kōnosu, *Japan* 55 F9
Konotop, *Ukraine* 47 G7
Konsankoro, *Guinea* 82 D3
Końskie, *Poland* 45 G7
Konstancin-Jeziorna, *Poland* 45 F8
Konstantinovka = Kostyantynivka, *Ukraine* 47 H9
Konstantinovsk, *Russia* 49 G5
Konstantynów Łódźki, *Poland* 45 G6
Konstanz, *Germany* 25 H5
Kont, *Iran* 71 E9
Kontagora, *Nigeria* 83 C6
Kontcha, *Cameroon* 83 D7
Konya, *Turkey* 70 B2
Konya Ovası, *Turkey* 72 C5
Konz, *Germany* 25 F2
Konza, *Kenya* 86 C4
Koocanusa, L., *Canada* 114 B6
Kookynie, *Australia* 93 E3
Koolyanobbing, *Australia* 93 F2
Koonibba, *Australia* 95 E1
Koorawatha, *Australia* 95 E4
Koorda, *Australia* 93 F2
Kooskia, *U.S.A.* 114 C6
Kootenay →, *U.S.A.* 104 D5
Kootenay L., *Canada* 104 D5
Kootenay Nat. Park, *Canada* 104 C5
Kootjieskolk, *S. Africa* 88 E3
Kopanovka, *Russia* 49 G8
Kopaonik, *Yugoslavia* 40 C4
Kópavogur, *Iceland* 8 D3
Koper, *Slovenia* 29 C10
Kopervik, *Norway* 9 G11
Kopet Dagh, *Asia* 71 B8
Kopi, *Australia* 95 E2
Köping, *Sweden* 10 E10
Köpingsvik, *Sweden* 11 H10
Kopište, *Croatia* 29 F13
Koplik, *Albania* 40 D3
Köpmanholmen, *Sweden* 10 A12
Kopparberg, *Sweden* 10 E9
Koppeh Dāgh = Kopet Dagh, *Asia* 71 B8
Koppies, *S. Africa* 89 D4
Koppom, *Sweden* 10 E6
Koprivlen, *Bulgaria* 40 E7
Koprivnica, *Croatia* 29 B13
Kopřivnice, *Czech Rep.* 27 B11
Koprivshtitsa, *Bulgaria* 41 D8
Köprübaşı, *Turkey* 39 C10
Kopychyntsi, *Ukraine* 47 H3
Korab, *Macedonia* 40 E4
Korakiána, *Greece* 36 A3
Koral, *India* 68 J5
Korarou, L., *Mali* 82 B4
Korba, *India* 69 H10
Korbach, *Germany* 24 D4
Korbu, G., *Malaysia* 65 K3
Korce = Korçë, *Albania* 40 F4
Korçë, *Albania* 40 F4
Korčula, *Croatia* 29 F13
Korčulanski Kanal, *Croatia* 29 E13
Kord Kūy, *Iran* 71 B7
Kord Sheykh, *Iran* 71 D7
Kordestān □, *Iran* 70 C5
Kordofân, *Sudan* 79 F11
Koré Mayroua, *Niger* 83 C5
Korea, North ■, *Asia* 57 E14
Korea, South ■, *Asia* 57 G15
Korea Bay, *Korea* 57 E13
Korea Strait, *Asia* 57 H15
Korem, *Ethiopia* 81 E4
Korenevo, *Russia* 47 G8
Korenovsk, *Russia* 49 H4
Korets, *Ukraine* 47 G4
Korfantów, *Poland* 45 H4
Korgan, *Turkey* 72 B7
Korgus, *Sudan* 80 D3
Korhogo, *Ivory C.* 82 D3
Koribundu, *S. Leone* 82 D2
Korienzé, *Mali* 82 B4
Korinthía □, *Greece* 38 D4
Korinthiakós Kólpos, *Greece* 38 C4
Kórinthos, *Greece* 38 D4
Korioumé, *Mali* 82 B4
Korissa, Límni, *Greece* 36 B3
Kōriyama, *Japan* 54 F10
Korkuteli, *Turkey* 39 D12
Kormakiti, C., *Cyprus* 36 D11
Körmend, *Hungary* 42 C1
Kornat, *Croatia* 29 E12
Korneshty = Corneşti, *Moldova* 43 C13
Korneuburg, *Austria* 27 C9
Kórnik, *Poland* 45 F4
Koro, *Fiji* 91 C8
Koro, *Ivory C.* 82 D3
Koro, *Mali* 82 C4
Koro Sea, *Fiji* 91 C9
Korocha, *Russia* 47 G9
Köroğlu Dağları, *Turkey* 72 B5
Korogwe, *Tanzania* 86 D4
Koronadal, *Phil.* 61 H6
Koróni, *Greece* 38 E3
Korónia, Limni, *Greece* 40 F7
Koronís, *Greece* 39 D7
Koronowo, *Poland* 45 E4
Koror, *Palau* 63 C8
Körös →, *Hungary* 42 D5
Köröstarcsa, *Hungary* 42 D6
Korosten, *Ukraine* 47 G5
Korostyshev, *Ukraine* 47 G5
Korotoyak, *Russia* 47 G10
Korraraika, Helodranon' i, *Madag.* 89 B7
Korsakov, *Russia* 51 E15
Korsberga, *Sweden* 11 G9
Korshunovo, *Russia* 51 D12
Korsør, *Denmark* 11 J5
Korsun Shevchenkovskiy, *Ukraine* 47 H6
Korsze, *Poland* 44 D8
Korti, *Sudan* 80 D3
Kortrijk, *Belgium* 17 D3
Korucu, *Turkey* 39 B9
Korwai, *India* 68 G8
Koryakskoye Nagorye, *Russia* 51 C18
Koryŏng, *S. Korea* 57 G15
Koryukovka, *Ukraine* 47 G7
Kos, *Greece* 39 E9
Kosa, *Ethiopia* 81 F4
Kosaya Gora, *Russia* 46 E9
Kościan, *Poland* 45 F3
Kościerzyna, *Poland* 44 D4
Kosciusko, *U.S.A.* 113 J10
Kosciuszko, Mt., *Australia* 95 F4
Kösély →, *Hungary* 42 C6
Kosha, *Sudan* 80 C3
Koshava, *Bulgaria* 40 B7
K'oshih = Kashi, *China* 60 C2
Koshiki-Rettō, *Japan* 55 J4
Kosi, *India* 68 F7
Kosi →, *India* 69 E8
Košice, *Slovak Rep.* 27 C14
Košický □, *Slovak Rep.* 27 C14
Kosjerić, *Serbia, Yug.* 40 B3
Köşk, *Turkey* 39 D10
Koskhinoú, *Greece* 36 C10
Koslan, *Russia* 50 C5
Kosŏng, *N. Korea* 57 E15
Kosovo □, *Yugoslavia* 40 D4
Kosovo Polje, *Kosovo, Yug.* 40 D5
Kosovska Kamenica, *Kosovo, Yug.* 40 D5
Kosovska Mitrovica, *Kosovo, Yug.* 40 D4
Kossou, L. de, *Ivory C.* 82 D3
Kosta, *Sweden* 11 H9
Kostajnica, *Croatia* 29 C13
Kostanjevica, *Slovenia* 29 C12
Kostenets, *Bulgaria* 40 D7
Koster, *S. Africa* 88 D4
Kôstî, *Sudan* 81 E3
Kostinbrod, *Bulgaria* 40 D7
Kostolac, *Serbia, Yug.* 40 B5
Kostopil, *Ukraine* 47 G4
Kostroma, *Russia* 46 D11
Kostromskoye Vdkhr., *Russia* 46 D11
Kostrzyn, *Lubuskie, Poland* 45 F1
Kostrzyn, *Wielkopolskie, Poland* 45 F4
Kostyantynivka, *Ukraine* 47 H9
Kostyukovichi = Kastsyukovichy, *Belarus* 46 F7
Koszalin, *Poland* 44 D3
Kőszeg, *Hungary* 42 C1
Kot Addu, *Pakistan* 68 D4
Kot Kapura, *India* 68 D6
Kot Moman, *Pakistan* 68 C5
Kot Sultan, *Pakistan* 68 D4
Kota, *India* 68 G6
Kota Baharu, *Malaysia* 65 J4
Kota Barrage, *India* 68 G6
Kota Belud, *Malaysia* 62 C5
Kota Kinabalu, *Malaysia* 62 C5
Kota Kubu Baharu, *Malaysia* 65 L3
Kota Tinggi, *Malaysia* 65 M4
Kotaagung, *Indonesia* 62 F2
Kotabaru, *Indonesia* 62 E5
Kotabumi, *Indonesia* 62 E2
Kotamobagu, *Indonesia* 63 D6
Kotcho L., *Canada* 104 B4
Kotdwara, *India* 69 E8
Kotel, *Bulgaria* 41 D10
Kotelnich, *Russia* 48 A9
Kotelnikovo, *Russia* 49 G6
Kotelnyy, Ostrov, *Russia* 51 B14
Kothari →, *India* 68 G6
Köthen, *Germany* 24 D7
Kothi, *Mad. P., India* 69 H10
Kothi, *Mad. P., India* 69 G9
Kotiro, *Pakistan* 68 F2
Kotka, *Finland* 9 F22
Kotlas, *Russia* 50 C5
Kotlenska Planina, *Bulgaria* 41 D10
Kotli, *Pakistan* 68 C5
Kotma, *India* 69 H9
Kotmul, *Pakistan* 69 B6
Koton-Karifi, *Nigeria* 83 D6
Kotonkoro, *Nigeria* 83 C6
Kotor, *Montenegro, Yug.* 40 D2
Kotor Varoš, *Bos.-H.* 42 F2
Kotoriba, *Croatia* 29 B13
Kotovo, *Russia* 48 E7
Kotovsk, *Russia* 48 D5
Kotovsk, *Ukraine* 47 J5
Kotputli, *India* 68 F7
Kotri, *Pakistan* 68 G3
Kótronas, *Greece* 38 E4
Kötschach-Mauthen, *Austria* 26 E6
Kotturu, *India* 66 M10
Kotuy →, *Russia* 51 B11
Kotzebue, *U.S.A.* 100 B3
Koudougou, *Burkina Faso* 82 C4
Koufonísi, *Greece* 36 E8
Koufonísia, *Greece* 39 E7
Kougaberge, *S. Africa* 88 E3
Kouibli, *Ivory C.* 82 D3
Kouilou →, *Congo* 84 E2
Koula Moutou, *Gabon* 84 E2
Koulen = Kulen, *Cambodia* 64 F5
Koulikoro, *Mali* 82 C3
Kouloúra, *Greece* 36 A3
Koúm-bournoú, Ákra, *Greece* 36 C10
Koumala, *Australia* 94 C4
Koumankou, *Mali* 82 C3
Koumbia, *Burkina Faso* 82 C4
Koumbia, *Guinea* 82 C2
Koumboum, *Guinea* 82 C2
Koumpenntoum, *Senegal* 82 C2
Koumra, *Chad* 79 G9
Koun-Fao, *Ivory C.* 82 D4
Koundara, *Guinea* 82 C2
Koundian, *Guinea* 82 C3
Koungheul, *Senegal* 82 C2
Kounradskiy, *Kazakstan* 50 E8
Kountze, *U.S.A.* 113 K7
Koupéla, *Burkina Faso* 83 C4
Kourémalé, *Mali* 82 C3
Kouris →, *Cyprus* 36 E11
Kourou, *Fr. Guiana* 125 B8
Kourouba, *Mali* 82 C2
Kouroukoto, *Mali* 82 C2
Kourouma, *Burkina Faso* 82 C4
Kourouninkoto, *Mali* 82 C3
Kouroussa, *Guinea* 82 C3
Koussanar, *Senegal* 82 C2
Koussané, *Mali* 82 C2
Koussane, *Senegal* 82 C2
Kousseri, *Cameroon* 79 F8
Koutiala, *Mali* 82 C3
Kouto, *Ivory C.* 82 D3
Kouvé, *Togo* 83 D5
Kouvola, *Finland* 9 F22
Kovačica, *Serbia, Yug.* 42 E5
Kovel, *Ukraine* 47 G3
Kovin, *Serbia, Yug.* 42 F5
Kovrov, *Russia* 48 B5
Kowal, *Poland* 45 F6
Kowalewo Pomorskie, *Poland* 45 E5
Kowanyama, *Australia* 94 B3
Kowloon, *H.K.* 59 F10
Kowŏn, *N. Korea* 57 E14
Köyceğiz, *Turkey* 39 E10
Köyceğiz Gölü, *Turkey* 39 E10
Koyulhisar, *Turkey* 72 B7
Koyunyeri, *Turkey* 41 F10
Koza, *Japan* 55 L3
Kozak, *Turkey* 39 B9
Kozan, *Turkey* 70 B2
Kozáni, *Greece* 40 F5
Kozáni □, *Greece* 40 F5
Kozara, *Bos.-H.* 29 D14
Kozarac, *Bos.-H.* 29 D13
Kozelets, *Ukraine* 47 G6
Kozelsk, *Russia* 46 E8
Kozhikode = Calicut, *India* 66 P9
Koziegłowy, *Poland* 45 H6
Kozienice, *Poland* 45 G8
Kozje, *Slovenia* 29 B12
Kozloduy, *Bulgaria* 40 C7
Kozlovets, *Bulgaria* 41 C9
Kozlovka, *Russia* 48 C9
Kozlu, *Turkey* 72 B4
Kozluk, *Turkey* 73 C9
Koźmin, *Poland* 45 G4
Kozmodemyansk, *Russia* 48 B8
Kożuchów, *Poland* 45 G2
Kozyatyn, *Ukraine* 47 H5
Kpabia, *Ghana* 83 D4
Kpalimé, *Togo* 83 D5
Kpandae, *Ghana* 83 D4
Kpessi, *Togo* 83 D5
Kra, Isthmus of = Kra, Kho Khot, *Thailand* 65 G2
Kra, Kho Khot, *Thailand* 65 G2
Kra Buri, *Thailand* 65 G2
Kraai →, *S. Africa* 88 E4
Krabi, *Thailand* 65 H2
Kracheh, *Cambodia* 64 F6
Kragan, *Indonesia* 63 G14
Kragerø, *Norway* 9 G13
Kragujevac, *Serbia, Yug.* 40 B4
Krajenka, *Poland* 45 E3
Krajina, *Bos.-H.* 29 D13
Krakatau = Rakata, Pulau, *Indonesia* 62 F3
Krakatoa = Rakata, Pulau, *Indonesia* 62 F3
Krakor, *Cambodia* 64 F5
Kraków, *Poland* 45 H6
Kralanh, *Cambodia* 64 F4
Králíky, *Czech Rep.* 27 A9
Kraljevo, *Serbia, Yug.* 40 C4
Královéhradecký □, *Czech Rep.* 26 A8
Královský Chlmec, *Slovak Rep.* 27 C14
Kralupy nad Vltavou, *Czech Rep.* 26 A7
Kramatorsk, *Ukraine* 47 H9
Kramfors, *Sweden* 10 B11
Kraniá, *Greece* 40 G5
Kranía Elassónas, *Greece* 38 B4
Kranídhion, *Greece* 38 D5
Kranj, *Slovenia* 29 B11
Kranjska Gora, *Slovenia* 29 B10
Kranskop, *S. Africa* 89 D5
Krapina, *Croatia* 29 B12
Krapina →, *Croatia* 29 C12
Krapkowice, *Poland* 45 H4
Kras, *Croatia* 29 C10
Kraskino, *Russia* 51 E14
Krāslava, *Latvia* 46 E4
Kraslice, *Czech Rep.* 26 A5
Krasnaya Gorbatka, *Russia* 48 C5
Krasnaya Polyana, *Russia* 49 J5
Kraśnik, *Poland* 45 H9
Krasnoarmeisk, *Ukraine* 47 H9
Krasnoarmeysk, *Russia* 48 E7
Krasnoarmeyskiy, *Russia* 49 G6
Krasnobrod, *Poland* 45 H10
Krasnodar, *Russia* 49 H4
Krasnodon, *Ukraine* 47 H10
Krasnogorskiy, *Russia* 48 B9
Krasnograd = Krasnohrad, *Ukraine* 47 H8
Krasnogvardeyskoye, *Russia* 49 H5
Krasnogvardyesk, *Ukraine* 47 K8
Krasnohrad, *Ukraine* 47 H8
Krasnokutsk, *Ukraine* 47 G8
Krasnolesnyy, *Russia* 47 G10
Krasnoperekopsk, *Ukraine* 47 J7
Krasnorechenskiy, *Russia* 54 B7
Krasnoselkup, *Russia* 50 C9
Krasnoslobodsk, *Mordvinia, Russia* 48 C6
Krasnoslobodsk, *Volgograd, Russia* 49 F7
Krasnoturinsk, *Russia* 50 D7
Krasnovodsk = Türkmenbashi, *Turkmenistan* 50 E6
Krasnoyarsk, *Russia* 51 D10
Krasnoye = Krasnyy, *Russia* 46 E6
Krasnozavodsk, *Russia* 46 D10
Krasny Sulin, *Russia* 47 J11
Krasnystaw, *Poland* 45 H10
Krasnyy, *Russia* 46 E6
Krasnyy Kholm, *Russia* 46 C9
Krasnyy Kut, *Russia* 48 E8
Krasnyy Liman, *Ukraine* 47 H9
Krasnyy Luch, *Ukraine* 47 H10
Krasnyy Profintern, *Russia* 46 D11
Krasnyy Yar, *Astrakhan, Russia* 49 G9
Krasnyy Yar, *Samara, Russia* 48 D10
Krasnyy Yar, *Volgograd, Russia* 48 E7
Krasnyye Baki, *Russia* 48 B7
Krasnyyoskolske Vdskh., *Ukraine* 47 H9
Kraszna →, *Hungary* 42 B7
Kratie = Kracheh, *Cambodia* 64 F6
Kratovo, *Macedonia* 40 D6
Krau, *Indonesia* 63 E10
Kravanh, Chuor Phnum, *Cambodia* 65 G4
Krefeld, *Germany* 24 D2
Krémaston, Límni, *Greece* 38 C3
Kremen, *Croatia* 29 D12
Kremenchug = Kremenchuk, *Ukraine* 47 H7
Kremenchuk, *Ukraine* 47 H7
Kremenchuksk Vdskh., *Ukraine* 47 H7
Kremenets, *Ukraine* 47 G3
Kremennaya, *Ukraine* 47 H10
Kremges = Svitlovodsk, *Ukraine* 47 H7
Kremmen, *Germany* 24 C9
Kremmling, *U.S.A.* 114 F10
Kremnica, *Slovak Rep.* 27 C11
Krems, *Austria* 26 C8
Kremsmünster, *Austria* 26 C7
Kretinga, *Lithuania* 9 J19
Krettsy, *Russia* 46 C7
Kreuzberg, *Germany* 25 E5
Kreuztal, *Germany* 24 E4
Kría Vrísi, *Greece* 40 F6
Kribi, *Cameroon* 83 E6
Krichem, *Bulgaria* 41 D8
Krichev = Krychaw, *Belarus* 46 F6
Krim, *Slovenia* 29 C11
Kriós, Ákra, *Greece* 36 D5
Krishna →, *India* 67 M12
Krishnanagar, *India* 69 H13
Kristdala, *Sweden* 11 G10
Kristiansand, *Norway* 9 G13
Kristianstad, *Sweden* 11 H8
Kristiansund, *Norway* 8 E12
Kristiinankaupunki, *Finland* 9 E19
Kristinehamn, *Sweden* 10 E8
Kristinestad = Kristiinankaupunki, *Finland* 9 E19
Kríti, *Greece* 36 D7
Kritsá, *Greece* 36 D7
Kriva →, *Macedonia* 40 D5
Kriva Palanka, *Macedonia* 40 D6
Krivaja →, *Bos.-H.* 42 F3
Krivelj, *Serbia, Yug.* 40 B6
Krivoy Rog = Kryvyy Rih, *Ukraine* 47 J7
Križevci, *Croatia* 29 B13
Krk, *Croatia* 29 C11
Krka →, *Slovenia* 29 C12
Krkonoše, *Czech Rep.* 26 A8
Krnov, *Czech Rep.* 27 A10
Krobia, *Poland* 45 G3
Krokeaí, *Greece* 38 E4
Krokek, *Sweden* 11 F10
Krokodil →, *Mozam.* 89 D5
Krokom, *Sweden* 10 A8
Krokowa, *Poland* 44 D5
Krolevets, *Ukraine* 47 G7
Kroměříž, *Czech Rep.* 27 B10
Krompachy, *Slovak Rep.* 27 C13
Kromy, *Russia* 47 F8
Kronach, *Germany* 25 E7
Krong Kaoh Kong, *Cambodia* 62 B2
Kronobergs län □, *Sweden* 11 H8
Kronprins Olav Kyst, *Antarctica* 5 C5
Kronshtadt, *Russia* 46 C5
Kroonstad, *S. Africa* 88 D4
Kröpelin, *Germany* 24 A7
Kropotkin, *Russia* 49 H5
Kropp, *Germany* 24 A5
Krosna, *Lithuania* 44 D10
Krośniewice, *Poland* 45 F6
Krosno, *Poland* 45 J8
Krosno Odrzańskie, *Poland* 45 F2
Krotoszyn, *Poland* 45 G4
Krotovka, *Russia* 48 D10
Kroussón, *Greece* 36 D6
Krrabë, *Albania* 40 E3
Krško, *Slovenia* 29 C12
Krstača, *Serbia, Yug.* 40 D4
Kruger Nat. Park, *S. Africa* 89 C5
Krugersdorp, *S. Africa* 89 D4
Kruisfontein, *S. Africa* 88 E3
Krujë, *Albania* 40 E3
Krulevshchina = Krulyewshchyna, *Belarus* 46 E4
Krulyewshchyna, *Belarus* 46 E4
Krumbach, *Germany* 25 G6
Krumë, *Albania* 40 D4
Krumovgrad, *Bulgaria* 41 E9
Krung Thep = Bangkok, *Thailand* 64 F3
Krupanj, *Serbia, Yug.* 40 B3
Krupina, *Slovak Rep.* 27 C12
Krupinica →, *Slovak Rep.* 27 C11
Krupki, *Belarus* 46 E5
Kruševac, *Serbia, Yug.* 40 C5
Kruševo, *Macedonia* 40 E5
Kruszwica, *Poland* 45 F5
Krychaw, *Belarus* 46 F6
Krymsk, *Russia* 47 K10
Krymskiy Poluostrov = Krymskyy Pivostriv, *Ukraine* 47 K8
Krymskyy Pivostriv, *Ukraine* 47 K8
Krynica, *Poland* 45 J7
Krynica Morska, *Poland* 44 D6
Krynki, *Poland* 45 E10
Kryvyy Rih, *Ukraine* 47 J7
Krzepice, *Poland* 45 H5
Krzeszów, *Poland* 45 H9
Krzna →, *Poland* 45 F10
Krzywiń, *Poland* 45 G3
Krzyż Wielkopolski, *Poland* 45 F2
Ksar el Kebir, *Morocco* 78 B4
Ksar es Souk = Er Rachidia, *Morocco* 78 B5
Książ Wielkopolski, *Poland* 45 F4
Kstovo, *Russia* 48 B7
Ku, W. el →, *Sudan* 81 E2
Kuala Belait, *Malaysia* 62 D4
Kuala Berang, *Malaysia* 65 K4
Kuala Dungun = Dungun, *Malaysia* 65 K4
Kuala Kangsar, *Malaysia* 65 K3
Kuala Kelawang, *Malaysia* 65 L4
Kuala Kerai, *Malaysia* 65 K4
Kuala Lipis, *Malaysia* 65 K4
Kuala Lumpur, *Malaysia* 65 L3
Kuala Nerang, *Malaysia* 65 J3
Kuala Pilah, *Malaysia* 65 L4
Kuala Rompin, *Malaysia* 65 L4
Kuala Selangor, *Malaysia* 65 L3
Kuala Sepetang, *Malaysia* 65 K3
Kuala Terengganu, *Malaysia* 65 K4
Kualajelai, *Indonesia* 62 E4
Kualakapuas, *Indonesia* 62 E4
Kualakurun, *Indonesia* 62 E4
Kualapembuang, *Indonesia* 62 E4
Kualasimpang, *Indonesia* 62 D1
Kuancheng, *China* 57 D10
Kuandang, *Indonesia* 63 D6
Kuandian, *China* 57 D13
Kuangchou = Guangzhou, *China* 59 F9
Kuanshan, *Taiwan* 59 F13
Kuantan, *Malaysia* 65 L4
Kuba = Quba, *Azerbaijan* 49 K9
Kuban →, *Russia* 47 K9
Kubenskoye, Ozero, *Russia* 46 C10
Kubokawa, *Japan* 55 H6
Kubrat, *Bulgaria* 41 C10
Kučevo, *Serbia, Yug.* 40 B5
Kucha Gompa, *India* 69 B7
Kuchaman, *India* 68 F6
Kuchenspitze, *Austria* 26 D3
Kuchinda, *India* 69 J11
Kuching, *Malaysia* 62 D4
Kuchino-eruba-Jima, *Japan* 55 J5
Kuchino-Shima, *Japan* 55 K4
Kuchinotsu, *Japan* 55 H5
Kuchl, *Austria* 26 D6
Kucing = Kuching, *Malaysia* 62 D4
Kuçovë, *Albania* 40 F3
Küçükbahçe, *Turkey* 39 C8
Küçükköy, *Turkey* 39 B8
Küçükkuyu, *Turkey* 39 B8
Küçükmenderes →, *Turkey* 39 D9
Kud →, *Pakistan* 68 F2
Kuda, *India* 66 H7

Kudat


Kudat, *Malaysia* 62 C5
Kudirkos Naumiestis, *Lithuania* 44 D9
Kudowa-Zdrój, *Poland* 45 H3
Kudus, *Indonesia* 63 G14
Kudymkar, *Russia* 50 D6
Kueiyang = Guiyang, *China* 58 D6
Kufra Oasis = Al Kufrah, *Libya* 79 D10
Kufstein, *Austria* 26 D5
Kugluktuk, *Canada* 100 B8
Kugong I., *Canada* 102 A4
Kūhak, *Iran* 66 F3
Kuhan, *Pakistan* 68 E2
Kūhbonān, *Iran* 71 D8
Kūhestak, *Iran* 71 E8
Kuhin, *Iran* 71 B6
Kūhīrī, *Iran* 71 E9
Kuhnsdorf, *Austria* 26 E7
Kūhpāyeh, *Eşfahan, Iran* 71 C7
Kūhpāyeh, *Kermān, Iran* 71 D8
Kūhrān, Kūh-e, *Iran* 71 E8
Kui Buri, *Thailand* 65 F2
Kuiseb →, *Namibia* 88 B2
Kuito, *Angola* 85 G3
Kuiu I., *U.S.A.* 104 B2
Kujang, *N. Korea* 57 E14
Kujawsko-Pomorskie □, *Poland* 44 E5
Kuji, *Japan* 54 D10
Kujū-San, *Japan* 55 H5
Kukavica, *Serbia, Yug.* 40 D5
Kukawa, *Nigeria* 83 C7
Kukës, *Albania* 40 D4
Kukmor, *Russia* 48 B10
Kukup, *Malaysia* 65 M4
Kukvidze, *Russia* 48 E6
Kula, *Bulgaria* 40 C6
Kula, *Serbia, Yug.* 42 E4
Kula, *Turkey* 39 C10
Kulachi, *Pakistan* 68 D4
Kulai, *Malaysia* 65 M4
Kulal, Mt., *Kenya* 86 B4
Kulaly, Ostrov, *Kazakstan* 49 H10
Kulasekarappattinam, *India* 66 Q11
Kulautuva, *Lithuania* 44 D10
Kuldīga, *Latvia* 9 H19
Kuldīga □, *Latvia* 44 B8
Kuldja = Yining, *China* 50 E9
Kuldu, *Sudan* 81 E2
Kulebaki, *Russia* 48 C6
Kulen, *Cambodia* 64 F5
Kulen Vakuf, *Bos.-H.* 29 D13
Kulgam, *India* 69 C6
Kulgera, *Australia* 94 D1
Kulim, *Malaysia* 65 K3
Kulin, *Australia* 93 F2
Kullen, *Sweden* 11 H6
Kulmbach, *Germany* 25 E7
Kŭlob, *Tajikistan* 50 F7
Kulp, *Turkey* 73 C9
Kulpawn →, *Ghana* 83 D4
Kulsary, *Kazakstan* 50 E6
Kulti, *India* 69 H12
Kulu, *India* 68 D7
Kulu, *Turkey* 72 C5
Kulumbura, *Australia* 92 B4
Kulunda, *Russia* 50 D8
Kulungar, *Afghan.* 68 C3
Kūlvand, *Iran* 71 D7
Kulwin, *Australia* 95 F3
Kulyab = Kŭlob, *Tajikistan* 50 F7
Kuma →, *Russia* 49 H8
Kumafşarı, *Turkey* 39 D11
Kumaganum, *Nigeria* 83 C7
Kumagaya, *Japan* 55 F9
Kumai, *Indonesia* 62 E4
Kumalar Dağı, *Turkey* 39 C12
Kumamba, Kepulauan, *Indonesia* 63 E9
Kumamoto, *Japan* 55 H5
Kumamoto □, *Japan* 55 H5
Kumanovo, *Macedonia* 40 D5
Kumara, *N.Z.* 91 K3
Kumarina, *Australia* 93 D2
Kumasi, *Ghana* 82 D4
Kumayri = Gyumri, *Armenia* 49 K6
Kumba, *Cameroon* 83 E6
Kumbağ, *Turkey* 41 F11
Kumbakonam, *India* 66 P11
Kumbarilla, *Australia* 95 D5
Kumbhraj, *India* 68 G7
Kumbia, *Australia* 95 D5
Kumbo, *Cameroon* 83 D7
Kŭmch'ŏn, *N. Korea* 57 E14
Kumdok, *India* 69 C8
Kume-Shima, *Japan* 55 L3
Kumeny, *Russia* 48 A9
Kumharsain, *India* 68 D7
Kŭmhwa, *S. Korea* 57 E14
Kumi, *Uganda* 86 B3
Kumkale, *Turkey* 41 G10
Kumla, *Sweden* 10 E9
Kumluca, *Turkey* 39 E12
Kummerower See, *Germany* 24 B8
Kumo, *Nigeria* 83 C7
Kumon Bum, *Burma* 67 F20
Kumylzhenskaya, *Russia* 48 F6
Kunágota, *Hungary* 42 D6
Kunashir, Ostrov, *Russia* 51 E15
Kunda, *Estonia* 9 G22
Kunda, *India* 69 G9
Kundar →, *Pakistan* 68 D3
Kundian, *Pakistan* 68 C4
Kundla, *India* 68 J4
Kunga →, *Bangla.* 69 J13
Kungälv, *Sweden* 11 G5
Kunghit I., *Canada* 104 C2
Kungrad = Qŭnghirot, *Uzbekistan* 50 E6
Kungsängen, *Sweden* 10 E11
Kungsbacka, *Sweden* 11 G6
Kungsgården, *Sweden* 10 D10
Kungshamn, *Sweden* 11 F5
Kungsör, *Sweden* 10 E10
Kungur, *Russia* 50 D6
Kunhar →, *Pakistan* 69 B5
Kunhegyes, *Hungary* 42 C5
Kuningan, *Indonesia* 63 G13
Kunlong, *Burma* 58 F2
Kunlun Shan, *Asia* 60 C3
Kunmadaras, *Hungary* 42 C5
Kunming, *China* 58 E4
Kunów, *Poland* 45 H8
Kunsan, *S. Korea* 57 G14
Kunshan, *China* 59 B13
Kunszentmárton, *Hungary* 42 D5
Kunszentmiklós, *Hungary* 42 C4
Kuntaur, *Senegal* 82 C2
Kununurra, *Australia* 92 C4
Kunwari →, *India* 69 F8
Kunya-Urgench = Köneürgench, *Turkmenistan* 50 E6
Künzelsau, *Germany* 25 F5
Kuopio, *Finland* 8 E22
Kupa →, *Croatia* 29 C13
Kupang, *Indonesia* 63 F6
Kupreanof I., *U.S.A.* 104 B2
Kupres, *Bos.-H.* 42 G2
Kupyansk, *Ukraine* 47 H9
Kupyansk-Uzlovoi, *Ukraine* 47 H9
Kuqa, *China* 60 B3
Kür →, *Azerbaijan* 73 C13
Kür Dili, *Azerbaijan* 71 B6
Kura = Kür →, *Azerbaijan* 73 C13
Kuranda, *Australia* 94 B4
Kuranga, *India* 68 H3
Kurashiki, *Japan* 55 G6
Kurayoshi, *Japan* 55 G6
Kürdämir, *Azerbaijan* 49 K9
Kurdistan, *Asia* 73 D10
Kŭrdzhali, *Bulgaria* 41 E9
Kure, *Japan* 55 G6
Küre, *Turkey* 72 B5
Küre Dağları, *Turkey* 72 B6
Kuressaare, *Estonia* 9 G20
Kurgan, *Russia* 50 D7
Kurganinsk, *Russia* 49 H5
Kurgannaya = Kurganinsk, *Russia* 49 H5
Kuri, *India* 68 F4
Kuria Maria Is. = Khurīyā Murīyā, Jazā'ir, *Oman* 74 D6
Kuridala, *Australia* 94 C3
Kurigram, *Bangla.* 67 G16
Kurikka, *Finland* 9 E20
Kuril Is. = Kurilskiye Ostrova, *Russia* 51 E15
Kuril Trench, *Pac. Oc.* 52 E19
Kurilsk, *Russia* 51 E15
Kurilskiye Ostrova, *Russia* 51 E15
Kurino, *Japan* 55 J5
Kurinskaya Kosa = Kür Dili, *Azerbaijan* 71 B6
Kurkur, *Egypt* 80 C3
Kurlovskiy, *Russia* 48 C5
Kurmuk, *Sudan* 81 E3
Kurnool, *India* 66 M11
Kuro-Shima, *Kagoshima, Japan* 55 J4
Kuro-Shima, *Okinawa, Japan* 55 M2
Kuror, J., *Sudan* 80 C3
Kurow, *N.Z.* 91 L3
Kurów, *Poland* 45 G9
Kurram →, *Pakistan* 68 C4
Kurri Kurri, *Australia* 95 E5
Kurrimine, *Australia* 94 B4
Kursavka, *Russia* 49 H6
Kurshskiy Zaliv, *Russia* 9 J19
Kursk, *Russia* 47 G9
Kuršumlija, *Serbia, Yug.* 40 C5
Kuršumlijska Banja, *Serbia, Yug.* 40 C5
Kurşunlu, *Bursa, Turkey* 41 F13
Kurşunlu, *Çankırı, Turkey* 72 B5
Kurtalan, *Turkey* 73 D9
Kurtbey, *Turkey* 41 E10
Kuru, *Sudan* 81 F2
Kuru, Bahr el →, *Sudan* 81 F2
Kurucaşile, *Turkey* 72 B5
Kuruçay, *Turkey* 70 B3
Kuruktag, *China* 60 B3
Kuruman, *S. Africa* 88 D3
Kuruman →, *S. Africa* 88 D3
Kurume, *Japan* 55 H5
Kurun →, *Sudan* 81 F3
Kurunegala, *Sri Lanka* 66 R12
Kurya, *Russia* 50 C6
Kus Gölü, *Turkey* 41 F11
Kuşadası, *Turkey* 72 D2
Kuşadası Körfezı, *Turkey* 39 D8
Kusatsu, *Japan* 55 F9
Kusawa L., *Canada* 104 A1
Kusel, *Germany* 25 F3
Kushaka, *Nigeria* 83 C6
Kushalgarh, *India* 68 H6
Kushchevskaya, *Russia* 49 G4
Kusheriki, *Nigeria* 83 C6
Kushikino, *Japan* 55 J5
Kushima, *Japan* 55 J5
Kushimoto, *Japan* 55 H7
Kushiro, *Japan* 54 C12
Kushiro-Gawa →, *Japan* 54 C12
Kūshk, *Iran* 71 D8
Kushka = Gushgy, *Turkmenistan* 50 F7
Kūshkī, *Iran* 70 C5
Kushol, *India* 69 C7
Kushtia, *Bangla.* 67 H16
Kushum →, *Kazakstan* 48 F10
Kuskokwim B., *U.S.A.* 100 C3
Kusmi, *India* 69 H10
Kussharo-Ko, *Japan* 54 C12
Kustanay = Qostanay, *Kazakstan* 50 D7
Kut, Ko, *Thailand* 65 G4
Kütahya, *Turkey* 39 B12
Kütahya □, *Turkey* 39 B11
Kutaisi, *Georgia* 49 J6
Kutaraja = Banda Aceh, *Indonesia* 62 C1
Kutch, Gulf of = Kachchh, Gulf of, *India* 68 H3
Kutch, Rann of = Kachchh, Rann of, *India* 68 H4
Kutina, *Croatia* 29 C13
Kutiyana, *India* 68 J4
Kutjevo, *Croatia* 42 E2
Kutkashen, *Azerbaijan* 49 K8
Kutná Hora, *Czech Rep.* 26 B8
Kutno, *Poland* 45 F6
Kutse, *Botswana* 88 C3
Kutu, *Dem. Rep. of the Congo* 84 E3
Kutum, *Sudan* 81 E1
Kúty, *Slovak Rep.* 27 C10
Kuujjuaq, *Canada* 101 C13
Kuujjuarapik, *Canada* 102 A4
Kuŭp-tong, *N. Korea* 57 D14
Kuusamo, *Finland* 8 D23
Kuusankoski, *Finland* 9 F22
Kuvshinovo, *Russia* 46 D8
Kuwait = Al Kuwayt, *Kuwait* 70 D5
Kuwait ■, *Asia* 70 D5
Kuwana, *Japan* 55 G8
Kuwana →, *India* 69 F10
Kuybyshev = Samara, *Russia* 48 D10
Kuybyshev, *Russia* 50 D8
Kuybyshevo, *Ukraine* 47 J9
Kuybyshevskoye Vdkhr., *Russia* 48 C9
Kuye He →, *China* 56 E6
Küyeh, *Iran* 70 B5
Küysanjaq, *Iraq* 70 B5
Kuyucak, *Turkey* 39 D10
Kuyumba, *Russia* 51 C10
Kuzey Anadolu Dağları, *Turkey* 72 B7
Kuzmin, *Serbia, Yug.* 42 E4
Kuznetsk, *Russia* 48 D8
Kuzomen, *Russia* 50 C4
Kvænangen, *Norway* 8 A19
Kværndrup, *Denmark* 11 J4
Kvaløy, *Norway* 8 B18
Kvänum, *Sweden* 11 F7
Kvareli = Qvareli, *Georgia* 49 K7
Kvarner, *Croatia* 29 D11
Kvarnerič, *Croatia* 29 D11
Kvicksund, *Sweden* 10 E10
Kvillsfors, *Sweden* 11 G9
Kvismare kanal, *Sweden* 10 E9
Kvissleby, *Sweden* 10 B11
Kwa-Nobuhle, *S. Africa* 85 L5
Kwabhaca, *S. Africa* 89 E4
Kwakhanai, *Botswana* 88 C3
Kwakoegron, *Surinam* 125 B7
Kwale, *Kenya* 86 C4
Kwale, *Nigeria* 83 D6
KwaMashu, *S. Africa* 89 D5
Kwando →, *Africa* 88 B3
Kwangdaeri, *N. Korea* 57 D14
Kwangju, *S. Korea* 57 G14
Kwango →, *Dem. Rep. of the Congo* 84 E3
Kwangsi-Chuang = Guangxi Zhuangzu Zizhiqu □, *China* 58 F7
Kwangtung = Guangdong □, *China* 59 F9
Kwara □, *Nigeria* 83 D6
Kwataboahegan →, *Canada* 102 B3
Kwatisore, *Indonesia* 63 E8
KwaZulu Natal □, *S. Africa* 89 D5
Kweichow = Guizhou □, *China* 58 D6
Kwekwe, *Zimbabwe* 87 F2
Kwidzyn, *Poland* 44 E5
Kwiha, *Ethiopia* 81 E4
Kwinana New Town, *Australia* 93 F2
Kwisa →, *Poland* 45 G2
Kwoka, *Indonesia* 63 E8
Kwolla, *Nigeria* 83 D6
Kyabra Cr. →, *Australia* 95 D3
Kyabram, *Australia* 95 F4
Kyaikto, *Burma* 64 D1
Kyakhta, *Russia* 51 D11
Kyancutta, *Australia* 95 E2
Kyaukpadaung, *Burma* 67 J19
Kyaukpyu, *Burma* 67 K18
Kyaukse, *Burma* 67 J20
Kybartai, *Lithuania* 44 D9
Kyburz, *U.S.A.* 116 G6
Kyelang, *India* 68 C7
Kyenjojo, *Uganda* 86 B3
Kyjov, *Czech Rep.* 27 B10
Kyle, *Canada* 105 C7
Kyle Dam, *Zimbabwe* 87 G3
Kyle of Lochalsh, *U.K.* 14 D3
Kyll →, *Germany* 25 F2
Kyllburg, *Germany* 25 E2
Kymijoki →, *Finland* 9 F22
Kyneton, *Australia* 95 F3
Kynuna, *Australia* 94 C3
Kyō-ga-Saki, *Japan* 55 G7
Kyoga, L., *Uganda* 86 B3
Kyogle, *Australia* 95 D5
Kyom →, *Sudan* 81 F2
Kyongju, *S. Korea* 57 G15
Kyongpyaw, *Burma* 67 L19
Kyŏngsŏng, *N. Korea* 57 D15
Kyōto, *Japan* 55 G7
Kyōto □, *Japan* 55 G7
Kyparissovouno, *Cyprus* 36 D12
Kyperounda, *Cyprus* 36 E11
Kyrenia, *Cyprus* 36 D12
Kyrgyzstan ■, *Asia* 50 E8
Kyritz, *Germany* 24 C8
Kyrkhult, *Sweden* 11 H8
Kyrönjoki →, *Finland* 8 E19
Kystatyam, *Russia* 51 C13
Kysucké Nové Mesto, *Slovak Rep.* 27 B11
Kythréa, *Cyprus* 36 D12
Kyunhla, *Burma* 67 H19
Kyuquot Sound, *Canada* 104 D3
Kyurdamir = Kürdämir, *Azerbaijan* 49 K9
Kyūshū, *Japan* 55 H5
Kyūshū □, *Japan* 55 H5
Kyūshū-Sanchi, *Japan* 55 H5
Kyustendil, *Bulgaria* 40 D6
Kyusyur, *Russia* 51 B13
Kyyiv, *Ukraine* 47 G6
Kyyivske Vdskh., *Ukraine* 47 G6
Kyzyl, *Russia* 51 D10
Kyzyl Kum, *Uzbekistan* 50 E7
Kyzyl-Kyya, *Kyrgyzstan* 50 E8
Kzyl-Orda = Qyzylorda, *Kazakstan* 50 E7


# L


La Albuera, *Spain* 35 G4
La Alcarria, *Spain* 32 E2
La Almarcha, *Spain* 32 F2
La Almunia de Doña Godina, *Spain* 32 D3
La Asunción, *Venezuela* 124 A6
La Baie, *Canada* 103 C5
La Banda, *Argentina* 126 B3
La Bañeza, *Spain* 34 C5
La Barca, *Mexico* 118 C4
La Barge, *U.S.A.* 114 E8
La Bastide-Puylaurent, *France* 20 D7
La Baule-Escoubiac, *France* 18 E4
La Belle, *U.S.A.* 109 M5
La Biche →, *Canada* 104 B4
La Biche, L., *Canada* 104 C6
La Bisbal d'Empordà, *Spain* 32 D8
La Bomba, *Mexico* 118 A1
La Brède, *France* 20 D3
La Bresse, *France* 19 D13
La Bureba, *Spain* 34 C7
La Calera, *Chile* 126 C1
La Campiña, *Spain* 35 H6
La Canal = Sa Canal, *Spain* 37 C7
La Cañiza = A Cañiza, *Spain* 34 C2
La Canourgue, *France* 20 D7
La Capelle, *France* 19 C10
La Carlota, *Argentina* 126 C3
La Carlota, *Phil.* 61 F5
La Carlota, *Spain* 35 H6
La Carolina, *Spain* 35 G7
La Cavalerie, *France* 20 D7
La Ceiba, *Honduras* 120 C2
La Chaise-Dieu, *France* 20 C7
La Chapelle d'Angillon, *France* 19 E9
La Chapelle-St-Luc, *France* 19 D11
La Chapelle-sur-Erdre, *France* 18 E5
La Charité-sur-Loire, *France* 19 E10
La Chartre-sur-le-Loir, *France* 18 E7
La Châtaigneraie, *France* 20 B3
La Châtre, *France* 19 F9
La Chaux-de-Fonds, *Switz.* 25 H2
La Chorrera, *Panama* 120 E4
La Ciotat, *France* 21 E9
La Clayette, *France* 19 F11
La Cocha, *Argentina* 126 B2
La Concepción = Ri-Aba, *Eq. Guin.* 83 E6
La Concepción, *Panama* 120 E3
La Concordia, *Mexico* 119 D6
La Coruña = A Coruña, *Spain* 34 B2
La Coruña □, *Spain* 34 B2
La Côte-St-André, *France* 21 C9
La Courtine-le-Trucq, *France* 20 C6
La Crau, *Bouches-du-Rhône, France* 21 E8
La Crau, *Var, France* 21 E10
La Crescent, *U.S.A.* 112 D9
La Crete, *Canada* 104 B5
La Crosse, *Kans., U.S.A.* 112 F5
La Crosse, *Wis., U.S.A.* 112 D9
La Cruz, *Costa Rica* 120 D2
La Cruz, *Mexico* 118 C3
La Désirade, *Guadeloupe* 121 C7
La Escondida, *Mexico* 118 C5
La Esmeralda, *Paraguay* 126 A3
La Esperanza, *Cuba* 120 B3
La Esperanza, *Honduras* 120 D2
La Estrada = A Estrada, *Spain* 34 C2
La Faouët, *France* 18 D3
La Fayette, *U.S.A.* 109 H3
La Fé, *Cuba* 120 B3
La Fère, *France* 19 C10
La Ferté-Bernard, *France* 18 D7
La Ferté-Gaucher, *France* 19 D10
La Ferté-Macé, *France* 18 D6
La Ferté-St-Aubin, *France* 19 E8
La Ferté-sous-Jouarre, *France* 19 D10
La Ferté-Vidame, *France* 18 D7
La Flèche, *France* 18 E6
La Follette, *U.S.A.* 109 G3
La Fregeneda, *Spain* 34 E4
La Fuente de San Esteban, *Spain* 34 E4
La Gacilly, *France* 18 E4
La Gineta, *Spain* 33 F2
La Grand-Combe, *France* 21 D8
La Grande, *U.S.A.* 114 D4
La Grande →, *Canada* 102 B5
La Grande Deux, Rés., *Canada* 102 B4
La Grande-Motte, *France* 21 E8
La Grande Quatre, Rés., *Canada* 102 B5
La Grande Trois, Rés., *Canada* 102 B4
La Grange, *Calif., U.S.A.* 116 H6
La Grange, *Ga., U.S.A.* 109 J3
La Grange, *Ky., U.S.A.* 108 F3
La Grange, *Tex., U.S.A.* 113 L6
La Grave, *France* 21 C10
La Guaira, *Venezuela* 124 A5
La Guardia = A Guarda, *Spain* 34 D2
La Gudiña = A Gudiña, *Spain* 34 C3
La Guerche-de-Bretagne, *France* 18 E5
La Guerche-sur-l'Aubois, *France* 19 F9
La Habana, *Cuba* 120 B3
La Haye-du-Puits, *France* 18 C5
La Horra, *Spain* 34 D7
La Independencia, *Mexico* 119 D6
La Isabela, *Dom. Rep.* 121 C5
La Jonquera, *Spain* 32 C7
La Junta, *U.S.A.* 113 F3
La Laguna, *Canary Is.* 37 F3
La Libertad, *Guatemala* 120 C1
La Libertad, *Mexico* 118 B2
La Ligua, *Chile* 126 C1
La Línea de la Concepción, *Spain* 35 J5
La Loche, *Canada* 105 B7
La Londe-les-Maures, *France* 21 E10
La Lora, *Spain* 34 C7
La Loupe, *France* 18 D8
La Louvière, *Belgium* 17 D4
La Machine, *France* 19 F10
La Maddalena, *Italy* 30 A2
La Malbaie, *Canada* 103 C5
La Mancha, *Spain* 33 F2
La Mariña, *Spain* 34 B3
La Martre, L., *Canada* 104 A5
La Mesa, *U.S.A.* 117 N9
La Misión, *Mexico* 118 A1
La Mothe-Achard, *France* 18 F5
La Motte, *France* 21 D10
La Motte-Chalançon, *France* 21 D9
La Motte-Servolex, *France* 21 C9
La Moure, *U.S.A.* 112 B5
La Muela, *Spain* 32 D3
La Mure, *France* 21 D9
La Negra, *Chile* 126 A1
La Oliva, *Canary Is.* 37 F6
La Orotava, *Canary Is.* 37 F3
La Oroya, *Peru* 124 F3
La Pacaudière, *France* 19 F10
La Palma, *Canary Is.* 37 F2
La Palma, *Panama* 120 E4
La Palma del Condado, *Spain* 35 H4
La Paloma, *Chile* 126 C1
La Pampa □, *Argentina* 126 D2
La Paragua, *Venezuela* 124 B6
La Paz, *Entre Ríos, Argentina* 126 C4
La Paz, *San Luis, Argentina* 126 C2
La Paz, *Bolivia* 124 G5
La Paz, *Honduras* 120 D2
La Paz, *Mexico* 118 C2
La Paz, *Phil.* 61 D4
La Paz Centro, *Nic.* 120 D2
La Pedrera, *Colombia* 124 D5
La Pérade, *Canada* 103 C5
La Perouse Str., *Asia* 54 B11
La Pesca, *Mexico* 119 C5
La Piedad, *Mexico* 118 C4
La Pine, *U.S.A.* 114 E3
La Plata, *Argentina* 126 D4
La Pobla de Lillet, *Spain* 32 C6
La Pocatière, *Canada* 103 C5
La Pola de Gordón, *Spain* 34 C5
La Porta, *France* 21 F13
La Porte, *Ind., U.S.A.* 108 E2
La Porte, *Tex., U.S.A.* 113 L7
La Presanella, *Italy* 28 B7
La Puebla = Sa Pobla, *Spain* 32 F8
La Puebla de Cazalla, *Spain* 35 H5
La Puebla de los Infantes, *Spain* 35 H5
La Puebla de Montalbán, *Spain* 34 F6
La Puebla del Río, *Spain* 35 H4
La Puerta de Segura, *Spain* 35 G8
La Purísima, *Mexico* 118 B2
La Push, *U.S.A.* 116 C2
La Quiaca, *Argentina* 126 A2
La Réole, *France* 20 D3
La Restinga, *Canary Is.* 37 G2
La Rioja, *Argentina* 126 B2
La Rioja □, *Argentina* 126 B2
La Rioja □, *Spain* 32 C2
La Robla, *Spain* 34 C5
La Roche-Bernard, *France* 18 E4
La Roche-Canillac, *France* 20 C5
La Roche-en-Ardenne, *Belgium* 17 D5
La Roche-sur-Foron, *France* 19 F13
La Roche-sur-Yon, *France* 18 F5
La Rochefoucauld, *France* 20 C4
La Rochelle, *France* 20 B2
La Roda, *Spain* 33 F2
La Roda de Andalucía, *Spain* 35 H6
La Romana, *Dom. Rep.* 121 C6
La Ronge, *Canada* 105 B7
La Rumorosa, *Mexico* 117 N10
La Sabina = Sa Savina, *Spain* 37 C7
La Sagra, *Spain* 33 H2
La Salle, *U.S.A.* 112 E10
La Sanabria, *Spain* 34 C4
La Santa, *Canary Is.* 37 E6
La Sarre, *Canada* 102 C4
La Scie, *Canada* 103 C8

Llangollen


Levuka, *Fiji* 91 C8
Lewes, *U.K.* 13 G8
Lewes, *U.S.A.* 108 F8
Lewin Brzeski, *Poland* 45 H4
Lewis, *U.K.* 14 C2
Lewis →, *U.S.A.* 116 E4
Lewis, Butt of, *U.K.* 14 C2
Lewis Ra., *Australia* 92 D4
Lewis Range, *U.S.A.* 114 C7
Lewis Run, *U.S.A.* 110 E6
Lewisburg, *Pa., U.S.A.* 110 F8
Lewisburg, *Tenn., U.S.A.* 109 H2
Lewisburg, *W. Va., U.S.A.* 108 G5
Lewisporte, *Canada* 103 C8
Lewiston, *Idaho, U.S.A.* 114 C5
Lewiston, *Maine, U.S.A.* 109 C11
Lewiston, *N.Y., U.S.A.* 110 C5
Lewistown, *Mont., U.S.A.* 114 C9
Lewistown, *Pa., U.S.A.* 110 F7
Lexington, *Ill., U.S.A.* 112 E10
Lexington, *Ky., U.S.A.* 108 F3
Lexington, *Mich., U.S.A.* 110 C2
Lexington, *Mo., U.S.A.* 112 F8
Lexington, *N.C., U.S.A.* 109 H5
Lexington, *N.Y., U.S.A.* 111 D10
Lexington, *Nebr., U.S.A.* 112 E5
Lexington, *Ohio, U.S.A.* 110 F2
Lexington, *Tenn., U.S.A.* 109 H1
Lexington, *Va., U.S.A.* 108 G6
Lexington Park, *U.S.A.* 108 F7
Leyburn, *U.K.* 12 C6
Leye, *China* 58 E6
Leyland, *U.K.* 12 D5
Leyre →, *France* 20 D2
Leyte □, *Phil.* 61 F6
Leyte Gulf, *Phil.* 61 F6
Leżajsk, *Poland* 45 H9
Lezay, *France* 20 B3
Lezhë, *Albania* 40 E3
Lezhi, *China* 58 B5
Lézignan-Corbières, *France* 20 E6
Lezoux, *France* 20 C7
Lgov, *Russia* 47 G8
Lhasa, *China* 60 D4
Lhazê, *China* 60 D3
Lhokkruet, *Indonesia* 62 D1
Lhokseumawe, *Indonesia* 62 C1
L'Hospitalet de Llobregat, *Spain* 32 D7
Li, *Thailand* 64 D2
Li Shui →, *China* 59 C9
Li Xian, *Gansu, China* 56 G3
Li Xian, *Hebei, China* 56 E8
Li Xian, *Hunan, China* 59 C8
Liádhoi, *Greece* 39 E8
Liancheng, *China* 59 E11
Lianga, *Phil.* 61 G7
Liangcheng, *Nei Monggol Zizhiqu, China* 56 D7
Liangcheng, *Shandong, China* 57 G10
Liangdang, *China* 56 H4
Lianghe, *China* 58 E2
Lianghekou, *China* 58 C7
Liangping, *China* 58 B6
Liangpran, *Indonesia* 62 D4
Lianhua, *China* 59 D9
Lianjiang, *Fujian, China* 59 D12
Lianjiang, *Guangdong, China* 59 G8
Lianping, *China* 59 E10
Lianshan, *China* 59 E9
Lianshanguan, *China* 57 D12
Lianshui, *China* 57 H10
Lianyuan, *China* 59 D8
Lianyungang, *China* 57 G10
Lianzhou, *China* 59 E9
Liao He →, *China* 57 D11
Liaocheng, *China* 56 F8
Liaodong Bandao, *China* 57 E12
Liaodong Wan, *China* 57 D11
Liaoning □, *China* 57 D12
Liaoyang, *China* 57 D12
Liaoyuan, *China* 57 C13
Liaozhong, *China* 57 D12
Liapádhes, *Greece* 38 B1
Liard →, *Canada* 104 A4
Liard River, *Canada* 104 B3
Liari, *Pakistan* 68 G2
Libau = Liepāja, *Latvia* 9 H19
Libby, *U.S.A.* 114 B6
Libenge, *Dem. Rep. of the Congo* 84 D3
Liberal, *U.S.A.* 113 G4
Liberec, *Czech Rep.* 26 A8
Liberecký □, *Czech Rep.* 26 A8
Liberia, *Costa Rica* 120 D2
Liberia ■, *W. Afr.* 82 D3
Liberty, *Mo., U.S.A.* 112 F7
Liberty, *N.Y., U.S.A.* 111 E10
Liberty, *Pa., U.S.A.* 110 E7
Liberty, *Tex., U.S.A.* 113 K7
Libiąż, *Poland* 45 H6
Lîbîya, Sahrâ', *Africa* 79 C10
Libo, *China* 58 E6
Libobo, Tanjung, *Indonesia* 63 E7
Libode, *S. Africa* 89 E4
Libohovë, *Albania* 40 F4
Libourne, *France* 20 D3
Libramont, *Belgium* 17 E5
Librazhd, *Albania* 40 E4
Libreville, *Gabon* 84 D1
Libya ■, *N. Afr.* 79 C9
Libyan Desert = Lîbîya, Sahrâ', *Africa* 79 C10
Libyan Plateau = Ed-Déffa, *Egypt* 80 A2
Licantén, *Chile* 126 D1
Licata, *Italy* 30 E6
Lice, *Turkey* 73 C9
Licheng, *China* 56 F7
Lichfield, *U.K.* 13 E6
Lichinga, *Mozam.* 87 E4
Lichtenburg, *S. Africa* 88 D4
Lichtenfels, *Germany* 25 E7
Lichuan, *Hubei, China* 58 B7
Lichuan, *Jiangxi, China* 59 D11
Licking →, *U.S.A.* 108 F3
Licosa, Punta, *Italy* 31 B7
Lida, *Belarus* 9 K21
Liden, *Sweden* 10 B10
Lidhoríkion, *Greece* 38 C4
Lidhult, *Sweden* 11 H7
Lidköping, *Sweden* 11 F7
Lido, *Italy* 29 C9
Lido, *Niger* 83 C5
Lido di Roma = Óstia, Lido di, *Italy* 29 G9
Lidzbark, *Poland* 45 E6
Lidzbark Warmiński, *Poland* 44 D7
Liebenwalde, *Germany* 24 C9
Lieberose, *Germany* 24 D10
Liebig, Mt., *Australia* 92 D5
Liebling, *Romania* 42 E6
Liechtenstein ■, *Europe* 25 H5
Liège, *Belgium* 17 D5
Liège □, *Belgium* 17 D5
Liegnitz = Legnica, *Poland* 45 G3
Lienart, *Dem. Rep. of the Congo* 86 B2
Lienyünchiangshih = Lianyungang, *China* 57 G10
Lienz, *Austria* 26 E5
Liepāja, *Latvia* 9 H19
Liepāja □, *Latvia* 44 B8
Liepājas ezers, *Latvia* 44 B8
Lier, *Belgium* 17 C4
Liernais, *France* 19 E11
Lieşti, *Romania* 43 E12
Liévin, *France* 19 B9
Lièvre →, *Canada* 102 C4
Liezen, *Austria* 26 D7
Liffey →, *Ireland* 15 C5
Lifford, *Ireland* 15 B4
Liffré, *France* 18 D5
Lifudzin, *Russia* 54 B7
Ligao, *Phil.* 61 E5
Lightning Ridge, *Australia* 95 D4
Lignano Sabbiadoro, *Italy* 29 C10
Ligny-en-Barrois, *France* 19 D12
Ligonier, *U.S.A.* 110 F5
Ligoúrion, *Greece* 38 D5
Ligueil, *France* 18 E7
Liguria □, *Italy* 28 D5
Ligurian Sea, *Medit. S.* 6 G7
Lihou Reefs and Cays, *Australia* 94 B5
Lihue, *U.S.A.* 106 H15
Lijiang, *China* 58 D3
Likasi, *Dem. Rep. of the Congo* 87 E2
Likenäs, *Sweden* 10 D8
Likhoslavl, *Russia* 46 D8
Likhovskoy, *Russia* 47 H11
Likoma I., *Malawi* 87 E3
Likumburu, *Tanzania* 87 D4
L'Île-Bouchard, *France* 18 E7
L'Île-Rousse, *France* 21 F12
Liling, *China* 59 D9
Lilla Edet, *Sweden* 11 F6
Lille, *France* 19 B10
Lille Bælt, *Denmark* 11 J3
Lillebonne, *France* 18 C7
Lillehammer, *Norway* 9 F14
Lillesand, *Norway* 9 G13
Lillhärdal, *Sweden* 10 C8
Lillian Pt., *Australia* 93 E4
Lillo, *Spain* 34 F7
Lillooet, *Canada* 104 C4
Lillooet →, *Canada* 104 D4
Lilongwe, *Malawi* 87 E3
Liloy, *Phil.* 63 C6
Lim →, *Bos.-H.* 40 C3
Lima, *Indonesia* 63 E7
Lima, *Peru* 124 F3
Lima, *Mont., U.S.A.* 114 D7
Lima, *Ohio, U.S.A.* 108 E3
Lima →, *Portugal* 34 D2
Liman, *Indonesia* 63 G14
Liman, *Russia* 49 H8
Limanowa, *Poland* 45 J7
Limassol, *Cyprus* 36 E12
Limavady, *U.K.* 15 A5
Limay →, *Argentina* 128 D3
Limay Mahuida, *Argentina* 126 D2
Limbach-Oberfrohna, *Germany* 24 E8
Limbang, *Brunei* 62 D5
Limbara, Mte., *Italy* 30 B2
Limbaži, *Latvia* 9 H21
Limbdi, *India* 68 H4
Limbe, *Cameroon* 83 E6
Limburg, *Germany* 25 E4
Limburg □, *Belgium* 17 C5
Limburg □, *Neths.* 17 C5
Limedsforsen, *Sweden* 10 D7
Limeira, *Brazil* 127 A6
Limenária, *Greece* 41 F8
Limerick, *Ireland* 15 D3
Limerick, *U.S.A.* 111 C14
Limerick □, *Ireland* 15 D3
Limestone, *U.S.A.* 110 D6
Limestone →, *Canada* 105 B10
Limfjorden, *Denmark* 11 H3
Limia = Lima →, *Portugal* 34 D2
Limín Khersonísou, *Greece* 39 F7
Limingen, *Norway* 8 D15
Limmared, *Sweden* 11 G7
Limmen Bight, *Australia* 94 A2
Limmen Bight →, *Australia* 94 B2
Límni, *Greece* 38 C5
Límnos, *Greece* 39 B7
Limoges, *Canada* 111 A9
Limoges, *France* 20 C5
Limón, *Costa Rica* 120 E3
Limon, *U.S.A.* 112 F3
Limone Piemonte, *Italy* 28 D4
Limousin, *France* 20 C5
Limousin, Plateaux du, *France* 20 C5
Limoux, *France* 20 E6
Limpopo →, *Africa* 89 D5
Limuru, *Kenya* 86 C4
Lin Xian, *China* 56 F6
Lin'an, *China* 59 B12
Linapacan I., *Phil.* 61 F3
Linapacan Str., *Phil.* 61 F3
Linares, *Chile* 126 D1
Linares, *Mexico* 119 C5
Linares, *Spain* 35 G7
Linaro, Capo, *Italy* 29 F8
Línas Mte., *Italy* 30 C1
Lincang, *China* 58 F3
Lincheng, *China* 56 F8
Linchuan, *China* 59 D11
Lincoln, *Argentina* 126 C3
Lincoln, *N.Z.* 91 K4
Lincoln, *U.K.* 12 D7
Lincoln, *Calif., U.S.A.* 116 G5
Lincoln, *Ill., U.S.A.* 112 E10
Lincoln, *Kans., U.S.A.* 112 F5
Lincoln, *Maine, U.S.A.* 109 C11
Lincoln, *N.H., U.S.A.* 111 B13
Lincoln, *N. Mex., U.S.A.* 115 K11
Lincoln, *Nebr., U.S.A.* 112 E6
Lincoln City, *U.S.A.* 114 D1
Lincoln Hav = Lincoln Sea, *Arctic* 4 A5
Lincoln Sea, *Arctic* 4 A5
Lincolnshire □, *U.K.* 12 D7
Lincolnshire Wolds, *U.K.* 12 D7
Lincolnton, *U.S.A.* 109 H5
L'Incudine, *France* 21 G13
Lind, *U.S.A.* 114 C4
Linda, *U.S.A.* 116 F5
Lindau, *Germany* 25 H5
Linden, *Guyana* 124 B7
Linden, *Ala., U.S.A.* 109 J2
Linden, *Calif., U.S.A.* 116 G5
Linden, *Tex., U.S.A.* 113 J7
Lindenhurst, *U.S.A.* 111 F11
Lindesberg, *Sweden* 10 E9
Lindesnes, *Norway* 9 H12
Líndhos, *Greece* 36 C10
Líndhos, Ákra, *Greece* 36 C10
Lindi, *Tanzania* 87 D4
Lindi □, *Tanzania* 87 D4
Lindi →, *Dem. Rep. of the Congo* 86 B2
Lindö, *Sweden* 11 F10
Lindome, *Sweden* 11 G6
Lindoso, *Portugal* 34 D2
Lindow, *Germany* 24 C8
Lindsay, *Canada* 102 D4
Lindsay, *Calif., U.S.A.* 116 J7
Lindsay, *Okla., U.S.A.* 113 H6
Lindsborg, *U.S.A.* 112 F6
Lindsdal, *Sweden* 11 H10
Linesville, *U.S.A.* 110 E4
Linfen, *China* 56 F6
Ling Xian, *Hunan, China* 59 D9
Ling Xian, *Shandong, China* 56 F9
Lingao, *China* 64 C7
Lingayen, *Phil.* 63 A6
Lingayen G., *Phil.* 61 C4
Lingbi, *China* 57 H9
Lingbo, *Sweden* 10 C10
Lingchuan, *Guangxi Zhuangzu, China* 59 E8
Lingchuan, *Shanxi, China* 56 G7
Lingen, *Germany* 24 C3
Lingga, *Indonesia* 62 E2
Lingga, Kepulauan, *Indonesia* 62 E2
Lingga Arch. = Lingga, Kepulauan, *Indonesia* 62 E2
Linghem, *Sweden* 11 F9
Lingle, *U.S.A.* 112 D2
Lingqiu, *China* 56 E8
Lingshan, *China* 58 F7
Lingshi, *China* 56 F6
Lingshou, *China* 56 E8
Lingshui, *China* 64 C8
Lingtai, *China* 56 G4
Linguère, *Senegal* 82 B1
Lingui, *China* 59 E8
Lingwu, *China* 56 E4
Lingyuan, *China* 57 D10
Lingyun, *China* 58 E6
Linhai, *China* 59 C13
Linhares, *Brazil* 125 G10
Linhe, *China* 56 D4
Linjiang, *China* 57 D14
Linköping, *Sweden* 11 F9
Linkou, *China* 57 B16
Linli, *China* 59 C8
Linnhe, L., *U.K.* 14 E3
Linqi, *China* 56 G7
Linqing, *China* 56 F8
Linqu, *China* 57 F10
Linru, *China* 56 G7
Lins, *Brazil* 127 A6
Linshui, *China* 58 B6
Linta →, *Madag.* 89 D7
Linth →, *Switz.* 25 H5
Linthal, *Switz.* 25 J5
Linton, *Ind., U.S.A.* 108 F2
Linton, *N. Dak., U.S.A.* 112 B4
Lintong, *China* 56 G5
Linwood, *Canada* 110 C4
Linwu, *China* 59 E9
Linxi, *China* 57 C10
Linxia, *China* 60 C5
Linxiang, *China* 59 C9
Linyanti →, *Africa* 88 B4
Linyi, *China* 57 G10
Linz, *Austria* 26 C7
Linz, *Germany* 24 E3
Linzhenzhen, *China* 56 F5
Linzi, *China* 57 F10
Lion, G. du, *France* 20 E7
Lionárisso, *Cyprus* 36 D13
Lioni, *Italy* 31 B8
Lions, G. of = Lion, G. du, *France* 20 E7
Lion's Den, *Zimbabwe* 87 F3
Lion's Head, *Canada* 110 B3
Liozno = Lyozna, *Belarus* 46 E6
Lipa, *Phil.* 61 E4
Lipali, *Mozam.* 87 F4
Lipany, *Slovak Rep.* 27 B13
Lípari, *Italy* 31 D7
Lípari, I., *Italy* 31 D7
Lípari, Is. = Eólie, Ís., *Italy* 31 D7
Lipcani, *Moldova* 43 B11
Lipetsk, *Russia* 47 F10
Lipiany, *Poland* 45 E1
Liping, *China* 58 D7
Lipkany = Lipcani, *Moldova* 43 B11
Lipljan, *Kosovo, Yug.* 40 D5
Lipník nad Bečvou, *Czech Rep.* 27 B10
Lipno, *Poland* 45 F6
Lipova, *Romania* 42 D6
Lipovcy Manzovka, *Russia* 54 B6
Lipovets, *Ukraine* 47 H5
Lippe →, *Germany* 24 D2
Lippstadt, *Germany* 24 D4
Lipscomb, *U.S.A.* 113 G4
Lipsk, *Poland* 44 E10
Lipsko, *Poland* 45 G8
Lipsói, *Greece* 39 D8
Liptovský Hrádok, *Slovak Rep.* 27 B12
Liptovský Milkuláš, *Slovak Rep.* 27 B12
Liptrap C., *Australia* 95 F4
Lipu, *China* 59 E8
Lira, *Uganda* 86 B3
Liri →, *Italy* 30 A6
Liria = Llíria, *Spain* 33 F4
Lisala, *Dem. Rep. of the Congo* 84 D4
Lisboa, *Portugal* 35 G1
Lisboa □, *Portugal* 35 F1
Lisbon = Lisboa, *Portugal* 35 G1
Lisbon, *N. Dak., U.S.A.* 112 B6
Lisbon, *N.H., U.S.A.* 111 B13
Lisbon, *Ohio, U.S.A.* 110 F4
Lisbon Falls, *U.S.A.* 109 D10
Lisburn, *U.K.* 15 B5
Liscannor B., *Ireland* 15 D2
Liscia →, *Italy* 30 A2
Lishe Jiang →, *China* 58 E3
Lishi, *China* 56 F6
Lishu, *China* 57 C13
Lishui, *Jiangsu, China* 59 B12
Lishui, *Zhejiang, China* 59 C12
Lisianski I., *Pac. Oc.* 96 E10
Lisichansk = Lysychansk, *Ukraine* 47 H10
Lisieux, *France* 18 C7
Liski, *Russia* 47 G10
L'Isle-Jourdain, *Gers, France* 20 E5
L'Isle-Jourdain, *Vienne, France* 20 B4
L'Isle-sur-la-Sorgue, *France* 21 E9
Lisle-sur-Tarn, *France* 20 E5
Lismore, *Australia* 95 D5
Lismore, *Ireland* 15 D4
Lista, *Norway* 9 G12
Lister, Mt., *Antarctica* 5 D11
Liston, *Australia* 95 D5
Listowel, *Canada* 102 D3
Listowel, *Ireland* 15 D2
Lit, *Sweden* 10 A8
Lit-et-Mixe, *France* 20 D2
Litang, *Guangxi Zhuangzu, China* 58 F7
Litang, *Sichuan, China* 58 B3
Litang Qu →, *China* 58 C3
Litani →, *Lebanon* 75 B4
Litchfield, *Calif., U.S.A.* 116 E6
Litchfield, *Conn., U.S.A.* 111 E11
Litchfield, *Ill., U.S.A.* 112 F10
Litchfield, *Minn., U.S.A.* 112 C7
Liteni, *Romania* 43 C11
Lithgow, *Australia* 95 E5
Líthinon, Ákra, *Greece* 36 E6
Lithuania ■, *Europe* 9 J20
Litija, *Slovenia* 29 B11
Lititz, *U.S.A.* 111 F8
Litókhoron, *Greece* 40 F6
Litoměřice, *Czech Rep.* 26 A7
Litomyšl, *Czech Rep.* 27 B9
Litschau, *Austria* 26 C8
Little Abaco I., *Bahamas* 120 A4
Little Barrier I., *N.Z.* 91 G5
Little Belt Mts., *U.S.A.* 114 C8
Little Blue →, *U.S.A.* 112 F6
Little Buffalo →, *Canada* 104 A6
Little Cayman, *Cayman Is.* 120 C3
Little Churchill →, *Canada* 105 B9
Little Colorado →, *U.S.A.* 115 H8
Little Current, *Canada* 102 C3
Little Current →, *Canada* 102 B3
Little Falls, *Minn., U.S.A.* 112 C7
Little Falls, *N.Y., U.S.A.* 111 C10
Little Fork →, *U.S.A.* 112 A8
Little Grand Rapids, *Canada* 105 C9
Little Humboldt →, *U.S.A.* 114 F5
Little Inagua I., *Bahamas* 121 B5
Little Karoo, *S. Africa* 88 E3
Little Lake, *U.S.A.* 117 K9
Little Laut Is. = Laut Kecil, Kepulauan, *Indonesia* 62 E5
Little Mecatina = Petit-Mécatina →, *Canada* 103 B8
Little Minch, *U.K.* 14 D2
Little Missouri →, *U.S.A.* 112 B3
Little Ouse →, *U.K.* 13 E9
Little Rann, *India* 68 H4
Little Red →, *U.S.A.* 113 H9
Little River, *N.Z.* 91 K4
Little Rock, *U.S.A.* 113 H8
Little Ruaha →, *Tanzania* 86 D4
Little Sable Pt., *U.S.A.* 108 D2
Little Scarcies →, *S. Leone* 82 D2
Little Sioux →, *U.S.A.* 112 E6
Little Smoky →, *Canada* 104 C5
Little Snake →, *U.S.A.* 114 F9
Little Valley, *U.S.A.* 110 D6
Little Wabash →, *U.S.A.* 108 G1
Little White →, *U.S.A.* 112 D4
Littlefield, *U.S.A.* 113 J3
Littlehampton, *U.K.* 13 G7
Littleton, *U.S.A.* 111 B13
Litvinov, *Czech Rep.* 26 A6
Liu He →, *China* 57 D11
Liu Jiang →, *China* 58 F7
Liuba, *China* 56 H4
Liucheng, *China* 58 E7
Liugou, *China* 57 D10
Liuhe, *China* 57 C13
Liuheng Dao, *China* 59 C14
Liujiang, *China* 58 E7
Liukang Tenggaja = Sabalana, Kepulauan, *Indonesia* 63 F5
Liuli, *Tanzania* 87 E3
Liuwa Plain, *Zambia* 85 G4
Liuyang, *China* 59 C9
Liuzhou, *China* 58 E7
Liuzhuang, *China* 57 H11
Livada, *Romania* 42 C8
Livadherón, *Greece* 40 F5
Livadhia, *Cyprus* 36 E12
Livádhion, *Greece* 38 A4
Livarot, *France* 18 D7
Live Oak, *Calif., U.S.A.* 116 F5
Live Oak, *Fla., U.S.A.* 109 K4
Liveras, *Cyprus* 36 D11
Livermore, *U.S.A.* 116 H5
Livermore, Mt., *U.S.A.* 113 K2
Livermore Falls, *U.S.A.* 109 C11
Liverpool, *Canada* 103 D7
Liverpool, *U.K.* 12 D4
Liverpool, *U.S.A.* 111 C8
Liverpool Bay, *U.K.* 12 D4
Liverpool Plains, *Australia* 95 E5
Liverpool Ra., *Australia* 95 E5
Livigno, *Italy* 28 B7
Livingston, *Guatemala* 120 C2
Livingston, *U.K.* 14 F5
Livingston, *Ala., U.S.A.* 109 J1
Livingston, *Calif., U.S.A.* 116 H6
Livingston, *Mont., U.S.A.* 114 D8
Livingston, *S.C., U.S.A.* 109 J5
Livingston, *Tenn., U.S.A.* 109 G3
Livingston, *Tex., U.S.A.* 113 K7
Livingston, L., *U.S.A.* 113 K7
Livingston Manor, *U.S.A.* 111 E10
Livingstone, *Zambia* 87 F2
Livingstone Mts., *Tanzania* 87 D3
Livingstonia, *Malawi* 87 E3
Livno, *Bos.-H.* 42 G2
Livny, *Russia* 47 F9
Livonia, *Mich., U.S.A.* 108 D4
Livonia, *N.Y., U.S.A.* 110 D7
Livorno, *Italy* 28 E7
Livramento, *Brazil* 127 C4
Livron-sur-Drôme, *France* 21 D8
Liwale, *Tanzania* 87 D4
Liwiec →, *Poland* 45 F8
Lixi, *China* 58 D3
Lixian, *China* 58 B4
Lixoúrion, *Greece* 38 C2
Liyang, *China* 59 B12
Lizard I., *Australia* 94 A4
Lizard Pt., *U.K.* 13 H2
Lizzano, *Italy* 31 B10
Ljig, *Serbia, Yug.* 40 B4
Ljubija, *Bos.-H.* 29 D13
Ljubinje, *Bos.-H.* 40 D2
Ljubljana, *Slovenia* 29 B11
Ljubno, *Slovenia* 29 B11
Ljubovija, *Serbia, Yug.* 40 B3
Ljugarn, *Sweden* 11 G12
Ljung, *Sweden* 11 G7
Ljungan →, *Sweden* 10 B11
Ljungaverk, *Sweden* 10 B10
Ljungby, *Sweden* 9 H15
Ljungbyholm, *Sweden* 11 H10
Ljungdalen, *Sweden* 10 B6
Ljungsbro, *Sweden* 11 F9
Ljungskile, *Sweden* 11 F5
Ljusdal, *Sweden* 10 C10
Ljusfallshammar, *Sweden* 11 F9
Ljusnan →, *Sweden* 10 C11
Ljusne, *Sweden* 10 C11
Ljutomer, *Slovenia* 29 B13
Llagostera, *Spain* 32 D7
Llancanelo, Salina, *Argentina* 126 D2
Llandeilo, *U.K.* 13 F4
Llandovery, *U.K.* 13 F4
Llandrindod Wells, *U.K.* 13 E4
Llandudno, *U.K.* 12 D4
Llanelli, *U.K.* 13 F3
Llanes, *Spain* 34 B6
Llangollen, *U.K.* 12 E4

Madrid


Lucena, Phil. 61 E4
Lucena, Spain 35 H6
Lučenec, Slovak Rep. 27 C12
Lucera, Italy 31 A8
Lucerne = Luzern, Switz. 25 H4
Lucerne, U.S.A. 116 F4
Lucerne Valley, U.S.A. 117 L10
Lucero, Mexico 118 A3
Luchena →, Spain 33 H3
Lucheng, China 56 F7
Lucheringo →, Mozam. 87 E4
Lüchow, Germany 24 C7
Luchuan, China 59 F8
Lucia, U.S.A. 116 J5
Lucinda, Australia 94 B4
Luckau, Germany 24 D9
Luckenwalde, Germany 24 C9
Luckhoff, S. Africa 88 D3
Lucknow, Canada 110 C3
Lucknow, India 69 F9
Luçon, France 20 B2
Lüda = Dalian, China 57 E11
Luda Kamchiya →, Bulgaria 41 C11
Ludbreg, Croatia 29 B13
Lüdenscheid, Germany 24 D3
Lüderitz, Namibia 88 D2
Lüderitzbaai, Namibia 88 D2
Ludhiana, India 68 D6
Ludian, China 58 D4
Luding Qiao, China 58 C4
Lüdinghausen, Germany 24 D3
Ludington, U.S.A. 108 D2
Ludlow, U.K. 13 E5
Ludlow, Calif., U.S.A. 117 L10
Ludlow, Pa., U.S.A. 110 E6
Ludlow, Vt., U.S.A. 111 C12
Ludus, Romania 43 D9
Ludvika, Sweden 10 D9
Ludwigsburg, Germany 25 G5
Ludwigsfelde, Germany 24 C9
Ludwigshafen, Germany 25 F4
Ludwigslust, Germany 24 B7
Ludza, Latvia 46 D4
Lueki, Dem. Rep. of the Congo 86 C2
Luena, Dem. Rep. of the Congo 87 D2
Luena, Zambia 87 E3
Lüeyang, China 56 H4
Lufeng, Guangdong, China 59 F10
Lufeng, Yunnan, China 58 E4
Lufira →, Dem. Rep. of the Congo 87 D2
Lufkin, U.S.A. 113 K7
Lufupa, Dem. Rep. of the Congo 87 E1
Luga, Russia 46 C5
Luga →, Russia 46 C5
Lugano, Switz. 25 J4
Lugano, L. di, Switz. 28 C6
Lugansk = Luhansk, Ukraine 47 H10
Lugard's Falls, Kenya 86 C4
Lugela, Mozam. 87 F4
Lugenda →, Mozam. 87 E4
Lugh Ganana, Somali Rep. 74 G3
Lugnaquilla, Ireland 15 D5
Lugo, Italy 29 D8
Lugo, Spain 34 B3
Lugo □, Spain 34 C3
Lugoj, Romania 42 E6
Lugovoy = Qulan, Kazakstan 50 E8
Luhansk, Ukraine 47 H10
Luhe, China 59 A12
Luhe →, Germany 24 B6
Luhuo, China 58 B3
Luiana, Angola 88 B3
Luimneach = Limerick, Ireland 15 D3
Luing, U.K. 14 E3
Luino, Italy 28 C5
Luís Correia, Brazil 125 D10
Luitpold Coast, Antarctica 5 D1
Luiza, Dem. Rep. of the Congo 84 F4
Luizi, Dem. Rep. of the Congo 86 D2
Luján, Argentina 126 C4
Lujiang, China 59 B11
Lukang, Taiwan 59 E13
Lukanga Swamp, Zambia 87 E2
Lukavac, Bos.-H. 42 F3
Lukenie →, Dem. Rep. of the Congo 84 E3
Lukhisaral, India 69 G12
Lŭki, Bulgaria 41 E8
Lukolela, Dem. Rep. of the Congo 86 D1
Lukosi, Zimbabwe 87 F2
Lukovë, Albania 40 G3
Lukovit, Bulgaria 41 C8
Łuków, Poland 45 G9
Lukoyanov, Russia 48 C7
Lule älv →, Sweden 8 D19
Luleå, Sweden 8 D20
Lüleburgaz, Turkey 41 E11
Luliang, China 58 E4
Luling, U.S.A. 113 L6
Lulong, China 57 E10
Lulonga →, Dem. Rep. of the Congo 84 D3
Lulua →, Dem. Rep. of the Congo 84 E4
Lumajang, Indonesia 63 H15
Lumbala N'guimbo, Angola 85 G4
Lumberton, U.S.A. 109 H6
Lumbwa, Kenya 86 C4
Lumsden, Canada 105 C8
Lumsden, N.Z. 91 L2
Lumut, Malaysia 65 K3
Lumut, Tanjung, Indonesia 62 E3
Luna, India 68 H3
Lunan, China 58 E4
Lunavada, India 68 H5
Lunca, Romania 43 C10
Lunca Corbului, Romania 43 F9
Lund, Sweden 11 J7
Lundazi, Zambia 87 E3
Lunderskov, Denmark 11 J3
Lundi →, Zimbabwe 87 G3
Lundu, Malaysia 62 D3
Lundy, U.K. 13 F3
Lune →, U.K. 12 C5
Lüneburg, Germany 24 B6
Lüneburg Heath = Lüneburger Heide, Germany 24 B6
Lüneburger Heide, Germany 24 B6
Lunel, France 21 E8
Lünen, Germany 24 D3
Lunenburg, Canada 103 D7
Lunéville, France 19 D13
Lunga →, Zambia 87 E2
Lungi Airport, S. Leone 82 D2
Lunglei, India 67 H18
Luni, India 68 G5
Luni →, India 68 G4
Luninets = Luninyets, Belarus 47 F4
Luning, U.S.A. 114 G4
Lunino, Russia 48 D7
Luninyets, Belarus 47 F4
Lunkaransar, India 68 E5
Lunsemfwa →, Zambia 87 E3
Lunsemfwa Falls, Zambia 87 E2
Luo He →, China 56 G6
Luocheng, China 58 E7
Luochuan, China 56 G5
Luoci, China 58 E4
Luodian, China 58 E6
Luoding, China 59 F8
Luofu, Dem. Rep. of the Congo 86 C2
Luohe, China 56 H8
Luojiang, China 58 B5
Luonan, China 56 G6
Luoning, China 56 G6
Luoshan, China 59 A10
Luotian, China 59 B10
Luoxiao Shan, China 59 D10
Luoyang, China 56 G7
Luoyuan, China 59 D12
Luozigou, China 57 C16
Lupanshui, China 58 D5
Lupeni, Romania 43 E8
Lupilichi, Mozam. 87 E4
Łupków, Poland 45 J9
Lupoing, China 58 E5
Luquan, China 58 E4
Luque, Paraguay 126 B4
Lúras, Italy 30 B2
Luray, U.S.A. 108 F6
Lure, France 19 E13
Lurgan, U.K. 15 B5
Lusaka, Zambia 87 F2
Lusambo, Dem. Rep. of the Congo 86 C1
Lusangaye, Dem. Rep. of the Congo 86 C2
Luseland, Canada 105 C7
Lushan, Henan, China 56 H7
Lushan, Sichuan, China 58 B4
Lushi, China 56 G6
Lushnjë, Albania 40 F3
Lushoto, Tanzania 86 C4
Lushui, China 58 E2
Lüshun, China 57 E11
Lusignan, France 20 B4
Lusigny-sur-Barse, France 19 D11
Lusk, U.S.A. 112 D2
Lussac-les-Châteaux, France 20 B4
Lustenau, Austria 26 D2
Lūt, Dasht-e, Iran 71 D8
Luta = Dalian, China 57 E11
Lutherstadt Wittenberg, Germany 24 D8
Luton, U.K. 13 F7
Luton □, U.K. 13 F7
Lutselke, Canada 105 A6
Lutsk, Ukraine 47 G3
Lützow Holmbukta, Antarctica 5 C4
Lutzputs, S. Africa 88 D3
Luverne, Ala., U.S.A. 109 K2
Luverne, Minn., U.S.A. 112 D6
Luvua, Dem. Rep. of the Congo 87 D2
Luvua →, Dem. Rep. of the Congo 86 D2
Luvuvhu →, S. Africa 89 C5
Luwegu →, Tanzania 87 D4
Luwuk, Indonesia 63 E6
Luxembourg, Lux. 17 E6
Luxembourg □, Belgium 17 E5
Luxembourg ■, Europe 7 F7
Luxeuil-les-Bains, France 19 E13
Luxi, Hunan, China 59 C8
Luxi, Yunnan, China 58 E4
Luxi, Yunnan, China 58 E2
Luxor = El Uqsur, Egypt 80 B3
Luy-de-Béarn →, France 20 E3
Luy-de-France →, France 20 E3
Luyi, China 56 H8
Luz-St-Sauveur, France 20 F4
Luzern, Switz. 25 H4
Luzern □, Switz. 25 H3
Luzhai, China 58 E7
Luzhi, China 58 D5
Luzhou, China 58 C5
Luziânia, Brazil 125 G9
Lužnice →, Czech Rep. 26 B7
Luzon, Phil. 61 D4
Luzy, France 19 F10
Luzzi, Italy 31 C9
Lviv, Ukraine 47 H3
Lvov = Lviv, Ukraine 47 H3
Lwówek, Poland 45 F3
Lwówek Śląski, Poland 45 G2
Lyakhavichy, Belarus 47 F4
Lyakhovskiye, Ostrova, Russia 51 B15
Lyaki = Läki, Azerbaijan 49 K8
Lyal I., Canada 110 B3
Lyallpur = Faisalabad, Pakistan 68 D5
Lyaskovets, Bulgaria 41 C9
Lybster, U.K. 14 C5
Lycaonia, Turkey 72 D5
Lychen, Germany 24 B9
Lychkova, Russia 46 D7
Lycia, Turkey 39 E11
Lyckebyån →, Sweden 11 H9
Lycksele, Sweden 8 D18
Lycosura, Greece 38 D4
Lydda = Lod, Israel 75 D3
Lydenburg, S. Africa 89 D5
Lydia, Turkey 39 C10
Łydynia →, Poland 45 F7
Lyell, N.Z. 91 J4
Lyell I., Canada 104 C2
Lyepyel, Belarus 46 E5
Lygnern, Sweden 11 G6
Lykens, U.S.A. 111 F8
Lyman, U.S.A. 114 F8
Lyme B., U.K. 13 G4
Lyme Regis, U.K. 13 G5
Lymington, U.K. 13 G6
Łyna →, Poland 9 J19
Lynchburg, U.S.A. 108 G6
Lynd →, Australia 94 B3
Lynd Ra., Australia 95 D4
Lynden, Canada 110 C4
Lynden, U.S.A. 116 B4
Lyndhurst, Australia 95 E2
Lyndon →, Australia 93 D1
Lyndonville, N.Y., U.S.A. 110 C6
Lyndonville, Vt., U.S.A. 111 B12
Lyngen, Norway 8 B19
Lynher Reef, Australia 92 C3
Lynn, U.S.A. 111 D14
Lynn Lake, Canada 105 B8
Lynnwood, U.S.A. 116 C4
Lynton, U.K. 13 F4
Lyntupy, Belarus 9 J22
Lynx L., Canada 105 A7
Lyon, France 21 C8
Lyonnais, France 21 C8
Lyons = Lyon, France 21 C8
Lyons, Ga., U.S.A. 109 J4
Lyons, Kans., U.S.A. 112 F5
Lyons, N.Y., U.S.A. 110 C8
Lyons →, Australia 93 E2
Lyons Falls, U.S.A. 111 C9
Lyozna, Belarus 46 E6
Lys = Leie →, Belgium 17 C3
Lysá nad Labem, Czech Rep. 26 A7
Lysekil, Sweden 11 F5
Lyskovo, Russia 48 B7
Lystrup, Denmark 11 H4
Lysvik, Sweden 10 D7
Lysychansk, Ukraine 47 H10
Lytham St. Anne's, U.K. 12 D4
Lyttelton, N.Z. 91 K4
Lytton, Canada 104 C4
Lyuban, Russia 46 C6
Lyubertsy, Russia 46 E9
Lyubim, Russia 46 C11
Lyubimets, Bulgaria 41 E10
Lyuboml, Ukraine 47 G3
Lyubotyn, Ukraine 47 H8
Lyubytino, Russia 46 C7
Lyudinovo, Russia 46 F8


# M


M.R. Gomez, Presa, Mexico 119 B5
Ma →, Vietnam 58 H5
Ma'adaba, Jordan 75 E4
Maamba, Zambia 88 B4
Ma'ān, Jordan 75 E4
Ma'ān □, Jordan 75 F5
Maanselkä, Finland 8 C23
Ma'anshan, China 59 B12
Maarianhamina, Finland 9 F18
Ma'arrat an Nu'mān, Syria 70 C3
Maas →, Neths. 17 C4
Maaseik, Belgium 17 C5
Maasin, Phil. 63 B6
Maastricht, Neths. 17 D5
Maave, Mozam. 89 C5
Mababe Depression, Botswana 88 B3
Mabalane, Mozam. 89 C5
Mabel L., Canada 104 C5
Mabenge, Dem. Rep. of the Congo 86 B1
Maberly, Canada 111 B8
Mabian, China 58 C4
Mabil, Ethiopia 81 E4
Mablethorpe, U.K. 12 D8
Mably, France 19 F11
Maboma, Dem. Rep. of the Congo 86 B2
Mabonto, S. Leone 82 D2
Mabrouk, Mali 83 B4
Mac Bac, Vietnam 65 H6
Macachín, Argentina 126 D3
Macaé, Brazil 127 A7
Macael, Spain 33 H2
McAlester, U.S.A. 113 H7
McAllen, U.S.A. 113 M5
MacAlpine L., Canada 100 B9
Macamic, Canada 102 C4
Macao = Macau □, China 59 F9
Macão, Portugal 35 F3
Macapá, Brazil 125 C8
McArthur →, Australia 94 B2
McArthur, Port, Australia 94 B2
Macau, Brazil 125 E11
Macau □, China 59 F9
McBride, Canada 104 C4
McCall, U.S.A. 114 D5
McCamey, U.S.A. 113 K3
McCammon, U.S.A. 114 E7
McCauley I., Canada 104 C2
McCleary, U.S.A. 116 C3
Macclenny, U.S.A. 109 K4
Macclesfield, U.K. 12 D5
M'Clintock Chan., Canada 100 A9
McClintock Ra., Australia 92 C4
McCloud, U.S.A. 114 F2
McCluer I., Australia 92 B5
McClure, U.S.A. 110 F7
McClure, L., U.S.A. 116 H6
M'Clure Str., Canada 4 B2
McClusky, U.S.A. 112 B4
McComb, U.S.A. 113 K9
McConaughy, L., U.S.A. 112 E4
McCook, U.S.A. 112 E4
McCreary, Canada 105 C9
McCullough Mt., U.S.A. 117 K11
McCusker →, Canada 105 B7
McDame, Canada 104 B3
McDermitt, U.S.A. 114 F5
McDonald, U.S.A. 110 F4
Macdonald, L., Australia 92 D4
McDonald Is., Ind. Oc. 3 G13
MacDonnell Ranges, Australia 92 D5
MacDowell L., Canada 102 B1
Macduff, U.K. 14 D6
Maceda, Spain 34 C3
Macedonia, U.S.A. 110 E3
Macedonia ■, Europe 40 E5
Maceió, Brazil 125 E11
Maceira, Portugal 34 F2
Macenta, Guinea 82 D3
Macerata, Italy 29 E10
McFarland, U.S.A. 117 K7
McFarlane →, Canada 105 B7
Macfarlane, L., Australia 95 E2
McGehee, U.S.A. 113 J9
McGill, U.S.A. 114 G6
Macgillycuddy's Reeks, Ireland 15 E2
McGraw, U.S.A. 111 D8
McGregor, U.S.A. 112 D9
McGregor Ra., Australia 95 D3
Mach, Pakistan 66 E5
Māch Kowr, Iran 71 E9
Machado = Jiparaná →, Brazil 124 E6
Machagai, Argentina 126 B3
Machakos, Kenya 86 C4
Machala, Ecuador 124 D3
Machanga, Mozam. 89 C6
Machattie, L., Australia 94 C2
Machault, France 19 C11
Machava, Mozam. 89 D5
Machece, Mozam. 87 F4
Machecoul, France 18 F5
Macheke, Zimbabwe 89 B5
Macheng, China 59 B10
Machero, Spain 35 F6
Machhu →, India 68 H4
Machias, Maine, U.S.A. 109 C12
Machias, N.Y., U.S.A. 110 D6
Machichi →, Canada 105 B10
Machico, Madeira 37 D3
Machilipatnam, India 67 L12
Machiques, Venezuela 124 A4
Machupicchu, Peru 124 F4
Machynlleth, U.K. 13 E4
Macia, Mozam. 89 D5
Maciejowice, Poland 45 G8
McIlwraith Ra., Australia 94 A3
Măcin, Romania 43 E13
Macina, Mali 82 C4
McInnes L., Canada 105 C10
McIntosh, U.S.A. 112 C4
McIntosh L., Canada 105 B8
Macintosh Ra., Australia 93 E4
Macintyre →, Australia 95 D5
Macizo Galaico, Spain 34 C3
Mackay, Australia 94 C4
Mackay, U.S.A. 114 E7
MacKay →, Canada 104 B6
Mackay, L., Australia 92 D4
McKay Ra., Australia 92 D3
McKeesport, U.S.A. 110 F5
McKellar, Canada 110 A5
McKenna, U.S.A. 116 D4
Mackenzie, Canada 104 B4
McKenzie, U.S.A. 109 G1
Mackenzie →, Australia 94 C4
Mackenzie →, Canada 100 B6
McKenzie →, U.S.A. 114 D2
Mackenzie Bay, Canada 4 B1
Mackenzie City = Linden, Guyana 124 B7
Mackenzie Mts., Canada 100 B6
Mackinaw City, U.S.A. 108 C3
McKinlay, Australia 94 C3
McKinlay →, Australia 94 C3
McKinley, Mt., U.S.A. 100 B4
McKinley Sea, Arctic 4 A7
McKinney, U.S.A. 113 J6
Mackinnon Road, Kenya 86 C4
McKittrick, U.S.A. 117 K7
Macklin, Canada 105 C7
Macksville, Australia 95 E5
McLaughlin, U.S.A. 112 C4
Maclean, Australia 95 D5
McLean, U.S.A. 113 H4
McLeansboro, U.S.A. 112 F10
Maclear, S. Africa 89 E4
Macleay →, Australia 95 E5
McLennan, Canada 104 B5
McLeod →, Canada 104 C5
MacLeod, B., Canada 105 A7
McLeod, L., Australia 93 D1
MacLeod Lake, Canada 104 C4
McLoughlin, Mt., U.S.A. 114 E2
McMechen, U.S.A. 110 G4
McMinnville, Oreg., U.S.A. 114 D2
McMinnville, Tenn., U.S.A. 109 H3
McMurdo Sd., Antarctica 5 D11
McMurray = Fort McMurray, Canada 104 B6
McMurray, U.S.A. 116 B4
Macodoene, Mozam. 89 C6
Macomb, U.S.A. 112 E9
Macomer, Italy 30 B1
Mâcon, France 19 F11
Macon, Ga., U.S.A. 109 J4
Macon, Miss., U.S.A. 109 J1
Macon, Mo., U.S.A. 112 F8
Macossa, Mozam. 87 F3
Macoun L., Canada 105 B8
Macovane, Mozam. 89 C6
McPherson, U.S.A. 112 F6
McPherson Pk., U.S.A. 117 L7
McPherson Ra., Australia 95 D5
Macquarie →, Australia 95 E4
Macquarie Harbour, Australia 94 G4
Macquarie Is., Pac. Oc. 96 N7
MacRobertson Land, Antarctica 5 D6
Macroom, Ireland 15 E3
MacTier, Canada 110 A5
Macubela, Mozam. 87 F4
Macugnaga, Italy 28 C4
Macuiza, Mozam. 87 F3
Macusani, Peru 124 F4
Macuse, Mozam. 87 F4
Macuspana, Mexico 119 D6
Macusse, Angola 88 B3
Mada →, Nigeria 83 D6
Madadeni, S. Africa 89 D5
Madagali, Nigeria 83 C7
Madagascar ■, Africa 89 C8
Madā'in Sālih, Si. Arabia 70 E3
Madama, Niger 79 D8
Madame I., Canada 103 C7
Madan, Bulgaria 41 E8
Madaoua, Niger 83 C6
Madara, Nigeria 83 C7
Madaripur, Bangla. 67 H17
Madauk, Burma 67 L20
Madawaska, Canada 110 A7
Madawaska →, Canada 102 C4
Madaya, Burma 67 H20
Madbar, Sudan 81 F3
Maddalena, Italy 30 A2
Maddaloni, Italy 31 A7
Madeira, Atl. Oc. 37 D3
Madeira →, Brazil 122 D5
Madeleine, Îs. de la, Canada 103 C7
Maden, Turkey 73 C8
Madera, Mexico 118 B3
Madera, Calif., U.S.A. 116 J6
Madera, Pa., U.S.A. 110 F6
Madha, India 66 L9
Madhavpur, India 68 J3
Madhepura, India 69 F12
Madhubani, India 69 F12
Madhupur, India 69 G12
Madhya Pradesh □, India 68 J8
Madidi →, Bolivia 124 F5
Madikeri, India 66 N9
Madill, U.S.A. 113 H6
Madimba, Dem. Rep. of the Congo 84 E3
Ma'din, Syria 70 C3
Madina, Mali 82 C3
Madinani, Ivory C. 82 D3
Madingou, Congo 84 E2
Madirovalo, Madag. 89 B8
Madison, Calif., U.S.A. 116 G5
Madison, Fla., U.S.A. 109 K4
Madison, Ind., U.S.A. 108 F3
Madison, Nebr., U.S.A. 112 E6
Madison, Ohio, U.S.A. 110 E3
Madison, S. Dak., U.S.A. 112 D6
Madison, Wis., U.S.A. 112 D10
Madison →, U.S.A. 114 D8
Madison Heights, U.S.A. 108 G6
Madisonville, Ky., U.S.A. 108 G2
Madisonville, Tex., U.S.A. 113 K7
Madista, Botswana 88 C4
Madiun, Indonesia 62 F4
Madoc, Canada 110 B7
Madol, Sudan 81 F2
Madon →, France 19 D13
Madona, Latvia 9 H22
Madonie, Italy 30 E6
Madonna di Campíglio, Italy 28 B7
Madra Dağı, Turkey 39 B9
Madrakah, Ra's al, Oman 74 D6
Madras = Chennai, India 66 N12
Madras = Tamil Nadu □, India 66 P10
Madras, U.S.A. 114 D3
Madre, Laguna, U.S.A. 113 M6
Madre, Sierra, Phil. 61 C5
Madre de Dios →, Bolivia 122 E4
Madre de Dios, I., Chile 122 J3
Madre del Sur, Sierra, Mexico 119 D5
Madre Occidental, Sierra, Mexico 118 B3
Madre Oriental, Sierra, Mexico 118 C5
Madri, India 68 G5
Madrid, Spain 34 E7

**Madrid**


Madrid, *U.S.A.* 111 B9
Madrid □, *Spain* 34 E7
Madridejos, *Spain* 35 F7
Madrigal de las Altas Torres, *Spain* 34 D6
Madrona, Sierra, *Spain* 35 G6
Madroñera, *Spain* 35 F5
Madu, *Sudan* 81 E2
Madura, *Australia* 93 F4
Madura, *Indonesia* 63 G15
Madura, Selat, *Indonesia* 63 G15
Madurai, *India* 66 Q11
Madurantakam, *India* 66 N11
Madzhalis, *Russia* 49 J8
Mae Chan, *Thailand* 64 B2
Mae Hong Son, *Thailand* 64 C2
Mae Khlong →, *Thailand* 64 F3
Mae Phrik, *Thailand* 64 D2
Mae Ramat, *Thailand* 64 D2
Mae Rim, *Thailand* 64 C2
Mae Sot, *Thailand* 64 D2
Mae Suai, *Thailand* 58 H2
Mae Tha, *Thailand* 64 C2
Maebashi, *Japan* 55 F9
Maella, *Spain* 32 D5
Maesteg, *U.K.* 13 F4
Maestra, Sierra, *Cuba* 120 B4
Maevatanana, *Madag.* 89 B8
Mafeking = Mafikeng, *S. Africa* 88 D4
Mafeking, *Canada* 105 C8
Maféré, *Ivory C.* 82 D4
Mafeteng, *Lesotho* 88 D4
Maffra, *Australia* 95 F4
Mafia I., *Tanzania* 86 D4
Mafikeng, *S. Africa* 88 D4
Mafra, *Brazil* 127 B6
Mafra, *Portugal* 35 G1
Mafungabusi Plateau, *Zimbabwe* 87 F2
Magadan, *Russia* 51 D16
Magadi, *Kenya* 86 C4
Magadi, L., *Kenya* 86 C4
Magaliesburg, *S. Africa* 89 D4
Magallanes, Estrecho de, *Chile* 122 J3
Magaluf, *Spain* 33 F7
Magangué, *Colombia* 124 B4
Magaria, *Niger* 83 C6
Magburaka, *S. Leone* 82 D2
Magdalen Is. = Madeleine, Îs. de la, *Canada* 103 C7
Magdalena, *Argentina* 126 D4
Magdalena, *Bolivia* 124 F6
Magdalena, *Mexico* 118 A2
Magdalena, *U.S.A.* 115 J10
Magdalena →, *Colombia* 122 B3
Magdalena →, *Mexico* 118 A2
Magdalena, B., *Mexico* 118 C2
Magdalena, Llano de la, *Mexico* 118 C2
Magdeburg, *Germany* 24 C7
Magdelaine Cays, *Australia* 94 B5
Magdub, *Sudan* 81 E2
Magee, *U.S.A.* 113 K10
Magelang, *Indonesia* 62 F4
Magellan's Str. = Magallanes, Estrecho de, *Chile* 122 J3
Magenta, *Italy* 28 C5
Magenta, L., *Australia* 93 F2
Magerøya, *Norway* 8 A21
Maggia →, *Switz.* 25 J4
Maggiorasca, Mte., *Italy* 28 D6
Maggiore, Lago, *Italy* 28 C5
Maghâgha, *Egypt* 80 B3
Maghama, *Mauritania* 82 B2
Magherafelt, *U.K.* 15 B5
Maghreb, *N. Afr.* 78 B5
Magione, *Italy* 29 E9
Magistralnyy, *Russia* 51 D11
Maglaj, *Bos.-H.* 42 F3
Magliano in Toscana, *Italy* 29 F8
Máglie, *Italy* 31 B11
Magnac-Laval, *France* 20 B5
Magnetic Pole (North) = North Magnetic Pole, *Canada* 4 B2
Magnetic Pole (South) = South Magnetic Pole, *Antarctica* 5 C9
Magnisía □, *Greece* 38 B5
Magnitogorsk, *Russia* 50 D6
Magnolia, *Ark., U.S.A.* 113 J8
Magnolia, *Miss., U.S.A.* 113 K9
Magny-en-Vexin, *France* 19 C8
Magog, *Canada* 103 C5
Magoro, *Uganda* 86 B3
Magosa = Famagusta, *Cyprus* 36 D12
Magouládhes, *Greece* 36 A3
Magoye, *Zambia* 87 F2
Magozal, *Mexico* 119 C5
Magpie, L., *Canada* 103 B7
Magrath, *Canada* 104 D6
Magre →, *Spain* 33 F4
Magrur, *Sudan* 81 E3
Magrur, Wadi →, *Sudan* 81 D2
Magta Lahjar, *Mauritania* 82 B2
Maguan, *China* 58 F5
Maguarinho, C., *Brazil* 125 D9
Magude, *Mozam.* 89 D5
Mağusa = Famagusta, *Cyprus* 36 D12
Maguse L., *Canada* 105 A9
Maguse Pt., *Canada* 105 A10
Magvana, *India* 68 H3
Magwe, *Burma* 67 J19
Magwe, *Sudan* 81 G3
Maha Sarakham, *Thailand* 64 D4
Mahābād, *Iran* 70 B5
Mahabharat Lekh, *Nepal* 69 E10
Mahabo, *Madag.* 89 C7
Mahadeo Hills, *India* 69 H8
Mahaffey, *U.S.A.* 110 F6
Mahagi, *Dem. Rep. of the Congo* 86 B3
Mahajamba →, *Madag.* 89 B8
Mahajamba, Helodranon' i, *Madag.* 89 B8
Mahajan, *India* 68 E5
Mahajanga, *Madag.* 89 B8
Mahajanga □, *Madag.* 89 B8
Mahajilo →, *Madag.* 89 B8
Mahakam →, *Indonesia* 62 E5
Mahalapye, *Botswana* 88 C4
Maḩallāt, *Iran* 71 C6
Māhān, *Iran* 71 D8
Mahan →, *India* 69 H10
Mahanadi →, *India* 67 J15
Mahananda →, *India* 69 G12
Mahanoro, *Madag.* 89 B8
Mahanoy City, *U.S.A.* 111 F8
Maharashtra □, *India* 66 J9
Mahari Mts., *Tanzania* 86 D3
Mahasham, W. →, *Egypt* 75 E3
Mahasoa, *Madag.* 89 C8
Mahasolo, *Madag.* 89 B8
Mahattat ash Shīdīyah, *Jordan* 75 F4
Mahattat 'Unayzah, *Jordan* 75 E4
Mahavavy →, *Madag.* 89 B8
Mahaxay, *Laos* 64 D5
Mahbubnagar, *India* 66 L10
Maḩḑah, *Oman* 71 E7
Mahdia, *Tunisia* 79 A8
Mahe, *India* 69 C8
Mahendragarh, *India* 68 E7
Mahenge, *Tanzania* 87 D4
Maheno, *N.Z.* 91 L3
Mahesana, *India* 68 H5
Maheshwar, *India* 68 H6
Mahgawan, *India* 69 F8
Mahi →, *India* 68 H5
Mahia Pen., *N.Z.* 91 H6
Mahilyow, *Belarus* 46 F6
Mahmiya, *Sudan* 81 D3
Mahmud Kot, *Pakistan* 68 D4
Mahmudia, *Romania* 43 E14
Mahmudiye, *Turkey* 39 B12
Mahmutbey, *Turkey* 41 E12
Mahnomen, *U.S.A.* 112 B7
Mahoba, *India* 69 G8
Mahón = Maó, *Spain* 37 B11
Mahone Bay, *Canada* 103 D7
Mahopac, *U.S.A.* 111 E11
Mahuta, *Nigeria* 83 C5
Mahuva, *India* 68 J4
Mahya Dağı, *Turkey* 41 E11
Mai-Ndombe, L., *Dem. Rep. of the Congo* 84 E3
Mai-Sai, *Thailand* 58 G2
Maia, *Portugal* 34 D2
Maia, *Spain* 32 B3
Maials, *Spain* 32 D5
Maîche, *France* 19 E13
Maicurú →, *Brazil* 125 D8
Máida, *Italy* 31 D9
Maidan Khula, *Afghan.* 68 C3
Maidenhead, *U.K.* 13 F7
Maidstone, *Canada* 105 C7
Maidstone, *U.K.* 13 F8
Maiduguri, *Nigeria* 83 C7
Măieruş, *Romania* 43 E10
Maigatari, *Nigeria* 83 C6
Maignelay Montigny, *France* 19 C9
Maigo, *Phil.* 61 G5
Maigudo, *Ethiopia* 81 F4
Maihar, *India* 69 G9
Maijdi, *Bangla.* 67 H17
Maikala Ra., *India* 67 J12
Mailani, *India* 69 E9
Maillezais, *France* 20 B3
Mailsi, *Pakistan* 68 E5
Main →, *Germany* 25 F4
Main →, *U.K.* 15 B5
Mainburg, *Germany* 25 G7
Maine, *France* 18 D6
Maine □, *U.S.A.* 109 C11
Maine →, *Ireland* 15 D2
Maine-et-Loire □, *France* 18 E6
Maïne-Soroa, *Niger* 83 C7
Maingkwan, *Burma* 67 F20
Mainit, L., *Phil.* 61 G6
Mainland, *Orkney, U.K.* 14 C5
Mainland, *Shet., U.K.* 14 A7
Mainoru, *Australia* 94 A1
Mainpuri, *India* 69 F8
Maintal, *Germany* 25 E4
Maintenon, *France* 19 D8
Maintirano, *Madag.* 89 B7
Mainz, *Germany* 25 E4
Maipú, *Argentina* 126 D4
Maiquetía, *Venezuela* 124 A5
Máira →, *Italy* 28 D4
Mairabari, *India* 67 F18
Maisí, *Cuba* 121 B5
Maisí, Pta. de, *Cuba* 121 B5
Maitland, *N.S.W., Australia* 95 E5
Maitland, *S. Austral., Australia* 95 E2
Maitland →, *Canada* 110 C3
Maiyema, *Nigeria* 83 C5
Maiyuan, *China* 59 E11
Maiz, Is. del, *Nic.* 120 D3
Maizuru, *Japan* 55 G7
Majalengka, *Indonesia* 63 G13
Majene, *Indonesia* 63 E5
Majevica, *Bos.-H.* 42 F3
Maji, *Ethiopia* 81 F4
Majiang, *China* 58 D6
Majorca = Mallorca, *Spain* 37 B10
Maka, *Senegal* 82 C2
Makaha, *Zimbabwe* 89 B5
Makak, *Cameroon* 83 E7
Makalamabedi, *Botswana* 88 C3
Makale, *Indonesia* 63 E5
Makamba, *Burundi* 86 C2
Makari, *Cameroon* 83 C7
Makarikari = Makgadikgadi Salt Pans, *Botswana* 88 C4
Makarovo, *Russia* 51 D11
Makarska, *Croatia* 29 E14
Makaryev, *Russia* 48 B6
Makasar = Ujung Pandang, *Indonesia* 63 F5
Makasar, Selat, *Indonesia* 63 E5
Makasar, Str. of = Makasar, Selat, *Indonesia* 63 E5
Makat, *Kazakstan* 50 E6
Makedonija = Macedonia ■, *Europe* 40 E5
Makeni, *S. Leone* 82 D2
Makeyevka = Makiyivka, *Ukraine* 47 H9
Makgadikgadi Salt Pans, *Botswana* 88 C4
Makhachkala, *Russia* 49 J8
Makharadze = Ozurgeti, *Georgia* 49 K5
Makhmūr, *Iraq* 70 C4
Makian, *Indonesia* 63 D7
Makindu, *Kenya* 86 C4
Makinsk, *Kazakstan* 50 D8
Makiyivka, *Ukraine* 47 H9
Makkah, *Si. Arabia* 74 C2
Makkovik, *Canada* 103 A8
Makó, *Hungary* 42 D5
Mako, *Senegal* 82 C2
Makokou, *Gabon* 84 D2
Makongo, *Dem. Rep. of the Congo* 86 B2
Makoro, *Dem. Rep. of the Congo* 86 B2
Maków Mazowiecki, *Poland* 45 F8
Maków Podhalański, *Poland* 45 J6
Makrá, *Greece* 39 E7
Makrai, *India* 66 H10
Makran Coast Range, *Pakistan* 66 G4
Makrana, *India* 68 F6
Mákri, *Greece* 41 F9
Makriyialos, *Greece* 36 D7
Mākū, *Iran* 70 B5
Makunda, *Botswana* 88 C3
Makung, *Taiwan* 59 F12
Makurazaki, *Japan* 55 J5
Makurdi, *Nigeria* 83 D6
Makūyeh, *Iran* 71 D7
Makwassie, *S. Africa* 88 D4
Makwiro, *Zimbabwe* 89 B5
Mâl, *Mauritania* 82 B2
Mal B., *Ireland* 15 D2
Mala, Pta., *Panama* 120 E3
Mala Belozërka, *Ukraine* 47 J8
Mala Kapela, *Croatia* 29 D12
Mała Panew →, *Poland* 45 H4
Mala Vyska, *Ukraine* 47 H6
Malabang, *Phil.* 61 H6
Malabar Coast, *India* 66 P9
Malabo = Rey Malabo, *Eq. Guin.* 83 E6
Malabon, *Phil.* 61 D4
Malabu, *Nigeria* 83 D7
Malacca, Str. of, *Indonesia* 65 L3
Malacky, *Slovak Rep.* 27 C10
Malad City, *U.S.A.* 114 E7
Maladeta, *Spain* 32 C5
Maladzyechna, *Belarus* 46 E4
Málaga, *Spain* 35 J6
Málaga □, *Spain* 35 J6
Malagarasi, *Tanzania* 86 D3
Malagarasi →, *Tanzania* 86 D3
Malagasy Rep. = Madagascar ■, *Africa* 89 C8
Malagón, *Spain* 35 F7
Malagón →, *Spain* 35 H3
Malahide, *Ireland* 15 C5
Malaimbandy, *Madag.* 89 C8
Malakâl, *Sudan* 81 F3
Malakand, *Pakistan* 68 B4
Malakwal, *Pakistan* 68 C5
Malamala, *Indonesia* 63 E6
Malanda, *Australia* 94 B4
Malang, *Indonesia* 62 F4
Malangen, *Norway* 8 B18
Malanje, *Angola* 84 F3
Mälaren, *Sweden* 10 E11
Malargüe, *Argentina* 126 D2
Malartic, *Canada* 102 C4
Malaryta, *Belarus* 47 G3
Malatya, *Turkey* 70 B3
Malawi ■, *Africa* 87 E3
Malawi, L. = Nyasa, L., *Africa* 87 E3
Malay Pen., *Asia* 65 J3
Malaya Belozërka = Mala Belozërka, *Ukraine* 47 J8
Malaya Vishera, *Russia* 46 C7
Malaya Viska = Mala Vyska, *Ukraine* 47 H6
Malaybalay, *Phil.* 61 G6
Malāyer, *Iran* 71 C6
Malaysia ■, *Asia* 65 K4
Malazgirt, *Turkey* 70 B4
Malbaza, *Niger* 83 C6
Malbon, *Australia* 94 C3
Malbooma, *Australia* 95 E1
Malbork, *Poland* 44 D6
Malcésine, *Italy* 28 C7
Malchin, *Germany* 24 B8
Malchow, *Germany* 24 B8
Malcolm, *Australia* 93 E3
Malcolm, Pt., *Australia* 93 F3
Malczyce, *Poland* 45 G3
Maldah, *India* 69 G13
Maldegem, *Belgium* 17 C3
Malden, *Mass., U.S.A.* 111 D13
Malden, *Mo., U.S.A.* 113 G10
Malden I., *Kiribati* 97 H12
Maldives ■, *Ind. Oc.* 52 J11
Maldonado, *Uruguay* 127 C5
Maldonado, Punta, *Mexico* 119 D5
Malè, *Italy* 28 B7
Malé, *Maldives* 53 J11
Malé Karpaty, *Slovak Rep.* 27 C10
Maléa, Ákra, *Greece* 38 E5
Malegaon, *India* 66 J9
Malei, *Mozam.* 87 F4
Malek, *Sudan* 81 F3
Malek Kandī, *Iran* 70 B5
Malela, *Dem. Rep. of the Congo* 86 C2
Malema, *Mozam.* 87 E4
Máleme, *Greece* 36 D5
Maleny, *Australia* 95 D5
Målerås, *Sweden* 11 H9
Malerkotla, *India* 68 D6
Máles, *Greece* 36 D7
Malesherbes, *France* 19 D9
Maleshevska Planina, *Europe* 40 E7
Malesína, *Greece* 38 C5
Malestroit, *France* 18 E4
Malfa, *Italy* 31 D7
Malgobek, *Russia* 49 J7
Malgomaj, *Sweden* 8 D17
Malgrat = Malgrat de Mar, *Spain* 32 D7
Malgrat de Mar, *Spain* 32 D7
Malha, *Sudan* 81 D2
Malhargarh, *India* 68 G6
Malheur →, *U.S.A.* 114 D5
Malheur L., *U.S.A.* 114 E4
Mali, *Guinea* 82 C2
Mali ■, *Africa* 82 B4
Mali →, *Burma* 67 G20
Mali Kanal, *Serbia, Yug.* 42 E4
Mali Kyun, *Burma* 64 F2
Malibu, *U.S.A.* 117 L8
Maliku, *Indonesia* 63 E6
Malili, *Indonesia* 63 E6
Målilla, *Sweden* 11 G9
Malimba, Mts., *Dem. Rep. of the Congo* 86 D2
Malin Hd., *Ireland* 15 A4
Malin Pen., *Ireland* 15 A4
Malindi, *Kenya* 86 C5
Malines = Mechelen, *Belgium* 17 C4
Malino, *Indonesia* 63 D6
Malinyi, *Tanzania* 87 D4
Malipo, *China* 58 F5
Maliq, *Albania* 40 F4
Malita, *Phil.* 63 C7
Maliwun, *Burma* 62 B1
Maliya, *India* 68 H4
Maljenik, *Serbia, Yug.* 40 C5
Malkara, *Turkey* 41 F10
Małkinia Górna, *Poland* 45 F9
Malko Tŭrnovo, *Bulgaria* 41 E11
Mallacoota Inlet, *Australia* 95 F4
Mallaig, *U.K.* 14 D3
Mallaoua, *Niger* 83 C6
Mallawan, *India* 69 F9
Mallawi, *Egypt* 80 B3
Mallemort, *France* 21 E9
Málles Venosta, *Italy* 28 B7
Mállia, *Greece* 36 D7
Mallión, Kólpos, *Greece* 36 D7
Mallorca, *Spain* 37 B10
Mallorytown, *Canada* 111 B9
Mallow, *Ireland* 15 D3
Malmbäck, *Sweden* 11 G8
Malmberget, *Sweden* 8 C19
Malmédy, *Belgium* 17 D6
Malmesbury, *S. Africa* 88 E2
Malmköping, *Sweden* 10 E10
Malmö, *Sweden* 11 J6
Malmslätt, *Sweden* 11 F9
Malmyzh, *Russia* 48 B10
Malnaş, *Romania* 43 D10
Malo Konare, *Bulgaria* 41 D8
Maloarkhangelsk, *Russia* 47 F9
Malolos, *Phil.* 63 B6
Malombe L., *Malawi* 87 E4
Małomice, *Poland* 45 G2
Malomir, *Bulgaria* 41 D10
Malone, *U.S.A.* 111 B10
Malong, *China* 58 E4
Małopolskie □, *Poland* 45 J7
Malorad, *Bulgaria* 40 C7
Måløy, *Norway* 9 F11
Maloyaroslovets, *Russia* 46 E9
Malpartida, *Spain* 35 F4
Malpaso, *Canary Is.* 37 G1
Malpelo, I. de, *Colombia* 124 C2
Malpica de Bergantiños, *Spain* 34 B2
Malpur, *India* 68 H5
Malpura, *India* 68 F6
Mals = Málles Venosta, *Italy* 28 B7
Malta, *Idaho, U.S.A.* 114 E7
Malta, *Mont., U.S.A.* 114 B10
Malta ■, *Europe* 36 D2
Maltahöhe, *Namibia* 88 C2
Maltepe, *Turkey* 41 F13
Malton, *Canada* 110 C5
Malton, *U.K.* 12 C7
Maluku, *Indonesia* 63 E7
Maluku □, *Indonesia* 63 E7
Maluku Sea = Molucca Sea, *Indonesia* 63 E6
Malumfashi, *Nigeria* 83 C6
Malung, *Sweden* 10 D7
Malungsfors, *Sweden* 10 D7
Maluwe, *Ghana* 82 D4
Malvan, *India* 66 L8
Malvern, *U.S.A.* 113 H8
Malvern Hills, *U.K.* 13 E5
Malvinas, Is. = Falkland Is. □, *Atl. Oc.* 128 G5
Malý Dunaj →, *Slovak Rep.* 27 D11
Malya, *Tanzania* 86 C3
Malyn, *Ukraine* 47 G5
Malyy Lyakhovskiy, Ostrov, *Russia* 51 B15
Mama, *Russia* 51 D12
Mamadysh, *Russia* 48 C10
Mamanguape, *Brazil* 125 E11
Mamarr Mitlā, *Egypt* 75 E1
Mamasa, *Indonesia* 63 E5
Mambasa, *Dem. Rep. of the Congo* 86 B2
Mamberamo →, *Indonesia* 63 E9
Mambilima Falls, *Zambia* 87 E2
Mambirima, *Dem. Rep. of the Congo* 87 E2
Mambo, *Tanzania* 86 C4
Mambrui, *Kenya* 86 C5
Mamburao, *Phil.* 61 E4
Mameigwess L., *Canada* 102 B2
Mamers, *France* 18 D7
Mamfé, *Cameroon* 83 D6
Mammoth, *U.S.A.* 115 K8
Mammoth Cave National Park, *U.S.A.* 108 G3
Mamoré →, *Bolivia* 122 E4
Mamou, *Guinea* 82 C2
Mampatá, *Guinea-Biss.* 82 C2
Mampikony, *Madag.* 89 B8
Mampong, *Ghana* 83 D4
Mamry, Jezioro, *Poland* 44 D8
Mamuju, *Indonesia* 63 E5
Mamuno, *Botswana* 88 C3
Mamuras, *Albania* 40 E3
Man, *Ivory C.* 82 D3
Man, I. of, *U.K.* 12 C3
Man-Bazar, *India* 69 H12
Man Na, *Burma* 67 H20
Mana →, *Fr. Guiana* 125 B8
Manaar, G. of = Mannar, G. of, *Asia* 66 Q11
Manacapuru, *Brazil* 124 D6
Manacor, *Spain* 37 B10
Manado, *Indonesia* 63 D6
Managua, *Nic.* 120 D2
Managua, L. de, *Nic.* 120 D2
Manakara, *Madag.* 89 C8
Manali, *India* 68 C7
Manama = Al Manāmah, *Bahrain* 71 E6
Manambao →, *Madag.* 89 B7
Manambato, *Madag.* 89 A8
Manambolo →, *Madag.* 89 B7
Manambolosy, *Madag.* 89 B8
Mananara, *Madag.* 89 B8
Mananara →, *Madag.* 89 C8
Mananjary, *Madag.* 89 C8
Manankoro, *Mali* 82 C3
Manantenina, *Madag.* 89 C8
Manaos = Manaus, *Brazil* 124 D7
Manapire →, *Venezuela* 124 B5
Manapouri, *N.Z.* 91 L1
Manapouri, L., *N.Z.* 91 L1
Manaqil, *Sudan* 81 E3
Manār, Jabal, *Yemen* 74 E3
Manaravolo, *Madag.* 89 C8
Manas, *China* 60 B3
Manas →, *India* 67 F17
Manaslu, *Nepal* 69 E11
Manasquan, *U.S.A.* 111 F10
Manassa, *U.S.A.* 115 H11
Manaung, *Burma* 67 K18
Manaus, *Brazil* 124 D7
Manavgat, *Turkey* 72 D4
Manawan L., *Canada* 105 B8
Manay, *Phil.* 61 H7
Manbij, *Syria* 70 B3
Mancha Real, *Spain* 35 H7
Manche □, *France* 18 C5
Manchegorsk, *Russia* 50 C4
Manchester, *U.K.* 12 D5
Manchester, *Calif., U.S.A.* 116 G3
Manchester, *Conn., U.S.A.* 111 E12
Manchester, *Ga., U.S.A.* 109 J3
Manchester, *Iowa, U.S.A.* 112 D9
Manchester, *Ky., U.S.A.* 108 G4
Manchester, *N.H., U.S.A.* 111 D13
Manchester, *N.Y., U.S.A.* 110 D7
Manchester, *Pa., U.S.A.* 111 F8
Manchester, *Tenn., U.S.A.* 109 H2
Manchester, *Vt., U.S.A.* 111 C11
Manchester L., *Canada* 105 A7
Manchhar L., *Pakistan* 68 F2
Manchuria = Dongbei, *China* 57 D13
Manchurian Plain, *China* 52 E16
Manciano, *Italy* 29 F8
Mancifa, *Ethiopia* 81 F5
Mand →, *India* 69 J10
Mand →, *Iran* 71 D7
Manda, *Ludewe, Tanzania* 87 E3
Manda, *Mbeya, Tanzania* 86 D3
Manda, *Mbeya, Tanzania* 87 D3
Mandabé, *Madag.* 89 C7
Mandaguari, *Brazil* 127 A5
Mandah = Töhöm, *Mongolia* 56 B5
Mandal, *Norway* 9 G12
Mandala, Puncak, *Indonesia* 63 E10
Mandalay, *Burma* 67 J20
Mandale = Mandalay, *Burma* 67 J20
Mandalgarh, *India* 68 G6
Mandalgovi, *Mongolia* 56 B4
Mandalī, *Iraq* 70 C5
Mandan, *U.S.A.* 112 B4
Mandaon, *Phil.* 61 E5

Marshūn


Mandar, Teluk, *Indonesia* 63 E5
Mándas, *Italy* 30 C2
Mandaue, *Phil.* 61 F5
Mandelieu-la-Napoule, *France* 21 E10
Mandera, *Kenya* 86 B5
Mandi, *India* 68 D7
Mandi Dabwali, *India* 68 E6
Mandiana, *Guinea* 82 C3
Mandimba, *Mozam.* 87 E4
Mandioli, *Indonesia* 63 E7
Mandla, *India* 69 H9
Mandø, *Denmark* 11 J2
Mandorah, *Australia* 92 B5
Mandoto, *Madag.* 89 B8
Mandoúdhion, *Greece* 38 C5
Mándra, *Greece* 38 C5
Mandra, *Pakistan* 68 C5
Mandrákhi, *Greece* 39 E9
Mandrare →, *Madag.* 89 D8
Mandritsara, *Madag.* 89 B8
Mandronarivo, *Madag.* 89 C8
Mandsaur, *India* 68 G6
Mandurah, *Australia* 93 F2
Mandúria, *Italy* 31 B10
Mandvi, *India* 68 H3
Mandya, *India* 66 N10
Mandzai, *Pakistan* 68 D2
Mané, *Burkina Faso* 83 C4
Maneh, *Iran* 71 B8
Manengouba, Mts., *Cameroon* 83 E6
Manera, *Madag.* 89 C7
Manérbio, *Italy* 28 C7
Maneroo Cr. →, *Australia* 94 C3
Manfalût, *Egypt* 80 B3
Manfredónia, *Italy* 29 G12
Manfredónia, G. di, *Italy* 29 G13
Manga, *Burkina Faso* 83 C4
Manga, *Niger* 83 C7
Mangabeiras, Chapada das, *Brazil* 125 F9
Mangalia, *Romania* 43 G13
Mangalore, *India* 66 N9
Mangan, *India* 69 F13
Mangaung, *S. Africa* 85 K5
Mangawan, *India* 69 G9
Mangaweka, *N.Z.* 91 H5
Manggar, *Indonesia* 62 E3
Manggawitu, *Indonesia* 63 E8
Mangindrano, *Madag.* 89 A8
Mangkalihat, Tanjung, *Indonesia* 63 D5
Mangla, *Pakistan* 68 C5
Mangla Dam, *Pakistan* 69 C5
Manglaur, *India* 68 E7
Mangnai, *China* 60 C4
Mango, *Togo* 83 C5
Mangoche, *Malawi* 87 E4
Mangoky →, *Madag.* 89 C7
Mangole, *Indonesia* 63 E6
Mangombe, *Dem. Rep. of the Congo* 86 C2
Mangonui, *N.Z.* 91 F4
Mangoro →, *Madag.* 89 B8
Mangrol, *Mad. P., India* 68 J4
Mangrol, *Raj., India* 68 G6
Mangualde, *Portugal* 34 E3
Mangueira, L. da, *Brazil* 127 C5
Mangum, *U.S.A.* 113 H5
Mangyshlak Poluostrov, *Kazakstan* 50 E6
Manhattan, *U.S.A.* 112 F6
Manhiça, *Mozam.* 89 D5
Mania →, *Madag.* 89 B8
Maniago, *Italy* 29 B9
Manica, *Mozam.* 89 B5
Manica □, *Mozam.* 89 B5
Manicaland □, *Zimbabwe* 87 F3
Manicoré, *Brazil* 124 E6
Manicouagan →, *Canada* 103 C6
Manicouagan, Rés., *Canada* 103 B6
Maniema □, *Dem. Rep. of the Congo* 86 C2
Manīfah, *Si. Arabia* 71 E6
Manifold, C., *Australia* 94 C5
Maniganggo, *China* 58 B2
Manigotagan, *Canada* 105 C9
Manigotagan →, *Canada* 105 C9
Manihari, *India* 69 G12
Manihiki, *Cook Is.* 97 J11
Manika, Plateau de la, *Dem. Rep. of the Congo* 87 E2
Manikpur, *India* 69 G9
Manila, *Phil.* 61 D4
Manila, *U.S.A.* 114 F9
Manila B., *Phil.* 61 D4
Manilla, *Australia* 95 E5
Manimpé, *Mali* 82 C3
Maningrida, *Australia* 94 A1
Maninian, *Ivory C.* 82 C3
Manipur □, *India* 67 G19
Manipur →, *Burma* 67 H19
Manisa, *Turkey* 39 C9
Manisa □, *Turkey* 39 C9
Manistee, *U.S.A.* 108 C2
Manistee →, *U.S.A.* 108 C2
Manistique, *U.S.A.* 108 C2
Manito L., *Canada* 105 C7
Manitoba □, *Canada* 105 B9
Manitoba, L., *Canada* 105 C9
Manitou, *Canada* 105 D9
Manitou, L., *Canada* 103 B6
Manitou Is., *U.S.A.* 108 C3
Manitou Springs, *U.S.A.* 112 F2
Manitoulin I., *Canada* 102 C3
Manitouwadge, *Canada* 102 C2
Manitowoc, *U.S.A.* 108 C2
Manizales, *Colombia* 124 B3
Manja, *Madag.* 89 C7
Manjacaze, *Mozam.* 89 C5
Manjakandriana, *Madag.* 89 B8
Manjhand, *Pakistan* 68 G3
Manjil, *Iran* 71 B6
Manjimup, *Australia* 93 F2
Manjra →, *India* 66 K10
Mankato, *Kans., U.S.A.* 112 F5
Mankato, *Minn., U.S.A.* 112 C8
Mankayane, *Swaziland* 89 D5
Mankera, *Pakistan* 68 D4
Mankim, *Cameroon* 83 D7
Mankono, *Ivory C.* 82 D3
Mankota, *Canada* 105 D7
Manlay = Üydzin, *Mongolia* 56 B4
Manlleu, *Spain* 32 C7
Manmad, *India* 66 J9
Mann Ranges, *Australia* 93 E5
Manna, *Indonesia* 62 E2
Mannahill, *Australia* 95 E3
Mannar, *Sri Lanka* 66 Q11
Mannar, G. of, *Asia* 66 Q11
Mannar I., *Sri Lanka* 66 Q11
Mannheim, *Germany* 25 F4
Manning, *Canada* 104 B5
Manning, *Oreg., U.S.A.* 116 E3
Manning, *S.C., U.S.A.* 109 J5
Manning Prov. Park, *Canada* 104 D4
Mannu →, *Italy* 30 C2
Mannu, C., *Italy* 30 B1
Mannum, *Australia* 95 E2
Mano, *S. Leone* 82 D2
Mano →, *Liberia* 82 D2
Mano River, *Liberia* 82 D2
Manoharpur, *India* 69 H11
Manokwari, *Indonesia* 63 E8
Manolás, *Greece* 38 C3
Manombo, *Madag.* 89 C7
Manono, *Dem. Rep. of the Congo* 86 D2
Manoppello, *Italy* 29 F11
Manosque, *France* 21 E9
Manotick, *Canada* 111 A9
Manouane →, *Canada* 103 C5
Manouane, L., *Canada* 103 B5
Manp'o, *N. Korea* 57 D14
Manpojin = Manp'o, *N. Korea* 57 D14
Manpur, *Mad. P., India* 68 H6
Manpur, *Mad. P., India* 69 H10
Manresa, *Spain* 32 D6
Mansa, *Gujarat, India* 68 H5
Mansa, *Punjab, India* 68 E6
Mansa, *Zambia* 87 E2
Månsåsen, *Sweden* 10 A8
Mansehra, *Pakistan* 68 B5
Mansel I., *Canada* 101 B11
Mansfield, *Australia* 95 F4
Mansfield, *U.K.* 12 D6
Mansfield, *La., U.S.A.* 113 J8
Mansfield, *Mass., U.S.A.* 111 D13
Mansfield, *Ohio, U.S.A.* 110 F2
Mansfield, *Pa., U.S.A.* 110 E7
Mansfield, Mt., *U.S.A.* 111 B12
Mansilla de las Mulas, *Spain* 34 C5
Mansle, *France* 20 C4
Mansoa, *Guinea-Biss.* 82 C1
Manson Creek, *Canada* 104 B4
Manta, *Ecuador* 124 D2
Mantalingajan, Mt., *Phil.* 61 G2
Mantare, *Tanzania* 86 C3
Manteca, *U.S.A.* 116 H5
Manteo, *U.S.A.* 109 H8
Mantes-la-Jolie, *France* 19 D8
Manthani, *India* 66 K11
Manti, *U.S.A.* 114 G8
Mantiqueira, Serra da, *Brazil* 127 A7
Manton, *U.S.A.* 108 C3
Mantorp, *Sweden* 11 F9
Mántova, *Italy* 28 C7
Mänttä, *Finland* 9 E21
Mantua = Mántova, *Italy* 28 C7
Manturovo, *Russia* 48 A7
Manu, *Peru* 124 F4
Manu →, *Peru* 124 F4
Manua Is., *Amer. Samoa* 91 B14
Manuel Alves →, *Brazil* 125 F9
Manui, *Indonesia* 63 E6
Manukau, *N.Z.* 91 G5
Manuripi →, *Bolivia* 124 F5
Many, *U.S.A.* 113 K8
Manyara, L., *Tanzania* 86 C4
Manyas, *Turkey* 41 F11
Manych →, *Russia* 49 G5
Manych-Gudilo, Ozero, *Russia* 49 G6
Manyonga →, *Tanzania* 86 C3
Manyoni, *Tanzania* 86 D3
Manzai, *Pakistan* 68 C4
Manzala, Bahra el, *Egypt* 80 H7
Manzanares, *Spain* 35 F7
Manzaneda, *Spain* 34 C3
Manzanillo, *Cuba* 120 B4
Manzanillo, *Mexico* 118 D4
Manzanillo, Pta., *Panama* 120 E4
Manzano Mts., *U.S.A.* 115 J10
Manzarīyeh, *Iran* 71 C6
Manzhouli, *China* 60 B6
Manzini, *Swaziland* 89 D5
Mao, *Chad* 79 F9
Maó, *Spain* 37 B11
Maoke, Pegunungan, *Indonesia* 63 E9
Maolin, *China* 57 C12
Maoming, *China* 59 G8
Maopi T'ou, *China* 59 G13
Maouri, Dallol →, *Niger* 83 C5
Maoxian, *China* 58 B4
Maoxing, *China* 57 B13
Mapam Yumco, *China* 60 C3
Mapastepec, *Mexico* 119 D6
Mapia, Kepulauan, *Indonesia* 63 D8
Mapimí, *Mexico* 118 B4
Mapimí, Bolsón de, *Mexico* 118 B4
Maping, *China* 59 B9
Mapinga, *Tanzania* 86 D4
Mapinhane, *Mozam.* 89 C6
Maple Creek, *Canada* 105 D7
Maple Valley, *U.S.A.* 116 C4
Mapleton, *U.S.A.* 114 D2
Mapuera →, *Brazil* 124 D7
Mapulanguene, *Mozam.* 89 C5
Maputo, *Mozam.* 89 D5
Maputo □, *Mozam.* 89 D5
Maputo, B. de, *Mozam.* 89 D5
Maqiaohe, *China* 57 B16
Maqnā, *Si. Arabia* 70 D2
Maqueda, *Spain* 34 E6
Maquela do Zombo, *Angola* 84 F3
Maquinchao, *Argentina* 128 E3
Maquoketa, *U.S.A.* 112 D9
Mar, Serra do, *Brazil* 127 B6
Mar Chiquita, L., *Argentina* 126 C3
Mar del Plata, *Argentina* 126 D4
Mar Menor, *Spain* 33 H4
Mara, *Tanzania* 86 C3
Mara □, *Tanzania* 86 C3
Maraã, *Brazil* 124 D5
Marabá, *Brazil* 125 E9
Maracá, I. de, *Brazil* 125 C8
Maracaibo, *Venezuela* 124 A4
Maracaibo, L. de, *Venezuela* 122 C3
Maracaju, *Brazil* 127 A4
Maracay, *Venezuela* 124 A5
Maracena, *Spain* 35 H7
Maradi, *Niger* 83 C6
Marāgheh, *Iran* 70 B5
Marāh, *Si. Arabia* 70 E5
Marajó, I. de, *Brazil* 122 D6
Marākand, *Iran* 70 B5
Maralal, *Kenya* 86 B4
Maralinga, *Australia* 93 F5
Maramaraereğlisi, *Turkey* 41 F11
Marampa, *S. Leone* 82 D2
Maramureş □, *Romania* 43 C9
Maran, *Malaysia* 65 L4
Marana, *U.S.A.* 115 K8
Maranboy, *Australia* 92 B5
Maranchón, *Spain* 32 D2
Marand, *Iran* 70 B5
Marang, *Malaysia* 65 K4
Maranguape, *Brazil* 125 D11
Maranhão = São Luís, *Brazil* 125 D10
Maranhão □, *Brazil* 125 E9
Marano, L. di, *Italy* 29 C10
Maranoa →, *Australia* 95 D4
Marañón →, *Peru* 122 D3
Marão, *Mozam.* 89 C5
Maraş = Kahramanmaraş, *Turkey* 70 B3
Mărăşeşti, *Romania* 43 E12
Maratea, *Italy* 31 C8
Marateca, *Portugal* 35 G2
Marathasa □, *Cyprus* 36 E11
Marathókambos, *Greece* 39 D8
Marathon, *Australia* 94 C3
Marathon, *Canada* 102 C2
Marathón, *Greece* 38 C5
Marathon, *N.Y., U.S.A.* 111 D8
Marathon, *Tex., U.S.A.* 113 K3
Marathóvouno, *Cyprus* 36 D12
Maratua, *Indonesia* 63 D5
Maravatío, *Mexico* 118 D4
Marawi City, *Phil.* 61 G6
Marāwih, *U.A.E.* 71 E7
Marbella, *Spain* 35 J6
Marble Bar, *Australia* 92 D2
Marble Falls, *U.S.A.* 113 K5
Marblehead, *U.S.A.* 111 D14
Marburg, *Germany* 24 E4
Marcal →, *Hungary* 42 C2
Marcali, *Hungary* 42 D2
Marcaria, *Italy* 28 C7
Mărcăuţi, *Moldova* 43 B12
March, *U.K.* 13 E8
Marche, *France* 20 B5
Marche □, *Italy* 29 E10
Marche-en-Famenne, *Belgium* 17 D5
Marchena, *Spain* 35 H5
Marches = Marche □, *Italy* 29 E10
Marciana Marina, *Italy* 28 F7
Marcianise, *Italy* 31 A7
Marcigny, *France* 19 F11
Marcillat-en-Combraille, *France* 19 F9
Marck, *France* 19 B8
Marckolsheim, *France* 19 D14
Marco, *U.S.A.* 109 N5
Marcos Juárez, *Argentina* 126 C3
Mărculeşti, *Moldova* 43 C13
Marcus I. = Minami-Tori-Shima, *Pac. Oc.* 96 E7
Marcus Necker Ridge, *Pac. Oc.* 96 F9
Marcy, Mt., *U.S.A.* 111 B11
Mardan, *Pakistan* 68 B5
Mardin, *Turkey* 70 B4
Mårdsjön, *Sweden* 10 A9
Marécchia →, *Italy* 29 D9
Maree, L., *U.K.* 14 D3
Mareeba, *Australia* 94 B4
Mareetsane, *S. Africa* 88 D4
Maremma, *Italy* 29 F8
Maréna, *Mali* 82 C2
Maréna, *Mali* 82 C3
Marengo, *U.S.A.* 112 E8
Marennes, *France* 20 C2
Marenyi, *Kenya* 86 C4
Marerano, *Madag.* 89 C7
Maréttimo, *Italy* 30 E5
Mareuil, *France* 20 C4
Marfa, *U.S.A.* 113 K2
Marfa Pt., *Malta* 36 D1
Marganets = Marhanets, *Ukraine* 47 J8
Margaret →, *Australia* 92 C4
Margaret Bay, *Canada* 104 C3
Margaret L., *Canada* 104 B5
Margaret River, *Australia* 93 F2
Margarita, I. de, *Venezuela* 122 B4
Margaritíon, *Greece* 38 B2
Margaritovo, *Russia* 54 C7
Margate, *S. Africa* 89 E5
Margate, *U.K.* 13 F9
Margeride, Mts. de la, *France* 20 D7
Margherita di Savóia, *Italy* 31 A9
Marghita, *Romania* 42 C7
Margonin, *Poland* 45 F4
Margosatubig, *Phil.* 61 H5
Mārgow, Dasht-e, *Afghan.* 66 D3
Marguerite, *Canada* 104 C4
Marhanets, *Ukraine* 47 J8
Mari El □, *Russia* 48 B8
Mari Indus, *Pakistan* 68 C4
Mari Republic = Mari El □, *Russia* 48 B8
María, Sa. de, *Spain* 33 H2
María Elena, *Chile* 126 A2
María Grande, *Argentina* 126 C4
Maria I., *N. Terr., Australia* 94 A2
Maria I., *Tas., Australia* 94 G4
Maria van Diemen, C., *N.Z.* 91 F4
Mariager, *Denmark* 11 H3
Mariager Fjord, *Denmark* 11 H4
Mariakani, *Kenya* 86 C4
Marian, *Australia* 94 C4
Marian L., *Canada* 104 A5
Mariana Trench, *Pac. Oc.* 52 H18
Marianao, *Cuba* 120 B3
Marianna, *Ark., U.S.A.* 113 H9
Marianna, *Fla., U.S.A.* 109 K3
Mariannelund, *Sweden* 11 G9
Mariánské Lázně, *Czech Rep.* 26 B5
Marias →, *U.S.A.* 114 C8
Mariato, Punta, *Panama* 120 E3
Mariazell, *Austria* 26 D8
Maribo, *Denmark* 11 K5
Maribor, *Slovenia* 29 B12
Marico →, *Africa* 88 C4
Maricopa, *Ariz., U.S.A.* 115 K7
Maricopa, *Calif., U.S.A.* 117 K7
Marîdî, *Sudan* 81 G2
Marîdî, Wadi →, *Sudan* 81 F2
Marié →, *Brazil* 124 D5
Marie Byrd Land, *Antarctica* 5 D14
Marie-Galante, *Guadeloupe* 121 C7
Mariecourt = Kangiqsujuaq, *Canada* 101 B12
Mariefred, *Sweden* 10 E11
Marieholm, *Sweden* 11 J7
Mariembourg, *Belgium* 17 D4
Marienbad = Mariánské Lázně, *Czech Rep.* 26 B5
Marienberg, *Germany* 24 E9
Mariental, *Namibia* 88 C2
Marienville, *U.S.A.* 110 E5
Mariestad, *Sweden* 11 F7
Marietta, *Ga., U.S.A.* 109 J3
Marietta, *Ohio, U.S.A.* 108 F5
Marieville, *Canada* 111 A11
Mariga →, *Nigeria* 83 C6
Marignane, *France* 21 E9
Marihatag, *Phil.* 61 G7
Mariinsk, *Russia* 50 D9
Mariinskiy Posad, *Russia* 48 B8
Marijampolė, *Lithuania* 9 J20
Marijampolės □, *Lithuania* 44 D10
Marília, *Brazil* 127 A6
Marín, *Spain* 34 C2
Marina, *U.S.A.* 116 J5
Marinduque, *Phil.* 63 B6
Marine City, *U.S.A.* 110 D2
Marineo, *Italy* 30 E6
Marinette, *U.S.A.* 108 C2
Maringá, *Brazil* 127 A5
Marinha Grande, *Portugal* 34 F2
Marino, *Italy* 29 G9
Marion, *Ala., U.S.A.* 109 J2
Marion, *Ill., U.S.A.* 113 G10
Marion, *Ind., U.S.A.* 108 E3
Marion, *Iowa, U.S.A.* 112 D9
Marion, *Kans., U.S.A.* 112 F6
Marion, *N.C., U.S.A.* 109 H5
Marion, *Ohio, U.S.A.* 108 E4
Marion, *S.C., U.S.A.* 109 H6
Marion, *Va., U.S.A.* 109 G5
Marion, L., *U.S.A.* 109 J5
Mariposa, *U.S.A.* 116 H7
Mariscal Estigarribia, *Paraguay* 126 A3
Maritime Alps = Maritimes, Alpes, *Europe* 21 D11
Maritimes, Alpes, *Europe* 21 D11
Maritsa = Évros →, *Greece* 72 B2
Maritsá, *Greece* 36 C10
Mariupol, *Ukraine* 47 J9
Marīvān, *Iran* 70 C5
Marj 'Uyûn, *Lebanon* 75 B4
Marka, *Si. Arabia* 80 D5
Markam, *China* 58 C2
Markaryd, *Sweden* 11 H7
Markazī □, *Iran* 71 C6
Markdale, *Canada* 110 B4
Marked Tree, *U.S.A.* 113 H9
Markelsdorfer Huk, *Germany* 24 A7
Market Drayton, *U.K.* 12 E5
Market Harborough, *U.K.* 13 E7
Market Rasen, *U.K.* 12 D7
Markham, *Canada* 110 C5
Markham, Mt., *Antarctica* 5 E11
Marki, *Poland* 45 F8
Markkleeberg, *Germany* 24 D8
Markleeville, *U.S.A.* 116 G7
Markoupoulon, *Greece* 38 D5
Markovac, *Serbia, Yug.* 40 B5
Markovo, *Russia* 51 C17
Markoye, *Burkina Faso* 83 C5
Marks, *Russia* 48 E8
Marksville, *U.S.A.* 113 K8
Markt Schwaben, *Germany* 25 G7
Marktoberdorf, *Germany* 25 H6
Marktredwitz, *Germany* 25 E8
Marl, *Germany* 24 D3
Marla, *Australia* 95 D1
Marlbank, *Canada* 110 B7
Marlboro, *Mass., U.S.A.* 111 D13
Marlboro, *N.Y., U.S.A.* 111 E11
Marlborough, *Australia* 94 C4
Marlborough, *U.K.* 13 F6
Marlborough Downs, *U.K.* 13 F6
Marle, *France* 19 C10
Marlin, *U.S.A.* 113 K6
Marlow, *Germany* 24 A8
Marlow, *U.S.A.* 113 H6
Marmagao, *India* 66 M8
Marmande, *France* 20 D4
Marmara, *Turkey* 41 F11
Marmara, Sea of = Marmara Denizi, *Turkey* 41 F12
Marmara Denizi, *Turkey* 41 F12
Marmara Gölü, *Turkey* 39 C10
Marmaris, *Turkey* 39 E10
Marmaris Limanı, *Turkey* 39 E10
Marmion, Mt., *Australia* 93 E2
Marmion L., *Canada* 102 C1
Marmolada, Mte., *Italy* 29 B8
Marmolejo, *Spain* 35 G6
Marmora, *Canada* 102 D4
Mármora, La, *Italy* 30 C2
Marnay, *France* 19 E12
Marne, *Germany* 24 B5
Marne □, *France* 19 D11
Marne →, *France* 19 D9
Marneuli, *Georgia* 49 K7
Maroala, *Madag.* 89 B8
Maroantsetra, *Madag.* 89 B8
Maroelaboom, *Namibia* 88 B2
Marofandilia, *Madag.* 89 C7
Marolambo, *Madag.* 89 C8
Maromandia, *Madag.* 89 A8
Marondera, *Zimbabwe* 87 F3
Maroni →, *Fr. Guiana* 125 B8
Marónia, *Greece* 41 F9
Maronne →, *France* 20 C5
Maroochydore, *Australia* 95 D5
Maroona, *Australia* 95 F3
Maros →, *Hungary* 42 D5
Marosakoa, *Madag.* 89 B8
Maroseranana, *Madag.* 89 B8
Maróstica, *Italy* 29 C8
Marotandrano, *Madag.* 89 B8
Marotaolano, *Madag.* 89 A8
Maroua, *Cameroon* 83 C7
Marovato, *Madag.* 89 B8
Marovoay, *Madag.* 89 B8
Marquard, *S. Africa* 88 D4
Marquesas Is. = Marquises, Is., *Pac. Oc.* 97 H14
Marquette, *U.S.A.* 108 B2
Marquise, *France* 19 B8
Marquises, Is., *Pac. Oc.* 97 H14
Marra, Djebel, *Sudan* 79 F10
Marra, Gebel, *Sudan* 81 F2
Marracuene, *Mozam.* 89 D5
Marradi, *Italy* 29 D8
Marrakech, *Morocco* 78 B4
Marratxi, *Spain* 32 F7
Marrawah, *Australia* 94 G3
Marree, *Australia* 95 D2
Marrero, *U.S.A.* 113 L9
Marrimane, *Mozam.* 89 C5
Marromeu, *Mozam.* 89 B6
Marroquí, Punta, *Spain* 35 K5
Marrowie Cr. →, *Australia* 95 E4
Marrubane, *Mozam.* 87 F4
Marrúbiu, *Italy* 30 C1
Marrupa, *Mozam.* 87 E4
Mars Hill, *U.S.A.* 109 B12
Marsá 'Alam, *Egypt* 80 B3
Marsá Matrûh, *Egypt* 80 A2
Marsá Sha'b, *Sudan* 80 C4
Marsabit, *Kenya* 86 B4
Marsala, *Italy* 30 E5
Marsalforn, *Malta* 36 C1
Mârşani, *Romania* 43 F9
Marsberg, *Germany* 24 D4
Marsciano, *Italy* 29 F9
Marsden, *Australia* 95 E4
Marseillan, *France* 20 E7
Marseille, *France* 21 E9
Marseilles = Marseille, *France* 21 E9
Marsh I., *U.S.A.* 113 L9
Marshall, *Liberia* 82 D2
Marshall, *Ark., U.S.A.* 113 H8
Marshall, *Mich., U.S.A.* 108 D3
Marshall, *Minn., U.S.A.* 112 C7
Marshall, *Mo., U.S.A.* 112 F8
Marshall, *Tex., U.S.A.* 113 J7
Marshall →, *Australia* 94 C2
Marshall Is. ■, *Pac. Oc.* 96 G9
Marshalltown, *U.S.A.* 112 D8
Marshbrook, *Zimbabwe* 89 B5
Marshfield, *Mo., U.S.A.* 113 G8
Marshfield, *Vt., U.S.A.* 111 B12
Marshfield, *Wis., U.S.A.* 112 C9
Marshūn, *Iran* 71 B6

**Mársico Nuovo**


Mársico Nuovo, *Italy* 31 B8
Märsta, *Sweden* 10 E11
Marstal, *Denmark* 11 K4
Marstrand, *Sweden* 11 G5
Mart, *U.S.A.* 113 K6
Marta →, *Italy* 29 F8
Martaban, *Burma* 67 L20
Martaban, G. of, *Burma* 67 L20
Martano, *Italy* 31 B11
Martapura, *Kalimantan, Indonesia* 62 E4
Martapura, *Sumatera, Indonesia* 62 E2
Marte, *Nigeria* 83 C7
Martel, *France* 20 D5
Martelange, *Belgium* 17 E5
Martellago, *Italy* 29 C9
Martés, Sierra, *Spain* 33 F4
Martfű, *Hungary* 42 C5
Martha's Vineyard, *U.S.A.* 111 E14
Martigné-Ferchaud, *France* 18 E5
Martigny, *Switz.* 25 J3
Martigues, *France* 21 E9
Martin, *Slovak Rep.* 27 B11
Martin, *S. Dak., U.S.A.* 112 D4
Martin, *Tenn., U.S.A.* 113 G10
Martín →, *Spain* 32 D4
Martin, L., *U.S.A.* 109 J3
Martina Franca, *Italy* 31 B10
Martinborough, *N.Z.* 91 J5
Martinez, *Calif., U.S.A.* 116 G4
Martinez, *Ga., U.S.A.* 109 J4
Martinique ■, *W. Indies* 121 D7
Martinique Passage, *W. Indies* 121 C7
Martínon, *Greece* 38 C5
Martinópolis, *Brazil* 127 A5
Martins Ferry, *U.S.A.* 110 F4
Martinsberg, *Austria* 26 C8
Martinsburg, *Pa., U.S.A.* 110 F6
Martinsburg, *W. Va., U.S.A.* 108 F7
Martinsicuro, *Italy* 29 F10
Martinsville, *Ind., U.S.A.* 108 F2
Martinsville, *Va., U.S.A.* 109 G6
Marton, *N.Z.* 91 J5
Martorell, *Spain* 32 D6
Martos, *Spain* 35 H7
Martuni, *Armenia* 49 K7
Maru, *Nigeria* 83 C6
Marudi, *Malaysia* 62 D4
Maruf, *Afghan.* 66 D5
Marugame, *Japan* 55 G6
Marunga, *Angola* 88 B3
Marungu, Mts., *Dem. Rep. of the Congo* 86 D3
Marv Dasht, *Iran* 71 D7
Marvast, *Iran* 71 D7
Marvejols, *France* 20 D7
Marvel Loch, *Australia* 93 F2
Marwar, *India* 68 G5
Mary, *Turkmenistan* 50 F7
Maryborough = Port Laoise, *Ireland* 15 C4
Maryborough, *Queens., Australia* 95 D5
Maryborough, *Vic., Australia* 95 F3
Maryfield, *Canada* 105 D8
Maryland □, *U.S.A.* 108 F7
Maryland Junction, *Zimbabwe* 87 F3
Maryport, *U.K.* 12 C4
Mary's Harbour, *Canada* 103 B8
Marystown, *Canada* 103 C8
Marysville, *Canada* 104 D5
Marysville, *Calif., U.S.A.* 116 F5
Marysville, *Kans., U.S.A.* 112 F6
Marysville, *Mich., U.S.A.* 110 D2
Marysville, *Ohio, U.S.A.* 108 E4
Marysville, *Wash., U.S.A.* 116 B4
Maryville, *Mo., U.S.A.* 112 E7
Maryville, *Tenn., U.S.A.* 109 H4
Marzūq, *Libya* 79 C8
Masahunga, *Tanzania* 86 C3
Masai Steppe, *Tanzania* 86 C4
Masaka, *Uganda* 86 C3
Masalembo, Kepulauan, *Indonesia* 62 F4
Masalima, Kepulauan, *Indonesia* 62 F5
Masallı, *Azerbaijan* 73 C13
Masamba, *Indonesia* 63 E6
Masan, *S. Korea* 57 G15
Masandam, Ra's, *Oman* 71 E8
Masasi, *Tanzania* 87 E4
Masaya, *Nic.* 120 D2
Masba, *Nigeria* 83 C7
Masbate, *Phil.* 61 E5
Máscali, *Italy* 31 E8
Mascara, *Algeria* 78 A6
Mascota, *Mexico* 118 C4
Masela, *Indonesia* 63 F7
Maseru, *Lesotho* 88 D4
Mashaba, *Zimbabwe* 87 G3
Mashābih, *Si. Arabia* 70 E3
Mashan, *China* 58 F7
Mashar, *Sudan* 81 F2
Mashegu, *Nigeria* 83 D6
Masherbrum, *Pakistan* 69 B7
Mashhad, *Iran* 71 B8
Mashi, *Nigeria* 83 C6
Mashīz, *Iran* 71 D8
Māshkel, Hāmūn-i-, *Pakistan* 66 E3
Mashki Chāh, *Pakistan* 66 E3
Mashonaland, *Zimbabwe* 85 H6
Mashonaland Central □, *Zimbabwe* 89 B5
Mashonaland East □, *Zimbabwe* 89 B5
Mashonaland West □, *Zimbabwe* 89 B4
Mashrakh, *India* 69 F11
Mashtaga = Maştağa, *Azerbaijan* 49 K10
Masindi, *Uganda* 86 B3
Masindi Port, *Uganda* 86 B3
Maşīrah, *Oman* 74 C6
Maşīrah, Khalīj, *Oman* 74 C6
Masisi, *Dem. Rep. of the Congo* 86 C2
Masjed Soleyman, *Iran* 71 D6
Mask, L., *Ireland* 15 C2
Maskin, *Oman* 71 F8
Maslen Nos, *Bulgaria* 41 D11
Maslinica, *Croatia* 29 E13
Masnou = El Masnou, *Spain* 32 D7
Masoala, Tanjon' i, *Madag.* 89 B9
Masoarivo, *Madag.* 89 B7
Masohi = Amahai, *Indonesia* 63 E7
Masomeloka, *Madag.* 89 C8
Mason, *Nev., U.S.A.* 116 G7
Mason, *Tex., U.S.A.* 113 K5
Mason City, *U.S.A.* 112 D8
Maspalomas, *Canary Is.* 37 G4
Maspalomas, Pta., *Canary Is.* 37 G4
Masqat, *Oman* 74 C6
Massa, *Italy* 28 D7
Massa Marítima, *Italy* 28 E7
Massachusetts □, *U.S.A.* 111 D13
Massachusetts B., *U.S.A.* 111 D14
Massafra, *Italy* 31 B10
Massakory, *Chad* 79 F9
Massanella, *Spain* 37 B9
Massangena, *Mozam.* 89 C5
Massango, *Angola* 84 F3
Massat, *France* 20 F5
Massawa = Mitsiwa, *Eritrea* 81 D4
Massena, *U.S.A.* 111 B10
Massénya, *Chad* 79 F9
Masset, *Canada* 104 C2
Masseube, *France* 20 E4
Massiac, *France* 20 C7
Massif Central, *France* 20 D7
Massigui, *Mali* 82 C3
Massillon, *U.S.A.* 110 F3
Massinga, *Mozam.* 89 C6
Massingir, *Mozam.* 89 C5
Mässlingen, *Sweden* 10 B6
Masson, *Canada* 111 A9
Masson I., *Antarctica* 5 C7
Maştağa, *Azerbaijan* 49 K10
Mastanli = Momchilgrad, *Bulgaria* 41 E9
Masterton, *N.Z.* 91 J5
Mastic, *U.S.A.* 111 F12
Mástikho, Ákra, *Greece* 39 C8
Mastuj, *Pakistan* 69 A5
Mastung, *Pakistan* 66 E5
Mastūrah, *Si. Arabia* 80 C4
Masty, *Belarus* 46 F3
Masuda, *Japan* 55 G5
Masvingo, *Zimbabwe* 87 G3
Masvingo □, *Zimbabwe* 87 G3
Maşyāf, *Syria* 70 C3
Maszewo, *Poland* 44 E2
Mat →, *Albania* 40 E3
Matabeleland, *Zimbabwe* 85 H5
Matabeleland North □, *Zimbabwe* 87 F2
Matabeleland South □, *Zimbabwe* 87 G2
Matachel →, *Spain* 35 G4
Matachewan, *Canada* 102 C3
Matadi, *Dem. Rep. of the Congo* 84 F2
Matagalpa, *Nic.* 120 D2
Matagami, *Canada* 102 C4
Matagami, L., *Canada* 102 C4
Matagorda B., *U.S.A.* 113 L6
Matagorda I., *U.S.A.* 113 L6
Matak, *Indonesia* 65 L6
Mátala, *Greece* 36 E6
Matam, *Senegal* 82 B2
Matameye, *Niger* 83 C6
Matamoros, *Campeche, Mexico* 119 D6
Matamoros, *Coahuila, Mexico* 118 B4
Matamoros, *Tamaulipas, Mexico* 119 B5
Ma'ţan as Sarra, *Libya* 79 D10
Matandu →, *Tanzania* 87 D3
Matane, *Canada* 103 C6
Matang, *China* 58 F5
Matankari, *Niger* 83 C5
Matanomadh, *India* 68 H3
Matanzas, *Cuba* 120 B3
Matapa, *Botswana* 88 C3
Matapan, C. = Taínaron, Ákra, *Greece* 38 E4
Matapédia, *Canada* 103 C6
Matara, *Sri Lanka* 66 S12
Mataram, *Indonesia* 62 F5
Matarani, *Peru* 124 G4
Mataranka, *Australia* 92 B5
Matarma, Râs, *Egypt* 75 E1
Mataró, *Spain* 32 D7
Matarraña →, *Spain* 32 D5
Mataruška Banja, *Serbia, Yug.* 40 C4
Matatiele, *S. Africa* 89 E4
Mataura, *N.Z.* 91 M2
Matehuala, *Mexico* 118 C4
Mateke Hills, *Zimbabwe* 87 G3
Matera, *Italy* 31 B9
Matese, Monti del, *Italy* 31 A7
Mátészalka, *Hungary* 42 C7
Matetsi, *Zimbabwe* 87 F2
Matfors, *Sweden* 10 B11
Matha, *France* 20 C3
Mathis, *U.S.A.* 113 L6
Mathráki, *Greece* 36 A3
Mathura, *India* 68 F7
Mati, *Phil.* 61 H7
Matiakoali, *Burkina Faso* 83 C5
Matiali, *India* 69 F13
Matías Romero, *Mexico* 119 D5
Matibane, *Mozam.* 87 E5
Matima, *Botswana* 88 C3
Matiri Ra., *N.Z.* 91 J4
Matjiesfontein, *S. Africa* 88 E3
Matla →, *India* 69 J13
Matlamanyane, *Botswana* 88 B4
Matli, *Pakistan* 68 G3
Matlock, *U.K.* 12 D6
Matna, *Sudan* 81 E4
Mato Grosso □, *Brazil* 125 F8
Mato Grosso, Planalto do, *Brazil* 122 E5
Mato Grosso do Sul □, *Brazil* 125 G8
Matochkin Shar, *Russia* 50 B6
Matopo Hills, *Zimbabwe* 87 G2
Matopos, *Zimbabwe* 87 G2
Matosinhos, *Portugal* 34 D2
Matour, *France* 19 F11
Matroosberg, *S. Africa* 88 E2
Maţruḩ, *Oman* 74 C6
Matsena, *Nigeria* 83 C7
Matsesta, *Russia* 49 J4
Matsu Tao, *Taiwan* 59 E13
Matsue, *Japan* 55 G6
Matsumae, *Japan* 54 D10
Matsumoto, *Japan* 55 F9
Matsusaka, *Japan* 55 G8
Matsuura, *Japan* 55 H4
Matsuyama, *Japan* 55 H6
Mattagami →, *Canada* 102 B3
Mattancheri, *India* 66 Q10
Mattawa, *Canada* 102 C4
Matterhorn, *Switz.* 25 K3
Mattersburg, *Austria* 27 D9
Matthew Town, *Bahamas* 121 B5
Matthew's Ridge, *Guyana* 124 B6
Mattice, *Canada* 102 C3
Mattituck, *U.S.A.* 111 F12
Mattō, *Japan* 55 F8
Mattoon, *U.S.A.* 108 F1
Matuba, *Mozam.* 89 C5
Matucana, *Peru* 124 F3
Matūn = Khowst, *Afghan.* 68 C3
Maturín, *Venezuela* 124 B6
Matveyev Kurgan, *Russia* 47 J10
Matxitxako, C., *Spain* 32 B2
Mau, *Mad. P., India* 69 F8
Mau, *Ut. P., India* 69 G10
Mau, *Ut. P., India* 69 G9
Mau Escarpment, *Kenya* 86 C4
Mau Ranipur, *India* 69 G8
Maubeuge, *France* 19 B10
Maubourguet, *France* 20 E4
Maud, Pt., *Australia* 92 D1
Maude, *Australia* 95 E3
Maudin Sun, *Burma* 67 M19
Maués, *Brazil* 124 D7
Mauganj, *India* 67 G12
Maughold Hd., *U.K.* 12 C3
Mauguio, *France* 20 E7
Maui, *U.S.A.* 106 H16
Maulamyaing = Moulmein, *Burma* 67 L20
Maule □, *Chile* 126 D1
Mauléon-Licharre, *France* 20 E3
Maumee, *U.S.A.* 108 E4
Maumee →, *U.S.A.* 108 E4
Maumere, *Indonesia* 63 F6
Maumusson, Pertuis de, *France* 20 C2
Maun, *Botswana* 88 C3
Mauna Kea, *U.S.A.* 106 J17
Mauna Loa, *U.S.A.* 106 J17
Maungmagan Kyunzu, *Burma* 64 E1
Maupin, *U.S.A.* 114 D3
Maure-de-Bretagne, *France* 18 E5
Maurepas, L., *U.S.A.* 113 K9
Maures, *France* 21 E10
Mauriac, *France* 20 C6
Maurice, L., *Australia* 93 E5
Mauricie, Parc Nat. de la, *Canada* 102 C5
Maurienne, *France* 21 C10
Mauritania ■, *Africa* 78 E3
Mauritius ■, *Ind. Oc.* 77 J9
Mauron, *France* 18 D4
Maurs, *France* 20 D6
Mauston, *U.S.A.* 112 D9
Mauterndorf, *Austria* 26 D6
Mauthen, *Austria* 26 E6
Mauvezin, *France* 20 E4
Mauzé-sur-le-Mignon, *France* 20 B3
Mavli, *India* 68 G5
Mavrovë, *Albania* 40 F3
Mavuradonha Mts., *Zimbabwe* 87 F3
Mawa, *Dem. Rep. of the Congo* 86 B2
Mawai, *India* 69 H9
Mawana, *India* 68 E7
Mawand, *Pakistan* 68 E3
Mawk Mai, *Burma* 67 J20
Mawlaik, *Burma* 67 H19
Mawlamyine = Moulmein, *Burma* 67 L20
Mawqaq, *Si. Arabia* 70 E4
Mawson Coast, *Antarctica* 5 C6
Max, *U.S.A.* 112 B4
Maxcanú, *Mexico* 119 C6
Maxesibeni, *S. Africa* 89 E4
Maxhamish L., *Canada* 104 B4
Maxixe, *Mozam.* 89 C6
Maxville, *Canada* 111 A10
Maxwell, *U.S.A.* 116 F4
Maxwelton, *Australia* 94 C3
May, C., *U.S.A.* 108 F8
May Pen, *Jamaica* 120 C4
Maya →, *Russia* 51 D14
Maya Mts., *Belize* 119 D7
Mayaguana, *Bahamas* 121 B5
Mayagüez, *Puerto Rico* 121 C6
Mayahi, *Niger* 83 C6
Mayals = Maials, *Spain* 32 D5
Mayāmey, *Iran* 71 B7
Mayang, *China* 58 D7
Mayanup, *Australia* 93 F2
Mayapan, *Mexico* 119 C7
Mayarí, *Cuba* 121 B4
Maybell, *U.S.A.* 114 F9
Maybole, *U.K.* 14 F4
Maychew, *Ethiopia* 81 E4
Maydān, *Iraq* 70 C5
Maydena, *Australia* 94 G4
Mayen, *Germany* 25 E3
Mayenne, *France* 18 D6
Mayenne □, *France* 18 D6
Mayenne →, *France* 18 E6
Mayer, *U.S.A.* 115 J7
Mayerthorpe, *Canada* 104 C5
Mayfield, *Ky., U.S.A.* 109 G1
Mayfield, *N.Y., U.S.A.* 111 C10
Mayhill, *U.S.A.* 115 K11
Maykop, *Russia* 49 H5
Maymyo, *Burma* 64 A1
Maynard, *Mass., U.S.A.* 111 D13
Maynard, *Wash., U.S.A.* 116 C4
Maynard Hills, *Australia* 93 E2
Mayne →, *Australia* 94 C3
Maynooth, *Ireland* 15 C5
Mayo, *Canada* 100 B6
Mayo □, *Ireland* 15 C2
Mayo Daga, *Nigeria* 83 D7
Mayo Faran, *Nigeria* 83 D7
Mayon Volcano, *Phil.* 61 E5
Mayor I., *N.Z.* 91 G6
Mayorga, *Spain* 34 C5
Mayotte, *Ind. Oc.* 85 G9
Mayraira Pt., *Phil.* 61 B4
Mayskiy, *Russia* 49 J7
Maysville, *U.S.A.* 108 F4
Mayu, *Indonesia* 63 D7
Mayville, *N. Dak., U.S.A.* 112 B6
Mayville, *N.Y., U.S.A.* 110 D5
Mayya, *Russia* 51 C14
Mazabuka, *Zambia* 87 F2
Mazagán = El Jadida, *Morocco* 78 B4
Mazagão, *Brazil* 125 D8
Mazamet, *France* 20 E6
Mazán, *Peru* 124 D4
Māzandarān □, *Iran* 71 B7
Mazapil, *Mexico* 118 C4
Mazara del Vallo, *Italy* 30 E5
Mazarrón, *Spain* 33 H3
Mazarrón, G. de, *Spain* 33 H3
Mazaruni →, *Guyana* 124 B7
Mazatán, *Mexico* 118 B2
Mazatenango, *Guatemala* 120 D1
Mazatlán, *Mexico* 118 C3
Mažeikiai, *Lithuania* 9 H20
Māzhān, *Iran* 71 C8
Mazīnān, *Iran* 71 B8
Mazoe, *Mozam.* 87 F3
Mazoe →, *Mozam.* 87 F3
Mazowe, *Zimbabwe* 87 F3
Mazowieckie □, *Poland* 45 F8
Mazrûb, *Sudan* 81 E2
Mazu Dao, *China* 59 D12
Mazurian Lakes = Mazurski, Pojezierze, *Poland* 44 E7
Mazurski, Pojezierze, *Poland* 44 E7
Mazyr, *Belarus* 47 F5
Mbaba, *Senegal* 82 C1
Mbabane, *Swaziland* 89 D5
Mbagne, *Mauritania* 82 B2
M'bahiakro, *Ivory C.* 82 D4
Mbaïki, *C.A.R.* 84 D3
Mbala, *Zambia* 87 D3
Mbalabala, *Zimbabwe* 89 C4
Mbale, *Uganda* 86 B3
Mbalmayo, *Cameroon* 83 E7
Mbam →, *Cameroon* 83 E7
Mbamba Bay, *Tanzania* 87 E3
Mbandaka, *Dem. Rep. of the Congo* 84 D3
Mbanga, *Cameroon* 83 E6
Mbanza Congo, *Angola* 84 F2
Mbanza Ngungu, *Dem. Rep. of the Congo* 84 F2
Mbarara, *Uganda* 86 C3
Mbashe →, *S. Africa* 89 E4
Mbatto, *Ivory C.* 82 D4
Mbenkuru →, *Tanzania* 87 D4
Mberengwa, *Zimbabwe* 87 G2
Mberengwa, Mt., *Zimbabwe* 87 G2
Mberubu, *Nigeria* 83 D6
Mbesuma, *Zambia* 87 E3
Mbeya, *Tanzania* 87 D3
Mbeya □, *Tanzania* 86 D3
M'bili, *Sudan* 81 F2
Mbinga, *Tanzania* 87 E4
Mbini □, *Eq. Guin.* 84 D2
Mboki, *C.A.R.* 81 F2
M'bonge, *Cameroon* 83 E6
Mboro, *Senegal* 82 B1
M'boukou Res., *Cameroon* 83 D7
Mboune, *Senegal* 82 C2
Mbour, *Senegal* 82 C1
Mbout, *Mauritania* 82 B2
Mbuji-Mayi, *Dem. Rep. of the Congo* 86 D1
Mbulu, *Tanzania* 86 C4
Mburucuyá, *Argentina* 126 B4
Mchinja, *Tanzania* 87 D4
Mchinji, *Malawi* 87 E3
Mdantsane, *S. Africa* 85 L5
Mead, L., *U.S.A.* 117 J12
Meade, *U.S.A.* 113 G4
Meadow Lake, *Canada* 105 C7
Meadow Lake Prov. Park, *Canada* 105 C7
Meadow Valley Wash →, *U.S.A.* 117 J12
Meadville, *U.S.A.* 110 E4
Meaford, *Canada* 102 D3
Mealhada, *Portugal* 34 E2
Mealy Mts., *Canada* 103 B8
Meander River, *Canada* 104 B5
Meares, C., *U.S.A.* 114 D2
Mearim →, *Brazil* 125 D10
Meath □, *Ireland* 15 C5
Meath Park, *Canada* 105 C7
Meaulne, *France* 19 F9
Meaux, *France* 19 D9
Mebechi-Gawa →, *Japan* 54 D10
Mecanhelas, *Mozam.* 87 F4
Mecca = Makkah, *Si. Arabia* 74 C2
Mecca, *U.S.A.* 117 M10
Mechanicsburg, *U.S.A.* 110 F8
Mechanicville, *U.S.A.* 111 D11
Mechara, *Ethiopia* 81 F5
Mechelen, *Belgium* 17 C4
Mecheria, *Algeria* 78 B5
Mechernich, *Germany* 24 E2
Mechetinskaya, *Russia* 49 G5
Mecidiye, *Turkey* 41 F10
Mecitözü, *Turkey* 72 B6
Mecklenburg-Vorpommern □, *Germany* 24 B8
Mecklenburger Bucht, *Germany* 24 A7
Meconta, *Mozam.* 87 E4
Mecsek, *Hungary* 42 D3
Meda, *Portugal* 34 E3
Medan, *Indonesia* 62 D1
Medanosa, Pta., *Argentina* 128 F3
Mede, *Italy* 28 C5
Médéa, *Algeria* 78 A6
Mededa, *Bos.-H.* 42 G4
Medellín, *Colombia* 124 B3
Medelpad, *Sweden* 10 B10
Medemblik, *Neths.* 17 B5
Mederdra, *Mauritania* 82 B1
Medford, *Mass., U.S.A.* 111 D13
Medford, *Oreg., U.S.A.* 114 E2
Medford, *Wis., U.S.A.* 112 C9
Medgidia, *Romania* 43 F13
Medi, *Sudan* 81 F3
Media Agua, *Argentina* 126 C2
Media Luna, *Argentina* 126 C2
Medianeira, *Brazil* 127 B5
Mediaş, *Romania* 43 D9
Medicina, *Italy* 29 D8
Medicine Bow, *U.S.A.* 114 F10
Medicine Bow Pk., *U.S.A.* 114 F10
Medicine Bow Ra., *U.S.A.* 114 F10
Medicine Hat, *Canada* 105 D6
Medicine Lake, *U.S.A.* 112 A2
Medicine Lodge, *U.S.A.* 113 G5
Medina = Al Madīnah, *Si. Arabia* 70 E3
Medina, *N. Dak., U.S.A.* 112 B5
Medina, *N.Y., U.S.A.* 110 C6
Medina, *Ohio, U.S.A.* 110 E3
Medina →, *U.S.A.* 113 L5
Medina de Pomar, *Spain* 34 C7
Medina de Ríoseco, *Spain* 34 D5
Medina del Campo, *Spain* 34 D6
Medina L., *U.S.A.* 113 L5
Medina Sidonia, *Spain* 35 J5
Medinaceli, *Spain* 32 D2
Medinipur, *India* 69 H12
Mediterranean Sea, *Europe* 6 H7
Médoc, *France* 20 C3
Medulin, *Croatia* 29 D10
Medveđa, *Serbia, Yug.* 40 D5
Medvedevo, *Russia* 48 B8
Medveditsa →, *Tver, Russia* 46 D9
Medveditsa →, *Volgograd, Russia* 48 F6
Medvedok, *Russia* 48 B10
Medvezhi, Ostrava, *Russia* 51 B17
Medvezhyegorsk, *Russia* 50 C4
Medway □, *U.K.* 13 F8
Medway →, *U.K.* 13 F8
Medzev, *Slovak Rep.* 27 C13
Medzilaborce, *Slovak Rep.* 27 B14
Medžitlija, *Macedonia* 40 F5
Meekatharra, *Australia* 93 E2
Meeker, *U.S.A.* 114 F10
Meelpaeg Res., *Canada* 103 C8
Meersburg, *Germany* 25 H5
Meerut, *India* 68 E7
Meeteetse, *U.S.A.* 114 D9
Mega, *Ethiopia* 81 G4
Megálo Khorío, *Greece* 39 E9
Megálo Petalí, *Greece* 38 D6
Megalópolis, *Greece* 38 D4
Meganísi, *Greece* 38 C2
Mégara, *Greece* 38 D5
Megasini, *India* 69 J12
Megdhova →, *Greece* 38 B3
Megève, *France* 21 C10
Meghalaya □, *India* 67 G17
Meghezez, *Ethiopia* 81 F4
Mégiscane, L., *Canada* 102 C4
Megiste, *Greece* 39 E11
Megra, *Russia* 46 B9
Mehadia, *Romania* 42 F7
Meharry, Mt., *Australia* 92 D2
Mehedeby, *Sweden* 10 D11
Mehedinţi □, *Romania* 42 F7
Meheisa, *Sudan* 80 D3
Mehlville, *U.S.A.* 112 F9
Mehndawal, *India* 69 F10
Mehr Jān, *Iran* 71 C7
Mehrābād, *Iran* 70 B5
Mehrān, *Iran* 70 C5

**Milford**


Mehrīz, *Iran* 71 D7
Mehun-sur-Yèvre, *France* 19 E9
Mei Jiang →, *China* 59 E11
Mei Xian, *China* 56 G4
Meicheng, *China* 59 C12
Meichengzhen, *China* 59 C8
Meichuan, *China* 59 B10
Meigu, *China* 58 C4
Meiktila, *Burma* 67 J19
Meinerzhagen, *Germany* 24 D3
Meiningen, *Germany* 24 E6
Meira, Serra de, *Spain* 34 B3
Meiringen, *Switz.* 25 J4
Meishan, *China* 58 B4
Meissen, *Germany* 24 D9
Meissner, *Germany* 24 D5
Meitan, *China* 58 D6
Meizhou, *China* 59 E11
Meja, *India* 69 G10
Mejillones, *Chile* 126 A1
Mekdela, *Ethiopia* 81 E4
Mekele, *Ethiopia* 81 E4
Mekhtar, *Pakistan* 66 D6
Meknès, *Morocco* 78 B4
Meko, *Nigeria* 83 D5
Mekong →, *Asia* 65 H6
Mekongga, *Indonesia* 63 E6
Mekrou →, *Benin* 83 C5
Mekvari = Kür →, *Azerbaijan* 73 C13
Mel, *Italy* 29 B9
Melagiri Hills, *India* 66 N10
Melaka, *Malaysia* 65 L4
Melalap, *Malaysia* 62 C5
Mélambes, *Greece* 36 D6
Melanesia, *Pac. Oc.* 96 H7
Melbourne, *Australia* 95 F4
Melbourne, *U.S.A.* 109 L5
Melchor Múzquiz, *Mexico* 118 B4
Melchor Ocampo, *Mexico* 118 C4
Méldola, *Italy* 29 D9
Meldorf, *Germany* 24 A5
Melegnano, *Italy* 28 C6
Melenci, *Serbia, Yug.* 42 E5
Melenki, *Russia* 48 C5
Mélèzes →, *Canada* 102 A5
Melfi, *Italy* 31 B8
Melfort, *Canada* 105 C8
Melfort, *Zimbabwe* 87 F3
Melgaço, *Portugal* 34 C2
Melgar de Fernamental, *Spain* 34 C6
Melhus, *Norway* 8 E14
Melide, *Spain* 34 C2
Meligalá, *Greece* 38 D3
Melilla, *N. Afr.* 78 A5
Melilli, *Italy* 31 E8
Melipilla, *Chile* 126 C1
Mélissa, Ákra, *Greece* 36 D6
Mélissa Óros, *Greece* 39 D8
Melita, *Canada* 105 D8
Mélito di Porto Salvo, *Italy* 31 E8
Melitopol, *Ukraine* 47 J8
Melk, *Austria* 26 C8
Mellan Fryken, *Sweden* 10 E7
Mellansel, *Sweden* 8 E18
Mellbystrand, *Sweden* 11 H6
Melle, *France* 20 B3
Melle, *Germany* 24 C4
Mellen, *U.S.A.* 112 B9
Mellerud, *Sweden* 11 F6
Mellette, *U.S.A.* 112 C5
Mellid = Melide, *Spain* 34 C2
Mellieha, *Malta* 36 D1
Mellit, *Sudan* 81 E2
Mellrichstadt, *Germany* 24 E6
Melnik, *Bulgaria* 40 E7
Mělník, *Czech Rep.* 26 A7
Melo, *Uruguay* 127 C5
Melolo, *Indonesia* 63 F6
Melouprey, *Cambodia* 64 F5
Melrose, *Australia* 95 E4
Melrose, *U.K.* 14 F6
Melrose, *Minn., U.S.A.* 112 C7
Melrose, *N. Mex., U.S.A.* 113 H3
Melstone, *U.S.A.* 114 C10
Melsungen, *Germany* 24 D5
Melton Mowbray, *U.K.* 12 E7
Melun, *France* 19 D9
Melut, *Sudan* 81 E3
Melville, *Canada* 105 C8
Melville, C., *Australia* 94 A3
Melville, L., *Canada* 103 B8
Melville B., *Australia* 94 A2
Melville I., *Australia* 92 B5
Melville I., *Canada* 4 B2
Melville Pen., *Canada* 101 B11
Mélykút, *Hungary* 42 D4
Memaliaj, *Albania* 40 F3
Memba, *Mozam.* 87 E5
Memboro, *Indonesia* 63 F5
Membrilla, *Spain* 35 G7
Memel = Klaipėda, *Lithuania* 9 J19
Memel, *S. Africa* 89 D4
Memmingen, *Germany* 25 H6
Mempawah, *Indonesia* 62 D3
Memphis, *Egypt* 80 J7
Memphis, *Mich., U.S.A.* 110 D2
Memphis, *Tenn., U.S.A.* 113 H10
Memphis, *Tex., U.S.A.* 113 H4
Memphremagog, L., *U.S.A.* 111 B12
Mena, *Ukraine* 47 G7
Mena, *U.S.A.* 113 H7
Mena →, *Ethiopia* 81 F5
Menai Strait, *U.K.* 12 D3
Ménaka, *Mali* 83 B5
Menan = Chao Phraya →, *Thailand* 64 F3
Menarandra →, *Madag.* 89 D7
Menard, *U.S.A.* 113 K5
Menawashei, *Sudan* 81 E1
Mendawai →, *Indonesia* 62 E4
Mende, *France* 20 D7
Mendebo, *Ethiopia* 81 F4
Menden, *Germany* 24 D3
Menderes, *Turkey* 39 C9
Mendez, *Mexico* 119 B5
Mendhar, *India* 69 C6
Mendi, *Ethiopia* 81 F4
Mendip Hills, *U.K.* 13 F5
Mendocino, *U.S.A.* 114 G2
Mendocino, C., *U.S.A.* 114 F1
Mendota, *Calif., U.S.A.* 116 J6
Mendota, *Ill., U.S.A.* 112 E10
Mendoza, *Argentina* 126 C2
Mendoza □, *Argentina* 126 C2
Mene Grande, *Venezuela* 124 B4
Menemen, *Turkey* 39 C9
Menen, *Belgium* 17 D3
Menfi, *Italy* 30 E5
Mengdingjie, *China* 58 F2
Mengeš, *Slovenia* 29 B11
Menggala, *Indonesia* 62 E3
Menghai, *China* 58 G3
Mengíbar, *Spain* 35 H7
Mengjin, *China* 56 G7
Mengla, *China* 58 G3
Menglian, *China* 58 F2
Mengshan, *China* 59 E8
Mengyin, *China* 57 G9
Mengzhe, *China* 58 F3
Mengzi, *China* 58 F4
Menihek, *Canada* 103 B6
Menihek L., *Canada* 103 B6
Menin = Menen, *Belgium* 17 D3
Menindee, *Australia* 95 E3
Menindee L., *Australia* 95 E3
Meningie, *Australia* 95 F2
Menlo Park, *U.S.A.* 116 H4
Menominee, *U.S.A.* 108 C2
Menominee →, *U.S.A.* 108 C2
Menomonie, *U.S.A.* 112 C9
Menongue, *Angola* 85 G3
Menorca, *Spain* 37 B11
Mentakab, *Malaysia* 65 L4
Mentawai, Kepulauan, *Indonesia* 62 E1
Menton, *France* 21 E11
Mentor, *U.S.A.* 110 E3
Menzies, *Australia* 93 E3
Meob B., *Namibia* 88 B2
Me'ona, *Israel* 75 B4
Meoqui, *Mexico* 118 B3
Mepaco, *Mozam.* 87 F3
Meppel, *Neths.* 17 B6
Meppen, *Germany* 24 C3
Mequinenza, *Spain* 32 D5
Mequinenza, Embalse de, *Spain* 32 D5
Mer, *France* 18 E8
Merabéllou, Kólpos, *Greece* 36 D7
Merak, *Indonesia* 63 F12
Meramangye, L., *Australia* 93 E5
Meran = Merano, *Italy* 29 B8
Merano, *Italy* 29 B8
Merate, *Italy* 28 C6
Merauke, *Indonesia* 63 F10
Merbein, *Australia* 95 E3
Merca, *Somali Rep.* 74 G3
Mercato Saraceno, *Italy* 29 E9
Merced, *U.S.A.* 116 H6
Merced →, *U.S.A.* 116 H6
Merced Pk., *U.S.A.* 116 H7
Mercedes, *Buenos Aires, Argentina* 126 C4
Mercedes, *Corrientes, Argentina* 126 B4
Mercedes, *San Luis, Argentina* 126 C2
Mercedes, *Uruguay* 126 C4
Mercedes, *U.S.A.* 113 M6
Merceditas, *Chile* 126 B1
Mercer, *N.Z.* 91 G5
Mercer, *U.S.A.* 110 E4
Mercer Island, *U.S.A.* 116 C4
Mercury, *U.S.A.* 117 J11
Mercy C., *Canada* 101 B13
Merdrignac, *France* 18 D4
Mere, *U.K.* 13 F5
Meredith, C., *Falk. Is.* 128 G4
Meredith, L., *U.S.A.* 113 H4
Merefa, *Ukraine* 47 H9
Merei, *Romania* 43 E11
Merga = Nukheila, *Sudan* 80 D2
Mergui, *Burma* 64 F2
Mergui Arch. = Myeik Kyunzu, *Burma* 65 G1
Meriç, *Turkey* 41 E10
Meriç →, *Turkey* 41 F10
Mérida, *Mexico* 119 C7
Mérida, *Spain* 35 G4
Mérida, *Venezuela* 124 B4
Mérida, Cord. de, *Venezuela* 122 C3
Meriden, *U.K.* 13 E6
Meriden, *U.S.A.* 111 E12
Meridian, *Calif., U.S.A.* 116 F5
Meridian, *Idaho, U.S.A.* 114 E5
Meridian, *Miss., U.S.A.* 109 J1
Mérignac, *France* 20 D3
Mérinaghène, *Senegal* 82 B1
Merinda, *Australia* 94 C4
Mering, *Germany* 25 G6
Meringa, *Nigeria* 83 C7
Merir, *Pac. Oc.* 63 D8
Merirumã, *Brazil* 125 C8
Merkel, *U.S.A.* 113 J5
Mermaid Reef, *Australia* 92 C2
Merowe, *Sudan* 80 D3
Merredin, *Australia* 93 F2
Merrick, *U.K.* 14 F4
Merrickville, *Canada* 111 B9
Merrill, *Oreg., U.S.A.* 114 E3
Merrill, *Wis., U.S.A.* 112 C10
Merrimack →, *U.S.A.* 111 D14
Merriman, *U.S.A.* 112 D4
Merritt, *Canada* 104 C4
Merritt Island, *U.S.A.* 109 L5
Merriwa, *Australia* 95 E5
Merry I., *Canada* 102 A4
Merryville, *U.S.A.* 113 K8
Mersa Fatma, *Eritrea* 81 E5
Mersch, *Lux.* 17 E6
Merse →, *Italy* 29 E8
Mersea I., *U.K.* 13 F8
Merseburg, *Germany* 24 D7
Mersey →, *U.K.* 12 D4
Merseyside □, *U.K.* 12 D4
Mersin, *Turkey* 70 B2
Mersing, *Malaysia* 65 L4
Merta, *India* 68 F6
Merta Road, *India* 68 F5
Merthyr Tydfil, *U.K.* 13 F4
Merthyr Tydfil □, *U.K.* 13 F4
Mértola, *Portugal* 35 H3
Mertzon, *U.S.A.* 113 K4
Méru, *France* 19 C9
Meru, *Kenya* 86 B4
Meru, *Tanzania* 86 C4
Merville, *France* 19 B9
Méry-sur-Seine, *France* 19 D10
Merzifon, *Turkey* 72 B6
Merzig, *Germany* 25 F2
Mesa, *U.S.A.* 115 K8
Mesa Verde National Park, *U.S.A.* 115 H9
Mesagne, *Italy* 31 B10
Mesanagrós, *Greece* 36 C9
Mesaoría □, *Cyprus* 36 D12
Mesarás, Kólpos, *Greece* 36 D6
Meschede, *Germany* 24 D4
Mescit, *Turkey* 73 B9
Mesfinto, *Ethiopia* 81 E4
Mesgouez, L., *Canada* 102 B5
Meshchovsk, *Russia* 46 E8
Meshed = Mashhad, *Iran* 71 B8
Meshoppen, *U.S.A.* 111 E8
Meshra er Req, *Sudan* 81 F2
Mesilinka →, *Canada* 104 B4
Mesilla, *U.S.A.* 115 K10
Meslay-du-Maine, *France* 18 E6
Mesocco, *Switz.* 25 J5
Mesolóngion, *Greece* 38 C3
Mesopotamia = Al Jazirah, *Iraq* 70 C5
Mesopotamia, *U.S.A.* 110 E4
Mesopótamon, *Greece* 38 B2
Mesoraca, *Italy* 31 C9
Mésou Volímais = Volímai, *Greece* 38 D2
Mesquite, *U.S.A.* 115 H6
Messaad, *Algeria* 78 B6
Messac, *France* 18 E5
Messalo →, *Mozam.* 87 E4
Méssaména, *Cameroon* 83 E7
Messeue, *Greece* 38 D3
Messina, *Italy* 31 D8
Messina, *S. Africa* 89 C5
Messina, Str. di, *Italy* 31 D8
Messíni, *Greece* 38 D4
Messínia □, *Greece* 38 D3
Messiniakós Kólpos, *Greece* 38 E4
Messkirch, *Germany* 25 H5
Messonghi, *Greece* 36 B3
Mesta →, *Bulgaria* 40 E7
Mestá, Ákra, *Greece* 39 C7
Mestanza, *Spain* 35 G6
Mestre, *Italy* 29 C9
Mesudiye, *Turkey* 72 B7
Meta →, *S. Amer.* 122 C4
Meta Incognita Peninsula, *Canada* 101 B13
Metabetchouan, *Canada* 103 C5
Metairie, *U.S.A.* 113 L9
Metalici, Munţii, *Romania* 42 D7
Metaline Falls, *U.S.A.* 114 B5
Metallifere, Colline, *Italy* 28 E8
Metán, *Argentina* 126 B3
Metangula, *Mozam.* 87 E3
Metauro →, *Italy* 29 E10
Metema, *Ethiopia* 81 E4
Metengobalame, *Mozam.* 87 E3
Méthana, *Greece* 38 D5
Methóni, *Greece* 38 E3
Methven, *N.Z.* 91 K3
Metil, *Mozam.* 87 F4
Metkovets, *Bulgaria* 40 C7
Metković, *Croatia* 29 E14
Metlakatla, *U.S.A.* 100 C6
Metlika, *Slovenia* 29 C12
Metropolis, *U.S.A.* 113 G10
Métsovon, *Greece* 38 B3
Metu, *Ethiopia* 81 F4
Metz, *France* 19 C13
Metzingen, *Germany* 25 G5
Meulaboh, *Indonesia* 62 D1
Meung-sur-Loire, *France* 19 E8
Meureudu, *Indonesia* 62 C1
Meurthe →, *France* 19 D13
Meurthe-et-Moselle □, *France* 19 D13
Meuse □, *France* 19 C12
Meuse →, *Europe* 17 D5
Meuselwitz, *Germany* 24 D8
Mexia, *U.S.A.* 113 K6
Mexiana, I., *Brazil* 125 D9
Mexicali, *Mexico* 117 N11
Mexican Plateau, *Mexico* 98 G9
Mexican Water, *U.S.A.* 115 H9
México, *Mexico* 119 D5
Mexico, *Maine, U.S.A.* 111 B14
Mexico, *Mo., U.S.A.* 112 F9
Mexico, *N.Y., U.S.A.* 111 C8
México □, *Mexico* 119 D5
Mexico ■, *Cent. Amer.* 118 C4
Mexico, G. of, *Cent. Amer.* 119 C7
Mexico B., *U.S.A.* 111 C8
Meydān-e Naftūn, *Iran* 71 D6
Meydani, Ra's-e, *Iran* 71 E8
Meyenburg, *Germany* 24 B8
Meymac, *France* 20 C6
Meymaneh, *Afghan.* 66 B4
Meyrueis, *France* 20 D7
Meyssac, *France* 20 C5
Meyzieu, *France* 21 C8
Mezdra, *Bulgaria* 40 C7
Mèze, *France* 20 E7
Mezen, *Russia* 50 C5
Mezen →, *Russia* 50 C5
Mézenc, Mt., *France* 21 D8
Mezeş, Munţii, *Romania* 42 C8
Mezha →, *Russia* 46 E6
Mezhdurechenskiy, *Russia* 50 D7
Mézidon-Canon, *France* 18 C6
Mézières-en-Brenne, *France* 20 B5
Mézilhac, *France* 21 D8
Mézin, *France* 20 D4
Mezőberény, *Hungary* 42 D6
Mezőfalva, *Hungary* 42 D3
Mezőhegyes, *Hungary* 42 D5
Mezőkövácsháza, *Hungary* 42 D5
Mezőkövesd, *Hungary* 42 C5
Mézos, *France* 20 D2
Mezőtúr, *Hungary* 42 C5
Mezquital, *Mexico* 118 C4
Mezzolombardo, *Italy* 28 B8
Mfolozi →, *S. Africa* 89 D5
Mgeta, *Tanzania* 87 D4
Mglin, *Russia* 47 F7
Mhlaba Hills, *Zimbabwe* 87 F3
Mhow, *India* 68 H6
Miahuatlán, *Mexico* 119 D5
Miajadas, *Spain* 35 F5
Miami, *Fla., U.S.A.* 109 N5
Miami, *Okla., U.S.A.* 113 G7
Miami, *Tex., U.S.A.* 113 H4
Miami Beach, *U.S.A.* 109 N5
Mian Xian, *China* 56 H4
Mianchi, *China* 56 G6
Mīāndarreh, *Iran* 71 C7
Mīāndowāb, *Iran* 70 B5
Miandrivazo, *Madag.* 89 B8
Mīāneh, *Iran* 70 B5
Mianning, *China* 58 C4
Mianwali, *Pakistan* 68 C4
Mianyang, *China* 58 B5
Mianzhu, *China* 58 B5
Miaoli, *Taiwan* 59 E13
Miarinarivo, *Antananarivo, Madag.* 89 B8
Miarinarivo, *Toamasina, Madag.* 89 B8
Miariravaratra, *Madag.* 89 C8
Miass, *Russia* 50 D7
Miasteczko Krajeńskie, *Poland* 45 E4
Miastko, *Poland* 44 E3
Mica, *S. Africa* 89 C5
Micăsasa, *Romania* 43 D9
Michalovce, *Slovak Rep.* 27 C14
Michigan □, *U.S.A.* 108 C3
Michigan, L., *U.S.A.* 108 D2
Michigan City, *U.S.A.* 108 E2
Michika, *Nigeria* 83 C7
Michipicoten I., *Canada* 102 C2
Michoacan □, *Mexico* 118 D4
Michurin, *Bulgaria* 41 D11
Michurinsk, *Russia* 48 D5
Mico, Pta., *Nic.* 120 D3
Micronesia, *Pac. Oc.* 96 G7
Micronesia, Federated States of ■, *Pac. Oc.* 96 G7
Midai, *Indonesia* 65 L6
Midale, *Canada* 105 D8
Middelburg, *Neths.* 17 C3
Middelburg, *Eastern Cape, S. Africa* 88 E4
Middelburg, *Mpumalanga, S. Africa* 89 D4
Middelfart, *Denmark* 11 J3
Middelpos, *S. Africa* 88 E3
Middelwit, *S. Africa* 88 C4
Middle Alkali L., *U.S.A.* 114 F3
Middle Bass I., *U.S.A.* 110 E2
Middle East, *Asia* 52 F7
Middle Fork Feather →, *U.S.A.* 116 F5
Middle I., *Australia* 93 F3
Middle Loup →, *U.S.A.* 112 E5
Middle Sackville, *Canada* 103 D7
Middleboro, *U.S.A.* 111 E14
Middleburg, *Fla., U.S.A.* 109 K5
Middleburg, *N.Y., U.S.A.* 111 D10
Middleburg, *Pa., U.S.A.* 110 F7
Middlebury, *U.S.A.* 111 B11
Middlemount, *Australia* 94 C4
Middleport, *N.Y., U.S.A.* 110 C6
Middleport, *Ohio, U.S.A.* 108 F4
Middlesboro, *U.S.A.* 109 G4
Middlesbrough, *U.K.* 12 C6
Middlesbrough □, *U.K.* 12 C6
Middlesex, *Belize* 120 C2
Middlesex, *N.J., U.S.A.* 111 F10
Middlesex, *N.Y., U.S.A.* 110 D7
Middleton, *Australia* 94 C3
Middleton, *Canada* 103 D6
Middleton Cr. →, *Australia* 94 C3
Middletown, *U.K.* 15 B5
Middletown, *Calif., U.S.A.* 116 G4
Middletown, *Conn., U.S.A.* 111 E12
Middletown, *N.Y., U.S.A.* 111 E10
Middletown, *Ohio, U.S.A.* 108 F3
Middletown, *Pa., U.S.A.* 111 F8
Midhurst, *U.K.* 13 G7
Mīdī, *Yemen* 81 D5
Midi, Canal du →, *France* 20 E5
Midi d'Ossau, Pic du, *France* 20 F3
Midi-Pyrénées □, *France* 20 E5
Midland, *Canada* 102 D4
Midland, *Calif., U.S.A.* 117 M12
Midland, *Mich., U.S.A.* 108 D3
Midland, *Pa., U.S.A.* 110 F4
Midland, *Tex., U.S.A.* 113 K3
Midlands □, *Zimbabwe* 87 F2
Midleton, *Ireland* 15 E3
Midlothian, *U.S.A.* 113 J6
Midlothian □, *U.K.* 14 F5
Midongy, Tangorombohitr' i, *Madag.* 89 C8
Midongy Atsimo, *Madag.* 89 C8
Midou →, *France* 20 E3
Midouze →, *France* 20 E3
Midsayap, *Phil.* 61 H6
Midu, *China* 58 E3
Midway Is., *Pac. Oc.* 96 E10
Midway Wells, *U.S.A.* 117 N11
Midwest, *U.S.A.* 114 E10
Midwest City, *U.S.A.* 113 H6
Midyat, *Turkey* 70 B4
Midžor, *Bulgaria* 40 C6
Mie □, *Japan* 55 G8
Miechów, *Poland* 45 H7
Miedwie, Jezioro, *Poland* 45 E1
Międzybórz, *Poland* 45 G4
Międzychód, *Poland* 45 F2
Międzylesie, *Poland* 45 H3
Międzyrzec Podlaski, *Poland* 45 G9
Międzyrzecz, *Poland* 45 F2
Międzyzdroje, *Poland* 44 E1
Miejska Górka, *Poland* 45 G3
Miélan, *France* 20 E4
Mielec, *Poland* 45 H8
Mienga, *Angola* 88 B2
Miercurea-Ciuc, *Romania* 43 D10
Miercurea Sibiului, *Romania* 43 E8
Mieres, *Spain* 34 B5
Mieroszów, *Poland* 45 H3
Mieso, *Ethiopia* 81 F5
Mieszkowice, *Poland* 45 F1
Mifflintown, *U.S.A.* 110 F7
Mifraz Hefa, *Israel* 75 C4
Migennes, *France* 19 E10
Migliarino, *Italy* 29 D8
Miguel Alemán, Presa, *Mexico* 119 D5
Miguelturra, *Spain* 35 G7
Mihăileni, *Romania* 43 C11
Mihăileşti, *Romania* 43 F10
Mihailovca, *Moldova* 43 D13
Mihalgazi, *Turkey* 39 A12
Mihaliççık, *Turkey* 72 C4
Mihara, *Japan* 55 G6
Miheşu de Cîmpie, *Romania* 43 D9
Mijas, *Spain* 35 J6
Mikese, *Tanzania* 86 D4
Mikha-Tskhakaya = Senaki, *Georgia* 49 J6
Mikhailovka = Mykhaylivka, *Ukraine* 47 J8
Mikhaylov, *Russia* 46 E10
Mikhaylovgrad = Montana, *Bulgaria* 40 C7
Mikhaylovka, *Russia* 48 E6
Mikhnevo, *Russia* 46 E9
Mikínai, *Greece* 38 D4
Mikkeli, *Finland* 9 F22
Mikkwa →, *Canada* 104 B6
Mikniya, *Sudan* 81 D3
Mikołajki, *Poland* 44 E8
Míkonos, *Greece* 39 D7
Mikrí Préspa, Límni, *Greece* 40 F5
Mikrón Dhérion, *Greece* 41 E10
Mikstat, *Poland* 45 G4
Mikulov, *Czech Rep.* 27 C9
Mikumi, *Tanzania* 86 D4
Milaca, *U.S.A.* 112 C8
Milagro, *Ecuador* 124 D3
Milagros, *Phil.* 61 E5
Milan = Milano, *Italy* 28 C6
Milan, *Mo., U.S.A.* 112 E8
Milan, *Tenn., U.S.A.* 109 H1
Milange, *Mozam.* 87 F4
Milano, *Italy* 28 C6
Milanoa, *Madag.* 89 A8
Milâs, *Turkey* 39 D9
Mílatos, *Greece* 36 D7
Milazzo, *Italy* 31 D8
Milbank, *U.S.A.* 112 C6
Milbanke Sd., *Canada* 104 C3
Milden, *Canada* 105 C7
Mildenhall, *U.K.* 13 E8
Mildmay, *Canada* 110 B3
Mildura, *Australia* 95 E3
Mile, *China* 58 E4
Miléai, *Greece* 38 B5
Miles, *Australia* 95 D5
Miles City, *U.S.A.* 112 B2
Mileşti, *Moldova* 43 C13
Milestone, *Canada* 105 D8
Mileto, *Italy* 31 D9
Miletto, Mte., *Italy* 31 A7
Miletus, *Turkey* 39 D9
Milevsko, *Czech Rep.* 26 B7
Milford, *Calif., U.S.A.* 116 E6
Milford, *Conn., U.S.A.* 111 E11
Milford, *Del., U.S.A.* 108 F8
Milford, *Mass., U.S.A.* 111 D13
Milford, *N.H., U.S.A.* 111 D13

Moshi


Molotov = Perm, *Russia* 50 **D6**
Molsheim, *France* 19 **D14**
Molson L., *Canada* 105 **C9**
Molteno, *S. Africa* 88 **E4**
Molu, *Indonesia* 63 **F8**
Molucca Sea, *Indonesia* 63 **E6**
Moluccas = Maluku, *Indonesia* 63 **E7**
Moma, *Dem. Rep. of the Congo* 86 **C1**
Moma, *Mozam.* 87 **F4**
Mombasa, *Kenya* 86 **C4**
Mombetsu, *Japan* 54 **B11**
Mombuey, *Spain* 34 **C4**
Momchilgrad, *Bulgaria* 41 **E9**
Momi, *Dem. Rep. of the Congo* 86 **C2**
Mompós, *Colombia* 124 **B4**
Møn, *Denmark* 11 **K6**
Mon □, *Burma* 67 **L20**
Mona, Canal de la, *W. Indies* 121 **C6**
Mona, Isla, *Puerto Rico* 121 **C6**
Mona, Pta., *Costa Rica* 120 **E3**
Monaca, *U.S.A.* 110 **F4**
Monaco ■, *Europe* 21 **E11**
Monadhliath Mts., *U.K.* 14 **D4**
Monadnock, Mt., *U.S.A.* 111 **D12**
Monaghan, *Ireland* 15 **B5**
Monaghan □, *Ireland* 15 **B5**
Monahans, *U.S.A.* 113 **K3**
Monapo, *Mozam.* 87 **E5**
Monar, L., *U.K.* 14 **D3**
Monarch Mt., *Canada* 104 **C3**
Monashee Mts., *Canada* 104 **C5**
Monasterevin, *Ireland* 15 **C4**
Monastir = Bitola, *Macedonia* 40 **E5**
Moncada, *Phil.* 61 **D4**
Moncalieri, *Italy* 28 **D4**
Moncalvo, *Italy* 28 **C5**
Moncão, *Portugal* 34 **C2**
Moncarapacho, *Portugal* 35 **H3**
Moncayo, Sierra del, *Spain* 32 **D3**
Mönchengladbach, *Germany* 24 **D2**
Monchique, *Portugal* 35 **H2**
Moncks Corner, *U.S.A.* 109 **J5**
Monclova, *Mexico* 118 **B4**
Moncontour, *France* 18 **D4**
Moncton, *Canada* 103 **C7**
Mondariz, *Spain* 34 **C2**
Mondego →, *Portugal* 34 **E2**
Mondego, C., *Portugal* 34 **E2**
Mondeodo, *Indonesia* 63 **E6**
Mondeville, *France* 18 **C6**
Mondolfo, *Italy* 29 **E10**
Mondoñedo, *Spain* 34 **B3**
Mondovì, *Italy* 28 **D4**
Mondragon, *Phil.* 61 **E6**
Mondragone, *Italy* 30 **A6**
Mondrain I., *Australia* 93 **F3**
Monemvasía, *Greece* 38 **E5**
Monessen, *U.S.A.* 110 **F5**
Monesterio, *Spain* 35 **G4**
Monestier-de-Clermont, *France* 21 **D9**
Monett, *U.S.A.* 113 **G8**
Moneymore, *U.K.* 15 **B5**
Monfalcone, *Italy* 29 **C10**
Monflanquin, *France* 20 **D4**
Monforte, *Portugal* 35 **F3**
Monforte de Lemos, *Spain* 34 **C3**
Mong Hsu, *Burma* 58 **G2**
Mong Kung, *Burma* 67 **J20**
Mong Nai, *Burma* 67 **J20**
Mong Pawk, *Burma* 67 **H21**
Mong Ping, *Burma* 58 **G2**
Mong Ton, *Burma* 67 **J21**
Mong Wa, *Burma* 67 **J22**
Mong Yai, *Burma* 67 **H21**
Mongalla, *Sudan* 81 **F3**
Mongers, L., *Australia* 93 **E2**
Monghyr = Munger, *India* 69 **G12**
Mongibello = Etna, *Italy* 31 **E7**
Mongo, *Chad* 79 **F9**
Mongo →, *S. Leone* 82 **D2**
Mongolia ■, *Asia* 51 **E10**
Mongonu, *Nigeria* 83 **C7**
Mongu, *Zambia* 85 **H4**
Môngua, *Angola* 88 **B2**
Monifieth, *U.K.* 14 **E6**
Monistrol-sur-Loire, *France* 21 **C8**
Monkey Bay, *Malawi* 87 **E4**
Monkey Mia, *Australia* 93 **E1**
Monkey River, *Belize* 119 **D7**
Mońki, *Poland* 44 **E9**
Monkoto, *Dem. Rep. of the Congo* 84 **E4**
Monkton, *Canada* 110 **C3**
Monmouth, *U.K.* 13 **F5**
Monmouth, *Ill., U.S.A.* 112 **E9**
Monmouth, *Oreg., U.S.A.* 114 **D2**
Monmouthshire □, *U.K.* 13 **F5**
Mono L., *U.S.A.* 116 **H7**
Monolith, *U.S.A.* 117 **K8**
Monólithos, *Greece* 36 **C9**
Monongahela, *U.S.A.* 110 **F5**
Monópoli, *Italy* 31 **B10**
Monor, *Hungary* 42 **C4**
Monóvar, *Spain* 33 **G4**
Monreal del Campo, *Spain* 32 **E3**
Monreale, *Italy* 30 **D6**
Monroe, *Ga., U.S.A.* 109 **J4**
Monroe, *La., U.S.A.* 113 **J8**
Monroe, *Mich., U.S.A.* 108 **E4**
Monroe, *N.C., U.S.A.* 109 **H5**
Monroe, *N.Y., U.S.A.* 111 **E10**
Monroe, *Utah, U.S.A.* 115 **G7**
Monroe, *Wash., U.S.A.* 116 **C5**
Monroe, *Wis., U.S.A.* 112 **D10**
Monroe City, *U.S.A.* 112 **F9**
Monroeton, *U.S.A.* 111 **E8**
Monroeville, *Ala., U.S.A.* 109 **K2**
Monroeville, *Pa., U.S.A.* 110 **F5**
Monrovia, *Liberia* 82 **D2**
Mons, *Belgium* 17 **D3**
Møns Klint, *Denmark* 11 **K6**
Monsaraz, *Portugal* 35 **G3**
Monse, *Indonesia* 63 **E6**
Monségur, *France* 20 **D4**
Monsélice, *Italy* 29 **C8**
Mönsterås, *Sweden* 11 **G10**
Mont Cenis, Col du, *France* 21 **C10**
Mont-de-Marsan, *France* 20 **E3**
Mont-Joli, *Canada* 103 **C6**
Mont-Laurier, *Canada* 102 **C4**
Mont-Louis, *Canada* 103 **C6**
Mont-roig del Camp, *Spain* 32 **D5**
Mont-St-Michel, Le = Le Mont-St-Michel, *France* 18 **D5**
Mont Tremblant, Parc Recr. du, *Canada* 102 **C5**
Montabaur, *Germany* 24 **E3**
Montagnac, *France* 20 **E7**
Montagnana, *Italy* 29 **C8**
Montagu, *S. Africa* 88 **E3**
Montagu I., *Antarctica* 5 **B1**
Montague, *Canada* 103 **C7**
Montague, I., *Mexico* 118 **A2**
Montague Ra., *Australia* 93 **E2**
Montague Sd., *Australia* 92 **B4**
Montaigu, *France* 18 **F5**
Montalbán, *Spain* 32 **E4**
Montalbano Iónico, *Italy* 31 **B9**
Montalbo, *Spain* 32 **F2**
Montalcino, *Italy* 29 **E8**
Montalegre, *Portugal* 34 **D3**
Montalto, *Italy* 31 **D8**
Montalto di Castro, *Italy* 29 **F8**
Montalto Uffugo, *Italy* 31 **C9**
Montalvo, *U.S.A.* 117 **L7**
Montamarta, *Spain* 34 **D5**
Montana, *Bulgaria* 40 **C7**
Montaña, *Peru* 124 **E4**
Montana □, *Bulgaria* 40 **C7**
Montana □, *U.S.A.* 114 **C9**
Montaña Clara, I., *Canary Is.* 37 **E6**
Montánchez, *Spain* 35 **F4**
Montargil, *Portugal* 35 **F2**
Montargis, *France* 19 **E9**
Montauban, *France* 20 **D5**
Montauk, *U.S.A.* 111 **E13**
Montauk Pt., *U.S.A.* 111 **E13**
Montbard, *France* 19 **E11**
Montbarrey, *France* 19 **E12**
Montbéliard, *France* 19 **E13**
Montblanc, *Spain* 32 **D6**
Montbrison, *France* 21 **C8**
Montcalm, Pic de, *France* 20 **F5**
Montceau-les-Mines, *France* 19 **F11**
Montcenis, *France* 21 **B8**
Montclair, *U.S.A.* 111 **F10**
Montcornet, *France* 19 **C11**
Montcuq, *France* 20 **D5**
Montdidier, *France* 19 **C9**
Monte Albán, *Mexico* 119 **D5**
Monte Alegre, *Brazil* 125 **D8**
Monte Azul, *Brazil* 125 **G10**
Monte Bello Is., *Australia* 92 **D2**
Monte-Carlo, *Monaco* 21 **E11**
Monte Caseros, *Argentina* 126 **C4**
Monte Comán, *Argentina* 126 **C2**
Monte Cristi, *Dom. Rep.* 121 **C5**
Monte Lindo →, *Paraguay* 126 **A4**
Monte Patria, *Chile* 126 **C1**
Monte Quemado, *Argentina* 126 **B3**
Monte Redondo, *Portugal* 34 **F2**
Monte Rio, *U.S.A.* 116 **G4**
Monte San Giovanni Campano, *Italy* 30 **A6**
Monte San Savino, *Italy* 29 **E8**
Monte Sant' Ángelo, *Italy* 29 **G12**
Monte Santu, C. di, *Italy* 30 **B2**
Monte Vista, *U.S.A.* 115 **H10**
Monteagudo, *Argentina* 127 **B5**
Montealegre del Castillo, *Spain* 33 **G3**
Montebello, *Canada* 102 **C5**
Montebello Iónico, *Italy* 31 **E8**
Montebelluna, *Italy* 29 **C9**
Montebourg, *France* 18 **C5**
Montecastrilli, *Italy* 29 **F9**
Montecatini Terme, *Italy* 28 **E7**
Montecito, *U.S.A.* 117 **L7**
Montecristo, *Italy* 28 **F7**
Montefalco, *Italy* 29 **F9**
Montefiascone, *Italy* 29 **F9**
Montefrío, *Spain* 35 **H7**
Montegiórgio, *Italy* 29 **E10**
Montego Bay, *Jamaica* 120 **C4**
Montehermoso, *Spain* 34 **E4**
Montejicar, *Spain* 35 **H7**
Montélimar, *France* 21 **D8**
Montella, *Italy* 31 **B8**
Montellano, *Spain* 35 **J5**
Montello, *U.S.A.* 112 **D10**
Montemor-o-Novo, *Portugal* 35 **G2**
Montemor-o-Velho, *Portugal* 34 **E2**
Montemorelos, *Mexico* 119 **B5**
Montendre, *France* 20 **C3**
Montenegro, *Brazil* 127 **B5**
Montenegro □, *Yugoslavia* 40 **D3**
Montenero di Bisáccia, *Italy* 29 **G11**
Montepuez, *Mozam.* 87 **E4**
Montepuez →, *Mozam.* 87 **E5**
Montepulciano, *Italy* 29 **E8**
Montereale, *Italy* 29 **F10**
Montereau-Faut-Yonne, *France* 19 **D9**
Monterey, *U.S.A.* 116 **J5**
Monterey B., *U.S.A.* 116 **J5**
Montería, *Colombia* 124 **B3**
Monteros, *Argentina* 126 **B2**
Monterotondo, *Italy* 29 **F9**
Monterrey, *Mexico* 118 **B4**
Montes Claros, *Brazil* 125 **G10**
Montesano, *U.S.A.* 116 **D3**
Montesano sulla Marcellana, *Italy* 31 **B8**
Montesárchio, *Italy* 31 **A7**
Montescaglioso, *Italy* 31 **B9**
Montesilvano, *Italy* 29 **F11**
Montevarchi, *Italy* 29 **E8**
Montevideo, *Uruguay* 127 **C4**
Montevideo, *U.S.A.* 112 **C7**
Montezuma, *U.S.A.* 112 **E8**
Montfaucon, *France* 18 **E5**
Montfaucon-d'Argonne, *France* 19 **C12**
Montfaucon-en-Velay, *France* 21 **C8**
Montfort, *France* 18 **D5**
Montfort-le-Gesnois, *France* 18 **D7**
Montgenèvre, *France* 21 **D10**
Montgomery = Sahiwal, *Pakistan* 68 **D5**
Montgomery, *U.K.* 13 **E4**
Montgomery, *Ala., U.S.A.* 109 **J2**
Montgomery, *Pa., U.S.A.* 110 **E8**
Montgomery, *W. Va., U.S.A.* 108 **F5**
Montgomery City, *U.S.A.* 112 **F9**
Montguyon, *France* 20 **C3**
Monthermé, *France* 19 **C11**
Monthey, *Switz.* 25 **J2**
Monthois, *France* 19 **C11**
Monti, *Italy* 30 **B2**
Monticelli d'Ongina, *Italy* 28 **C6**
Monticello, *Ark., U.S.A.* 113 **J9**
Monticello, *Fla., U.S.A.* 109 **K4**
Monticello, *Ind., U.S.A.* 108 **E2**
Monticello, *Iowa, U.S.A.* 112 **D9**
Monticello, *Ky., U.S.A.* 109 **G3**
Monticello, *Minn., U.S.A.* 112 **C8**
Monticello, *Miss., U.S.A.* 113 **K9**
Monticello, *N.Y., U.S.A.* 111 **E10**
Monticello, *Utah, U.S.A.* 115 **H9**
Montichiari, *Italy* 28 **C7**
Montier-en-Der, *France* 19 **D11**
Montignac, *France* 20 **C5**
Montigny-les-Metz, *France* 19 **C13**
Montigny-sur-Aube, *France* 19 **E11**
Montijo, *Portugal* 35 **G2**
Montijo, *Spain* 35 **G4**
Montilla, *Spain* 35 **H6**
Montivilliers, *France* 18 **C7**
Montluçon, *France* 19 **F9**
Montmagny, *Canada* 103 **C5**
Montmarault, *France* 19 **F9**
Montmartre, *Canada* 105 **C8**
Montmédy, *France* 19 **C12**
Montmélian, *France* 21 **C10**
Montmirail, *France* 19 **D10**
Montmoreau-St-Cybard, *France* 20 **C4**
Montmorillon, *France* 20 **B4**
Montmort-Lucy, *France* 19 **D10**
Monto, *Australia* 94 **C5**
Montoire-sur-le-Loir, *France* 18 **E7**
Montório al Vomano, *Italy* 29 **F10**
Montoro, *Spain* 35 **G6**
Montour Falls, *U.S.A.* 110 **D8**
Montoursville, *U.S.A.* 110 **E8**
Montpelier, *Idaho, U.S.A.* 114 **E8**
Montpelier, *Vt., U.S.A.* 111 **B12**
Montpellier, *France* 20 **E7**
Montpezat-de-Quercy, *France* 20 **D5**
Montpon-Ménestérol, *France* 20 **D4**
Montréal, *Canada* 102 **C5**
Montréal, *Aude, France* 20 **E6**
Montréal, *Gers, France* 20 **E4**
Montreal →, *Canada* 102 **C3**
Montreal L., *Canada* 105 **C7**
Montreal Lake, *Canada* 105 **C7**
Montredon-Labessonnié, *France* 20 **E6**
Montrésor, *France* 18 **E8**
Montret, *France* 19 **F12**
Montreuil, *Pas-de-Calais, France* 19 **B8**
Montreuil, *Seine-St-Denis, France* 19 **D9**
Montreuil-Bellay, *France* 18 **E6**
Montreux, *Switz.* 25 **J2**
Montrevel-en-Bresse, *France* 19 **F12**
Montrichard, *France* 18 **E8**
Montrose, *U.K.* 14 **E6**
Montrose, *Colo., U.S.A.* 115 **G10**
Montrose, *Pa., U.S.A.* 111 **E9**
Monts, Pte. des, *Canada* 103 **C6**
Montsalvy, *France* 20 **D6**
Montsant, Serra de, *Spain* 32 **D6**
Montsauche-les-Settons, *France* 19 **E11**
Montsec, Serra del, *Spain* 32 **C5**
Montserrat, *Spain* 32 **D6**
Montserrat ■, *W. Indies* 121 **C7**
Montuenga, *Spain* 34 **D6**
Montuiri, *Spain* 37 **B9**
Monywa, *Burma* 67 **H19**
Monza, *Italy* 28 **C6**
Monze, *Zambia* 87 **F2**
Monze, C., *Pakistan* 68 **G2**
Monzón, *Spain* 32 **D5**
Mooers, *U.S.A.* 111 **B11**
Mooi →, *S. Africa* 89 **D5**
Mooi River, *S. Africa* 89 **D4**
Moonah →, *Australia* 94 **C2**
Moonda, L., *Australia* 94 **D3**
Moonie, *Australia* 95 **D5**
Moonie →, *Australia* 95 **D4**
Moonta, *Australia* 95 **E2**
Moora, *Australia* 93 **F2**
Moorcroft, *U.S.A.* 112 **C2**
Moore →, *Australia* 93 **F2**
Moore, L., *Australia* 93 **E2**
Moore Park, *Australia* 94 **C5**
Moore Reefs, *Australia* 94 **B4**
Moorefield, *U.S.A.* 108 **F6**
Moores Res., *U.S.A.* 111 **B13**
Moorfoot Hills, *U.K.* 14 **F5**
Moorhead, *U.S.A.* 112 **B6**
Moormerland, *Germany* 24 **B3**
Moorpark, *U.S.A.* 117 **L8**
Moorreesburg, *S. Africa* 88 **E2**
Moosburg, *Germany* 25 **G7**
Moose →, *Canada* 102 **B3**
Moose →, *U.S.A.* 111 **C9**
Moose Creek, *Canada* 111 **A10**
Moose Factory, *Canada* 102 **B3**
Moose Jaw, *Canada* 105 **C7**
Moose Jaw →, *Canada* 105 **C7**
Moose Lake, *Canada* 105 **C8**
Moose Lake, *U.S.A.* 112 **B8**
Moose Mountain Prov. Park, *Canada* 105 **D8**
Moosehead L., *U.S.A.* 109 **C11**
Mooselookmeguntic L., *U.S.A.* 109 **C10**
Moosilauke, Mt., *U.S.A.* 111 **B13**
Moosomin, *Canada* 105 **C8**
Moosonee, *Canada* 102 **B3**
Moosup, *U.S.A.* 111 **E13**
Mopane, *S. Africa* 89 **C4**
Mopeia Velha, *Mozam.* 87 **F4**
Mopipi, *Botswana* 88 **C3**
Mopoi, *C.A.R.* 86 **A2**
Mopti, *Mali* 82 **C4**
Moqatta, *Sudan* 81 **E4**
Moqor, *Afghan.* 68 **C2**
Moquegua, *Peru* 124 **G4**
Mór, *Hungary* 42 **C3**
Mora, *Cameroon* 83 **C7**
Móra, *Portugal* 35 **G2**
Mora, *Spain* 35 **F7**
Mora, *Sweden* 10 **C8**
Mora, *Minn., U.S.A.* 112 **C8**
Mora, *N. Mex., U.S.A.* 115 **J11**
Mora →, *U.S.A.* 113 **H2**
Mora de Ebro = Mòra d'Ebre, *Spain* 32 **D5**
Mora de Rubielos, *Spain* 32 **E4**
Mòra d'Ebre, *Spain* 32 **D5**
Mòra la Nova, *Spain* 32 **D5**
Morača →, *Montenegro, Yug.* 40 **D3**
Moradabad, *India* 69 **E8**
Morafenobe, *Madag.* 89 **B7**
Morąg, *Poland* 44 **E6**
Moral de Calatrava, *Spain* 35 **G7**
Moraleja, *Spain* 34 **E4**
Moramanga, *Madag.* 89 **B8**
Moran, *Kans., U.S.A.* 113 **G7**
Moran, *Wyo., U.S.A.* 114 **E8**
Moranbah, *Australia* 94 **C4**
Morano Cálabro, *Italy* 31 **C9**
Morant Cays, *Jamaica* 120 **C4**
Morant Pt., *Jamaica* 120 **C4**
Morar, *India* 68 **F8**
Morar, L., *U.K.* 14 **E3**
Moratalla, *Spain* 33 **G3**
Moratuwa, *Sri Lanka* 66 **R11**
Morava →, *Slovak Rep.* 27 **C9**
Moravia, *U.S.A.* 111 **D8**
Moravian Hts. = Českomoravská Vrchovina, *Czech Rep.* 26 **B8**
Moravica →, *Serbia, Yug.* 40 **C4**
Moraviţa, *Romania* 42 **E6**
Moravská Třebová, *Czech Rep.* 27 **B9**
Moravské Budějovice, *Czech Rep.* 26 **B8**
Morawa, *Australia* 93 **E2**
Morawhanna, *Guyana* 124 **B7**
Moray □, *U.K.* 14 **D5**
Moray Firth, *U.K.* 14 **D5**
Morbach, *Germany* 25 **F3**
Morbegno, *Italy* 28 **B6**
Morbi, *India* 68 **H4**
Morbihan □, *France* 18 **E4**
Mörbylånga, *Sweden* 11 **H10**
Morcenx, *France* 20 **D3**
Morcone, *Italy* 31 **A7**
Mordelles, *France* 18 **D5**
Morden, *Canada* 105 **D9**
Mordoğan, *Turkey* 39 **C8**
Mordovian Republic = Mordvinia □, *Russia* 48 **C7**
Mordovo, *Russia* 48 **D5**
Mordvinia □, *Russia* 48 **C7**
Mordy, *Poland* 45 **F9**
Morea, *Greece* 6 **H10**
Moreau →, *U.S.A.* 112 **C4**
Morecambe, *U.K.* 12 **C5**
Morecambe B., *U.K.* 12 **C5**
Moree, *Australia* 95 **D4**
Morehead, *U.S.A.* 108 **F4**
Morehead City, *U.S.A.* 109 **H7**
Morel →, *India* 68 **F7**
Morelia, *Mexico* 118 **D4**
Morella, *Australia* 94 **C3**
Morella, *Spain* 32 **E4**
Morelos, *Mexico* 118 **B3**
Morelos □, *Mexico* 119 **D5**
Morena, *India* 68 **F8**
Morena, Sierra, *Spain* 35 **G7**
Moreni, *Romania* 43 **F10**
Moreno Valley, *U.S.A.* 117 **M10**
Moresby I., *Canada* 104 **C2**
Morestel, *France* 21 **C9**
Moreton I., *Australia* 95 **D5**
Moreuil, *France* 19 **C9**
Morey, *Spain* 37 **B10**
Morez, *France* 19 **F13**
Morgan, *U.S.A.* 114 **F8**
Morgan City, *U.S.A.* 113 **L9**
Morgan Hill, *U.S.A.* 116 **H5**
Morganfield, *U.S.A.* 108 **G2**
Morganton, *U.S.A.* 109 **H5**
Morgantown, *U.S.A.* 108 **F6**
Morgenzon, *S. Africa* 89 **D4**
Morges, *Switz.* 25 **J2**
Morghak, *Iran* 71 **D8**
Morgongåva, *Sweden* 10 **E10**
Morhange, *France* 19 **D13**
Morhar →, *India* 69 **G11**
Mori, *Italy* 28 **C7**
Moriarty, *U.S.A.* 115 **J10**
Moribaya, *Guinea* 82 **D3**
Morice L., *Canada* 104 **C3**
Moriki, *Nigeria* 83 **C6**
Morinville, *Canada* 104 **C6**
Morioka, *Japan* 54 **E10**
Moris, *Mexico* 118 **B3**
Morlaàs, *France* 20 **E3**
Morlaix, *France* 18 **D3**
Mörlunda, *Sweden* 11 **G9**
Mormanno, *Italy* 31 **C8**
Mormant, *France* 19 **D9**
Mornington, *Australia* 95 **F4**
Mornington, I., *Chile* 128 **F1**
Mornington I., *Australia* 94 **B2**
Mórnos →, *Greece* 38 **C3**
Moro, *Pakistan* 68 **F2**
Moro, *Sudan* 81 **E3**
Moro →, *Pakistan* 68 **E2**
Moro G., *Phil.* 61 **H5**
Morocco ■, *N. Afr.* 78 **B4**
Morogoro, *Tanzania* 86 **D4**
Morogoro □, *Tanzania* 86 **D4**
Moroleón, *Mexico* 118 **C4**
Morombe, *Madag.* 89 **C7**
Moron, *Argentina* 126 **C4**
Morón, *Cuba* 120 **B4**
Morón de Almazán, *Spain* 32 **D2**
Morón de la Frontera, *Spain* 35 **H5**
Morona →, *Peru* 124 **D3**
Morondava, *Madag.* 89 **C7**
Morondo, *Ivory C.* 82 **D3**
Morongo Valley, *U.S.A.* 117 **L10**
Moroni, *Comoros Is.* 77 **H8**
Moroni, *U.S.A.* 114 **G8**
Moronou, *Ivory C.* 82 **D4**
Morotai, *Indonesia* 63 **D7**
Moroto, *Uganda* 86 **B3**
Moroto Summit, *Kenya* 86 **B3**
Morozov, *Bulgaria* 41 **D9**
Morozovsk, *Russia* 49 **F5**
Morpeth, *U.K.* 12 **B6**
Morphou, *Cyprus* 36 **D11**
Morphou Bay, *Cyprus* 36 **D11**
Morrilton, *U.S.A.* 113 **H8**
Morrinhos, *Brazil* 125 **G9**
Morrinsville, *N.Z.* 91 **G5**
Morris, *Canada* 105 **D9**
Morris, *Ill., U.S.A.* 112 **E10**
Morris, *Minn., U.S.A.* 112 **C7**
Morris, *N.Y., U.S.A.* 111 **D9**
Morris, *Pa., U.S.A.* 110 **E7**
Morris, Mt., *Australia* 93 **E5**
Morrisburg, *Canada* 111 **B9**
Morristown, *Ariz., U.S.A.* 115 **K7**
Morristown, *N.J., U.S.A.* 111 **F10**
Morristown, *N.Y., U.S.A.* 111 **B9**
Morristown, *Tenn., U.S.A.* 109 **G4**
Morrisville, *N.Y., U.S.A.* 111 **D9**
Morrisville, *Pa., U.S.A.* 111 **F10**
Morrisville, *Vt., U.S.A.* 111 **B12**
Morro, Pta., *Chile* 126 **B1**
Morro Bay, *U.S.A.* 116 **K6**
Morro del Jable, *Canary Is.* 37 **F5**
Morro Jable, Pta. de, *Canary Is.* 37 **F5**
Morrosquillo, G. de, *Colombia* 120 **E4**
Mörrum, *Sweden* 11 **H8**
Morrumbene, *Mozam.* 89 **C6**
Mörrumsån →, *Sweden* 11 **H8**
Mors, *Denmark* 11 **H2**
Morshansk, *Russia* 48 **D5**
Mörsil, *Sweden* 10 **A7**
Mortagne →, *France* 19 **D13**
Mortagne-au-Perche, *France* 18 **D7**
Mortagne-sur-Gironde, *France* 20 **C3**
Mortagne-sur-Sèvre, *France* 18 **F6**
Mortain, *France* 18 **D6**
Mortara, *Italy* 28 **C5**
Morteau, *France* 19 **E13**
Morteros, *Argentina* 126 **C3**
Mortlach, *Canada* 105 **C7**
Mortlake, *Australia* 95 **F3**
Morton, *Tex., U.S.A.* 113 **J3**
Morton, *Wash., U.S.A.* 116 **D4**
Morundah, *Australia* 95 **E4**
Moruya, *Australia* 95 **F5**
Morvan, *France* 19 **E11**
Morven, *Australia* 95 **D4**
Morvern, *U.K.* 14 **E3**
Morwell, *Australia* 95 **F4**
Moryń, *Poland* 45 **F1**
Morzine, *France* 19 **F13**
Mosalsk, *Russia* 46 **E8**
Mosbach, *Germany* 25 **F5**
Mošćenice, *Croatia* 29 **C11**
Mosciano Sant' Ángelo, *Italy* 29 **F10**
Moscos Is., *Burma* 64 **E1**
Moscow = Moskva, *Russia* 46 **E9**
Moscow, *Idaho, U.S.A.* 114 **C5**
Moscow, *Pa., U.S.A.* 111 **E9**
Mosel →, *Europe* 19 **B14**
Moselle = Mosel →, *Europe* 19 **B14**
Moselle □, *France* 19 **D13**
Moses Lake, *U.S.A.* 114 **C4**
Mosgiel, *N.Z.* 91 **L3**
Moshaweng →, *S. Africa* 88 **D3**
Moshi, *Tanzania* 86 **C4**

North Syracuse


Newry, *U.K.* 15 B5
Newton, *Ill., U.S.A.* 112 F10
Newton, *Iowa, U.S.A.* 112 E8
Newton, *Kans., U.S.A.* 113 F6
Newton, *Mass., U.S.A.* 111 D13
Newton, *Miss., U.S.A.* 113 J10
Newton, *N.C., U.S.A.* 109 H5
Newton, *N.J., U.S.A.* 111 E10
Newton, *Tex., U.S.A.* 113 K8
Newton Abbot, *U.K.* 13 G4
Newton Aycliffe, *U.K.* 12 C6
Newton Falls, *U.S.A.* 110 E4
Newton Stewart, *U.K.* 14 G4
Newtonmore, *U.K.* 14 D4
Newtown, *U.K.* 13 E4
Newtownabbey, *U.K.* 15 B6
Newtownards, *U.K.* 15 B6
Newtownbarry = Bunclody, *Ireland* 15 D5
Newtownstewart, *U.K.* 15 B4
Newville, *U.S.A.* 110 F7
Nexon, *France* 20 C5
Neya, *Russia* 48 A6
Neyrīz, *Iran* 71 D7
Neyshābūr, *Iran* 71 B8
Nezhin = Nizhyn, *Ukraine* 47 G6
Nezperce, *U.S.A.* 114 C5
Ngabang, *Indonesia* 62 D3
Ngabordamlu, Tanjung, *Indonesia* 63 F8
N'Gage, *Angola* 84 F3
Ngala, *Nigeria* 83 C7
Ngambé, *Cameroon* 83 D7
Ngambé, *Cameroon* 83 E7
Ngami Depression, *Botswana* 88 C3
Ngamo, *Zimbabwe* 87 F2
Ngangala, *Sudan* 81 G3
Nganglong Kangri, *China* 67 C12
Ngao, *Thailand* 64 C2
Ngaoundéré, *Cameroon* 84 C2
Ngapara, *N.Z.* 91 L3
Ngara, *Tanzania* 86 C3
Ngawi, *Indonesia* 63 G14
Nghia Lo, *Vietnam* 58 G5
Ngoboli, *Sudan* 81 G3
Ngoma, *Malawi* 87 E3
Ngomahura, *Zimbabwe* 87 G3
Ngomba, *Tanzania* 87 D3
Ngop, *Sudan* 81 F3
Ngoring Hu, *China* 60 C4
Ngorkou, *Mali* 82 B4
Ngorongoro, *Tanzania* 86 C4
Ngozi, *Burundi* 86 C2
Ngudu, *Tanzania* 86 C3
Nguigmi, *Niger* 79 F8
Nguila, *Cameroon* 83 E7
Nguiu, *Australia* 92 B5
Ngukurr, *Australia* 94 A1
Ngulu Atoll, *Pac. Oc.* 63 C9
Ngunga, *Tanzania* 86 C3
Nguru, *Nigeria* 83 C7
Nguru Mts., *Tanzania* 86 D4
Nguyen Binh, *Vietnam* 58 F5
Nha Trang, *Vietnam* 65 F7
Nhacoongo, *Mozam.* 89 C6
Nhamaabué, *Mozam.* 87 F4
Nhamundá →, *Brazil* 125 D7
Nhangulaze, L., *Mozam.* 89 C5
Nhill, *Australia* 95 F3
Nho Quan, *Vietnam* 58 G5
Nhulunbuy, *Australia* 94 A2
Nia-nia, *Dem. Rep. of the Congo* 86 B2
Niafounké, *Mali* 82 B4
Niagara Falls, *Canada* 102 D4
Niagara Falls, *U.S.A.* 110 C6
Niagara-on-the-Lake, *Canada* 110 C5
Niah, *Malaysia* 62 D4
Niamey, *Niger* 83 C5
Niandan-Koro, *Guinea* 82 C3
Nianforando, *Guinea* 82 D2
Niangara, *Dem. Rep. of the Congo* 86 B2
Niangbo, *Ivory C.* 82 D3
Niangoloko, *Burkina Faso* 82 C4
Niantic, *U.S.A.* 111 E12
Niaro, *Sudan* 81 E3
Nias, *Indonesia* 62 D1
Niassa □, *Mozam.* 87 E4
Nibāk, *Si. Arabia* 71 E7
Nibe, *Denmark* 11 H3
Nicaragua ■, *Cent. Amer.* 120 D2
Nicaragua, L. de, *Nic.* 120 D2
Nicastro, *Italy* 31 D9
Nice, *France* 21 E11
Niceville, *U.S.A.* 109 K2
Nichicun, L., *Canada* 103 B5
Nichinan, *Japan* 55 J5
Nicholás, Canal, *W. Indies* 120 B3
Nicholasville, *U.S.A.* 108 G3
Nichols, *U.S.A.* 111 D8
Nicholson, *Australia* 92 C4
Nicholson, *U.S.A.* 111 E9
Nicholson →, *Australia* 94 B2
Nicholson L., *Canada* 105 A8
Nicholson Ra., *Australia* 93 E2
Nicholville, *U.S.A.* 111 B10
Nicobar Is., *Ind. Oc.* 52 J13
Nicola, *Canada* 104 C4
Nicolls Town, *Bahamas* 120 A4
Nicopolis, *Greece* 38 B2
Nicosia, *Cyprus* 36 D12
Nicosia, *Italy* 31 E7
Nicótera, *Italy* 31 D8
Nicoya, *Costa Rica* 120 D2
Nicoya, G. de, *Costa Rica* 120 E3
Nicoya, Pen. de, *Costa Rica* 120 E2
Nidd →, *U.K.* 12 D6
Nidda, *Germany* 25 E5
Nidda →, *Germany* 25 E4
Nidwalden □, *Switz.* 25 J4
Nidzica, *Poland* 45 E7
Niebüll, *Germany* 24 A4
Nied →, *Germany* 19 C13
Niederaula, *Germany* 24 E5
Niederbayern □, *Germany* 25 G8
Niederbronn-les-Bains, *France* 19 D14
Niedere Tauern, *Austria* 26 D7
Niederlausitz, *Germany* 24 D9
Niederösterreich □, *Austria* 26 C8
Niedersachsen □, *Germany* 24 C4
Niekerkshoop, *S. Africa* 88 D3
Niellé, *Ivory C.* 82 C3
Niemba, *Dem. Rep. of the Congo* 86 D2
Niemen = Neman →, *Lithuania* 9 J19
Niemodlin, *Poland* 45 H4
Nienburg, *Germany* 24 C5
Niepołomice, *Poland* 45 H7
Niers →, *Germany* 24 D1
Niesky, *Germany* 24 D10
Nieszawa, *Poland* 45 F5
Nieu Bethesda, *S. Africa* 88 E3
Nieuw Amsterdam, *Surinam* 125 B7
Nieuw Nickerie, *Surinam* 125 B7
Nieuwoudtville, *S. Africa* 88 E2
Nieuwpoort, *Belgium* 17 C2
Nieves, Pico de las, *Canary Is.* 37 G4
Nièvre □, *France* 19 E10
Niga, *Mali* 82 C3
Niğde, *Turkey* 70 B2
Nigel, *S. Africa* 89 D4
Niger □, *Nigeria* 83 D6
Niger ■, *W. Afr.* 83 B7
Niger →, *W. Afr.* 83 D6
Niger Delta, *Africa* 83 E6
Nigeria ■, *W. Afr.* 83 D6
Nighasin, *India* 69 E9
Nightcaps, *N.Z.* 91 L2
Nigríta, *Greece* 40 F7
Nii-Jima, *Japan* 55 G9
Niigata, *Japan* 54 F9
Niigata □, *Japan* 55 F9
Niihama, *Japan* 55 H6
Niihau, *U.S.A.* 106 H14
Niimi, *Japan* 55 G6
Niitsu, *Japan* 54 F9
Níjar, *Spain* 33 J2
Nijil, *Jordan* 75 E4
Nijkerk, *Neths.* 17 B5
Nijmegen, *Neths.* 17 C5
Nijverdal, *Neths.* 17 B6
Nīk Pey, *Iran* 71 B6
Nike, *Nigeria* 83 D6
Nikiniki, *Indonesia* 63 F6
Nikísiani, *Greece* 41 F8
Nikítas, *Greece* 40 F7
Nikki, *Benin* 83 D5
Nikkō, *Japan* 55 F9
Nikolayev = Mykolayiv, *Ukraine* 47 J7
Nikolayevsk, *Russia* 48 E7
Nikolayevsk-na-Amur, *Russia* 51 D15
Nikolsk, *Russia* 48 D8
Nikolskoye, *Russia* 51 D17
Nikopol, *Bulgaria* 41 C8
Nikopol, *Ukraine* 47 J8
Niksar, *Turkey* 72 B7
Nīkshahr, *Iran* 71 E9
Nikšić, *Montenegro, Yug.* 40 D2
Nîl, Nahr en →, *Africa* 80 H7
Nîl el Abyad →, *Sudan* 81 D3
Nîl el Azraq →, *Sudan* 81 D3
Nila, *Indonesia* 63 F7
Niland, *U.S.A.* 117 M11
Nile = Nîl, Nahr en →, *Africa* 80 H7
Niles, *Mich., U.S.A.* 108 E2
Niles, *Ohio, U.S.A.* 110 E4
Nilüfer →, *Turkey* 41 F12
Nim Ka Thana, *India* 68 F6
Nimach, *India* 68 G6
Nimbahera, *India* 68 G6
Nîmes, *France* 21 E8
Nimfaíon, Ákra = Pínnes, Ákra, *Greece* 41 F8
Nimmitabel, *Australia* 95 F4
Nimule, *Sudan* 81 G3
Nin, *Croatia* 29 D12
Nīnawá, *Iraq* 70 B4
Nindigully, *Australia* 95 D4
Nineveh = Nīnawá, *Iraq* 70 B4
Ning Xian, *China* 56 G4
Ning'an, *China* 57 B15
Ningbo, *China* 59 C13
Ningcheng, *China* 57 D10
Ningde, *China* 59 D12
Ningdu, *China* 59 D10
Ninggang, *China* 59 D9
Ningguo, *China* 59 B12
Ninghai, *China* 59 C13
Ninghua, *China* 59 D11
Ningi, *Nigeria* 83 C6
Ningjin, *China* 56 F8
Ningjing Shan, *China* 58 C2
Ninglang, *China* 58 D3
Ningling, *China* 56 G8
Ningming, *China* 58 F6
Ningnan, *China* 58 D4
Ningpo = Ningbo, *China* 59 C13
Ningqiang, *China* 56 H4
Ningshan, *China* 56 H5
Ningsia Hui A.R. = Ningxia Huizu Zizhiqu □, *China* 56 F4
Ningwu, *China* 56 E7
Ningxia Huizu Zizhiqu □, *China* 56 F4
Ningxiang, *China* 59 C9
Ningyang, *China* 56 G9
Ningyuan, *China* 59 E8
Ninh Binh, *Vietnam* 58 G5
Ninh Giang, *Vietnam* 64 B6
Ninh Hoa, *Vietnam* 64 F7
Ninh Ma, *Vietnam* 64 F7
Ninove, *Belgium* 17 D4
Nioaque, *Brazil* 127 A4
Niobrara, *U.S.A.* 112 D6
Niobrara →, *U.S.A.* 112 D6
Niono, *Mali* 82 C3
Nionsamoridougou, *Guinea* 82 D3
Nioro du Rip, *Senegal* 82 C1
Nioro du Sahel, *Mali* 82 B3
Niort, *France* 20 B3
Nipawin, *Canada* 105 C8
Nipfjället, *Sweden* 10 C6
Nipigon, *Canada* 102 C2
Nipigon, L., *Canada* 102 C2
Nipishish L., *Canada* 103 B7
Nipissing, L., *Canada* 102 C4
Nipomo, *U.S.A.* 117 K6
Nipton, *U.S.A.* 117 K11
Niquelândia, *Brazil* 125 F9
Nīr, *Iran* 70 B5
Nirasaki, *Japan* 55 G9
Nirmal, *India* 66 K11
Nirmali, *India* 69 F12
Niš, *Serbia, Yug.* 40 C5
Nisa, *Portugal* 35 F3
Nisāb, *Si. Arabia* 70 D5
Nişāb, *Yemen* 74 E4
Nišava →, *Serbia, Yug.* 40 C5
Niscemi, *Italy* 31 E7
Nishinomiya, *Japan* 55 G7
Nishino'omote, *Japan* 55 J5
Nishiwaki, *Japan* 55 G7
Nísíros, *Greece* 39 E9
Niška Banja, *Serbia, Yug.* 40 C6
Niskibi →, *Canada* 102 A2
Nisko, *Poland* 45 H9
Nisporeni, *Moldova* 43 C13
Nisqually →, *U.S.A.* 116 C4
Nissáki, *Greece* 36 A3
Nissan →, *Sweden* 11 H6
Nissum Bredning, *Denmark* 11 H2
Nissum Fjord, *Denmark* 11 H2
Nistru = Dnister →, *Europe* 47 J6
Nisutlin →, *Canada* 104 A2
Nitchequon, *Canada* 103 B5
Niterói, *Brazil* 127 A7
Nith →, *Canada* 110 C4
Nith →, *U.K.* 14 F5
Nitra, *Slovak Rep.* 27 C11
Nitra →, *Slovak Rep.* 27 D11
Nitriansky □, *Slovak Rep.* 27 C11
Nittenau, *Germany* 25 F8
Niuafo'ou, *Tonga* 91 B11
Niue, *Cook Is.* 97 J11
Niulan Jiang →, *China* 58 D4
Niut, *Indonesia* 62 D4
Niutou Shan, *China* 59 C13
Niuzhuang, *China* 57 D12
Nivala, *Finland* 8 E21
Nivelles, *Belgium* 17 D4
Nivernais, *France* 19 E10
Niwas, *India* 69 H9
Nixon, *U.S.A.* 113 L6
Nizamabad, *India* 66 K11
Nizamghat, *India* 67 E19
Nizhne Kolymsk, *Russia* 51 C17
Nizhnegorskiy = Nyzhnohirskyy, *Ukraine* 47 K8
Nizhnekamsk, *Russia* 48 C10
Nizhneudinsk, *Russia* 51 D10
Nizhnevartovsk, *Russia* 50 C8
Nizhniy Chir, *Russia* 49 F6
Nizhniy Lomov, *Russia* 48 D6
Nizhniy Novgorod, *Russia* 48 B7
Nizhniy Tagil, *Russia* 50 D6
Nizhyn, *Ukraine* 47 G6
Nizina Mazowiecka, *Poland* 45 F8
Nizip, *Turkey* 70 B3
Nízké Tatry, *Slovak Rep.* 27 C12
Nízký Jeseník, *Czech Rep.* 27 B10
Nizza Monferrato, *Italy* 28 D5
Njakwa, *Malawi* 87 E3
Njanji, *Zambia* 87 E3
Njegoš, *Montenegro, Yug.* 40 D2
Njinjo, *Tanzania* 87 D4
Njombe, *Tanzania* 87 D3
Njombe →, *Tanzania* 86 D4
Njurundabommen, *Sweden* 10 B11
Nkambe, *Cameroon* 83 D7
Nkana, *Zambia* 87 E2
Nkandla, *S. Africa* 89 D5
Nkawkaw, *Ghana* 83 D4
Nkayi, *Zimbabwe* 87 F2
Nkhotakota, *Malawi* 87 E3
Nkongsamba, *Cameroon* 83 E6
Nkurenkuru, *Namibia* 88 B2
Nkwanta, *Ghana* 82 D4
Nmai →, *Burma* 58 F2
Noakhali = Maijdi, *Bangla.* 67 H17
Nobel, *Canada* 110 A4
Nobeoka, *Japan* 55 H5
Noblejas, *Spain* 34 F7
Noblesville, *U.S.A.* 108 E3
Noce →, *Italy* 28 B8
Nocera Inferiore, *Italy* 31 B7
Nocera Umbra, *Italy* 29 E9
Noci, *Italy* 31 B10
Nocona, *U.S.A.* 113 J6
Nocrich, *Romania* 43 E9
Noda, *Japan* 55 G9
Nogales, *Mexico* 118 A2
Nogales, *U.S.A.* 115 L8
Nogaro, *France* 20 E3
Nogat →, *Poland* 44 D6
Nōgata, *Japan* 55 H5
Nogent, *France* 19 D12
Nogent-le-Rotrou, *France* 18 D7
Nogent-sur-Seine, *France* 19 D10
Noggerup, *Australia* 93 F2
Noginsk, *Moskva, Russia* 46 E10
Noginsk, *Tunguska, Russia* 51 C10
Nogoa →, *Australia* 94 C4
Nogoyá, *Argentina* 126 C4
Nógrád □, *Hungary* 42 C4
Noguera Pallaresa →, *Spain* 32 D5
Noguera Ribagorzana →, *Spain* 32 D5
Nohar, *India* 68 E6
Nohfelden, *Germany* 25 F3
Nohta, *India* 69 H8
Noia, *Spain* 34 C2
Noire, Montagne, *France* 20 E6
Noires, Mts., *France* 18 D3
Noirétable, *France* 20 C7
Noirmoutier, Î. de, *France* 18 F4
Noirmoutier-en-l'Île, *France* 18 F4
Nojane, *Botswana* 88 C3
Nojima-Zaki, *Japan* 55 G9
Nok Kundi, *Pakistan* 66 E3
Nokaneng, *Botswana* 88 B3
Nokia, *Finland* 9 F20
Nokomis, *Canada* 105 C8
Nokomis L., *Canada* 105 B8
Nol, *Sweden* 11 G6
Nola, *C.A.R.* 84 D3
Nola, *Italy* 31 B7
Nolay, *France* 19 F11
Noli, C. di, *Italy* 28 D5
Nolinsk, *Russia* 48 B9
Noma Omuramba →, *Namibia* 88 B3
Nombre de Dios, *Panama* 120 E4
Nome, *U.S.A.* 100 B3
Nomo-Zaki, *Japan* 55 H4
Nonacho L., *Canada* 105 A7
Nonancourt, *France* 18 D8
Nonda, *Australia* 94 C3
None, *Italy* 28 D4
Nong Chang, *Thailand* 64 E2
Nong Het, *Laos* 64 C4
Nong Khai, *Thailand* 64 D4
Nong'an, *China* 57 B13
Nongoma, *S. Africa* 89 D5
Nonoava, *Mexico* 118 B3
Nonoava →, *Mexico* 118 B3
Nonthaburi, *Thailand* 64 F3
Nontron, *France* 20 C4
Nonza, *France* 21 F13
Noonamah, *Australia* 92 B5
Noord Brabant □, *Neths.* 17 C5
Noord Holland □, *Neths.* 17 B4
Noordbeveland, *Neths.* 17 C3
Noordoostpolder, *Neths.* 17 B5
Noordwijk, *Neths.* 17 B4
Nootka I., *Canada* 104 D3
Nopiming Prov. Park, *Canada* 105 C9
Nora, *Eritrea* 81 D5
Nora, *Sweden* 10 E9
Noralee, *Canada* 104 C3
Noranda = Rouyn-Noranda, *Canada* 102 C4
Norberg, *Sweden* 10 D9
Nórcia, *Italy* 29 F10
Norco, *U.S.A.* 117 M9
Nord □, *France* 19 B10
Nord-Kivu □, *Dem. Rep. of the Congo* 86 C2
Nord-Ostsee-Kanal, *Germany* 24 A5
Nord-Pas-de-Calais □, *France* 19 B9
Nordaustlandet, *Svalbard* 4 B9
Nordborg, *Denmark* 11 J3
Nordby, *Denmark* 11 J2
Norddeich, *Germany* 24 B3
Nordegg, *Canada* 104 C5
Norden, *Germany* 24 B3
Nordenham, *Germany* 24 B4
Norderney, *Germany* 24 B3
Norderstedt, *Germany* 24 B6
Nordfjord, *Norway* 9 F11
Nordfriesische Inseln, *Germany* 24 A4
Nordhausen, *Germany* 24 D6
Nordhorn, *Germany* 24 C3
Norðoyar, *Færoe Is.* 8 E9
Nordingrå, *Sweden* 10 B12
Nordjyllands Amtskommune □, *Denmark* 11 G4
Nordkapp, *Norway* 8 A21
Nordkapp, *Svalbard* 4 A9
Nordkinn = Kinnarodden, *Norway* 6 A11
Nordkinn-halvøya, *Norway* 8 A22
Nördlingen, *Germany* 25 G6
Nordrhein-Westfalen □, *Germany* 24 D3
Nordstrand, *Germany* 24 A4
Nordvik, *Russia* 51 B12
Nore →, *Ireland* 15 D4
Norfolk, *Nebr., U.S.A.* 112 D6
Norfolk, *Va., U.S.A.* 108 G7
Norfolk □, *U.K.* 13 E8
Norfolk I., *Pac. Oc.* 96 K8
Norfork L., *U.S.A.* 113 G8
Norilsk, *Russia* 51 C9
Norma, Mt., *Australia* 94 C3
Normal, *U.S.A.* 112 E10
Norman, *U.S.A.* 113 H6
Norman →, *Australia* 94 B3
Norman Wells, *Canada* 100 B7
Normanby →, *Australia* 94 A3
Normandin, *Canada* 102 C5
Normanhurst, Mt., *Australia* 93 E3
Normanton, *Australia* 94 B3
Normétal, *Canada* 102 C4
Norquay, *Canada* 105 C8
Norquinco, *Argentina* 128 E2
Norra Dellen, *Sweden* 10 C10
Norra Ulvön, *Sweden* 10 A12
Norrahammar, *Sweden* 11 G8
Norrbotten □, *Sweden* 8 C19
Nørre Åby, *Denmark* 11 J3
Nørre Alslev, *Denmark* 11 K5
Nørresundby, *Denmark* 11 G3
Norrhult, *Sweden* 11 G9
Norris Point, *Canada* 103 C8
Norristown, *U.S.A.* 111 F9
Norrköping, *Sweden* 11 F10
Norrland, *Sweden* 9 E16
Norrsundet, *Sweden* 10 D11
Norrtälje, *Sweden* 10 E12
Norseman, *Australia* 93 F3
Norsk, *Russia* 51 D14
Norte, Pta. del, *Canary Is.* 37 G2
Norte, Serra do, *Brazil* 124 F7
North, C., *Canada* 103 C7
North Adams, *U.S.A.* 111 D11
North Arm, *Canada* 104 A5
North Augusta, *U.S.A.* 109 J5
North Ayrshire □, *U.K.* 14 F4
North Bass I., *U.S.A.* 110 E2
North Battleford, *Canada* 105 C7
North Bay, *Canada* 102 C4
North Belcher Is., *Canada* 102 A4
North Bend, *Oreg., U.S.A.* 114 E1
North Bend, *Pa., U.S.A.* 110 E7
North Bend, *Wash., U.S.A.* 116 C5
North Bennington, *U.S.A.* 111 D11
North Berwick, *U.K.* 14 E6
North Berwick, *U.S.A.* 111 C14
North C., *Canada* 103 C7
North C., *N.Z.* 91 F4
North Canadian →, *U.S.A.* 113 H7
North Canton, *U.S.A.* 110 F3
North Cape = Nordkapp, *Norway* 8 A21
North Cape = Nordkapp, *Svalbard* 4 A9
North Caribou L., *Canada* 102 B1
North Carolina □, *U.S.A.* 109 H6
North Cascades National Park, *U.S.A.* 114 B3
North Channel, *Canada* 102 C3
North Channel, *U.K.* 14 F3
North Charleston, *U.S.A.* 109 J6
North Chicago, *U.S.A.* 108 D2
North Creek, *U.S.A.* 111 C11
North Dakota □, *U.S.A.* 112 B5
North Downs, *U.K.* 13 F8
North East, *U.S.A.* 110 D5
North East Frontier Agency = Arunachal Pradesh □, *India* 67 F19
North East Lincolnshire □, *U.K.* 12 D7
North Eastern □, *Kenya* 86 B5
North Esk →, *U.K.* 14 E6
North European Plain, *Europe* 6 E10
North Foreland, *U.K.* 13 F9
North Fork, *U.S.A.* 116 H7
North Fork American →, *U.S.A.* 116 G5
North Fork Feather →, *U.S.A.* 116 F5
North Fork Grand →, *U.S.A.* 112 C3
North Fork Red →, *U.S.A.* 113 H5
North Frisian Is. = Nordfriesische Inseln, *Germany* 24 A4
North Gower, *Canada* 111 A9
North Hd., *Australia* 93 F1
North Henik L., *Canada* 105 A9
North Highlands, *U.S.A.* 116 G5
North Horr, *Kenya* 86 B4
North I., *Kenya* 86 B4
North I., *N.Z.* 91 H5
North Kingsville, *U.S.A.* 110 E4
North Knife →, *Canada* 105 B10
North Koel →, *India* 69 G10
North Korea ■, *Asia* 57 E14
North Lakhimpur, *India* 67 F19
North Lanarkshire □, *U.K.* 14 F5
North Las Vegas, *U.S.A.* 117 J11
North Lincolnshire □, *U.K.* 12 D7
North Little Rock, *U.S.A.* 113 H8
North Loup →, *U.S.A.* 112 E5
North Magnetic Pole, *Canada* 4 B2
North Minch, *U.K.* 14 C3
North Moose L., *Canada* 105 C8
North Myrtle Beach, *U.S.A.* 109 J6
North Nahanni →, *Canada* 104 A4
North Olmsted, *U.S.A.* 110 E3
North Ossetia □, *Russia* 49 J7
North Pagai, I. = Pagai Utara, Pulau, *Indonesia* 62 E2
North Palisade, *U.S.A.* 116 H8
North Platte, *U.S.A.* 112 E4
North Platte →, *U.S.A.* 112 E4
North Pole, *Arctic* 4 A
North Portal, *Canada* 105 D8
North Powder, *U.S.A.* 114 D5
North Pt., *U.S.A.* 110 A1
North Rhine Westphalia = Nordrhein-Westfalen □, *Germany* 24 D3
North River, *Canada* 103 B8
North Ronaldsay, *U.K.* 14 B6
North Saskatchewan →, *Canada* 105 C7
North Sea, *Europe* 6 D6
North Seal →, *Canada* 105 B9
North Somerset □, *U.K.* 13 F5
North Sporades = Vóriai Sporádhes, *Greece* 38 B5
North Sydney, *Canada* 103 C7
North Syracuse, *U.S.A.* 111 C8

# Orava, Vodna nádriž



Orava, Vodna nádriž, *Slovak Rep.* 27 B12
Oraviţa, *Romania* 42 E6
Orb →, *France* 20 E7
Orba →, *Italy* 28 D5
Ørbæk, *Denmark* 11 J4
Orbe, *Switz.* 25 J2
Orbec, *France* 18 C7
Orbetello, *Italy* 29 F8
Órbigo →, *Spain* 34 C5
Orbisonia, *U.S.A.* 110 F7
Orbost, *Australia* 95 F4
Örbyhus, *Sweden* 10 D11
Orcas I., *U.S.A.* 116 B4
Orce, *Spain* 33 H2
Orce →, *Spain* 33 H2
Orchard City, *U.S.A.* 115 G10
Orchies, *France* 19 B10
Orchila, I., *Venezuela* 121 D6
Órcia →, *Italy* 29 F8
Orco →, *Italy* 28 C4
Orcutt, *U.S.A.* 117 L6
Ord, *U.S.A.* 112 E5
Ord →, *Australia* 92 C4
Ord, Mt., *Australia* 92 C4
Ordenes = Ordes, *Spain* 34 B2
Orderville, *U.S.A.* 115 H7
Ordes, *Spain* 34 B2
Ording = St-Peter-Ording, *Germany* 24 A4
Ordos = Mu Us Shamo, *China* 56 E5
Ordu, *Turkey* 72 B7
Ordubad, *Azerbaijan* 73 C12
Orduña, *Álava, Spain* 32 C2
Orduña, *Granada, Spain* 35 H7
Ordway, *U.S.A.* 112 F3
Ordzhonikidze = Vladikavkaz, *Russia* 49 J7
Ordzhonikidze, *Ukraine* 47 J8
Ore, *Dem. Rep. of the Congo* 86 B2
Ore Mts. = Erzgebirge, *Germany* 24 E8
Orebić, *Croatia* 29 F14
Örebro, *Sweden* 10 E9
Örebro län □, *Sweden* 10 E8
Oregon, *U.S.A.* 112 D10
Oregon □, *U.S.A.* 114 E3
Oregon City, *U.S.A.* 116 E4
Öregrund, *Sweden* 10 D12
Öregrundsgrepen, *Sweden* 10 D12
Orekhov = Orikhiv, *Ukraine* 47 J8
Orekhovo-Zuyevo, *Russia* 46 E10
Orel, *Russia* 47 F9
Orel →, *Ukraine* 47 H8
Orellana, *Spain* 35 F5
Orellana, Canal de, *Spain* 35 F5
Orellana, Embalse de, *Spain* 35 F5
Orem, *U.S.A.* 114 F8
Ören, *Turkey* 39 D9
Orenburg, *Russia* 50 D6
Örencik, *Turkey* 39 B11
Orense = Ourense, *Spain* 34 C3
Orense □, *Spain* 34 C3
Orepuki, *N.Z.* 91 M1
Orestiás, *Greece* 41 E10
Orestos Pereyra, *Mexico* 118 B3
Øresund, *Europe* 11 J6
Orford Ness, *U.K.* 13 E9
Organà = Organyà, *Spain* 32 C6
Organos, Pta. de los, *Canary Is.* 37 F2
Organyà, *Spain* 32 C6
Orgaz, *Spain* 35 F7
Orgeyev = Orhei, *Moldova* 43 C13
Orhaneli, *Turkey* 41 G12
Orhaneli →, *Turkey* 41 G12
Orhangazi, *Turkey* 41 F13
Orhei, *Moldova* 43 C13
Orhon Gol →, *Mongolia* 60 A5
Ória, *Italy* 31 B10
Oriental, Cordillera, *Colombia* 122 C3
Orientale □, *Dem. Rep. of the Congo* 86 B2
Oriente, *Argentina* 126 D3
Orihuela, *Spain* 33 G4
Orihuela del Tremedal, *Spain* 32 E3
Orikhiv, *Ukraine* 47 J8
Orikum, *Albania* 40 F3
Orillia, *Canada* 102 D4
Orinoco →, *Venezuela* 122 C4
Orion, *Canada* 105 D6
Oriskany, *U.S.A.* 111 C9
Orissa □, *India* 67 K14
Orissaare, *Estonia* 9 G20
Oristano, *Italy* 30 C1
Oristano, G. di, *Italy* 30 C1
Orizaba, *Mexico* 119 D5
Orizare, *Bulgaria* 41 D11
Orjen, *Bos.-H.* 40 D2
Orjiva, *Spain* 35 J7
Orkanger, *Norway* 8 E13
Örkelljunga, *Sweden* 11 H7
Örken, *Sweden* 11 G9
Örkény, *Hungary* 42 C4
Orkla →, *Norway* 8 E13
Orkney, *S. Africa* 88 D4
Orkney □, *U.K.* 14 B5
Orkney Is., *U.K.* 14 B6
Orland, *U.S.A.* 116 F4
Orlando, *U.S.A.* 109 L5
Orlando, C. d', *Italy* 31 D7
Orléanais, *France* 19 E9
Orléans, *France* 19 E8
Orleans, *U.S.A.* 111 B12
Orléans, I. d', *Canada* 103 C5
Orlice →, *Czech Rep.* 26 A8
Orlov, *Slovak Rep.* 27 B13
Orlov Gay, *Russia* 48 E9
Orlová, *Czech Rep.* 27 B11
Orlovat, *Serbia, Yug.* 42 E5
Ormara, *Pakistan* 66 G4
Ormea, *Italy* 28 D4
Ormília, *Greece* 40 F7
Ormoc, *Phil.* 61 F6
Ormond, *N.Z.* 91 H6
Ormond Beach, *U.S.A.* 109 L5
Ormož, *Slovenia* 29 B13
Ormskirk, *U.K.* 12 D5
Ormstown, *Canada* 111 A11
Ornans, *France* 19 E13
Orne □, *France* 18 D7
Orne →, *France* 18 C6
Orneta, *Poland* 44 D7
Ornö, *Sweden* 10 E12
Örnsköldsvik, *Sweden* 10 A12
Oro, *N. Korea* 57 D14
Oro →, *Mexico* 118 B3
Oro Grande, *U.S.A.* 117 L9
Oro Valley, *U.S.A.* 115 K8
Orobie, Alpi, *Italy* 28 B6
Orocué, *Colombia* 124 C4
Orodara, *Burkina Faso* 82 C4
Orodo, *Nigeria* 83 D6
Orofino, *U.S.A.* 114 C5
Orol Dengizi = Aral Sea, *Asia* 50 E7
Oromocto, *Canada* 103 C6
Oron, *Nigeria* 83 E6
Orono, *Canada* 110 C6
Orono, *U.S.A.* 109 C11
Oronsay, *U.K.* 14 E2
Oropesa, *Spain* 34 F5
Oroquieta, *Phil.* 61 G5
Orosei, *Italy* 30 B2
Orosei, G. di, *Italy* 30 B2
Orosháza, *Hungary* 42 D5
Oroszlány, *Hungary* 42 C3
Orotukan, *Russia* 51 C16
Oroville, *Calif., U.S.A.* 116 F5
Oroville, *Wash., U.S.A.* 114 B4
Oroville, L., *U.S.A.* 116 F5
Orrefors, *Sweden* 11 H9
Orroroo, *Australia* 95 E2
Orrviken, *Sweden* 10 A8
Orrville, *U.S.A.* 110 F3
Orsa, *Sweden* 10 C8
Orsara di Púglia, *Italy* 31 A8
Orsasjön, *Sweden* 10 C8
Orsha, *Belarus* 46 E6
Örsjö, *Sweden* 11 H9
Orsk, *Russia* 50 D6
Orşova, *Romania* 42 F7
Ørsted, *Denmark* 11 H4
Örsundsbro, *Sweden* 10 E11
Orta, L. d', *Italy* 28 C5
Orta Nova, *Italy* 31 A8
Ortaca, *Turkey* 39 E10
Ortakent, *Turkey* 39 D9
Ortaklar, *Turkey* 39 D9
Ortaköy, *Çorum, Turkey* 72 B6
Ortaköy, *Niğde, Turkey* 72 C6
Orte, *Italy* 29 F9
Ortegal, C., *Spain* 34 B3
Orthez, *France* 20 E3
Ortigueira, *Spain* 34 B3
Orting, *U.S.A.* 116 C4
Ortisei, *Italy* 29 B8
Ortles, *Italy* 28 B7
Ortón →, *Bolivia* 124 F5
Ortona, *Italy* 29 F11
Ortonville, *U.S.A.* 112 C6
Orūmīyeh, *Iran* 70 B5
Orūmīyeh, Daryācheh-ye, *Iran* 70 B5
Orune, *Italy* 30 B2
Oruro, *Bolivia* 124 G5
Orust, *Sweden* 11 F5
Oruzgān □, *Afghan.* 66 C5
Orvault, *France* 18 E5
Orvieto, *Italy* 29 F9
Orwell, *N.Y., U.S.A.* 111 C9
Orwell, *Ohio, U.S.A.* 110 E4
Orwell →, *U.K.* 13 F9
Orwigsburg, *U.S.A.* 111 F8
Oryakhovo, *Bulgaria* 40 C7
Orzinuovi, *Italy* 28 C6
Orzyc →, *Poland* 45 F8
Orzysz, *Poland* 44 E8
Osa →, *Poland* 44 E5
Osa, Pen. de, *Costa Rica* 120 E3
Osage, *U.S.A.* 112 D8
Osage →, *U.S.A.* 112 F9
Osage City, *U.S.A.* 112 F7
Ōsaka, *Japan* 55 G7
Osan, *S. Korea* 57 F14
Osawatomie, *U.S.A.* 112 F7
Osborne, *U.S.A.* 112 F5
Osby, *Sweden* 11 H7
Osceola, *Ark., U.S.A.* 113 H10
Osceola, *Iowa, U.S.A.* 112 E8
Oschatz, *Germany* 24 D9
Oschersleben, *Germany* 24 C7
Óschiri, *Italy* 30 B2
Oscoda, *U.S.A.* 110 B1
Osečina, *Serbia, Yug.* 40 B3
Ösel = Saaremaa, *Estonia* 9 G20
Osery, *Russia* 46 E10
Osgoode, *Canada* 111 A9
Osh, *Kyrgyzstan* 50 E8
Oshakati, *Namibia* 85 H3
Oshawa, *Canada* 102 D4
Oshigambo, *Namibia* 88 B2
Oshkosh, *Nebr., U.S.A.* 112 E3
Oshkosh, *Wis., U.S.A.* 112 C10
Oshmyany = Ashmyany, *Belarus* 9 J21
Oshnovīyeh, *Iran* 70 B5
Oshogbo, *Nigeria* 83 D5
Oshtorīnān, *Iran* 71 C6
Oshwe, *Dem. Rep. of the Congo* 84 E3
Osi, *Nigeria* 83 D6
Osieczna, *Poland* 45 G3
Osijek, *Croatia* 42 E3
Ósilo, *Italy* 30 B1
Ósimo, *Italy* 29 E10
Osintorf, *Belarus* 46 E6
Osipenko = Berdyansk, *Ukraine* 47 J9
Osipovichi = Asipovichy, *Belarus* 46 F5
Osiyan, *India* 68 F5
Osizweni, *S. Africa* 89 D5
Oskaloosa, *U.S.A.* 112 E8
Oskarshamn, *Sweden* 11 G10
Oskarström, *Sweden* 11 H6
Oskélanéo, *Canada* 102 C4
Öskemen, *Kazakstan* 50 E9
Oskol →, *Ukraine* 47 H9
Oslo, *Norway* 9 G14
Oslob, *Phil.* 61 G5
Oslofjorden, *Norway* 9 G14
Osmanabad, *India* 66 K10
Osmancık, *Turkey* 72 B6
Osmaniye, *Turkey* 70 B3
Osmanlı, *Turkey* 41 E10
Ösmo, *Sweden* 10 F11
Osnabrück, *Germany* 24 C4
Ośno Lubuskie, *Poland* 45 F1
Osoblaha, *Czech Rep.* 27 A10
Osogovska Planina, *Macedonia* 40 D6
Osor, *Italy* 29 D11
Osorio, *Brazil* 127 B5
Osorno, *Chile* 128 E2
Osorno, *Spain* 34 C6
Osoyoos, *Canada* 104 D5
Osøyro, *Norway* 9 F11
Ospika →, *Canada* 104 B4
Osprey Reef, *Australia* 94 A4
Oss, *Neths.* 17 C5
Ossa, Mt., *Australia* 94 G4
Óssa, Óros, *Greece* 38 B4
Ossa de Montiel, *Spain* 33 G2
Ossabaw I., *U.S.A.* 109 K5
Osse →, *France* 20 D4
Osse →, *Nigeria* 83 D6
Ossi, *Italy* 30 B1
Ossining, *U.S.A.* 111 E11
Ossipee, *U.S.A.* 111 C13
Ossokmanuan L., *Canada* 103 B7
Ossora, *Russia* 51 D17
Ostashkov, *Russia* 46 D7
Östavall, *Sweden* 10 B9
Oste →, *Germany* 24 B5
Ostend = Oostende, *Belgium* 17 C2
Oster, *Ukraine* 47 G6
Osterburg, *Germany* 24 C7
Osterburg, *U.S.A.* 110 F6
Osterburken, *Germany* 25 F5
Österbybruk, *Sweden* 10 D11
Österbymo, *Sweden* 11 G9
Österdalälven, *Sweden* 10 C7
Østerdalen, *Norway* 9 F14
Österfärnebo, *Sweden* 10 D10
Österforse, *Sweden* 10 A11
Östergötlands län □, *Sweden* 11 F9
Osterholz-Scharmbeck, *Germany* 24 B4
Østerild, *Denmark* 11 G2
Osterode, *Germany* 24 D6
Östersund, *Sweden* 10 A8
Östervåla, *Sweden* 10 D11
Ostfriesische Inseln, *Germany* 24 B3
Ostfriesland, *Germany* 24 B3
Östhammar, *Sweden* 10 D12
Óstia, Lido di, *Italy* 29 G9
Ostíglia, *Italy* 29 C8
Östmark, *Sweden* 10 D6
Östra Husby, *Sweden* 11 F10
Ostrava, *Czech Rep.* 27 B11
Ostravský □, *Czech Rep.* 27 B10
Ostróda, *Poland* 44 E6
Ostrogozhsk, *Russia* 47 G10
Ostroh, *Ukraine* 47 G4
Ostrołęka, *Poland* 45 E8
Ostrov, *Bulgaria* 41 C8
Ostrov, *Czech Rep.* 26 A5
Ostrov, *Romania* 43 F12
Ostrov, *Russia* 46 D5
Ostrów Lubelski, *Poland* 45 G9
Ostrów Mazowiecka, *Poland* 45 F8
Ostrów Wielkopolski, *Poland* 45 G4
Ostrowiec-Świętokrzyski, *Poland* 45 H8
Ostrožac, *Bos.-H.* 42 G2
Ostrzeszów, *Poland* 45 G4
Ostseebad Kühlungsborn, *Germany* 24 A7
Osttirol □, *Austria* 26 E5
Ostuni, *Italy* 31 B10
Osum →, *Albania* 40 F4
Osŭm →, *Bulgaria* 41 C8
Ōsumi-Kaikyō, *Japan* 55 J5
Ōsumi-Shotō, *Japan* 55 J5
Osun □, *Nigeria* 83 D5
Osuna, *Spain* 35 H5
Oswegatchie →, *U.S.A.* 111 B9
Oswego, *U.S.A.* 111 C8
Oswego →, *U.S.A.* 111 C8
Oswestry, *U.K.* 12 E4
Oświęcim, *Poland* 45 H6
Otaci, *Moldova* 43 B12
Otago □, *N.Z.* 91 L2
Otago Harbour, *N.Z.* 91 L3
Ōtake, *Japan* 55 G6
Otaki, *N.Z.* 91 J5
Otaru, *Japan* 54 C10
Otaru-Wan = Ishikari-Wan, *Japan* 54 C10
Otava →, *Czech Rep.* 26 B7
Otavalo, *Ecuador* 124 C3
Otavi, *Namibia* 88 B2
Otchinjau, *Angola* 88 B1
Otelec, *Romania* 42 E5
Otelnuk L., *Canada* 103 A6
Oţelu Roşu, *Romania* 42 E7
Otero de Rey = Outeiro de Rei, *Spain* 34 B3
Othello, *U.S.A.* 114 C4
Othonoí, *Greece* 38 B1
Óthris, Óros, *Greece* 38 B4
Otjiwarongo, *Namibia* 88 C2
Otmuchów, *Poland* 45 H4
Otočac, *Croatia* 29 D12
Otoineppu, *Japan* 54 B11
Otok, *Croatia* 29 E13
Otorohanga, *N.Z.* 91 H5
Otoskwin →, *Canada* 102 B2
Otra →, *Norway* 9 G13
Otradnyy, *Russia* 48 D10
Otranto, *Italy* 31 B11
Otranto, C. d', *Italy* 31 B11
Otranto, Str. of, *Italy* 31 B11
Otrokovice, *Czech Rep.* 27 B10
Otse, *S. Africa* 88 D4
Ōtsu, *Japan* 55 G7
Ōtsuki, *Japan* 55 G9
Ottawa = Outaouais →, *Canada* 102 C5
Ottawa, *Canada* 102 C4
Ottawa, *Ill., U.S.A.* 112 E10
Ottawa, *Kans., U.S.A.* 112 F7
Ottawa Is., *Canada* 101 C11
Ottélé, *Cameroon* 83 E7
Ottensheim, *Austria* 26 C7
Otter Cr. →, *U.S.A.* 111 B11
Otter L., *Canada* 105 B8
Otterndorf, *Germany* 24 B4
Otterup, *Denmark* 11 J4
Otterville, *Canada* 110 D4
Ottery St. Mary, *U.K.* 13 G4
Otto Beit Bridge, *Zimbabwe* 87 F2
Ottosdal, *S. Africa* 88 D4
Ottumwa, *U.S.A.* 112 E8
Otu, *Nigeria* 83 D5
Otukpa, *Nigeria* 83 D6
Oturkpo, *Nigeria* 83 D6
Otway, B., *Chile* 128 G2
Otway, C., *Australia* 95 F3
Otwock, *Poland* 45 F8
Ötztaler Ache →, *Austria* 26 D3
Ötztaler Alpen, *Austria* 26 E3
Ou →, *Laos* 64 B4
Ou Neua, *Laos* 58 F3
Ou-Sammyaku, *Japan* 54 E10
Ouachita →, *U.S.A.* 113 K9
Ouachita, L., *U.S.A.* 113 H8
Ouachita Mts., *U.S.A.* 113 H7
Ouagadougou, *Burkina Faso* 83 C4
Ouahigouya, *Burkina Faso* 82 C4
Ouahran = Oran, *Algeria* 78 A5
Oualâta, *Mauritania* 82 B3
Ouallam, *Niger* 83 C5
Ouallene, *Algeria* 78 D6
Ouargaye, *Burkina Faso* 83 C5
Ouargla, *Algeria* 78 B7
Ouarkoye, *Burkina Faso* 82 C4
Ouarzazate, *Morocco* 78 B4
Ouassouas, *Mali* 83 B5
Ouatagouna, *Mali* 83 B5
Oubangi →, *Dem. Rep. of the Congo* 84 E3
Ouche →, *France* 19 E12
Ouddorp, *Neths.* 17 C3
Oude Rijn →, *Neths.* 17 B4
Oudeïka, *Mali* 83 B4
Oudenaarde, *Belgium* 17 D3
Oudon →, *France* 18 E6
Oudtshoorn, *S. Africa* 88 E3
Ouellé, *Ivory C.* 82 D4
Ouéme →, *Benin* 83 D5
Ouessa, *Burkina Faso* 82 C4
Ouessant, Î. d', *France* 18 D1
Ouesso, *Congo* 84 D3
Ouest, Pte. de l', *Canada* 103 C7
Ouezzane, *Morocco* 78 B4
Ougarou, *Burkina Faso* 83 C5
Oughterard, *Ireland* 15 C2
Ouidah, *Benin* 83 D5
Ouidi, *Niger* 83 C7
Ouistreham, *France* 18 C6
Oujda, *Morocco* 78 B5
Oujeft, *Mauritania* 82 A2
Oulainen, *Finland* 8 D21
Ould Yenjé, *Mauritania* 82 B2
Oullins, *France* 21 C8
Oulu, *Finland* 8 D21
Oulujärvi, *Finland* 8 D22
Oulujoki →, *Finland* 8 D21
Oulx, *Italy* 28 C3
Oum Chalouba, *Chad* 79 E10
Oum Hadjer, *Chad* 79 F9
Oumé, *Ivory C.* 82 D3
Ounasjoki →, *Finland* 8 C21
Ounguati, *Namibia* 88 C2
Ounianga Sérir, *Chad* 79 E10
Our →, *Lux.* 17 E6
Ouranópolis, *Greece* 40 F7
Ourârene, *Niger* 83 B6
Ouray, *U.S.A.* 115 G10
Ourcq →, *France* 19 C10
Ourense, *Spain* 34 C3
Ouricuri, *Brazil* 125 E10
Ourinhos, *Brazil* 127 A6
Ourique, *Portugal* 35 H2
Ouro Fino, *Brazil* 127 A6
Ouro-Ndia, *Mali* 82 B4
Ouro Prêto, *Brazil* 127 A7
Ouro Sogui, *Senegal* 82 B2
Oursi, *Burkina Faso* 83 C4
Ourthe →, *Belgium* 17 D5
Ouse →, *E. Susx., U.K.* 13 G8
Ouse →, *N. Yorks., U.K.* 12 D7
Oust, *France* 20 F5
Oust →, *France* 18 E4
Outaouais →, *Canada* 102 C5
Outardes →, *Canada* 103 C6
Outeiro de Rei, *Spain* 34 B3
Outer Hebrides, *U.K.* 14 D1
Outes = Serra de Outes, *Spain* 34 C2
Outjo, *Namibia* 88 C2
Outlook, *Canada* 105 C7
Outokumpu, *Finland* 8 E23
Outreau, *France* 19 B8
Ouvèze →, *France* 21 E8
Ouyen, *Australia* 95 F3
Ouzouer-le-Marché, *France* 19 E8
Ovada, *Italy* 28 D5
Ovalau, *Fiji* 91 C8
Ovalle, *Chile* 126 C1
Ovamboland, *Namibia* 88 B2
Ovar, *Portugal* 34 E2
Overath, *Germany* 24 E3
Overflakkee, *Neths.* 17 C4
Overijssel □, *Neths.* 17 B6
Overland Park, *U.S.A.* 112 F7
Overton, *U.S.A.* 117 J12
Övertorneå, *Sweden* 8 C20
Överum, *Sweden* 11 F10
Ovid, *U.S.A.* 111 D8
Ovidiopol, *Ukraine* 47 J6
Ovidiu, *Romania* 43 F13
Oviedo, *Spain* 34 B5
Oviksfjällen, *Sweden* 10 A7
Oviši, *Latvia* 9 H19
Ovoot, *Mongolia* 56 B7
Övör Hangay □, *Mongolia* 56 B2
Ovoro, *Nigeria* 83 D6
Øvre Ardal, *Norway* 9 F12
Övre Fryken, *Sweden* 10 E7
Ovruch, *Ukraine* 47 G5
Owaka, *N.Z.* 91 M2
Owambo = Ovamboland, *Namibia* 88 B2
Owasco L., *U.S.A.* 111 D8
Owase, *Japan* 55 G8
Owatonna, *U.S.A.* 112 C8
Owbeh, *Afghan.* 66 B3
Owego, *U.S.A.* 111 D8
Owen Falls Dam, *Uganda* 86 B3
Owen Sound, *Canada* 102 D3
Owens →, *U.S.A.* 116 J9
Owens L., *U.S.A.* 117 J9
Owensboro, *U.S.A.* 108 G2
Owerri, *Nigeria* 83 D6
Owl →, *Canada* 105 B10
Owo, *Nigeria* 83 D6
Owosso, *U.S.A.* 108 D3
Owyhee, *U.S.A.* 114 F5
Owyhee →, *U.S.A.* 114 E5
Owyhee, L., *U.S.A.* 114 E5
Ox Mts. = Slieve Gamph, *Ireland* 15 B3
Öxarfjörður, *Iceland* 8 C5
Oxbow, *Canada* 105 D8
Oxelösund, *Sweden* 11 F11
Oxford, *N.Z.* 91 K4
Oxford, *U.K.* 13 F6
Oxford, *Mass., U.S.A.* 111 D13
Oxford, *Miss., U.S.A.* 113 H10
Oxford, *N.C., U.S.A.* 109 G6
Oxford, *N.Y., U.S.A.* 111 D9
Oxford, *Ohio, U.S.A.* 108 F3
Oxford L., *Canada* 105 C9
Oxfordshire □, *U.K.* 13 F6
Oxía, *Greece* 38 C3
Oxie, *Sweden* 11 J7
Oxílithos, *Greece* 38 C6
Oxnard, *U.S.A.* 117 L7
Oxsjövålen, *Sweden* 10 B7
Oxus = Amudarya →, *Uzbekistan* 50 E6
Oya, *Malaysia* 62 D4
Oyama, *Japan* 55 F9
Oyem, *Gabon* 84 D2
Oyen, *Canada* 105 C6
Oykel →, *U.K.* 14 D4
Oymyakon, *Russia* 51 C15
Oyo, *Nigeria* 83 D5
Oyo □, *Nigeria* 83 D5
Oyonnax, *France* 19 F12
Oyster Bay, *U.S.A.* 111 F11
Öyübari, *Japan* 54 C11
Ozalp, *Turkey* 73 C10
Ozamiz, *Phil.* 61 G5
Ozark, *Ala., U.S.A.* 109 K3
Ozark, *Ark., U.S.A.* 113 H8
Ozark, *Mo., U.S.A.* 113 G8
Ozark Plateau, *U.S.A.* 113 G9
Ozarks, L. of the, *U.S.A.* 112 F8
Ożarów, *Poland* 45 H8
Ózd, *Hungary* 42 B5
Ozernoye, *Russia* 48 E10
Ozette L., *U.S.A.* 116 B2
Ozieri, *Italy* 30 B2
Ozimek, *Poland* 45 H5
Ozinki, *Russia* 48 E9
Ozona, *U.S.A.* 113 K4
Ozorków, *Poland* 45 G6
Ozren, *Bos.-H.* 42 G3
Ozuluama, *Mexico* 119 C5
Ozun, *Romania* 43 E10
Ozurgeti, *Georgia* 49 K5

Pasaje

# P


Pa, *Burkina Faso* 82 C4
Pa-an, *Burma* 67 L20
Pa Mong Dam, *Thailand* 64 D4
Pa Sak →, *Thailand* 62 B2
Paamiut, *Greenland* 4 C5
Paar →, *Germany* 25 G7
Paarl, *S. Africa* 88 E2
Pab Hills, *Pakistan* 68 F2
Pabbay, *U.K.* 14 D1
Pabianice, *Poland* 45 G6
Pabna, *Bangla.* 67 G16
Pabo, *Uganda* 86 B3
Pacaja →, *Brazil* 125 D8
Pacaraima, Sa., *S. Amer.* 122 C4
Pacasmayo, *Peru* 124 E3
Paceco, *Italy* 30 E5
Pachhar, *India* 68 G7
Pachino, *Italy* 31 F8
Pachitea →, *Peru* 124 E4
Pachmarhi, *India* 69 H8
Pachpadra, *India* 66 G8
Pachuca, *Mexico* 119 C5
Pacific, *Canada* 104 C3
Pacific-Antarctic Ridge, *Pac. Oc.* 97 M16
Pacific Grove, *U.S.A.* 116 J5
Pacific Ocean, *Pac. Oc.* 97 G14
Pacific Rim Nat. Park, *Canada* 116 B2
Pacifica, *U.S.A.* 116 H4
Pacitan, *Indonesia* 63 H14
Packwood, *U.S.A.* 116 D5
Pacov, *Czech Rep.* 26 B8
Pacy-sur-Eure, *France* 18 C8
Padaido, Kepulauan, *Indonesia* 63 E9
Padang, *Indonesia* 62 E2
Padang Endau, *Malaysia* 65 L4
Padangpanjang, *Indonesia* 62 E2
Padangsidempuan, *Indonesia* 62 D1
Padborg, *Denmark* 11 K3
Paddle Prairie, *Canada* 104 B5
Paddockwood, *Canada* 105 C7
Paderborn, *Germany* 24 D4
Padeş, Vf., *Romania* 42 E7
Padina, *Romania* 43 F12
Padma, *India* 69 G11
Pádova, *Italy* 29 C8
Padra, *India* 68 H5
Padrauna, *India* 69 F10
Padre I., *U.S.A.* 113 M6
Padrón, *Spain* 34 C2
Padstow, *U.K.* 13 G3
Padua = Pádova, *Italy* 29 C8
Paducah, *Ky., U.S.A.* 108 G1
Paducah, *Tex., U.S.A.* 113 H4
Padul, *Spain* 35 H7
Paengnyŏng-do, *S. Korea* 57 F13
Paeroa, *N.Z.* 91 G5
Paesana, *Italy* 28 D4
Pafúri, *Mozam.* 89 C5
Pag, *Croatia* 29 D12
Paga, *Ghana* 83 C4
Pagadian, *Phil.* 61 H5
Pagai Selatan, Pulau, *Indonesia* 62 E2
Pagai Utara, Pulau, *Indonesia* 62 E2
Pagalu = Annobón, *Atl. Oc.* 77 G4
Pagara, *India* 69 G9
Pagastikós Kólpos, *Greece* 38 B5
Pagatan, *Indonesia* 62 E5
Page, *U.S.A.* 115 H8
Pagėgiai, *Lithuania* 44 C8
Pago Pago, *Amer. Samoa* 91 B13
Pagosa Springs, *U.S.A.* 115 H10
Pagwa River, *Canada* 102 B2
Pahala, *U.S.A.* 106 J17
Pahang →, *Malaysia* 65 L4
Pahiatua, *N.Z.* 91 J5
Pahokee, *U.S.A.* 109 M5
Pahrump, *U.S.A.* 117 J11
Pahute Mesa, *U.S.A.* 116 H10
Pai, *Thailand* 64 C2
Paicines, *U.S.A.* 116 J5
Paide, *Estonia* 9 G21
Paignton, *U.K.* 13 G4
Paiho, *Taiwan* 59 F13
Päijänne, *Finland* 9 F21
Pailani, *India* 69 G9
Pailin, *Cambodia* 64 F4
Paimpol, *France* 18 D3
Painan, *Indonesia* 62 E2
Painesville, *U.S.A.* 110 E3
Paint Hills = Wemindji, *Canada* 102 B4
Paint L., *Canada* 105 B9
Painted Desert, *U.S.A.* 115 J8
Paintsville, *U.S.A.* 108 G4
País Vasco □, *Spain* 32 C2
Paisley, *Canada* 110 B3
Paisley, *U.K.* 14 F4
Paisley, *U.S.A.* 114 E3
Paita, *Peru* 124 E2
Paiva →, *Portugal* 34 D2
Paizhou, *China* 59 B9
Pajares, *Spain* 34 B5
Pajares, Puerto de, *Spain* 34 C5
Pajęczno, *Poland* 45 G5
Pak Lay, *Laos* 64 C3
Pak Phanang, *Thailand* 65 H3
Pak Sane, *Laos* 64 C4
Pak Song, *Laos* 64 E6
Pak Suong, *Laos* 58 H4
Pakaur, *India* 69 G12
Pakenham, *Canada* 111 A8
Pákhnes, *Greece* 36 D6
Pakhuis, *S. Africa* 88 E2
Pakistan ■, *Asia* 68 E4
Pakkading, *Laos* 64 C4
Pakokku, *Burma* 67 J19
Pakość, *Poland* 45 F5
Pakowki L., *Canada* 105 D6
Pakpattan, *Pakistan* 68 D5
Pakrac, *Croatia* 42 E2
Pakruojis, *Lithuania* 44 C10
Paks, *Hungary* 42 D3
Paktīā □, *Afghan.* 66 C6
Paktīkā □, *Afghan.* 66 C6
Pakwach, *Uganda* 86 B3
Pakxe, *Laos* 64 E5
Pal Lahara, *India* 69 J11
Pala, *Chad* 79 G9
Pala, *Dem. Rep. of the Congo* 86 D2
Pala, *U.S.A.* 117 M9
Palabek, *Uganda* 86 B3
Palacios, *U.S.A.* 113 L6
Palafrugell, *Spain* 32 D8
Palagiano, *Italy* 31 B10
Palagonía, *Italy* 31 E7
Palagruža, *Croatia* 29 F13
Palaiókastron, *Greece* 36 D8
Palaiokhóra, *Greece* 36 D5
Pálairos, *Greece* 38 C2
Palaiseau, *France* 19 D9
Palam, *India* 66 K10
Palamás, *Greece* 38 B4
Palamòs, *Spain* 32 D8
Palampur, *India* 68 C7
Palamut, *Turkey* 39 C9
Palana, *Australia* 94 F4
Palana, *Russia* 51 D16
Palanan, *Phil.* 61 C5
Palanan Pt., *Phil.* 61 C5
Palandri, *Pakistan* 69 C5
Palanga, *Lithuania* 9 J19
Palangkaraya, *Indonesia* 62 E4
Palani Hills, *India* 66 P10
Palanpur, *India* 68 G5
Palapye, *Botswana* 88 C4
Palas, *Pakistan* 69 B5
Palas de Rei, *Spain* 34 C3
Palashi, *India* 69 H13
Palasponga, *India* 69 J11
Palatka, *Russia* 51 C16
Palatka, *U.S.A.* 109 L5
Palau, *Italy* 30 A2
Palau ■, *Pac. Oc.* 52 J17
Palauk, *Burma* 64 F2
Palawan, *Phil.* 61 G3
Palayankottai, *India* 66 Q10
Palazzo, Pte., *France* 21 F12
Palazzo San Gervásio, *Italy* 31 B8
Palazzolo Acréide, *Italy* 31 E7
Paldiski, *Estonia* 9 G21
Pale, *Bos.-H.* 42 G3
Paleleh, *Indonesia* 63 D6
Palembang, *Indonesia* 62 E2
Palencia, *Spain* 34 C6
Palencia □, *Spain* 34 C6
Palenque, *Mexico* 119 D6
Paleokastrítsa, *Greece* 36 A3
Paleometokho, *Cyprus* 36 D12
Palermo, *Italy* 30 D6
Palermo, *U.S.A.* 114 G3
Palestina, *Chile* 128 A3
Palestine, *Asia* 75 D4
Palestine, *U.S.A.* 113 K7
Palestrina, *Italy* 29 G9
Paletwa, *Burma* 67 J18
Palghat, *India* 66 P10
Palgrave, Mt., *Australia* 92 D2
Pali, *India* 68 G5
Palikir, *Micronesia* 96 G7
Palinuro, *Italy* 31 B8
Palinuro, C., *Italy* 31 B8
Palioúrion, Ákra, *Greece* 40 G7
Palisades Reservoir, *U.S.A.* 114 E8
Paliseul, *Belgium* 17 E5
Palitana, *India* 68 J4
Palizada, *Mexico* 119 D6
Palk Bay, *Asia* 66 Q11
Palk Strait, *Asia* 66 Q11
Palkānah, *Iraq* 70 C5
Palkot, *India* 69 H11
Palla Road = Dinokwe, *Botswana* 88 C4
Pallanza = Verbánia, *Italy* 28 C5
Pallarenda, *Australia* 94 B4
Pallasovka, *Russia* 48 E8
Pallës, Bishti i, *Albania* 40 E3
Pallinup →, *Australia* 93 F2
Pallisa, *Uganda* 86 B3
Pallu, *India* 68 E6
Palm Bay, *U.S.A.* 109 L5
Palm Beach, *U.S.A.* 109 M6
Palm Coast, *U.S.A.* 109 L5
Palm Desert, *U.S.A.* 117 M10
Palm Is., *Australia* 94 B4
Palm Springs, *U.S.A.* 117 M10
Palma, *Mozam.* 87 E5
Palma, B. de, *Spain* 37 B9
Palma de Mallorca, *Spain* 37 B9
Palma del Río, *Spain* 35 H5
Palma di Montechiaro, *Italy* 30 E6
Palma Soriano, *Cuba* 120 B4
Palmares, *Brazil* 125 E11
Palmarola, *Italy* 30 B5
Palmas, *Brazil* 127 B5
Palmas, C., *Liberia* 82 E3
Pálmas, G. di, *Italy* 30 D1
Palmdale, *U.S.A.* 117 L8
Palmeira das Missões, *Brazil* 127 B5
Palmeira dos Índios, *Brazil* 125 E11
Palmela, *Portugal* 35 G2
Palmer, *U.S.A.* 100 B5
Palmer →, *Australia* 94 B3
Palmer Arch., *Antarctica* 5 C17
Palmer Lake, *U.S.A.* 112 F2
Palmer Land, *Antarctica* 5 D18
Palmerston, *Canada* 110 C4
Palmerston, *N.Z.* 91 L3
Palmerston North, *N.Z.* 91 J5
Palmerton, *U.S.A.* 111 F9
Palmetto, *U.S.A.* 109 M4
Palmi, *Italy* 31 D8
Palmira, *Argentina* 126 C2
Palmira, *Colombia* 124 C3
Palmyra = Tudmur, *Syria* 70 C3
Palmyra, *Mo., U.S.A.* 112 F9
Palmyra, *N.J., U.S.A.* 111 F9
Palmyra, *N.Y., U.S.A.* 110 C7
Palmyra, *Pa., U.S.A.* 111 F8
Palmyra Is., *Pac. Oc.* 97 G11
Palo Alto, *U.S.A.* 116 H4
Palo Verde, *U.S.A.* 117 M12
Paloich, *Sudan* 81 E3
Palompon, *Phil.* 61 F6
Palopo, *Indonesia* 63 E6
Palos, C. de, *Spain* 33 H4
Palos de la Frontera, *Spain* 35 H4
Palos Verdes, *U.S.A.* 117 M8
Palos Verdes, Pt., *U.S.A.* 117 M8
Pålsboda, *Sweden* 10 E9
Palu, *Indonesia* 63 E5
Palu, *Turkey* 70 B3
Paluke, *Liberia* 82 D3
Paluzza, *Italy* 29 B10
Palwal, *India* 68 E7
Pama, *Burkina Faso* 83 C5
Pamanukan, *Indonesia* 63 G12
Pamiers, *France* 20 E5
Pamir, *Tajikistan* 50 F8
Pamlico →, *U.S.A.* 109 H7
Pamlico Sd., *U.S.A.* 109 H8
Pampa, *U.S.A.* 113 H4
Pampa de las Salinas, *Argentina* 126 C2
Pampanua, *Indonesia* 63 E6
Pampas, *Argentina* 126 D3
Pampas, *Peru* 124 F4
Pamphylia, *Turkey* 72 D4
Pamplona, *Colombia* 124 B4
Pamplona, *Spain* 32 C3
Pampoenpoort, *S. Africa* 88 E3
Pamukçu, *Turkey* 39 B9
Pamukkale, *Turkey* 39 D11
Pan Xian, *China* 58 E5
Pana, *U.S.A.* 112 F10
Panabo, *Phil.* 61 H6
Panaca, *U.S.A.* 115 H6
Panagyurishte, *Bulgaria* 41 D8
Panaitan, *Indonesia* 63 G11
Panaji, *India* 66 M8
Panamá, *Panama* 120 E4
Panama ■, *Cent. Amer.* 120 E4
Panamá, G. de, *Panama* 120 E4
Panama Canal, *Panama* 120 E4
Panama City, *U.S.A.* 109 K3
Panamint Range, *U.S.A.* 117 J9
Panamint Springs, *U.S.A.* 117 J9
Panão, *Peru* 124 E3
Panaon I., *Phil.* 61 F6
Panare, *Thailand* 65 J3
Panarea, *Italy* 31 D8
Panaro →, *Italy* 29 D8
Panay, *Phil.* 61 F5
Panay, G., *Phil.* 63 B6
Pančevo, *Serbia, Yug.* 42 F5
Panch'iao, *Taiwan* 59 E13
Panciu, *Romania* 43 E12
Pancorbo, Desfiladero, *Spain* 34 C7
Pâncota, *Romania* 42 D6
Panda, *Mozam.* 89 C5
Pandan, *Antique, Phil.* 61 F5
Pandan, *Catanduanes, Phil.* 61 D6
Pandegelang, *Indonesia* 63 G12
Pandhana, *India* 68 J7
Pandharpur, *India* 66 L9
Pando, *Uruguay* 127 C4
Pando, L. = Hope, L., *Australia* 95 D2
Pandokrátor, *Greece* 36 A3
Pandora, *Costa Rica* 120 E3
Pandrup, *Denmark* 11 G3
Panevėžys, *Lithuania* 9 J21
Panfilov, *Kazakstan* 50 E8
Panfilovo, *Russia* 48 E6
Pang-Long, *Burma* 67 H21
Pang-Yang, *Burma* 67 H21
Panga, *Dem. Rep. of the Congo* 86 B2
Pangaíon Óros, *Greece* 41 F8
Pangalanes, Canal des = Ampangalana, Lakandranon', *Madag.* 89 C8
Pangani, *Tanzania* 86 D4
Pangani →, *Tanzania* 86 D4
Pangfou = Bengbu, *China* 57 H9
Pangil, *Dem. Rep. of the Congo* 86 C2
Pangkah, Tanjung, *Indonesia* 63 G15
Pangkajene, *Indonesia* 63 E5
Pangkalanbrandan, *Indonesia* 62 D1
Pangkalanbuun, *Indonesia* 62 E4
Pangkalpinang, *Indonesia* 62 E3
Pangnirtung, *Canada* 101 B13
Pangong Tso, *India* 68 B8
Panguitch, *U.S.A.* 115 H7
Pangutaran Group, *Phil.* 61 H4
Panhandle, *U.S.A.* 113 H4
Pani Mines, *India* 68 H5
Pania-Mutombo, *Dem. Rep. of the Congo* 86 D1
Panikota I., *India* 68 J4
Panipat, *India* 68 E7
Panjal Range, *India* 68 C7
Panjang, Hon, *Vietnam* 65 H4
Panjgur, *Pakistan* 66 F4
Panjim = Panaji, *India* 66 M8
Panjin, *China* 57 D12
Panjinad Barrage, *Pakistan* 66 E7
Panjnad →, *Pakistan* 68 E4
Panjwai, *Afghan.* 68 D1
Pankshin, *Nigeria* 83 D6
Panmunjŏm, *N. Korea* 57 F14
Panna, *India* 69 G9
Panna Hills, *India* 69 G9
Pannawonica, *Australia* 92 D2
Pannirtuuq = Pangnirtung, *Canada* 101 B13
Pano Akil, *Pakistan* 68 F3
Pano Lefkara, *Cyprus* 36 E12
Pano Panayia, *Cyprus* 36 E11
Panorama, *Brazil* 127 A5
Pánormon, *Greece* 36 D6
Pansemal, *India* 68 J6
Panshan = Panjin, *China* 57 D12
Panshi, *China* 57 C14
Pantanal, *Brazil* 124 H7
Pantar, *Indonesia* 63 F6
Pante Macassar, *E. Timor* 63 F6
Pante Makasar = Pante Macassar, *E. Timor* 63 F6
Pantelleria, *Italy* 30 F4
Pantón, *Spain* 34 C3
Pánuco, *Mexico* 119 C5
Panyam, *Nigeria* 83 D6
Panyu, *China* 59 F9
Panzhihua, *China* 58 D3
Páola, *Italy* 31 C9
Paola, *Malta* 36 D2
Paola, *U.S.A.* 112 F7
Paonia, *U.S.A.* 115 G10
Paoting = Baoding, *China* 56 E8
Paot'ou = Baotou, *China* 56 D6
Paoua, *C.A.R.* 84 C3
Pápa, *Hungary* 42 C2
Papa Stour, *U.K.* 14 A7
Papa Westray, *U.K.* 14 B6
Papagayo →, *Mexico* 119 D5
Papagayo, G. de, *Costa Rica* 120 D2
Papakura, *N.Z.* 91 G5
Papantla, *Mexico* 119 C5
Papar, *Malaysia* 62 C5
Pápas, Ákra, *Greece* 38 C3
Papeete, *Tahiti* 97 J13
Papenburg, *Germany* 24 B3
Paphlagonia, *Turkey* 72 B5
Paphos, *Cyprus* 36 E11
Papien Chiang = Da →, *Vietnam* 58 G5
Papigochic →, *Mexico* 118 B3
Paposo, *Chile* 126 B1
Papoutsa, *Cyprus* 36 E12
Papua New Guinea ■, *Oceania* 96 H6
Papudo, *Chile* 126 C1
Papuk, *Croatia* 42 E2
Papun, *Burma* 67 K20
Papunya, *Australia* 92 D5
Pará = Belém, *Brazil* 125 D9
Pará □, *Brazil* 125 D8
Paraburdoo, *Australia* 92 D2
Paracale, *Phil.* 61 D5
Paracatu, *Brazil* 125 G9
Paracel Is., *S. China Sea* 62 A4
Parachilna, *Australia* 95 E2
Parachinar, *Pakistan* 68 C4
Paraćin, *Serbia, Yug.* 40 C5
Paradas, *Spain* 35 H5
Paradela, *Spain* 34 C3
Paradhísi, *Greece* 36 C10
Paradip, *India* 67 J15
Paradise, *Calif., U.S.A.* 116 F5
Paradise, *Nev., U.S.A.* 117 J11
Paradise →, *Canada* 103 B8
Paradise Hill, *Canada* 105 C7
Paradise River, *Canada* 103 B8
Paradise Valley, *U.S.A.* 114 F5
Parado, *Indonesia* 63 F5
Paragould, *U.S.A.* 113 G9
Paragua →, *Venezuela* 124 B6
Paraguaçu →, *Brazil* 125 F11
Paraguaçu Paulista, *Brazil* 127 A5
Paraguaná, Pen. de, *Venezuela* 124 A5
Paraguarí, *Paraguay* 126 B4
Paraguarí □, *Paraguay* 126 B4
Paraguay ■, *S. Amer.* 126 A4
Paraguay →, *Paraguay* 126 B4
Paraíba = João Pessoa, *Brazil* 125 E12
Paraíba □, *Brazil* 125 E11
Paraíba do Sul →, *Brazil* 127 A7
Parainen, *Finland* 9 F20
Paraiso, *Mexico* 119 D6
Parak, *Iran* 71 E7
Parakhino Paddubye, *Russia* 46 C7
Parakou, *Benin* 83 D5
Paralimni, *Cyprus* 36 D12
Parálion-Astrous, *Greece* 38 D4
Paramaribo, *Surinam* 125 B7
Paramithiá, *Greece* 38 B2
Paramushir, Ostrov, *Russia* 51 D16
Paran →, *Israel* 75 E4
Paraná, *Argentina* 126 C3
Paranã, *Brazil* 125 F9
Paraná □, *Brazil* 127 A5
Paraná →, *Argentina* 126 C4
Paranaguá, *Brazil* 127 B6
Paranaíba, *Brazil* 125 G8
Paranaíba →, *Brazil* 125 H8
Paranapanema →, *Brazil* 127 A5
Paranapiacaba, Serra do, *Brazil* 127 A6
Paranas, *Phil.* 61 F6
Paranavaí, *Brazil* 127 A5
Parang, *Maguindanao, Phil.* 63 C6
Parang, *Sulu, Phil.* 61 J4
Parângul Mare, Vf., *Romania* 43 E8
Paraparaumu, *N.Z.* 91 J5
Parapóla, *Greece* 38 E5
Paraspóri, Ákra, *Greece* 39 F9
Paray-le-Monial, *France* 19 F11
Parbati →, *Mad. P., India* 68 G7
Parbati →, *Raj., India* 68 F7
Parbhani, *India* 66 K10
Parchim, *Germany* 24 B7
Parczew, *Poland* 45 G9
Pardes Hanna-Karkur, *Israel* 75 C3
Pardilla, *Spain* 34 D7
Pardo →, *Bahia, Brazil* 125 G11
Pardo →, *Mato Grosso, Brazil* 127 A5
Pardubice, *Czech Rep.* 26 A8
Pardubický □, *Czech Rep.* 26 B8
Pare, *Indonesia* 63 G15
Pare Mts., *Tanzania* 86 C4
Parecis, Serra dos, *Brazil* 124 F7
Paredes de Nava, *Spain* 34 C6
Paren, *Russia* 51 C17
Parent, *Canada* 102 C5
Parent, L., *Canada* 102 C4
Parentis-en-Born, *France* 20 D2
Parepare, *Indonesia* 63 E5
Parfino, *Russia* 46 D6
Párga, *Greece* 38 B2
Pargo, Pta. do, *Madeira* 37 D2
Pariaguán, *Venezuela* 124 B6
Paricutín, Cerro, *Mexico* 118 D4
Parigi, *Indonesia* 63 E6
Parika, *Guyana* 124 B7
Parikkala, *Finland* 46 B5
Parima, Serra, *Brazil* 124 C6
Parinari, *Peru* 124 D4
Pariñas, Pta., *S. Amer.* 122 D2
Parincea, *Romania* 43 D12
Parintins, *Brazil* 125 D7
Pariparit Kyun, *Burma* 67 M18
Paris, *Canada* 110 C4
Paris, *France* 19 D9
Paris, *Idaho, U.S.A.* 114 E8
Paris, *Ky., U.S.A.* 108 F3
Paris, *Tenn., U.S.A.* 109 G1
Paris, *Tex., U.S.A.* 113 J7
Paris, Ville de □, *France* 19 D9
Parish, *U.S.A.* 111 C8
Parishville, *U.S.A.* 111 B10
Park, *U.S.A.* 116 B4
Park City, *U.S.A.* 113 G6
Park Falls, *U.S.A.* 112 C9
Park Head, *Canada* 110 B3
Park Hills, *U.S.A.* 113 G9
Park Range, *U.S.A.* 114 G10
Park Rapids, *U.S.A.* 112 B7
Park River, *U.S.A.* 112 A6
Park Rynie, *S. Africa* 89 E5
Parkā Bandar, *Iran* 71 E8
Parkano, *Finland* 9 E20
Parker, *Ariz., U.S.A.* 117 L12
Parker, *Pa., U.S.A.* 110 E5
Parker Dam, *U.S.A.* 117 L12
Parkersburg, *U.S.A.* 108 F5
Parkes, *Australia* 95 E4
Parkfield, *U.S.A.* 116 K6
Parkhill, *Canada* 110 C3
Parkland, *U.S.A.* 116 C4
Parkston, *U.S.A.* 112 D6
Parksville, *Canada* 104 D4
Parla, *Spain* 34 E7
Pârliţa, *Moldova* 43 C12
Parma, *Italy* 28 D7
Parma, *Idaho, U.S.A.* 114 E5
Parma, *Ohio, U.S.A.* 110 E3
Parma →, *Italy* 28 D7
Parnaguá, *Brazil* 125 F10
Parnaíba, *Brazil* 125 D10
Parnaíba →, *Brazil* 122 D6
Parnassós, *Greece* 38 C4
Párnis, *Greece* 38 C5
Párnon Óros, *Greece* 38 D4
Pärnu, *Estonia* 9 G21
Paroo →, *Australia* 95 E3
Páros, *Greece* 39 D7
Parowan, *U.S.A.* 115 H7
Parpaillon, *France* 21 D10
Parral, *Chile* 126 D1
Parras, *Mexico* 118 B4
Parrett →, *U.K.* 13 F4
Parris I., *U.S.A.* 109 J5
Parrsboro, *Canada* 103 C7
Parry I., *Canada* 110 A4
Parry Is., *Canada* 4 B2
Parry Sound, *Canada* 102 C4
Parsberg, *Germany* 25 F7
Parsęta →, *Poland* 44 D2
Parsnip →, *Canada* 104 B4
Parsons, *U.S.A.* 113 G7
Parsons Ra., *Australia* 94 A2
Partanna, *Italy* 30 E5
Parthenay, *France* 18 F6
Partinico, *Italy* 30 D6
Partizánske, *Slovak Rep.* 27 C11
Partridge I., *Canada* 102 A2
Paru →, *Brazil* 125 D8
Parvān □, *Afghan.* 66 B6
Parvatipuram, *India* 67 K13
Parvatsar, *India* 68 F6
Påryd, *Sweden* 11 H9
Parys, *S. Africa* 88 D4
Pas, Pta. des, *Spain* 37 C7
Pas-de-Calais □, *France* 19 B9
Pasada, *Spain* 34 B5
Pasadena, *Canada* 103 C8
Pasadena, *Calif., U.S.A.* 117 L8
Pasadena, *Tex., U.S.A.* 113 L7
Pasaje →, *Argentina* 126 B3

Petília Policastro, *Italy* 31 C9
Petit Goâve, *Haiti* 121 C5
Petit Jardin, *Canada* 103 C8
Petit Lac Manicouagan, *Canada* 103 B6
Petit-Mécatina →, *Canada* 103 B8
Petit-Mécatina, I. du, *Canada* 103 B8
Petit Saint Bernard, Col du, *Italy* 21 C10
Petitcodiac, *Canada* 103 C6
Petite Baleine →, *Canada* 102 A4
Petite Saguenay, *Canada* 103 C5
Petitot →, *Canada* 104 A4
Petitsikapau L., *Canada* 103 B6
Petlad, *India* 68 H5
Peto, *Mexico* 119 C7
Petone, *N.Z.* 91 J5
Petorca, *Chile* 126 C1
Petoskey, *U.S.A.* 108 C3
Petra, *Jordan* 75 E4
Petra, *Spain* 37 B10
Petra, Ostrova, *Russia* 4 B13
Petra Velikogo, Zaliv, *Russia* 54 C6
Petrel = Petrer, *Spain* 33 G4
Petrella, Monte, *Italy* 30 A6
Petrer, *Spain* 33 G4
Petreto-Bicchisano, *France* 21 G12
Petrich, *Bulgaria* 40 E7
Petrified Forest National Park, *U.S.A.* 115 J9
Petrijanec, *Croatia* 29 B13
Petrikov = Pyetrikaw, *Belarus* 47 F5
Petrila, *Romania* 43 E8
Petrinja, *Croatia* 29 C13
Petrodvorets, *Russia* 46 C5
Petrograd = Sankt-Peterburg, *Russia* 46 C6
Petrolândia, *Brazil* 125 E11
Petrolia, *Canada* 102 D3
Petrolina, *Brazil* 125 E10
Petropavl, *Kazakstan* 50 D7
Petropavlovsk = Petropavl, *Kazakstan* 50 D7
Petropavlovsk-Kamchatskiy, *Russia* 51 D16
Petropavlovskiy = Akhtubinsk, *Russia* 49 F8
Petrópolis, *Brazil* 127 A7
Petroşani, *Romania* 43 E8
Petrova Gora, *Croatia* 29 C12
Petrovac, *Montenegro, Yug.* 40 D2
Petrovac, *Serbia, Yug.* 40 B5
Petrovaradin, *Serbia, Yug.* 42 E4
Petrovsk, *Russia* 48 D7
Petrovsk-Zabaykalskiy, *Russia* 51 D11
Petrovskaya, *Russia* 47 K9
Petrovskoye = Svetlograd, *Russia* 49 H6
Petrozavodsk, *Russia* 46 B8
Petrus Steyn, *S. Africa* 89 D4
Petrusburg, *S. Africa* 88 D4
Petzeck, *Austria* 26 E5
Peumo, *Chile* 126 C1
Peureulak, *Indonesia* 62 D1
Pevek, *Russia* 51 C18
Peveragno, *Italy* 28 D4
Peyrehorade, *France* 20 E2
Peyruis, *France* 21 D9
Pézenas, *France* 20 E7
Pezinok, *Slovak Rep.* 27 C10
Pfaffenhofen, *Germany* 25 G7
Pfarrkirchen, *Germany* 25 G8
Pfeffenhausen, *Germany* 25 G7
Pforzheim, *Germany* 25 G4
Pfullendorf, *Germany* 25 H5
Pfungstadt, *Germany* 25 F4
Phagwara, *India* 66 D9
Phaistós, *Greece* 36 D6
Phala, *Botswana* 88 C4
Phalera = Phulera, *India* 68 F6
Phalodi, *India* 68 F5
Phalsbourg, *France* 19 D14
Phan, *Thailand* 64 C2
Phan Rang, *Vietnam* 65 G7
Phan Ri = Hoa Da, *Vietnam* 65 G7
Phan Thiet, *Vietnam* 65 G7
Phanae, *Greece* 39 C7
Phanat Nikhom, *Thailand* 64 F3
Phangan, Ko, *Thailand* 65 H3
Phangnga, *Thailand* 65 H2
Phanom Sarakham, *Thailand* 64 F3
Phaphund, *India* 69 F8
Pharenda, *India* 69 F10
Pharr, *U.S.A.* 113 M5
Phatthalung, *Thailand* 65 J3
Phayao, *Thailand* 64 C2
Phelps, *U.S.A.* 110 D7
Phelps L., *Canada* 105 B8
Phenix City, *U.S.A.* 109 J3
Phet Buri, *Thailand* 64 F2
Phetchabun, *Thailand* 64 D3
Phetchabun, Thiu Khao, *Thailand* 64 E3
Phetchaburi = Phet Buri, *Thailand* 64 F2
Phi Phi, Ko, *Thailand* 65 J2
Phiafay, *Laos* 64 E6
Phibun Mangsahan, *Thailand* 64 E5
Phichai, *Thailand* 64 D3
Phichit, *Thailand* 64 D3
Philadelphia, *Miss., U.S.A.* 113 J10
Philadelphia, *N.Y., U.S.A.* 111 B9
Philadelphia, *Pa., U.S.A.* 111 G9
Philip, *U.S.A.* 112 C4
Philippeville, *Belgium* 17 D4
Philippi, *Greece* 41 E8
Philippi, *U.S.A.* 108 F5
Philippi L., *Australia* 94 C2
Philippines ■, *Asia* 61 F5
Philippolis, *S. Africa* 88 E4
Philippopolis = Plovdiv, *Bulgaria* 41 D8
Philipsburg, *Canada* 111 A11
Philipsburg, *Mont., U.S.A.* 114 C7
Philipsburg, *Pa., U.S.A.* 110 F6
Philipstown = Daingean, *Ireland* 15 C4
Philipstown, *S. Africa* 88 E3
Phillip I., *Australia* 95 F4
Phillips, *U.S.A.* 112 C9
Phillipsburg, *Kans., U.S.A.* 112 F5
Phillipsburg, *N.J., U.S.A.* 111 F9
Philmont, *U.S.A.* 111 D11
Philomath, *U.S.A.* 114 D2
Phimai, *Thailand* 64 E4
Phitsanulok, *Thailand* 64 D3
Phnom Dangrek, *Thailand* 62 B2
Phnom Penh, *Cambodia* 65 G5
Phnum Penh = Phnom Penh, *Cambodia* 65 G5
Phoenicia, *U.S.A.* 111 D10
Phoenix, *Ariz., U.S.A.* 115 K7
Phoenix, *N.Y., U.S.A.* 111 C8
Phoenix Is., *Kiribati* 96 H10
Phoenixville, *U.S.A.* 111 F9
Phon, *Thailand* 64 E4
Phon Tiou, *Laos* 64 D5
Phong →, *Thailand* 64 D4
Phong Saly, *Laos* 58 G4
Phong Tho, *Vietnam* 64 A4
Phonhong, *Laos* 64 C4
Phonum, *Thailand* 65 H2
Phosphate Hill, *Australia* 94 C2
Photharam, *Thailand* 64 F2
Phra Nakhon Si Ayutthaya, *Thailand* 64 E3
Phra Thong, Ko, *Thailand* 65 H2
Phrae, *Thailand* 64 C3
Phrom Phiram, *Thailand* 64 D3
Phrygia, *Turkey* 72 C4
Phu Dien, *Vietnam* 64 C5
Phu Loi, *Laos* 64 B4
Phu Ly, *Vietnam* 58 G5
Phu Quoc, Dao, *Vietnam* 65 G4
Phu Tho, *Vietnam* 58 G5
Phuc Yen, *Vietnam* 58 G5
Phuket, *Thailand* 65 J2
Phuket, Ko, *Thailand* 65 J2
Phul, *India* 68 D6
Phulad, *India* 68 G5
Phulchari, *Bangla.* 69 G13
Phulera, *India* 68 F6
Phulpur, *India* 69 G10
Phun Phin, *Thailand* 65 H2
Piacenza, *Italy* 28 C6
Pian Cr. →, *Australia* 95 E4
Piana, *France* 21 F12
Pianella, *Italy* 29 F11
Pianosa, *Puglia, Italy* 29 F12
Pianosa, *Toscana, Italy* 28 F7
Piapot, *Canada* 105 D7
Pias, *Portugal* 35 G3
Piaseczno, *Poland* 45 F8
Piaski, *Poland* 45 G9
Piastów, *Poland* 45 F7
Piatra, *Romania* 43 G10
Piatra Neamţ, *Romania* 43 D11
Piatra Olt, *Romania* 43 F9
Piauí □, *Brazil* 125 E10
Piauí →, *Brazil* 125 E10
Piave →, *Italy* 29 C9
Piazza Ármerina, *Italy* 31 E7
Pibor →, *Sudan* 81 F3
Pibor Post, *Sudan* 81 F3
Picardie, *France* 19 C10
Picardie, Plaine de, *France* 19 C9
Picardy = Picardie, *France* 19 C10
Picayune, *U.S.A.* 113 K10
Picerno, *Italy* 31 B8
Pichhor, *India* 69 G8
Pichilemu, *Chile* 126 C1
Pichor, *India* 68 G8
Pickerel L., *Canada* 102 C1
Pickering, *U.K.* 12 C7
Pickering, Vale of, *U.K.* 12 C7
Pickle Lake, *Canada* 102 B1
Pickwick L., *U.S.A.* 109 H1
Pico Truncado, *Argentina* 128 F3
Picos, *Brazil* 125 E10
Picton, *Australia* 95 E5
Picton, *Canada* 102 D4
Picton, *N.Z.* 91 J5
Pictou, *Canada* 103 C7
Picture Butte, *Canada* 104 D6
Picún Leufú, *Argentina* 128 D3
Pidurutalagala, *Sri Lanka* 66 R12
Piechowice, *Poland* 45 H2
Piedmont = Piemonte □, *Italy* 28 D5
Piedmont, *Ala., U.S.A.* 109 J3
Piedmont, *S.C., U.S.A.* 107 D10
Piedmonte Matese, *Italy* 31 A7
Piedra →, *Spain* 32 D3
Piedrabuena, *Spain* 35 G6
Piedrahita, *Spain* 34 E5
Piedralaves, *Spain* 34 E6
Piedras Blancas, *Spain* 34 B5
Piedras Negras, *Mexico* 118 B4
Piekary Śląskie, *Poland* 45 H5
Pieksämäki, *Finland* 9 E22
Piemonte □, *Italy* 28 D5
Pienaarsrivier, *S. Africa* 89 D4
Pieniężno, *Poland* 44 D7
Pieńsk, *Poland* 45 G2
Piercefield, *U.S.A.* 111 B10
Pierceland, *Canada* 105 C7
Piería □, *Greece* 40 F6
Pierpont, *U.S.A.* 110 E4
Pierre, *U.S.A.* 112 C4
Pierre-Buffière, *France* 20 C5
Pierre-de-Bresse, *France* 19 F12
Pierre E. Trudeau, Mt. = Logan, Mt., *Canada* 100 B5
Pierrefontaine-les-Varans, *France* 19 E13
Pierrefort, *France* 20 D6
Pierrelatte, *France* 21 D8
Pieštany, *Slovak Rep.* 27 C10
Piesting →, *Austria* 27 C9
Pieszyce, *Poland* 45 H3
Piet Retief, *S. Africa* 89 D5
Pietarsaari, *Finland* 8 E20
Pietermaritzburg, *S. Africa* 89 D5
Pietersburg, *S. Africa* 89 C4
Pietragalla, *Italy* 31 B8
Pietrasanta, *Italy* 28 E7
Pietroşiţa, *Romania* 43 E10
Pietrosul, Vf., *Maramureş, Romania* 43 C9
Pietrosul, Vf., *Suceava, Romania* 43 C10
Pieve di Cadore, *Italy* 29 B9
Pieve di Teco, *Italy* 28 D4
Pievepélago, *Italy* 28 D7
Pigadhítsa, *Greece* 40 G5
Pigeon L., *Canada* 110 B6
Piggott, *U.S.A.* 113 G9
Pigna, *Italy* 28 E4
Pigüe, *Argentina* 126 D3
Pihani, *India* 69 F9
Pihlajavesi, *Finland* 9 F23
Pijijiapan, *Mexico* 119 D6
Pikalevo, *Russia* 46 C8
Pikangikum Berens, *Canada* 105 C10
Pikes Peak, *U.S.A.* 112 F2
Piketberg, *S. Africa* 88 E2
Pikeville, *U.S.A.* 108 G4
Pikou, *China* 57 E12
Pikwitonei, *Canada* 105 B9
Piła, *Poland* 45 E3
Pila, *Spain* 33 G3
Pilaía, *Greece* 40 F6
Pilani, *India* 68 E6
Pilar, *Paraguay* 126 B4
Pilar de la Horadada, *Spain* 33 H4
Pilawa, *Poland* 45 G8
Pilaya →, *Bolivia* 124 H6
Pilbara, *Australia* 92 D2
Pilcomayo →, *Paraguay* 126 B4
Pilgrim's Rest, *S. Africa* 89 C5
Pilgrimstad, *Sweden* 10 B9
Píli, *Greece* 39 E9
Pilibhit, *India* 69 E8
Pilica →, *Poland* 45 G8
Pilion, *Greece* 38 B5
Pilis, *Hungary* 42 C4
Pilisvörösvár, *Hungary* 42 C3
Pilkhawa, *India* 68 E7
Pilliga, *Australia* 95 E4
Pílos, *Greece* 38 E3
Pilot Mound, *Canada* 105 D9
Pilot Point, *U.S.A.* 113 J6
Pilot Rock, *U.S.A.* 114 D4
Pilsen = Plzeň, *Czech Rep.* 26 B6
Pilštanj, *Slovenia* 29 B12
Piltene, *Latvia* 44 A8
Pilzno, *Poland* 45 J8
Pima, *U.S.A.* 115 K9
Pimba, *Australia* 95 E2
Pimenta Bueno, *Brazil* 124 F6
Pimentel, *Peru* 124 E3
Pina de Ebro, *Spain* 32 D4
Pinamalayan, *Phil.* 61 E4
Pinang, *Malaysia* 65 K3
Pinar, C. des, *Spain* 37 B10
Pinar del Río, *Cuba* 120 B3
Pınarbaşı, *Çanakkale, Turkey* 39 B8
Pınarbaşı, *Kayseri, Turkey* 72 C7
Pınarhisar, *Turkey* 41 E11
Pinatubo, Mt., *Phil.* 61 D3
Pincehely, *Hungary* 42 D3
Pinchang, *China* 58 B6
Pincher Creek, *Canada* 104 D6
Pinchi L., *Canada* 104 C4
Pinckneyville, *U.S.A.* 112 F10
Pińczów, *Poland* 45 H7
Pindar, *Australia* 93 E2
Pindi Gheb, *Pakistan* 68 C5
Pindiga, *Nigeria* 83 D7
Pindos Óros, *Greece* 38 B3
Pindus Mts. = Pindos Óros, *Greece* 38 B3
Pine →, *B.C., Canada* 104 B4
Pine →, *Sask., Canada* 105 B7
Pine, C., *Canada* 103 C9
Pine Bluff, *U.S.A.* 113 H9
Pine Bluffs, *U.S.A.* 112 E2
Pine City, *U.S.A.* 112 C8
Pine Cr. →, *U.S.A.* 110 E7
Pine Creek, *Australia* 92 B5
Pine Falls, *Canada* 105 C9
Pine Flat Res., *U.S.A.* 116 J7
Pine Grove, *U.S.A.* 111 F8
Pine Pass, *Canada* 104 B4
Pine Point, *Canada* 104 A6
Pine Ridge, *U.S.A.* 112 D3
Pine River, *Canada* 105 C8
Pine River, *U.S.A.* 112 B7
Pine Valley, *U.S.A.* 117 N10
Pinecrest, *U.S.A.* 116 G6
Pineda de Mar, *Spain* 32 D7
Pinedale, *Calif., U.S.A.* 116 J7
Pinedale, *Wyo., U.S.A.* 114 E9
Pinega →, *Russia* 50 C5
Pinehill, *Australia* 94 C4
Pinehouse L., *Canada* 105 B7
Pineimuta →, *Canada* 102 B1
Pinerolo, *Italy* 28 D4
Pineto, *Italy* 29 F11
Pinetop, *U.S.A.* 115 J9
Pinetown, *S. Africa* 89 D5
Pineville, *U.S.A.* 113 K8
Piney, *France* 19 D11
Ping →, *Thailand* 64 E3
Pingaring, *Australia* 93 F2
Pingba, *China* 58 D6
Pingbian, *China* 58 F4
Pingchuan, *China* 58 D3
Pingding, *China* 56 F7
Pingdingshan, *China* 56 H7
Pingdong, *Taiwan* 59 F13
Pingdu, *China* 57 F10
Pingelly, *Australia* 93 F2
Pingguo, *China* 58 F6
Pinghe, *China* 59 E11
Pinghu, *China* 59 B13
Pingjiang, *China* 59 C9
Pingle, *China* 59 E8
Pingli, *China* 58 A7
Pingliang, *China* 56 G4
Pinglu, *China* 56 E7
Pingluo, *China* 56 E4
Pingnan, *Fujian, China* 59 D12
Pingnan, *Guangxi Zhuangzu, China* 59 F8
Pingquan, *China* 57 D10
Pingrup, *Australia* 93 F2
Pingshan, *China* 58 C5
Pingtan, *China* 59 E12
Pingtang, *China* 58 E6
P'ingtung, *Taiwan* 59 F13
Pingwu, *China* 56 H3
Pingxiang, *Guangxi Zhuangzu, China* 58 F6
Pingxiang, *Jiangxi, China* 59 D9
Pingyao, *China* 56 F7
Pingyi, *China* 57 G9
Pingyin, *China* 56 F9
Pingyuan, *Guangdong, China* 59 E10
Pingyuan, *Shandong, China* 56 F9
Pingyuanjie, *China* 58 F4
Pinhal, *Brazil* 127 A6
Pinhal Novo, *Portugal* 35 G2
Pinheiro, *Brazil* 125 D9
Pinheiro Machado, *Brazil* 127 C5
Pinhel, *Portugal* 34 E3
Pini, *Indonesia* 62 D1
Piniós →, *Ilía, Greece* 38 D3
Piniós →, *Trikkala, Greece* 38 B4
Pinjarra, *Australia* 93 F2
Pink Mountain, *Canada* 104 B4
Pinkafeld, *Austria* 27 D9
Pinnacles, *U.S.A.* 116 J5
Pinnaroo, *Australia* 95 F3
Pinneberg, *Germany* 24 B5
Pínnes, Ákra, *Greece* 41 F8
Pinon Hills, *U.S.A.* 117 L9
Pinos, *Mexico* 118 C4
Pinos, Mt., *U.S.A.* 117 L7
Pinos Pt., *U.S.A.* 115 H3
Pinos Puente, *Spain* 35 H7
Pinotepa Nacional, *Mexico* 119 D5
Pinrang, *Indonesia* 63 E5
Pins, Pte. aux, *Canada* 110 D3
Pinsk, *Belarus* 47 F4
Pintados, *Chile* 124 H5
Pinyang, *China* 59 D13
Pinyug, *Russia* 50 C5
Pioche, *U.S.A.* 115 H6
Piombino, *Italy* 28 F7
Piombino, Canale di, *Italy* 28 F7
Pioner, Ostrov, *Russia* 51 B10
Pionki, *Poland* 45 G8
Piorini, L., *Brazil* 124 D6
Piotrków Trybunalski, *Poland* 45 G6
Piove di Sacco, *Italy* 29 C9
Pip, *Iran* 71 E9
Pipar, *India* 68 F5
Pipar Road, *India* 68 F5
Piparia, *Mad. P., India* 68 H8
Piparia, *Mad. P., India* 68 J7
Pipéri, *Greece* 38 B6
Pipestone, *U.S.A.* 112 D6
Pipestone →, *Canada* 102 B2
Pipestone Cr. →, *Canada* 105 D8
Piplan, *Pakistan* 68 C4
Piploda, *India* 68 H6
Pipmuacan, Rés., *Canada* 103 C5
Pippingarra, *Australia* 92 D2
Pipriac, *France* 18 E5
Piqua, *U.S.A.* 108 E3
Piquiri →, *Brazil* 127 A5
Pīr Sohrāb, *Iran* 71 E9
Pira, *Benin* 83 D5
Piracicaba, *Brazil* 127 A6
Piracuruca, *Brazil* 125 D10
Piræus = Piraiévs, *Greece* 38 D5
Piraiévs, *Greece* 38 D5
Pirajuí, *Brazil* 127 A6
Piram I., *India* 68 J5
Piran, *Slovenia* 29 C10
Pirané, *Argentina* 126 B4
Pirano = Piran, *Slovenia* 29 C10
Pirapora, *Brazil* 125 G10
Pirawa, *India* 68 G7
Pirdop, *Bulgaria* 41 D8
Pírgos, *Ilía, Greece* 38 D3
Pírgos, *Kríti, Greece* 39 F7
Pirgovo, *Bulgaria* 41 C9
Piribebuy, *Paraguay* 126 B4
Pirimapun, *Indonesia* 63 F9
Pirin Planina, *Bulgaria* 40 E7
Píríneos = Pyrénées, *Europe* 20 F4
Piripiri, *Brazil* 125 D10
Pirmasens, *Germany* 25 F3
Pirna, *Germany* 24 E9
Pirot, *Serbia, Yug.* 40 C6
Piru, *Indonesia* 63 E7
Piru, *U.S.A.* 117 L8
Piryatin = Pyryatyn, *Ukraine* 47 G7
Piryí, *Greece* 39 C7
Pisa, *Italy* 28 E7
Pisa →, *Poland* 45 E8
Pisagne, *Italy* 28 C7
Pisagua, *Chile* 124 G4
Pisarovina, *Croatia* 29 C12
Pisco, *Peru* 124 F3
Piscu, *Romania* 43 E12
Písek, *Czech Rep.* 26 B7
Pishan, *China* 60 C2
Pīshīn, *Iran* 71 E9
Pishin, *Pakistan* 68 D2
Pishin Lora →, *Pakistan* 68 E1
Pisidia, *Turkey* 72 D4
Pising, *Indonesia* 63 F6
Pismo Beach, *U.S.A.* 117 K6
Piso, L., *Liberia* 82 D2
Pissila, *Burkina Faso* 83 C4
Pissis, Cerro, *Argentina* 126 B2
Pissos, *France* 20 D3
Pissouri, *Cyprus* 36 E11
Pisticci, *Italy* 31 B9
Pistóia, *Italy* 28 E7
Pistol B., *Canada* 105 A10
Pisuerga →, *Spain* 34 D6
Pisz, *Poland* 44 E8
Pit →, *U.S.A.* 114 F2
Pita, *Guinea* 82 C2
Pitarpunga, L., *Australia* 95 E3
Pitcairn I., *Pac. Oc.* 97 K14
Pite älv →, *Sweden* 8 D19
Piteå, *Sweden* 8 D19
Piterka, *Russia* 48 E8
Piteşti, *Romania* 43 F9
Pithapuram, *India* 67 L13
Pithara, *Australia* 93 F2
Píthion, *Greece* 41 E10
Pithiviers, *France* 19 D9
Pithoragarh, *India* 69 E9
Pithoro, *Pakistan* 68 G3
Pitigliano, *Italy* 29 F8
Pitkyaranta, *Russia* 46 B6
Pitlochry, *U.K.* 14 E5
Pitsilia □, *Cyprus* 36 E12
Pitt I., *Canada* 104 C3
Pittsburg, *Calif., U.S.A.* 116 G5
Pittsburg, *Kans., U.S.A.* 113 G7
Pittsburg, *Tex., U.S.A.* 113 J7
Pittsburgh, *U.S.A.* 110 F5
Pittsfield, *Ill., U.S.A.* 112 F9
Pittsfield, *Maine, U.S.A.* 109 C11
Pittsfield, *Mass., U.S.A.* 111 D11
Pittsfield, *N.H., U.S.A.* 111 C13
Pittston, *U.S.A.* 111 E9
Pittsworth, *Australia* 95 D5
Pituri →, *Australia* 94 C2
Piura, *Peru* 124 E2
Piva →, *Montenegro, Yug.* 40 C2
Piwniczna, *Poland* 45 J7
Pixley, *U.S.A.* 116 K7
Piyai, *Greece* 38 B3
Pizarra, *Spain* 35 J6
Pizhou, *China* 56 G9
Pizzo, *Italy* 31 D9
Placentia, *Canada* 103 C9
Placentia B., *Canada* 103 C9
Placer, *Masbate, Phil.* 61 F5
Placer, *Surigao N., Phil.* 61 G6
Placerville, *U.S.A.* 116 G6
Placetas, *Cuba* 120 B4
Plačkovica, *Macedonia* 40 E6
Plainfield, *N.J., U.S.A.* 111 F10
Plainfield, *Ohio, U.S.A.* 110 F3
Plainfield, *Vt., U.S.A.* 111 B12
Plains, *Mont., U.S.A.* 114 C6
Plains, *Tex., U.S.A.* 113 J3
Plainview, *Nebr., U.S.A.* 112 D6
Plainview, *Tex., U.S.A.* 113 H4
Plainwell, *U.S.A.* 108 D3
Plaisance, *France* 20 E4
Plaistow, *U.S.A.* 111 D13
Pláka, *Greece* 39 B7
Pláka, Ákra, *Greece* 36 D8
Plakenska Planina, *Macedonia* 40 E5
Planá, *Czech Rep.* 26 B5
Plana Cays, *Bahamas* 121 B5
Planada, *U.S.A.* 116 H6
Plancoët, *France* 18 D4
Plandište, *Serbia, Yug.* 42 E6
Plano, *U.S.A.* 113 J6
Plant City, *U.S.A.* 109 M4
Plaquemine, *U.S.A.* 113 K9
Plasencia, *Spain* 34 E4
Plaški, *Croatia* 29 C12
Plaster City, *U.S.A.* 117 N11
Plaster Rock, *Canada* 103 C6
Plastun, *Russia* 54 B8
Plasy, *Czech Rep.* 26 B6
Plata, Río de la, *S. Amer.* 126 C4
Plátani →, *Italy* 30 E6
Plátanos, *Greece* 36 D5
Plateau □, *Nigeria* 83 D6
Platí, Ákra, *Greece* 41 F8
Platte, *U.S.A.* 112 D5
Platte →, *Mo., U.S.A.* 112 F7
Platte →, *Nebr., U.S.A.* 112 E7
Platteville, *U.S.A.* 112 D9
Plattling, *Germany* 25 G8
Plattsburgh, *U.S.A.* 111 B11
Plattsmouth, *U.S.A.* 112 E7
Plau, *Germany* 24 B8

Puerto Pollensa


Porthill, *U.S.A.* **114 B5**
Porthmadog, *U.K.* **12 E3**
Portile de Fier, *Europe* **42 F7**
Portimão, *Portugal* **35 H2**
Portishead, *U.K.* **13 F5**
Portiţei, Gura, *Romania* **43 F14**
Portknockie, *U.K.* **14 D6**
Portland, *N.S.W., Australia* **95 E5**
Portland, *Vic., Australia* **95 F3**
Portland, *Canada* **111 B8**
Portland, *Conn., U.S.A.* **111 E12**
Portland, *Maine, U.S.A.* **101 D12**
Portland, *Mich., U.S.A.* **108 D3**
Portland, *Oreg., U.S.A.* **116 E4**
Portland, *Pa., U.S.A.* **111 F9**
Portland, *Tex., U.S.A.* **113 M6**
Portland, I. of, *U.K.* **13 G5**
Portland B., *Australia* **95 F3**
Portland Bill, *U.K.* **13 G5**
Portland Canal, *U.S.A.* **104 B2**
Portmadoc = Porthmadog, *U.K.* **12 E3**
Porto, *France* **21 F12**
Porto, *Portugal* **34 D2**
Porto □, *Portugal* **34 D2**
Porto, G. de, *France* **21 F12**
Pôrto Alegre, *Brazil* **127 C5**
Porto Amboim = Gunza, *Angola* **84 G2**
Porto Azzurro, *Italy* **28 F7**
Porto Cristo, *Spain* **37 B10**
Pôrto de Móz, *Brazil* **125 D8**
Porto Empédocle, *Italy* **30 E6**
Pôrto Esperança, *Brazil* **124 G7**
Pôrto Franco, *Brazil* **125 E9**
Pórto Lágos, *Greece* **41 E9**
Porto Mendes, *Brazil* **127 A5**
Porto Moniz, *Madeira* **37 D2**
Pôrto Murtinho, *Brazil* **124 H7**
Pôrto Nacional, *Brazil* **125 F9**
Porto-Novo, *Benin* **83 D5**
Porto Petro, *Spain* **37 B10**
Porto San Giórgio, *Italy* **29 E10**
Porto Sant' Elpídio, *Italy* **29 E10**
Porto Santo, I. de, *Madeira* **78 B2**
Porto Santo Stéfano, *Italy* **28 F8**
Pôrto São José, *Brazil* **127 A5**
Pôrto Seguro, *Brazil* **125 G11**
Porto Tolle, *Italy* **29 D9**
Porto Tórres, *Italy* **30 B1**
Pôrto União, *Brazil* **127 B5**
Pôrto Válter, *Brazil* **124 E4**
Porto-Vecchio, *France* **21 G13**
Pôrto Velho, *Brazil* **124 E6**
Portobelo, *Panama* **120 E4**
Portoferráio, *Italy* **28 F7**
Portogruaro, *Italy* **29 C9**
Portola, *U.S.A.* **116 F6**
Portomaggiore, *Italy* **29 D8**
Portoscuso, *Italy* **30 C1**
Portovénere, *Italy* **28 D6**
Portoviejo, *Ecuador* **124 D2**
Portpatrick, *U.K.* **14 G3**
Portree, *U.K.* **14 D2**
Portrush, *U.K.* **15 A5**
Portsmouth, *Domin.* **121 C7**
Portsmouth, *U.K.* **13 G6**
Portsmouth, *N.H., U.S.A.* **109 D10**
Portsmouth, *Ohio, U.S.A.* **108 F4**
Portsmouth, *R.I., U.S.A.* **111 E13**
Portsmouth, *Va., U.S.A.* **108 G7**
Portsmouth □, *U.K.* **13 G6**
Portsoy, *U.K.* **14 D6**
Portstewart, *U.K.* **15 A5**
Porttipahtan tekojärvi, *Finland* **8 B22**
Portugal ■, *Europe* **34 F3**
Portugalete, *Spain* **32 B1**
Portumna, *Ireland* **15 C3**
Portville, *U.S.A.* **110 D6**
Porvenir, *Chile* **128 G2**
Porvoo, *Finland* **9 F21**
Porzuna, *Spain* **35 F6**
Posada, *Italy* **30 B2**
Posada →, *Italy* **30 B2**
Posadas, *Argentina* **127 B4**
Posadas, *Spain* **35 H5**
Poschiavo, *Switz.* **25 J6**
Posets, *Spain* **32 C5**
Poshan = Boshan, *China* **57 F9**
Posht-e-Badam, *Iran* **71 C7**
Posídhion, Ákra, *Greece* **40 G7**
Posidium, *Greece* **39 F9**
Poso, *Indonesia* **63 E6**
Posong, *S. Korea* **57 G14**
Posse, *Brazil* **125 F9**
Possession I., *Antarctica* **5 D11**
Pössneck, *Germany* **24 E7**
Possum Kingdom L., *U.S.A.* **113 J5**
Post, *U.S.A.* **113 J4**
Post Falls, *U.S.A.* **114 C5**
Postavy = Pastavy, *Belarus* **9 J22**
Poste-de-la-Baleine = Kuujjuarapik, *Canada* **102 A4**
Postmasburg, *S. Africa* **88 D3**
Postojna, *Slovenia* **29 C11**
Poston, *U.S.A.* **117 M12**
Postville, *Canada* **103 B8**
Potamós, *Andikíthira, Greece* **38 F5**
Potamós, *Kíthira, Greece* **38 E4**
Potchefstroom, *S. Africa* **88 D4**
Potcoava, *Romania* **43 F9**
Poteau, *U.S.A.* **113 H7**
Poteet, *U.S.A.* **113 L5**
Potenza, *Italy* **31 B8**
Potenza →, *Italy* **29 E10**
Potenza Picena, *Italy* **29 E10**
Poteriteri, L., *N.Z.* **91 M1**
Potgietersrus, *S. Africa* **89 C4**
Poti, *Georgia* **49 J5**
Potiskum, *Nigeria* **83 C7**
Potlogi, *Romania* **43 F10**
Potomac →, *U.S.A.* **108 G7**
Potosí, *Bolivia* **124 G5**
Potosi Mt., *U.S.A.* **117 K11**
Pototan, *Phil.* **61 F5**
Potrerillos, *Chile* **126 B2**
Potsdam, *Germany* **24 C9**
Potsdam, *U.S.A.* **111 B10**
Pottenstein, *Germany* **25 F7**
Pottersville, *U.S.A.* **111 C11**
Pottery Hill = Abu Ballas, *Egypt* **80 C2**
Pottstown, *U.S.A.* **111 F9**
Pottsville, *U.S.A.* **111 F8**
Pottuvil, *Sri Lanka* **66 R12**
P'otzu, *Taiwan* **59 F13**
Pouancé, *France* **18 E5**
Pouce Coupé, *Canada* **104 B4**
Poughkeepsie, *U.S.A.* **111 E11**
Pouilly-sur-Loire, *France* **19 E9**
Poulaphouca Res., *Ireland* **15 C5**
Poulsbo, *U.S.A.* **116 C4**
Poultney, *U.S.A.* **111 C11**
Poulton-le-Fylde, *U.K.* **12 D5**
Pouso Alegre, *Brazil* **127 A6**
Pout, *Senegal* **82 C1**
Pouthisat, *Cambodia* **64 F4**
Pouzauges, *France* **18 F6**
Pova de Sta. Iria, *Portugal* **35 G1**
Považská Bystrica, *Slovak Rep.* **27 B11**
Poverty B., *N.Z.* **91 H7**
Povlen, *Serbia, Yug.* **40 B3**
Póvoa de Lanhosa, *Portugal* **34 D2**
Póvoa de Varzim, *Portugal* **34 D2**
Povorino, *Russia* **48 E6**
Povungnituk = Puvirnituq, *Canada* **101 B12**
Powassan, *Canada* **102 C4**
Poway, *U.S.A.* **117 N9**
Powder →, *U.S.A.* **112 B2**
Powder River, *U.S.A.* **114 E10**
Powell, *U.S.A.* **114 D9**
Powell, L., *U.S.A.* **115 H8**
Powell River, *Canada* **104 D4**
Powers, *U.S.A.* **108 C2**
Powys □, *U.K.* **13 E4**
Poyang Hu, *China* **59 C11**
Poyarkovo, *Russia* **51 E13**
Poysdorf, *Austria* **27 C9**
Poza de la Sal, *Spain* **34 C7**
Poza Rica, *Mexico* **119 C5**
Pozanti, *Turkey* **72 D6**
Požarevac, *Serbia, Yug.* **40 B5**
Pozazal, Puerto, *Spain* **34 C6**
Požega, *Croatia* **42 E2**
Požega, *Serbia, Yug.* **40 C4**
Poznań, *Poland* **45 F3**
Pozo, *U.S.A.* **117 K6**
Pozo Alcón, *Spain* **35 H8**
Pozo Almonte, *Chile* **124 H5**
Pozo Colorado, *Paraguay* **126 A4**
Pozoblanco, *Spain* **35 G6**
Pozzallo, *Italy* **31 F7**
Pozzomaggiore, *Italy* **30 B1**
Pozzuoli, *Italy* **31 B7**
Pra →, *Ghana* **83 D4**
Prabuty, *Poland* **44 E6**
Prača, *Bos.-H.* **42 G3**
Prachatice, *Czech Rep.* **26 B6**
Prachin Buri, *Thailand* **64 E3**
Prachuap Khiri Khan, *Thailand* **65 G2**
Pradelles, *France* **20 D7**
Prades, *France* **20 F6**
Prado, *Brazil* **125 G11**
Prado del Rey, *Spain* **35 J5**
Præstø, *Denmark* **11 J6**
Pragersko, *Slovenia* **29 B12**
Prague = Praha, *Czech Rep.* **26 A7**
Praha, *Czech Rep.* **26 A7**
Prahecq, *France* **20 B3**
Prahova □, *Romania* **43 E10**
Prahova →, *Romania* **43 F10**
Prahovo, *Serbia, Yug.* **40 B6**
Praia, *C. Verde Is.* **77 E1**
Práia a Mare, *Italy* **31 C8**
Praid, *Romania* **43 D10**
Prainha, *Amazonas, Brazil* **124 E6**
Prainha, *Pará, Brazil* **125 D8**
Prairie, *Australia* **94 C3**
Prairie City, *U.S.A.* **114 D4**
Prairie Dog Town Fork →, *U.S.A.* **113 H5**
Prairie du Chien, *U.S.A.* **112 D9**
Prairies, L. of the, *Canada* **105 C8**
Pramánda, *Greece* **38 B3**
Prampram, *Ghana* **83 D5**
Pran Buri, *Thailand* **64 F2**
Prang, *Ghana* **83 D4**
Prapat, *Indonesia* **62 D1**
Prasonísi, Ákra, *Greece* **36 D9**
Prästmon, *Sweden* **10 A11**
Praszka, *Poland* **45 G5**
Prata, *Brazil* **125 G9**
Pratabpur, *India* **69 H10**
Pratapgarh, *Raj., India* **68 G6**
Pratapgarh, *Ut. P., India* **69 G9**
Prato, *Italy* **28 E8**
Prátola Peligna, *Italy* **29 F10**
Prats-de-Mollo-la-Preste, *France* **20 F6**
Pratt, *U.S.A.* **113 G5**
Prattville, *U.S.A.* **109 J2**
Pravdinsk, *Russia* **48 B6**
Pravets, *Bulgaria* **40 D7**
Pravia, *Spain* **34 B4**
Praya, *Indonesia* **62 F5**
Pré-en-Pail, *France* **18 D6**
Precordillera, *Argentina* **126 C2**
Predáppio, *Italy* **29 D8**
Predazzo, *Italy* **29 B8**
Predeal, *Romania* **43 E10**
Predejane, *Serbia, Yug.* **40 D6**
Preeceville, *Canada* **105 C8**
Preetz, *Germany* **24 A6**
Pregrada, *Croatia* **29 B12**
Preiļi, *Latvia* **9 H22**
Preko, *Croatia* **29 D12**
Prelog, *Croatia* **29 B13**
Prémery, *France* **19 E10**
Premià de Mar, *Spain* **32 D7**
Premont, *U.S.A.* **113 M5**
Premuda, *Croatia* **29 D11**
Prentice, *U.S.A.* **112 C9**
Prenzlau, *Germany* **24 B9**
Preobrazheniye, *Russia* **54 C6**
Preparis North Channel, *Ind. Oc.* **67 M18**
Preparis South Channel, *Ind. Oc.* **67 M18**
Přerov, *Czech Rep.* **27 B10**
Prescott, *Canada* **102 D4**
Prescott, *Ariz., U.S.A.* **115 J7**
Prescott, *Ark., U.S.A.* **113 J8**
Prescott Valley, *U.S.A.* **115 J7**
Preservation Inlet, *N.Z.* **91 M1**
Preševo, *Serbia, Yug.* **40 D5**
Presho, *U.S.A.* **112 D4**
Presicce, *Italy* **31 C11**
Presidencia de la Plaza, *Argentina* **126 B4**
Presidencia Roque Saenz Peña, *Argentina* **126 B3**
Presidente Epitácio, *Brazil* **125 H8**
Presidente Hayes □, *Paraguay* **126 A4**
Presidente Prudente, *Brazil* **127 A5**
Presidio, *Mexico* **118 B4**
Presidio, *U.S.A.* **113 L2**
Preslav, *Bulgaria* **41 C10**
Preslavska Planina, *Bulgaria* **41 C10**
Prešov, *Slovak Rep.* **27 B14**
Prešovský □, *Slovak Rep.* **27 B13**
Prespa, *Bulgaria* **41 E8**
Prespa, L. = Prespansko Jezero, *Macedonia* **40 F5**
Prespansko Jezero, *Macedonia* **40 F5**
Presque I., *U.S.A.* **110 D4**
Presque Isle, *U.S.A.* **109 B12**
Prestatyn, *U.K.* **12 D4**
Prestea, *Ghana* **82 D4**
Presteigne, *U.K.* **13 E5**
Přeštice, *Czech Rep.* **26 B6**
Preston, *Canada* **110 C4**
Preston, *U.K.* **12 D5**
Preston, *Idaho, U.S.A.* **114 E8**
Preston, *Minn., U.S.A.* **112 D8**
Preston, C., *Australia* **92 D2**
Prestonburg, *U.S.A.* **108 G4**
Prestwick, *U.K.* **14 F4**
Pretoria, *S. Africa* **89 D4**
Preuilly-sur-Claise, *France* **18 F7**
Préveza, *Greece* **38 C2**
Préveza □, *Greece* **38 B2**
Prey Veng, *Cambodia* **65 G5**
Priazovskoye, *Ukraine* **47 J8**
Pribilof Is., *U.S.A.* **100 C2**
Priboj, *Serbia, Yug.* **40 C3**
Příbram, *Czech Rep.* **26 B7**
Price, *U.S.A.* **114 G8**
Price I., *Canada* **104 C3**
Prichard, *U.S.A.* **109 K1**
Priego, *Spain* **32 E2**
Priego de Córdoba, *Spain* **35 H6**
Priekule, *Latvia* **9 H19**
Prien, *Germany* **25 H8**
Prienai, *Lithuania* **9 J20**
Prieska, *S. Africa* **88 D3**
Priest L., *U.S.A.* **114 B5**
Priest River, *U.S.A.* **114 B5**
Priest Valley, *U.S.A.* **116 J6**
Prievidza, *Slovak Rep.* **27 C11**
Prignitz, *Germany* **24 B7**
Prijedor, *Bos.-H.* **29 D13**
Prijepolje, *Serbia, Yug.* **40 C3**
Prikaspiyskaya Nizmennost = Caspian Depression, *Eurasia* **49 G9**
Prikro, *Ivory C.* **82 D4**
Prikubanskaya Nizmennost, *Russia* **49 H4**
Prilep, *Macedonia* **40 E5**
Priluki = Pryluky, *Ukraine* **47 G7**
Prime Seal I., *Australia* **94 G4**
Primorsk, *Russia* **46 B5**
Primorsko, *Bulgaria* **41 D11**
Primorsko-Akhtarsk, *Russia* **47 J10**
Primorskoye, *Ukraine* **47 J9**
Primrose L., *Canada* **105 C7**
Prince Albert, *Canada* **105 C7**
Prince Albert, *S. Africa* **88 E3**
Prince Albert Mts., *Antarctica* **5 D11**
Prince Albert Nat. Park, *Canada* **105 C7**
Prince Albert Pen., *Canada* **100 A8**
Prince Albert Sd., *Canada* **100 A8**
Prince Alfred, C., *Canada* **4 B1**
Prince Charles I., *Canada* **101 B12**
Prince Charles Mts., *Antarctica* **5 D6**
Prince Edward I. □, *Canada* **103 C7**
Prince Edward Is., *Ind. Oc.* **3 G11**
Prince Edward Pt., *Canada* **110 C8**
Prince George, *Canada* **104 C4**
Prince of Wales, C., *U.S.A.* **98 C3**
Prince of Wales I., *Australia* **94 A3**
Prince of Wales I., *Canada* **100 A10**
Prince of Wales I., *U.S.A.* **100 C6**
Prince Patrick I., *Canada* **4 B2**
Prince Regent Inlet, *Canada* **4 B3**
Prince Rupert, *Canada* **104 C2**
Princess Charlotte B., *Australia* **94 A3**
Princess May Ranges, *Australia* **92 C4**
Princess Royal I., *Canada* **104 C3**
Princeton, *Canada* **104 D4**
Princeton, *Calif., U.S.A.* **116 F4**
Princeton, *Ill., U.S.A.* **112 E10**
Princeton, *Ind., U.S.A.* **108 F2**
Princeton, *Ky., U.S.A.* **108 G2**
Princeton, *Mo., U.S.A.* **112 E8**
Princeton, *N.J., U.S.A.* **111 F10**
Princeton, *W. Va., U.S.A.* **108 G5**
Principe, I. de, *Atl. Oc.* **76 F4**
Principe da Beira, *Brazil* **124 F6**
Prineville, *U.S.A.* **114 D3**
Prins Harald Kyst, *Antarctica* **5 D4**
Prinsesse Astrid Kyst, *Antarctica* **5 D3**
Prinsesse Ragnhild Kyst, *Antarctica* **5 D4**
Prinzapolca, *Nic.* **120 D3**
Prior, C., *Spain* **34 B2**
Priozersk, *Russia* **46 B6**
Pripet = Prypyat →, *Europe* **47 G6**
Pripet Marshes, *Europe* **47 F5**
Pripyat Marshes = Pripet Marshes, *Europe* **47 F5**
Pripyats = Prypyat →, *Europe* **47 G6**
Prislop, Pasul, *Romania* **43 C9**
Pristen, *Russia* **47 G9**
Priština, *Kosovo, Yug.* **40 D5**
Pritzwalk, *Germany* **24 B8**
Privas, *France* **21 D8**
Priverno, *Italy* **30 A6**
Privolzhsk, *Russia* **48 B5**
Privolzhskaya Vozvyshennost, *Russia* **48 E7**
Privolzhskiy, *Russia* **48 E8**
Privolzhye, *Russia* **48 D9**
Priyutnoye, *Russia* **49 G6**
Prizren, *Kosovo, Yug.* **40 D4**
Prizzi, *Italy* **30 E6**
Prnjavor, *Bos.-H.* **42 F2**
Probolinggo, *Indonesia* **63 G15**
Prochowice, *Poland* **45 G3**
Proctor, *U.S.A.* **111 C11**
Proddatur, *India* **66 M11**
Prodhromos, *Cyprus* **36 E11**
Proença-a-Nova, *Portugal* **34 F3**
Profítis Ilías, *Greece* **36 C9**
Profondeville, *Belgium* **17 D4**
Progreso, *Coahuila, Mexico* **118 B4**
Progreso, *Yucatán, Mexico* **119 C7**
Prokhladnyy, *Russia* **49 J7**
Prokletije, *Albania* **40 D3**
Prokopyevsk, *Russia* **50 D9**
Prokuplje, *Serbia, Yug.* **40 C5**
Proletarsk, *Russia* **49 G5**
Proletarskaya = Proletarsk, *Russia* **49 G5**
Prome = Pyè, *Burma* **67 K19**
Prophet →, *Canada* **104 B4**
Prophet River, *Canada* **104 B4**
Propriá, *Brazil* **125 F11**
Propriano, *France* **21 G12**
Proserpine, *Australia* **94 C4**
Prosna →, *Poland* **45 F4**
Prospect, *U.S.A.* **111 C9**
Prosser, *U.S.A.* **114 C4**
Prostějov, *Czech Rep.* **27 B10**
Prostki, *Poland* **44 E9**
Proston, *Australia* **95 D5**
Proszowice, *Poland* **45 H7**
Próti, *Greece* **38 D3**
Provadiya, *Bulgaria* **41 C11**
Provence, *France* **21 E9**
Provence-Alpes-Côte d'Azur □, *France* **21 D10**
Providence, *Ky., U.S.A.* **108 G2**
Providence, *R.I., U.S.A.* **111 E13**
Providence Bay, *Canada* **102 C3**
Providence Mts., *U.S.A.* **117 K11**
Providencia, I. de, *Colombia* **120 D3**
Provideniya, *Russia* **51 C19**
Provins, *France* **19 D10**
Provo, *U.S.A.* **114 F8**
Provost, *Canada* **105 C6**
Prozor, *Bos.-H.* **42 G2**
Prrenjas, *Albania* **40 E4**
Prudhoe Bay, *U.S.A.* **100 A5**
Prudhoe I., *Australia* **94 C4**
Prud'homme, *Canada* **105 C7**
Prudnik, *Poland* **45 H4**
Prüm, *Germany* **25 E2**
Prundu, *Romania* **43 F11**
Pruszcz Gdański, *Poland* **44 D5**
Pruszków, *Poland* **45 F7**
Prut →, *Romania* **43 E13**
Pruzhany, *Belarus* **47 F3**
Prvič, *Croatia* **29 D11**
Prydz B., *Antarctica* **5 C6**
Pryluky, *Ukraine* **47 G7**
Pryor, *U.S.A.* **113 G7**
Prypyat →, *Europe* **47 G6**
Przasnysz, *Poland* **45 E7**
Przedbórz, *Poland* **45 G6**
Przedecz, *Poland* **45 F5**
Przemków, *Poland* **45 G2**
Przemyśl, *Poland* **45 J9**
Przeworsk, *Poland* **45 H9**
Przewóz, *Poland* **45 G1**
Przhevalsk = Karakol, *Kyrgyzstan* **50 E8**
Przysucha, *Poland* **45 G7**
Psakhná, *Greece* **38 C5**
Psará, *Greece* **39 C7**
Psathoúra, *Greece* **38 B6**
Psel →, *Ukraine* **47 H7**
Pserimos, *Greece* **39 E9**
Psíra, *Greece* **36 D7**
Pskov, *Russia* **46 D5**
Pskovskoye, Ozero, *Russia* **46 D5**
Psunj, *Croatia* **42 E2**
Pteleón, *Greece* **38 B4**
Ptich = Ptsich →, *Belarus* **47 F5**
Ptolemaís, *Greece* **40 F5**
Ptsich →, *Belarus* **47 F5**
Ptuj, *Slovenia* **29 B12**
Ptujska Gora, *Slovenia* **29 B12**
Pu Xian, *China* **56 F6**
Pua, *Thailand* **64 C3**
Puán, *Argentina* **126 D3**
Pu'an, *China* **58 E5**
Puan, *S. Korea* **57 G14**
Pubei, *China* **58 F7**
Pucallpa, *Peru* **124 E4**
Pucheng, *China* **59 D12**
Pucheni, *Romania* **43 E10**
Puchheim, *Germany* **25 G7**
Púchov, *Slovak Rep.* **27 B11**
Pucioasa, *Romania* **43 E10**
Pučišća, *Croatia* **29 E13**
Puck, *Poland* **44 D5**
Pucka, Zatoka, *Poland* **44 D5**
Puçol, *Spain* **33 F4**
Pudasjärvi, *Finland* **8 D22**
Puding, *China* **58 D5**
Pudozh, *Russia* **46 B9**
Pudukkottai, *India* **66 P11**
Puebla, *Mexico* **119 D5**
Puebla □, *Mexico* **119 D5**
Puebla de Alcocer, *Spain* **35 G5**
Puebla de Don Fadrique, *Spain* **33 H2**
Puebla de Don Rodrigo, *Spain* **35 F6**
Puebla de Guzmán, *Spain* **35 H3**
Puebla de la Calzada, *Spain* **35 G4**
Puebla de Sanabria, *Spain* **34 C4**
Puebla de Trives = Pobra de Trives, *Spain* **34 C3**
Pueblo, *U.S.A.* **112 F2**
Pueblo Hundido, *Chile* **126 B1**
Puelches, *Argentina* **126 D2**
Puelén, *Argentina* **126 D2**
Puente Alto, *Chile* **126 C1**
Puente-Genil, *Spain* **35 H6**
Puente la Reina, *Spain* **32 C3**
Puenteareas = Ponteareas, *Spain* **34 C2**
Puentedeume = Pontedeume, *Spain* **34 B2**
Puentes de Garcia Rodriguez = As Pontes de García Rodríguez, *Spain* **34 B3**
Pu'er, *China* **58 F3**
Puerco →, *U.S.A.* **115 J10**
Puerto, *Canary Is.* **37 F2**
Puerto Aisén, *Chile* **128 F2**
Puerto Ángel, *Mexico* **119 D5**
Puerto Arista, *Mexico* **119 D6**
Puerto Armuelles, *Panama* **120 E3**
Puerto Ayacucho, *Venezuela* **124 B5**
Puerto Barrios, *Guatemala* **120 C2**
Puerto Bermejo, *Argentina* **126 B4**
Puerto Bermúdez, *Peru* **124 F4**
Puerto Bolívar, *Ecuador* **124 D3**
Puerto Cabello, *Venezuela* **124 A5**
Puerto Cabezas, *Nic.* **120 D3**
Puerto Cabo Gracias á Dios, *Nic.* **120 D3**
Puerto Carreño, *Colombia* **124 B5**
Puerto Castilla, *Honduras* **120 C2**
Puerto Chicama, *Peru* **124 E3**
Puerto Coig, *Argentina* **128 G3**
Puerto Cortés, *Costa Rica* **120 E3**
Puerto Cortés, *Honduras* **120 C2**
Puerto Cumarebo, *Venezuela* **124 A5**
Puerto de Alcudia = Port d'Alcúdia, *Spain* **37 B10**
Puerto de Andraitx, *Spain* **37 B9**
Puerto de Cabrera, *Spain* **37 B9**
Puerto de Gran Tarajal, *Canary Is.* **37 F5**
Puerto de la Cruz, *Canary Is.* **37 F3**
Puerto de Mazarrón, *Spain* **33 H3**
Puerto de Pozo Negro, *Canary Is.* **37 F6**
Puerto de Sóller = Port de Sóller, *Spain* **37 B9**
Puerto de Somosierra, *Spain* **34 D7**
Puerto del Carmen, *Canary Is.* **37 F6**
Puerto del Rosario, *Canary Is.* **37 F6**
Puerto Deseado, *Argentina* **128 F3**
Puerto Escondido, *Mexico* **119 D5**
Puerto Heath, *Bolivia* **124 F5**
Puerto Inírida, *Colombia* **124 C5**
Puerto Juárez, *Mexico* **119 C7**
Puerto La Cruz, *Venezuela* **124 A6**
Puerto Leguízamo, *Colombia* **124 D4**
Puerto Limón, *Colombia* **124 C4**
Puerto Lobos, *Argentina* **128 E3**
Puerto Lumbreras, *Spain* **33 H3**
Puerto Madryn, *Argentina* **128 E3**
Puerto Maldonado, *Peru* **124 F5**
Puerto Manotí, *Cuba* **120 B4**
Puerto Mazarrón = Puerto de Mazarrón, *Spain* **33 H3**
Puerto Montt, *Chile* **128 E2**
Puerto Morazán, *Nic.* **120 D2**
Puerto Morelos, *Mexico* **119 C7**
Puerto Natales, *Chile* **128 G2**
Puerto Padre, *Cuba* **120 B4**
Puerto Páez, *Venezuela* **124 B5**
Puerto Peñasco, *Mexico* **118 A2**
Puerto Pinasco, *Paraguay* **126 A4**
Puerto Plata, *Dom. Rep.* **121 C5**
Puerto Pollensa = Port de Pollença, *Spain* **37 B10**

Resht


Radnevo, *Bulgaria* 41 D9
Radnice, *Czech Rep.* 26 B6
Radnor Forest, *U.K.* 13 E4
Radolfzell, *Germany* 25 H4
Radom, *Poland* 45 G8
Radomir, *Bulgaria* 40 D6
Radomka →, *Poland* 45 G8
Radomsko, *Poland* 45 G6
Radomyshl, *Ukraine* 47 G5
Radomyśl Wielki, *Poland* 45 H8
Radoszyce, *Poland* 45 G7
Radoviš, *Macedonia* 40 E6
Radovljica, *Slovenia* 29 B11
Radstadt, *Austria* 26 D6
Radstock, C., *Australia* 95 E1
Răducăneni, *Romania* 43 D12
Raduša, *Macedonia* 40 D5
Radviliškis, *Lithuania* 9 J20
Radville, *Canada* 105 D8
Raḍwá, J., *Si. Arabia* 80 C4
Radymno, *Poland* 45 J9
Radzanów, *Poland* 45 F7
Radziejów, *Poland* 45 F5
Radzyń Chełmiński, *Poland* 44 E5
Radzyń Podlaski, *Poland* 45 G9
Rae, *Canada* 104 A5
Rae Bareli, *India* 69 F9
Rae Isthmus, *Canada* 101 B11
Raeren, *Belgium* 17 D6
Raeside, L., *Australia* 93 E3
Raetihi, *N.Z.* 91 H5
Rafaela, *Argentina* 126 C3
Rafah, *Gaza Strip* 75 D3
Rafai, *C.A.R.* 86 B1
Raffadali, *Italy* 30 E6
Raffili, *Sudan* 81 F2
Rafḥā, *Si. Arabia* 70 D4
Rafsanjān, *Iran* 71 D8
Raft Pt., *Australia* 92 C3
Râgâ, *Sudan* 81 F2
Raga →, *Sudan* 81 F2
Ragachow, *Belarus* 47 F6
Ragag, *Sudan* 81 E1
Ragama, *Sri Lanka* 66 R11
Ragged, Mt., *Australia* 93 F3
Raghunathpalli, *India* 69 H11
Raghunathpur, *India* 69 H12
Raglan, *N.Z.* 91 G5
Ragusa, *Italy* 31 F7
Raha, *Indonesia* 63 E6
Rahad, Nahr ed →, *Sudan* 81 E3
Rahaeng = Tak, *Thailand* 64 D2
Rahatgarh, *India* 69 H8
Rahden, *Germany* 24 C4
Raheita, *Eritrea* 81 E5
Rahimyar Khan, *Pakistan* 68 E4
Rāhjerd, *Iran* 71 C6
Rahon, *India* 68 D7
Raichur, *India* 66 L10
Raiganj, *India* 69 G13
Raigarh, *India* 67 J13
Raijua, *Indonesia* 63 F6
Raikot, *India* 68 D6
Railton, *Australia* 94 G4
Rainbow Lake, *Canada* 104 B5
Rainier, *U.S.A.* 116 D4
Rainier, Mt., *U.S.A.* 116 D5
Rainy L., *Canada* 105 D10
Rainy River, *Canada* 105 D10
Raippaluoto, *Finland* 8 E19
Raipur, *India* 67 J12
Ra'is, *Si. Arabia* 80 C4
Raisen, *India* 68 H8
Raisio, *Finland* 9 F20
Raj Nandgaon, *India* 67 J12
Raj Nilgiri, *India* 69 J12
Raja, Ujung, *Indonesia* 62 D1
Raja Ampat, Kepulauan, *Indonesia* 63 E7
Rajahmundry, *India* 67 L12
Rajang →, *Malaysia* 62 D4
Rajanpur, *Pakistan* 68 E4
Rajapalaiyam, *India* 66 Q10
Rajasthan □, *India* 68 F5
Rajasthan Canal, *India* 68 F5
Rajauri, *India* 69 C6
Rajgarh, *Mad. P., India* 68 G7
Rajgarh, *Raj., India* 68 F7
Rajgarh, *Raj., India* 68 E6
Rajgir, *India* 69 G11
Rajgród, *Poland* 44 E9
Rajkot, *India* 68 H4
Rajmahal Hills, *India* 69 G12
Rajpipla, *India* 66 J8
Rajpur, *India* 68 H6
Rajpura, *India* 68 D7
Rajshahi, *Bangla.* 67 G16
Rajshahi □, *Bangla.* 69 G13
Rajula, *India* 68 J4
Rakaia, *N.Z.* 91 K4
Rakaia →, *N.Z.* 91 K4
Rakan, Ra's, *Qatar* 71 E6
Rakaposhi, *Pakistan* 69 A6
Rakata, Pulau, *Indonesia* 62 F3
Rakhiv, *Ukraine* 47 H3
Rakhni, *Pakistan* 68 D3
Rakhni →, *Pakistan* 68 E3
Rakitnoye, *Russia* 54 B7
Rakitovo, *Bulgaria* 41 E8
Rakoniewice, *Poland* 45 F3
Rakops, *Botswana* 88 C3
Rakovica, *Croatia* 29 D12
Rakovník, *Czech Rep.* 26 A6
Rakovski, *Bulgaria* 41 D8
Rakvere, *Estonia* 9 G22
Raleigh, *U.S.A.* 109 H6
Ralja, *Serbia, Yug.* 40 B4
Ralls, *U.S.A.* 113 J4
Ralston, *U.S.A.* 110 E8
Ram →, *Canada* 104 A4
Rām Allāh, *West Bank* 75 D4
Rama, *Nic.* 120 D3
Ramacca, *Italy* 31 E7
Ramakona, *India* 69 J8
Ramales de la Victoria, *Spain* 34 B7
Raman, *Thailand* 65 J3
Ramanathapuram, *India* 66 Q11
Ramanetaka, B. de, *Madag.* 89 A8
Ramanujganj, *India* 69 H10
Ramat Gan, *Israel* 75 C3
Ramatlhabama, *S. Africa* 88 D4
Ramban, *India* 69 C6
Rambervillers, *France* 19 D13
Rambipuji, *Indonesia* 63 H15
Rambouillet, *France* 19 D8
Rame Hd., *Australia* 95 F4
Ramechhap, *Nepal* 69 F12
Ramenskoye, *Russia* 46 E10
Ramganga →, *India* 69 F8
Ramgarh, *Bihar, India* 69 H11
Ramgarh, *Raj., India* 68 F6
Ramgarh, *Raj., India* 68 F4
Rāmhormoz, *Iran* 71 D6
Ramīān, *Iran* 71 B7
Ramingining, *Australia* 94 A2
Ramla, *Israel* 75 D3
Ramlu, *Eritrea* 81 E5
Râmna →, *Romania* 43 E12
Ramnad = Ramanathapuram, *India* 66 Q11
Ramnagar, *Jammu & Kashmir, India* 69 C6
Ramnagar, *Ut. P., India* 69 E8
Ramnäs, *Sweden* 10 E10
Râmnicu Sărat, *Romania* 43 E12
Râmnicu Vâlcea, *Romania* 43 E9
Ramon, *Russia* 47 G10
Ramona, *U.S.A.* 117 M10
Ramonville-St-Agne, *France* 20 E5
Ramore, *Canada* 102 C3
Ramos →, *Nigeria* 83 D6
Ramotswa, *Botswana* 88 C4
Rampur, *H.P., India* 68 D7
Rampur, *Mad. P., India* 68 H5
Rampur, *Ut. P., India* 69 E8
Rampur Hat, *India* 69 G12
Rampura, *India* 68 G6
Ramrama Tola, *India* 69 J8
Ramree I., *Burma* 67 K19
Rāmsar, *Iran* 71 B6
Ramsey, *U.K.* 12 C3
Ramsey, *U.S.A.* 111 E10
Ramsey L., *Canada* 102 C3
Ramsgate, *U.K.* 13 F9
Ramsjö, *Sweden* 10 B9
Ramstein, *Germany* 25 F3
Ramtek, *India* 66 J11
Ramvik, *Sweden* 10 B11
Rana Pratap Sagar Dam, *India* 68 G6
Ranaghat, *India* 69 H13
Ranahu, *Pakistan* 68 G3
Ranau, *Malaysia* 62 C5
Rancagua, *Chile* 126 C1
Rance →, *France* 18 D5
Rancheria →, *Canada* 104 A3
Ranchester, *U.S.A.* 114 D10
Ranchi, *India* 69 H11
Rancho Cucamonga, *U.S.A.* 117 L9
Randalstown, *U.K.* 15 B5
Randan, *France* 19 F10
Randazzo, *Italy* 31 E7
Randers, *Denmark* 11 H4
Randers Fjord, *Denmark* 11 H4
Randfontein, *S. Africa* 89 D4
Randle, *U.S.A.* 116 D5
Randolph, *Mass., U.S.A.* 111 D13
Randolph, *N.Y., U.S.A.* 110 D6
Randolph, *Utah, U.S.A.* 114 F8
Randolph, *Vt., U.S.A.* 111 C12
Randsburg, *U.S.A.* 117 K9
Råne älv →, *Sweden* 8 D20
Rangae, *Thailand* 65 J3
Rangaunu B., *N.Z.* 91 F4
Rangeley, *U.S.A.* 111 B14
Rangeley L., *U.S.A.* 111 B14
Rangely, *U.S.A.* 114 F9
Ranger, *U.S.A.* 113 J5
Rangia, *India* 67 F17
Rangiora, *N.Z.* 91 K4
Rangitaiki →, *N.Z.* 91 G6
Rangitata →, *N.Z.* 91 K3
Rangkasbitung, *Indonesia* 63 G12
Rangon →, *Burma* 67 L20
Rangoon, *Burma* 67 L20
Rangpur, *Bangla.* 67 G16
Rangsit, *Thailand* 64 F3
Ranibennur, *India* 66 M9
Raniganj, *Ut. P., India* 69 F9
Raniganj, *W. Bengal, India* 67 H15
Ranikhet, *India* 69 E8
Raniwara, *India* 66 G8
Rāniyah, *Iraq* 70 B5
Ranka, *India* 69 H10
Ranken →, *Australia* 94 C2
Rankin, *U.S.A.* 113 K4
Rankin Inlet, *Canada* 100 B10
Rankins Springs, *Australia* 95 E4
Rankweil, *Austria* 26 D2
Rannoch, L., *U.K.* 14 E4
Rannoch Moor, *U.K.* 14 E4
Ranobe, Helodranon' i, *Madag.* 89 C7
Ranohira, *Madag.* 89 C8
Ranomafana, *Toamasina, Madag.* 89 B8
Ranomafana, *Toliara, Madag.* 89 C8
Ranomena, *Madag.* 89 C8
Ranong, *Thailand* 65 H2
Ranotsara Nord, *Madag.* 89 C8
Rānsa, *Iran* 71 C6
Ransiki, *Indonesia* 63 E8
Rantabe, *Madag.* 89 B8
Rantauprapat, *Indonesia* 62 D1
Rantemario, *Indonesia* 63 E5
Rantoul, *U.S.A.* 108 E1
Ranum, *Denmark* 11 H3
Ranyah, W. →, *Si. Arabia* 80 C5
Raon l'Étape, *France* 19 D13
Raoping, *China* 59 F11
Raoyang, *China* 56 E8
Rapa, *Pac. Oc.* 97 K13
Rapallo, *Italy* 28 D6
Rapar, *India* 68 H4
Rāpch, *Iran* 71 E8
Raper, C., *Canada* 101 B13
Rapid City, *U.S.A.* 112 D3
Rapid River, *U.S.A.* 108 C2
Rapla, *Estonia* 9 G21
Rapti →, *India* 69 F10
Rapu Rapu I., *Phil.* 61 E6
Raqaba ez Zarqa →, *Sudan* 81 F2
Raquette →, *U.S.A.* 111 B10
Raquette Lake, *U.S.A.* 111 C10
Rarotonga, *Cook Is.* 97 K12
Ra's al 'Ayn, *Syria* 70 B4
Ra's al Khaymah, *U.A.E.* 71 E7
Râs el Mâ, *Mali* 82 B4
Ras Ghârib, *Egypt* 80 B3
Ras Mallap, *Egypt* 80 B3
Rasca, Pta. de la, *Canary Is.* 37 G3
Rășcani, *Moldova* 43 C12
Raseiniai, *Lithuania* 9 J20
Rashad, *Sudan* 81 E3
Rashîd, *Egypt* 80 H7
Rashîd, Masabb, *Egypt* 80 H7
Rashmi, *India* 68 G6
Rasht, *Iran* 71 B6
Rasi Salai, *Thailand* 64 E5
Raška, *Serbia, Yug.* 40 C4
Râsnov, *Romania* 43 E10
Rason L., *Australia* 93 E3
Rașova, *Romania* 43 F12
Rasovo, *Bulgaria* 40 C7
Rasra, *India* 69 G10
Rasskazovo, *Russia* 48 D5
Rast, *Romania* 43 G8
Rastatt, *Germany* 25 G4
Rastede, *Germany* 24 B4
Răstolița, *Romania* 43 D9
Rasul, *Pakistan* 68 C5
Raszków, *Poland* 45 G4
Rat Buri, *Thailand* 64 F2
Rat Islands, *U.S.A.* 100 C1
Rat L., *Canada* 105 B9
Ratangarh, *India* 68 E6
Rätansbyn, *Sweden* 10 B8
Raṭāwī, *Iraq* 70 D5
Rath, *India* 69 G8
Rath Luirc, *Ireland* 15 D3
Rathdrum, *Ireland* 15 D5
Rathenow, *Germany* 24 C8
Rathkeale, *Ireland* 15 D3
Rathlin I., *U.K.* 15 A5
Rathmelton, *Ireland* 15 A4
Ratibor = Racibórz, *Poland* 45 H5
Rätikon, *Austria* 26 D2
Ratingen, *Germany* 24 D2
Ratlam, *India* 68 H6
Ratnagiri, *India* 66 L8
Ratodero, *Pakistan* 68 F3
Raton, *U.S.A.* 113 G2
Rattaphum, *Thailand* 65 J3
Ratten, *Austria* 26 D8
Rattray Hd., *U.K.* 14 D7
Rättvik, *Sweden* 10 D9
Ratz, Mt., *Canada* 104 B2
Ratzeburg, *Germany* 24 B6
Raub, *Malaysia* 65 L3
Rauch, *Argentina* 126 D4
Raudales de Malpaso, *Mexico* 119 D6
Raufarhöfn, *Iceland* 8 C6
Raufoss, *Norway* 9 F14
Raukumara Ra., *N.Z.* 91 H6
Rauma, *Finland* 9 F19
Raurkela, *India* 69 H11
Rausu-Dake, *Japan* 54 B12
Răut →, *Moldova* 43 C14
Rava-Ruska, *Poland* 47 G2
Rava Russkaya = Rava-Ruska, *Poland* 47 G2
Ravalli, *U.S.A.* 114 C6
Ravānsar, *Iran* 70 C5
Ravanusa, *Italy* 30 E6
Rāvar, *Iran* 71 D8
Ravena, *U.S.A.* 111 D11
Ravenna, *Italy* 29 D9
Ravenna, *Nebr., U.S.A.* 112 E5
Ravenna, *Ohio, U.S.A.* 110 E3
Ravensburg, *Germany* 25 H5
Ravenshoe, *Australia* 94 B4
Ravensthorpe, *Australia* 93 F3
Ravenswood, *Australia* 94 C4
Ravenswood, *U.S.A.* 108 F5
Ravi →, *Pakistan* 68 D4
Ravna Gora, *Croatia* 29 C11
Ravna Reka, *Serbia, Yug.* 40 B5
Ravne na Koroškem, *Slovenia* 29 B11
Rawa Mazowiecka, *Poland* 45 G7
Rawalpindi, *Pakistan* 68 C5
Rawāndūz, *Iraq* 70 B5
Rawang, *Malaysia* 65 L3
Rawene, *N.Z.* 91 F4
Rawicz, *Poland* 45 G3
Rawka →, *Poland* 45 F7
Rawlinna, *Australia* 93 F4
Rawlins, *U.S.A.* 114 F10
Rawlinson Ra., *Australia* 93 D4
Rawson, *Argentina* 128 E3
Raxaul, *India* 69 F11
Ray, *U.S.A.* 112 A3
Ray, C., *Canada* 103 C8
Rayadurg, *India* 66 M10
Rayagada, *India* 67 K13
Raychikhinsk, *Russia* 51 E13
Rāyen, *Iran* 71 D8
Rayleigh, *U.K.* 13 F8
Raymond, *Canada* 104 D6
Raymond, *Calif., U.S.A.* 116 H7
Raymond, *N.H., U.S.A.* 111 C13
Raymond, *Wash., U.S.A.* 116 D3
Raymondville, *U.S.A.* 113 M6
Raymore, *Canada* 105 C8
Rayón, *Mexico* 118 B2
Rayong, *Thailand* 64 F3
Rayville, *U.S.A.* 113 J9
Raz, Pte. du, *France* 18 D2
Razan, *Iran* 71 C6
Ražana, *Serbia, Yug.* 40 B3
Ražanj, *Serbia, Yug.* 40 C5
Razdelna, *Bulgaria* 41 C11
Razdel'naya = Rozdilna, *Ukraine* 47 J6
Razdolnoye, *Russia* 54 C5
Razdolnoye, *Ukraine* 47 K7
Razeh, *Iran* 71 C6
Razgrad, *Bulgaria* 41 C10
Razim, Lacul, *Romania* 43 F14
Razlog, *Bulgaria* 40 E7
Razmak, *Pakistan* 68 C3
Ré, Î. de, *France* 20 B2
Reading, *U.K.* 13 F7
Reading, *U.S.A.* 111 F9
Reading □, *U.K.* 13 F7
Realicó, *Argentina* 126 D3
Réalmont, *France* 20 E6
Ream, *Cambodia* 65 G4
Reata, *Mexico* 118 B4
Reay Forest, *U.K.* 14 C4
Rebais, *France* 19 D10
Rebi, *Indonesia* 63 F8
Rebiana, *Libya* 79 D10
Rebun-Tō, *Japan* 54 B10
Recanati, *Italy* 29 E10
Recaș, *Romania* 42 E6
Recco, *Italy* 28 D6
Recherche, Arch. of the, *Australia* 93 F3
Rechna Doab, *Pakistan* 68 D5
Rechytsa, *Belarus* 47 F6
Recife, *Brazil* 125 E12
Recklinghausen, *Germany* 17 C7
Reconquista, *Argentina* 126 B4
Recreo, *Argentina* 126 B2
Recz, *Poland* 45 E2
Red →, *La., U.S.A.* 113 K9
Red →, *N. Dak., U.S.A.* 100 C10
Red Bank, *U.S.A.* 111 F10
Red Bay, *Canada* 103 B8
Red Bluff, *U.S.A.* 114 F2
Red Bluff L., *U.S.A.* 113 K3
Red Cliffs, *Australia* 95 E3
Red Cloud, *U.S.A.* 112 E5
Red Creek, *U.S.A.* 111 C8
Red Deer, *Canada* 104 C6
Red Deer →, *Alta., Canada* 105 C7
Red Deer →, *Man., Canada* 105 C8
Red Deer L., *Canada* 105 C8
Red Hook, *U.S.A.* 111 E11
Red Indian L., *Canada* 103 C8
Red L., *Canada* 105 C10
Red Lake, *Canada* 105 C10
Red Lake Falls, *U.S.A.* 112 B6
Red Lake Road, *Canada* 105 C10
Red Lodge, *U.S.A.* 114 D9
Red Mountain, *U.S.A.* 117 K9
Red Oak, *U.S.A.* 112 E7
Red Rock, *Canada* 102 C2
Red Rock, L., *U.S.A.* 112 E8
Red Rocks Pt., *Australia* 93 F4
Red Sea, *Asia* 74 C2
Red Slate Mt., *U.S.A.* 116 H8
Red Sucker L., *Canada* 102 B1
Red Tower Pass = Turnu Roșu, P., *Romania* 43 E9
Red Wing, *U.S.A.* 112 C8
Reda, *Poland* 44 D5
Redang, *Malaysia* 62 C2
Redange, *Lux.* 17 E5
Redcar, *U.K.* 12 C6
Redcar & Cleveland □, *U.K.* 12 C7
Redcliff, *Canada* 105 C6
Redcliffe, *Australia* 95 D5
Redcliffe, Mt., *Australia* 93 E3
Reddersburg, *S. Africa* 88 D4
Redding, *U.S.A.* 114 F2
Redditch, *U.K.* 13 E6
Redfield, *U.S.A.* 112 C5
Redford, *U.S.A.* 111 B11
Redkino, *Russia* 46 D9
Redlands, *U.S.A.* 117 M9
Redmond, *Oreg., U.S.A.* 114 D3
Redmond, *Wash., U.S.A.* 116 C4
Redon, *France* 18 E4
Redonda, *Antigua* 121 C7
Redondela, *Spain* 34 C2
Redondo, *Portugal* 35 G3
Redondo Beach, *U.S.A.* 117 M8
Redruth, *U.K.* 13 G2
Redvers, *Canada* 105 D8
Redwater, *Canada* 104 C6
Redwood, *U.S.A.* 111 B9
Redwood City, *U.S.A.* 116 H4
Redwood Falls, *U.S.A.* 112 C7
Redwood National Park, *U.S.A.* 114 F1
Ree, L., *Ireland* 15 C3
Reed, L., *Canada* 105 C8
Reed City, *U.S.A.* 108 D3
Reedley, *U.S.A.* 116 J7
Reedsburg, *U.S.A.* 112 D9
Reedsport, *U.S.A.* 114 E1
Reedsville, *U.S.A.* 110 F7
Reefton, *N.Z.* 91 K3
Rees, *Germany* 24 D2
Reese →, *U.S.A.* 114 F5
Refahiye, *Turkey* 73 C8
Reftele, *Sweden* 11 G7
Refugio, *U.S.A.* 113 L6
Rega →, *Poland* 44 D2
Regalbuto, *Italy* 31 E7
Regen, *Germany* 25 G9
Regen →, *Germany* 25 F8
Regensburg, *Germany* 25 F8
Regenstauf, *Germany* 25 F8
Reggâne = Zaouiet Reggâne, *Algeria* 78 C6
Reggello, *Italy* 29 E8
Réggio di Calábria, *Italy* 31 D8
Réggio nell'Emília, *Italy* 28 D7
Reghin, *Romania* 43 D9
Regina, *Canada* 105 C8
Regina Beach, *Canada* 105 C8
Registro, *Brazil* 127 A6
Reguengos de Monsaraz, *Portugal* 35 G3
Rehar →, *India* 69 H10
Rehli, *India* 69 H8
Rehoboth, *Namibia* 88 C2
Rehovot, *Israel* 75 D3
Reichenbach, *Germany* 24 E8
Reid, *Australia* 93 F4
Reidsville, *U.S.A.* 109 G6
Reigate, *U.K.* 13 F7
Reillo, *Spain* 32 F3
Reims, *France* 19 C11
Reina Adelaida, Arch., *Chile* 128 G2
Reinbek, *Germany* 24 B6
Reindeer →, *Canada* 105 B8
Reindeer I., *Canada* 105 C9
Reindeer L., *Canada* 105 B8
Reinga, C., *N.Z.* 91 F4
Reinosa, *Spain* 34 B6
Reitz, *S. Africa* 89 D4
Reivilo, *S. Africa* 88 D3
Rejaf, *Sudan* 81 G3
Rejmyre, *Sweden* 11 F9
Rejowiec Fabryczny, *Poland* 45 G10
Reka →, *Slovenia* 29 C11
Rekovac, *Serbia, Yug.* 40 C5
Reliance, *Canada* 105 A7
Rémalard, *France* 18 D7
Remarkable, Mt., *Australia* 95 E2
Rembang, *Indonesia* 63 G14
Remedios, *Panama* 120 E3
Remeshk, *Iran* 71 E8
Remetea, *Romania* 43 D10
Remich, *Lux.* 17 E6
Remiremont, *France* 19 D13
Remo, *Ethiopia* 81 F5
Remontnoye, *Russia* 49 G6
Remoulins, *France* 21 E8
Remscheid, *Germany* 17 C7
Ren Xian, *China* 56 F8
Rende, *Italy* 31 C9
Rendína, *Greece* 38 B3
Rendsburg, *Germany* 24 A5
Renfrew, *Canada* 102 C4
Renfrewshire □, *U.K.* 14 F4
Rengat, *Indonesia* 62 E2
Rengo, *Chile* 126 C1
Renhua, *China* 59 E9
Renhuai, *China* 58 D6
Reni, *Ukraine* 47 K5
Renk, *Sudan* 81 E3
Renmark, *Australia* 95 E3
Rennell Sd., *Canada* 104 C2
Renner Springs, *Australia* 94 B1
Rennes, *France* 18 D5
Rennie L., *Canada* 105 A7
Reno, *U.S.A.* 116 F7
Reno →, *Italy* 29 D9
Renovo, *U.S.A.* 110 E7
Renqiu, *China* 56 E9
Rens, *Denmark* 11 K3
Renshou, *China* 58 C5
Rensselaer, *Ind., U.S.A.* 108 E2
Rensselaer, *N.Y., U.S.A.* 111 D11
Rentería, *Spain* 32 B3
Renton, *U.S.A.* 116 C4
Réo, *Burkina Faso* 82 C4
Reocín, *Spain* 34 B6
Reotipur, *India* 69 G10
Répcelak, *Hungary* 42 C2
Republic, *Mo., U.S.A.* 113 G8
Republic, *Wash., U.S.A.* 114 B4
Republican →, *U.S.A.* 112 F6
Repulse Bay, *Canada* 101 B11
Requena, *Peru* 124 E4
Requena, *Spain* 33 F3
Réquista, *France* 20 D6
Reşadiye = Datça, *Turkey* 39 E9
Reşadiye, *Turkey* 72 B7
Reşadiye Yarımadası, *Turkey* 39 E9
Resavica, *Serbia, Yug.* 40 B5
Resen, *Macedonia* 40 E5
Reserve, *U.S.A.* 115 K9
Resht = Rasht, *Iran* 71 B6

203

# Selemdzha

# Siniscóla

211

Thrakikón Pélagos


Thrakikón Pélagos, *Greece* 41 F8
Three Forks, *U.S.A.* 114 D8
Three Gorges Dam, *China* 59 B8
Three Hills, *Canada* 104 C6
Three Hummock I., *Australia* 94 G3
Three Points, C., *Ghana* 82 E4
Three Rivers, *Calif., U.S.A.* 116 J8
Three Rivers, *Tex., U.S.A.* 113 L5
Three Sisters, *U.S.A.* 114 D3
Three Springs, *Australia* 93 E2
Throssell, L., *Australia* 93 E3
Throssell Ra., *Australia* 92 D3
Thuan Hoa, *Vietnam* 65 H5
Thubun Lakes, *Canada* 105 A6
Thueyts, *France* 21 D8
Thuin, *Belgium* 17 D4
Thuir, *France* 20 F6
Thule = Qaanaaq, *Greenland* 4 B4
Thun, *Switz.* 25 J3
Thunder B., *U.S.A.* 110 B1
Thunder Bay, *Canada* 102 C2
Thunersee, *Switz.* 25 J3
Thung Song, *Thailand* 65 H2
Thunkar, *Bhutan* 67 F17
Thuong Tra, *Vietnam* 64 D6
Thur →, *Switz.* 25 H5
Thurgau □, *Switz.* 25 H5
Thüringen □, *Germany* 24 D6
Thüringer Wald, *Germany* 24 E6
Thurles, *Ireland* 15 D4
Thurn P., *Austria* 26 D5
Thurrock □, *U.K.* 13 F8
Thursday I., *Australia* 94 A3
Thurso, *Canada* 102 C4
Thurso, *U.K.* 14 C5
Thurso →, *U.K.* 14 C5
Thurston I., *Antarctica* 5 D16
Thury-Harcourt, *France* 18 D6
Thutade L., *Canada* 104 B3
Thy, *Denmark* 11 H2
Thyborøn, *Denmark* 11 H2
Thyolo, *Malawi* 87 F4
Thysville = Mbanza Ngungu, *Dem. Rep. of the Congo* 84 F2
Ti-n-Amzi →, *Niger* 83 B5
Ti-n-Barraouene, O. →, *Africa* 83 B5
Ti-n-Zaouatene, *Algeria* 83 B5
Ti Tree, *Australia* 94 C1
Tiadiaye, *Senegal* 82 C1
Tian Shan, *Asia* 60 B3
Tianchang, *China* 59 A12
Tiandeng, *China* 58 F6
Tiandong, *China* 58 F6
Tian'e, *China* 58 E6
Tianhe, *China* 58 E7
Tianjin, *China* 57 E9
Tiankoura, *Burkina Faso* 82 C4
Tianlin, *China* 58 E6
Tianmen, *China* 59 B9
Tianquan, *China* 58 B4
Tianshui, *China* 56 G3
Tiantai, *China* 59 C13
Tianyang, *China* 58 F6
Tianzhen, *China* 56 D8
Tianzhu, *China* 58 D7
Tianzhuangtai, *China* 57 D12
Tiaret, *Algeria* 78 A6
Tiassalé, *Ivory C.* 82 D4
Tibagi, *Brazil* 127 A5
Tibagi →, *Brazil* 127 A5
Tibati, *Cameroon* 83 D7
Tibe, *Ethiopia* 81 F4
Tiber = Tevere →, *Italy* 29 G9
Tiberias = Teverya, *Israel* 75 C4
Tiberias, L. = Yam Kinneret, *Israel* 75 C4
Tibesti, *Chad* 79 D9
Tibet = Xizang Zizhiqu □, *China* 60 C3
Tibet, Plateau of, *Asia* 52 F12
Tibiao, *Phil.* 61 F5
Tibiri, *Niger* 83 C6
Ţibleş, Vf., *Romania* 43 C9
Ţibleşului, Munţii, *Romania* 43 C9
Tībnī, *Syria* 70 C3
Tibooburra, *Australia* 95 D3
Tibro, *Sweden* 11 F8
Tiburón, I., *Mexico* 118 B2
Ticao I., *Phil.* 61 E5
Tîchît, *Mauritania* 82 B3
Ticho, *Ethiopia* 81 F4
Ticino □, *Switz.* 25 J4
Ticino →, *Italy* 25 K5
Ticleni, *Romania* 43 F8
Ticonderoga, *U.S.A.* 111 C11
Ticul, *Mexico* 119 C7
Tidaholm, *Sweden* 11 F7
Tidan, *Sweden* 11 F8
Tiddim, *Burma* 67 H18
Tidioute, *U.S.A.* 110 E5
Tidjikja, *Mauritania* 82 B2
Tidore, *Indonesia* 63 D7
Tiébissou, *Ivory C.* 82 D3
Tiel, *Neths.* 17 C5
Tiel, *Senegal* 82 C1
Tieling, *China* 57 C12
Tielt, *Belgium* 17 C3
Tien Shan = Tian Shan, *Asia* 60 B3
Tien-tsin = Tianjin, *China* 57 E9
Tien Yen, *Vietnam* 64 B6
T'ienching = Tianjin, *China* 57 E9
Tienen, *Belgium* 17 D4
Tiénigbé, *Ivory C.* 82 D3
Tientsin = Tianjin, *China* 57 E9
Tieri, *Australia* 94 C4
Tierp, *Sweden* 10 D11
Tierra Amarilla, *Chile* 126 B1
Tierra Amarilla, *U.S.A.* 115 H10
Tierra Colorada, *Mexico* 119 D5
Tierra de Barros, *Spain* 35 G4
Tierra de Campos, *Spain* 34 C6
Tierra del Fuego, I. Gr. de, *Argentina* 122 J4
Tiétar →, *Spain* 34 F4
Tieté →, *Brazil* 127 A5
Tiffin, *U.S.A.* 108 E4
Tiflis = Tbilisi, *Georgia* 49 K7
Tifton, *U.S.A.* 109 K4
Tifu, *Indonesia* 63 E7
Tighina, *Moldova* 43 D14
Tigil, *Russia* 51 D16
Tignish, *Canada* 103 C7
Tigray □, *Ethiopia* 81 E4
Tigre →, *Peru* 124 D4
Tigre →, *Venezuela* 124 B6
Tigris = Dijlah, Nahr →, *Asia* 70 D5
Tigveni, *Romania* 43 E9
Tigyaing, *Burma* 67 H20
Tîh, Gebel el, *Egypt* 80 B3
Tijara, *India* 68 F7
Tijuana, *Mexico* 117 N9
Tikal, *Guatemala* 120 C2
Tikamgarh, *India* 69 G8
Tikaré, *Burkina Faso* 83 C4
Tikhoretsk, *Russia* 49 H5
Tikhvin, *Russia* 46 C7
Tiko, *Cameroon* 83 E6
Tikrīt, *Iraq* 70 C4
Tiksi, *Russia* 51 B13
Tilamuta, *Indonesia* 63 D6
Tilburg, *Neths.* 17 C5
Tilbury, *Canada* 102 D3
Tilbury, *U.K.* 13 F8
Tilcara, *Argentina* 126 A2
Tilden, *U.S.A.* 112 D6
Tilemses, *Niger* 83 B5
Tilemsi, Vallée du, *Mali* 83 B5
Tilhar, *India* 69 F8
Tilichiki, *Russia* 51 C17
Tílissos, *Greece* 36 D7
Till →, *U.K.* 12 B5
Tillabéri, *Niger* 83 C5
Tillamook, *U.S.A.* 114 D2
Tillberga, *Sweden* 10 E10
Tillia, *Niger* 83 B5
Tillsonburg, *Canada* 102 D3
Tillyeria □, *Cyprus* 36 D11
Tilogne, *Senegal* 82 B2
Tílos, *Greece* 39 E9
Tilpa, *Australia* 95 E3
Tilsit = Sovetsk, *Russia* 9 J19
Tilt →, *U.K.* 14 E5
Tilton, *U.S.A.* 111 C13
Tiltonsville, *U.S.A.* 110 F4
Tim, *Denmark* 11 H2
Timagami, L., *Canada* 102 C3
Timaru, *N.Z.* 91 L3
Timashevo, *Russia* 48 D10
Timashevsk, *Russia* 49 H4
Timau, *Kenya* 86 B4
Timbákion, *Greece* 36 D6
Timbedgha, *Mauritania* 82 B3
Timber Creek, *Australia* 92 C5
Timber Lake, *U.S.A.* 112 C4
Timber Mt., *U.S.A.* 116 H10
Timbo, *Guinea* 82 C2
Timbo, *Liberia* 82 D3
Timbuktu = Tombouctou, *Mali* 82 B4
Timeiaouine, *Algeria* 83 A5
Timétrine, Mts., *Mali* 83 B4
Timfi Óros, *Greece* 38 B2
Timfristós, Óros, *Greece* 38 C3
Timi, *Cyprus* 36 E11
Tîmia, *Niger* 83 B6
Timimoun, *Algeria* 78 C6
Timirist, Râs, *Mauritania* 82 B1
Timiş = Tamis →, *Serbia, Yug.* 42 E5
Timiş □, *Romania* 42 E6
Timişoara, *Romania* 42 E6
Timmersdala, *Sweden* 11 F7
Timmins, *Canada* 102 C3
Timok →, *Serbia, Yug.* 40 B6
Timor, *Indonesia* 63 F7
Timor Sea, *Ind. Oc.* 92 B4
Timor Timur = East Timor ■, *Asia* 63 F7
Timrå, *Sweden* 10 B11
Tin Can Bay, *Australia* 95 D5
Tin Ethisane, *Mali* 83 B4
Tin Gornai, *Mali* 83 B4
Tin Mt., *U.S.A.* 116 J9
Tina →, *S. Africa* 89 E4
Tîna, Khalîg el, *Egypt* 80 A3
Tinaca Pt., *Phil.* 61 J6
Tinajo, *Canary Is.* 37 E6
Tinca, *Romania* 42 D6
Tindal, *Australia* 92 B5
Tindouf, *Algeria* 78 C4
Tinée →, *France* 21 E11
Tineo, *Spain* 34 B4
Ting Jiang →, *China* 59 E11
Tinggi, Pulau, *Malaysia* 65 L5
Tinglev, *Denmark* 11 K3
Tingo Maria, *Peru* 124 E3
Tingrela, *Ivory C.* 82 C3
Tingsryd, *Sweden* 11 H9
Tingstäde, *Sweden* 11 G12
Tinh Bien, *Vietnam* 65 G5
Tinnevelly = Tirunelveli, *India* 66 Q10
Tinogasta, *Argentina* 126 B2
Tínos, *Greece* 39 D7
Tiñoso, C., *Spain* 33 H3
Tinpahar, *India* 69 G12
Tintina, *Argentina* 126 B3
Tintinara, *Australia* 95 F3
Tintioulé, *Guinea* 82 C3
Tinto →, *Spain* 35 H4
Tioga, *N. Dak., U.S.A.* 112 A3
Tioga, *Pa., U.S.A.* 110 E7
Tioman, Pulau, *Malaysia* 65 L5
Tione di Trento, *Italy* 28 B7
Tionesta, *U.S.A.* 110 E5
Tior, *Sudan* 81 F3
Tipongpani, *India* 67 F19
Tipperary, *Ireland* 15 D3
Tipperary □, *Ireland* 15 D4
Tipton, *Calif., U.S.A.* 116 J7
Tipton, *Iowa, U.S.A.* 112 E9
Tipton Mt., *U.S.A.* 117 K12
Tiptonville, *U.S.A.* 113 G10
Tīrān, *Iran* 71 C6
Tīrān, *Si. Arabia* 80 B3
Tiranë, *Albania* 40 E3
Tirano, *Italy* 28 B7
Tiraspol, *Moldova* 43 D14
Tirdout, *Mali* 83 B4
Tire, *Turkey* 39 C9
Tirebolu, *Turkey* 73 B8
Tiree, *U.K.* 14 E2
Tiree, Passage of, *U.K.* 14 E2
Tîrgovişte = Târgovişte, *Romania* 43 F10
Tîrgu-Jiu = Târgu-Jiu, *Romania* 43 E8
Tîrgu Mureş = Târgu Mureş, *Romania* 43 D9
Tirich Mir, *Pakistan* 66 A7
Tiriolo, *Italy* 31 D9
Tiriro, *Guinea* 82 C3
Tírnavos, *Greece* 38 B4
Tirodi, *India* 66 J11
Tirol □, *Austria* 26 D3
Tirschenreuth, *Germany* 25 F8
Tirso →, *Italy* 30 C1
Tirstrup, *Denmark* 11 H4
Tiruchchirappalli, *India* 66 P11
Tirunelveli, *India* 66 Q10
Tirupati, *India* 66 N11
Tiruppur, *India* 66 P10
Tiruvannamalai, *India* 66 N11
Tisa, *India* 68 C7
Tisa →, *Serbia, Yug.* 42 E5
Tisdale, *Canada* 105 C8
Tishomingo, *U.S.A.* 113 H6
Tisjön, *Sweden* 10 D7
Tisnaren, *Sweden* 11 F9
Tišnov, *Czech Rep.* 27 B9
Tisovec, *Slovak Rep.* 27 C12
Tisza = Tisa →, *Serbia, Yug.* 42 E5
Tiszaföldvár, *Hungary* 42 D5
Tiszafüred, *Hungary* 42 C5
Tiszalök, *Hungary* 42 B6
Tiszavasvári, *Hungary* 42 C6
Tit-Ary, *Russia* 51 B13
Titaguas, *Spain* 32 F3
Titao, *Burkina Faso* 83 C4
Titel, *Serbia, Yug.* 42 E5
Tithwal, *Pakistan* 69 B5
Titicaca, L., *S. Amer.* 122 E4
Titisee, *Germany* 25 H4
Titiwa, *Nigeria* 83 C7
Tito, *Italy* 31 B8
Titograd = Podgorica, *Montenegro, Yug.* 40 D3
Titova Korenica, *Croatia* 29 D12
Titu, *Romania* 43 F10
Titule, *Dem. Rep. of the Congo* 86 B2
Titusville, *Fla., U.S.A.* 109 L5
Titusville, *Pa., U.S.A.* 110 E5
Tivaouane, *Senegal* 82 C1
Tivat, *Montenegro, Yug.* 40 D2
Tiverton, *U.K.* 13 G4
Tívoli, *Italy* 29 G9
Tiyo, *Eritrea* 81 E5
Tizi-Ouzou, *Algeria* 78 A6
Tizimín, *Mexico* 119 C7
Tjæreborg, *Denmark* 11 J2
Tjällmo, *Sweden* 11 F9
Tjeggelvas, *Sweden* 8 C17
Tjirebon = Cirebon, *Indonesia* 62 F3
Tjörn, *Sweden* 11 F5
Tkibuli = Tqibuli, *Georgia* 49 J6
Tkvarcheli = Tqvarcheli, *Georgia* 49 J5
Tlacotalpan, *Mexico* 119 D5
Tlahualilo, *Mexico* 118 B4
Tlaquepaque, *Mexico* 118 C4
Tlaxcala, *Mexico* 119 D5
Tlaxcala □, *Mexico* 119 D5
Tlaxiaco, *Mexico* 119 D5
Tlemcen, *Algeria* 78 B5
Tłuszcz, *Poland* 45 F8
Tlyarata, *Russia* 49 J8
To Bong, *Vietnam* 64 F7
Toad →, *Canada* 104 B4
Toad River, *Canada* 104 B3
Toamasina, *Madag.* 89 B8
Toamasina □, *Madag.* 89 B8
Toay, *Argentina* 126 D3
Toba, *China* 58 B1
Toba, *Japan* 55 G8
Toba, Danau, *Indonesia* 62 D1
Toba Kakar, *Pakistan* 68 D3
Toba Tek Singh, *Pakistan* 68 D5
Tobago, *Trin. & Tob.* 121 D7
Tobarra, *Spain* 33 G3
Tobelo, *Indonesia* 63 D7
Tobermory, *Canada* 102 C3
Tobermory, *U.K.* 14 E2
Tobi, *Pac. Oc.* 63 D8
Tobin, *U.S.A.* 116 F5
Tobin, L., *Australia* 92 D4
Tobin L., *Canada* 105 C8
Toblach = Dobbiaco, *Italy* 29 B9
Toboali, *Indonesia* 62 E3
Tobol →, *Russia* 50 D7
Toboli, *Indonesia* 63 E6
Tobolsk, *Russia* 50 D7
Tobor, *Senegal* 82 C1
Tobruk = Tubruq, *Libya* 79 B10
Tobyhanna, *U.S.A.* 111 E9
Tobyl = Tobol →, *Russia* 50 D7
Tocantinópolis, *Brazil* 125 E9
Tocantins □, *Brazil* 125 F9
Tocantins →, *Brazil* 122 D6
Toccoa, *U.S.A.* 109 H4
Toce →, *Italy* 28 C5
Tochi →, *Pakistan* 68 C4
Tochigi, *Japan* 55 F9
Tochigi □, *Japan* 55 F9
Tocina, *Spain* 35 H5
Töcksfors, *Sweden* 10 E5
Toconao, *Chile* 126 A2
Tocopilla, *Chile* 126 A1
Tocumwal, *Australia* 95 F4
Tocuyo →, *Venezuela* 124 A5
Todd →, *Australia* 94 C2
Todeli, *Indonesia* 63 E6
Todenyang, *Kenya* 86 B4
Todgarh, *India* 68 G5
Todi, *Italy* 29 F9
Todos os Santos, B. de, *Brazil* 125 F11
Todos Santos, *Mexico* 118 C2
Todtnau, *Germany* 25 H3
Toe Hd., *U.K.* 14 D1
Toecé, *Burkina Faso* 83 C4
Tofield, *Canada* 104 C6
Tofino, *Canada* 104 D3
Tofua, *Tonga* 91 D11
Tōgane, *Japan* 55 G10
Togba, *Mauritania* 82 B2
Togian, Kepulauan, *Indonesia* 63 E6
Togliatti, *Russia* 48 D9
Togo ■, *W. Afr.* 83 D5
Togtoh, *China* 56 D6
Tohma →, *Turkey* 72 C7
Tōhoku □, *Japan* 54 E10
Töhöm, *Mongolia* 56 B5
Toinya, *Sudan* 81 F2
Toiyabe Range, *U.S.A.* 114 G5
Tojikiston = Tajikistan ■, *Asia* 50 F8
Tojo, *Indonesia* 63 E6
Tōjō, *Japan* 55 G6
Tok, *U.S.A.* 100 B5
Tok-do, *Japan* 55 F5
Tokachi-Dake, *Japan* 54 C11
Tokachi-Gawa →, *Japan* 54 C11
Tokaj, *Hungary* 42 B6
Tokala, *Indonesia* 63 E6
Tōkamachi, *Japan* 55 F9
Tokanui, *N.Z.* 91 M2
Tokar, *Sudan* 80 D4
Tokara-Rettō, *Japan* 55 K4
Tokarahi, *N.Z.* 91 L3
Tokashiki-Shima, *Japan* 55 L3
Tokat, *Turkey* 72 B7
Tŏkch'ŏn, *N. Korea* 57 E14
Tokeland, *U.S.A.* 116 D3
Tokelau Is., *Pac. Oc.* 96 H10
Tokmak, *Kyrgyzstan* 50 E8
Tokmak, *Ukraine* 47 J8
Toko Ra., *Australia* 94 C2
Tokoro-Gawa →, *Japan* 54 B12
Tokuno-Shima, *Japan* 55 L4
Tokushima, *Japan* 55 G7
Tokushima □, *Japan* 55 H7
Tokuyama, *Japan* 55 G5
Tōkyō, *Japan* 55 G9
Tolaga Bay, *N.Z.* 91 H7
Tolbukhin = Dobrich, *Bulgaria* 41 C11
Toledo, *Brazil* 127 A5
Toledo, *Spain* 34 F6
Toledo, *Ohio, U.S.A.* 108 E4
Toledo, *Oreg., U.S.A.* 114 D2
Toledo, *Wash., U.S.A.* 114 C2
Toledo, Montes de, *Spain* 35 F6
Toledo Bend Reservoir, *U.S.A.* 113 K8
Tolentino, *Italy* 29 E10
Tolfa, *Italy* 29 F8
Tolga, *Australia* 94 B4
Toliara, *Madag.* 89 C7
Toliara □, *Madag.* 89 C8
Tolima, *Colombia* 124 C3
Tolitoli, *Indonesia* 63 D6
Tolkmicko, *Poland* 44 D6
Tollarp, *Sweden* 11 J7
Tollensesee, *Germany* 24 B9
Tollhouse, *U.S.A.* 116 H7
Tolmachevo, *Russia* 46 C5
Tolmezzo, *Italy* 29 B10
Tolmin, *Slovenia* 29 B10
Tolna, *Hungary* 42 D3
Tolna □, *Hungary* 42 D3
Tolo, Teluk, *Indonesia* 63 E6
Tolochin = Talachyn, *Belarus* 46 E5
Tolosa, *Spain* 32 B2
Tolox, *Spain* 35 J6
Toluca, *Mexico* 119 D5
Tom Burke, *S. Africa* 89 C4
Tom Price, *Australia* 92 D2
Toma, *Burkina Faso* 82 C4
Tomah, *U.S.A.* 112 D9
Tomahawk, *U.S.A.* 112 C10
Tomai, *Moldova* 43 D13
Tomakomai, *Japan* 54 C10
Tomales, *U.S.A.* 116 G4
Tomales B., *U.S.A.* 116 G3
Tomar, *Portugal* 35 F2
Tómaros, Óros, *Greece* 38 B2
Tomarza, *Turkey* 72 C6
Tomaszów Lubelski, *Poland* 45 H10
Tomaszów Mazowiecki, *Poland* 45 G7
Tomatlán, *Mexico* 118 D3
Tombadonkéa, *Guinea* 82 C2
Tombador, Serra do, *Brazil* 124 F7
Tombe, *Sudan* 81 F3
Tombigbee →, *U.S.A.* 109 K2
Tombouctou, *Mali* 82 B4
Tombstone, *U.S.A.* 115 L8
Tombua, *Angola* 88 B1
Tomé, *Chile* 126 D1
Tomelilla, *Sweden* 11 J7
Tomelloso, *Spain* 35 F7
Tomini, *Indonesia* 63 D6
Tomini, Teluk, *Indonesia* 63 E6
Tominian, *Mali* 82 C4
Tomiño, *Spain* 34 D2
Tomintoul, *U.K.* 14 D5
Tomislavgrad, *Bos.-H.* 42 G2
Tomkinson Ranges, *Australia* 93 E4
Tommot, *Russia* 51 D13
Tomnop Ta Suos, *Cambodia* 65 G5
Tomo →, *Colombia* 124 B5
Toms Place, *U.S.A.* 116 H8
Toms River, *U.S.A.* 111 G10
Tomsk, *Russia* 50 D9
Tomtabacken, *Sweden* 11 G8
Tona, *Spain* 32 D7
Tonalá, *Mexico* 119 D6
Tonale, Passo del, *Italy* 28 B7
Tonantins, *Brazil* 124 D5
Tonasket, *U.S.A.* 114 B4
Tonawanda, *U.S.A.* 110 D6
Tonbridge, *U.K.* 13 F8
Tondano, *Indonesia* 63 D6
Tondela, *Portugal* 34 E2
Tønder, *Denmark* 11 K2
Tondi Kiwindi, *Niger* 83 C5
Tondibi, *Mali* 83 B4
Tondoro, *Namibia* 88 B2
Tone →, *Australia* 93 F2
Tone-Gawa →, *Japan* 55 F9
Tonekābon, *Iran* 71 B6
Tong Xian, *China* 56 E9
Tongā, *Sudan* 81 F3
Tonga ■, *Pac. Oc.* 91 D11
Tonga Trench, *Pac. Oc.* 96 J10
Tongaat, *S. Africa* 89 D5
Tong'an, *China* 59 E12
Tongareva, *Cook Is.* 97 H12
Tongatapu Group, *Tonga* 91 E12
Tongbai, *China* 59 A9
Tongcheng, *Anhui, China* 59 B11
Tongcheng, *Hubei, China* 59 C9
Tongchŏn-ni, *N. Korea* 57 E14
Tongchuan, *China* 56 G5
Tongdao, *China* 58 D7
Tongeren, *Belgium* 17 D5
Tonggu, *China* 59 C10
Tongguan, *China* 56 G6
Tonghai, *China* 58 E4
Tonghua, *China* 57 D13
Tongjiang, *China* 58 B6
Tongjosŏn Man, *N. Korea* 57 E15
Tongking, G. of = Tonkin, G. of, *Asia* 60 E5
Tongliang, *China* 58 C6
Tongliao, *China* 57 C12
Tongling, *China* 59 B11
Tonglu, *China* 59 C12
Tongnae, *S. Korea* 57 G15
Tongnan = Anyue, *China* 58 B5
Tongobory, *Madag.* 89 C7
Tongoy, *Chile* 126 C1
Tongren, *China* 58 D7
Tongres = Tongeren, *Belgium* 17 D5
Tongsa Dzong, *Bhutan* 67 F17
Tongue, *U.K.* 14 C4
Tongue →, *U.S.A.* 112 B2
Tongwei, *China* 56 G3
Tongxiang, *China* 59 B13
Tongxin, *China* 56 F3
Tongyang, *N. Korea* 57 E14
Tongyu, *China* 57 B12
Tongzi, *China* 58 C6
Tonj, *Sudan* 81 F2
Tonj →, *Sudan* 81 F2
Tonk, *India* 68 F6
Tonkawa, *U.S.A.* 113 G6
Tonkin = Bac Phan, *Vietnam* 64 B5
Tonkin, G. of, *Asia* 60 E5
Tonle Sap, *Cambodia* 64 F4
Tonnay-Charente, *France* 20 C3
Tonneins, *France* 20 D4
Tonnerre, *France* 19 E10
Tönning, *Germany* 24 A4
Tono, *Japan* 54 E10
Tonopah, *U.S.A.* 115 G5
Tonosí, *Panama* 120 E3
Tons →, *Haryana, India* 68 D7
Tons →, *Ut. P., India* 69 F10
Tønsberg, *Norway* 9 G14
Tonya, *Turkey* 73 B8
Toobanna, *Australia* 94 B4
Toodyay, *Australia* 93 F2
Tooele, *U.S.A.* 114 F7
Toompine, *Australia* 95 D3
Toora, *Australia* 95 F4
Toora-Khem, *Russia* 51 D10
Toowoomba, *Australia* 95 D5
Top Springs, *Australia* 92 C5
Topalu, *Romania* 43 F13
Topaz, *U.S.A.* 116 G7
Topeka, *U.S.A.* 112 F7
Topl'a →, *Slovak Rep.* 27 C14
Topley, *Canada* 104 C3
Toplica →, *Serbia, Yug.* 40 C5

215

## U

**Vangaindrano**


Umka, *Serbia, Yug.* 40 B4
Umkomaas, *S. Africa* 89 E5
Umlazi, *S. Africa* 85 L6
Umm ad Daraj, J., *Jordan* 75 C4
Umm al Qaywayn, *U.A.E.* 71 E7
Umm al Qittayn, *Jordan* 75 C5
Umm Arda, *Sudan* 81 D3
Umm Bāb, *Qatar* 71 E6
Umm Badr, *Sudan* 81 E2
Umm Baiyud, *Sudan* 81 E3
Umm Bel, *Sudan* 81 E2
Umm Birkah, *Si. Arabia* 80 B4
Umm Boim, *Sudan* 81 E2
Umm Dam, *Sudan* 81 E3
Umm Debi, *Sudan* 81 E3
Umm Dubban, *Sudan* 81 D3
Umm el Fahm, *Israel* 75 C4
Umm Gafala, *Sudan* 81 E2
Umm Gimala, *Sudan* 81 E2
Umm Inderaba, *Sudan* 80 D3
Umm Keddada, *Sudan* 81 E2
Umm Koweika, *Sudan* 81 E3
Umm Lajj, *Si. Arabia* 70 E3
Umm Merwa, *Sudan* 80 D3
Umm Qantur, *Sudan* 81 E3
Umm Qurein, *Sudan* 81 F2
Umm Ruwaba, *Sudan* 81 E3
Umm Saiyala, *Sudan* 81 E3
Umm Shanqa, *Sudan* 81 E2
Umm Shutur, *Sudan* 81 F3
Umm Sidr, *Sudan* 81 E2
Umm Zehetir, *Egypt* 80 J8
Umnak I., *U.S.A.* 100 C3
Umniati →, *Zimbabwe* 87 F2
Umpqua →, *U.S.A.* 114 E1
Umreth, *India* 68 H5
Umtata, *S. Africa* 89 E4
Umuahia, *Nigeria* 83 D6
Umuarama, *Brazil* 127 A5
Umurbey, *Turkey* 41 F10
Umvukwe Ra., *Zimbabwe* 87 F3
Umzimvubu, *S. Africa* 89 E4
Umzingwane →, *Zimbabwe* 87 G2
Umzinto, *S. Africa* 89 E5
Una, *India* 68 J4
Una →, *Bos.-H.* 29 D13
Unac →, *Bos.-H.* 29 D13
Unadilla, *U.S.A.* 111 D9
Unalakleet, *U.S.A.* 100 B3
Unalaska, *U.S.A.* 100 C3
Unalaska I., *U.S.A.* 100 C3
'Unayzah, *Si. Arabia* 70 E4
'Unāzah, J., *Asia* 70 C3
Uncastillo, *Spain* 32 C3
Uncía, *Bolivia* 124 G5
Uncompahgre Peak, *U.S.A.* 115 G10
Uncompahgre Plateau, *U.S.A.* 115 G9
Unden, *Sweden* 11 F8
Underbool, *Australia* 95 F3
Undersaker, *Sweden* 10 A7
Unecha, *Russia* 47 F7
Ungarie, *Australia* 95 E4
Ungarra, *Australia* 95 E2
Ungava, Pén. d', *Canada* 101 C12
Ungava B., *Canada* 101 C13
Ungeny = Ungheni, *Moldova* 43 C12
Unggi, *N. Korea* 57 C16
Ungheni, *Moldova* 43 C12
Unguala →, *Ethiopia* 81 F5
Ungwatiri, *Sudan* 81 D4
Uni, *Russia* 48 B10
União da Vitória, *Brazil* 127 B5
Uničov, *Czech Rep.* 27 B10
Uniejów, *Poland* 45 G5
Unije, *Croatia* 29 D11
Unimak I., *U.S.A.* 100 C3
Union, *Miss., U.S.A.* 113 J10
Union, *Mo., U.S.A.* 112 F9
Union, *S.C., U.S.A.* 109 H5
Union City, *Calif., U.S.A.* 116 H4
Union City, *N.J., U.S.A.* 111 F10
Union City, *Pa., U.S.A.* 110 E5
Union City, *Tenn., U.S.A.* 113 G10
Union Gap, *U.S.A.* 114 C3
Union Springs, *U.S.A.* 109 J3
Uniondale, *S. Africa* 88 E3
Uniontown, *U.S.A.* 108 F6
Unionville, *U.S.A.* 112 E8
Unirea, *Romania* 43 F12
United Arab Emirates ■, *Asia* 71 F7
United Kingdom ■, *Europe* 7 E5
United States of America ■, *N. Amer.* 106 C7
Unity, *Canada* 105 C7
Universales, Mtes., *Spain* 32 E3
University Park, *U.S.A.* 115 K10
Unjha, *India* 68 H5
Unna, *Germany* 24 D3
Unnao, *India* 69 F9
Uno, Ilha, *Guinea-Biss.* 82 C1
Unst, *U.K.* 14 A8
Unstrut →, *Germany* 24 D7
Unterfranken □, *Germany* 25 F5
Unterschleissheim, *Germany* 25 G7
Unuk →, *Canada* 104 B2
Ünye, *Turkey* 72 B7
Unzha, *Russia* 48 A7
Unzha →, *Russia* 48 B6
Uozu, *Japan* 55 F8
Upata, *Venezuela* 124 B6
Upemba, L., *Dem. Rep. of the Congo* 87 D2
Upernavik, *Greenland* 4 B5
Upington, *S. Africa* 88 D3
Upleta, *India* 68 J4
Upolu, *Samoa* 91 A13
Upper □, *Ghana* 83 C4
Upper Alkali L., *U.S.A.* 114 F3
Upper Arrow L., *Canada* 104 C5
Upper Austria = Oberösterreich □, *Austria* 26 C7
Upper Foster L., *Canada* 105 B7
Upper Hutt, *N.Z.* 91 J5
Upper Klamath L., *U.S.A.* 114 E3
Upper Lake, *U.S.A.* 116 F4
Upper Musquodoboit, *Canada* 103 C7
Upper Red L., *U.S.A.* 112 A7
Upper Sandusky, *U.S.A.* 108 E4
Upper Volta = Burkina Faso ■, *Africa* 82 C4
Upphärad, *Sweden* 11 F6
Uppland, *Sweden* 10 E11
Upplands-Väsby, *Sweden* 10 E11
Uppsala, *Sweden* 10 E11
Uppsala län □, *Sweden* 10 D11
Upshi, *India* 69 C7
Upstart, C., *Australia* 94 B4
Upton, *U.S.A.* 112 C2
Ur, *Iraq* 70 D5
Urad Qianqi, *China* 56 D5
Urakawa, *Japan* 54 C11
Ural = Zhayyq →, *Kazakstan* 50 E6
Ural, *Australia* 95 E4
Ural Mts. = Uralskie Gory, *Eurasia* 50 D6
Uralla, *Australia* 95 E5
Uralsk = Oral, *Kazakstan* 48 E10
Uralskie Gory, *Eurasia* 50 D6
Urambo, *Tanzania* 86 D3
Urandangi, *Australia* 94 C2
Uranium City, *Canada* 105 B7
Uraricoera →, *Brazil* 124 C6
Urawa, *Japan* 55 G9
Uray, *Russia* 50 C7
'Uray'irah, *Si. Arabia* 71 E6
Urbana, *Ill., U.S.A.* 108 E1
Urbana, *Ohio, U.S.A.* 108 E4
Urbánia, *Italy* 29 E9
Urbel →, *Spain* 34 C7
Urbino, *Italy* 29 E9
Urbión, Picos de, *Spain* 32 C2
Urcos, *Peru* 124 F4
Urdinarrain, *Argentina* 126 C4
Urdos, *France* 20 F3
Urdzhar, *Kazakstan* 50 E9
Ure →, *U.K.* 12 C6
Uren, *Russia* 48 B7
Ures, *Mexico* 118 B2
Urfa = Sanliurfa, *Turkey* 70 B3
Urganch, *Uzbekistan* 50 E7
Urgench = Urganch, *Uzbekistan* 50 E7
Ürgüp, *Turkey* 70 B2
Uri, *India* 69 B6
Uri □, *Switz.* 25 J4
Uribia, *Colombia* 124 A4
Uricani, *Romania* 42 E8
Uriondo, *Bolivia* 126 A3
Urique, *Mexico* 118 B3
Urique →, *Mexico* 118 B3
Urk, *Neths.* 17 B5
Urla, *Turkey* 39 C8
Urlaţi, *Romania* 43 F11
Urmia = Orūmīyeh, *Iran* 70 B5
Urmia, L. = Orūmīyeh, Daryācheh-ye, *Iran* 70 B5
Uroševac, *Kosovo, Yug.* 40 D5
Urshult, *Sweden* 11 H8
Uruaçu, *Brazil* 125 F9
Uruapan, *Mexico* 118 D4
Urubamba →, *Peru* 124 F4
Uruçara, *Brazil* 124 D7
Uruçuí, *Brazil* 125 E10
Uruguai →, *Brazil* 127 B5
Uruguaiana, *Brazil* 126 B4
Uruguay ■, *S. Amer.* 126 C4
Uruguay →, *S. Amer.* 126 C4
Urumchi = Ürümqi, *China* 50 E9
Ürümqi, *China* 50 E9
Urup →, *Russia* 49 H5
Urup, Ostrov, *Russia* 51 E16
Uryupinsk, *Russia* 48 E5
Urzhum, *Russia* 48 B9
Urziceni, *Romania* 43 F11
Usa →, *Russia* 50 C6
Uşak, *Turkey* 39 C11
Uşak □, *Turkey* 39 C11
Usakos, *Namibia* 88 C2
Ušće, *Serbia, Yug.* 40 C4
Usedom, *Germany* 24 B10
Useless Loop, *Australia* 93 E1
'Usfān, *Si. Arabia* 80 C4
Ush-Tobe, *Kazakstan* 50 E8
Ushakova, Ostrov, *Russia* 4 A12
Ushant = Ouessant, Î. d', *France* 18 D1
Ushashi, *Tanzania* 86 C3
Ushat, *Sudan* 81 F2
'Ushayrah, *Si. Arabia* 80 C5
Ushibuka, *Japan* 55 H5
Ushuaia, *Argentina* 128 G3
Ushumun, *Russia* 51 D13
Usk, *Canada* 104 C3
Usk →, *U.K.* 13 F5
Uska, *India* 69 F10
Üsküdar, *Turkey* 41 F13
Uslar, *Germany* 24 D5
Usman, *Russia* 47 F10
Usoke, *Tanzania* 86 D3
Usolye Sibirskoye, *Russia* 51 D11
Usoro, *Nigeria* 83 D6
Uspallata, P. de, *Argentina* 126 C2
Uspenskiy, *Kazakstan* 50 E8
Ussel, *France* 20 C6
Usson-du-Poitou, *France* 20 B4
Ussuri →, *Asia* 54 A7
Ussuriysk, *Russia* 51 E14
Ussurka, *Russia* 54 B6
Ust-Aldan = Batamay, *Russia* 51 C13
Ust-Amginskoye = Khandyga, *Russia* 51 C14
Ust-Bolsheretsk, *Russia* 51 D16
Ust-Buzulukskaya, *Russia* 48 E6
Ust-Chaun, *Russia* 51 C18
Ust-Donetskiy, *Russia* 49 G5
Ust-Ilimpeya = Yukta, *Russia* 51 C11
Ust-Ilimsk, *Russia* 51 D11
Ust-Ishim, *Russia* 50 D8
Ust-Kamchatsk, *Russia* 51 D17
Ust-Kamenogorsk = Öskemen, *Kazakstan* 50 E9
Ust-Khayryuzovo, *Russia* 51 D16
Ust-Kut, *Russia* 51 D11
Ust-Kuyga, *Russia* 51 B14
Ust-Labinsk, *Russia* 49 H4
Ust-Luga, *Russia* 46 C5
Ust-Maya, *Russia* 51 C14
Ust-Mil, *Russia* 51 D14
Ust-Nera, *Russia* 51 C15
Ust-Nyukzha, *Russia* 51 D13
Ust-Olenek, *Russia* 51 B12
Ust-Omchug, *Russia* 51 C15
Ust-Port, *Russia* 50 C9
Ust-Tsilma, *Russia* 50 C6
Ust Urt = Ustyurt Plateau, *Asia* 50 E6
Ustaritz, *France* 20 E2
Ustecký □, *Czech Rep.* 26 A7
Uster, *Switz.* 25 H4
Ústí nad Labem, *Czech Rep.* 26 A7
Ústí nad Orlicí, *Czech Rep.* 27 B9
Ústica, *Italy* 30 D6
Ustinov = Izhevsk, *Russia* 50 D6
Ustka, *Poland* 44 D3
Ustroń, *Poland* 45 J5
Ustrzyki Dolne, *Poland* 45 J9
Ustyurt Plateau, *Asia* 50 E6
Ustyuzhna, *Russia* 46 C9
Usu, *China* 60 B3
Usuki, *Japan* 55 H5
Usulután, *El Salv.* 120 D2
Usumacinta →, *Mexico* 119 D6
Usumbura = Bujumbura, *Burundi* 86 C2
Usure, *Tanzania* 86 C3
Usutuo →, *Mozam.* 89 D5
Uta, *Indonesia* 63 E9
Utah □, *U.S.A.* 114 G8
Utah L., *U.S.A.* 114 F8
Utansjö, *Sweden* 10 B11
Utarni, *India* 68 F4
Utatlan, *Guatemala* 120 C1
Ute Creek →, *U.S.A.* 113 H3
Utebo, *Spain* 32 D3
Utena, *Lithuania* 9 J21
Utete, *Tanzania* 86 D4
Uthai Thani, *Thailand* 64 E3
Uthal, *Pakistan* 68 G2
Utiariti, *Brazil* 124 F7
Utica, *N.Y., U.S.A.* 111 C9
Utica, *Ohio, U.S.A.* 110 F2
Utiel, *Spain* 33 F3
Utikuma L., *Canada* 104 B5
Utö, *Sweden* 10 F12
Utopia, *Australia* 94 C1
Utraula, *India* 69 F10
Utrecht, *Neths.* 17 B5
Utrecht, *S. Africa* 89 D5
Utrecht □, *Neths.* 17 B5
Utrera, *Spain* 35 H5
Utsjoki, *Finland* 8 B22
Utsunomiya, *Japan* 55 F9
Uttar Pradesh □, *India* 69 F9
Uttaradit, *Thailand* 64 D3
Uttaranchal □, *India* 69 D8
Uttoxeter, *U.K.* 12 E6
Uummannarsuaq = Nunap Isua, *Greenland* 101 C15
Uusikaarlepyy, *Finland* 8 E20
Uusikaupunki, *Finland* 9 F19
Uva, *Russia* 48 B11
Uvac →, *Serbia, Yug.* 40 C3
Uvalde, *U.S.A.* 113 L5
Uvarovo, *Russia* 48 E6
Uvat, *Russia* 50 D7
Uvinza, *Tanzania* 86 D3
Uvira, *Dem. Rep. of the Congo* 86 C2
Uvs Nuur, *Mongolia* 60 A4
'Uwairidh, Ḥarrat al, *Si. Arabia* 70 E3
Uwajima, *Japan* 55 H6
Uweinat, Jebel, *Sudan* 80 C1
Uxbridge, *Canada* 110 B5
Uxin Qi, *China* 56 E5
Uxmal, *Mexico* 119 C7
Üydzin, *Mongolia* 56 B4
Uyo, *Nigeria* 83 D6
Üyüklü Tepe, *Turkey* 39 D9
Uyûn Mûsa, *Egypt* 75 F1
Uyuni, *Bolivia* 124 H5
Uzbekistan ■, *Asia* 50 E7
Uzen, Bolshoi →, *Kazakstan* 49 F9
Uzen, Mal →, *Kazakstan* 49 F9
Uzerche, *France* 20 C5
Uzès, *France* 21 D8
Uzh →, *Ukraine* 47 G6
Uzhgorod = Uzhhorod, *Ukraine* 47 H2
Uzhhorod, *Ukraine* 47 H2
Užice, *Serbia, Yug.* 40 C3
Uzlovaya, *Russia* 46 F10
Üzümlü, *Turkey* 39 E11
Uzunköprü, *Turkey* 41 E10
Uzunkuyu, *Turkey* 39 C8


# V


Vaal →, *S. Africa* 88 D3
Vaal Dam, *S. Africa* 89 D4
Vaalwater, *S. Africa* 89 C4
Vaasa, *Finland* 8 E19
Vabre, *France* 20 E6
Vác, *Hungary* 42 C4
Vacaria, *Brazil* 127 B5
Vacaville, *U.S.A.* 116 G5
Vaccarès, Étang de, *France* 21 E8
Vach = Vakh →, *Russia* 50 C8
Vache, Î. à, *Haiti* 121 C5
Väckelsång, *Sweden* 11 H8
Väddö, *Sweden* 10 D12
Väderstad, *Sweden* 11 F8
Vadnagar, *India* 68 H5
Vado Lígure, *Italy* 28 D5
Vadodara, *India* 68 H5
Vadsø, *Norway* 8 A23
Vadstena, *Sweden* 11 F8
Vaduz, *Liech.* 25 H5
Værøy, *Norway* 8 C15
Vágar, *Færoe Is.* 8 E9
Vaggeryd, *Sweden* 11 G8
Vagney, *France* 19 D13
Vagnhärad, *Sweden* 11 F11
Vagos, *Portugal* 34 E2
Vågsfjorden, *Norway* 8 B17
Váh →, *Slovak Rep.* 27 D11
Vahsel B., *Antarctica* 5 D1
Váï, *Greece* 36 D8
Vaigach, *Russia* 50 B6
Vaiges, *France* 18 D6
Vaihingen, *Germany* 25 G4
Vail, *U.S.A.* 106 C5
Vailly-sur-Aisne, *France* 19 C10
Vaisali →, *India* 69 F8
Vaison-la-Romaine, *France* 21 D9
Vakarel, *Bulgaria* 40 D7
Vakfıkebir, *Turkey* 73 B8
Vakh →, *Russia* 50 C8
Vakhtan, *Russia* 48 B8
Vál, *Hungary* 42 C3
Val-de-Marne □, *France* 19 D9
Val-d'Isère, *France* 21 C10
Val-d'Oise □, *France* 19 C9
Val-d'Or, *Canada* 102 C4
Val Marie, *Canada* 105 D7
Valaam, *Russia* 46 B6
Valadares, *Portugal* 34 D2
Valahia, *Romania* 43 F9
Valais □, *Switz.* 25 J3
Valais, Alpes du, *Switz.* 25 J3
Valandovo, *Macedonia* 40 E6
Valašské Meziříčí, *Czech Rep.* 27 B10
Valáxa, *Greece* 38 C6
Vålberg, *Sweden* 10 E7
Valbo, *Sweden* 10 D10
Valbondione, *Italy* 28 B7
Vălcani, *Romania* 42 D5
Vâlcea □, *Romania* 43 F9
Valcheta, *Argentina* 128 E3
Valdagno, *Italy* 29 C8
Valdahon, *France* 19 E13
Valday, *Russia* 46 D7
Valdayskaya Vozvyshennost, *Russia* 46 D7
Valdeazogues →, *Spain* 35 G6
Valdecañas, Embalse de, *Spain* 34 F5
Valdemarsvik, *Sweden* 11 F10
Valdemoro, *Spain* 34 E7
Valdepeñas, *Spain* 35 G7
Valderaduey →, *Spain* 34 D5
Valdérice, *Italy* 30 D5
Valderrobres, *Spain* 32 E5
Valdés, Pen., *Argentina* 122 H4
Valdez, *U.S.A.* 100 B5
Valdivia, *Chile* 128 D2
Valdobbiádene, *Italy* 29 C8
Valdosta, *U.S.A.* 109 K4
Valdoviño, *Spain* 34 B2
Valdres, *Norway* 9 F13
Vale, *Georgia* 49 K6
Vale, *U.S.A.* 114 E5
Vale of Glamorgan □, *U.K.* 13 F4
Valea lui Mihai, *Romania* 42 C7
Valea Mărului, *Romania* 43 E12
Valemount, *Canada* 104 C5
Valença, *Brazil* 125 F11
Valença, *Portugal* 34 C2
Valença do Piauí, *Brazil* 125 E10
Valençay, *France* 19 E8
Valence = Valence d'Agen, *France* 20 D4
Valence, *France* 21 D8
Valence d'Agen, *France* 20 D4
Valencia, *Spain* 33 F4
Valencia, *U.S.A.* 115 J10
Valencia, *Venezuela* 124 A5
Valencia □, *Spain* 33 F4
Valencia, G. de, *Spain* 33 F5
Valencia de Alcántara, *Spain* 35 F3
Valencia de Don Juan, *Spain* 34 C5
Valencia I., *Ireland* 15 E1
Valenciennes, *France* 19 B10
Văleni, *Romania* 43 F9
Vălenii de Munte, *Romania* 43 E11
Valensole, *France* 21 E9
Valentigney, *France* 19 E13
Valentim, Sa. do, *Brazil* 125 E10
Valentin, *Russia* 54 C7
Valentine, *U.S.A.* 113 K2
Valenza, *Italy* 28 C5
Valera, *Venezuela* 124 B4
Valga, *Estonia* 9 H22
Valguarnera Caropepe, *Italy* 31 E7
Valier, *U.S.A.* 114 B7
Valinco, G. de, *France* 21 G12
Valjevo, *Serbia, Yug.* 40 B3
Valka, *Latvia* 9 H21
Valkeakoski, *Finland* 9 F20
Valkenswaard, *Neths.* 17 C5
Vall de Uxó = La Vall d'Uixó, *Spain* 32 F4
Valla, *Sweden* 10 E10
Valladolid, *Mexico* 119 C7
Valladolid, *Spain* 34 D6
Valladolid □, *Spain* 34 D6
Vallata, *Italy* 31 A8
Valldemossa, *Spain* 37 B9
Valle d'Aosta □, *Italy* 28 C4
Valle de Arán, *Spain* 32 C5
Valle de la Pascua, *Venezuela* 124 B5
Valle de las Palmas, *Mexico* 117 N10
Valle de Santiago, *Mexico* 118 C4
Valle de Suchil, *Mexico* 118 C4
Valle de Zaragoza, *Mexico* 118 B3
Valle Fértil, Sierra del, *Argentina* 126 C2
Valle Hermoso, *Mexico* 119 B5
Valledupar, *Colombia* 124 A4
Vallehermoso, *Canary Is.* 37 F2
Vallejo, *U.S.A.* 116 G4
Vallenar, *Chile* 126 B1
Vallentuna, *Sweden* 10 E12
Valleraugue, *France* 20 D7
Vallet, *France* 18 E5
Valletta, *Malta* 36 D2
Valley Center, *U.S.A.* 117 M9
Valley City, *U.S.A.* 112 B6
Valley Falls, *Oreg., U.S.A.* 114 E3
Valley Falls, *R.I., U.S.A.* 111 E13
Valley Springs, *U.S.A.* 116 G6
Valley View, *U.S.A.* 111 F8
Valley Wells, *U.S.A.* 117 K11
Valleyview, *Canada* 104 B5
Valli di Comácchio, *Italy* 29 D9
Vallimanca, Arroyo, *Argentina* 126 D4
Vallo della Lucánia, *Italy* 31 B8
Vallon-Pont-d'Arc, *France* 21 D8
Vallorbe, *Switz.* 25 J2
Valls, *Spain* 32 D6
Valmaseda = Balmaseda, *Spain* 32 B1
Valmiera, *Latvia* 9 H21
Valnera, *Spain* 34 B7
Valognes, *France* 18 C5
Valona = Vlorë, *Albania* 40 F3
Valongo, *Portugal* 34 D2
Valozhyn, *Belarus* 46 E4
Valpaços, *Portugal* 34 D3
Valparaíso, *Chile* 126 C1
Valparaíso, *Mexico* 118 C4
Valparaiso, *U.S.A.* 108 E2
Valparaíso □, *Chile* 126 C1
Valpovo, *Croatia* 42 E3
Valréas, *France* 21 D9
Vals, *Switz.* 25 J5
Vals →, *S. Africa* 88 D4
Vals, Tanjung, *Indonesia* 63 F9
Vals-les-Bains, *France* 21 D8
Valsad, *India* 66 J8
Valtellina, *Italy* 28 B6
Valuyki, *Russia* 47 G10
Valverde, *Canary Is.* 37 G2
Valverde del Camino, *Spain* 35 H4
Valverde del Fresno, *Spain* 34 E4
Vama, *Romania* 43 C10
Vamdrup, *Denmark* 11 J3
Våmhus, *Sweden* 10 C8
Vammala, *Finland* 9 F20
Vámos, *Greece* 36 D6
Van, *Turkey* 70 B4
Van, L. = Van Gölü, *Turkey* 70 B4
Van Alstyne, *U.S.A.* 113 J6
Van Blommestein Meer, *Surinam* 125 C7
Van Buren, *Canada* 103 C6
Van Buren, *Ark., U.S.A.* 113 H7
Van Buren, *Maine, U.S.A.* 109 B11
Van Buren, *Mo., U.S.A.* 113 G9
Van Canh, *Vietnam* 64 F7
Van Diemen, C., *N. Terr., Australia* 92 B5
Van Diemen, C., *Queens., Australia* 94 B2
Van Diemen G., *Australia* 92 B5
Van Gölü, *Turkey* 70 B4
Van Horn, *U.S.A.* 113 K2
Van Ninh, *Vietnam* 64 F7
Van Rees, Pegunungan, *Indonesia* 63 E9
Van Wert, *U.S.A.* 108 E3
Van Yen, *Vietnam* 58 G5
Vanadzor, *Armenia* 49 K7
Vanavara, *Russia* 51 C11
Vancouver, *Canada* 104 D4
Vancouver, *U.S.A.* 116 E4
Vancouver, C., *Australia* 93 G2
Vancouver I., *Canada* 104 D3
Vandalia, *Ill., U.S.A.* 112 F10
Vandalia, *Mo., U.S.A.* 112 F9
Vandenburg, *U.S.A.* 117 L6
Vanderbijlpark, *S. Africa* 89 D4
Vandergrift, *U.S.A.* 110 F5
Vanderhoof, *Canada* 104 C4
Vanderkloof Dam, *S. Africa* 88 E3
Vanderlin I., *Australia* 94 B2
Vänern, *Sweden* 11 F7
Vänersborg, *Sweden* 11 F6
Vang Vieng, *Laos* 64 C4
Vanga, *Kenya* 86 C4
Vangaindrano, *Madag.* 89 C8

# KEY TO WORLD MAP PAGES

**NORTH AMERICA**

**ARCTIC OCEAN** 4

8

Arctic Circle

8

14

15

12-13

18-19

34-35

20-21    28-

37    37

32-33

37

37

100-101

104-105

102-103

108-109

110-111

116-117

114-115    112-113

118-119

120-121

ATLANTIC

OCEAN

Tropic of Cancer

106

**PACIFIC OCEAN** 96-97

78-79

Equator

**AFRICA**

**SOUTH AMERICA**

124-125

Tropic of Capricorn

126-127

PACIFIC OCEAN

128